# Handbook of
# Treatment Approaches
# in Childhood
# Psychopathology

# APPLIED CLINICAL PSYCHOLOGY

Series Editors:
Alan S. Bellack, *Medical College of Pennsylvania at EPPI, Philadelphia, Pennsylvania,* and Michel Hersen, *University of Pittsburgh, Pittsburgh, Pennsylvania*

A Continuation Order Plan is available for this series. A continuation order will bring delivery of each new volume immediately upon publication. Volumes are billed only upon actual shipment. For further information please contact the publisher.

# Handbook of Treatment Approaches in Childhood Psychopathology

Edited by

## JOHNNY L. MATSON

*Louisiana State University*
*Baton Rouge, Louisiana*

PLENUM PRESS • NEW YORK AND LONDON

Library of Congress Cataloging in Publication Data

Handbook of treatment approaches in childhood psychopathology.

(Applied clinical psychology)
Includes bibliographies and index.
1. Child psychopathology. 2. Child psychotherapy. I. Matson, Johnny L. II. Series.
[DNLM: 1. Psychopathology—in infancy & childhood. 2. Psychotherapy—in infancy
and childhood. WS 350 H2365]
RJ499.H334   1988                    618.92′89                          88-19648
ISBN 0-306-42844-X

© 1988 Plenum Press, New York
A Division of Plenum Publishing Corporation
233 Spring Street, New York, N.Y. 10013

Printed in the United States of America

# Contributors

*Anna Accardi,* Department of Educational Psychology, University of Wisconsin— Madison, Madison, Wisconsin 53706

*Martin Agran,* Department of Special Education, Utah State University, Logan, Utah 84322

*Robert T. Ammerman,* Western Pennsylvania School for Blind Children, Pittsburgh, Pennsylvania 15213

*Frank Andrasik,* Department of Psychology, University of West Florida, Pensacola, Florida 32514-5751

*Ivan L. Beale,* Department of Psychology, University of Auckland, Auckland, New Zealand

*Dudley David Blake,* Veterans Administration Medical Center, Boston, Massachusetts 02130

*Daniel J. Burbach,* Department of Psychology, University of Missouri—Columbia, Columbia, Missouri 65201

*Jennifer Burkhart,* Western Psychiatric Institute and Clinic, University of Pittsburgh, School of Medicine, Pittsburgh, Pennsylvania 15213

*Michael Carey,* Department of Psychology, Louisiana State University, Baton Rouge, Louisiana 70803-5501

*Gabrielle A. Carlson,* Department of Psychiatry and Behavioral Sciences, State University of New York at Stony Brook, Stony Brook, New York 11794

*Christine L. Cole,* Waisman Center on Mental Retardation and Human Development, University of Wisconsin—Madison, Madison, Wisconsin

*Thomas M. DiLorenzo,* Department of Psychology, University of Missouri-Columbia, Columbia, Missouri 65201

*Sharon L. Foster,* Department of Psychology, West Virginia University, Morgantown, West Virginia 26506

*Cynthia L. Frame,* Department of Psychology, University of Georgia, Athens, Georgia 30601

*Kenneth D. Gadow,* Department of Psychiatry and Behavioral Science, SUNY at Stony Brook, Stony Brook, New York 11794-8790

*William I. Gardner,* Waisman Center on Mental Retardation and Human Development, University of Wisconsin—Madison, Madison, Wisconsin 53706

*Markham S. Giblin,* Department of Psychology, University of Georgia, Athens, Georgia 30601

*David C. Guevremant*, Department of Psychology, West Virginia University, Morgantown, West Virginia 26506

*Sandra L. Harris*, Graduate School of Applied and Professional Psychology, Rutgers University, Piscataway, New Jersey 08854

*Robert W. Heffer*, Department of Psychology, Louisiana State University, Baton Rouge, Louisiana 70803

*George R. Johnstone*, Department of Psychology, University of Georgia, Athens, Georgia 30601

*Elise Kabela*, Center for Stress and Anxiety Disorders, State University of New York at Albany, Albany, New York 12203

*Mary L. Kelley*, Department of Psychology, Louisiana State University, Baton Rouge, Louisiana 70803

*Philip C. Kendall*, Department of Psychology, Temple University, Philadelphia, Pennsylvania 19122

*Thomas R. Kratochwill*, Department of Educational Psychology, University of Wisconsin—Madison, Madison, Wisconsin 53706

*Benjamin B. Lahey*, Department of Psychology, University of Georgia, Athens, Georgia 30602

*Robert D. Lyman*, Department of Psychology, University of Alabama, Tuscaloosa, Alabama 35486

*James E. Martin*, School of Education, University of Colorado at Colorado Springs, Colorado Springs, Colorado 80933-9150

*Johnny L. Matson*, Department of Psychology, Louisiana State University, Baton Rouge, Louisiana 70803-5501

*Karen Meiselas*, Department of Psychiatry, New York University Medical Center, New York, New York 10016

*Richard J. Morris*, Department of Educational Psychology, University of Arizona, Tucson, Arizona 85721

*Edward J. Nuffield*, Box 57, P. O. Lindfield, 2070 N. S. W., Sydney, Australia

*Richard Perry*, Department of Psychiatry, New York University Medical Center, New York, New York 10016

*Lizette Peterson*, Department of Psychology, University of Missouri—Columbia, Columbia, Missouri 65201

*Rita C. Prather*, Department of Psychology, Louisiana State University, Baton Rouge, Louisiana 70803

*Michael C. Roberts*, Department of Psychology, University of Alabama, Tuscaloosa, Alabama 35486

*Johannes Rojahn*, Western Psychiatric Institute and Clinic, University of Pittsburgh School of Medicine, Pittsburgh, Pennsylvania 15213

*Elizabeth A. Schaughency*, Department of Psychology, University of Oregon, Eugene, Oregon 97403

*James P. Schierberl*, St. Vincent Health Center, Erie, Pennsylvania 16544

*Nirbhay N. Singh*, Educational Research and Services Center, DeKalb, Illinois 60115

*Lori A. Sisson*, Department of Psychiatry, University of Pittsburgh School of Medicine, Pittsburgh, Pennsylvania 15213

*Marie de Fatima Thomas*, Department of Psychiatry, University of Missouri-Columbia, Columbia, Missouri 65212

*Vincent B. Van Hasselt*, Department of Psychiatry and Human Behavior, University of California—Irvine, Medical Center, Orange, California 92668

*Jason Walker*, Department of Psychology, University of Georgia, Athens, Georgia 30602

*Karen C. Wells*, Children's Hospital National Medical Center and George Washington University, School of Medicine, Washington, D.C. 20010

*Donald A. Williamson*, Department of Psychology, Louisiana State University, Baton Rouge, Louisiana 70803

# *Preface*

The treatment of psychopathology in children has been a centerpiece of the overall field of problem behaviors in children. Therefore, a considerable number of data have been accumulated, particularly in recent years. These efforts have expanded at such a rate as to result in the publication of several new journals, such as the *Journal of Clinical Child Psychology* and *Education and Treatment of Children*. Similarly, many standard general clinical journals have begun to devote more attention to children. Despite these efforts, few books have emerged that are devoted directly and specifically to treatment in childhood psychopathology.

This volume's scope is broad in that it reviews not only behavior therapy, but also the rapidly expanding efforts in psychopathology and traditional psychotherapy, and at an advanced level. It is designed to provide an in-depth scholarly review of the empirical evidence, including an overview and analysis of the available techniques, their effectiveness, and the limitations and complications arising from the use of these treatment methods with the full range of psychopathology displayed by children. Many nationally and internationally recognized experts have agreed to contribute chapters to this book, and we hope that what has emerged is an up-to-date and authoritative volume.

The book is geared to the graduate student in clinical child psychology, school psychology, child psychiatry, special education, and related areas in which interest is likely to be considerable. This book should also serve as a source book for practicing professionals in the field. Illustrations and examples of various techniques are provided to further enhance the utility and appeal of the book. An effort was made to produce a book that is both scholarly and of practical utility.

Some features of this book include its coverage of major psychological and pharmacological approaches. Also, it is this author's view that far too many handicapped groups have not received the attention they deserve from mental health professionals. Therefore, specific attention is directed to mentally retarded, visually impaired, and hearing-impaired children, as well as more frequently discussed childhood groups. It is hoped that this book will highlight areas for futher consideration, study, and intervention. It is also hoped that this volume will not only serve to define where we currently are as mental health professionals but will also serve as a springboard to a better understanding of how best to and where we most urgently need to further advance our knowledge.

Johnny L. Matson

*Baton Rouge, Louisiana*

# Contents

PART IV. TREATMENT APPROACHES: SEVERE MENTAL DISORDERS

PART V. TREATMENT APPROACHES: MEDICAL PSYCHOLOGY

PART VI. TREATMENT APPROACHES: PHYSICAL AND LEARNING DISABILITIES

# Handbook of
# Treatment Approaches
# in Childhood
# Psychopathology

# I  History, Systems, and Methods

A number of general issues deserve discussion in a treatment book on child psychopathology. Thus, this book begins with an overview of past views of childhood emotional disorders. Certainly, a major issue is the very rapid (from a historical view) positive advances in this area. This chapter is followed by one on classification. Obviously, this topic is important for the selection of treatments. Movement in this area has been considerable and substantial, and important research has occurred of late. The final chapter in this section is on family therapy. It was felt that any treatment book on children would need to include this topic. However, as this area does not fit conveniently into the format used in the remainder of the volume, it was placed here. The methods used are well founded in the best available research. Hopefully, these initial chapters will set up the remainder of the book in describing some of the broad and very important topics in the field.

# 1    *Historical Trends*

LIZETTE PETERSON AND DANIEL J. BURBACH

The primary purpose of this chapter is to describe the history of child psychopathology and its treatment. In order to accomplish this task, ancient to modern-day awareness of children and their psychological dysfunctions are considered. As this chapter begins to unfold, it will become clear that nothing resembling current conceptualizations and treatments of child psychopathology existed before this century. Nevertheless, it seems useful to explore earlier notions about the psychological disorders of children in order to gain insight into how modern-day treatment modalities, many of which are described in this book, evolved.

Because we wish to provide a broad overview of this subject, it will be necessary to sample only briefly the numerous ways in which child psychopathology has been approached over the course of history. Thus, rather than attempting to provide exhaustive coverage, we will identify and discuss representative historical beliefs and events, as well as current treatments. The goal is to provide the reader with a background for interpreting current and future trends in the treatment of psychopathology in children.

## HISTORY BEFORE THE 20TH CENTURY

Before this century, childhood was almost never conceptualized as a separate developmental period (Senn, 1975). In classical China and ancient Greece, words connoting childhood (i.e., individuals in the first decade of life) simply did not exist. For example, words like *child* and *boy* suggested a kinship relation and an economically dependent relationship, respectively (Aries, 1962). There were no available words to describe the period of early development now known as *childhood*. Thus, children were most often viewed as inferior or inadequate adults who, if tolerated and provided for, might eventually develop out of their current worthless state (Kessen, 1965). The decision about whether to tolerate or provide for children was by no means automatic and, as will be demonstrated later, depended on the economic and political needs of society. In fact, in most early cultures, even the soundest child was considered a most expendable item, and not surprisingly, a maladaptive child was viewed as a detriment to both society and the family. It was not until the 17th century that childhood was regarded as a special time for learning. The notion that childhood was a time for nurturance and love came even later (Gelfand & Peterson, 1985).

LIZETTE PETERSON AND DANIEL J. BURBACH • Department of Psychology, University of Missouri—Columbia, Columbia, Missouri 65201.

With no systematic study or knowledge of childhood, it was impossible to identify typical or normal development, and thus, there was no way to determine what was pathological in children. Of course, at the beginning of our history, there was limited scientific understanding of either physical or mental disorder. What little understanding there was almost always concerned dysfunction in adults (Rie, 1971), for several reasons. Adults' dysfunction is usually more interpretable, as it is set against a more static developmental course than is childhood dysfunction. More important, the economic impact of psychological disorder in an adult is more immediately apparent and serious than of that in a child. For whatever reason, society's concern for the child has always lagged behind that for the adult (Wenar, 1982). Furthermore, the earliest interventions applied to children were merely downward extensions of treatments created for adults (Roberts & Peterson, 1984). These treatments, although frequently inappropriate, represented a substantial improvement over the brutal methods that had been used by earlier societies to deal with dysfunctional children. Some of these methods are discussed below.

## Children of the Old Testament

The writings contained in the Old Testament of the Bible (authorized King James version) provide some of the earliest recorded references to children and their difficulties (Despert, 1965). Although there appeared to be some recognition of the physical and emotional limitations of young children at this time (e.g., Genesis 33:13), it is clear that even preadolescent children were often expected to assume major responsibilities. For example, Manessah (II Kings 21:1) became the king of Judah at the age of 12. Josiah (II Kings 22:1) took over this task at the age of 8. Furthermore, although children were referred to as "a gift from God" in the Book of Psalms (127:3), it is clear that they were often tortured or executed during times of political unrest and familial discord (e.g., Gensis 21:10; II Kings 11:1). Unfortunately, children were treated in similar ways for many years to follow.

## Ancient Greece: Sparta and Athens

Infanticide was commonly accepted in ancient Greece as a method of dealing with unwanted children. In deciding on the survival of children, the primary determinant was their physical intactness, that is, their ability to serve the state (Nathan & Harris, 1975). In Sparta, boys were expected to develop as laborers and soldiers. The boys of Athens were expected to develop into loyal and peaceful leaders. The major contribution of girls in both societies was considered the bearing of male children. Minimal attention was paid to psychological functioning, especially in Sparta, although a child with clearly aberrant psychological functioning or psychopathological symptomatology was likely to be judged a poor physical specimen and thus was eliminated. In Sparta, this decision was made by the leaders of the state. In Athens, this decision was made by the father. The most common method of putting a child to death was abandonment; the child would die of exposure or would be killed by wild animals (Despert, 1965). Some methods were more artistic, however: infants were sometimes asphyxiated within large, ornamental clay pots.

Gainful employment typically began at approximately age 7, and it was anticipated that, by this time, children would be relatively physically self-sufficient and able to perform rudimentary manual labor and domestic tasks (Despert, 1965). There was no special spokesperson or protector of working children. Instead, children were expected to serve the state. This was a primary difference between the Greek culture and the later Roman Empire.

## Roman Empire

The Roman Empire was a patriarchal society. Fathers were considered the only citizens of the state and the major controlling force in their respective families. Thus, within a family unit, the father made several choices regarding the children. First, like the Athenian father, he alone determined which of his children would live or die. Further, if the decision was to raise the child, there remained the question of whether the child would live within the family or be sold to others later as a slave. This decision often depended on the child's value to the family (Goodsell, 1934).

Despite the apparent harshness of a culture with no provision for the protection of its children, the Roman Empire exhibited a much more liberal attitude toward children than had previous cultures. This was one of the first societies to overindulge children and adolescents. Some authors have suggested that children were overindulged in exciting sports and games at the expense of lessons concerning labor and duty and that this practice contributed to the fall of the Roman Empire (Goodsell, 1934).

Despite great regard for sports, art, and poetry, there was also a continuing disregard of individual differences in children and a relative intolerance of children who were physically, emotionally, or intellectually atypical. The treatment of emotional disorders in adults typically involved physical interventions such as trephining, bloodletting, and laxatives to restore the balance of humoral substances in the body. There is little record of any treatment being applied to children, other than abandonment. However, given the later treatment methods, such as torture and burning, seen in the Middle Ages and the Renaissance, the absence of child treatment modalities may have proved a blessing to children.

## Middle Ages (A.D. 500–1300)

This time period has been called the Middle Ages, or the Dark Ages. The latter term may be a more accurate depiction of reality, as this period was characterized by a strong, repressive interlocking of Church and State that proved detrimental to the freedom of individual citizens. The Catholic church's primary dictum relevant to children at this time was that of original sin (Aries, 1962). Basically, this point of view suggested that humankind is born in a state of sin and that children will remain inherently evil if not led toward a life of piety. Infanticide was regarded by the Church as a major sin, but it was not until the 12th century that secular legislation equated infanticide with murder. Even then, very few illegitimate children survived to be baptized, and the ratio of baptized boys to girls exceeded three to two. Thus, it seems likely that the number of unwanted illegitimate or female children who were murdered was relatively high (Holmes & Morrison, 1979). It is said that Pope Innocent III began his efforts to establish orphanages in Italy after being appalled at the sight of "countless" bodies of newborns floating in the Tiber (deMause, 1974; McLaughlin, 1974).

Children continued to have no legal rights in this culture. Beating and neglect were common. One 13th-century law read, "If one beats a child until it bleeds, then it will remember, but if one beats it to death, then the law applies" (deMause, 1974, p. 42), suggesting that severe beating was desirable, even if murder was not. At about age 7, children were often removed from their mothers. A child could be legally sold into slavery only before age 7, although it seems clear that many families disobeyed the law, selling their children at a later age. Even in wealthy families, children were often sent to serve still wealthier gentry in nearby castles and were treated as slaves or servants (Despert, 1965). A child might also be given as an oblate or religious offering to the Church for the betterment of the parent's soul. The child was then obligated to serve the rest of his or her life in a monastery or a convent, excommunication being the penalty for leaving the Church.

During this time, the Church also became involved in a search for the followers of Satan in an attempt to eliminate the evils and wickedness that existed in society. It was thought that such individuals were often easily recognizable by their bizarre behavior and beliefs. Thus, children experiencing outward manifestations of psychopathology became easy targets of the Inquisition. Interestingly, the families of such children were often among the first to condemn them, lest the family be regarded by others as also being followers of Satan. It is difficult to estimate the number of children who were tortured to confess their allegiance to the devil or who were burned at the stake as witches because of their disordered behavior. Some historians have suggested that their number may have been quite high (Zilboorg, 1941), whereas others believe that this number remained quite small, at least until the Renaissance (Kroll, 1973; Neugebauer, 1979).

## Renaissance (1300–1600)

The term *renaissance* implies a societal enlightenment. Unfortunately, this enlightenment led to only limited improvements in the ways in which children were treated by society. Up through 1600, professionals still used demonic possession as an explanation for childhood psychopathology (Hunter & Macalpine, 1963). Although some began to advocate more nurturant forms of discipline, physical punishment was still routinely applied. Often, very severe punishment was used in the most elite families. For example, John Milton's wife commented on how she hated to hear her nephews scream as Milton beat them. Louis XIII of France was whipped routinely from the time he was 2 years old, and as an adult, he reported continued nightmares about the beatings (deMause, 1974).

By this time, putting children to death was condemned; however, it was still considered acceptable to abandon a child to the Church or to an orphanage. In terms of actual outcome, this practice amounted to infanticide in many cases, as most infants abandoned in this manner died. In one French orphanage, for example, not a single child admitted survived into adulthood (Marvick, 1974). In one Russian orphanage, 1,000 children were eventually adopted, and 6,100 remained living at the orphanage. However, the majority (over 30,000 children) died before puberty (Dunn, 1974).

Whereas poor families were inclined to abandon their children to orphanages, wealthier individuals sent their children to a wet nurse until the child was of preschool age. Some estimates suggest that as few as 3% of the infants born in Paris as late as 1700 were nursed by their own mothers (deMause, 1974). In total, one of every three children during this time period died during childhood.

There were some positive trends in the treatment of children toward the end of this period. With John Locke's doctrine of the *tabula rasa* came an increased focus on the need to educate children. Although this resulted in very strict educational practices, it also removed some children from a life devoted exclusively to labor. There is evidence that the educational materials used at the time emphasized pictures and toys for educational purposes.

The first English book on pediatrics was written in 1545. Thomas Phaire's *The Boke of Chyldren* (1545/1955) considered such child problems as "Terrible Dreames and Feare in the Slepe" and "of pissing in the Bedde," and it represented one of the first formal treatments of problems that are unique to children. Thus, by the end of this period, at least in Europe, the scene was set for a change in attitude and in emphasis in the treatment of children.

## Colonial North America (1600–1700)

Just as the tide in Europe was turning toward more nurturant treatment of children, with a greater focus on education, the demands of the New World were rendering childhood an even more arduous experience than in earlier European society. Public health officials have estimated that as many as two thirds of all children in colonial America died before they were 4 years old (Duffy, 1976). Infanticide itself was rare, but common practices such as "toughening" infants with icy baths in the winter and rampant disease contributed to their mortality. Also, children and youth were more often than adults the targets of witch hunts, such as in the trials held in Salem in 1692.

There were also laws, such as the 1654 Stubborn Child Law, that allowed a parent to put a child to death as an ultimate penalty for disobedience (Katz, Schroeder, & Sidman, 1973). However, because children were economically very important, there was a clear cost in using disciplines severe enough to maim or kill. Despite children's economic value, however, parents continued to employ corporal punishment: "Thou shall beat the child with the rod and deliver his soul from hell" (John Elliot, quoted in Illick, 1974).

It was not uncommon for children under 6 years old to work in shops and on farms. Children could be bound out as apprentices if the family business did not necessitate their labor, if their families could not afford to keep them, or if they were atypical in some respect. Even with the economic value of children recognized, there were few advances in the treatment of physical illness beyond the bleeding and purging that characterized much more ancient times. There was even less explicit treatment of child psychopathology.

LIZETTE PETERSON AND
DANIEL J. BURBACH

Although a modern conceptualization of childhood was not articulated during this period, there were many changes in attitude regarding children during these two centuries. Part of this change was facilitated by Locke's *tabula rasa* doctrine, which implicitly suggested that, because the later adult will be a product of learning that takes place in childhood, such learning early in life is of monumental importance. Curiously, the movement was also furthered by Jean-Jacques Rousseau, who had a very dissimilar attitude toward childhood. Rousseau believed that, rather than being born completely *tabula rasa*, children were born innately good. He advocated a simple recording of children's developmental progress (Kanner, 1973) and suggested that children would come to love learning and to learn spontaneously if given the appropriate environment (i.e., the "noble savage" concept). Both Rousseau and Locke produced data relevant to child development by maintaining records on the development of their own children.

This was an age of many firsts. Although the bulk of deviant children continued to be indentured or cared for in almshouses with the elderly, the diseased, and the insane, there were several reports of the use of hospital-based interventions for children's medical and psychopathological conditions (Stone, 1979). Benjamin Rush, the founder of modern-day psychiatry, first described cholera symptoms in infants, and his student, Charles Caldwell, wrote the first medical degree dissertation on pediatrics. Duffy (1976) described one of the first admittances of a child to Pennsylvania Hospital in 1765. The 13-year-old child had experienced a severe negative reaction to the death of her mother and sibling. At this time, she was "seized with so violent a grief as would not yield to any comfort, her Mind was disturbed and she cried Day and Night" (Duffy, 1976, p. 94). The commander of the ship on which the girl was traveling had recommended hospitalization, and the hospital had accepted her for treatment.

Nearly a century later, Henry Maudsley (1867) included a chapter in his psychiatric text on *Insanity of Early Life* (although the chapter was so severely criticized that the second volume began the chapter with an apologetic explanation). In contrast to this early reluctance to describe child psychopathology, by the late 1800s, there were whole textbooks on the subject published in Germany, France, and Great Britain (Kanner, 1973).

The first institutions for the mentally retarded also began to be formed at this time (Stone, 1979). Johann Jakob Duggenbuhl founded an institute in Abendberg, Switzerland, which served, among others, those individuals from Alpine areas suffering from endemic cretinism. Samuel Gridley Howe was influenced by such endeavors and persuaded the Commonwealth of Massachusetts to begin similar programs in 1848.

In a similar spirit, the first Board of Charities and Corrections was organized in 1863 in Massachusetts, and it assumed public responsibility for children who were "dependent, defective, and delinquent." By the end of the century, 16 states had similar boards, and 92 cities had family service agencies (Kideneigh, 1965). The first case charging child abuse was also heard in 1870, although at the time there were no laws prohibiting the beating of a child. The case was tried under the auspices of the American Society for the Prevention of Cruelty to Animals, the prosecution arguing that the child should be entitled to the same rights as other animals (Brown, Rox & Hubbard, 1974). Although this may not sound like much of a triumph, it should be recalled that it was the first time that the family's right to inflict injury on a child was publicly challenged.

Finally, by the end of the 19th century, the first attempts to systematically study children were being made. Alfred Binet's early work on the measurement of French children's intelligence and G. Stanley Hall's work measuring typical motor and emotional development in the United States typified these efforts. They would soon be joined by Arnold Gesell, who conducted numerous studies of children at the Yale Child Study Clinic. It is fortunate that, as large institutions and associations were being formed to provide services and treatment to child populations, simultaneous efforts were being made to explicitly study the development and difficulties of children. Because of these efforts, it became possible to begin to establish a scientific basis for the many treatments that were to be used with children. However, as will be seen, the study and treatment of children remained relatively separate for the next several decades (Gelfand & Peterson, 1985).

## Early 20th Century (1900–1950)

Throughout this period, there were specific political reform movements oriented toward protecting and bettering the lot of children, particularly poor children. In 1909, President Theodore Roosevelt organized the first White House Conference on Children and renounced the commonly accepted Elizabethan Poor Law, which suggested that children could be removed from their homes solely on the basis of their family's poverty. The federally funded Children's Bureau was formed in 1912 to serve in an advocacy capacity, to support child protective legislation and child welfare services, and to provide aid to dependent children. This support fostered the growth of still other, voluntary organizations, such as the Child Welfare League of American, formed in 1920 (Hetznecker & Forman, 1971).

The formation in 1922 of the National Committee on Mental Hygiene was an outgrowth of Clifford Beer's mental hygiene movement. The description by this group of the link between childhood difficulties and later mental health problems was instrumental in establishing the child guidance movement (Rie, 1971), which will be described in the next section. Legislation and funding for childhood disorders was also influenced by the 1946 National Mental Health Act, which contained explicit provisions for the prevention of mental health problems. This act focused additional attention on early childhood and family interventions. Although the primary intent of the act was to guarantee the delivery of preventive services, training and treatment aspects gradually overshadowed the emphasis on prevention.

The formation of the National Institute of Mental Health in 1949 marked another turning point in governmental support for mental health services, but this was directed largely toward adult-based research and training. The controversy surrounding the advisability of primary prevention, with its accompanying explicit focus on the child, has continued since the first report of the Joint Commission on Mental Illness and Health in 1961. In this document, the commission discouraged applied primary prevention and research on primary prevention. As a consequence, the Community Mental Health Centers Act did not include prevention in its list of essential services. It should be noted, however, that the consultation and educational services provided for by this act were often interpreted as having a preventive component. The explicit partitioning of services and facilities for children was not a part of any of these bodies, however, and children have remained underserved in terms of federal mental-health dollars to the present time (Meyers, 1985).

The interest in political reform was accompanied by an increase in the number of volumes devoted to the assessment and treatment of child psychopathology. One of the first texts in this area was Ireland's *Mental Affections of Children* (1898). This was followed by Freud's *The Case of Little Hans* (1950), originally published in 1909. In 1918, Cameron published *The Nervous Child*. Several years later (in 1935), the first American textbook on child psychiatry was published by Kanner (1957).

Several useful chapters and articles also appeared at this time. For example, Hutchinson's *Lectures on Diseases of Children* (1904) contained two chapters on the functional disorders of children. Kenworthy (1930) outlined the social maladjustments of children in an article that appeared in *Mental Hygiene*.

Despite the absence of large-scale political advocacy and detailed publications concerning the assessment and treatment of child psychopathology, this was the time period in which treatment centers began to be formed specifically for children. These early clinics began with an explicit focus on educational problems, social dysfunction, or behavioral ("habit") disorders, as will be seen below.

*Child Treatment Centers*

The mental hygiene movement was seen as the impetus for Lightner Witmer's establishing the first psychology clinic in 1896 at the University of Pennsylvania. It was Witmer who first coined the term *clinical psychologist* (Achenbach, 1982) to describe his psychoeducational methods. These methods were directed toward children with school adjustment problems such as stuttering and spelling difficulties, as well as toward children who were intellectually atypical. Thus, Witmer's efforts resulted in the first treatment center that focused primarily on the difficulties of children.

A little over a decade later, with the support of the Hull House reformer group, William Healy founded the Juvenile Psychopathic Institute in Chicago in 1909. The first juvenile court had been established in Chicago a decade earlier (1899) and Healy's institute focused specifically on juvenile delinquency and other socially unacceptable behavior. Together, psychiatrist Healy and his wife, psychologist Augusta Bronner, created an interdisciplinary approach in which the psychiatrist, the psychologist, and the social worker contributed equally to the diagnosis of the child. The couple went on to organize a second clinic in Boston, and this clinic, the Judge Baker Guidance Center, came to epitomize the child guidance approach in this country.

Shakow (1968) contrasted the contributions of Witmer and Healy by noting the basic differences in the patients they served, the techniques they used, and the conceptualizations that they formulated. Witmer was strongly influenced by the more traditional Wundtian-Kraepelinian theories, whereas Healy was more influenced by Freud's, James's, and Meyer's concepts of prevention. Witmer's clinics tended to serve primarily the retarded, the gifted, and children with speech difficulty or those requiring vocational adjustment. The emphasis was on the intellectual and cognitive aspects of personality, which led to frequent contact with schoolteachers or institutions for the mentally retarded. In contrast, Healy treated juvenile delinquents, sociopaths, and conduct-disordered children, with an emphasis on the social-affective aspects of development. This approach led more often to contact with social agencies and legal bodies.

Although it is Healy whom most credit with the "real" beginning of the child guidance movement, it is important to acknowledge some of the areas of initial and eventual overlap between the approaches used by Healy and Witmer. Initially, Adolph Meyer, an influential member of the National Committee on Mental Hygiene, urged consideration of the disturbed child (more typically treated by Healy) in the context of the educational situation (more typically served by Witmer). Meyer urged that psychiatrists be placed within the schools and that they actively work with teachers and parents to prevent problems, a viewpoint that typifies today's approach to primary prevention.

Eventually, the overlap between the two methods occurred in a different fashion, through the gradual shift away from the treatment of the juvenile offender. The Commonwealth Fund Report of 1921 provided for the creation of demonstration child-guidance clinics, and such clinics were established in dozens of teaching hospitals and laboratories (Duffy, 1974). In their early history, the majority of referrals to child guidance clinics came from juvenile courts, but gradually, more children were referred by families and schools. Studies in the late 1920s showed that the clinics gradually accepted more non-foreign-born children of higher intelligence and from middle-class homes, who were being raised by their natural parents (Stevenson & Smith, 1934). State outpatient clinics came to be the recipient of most court referrals, and they treated not only the mentally retarded and the neurologically disabled but the severely delinquent as well. Eventually, even with the selective accepting of cases, the large case load, in conjuction with the limited resources, led clinics to advocate education as a possible solution. Consequently, mental health professionals began to devote energy to teaching mental hygiene principles to parents, teachers, court workers, and social workers (Hetznecker & Forman, 1971).

By 1932, there were over 200 child guidance clinics that operated on one of two therapeutic models. The first was concerned with the individuality of the child and with methods of helping him or her adjust to his or her environment. This approach focused on the child, his or her unique history, and his or her emotional difficulty. The second viewed the child as a product of the educational and social environment, and this method was more interested in community involvement and social reform. It seems noteworthy that both philosophies are mirrored in current approaches to child psychopathology.

A third movement, relatively separate from the other two and far less involved in the formation of psychiatry as a discipline, was the early behavioral movement. This movement influenced many clinicians, including psychiatrist Douglas Thom, who used behavioral methods in his Habit Clinic in Boston. In fact, some credit Thom's success with his Habit Clinic, rather than Witmer or Healy, with the funding for the Demonstration Child Guidance Clinics (Kanner, 1973). These clinics accepted any child whose behavior puzzled, worried, or

LIZETTE PETERSON AND
DANIEL J. BURBACH

annoyed parents and teachers, whether or not the behavior was likely to lead to later dysfunction. The basic approach was to influence the child's typical behaviors and habits by working not only with the child, but also with the adults in the child's immediate environment in order to alter their attitudes toward and beliefs about the child. This approach was continued in academic and research settings by individuals like John Watson and Mary Cover Jones and reappeared as a major treatment force only in the later part of this century.

## Parallel Contributions

There were several contributions from many diverse groups, such as radical behaviorism, developmental and educational psychology, and adult psychiatry, that laid the foundation for the development of child-focused interventions. Some of these events did not have an immediate and direct influence on child treatment. Instead, they continued to evolve as separate, nonoverlapping phenomena. We will consider three such examples briefly.

One sample of such an event began with Watson's essay "Psychology as a Behaviorist Sees It" (1913). Behavioral psychology had important implications for child rearing and treatment, but for the next two decades, it remained primarily within the province of academic psychology and basic research. Of course, there were (as noted above) early examples of child treatment using behavioral methods, but for the most part, these techniques were not yet widely applied to children.

Similarly, Freud's "Three Essays on the Theory of Sexuality" (1905) suggested that various childhood events were the source of adult neuroticism and maladjustment. Although some aspects of a healthy and normal childhood were spelled out by this theory, more attention was given to the many ways in which parental errors could lead to long-lasting pathology. For example, parents could err by giving the child either too little or too much gratification. Freud thought that such errors condemned the child to serious dysfunction as an adult unless the developmental shortcomings could be analyzed and worked through in later life. Interestingly, although Freud's theory underlined the importance of childhood, Freud never treated a child directly. It is true that one of his earlier mentioned, most famous illustrative cases was the treatment of a child's phobia of horses ("little Hans"). However, Freud treated Hans only through the child's father, and he commented at the conclusion of the case that he had learned nothing that he had not already known from treating adults. As will be noted in the next section, on modern-day treatment, psychoanalysis did not become relevant to child treatment until it was later modified by Anna Freud.

A third sample of parallel contribution was the assessment of intellectual abilities begun in France during the 19th century. It was not until the first half of the 20th century, however, that this contribution began to have a major impact on children. In 1838, the French physician J. D. Esquirol, was one of the first professionals to define mental subnormality (Goodenough, 1949). By the 1890s, there were a few specific tests of intellectual performance in existence (e.g., Gilbert, 1894; Munsterberg, 1891). Binet and Simon's early efforts in this area (1905) are among the best known. The work of these and other professionals eventually made possible the valid assessment of intellectual ability, which, in turn, facilitated large-scale compulsory education for intellectually normal children. Although the examination of children's intellectual abilities had clear implications for treatment, the province of assessment per se remained within the domain of psychometricians and developmental psychologists. Their concerns about the statistical properties and the developmental stability of the tests differed from the clinicians' desire to use the tests to diagnose specific deficits, and they characterize what some clinicians continue to perceive as the inadequacies of standardized intellectual assessment.

There were many other parallel trends, such as the description of self-directed speech for self-regulation by neuropsychologists L. S. Vygotsky and A. R. Luria (Zivin, 1979) and findings concerning the importance of early parent–child bonding by numerous developmental psychologists (Lamb, 1981), both of which could be discussed here but will not be because of lack of space. Gelfand and Peterson (1985) considered some of these trends further and pointed out the problems that result from separate and parallel, rather than cooperative and multidisciplinary, contributions to the child area. Hopefully, some of the gaps between research on the treatment of child psychopathology and other contributing areas of research will diminish by the end of the current decade. This notion will be considered later, when future trends are discussed.

## THERAPIES OF THE MODERN ERA

We have thus far described the historical roots of what appears to be a jungle of competing therapeutic approaches to child psychopathology. In this section, we sample from four major current approaches to child psychotherapy, and we introduce a brief history of pediatric pharmacotherapy.

### Child Pharmacotherapy

Although there were some scattered investigations of the treatment of child psychopathology with organic agents such as nonspecific sedatives and dietary manipulation before the late 1930s, there is a consensus that there was little systematic study or use of drug therapy in children before that time (Rapoport & Kruesi, 1985). In Wiener and Jaffe's detailed history of childhood psychopharmacology (1977), they described only a handful of relevant studies that bridge the 1930s and 1950s. This early work began with Bradley's landmark study (1937) concerning the use of Benzedrine at the Emma Pendleton Bradley Home, the first residential home for children in the United States. This report suggested that "spectacular" improvement in school performance, involving increased interest, accuracy, and speed of comprehension, could be obtained with this medication. Molitch and Sullivan (1937) also reported improvements in verbal intelligence scores after the use of Benzedrine with preadolescent and adolescent boys residing at the New Jersey State Home for Boys. Two years later, Cutts and Jasper (1939) described the positive effects of Benzedrine and the negative effects of phenobarbital (e.g., increased irritability, impulsivity, and destructiveness) in 7- to 10-year-old children at the Bradley Home.

Benzedrine continued to be studied by Bradley at the Bradley Home and by Bender at Bellevue Hospital throughout the 1940s. This drug, the first used in formal research work with children, was gradually replaced in the late 1940s by other stimulant drugs. For example, Bradley (1950) described a comparative study on the use of Benzedrine and dextroamphetamine in a population of over 350 preadolescent children. He reported the drugs to be equally effective. Bender and Nichtern (1956) similarly reported Dexedrine to be as effective as Benzedrine, even at much lower doses. Ritalin was synthesized in 1954, and preliminary studies noted clinical improvements in subjects from age 4 years to young adulthood (Zimmerman & Burgemeister, 1958).

Major tranquilizers such as chlorpromazine were also investigated during this time for use with emotionally disturbed, mentally retarded, and cerebral-palsied children, with varying degrees of effectiveness (e.g., Bair & Herold, 1955; Gatski, 1955). Other studies outlined the successful use of meprobamate for problems as varied as enuresis (Breger, 1961) and prepsychotic symptoms (Litchfield, 1957). Freedman (1958) reviewed the literature at that time and stated that "one is appalled at the number of drugs recommended and the conflicting claims both as to efficacy and absence of toxicity" (p. 573). He noted the methodological inadequacy of the majority of studies, including poor descriptions of diagnostic procedures and lack of adequate control strategies. Thus, this early period provided only a rudimentary foundation for the study of pediatric pharmacotherapy.

Wiener and Jaffe (1977) identified five major developments that characterize progress in this field in the 1960s. First, they noted "an almost quantum leap forward in the study of stimulants in children with hyperkinetic symptoms" (p. 18). These studies were characterized by a focus on specific drugs, such as Ritalin and Dexedrine, and on improved methodologies, such as double-blind, placebo-controlled, cross-over designs (e.g., Conners, Eisenberg, & Barcai, 1967). The first reports of negative side effects of stimulants, such as toxic psychosis (Ney, 1967) and dyskinesia (Mattson & Calverlez, 1968), were also published at this time.

The second major development was the use of two additional classes of major tranquilizers, including the piperazines, such as Stelazine (trifluoperazine), Prolixin (fluphenazine), and Compazine (prochlorperazine), and the piperidine compounds, such as Mellaril (thioridazine). The third major development, related to the second, was the use of major tranquilizers, such as thiothixene (e.g., Navane) and the butyrophenones (e.g., Haldol). Unfortunately, the early studies in this area were also poorly controlled and overenthusiastic in their claims, but they were later joined by better controlled studies. For example, later studies compared the major tranquilizers to both stimulants and placebos, in double-blind administration (e.g., Alexandris & Lundell, 1968). More attention to diagnosing subtypes of childhood problems also occurred during this era. For instance, Fish and Shapiro (1965) separated children into four subtypes and noted that Types I and II, who were of lower intellectual functioning, improved with chlorpromazine more than Types III and IV, who were intellectually intact but had behavioral disorders. Finally, extended concern about the side effects of these drugs occurred during this time. In a typical study, Ucer and Kreger (1969) noted that Haldol (haloperidol) was more effective in controlling disturbed behavior in mentally retarded children than thioridazine, but that it also resulted in greater agitation, ataxia, and extrapyramidal reactions.

The fourth development noted by Wiener and Jaffe (1977) was the use of antidepressant drugs for a variety of child problems. The first reports described

TABLE 1. History of Childhood Pharmacotherapy[a]

| Years study began | Drug and current status[b] |
|---|---|
| 1935–1940 | Benzedrine, N |
| 1945–1950 | Dilantin, C; Dexedrine, O |
| 1950–1955 | Chlorpromazine, O; reserpine, N; Benadryl, O |
| 1955–1957 | Ritalin, O; meprobamate, N; thioridazine, O; lithium, C |
| 1957–1960 | Imipramine, O; Trilafon, C; Compazine, C; Prolixin, C; Stelazine, O; LSD, N; Taractan, C |
| 1960–1965 | Cylert, C; Elavil, C; Navane, C; Haldol, O |
| 1965–1970 | Phenylzine, C; Triperidol, O |

[a]Abstracted from Wiener and Jaffe (1977).
[b]N = no longer in use; C = controversial or experimental use; O = ongoing use.

the use of Tofranil (imipramine) for the successful treatment of enuresis (e.g., Breger, 1961; MacLean, 1960). Elavil (amitriptyline) also began to be used to treat depression in hyperkinetic children (e.g., Lucas, Lockett, & Grimm, 1965; Rapoport, 1965) during this decade.

The fifth development was an increased attention to improved methodology in research studies on children's reactions to drug therapy. With so many parameters to consider, including the diagnostic groups, the developmental status and the intellectual level of the subjects, the drug dosage, the timing of the dosage, the drug type, the target behavior, and the potential drug side effects, it became crucial to control for as many sources of error as possible.

Table 1 summarizes this abbreviated history of child pharmacotherapy from 1930 to 1970. As can be seen, the 1960s were marked by increased attention to stimulant, tranquilizer, and antidepressant drugs in comparative, controlled studies. However, many experts still note that pediatric psychopharmacology is far less advanced than adult psychopharmacology (e.g., Werry, 1982), although much exciting progress has been made in the 1970s and 1980s (e.g., Rapoport & Kruesi, 1985; Wiener & Jaffe, 1977). Later chapters in this volume outline modern contributions to this rapidly developing area. We turn our attention next to four different types of psychotherapy.

## Dynamic Psychotherapy

The two primary types of dynamic therapy that have been applied to children are psychoanalytic therapy and nondirective play therapy. Psychoanalytically oriented therapy for children uses some of the same techniques as are used in adult psychoanalysis, but it differs in several important respects. Full-scale analysis requires multiple sessions per week over a period of years and thus is impractical for most children, who are likely to leave childhood before leaving analysis. Also, children's "weak ego structures," placed on a background of continuing development, make them poor analytic subjects (A. Freud, 1968). Thus, the basic goal of analytically oriented child therapy is the loosening of fixations and the increasing of children's capacity for reality testing (Brody, 1964). These goals are typically accomplished by bringing unconscious conflicts into conscious awareness through dramatic play and artwork (Bornstein, 1949).

LIZETTE PETERSON AND
DANIEL J. BURBACH

Nondirective therapy for children (Axline, 1976) also uses play materials and art, but with a somewhat different aim. This form of child therapy developed from Carl Rogers's nondirective, client-centered therapy for adults (1951), which was, in turn, strongly influenced by Frederick Allen's developmental theory. Allen suggested that if the therapist conveyed clear respect for and confidence in children's abilities to help themselves, children would develop adaptive abilities and faith in their own problem-solving. Thus, Rogers's approach is imminently relevant to children. Axline (1976) advocated the use of common child activities like play and art as vehicles for forming an alliance with the child, which allows the child a greater ability to express feelings. In this fashion, where feelings can be expressed without judgment or censure, the child can learn to control or give up feelings while experiencing a sense of self-acceptance.

Dynamic therapies are still used for special populations, such as medically ill children (e.g., Abbott, Hansen, & Lewis, 1970) and emotionally disturbed children (e.g., Abramson, Hoffman, & Johns, 1979), but in general they are regarded as less efficacious than behavioral techniques (Gelfand, Jenson, & Drew, 1982). It remains to be seen whether these therapy forms will gain more research support or whether they will continue to decline in popularity.

### Family Therapy

The historical beginnings of current forms of family therapy are less clear than those of many other currently espoused therapies. Apparently, in the late 1940s and the early 1950s, several therapists in differing locations around this country and in Great Britain began to treat their adult clients within the context of the entire family, rather than treating the client individually. Some have suggested that this shift in focus can be traced back to the lack of success that professionals had had in treating schizophrenia as well as juvenile delinquency and other behavior difficulties in children by using traditional forms of psychotherapy (Guerin, 1976). Others believe that the reasons therapists began to use family-based interventions are not entirely clear, especially given the resulting professional isolation (Haley, 1971). In any case, such techniques were initially subjected to much criticism. However, these methods were later strengthened by family studies of schizophrenia such as Bateson's Stanford-based study of communication patterns in the early 1950s and Laing's later work in the late 1950s at the Tavistock London Clinic.

These early studies produced new concepts about the family, such as *homeostasis* and the *double bind*. *Homeostasis* refers to the existence of a steady state and a sense of balance within the family. According to this theory, a family seeks to preserve even a maladaptive, uncomfortable state if that state produces a sense of balance within the family. Furthermore, if change does occur in one part of the family, it is likely to cause a corresponding change in another part, as the family is motivated to maintain its balance. The concept of the *double bind* suggests that the family places the "sick" member or the "identified patient" of the family in a no-win situation by sending him or her mixed messages. For example, if the member is competent, she or he is seen as abandoning the helpful parent; if not, she or he is incompetent and a drain on the family. It is thought that the member placed in the double-bind situation is often sacrificed in order to maintain the homeostatic functioning of the family.

As can be seen in these examples, this early research was instrumental in altering thinking about the functioning of the family. Rather than continuing to treat individuals in the context of their families (also made up of separate individuals in separate roles), Bell and others began to treat the family as an intact system in which the sum of the family was viewed as greater than the group made up of the individual members (Taschman, 1975). More recently, investigators have also begun to consider the other systems in which individuals function (e.g., peer systems and school) and how these various systems interact with one another (Henggeler, 1982).

The early work on family therapy was conducted primarily with adult-identified patients, however. Early forms of family therapy directed toward children often began with treatment through the mother, with the child occasionally attending, too, in order to provide the therapist with an opportunity to observe the child–parent interaction. This approach gradually developed into "conjoint therapy," in which a parent and child or several other selected members of the family work together. Still, because traditional family therapy involves a complex interchange typically conducted through verbal exercises and examples, it may be inappropriate for very young children and is viewed as more appropriate for adolescent clients (Korchin, 1976). Although some attempts have been made to use play and other developmentally appropriate vehicles for child–family–therapist communication (e.g., Zillbach, Bergel, & Gass, 1972), these have remained outside the mainstream of most family therapy interventions.

This mainstream includes a variety of different approaches, some of which are more similar than others. In fact, there are even several different ways of classifying family therapists based on the similarities of their approaches, including one delineated by the Group for Advancement of Psychiatry, and others by theorists such as Foley, Guerin, and Beels and Ferber (Jones, 1980). We will use Beels and Ferber to very briefly characterize the divergent approaches in this rapidly developing area.

Beels and Ferber (1973) suggested three major types of family therapists. They differ in the degree to which they believe that the therapist should actively direct the session, rather than following the direction of the family, and the degree to which internal processes, as opposed to external power, should be the focus of intervention. Beels and Ferber labeled the first group *conductors*. These individuals believe that the therapist should lead the discussion in the directions where it will be most therapeutic for the family and should assume responsibility for the direction of the sessions. Theorists such as N. Ackerman, J. Alexander, M. Bowen, S. Minuchin, and V. Satir espouse this approach. Next, Beels and Ferber described *reactor analysts*. These individuals believe that the family should determine the direction of therapy sessions and that the therapist's primary function is to react to the material presented by the family. The important material, as viewed by this group, is not the content of the sessions per se, but the internal functioning of the family members. This conceptualization characterizes therapists such as J. Framo, H. Searles, C. Whittaker, and L. Wynne. Finally, the third group is identified by Beels and Ferber as *reactor purists*. These therapists also allow the family to determine the direction of the sessions, and in addition, they explicitly focus on the balance of power within the family, attempting to identify the degree to which the family members adaptively or coercively influence one another. This conceptualization is typified by J. Haley, O. Jackson, and G. Zuk.

Family therapy is a good example of a method of intervention that was largely nonexistent during the first half of this century and that has rapidly proliferated only since the mid-1960s. As is frequently true of clinical techniques that develop to fill a therapeutic need, research on the efficacy of these methods has lagged far behind conceptualizations and practice. In the 1950s, only 60 articles were published on family therapy. During the 1960s, this number increased to 250. Few of these, however, contained empirical research (Olson, 1970). Wells, Dilkes, and Trivelli (1972) found only 18 studies that offered outcome data, and 15 of these were considered methodologically inadequate. Although additional research support has accumulated since the mid-1970s, family therapy remains an intervention much in need of experimental investigation. This is also true of intervention methods that have viewed the community rather than family as the relevant target for intervention, as is seen in the next section.

## Community-Based Diversion Programs

No other area of intervention for children and youth has generated more controversy than community-based treatments for juvenile offenders. Some, like Orlando and Black (1975), have suggested that treatments that originate in the courts are ineffective or even harmful: "It would probably be better for all concerned if young delinquents were not detected, apprehended, or institutionalized. Many of them get worse in our care" (p. 370). Others have claimed that there is evidence that interventions can be effective if individual differences are recognized, if enough treatment is available, and if interdisciplinary intervention is the rule (Gendreau & Ross, 1979).

The immediate history of the area is fraught with challenges to community-based approaches. One of the best known and earliest interventions for delinquency was the Cambridge–Sommerville Youth Study begun in 1935 (McCord, 1982). A control group of boys 5–11 years old, matched for age, socioeconomic status, and possibility of delinquency, received no treatment. The boys in the experimental group were each assigned a counselor, who was to develop a special relationship with each boy, taking trips, arranging for medical or dental care, and coordinating attendance at summer camps and church. There were a number of procedural problems with the treatment application, including maintaining the one-to-one counselor–child ratio. A decade later, only 75 of the original 325 boys in the experimental group had maintained counselor contact. Disappointingly, a 10-year follow-up showed no effects for the program (McCord, McCord, & Zola, 1959), and what was even more devastating, a 30-year follow-up showed that the experimental group had had more negative outcomes than the control group in terms of criminal convictions, major psychopathology, and alcoholism (McCord, 1982). The reasons for these negative effects have never been completely elucidated, but with such findings, the reasons for the controversy surrounding community-based treatments for delinquency are clear.

Like family therapy, interventions with this population have been based more on common sense than on an empirical research. Lipton, Martinson, and Wilks (1975) reviewed 231 treatment studies published between 1945 and 1967. Only 138 used a measure of recidivism to crime as an outcome criterion, and only 65 showed even minimal methodological strength. Fewer than half indicated positive results. Yet, the field has continued to expand; partly, at least, because of the continued increase in juvenile crime, as well as increased governmental and societal concern about this issue.

The model set by the Cambridge–Sommerville program of establishing a one-to-one relationship with the troubled child was repeated in other earlier programs and continued through the late 1960s and early 1970s. Many of these programs attempted to engineer supportive contacts for the child and to alter basic resources within the community (e.g., the Chicago project) or to focus on the child's own skills and abilities, such as communications and problem solving (e.g., Project CREST in Florida). However, individual counseling still provided the foundation for these programs.

The Juvenile Justice and Delinquency Prevention Act of 1974 marked a turning point for treatment in this area. Specific funding was made available for the deinstitutionalization of status offenders (DSO; Kobrin & Klein, 1983) and to promote the diversion of juvenile offenders from the juvenile justice system. The latter aim was based on the notion that status offenders should be treated differently from delinquent offenders. Status offenders are youths whose only misdeed involves a behavior that would not be a problem in an adult (e.g., running away, being "uncontrollable," or smoking cigarettes). These individuals are slightly more often female than male (perhaps because parents tolerate more "wild" behavior in males), more often 15–16 years old (as opposed to younger or older), and are most often charged with being incorrigible or with running away. Once charged, they have a one-in-six chance of being charged again, higher if they are from single-parent families (Hellum & Corry, 1983). For such individuals, placement in community-based services without the stigma of a court hearing was the goal. The 12 prototype programs funded by the federal government to demonstrate such treatment were summarized by Kobrin and Klein (1983).

The other major goal of the Juvenile and Delinquency Prevention Act was to promote the "diversion" of juvenile offenders. Like the DSO interventions, the goal here was to prevent the stigma of a juvenile record, to prevent association with other delinquents, and to maintain close community ties. Although a large number of such programs have been evaluated, there has been a surprising lack of specificity in the research reports regarding the actual services provided. For the most part, it appears that services are tailored to the individual case and include such components as academic tutoring, vocational counseling, and training (e.g., Quay & Love, 1977; Shore & Massimo, 1964). The use of special one-to-one relationships and counseling also appears common (e.g., O'Donnell, Lydgate, & Fo, 1979).

The most effective interventions established thus far have used combinations of behavioral techniques and family therapy (e.g., Alexander & Parsons, 1973; Wade, Morton, Lind, & Ferris, 1977). These methods have demonstrated an enduring impact on positive behaviors such as school achievement and negative behaviors such as recidivism to crime. Further, behaviorally based residen-

tial centers whose staffs operate as a teaching "family" have shown very promising results (Phillips, Phillips, Fixsen, & Wolf, 1973). Thus, other more recently
validated methods are being increasingly used across populations.

The rapid growth of behavioral and cognitive behavioral techniques in recent years and the rapidly accruing evidence of their effectiveness with children
exceeds those of any other therapeutic method. Thus, we conclude this section
with a discussion of the development of behavior modification and behavior
therapy in children.

## Behavioral Techniques

### Behavior Modification

As was noted earlier, in the beginning of the behavioral movement there
were successful demonstration projects concerning the treatment of child psychopathology. However, from Watson's time to the formative period under B. F.
Skinner, behaviorism remained largely the province of the laboratory. It was not
that behaviorists doubted the efficacy or applicability of behavioral techniques to
children. Far from it. Rather, behaviorists were certain that the rules they investigated applied to any species. Furthermore, behaviorists felt that research with
children required the control of many extraneous variables, whereas research
with rats or pigeons would allow the same conclusions with less effort. The early
scientific investigation of behavior relied on subjects whose behavioral history
and ongoing level of deprivation and reward could be tightly controlled. Thus,
animal subjects were preferred, even for research on normally child-based tasks,
such as the acquisition of arithmetic skills (e.g., Ferster & Hammer, 1966).

With movements such as the founding of the *Journal of Applied Behavior
Analysis* in the late 1960s, however, behaviorism came increasingly to be used as
the treatment of choice with children. Early studies established the credibility of
behavioral methods by demonstrating success with severe problems that traditional interventions had failed to solve. These included studies that illustrated
the ability of behavioral techniques to decrease life-threatening ruminative
vomiting in an infant (Lang & Melamed, 1969) and self-injurious behavior in
psychotic children (Lovaas, Young, & Newsom, 1978). Behavioral techniques
also showed a successful impact on language training in psychotic and severely
mentally retarded children (Lovaas, Berberich, Perloff, & Schaeffer, 1966; Miller
& Yoder, 1972) and on increasing parent–child interaction in autistic children
(Kozloff, 1973).

Behavior modification also demonstrated its efficacy in influencing less serious but often intractable problems in normal populations of children, reducing
thumb sucking (Knight & McKenzie, 1974), enuresis (Kimmel & Kimmel, 1970;
Mowrer & Mowrer, 1938), and excessive bedtime crying (Williams, 1959). Suggestions for regular parenting techniques were eventually formulated from this
basis, and they dealt with the entire range of early behavioral disturbances.

One aspect of the behavioral tradition that contributes to our somewhat
arbitrary distinction between behavior modification and behavior therapy was
the earlier limiting of appropriate targets of intervention to explicit external
events. As the field grew, however, some behaviorists increased their use of

cognitive techniques, such as self-instruction, and began to focus on problems involving self-control or self-regulation. This attention to internal events became recognized by many as a valuable feature of behavioral interventions for children.

*Behavior Therapy*

As noted earlier, the Soviet psychologists Vygotsky and Luria described the process in which physical intervention and verbal instruction from others lead to the child's own overt self-instructional speech and eventually to covert self-instruction. In this way, techniques of external control can be used to facilitate internal control in children. Behavioral psychologists (e.g., Meichenbaum & Goodman, 1971) demonstrated that this sequence of events could be accelerated and trained through modeling and reinforcement, and that it could be successfully applied to children who lacked impulse control. Such techniques are now used frequently with a variety of clinical problems, such as hyperactivity, learning problems, social withdrawal, and aggression (Gelfand & Hartman, 1984).

Currently, behavioral techniques are used to treat the entire range of childhood disturbances (Kazdin & Bornstein, 1985). Just to give a sample of this range, children's gender-appropriate behavior and concept of their own gender have been improved through modeling and reinforcement (Rekers, 1981); children's inadequate social skills have been improved through the use of popular peers as models and agents of reinforcement (Axelrod, Hall, & Maxwell, 1972); and children's problem eating and exercise habits have been influenced by contracting, self-monitoring, and reward (Epstein, Wing, Koeske, Andrasik, & Ossip, 1981). Broad-spectrum programs improve general skills such as a child's ability to problem-solve (Kendall & Zupan, 1981). Also, as will be seen in our final section, behavioral treatments form the basis for most preventive endeavors with children.

## INTERLOCKING FUTURE TRENDS

It seems appropriate to give some consideration to the future of the treatment of child psychopathology, if only to demonstrate that several recurrent themes are currently receiving the recognition that they have always deserved, whereas other unfortunate trends continue. For example, children are now protected from physical abuse, from child labor, and from physically harmful substances such as lead, alcohol, and tobacco, in explicit recognition of their vulnerable developmental state. Parents are legally obligated to provide for the child's physical welfare, although there are still alarmingly high rates of the physical and sexual abuse of children in the United States (Broadhurst, Edmunds, & MacDicken, 1979), and children with serious illnesses like AIDS are still abandoned by their parents and ostracized by others (Goodman, 1986). Special laws (e.g., Public Law 94-142) have also been passed to ensure that children will receive the best and most appropriate educational and mental health interventions.

However, the historical emphasis on adult as opposed to child psychopathology noted by Wenar (1982) continues. Children and adolescents currently represent nearly half the population in the United States, yet only one of every nine mental health dollars is spent on services for children (Hobbs, 1982). If this situation is to improve in the future, attempts must be made to increase political lobbying efforts on behalf of children. The belief that children will "grow out" of problems without interventions, that children are unusually resilient, and that child dysfunctions do not have serious long-term consequences all currently militate against such efforts, as does children's economic dependence on adults.

One factor that may turn the tide of public opinion is the increasing recognition of the importance of developmental factors in understanding and treating childhood psychopathology (Gelfand & Peterson, 1985). The recent emergence of a separate field calling itself *developmental psychopathology* demonstrates this trend (Cicchetti, 1984). As it becomes clearer that childhood is the essential time period for the formation of social and language skills (Curtiss, 1977), and that serious behavior disorders are generally long-lasting and rarely remit spontaneously with increasing age (Gelfand *et al.*, 1982), funding for mental health services for children may indeed improve.

The gap between clinical child psychology and other disciplines, particularly developmental psychology, has been noted throughout this chapter as an unfortunate historical trend. Now, there is increasing recognition of the importance of joining relevant professionals together to maximize the possibility of solving the most intractable problems in child psychopathology.

There is also an increasing emphasis on the utility of considering multisystem approaches in which biological, affective, cognitive, familial, and social factors are all considered. With such complexity has come an appreciation of multidisciplinary teams, with members from within psychology, including clinical, developmental, educational, social, and experimental psychology, and members from disparate other fields, such as medicine; speech and language; occupational, physical, and recreational therapy; law; anthropology; and social work. These trends, because they are likely to meet with success, should continue and intensify in the future.

The other major impact of the increased recognition of the importance of developmental factors has been a renewed appreciation of prevention. The concept of prevention has reoccurred historically since ancient times, first in the societal practice of eliminating children who were or who were likely to become dysfunctional, and later as a prominent part of the mental hygiene movement. Prevention is now an explicit or at least implicit focus of most modern therapies for children in the form of relapse prevention. Yet, it is noteworthy that the primary prevention of childhood disorders has not received strong support until recently. It is currently recognized that because the prevention of disorders must occur before the onset of the disorder, it is most logical to intervene in childhood before reading problems, social skill deficits, eating disorders, substance abuse, or depression have even had a chance to begin (Roberts & Peterson, 1984). Children are also an ideal population for milestone prevention; because of compulsory education, they are frequently brought together to remediate deficits, they go through clear developmental transitions, and they show good sensitivity to preventive interventions.

Prevention programs have been successfully used with a very wide range of problems, including elevating IQ in high-risk premature infants through psychosocial stimulation, preventing school problems in preschoolers through early remedial education, preventing negative reactions to life stresses such as school transition or divorce, preventing substance abuse and injury during automobile accidents, and increasing the ability to cope with and cooperate in stressful medical situations (Roberts & Peterson, 1984). Future research is likely to continue to focus on preventive interventions where possible as an economically and emotionally preferable alternative to intervening in cases of existing psychopathology.

## SUMMARY

This chapter has described the history of the treatment of child psychopathology. For most of recorded history, both normal and atypical children have been the victims of murder and abuse as a result of the political and economic needs of society. Those children who were maladjusted in any way were likely to fare the worst from the typically brutal societal practices that characterized earlier time periods. For the most part, the treatment of psychopathology in adults before the last two centuries involved crude physical remedies such as trephining, bleeding, fasting, and purging, but these appear to have been infrequently applied to children. The 17th and 18th centuries brought the beginnings of scientific curiosity about the child, a focus on the child's need to learn, and the protection of the unwanted child's life through the founding of almshouses and orphanages. More often than not, however, the child was regarded as an inferior, second-class adult, and the status of disturbed children was even worse.

The turn of the century brought many changes in regard to children. Children began to have legal rights, such as the right not to be removed from their home solely on the basis of poverty and the right not to be physically abused. The availability of treatments designed specifically for educational and emotional dysfunction increased rapidly over the first three decades of this century. The accompanying research interest in the child began to allow for the possibility that treatments used for child psychopathology could be empirically validated.

A variety of therapeutic modalities are currently used to treat child psychopathology. These include, but are not limited to, those methods discussed here: dynamic therapy, family therapy, diversion programs, and behavioral treatments. As this chapter has illustrated, the methods, research bases, and problems targeted vary greatly across these treatments, and additional variation in treatment methodology is added every year.

Because the modern treatment of child psychopathology has such a brief history, future trends in this area are somewhat uncertain. Much will depend on improvements in funding for mental health services, continued support for multisystem and multidisciplinary approaches, and the amount of vision and energy that is devoted to remediating and preventing child psychopathology. We can make predictions only by examining past and current practices. The historical events and current trends examined in this chapter suggest that, after a long time in the shadows, the treatment of psychopathology in children is finally approaching the light.

REFERENCES

LIZETTE PETERSON AND
DANIEL J. BURBACH

Abbott, N. C., Hansen, P., & Lewis, K. (1970). Dress rehearsal for the hospital. *American Journal of Nursing, 70*, 23–60.

Abramson, R. M., Hoffman, L. & Johns, C. A. (1979). Play group psychotherapy for early latency-age children on an inpatient psychiatric unit. *International Journal of Group Psychotherapy, 29*, 383–392.

Achenbach, T. M. (1982). *Developmental psychotherapy* (2nd ed.). New York: Wiley.

Alexander, J. J., & Parsons, B. V. (1973). Short-term intervention with delinquent families: Impact on family process and recidivism. *Journal of Abnormal Psychology, 81*, 219–225.

Alexandris, A., & Lundell, F. W. (1968). Effect of thioridazine, amphetamine, and placebo on the hyperkinetic syndrome and cognitive area in mentally deficient children. *Canadian Medical Association Journal, 98*, 92–96.

Aries, P. (1962). *Centuries of childhood* (R. Baldick, trans.). New York: Knopf.

Axelrod, S., Hall, R. V., & Maxwell, A. (1972). Use of peer attention to increase study behavior. *Behavior Therapy, 3*, 349–351.

Axline, V. (1976). Play therapy procedures and results. In C. Schaefer (Ed.), *The therapeutic use of child's play* (pp. 209–218). New York: Jason Aronson.

Bair, H. V., & Herold, W. (1955). Efficacy of chlorpromazine in hyperactive mentally retarded children. *Archives of Neurology and Psychiatry, 74*, 363.

Beels, C., & Ferber, A. (1973). What family therapists do. In A. Ferber, M. Mendelsohn. & A. Napier (Eds.), *The book of family therapy* (pp. 168–232). New York: Houghton Mifflin.

Bender, L., & Nichtern. S. (1956). Chemotherapy in child psychiatry. *New York State Journal of Medicine, 56*, 2791–2796.

Binet, A., & Simon, T. (1905). Méthodes nouvelles pour 6 diagnostic du niveau intellectual chez les infants normaux et anormaux, d'hospice et d'école primaire. *L'Anée Psychologique, 11*, 245–263.

Bornstein, B. (1949). Analysis of a phobic child. *Psychoanalytic Study of the Child, 3*, 181–226.

Bradley, C. (1937). The behavior of children receiving Benzedrine. *American Journal of Psychiatry, 94*, 577–585.

Bradley, C. (1950). Benzedrine and Dexedrine in the treatment of children's behavior disorders. *Pediatrics, 5*, 24–37.

Breger, E. (1961, October). Meprobamate in the management of enuresis. *Journal of Pediatrics*, 571–576.

Broadhurst, D. D., Edmunds, M., & MacDicken, R. A. (1979). *Early childhood programs and the prevention and treatment of child abuse and neglect.* National Center on Child Abuse and Neglect, Children's Bureau. (DHEW Publication No. DADS 79-20198). Washington, DC: U.S. Government Printing Office.

Brody, S. (1964). Aims and methods in child psychotherapy. *Journal of the American Academy of Child Psychiatry, 3*, 385–412.

Brown, R. H., Rox, E. S., & Hubbard, E. L. (1974). Medical and legal aspects of the battered child syndrome. *Chicago-Kent Law Review, 50*, 45–84.

Cameron, H. (1918). *The nervous child.* London: Oxford University Press.

Cicchetti, D. (1984). The emergence of developmental psychopathology. *Child Development, 55*, 1–7.

Conners, C. K., Eisenberg, L., & Barcai, A. (1967). Effect of dextroamphetamine on children. *Archives of General Psychiatry, 17*, 478–485.

Curtiss, S. (1977). *Genie: A psycholinguistic study of a modern day "wild child."* New York: Academic Press.

Cutts, K. K., & Jasper, H. H. (1939). Effect of benzedrine sulfate and phenobarbital on behavior problem children with abnormal electroencephalograms. *Archives of Neurology and Psychiatry, 41*, 1138–1145.

deMause, L. (1974). The evolution of childhood. In L. deMause (Ed.), *The history of childhood* (pp. 1–74). New York: Harper & Row.

Despert, J. L. (1965). *The emotionally disturbed child: Then and now.* New York: Brunner.

Duffy, J. C. (1974). *Child psychiatry: Medical outline series.* Flushing, NY: Medical Examination Publishing Company.

Duffy, J. C. (1976). "Special article" in honor of the bicentennial year, 1776–1976. *Child Psychiatry and Human Development, 6*, 189–197.

Dunn, P. P. (1974). "That enemy is the baby": Childhood in imperial Russia. In L. deMause (Ed.), *The history of childhood* (pp. 383–406). New York: Harper & Row.

Epstein, L. H., Wing, R. R., Koeske, R., Andrasik, F., & Ossip, D. J. (1981). Child and parent weight loss programs. *Journal of Consulting and Clinical Psychology, 49*, 674–685.

Ferster, C. B., & Hammer, C. E. (1966). Synthesizing the components of arithmetic behavior. In W. K. Honig (Ed.), *Operant behavior: Areas of research and application* (pp. 634–676). New York: Appleton-Century-Crofts.

Fish, B., & Shapiro, T. (1965). A typology of children's psychiatric disorders: 1. Its application to a controlled evaluation of treatment. *Journal of the American Academy of Child Psychiatry, 4*, 32–52.

Freedman, A. M. (1958). Drug therapy in behavior disorders. *Pediatric Clinics of North America, 5*, 573–594.

Freud, A. (1968). Indications and contraindications for child analysis. *Psychoanalytic Study of the Child, 23*, 37–46.

Freud, S. (1905). Three essays on the theory of sexuality. In J. Strachey (Ed.), *Standard edition of the complete psychological works of Sigmund Freud*, London: Hogarth Press.

Freud, S. (1950). *Collected papers*, (Vol. 3). London: Hogarth Press.

Gatski, R. L. (1955). Chlorpromazine in the treatment of emotionally maladjusted children. *Journal of the American Medical Association, 157*, 1298–1300.

Gelfand, D. M., & Hartman, D. P. (1984). *Child behavior analysis and therapy* (2nd ed.). New York: Pergamon Press.

Gelfand, D. M., & Peterson, L. (1985). *Child development and psychopathology*. Beverly Hills, CA: Sage.

Gelfand, D. M., Jenson, W. R., & Drew, C. J. (1982). *Understanding children's behavior disorders*. New York: Holt, Rinehart, & Winston.

Gendreau, P., & Ross, R. R. (Eds.). (1979). *Effective correctional treatment*. Toronto: Butterworths.

Gilbert, J. A. (1894). Research on the mental and physical development of school children. *Studies of Yale Psychological Laboratory, 2*, 40–50.

Goodenough, F. L. (1949). *Mental testing*. New York: Holt, Rinehart, & Winston.

Goodman, E. (1986). Aids: Beneath the sign of the cross. *Life, 9*(2), 27.

Goodsell, W. (1934). *A history of marriage and the family*. New York: Macmillan.

Guerin, P. J. (1976). Family therapy: The first twenty-five years. In P. J. Guerin (Ed.), *Family therapy: Theory and practice* (pp. 2–22). New York: Gardner Press.

Haley, J. (1971). *Changing families*. New York: Grune & Stratton.

Hellum, F. R., & Corry, E. M. (1983). Characteristics of status offenders. In S. Kobrin & M. W. Klein (Eds.), *Community treatment of juvenile offenders: The DSO experiments* (pp. 58–83). Beverly Hills, CA: Sage.

Henggeler, S. W. (1982). The family-ecological systems theory. In S. W. Henggeler (Ed.), *Delinquency and adolescent psychopathology: A family-ecological systems approach* (pp. 1–10). Littleton, MA: John Wright.

Hetznecker, W., & Forman, M. A. (1971). Community child psychiatry: Evolution and direction. *American Journal of Orthopsychiatry, 41*, 350–370.

Hobbs, N. (1982). *The troubling child*. San Francisco: Jossey-Bass.

Holmes, D. L., & Morrison, F. J. (1979). *The child: An introduction to developmental psychology*. Monterey, CA: Brooks/Cole.

Hunter, R., & Macalpine, I. (1963). *Three hundred years of psychiatry*. New York: Oxford University Press.

Hutchinson, R. (1904). *Lectures on diseases of children*. London: Arnold.

Illick, J. E. (1974) Childrearing in 17th century England and America. In L. deMause (Ed.), *The history of childhood* (pp. 303–350). New York: Harper & Row.

Ireland, W. W. (1898). *The mental affections of children*. Philadelphia: Blackiston.

Jones, S. L. (1980). *Family therapy: A comparison of approaches*. Bowie, MD: Prentice-Hall.

Joint Commission on Mental Illness and Health (1961) Action for mental health. New York: Basic Books.

Kanner, L. (1957). *Child psychiatry*. Springfield, IL: Thomas. (Originally published, 1935.)

Kanner, L. (1973). Historical perspective on developmental deviations. *Journal of Autism and Childhood Schizophrenia, 3*, 187–198.

Katz, S. N., Schroeder, W. A., & Sidman, L. R. (1973). Emancipating our children—Coming of legal age in America. *Family Law Quarterly, 7*, 211–241.

Kazdin, A. E., & Bornstein, P. (Eds.). (1985). *Handbook of clinical behavior therapy with children*. New York: Dorsey.

Kendall, P. C., & Zupan, B. A. (1981). Individual versus group application of cognitive behavioral self-control procedures with children. *Behavior Therapy, 12*, 344–359.

Kenworthy, M. (1930). Social maladjustments in the intellectually normal. *Mental Hygiene, 14*, 837–852.

Kessen, W. (1965). *The child*. New York: Wiley.

Kideneigh, J. (1965). History of American social work. In *Encyclopedia of Social Work* (pp. 3–18). New York: National Association of Social Workers.

Kimmel, H. D., & Kimmel, E. (1970). An instrumental conditioning method for the treatment of enuresis. *Journal of Behavior Therapy and Experimental Psychiatry, 1*, 121–122.

Knight, M. F., & McKenzie, H. S. (1974). Elimination of bedtime thumbsucking in the home setting through contingent reading. *Journal of Applied Behavior Analysis, 7*, 33–38.

Kobrin, S., & Klein, M. W. (1983). *Community treatment of juvenile offenders: The DSO experiments*. Beverly Hills, CA: Sage.

Korchin, S. J. (1976). *Modern clinical psychology*. New York: Basic Books.

Kozloff, M. (1973). *Reaching the autistic child*. Champaign, IL: Research Press.

Kroll, J. (1973). A reappraisal of psychiatry in the Middle Ages. *Archives of General Psychiatry, 29*, 276–283.

Lamb, M. E. (1981). Fathers and child development: An integrative overview. In M. E. Lamb (Ed.), *The role of the father in child development* (2nd ed., pp. 1–70). New York: Wiley.

Lang, P. J., & Melamed, B. G. (1969). Avoidance conditioning therapy of an infant with chronic ruminative vomiting: Case report. *Journal of Abnormal Psychology, 74*, 1–8.

Lipton, D., Martinson, R., & Wilks, J. (1975). *The effectiveness of correctional treatment*. New York: Praeger.

Litchfield, H. R. (1957). Clinical evaluation of meprobamate in disturbed and prepsychotic children. *Annals of the New York Academy of Sciences, 67*, 828–832.

Lovaas, O. I., Berberich, J. P., Perloff, B. F., & Schaeffer, B. (1966). Acquisition of imitative speech by schizophrenic children. *Science, 151*, 705–707.

Lovaas, O. I., Young, D. B., & Newsom, C. D. (1978). Childhood psychosis: Behavior treatment. *Treatment of mental disorders in childhood and adolescence* (pp. 121–188). Englewood Cliffs, NJ: Prentice-Hall.

Lucas, A. P., Lockett, H. J., & Grimm, F. (1965). Amitriptyline in childhood depression. *Diseases of the Nervous System, 28*, 105–113.

McCord, J. (1982). The Cambridge-Sommerville Youth study: A sobering lesson on treatment, prevention, and evaluation. In A. J. McSweeny, W. J. Fremouw, & R. P. Hawkins (Eds.), *Practice program evaluation for youth treatment* (pp. 11–23). Springfield, IL: Thomas.

McCord, W., McCord, J., & Zola, I. K. (1959). *Origins of crime*. New York: Columbia University Press.

McLaughlin, M. M. (1974). Survivors and surrogates: Children and parents from the ninth to the thirteenth centuries. In L. deMause (Ed.), *The history of childhood* (pp. 101–182). New York: Harper & Row.

MacLean, R. E. G. (1960). Imipramine hydrochloride (Tofranil) and enuresis. *American Journal of Psychiatry, 117*, 551.

Marvick, E. W. (1974). Nature versus nurture: Patterns and trends in seventeenth-century French child-rearing. In L. deMause (Ed.), *The history of childhood* (pp. 259–302). New York: Harper & Row.

Mattson, R. H., & Calverlez, J. R. (1968). Dextroamphetamine sulfate induced dyskinesias. *Journal of the American Medical Association, 205*, 400–402.

Maudsley, H. (1867). *Physiology and pathology of the mind*. London: Oxford University Press.

Meichenbaum, D., & Goodman, J. (1971). Training impulsive children to talk to themselves: A means of developing self-control. *Journal of Abnormal Psychology, 77*, 115–126.

Meyers, J. C. (1985). Federal efforts to improve mental health services for children: Breaking a cycle of failure. *Journal of Clinical Child Psychology, 14*, 182–187.

Miller, J., & Yoder, D. (1972). A syntax teaching program. In J. E. McLean, D. E. Yoder, & R. L. Schiefelbusch (Eds.), *Language intervention with the retarded: Developing strategies* (pp. 191–211). Baltimore: University Park Press.

Molitch, M., & Sullivan, J. P. (1937). The effects of benzedrine sulfate on children taking the new Stanford Achievement Test. *American Journal of Orthopsychiatry, 7*, 519–522.

Mowrer, O. H., & Mowrer, W. A. (1938). Enuresis: A method for its study and treatment. *American Journal of Orthopsychiatry, 8,* 436–447.

Munsterberg, H. (1891). Zur individual psychologie. *Centralblatt für Nervenheilkunde und Psychiatrie,* 14.

Nathan, P. E., & Harris, S. L. (1975). *Psychopathology and society.* New York: McGraw-Hill.

Neugebauer, R. (1979). Medieval and early modern theories of mental illness. *Archives of General Psychiatry, 36,* 477–483.

Ney, P. G. (1967). Psychosis in a child associated with amphetamine administration. *Canadian Medical Association Journal, 97,* 1026–1029.

O'Donnell, C. R., Lydgate, T., & Fo, W. S. O. (1979). The buddy system: Review and follow-up. *Child Behavior Therapy, 1,* 161–169.

Olson, D. H. (1970). Marriage and family therapy: Integrative review and critique. *Journal of Marriage and the Family, 32,* 501–538.

Orlando, F. A., & Black, J. P. (1975). The juvenile court. In N. Hobbs (Ed.), *Issues in the classification of children* (pp. 166–198). San Francisco: Jossey-Bass.

Phaire, T. (1955). *The boke of chyldren.* London: Livingston. (Originally published 1545.)

Phillips, E. L., Phillips, E. A., Fixsen, D. L., & Wolf, M. M. (1973). Achievement place: Behavior shaping works for delinquents. *Psychology Today Magazine, 6,* 75–79.

Quay, H. C., & Love, C. T. (1977). The effect of a juvenile diversion program on rearrests. *Criminal Justice and Behavior, 4,* 377–396.

Rapoport, J. (1965). Childhood behavior and learning problems treated with imipramine. *International Journal of Neuropsychiatry, 1,* 635–642.

Rapoport, J. L., & Kruesi, M. J. P. (1985). Organic therapies. In H. I. Kaplan & B. J. Sadock (Eds.), *Comprehensive textbook of psychiatry* (Vol. 4, pp. 1793–1798). Baltimore: Williams & Wilkins.

Rekers, G. A. (1981). Psychosexual and gender problems. In E. J. Mash & L. G. Terdal (Eds.), *Behavioral assessment of childhood disorders* (pp. 483–528). New York: Guildford Press.

Rie, H. E. (1971). *Perspectives in child psychopathology.* Chicago: Aldine-Atherton.

Roberts, M. C., & Peterson, L. (1984). *Prevention of problems in childhood: Psychological research and applications.* New York: Wiley-Interscience.

Rogers, C. R. (1951). *Client-centered therapy: Its current practice, implications, and theory.* Boston: Houghton Mifflin.

Senn, M. J. E. (1975). Insights on the child development movement in the United States. *Monographs of the Society for Research in Child Development, 40*(3–4, Serial No. 161).

Shakow, D. (1968). The development of orthopsychiatry: The contributions of Levy, Menninger, and Stevenson. *American Journal of Orthopsychiatry, 38,* 804–809.

Shore, M. F., & Massimo, J. L. (1964). Job-focused treatment for anti-social youth. *Children, 11,* 143–147.

Stevenson, G., & Smith, G. (1934). *Child guidance clinics: A quarter of a century of development.* New York: Commonwealth Fund.

Stone, L. A. (1979). Residential treatment. In J. D. Noshpitz (Ed.), *Basic handbook of child psychiatry,* (Vol. 3, pp. 231–262). New York: Basic Books.

Taschman, H. A. (1975). Developments and innovations in family therapy in a changing society. In V. Satir, J. Stachowiak, & H. A. Taschman (Eds.), *Helping families to change* (pp. 127–162). New York: Aronson.

Ucer, E., & Kreger, K. C. (1969). A double-blind study comparing haloperidol and thioridazine in emotionally disturbed, mentally retarded children. *Current Therapy Research, 11,* 278–283.

Wade, T. C., Morton, T. L., Lind, J. E., & Ferris, N. R. (1977). A family crisis intervention approach to diversion from the juvenile justice system. *Juvenile Justice Journal, 28*(3), 43–51.

Watson, J. B. (1913). Psychology as a behaviorist sees it. *Psychological Review, 20,* 158–177.

Wells, R. A., Dilkes, T., & Trivelli, N. (1972). The results of family therapy: A critical review of the literature. *Family Process, 7,* 189–207.

Wenar, C. (1982). *Psychopathology from infancy through adolescence.* New York: Random House.

Werry, J. S. (1982). An overview of pediatric psychopharmacology. *Journal of the American Academy of Child Psychiatry, 21,* 3–9.

Wiener, J. M., & Jaffe, S. (1977). History of drug therapy in childhood and adolescent psychiatric disorders. In J. M. Wiener (Ed.), *Psychopharmacology in childhood and adolescence* (pp. 9–40). New York: Basic Books.

Williams, C. D. (1959). The elimination of tantrum behavior by extinction procedures. *Journal of Abnormal and Social Psychology, 59,* 269.

Zilboorg, G. A. (1941). *A history of medical psychology.* New York: Norton.

Zillbach, J. J., Bergel, E., & Gass, C. (1972). The role of the young child in family therapy. In C. J. Sager & H. S. Kaplan (Eds.), *Progress in group and family therapy* (pp. 385–399). New York: Brunner/Mazel.

Zimmerman, F. T., & Burgemeister, B. B. (1958). Action of methyl-phenidate (Ritalin) and reserpine in behavior disorders in children and adults. *American Journal of Psychiatry, 115,* 323–328.

Zivin, G. (1979). Removing common confusions about egocentric speech, private speech, and self-regulation. In G. Zivin (Ed.), *The development of self-regulation through private speech* (pp. 13–50). New York: Wiley

# 2  *Diagnostic Classification Systems*

CYNTHIA L. FRAME,
MARKHAM S. GIBLIN, AND GEORGE R. JOHNSTONE

It has not been until within the past several decades that significant advances have been made in the development of diagnostic classification systems for childhood psychopathology. Several important factors throughout history seem to have contributed to the failure to develop any such system (see Frame & Matson, 1987; Nathan & Harris, 1983), the most important factor possibly being the relatively insignificant attention paid to the study of psychopathology in general until the late 1800s. Because there was little interest in psychopathology in general, there was no perceived need for diagnosis or classification. Second, it was not truly until the turn of this century that children were viewed as being different from adults. Therfore, little attention was given to issues pertaining to children or their development. A third factor that diverted attention away from childhood psychopathology involved the work of Alfred Binet. He and his associates, using extensive normative and developmental data, developed a test that was very successful in assessing intellectual functioning. The utility and popularity of their test turned attention toward intellectual assessment and away from other psychological problems of children. Finally, a movement of American psychiatrists led by Adolf Meyer in the first half of this century stressed the unimportance of diagnostic labels and classification systems and stated that, instead of assigning meaningless labels, one should focus on each individual's symptoms and ways of responding to the environment. Needless to say, the influence of this movement further hindered the development of classification systems.

## HISTORICAL PERSPECTIVES

Although advances in the assessment of childhood psychopathology have been lacking until recently, the assessment of adult psychopathology was also neglected until the second half of the nineteenth century. Because the assessment of childhood psychopathology has obviously been directly influenced by

CYNTHIA L. FRAME, MARK S. GIBLIN, AND GEORGE R. JOHNSTONE • Department of Psychology, University of Georgia, Athens, Georgia 30601.

advances in the study of adult psychopathology, it is worthwhile to mention a few of these now.

During the late 1800s, it was discovered that certain organic factors and infections sometimes caused mental symptoms such as delusions, hallucinations, mood swings, and memory loss. These findings led to the development of a medical model of mental disorders and therefore, to a classification system for such disorders. At about the same time, the psychiatrist Emil Kraepelin attempted to identify psychopathological conditions in his patients by the systematic documentation of various conditions. Noting the etiology, the symptomatology, the course, and the outcome of each of his patients' conditions, Kraepelin contributed greatly to the study of classification by emphasizing the importance of the careful description of each of these factors.

Still lacking at the time, however, were adequate theories of abnormal behavior. Although proposing two very different orientations, Sigmund Freud and John B. Watson were two of the first individuals to provide such theoretical frameworks. Freud emphasized symptomatic behavior as being indicative of an underlying psychological conflict, whereas Watson and his fellow learning theorists proposed that abnormal behaviors could be learned by operant or classical conditioning. Nonetheless, from that time on, scientists had several theoretical propositions to draw from in their study of psychopathology.

Freud made another significant contribution to the study of childhood psychopathology by describing psychosexual stages of childhood and suggesting that various developmental delays characterized by specific symptoms may occur in the different stages of childhood. Thus, Freud proposed a theory that not only provided a foundation for theories of psychopathology, but also implied that children may have distinct psychopathological disorders and, as a result, special assessment needs.

In the United States, the study of children and their development was formally begun with the founding of child development institutes during the early 1900s. The Iowa Child Welfare Research Station, founded in 1916, set the precedent for future institutes by becoming a center for the study of the physiological and mental growth of children. Soon, other states founded similar institutes, which studied such areas as the social, physical, cognitive, intellectual, and behavioral development of children. The information generated by these institutes concerning normal child development permitted a better understanding of abnormal behavior at various ages of childhood.

Two individuals who made significant contributions to the child mental-health movement at the turn of the century were Lightner Witmer and William Healy. Witmer founded a clinic at the University of Pennsylvania dedicated solely to the assessment, treatment, and study of childhood disorders. Similarly, Healy founded the Institute for Juvenile Research in 1909 to learn about the causes and prevention of juvenile delinquency and to assess and treat delinquents. Largely because of these two men, awareness of the need for psychological services for children grew, so that by 1921, and continuing into the present time, the government has provided funding for the development and support of child guidance clinics across the country.

Finally, although the work of Alfred Binet on intellectual assessment may have hindered the study of childhood psychopathology as previously stated, his work also had several positive effects. First, it focused attention on children and issues pertaining to their intellectual development. Second, it produced a measure that could predict which children might need special assistance in school. Third, and probably most important, it set a precedent for future research on children both by using extensive normative and developmental data for prediction and by highlighting the importance of psychometric properties in assessment.

Today, significant advances in the assessment of childhood psychopathology are being made because of an increased interest in issues pertaining to childhood. Several fields, including learning theory, psychoanalysis, criminal justice, and child development, have enhanced the study of child psychopathology by developing special assessment and treatment techniques for children. The American Psychiatric Association's third edition of the *Diagnostic and Statistical Manual of Mental Disorders* (DSM-III, 1980) represents the culmination of an awareness of the advantages of psychiatric diagnosis and the need to make such classification reliable and valid. (This manual is discussed at length in a later section of this chapter.)

## THE MEANING AND PURPOSES OF DIAGNOSIS

Now that the history of childhood classification systems has been briefly reviewed, it is important to turn our attention to the meaning and purposes of diagnosis. As Mezzich and Mezzich (1987) noted, the term *diagnosis* has two meanings, both of which are essential to an understanding of the important role of diagnosis and classification in the study of psychopathology. First, *diagnosis* means "distinguishing." This definition underscores the necessity of accurately differentiating between various categories of disorders in order to successfully identify, and thus treat, different disorders. Second, the Greek *diagignoskein* means "to know thoroughly," or to provide a careful, comprehensive description of an individual's condition. By providing such descriptive information, diagnosis can reflect vast information concerning different aspects of an individual's disorder, most notably its etiology, the symptomatology, the prognosis, and the probable treatment response. In simple terms, a diagnosis is a label assigned to an individual by a clinician "so as to convey to himself and others as much as possible about etiology, the immediate manifestations, and the prognosis of the patient's condition" (Shepard, Brooke, Cooper, & Lin, 1968, p. 13).

Diagnostic systems in general are based on scientific classification schemes that involve the systematic description of observable data. By means of classification, diagnostic systems have been used in an attempt to organize the pertinent data into the concise categories that are best suited to describing the condition of an individual. In this sense, diagnosis can be viewed simply as the organization of an individual's symptoms into a known category that reflects the symptoms common to that individual's disorder. Thus, the utility of diagnosis can best be understood when these diagnostic categories are viewed as the focal point of thought: using the diagnosis, one can go back to the possible etiology and forward to prognosis and treatment.

Morey, Skinner and Blashfield (1986) discussed in detail five main purposes of psychiatric classification. The first is *communication*. Classification provides a nosology that serves as a basis for communication among the professionals in a given field. Thus, the use of standard terminology permits the exchange of understandable, clear, and consistent information regarding an individual's disorder. A second goal is *information retrieval*. As previously stated, classification organizes information within a given field of science. Because of this categorization of information, one has only to go to the literature in order to gain information on differing aspects of the disorder. The third primary purpose of classification is the accurate *description* of the significant similarities and differences between disordered individuals. Careful description serves the purpose of presenting us with homogeneous categories that provide a concise summary of the important factors in a disorder.

Perhaps the most important function of diagnosis and classification is *prediction* concerning etiology, prognosis, and differential response to treatment. Knowing the descriptive symptoms of a disorder can be useful, but it does not directly benefit the individual. A good classification system allows one to predict which treatment strategies may be most beneficial to a person; in this manner, prediction serves as a link between classification and intervention.

Finally, the classification of disordered behavior can serve as a foundation for *theory formulation* in psychopathology research. The characteristics of a classification system can limit the type of theory that evolves from it, and vice versa. Similarly, the choice of classificatory concepts serves as a guide for research and organizes the explanatory principles.

It is apparent that classification systems optimally attempt to achieve several purposes. The DSM-III has attempted to fulfill all of these purposes by means of the innovative use of a multiaxial diagnostic system. The multiaxial diagnostic system was incorporated to meet one of the most common criticisms of the DSM-II (1968), which was that its diagnoses were of little help in treatment planning. The DSM-III attempted to correct this fault by linking diagnostic judgments to their environmental determinants via a multiaxial system.

Generally using two components (categorical and dimensional), multiaxial systems utilize separate axes, which are thought to have high clinical information value and are conceptualized as being as independent from one another as possible. Drawn from numerous multiaxial models from around the world, the following themes seem to be incorporated into the majority of multiaxial systems: phenomenology; etiology; a time frame, including information regarding onset and duration; and social functioning.

## Requisite Psychometric Properties

In the evaluation of classification systems, it is essential to discuss several psychometric properties that are mandatory in a useful and meaningful approach to classification. The first concept is *reliability*. In its broadest sense, *reliability* refers to the "repeatability" of a finding across persons, time, and situations. For example, a patient diagnosed as depressed by one professional should also be given that diagnosis by a different professional on the next day in another hospital. Because the process of diagnosis can be complex, there is ample opportunity for error. Two major sources of diagnostic unreliability are the variability produced while obtaining clinical information and the variability produced while formulating diagnoses. Structured clinical interviews are frequently used in an attempt to reduce the variability that develops while gaining clinical information. The structured interview achieves this aim by specifying the areas to be assessed, by providing precise definitions of terms, by presenting the actual questions to be asked, and by giving instructions for rating the presence and the severity of the symptoms.

On the other hand, reliability associated with the actual process of assigning a diagnosis has been increased through the development and use of explicit diagnostic criteria. The use of diagnostic criteria has served to set clear and objective rules for assigning diagnostic categories, instead of permitting clinicians to formulate diagnoses based on idiosyncratic reasoning. These concepts are examined in greater detail in the next section.

The reliability of a diagnosis places an upper limit on its *validity*, or the extent to which a label can be thought to explain a true phenomenon. That is, if no two people can agree on whether any patients are schizophrenic, for instance (poor reliability), then it is unclear whether there can be such a diagnostic entity as schizophrenia. In a valid diagnostic system, the diagnostic labels must clearly represent distinct disorders, each of which has its own symptomatology, etiology, and course. If a diagnosis is not both valid and reliable, then it serves none of the five previously described purposes of classification systems and therefore, is worse than useless; it would have the potential to hinder both careful research on and the choice of effective treatments for psychiatric disorders.

Finally, it should go without saying that all assessment measures, such as tests and questionnaires used during the diagnostic process, need to be reliable and valid themselves. As previously stated, and as evinced by Kraepelin and Binet in their work, the collection of extensive normative and developmental data is very useful in establishing reliability and validity.

## ASSESSMENT METHODS

A number of assessment methods are used to gather diagnostic information, including unstructured clinical interviews, structured interview schedules, written questionnaires, direct observations of behavior, role-playing and self-monitoring procedures, and physiological response measures. Some of these methods have adequate reliability and validity, whereas others do not. Given the critical role that assessment plays in the diagnostic process, each of these methods is discussed briefly below. For a more comprehensive listing of assessment procedures and a more detailed accounting of specific assessment methods, the reader is referred to the updated *Handbook of Behavioral Assessment* (Ciminero, Calhoun, & Adams, 1986).

One of the most frequently used assessment methods is the unstructured clinical interview. During a typical clinical interview, the clinician or interviewer inquires about the patient's functioning in a variety of areas by asking the patient or significant others in the patient's life (e.g., parents and teachers) about specific symptoms and behaviors. With no specified format to follow, the interviewer must frequently rely on his or her clinical experience to decide which are the most appropriate areas to assess, given a patient's appearance and presenting concerns. Although most interviewers routinely assess areas such as mood, affect, and thought processes, the wording of specific questions and the depth and breadth of assessment often vary greatly from one interviewer to another. These differences can result in two interviewers' obtaining different diagnostic information about the same patient during separate interviews. As can be seen, the unspecified format of the typical clinical interview produces variability in the type and amount of diagnostic information obtained by different interviewers, which, in turn, decreases diagnostic reliability.

In recent years, a number of structured interview schedules have been developed in an attempt to reduce variability in the interview process and thereby to increase diagnostic reliability. In general, structured interview schedules contain lists of questions pertaining to specific disorders that are to be asked in a specified manner and order. Additionally, structured interviews usually provide instructions for rating the severity of the endorsed items and for assigning diagnoses. These innovations greatly reduce variability in the type and amount of information obtained during clinical interviews. A few of the more commonly used interview schedules include the Present State Exam (PSE; Wing, Cooper, & Sartorious, 1974); the Schedule for Affective Disorders and Schizophrenia (SADS; Endicott & Spitzer, 1978); and the reformulated children's version of the SADS (Kiddie SADS; Puig-Antich & Chambers, 1970).

While these schedules help to increase diagnostic reliability, they do have limitations. The PSE and the SADS yield a relatively small subset of clinical diagnoses, for example, and still require the interviewer to use his or her clinical experience to determine when and how to probe certain issues. The more recently developed Diagnostic Interview Schedule (DIS; Robins, Helzer, Croughan, & Ratcliff, 1981) takes the process a step further. The DIS attempts to eliminate the need for judgments based on clinical experience by providing standard probes that can be used to clarify or to further explore certain items. Additionally, the DIS uses computer algorithms to help make diagnostic decisions and yields a greater number of psychiatric diagnoses, including a number of DSM-III Axis I and Axis II diagnoses. Although research findings have suggested that some of the probes are inadequate and still sometimes require the interviewer to make judgments based on clinical experience (Ganguli & Saul, 1982), the DIS greatly reduces variability in the assessment process and represents a significant improvement over the unstructured clinical interview.

Another common method of assessing psychopathology is the written questionnaire. Assessment questionnaires typically contain questions about specific behaviors and symptoms that require forced-choice answers. Many questionnaires use true–false or multiple-choice formats, and others require the respondent to answer items on a Likert rating scale. Typically, the patient or the significant-other respondent is able to read the questions and mark the appropriate responses without assistance. However, it is often necessary to read the questions aloud to young children or individuals who have difficulties in reading. In any case, questionnaires are usually easy to administer and require relatively little time to complete. Most of the commonly used questionnaires have been standardized and offer normative data for comparing individual scores and assessing psychopathological deviance. Reliability and validity coefficients are reported for most scales, as well. There are questionnaires that provide a global assessment of psychopathology, such as the Child Behavior Profile (Achenbach, 1978), and there are questionnaires that are designed to assess specific disorders, such as the Childhood Depression Inventory (Kovacs & Beck,

forced-choice nature of most scales can sometimes obscure valuable information.
As a result, other assessment methods are frequently used in conjunction with
questionnaires to provide more detailed information about symptoms and
behaviors.

One of the major problems with interviews and written questionnaires is
that they rely on others' recollections of symptoms and behaviors to provide
diagnostic information. This reliance reduces the reliability and validity of the
information obtained, as research has demonstrated that retrospective reports
tend to be unreliable and distorted in the direction of social desirability (Evans &
Nelson, 1977). That is, people have a tendency to respond to questions in a
socially conforming and approving manner, which can obscure real problems
that they may be experiencing. In order to obtain a more accurate indication of
symptoms, direct observation of the patient's behavior is frequently required.

Behavioral observation techniques typically involve training two or more
independent observers to identify and code specific behaviors displayed by the
patient during a given period of time. To increase the reliability and validity of
information obtained through observational procedures, several steps should be
taken. First, the observers must be given precise definitions of the behaviors
they are to observe, as well as specific criteria for determining the occurrence or
nonoccurrence of the identified behaviors.

Second, the observers should practice identifying and coding the targeted
behaviors until they have attained an acceptable rate of agreement among them.
In this way, adequate reliability may be demonstrated. If repeated observations
are to take place over an extended period of time, the observers should be
retrained periodically to ensure that they will not inadvertently alter the definitions of the targeted behaviors over time.

Third, as behaviors can be scored in a number of ways, the method of
coding the targeted behaviors must be decided on in advance. Some common
coding methods include timing the duration of the behavioral occurrences, tab-
ulating the number of times a behavior occurs during a given period of time, and
dividing the time period into segments and recording whether the behavior
occurs during each segment.

Steps should also be taken to reduce the possibility of subject reactivity, as it
is not uncommon for a patient who knows that he or she is being observed to
exhibit atypical behavior. One method of reducing reactivity is to allow the
patient to become accustomed to the presence of the observers by having them
practice observations in the presence of the patient for a time before the
assessment.

As training, practicing, and retraining take time, observational techniques
can be both costly and time-consuming. However, direct behavioral observation
is frequently invaluable to the diagnostic process; when it is properly performed,
it can provide reliable and valid diagnostic information that cannot be obtained
in any other manner.

Another method of obtaining information is to instruct the patient to
monitor and record his or her own behaviors and feelings. Using a self-monitoring procedure, it is possible to obtain information about personal feelings and
covert behaviors that independent observers cannot identify. However, self-
monitoring is subject to a number of problems that make its utility questionable.

First, patients tend to be inaccurate in their reporting and thus reduce its reliability. Additionally, the monitoring process itself inevitably makes the patient more aware of his or behavior and tends to reduce the frequency of inappropriate behaviors. Although training individuals in the practice of self-monitoring and reinforcing accurate recordings when possible have been shown to increase accuracy to some extent (Nelson, 1977), the reliability and validity of self-monitoring procedures remain questionable.

Another assessment method involves asking the patient to act out or "role-play" a situation while observers rate the appropriateness of his or her responses. This method is most frequently used to obtain information about an individual's social skills. Like those of self-monitoring procedures, the reliability and validity of role-playing methods appear to be questionable (Van Hasselt, Hersen, & Bellack, 1981).

A final method of obtaining diagnostic information involves using sophisticated instruments to monitor the physiological responses of a patient in particular situations or in reaction to specific stimuli. Physiological response measures are most commonly used to assess specific phobias or fear reactions. The use of psychopysiological measures generally requires specialized training, and their expense places limits on their availability at the present time. However, because they do not rely on reported information or analogue procedures and directly measure physiological responding, psychophysiological measures can provide important, reliable, and valid diagnostic information when they are properly and appropriately used.

## CLINICAL DIAGNOSTIC SYSTEMS

As previously mentioned, two of the major sources of diagnostic unreliability are the variability present in the information-gathering process and the variability associated with the assignment of diagnoses. Recent improvements in assessment procedures, such as the development of structured interview schedules, have served to reduce variability in the information-gathering process. Similarly, the development and use of explicit diagnostic criteria have served to reduce variability in the diagnostic process.

One of the earliest sets of explicit diagnostic criteria was developed primarily for research purposes (Feighner, Robins, Guze, Woodruff, Winokur, & Munoz, 1972). These criteria specify explicit features that must be present for a given diagnosis to be made, and they specify other features that, when present, rule out the possibility of a particular diagnosis. Although they cover only 15 psychiatric disorders, these criteria set the stage for the development of more comprehensive diagnostic systems in later years.

The Research Diagnostic Criteria (RDC), developed by Spitzer, Endicott, and Robins in 1978, improved on the Feighner *et al.* criteria by adding eight diagnostic categories. In addition to specifying the necessary and sufficient diagnostic criteria, the RDC provides methods of subtyping some of the more important categories. Like the Feighner criteria, however, the RDC was developed for research purposes and consequently ignores many of the disorders which are encountered in clinical settings.

The Third Edition of the Diagnostic and Statistical Manual of Mental Disorders (DSM-III), which was published by the American Psychiatric Association in 1980, extended the use of explicit diagnostic criteria even further. Because the DSM-III was developed for use in clinical settings, it covered a broad range of psychopathology, including developmental disorders and psychiatric disorders of childhood. Additionally, the DSM-III used a multiaxial system of evaluation to provide more comprehensive diagnostic information and help with treatment planning and outcome prediction for individual patients. The DSM-III provided information about the features, age of onset, course, impairment, complications, predisposing factors, prevalence, sex ratio, and familial patterns that are associated with each disorder. Finally, the DSM-III employed a hierarchical organization of diagnostic classes, such that disorders which place high in the hierarchy may have features found in lower disorders, but the presence of features associated with higher order diagnoses rules out the assignment of lower order diagnoses. This enabled differential diagnoses to be made using a decision tree format.

The multiaxial system in DSM-III contained five "axes," each of which referred to a different class of information. The DSM-III required that every case be assessed on each of the five axes. The first three axes were categorical in nature and comprised the official diagnostic assessment. The remaining two axes were dimensional and provided supplemental information which might be useful in planning treatment and predicting treatment outcome. The classes of information covered by each of the five axes are listed below:

Axis I      Clinical Syndromes
             Conditions Not Attributable to a Mental Disorder That Are a
                Focus of Attention or Treatment
             Additional Codes
Axis II     Personality Disorders
             Specific Developmental Disorders
Axis III    Physical Disorders and Conditions
Axis IV     Severity of Psychosocial Stressors
Axis V      Highest Level of Adaptive Functioning Past Year

All of the mental disorder classifications were listed on Axes I and II. Disorders contained on Axis I included organic mental disorders, substance abuse disorders, affective disorders, schizophrenic and psychotic disorders, anxiety disorders, somatoform disorders, psychosexual disorders, and dissociative disorders, as well as a number of disorders of interest to readers of this volume which commonly onset during childhood or adolescence. Axis II, which focused on more stable or longstanding behavior handicaps, listed personality disorders and specific developmental disorders. When indicated, individuals could be assigned Axis I and Axis II diagnoses concomitantly. For example, a child could be given an Axis I diagnosis of Conduct Disorder while receiving a diagnosis of Developmental Reading Disorder on Axis II. Multiple diagnoses were also acceptable within Axes I and II.

Axis III permitted the clinician to communicate information about current physical disorders or conditions which may be relevant to the understanding or management of an individual. As with Axes I and II, multiple diagnoses could be assigned within Axis III.

Axis IV assessed psychosocial stressors which may have contributed to the development or exacerbation of a current disorder. Psychosocial stressors, such as the death of a family member, were listed in order of their importance. The severity of the overall stressor (i.e., the combination of specific psychosocial stressors when two or more stressors are identified) was then rated, using a seven point rating scale. The DSM-III provided instructions and examples for rating the severity of psychosocial stressors.

Axis V permitted the clinician to communicate his or her judgment of an individual's highest level of adaptive functioning during the past year. Adaptive functioning was conceptualized as a composite of three major areas: social relations, which focused on relations with family members and friends; occupational functioning, which consisted of consistency and quality of performance as an employee, student or homemaker; and use of leisure time. The highest level of adaptive functioning was rated on a seven point scale. Instructions and examples for assigning ratings were provided in the DSM-III.

DSM-III represented a significant improvement over its predecessors, DSM-I (APA, 1953) and DSM-II (APA, 1968), as these early editions of the Diagnostic and Statistical Manual of Mental Disorders did not provide explicit diagnostic criteria and consequently left the content and boundaries of diagnostic categories for clinicians to decide upon individually. Additionally, the DSM-III encompassed a much broader range of psychopathology, particularly with respect to child disorders, which increased its utility to clinicians and mental health professionals.

Since its publication, the DSM-III has attracted an enormous amount of attention. Experts in the field of child psychopathology praised it for (a) utilizing a multiaxial format; (b) specifying necessary and sufficient diagnostic criteria; (c) providing additional descriptive information about disorders; (d) including ways of communicating information about stressors and adaptational functioning; and (e) providing a more comprehensive listing of child psychiatric disorders (e.g., Achenbach, 1980; Rutter and Shaffer, 1980; Mezzich and Mezzich, 1985). At the same time, criticisms were made regarding its reliance on the medical model of classification and its inclusion of diagnostic categories which have yet to be validated (Achenbach, 1980; Rutter *et al.*, 1980; Werry, Methven, Fitzpatrick, & Dixon, 1983; Werry, 1985).

In response to these criticisms, a revised version of DSM-III began to be developed in May 1983 under the supervision of Robert L. Spitzer as Chairman of the Work Group to Revise DSM-III. This recently published revision (DSM-III-R; American Psychiatric Association, 1987) was circulated for comment among mental health professionals with the aims of improving its clarity, clinical descriptions, and specific diagnostic criteria for each disorder. Perhaps the most notable change from DSM-III with regard to childhood disorders involves a reconceptualization of the organization of the diagnostic system. In DSM-III, Axis I Disorders Usually First Evident in Infancy, Childhood, or Adolescence included Mental Retardation; Attention Deficit Disorders; Conduct Disorders; Anxiety Disorders; Other Disorders of Infancy, Childhood, or Adolescence; Eating Disorders; Stereotyped Movement Disorders; Other Disorders with Physical Manifestations; and Pervasive Developmental Disorders. In contrast, the DSM-III-R considers Mental Retardation, Articulation Disorder, and Pervasive Developmental Disorder to be subtypes of Developmental Disorders, all of which are to be coded on Axis II. The new Axis I childhood disorder section consists of eight types of problems: (1) Disruptive Behavior Disorders, which include Attention Deficit Disorder–Hyperactivity, Conduct Disorder, and Oppositional Disorder, (2) Eating Disorders; (3) Tic Disorders; (4) Disorders of Elimination; (5) Anxiety Disorders; (6) Gender Identity Disorders; (7) Speech Disorders; and (8) Other Disorders of Infancy, Childhood, or Adolescence, which include Reactive Attachment Disorder, Stereotypy/Habit Disorder, Elective Childhood Mutism, Identity Disorder, and Undifferentiated Attention Deficit Disorder. Childhood categories that were eliminated in DSM-III-R include the Schizoid and Sleep Terror/Sleepwalking Disorders, the latter of which is now classified under Sleep Disorders that may occur in adults or children.

These changes were all made in response to input from both researchers and clinicians in the field of childhood psychopathology. The final version represents an attempt to satisfy both groups of users through compromise regarding the inclusion of specific categories and criteria. Thus, while it should be an improvement over the old DSM-III, without a clear emphasis on empirical findings, DSM-III-R may still be subject to problems of poor validity and reliability.

## STATISTICAL CLASSIFICATION SYSTEMS

Another approach to the classification of childhood behavior problems has gained popularity over the last two decades, due largely to the early work of Peterson (1961) and the more recent research by Thomas Achenbach and his colleagues (Achenbach, 1966; Achenbach & Edelbrock, 1978, 1983). These writers have combined information about the presence of specific symptoms in hundreds of children of both sexes across all possible ages with the use of sophisticated statistical techniques to develop a quantitive classification system with excellent psychometric properties.

Quay (1986) provides an extensive review of research findings pertaining to the statistical classification of childhood disorders. He proposes that these data indicate the presence of several reliable dimensions of childhood behavior problems. Most commonly found is a factor comprised of aggressive, noncompliant, disruptive, and sometimes hyperactive behaviors, which would appear to correspond closely with DSM-III-R Disruptive Behavior Disorders. A second dimension, found to occur primarily in older children and adolescents, involves non-aggressive, norm-violating behavior such as stealing, lying, and truancy, and would also be subsumed under DSM-III-R's Disruptive Behavior Disorders.

Two other patterns of deviant behavior that Quay proposes deviate somewhat from DSM-III and DSM-III-R, however. First, statistical studies have strongly supported the notion of attention problems as an entity separate from conduct and hyperactivity problems. In fact, the attention problem syndrome contains symptoms of *underactivity* such as daydreaming and sluggishness, as well as impulsivity, distractibility, and poor concentration. By contrast, DSM-III-R classifies attention deficit-hyperactivity disorder as a Disruptive Behavior Disorder. After considerable controversy about whether attention problems and hyperactivity would be separable under DSM-III-R, the Undifferentiated Attention Deficit Disorder diagnosis was included. Likewise, DSM-III-R provides no category that is equivalent to the clearly established childhood multivariate dimension of Anxiety–Withdrawal–Dysphoria that includes fearfulness, tension, sadness, shyness, and low self-esteem. However, the final version of DSM-III-R does contain three types of childhood anxiety disorders that may be accompanied by depressed mood.

Finally, the statistical approach provides some tentative support for four other possible patterns of childhood problems. These include a schizoid dimension, consisting of aloofness, withdrawal, and lack of interest; a social ineptness pattern characterized by poor peer relations; a psychotic disorder involving hallucinations and odd speech and behavior; and a motor overactivity dimension, which consists of excess motor behaviors in the absence of attention or conduct problems. DSM-III-R contains no parallels for the first two of these tentative categories, while the pychotic disorders would be classified under Axis II Pervasive Developmental Disorder or Axis I Schizophrenic Disorder (childhood or adolescent onset). The motor overactivity dimension, like the attention problem dimension, would be subsumed under the DSM-III-R Disruptive Behavior Disorders, but without a clear differentiation from Attention Deficit Disorder.

The advantages of the statistical approach to classification are obvious. These findings represent disorders with symptoms that are clearly, observably, related to each other across hundreds of individuals. The procedure is also free from the influence of biases or idosyncratic approaches on the part of the person assigning the diagnosis, thereby increasing reliability.

On the other hand, the statistical method currently exhibits one major limitation. Studies using this approach have concentrated almost exclusively on symptomatology, to the neglect of etiology, course, prognosis, and response to treatment. Although such a limitation is understandable given our current lack of knowledge about childhood psychopathology in general, the statistical classification approach must demonstrate its relationship to these important characteristics before its final value can be determined.

## SPECIAL CONSIDERATIONS

Although this chapter has provided a great deal of information regarding the rationale and methodology for using psychiatric diagnoses with children, several caveats are still in order for the researcher and the clinician alike. These warnings involve common assessment pitfalls that are related to a failure to evaluate childhood symptoms in context.

The first factor that must be considered in the assessment and diagnosis of children and adolescents is the child's developmental level, both chronologically and mentally. Familiarity with normal developmental processes is a prerequisite to understanding deviant behaviors in children. For instance, almost all children might be viewed by their parents as qualifying for a diagnosis of Oppositional Disorder during their second year of life! This is the time when normal children are likely to become negative and/or noncompliant, as they come to recognize their control over their own behavior. Yet this is hardly a mental disorder. Likewise, the mentally retarded adolescents who cry frequently may be displaying normal tendencies typical of a child of their low cognitive developmental level, rather than of their chronological age, making it inappropriate to diagnose depression or dysphoria.

Second, all children being assessed must be screened initially for other handicaps that could result in misdiagnosis. Hearing impairments, speech disorders, visual problems, and motor disorders can all lead the unwary diagnostician toward impressions of psychopathology. In fact, we are aware of one preschool child who was labeled depressed and regressed because she was unable to learn color names, when later tests indicated that she was color-blind. Another child was labeled mentally retarded because the assessor neglected to ascertain that the child's native language was not English. The ramifications of such misdiagnoses can have a lifelong impact on the individual and must be avoided at all costs.

Finally, the diagnostician must attend to the family characteristics of the child being assessed. In some cases, reliance on the report of a parent who is suffering from psychopathology can lead to an inappropriate diagnosis of the offspring. For instance, depressed mothers are much more likely than nondepressed mothers to endorse disruptive behavior problems in their child (Wells, McMahon, Griest, & Rogers, 1982; Griest, Wells, & Forehand, 1979; Griest, Forehand, Wells, & McMahon, 1980). Furthermore, home environment factors, including the parents' marital problems may be related to the onset and/or maintenance of various child behavior problems, sometimes rendering the assignment of a clinical diagnosis to the child questionable. These facts underscore the necessity of considering etiology as well as symptomatology during childhood assessment. Although the diagnosis may be the same based on the presenting symptoms, the most effective treatment may be determined in some cases by differing etiological factors.

In summary, the good diagnostician reviews critically all the characteristics of a child or adolescent, as well as those of his or her environment, before assigning a diagnosis. Careful diagnoses of child disorders are necessary to enhance our understanding of childhood psychopathology and to permit more effective intervention and prevention. Although our current practices are far from perfect, the field has progressed remarkably since the early 1960s, giving conscientious clinicians and researchers an increased number of valuable tools for their work.

# REFERENCES

Achenbach, T. M. (1966). The classification of children's psychiatric symptoms: A factor analytic study. *Psychological Monographs, 80,* 1–37.
Achenbach, T. M. (1978). The child behavior profile: Boys aged 6–11. *Journal of Consulting and Clinical Psychology, 46,* 478–488.
Achenbach, T. M. (1980). DSM-III in light of empirical research on the classification of child psychopathology. *Journal of American Academy of Child Psychiatry, 19,* 395–412.
Achenbach, T. M., & Edelbrock, C. S. (1978). The classification of child psychopathology: A review and analysis of empirical efforts. *Psychological Bulletin, 85,* 1275–1301.
Achenbach, T. M., & Edelbrock, C. S. (1983). *Manual for the Child Behavior Checklist and Revised Child Behavior Profile.* Burlington, VT: Queen City Printers.
American Psychiatric Association (1953). *Diagnostic and statistical manual of mental disorders.* Washington, D.C.: Author.
American Psychiatric Association (1968). *Diagnostic and statistical manual of mental disorders,* (2nd ed.). Washington, D.C.: Author.
American Psychiatric Association. (1980). *Diagnostic and statistical manual of mental disorders* (3rd. ed.). Washington, D.C.: Author.

American Psychiatric Association (1987). *Diagnostic and statistical manual of mental disorders*, (3rd ed.–rev.). Washington, D.C.: Author.

Ciminero, A. R., Calhoun, K. S., & Adams, H. E. (Eds.). (1986). *Handbook of Behavioral Assessment* (2nd ed.). New York: Wiley.

Endicott, J., & Spitzer, R. L. (1978). A diagnostic interview: the schedule of affective disorders and schizophrenia. *Archives of General Psychiatry, 35,* 837–844.

Evans, I. M., & Nelson, R. O. (1977). Assessment of child behavior problems. In A. R. Ciminero, K. S. Calhoun, & H. E. Adams (Eds.), *Handbook of behavioral assessment.* New York: Wiley.

Feighner, J. P., Robins, E., Guze, S. B., Woodruff, R. A., Winokur, G., & Munoz, R. (1972). Diagnostic criteria for use in research. *Archives of General Psychiatry, 26,* 57–63.

Forehand, R., Wells, K. C., McMahon, R. J., Griest, D. C., & Rogers, T. (1982). Maternal perception of maladjustment in clinic-referred children: An extension of earlier research. *Journal of Behavior Assessment, 4,* 145–151.

Frame, C. L., & Matson, J. L. (1987). Historical trends in the recognition and assessment of childhood psychopathology. In C. L. Frame & J. L. Matson (Eds.), *Handbook of assessment in childhood psychopathology: Applied issues in differential diagnosis and treatment evaluation.* New York: Plenum Press.

Ganguli, M., & Saul, M. C. (1982). On the Diagnostic Interview Schedule (letter to the editor). *Archives of General Psychiatry, 39,* 1442–1443.

Griest, D., Wells, K., & Forehand, R. (1979). An examination of predictors of maternal perceptions of maladjustment in clinic-referred children. *Journal of Abnormal Psychology, 88,* 277–281.

Griest, D., Forehand, R., Wells, K. C., & McMahon, R. S. (1980). An examination of differences between nonclinic and behavior-problem clinic-reffered children and their mothers. *Jounral of Abnormal Psychology, 89,* 497–500.

Kovacs, M., & Beck, A. T. (1977). An empirical-clinical approach toward a definition of childhood depression. In J. G. Schulterbrandt & A. Raskin (Eds.), *Depression in childhood: Diagnosis, treatment, and conceptual models.* New York: Raven Press.

Mezzich, A. C., & Mezzich, J. E. (1985). Perceived suitability and usefulness of DSM-III vs. DSM-II in child psychopathology. *Journal of the American Academy of Child Psychiatry, 24,* 281–285.

Mezzich, J. E., & Mezzich, A. C. (1987). Diagnostic classification systems in child psychopathology. In C. L. Frame & J. L. Matson (Eds.), *Handbook of assessment in child psychopathology: Applied issues in differential diagnosis and treatment evaluation.* New York: Plenum Press.

Morey, C. C., Skinner, H. A., & Blashfield, R. K. (1986). Trends in the classification of abnormal behavior. In A. R. Ciminero, K. S. Calhoun, & H. E. Adams (Eds.), *Handbook of behavior assessment* (2nd ed.). New York: Wiley.

Nathan, P. E., & Harris, S. L. (1983). The Diagnostic and Statistical Manual of Mental Disorders: History, comparative analysis, current status, and appraisal. In C. E. Walker (Ed.), *The handbook of clinical psychology: Theory, research, and practice.* (pp. 303–434) Homewood, IL: Dow Jones-Irwin.

Nelson, R. O. (1977). Methodological issues in assessment via self-monitoring. In J. D. Cone & R. P. Hawkins (Eds.), *Behavioral assessment.* New York: Brunner/Mazel.

Peterson, D. R. (1961). Behavior problems of middle childhood. *Journal of Consulting Psychology, 25,* 205–209.

Puig-Antich, J., & Chambers, W. (1978). *The schedule for affective disorders and schizophrenia for school-aged children.* New York: New York State Psychiatric Institute.

Quay, H. C. (1986). Classification. In H. C. Quay & J. S. Werry (Eds.), *Psychopathological disorders of childhood* (3rd ed.). New York: Wiley.

Robins, L. N., Helzer, J. E., Croughan, J., & Ratcliff, K. S. (1981). National Institute of Mental Health Diagnostic Interview Schedule: Its history, characteristics and validity. *Archives of General Psychiatry, 38,* 381–389.

Rutter, M., & Shaffer, D. (1980). DSM-III: A step forward or back in terms of classification of child psychiatric disorders? *Journal of the American Academy of Child Psychiatry, 19,* 371–394.

Shepard, M., Brooke, E. M., Cooper, J. E., & Lin, T. (1968). An experimental approach to psychiatric diagnosis. *Acta Psychiatrica Scandinavica, 44,* 7–89 (Suppl. No. 201).

Spitzer, R. L., Endicott, J., & Robins. (1978). Research diagnostic criteria. *Archives of General Psychiatry, 35,* 773–782.

Van Hasselt, V. B., Hersen, M., & Bellack, A. S. (1981). The validity of role play tests for assessing social skills in children. *Behavior Therapy, 12,* 202–216.

Werry, J. S. (1985). ICD-9 and DSM-III classification for the clinician. *Journal of Child Psychology and Psvchiatry, 26,* 1–6.

Werry, J. S., Methven, R. J., Fitzpatrick, J., & Dixon, H. (1983). The Interrater Reliability of DSM-III in children. *Journal of Abnormal Child Psychology, 11,* 341–355.

Wing, J. K., Cooper, J. E., & Sartorious, N. (1974). *The measurement and classification of psychiatric symptoms.* Cambridge, England: University Press.

# 3    *Family Therapy*

KAREN C. WELLS

## INTRODUCTION

Family therapy for children and adolescents has its historical roots in the child guidance movement of the 1920s, when it was first recognized that, in addition to the individual treatment of the child, some form of collateral counseling was needed by the parents of children with behavioral and emotional disturbances (Korchin, 1976). Before that time, contact with the families of patients was often avoided, based in large part on the theories of Freud, who emphasized that neurotic conflicts were acquired in the early relationships of children with their parents. Although this theory would appear to imply family treatment, Freud took the position that, because of the family's pathological influence, the patient must be isolated from the family if improvement was to occur. In addition, early in the development of his ideas, Freud adopted the position that it is not factual events, but the patient's subjective perceptions, opinions, and fantasies about those events, that is of primary therapeutic importance. Therefore, observing and intervening in overt family interactions were considered not only unimportant but, potentially, counterproductive to the therapeutic process.

With the advent of the child guidance movement in Vienna and later in the United States, there was for the first time a recognition that, in addition to work with the child, some form of intervention with the parents, usually the mother, was of potential benefit. However, under the dominating influence of psychoanalysis, mother and child were seen in separate sessions by separate therapists, and the individual analysis of the child continued to be of primary importance. Work with the mother was viewed as collateral or adjunctive treatment. Joint sessions did not occur, and often, the child's and the mother's therapists assiduously avoided discussion of the case in order to protect the privacy of the respective therapeutic relationships.

Eventually, under the influence of such psychoanalytically oriented psychiatrists as John Bowlby and Nathan Ackerman, who had begun to develop interactional theories of psychopathology, a shift of emphasis began to occur from the view of parents as disturbed and disturbing influences on their children's mental development to the view that the *interactional relationship* between parent and child was at least part of the problem. This shift set the stage for studying the family—and the interactions among its members—as a means of under-

KAREN C. WELLS • Children's Hospital National Medical Center, George Washington University School of Medicine, Washington, D.C. 20010.

standing the child's presenting symptoms, and it allowed for the development of family intervention techniques.

In more recent times, since the advent of systems, communications, and behavioral theories of symptom development and maintenance, family theory and therapy have achieved a strong foothold in the conceptualization and treatment of child and adolescent psychological disturbances. However, with the exception of behavioral family therapy, theory and technology development have far outdistanced empirical demonstrations of efficacy. Gurman (1971) has pointed out that family therapists developed largely in child guidance centers, where psychologists, whose degrees prepared them for behavioral research, were less actively involved than psychiatrists and social workers. Consequently, by 1978, there were only approximately 38 studies of family therapy, involving children or adolescents as the identified patients, in which even gross rates of improvement were reported (Gurman & Kniskern, 1978). With the exception of behavioral family therapy, this state of affairs remains largely unchanged today.

Even without a strong research base, family therapy is increasingly being used as a treatment for children and adolescents (Johnson, 1986; Masten, 1979; Nichols, 1984). The proliferation of family therapy has been based largely on the theoretical/anecdotal writings of compelling, charismatic leaders in the field and by the creation of numerous training programs for family therapy. Paralleling these developments, behavioral therapy has advanced from the S-R-C (stimulus–response–consequences) paradigms of Skinner and others to theories emphasizing the reciprocal influences imposed by each member of an interacting dyad on the behavior of the other in highly interdependent reinforcement and punishment systems (Patterson, 1982). These advances in behavioral theory have influenced and have been influenced by a proliferation of research in the literature on behavioral family therapy.

In the remainder of this chapter, I will review some of the major schools of family therapy that have dealt with the problems of children and adolescents. Where it exists, I will review some of the relevant outcome research on family therapy, and I will point out which approaches to family therapy are most appropriate for specific disorders when such information is available.

## STRUCTURAL FAMILY THERAPY

Perhaps the leading figure in structural family therapy is Salvador Minuchin, a child psychiatrist who first began seeing families in the 1960s. Although not among the first wave of family theoreticians and therapists, Minuchin has had a tremendous impact on the field of family therapy, largely because of his reputation as a clinician, and because of the excellent training programs at the Philadelphia Child Guidance Clinic, which he directed in the 1960s and 1970s. Along with Montalvo, Rosman, and Haley, Minuchin transformed what had been a traditional child guidance center into a world-renowned family therapy training and treatment center with excellent physical facilities, including videotaping equipment and even small apartments so that whole families could be "hospitalized" together. Literally thousands of family therapists have been trained in structural family therapy at the Philadelphia Child Guidance Clinic.

In addition to the personal renown of Minuchin, the success of structural family therapy can be related to the simple, practical theory that underlies the treatment. The theory describes families as having an underlying organization or structure. This structure is homeostatically maintained and regulated by repeated transactional patterns among and within its subsystems, which are separated from each other by boundaries. Thus, the three key concepts in structural family therapy are *structure, subsystems,* and *boundaries* (Nichols, 1984).

Family organization or structure is an organized pattern of interpersonal transactions that are repeated and that become established modes of interacting within the family. Such predictable, repetitive sequences of behavior can involve two or more family members. For example, a husband–wife dyad experiencing marital conflict may begin to argue. As the argument escalates, the two children begin to fight with each other in the next room. The parents terminate their argument in order to attend to the children. If this sequence is repeated, it creates a structure in which child acting-out becomes a (short-term) solution for marital conflict.

Family structure also involves covert rules that develop as family members learn to accommodate to each other. Sometimes, these rules are adaptive in terms of promoting the positive development of all family members. For example, there may be a family rule that the parents are responsible for cooking dinner, and the children are responsible for after-dinner clean-up. This rule regarding division of labor reduces conflict around dinnertime by making clear the expectations of all family members and promoting a sense of contribution and responsibility in the children. On the other hand, covert rules can also promote maladaptive patterns of behavior. For example, in a family with an asthmatic child, a rule may develop that because he or she is sick, the affected child does not have to conform to the expectations of the other children in the family, such as performing chores, obeying the parents, and socializing with peers. This rule retards the social development of the child and promotes conflict and resentment among the siblings and/or the parents.

Family dysfunction also can develop when covert rules are not created by the family when they are necessary to meet the demands of a new situation. For example, in the same asthmatic family, there may be no rules regarding the division of emergency tasks by the parents when an asthmatic attack requires hospitalization. Consequently, panic and chaos break out, delaying effective action and exacerbating the child's attack.

Other aspects of family structure involve the hierarchial organization of the family or how parents and children share authority. In some families, children are given more power and authority than they are developmentally capable of managing, and the result is often anxiety or acting-out behavior.

An early task in family therapy is discerning the family structure. According to Minuchin, this can only be done by observing over time the repeated sequences of family behavior that reveal structural patterns.

A second key idea in structural family therapy is that families group themselves into subsystems of members who join together to perform various functions (Nichols, 1984). Subsystems can be obvious groupings, such as "the parents" or "the teenagers," but they can also involve more covert coalitions (e.g., the father and the oldest daughter form a coalition that excludes the mother).

A final concept in structural therapy is the notion that the individuals within a family, the subsystems, and whole families are separated by interpersonal boundaries that regulate the amount of contact with others inside and outside the family. In functional families, the boundaries around certain subsystems are clear, but they are flexible enough to allow adaptive input into other subsystems when necessary. For example, the boundaries around the marital subsystem may provide certain times for husband and wife to spend away from the children, but they are flexible enough to allow for effective parenting.

On the other hand, boundaries can be overly rigid or overly diffuse. Diffuse boundaries invite enmeshment among subsystems, in which there is often a sense of mutual support, but at the expense of promoting independence and autonomy (Nichols, 1984). In addition, in enmeshed families, the executive hierarchies are confused, so that the children may join one parent in criticizing the other, or the children may take inappropriate parental roles toward each other. Rigid boundaries limit contact among family members or subsystems and often result in the development of autonomy, but at the expense of warmth, affection, nuturance, and a sense of support from the family.

Children involved in enmeshed subsystems with their parents tend to grow up to be dependent and unsure of themselves. They often do not function well when society's conventions force a separation from their parents, and they have trouble relating to non-family-members. Children growing up in disengaged families (i.e., those with rigid boundaries) often develop a fierce sense of independence and autonomy but may have difficulty in forming close affective relationships with and attachments to other people. In either case, the children often display oppositional or acting-out behavior problems because their parents cannot or do not perform the executive parenting functions that are necessary to promote adaptive, socialized behavior in their children, although for different reasons in enmeshed and in disengaged families.

Structural family therapy is predicated on the assumption that presenting problems or symptoms are maintained by dysfunctional family structures, that is, structures that have not adjusted adequately to the maturational, developmental, or situational challenges faced bv the family or one or more of its members. Therapy is therefore directed to an alteration in family structure, which has, as its by-product, symptom change.

Some aspects of family structure are thought to be generally important in families, for example, creating an appropriate power hierarchy in which the parents, as a cohesive executive subsystem, are in positions of authority over, not equal with, their children; promoting differentiation in enmeshed families; and increasing interaction in disengaged families. Other aspects of family structure are idiosyncratic and must be assessed case by case.

Therapy often begins with a process in which the therapist "joins" with a family by listening to each member in a balanced fashion, by finding a common ground or a common goal with people in the family, and by supporting the needs of individuals in the family, if not necessarily the actions taken to meet those needs (Howe, 1986). Joining the family is considered a necessary condition for restructuring to take place.

After joining the family, the therapist attempts to understand the family's structure and to reframe the family's presentation of its problems into one that is based on this understanding. To accomplish this, the therapist focuses on spontaneous behavior sequences that occur naturally in the therapy session or on enactments in which the therapist directs the family to demonstrate how they handle a particular type of problem. In both spontaneous behavior sequences and enactments, the therapist observes the family process, looking for evidence of relevant enmeshed or disengaged subsystems, covert coalitions, imbalanced hierarchies, repetitive maladaptive behavior sequences, and/or the use of conflict avoidance tactics. The therapist may often direct the enactment in such a way as to stimulate more adaptive family structures. This process often requires forceful interventions involving intensity on the part of the therapist (e.g., to the mother of a child behaving disruptively in a therapy session: "Do you really want your child disobeying you like that? What are you going to do about it?").

Family therapists are also boundary menders. For example, in enmeshed families, the therapist will invoke boundaries by directly blocking interruptions, urging family members to speak for themselves, and allowing relevant dyads to finish an interaction without intrusions from others. In disengaged families, therapists may direct distant family members to interact or even argue in a therapy session because disengagement is usually maintained as a way of avoiding arguments or conflicts. Subsequently, the therapist may prompt more effective problem-solving and may have family members plan pleasant activites together.

Another reason for the widespread use of structural family therapy with children and adolescents is that Minuchin has published a number of papers in respected psychiatric journals both outlining his conceptual model and presenting data on the outcome of treatment. Minuchin's first outcome study was conducted at Wiltwyck School for Boys, a school for low-SES urban delinquents. Although this study did not meet the criteria of a true experiment, 7 of 11 boys were judged to be significantly improved after 6–12 months of treatment. Interestingly, none of the families rated as disengaged improved. Treatment appeared to be more successful with enmeshed families (Minuchin, Mantalvo, Guerney, Rosman, & Schumer, 1967).

After his work with delinquents Minuchin developed a strong interest in working with families of children and adolescents with "psychosomatic" illness, such as superlabile diabetes, intractable asthma, and anorexia nervosa.

In two interesting papers, (Liebman, Minuchin, & Baker, 1974b; Minuchin et al., 1975) Minuchin and colleagues argued for the importance of moving beyond linear models of psychosomatic illness, in which the child is seen as a passive recipient of noxious environmental influence, to an open systems model, in which the child is examined in his or her social context. In this model, it is assumed that multiple feedback processes occur among the child and subsystems in the family, with the child as much the influencer as the influenced. These feedback processes, as well as certain family characteristics associated with them, often serve to escalate and maintain asthma attacks, noncompliance with medical regimens in diabetics, and self-imposed starvation in anorectics (Liebman, Minuchin & Baker, 1974a,b,c; Minuchin, Baker, Rosman, Liebman, Milman, & Todd, 1975).

Minuchin et al. (1975) presented data from the treatment of 13 diabetics, 10 asthmatics, and 25 anorectic patients using a structural family therapy approach. In almost all of the cases, rather dramatic improvement was reported after treatment in terms of substantial decreases in hospital admissions; an absence of recurrent ketosis and chronic acetonuria in diabetics; a reduction in the scaled grade of clinical severity in asthmatics; and either full or partial recovery (in terms of weight gain) for 22 of 25 anorectics at 1- to 4-year follow-up. Again, no control groups were used. Thus, alternative explanations for improvement were not ruled out.

There is at least one experimental evaluation of the effects of "family psychotherapy" on childhood asthma (Lask & Matthew, 1979). Although the therapy model used was not specifically identified as structured family therapy, the conceptual focus was described as emphasizing "understanding the individual's symptoms and behavior as arising from and feeding back into the general family system of interaction" (p. 117), certainly consistent with an open systems model. In this study, 29 asthmatic children, between 4 and 14 years years old, and their families were randomly assigned to receive medical management alone or medical management plus family therapy. There were no differences at follow-up between the groups on peak expiratory flow rates or on activity limitation. However, the group that received family therapy was significantly more improved on a daily wheeze score and on thoracic gas volume, compared to the group that did not receive family therapy. These results, along with the work of Minuchin and colleagues, lend some empirical support to the popularity of structural family therapy in the treatment of children and adolescents.

## STRATEGIC FAMILY THERAPY

There are several prominent writers and practitioners of strategic family therapy, including Haley and Madanes, Palazzoli and her colleagues in Milan, Hoffman and her colleagues at the Ackerman Institute, and Fisch, Weakland, Watzlawick, and colleagues at the Mental Research Institute in Palo Alto. Although these groups may represent slightly different approaches to strategic family therapy, they have in common a general theoretical foundation in general systems theory, cybernetics, and communications theory.

In applying cybernetics theory to families, strategic therapists view families as systems that strive to maintain equilibrium or balance. Whenever the family system is disturbed, it initiates moves to return to a homeostatic balance. Viewed in this context, symptomatic behavior by one family member serves the cybernetic function of returning the family to equilibrium; that is, symptoms are homeostatic mechanisms.

Strategic theorists also view cybernetic processes within the context of general systems theory, which postulates that "living systems are characterized by a dynamic tension between homeostasis and change. That is, they operate to maintain a pattern of stability, but also are able to grow and adapt. Pathological families are systems in which homeostasis begins to take precedence over change and transformation" (Nichols, 1984, p. 434).

Viewed in the context of cybernetics and general systems theory, developmental, maturational, or situational events may challenge a family system in a way that disturbs the ongoing equilibrium. The family can react by facing the challenge and adapting to it, reaching a new homeostatic balance in the process. On the other hand, the family may create ways to avoid confronting the challenge, thereby maintaining the present homeostatic balance. In this way, families maintain outmoded patterns of behavior that once worked but are no longer functional.

For example, a couple decide to separate, and the husband moves out of the family home. Shortly thereafter, one of the children develops severe tantrums and disobedience to his mother, who calls the father to come over and "deal with his son." This happens two or three times a week. The son's tantrums do not diminish.

In this scenario, the father's moving out represents a severe challenge to the ongoing equilibrium of the family. Rather than adapting to the challenge in more constructive ways (e.g., the mother's moving into the disciplinary role and the mother and father's taking steps to develop new lives for themselves), the son displays behavior problems that bring the father, the disciplinarian, back into the intimate family system. This "maneuver" seeks to reestablish the former homeostatic balance. However, it results in a pathological situation in which the son must continue to act out, the mother is not motivated to develop executive parental functions, and the mother and the father are blocked from effecting the kind of separation that would allow them to make the transition from marital couple to separate, independent adults. Strategic family therapy uses therapeutic techniques that are designed to blast families such as this one out of outmoded, repetitive, pathological patterns of behavior, and to create new behavior patterns in place of the vicious circles.

In recent years, there has been some overlap between strategic and structural family therapy, especially as practiced by Haley. As mentioned in an earlier section, Haley worked with, and was strongly influenced by, Minuchin. In his more contemporary writings, Haley has discussed the application of strategic techniques within the context of the structural model of family organization. For example, Haley believes that normal families are hierarchially organized and that problems arise when the hierarchy is unbalanced or unclear, or when covert coalitions occur across generational boundaries (e.g., a father and a daughter in a coalition that keeps the mother at a distance).

The term *strategic therapy* was coined by Haley to emphasize a planned, problem-focused orientation to change. In this therapy, the first step is to identify the problem, as well as the interactive sequence that is maintaining it. The latter may be accomplished by asking the family what "solutions" they have tried. The major techniques involve "reframing" or relabeling the problem in such a way that the conceptual or emotional viewpoint of the problem is changed, and this change allows for new and creative solutions. For example, in a case involving the family treatment of an epileptic 12-year-old child, it became apparent to the therapist that the child's provocative, disobedient behavior resulted from the overindulgence of the parents and their failure to act as an effective, executive parental unit. Furthermore, it was clear that the parents believed that their posture toward the child represented good, caring parenting because, after all, the boy was so sick. Once the therapist understood this emotional viewpoint of the parents, he attempted to reframe it with the comment, "Of course, he is sick. Why, then, do you handicap him further by providing poor parenting?" This statement jolted the parents into more effective executive action toward the son, with further input from the therapist.

Another set of techniques in strategic family therapy involves the use of either straightforward or paradoxical directives. Paradoxical directives often involve "prescribing the symptom," that is, identifying an ongoing sequence that appears to be maintaining problem behavior and then instructing the family to do it more and harder. This process sets up a situation in which the family either complies with the therapist (thus bringing the family's out-of-control behavior under the therapist's control) or doesn't comply, in which case change is necessary.

Although some strategic therapists are very quick to use paradoxical directives, others use straightforward directives first and then move to the use of paradox only when resistance is encountered. Other therapists use *pretend techniques*, in which children may be instructed to pretend to have a tantrum and parents may be asked to pretend to stop it, thereby bringing the behavior sequence under control.

Other paradoxical maneuvers include the use of *restraining* if change has begun, that is, warning the family that they should not move too quickly. This paradoxical instruction is intended to promote and maintain change by provoking resistant families into proving the therapist wrong. Relapse is often predicted for the same reason.

There is a large theoretical-anecdotal literature advocating the use of strategic family therapy (Fisch, Weakland, & Segal, 1982; Haley, 1963, 1973, 1976, 1980; Hoffman, 1981; Madanes, 1981; Palazzoli, Boscolo, Cecchin, & Prata, 1978). However, there are very few experimental investigations of the outcome of the use of this form of therapy with children. Without empirical support for its efficacy, strategic family therapy will remain a popular but unproven approach to the treatment of children and adolescents.

## BEHAVIORAL APPROACHES TO FAMILY THERAPY

### Parent Training

Behavioral approaches to family therapy with children initially developed within a parent-training model and were focused primarily on the treatment of childhood conduct and oppositional disorders. The parent-training model is based on the assumption that child behavior is largely a function of naturally occurring environmental contingencies of positive and negative reinforcement and punishment. Specifically, the interactions occurring in the family among parents and children contain social influence and learning processes that result in the escalation and maintenance of disruptive child behavior (Griest & Wells, 1983; Patterson, 1982).

In the early parent-training work, the force of influence was thought to be linear and unidirectional; that is, certain parent behaviors, when displayed in interactions with children, were thought to evoke problem child behaviors following the laws of learning. The basic process contributing to children's disruptive behavior was assumed to be a parenting-skills deficit. Some parents did not have appropriate skills for developing and promoting prosocial behavior in their children and therefore resorted to inappropriate, usually coercive, methods that served to escalate and maintain oppositional, aggressive child behavior.

As a consequence of this early unidirectional model (parent skills deficits → child misbehavior), the parent-training approach has proliferated since the mid-1960s and has focused almost exclusively on teaching parents new skills for managing positive and negative child behavior (for reviews, see Wells & Forehand, 1981, 1985). Consistent with the empirical tradition in behavior therapy, the teaching of the parents focused on increasing the positive parent behaviors empirically identified as occurring at a lower rate than normal in the parents of conduct-problem children, and on decreasing the coercive parent behaviors identified as occurring at a higher rate than normal (Patterson, 1982). Positive parent behaviors include such skills as attending to and rewarding prosocial child behavior in microscopic parent–child interactions, as well as the institution of macroscopic family-management practices, such as clearly specified house rules, clearly delineated schedules for individual and family activities, rules governing the social behavior among family members, parental monitoring of the child's whereabouts, parental monitoring of the child's performance of basic expectations, and the use of contingent consequences (Forehand & McMahon, 1981; Patterson, 1982). Negative parent behaviors to be decreased include the use of poor commands (commands that are vague, nonspecific, interrupted by superfluous information, stated in question form, or delivered in a threatening, nagging manner), criticisms, and ambient and contingent aversive behavior directed toward the child (Wells & Forehand, 1985).

In parent-training therapy sessions, parenting skills are introduced one at a time. The therapist first provides a rationale for the use of the skill; then carefully defines the skill, giving examples; and finally, models the use of the skill for the parent. The parent practices the skill (e.g., attending) with the therapist, who plays the part of the child. Subsequently, the parent practices with the child, with feedback from the therapist. Homework assignments are given for extra-session home practice (see Forehand & McMahon, 1981).

In contrast to other forms of family therapy for children and adolescents, parent training for the treatment of child aggressive disorders has been evaluated empirically in a number of studies using quasi-experimental and experimental designs. Illustrative of the former were a number of studies in the 1960s and the early 1970s using small numbers of subjects and no control groups (Bernal, 1969; Bernal, Duryee, Pruett & Burns, 1968; Forehand & King, 1974; 1977; O'Leary, O'Leary, & Becker, 1967; Patterson, 1974; Patterson, Cobb, & Ray, 1973; Patterson & Reid, 1973). In each of these clinical demonstration studies, positive effects of parent training were found on a number of parent and child behavioral and attitudinal measures from pre- to posttreatment. Subsequent experimental studies used waiting-list control groups (Karoly & Rosenthal, 1977; Peed, Roberts & Forehand, 1977; Wiltz & Patterson, 1974) or attention-placebo control groups (Walter & Gilmore, 1973) and, generally, demonstrated that behavioral parent training was more effective than no treatment or inert treatments for conduct-problem children (for review, see Wells & Forehand, 1981).

Since 1980, three studies have been conducted comparing behavioral parent training to active nonbehavioral treatments (Bernal, Klinnert & Schultz, 1980; Patterson, Chamberlain, & Reid, 1982; Wells & Egan, in press). In two of these studies, the nonbehavioral comparison groups represented other forms of family interventions (Bernal *et al.*, 1980; Wells & Egan, in press).

In the first of these studies, Bernal *et al.* (1980) compared parent training to "client-centered parent counseling," involving the exploration of feelings, attitudes, and experiences in the family and using student therapists. Parent report measures, parent-completed behavior-rating scales, and parent satisfaction measures showed superior treatment effects for behavioral parent training compared to client-centered counseling at posttreatment. No differential treatment effects were found on behavioral measures collected in the home by trained observers.

In the second study, Patterson and his colleagues (1982) compared behavioral parent training conducted by experienced professional therapists with community-based treatment. Families in the comparison group were randomly referred to community agencies or psychologists and psychiatrists in private practice. The results showed that behavioral parent training was clearly superior to community-based treatment on behavioral measures collected in the home by trained observers and on the parents' general level of satisfaction with treatment. Differences in parents' daily reports were generally in favor of parent training, but were not statistically significant.

In the final experimental study, Wells and Egan (in press) compared behavioral parent training to systems-oriented family therapy. The systems treatment was consistent with the contemporary approach of Haley, using a structural model of family organization and a strategic approach to planning interventions. In this study, parent training was significantly superior to systems family therapy on behavioral measures of disobedient, noncompliant behavior displayed by children with oppositional-behavior-disorder diagnoses. No differences were noted between treatments on measures of parent anxiety, depression, and marital satisfaction.

In summary, the rather extensive treatment-outcome literature clearly demonstrates that parent training is significantly more effective than no treatment for child aggressive behavior disorders. In studies comparing behavioral parent training to other forms of active therapy, parent training has been demonstrated to be equally efficacious or superior, depending upon the outcome measure being evaluated and the assessment interval (i.e., posttreatment or follow-up). In no case have other forms of therapy been found to be superior to parent training for child oppositional and aggressive behavior disorders (Forehand & McMahon, 1981; Wells & Forehand, 1985).

## Behavioral Family Therapy

In spite of the positive effects of parent training, it has become apparent in recent years that parent training alone may represent incomplete or inadequate treatment for a subset of families with aggressive and oppositional children. This conclusion is based on the fact that, in group outcome studies, up to one third of the families in the parent-training group do not change their behavior in the expected direction even though the group as a whole may show a statistically significant improvement. For those families that do change, positive treatment effects may erode with the passage of time, as attested to by the relapse rates reported in some studies, by the number of families who require "booster sessions" or other adjunctive interventions to maintain treatment acquired gains, and by studies documenting the failure of many families to cooperate fully with therapy (Wells, 1984).

These observations converge with the recent model of behavioral family therapy for conduct disorders in children explicated by Griest and Wells (1983; Wells, 1985). In this model, we reviewed evidence showing that, in addition to or instead of parenting-skills deficits, families of conduct-disordered children differ from normals on a number of important dimensions. Parents of aggressive children differ from parents of normals in their perceptions of their children's behavior, in their own (the parents') psychological adjustment, in their marital satisfaction, and in their social and community adjustments; the parents of aggressive children display more maladjustment on these measures. Furthermore, there is reason to believe that parent maladjustment on one or more of these dimensions is related to the short- and long-term outcome of parent training. Maladjusted parents are less likely to remain in treatment, to benefit from treatment, and to maintain any positive treatment effects that may occur (Griest & Wells, 1983). We have hypothesized that parent-training programs that fail to address the parental cognitive-psychological-marital-social maladjustment contributing to perceived or actual child deviance represent incomplete treatment. For such families, an expanded behavioral family-therapy model is advocated (Wells, 1985).

In behavioral family therapy, areas of parent maladjustment are assessed before treatment. For families in which the parents display significant evidence of depression, anxiety, marital maladjustment, and social insularity, treatment is expanded to include interventions in these problem areas. Because this approach to therapy has arisen out of a behavioral model, proven behavioral and cognitive-behavioral approaches to the treatment of these dimensions have been advocated. Such treatment can occur in the context of family meetings (e.g., all family members learn relaxation training together as an anxiety reduction strategy) or with subunits of the family system (e.g., husband and wife meet in sessions without the children to work on marital and communication issues). Such treatments occur during or after parent-skills-training sessions.

There is currently one study providing empirical evidence that the expanded behavioral family-therapy model results in significantly greater improvement in the behavior of conduct-disordered children than parent training alone (Griest, Forehand, Rogers, Breiner, Furey, & Williams, 1982). In this study, families of parents who, in addition to parent training, received adjunctive therapies designed to address their expectations and perceptions of their children, their own mood and psychological adjustment, their marital communication and problem-solving skills, and their social interactions were compared with families in which parent training was the sole intervention. In this study, behavioral family therapy was more effective than parent training alone in decreasing child deviant behavior at posttreatment. At 2-month follow-up, behavioral family therapy resulted in greater use of positive parent skills than did parent training alone. This study was the first empirical demonstration that addressing variables other than parenting skills deficits alone is important to consider in the treatment of conduct-disordered children. Other studies have also shown that incorporating adjunctive treatment strategies can enhance the effects of parent training (Wells, Griest, & Forehand, 1980).

In summary, behavioral parent training clearly has been demonstrated to be an effective treatment approach for children with oppositional and aggressive conduct disorders; comparative outcome studies suggest that it may very well be the treatment of choice for these disorders. When parent training is incorporated into a more comprehensive "behavioral family therapy" model in which parental psychological, marital, and social maladjustment are also addressed, evidence suggests that even more beneficial short- and long-term effects are obtained.

The effects of parent training and behavioral family therapy on other childhood and adolescent disorders have not been systematically evaluated; however, using parents as the administrators or mediators of the behavioral treatment of a variety of childhood disorders, such as enuresis, encopresis, and obesity, is a frequently employed treatment tactic in child behavior therapy (Ollendick & Cerney, 1981).

## Functional Family Therapy

Functional family therapy (FFT) is a therapeutic model that has evolved out of the behavioral-systems work of James Alexander and his colleagues, notably, Barton, and Parsons, at the University of Utah. FFT represents an integration and extension of behavioral psychology and systems theory that has resulted in an interesting theoretical model for explaining human action in a family context, and for selecting treatment strategies.

Like many of the systems theorists, functional family therapists derive the meaning of behavior from an examination of the relational process in which it is embedded. Like many behaviorists, functional family therapists also assume that behavior is best understood in terms of the outcomes that the behavior functionally evokes from others (Barton & Alexander, 1980). In this approach, presenting symptoms are viewed as sometimes maladaptive but, nevertheless, legitimate in terms of their functional significance; that is, the ultimate interpersonal outcome of behavior is adaptive, whereas the behavior that produces that outcome may be inefficient or maladaptive. For example, a child's tantrums may produce a legitimate short-term outcome (contact and closeness with the mother), but in a way that is maladaptive to harmonious family life.

Functional family therapists tend to emphasize the *relationship outcomes* produced in family interaction sequences. In this regard, they have hypothesized that interpersonal intimacy, interpersonal distance, and interpersonal midpointing (a phenomenological and behavioral blend of the first two) are the functions of much behavior occurring within a family context. Furthermore, these functional outcomes may be consistent with or directly contrary to the stated wishes of the people involved; for example, a wife may state that she wants more contact with her husband and may simultaneously engage in behavior that repeatedly results in his leaving the house.

Functional family therapy assumes that problem behavior arises when such behavior is the only course through which interpersonal functions can be met; that is, "problem behavior represents the most presently available means to attain interpersonal functions or outcomes" (Barton & Alexander, 1980, p. 31). Furthermore, this model assumes that family life constitutes a series of developmental epochs in which the interpersonal needs of respective family members change over the course of their own individual development. For example, most would agree that infancy is a time when interpersonal intimacy is necessary and adaptive, whereas adolescence is a time when interpersonal distancing becomes an issue. Problems are assumed to arise when the family and/or its subunits do not recognize and adapt well to the changing interpersonal outcomes sought by the members over the course of development.

In functional family therapy, the therapist has two major tasks. The first is to assess and understand what are the interpersonal outcomes of particular sequences of problem behavior. The second is to select and implement treatment strategies that *maintain* the interpersonal outcome, but in a more efficient, less disruptive fashion. In this regard, the functional-family-therapy model dichotomizes intervention into two phases: a "therapy" phase and an "education" phase (Barton & Alexander, 1980). *Therapy* is conceptualized as the phase of intervention that motivates families to change. *Education* has to do with the selection and implementation of well-known and evaluated behavioral technologies (e.g., contracting and contingency management) that replace problem behavior with more adaptive, efficient forms of behavior, while maintaining relevant interpersonal outcomes for family members.

In the therapy phase of intervention, the therapist attempts to assist the family in relabeling some of their attributions about the nature of the problem. Families often come to therapy with person-specific definitions of problems (e.g., "Our problem is that he is a lazy teenager"). The therapist helps the family to redefine the problem in relational terms. This is done by asking questions of everyone in the family, by asking questions designed to elicit information on relationship outcomes (e.g., "After he did that what did you do?"), and by making *relationship*-oriented comments (e.g., "You two don't spend much time talking about your differences of opinion"), rather than *content*-oriented comments (e.g., "You want a 1:00 A.M. curfew, whereas he wants you to have an 11:00 P.M. curfew"), in the beginning. Therapists also attempt to provide new labels that "revalence" behavior in ways that reduce anger and defensiveness and create a new value or affect toward the behavior. For example, a family that labels a 6-year-old tantruming child as "bad" might be told that the child is seeking the attention of the family in a 3-year-old way. This new label (1) helps the family to see the child in a more positive light (he's "attention seeking" rather than "bad"); (2) focuses them on the task of helping him behave in a more mature fashion; and (3) emphasizes the relational aspect of the child's problem (e.g., the family's attention is involved in the child's problem behavior). According to Barton and Alexander (1980), effective relabeling always revalences behavior in benign ways that decrease resistance and increase the motivation to work on the relational aspects of the problem.

In the "educational" phase of intervention, the therapist must select system-change strategies that are consistent with the functional outcomes of family members' behavior, and with the new labels that the therapist has provided in the therapy phase. For example, an adolescent daughter who has been staying out late at night without telephoning home (distancing function) may be greatly upsetting her legitimately concerned yet smothering mother, who wants to control all aspects of her daughter's behavior (intimacy function). The therapist might initiate a contingency contract approach that includes a message board for communicating the daughter's whereabouts. Both of these techniques allow for a midpointing function in which the mother has some control over her daughter's activities or whereabouts, and the daughter is allowed to maintain some distance from her mother.

The behavioral-systems family therapy model, from which functional family therapy evolved, has received empirical support for its use with conduct-disordered delinquent adolescents and their families in a series of studies conducted at the University of Utah. The series was based on work with 86 families referred by the Salt Lake Juvenile Court or the Utah Youth Services Bureau to the family clinic administered by James Alexander and his colleagues. The families were largely upper-lower to middle class, and the adolescents were involved in status offenses such as shoplifting, running away, and truancy.

The first set of studies demonstrated the effectiveness of treatment on certain processes of communication identified empirically as differentiating between delinquent and nondelinquent families (Alexander, 1973; Parsons & Alexander, 1973). Subsequently, the effects of treatment on recidivism and other measures of outcome were evaluated by means of powerful experimental designs that controlled for maturational, attention–placebo, and test–retest influences (Alexander & Parsons, 1973) and that compared the treatment with other forms of family intervention, for example, client-centered family counseling, and psychodynamic family therapy (Alexander & Barton, 1976; Klein, Alexander, & Parsons, 1977). The latter study also looked at the rates of court contact for *siblings* of the delinquents originally referred 3 years earlier, based on the assumption that, as the focus of treatment was the family system and not just the identified patient, the program could be expected to assist the family in dealing more effectively with subsequent developmental changes in younger siblings.

These studies showed that behavioral-systems family therapy resulted in 50%–66% lower rates of recidivism in the referred delinquents than that achieved with client-centered therapy or psychodynamic psychotherapy. The order of treatment effectiveness from most to least effective was behavioral-systems family therapy, client-oriented family therapy, no-treatment control, and psychodynamic family therapy. Furthermore, the reduction in recidivism rates in the behavioral systems group was found to be statistically related to changes in the family process (Alexander & Parsons, 1973).

The siblings of delinquent youths whose families were in behavioral-systems family therapy also showed lower rates of contact with the court 3 years after treatment than siblings in families receiving other forms of treatment or no treatment. The behavioral-systems treatment produced an incidence of sibling delinquency one third to one half lower than the sibling delinquency rates in the other treatment and control groups (Klein *et al.*, 1977).

The results of the studies by Alexander and colleagues lend strong empirical support to the use of behavioral-systems therapy with conduct-disordered delinquent adolescents and their families. Strictly speaking, this conclusion cannot be generalized to other patient populations or diagnostic categories because efficacy has not yet been demonstrated with other groups. However, as conduct-disordered and delinquent youths are notoriously difficult to treat, the results obtained by Alexander and his colleagues lend strong support to the use of this approach and suggest that it should be evaluated with other populations as well.

## CONCLUSIONS

In preparing this overview of family therapy models for children and adolescents, I was guided by the comprehensive review by Gurman, Kniskern, and Pinsof (1986). These authors presented a table (Gurman *et al.*, 1986, p. 595) that provides estimates of the effectiveness of family therapies for specific child and adolescent disorders. Because behavioral, structural, and functional approaches to family therapy have probable or established effectiveness with some disorders of childhood and adolescence, these approaches were emphasized in this chapter. Strategic family therapy was also reviewed because of its frequent use with children. Other approaches to family therapy that have uncertain or untested effectiveness for childhood disorders were not presented here (e.g., Bowenian, humanistic, and psychodynamic), although these approaches have demonstrated effectiveness with adult disorders and may, in the future, be tested with childhood disorders as well. It is incumbent on practitioners of other models to design and carry out studies of the outcome of these models so that the clinical practice of family therapy with children can be guided by empirical demonstrations of efficacy. At present, behavioral and structural family therapy show the greatest evidence of effectiveness, particularly for conduct, delinquent, and psychosomatic disorders (Gurman et al., 1986).

In reviewing these models of family therapy, the reader may have noted the similarities among them, particularly among the structural, strategic, and functional family models. Structural and strategic therapy are both offspring of systems theory. Both incorporate concepts of homeostasis, stability, and change in the face of normal and extreme challenges from within or outside the family. Both focus on repetitive, interpersonal transactions among various members of a family as a target of both assessment and intervention. Functional family therapy also focuses on interpersonal transactions among family members but views these with a behaviorist's eye, looking at the interpersonal outcomes for various family members as being of central importance.

Unlike structural and strategic therapy, which arose directly out of the study of family process, behavioral family therapy arose from a theory developed from work with individuals and was only later applied to family problems. Early applications of behavior therapy to the problems of children in the family were based on a unidirectional model in which parents were thought to shape and maintain problem child behavior by the way they dispensed reinforcers and punishers. More contemporary approaches to behavior therapy and the family have analyzed reciprocal influence processes in which two members of an interacting dyad (e.g., parent and child) both influence and are influenced by the behavior of each other (Patterson, 1982). In addition, modern behavior therapy has identified parent-controlled "family management practices," which sound very similar to the "executive functions" discussed in structural theory. Behavior therapy has done a more meticulous job of identifying exactly which parenting functions and skills discriminate strong from weak executive parental units and the consequences in children's development of the absence of these functions. The two approaches (structural and behavioral) still differ in the techniques used for addressing those absent functions. In addition, behavior therapy has not yet advanced beyond an analysis of dyadic interactions, whereas structural and strategic theories easily incorporate the evaluation of triadic influence processes.

It seems that, although there are clear differences among the models of family therapy, there are also areas of overlap and movement in the direction of a greater assimilation of concepts and techniques. This has occurred most notably in the work of Jay Haley, who has blended structural concepts with strategic intervention techniques. As noted above, there is an increasing similarity in some of the concepts and techniques of behavioral and systems family therapies as well.

In spite of the explosion of interest in family therapy, there has been a lamentable lack of empirical research on both the process and the outcome of strategic and structural family therapies. The need for such work is evident in the calls to document the effectiveness of all forms of psychotherapy, and one hopes that the future will find family therapists more willing to submit their ideas and strategies to the empirical test.

# REFERENCES

Alexander, J. F. (1973). Defensive and supportive communications in normal and deviant families. *Journal of Consulting and Clinical Psychology, 40,* 223–231.

Alexander, J. F., & Barton, C. (1976). Behavioral systems therapy for families. In D. H. Olson (Ed.), *Treating relationships.* Lake Mills, IA: Graphic Publishing.

Alexander, J. F., & Parsons, B. V. (1973). Short-term behavioral intervention with delinquent families: Impact on family process and recidivism. *Journal of Abnormal Psychology, 81,* 219–225.

Barton, C. V., & Alexander, J. F. (1980). Functional family therapy. In A. S. Gurman & D. P. Kniskern (Eds.), *Handbook of family therapy.* New York: Brunner/Mazel.

Bernal, M. E. (1969). Behavioral feedback in the modification of brat behaviors. *Journal of Nervous and Mental Disease, 148,* 375–385.

Bernal, M. E., Duryee, J. S., Pruett, H. L., & Burns, B. J. (1968). Behavioral modification and the brat syndrome. *Journal of Consulting and Clinical Psychology, 32,* 447–455.

Bernal, M. E., Klinnert, M. D., & Schultz, L. A. (1980). Outcome evaluation of behavioral parent training and client centered parent counseling for children with conduct problems. *Journal of Applied Behavior Analysis, 13,* 677–691.

Fisch, R., Weakland, J. H., & Segal, L. (1982). *The tactics of change: Doing therapy briefly.* San Francisco: Jossey-Bass.

Forehand, R., & King, H. E. (1974). Preschool children's noncompliance: Effects of short-term therapy. *Journal of Community Psychology, 2,* 42–44.

Forehand, R., & King, H. E. (1977). Noncompliant children: Effects of parent training on behavior and attitude change. *Behavior Modification, 1,* 93–108.

Forehand, R., & McMahon, R. J. (1981). *Helping the noncompliant child: A clinician's guide to parent training.* New York: Guilford Press.

Griest, D. L., & Wells, K. C. (1983). Behavioral family therapy for conduct disorders in children. *Behavior Therapy, 14,* 37–53.

Griest, D. L., Forehand, R., Rogers, T., Breiner, J., Furey, W., & Williams, C. A. (1982). Effects of parent enhancement therapy on the treatment outcome and generalization of a parent training program. *Behaviour Research and Therapy, 20,* 429–436.

Gurman, A. S. (1971). Group-marital therapy: Clinical and empirical implications for outcome research. *International Journal of Group Psychotherapy, 21,* 174–189.

Gurman, A. S., & Kniskern, D. P. (1978). Research on marital and family therapy: Progress, perspective, and prospect. In S. Garfield & A. Bergin (Eds.), *Handbook of psychotherapy and behavior change* (2nd ed.). New York: Wiley.

Gurman, A. S., Kniskern, D. P., & Pinsof, W. M. (1986). Research on marital and family therapies. In S. Garfield & A. Bergin (Eds.)., *Handbook of psychotherapy and behavior change* (3rd ed.). New York: Wiley.

Haley, J. (1963). *Strategies of psychotherapy.* New York: Grune & Stratton.

Haley, J. (1973). *Uncommon therapy.* New York: Norton.

Haley, J. (1976). *Problem solving therapy.* San Francisco: Jossey-Bass.

Haley, J. (1980). *Leaving home.* New York: McGraw-Hill.

Hoffman, L. (1981). *Foundations of family therapy.* New York: Basic Books.

Howe, G. (1986). *Structural and strategic family therapy.* Washington, DC: Children's Hospital National Medical Center.

Johnson, H. C. (1986). Emerging concerns in family therapy. *Social Work, 37,* 299–305.

Karoly, P., & Rosenthal, M. (1977). Training parents in behavior modification: Effects on perceptions of family interaction and deviant child behavior. *Behavior Therapy, 8,* 406–410.

Klein, N. C., Alexander, J. F., & Parsons, B. V. (1977). Impact of family systems intervention on recidivism and sibling delinquency: A model of primary prevention and program evaluation. *Journal of Consulting and Clinical Psychology, 45,* 469–474.

Korchin, S. J. (1976). *Modern clinical psychology: Principles of intervention in the clinic and community.* New York: Basic Books.

Lask, B., & Matthew, D. (1979). Childhood asthma: A controlled trial of family psychotherapy. *Archives of Diseases of Childhood, 54,* 116–119.

Liebman, R., Minuchin, S., & Baker, L. (1974a). An integrated treatment program for anorexia nervosa. *American Journal of Psychiatry, 131,* 432–436.

Liebman, R., Minuchin, S., & Baker, L. (1974b). The role of the family in the treatment of anorexia nervosa. *Journal of the American Academy of Child Psychiatry, 13,* 264–274.

Liebman, R., Minuchin, S., & Baker, L. (1974c). The use of structural family therapy in the treatment of intractable asthma. *American Journal of Psychiatry, 131,* 535–540.

Madanes, C. (1981). *Strategic family therapy.* San Francisco: Jossey-Bass.

Masten, A. S. (1979). Family therapy as a treatment for children: A critical review of outcome research. *Family Process, 14,* 323–335.

Minuchin, S., Montalvo, B., Guerney, B., Rosman, B., & Schumer, F. (1967). *Families of the slums.* New York: Basic Books.

Minuchin, S., Baker, L., Rosman, B., Liebman, R., Milman, L., & Todd, T. C. (1975) A conceptual model of psychosomatic illness in children. *Archives of General Psychiatry, 32,* 1031–1038.

Nichols, M. (1984). *Family therapy: Concepts and methods.* New York: Gardner Press.

O'Leary, K. D., O'Leary, S. G., & Becker, W. C. (1967). Modification of a deviant sibling interaction in the home. *Behaviour Research and Therapy, 5,* 113–120.

Ollendick, T. H., & Cerney, J. A. (1981). *Clinical behavior therapy with children.* New York: Plenum Press.

Palazzoli, S., Boscolo, M., Cecchin, G., & Prata, G. (1978). *Paradox and counterparadox.* New York: Jason Aronson.

Parsons, B. V., & Alexander J. F. (1973). Short-term family intervention: A therapy outcome study. *Journal of Consulting and Clinical Psychology, 41,* 195–201.

Patterson, G. R. (1974). Interventions for boys with conduct problems: Multiple settings, treatments, and criteria. *Journal of Consulting and Clinical Psychology, 42,* 471–481.

Patterson, G. R. (1982). *Coercive family process.* Eugene, OR: Castalia.

Patterson, G. R., & Reid, J. B. (1973). Intervention for families of aggressive boys: A replication study. *Behaviour Research and Therapy, 11,* 383–394.

Patterson, G. R., Cobb, J. A., & Ray, R. S. (1973). A social engineering technology for retraining aggressive boys. In H. E. Adams & P. Unikel (Eds.), *Issues and trends in behavior therapy.* Springfield, IL: Thomas.

Patterson, G. R., Chamberlain, P., & Reid, J. B. (1982). A comparative evaluation of a parent training program. *Behavior Therapy, 10,* 168–185.

Peed, S., Roberts, M., & Forehand, R. (1977). Evaluation of the effectiveness of a standardized parent training program in altering the interactions of mothers and their noncompliant children. *Behavior Modification, 1,* 323–350.

Walter, H., & Gilmore, S. D. (1973). Placebo versus social learning effects in parent training procedures designed to alter the behaviors of aggressive boys. *Behavior Therapy, 4,* 361–377.

Wells, K. C. (1984). *Treatment of oppositional behavior disorder.* Presented at the annual meeting of the American Psychological Association, Toronto.

Wells, K. C. (1985). Behavioral family therapy. In A. S. Bellack & M. Hersen (Eds.), *Dictionary of behavior therapy techniques.* New York: Pergamon Press.

Wells, K. C., & Egan, J. (in press). Behavioral parent training and systems family therapy for oppositional disorder: A comparative treatment outcome study. *Comprehensive Psychiatry.*

Wells, K. C., & Forehand, R. (1981). Childhood behavior problems in the home. In S. M. Turner, K. S. Calhoun, & H. E. Adams, (Eds.), *Handbook of clinical behavior therapy.* New York: Wiley.

Wells, K. C., & Forehand, R. (1985). Conduct and oppositional disorders. In P. H. Bornstein & A. S. Kazdin (Eds.), *Handbook of clinical behavior therapy with children.* New York: Dorsey.

Wells, K. C., Griest, D. L., & Forehand, R. (1980). The use of a self-control package to enhance temporal generality of a parent training program. *Behavior Research and Therapy, 18,* 347–358.

Wiltz, N. A., & Patterson, G. R. (1974). An evaluation of parent training procedures designed to alter inappropriate aggressive behavior of boys. *Behavior Therapy, 5,* 215–221.

# II     *Treatment Methods:*
# *Overview*

Numerous methods have been proposed and described to treat psychopathology in children. And within this framework are major theoretical formulations that support this array of methods. There are, of course, many theories of child psychopathology, and entire volumes have been written on the available empirically supported and generally most frequently used treatments. Obviously, the selections that are made in this regard still rely in part on judgments and personal bias. The reader should, of course, be aware of this factor.

Four general areas have been selected and formulated into chapters. Because most research in the treatment of children involves behavioral learning theory, two of the four chapters are devoted to this area. The first chapter deals with operant and classical conditioning. The operant and behavioral methods have traditionally used techniques that fall into this general category. The operant method in particular is popular and well documented in its use with young children and the multiply handicapped, especially the mentally retarded–emotionally disturbed. A major new trend is cognitive and social learning approaches to the treatment of children, which are discussed in the second chapter in this section. The interface of modeling, vicarious learning, and the modification of thoughts is among the areas that are being given the most attention in this regard.

Pharmacotherapy certainly has a number of biological rationales and is therefore approached more from the standpoint of describing various principles. This method follows the style we have discussed in the two previous chapters, which have been briefly mentioned above. Pharmacotherapy has become quite popular with adults, but except for drugs that have received special attention in their use with children, such as stimulants, progress has been made more slowly. Only recently, for example, have antidepressant medications been experimentally tested for affective disorders in children. And as with some of the aversive behavior modification procedures used with children, there has been controversy about the use of many of these drugs. In the next few years, it is hoped that professionals will be better able to agree on when and how these behavioral and pharmacological interventions should be used. As yet, the debate rages and, in fact, has intensified.

The final chapter in this section is entitled "Psychotherapy." Obviously, this is a very broad category; thus, only the major formulations are reviewed. Psychotherapy has been used as a treatment technique longer than any other general method, and it is still widely employed. However, research in this area has lagged far behind what has been reported in the previous three chapters in this section. As a result, the popularity of this approach with children, as compared to adults, has lost ground in recent years. Even so, psychotherapy is still a very influential approach with emotionally disturbed children. The acceptability of this approach will continue for some time to come and warrants attention in any broadly developed treatment-oriented book.

# 4  *Operant and Classical Conditioning*

## THOMAS M. DiLORENZO

This chapter is the first of two that outlines behavioral treatment strategies for children. The behavioral approach to treating childhood problems has been characterized by some researchers as a very simplistic type of therapy (i.e., the focus is only on environmental or situational variables). Other researchers characterize the approach as quite complex (i.e., the focus encompasses not only environmental, person, and cognitive variables but also the interaction among the variables). However, a fairly clear consensus has been obtained on how the behavioral approach is different from other psychological theories of personality. Kazdin (1984) cogently summarized these differences:

> The behavioral approach departs from the traditional conception of behavior by rejecting inferred motives, hypothesized needs, impulses, and drives, which supposedly explain behavior. Rather, emphasis is placed upon environmental, situational, and social determinants that influence behavior. Other events within the individual, including various cognitive processes, often serve as the focus of behavioral treatment. However, these processes are specified as measurable events, and their connection to overt behavior can be evaluated empirically rather than only presumed. (pp. 13–14)

Furthermore, learning plays a critical role in the development of both normal and abnormal behavior. Three types of learning have been specified (i.e., operant conditioning, classical conditioning, and observational learning, or modeling), as well as the formulation of a theory that integrates the three around cognitive processes (i.e., social learning theory) (Kazdin, 1984).

## BEHAVIORAL ASSESSMENT

The cornerstone of the behavioral approach to the treatment of problem behaviors has been the link between assessment and treatment. Indeed, the majority of behavioral researchers would agree that behavioral assessment and treatment go hand in hand and that treatment is not possible without a good assessment phase. Hersen (1976) noted that

> contrary to the practice of traditional psychotherapy, where there is a tendency to apply a rather uniform therapy irrespective of the presenting problem(s), the choice of

THOMAS M. DiLORENZO • Department of Psychology, University of Missouri—Columbia, Columbia, Missouri 65201.

treatment in behavior modification [or therapy] is determined on the basis of the findings derived from the behavioral analysis [or assessment]. (p. 13)

Because this assessment–treatment link is such an indigenous part of the approach, behavioral treatments can be discussed only after a thorough but brief presentation of behavioral assessment.

Bornstein and van den Pol (1985) indicated that no single model of behavioral assessment has emerged as the one most widely used. They cited five models that have been developed to guide the practitioner or are used as conceptual or taxonomic classification systems: (1) the functional analysis of behavior model (Peterson, 1968); (2) the S-O-R-K-C model (Kanfer & Saslow, 1969); (3) the BASIC ID model (Lazarus, 1985); (4) the behavioral assessment grid model (Cone, 1978); and (5) the multimethod assessment model (Nay, 1979). The functional analysis of behavior and S-O-R-K-C models appear to have the greatest utility for the practicing clinician, so they will be discussed in some detail.

A basic component of behavioral assessment is a functional analysis (sometimes referred to as a *behavioral analysis*). Bornstein and van den Pol (1985) considered this approach somewhat inadequate because of its lack of emphasis on cognitive factors. However, the generic approach can be applied to a wide range of behaviors, cognitions, situations, and person variables. The importance of performing a functional analysis before the initiation of specified treatment cannot be overemphasized. A functional analysis is defined as a thorough assessment of the problem behavior and its interrelationship with the variables that control its emission (DiLorenzo, 1987) to determine cause–effect relationships. The variables are located in a chain or series of behaviors, with the problem behavior juxtaposed to antecedent and consequent events. This interactional sequence may be analyzed from within a molecular framework (e.g., antecedent discriminative cues–response–consequences) or within a molar framework (e.g., matching the rate of responses with the rate of reinforcement).

This functional analysis (leading to the specification of controlling variables) would tie the assessment procedure directly to specific treatment implications (i.e., modifying the controlling variables). Effective interventions rely on a comprehensive analysis of the functional relationships among behaviors in child–environment interactions. Without this process, treatments are very often adopted uncritically (Phillips & Ray, 1980).

In the interest of developing a treatment plan, several steps should be followed in the functional analysis. First, the problem must be specified, and the behavior of interest must be defined. Second, the variables that control the problem must be identified. Third, Schreibman and Koegel (1981) suggested grouping the behaviors according to common controlling variables. In this way, as with every functional analysis or assessment performed, the treatment is specified automatically (Matson & DiLorenzo, 1984). Fourth, a procedure should be selected that will manipulate the controlling variables in the most efficacious way to change the behavior in a desirable and predictable direction (Schreibman & Koegel, 1981). Throughout this process, data or assessments must be collected to determine whether treatment goals are being met (Mash & Terdal, 1981).

The S-O-R-K-C model (Kanfer & Saslow, 1969) of behavioral assessment is an extension of Lindsley's (1964) earlier S-R-K-C model. Each letter represents an important area that needs to be assessed in a full behavioral analysis (i.e., S—

stimulus or antecedent events; O—organism or biological conditions; R—response or observed behaviors; K—contingency, refers to contingency-related conditions; and C—consequences, refers to environmental or organismic events that follow R or events). Actually, this model serves as a nice extention of the functional analysis model by using the above criteria to help specify controlling variables.

Kanfer and Saslow (1969) added a seven-part analysis or assessment to the model. They noted that this analysis

> should serve as a basis for making decisions about specific therapeutic interventions, regardless of the presenting problem. The compilation of data under as many headings as are relevant should yield a good basis for decisions about the areas in which intervention is needed, the particular targets of the intervention, the treatment methods to be used, and the series of goals at which treatment should aim. (p. 430)

The areas to be assessed are as follows. First, an initial analysis of the problem situation is conducted with special reference to whether the problem behavior could be considered a behavioral excess or deficit. Further assessment would be aimed at defining (1) the frequency, (2) the intensity, (3) the duration or form, and/or (4) the stimulus conditions of the problem behavior. Finally, behavioral assets (i.e., nonproblem or adaptive behaviors) should be assessed to aid in the execution of the therapeutic program.

The second step involves a clarification of the problem situation. Behavior does not occur in a vacuum, and changes will inevitably affect other areas of the child's life, including the family situation.

The third step involves a motivational analysis of the ongoing behavior and situation. Two important component parts of this analysis are identifying the reinforcement contingencies of the problem behavior and the major aversive stimuli present for the child.

The fourth part of the overall behavioral analysis or assessment involves a developmental analysis. Biological, sociological, and behavioral restrictions are assessed that contribute to the ongoing problem(s). Also, the potential for changes in each area are assessed as precursors of the implementation of a treatment strategy or strategies.

The fifth step involves an analysis of self-control. A goal of the treatment program would be to get the child involved in whatever way possible rather than relying solely on external controls.

The sixth step involves an analysis of the social relationships that are currently important to the child. Not only are the significant people in the child's current environment important, but the expectations of the child and significant others should also be assessed.

The final step involves an analysis of the social-cultural-physical environment. Several questions that are asked in this part of the assessment are

> What are the norms in the [child's] social milieu for the behaviors about which there is a complaint? . . . Are these norms similar in various environments in which the [child] interacts, e.g., home and school, friends and parents, work and social milieu, etc.? (Kanfer & Saslow, 1969, p. 436)

As noted earlier, the concepts of behavioral assessment and behavior therapy are inextricably interwoven. A thorough and complete assessment and analysis must be conducted before a treatment strategy is selected. The next section describes and defines the operant strategies that would be applied to ameliorate the problem behavior.

## Operant Conditioning

The procedures that are defined as operant conditioning fall into three general categories: reinforcement, extinction, and punishment programs. Although these procedures are often used together in comprehensive programs, they are presented below individually.

### Reinforcement Procedures

The intervention of choice varies as a function of how the target behavior is defined (Bellack & Hersen, 1977). If the problem behavior is conceptualized as a behavioral deficit, reinforcement programs are implicated as the treatment of choice. Conversely, if the problem behavior is conceptualized as a behavioral excess, extinction or punishment programs are implicated as the treatment of choice. (The reader may remember that, in the assessment phase, one specific guideline called for the assessor to define the problem behavior as a behavioral deficit or excess.) The clinician should attempt to define most problem behaviors as deficits so that reinforcement programs may be designed. This does not appear to be a problem in many cases. Even some problems defined as behavioral excesses can be reconceptualized as behavioral deficits. For example, disruptive out-of-seat behavior (i.e., a behavioral excess) could be redefined as infrequent in-seat behavior (i.e., a behavioral deficit). The reason for this emphasis on defining problems as deficits is that reinforcement programs are generally more positive and therefore easier and more acceptable to design.

Bellack and Hersen (1977) defined at least three of the innumerable factors that may categorize deficits:

> *First*, the environment might not provide adequate prompts (S$^D$s) for the child to emit a response in his [or her] repertoire. *Second*, a response in the repertoire might be prompted, but fails to appear because its occurrence is not maintained by reinforcement. *Third*, the response simply might not be in the child's repertoire (i.e., a skill deficit). Frequently, two or all three of these factors appear in combination. (p. 174)

These factors should be assessed in each child when the program development phase is initiated. If the problem behavior can be defined as a behavioral deficit, then a reinforcement program may be used. Reinforcement contingencies are designed to define and accelerate positive behaviors:

> The word *reinforcement* refers to the effect of an operation; it does not describe an independent variable but is the interaction of an independent variable with behavior. By *reinforcement* is meant an increase in responding as a function of a stimulus event following the response. The stimuli having these effects are *reinforcing stimuli* or *reinforcers*. *Schedules of reinforcement* are the rules used to present reinforcing stimuli. (Zeiler, 1977, p. 202)

In addition, contingencies of reinforcement have been defined as the interrelations among a discriminative stimulus, a response, and reinforcement (Skinner, 1969). Clear indications of the effective control of behavior using contingent reinforcement (as opposed to noncontingent reinforcement using the same stimulus) have been demonstrated (Hart, Reynolds, Baer, Brawley, & Harris, 1969; Redd, 1969). Similarly, the contingent application of a stimulus not demonstrated to be a reinforcer is ineffective in increasing the targeted behavior (Bassett, Blanchard, & Koshland, 1977; Kelleher, 1966).

Ten parameters of reinforcement are delineated that increase the probability of effectively using stimuli to increase behavior. First, the selection of effective reinforcers is critical. Bellack and Hersen (1977) suggested that the reinforcing value of a stimulus cannot "be determined on an ipso facto basis" (p. 177). Observations must be made as a stimulus is presented to assess the reinforcing value, quality, or preference (Kazdin, 1980) of the individual. Too often, we assume that specific stimuli act as universal reinforcers.

Second, after demonstration of the stimulus's reinforcing value, it should be given only contingently.

Third, the greater the amount of a reinforcer delivered for a response, the more frequent the response. However, limits on the quantity of the stimulus are defined by the fourth parameter: The reinforcer should not be so large that satiation occurs. The effect that magnitude has on reinforcement is limited by the point at which the individual becomes satiated (Kazdin, 1980).

The fifth parameter has been termed the *temporal gradient* of reinforcement. Immediate presentation of the reinforcing stimulus after the desired response is emitted leads to the greatest effect (Hull, 1952; Terrell & Ware, 1961).

If a response is not exhibited, it cannot be reinforced. The sixth and seventh points involve various aspects of this statement. If the response is in the individual's repertoire, it may need to be prompted. The prompt may involve the verbalization of the specific if-then contingency ("If the desired behavior is performed, then you will receive the reinforcing stimulus"). If the behavior is not in the individual's repertoire, it may need to be shaped. This process involves the reinforcement of successive approximations of the target behavior.

To prevent satiation, different reinforcers should be available to the individual. This is the eighth parameter. Effective reinforcers can be outlined by using a reinforcement menu (Homme, 1971), which is simply a list of reinforcers and dispensing media.

The ninth and tenth parameters involve the scheduling of reinforcers. The beginning stages of a program should be operating on a continuous reinforcement schedule (e.g., each time the behavior is emitted, it should be reinforced). However, the tenth parameter suggests that the contingency should be faded into a specific intermittent schedule because this schedule is the most resistant to extinction. (Several types of schedules are presented later.)

Many stimuli may serve as effective reinforcers for different individuals. Several classes or types have been delineated in the behavioral literature. Five global categories are material reinforcers, social reinforcers, activity reinforcers, token reinforcers, and covert reinforcers.

Material reinforcers include such things as food, drink, money, and toys. This type of reinforcer appears to be most effective for young children. Rimm and Masters (1979) suggested that most reinforcers in the natural environment are social (e.g., smiles, praises, and physical closeness). Therefore, it is often suggested that social reinforcers be incorporated into reinforcement programs from the beginning. If a person is not responsive to typical social reinforcers, a suggestion is made to pair material reinforcers (if effective) with social reinforcers and then gradually to fade the material reinforcers.

The third type of reinforcers is preferred activities. Researchers and clinicians (Becker, 1971; Homme, 1971) have referred repeatedly to "grandma's rule," or "if-then" contingencies. For example, "If you do your homework first, then you can watch television." The fourth type of reinforcer is a token (Kazdin, 1977). A token reinforcer is presented to the individual, contingent on performance. The token is redeemable later for other "backup reinforcers," including any of the first three defined (i.e., material, social, and activity). Finally, covert reinforcers are covert stimuli (i.e., thoughts or cognitions) that take the form of positive self-evaluations that an individual may engage in contingent on his or her own behavior (Cautela, 1977; Masters, Furman, & Barden, 1977; Masters & Santrock, 1976).

## Extinction

Although, in a technical sense, extinction is not considered a punishment procedure because a specific stimulus is not applied (Azrin & Holz, 1966; Matson & DiLorenzo, 1984), it is considered a reductive procedure because a reduction in the future probability of a response is observed when the procedure is used correctly. Harris and Ersner-Hershfield (1978) defined extinction as the

> withholding of previously given positive reinforcement following the emission of the target behavior. No discriminative cues, such as environmental changes or verbal warnings, are given. For example, in using an extinction procedure to treat tantrums, the therapist simply ignores the tantrum behavior and proceeds as though nothing has happened. (pp. 1355–1356)

Extinction is probably one of the most widely attempted procedures and also one of the most widely misunderstood. Clear and serious associated effects accompany and probably outweigh its use in most circumstances.

DiLorenzo and Ollendick (1986) outlined several treatment considerations that should be included in attempts to use extinction. First, the ease with which a response is extinguished is directly related to the frequency of the response–reinforcement relationship. That is, those responses that are continuously reinforced are easier to extinguish than intermittently reinforced responses (Kazdin, 1980). However, most responses in everyday life are intermittently reinforced. Second, every response must be consequated. If it is not, an intermittent reinforcement schedule is produced, and the response is maintained indefinitely. Third, responses are harder to extinguish if (1) the behavior has been greatly reinforced; (2) the behavior has been in existence a long time; and (3) the behavior has been exposed to extinction repeatedly. All three of the preceding conditions are typical of resistant high-rate maladaptive behaviors. Fourth, extinction is a gradual process. It usually takes a long time for extinction to work. Fifth, extinction bursts should be expected. Extinction bursts are defined as increases in the maladaptive behavior to above baseline levels after an initial decrease has been observed.

For the above reasons, extinction is simply not suggested as a treatment of choice in most instances. It is simply too difficult to ignore extremely problematic behaviors for long periods of time. It is not being suggested that extinction is not an effective procedure if the preceding treatment considerations are observed. However, in most applied settings, it is virtually impossible to gain the amount of control necessary to make the procedure effective.

## Punishment

When a problem behavior is defined as a behavioral excess, then punishment is the treatment of choice. Azrin and Holz (1966) define punishment as

> a reduction of the future probability of a specific response as a result of the immediate delivery of a stimulus for that response. The stimulus is designated as a punishing stimulus; the entire process is designated as punishment. (p. 381)

Note that the behavioral definition describes a process in which three essential components are outlined; (1) a behavior is defined; (2) a punishing stimulus is administered; and (3) a decrease is observed in the behavior. Several specific types of punishment procedures are detailed next.

### Overcorrection

Azrin and Foxx introduced overcorrection in the early 1970s as a viable method of reducing maladaptive behavior (Azrin & Foxx, 1971; Foxx & Azrin, 1972, 1973). As originally conceptualized,

> the general rationale of the proposed restitution procedure is to educate the offender to assume individual responsibility for the disruption caused by his misbehavior by requiring him to restore the disturbed situation to a greatly improved state. (Foxx & Azrin, 1972, p. 16)

Although overcorrection has been defined as an educative procedure or as a type of reinforcement, Axelrod, Brantner, and Meddock (1978) noted that, because the purpose of overcorrection is to decrease the frequency, duration, and/or intensity of the inappropriate behavior that precedes the application of the overcorrection technique, it is, by definition, punishment.

Overcorrection has been defined as a two-stage process in which the child must provide some work and expend some effort for some disruption. The first stage, referred to as *restitution overcorrection,* requires the child to restore the area that was disturbed to its original condition. For example, if a child pushed a glass of water off a table, he or she would be required to clean the mess (restitution) as well as to clean other adjoining areas (overcorrection). Therefore, the required work would result in considerably more effort than merely reversing the original disruptive behavior. The purpose for the extended effort is to make the task particularly aversive by requiring additional repetitive tasks that result in an increased expenditure of effort (Matson & DiLorenzo, 1984).

The second stage, defined as *positive practice overcorrection,* requires the child to practice appropriate modes of responding in situations where he or she normally misbehaves (Azrin & Powers, 1975; Foxx & Martin, 1975). For example, after the child completes the restitution overcorrection, the glass would be set up again in the disrupted area, and the child would be required to walk past the glass appropriately (positive practice). This task would be repeated 10–20 times (overcorrection) (Matson & DiLorenzo, 1984).

Thomas M. DiLorenzo

Time-out from reinforcement, or simply time-out, has been defined in a number of ways. Some researchers have defined time-out as the removal of all positive reinforcers for a certain period of time (Kazdin, 1980; Wells & Forehand, 1981). Others have defined time-out as removing an individual from positively reinforcing events (Bellack & Hersen, 1977). Still others have defined it as a combination of the preceding (Harris & Ersner-Hershfield, 1978; Plummer, Baer, & LeBlanc, 1977; Rimm & Masters, 1979).

Harris and Ersner-Hershfield's definition (1978) appears to be rather comprehensive and will be used here. Time-out is defined as

> removing attention or another reinforcing event upon emission of the target behavior. This removal is marked clearly by such events as removing the subject from the room, physical withdrawal of the therapist, or other discrete acts that signal the withdrawal of reinforcement. Return of access to reinforcement may be contingent upon cessation of the target behavior. This procedure is often called time-out but is more actively punishing than most definitions of time-out permit. (p. 1356)

## Punishing Stimuli

Researchers originally considered punishing stimuli to be quite specific, as opposed to elaborate procedures (i.e., overcorrection or time-out). Therefore, any specific stimulus that reduces the future probability that a response will occur would be considered a punishing stimulus. Contingent electric shock was the first punishing stimulus that was thoroughly researched with humans.

Other stimuli that have been administered contingent on the emission of maladaptive behaviors and that have resulted in the reduction of the behavior include noxious substances. Noxious substances are defined as any substances that are not physically harmful but that are unpleasant for the child to either hear, ingest, or smell (Matson & DiLorenzo, 1984). In addition, for a noxious substance to be considered a punishing stimulus, it must fulfill all the other properties of punishing stimuli (e.g., consistent application and reduction in the behavior observed). Some examples are lemon juice, aromatic ammonia, ice, noise, water squirts, and mouthwash.

Finally, a number of other stimuli have been used to decrease the frequency of problem behaviors. Some of these punishing stimuli are reprimands or verbal commands, slaps, and shaking.

## Physical Restraint

Traditionally, the term *physical restraint* has referred to the use of leather or cloth bracelets to restrict the movement of a client's limbs (Rosen & DiGiacomo, 1978). Physical restraint had been used primarily with psychotic clients to control violent behavior (Abroms, 1968; Bursten, 1975; Wells, 1972). However, the term *physical restraint* in the behavior modification literature refers to a very different procedure. Matson and DiLorenzo (1984) referred to physical restraint as a special case of time-out in which a client is removed from an environment that is highly reinforcing. These authors defined physical restraint as the physical restriction of the movement of a person's limbs (e.g., holding the limb behind the person's back) for a specified brief period of time. The procedure is initiated contingent on the emission of a specific behavior that is functionally related to the limbs involved in the procedure. Finally, the expressed purpose of the procedure is to decrease the future probability of the occurrence of the targeted behavior. This procedure is a relatively new advancement in the behavioral literature, and therefore, little research has been conducted on the use of physical restraint.

### Response Cost

Response cost is a punishment procedure based primarily on assessing fines or withdrawing positive reinforcers. Typically, response cost is one part of token economy systems. In the reinforcement component of a token economy, individuals earn tokens or some other form of tangible product for exhibiting appropriate behavior. At some later time, they are given the opportunity to trade the tokens for reinforcers. If the individual exhibits inappropriate or maladaptive behavior, tokens will be removed or fines assessed.

### Reinforcement and Punishment

One of the justifiable criticisms of punishment is that it teaches the child what behaviors not to exhibit but does not teach what behaviors to exhibit. Therefore, alternative adaptive responses should be prompted and reinforced. This point cannot be overstated. *No punishment program should ever be initiated without a reinforcement program overtly expressed and initiated either before or in addition to the punishment program.* There is no reason to expect that an adaptive behavior that is not being emitted at the present time will increase unless reinforcement for the desired response occurs. This statement is a simple principle of learning, and yet, it is often ignored.

Several specific types of reinforcement schedules have been used in punishment programs. These schedules have been referred to as *differentiation schedules* or *differential reinforcement* of positive and/or neutral behaviors.

"In differentiation schedules reinforcers are presented when a response or a group of responses displays a specified property" (Zeiler, 1977, p. 203). At least four differentiation schedules have been defined in the behavioral literature. Differential reinforcement of other behavior (DRO) is defined as the delivery of reinforcement when the targeted behavior has not been emitted for a specified interval. Differential reinforcement of low rates of responding (DRL) is defined as the delivery of reinforcement when the rate of the targeted behavior is less than or equal to some specified criterion. Differential reinforcement of incompatible responding (DRI) is defined as the delivery of reinforcement for responses that are topographically incompatible with the targeted behavior. Differential reinforcement of alternative behavior (DRA) is defined as the delivery of reinforcement for adaptive behaviors that are not necessarily topographically incompatible with the targeted behavior (Repp & Brulle, 1981).

## CLASSICAL CONDITIONING

The second form of learning that is discussed in this chapter is classical conditioning (also called *Pavlovian conditioning* or *respondent conditioning*). This form of conditioning has not been used as extensively in the behavioral literature as operant conditioning.

This form of conditioning is concerned with stimuli that automatically elicit reflexive responses (Kazdin, 1984). These stimuli are called *unconditioned stimuli,* and the responses are called *unconditioned responses.* In classical conditioning, a neutral stimulus is conditioned to elicit the same type of response that the unconditioned stimulus elicits by being paired repeatedly with the unconditioned stimulus. When this occurs, the neutral stimulus is called the *conditioned stimulus,* and the response that it elicits is called the *conditioned response.* In classical conditioning, the conditioned stimulus controls the response, whereas in operant conditioning, the consequence usually controls the emission of the response (Kazdin, 1984).

However, Kazdin (1984) noted that the distinction between classical conditioning and operant conditioning is blurred in at least two important respects. First, the distinction between the types of responses that are considered in each approach is difficult to make. At one time, it was thought that the responses that were changed by operant conditioning were exclusively voluntary, and that the responses that were changed by classical conditioning were involuntary. However, some involuntary responses (e.g., heart rate and blood pressure) have been manipulated or changed by operant consequences. Second, operant behavior can also be controlled by antecedent stimuli (i.e., stimulus control procedures). It is noted that, in operant conditioning, the stimulus does not elicit the response as in classical conditioning, but the stimulus does occasion the response or increase the probability that the response will be performed (Kazdin, 1984). Kazdin (1984) summarized as follows:

> Even though these and other reasons point to the difficulties in distinguishing [classical] and operant conditioning, it is important to keep the major difference in mind. In [classical] conditioning, the primary result is a change in the power of a stimulus to elicit a reflex response. In operant conditioning, the primary result is a change in the frequency of the response emitted or a change in some other aspect of the response such as intensity, speed, or magnitude. (p. 17)

Therefore, from this account, the clinician should be interested in elicited responses when using classical conditioning. Responses produced from fears and phobias seem to fit into this category, and therefore, desensitization procedures are implicated as the most well-known behavioral technique that operates (or may operate) within the classical conditioning paradigm.

### Desensitization Procedures

Two types of desensitization procedures are explained briefly here: systematic and *in vivo.* Wolpe (1958) developed the desensitization procedure known as *systematic desensitization.* In this procedure, the client is first trained to relax. When proficiency has been gained in this technique, the client is asked to use this procedure during the desensitization therapy. As originally conceptualized, the client would be asked to relax and then imagine anxiety-provoking stimuli or situations. Often, a hierarchy is used, in which the client starts with imagining low-anxiety situations and moves up through the hierarchy to high-anxiety situations. The client is instructed to use relaxation to counter the anxiety.

More recently, *in vivo* desensitization has been developed, in which the actual environment is manipulated to reduce fear and anxiety (Rickard & Elkins, 1983). This technique has been used to treat school phobias and fears of dogs, buses, water, and darkness.

As mentioned earlier, techniques derived from the classical conditioning paradigm do not appear often in the behavioral literature. Although a number of successes have been documented with the desensitization procedures, the basic premises have been questioned. The procedures used currently for fears and phobias would appear to be more exposure-based than grounded in the original conceptualization of how desensitization works.

## MAINTENANCE AND GENERALIZATION

In this chapter, operant and classical conditioning behavior-change methods have been delineated. However, of equal importance is the maintainance of treatment gains. Stokes and Baer (1977) noted:

> Traditionally, many theorists have considered generalization to be a *passive* phenomenon. Generalization was not seen as an operant response that could be programmed, but as a description of a "natural" outcome of any behavior-change process. . . . Even though the literature shows many instances of generalization, it is still frequently observed that when a change in behavior has been accomplished through experimental contingencies, then that change is manifest where and when those contingencies operate, and is often seen in only transitory forms in other places and at other times. The frequent need for generalization of therapeutic behavior change is widely accepted, but it is not always realized that generalization does not automatically occur simply because a behavior change is accomplished. Thus, the need actively to *program* generalization, rather than passively to expect it as an outcome of certain training procedures, is a point requiring both emphasis and effective techniques. (pp. 349–350)

Kazdin (1984) referred to two types of generalization: (1) response maintenance, defined as the degree to which behaviors are maintained after the program has been terminated, and (2) transfer of training, defined as the degree to which behaviors transfer to situations and settings other than the training situation. He suggested at least eight pragmatic techniques for helping to ensure maintenance and transfer.

The first procedure is to bring the changed behavior under the control of natural contingencies. During training, the target behavior should be reinforced or punished with naturally occurring consequences (e.g., praise or reprimands). Also, behaviors should be chosen that are naturally consequated.

Second, naturally occurring reinforcers should be used. This procedure consists of developing a program that takes advantage of events and resources in the natural environment.

Third, the programmed contingencies should be removed or faded gradually. An abrupt withdrawal will produce the baseline condition too quickly and can be discriminated easily by the child.

Fourth, stimulus control should be expanded. The term *stimulus control* refers to the control obtained by associating certain stimuli with programmed contingencies or conditions. If a narrow range of cues is programmed, the desired behavior will occur only when the circumscribed cues are presented. With a broader range of cues, the behavior will occur in a greater number of situations.

The fifth technique that aids in generalization involves schedules of reinforcement. After the targeted behavior is well established, it should be reinforced intermittently, as behavior controlled under this schedule is most resistant to extinction.

The sixth procedure involves delaying reinforcement. Because most reinforcers in the natural environment are delayed (e.g., an allowance at the end of the week), it is important to fade from immediate reinforcement. One caution is to be sure that the behavior is well established before instituting a delay.

The seventh technique is to use peers or other behavior-change agents in the program, as they may have contact with the child across a variety of situations.

The final technique is the designing of self-control procedures. Kazdin (1984) noted that performance may not be restricted to a narrow set of stimulus conditions (i.e., involving external behavior-change agents) if children can be trained to control their own behavior.

Response maintenance and programming generalization should be critical aspects of every behavioral program. Some of the practical considerations and procedures presented exemplify methods that should ensure this process.

## REFERENCES

Abroms, G. M. (1968). Setting limits. *Archives of General Psychiatry, 19*, 113–119.

Axelrod, S., Brantner, J. P., & Meddock, T. D. (1978). Overcorrection: A review and critical analysis. *The Journal of Special Education, 12*, 367–391.

Azrin, N. H., & Foxx, R. M. (1971). A rapid method of toilet training the institutionalized retarded. *Journal of Applied Behavior Analysis, 4*, 89–99.

Azrin, N. H., & Holz, W. C. (1966). Punishment. In W. K. Honig (Ed.), *Operant behavior: Areas of research and application*. New York: Appleton-Century-Crofts.

Azrin, N. H., & Powers, M. A. (1975). Eliminating classroom disturbances of emotionally disturbed children by positive practice procedures. *Behavior Therapy, 6*, 525–534.

Bassett, J. E., Blanchard, E. B., & Koshland, E. (1977). On determining reinforcing stimuli: Armchair versus empirical procedures. *Behavior Therapy, 8*, 205–212.

Becker, W. C. (1971). *Parents are teachers*. Champaign, IL: Research Press.

Bellack, A. S., & Hersen, M. (1977). *Behavior modification: An introductory textbook*. New York: Oxford University Press.

Bornstein, P. H., & van den Pol, R. A. (1985). Models of assessment and treatment in child behavior therapy. In P. H. Bornstein & A. E. Kazdin (Eds.), *Handbook of clinical behavior therapy with children*. Homewood, IL: The Dorsey Press.

Bursten, B. (1975). Using mechanical restraints on acutely disturbed psychiatric patients. *Hospital and Community Psychiatry, 26*, 757–759.

Cautela, J. R. (1977). The use of covert conditioning in modifying pain behavior. *Journal of Behavior Therapy and Experimental Psychiatry, 8*, 45–52.

Cone, J. D. (1978). The behavioral assessment grid (BAG): A conceptual framework and taxonomy. *Behavior Therapy, 9*, 882–888.

DiLorenzo, T. M. (1987). Methods of assessment II: Standardized and projective tests. In C. Frame & J. L. Matson (Eds.), *Handbook of assessment in childhood psychopathology: Applied issues in differential diagnosis and treatment evaluation*. New York: Plenum Press.

DiLorenzo, T. M., & Ollendick, T. H. (1986). Behavior modification: Punishment. In R. P. Barrett (Ed.), *Severe behavior disorders in the mentally retarded: Nondrug approaches to treatment*. New York: Plenum Press.

Foxx, R. M., & Azrin, N. H. (1972). Restitution: A method of eliminating aggressive-disruptive behavior of retarded and brain damaged patients. *Behaviour Research and Therapy, 10*, 15–27.

Foxx, R. M., & Azrin, N. H. (1973). The elimination of autistic self-stimulatory behavior by overcorrection. *Journal of Applied Behavior Analysis, 6*, 1–14.

Foxx, R. M., & Martin, E. D. (1975). Treatment of scavenging behavior (coprophagy and pica) by overcorrection. *Behaviour Research and Therapy, 13,* 153–163.

Harris, S. L., & Ersner-Hershfield, R. (1978). Behavioral suppression of seriously disruptive behavior in psychotic and retarded patients: A review of punishment and its alternatives. *Psychological Bulletin, 85,* 1352–1375.

Hart, B. M., Reynolds, N. J., Baer, D. M., Brawley, E. R., & Harris, F. R. (1968). Effect of contingent and non-contingent social reinforcement on the cooperative play of a preschool child. *Journal of Applied Behavior Analysis, 1,* 73–76.

Hersen, M. (1976). Historical perspectives in behavioral assessment. In M. Hersen & A. S. Bellack (Eds.), *Behavioral assessment: A practical handbook.* New York: Pergamon Press.

Homme, L. E. (1971). *How to use contingency contracting in the classroom.* Champaign, IL: Research Press.

Hull, C. L. (1952). *A behavior system.* New Haven, CT: Yale University Press.

Kanfer, F. H., & Saslow, G. (1969). Behavioral diagnosis. In C. M. Franks (Ed.), *Behavior therapy: Appraisal and status.* New York: McGraw-Hill.

Kazdin, A. E. (1977). *The token economy: A review and evaluation.* New York: Plenum Press.

Kazdin, A. E. (1980). *Behavior modification in applied settings* (2nd ed.). Homewood, IL: Dorsey Press.

Kazdin, A. E. (1984). *Behavior modification in applied settings* (3rd ed.). Homewood, IL: Dorsey Press.

Kelleher, R. T. (1966). Chaining and conditioned reinforcement. In W. K. Honig (Ed.), *Operant behavior: Areas of research and application.* New York: Appleton.

Lazarus, A. A. (1985). A brief overview of multimodal therapy. In A. A. Lazarus (Ed.), *Casebook of multimodal therapy.* New York: Guilford Press.

Lindsley, O. R. (1964). Direct measurement and prosthesis of retarded behavior. *Journal of Education, 147,* 62–81.

Mash, E. J., & Terdal, L. G. (1981). Behavioral assessment of childhood disturbance. In E. J. Mash & L. G. Terdal (Eds.), *Behavioral assessment of childhood disorders.* New York: Guilford Press.

Masters, J. C., & Santrock, J. (1976). Studies in the self-regulation of behavior: Effects of contingent cognitive and affective events. *Development Psychology, 12,* 334–348.

Masters, J. C., Furman, W., & Barden, R. C. (1977). Effects of achievement standards, tangible rewards, and self-dispensed achievement evaluations on children's task mastery. *Child Development, 48,* 217–224.

Matson, J. L., & DiLorenzo, T. M. (1984). *Punishment and its alternatives: A new perspective for behavior modification.* New York: Springer.

Nay, W. R. (1979). *Multimodal clinical assessment.* New York: Gardner Press.

Peterson, D. R. (1968). *The clinical study of social behavior.* New York: Appleton-Century-Crofts.

Phillips, J. S., & Ray, R. S. (1980). Behavioral approaches to childhood disorders. *Behavior Modification, 4,* 3–34.

Plummer, S., Baer, D. M., & LeBlanc, J. M. (1977). Functional considerations in the use of procedural time-out and an effective alternative. *Journal of Applied Behavior Analysis, 10,* 689–705.

Redd, W. H. (1969). Effects of mixed reinforcement contingencies on adults' control of children's behavior. *Journal of Applied Behavior Analysis, 2,* 249–254.

Repp, A. C., & Brulle, A. R. (1981). Reducing aggressive behavior of mentally retarded persons. In J. L. Matson & J. R. McCartney (Eds.), *Handbook of behavior modification with the mentally retarded.* New York: Plenum Press.

Rickard, H. C., & Elkins, P. D. (1983). Behavior therapy with children. In C. E. Walker & M. C. Roberts (Eds.), *Handbook of clinical child psychology.* New York: Wiley.

Rimm, D. C., & Masters, J. C. (1979). *Behavior therapy: Techniques and empirical findings* (2nd ed.). New York: Academic Press.

Rosen, H., & DiGiacomo, J. N. (1978). The role of physical restraint in the treatment of psychiatric illness. *The Journal of Clinical Psychiatry, 135,* 325–328.

Schreibman, L., & Koegel, R. L. (1981). A guideline for planning behavior modification programs for autistic children. In S. M. Turner, K. S. Calhoun, & H. E. Adams (Eds.), *Handbook of clinical behavior therapy.* New York: Wiley.

Skinner, B. F. (1969). *Contingencies of reinforcement: A theoretical analysis.* New York: Appleton-Century-Crofts.

Stokes, T. F., & Baer, D. M. (1977). An implicit technology of generalization. *Journal of Applied Behavior Analysis, 10,* 349–367.

Terrell, G., & Ware, R. (1961). Role of delay of reward in speed of size and form discrimination learning in children. *Child Development, 32,* 409–415.

Wells, D. A. (1972). The use of seclusion on a university hospital psychiatric floor. *Archives of General Psychiatry, 26,* 410–413.

Wells, K. C., & Forehand, R. (1981). Childhood behavior problems in the home. In S. M. Turner, K. S. Calhoun, & H. E. Adams (Eds.), *Handbook of clinical behavior therapy.* New York: Wiley.

Wolpe, J. (1958). *Psychotherapy by reciprocal inhibition.* Stanford, CA: Stanford University Press.

Zeiler, M. (1977). Schedules of reinforcement: The controlling variables. In W. K. Honig & J. E. R. Staddon (Eds.), *Handbook of operant behavior.* Englewood Cliffs, NJ: Prentice-Hall.

# 5    Cognitive and Social Learning Theories

SHARON L. FOSTER, PHILIP C. KENDALL, AND
DAVID C. GUEVREMONT

Theoretical and therapeutic approaches falling under the general heading of "cognitive" and "social learning" have gained wide popularity since 1960. No single "cognitive" or "social learning theory" is uniformly accepted, although numerous approaches fit these general descriptive terms. These theories share an emphasis on the complex interaction among cognitive events and processes, affect, overt behavior, and environmental contexts and events as underlying various facets of dysfunctional behavior. Similarly, these different theories agree that learning has a pivotal role in the acquisition and maintenance of deviant and adaptive behavior, and like operant theories (but to a lesser degree), they recognize the importance of environmental consequences—particularly those provided by the social environment—in these processes. Unlike operant theories, however, cognitive social learning (CSL) theories postulate that most learning is a function of how the individual cognitively processes stimulus and consequence information. Possibly because these mediating processes are assumed to explain deviant behavior more adequately than the principles of operant and classical conditioning alone, much of CSL research and writing has been devoted to defining, examining, and defending their nature. It is in this arena that different CSL theories diverge most widely (cf. Meichenbaum & Cameron, 1982).

Cognitive-behavioral treatment approaches, like social learning theories, are not defined by a single technique or set of strategies. Nonetheless, most interventions have a common conceptual framework of the change process underlying effective therapeutic procedures (Meichenbaum, 1985). In accord with cognitive and social learning models, change may be induced through various methods, including direct, vicarious, or symbolically represented experience. Regardless of the procedures producing change, though, the mechanisms assumed to be responsible for the change lie in the cognitive events or processes producing behavior. Possibly as a result, many cognitive-behavioral interventions with children recognize the importance of the learning process and of the

SHARON L. FOSTER • Department of Psychology, West Virginia University, Morgantown, West Virginia 26506.    PHILIP C. KENDALL • Department of Psychology, Temple University, Philadelphia, Pennsylvania 19122.    DAVID C. GUEVREMONT • Department of Psychology, West Virginia University, Morgantown, West Virginia 26506.

influence of contingencies and models in the environment, while underscoring the centrality of mediating and information-processing factors in both the development and the remediation of childhood disorders (Kendall, 1985a).

This chapter first overviews major cognitive and social learning theoretical stances toward psychopathology in general and deviant child behavior in particular. We then highlight major tenets of these approaches that should be included in a unified theoretical system for explaining the etiology and maintenance of childhood disturbance. Finally, we summarize and critique important treatment modalities that have emerged within this tradition, describing their typical procedures and use.

## SOCIAL LEARNING AND COGNITIVE THEORIES

Most social learning and cognitive theories of psychopathology were developed without an explicit focus on children. Rather, they initially either addressed adult disorders or assumed that the same principles applied equally to children, with little discussion of the role of development in the processes underlying adaptive and disordered behavior. Here we review several influential theoretical frameworks proposed to account for deviant behavior, recognizing that many have been uncritically extrapolated to children.

### Bandura's Formulations of Social Learning Theory

Although developmental psychologists speculated on and investigated the role of learning processes in the family in the 1950s, using social learning models (e.g., Sears, Maccoby, & Levin, 1957), the seminal work describing a coherent, extensive theory with an explicit focus on modifying deviant behavior is generally held to be Albert Bandura's *Principles of Behavior Modification* (1969). Bandura conceptualized psychopathology in terms of behavioral excesses and deficits, defined and labeled by the social environment. Behavior resulted from learning processes that operated, not unidirectionally from an active environment's shaping passive organisms, but in reciprocal, mutually influenced interactions between the individual and the environment. Bandura (1969) described the critical components of these interactions: "Human functioning . . . involves interrelated control systems in which behavior is determined by external stimulus events, by internal information-processing systems and regulatory codes, and by reinforcing response-feedback processes" (p. 19).

In later publications (e.g., 1973, 1977a,b, 1986), Bandura further developed his version of social learning theory, explicating in particular the nature and workings of cognitive processes, but still emphasizing the notion of reciprocal determinism, in which behavior, environment, and cognitive processes operate together, each element influencing and influenced by the others (Bandura, 1986). The relative influence of each of these factors at any given point depends on both the situation and the behavior in question (Bandura, 1977b). The interdependence of internal and external events can be illustrated in a socially anxious adolescent who believes adamantly that his peers dislike him. His negative cognitions (e.g., "No one will talk to me") lead him to behave in a cold, aloof manner when he encounters his peers. Consequently, few peers interact with him, strengthening his conviction that he is disliked and maintaining the chain of biased thinking (distorted information processing), social aloofness, and rejection. Here, cognitions, behavior, and the environmental outcomes of these events are interlocked in a self-perpetuating cycle of defeat (Kendall, 1985b).

From the notion of reciprocal interactive processes came Bandura's dual emphasis on the roles of both the environment and internal processes in the development and maintenance of devant behavior. Like Mischel (1968), Bandura (1969) rejected trait theories in favor of more situational accounts of behavior. His early descriptions of the role of the environment in learning relied heavily on the importance of contiguous associations between events, stimulus control, and the kind of response–environment relations described in classical and operant conditioning.

Bandura's social learning theory differs from operant approaches in his stance toward cognitive, internal events. Although not disputing the powerful effects that external contingencies exert on behavior, Bandura has maintained that these effects are mediated by cognitive events and processes that are critical links in causal chains producing behavior. He has defined covert events broadly to include verbal mediators, imaginal mediators (images), and arousal mediators (reactions with physiological components). These can serve as stimuli and consequences for other covert and overt responses. Cognitive events are critical components of the mediational processes that comprise what Bandura (1986) postulated are basic capabilities of humans: representing events and ideas symbolically, thinking about the future, learning vicariously (without direct personal experience of consequences), using internal standards and self-generated activities to regulate one's actions, and consciously reflecting on the self. These capabilities, together with the concepts of attention to relevant stimuli, memory of experience, conversion of symbolic representation into specific actions, and motivational states, are used to explain the acquisition and performance of learned behavior (Bandura, 1986).

Cognitive events and processes are integral to Bandura's formulations of learning, which he assumed to be mediated through symbolic activity. Learning processes involve the association of environmental events with other events and with outcomes through direct and vicarious experience, with modeling emphasized as a particularly potent form of vicarious learning. Once an individual is capable of performing a particular response, its performance at a particular point in time depends on the stimulus cues present in the environment and the expected outcome of the behavior.

According to Bandura, the outcomes of behavior influence future actions through their informational and motivational properties rather than via a direct strengthening of responses. By directly or vicariously experiencing particular outcomes, the individual acquires information (which may or may not be subject to awareness) about the response–consequence relations operating in particular situations. Over time, the individual translates this accumulating information into expectations, which, together with the value the individual attaches to the outcomes associated with the action, influence the likelihood that the response will be reproduced in similar and related situations in the future. Thus, expected consequences are assumed to influence an individual's behavior more than actual consequences, until new experiences change the person's expectations (Bandura, 1986). Consequences are cognitively represented and are translated into incentives, which are symbolically depicted as potential future outcomes.

Self-regulatory processes are also postulated to be crucial to learning. These processes include setting standards for one's own behavior, evaluating one's performance relative to these standards, and providing self-administered consequences, such as self-praise or self-criticism. Self-administered consequences function as do external consequences by providing information about the outcomes of behavior.

Bandura (1977a) also explained the influence of planned therapeutic intervention on behavior via cognitive processes, speculating that a variety of mechanisms, including performance accomplishments, vicarious experience, persuasion, and emotional arousal, induce individuals' expectations that they can perform in ways that will produce positive outcomes. These efficacy expectations, together with relevant behavioral skills and appropriate incentives, determine whether a client will engage in new behavior patterns.

Numerous mechanisms by which deviant behavior can be produced and maintained can be derived from social learning theory (Bandura, 1969, 1977b). Dysfunctional learning can result from adventitious association among stimuli, behavior, and outcome, which the individual mistakenly construes as a causal relationship, as when a child who has a bad dream at night comes to fear the dark as the source of the dream. Faulty information-processing can also result in defective association of responses with outcomes, inappropriate or inadequate linking of responses with relevant social cues, or inappropriate generalization from aversive to nonthreatening circumstances (e.g., withdrawing from all encounters with peers after being rudely teased by the local bully). Dysfunctional self-evaluation systems, too, can produce overly high standards of performance, leading to insufficient self-commendation and excessive self-criticism, with correspondingly low self-esteem.

Mahoney (1974) described several processes that specify potential cognitive and behavioral determinants of deviant behavior in greater detail and that are compatible with Bandura's theoretical framework. One set of mechanisms involves attentional processes; misguided cognition in this area includes ignoring relevant environmental stimuli, perceiving but inaccurately labeling these stimuli, and focusing on or generating irrelevant stimuli that interfere with performance. In processing stimuli, individuals can make errors in classifying information (as when events are classified dichotomously into "good" and "bad," with no middle ground), errors in comparisons (as when performance is always evaluated as falling short of goals), and errors in inference (as when negative consequences are incorrectly predicted). An inadequate storage of information about relations among environmental events can also lead to behavior that fails to capitalize on positive environmental outcomes in appropriate situations. Finally, an inadequate repertoire of responses appropriate to particular situations will lead to inappropriate behavior, even if the cognitive processes function adaptively.

Certain environmental factors could also enhance the likelihood of deviant behavior. Although less often emphasized by social learning theorists than are cognitive processes, these may be particularly important for children who are presumably in the process of forming important connections between their behavior and its outcomes. Erratic or insufficient positive familial and peer consequences for adaptive behavior, coupled with highly valued consequences regularly paired with deviant behavior, would be likely to produce and sustain negative behavior. Environments where prosocial behavior is rarely seen or rewarded and where deviant behavior is modeled and reinforced would also encourage the development of maladaptive behavior.

Although Bandura's theory does not explicitly focus on children, he recently speculated on cognitive development (Bandura, 1986). Acquiring increased knowledge and cognitive skills in childhood, like other kinds of response acquisition, results from experience (both direct and vicarious), as well as from guided teaching, and depends heavily on the child's social environment. As in other forms of behavior, the cross-situational use of acquired skills is not assumed, nor is development assumed to take a uniform course for all individuals across all situations.

Because social learning theory is a general framework for explaining the development of all behavior, not just deviant responding, it includes relatively little explicit consideration of the mechanisms underlying specific patterns of maladjustment (with the exception of aggression; see Bandura, 1973). Similarly, with the exception of modeling, Bandura has not developed specific therapeutic procedures based on this theoretical framework. Instead, social learning theory appears to have been formulated as a comprehensive system to explain various data on behavior and treatment outcome within a coherent theoretical framework.

## Cognitive Models of Adult Psychopathology

Several models of adult psychopathology offer cognitive theories with explicit statements about the relation of dysfunctional thinking to deviant behavior and to intervention efforts. Among the most prominent of these are those offered by Albert Ellis, Aaron T. Beck, and their colleagues, which have had major influences on cognitive-behavioral theory and practice.

A fundamental premise underlying both Ellis's and Beck's cognitive-behavioral theories as applied to adults is that much maladaptive behavior and negative emotion arises from distorted, cognitively mediated representations of external events. Distorted processing and worldviews are causally linked to problems of depression, anger, anxiety, and other disturbances of thought and behavior (e.g., Beck, 1976; Beck, Rush, Shaw, & Emery, 1979; Ellis & Grieger, 1977). Faulty cognitive styles are generally assumed to have been acquired through experience, both direct and vicarious. Cognitions play a critical role in mediating responses to external events and are themselves influenced by external events and behavior in a continuous reciprocal interplay.

At the core of Ellis's rational-emotive therapy (RET; Ellis, 1970; Ellis & Bernard, 1983) lies the assumption that certain kinds of irrational beliefs, and not environmental events, directly produce emotional upsets. One prominent form that these beliefs take is characterized as self-statements (self-talk). Self-statements that result in negative emotional reactions have several distinctive characteristics. First, they may not follow logically from the precipitating external event. Second, they are irrational and are often based on unverifiable faulty assumptions. Finally, problem self-statements frequently involve an exceedingly strong moralistic and inflexible sense of duty (e.g., "I must" and "I have to"). Although irrational beliefs can take numerous forms, Ellis and Bernard (1983; Bernard, 1984) speculated that, in children, these irrational self-statements revolve around three general themes: an overemphasis on approval and perfect performance, the distorted importance of getting what one wants, and a perceived inability to tolerate negative experience.

Beck and his colleagues have identified three interrelated types of cognition that contribute to the development and maintenance of emotional disorders: cognitive events, cognitive processes, and cognitive schemas. Cognitive events, defined by the content of thoughts and images, are automatic, are rapidly shifting, and, in disturbed individuals, are idiosyncratic and are often adamantly believed despite available contradictory evidence. These thoughts describe the personal meanings that individuals attach to events, and they take the forms of self-instructions and self-monitoring, anticipation, and rules for guiding one's behavior (Beck, 1976). Different types of self-defeating thoughts are associated with different emotional reactions. For example, negative self-evaluations, misconceptions of others' perceptions or evaluations, and pessimistic hopes and ideas about the future characterize the cognitive events common to depressed individuals (Beck *et al.*, 1979; Hollon & Kendall, 1980; Hollon, Kendall, & Lumry, 1986), whereas anxious people are prone to repetitive thoughts about danger (Beck, Emergy, & Greenberg, 1985) and automatic questioning (Kendall & Ingram, 1987).

Faulty cognitive processes, or the mechanisms by which individuals make sense of and interpret external events, can also predispose an individual to emotional problems. Beck *et al.* (1979) specified six biased ways in which depressed individuals are likely to process information: (1) dichotomous reasoning (thinking in extremes or in all-or-none ways); (2) overgeneralization (drawing unjustified conclusions based on a single incident or limited evidence); (3) magnification and minimization (grossly over- or underestimating the significance of an event); (4) arbitrary inference (drawing conclusions based on inadequate or even contradictory evidence); (5) selective abstraction (drawing conclusions based on details taken out of context); and (6) personalization (drawing conclusions about the self from irrelevant external events).

The cognitive events and cognitive processes elicited by particular situations are knit together by an individual's cognitive structures or schemas, which are relatively stable, learned cognitive patterns. These provide the basic filters through which individuals selectively focus on, differentiate, and organize certain aspects of the environment while ignoring others. Established via experience, schemas are hypothesized to be situationally linked and vary in terms of their generality and in the likelihood that they will be activated in particular situations (Beck *et al.*, 1985). When overly active, idiosyncratic, and negatively biased, these can dominate more rational schemas, filtering new information in ways that maintain the fundamental distortions by which they operate. As a net result, the individual both experiences emotional disturbance and is relatively immune to the kinds of environmental input that could, if attended to, challenge the inferences, beliefs, and processes that create and sustain the schemas (see also Ingram, 1986).

The emphases on cognition and learning evident in both Ellis's and Beck's models of psychopathology are also evident in the therapies derived from both theoretical frameworks. Although there are many variants on both approaches, most endorse the role of learning as a foundation for interventions and are typically considered cognitive-behavioral (Kendall, 1984b, 1985a). By structuring a series of vicarious, instructional, competency and performance-based, and direct experiences, therapists teach clients to challenge their current thinking patterns and to create and use alternative forms of thinking and behavior, thus interrupting the chain of events (external, cognitive, and behavioral) controlling maladaptive behavior. Therapy generally involves teaching clients to (1) observe their self-denigrating or distorted thoughts; (2) relate these to emotional distress and dysfunctional performance; (3) gather data and/or challenge the premises underlying distorted thinking; and (4) alter or restructure maladaptive thoughts and thought processes by replacing them with incompatible, adaptive cognitions and behaviors (e.g., Beck *et al.*, 1979; Kendall & Hollon, 1979; Meichenbaum, 1985). Clients participate as active collaborators in the change process by collecting information from their everyday lives to help them recognize their own problem thought processes and how these relate to the presenting complaints and by implementing interventions to challenge and change maladaptive thoughts and behavior.

In the same way that confirmatory outcomes may reinforce distorted cognitive patterns, disconfirmatory outcomes may contribute to changes in cognitive appraisals of external events. Thus, it is not surprising that cognitive-behavior therapists sometimes attempt to alter overt behavior directly in addition to targeting faulty thought processes, recognizing their ongoing mutual influence. Techniques such as behavior rehearsal, homework assignments, and self-monitoring are used extensively to promote cognitive and behavior change (see also Jacobson, 1987; Kendall, 1984b; Kendall & Bemis, 1984).

## Cognitive-Behavioral Models of Child Psychopathology

The theoretical and treatment approaches of Ellis and Beck evolved in efforts to understand and alter various forms of adult psychopathology, both views stressing the pivotal role of cognition as a determinant of behavior and emotion and as a critical element in therapeutic change processes. Cognitive-behavioral models of childhood maladjustment and therapy overlap considerably with adult models in both theory and technique. Both adult and child cognitive-behavioral approaches emphasize the relationship between thinking processes and dysfunctional behavior, endorse the notion of reciprocal determinism, and acknowledge the role of the environment and learning processes in the etiology and maintenance of behavior.

Despite these similarities, cognitive-behavioral applications with children are not merely a downward simplification of the approaches used in conceptualizing adult behavior (Kendall, 1981b). One reason lies in the difference between why children and why adults seek mental health professionals for help. Whereas adult problems, such as anxiety and depression, are often coupled with subjective distress, child problems, such as inattentiveness, aggression, and impulsivity, are frequently targeted not because they are personally distressing, but because they are disturbing to others, such as parents and teachers. As a consequence, cognitive theories and therapies with adults are most often applied to problems with major affective components ("internalizing problems"), whereas cognitive-behavioral approaches with children have more often addressed "externalizing" behavior problems. In adult-oriented theories, affective distress is believed to be a major outcome of distorted (dysfunctional) thought;

in childhood, unwanted behavioral reactions are thought to result from an absence of or a deficiency in various cognitive processes.

Although several types of adult psychopathology (e.g., depression and anxiety) are thought to derive from *distorted* or erroneous cognitions, theories of childhood disturbances such as impulsivity, attention deficits, and/or acting out often emphasize cognitive *deficiencies,* or the absence of certain forms of cognitive activities that are assumed to be prerequisites for effective and adaptive behavior (e.g., Kendall, 1985b; Kendall & Braswell, 1985). One of the primary deficiencies postulated as underlying child behavior problems is the absence of self-guiding private speech. Private speech is assumed to serve an important self-regulatory function by guiding behavior via covert self-instruction (e.g., Meichenbaum, 1977). Other theorists speculate that deficiencies in interpersonal problem-solving skills, including problem recognition, means–end thinking, the generation of alternative solutions, and the analysis of cause–effect relations may be central to acting-out problems in childhood (e.g., Spivak, Platt, & Shure, 1976). Spivak *et al.* (1976) also suggested that deficiencies in role-taking skills, or the ability to see events from the perspective of others, may be related to childhood deviance, a speculation echoed by some developmental psychologists (e.g., Chandler, 1973; Selman, Lavin, & Brion-Meisels, 1982).

Although cognitive deficiency (i.e., not actively processing) is thought to be a primary component of certain types of child deviance, Ellis and Beck-type distortions are associated with other disturbed child behaviors. Dodge (1980; Dodge & Frame, 1982; Dodge, Murphy, & Buschbaum, 1984) and Asher and his colleagues (Renshaw & Asher, 1982; Taylor & Asher, 1984) have each postulated and provided data to support the hypothesis that distorted processing underlies socially incompetent performance. Dodge endorsed the hypothesis that aggressive children misattribute neutral circumstances as reflecting peer hostility, a misattribution leading them to retaliate inappropriately. Asher postulated that socially incompetent children hold inappropriate goals for interpersonal tasks and thus fail to work cooperatively, a process producing behavior that alienates others and leads to peer rejection.

Different emphases on cognitive distortions versus deficiencies also produce distinct cognitive-behavioral treatment approaches. As will be described in more detail in a later part of the chapter, cognitive-behavioral interventions with children that derive from deficit models, while stressing learning and the active-directive methods that characterize adult-oriented approaches, generally proceed by teaching various cognitive self-control activities. When new cognitions are taught, they often take the form of self-instructional or coping self-statements, sometimes sequenced into a series of steps that accumulate to teach the child a complete decision-making process to guide behavior, such as problem solving. As in the adult cognitive-behavioral approaches, a variety of strategies, including modeling, instruction, behavior rehearsal, and homework, are used to produce cognitive and behavioral change.

The cognitive approaches used with adults and children also differ in the need to consider developmental factors. Although only a few of the early descriptions of cognitive-behavioral treatment devoted explicit attention to the child's developing cognitive and behavioral repertoires, more recent writings have begun to describe how this development might be considered in the planning of assessment and intervention strategies (e.g., Cole & Kazdin, 1980;

Copeland, 1983; Kendall, 1977, 1984c). Among the factors highlighted by various writers are (1) differences in the sorts of situations that children encounter and must master as they grow up (e.g., Mize & Ladd, in press); (2) qualitative changes in the ways children selectively attend to and remember environmental stimuli (Cohen & Schleser, 1984; Mize & Ladd, in press); (3) increases in the ability to manipulate symbolic information and to reason (Bernard, 1984; Bierman, 1983; Ellis & Bernard, 1983); (4) the increased ability to process different concepts simultaneously and to use strategic planning and problem-solving (Bierman, 1983; Cohen & Schleser, 1984); (5) the effects that different forms of rewards and punishments may have at different ages (Robinson, 1985); and (6) differences in the cognitive conceptual abilities needed to generalize acquired skills. The fact that children differ in each of these areas as they age implies that the intervention materials, procedures, and skills selected as intervention targets should be chosen with careful consideration of both the children's current cognitive skills and the types of environmental situations with which they must cope at their particular stage of development.

## Recent Developments in Social Learning and Cognitive Theories

We have overviewed the major social learning and cognitive theoretical frameworks explicitly aimed at explaining psychopathology and behavior change, integrating recent developments into our description of these frameworks. Several additional models have joined the ranks of those summarized above. Although most of these are not new to psychology, their extension to child behavior problems is relatively recent.

### Self-Efficacy Expectations

Recent developments in cognitive social learning theory have focused largely on the cognitive side of the label. For example, Bandura's description of *self-efficacy* theory (1977a) is firmly placed within an expectational analysis of human behavior. The degree to which individuals develop the expectancy that they will be able to perform desired behaviors is an important facet of this extension of cognitive social learning theory, and it can be divided into two components: self-efficacy expectations and response outcome expectations. Response outcome expectancies have to do with the likelihood that a behavior (performed by *anyone*) will have a given effect. The more important expectational factor is the self-efficacy expectation, that is, the person's own sense that he or she can master a particular situation or perform a particular action. According to self-efficacy theory, individuals' changes in self-efficacy expectations (i.e., changes in their beliefs that they can perform desired actions) are crucial determinants of whether behavior change will occur.

A central feature of the notion of self-efficacy is its claim to providing a unified theory of behavior change. That is, self-efficacy theory is said to be a conceptual framework for understanding the effectiveness of different treatments. Independent of the method of treatment used, increased self-efficacy expectations are required for behavioral improvement at the end point. Data presented by Bandura and colleagues (Bandura, Reese, & Adams, 1982) support self-efficacy theory by demonstrating associations between improvements in formerly snake-phobic subjects and enhanced perceptions of self-efficacy. Other studies also document the predicted relationship between self-efficacy increases and desired behavioral gains (see Kendall, 1984c). In the words of a colleague, for therapy to be effective, "You gotta believe."

### Social Information-Processing

Dodge (1983, 1986) offered a model that incorporates many of the elements described earlier into a sequential process that he believes describes the cognitive substrate of social behavior in childhood. Influenced by literature addressing social cognitive development (e.g., Flavell, 1974) as well as adult models of social competence and problem solving (D'Zurilla & Goldfried, 1971; McFall, 1982), Dodge (1983) described several processes that he believes proceed in a lockstep fashion to determine the child's social behavior. The task or social situation provides a variety of complex but coherent cues to the child, eliciting filters for processing that information. These filters, which Dodge called "unconscious influences," are similar conceptually to Beck *et al.*'s schemas (1979, 1985) and to cognitive structures (Ingram & Kendall, 1986) and are assumed to be learned and to determine how a sequence of specific cognitive processes will be used to process situational information. This sequence consists of encoding environmental cues, representing and interpreting those cues, searching for potential behavioral responses, evaluating and selecting from these alternatives, and enacting the behavior that has been selected.

Dodge (1986) described several ways in which problems at stages in this process can produce deviant behavior, including (1) the inefficient or inaccurate encoding of stimulus information; (2) the inaccurate or biased interpretation of this information; (3) an inadequate or biased response search, possibly as a function of errors in the previous processing steps; (4) misinterpretations or misjudgments of the possible consequences of responses, resulting in poor selection of the behavior to perform; and (5) an inability to monitor and alter one's own behavior as a function of its immediate results.

Dodge proposed his model as an explication of the sequential processes involved in socially inadequate performance, particularly aggression, rather than as a comprehensive model of psychopathology and behavior change. Nonetheless, this model is compatible with the more comprehensive theories described earlier. Its description of the specific steps hypothesized as occurring in an invariant sequence is appealing because the framework can be evaluated empirically (i.e., is subject to disconfirmatory data). Furthermore, although not developed into a specific behavior change package, Dodge's model specifies different cognitive skills that could form the basis for assessment and intervention efforts.

### Social-Cognitive Developmental Approaches

Developmental psychologists concerned with the interface between social cognition and social behavior have amassed an impressive amount of data about the ways in which children's knowledge and thoughts related to social interaction change as they grow older. Most of this research has attempted to examine the relationship in normal children between the emergence of various types of cognition and social behavior, in a search for answers to questions about whether specific types of social cognition are related to specific classes of social behavior in causal or correlational ways (cf. Serafica, 1982). Thus, there appears to be no unified "social-cognitive developmental theory"; rather, there is a collection of theoretical and empirical literature revolving around questions of the relationship between the development of social thought and action. The development of child psychopathology is not a central concern of these researchers, although some research in this area deals with disturbed children (e.g., Selman *et al.*, 1982).

The literature on social-cognitive development contributes to CSL theories of child deviance in two major ways. First, its focus of investigation involves domains very different from those typically explored by more clinically oriented researchers, often targeting children's knowledge and understanding of social phenomena such as affect and trait labels (e.g., Harter, 1982), friendship (e.g., Bigelow, 1977), and social norms and rules (e.g., Shantz, 1982). Second, the data generated from such studies provide normative indications of the kinds of skills and knowledge that children commonly display at different ages. These provide an important descriptive data base for normative comparisons and ultimately for an understanding of the role of cognitive development in the etiology of child behavior problems. Moreover, such data are necessary for intervention agents to evaluate properly how their change efforts should be modified for children of different skill levels.

## Unifying and Critiquing Cognitive Social Learning Theories

One apparent consistency across various cognitive social learning perspectives is the dual focus on the learning processes and on the internal information-processing factors that influence this learning. Many of the essential ingredients of a more operant learning model are retained, but within a less doctrinaire context, allowing the needed focus on and inquiry into individuals' internal and contextual representations.

The analysis of "cognition" has played an important role in the recent advances in theory; yet, there are inconsistencies in the terminology used to describe the various features of cognition. One general system for conceptualizing cognition involves cognitive content (propositions), cognitive processes, cognitive products, and cognitive structures (e.g., Ingram & Kendall, 1986). Cognitive content is defined by the actual sentences (self-talk) and information represented in the organism's mental activity. Cognitive processes are the various procedures operating on the content, including such general processes as attentional focusing, remembering, active problem-solving, and processing biases (e.g., confirmatory bias). Cognitive processing may be distorted, as in illogical and irrational thinking, and/or deficient, as in instances in which behavior emerges without the benefit of prospective processing. Cognitive products are the cognitions that result from the interaction of information and processes.[1]

---

[1]Because the interaction of cognitive process, cognitive content, and cognitive product is ongoing, whether a cognitive event is labeled as cognitive content or cognitive product depends on the focus and punctuation used to describe cognitive sequences. Thus, a child who is the victim of peer ridicule may think about the ridicule, remember the last

Cognitive structures are organized systems of internally represented experiences, and they derive from repeated interactions among cognitive content, processes, and related products.[2] After structures develop sufficiently, they, too, come to influence the manner in which content is processed, serving as a background or template that influences current processing. Self-statements illustrate cognitive content, distorted thinking represents cognitive processing, attributions reflect cognitive products, and a negative view of the self, the world, and the future comprised of a complex system of negative self-statements and processing biases depicts an illustrative cognitive structure. These cognitive features interact and, in different ways, contribute to the development of distinct psychopathologies and to the most effective means of their remediation. Even within this classification system, however, specific schemes for describing crucial contents, processes, and structures and their relationships to specific child problems will remain to be organized into a coherent and comprehensive descriptive framework.

The distinction between cognitive deficits and cognitive distortions may provide the beginnings of a more in-depth framework of this sort for understanding child psychopathology. Kendall (1986), for example, postulated that cognitive deficiencies may predispose a child to externalizing behavior problems, whereas internalizing problems, such as anxiety, depression, and social withdrawal, may be more closely linked to the types of cognitive distortions found with similar adult difficulties. It will be particularly important for future research to identify the types of cognitive deficits and distortions common to particular child problems, and to demonstrate empirically their relationships to maladaptive behavior and to environmental antecedents and consequences.

Another area in need of additional theoretical development concerns the manner by which cognitive structures (schemas) develop. An initial explication of the development of cognitive schemas (Kendall & Braswell, 1982b) used a temporal model and included both cognitive and behavioral components. Cen-

---

time it happened, and attribute the event to his unpopularity with peers. These thoughts lead the child to notice other negative incidents, concluding that no one likes him. In this instance, the attribution of unpopularity as a cause of the ridicule is the cognitive product of the thoughts and the remembering process that preceded it. The attribution can also be seen as a cognitive content that, together with the child's selective attention and thought processes, leads to another cognitive product: the conclusion that no one likes him.

[2]As an alternative, it is possible to define cognitive structures as content-free architectures that define abstractly the relationships among component bits of cognitive content, process, and product. Although this definition has some theoretical appeal, in practice cognitive structures always contain content. Whether, in fact, structure and content are relatively independent or are mutually determined, each constrained by and constraining the other, is a theoretical and empirical question. In the meantime, we use the term *cognitive structures* to refer to organized systems of related cognitive contents, processes, and products that have both content and organizational characteristics. From a clinical perspective, this definition implies that assessing a cognitive structure involves examining the network of thoughts, beliefs, attributions, processes, and so on that relates to the target behaviors (i.e., the content of the structure), specifying the connections among these factors (i.e., the organization or architecture of the structure), and determining the situations in which the cognitive structure appears to be elicited.

tral to the model are behavioral events that vary in their impact and meaningfulness for the individual. Preceding these behavioral events, expectational factors are important; during the behavioral events, one's ongoing cognitive content and processing take charge; following the behavioral events, attributional explanations for the preceding behavioral events contribute to persons' understanding of the causes of their own behavior and its outcome.

Behavioral events retain a central role in Kendall and Braswell's cognitive-behavioral model (1982b), as cognitive structures are said to be affected to varying degrees, according to the potency of diverse behavioral events. More potent behavioral experiences become associated with more influential cognitive events and processes than do less salient behavioral events. For example, the impact of a broken toy on a child's developing cognitive structures should be less than the impact of a parent's illness. The emotional state of the child at the time, the presence or absence of significant others in the situation, the existing cognitive structure(s) associated with an event, and the degree to which the child focuses attention on the event all influence its potency. The relative salience of experiences changes as a child grows older, so that many key behavioral events for younger children lose their importance as different situations become more compelling for older children.

Social learning processes provide additional speculations that supplement Kendall and Braswell's hypotheses about how cognitive structures develop. Environmental situations and consequences undoubtedly assist in the acquisition and maintenance of cognitive structures. The child is only one actor in an environment peopled primarily by parents, teachers, and peers who provide consequences contingent on the child's behavior in particular situations. These individuals also model the use of language to describe, organize, and communicate about experience. This modeling contributes to individual differences in the ways children use language, both publicly and in creating the semantically based structures through which stimulus information is selectively attended to and organized cognitively.

Cognitive structures are entrenched as a result of multiple behavioral events in which the individual's expectational, ongoing, and attributional cognitions are exposed to consequences provided by the self and/or others. After a repetition of particular kinds of cognitive information-processing, after repeated behavioral events, and after some degree of consistent consequences, the individual acquires a cognitive representation of similar and related situations. This structure then contributes to how related information is processed, as well as to the person's actions in those situations.

Cognitive social learning theories could also benefit from increased attention to two curious omissions. These are not omissions in the sense that they are totally missing in the conceptual system; rather, they are factors that have been mentioned but insufficiently integrated. First, variations in children's cognitive abilities and the role that these differences play in the development of psychopathology and/or the coping skills needed to adjust to challenging personal and social contexts have received insufficient attention. The plurality of children's cognitive skills has been addressed more in the applied arena, where intervention strategies are moderated by and modified for individual differences in cognitive skills, than in the theoretical treatises on the development and maintenance of psychological difficulties. Related to cognitive ability factors are cognitive developmental features in general. Greater emphasis on a theoretical analysis of individual differences in the development of cognitive processing and structures could enhance CSL contributions to child and adolescent psychopathology.

A second omission in CSL theories concerns the role of the environment, which appears to have been downplayed to an undesirable degree. The social environment is the context in which learning takes place, and an individual's cognitive structures are inextricably related to social situations. For children, in particular, social relations constitute an especially potent environment. It is not outrageous nor new to point to the crucial influence of peers (Hartup, 1984) and the family in a child's social functioning. Although most CSL theorists would agree that environmental factors contribute to the development of individual differences in cognitive structures, and that these, in turn, modify the effects of the environment on behavior, the precise mechanisms by which these factors interact in specific situations sorely beg explication.

Thus, CSL theories could be improved by directing greater attention to the mechanisms by which environmental (e.g., family and peer) influences contribute to the development of faulty (or adaptive) cognitive events, processes, products, and structures. Perhaps the neglect of the environment is benign, as no one in the entire cast of cognitive social learning theorists disputes the notion that environmental consequences influence behavior. It may be that these behavioral processes are simply assumed to be a part of the method by which cognitive influences come to be acquired and maintained. Indeed, Beck and Bandura have postulated that schemas and self-efficacy expectations develop through interactions with the social environment. Nevertheless, the development of a unified CSL theory would profit from a more detailed reflection both on the processes influencing the development of the proposed cognitive processes and structures and on how and in what circumstances cognitive processes override environmental consequences and/or work in concert with these factors to contribute to pathological behavior. Family and peer contexts are viewed as important (e.g., Kendall, 1985b), but it is surprising that the consequences that parents, teachers, and peers provide for children's behavior have received so little attention within cognitive-behavioral theories of child psychopathology. The work of Patterson (1982; Patterson & Bank, 1986), in which deviant parenting styles have been empirically linked to various types of child problems, seems sufficient to spur and speed continued theoretical analysis (see also Robinson, 1985).

Contributing to a reasonable degree of consensus among theoreticians is an often unstated agreement on a set of basic tenets or guiding principles (see Mahoney, 1977), and these form a general foundation on which a unified CSL theory might stand and build. Basic to cognitive social learning theories is the assumption that the human organism responds primarily to cognitive representations of the environment and not to the environment per se. Similarly, there is a reasonable consensus that most human learning is cognitively mediated. There is also agreement, though inconsistent terminology dominates, that "cognition" can be broken down into subfactors such as cognitive content, processes, products, and structures. Thoughts, feelings, and behaviors are causally interrelated, a statement with which cognitive social learning theorists would agree, and a statement that reflects the absence of a simple "cognition-causes-all" formulation.

Scientist–practitioners, researchers, and clinicians have developed a range of therapeutic strategies aligned with social learning and cognitive traditions. Although some are closely tied to theoretical frameworks, others are less tightly connected to formal theory. Here, we describe illustrative intervention strategies that, in part or in whole, are believed to rely on cognitive and social learning processes. Three strategies—modeling, coaching, and teaching self-regulation —explicitly attempt to influence behavior but explain their impact via cognitive mechanisms. The remaining cognitive strategies directly target cognitive skills, with the assumption that changes at the cognitive level will produce changes in children's behavior.

Like CSL approaches in general, CSL interventions with children are not defined by specific *techniques*. Nor are they defined by *content*, as CSL interventions can address cognitive or behavioral targets. Rather, these interventions are unified by a common belief in cognitive *mechanisms* and *processes* as being the crucial factors underlying change. Accordingly, the content and techniques of CSL interventions rely primarily on strategies designed to get the child to think differently and to translate these new thought processes into action. Because new learning is assumed to be cognitively mediated, generalization and mainte- nance are often presumed to follow spontaneously from cognitive change with- out requiring explicit intervention. As we will discuss later, this assumption appears to be mistaken: generalization is not a magical positive side effect of cognitive behavioral treatment; rather, it is a specific target of intervention planning.

The distinctions among content, technique, and mechanisms of change, together with the strong relationship between cognitive and behavior change emphasized by many CSL approaches, underscore the importance of evaluating several different potential outcomes of CSL interventions with children. First, it is important to assess whether treatment affects the child's presenting problems, which are often defined in terms of behavior problems such as disruption, inattention, and aggression. These changes are what Rosen and Proctor (1981) called "ultimate outcomes": their attainment is necessary and sufficient to call the therapy successful, and they are defined by the client's (or the referral agent's) wishes rather than the therapist's orientation. At another level of eval- uation are instrumental outcomes, or those steps dictated by the therapist's theoretical framework as the prerequisites for achieving the ultimate outcomes. These are chosen by the therapist and are closely related to the mechanisms that the theory postulates as necessary and sufficient for change; in cognitive-behav- ioral approaches, they generally comprise changes in the child's thoughts or cognitive processes. Their presumed relationship to ultimate outcomes is an empirical question. Thus, for example, the ultimate outcome for an impulsive child may be improved academic performance and reduced disruptiveness in the classroom, whereas the instrumental outcomes that achieve this aim may be an increased ability to provide covert self-guidance via self-instruction. An eval- uation of both types of outcomes allows the clinician to assess whether the instrumental goals were met and to examine the relationship between the attain- ment of the instrumental goals and the attainment of the ultimate goals.

The latter is important because the basic premises underlying the theory are supported only if measures of instrumental and ultimate outcome both change during the course of treatment. When changes in presenting problems occur without changes in the measures of instrumental outcomes, the proposed mechanisms by which change is presumed to occur can be called into question. When changes in the measures of instrumental goals occur without changes in the measures of ultimate goals, the issue is more complex. On the one hand, the instrumental targets may not play a pivotal role in causing the child's behavior. On the other hand, these skills may be necessary but not sufficient to produce behavior change. If, for example, the specific cognitive skills targeted in treatment are part of a broader set of cognitive skills required for successful performance, simply training these skills per se will not produce behavior change. Instead, additional components should be added to the therapy package. Lack of change on both instrumental and ultimate outcomes should lead to questions about the efficacy of the therapeutic procedures used to induce change, rather than to questions about the relevance of the instrumental goals.

The distinction between instrumental and ultimate outcomes is particularly important for cognitive behavioral approaches, because methods designed to change behavior in addition to cognition are often used based on the assumption that inducing new behavior will interrupt problem cognition–behavior cycles. For example, a child might be taught a series of problem-solving skills with treatment culminating in role-played practice of the new and better solutions that the child had arrived at to handle interpersonal conflict. Assessing only a child's handling of conflict without also assessing changes in problem-solving skills would be less than optimal. Suppose that the child handled conflict with peers more adaptively (a behavior change representing an ultimate outcome) after treatment. This approach would not establish that changes in problem-solving skills (instrumental outcomes) were responsible for the change, as behavior change may have been achieved via the enactment procedures without altering the child's problem-solving skills. To support a cognitive interpretation of the mechanism by which the behavior changed, it would be necessary to demonstrate that (1) the child had acquired the problem-solving skills; (2) the child had used them in relevant circumstances; and (3) the child's identified target problems had improved.

Assessing the acquisition and generalization of problem-solving skills without assessing behavior change would be insufficient, as the *impact* of altered cognitive performance cannot be determined. Thus, a complete assessment of cognitive-behavioral interventions should include assessments of the acquisition of those cognitions presumed to change as a function of therapy (cf. Kendall, 1981a; Kendall & Korgeski, 1979), of the generality of that change, and of changes in the child's presenting problems (see Kendall, Pellegrini, & Urbain, 1981). Unfortunately, as we shall see, few studies have assessed change at all three levels; thus, the possible conclusions about the impact and mechanisms of cognitive-behavioral interventions with children are considerably limited.

## *Modeling*

Modeling approaches rely on imitative learning and involve exposing the child to a model performing the desired behavior; the performance may be live, filmed, or imagined, and it is often accompanied by a commentary pointing out features of the model's behavior or describing the model's coping self-statements. Modeled scenes may be sequenced so that the easiest behaviors are depicted initially, and more complex or difficult behaviors are presented in later scenes. Modeling by others is sometimes followed by participant modeling, in which the child is encouraged to engage in the target behavior under adult supervision and is praised for his or her performance attempts. Modeling has been used both alone and as a component of other strategies, such as coaching. Here, we describe its use as a primary intervention strategy; later sections show how modeling is integrated into multicomponent treatment approaches.

Because most CSL theories agree that imitation is a basic mechanism by which information is acquired, modeling has obvious ties to theory. Modeling can operate via several mechanisms (Bandura, 1986; Rosenthal & Bandura, 1978): (1) teaching the child responses not currently in his or her repertoire; (2) reducing or increasing the probability that responses already in the child's repertoire will be displayed, presumably as a function of the consequences that the child observes for the modeled behavior; (3) eliciting responses already in the child's repertoire; (4) providing new information that changes the child's self-regulatory processes (e.g., by increasing or decreasing the standards the child sets for himself or herself); (5) directing the child's attention to particular aspects of the environment; and (6) altering emotional arousal.

Modeling has been used as a treatment for socially isolated preschool children displaying low rates of interaction and has shown some success in producing increases in rates of interaction, assessed via direct observation (Evers & Schwartz, 1973; Keller & Carlson, 1974; O'Connor, 1969, 1972). These approaches generally use a varying number of films of same-aged children interacting positively with peers, the modeled behaviors including responses like joining others' play, smiling, giving objects, and displaying physical affection. The films often include commentaries describing the models' behavior to heighten its salience for the children; the films also show positive peer responses to the modeled behavior. Modeling appears to lead to greater increases in social behavior if the child highly values peer interaction (Evers-Pasquale, 1978; Evers-Pasquale & Sherman, 1975) and if the film is accompanied by coping self-statements, voiced as though the model child is providing self-instructions for his or her interaction attempts (Jakibchuk & Smeriglio, 1976). Interestingly, two studies that assessed whether positive adult consequences provided after increased interaction enhanced the effects of modeling found that they did not (Evers & Schwartz, 1973; O'Connor, 1972). However, most positive outcomes of interaction are presumably provided by peers, not adults, and in neither study was the effect of the modeled behavior on peers assessed for a determination of whether sufficient reinforcement for changed behavior without experimental programming made the adult rewards superfluous. Providing some support for this hypothesis are two studies that included observations of peer behavior toward models which found significant increases in positive peer behavior toward children who increased their own positive interactions (Jakibchuk & Smeriglio, 1976; Keller & Carlson, 1974).

Positive results of modeling have been maintained in several studies for up to 4 weeks (Evers-Pasquale & Sherman, 1975; O'Connor, 1972), although maintenance failures have been noted as well (Gottman, 1977; Keller & Carlson, 1974). Geller and Scheirer (1978) failed to replicate earlier results in a series of carefully designed studies aimed at increasing cooperative play with Head Start children, although their efforts were more successful with middle-class pre-schoolers, a finding suggesting that modeling may not be as effective with disadvantaged children as with children from more privileged environments. Interestingly, Geller and Scheirer (1978) found that only videotapes with sound-tracks containing extensive descriptions of the models' behavior were effective, a finding that may indicate that this component elicits new thoughts and/or helps to sustain young children's attention and to focus it on the models' responses.

Although numerous studies demonstrate that modeling can be effective with young children who interact infrequently with peers, they have been crit-icized on several grounds. First, many writers have questioned the relevance of increases in interaction rate to the child's long-term adjustment (e.g., Asher, Markel, & Hymel, 1981) or the use of increases in interaction rate as an index of immediate peer acceptance (Conger & Keane, 1981; Foster & Ritchey, 1979). Second, as Conger and Keane noted, the observation categories used to assess the effects of modeling generally appraise rates of interaction rather than the specific behaviors modeled in the films, and thus, they do not establish the extent to which children actually imitate what they have seen. In two studies that carefully assessed children's performance of the behaviors emphasized in modeling films, few (Keller & Carlson, 1974) or none (Jakibchuk & Smeriglio, 1976) of the emphasized behaviors changed significantly. Instead, in both stud-ies, the increased rates of interaction appeared to be due to increases in the category *verbalization*, which was displayed in the videotapes but not empha-sized in the commentaries. This finding points to the importance of assessing those instrumental outcomes that the strategy is designed to produce as a critical part of evaluating the mechanism of change that operates in the ultimate out-comes. Finally, Kendall and Morison (1984) pointed out that, as investigators do not report the specific skill deficits of low-rate interactors, it is unclear whether the modeling films contained examples of the specific behaviors that these chil-dren failed to perform.

A second application of modeling has been its use with fearful children to encourage approach to feared objects or situations, such as dogs (Bandura, Grusec, & Menlove, 1967; Bandura & Menlove, 1968), snakes (Kornhaber & Schroeder, 1975), and water (Lewis, 1974), based on the assumption that dis-plays of fearless behavior serve both to teach approach behavior and to ex-tinguish fear vicariously. These studies have often compared various forms of modeling and have evaluated the treatment effects in terms of the children's willingness to approach and engage in feared situations that are analogues of the modeled situations. Based on these studies, participant modeling appears to be superior to filmed modeling in promoting approach behavior, and follow-ups usually show maintenance 1 month after treatment (see Ollendick, 1979, and Graziano, DeGiovanni, & Garcia, 1979, for reviews). As Ollendick (1979) and Graziano, DeGiovanni, and Garcia (1979) have pointed out, however, most of these studies used volunteer populations with isolated fears, thus raising ques-tions regarding the generalizability of these findings to clinical populations. Further, evaluations of treatment gains have generally been conducted via struc-tured behavioral avoidance tests without assessing whether gains on these tasks generalize to the child's behavior in his or her daily environment, the ultimate goal of most studies.

A related use of modeling is geared toward reducing fear and disruptive behavior in preadolescent children experiencing frightening or unfamiliar medical procedures, such as surgery (e.g., Peterson, Schutheis, Ridley-Johnson, Miller, & Tracy, 1984) and dental work (e.g., Melamed, Yurcheson, Fleece, Hutcherson, & Hawes, 1978). Effective models in these circumstances have involved filmed children (e.g., Melamed & Siegel, 1975), live models (White & Davis, 1974), and puppets (Peterson *et al.*, 1984). Many of these approaches have been preventive, being used with all children as a part of the medical preparation procedure. The findings are that children experiencing the procedure for the first time display less self-reported fear and directly observed uncooperative and/or anxious behavior than children exposed to a placebo control experience (e.g., Klingman, Melamed, Cuthbert, & Hermecz, 1984; Melamed & Siegel, 1975; Peterson *et al.*, 1984). As in the reduction of other types of fearful behavior, involving children as active participants by encouraging them to practice coping strategies while viewing a model who is demonstrating these tactics appears to enhance the treatment effects (Klingman *et al.*, 1984). Interestingly, Klorman, Hilpert, Michael, LaGana, and Sveen's data (1980) failed to support the oft-noted recommendation based on research with adults to use "coping" models (who demonstrate initial fear but cope effectively with the situation) rather than mastery models (who are fearless from the outset): both were equally effective in reducing disruptiveness in children going to the dentist for the first time.

Although the effects of modeling are generally positive on children who have not experienced a medical procedure before, its impact on children who have previously experienced the medical procedure is less clear. Some investigators have found modeling to have no significant effects on this population (Klorman *et al.*, 1980), and others have noted different patterns of effects for experienced and inexperienced youngsters (Klingman *et al.*, 1984; Melamed *et al.*, 1978). Both White and Davis (1974) and Klingman *et al.* (1984) found positive effects of modeling on children who had previously been to the dentist. Interestingly, both of these studies selected children who were either more fearful than average (Klingman *et al.*, 1984), or who had been extremely disruptive on previous dental visits (White & Davis, 1974).

A final focus of modeling interventions involves teaching autistic and severely mentally retarded children to imitate verbal and/or motor behaviors (e.g., Baer, Peterson, & Sherman, 1967; Lovaas, Berberich, Perloff, & Schaeffer, 1966; Lovaas, Freitas, Nelson, & Whalen, 1967). Once generalized imitation has been established, it can then be used as a convenient means of teaching more complex skills. Establishing imitation generally involves establishing stimulus control for command verbalizations via shaping, prompting, and immediate reinforcement. In teaching nonverbal psychotic children to imitate sounds and words, for example, food reinforcers are first delivered contingent on any verbalization, then only when the verbalization occurs soon after the therapist's command. This procedure is followed by reinforcing successively closer approximations to the therapist's verbalizations, which gradually increase in complexity (Lovaas & Newsom, 1976). Teaching motor imitation follows a similar process, using prompting (via physical guidance) to elicit initial imitation and then fading the prompt (e.g., Baer *et al.*, 1967; Lovaas *et al.*, 1967).

There is no doubt that modeling can affect behavioral performance. However, questions remain regarding the conditions under which it is successful as a sole treatment strategy. Its widest use has been with two "internalizing" problems—social withdrawal and fearful behavior—where presumably the modeled behaviors are already in the child's repertoire and will be supported by their natural environmental consequences. Although modeling appears to be effective in lowering the probability of disruptiveness during medical procedures, whether it is as effective in reducing more pervasive acting-out, disruptive behaviors in home and school settings is more questionable. Gresham and Nagle (1980) found that a modeling intervention for socially unskilled third- and fourth-graders was effective in increasing positive behavior, but not in decreasing negative behavior, although the rates of negative behavior had been fairly low before treatment and were perhaps less susceptible to reduction.

From a social learning vantage point, the consequences that the child encounters when imitating a model's prosocial behavior should be the critical determinants of whether the child will continue to perform the response: a child who imitates a model's initiations to peers but is rebuffed will be unlikely to continue that behavior, regardless of its positive effects for a child in a film. With the exception of two of the social withdrawal studies (Jakibchuk & Smeriglio, 1976; Keller & Carlson, 1974), most investigations have not assessed peer responses to engagement in the modeled behavior. This finding may be particularly important for children with histories of rich reinforcement for deviant social behavior, whose newly acquired prosocial repertoires at first produce negative or neutral consequences because of the child's long-standing negative reputation.

From a more cognitive vantage point, the child's internal dialogue preceding and during the desired prosocial behavior should be a critical determinant of continued prosocial action. The focus on cognitive, social, and environmental antecedent and consequent events together results in an apparently potent strategy. All of these factors point to the importance, in the clinical use of modeling, of assessing the child's performance of the modeled behavior and its impact in relevant environmental situations, so that additional strategies can be planned, if needed, to improve performance (Rosenthal & Bandura, 1978). In addition, the therapist should be concerned with the child's self-talk (e.g., Meichenbaum, 1977) and should ensure that positive consequences for the modeled responses are likely in the child's environment, are valued by the child, and outweigh the rewards for competing responses.

## Coaching

Coaching is a multicomponent approach that relies on a variety of techniques to teach a child new behaviors, including instruction, modeling, behavior rehearsal, and feedback. Widely used in social skills training with children, coaching generally involves several specific steps: (1) instructing the child in the target skill concept and its relation to the behavior to be performed; (2) providing a rationale for the behavior; (3) modeling the response; (4) prompting the child to rehearse the response; (5) providing feedback; and (6) recycling through rehearsal and feedback until the child can perform well. Coaching is used in one-to-one treatment or small groups, sometimes involving children with similar problems, sometimes involving nonclinic peers.

Ladd and Mize (1983) described the potential types of learning that coaching promotes. Like modeling, coaching conveys information about responses and their likely consequences through verbal instructions, discussion, and modeling. Through practice, the child refines and develops the appropriate responses, distinguishes the relevant aspects of performance, and matches his or her behavior to the knowledge acquired through instruction. Feedback assists the child in matching behavior to a criterion. Ladd and Mize further speculated that using rehearsal situations that approximate actual social situations, creating opportunities for the child to practice skills in the natural environment, teaching persistence in skill use, and instructing the child in how to monitor cognitively the outcomes of skill use and to adjust performance when necessary will enhance the maintenance and the generalization of the skills learned during coaching sessions. Unfortunately, these last steps are rarely explicitly described as components of coaching packages (but see Ladd, 1981, for an exception).

As will be seen in later sections of this chapter, strategies akin to coaching have also been used successfully to teach cognitive skills such as problem solving and self-instruction. As a means of directly teaching behavioral skills, coaching has been widely applied in social skills training with elementary-school children in Grades 3–6. Although specific treatments and their results have varied, coaching procedures have resulted in (1) changes in the coached behaviors in analogue settings and/or role-played performance (Berler, Gross, & Drabman, 1982; Bornstein, Bellack, & Hersen, 1977; Whitehill, Hersen, & Bellack, 1980); (2) increases in knowledge about the coached behaviors (LaGreca & Santogrossi, 1980); and (3) increases in coached behavior in the child's natural environment which have been maintained at 4-week (Ladd, 1981) and 6-week follow-up (Bierman & Furman, 1984).

Despite these positive results, some investigators have not demonstrated changes in behavior in analogue settings (Oden & Asher, 1977), and others have found that, although children show improvement in role-play situations, their behavior in their daily environments has not improved (Berler *et al.*, 1982). Further, most studies have not used populations referred for mental health services; instead, they have selected children receiving low scores on sociometric measures in their classrooms. In the one study on a clinic-referred population, Michelson, Mannarino, Marchione, Stern, Figueroa, and Beck (1983) found fewer and less extensive changes after outpatient group coaching in social skills than had been reported in apparently less disturbed populations.

Thus, although coaching has a substantial track record of producing behavior change during intervention sessions, its impact on behavior in the natural environment is less clear. This issue has been complicated by the fact that only a few studies have included observations of children's performance of specific coached skills in their ongoing peer interactions, so that it is difficult to assess whether the behavior change, when it does occur, is a function of changes in coached behavior. Furthermore, many writers question whether coaching programs target the skills most pivotal in peer acceptance (e.g., Foster, DeLawyer, & Guevremont, 1985; Putallaz & Gottman, 1983) in light of the repeated finding that behavior change after coaching is not always associated with widespread or lasting gains in peer acceptance (e.g., Bierman & Furman, 1984; Gresham & Nagle, 1980; LaGreca & Santogrossi, 1980), the ultimate goal of many of these programs. In addition, most coaching studies have been more concerned with producing behavior change than with assessing the mechanisms by which it is produced and thus have not included measures that assess whether the processes offered by Ladd and Mize (1983), or related cognitive processes, occur during successful coaching.

Finally, as with modeling, coaching advocates have paid little attention to the outcome of coached behavior when children attempt to change the quality of their peer interactions by behaving differently. Bierman's finding (1986) that positive peer responses to treated children's display of target conversation skills during coaching sessions positively correlated between .37 and .48 with peer acceptance after treatment underscore the importance of focusing on whether trained behaviors produce positive peer outcomes. Thus, assessments of both the degree to which the child generalizes coached behaviors and the consequences provided by the social environment for these behaviors may be necessary if we are to understand and enhance the effects of coaching.

## Teaching Role-Taking Skills

Role taking—and its cousin, empathy—refer to the child's ability to understand (role-take) and emotionally experience situations (empathize) from the perspectives of other individuals. Developmental psychologists' interest in the relationship between social cognition and social behavior has provided a greater impetus for the study of these skills than have CSL theories of abnormal behavior. Initially stimulated by Piagetian observations related to egocentrism in childhood, investigators of role taking explored the possibilities that these skills mediate prosocial behavior, that deficits in role taking and/or empathy may underlie the development of aggressive and antisocial behavior, and that improved role-taking skills would enhance adjustment.

Unfortunately, studies of the relationship between role taking, empathy, and measures of social behavior and adjustment have yielded mixed findings, and writers sometimes disagree about the conclusions that can be reached from this body of literature (Kurdek, 1978; Underwood & Moore, 1982). These issues are further complicated by unclear definitions of the role-taking construct and researchers' use of numerous different measures of role taking that may lack sufficient psychometric investigation, particularly of their validity (Enright & Lapsley, 1980).

The same difficulties unfortunately plague the literature related to the effects of teaching children to be better role-takers. Role-taking interventions have varied considerably, but most have used a series of group experiences for children involving tasks designed to encourage practice in role taking, such as making a series of videotapes in which each skit is replayed several times, with the group members switching roles. Some have also involved discussion of and/or practice in understanding the feelings of others (see Urbain & Kendall, 1980, for a detailed review).

Because of the relatively few studies in this area, the wide variety of curricula and methods used to teach role taking, the large variations in the ages (preschool through adolescence) and the degree of disturbance of the participating children (from not identified as disturbed to institutionalized, emotionally disturbed), and the lack of generalization and follow-up data in most of these studies, it is difficult to draw firm conclusions from this literature. Nonetheless, various methods of training perspective-taking appear to lead to improvements in analogue measures of trained skills (e.g., Chandler, 1973; Chandler, Green-span, & Barenboim, 1974), but fewer gains in adjustment have been noted (see Urbain & Kendall, 1980). Further, it is not clear what the active ingredients of the therapeutic procedures actually are: Iannotti (1978) found that switching roles did not heighten the improvement in role taking produced when 6- and 9-year-old boys read, discussed, and acted out how they would handle mock situations, whereas Little (1979, described by Urbain & Kendall, 1980) found equal changes in role taking for a group of delinquent adolescent girls who switched roles while making a series of videotapes and a control group that also created a videotape but did not appear in it. These studies raise questions about whether the cooperative group effort, rather than role-taking training per se, was responsible for the treatment outcomes, and they highlight the need for more systematic outcome research on the effects and parameters of interventions designed to improve various forms of children's role-taking and empathy.

## Problem-Solving Training

Problem-solving training is a strategy for generating a variety of alternatives to deal with a problem and for increasing the probability of selecting the most appropriate and effective response from among these alternatives (D'Zurilla & Goldfried, 1971). Several models of problem solving have been described, although the component skills common to most include (1) defining the problem; (2) specifying a goal; (3) generating multiple solutions (alternative thinking); (4) evaluating the probable consequences (consequential thinking); (5) sequentially planning a strategy for achieving the goal (means–ends thinking); and (6) evaluating the outcome (e.g., D'Zurilla & Goldfried, 1971; Mahoney, 1977; Spivack & Shure, 1974).

Deficiencies in one or more of these problem-solving skills have been linked to a variety of childhood adjustment problems. In general, researchers have demonstrated poorer performance by maladjusted children than by their better adjusted peers on measures of social goal-setting (Renshaw & Asher, 1982), alternative thinking (e.g., Kendall & Fischler, 1984), consequential thinking (e.g., Spivack & Shure, 1974), and means–end thinking (e.g., Asarnow & Callan, 1985).

Problem-solving training directly targets those cognitive skills assumed to mediate overt behavior (Kendall, 1984a). Through an extensive use of modeling and rehearsal, children are taught to apply component problem-solving skills to real-life problems, with the ultimate goals of either reducing current behavior problems, enhancing peer relations and interpersonal sensitivity, or preventing later maladjustment.

Much of the rationale for teaching children problem-solving skills is based on the CSL emphasis on the cognitive-mediational processes thought to govern human action. Although alternative theories of problem solving have been described (e.g., Skinner, 1984), a basic premise of cognitive social learning theories is that individuals can learn effective ways of behaving both through cognitive or symbolic appraisals of a situation and the potential outcomes of their behavior and through direct experience (e.g., Bandura, 1977b). Learning through cognitive appraisal makes unnecessary the performance of an endless series of actions to test potential outcomes (Bandura, 1977b) by permitting cognitive explorations of probable response–consequence relations without direct experience of the consequences of specific actions. Thus, altering the manner in which children think about a problem by developing systematic cognitive strategies would presumably result in more favorable ways of behaving.

Problem-solving training has been used with nonclinic preschool, preadolescent, and adolescent populations, as well as with children exhibiting dysfunctional behavior and referred for treatment (Urbain & Kendall, 1980). Many of the programs tested to date have been part of large-scale classroom-based curricula (e.g., Allen, Chinsky, Larcen, Lochman, & Selinger, 1976; Weissberg, Gesten, Rapkin, Cowen, Davidson, Flores deApodaca, & McKim, 1981) geared to enhancing interpersonal relations and preventing later maladjustments in normal children. Prevention-oriented problem-solving programs have been extended to disadvantaged children, such as those from lower-income families, because these children are often identified as being at risk for developing behavioral problems (e.g., Richel & Burgio, 1982).

Fewer training programs have targeted children with adjustment problems. This situation is somewhat surprising, given that much of the research on children's problem-solving has focused on the deficits of maladjusted populations. When problem-solving training has been used as a treatment strategy, children identified with "externalizing" disorders (e.g., acting-out or aggressive) have most often been targeted (e.g., Camp, Blom, Herbert, & van Doorninck, 1977), usually with the ultimate goal of altering these children's social behaviors. Problem-solving training has also been used to teach coping skills to child psychiatric outpatients (Yu, Harris, Solovitz, & Franklin, 1986), and to enhance the assertive social skills of shy young adolescents (Christoff, Scott, Kelley, Schlundt, Baer, & Kelly, 1985).

Evaluations of problem-solving training have yielded promising but equivocal results. The most consistent and robust finding is that the training results in improved problem-solving skills as measured by hypothetical problem vignettes (Urbain & Kendall, 1980). Trained children of varying ages and presenting problems, relative to untrained controls, have been shown to have improved significantly in problem identification (e.g., Weissberg *et al.*, 1981b), the number of solutions they generate (e.g., Camp *et al.*, 1977), the quality of their solutions (e.g., Sarason & Sarason, 1981), and consequential and means–end thinking (e.g., Spivack & Shure, 1974) after training.

Of pivotal importance, however, is the relationship between the acquisition of problem-solving skills and the ultimate goals of most clinical interventions: enhanced behavioral adjustment. A fundamental premise underlying problem-solving training is that the development of more sophisticated cognitive strategies will mediate changes in behavior, but on this score, the results have not been conclusive (Kendall, 1986). Spivack and Shure (1974) reported that problem-solving training led to significant improvements in the behavioral adjustment of behavior problem preschoolers and that these gains were maintained at a 1-year follow-up. Attempts to replicate these findings, however, have produced mixed results. Some studies using comparable training methods and outcome measures have documented children's acquisition of problem-solving skills while failing to find clear concomitant changes in behavioral adjustment (e.g., Allen *et al.*, 1976; Camp *et al.*, 1977; Richel, Eshelman, & Loigman, 1983). Other studies have reported improvements in both problem-solving skills and behavioral adjustment, but little systematic relationship between the two (e.g., Elardo & Caldwell, 1979; Weissberg, Gesten, Carnrike, Toro, Rapkin, Davidson, & Cowen, 1981). Equally disconcerting are failures to find a reliable relationship between responses to hypothetical problem-solving assessments and actual behavior in analogue or simulated problem-solving tasks (e.g., Kendall & Fischler, 1984; Krasnor & Rubin, 1981).

Several factors may account for these mixed findings. It is possible that problem solving, as it is now conceptualized and measured, has little meaningful relationship to children's social behavior. Alternative explanations are viable as well, however. The use of hypothetical vignettes to assess problem-solving skills may produce data of limited generalizability, as the vignettes are often generated on the basis of face validity and are rarely tied empirically to problems that children may actually encounter. It is equally plausible that the commonly used measures of adjustment (e.g., teacher ratings) may not sufficiently tap more subtle or delayed benefits of problem-solving training interventions (Krasnor & Rubin, 1981). Furthermore, whether children actually use the problem-solving strategies after training in their day-to-day encounters is rarely assessed in problem-solving studies but would be important to know if we are to ascertain that the skills learned in therapy are being used in the child's daily life.

Weaknesses in the training programs may also account for the mixed findings. It is becoming increasingly apparent that generating more solutions without careful consideration of the quality of these solutions may not be sufficient to produce significant behavior change. In a large-scale study of the relationship between problem solving and children's adjustment, using both hypothetical and direct observational measures, Kendall and Fischler (1984) found that only qualitative and not quantitative measures of problem-solving performance were related to adjustment ratings. Thus, it is not surprising that studies failing to alter behavioral adjustment either have not specifically assessed the quality of the solutions that the children generate or have noted little improvement on qualitative measures of alternative thinking (e.g., Camp et al., 1977; Seaman & Sloane, 1984). In addition, active efforts to program the generalization of cognitive and behavior change are notably absent in problem-solving studies. Learning problem-solving skills would not be expected to lead automatically to improved social performance unless the skills are actually used in relevant circumstances (e.g., in the classroom).

Finally, factors such as age, developmental level, intelligence, and other subject variables may play a moderating role in the efficacy of problem-solving training and may explain some of the inconsistencies in outcome (Kendall, 1984c, 1986). Similarly, attention to the relationship between the nature of the disorder (e.g., aggression or withdrawal) and the impact of training may prove useful for ascertaining the optimal applications for problem-solving training. As noted by Kendall (1986), the proper matching of treatments to disorders would be facilitated by the identification of specific childhood psychopathologies in which problem-solving deficits are documented as being pivotal to the disorder.

## Self-Instructional Training

Self-instructional training is designed to enhance children's self-control through verbalizations that prompt, guide, and maintain performance. Although earlier theory and research examined the development of relationships between children's verbal and nonverbal behaviors (e.g., Bem, 1967), Meichenbaum and Goodman (1971) were among the first to apply training in self-instructional procedures to clinical problems. Like problem-solving interventions, self-instructional training teaches children a systematic and reflective method for approaching a problem. It is distinguished from other strategies by its emphasis on developing self-verbalizations to control performance.

In self-instructional training, children learn to verbalize a sequence of steps designed to facilitate their performance on a task. Most researchers use modified versions of the steps described initially by Meichenbaum and Goodman (1971), teaching children self-statements related to (1) defining the nature of the problem (e.g., "What is it that I have to do first?"); (2) guiding nonverbal actions (e.g., "This one is the same so I'll circle it"); (3) focusing attention (e.g., "I have to look at one problem at a time"); (4) coping (e.g., "I missed that one. I should go slower"); and (5) providing self-acknowledgment or self-reward (e.g., "I did a good job").

Children are taught during training to use the self-instructional steps aloud while performing a task. Gradually overt verbalizations are faded to a whisper, and finally, the children say the instructions covertly. Modeling, rehearsal, and social reinforcement are used extensively. Response–cost techniques can supplement these techniques with especially difficult or impulsive children to cue off-task and inappropriate behavior and to facilitate learning the self-instructional steps and the related nonverbal responses (e.g., Kendall & Braswell, 1985). Self-instructional training is also often used as one component in more comprehensive cognitive-behavioral interventions with children (see Urbain & Kendall, 1980) and is thought to enhance impulse control by increasing the child's use of adaptive cognitive strategies.

The theoretical basis for self-instructional training lies in the prominent role ascribed to self-regulatory processes and the use of "cognitive aids" in exercising control over one's own behavior (e.g., Bandura, 1977b). Presumably, children manifesting problems related to self-control are often deficient in their use of adaptive cognitive strategies. Self-instructional training facilitates the use of helpful thinking strategies by developing a repertoire of covert self-talk. Like cognitive-behavioral approaches in general, self-verbalizations are linked directly to thinking processes, and thus, inner speech is a vehicle for developing adaptive cognitions. The role of cognitive controlling factors and the development of self-regulatory skills is relevant to the social learning principles emphasizing children's ability to alter their behavior in accordance with social or situational constraints, independent of adult-mediated influences (e.g., Mischel, Ebbesen, & Zeiss, 1972). The link between linguistic, cognitive, and behavioral processes highlights the CSL emphases on higher learning capacities and the interdependence of thinking and overt behavior.

Self-instructional training has been used widely with impulsive, hyperactive, and acting-out preschoolers and preadolescents (e.g., Bryant & Budd, 1982; Kendall & Braswell, 1982a; Kendall & Finch, 1978). Fewer studies have been conducted with adolescents (e.g., Williams & Akamatsu, 1978). Children identified as "externalizers" or as being deficient in self-control often share the characteristics of attentional difficulties, excitability, and impulsive behavioral styles. Essentially, these are children who act before thinking, who have difficulty initiating the required activity because they are easily distracted, and who fail to sustain focused attention for sufficient periods of time to accomplish important tasks.

Because these problems are often most evident in educational settings, it is not surprising that self-instructional training has been almost exclusively applied to the ultimate goals of improved academic performance, sustained attention, and general classroom behavior. Self-instructional procedures have also been used to enhance the academic achievement of normal (e.g., Schleser, Meyers, Cohen, & Rodick, 1984), mentally retarded (e.g., Whitman & Johnson, 1983), and learning-disabled (e.g., Swanson & Scarpati, 1984) school-aged children.

To date, few studies have used self-instructional training in isolation as the primary intervention for nonacademic problem behaviors. Self-instructions have, however, been incorporated into larger treatment packages targeting social behavior (e.g., Camp *et al.*, 1977; Kendall & Braswell, 1982a), anxiety (e.g., Kanfer, Karoly, & Newman, 1975), and anger (e.g., Blue, Madsen, & Heimberg, 1981). Common to these treatment programs is the emphasis on teaching children to use adaptive, coping self-statements to regulate their behavior.

Numerous studies have found self-instructional training to be effective in enhancing impulsive and hyperactive children's performance on standardized educational tasks similar or identical to those used in the training (e.g., Kendall & Finch, 1978; Palkes, Stewart, & Kahana, 1968). Increases in the performance accuracy of trained subjects relative to untrained controls suggests that the training may indeed lead to improved cognitive and behavioral strategies. Furthermore, component analyses of self-instructional training packages show that self-instructional steps are critical to achieving positive gains (e.g., Arnold & Forehand, 1978; Kendall & Braswell, 1982a), although modeling and self-reinforcement procedures may also facilitate the change process (e.g., Kendall & Zupan, 1981; Nelson & Birkimer, 1978).

Studies evaluating the effects of training on various aspects of children's classroom performance have produced encouraging but inconclusive findings. Some studies have reported improvements in on-task behavior (e.g., Bornstein & Quevillon, 1976; Burgio, Whitman, & Johnson, 1980), whereas others have not found significant changes (e.g., Billings & Wasik, 1985; Friedling & O'Leary, 1979). Similarly, although a number of researchers have documented improved performance on some educational tasks (e.g., Guevremont, Tishelman, & Hull, 1985; Kendall & Braswell, 1982a; Whitman & Johnson, 1983), others have not (e.g., Burgio *et al.*, 1980; Robin, Arnel, & O'Leary, 1975). Mixed findings have also been reported when investigators have assessed changes in parent and teacher ratings of the child's behavior, with some studies demonstrating positive gains on ratings of self-control and hyperactivity (e.g., Guevremont *et al.*, 1985; Kendall & Wilcox, 1980) and others finding few changes in the reports of others (e.g., Kendall & Finch, 1978; Moore & Cole, 1978).

Altogether, these findings suggest that self-instructional training may be effective for some of the children some of the time (Hobbs, Molguin, Tyroler, & Lahey, 1980). As a result, researchers have begun to examine the training and subject variables that may account for the mixed findings. Of particular importance is generalization of the training to children's natural environments. Teaching self-instructional skills is founded, in part, on the assumption that children will use these strategies in nontraining conditions and that these self-instructions will continue to have a self-controlling function. Preliminary efforts to understand the training parameters that facilitate generalization across settings and responses suggest that teaching conceptual rather than concrete or task-specific self-instructions (e.g., Kendall & Wilcox, 1980; Schleser, Meyers, & Cohen, 1981), involving children in the generation of self-instructional statements (e.g., Schleser *et al.*, 1984), using naturalistic training material (Bryant & Budd, 1982), and incorporating natural change agents—for example, parents —into training (e.g., Guevremont *et al.*, 1985) may lead to more generalized effects.

With respect to subject variables, equivocal findings with preschoolers suggest that younger children may require more structured and concrete training than older subjects. Kendall (1977) hypothesized that factors such as IQ and developmental stage may play crucial roles in training outcome, and indeed, several investigators have found interactions among cognitive-developmental level and treatment gains (e.g., Schleser *et al.*, 1984). Children's attributional styles (e.g., internal versus external locus of control) may also play a role in the effects of self-instructional training (e.g., Bugenthal, Whalen, & Henker, 1977)—and/or cognitive-behavior therapy in general—although such hypotheses require further examination. Finally, children's involvement in the training appears to predict treatment success; those who are more active in therapy sessions display the greatest improvements on teacher ratings of classroom behavior (Braswell, Kendall, Braith, Carey, & Vye, 1985).

## Other Self-Regulation Models

Problem-solving training and self-instructional training are characterized by a multitude of component skills (e.g., alternative thinking and self-reinforcement) combined into treatment packages aimed at enhancing children's self-control. Other self-regulation processes have been examined that focus on more specific cognitive-mediational devices or self-produced behavioral responses assumed to facilitate children's self-regulatory capacities.

In laboratory settings, researchers have extensively examined children's use of cognitive-mediational strategies in delaying gratification and resisting temptation (e.g., Hartig & Kanfer, 1973; Mischel *et al.*, 1972; Monahan & O'Leary, 1971). In the delay-of-gratification paradigm, children must choose between an immediately available but less valued reward (e.g., a cookie) and a delayed reward of greater value (e.g., three cookies). Similarly, in temptation resistance studies, children are instructed to perform a task in the presence of more attractive options (e.g., watching a toy clown or cheating to obtain an available reward). Delayed rewards are contingent on completing the task and following the rules. Self-regulatory tactics must presumably be invoked to comply with the instructional demands.

Children using mediational strategies, either spontaneously or as a result of instruction, demonstrate greater self-control (e.g., fewer rule infractions) than children not using these strategies. In general, cognitive activities that distract attention from the arousing qualities of the tempting goal-object appear to facilitate self-control. These strategies include transforming (in imagination) external stimuli into less attractive objects (e.g., Mischel & Baker, 1975), thinking "fun things" to reduce the aversiveness of the delay periods (e.g., Mischel *et al.*,

1972), and verbalizing the rules related to the task demands or the benefits of resisting (e.g., Patterson & Mischel, 1975).

These studies support social learning accounts of self-regulation, emphasizing the cognitive representational mechanisms mediating responses to external stimuli. In contrast to self-control strategies directing children's attention to relevant stimulus information to enhance adaptive responding (e.g., self-instruction), cognitive distraction techniques appear to reduce the controlling effects of the external stimuli associated with maladaptive responding.

Surprisingly few studies have systematically evaluated cognitive distraction and imagery techniques with clinical samples of children. Several investigators have, however, reported positive effects when these procedures are used in conjunction with other interventions (e.g., relaxation training) in reducing children's nighttime fears (e.g., Graziano, Mooney, Huber, & Ignasiak, 1979b; Kanfer *et al.*, 1975), disruptive behavior and fear during visits to the dentist (Siegel & Peterson, 1980, 1981), and aggressive behavior (e.g., Robin, Schneider, & Dolnick, 1976).

Another self-regulation paradigm involves teaching children self-management skills. This approach is based on the assumption that teaching children to manipulate the antecedent and consequent events surrounding their behavior will increase the occurrence of positive behaviors in the absence of adult control. Three interrelated processes are commonly included in this process: self-evaluation, self-reinforcement, and self-determined standard setting (e.g., Kanfer & Karoly, 1972).

Self-evaluation involves comparing one's performance with some standard, usually externally imposed (Bandura, 1977b; O'Leary & Dubey, 1979). Several studies have examined whether using self-evaluation procedures affects children's classroom behavior (e.g., disruptive activity or on-task behavior) and academic productivity, with mixed results (e.g., Nelson, Lipinski, & Boykin, 1978; Santogrossi, O'Leary, Romanczyk, & Kaufman, 1973). When used as a isolated procedure, self-evaluation does not appear to produce marked or durable changes. Self-evaluation procedures may be as effective as evaluation by others, however, when they are accompanied by external rewards for accurate assessment and for achieving externally established criteria. Furthermore, the durability of the behavior change after adult-delivered contingencies are withdrawn appears to be enhanced once children accurately use these skills, supporting the contribution of self-evaluation to the self-regulation process (e.g., O'Leary & Dubey, 1979; Wood & Flynn, 1978).

Self-reinforcement, judged by CSL theorists to be a critical component of self-regulation, refers to processes by which individuals increase and maintain their own behavior by self-produced consequences (Bandura, 1976; Catania, 1975). When examined in laboratory settings, children's use of self-administered rewards has been as effective as (e.g., Bandura & Perloff, 1967; Switzky & Haywood, 1974) or more effective than (e.g., Bolstad & Johnson, 1972; Glynn, 1970) externally delivered rewards. Although not extensively examined as an isolated procedure, the application of self-reinforcement to clinical problems has produced comparable findings (e.g., Ballard & Glynn, 1975). The effectiveness of self-reinforcement procedures as used by children appears to be tied to the accuracy of their self-evaluation (e.g., Drabman, Spitalnik, & O'Leary, 1973), a finding highlighting the interdependence of various self-regulation processes.

Thus, the potency of self-reinforcement and its regulating function is predicated on children's accurate assessment of their own behavior and the contingent administration of rewards.

A final related approach to teaching children to regulate their behavior involves teaching them to set self-determined standards of performance. Viewed by CSL theorists as a cognitively based source of motivation (Bandura, 1977b), self-determined performance standards are believed to have instructional or attentional functions, to provide information regarding the level of performance required to earn a reward, and to prompt self-evaluations in the form of overt or covert consequences for achievement (O'Leary & Dubey, 1979). Thus, these procedures are integrally related to self-evaluation, goal setting, and self-reinforcement.

On laboratory tasks and measures of academic achievement, setting self-determined criteria in isolation does not appear to lead to significant or long-term behavior change (e.g., Bandura & Perloff, 1967; Felixbrod & O'Leary, 1974). When combined with rewards for achieving the performance standards, however, self-selected goals lead to as much improvement as externally controlled criteria and may enhance maintenance when external influences are withdrawn (e.g., Brownell, Coletti, Ersner-Hershfield, Hershfield, & Wilson, 1977; Weiner & Dubanowski, 1975). The stringency of the standards that children select appears to be tied directly to performance gains. As one would expect, children setting higher standards (either spontaneously or through external prompts) demonstrate more desirable performance than children setting standards below their capabilities (e.g., Brownell *et al.*, 1977).

All of these data suggest that children can control their behavior by applying cognitive and behavioral strategies to inhibit maladaptive responses and to activate and maintain desirable behavior. Children often have to be taught how to use self-control tactics effectively, however, to achieve maximum benefits. The gradual transition from adult-controlled to child-controlled standards and evaluation appears to be essential to achieving clinically significant behavior change. Moreover, increasing the involvement of the child in the learning process may further enhance treatment gains.

### Toward Further Advancements

One major impetus for the movement toward integrating cognitive factors into social learning interventions was the widespread belief that attending to the children's cognitive functioning would yield increased generalization and greater clinical improvement. The expectation regarding generalization has not received unilateral support, and inconsistent evidence for generalization seems to be a relatively consistent conclusion (see Braswell & Kendall, 1988). For example, Abikoff and Gittelman (1985) reported that adding a cognitive training regimen to a medication program with hyperactive children neither enhanced the effects of the medication nor contributed to an increased generalization of behavior change.

If cognitive processes are assumed to have a certain situational specificity (and not to have traitlike cross-situational power), however, why would generalization be in any way primed by cognitive training? It seems reasonable to return to more behavioral notions and to restate the generalization issue as aiming direct effort at behavioral change in different situations (e.g., Stokes & Baer, 1977). What may be a reasonable explanation is that cognitive strategies are more efficient to teach because they have broad applicability, but that they do not necessarily generalize more readily than behavioral skills. Newly acquired behavioral skills and newly acquired cognitive functioning both appear to require generalization programming. It may also be that focusing on the development of cognitive structures in addition to cognitive content (the major target of most cognitive-behavioral interventions with children) improves generalization.

If cognitive structures play crucial roles in cognitive social learning applications, it is entirely reasonable to ask, "How modifiable are cognitive structures?" and, if they are modifiable at all, "How are they best modified?" An emerging consensus seems to be that cognitive structures are plastic, but that they are not as readily modifiable as discrete behaviors. Once influenced by interventions, cognitive structures are subject to new input and further refinements. For the clinician, the question then becomes how to proceed in describing, assessing, and modifying cognitive structures.

Ingram and Kendall (1987) and Kendall and Ingram (1987) have described various procedures for schematic modification. The methods proposed contrast surgeons, mechanics, and carpenters. In the surgical approach, the therapeutic goal is the removal of an unwanted structure (e.g., eliminating the anxious person's schema for threat and, as a consequence, reducing anxiety). In depression, removing the negative schematic view of the self, the future, and the world should elevate the depressed mood.

But is it genuinely likely that cognitive structures, which represent individuals' cumulative experiences of their history, can be removed? A second model suggests that structures are not removed; rather, they are altered in meaningful ways through therapy. Here, the therapist is the mechanic, fixing troubled and dysfunctional cognitive schemas. The therapeutic procedures would be designed to decrease the activation of dysfunctional schemas in key situations, to reduce the number of associations between environmental events and the existing schemas, and to increase the associations with altered and more adaptive schemas.

The cognitive carpenter model proposes that the task of the therapist is to create or construct new schematic structures. These new procedural structures are essentially a series of cognitive contents, processes, and products that enable the individual to actively and adaptively cope with the environmental situations that have previously been the source of the disproportionate, maladaptive, and unwanted emotional and behavioral reactions.

The challenge facing cognitive social learning interventionists is first to develop useful, generalizable, empirically based models of the specific kinds of cognitive structures that accompany different types of child disorders, with particular attention to the interaction among the child's environment and the child's developing cognitive and behavioral repertoires. It is then necessary to design psychometrically sound methods for assessing cognitive structures and to further develop effective procedures for modifying the various components of cognitive functioning, especially those structures that pose the greatest difficulty for distressed children. Consistent with what has been learned to date from evaluations of behavioral and cognitive-behavioral treatments with children, it seems quite reasonable to recommend that performance-based interventions, concerns about the personal and social consequences of action, emphases on generalized cognitive and behavioral change, and a focus on the organism's active information-processing of the therapeutic experiences may collectively contribute to maximal gains.

## REFERENCES

Abikoff, H., & Gittelman, R. (1985). Hyperactive children treated with stimulants: Is cognitive training a useful adjunct? *Archives of General Psychiatry, 42,* 953–961.

Allen, G., Chinsky, J., Larcen, S., Lochman, J. E., & Selinger, H. (1976). *Community psychology and the schools: A behaviorally-oriented multi-level preventive approach.* Hillsdale, NJ: Erlbaum.

Arnold, S. C., & Forehand, R. A. (1978). A comparison of cognitive training and response-cost in modifying cognitive styles of impulsive children. *Cognitive Therapy and Research, 2,* 183–187.

Asarnow, J. R., & Callan, J. W. (1985). Boys with peer adjustment problems: Social cognitive processes. *Journal of Consulting and Clinical Psychology, 53,* 80–87.

Asher, S. R., Markel, R. A., & Hymel, S. (1981). Identifying children at risk in peer relations: A critique of the rate of interaction approach to assessment. *Child Development, 52,* 1239–1245.

Baer, D. M., Peterson, R. F., & Sherman, J. A. (1967). The development of imitation by reinforcing behavioral similarity to a model. *Journal of the Experimental Analysis of Behavior, 10,* 405–416.

Ballard, K. D., & Glynn, E. L. (1975). Behavioral self-management in story-writing with elementary school children. *Journal of Applied Behavior Analysis, 8,* 387–398.

Bandura, A. (1969). *Principles of behavior modification.* New York: Holt, Rinehart, & Winston.

Bandura, A. (1973). *Aggression: A social learning analysis.* Englewood Cliffs, NJ: Prentice-Hall.

Bandura, A. (1976). Self-reinforcement: Theoretical and methodological considerations. *Behaviorism, 4,* 135–155.

Bandura, A. (1977a). Self-efficacy: Toward a unifying theory of behavior change. *Psychological Review, 84,* 191–215.

Bandura, A. (1977b). *Social learning theory.* Englewood Cliffs, NJ: Prentice-Hall.

Bandura, A. (1986). *Social foundations of thought and action: A social cognitive theory.* Englewood Cliffs, NJ: Prentice-Hall.

Bandura, A., & Menlove, F. L. (1968). Factors determining vicarious extinction of avoidance behavior. *Journal of Personality and Social Psychology, 8,* 99–108.

Bandura, A., & Perloff, B. (1967). Relative efficacy of self-monitored and externally-imposed reinforcement systems. *Journal of Personality and Social Psychology, 3,* 54–62.

Bandura, A., Grusec, J. E., & Menlove, F. L. (1967). Vicarious extinction of avoidance behavior. *Journal of Personality and Social Psychology, 5,* 16–23.

Bandura, A., Reese, L., & Adams, N. (1982). Microanalysis of action and fear arousal as a function of differential levels of perceived self-efficacy. *Journal of Personality and Social Psychology, 43,* 5–21.

Beck, A. (1976). *Cognitive therapy and the emotional disorders.* New York: International Universities Press.

Beck, A. T., Rush, A. J., Shaw, B. F., & Emery, G. (1979). *Cognitive therapy of depression.* New York: Guilford Press.

Beck, A. T., Emery, G., & Greenberg, R. (1985). *Anxiety disorders and phobias: A cognitive perspective.* New York: Basic Books.

Bem, S. L. (1967). Verbal self-control: The establishment of effective self-instruction. *Journal of Experimental Psychology, 74,* 485–491.

Berler, E. S., Gross, A. M., & Drabman, R. S. (1982). Social skills training with children: Proceed with caution. *Journal of Applied Behavior Analysis, 15,* 41–53.

Bernard, M. E. (1984). Childhood emotion and cognitive behavior therapy: A rational-emotive perspective. In P. C. Kendall (Ed.), *Advances in cognitive-behavioral research and therapy* (Vol. 3). New York: Academic Press.

Bierman, K. L. (1983). Cognitive development and clinical interviews with children. In B. B. Lahey & A. E. Kazdin (Eds.), *Advances in clinical child psychology* (Vol. 6). New York: Plenum Press.

Bierman, K. L. (1986). Process of change during social skills training with preadolescents and its relation to treatment outcome. *Child Development, 57,* 230–240.

Bierman, K. L., & Furman, W. (1984). The effects of social skills training and peer involvement on the social adjustment of preadolescents. *Child Development, 55,* 151–162.

Bigelow, B. J. (1977). Children's friendship expectations: A cognitive developmental study. *Child Development, 48,* 246–253.

Billings, D. C., & Wasik, B. H. (1985). Self-instructional training with preschoolers: An attempt to replicate. *Journal of Applied Behavior Analysis, 18,* 61–67.

Blue, S. W., Madsen, C. H., & Heimberg, R. G. (1981). Increasing coping behavior in children with aggressive behavior: Evaluation of the relative efficacy of the components of a treatment package. *Child Behavior Therapy, 3,* 51–60.

Bolstad, O. D., & Johnson, S. M. (1972). Self-regulation in the modification of disruptive classroom behavior. *Journal of Applied Behavior Analysis, 5,* 443–454.

Bornstein, M. R., Bellack, A. S., & Hersen, M. (1977). Social-skills training for unassertive children: A multiple-baseline analysis. *Journal of Applied Behavior Analysis, 10,* 183–195.

Bornstein, P. H., & Quevillon, R. P. (1976). The effects of a self-instructional package on overactive preschool boys. *Journal of Applied Behavior Analysis, 9,* 179–188.

Braswell, L., & Kendall, P. C. (1988). Cognitive-behavioral therapies for children. In K. Dobson (Ed.), *Handbook of cognitive-behavioral therapies.* New York: Guilford Press.

Braswell, L., Kendall, P. C., Braith, J., Carey, M. P., & Vye, C. S. (1985). "Involvement" in cognitive-behavioral therapy with children: Process and its relationship to outcome. *Cognitive Therapy and Research, 9,* 611–630.

Brownell, K. D., Coletti, G., Ersner-Hershfield, R., Hershfield, S. M., & Wilson, G. T. (1977). Self-control in school children: Stringency and leniency in self-determined and externally imposed performance standards. *Behavior Therapy, 8,* 442–455.

Bryant, L. E., & Budd, K. S. (1982). Self-instructional training to increase independent work performance in preschoolers. *Journal of Applied Behavior Analysis, 15,* 259–271.

Bugenthal, D. B., Whalen, C. K., & Henker, B. (1977). Causal attributions of hyperactive children and motivational assumptions of two behavior-change approaches: Evidence for an interactionist position. *Child Development, 48,* 874–884.

Burgio, L. D., Whitman, T. L., & Johnson, M. R. (1980). A self-instructional package for increasing attending behavior in educable mentally retarded children. *Journal of Applied Behavior Analysis, 13,* 443–459.

Camp, B. W., Blom, G., Herbert, F., & van Doorninck, W. (1977). "Think Aloud": A program for developing self-control in young aggressive boys. *Journal of Abnormal Child Psychology, 5,* 157–168.

Catania, A. C. (1975). The myth of self-reinforcement. *Behaviorism, 3,* 192–199.

Chandler, M. J. (1973). The assessment and training of social perspective-taking skills. *Developmental Psychology, 9,* 326–332.

Chandler, M. J., Greenspan, S., & Barenboim, C. (1974). Assessment and training of role-taking and referential communication skills in institutionalized emotionally disturbed children. *Developmental Psychology, 10,* 546–553.

Christoff, K. A., Scott, W. O. N., Kelley, M. L., Schlundt, D., Baer, G., & Kelly, J. A. (1985). Social skills and social problem-solving training for shy young adolescents. *Behavior Therapy, 16,* 468–477.

Cohen, R., & Schleser, R. (1984). Cognitive development and clinical interventions. In A. W. Myers & W. E. Craighead (Eds.), *Cognitive behavior therapy with children.* New York: Plenum Press.

Cole, P. M., & Kazdin, A. E. (1980). Critical issues in self-instructional training with children. *Child Behavior Therapy, 2,* 1–21.

Conger, J. C., & Keane, S. P. (1981). Social skills intervention in the treatment of isolated or withdrawn children. *Psychological Bulletin, 90,* 478–495.

Copeland, A. P. (1983). Children's talking to themselves: Its developmental significance, function, and therapeutic promise. In P. C. Kendall (Ed.), *Advances in cognitive-behavioral research and therapy* (Vol. 2). New York: Academic Press.

Dodge, K. A. (1980). Social cognition and children's aggressive behavior. *Child Development, 51,* 162–170.

Dodge, K. A. (1983). Facets of social interaction and the assessment of social competence in children. In B. H. Schneider, K. H. Rubin, & J. E. Ledingham (Eds.), *Childhood peer relations: Issues in assessment and intervention.* New York: Springer-Verlag.

Dodge, K. A. (1988). A social information processing model of social competence in children. In M. Perlmutter (Ed.), *Minnesota Symposium on Child Psychology* (Vol. 18). Hillsdale, NJ: Erlbaum.

Dodge, K. A., & Frame, C. M. (1982). Social cognitive biases and deficits in aggressive boys. *Child Development, 53,* 620–635.

Dodge, K. A., Murphy, R. R., & Buchsbaum, K. (1984). The assessment of intention-cue detection skills in children: Implications for developmental psychopathology. *Child Development, 55,* 163–173.

Drabman, R. S., Spitalnik, R., & O'Leary, K. D. (1973). Teaching self-control to disruptive children. *Journal of Abnormal Psychology, 82,* 10–16.

D'Zurilla, T., & Goldfried, M. (1971). Problem-solving and behavior modification. *Journal of Abnormal Psychology 78,* 107–126.

Elardo, P., & Caldwell, B. (1979). The effects of an experimental social development program on children in the middle childhood period. *Psychology in the Schools, 16,* 93–100.

Ellis, A. (1970). *The essence of rational psychotherapy: A comprehensive approach in treatment.* New York: Institute for Rational Living.

Ellis, A., & Bernard, M. E. (1983). An overview of rational-emotive approaches to the problems of childhood. In A. Ellis & M. E. Bernard (Eds.), *Rational-emotive approaches to the problems of childhood.* New York: Plenum Press.

Ellis, A., & Grieger, R. (1977). *Handbook of rational-emotive therapy.* New York: Springer.

Enright, R. D., & Lapsley, D. K. (1980). Social role-taking: A review of the constructs, measures, and measurement properties. *Review of Educational Research, 50,* 647–674.

Evers, W. L., & Schwartz, J. C. (1973). Modifying social withdrawal in preschoolers: The effects of filmed modeling and teacher praise. *Journal of Abnormal Child Psychology, 1,* 248–256.

Evers-Pasquale, W. L. (1978). The Peer Preference Test, a measure of reward value: Item analysis, cross validation, concurrent validation, and replication. *Journal of Abnormal Child Psychology, 6,* 175–188.

Evers-Pasquale, W., & Sherman, M. (1975). The reward value of peers: A variable influencing the efficacy of filmed modeling in modifying social isolation in preschoolers. *Journal of Abnormal Child Psychology, 3,* 179–189.

Felixbrod, J. J., & O'Leary, K. D. (1974). Self-determination of academic standards by children: Toward freedom from external control. *Journal of Educational Psychology, 66,* 845–850.

Flavell, J. H. (1974). The development of inferences about others. In T. Mischel (Ed.), *Understanding other persons* (pp. 66–116). Oxford, England: Blackwell.

Foster, S. L., & Ritchey, W. L. (1979). Issues in the assessment of social competence in children. *Journal of Applied Behavior Analysis, 12,* 625–638.

Foster, S. L., DeLawyer, D. D., & Guevremont, D. C. (1985). Selecting targets for social skills training with children and adolescents. In K. D. Gadow (Ed.), *Advances in learning and behavioral disabilities* (Vol. 4). Greenwich, CT: JAI Press.

Friedling, C., & O'Leary, S. G. (1979). Effects of self-instructional training on second- and third-grade hyperactive children. *Journal of Applied Behavior Analysis, 12,* 211–219.

Geller, M. I., & Scheirer, C. J. (1978). The effect of filmed modeling on cooperative play in disadvantaged preschoolers. *Journal of Abnormal Child Psychology, 6,* 71–87.

Gilbert, B. O. (1982). The effects of a peer-modeling film on children learning to self-inject insulin. *Behavior Therapy, 13,* 186–193.

Glynn, E. L. (1970). Classroom applications of self-determined reinforcement. *Journal of Applied Behavior Analysis, 3,* 123–132.

Gottman, J. (1977). The effects of a modeling film on social isolation in preschool children: A methodological investigation. *Journal of Abnormal Child Psychology, 5,* 69–78.

Graziano, A. M., DeGiovanni, I. S., & Garcia, K. A. (1979). Behavioral treatment of children's fears: A review. *Psychological Bulletin, 86,* 804–830.

Graziano, A. M., Mooney, K. C., Huber, C., & Ignasiak, D. (1979). Self-control instruction for children's fear reduction. *Journal of Behavior Therapy and Experimental Psychiatry, 10,* 221–227.

Gresham, F. M., & Nagle, R. J. (1980). Social skills training with children: Responsiveness to modeling and coaching as a function of peer orientation. *Journal of Consulting and Clinical Psychology, 48,* 718–729.

Guevremont, D. C., Tishelman, A. C., & Hull, D. B. (1985). Teaching generalized self-control to attention-deficit boys with mothers as adjunct therapists. *Child and Family Behavior Therapy, 7,* 23–37.

Harter, S. (1982). A cognitive-developmental approach to children's understanding of affect and trait labels. In F. C. Serafica (Ed.), *Social-cognitive development in context.* New York: Guilford Press.

Hartig, M., & Kanfer, F. H. (1973). The role of verbal self-instructions in children's resistance to temptation. *Journal of Personality and Social Psychology, 25,* 259–267.

Hartup, W. W. (1984). Peer relations. In P. H. Mussen (Ed.), *Handbook of child psychology: Vol. 4. Socialization, personality, and social development.* New York: Wiley.

Hobbs, S. A., Molguin, L. E., Tyroler, M., & Lahey, B. B. (1980). Cognitive behavior therapy with children: Has clinical utility been demonstrated? *Psychological Bulletin, 87*, 147–165.

Hollon, S. D., & Kendall, P. C. (1980). Cognitive self-statements in depression: Development of an Automatic Thoughts Questionnaire. *Cognitive Therapy and Research, 4*, 384–395.

Hollon, S. D., Kendall, P. C., & Lumry, A. (1986). The specificity of depressotypic cognitions in clinical depression. *Journal of Abnormal Psychology, 95*, 52–60.

Iannotti, R. J. (1978). Effect of role-taking experiences on role-taking, empathy, altruism, and aggression. *Developmental Psychology, 14*, 119–124.

Ingram, R. (Ed.) (1986). *Information processing approaches to clinical psychology.* New York: Academic Press.

Ingram, R., & Kendall, P. C. (1986). Cognitive clinical psychology. In R. Ingram (Ed.), *Information processing approaches to clinical psychology.* New York: Academic Press.

Jacobson, N. (Ed.) (1987). *Cognitive and behavioral therapists in practice.* New York: Guilford Press.

Jakibchuk, Z., & Smeriglio, V. L. (1976). The influence of symbolic modeling on the social behavior of preschool children with low levels of social responsiveness. *Child Development, 47*, 838–841.

Kanfer, F. H., & Karoly, P. (1972). Self-control: A behavioristic excursion into the lion's den. *Behavior Therapy, 3*, 398–416.

Kanfer, F. H., Karoly, P., & Newman, A. (1975). Reduction of children's fear of the dark by competence-related and situational threat-related verbal cues. *Journal of Consulting and Clinical Psychology, 43*, 251–258.

Keller, M. F., & Carlson, P. M. (1974). The use of symbolic modeling to promote social skills in preschool children with low levels of social responsiveness. *Child Development, 45*, 912–919.

Kendall, P. C. (1977). On the efficacious use of verbal self-instructional procedures with children. *Cognitive Therapy and Research, 1*, 331–341.

Kendall, P. C. (1981a). Assessment and cognitive-behavioral interventions: Purposes, proposals, and problems. In P. C. Kendall & S. D. Hollon (Eds.), *Assessment strategies for cognitive-behavioral interventions.* New York: Academic Press.

Kendall, P. C. (1981b). Cognitive-behavioral interventions with children. In B. B. Lahey & A. E. Kazdin (Eds.), *Advances in clinical child psychology* (Vol. 4). New York: Plenum Press.

Kendall, P. C. (1984a). Behavioral assessment and methodology. In G. T. Wilson, C. M. Franks, K. D. Brownell, & P. C. Kendall (Eds.), *Annual review of behavior therapy: Theory and practice* (Vol. 9). New York: Guilford Press.

Kendall, P. C. (1984b). Cognitive processes and procedures in behavior therapy. In G. T. Wilson, C. M. Franks, K. D. Brownell, & P. C. Kendall (Eds.), *Annual review of behavior therapy* (Vol. 9). New York: Guilford Press.

Kendall, P. C. (1984c). Social cognition and problem-solving: A developmental and child-clinical interface. In B. Gholson & T. L. Rosenthal (Eds.), *Applications of cognitive-developmental theory.* New York: Pergamon Press.

Kendall, P. C. (1985a). Cognitive processes and procedures in behavior therapy. In G. T. Wilson, C. M. Franks, K. D. Brownell, & P. C. Kendall (Eds.), *Annual review of behavior therapy* (Vol. 10). New York: Guilford Press.

Kendall, P. C. (1985b). Toward a cognitive-behavioral model of child psychopathology and a critique of related interventions. *Journal of Abnormal Child Psychology, 13*, 357–372.

Kendall, P. C. (1986). Comments on Rubin and Krasnor: Solutions and problems in research on problem-solving. In N. Perlmutter (Ed.), *Minnesota Symposium on Child Psychology* (Vol. 18). Hillsdale, NJ: Erlbaum.

Kendall, P. C., & Bemis, K. M. (1984). Thought and action in psychotherapy: The cognitive-behavioral approaches. In M. Hersen, A. E. Kazdin, & A. S. Bellack (Eds.), *Handbook of clinical psychology.* New York: Pergamon Press.

Kendall, P. C., & Braswell, L. (1982a). Cognitive-behavioral self-control therapy for children: A component analysis. *Journal of Consulting and Clinical Psychology, 50*, 672–689.

Kendall, P. C., & Braswell, L. (1982b). On cognitive-behavioral assessment: Model, measures, and madness. In C. D. Spielberger & J. N. Butcher (Eds.), *Advances in personality assessment* (Vol. 1). Hillsdale, NJ: Erlbaum.

Kendall, P. C., & Braswell, L. (1985). *Cognitive-behavioral therapy for impulsive children.* New York: Guilford Press.

Kendall, P. C., & Finch, A. J., Jr. (1978). A cognitive-behavioral treatment for impulsivity: A group comparison study. *Journal of Consulting and Clinical Psychology, 46*, 110–118.

Kendall, P. C., & Fischler, G. L. (1984). Behavioral and adjustment correlates of problem-solving:

Validational analyses of interpersonal cognitive problem-solving measures. *Child Development,* *55*, 879–892.

Kendall, P. C., & Hollon, S. D. (Eds.). (1979). *Cognitive-behavioral interventions: Theory, research, and procedures.* New York: Academic Press.

Kendall, P. C., & Ingram, R. (1987). The future for cognitive assessment of anxiety: Let's get specific. In L. Michelson & M. Asher (Eds.), *Cognitive-behavioral approaches to the anxiety disorders.* New York: Guilford Press.

Kendall, P. C., & Korgeski, G. P. (1979). Assessment and cognitive-behavioral interventions. *Cognitive Therapy and Research, 3,* 1–21.

Kendall, P. C., & Morison, P. (1984). Integrating cognitive and behavioral procedures for the treatment of socially isolated children. In A. W. Myers & W. E. Craighead (Eds.), *Cognitive behavior therapy with children.* New York: Plenum Press.

Kendall, P. C., & Reber, M. (1987). Cognitive therapy in the treatment of hyperactivity in children. *Archives of General Psychiatry, 44,* 296.

Kendall, P. C. & Wilcox, L. E. (1980). A cognitive-behavioral treatment for impulsivity: Concrete and conceptual training in non-self-controlled problem children. *Journal of Consulting and Clinical Psychology, 48,* 80–91.

Kendall, P. C., & Zupan, B. A. (1981). Individual versus group application of cognitive-behavioral strategies for developing self-control in children. *Behavior Therapy, 12,* 344–359.

Kendall, P. C., Pellegrini, D. S., & Urbain, E. S. (1981). Approaches to assessment for cognitive-behavioral interventions with children. In P. C. Kendall & S. D. Hollon (Eds.), *Assessment strategies and cognitive-behavioral interventions.* New York: Academic Press.

Klingman, A., Melamed, B. G., Cuthbert, M. I., & Hermecz, D. A. (1984). Effects of participant modeling on information acquisition and skill utilization. *Journal of Consulting and Clinical Psychology, 52,* 414–422.

Klorman, R., Hilpert, P. L., Michael, R., LaGana, C., & Sveen, O. B. (1980). Effects of coping and mastery modeling on experienced and inexperienced pedodontic patients' disruptiveness. *Behavior Therapy, 11,* 156–168.

Kornhaber, R., & Schroeder, H. (1975). Importance of model similarity on extinction of avoidance behavior in children. *Journal of Consulting and Clinical Psychology, 43,* 601–607.

Krasnor, L. R., & Rubin, K. H. (1981). The assessment of social problem-solving skills in young children. In T. V. Merluzzi, C. R. Glass, & T. M. Genest (Eds.), *Cognitive assessment.* New York: Guilford Press.

Kurdek, L. A. (1978). Perspective-taking as the cognitive basis for children's moral development: A review of the literature. *Merrill-Palmer Quarterly, 24,* 3–28.

Ladd, G. W. (1981). Effectiveness of a social learning method for enhancing children's social interaction and peer acceptance. *Child Development, 52,* 171–178.

Ladd, G. W., & Mize, J. (1983). A cognitive social-learning model of social-skill training. *Psychological Review, 90,* 127–157.

LaGreca, A. M., & Santogrossi, D. A. (1980). Social skills training with elementary school students: A behavioral group approach. *Journal of Consulting and Clinical Psychology, 48,* 220–227.

Lewis, S. (1974). A comparison of behavior therapy techniques in reduction of fearful avoidance behavior. *Behavior Therapy, 5,* 648–655.

Lovaas, O. I., & Newsom, C. D. (1976). Behavior modification with psychotic children. In H. Leitenberg (Ed.), *Handbook of behavior modification and behavior therapy.* Englewood Cliffs, NJ: Prentice-Hall.

Lovaas, O. I., Berberich, J. P., Perloff, B. F., & Schaeffer, B. (1966). Acquisition of imitative speech by schizophrenic children. *Science, 151,* 705–707.

Lovaas, O. I., Freitas, L., Nelson, K., & Whalen, C. (1967). The establishment of imitation and its use for the development of complex behavior in schizophrenic children. *Behaviour Research and Therapy, 5,* 171–181.

McFall, R. M. (1982). A review and reformulation of the concept of social skills. *Behavioral Assessment, 4,* 1–35.

Mahoney, M. J. (1974). *Cognition and behavior modification.* Cambridge, MA: Balinger.

Mahoney, M. J. (1977). Personal science: A cognitive-learning therapy. In A. Ellis & R. Grieger (Eds.), *Handbook of rational-emotive psychotherapy.* New York: Springer.

Meichenbaum, D. (1977). *Cognitive-behavior modification: An integrative approach.* New York: Plenum Press.

Meichenbaum, D. (1985). Cognitive-behavioral therapies. In S. J. Lynn & J. P. Garske (Eds.), *Contemporary psychotherapies: Models and methods.* Columbus, OH: Charles E. Merrill.

Meichenbaum, D., & Cameron, R. (1982). Cognitive behavior therapy. In G. T. Wilson & C. M. Franks (Eds.), *Contemporary behavior therapy: Conceptual and empirical foundations.* New York: Guilford Press.

Meichenbaum, D., & Goodman, J. (1971). Teaching impulsive children to talk to themselves: A means of developing self-control. *Journal of Abnormal Psychology, 77,* 115–126.

Melamed, B., & Siegel, L. (1975). Reduction of anxiety in children facing hospitalization and surgery by use of filmed modeling. *Journal of Consulting and Clinical Psychology, 43,* 511–521.

Melamed, B. G., Yurcheson, R., Fleece, E. L., Hutcherson, S., & Hawes, R. (1978). Effects of film modeling on the reduction of anxiety-related behaviors in individuals varying in levels of previous experience in the stress situation. *Journal of Consulting and Clinical Psychology, 46,* 1357–1367.

Michelson, L., Mannarino, A. P., Marchione, K. E., Stern, M., Figueroa, J., & Beck, S. (1983). A comparative outcome study of behavioral social skills training, interpersonal problem-solving and nondirective control treatments with child psychiatric outpatients. *Behaviour Research and Therapy, 21,* 545–556.

Mischel, W. (1968). *Personality and assessment.* New York: Wiley.

Mischel, W., & Baker, N. (1975). Cognitive appraisals and transformations in delay behavior. *Journal of Personality and Social Psychology, 31,* 254–261.

Mischel, W., Ebbesen, E. B., & Zeiss, A. R. (1972). Cognitive and attentional mechanisms in delay of gratification. *Journal of Personality and Social Psychology, 34,* 942–950.

Mize, J., & Ladd, G. W. (In press). Developmental issues in social skill training. In S. R. Asher & J. D. Coie (Eds.), *Children's status in the peer group.* New York: Cambridge University Press.

Monahan, J., & O'Leary, K. D. (1971). Effects of self-instruction on rule-breaking behavior. *Psychological Reports, 29,* 1059–1066.

Moore, S. G., & Cole, S. D. (1978). Cognitive self-mediation training with hyperkinetic children. *Bulletin of the Psychonomic Society, 12,* 18–20.

Nelson, R. O., Lipinski, D. P., & Boykin, R. A. (1978). The effects of self-recorders' training and the obtrusiveness of the self-recording device on the accuracy and reactivity of self-monitoring. *Behavior Therapy, 9,* 220–208.

Nelson, W., & Birkimer, J. C. (1978). Role of self-instruction and self-reinforcement in the modification of impulsivity. *Journal of Consulting and Clinical Psychology, 46,* 183.

O'Connor, R. D. (1969). Modification of social withdrawal through symbolic modeling. *Journal of Applied Behavior Analysis, 2,* 15–22.

O'Connor, R. D. (1972). The relative efficacy of modeling, shaping, and the combined procedures for the modification of social withdrawal. *Journal of Abnormal Psychology, 79,* 327–334.

Oden, S., & Asher, S. R. (1977). Coaching children in social skills for friendship making. *Child Development, 48,* 495–506.

O'Leary, S. G., & Dubey, D. R. (1979). Applications of self-control procedures by children: A review. *Journal of Applied Behavior Analysis, 12,* 449–465.

Ollendick, T. H. (1979). Fear reduction techniques with children. In M. Hersen, R. M. Eisler, & P. M. Miller (Eds.), *Progress in behavior modification* (Vol. 8). New York: Academic Press.

Palkes, H., Stewart, M., & Kahana, B. (1968). Porteus maze performance of hyperactive boys after training in self-directed verbal commands. *Child Development, 39,* 817–826.

Patterson, C., & Mischel, W. (1975). Plans to resist distraction. *Developmental Psychology, 11,* 369–378.

Patterson, G. R. (1982). *Coercive family process.* Eugene, OR: Castalia.

Patterson, G. R., & Bank, L. (1986). Bootstrapping your way in the nomological thicket. *Behavioral Assessment, 8,* 49–73.

Peterson, L., Schutheis, K., Ridley-Johnson, R., Miller, D. J., & Tracy, K. (1984). Comparison of three modeling procedures on the presurgical and postsurgical reactions of children. *Behavior Therapy, 15,* 197–203.

Putallaz, M., & Gottman, J. (1983). Social relationship problems in children: An approach to intervention. In B. B. Lahey & A. E. Kazdin (Eds.), *Advances in clinical child psychology* (Vol. 6). New York: Plenum Press.

Renshaw, P. D., & Asher, S. R. (1982). Social competence and peer status: The distinction between goals and strategies. In K. H. Rubin & H. S. Ross (Eds.), *Peer relationships and social skills in childhood.* New York: Springer-Verlag.

Richel, A., & Burgio, J. (1982). Assessing social competencies in lower-income preschool children. *American Journal of Community Psychology, 10,* 635–654.

Richel, A., Eshelman, A., & Loigman, G. (1983). Social problem-solving training: A follow-up study of cognitive and behavioral effects. *Journal of Abnormal Child Psychology, 2,* 15–28.

Robin, A. L., Arnel, S., & O'Leary, K. D. (1975). The effects of self-instruction in writing deficiencies. *Behavior Therapy, 6,* 178–187.

Robin, A. L., Schneider, M., & Dolnick, M. (1976). The turtle technique: An extended case study of self-control in the classroom. *Psychology in the Schools, 13,* 449–453.

Robinson, E. A. (1985). Coercion theory revisited: Toward a new theoretical perspective on the etiology of conduct disorders. *Clinical Psychology Review, 5,* 597–626.

Rosen, A., & Proctor, E. K. (1981). Distinctions between treatment outcomes and their implications for treatment evaluation. *Journal of Consulting and Clinical Psychology, 49,* 418–425.

Rosenthal, T., & Bandura, A. (1978). Psychological modeling: Theory and practice. In S. L. Garfield & A. E. Bergin (Eds.), *Handbook of psychotherapy and behavior change* (2nd ed.). New York: Wiley.

Santogrossi, D. A., O'Leary, K. D., Romanczyk, R. G., & Kaufman, K. F. (1973). Self-evaluation by adolescents in a psychiatric hospital school token program. *Journal of Applied Behavior Analysis, 6,* 277–287.

Sarason, I. G., & Sarason, B. R. (1981). Teaching cognitive and social skills to high school students. *Journal of Consulting and Clinical Psychology, 49,* 908–918.

Schleser, R., Meyers, A. W., & Cohen, R. (1981). Generalization of self-instructions: Effects of general versus specific content, active rehearsal, and cognitive level. *Child Development, 52,* 335–340.

Schleser, R., Meyers, A. W., Cohen, R., & Rodick, J. D. (1984). The effects of cognitive level and training procedures on the generalization of self-instructions. *Cognitive Therapy and Research, 8,* 187–200.

Seaman, J. M., & Sloane, H. M. (1984). Evaluation of a cognitive interpersonal problem-solving program. *Cognitive Therapy and Research, 8,* 187–200.

Sears, R. R., Maccoby, E. E., & Levin, H. (1957). *Patterns of child rearing.* Evanston, IL: Row, Peterson.

Selman, R. L., Lavin, D. R., & Brion-Meisels, S. (1982). Troubled children's use of self-reflection. In F. C. Serafica (Ed.), *Social-cognitive development in context.* New York: Guilford Press.

Serafica, F. C. (1982). Introduction. In F. C. Serafica (Ed.), *Social-cognitive development in context.* New York: Guilford Press.

Shantz, C. U. (1982). Children's understanding of social rules and the social context. In F. C. Serafica (Ed.), *Social-cognitive development in context.* New York: Guilford Press.

Siegel, L. J., & Peterson, L. (1980). Stress reduction in young dental patients through coping skills and sensory information. *Journal of Consulting and Clinical Psychology, 48,* 785–787.

Siegel, L. J., & Peterson, L. (1981). Maintenance effects of coping skills and sensory information on young children's response to repeated dental procedures. *Behavior Therapy, 12,* 530–535.

Skinner, B. F. (1984). An operant analysis of problem-solving. *The Behavioral and Brain Sciences, 7,* 583–613.

Spivack, G., & Shure, M. B. (1974). *Social adjustment of young children: A cognitive approach to solving real-life problems.* San Francisco: Jossey-Bass.

Spivack, G., Platt, J. J., & Shure, M. B. (1976). *The problem-solving approach to adjustment.* San Francisco: Jossey-Bass.

Stokes, T. F., & Baer, D. M. (1977). An implicit technology of generalization. *Journal of Applied Behavior Analysis, 10,* 349–368.

Swanson, H. L., & Scarpati, S. (1984). Self-instructional training to increase academic performance of educationally handicapped children. *Child and Family Behavior Therapy, 6,* 23–39.

Switsky, H. N., & Haywood, H. C. (1974). Motivational orientation and the relative efficacy of self-monitored and externally imposed reinforcement systems in children. *Journal of Personality and Social Psychology, 30,* 360–336.

Taylor, A. R., & Asher, S. R. (1984). Children's goals and social competence: Individual differences in a game-playing context. In T. Field, J. L. Roopnarine, & M. Segal (Eds.), *Friendships in normal and handicapped children.* Norwood, NJ: Ablex.

Underwood, B., & Moore, B. (1982). Perspective-taking and altruism. *Psychological Bulletin, 91,* 143–173.

Urbain, E. S., & Kendall, P. C. (1980). Review of social-cognitive problem-solving interventions with children. *Psychological Bulletin, 88,* 109–143.

Weiner, H. R., & Dubanowski, R. A. (1975). Resistance to extinction as a function of self- or externally determined schedules of reinforcement. *Journal of Personality and Social Psychology, 31,* 905–910.

Weissberg, R. P., Gesten, E. L., Carnrike, C. L., Toro, P. A., Rapkin, B. D., Davidson, E., & Cowen,

E. L. (1981). Social problem-solving skills training: A competence-building intervention with second- to fourth-grade children. *American Journal of Community Psychology, 9*, 411–423.

Weissberg, R. P., Gesten, E. L., Rapkin, B. D., Cowen, E. L., Davidson, E., Flores deApodaca, R., & McKim, B. J. (1981). Evaluation of a social-problem-solving training program for suburban and inner-city third-grade children. *Journal of Consulting and Clinical Psychology, 48*, 251–261.

White, W., & Davis, M. (1974). Vicarious extinction of phobic behavior in early childhood. *Journal of Abnormal Child Psychology, 2*, 25–33.

Whitehall, M. B., Hersen, M., & Bellack, A. S. (1980). Conversation skills training for socially isolated children. *Behavior Research and Therapy, 18*, 217–225.

Whitman, T. & Johnson, M. B. (1983). Teaching addition and subtraction with regrouping to educable mentally retarded children: A group self-instructional training program. *Behavior Therapy, 14*, 127–143.

Williams, D. Y., & Akamatsu, J. J. (1978). Cognitive self-guidance training with juvenile delinquents: Applicability and generalization. *Cognitive Therapy and Research, 2*, 285–288.

Wood, R., & Flynn, J. M. (1978). A self-evaluation token system versus an external evaluation token system alone in a residential setting with predelinquent youths. *Journal of Applied Behavior Analysis, 11*, 503–512.

Yu, P., Harris, G. E., Solovitz, B. L., & Franklin, J. L. (1986). A social problem-solving intervention for children at high risk for later psychopathology. *Journal of Clinical Child Psychology, 15*, 30–40.

# 6    *Pharmacotherapy*

JAMES E. MARTIN AND MARTIN AGRAN

Psychotropic drugs are those prescribed by a medical doctor to alter the behavior or emotions of children with severe childhood disorders (Gadow, 1986a; Sprague & Ullmann, 1981). Pharmacotherapy is the active use of psychotropic drugs to change behavior or emotions, and it has enabled many children to function well in school and to live fuller, happier lives (Aman, 1978, 1980; Kauffman, 1985). Although generally useful, the effects of psychotropic drugs need to be monitored closely because children's learning ability and social performance can be adversely affected (DiMascio & Shader, 1970). Therapists, teachers, and others who work with disturbed children need to understand both the benefits and the costs associated with the use of psychotropic drugs. The purpose of this chapter is to explain basic pharmacotherapy concepts and to discuss the effects of psychotropic drugs.

## CONCEPTS

### Classification

The psychotropic drugs used with children are generally grouped into four categories: (1) major tranquilizers; (2) minor tranquilizers; (3) antidepressants; and (4) stimulants. Each of these drug groups is discussed in detail. The most common trade names are used to describe each drug. When a drug is first introduced, the generic name is also included.

### Major Tranquilizers

These drugs, also called *neuroleptics* or *antipsychotics*, are used to treat psychotic disorders and to manage hyperactive, aggressive, self-injurious, self-stimulatory, and delusionary behaviors. The major tranquilizers are divided into three main groups: (1) the *phenothiazines*, which include Mellaril (thioridazine), Thorazine (chlorpromazine), and Stelazine (trifluoperazine); (2) the *butyrophenones*, which include Haldol (haloperidol); and (3) the *thioxanthenes*, which include Navane (thiothixene). The phenothiazines are the major tranquilizers

JAMES E. MARTIN • School of Education, University of Colorado at Colorado Springs, Colorado Springs, Colorado 80933.    MARTIN AGRAN • Department of Special Education, Utah State University, Logan, Utah 84322.

most often used to treat childhood problems (Gadow, 1986a). Thorazine, the first psychotropic drug, was introduced in the early 1950s (Spiegel & Aebi, 1983). Generally, children who use these drugs are attending special education programs for students with emotional problems or mental retardation (Gadow, 1986b).

## Minor Tranquilizers

These drugs, also called *antianxiety-sedative drugs* or *anxiolytics*, are used to treat anxiety disorders. However, the ability of Valium (diazepam) to relax skeletal muscles promotes its use with children who have cerebral palsy. Valium and Clonopin (clonazepam) are also frequently used to help control seizures in epileptic children. The minor tranquilizers are grouped into three classifications based on their chemical makeup. The first group is the *benzodiazepines*, which include Valium, Librium (chlordiazepoxide), and Clonopin; all of these drugs have some antiepileptic properties. The second group is the *diphenylmethane derivatives*, which include Atarax (hydroxyzine) and Benadryl (diphenhydramine). In young children Atarax is used occasionally to help manage hyperactivity and to promote sleep. The third group is the *propanediols*, which includes Equanil (meprobamate). This last group must be used with caution, as the drugs have been associated with suicide attempts and accidental poisonings (Gadow, 1986a).

## Antidepressant Drugs

These drugs are divided into two categories: the *tricyclics* and the *monoamine oxidase inhibitors* (MAOIs). The MAO inhibitors are used less often than the tricyclics because they are less effective and more toxic. The drugs in the tricyclic category include Tofranil (imipramine) and Elavil (amitriptyline). These drugs are used to treat severe, chronic childhood depression. As Gadow (1986a) indicated, however, the term *antidepressant* is somewhat misused, as these drugs are used to treat a variety of childhood problems. Tofranil is often prescribed to treat enuresis (bedwetting) and, at times, hyperactivity. Elavil is also used to treat hyperactivity. Lithium is the only known drug that can be used to treat individuals who are manic-depressive. Fortunately, very few children need to be treated for this disorder.

## Stimulants

These drugs appear to be the most-often-used childhood psychotropic drugs. They are used to treat attention-deficit disorders with or without hyperactivity. Ritalin (methylphenidate), Dexedrine (dextroamphetamine), and Cylert (pemoline) are the most-often-used stimulants. Like other drugs, stimulants can be used to treat other disorders. At times, they may be used to treat the drowsiness caused by antiepileptic drugs and to control narcolepsy. Narcolepsy, a disorder marked by sudden sleep, is rare and seldom develops in children under the age of 12 (Gadow, 1986a).

Psychotropic drugs are often used to treat various childhood disorders; yet, the majority of children with these problems do not take medication. The exact number of children prescribed psychotropic drugs is difficult to determine, as only a few prevalence studies have been completed. However, several estimates of drug use have been reported; and it appears that the use of psychotropic drugs varies by the type of disorder. About 15%–30% of children who have been labeled by the schools as being emotionally disturbed use psychotropic drugs (Gadow, 1986a; Safer & Krager, 1984). Of *all* elementary-school-aged children, 1%–2% receive psychotropic drugs to control hyperactivity (Gadow, 1986a). About 5% of students who are moderately mentally retarded and 13% of students who are mildly mentally retarded are prescribed psychotropic drugs (Aman, Field, & Bridgman, 1985; Gadow, 1986a; Gadow & Kalachnik, 1981). Of the 5% of the moderately mentally retarded students prescribed psychotropics, about 37% use major tranquilizers; of this group, a third are 13 years of age or younger (Gadow & Kalachnik, 1981). This rate of use is well below the figures for public residential institutions (Hill, Balow, & Bruininks, 1985) and adult community programs (Martin & Agran, 1985).

## Administration

Psychotropic drugs are usually administered orally. The drug—once dissolved by the stomach and intestinal fluids—passes through the intestinal walls, goes into the blood stream (after being processed by the liver), and is delivered to the brain. Once past the blood–brain barrier, the drug molecules affect brain cell activity. The amount of food and time when food is eaten, the supply of blood, stomach acidity levels, and other factors can all affect the rate of absorption into the blood stream (Leavitt, 1982). The drug is primarily removed from the blood stream by the kidney and is excreted with the passage of urine. A stable concentration of drug in the blood stream is achieved when the amount of drug intake equals the amount of drug output.

The half-life of a drug is the time the body takes to decrease the amount of the drug by half. Extreme fluctuations in the amount of drug in the blood stream can generally be prevented by administering another dosage each half-life. (See Gadow, 1986a,b, for a more detailed discussion of the administration of psychotropic drugs.) In an emergency, psychotropic drugs can also be administered intramuscularly. A needle passes the drug directly into muscle, where absorption into the blood stream is much quicker than when pills are taken orally.

## Dosage

*Titration* is the most common method of determining an effective medication dosage. A small amount of medication, often below the recommended effective level, is first prescribed. The amount is increased slowly until the desired effect is obtained. During titration, a different drug may be substituted or another added. Titration requires that each person's dosage be monitored

JAMES E. MARTIN AND
MARTIN AGRAN

individually, as two individuals who have similar physical characteristics may respond differently to the same amount of medication.

The titration process requires input from significant others to ensure that the physician will have adequate information. For example, Sleator and Ullmann (1981) reported that only 20% of children who are hyperactive can be accurately diagnosed based on observations completed only in the medical office. Consequently, other individuals (e.g., teachers) who interact with these children for extended periods of the day need to be asked to provide their observations. When teacher-completed observational checklists are given to the physician, the accuracy of diagnosis and follow-up drug monitoring improve dramatically. In the case of attention-deficit disorders with hyperactivity, a completed scale, like the one called ACTeRs developed by Ullmann, Sleator, and Sprague (1985), can be sent to the physician by the child's classroom teacher weekly or monthly. This additional information would ensure effective monitoring.

## Dose Response

Psychotropic drugs are prescribed to modify a specific target behavior. Various dosages of a drug have differing effects on the target behavior. The relationship between the dosage and its effect on the target behavior is called the *dose response*. When the desired results have been obtained, the threshold response has been reached (Ray, 1978). Marholin and Phillips (1976) discussed psychotropic drug effects in relation to the acquisition of skills. In their view, a therapeutic effect is obtained when symptomatic or deviant behavior is reduced *concurrently* with the demonstrated acquisition of new skills. To achieve this level of therapeutic effect, one must monitor the target behavior closely (Agran & Martin, 1982).

Besides affecting the target behavior, psychotropic drugs may also affect other behaviors. When collateral behavior becomes adversely affected, the drug is regarded as having toxic effects (DiMascio & Shader, 1970). A study completed by Sprague and Sleator (1975) illustrated the dose–response relationship between the target behavior and collateral behavior. As the dosage of stimulant medication was increased to control hyperactive behavior, academic behavior was negatively influenced. If the amount of drug was reduced from the level that best controlled the hyperactive behavior, academic behavior improved, but the level of hyperactive behavior increased. Whalen and Henker (1984) reported, however, that Sprague and Sleator's dose-response pattern across different behavioral domains (1975) has not been replicated. Whalen and Henker (1984) summarized by indicating that no definitive answer about temporary cognitive impairment is possible. The physician, in consultation with the family and the educational staff, must determine a dosage that will achieve the most positive control over the target behavior with as little effect on academic abilities as possible.

## Tolerance

Children may develop *tolerance* for any psychotropic drug. The same dosage of a drug that had successfully managed the target behavior may no longer control the child's problem behavior (Gadow, 1986a). The exact point during treatment when a child develops a tolerance for any particular drug is unknown. When tolerance is reached, a slight increase in the dosage level may often reestablish the threshold response. Sleator, von Neumann, and Sprague (1974) reported, for instance, that a slight increase in Ritalin usually reestablishes the treatment threshold. Gadow (1986a) warned of possible serious side effects when the dosage level of a drug is repeatedly increased to reestablish lost treatment effects, as heightened amounts of the drug may still be in the child's blood stream. After a brief period in which there may be a dramatic effect, a few children will develop complete tolerance (Gross & Wilson, 1974; Spiegel & Aebi, 1983). For instance, Shaywitz and Shaywitz (1984) estimated that 20%–30% of the children given stimulant medication for attention-deficit disorder do not show significant improvement.

## Polypharmacy

Children who receive psychotropic drugs to help manage their emotional or behavior problems often receive more than one type of drug. This practice is called *polypharmacy*, or *multiple-drug treatment*. A potential problem may arise when one drug alters or negates the effect of another. Gadow and Kalachnik (1981) estimated that 7%–10% of the children in special education classes who receive medication are given drugs to control their behavior and seizure disorders. Hill *et al.* (1985) reported that 54% of the residents (including children and adults) of community residential programs for mentally retarded individuals were regularly given more than one psychotropic or anticonvulsant drug. Although several researchers have attempted to determine the prevalence of polypharmacy, the effects of multiple-drug therapy on behavior have received little attention (Agran & Martin, 1982). Gadow (1986a) indicated that the negative effect of drug interactions warrants multiple-psychotropic-drug therapy only in unique cases.

## Drug-Free Periods

Children who receive psychotropic drugs on a long-term basis should occasionally undergo a brief drug-free period. This recommendation is derived from research suggesting that up to 30% of the children who are on psychotropic drugs could be removed from them with no recurrence of the deviant or symptomatic behavior. The drug-free period should be long enough to ensure that significant others, especially teachers or mental health workers, will be able to note any changes in behavior. For the facilitation of unbiased feedback, these individuals should not be told that the child is in a drug-free period. A study by Sleator *et al.* (1974) illustrates this point. During the course of a long-term investigation to determine the effects of stimulant medication on hyperactive behavior, the children were taken off medication. Before treatment, these children had displayed high levels of hyperactive behavior. Once the drug was removed, the children's teachers reported that 26% of the sample no longer had unacceptable behaviors. This unexpected finding is remarkable, as the teachers were not given information about the drug's being discontinued. The reasons behind the findings are unclear, and explanations range from environmental modifications to spontaneous remission. The point remains that, after continuous drug treatment, many children no longer needed the medication. If the drugs had not been withdrawn for a brief trial period, the behavior of these children in drug-free conditions would not have been known.

## Effects of Psychotropic Drugs

Psychotropic drugs almost always effect changes in a child's behavior. These changes may be wanted, unwanted, or both. In other words, deviant or symptomatic behavior may be reduced or brought under control, and at the same time, desired behavior may be impaired (Aman, 1980). Interestingly, an unwanted effect for one person may be the desired effect for another (Gadow, 1986a).

Drug-induced side effects are generally manifested through impairments in adaptive behavior or physical symptoms (Engelhardt & Polizos, 1978). Behavioral toxicity, discussed in the dose response section, may impair a child's adaptive functioning or learning ability. Physical side effects vary along a continuum from less to very serious, and they range from a transitory change in speech, coordination, or clarity of thought to permanent damage to an organ, such as the liver or the heart. The major and minor tranquilizers, the antidepressants, and the stimulants all have the potential to induce desired as well as unwanted side effects. Fortunately, some of these negative conditions may improve when the dosage is reduced or the drug is discontinued.

### Major Tranquilizers

#### Desired Effects

Thorazine, Mellaril, and Haldol are the major tranquilizers most often prescribed to assist in the management of childhood aggressive, destructive, and antisocial behavior. The major tranquilizers have been used to treat almost all childhood psychiatric disorders (including schizophrenia, autism, severe behavior problems, and conduct disorders). Although many studies examining the effects of these drugs on adult behavior have been completed, little research has been conducted on children (Gadow, 1986b). Most research information has been derived from studies conducted on mentally retarded children. Also, the overall lack of well-controlled studies limits the conclusions that can be drawn from the available reports (see Aman & Singh, 1980; Sprague & Werry, 1971).

In early and middle childhood, the major tranquilizers are used for the behavior management of severe conduct problems. Gadow (1986b), however, indicated that these drugs do not seem to help in treating autism. For adolescent psychotic problems, such as schizophrenia and severe affective disorders, these drugs are often successful. The drugs appear to manage the person's acute crisis and to calm agitated states. Usually, these drugs are prescribed on a short-term basis, but those few children diagnosed as having schizophrenia may receive long-term treatment.

Several well-controlled studies have suggested the usefulness of the major tranquilizers in reducing stereotypical behaviors (Davis, Sprague, & Werry,

1969; Singh & Aman, 1981; Zimmerman & Heistad, 1982). These studies targeted stereotypical behaviors as their major dependent measure. Other studies that have used broad-based clinical measures have found that the major tranquilizers did not reduce the frequency of occurrence of these behaviors (Aman & Singh, 1983). Because the subjects in these studies were children who were mentally retarded, generalization to children who are autistic, in whom stereotypical behaviors are also common, should be done in a cautious manner.

Among students who are mentally retarded, the usefulness of these drugs in helping to manage such behaviors as aggressiveness, destructiveness, and hyperactivity is still uncertain. However, clinical practice and a few well-controlled studies seem to suggest the usefulness of these drugs in certain cases. Aman and Singh (1983) indicated that Mellaril and Haldol can be used to control aggressive and other hostile behaviors. Menolascino, Ruedrich, Golden, and Wilson (1985) reported that Navane and Mellaril were used to successfully treat schizophrenic mentally retarded adults. Interestingly, the dosages prescribed were lower than those needed to treat patients who were not mentally retarded. Mellaril, Thorazine, and Haldol have also been used to successfully treat self-injurious behavior (Burk & Menolascino, 1968; Singh & Millichamp, 1985).

*Duration of Effect*

Usually, the major tranquilizers are given in one daily oral dose. Their maximum effect is reached in 1–4 hours and is maintained for up to 24 hours. Prolixin (fluphenazine decanoate), a drug that can be given intramuscularly, is given for long-term treatment, especially for individuals who can't manage their own medications. Its half-life—that is, the time at which its therapeutic action begins to lessen—is from 2 to 3 weeks. A child's body will take about 4 weeks to eliminate all traces of the drug.

*Side Effects*

The major tranquilizers can cause varied physical side effects, perhaps the most serious being extrapyramidal (a motor area of the brain) disturbances (Charalampous & Keepers, 1978). About 20% of the individuals on Mellaril and Thorazine complain of drowsiness and dry mouth. In addition, about 10% of the cases experience visual problems and constipation. For low dosages, these side effects are often short-term. However, as the dosage increases, adverse effects become more likely. Certain major tranquilizers have unique effects. Mellaril may inhibit ejaculation while not affecting the ability to have an erection. Thorazine is often associated with weight increase.

Four extrapyramidal syndromes are associated with major tranquilizer use: Parkinsonian syndrome, akathisia, acute dystonic reaction, and tardive dyskinesia. According to Gadow (1986b), these side effects occur most often with Haldol, Stelazine, and Compazine (prochlorperazine). Mellaril seems to cause the least extrapyramidal complications of all the major tranquilizers.

*Parkinsonian Syndrome.* This side effect causes the person to look "drugged out" or to have masked facial expressions. Other symptoms include rigid muscles, poor posture, involuntary quivering, and finger rubbing (i.e., pill rolling). A decrease in the amount of drug or the adminstration of anticholinergic drugs—that is, Artane (trihexyphenidyl) or Cogentin (benztropine)—may help reduce the frequency and intensity of the Parkinsonian reaction.

*Akathisia.* The major characteristic of this disorder is restless behavior. The person is always fidgeting, appears agitated, and has difficulty sitting still. At times, dosage reduction or taking anticholinergic drugs helps control this problem.

*Acute Dystonic Reaction.* This disorder is characterized by facial grimacing, an upward gaze, protruding tongue, or clenched teeth. Gadow (1986a) indicated that these symptoms usually occur in younger individuals and near the start of drug treatment. Anticholinergic drugs are of great help.

*Tardive Dyskinesia.* This disorder is usually noticed after months of treatment with high dosages of a major tranquilizer, and it is often observed only when the drug has been stopped. This syndrome is characterized by sterotyped involuntary movements: smacking of the lips, movement of the chin, movement of the fingers, and jerky body movements. Gadow (1986a) estimated that 15%–30% of the people who receive long-term treatment develop tardive dyskinesia. Schroeder and Gualtieri (1985) suggested that gradual withdrawal of the major tranquilizer will produce fewer instances of dyskinesia than immediate cessation. Unfortunately, some people never seem to stop having symptoms, even though the symptoms lessen. At times, the only way to provide symptom relief is to resume drug treatment.

Even though the major tranquilizers have been used to treat childhood disorders for several years, little is known about the effects of these drugs on learning (Aman, 1980), in part, because many of the studies have relied on insensitive instruments to measure the dependent variables (Gadow & Swanson, 1985). The few studies that have been conducted with non-mentally-retarded subjects suggest that the major tranquilizers do not produce consistent cognitive gains and, in fact, seem to worsen cognitive performance, especially at higher doses (Aman, 1978). When these drugs do appear to help cognitive performance, the dosages are relatively low (Aman, 1980). Several studies suggest that certain major tranquilizers are inimical to the cognitive performance of mentally retarded individuals (Wysocki, Fuqua, Davis, & Breuning, 1981).

## Minor Tranquilizers

### Desired Effects

This group of drugs is primarily used to treat anxiety disorders. However, little information is available about the use of these drugs in the treatment of children (Gittelman-Klein, 1978). This situation exists for several reasons. No data exist on the prevalence of the use of minor tranquilizers among children under 13 years old. The few studies that have investigated childhood prevalence rates have found little, if any, use of these drugs. The development of the recent

DSM-III childhood anxiety disorder categories (avoidance and separation disorders) have not allowed time for detailed studies to be completed (American Psychiatric Association, 1980). Even though the overanxious disorder was included in DSM-II, to date few research studies have examined the use of drugs to treat this disorder. Finally, the rarity of obsessive-compulsive disorders creates a situation in which subjects are very difficult to find. In contrast, several studies have been completed that have decreased childhood phobias (for a change), but drugs are seldom used in these cases (Schwartz & Johnson, 1985).

Pomeroy and Gadow (1986) indicated that few children under the age of 13 are treated with drugs for anxiety disorders, as the age of onset usually occurs during adolescence. Clinical practice with adolescents and young adults suggests that short-term drug therapy, coupled with psychological treatment, is the most effective approach. In these cases, Valium and Librium have been the most-often-used drug. Gittelman-Klein and Klein (1971) reported that Tofranil (an antidepressant) reduced children's fear of going to school and made them less depressed.

Instead of being used to help treat anxiety problems, the minor tranquilizers seem to be used more with children to help manage other problems. Valium and Clonopin are often used as antiepileptic drugs. Children who have cerebral palsy are frequently given Valium to help relax their skeletal muscles, although its use is of limited value because of its sedative nature and its weakening effect on the muscles. Dantrium (dantrolene sodium) is also used as a muscle relaxant, but its use may lower the seizure threshold (Denhoff, Feldman, Smith, Litchman, & Holden, 1975). Atarax is used at times to help control hyperactivity.

## Duration of Effect

The effects of the minor tranquilizers can be observed within 15–60 minutes after they have been taken. The maximum therapeutic effect begins to wear off in 2–6 hours; in other words, their half-lives are short. Because of this short duration, the drugs are usually administered three to four times a day.

## Side Effects

Sedation is the most frequent side effect. Less frequent is blurred vision, urinary incontinence, and constipation. Baldessarini (1980) reported that central nervous system activity is slowed and responsiveness to external stimuli is reduced. Increased aggressiveness and irritability have been observed to be associated with the use of Librium and other benzodiazepines. LaVeck and Buckley (1961) reported that behavior problems increased and the degree of play behavior decreased when children were prescribed this medication. Other side effects include failure to ovulate, headaches, nausea, skin rashes, and impaired sexual ability. Unfortunately, dependency can be developed when the minor tranquilizers are used for a long period of time. Gradual reduction and short-term use of these drugs can limit or impede the development of side effects.

Investigation of the effects of these drugs on cognition remains limited. However, the drugs do appear to limit the responsiveness to stimuli and, as a result, would seem to impair learning. Although somewhat dated, the conclusion reached by McNair (1973) that these drugs depress learning still seems to be relevant.

## Antidepressants

### Desired Effects

Little information has been reported on the effects of the antidepressants. Pomeroy and Gadow (1986) indicated that Tofranil and Elavil are used to help treat childhood depression, and their use is almost always limited to individuals who are not mentally retarded. Clinical practice suggests that the tricyclics are useful in helping children recover from the hurt and sadness associated with severe depression. Tofranil is also used to help stop bed-wetting.

### Duration of Effect

The maximum therapeutic effect, or half-life, of the tricyclic antidepressants is 10–18 hours. Usually, the drugs take 4–9 hours to reach peak effectiveness. Because of a delay in the onset of the primary effect, Tofranil must be taken for at least 4 weeks before its effect can be evaluated (Pomeroy & Gadow, 1986). Drug treatment should generally last from 3 to 6 months. As the MAO inhibitors are seldom used, this drug group will not be discussed.

### Side Effects

The tricyclics frequently produce physical side effects, including nausea, blurred vision, constipation, drowsiness, and dry mouth. Infrequently, the drugs cause the heart to race or to develop unusual rhythms. As a result, an overdose can be lethal. In rare cases, the drugs may be associated with the onset of epileptic seizures. The effects of these drugs on learning and adaptive environmental functioning have not been well studied (Aman, 1980). The little research available suggests that the antidepressants do not impair cognitive ability and may, in some instances, help.

## Stimulants

### Desired Effects

Stimulant medication, usually Ritalin or Cylert, is used to treat most children who are diagnosed as having an attention-deficit disorder with hyperactivity (Schwartz & Johnson, 1985). The effects of stimulant medication are by far the best researched of all of the psychotropic drugs (Aman, 1980; see the recent reviews completed by Barkley, 1981; Ross & Ross, 1982). The effects of the medication have been assessed across many different dependent variables, most of which have been in an analogue setting (i.e., a laboratory) rather than in the children's natural environment.

Before the effects of the stimulants are examined in relation to hyperactive children, the effects of these drugs on normal children will be discussed.

Rapoport, Buschbaum, Weingartner, Zahn, and Ludlow (1980) administered Dexedrine and placebos to 14 normal boys. These children responded in much the same way as hyperactive children. When on the medication, the boys were less active, made fewer errors on a cognitive task, were able to learn and re-member more on a memory task, and improved their language performance. In summary, the drug seemed to enable the children to focus their attention better.

Even though not all hyperactive children have conduct problems, those who do are most likely to be treated for hyperactivity (Sleator, 1982). Many studies have demonstrated that stimulants can suppress aggression, noncompliance, and other nonsocial behaviors (Ross & Ross, 1982). The use of Ritalin appears to help hyperactive children acquire both fine and gross motor skills. Wade (1976) reported that hyperactive children could do better on a gross-motor beam task when they were on medication. Lerer, Lerer, and Artner (1977) found that over half the hyperactive children in their sample of 50 had a better quality of handwrit-ing when on Ritalin than when on a placebo, and that the improvement was maintained as long as the children were on medication. Ritalin has also been found to produce better reaction time (Reid & Borkowski, 1984), to reduce errors in sustained-attention tasks (Michael, Klorman, Salzman, Borgstedt, & Painer, 1981), to reduce impulsivity (Brown & Sleator, 1979), to aid in memory (Sprague & Sleator, 1977), and to help with problem solving (Sprague, 1984). Finally, the effects, if any, of stimulants on academic performance (e.g., reading and writing) seem small (Gadow, 1983).

## Duration of Effect

In comparison to the other psychotropic drugs, the duration of effectiveness for some stimulants is rather short. For children, the half-life varies for different stimulants. The half-life of Ritalin is 4–5 hours (Safer & Allen, 1976). The half-life of Cylert, a long-lasting drug, is about 10 hours. Ritalin-SR, a long-lasting drug, has a half-life of about 8 hours. The advantage of using a long-lasting drug is that it eliminates the need of a noontime dose during the school day (Whitehouse, Shah, & Palmer, 1980). Usually, the effects of these drugs can be seen 30 minutes after they have been taken.

## Side Effects

Stimulant medication produces few physical side effects, and those associ-ated with proper moderate dosages are seldom serious (Safer & Allen, 1975). At the start of stimulant treatment, difficulty in sleeping and loss of appetite are the two most common side effects. Because the stimulant medications are typically given to a child at breakfast and at lunch, the possibility of any loss of appetite is reduced. The effect of the drugs taken in the morning and at lunch usually wear off by bedtime, and thus, potential sleep problems are limited. Minor side ef-fects, which are usually only experienced at the start of treatment, include headaches, moodiness, and irritability. At times, the dosage needs to be reduced to eliminate these effects. Whalen and Henker (1984) reported that, in their clinical work and review of the research literature, many children become sad or depressed while on stimulant medication. Finally, Safer, Allen, and Barr (1972) reported that long-term stimulant treatment may cause some children to gain less weight and height. However, when the drug treatment is stopped, these children catch up in their growth rates (Safer, Allen, & Barr, 1975).

Stimulant medication may have a detrimental effect on cognitive performance when the dosage is too high. When this occurs, Gadow (1986a) indicated the medication may improve the child's attention span to the point where he or she may be overfocused. On cognitive tasks, the overdosed child will make the same mistake over and over again. When the medication is reduced, performance improves. Whalen and Henker (1984) suggested that only complex cognitive tasks may be impaired by higher levels of stimulants, and that more routine tasks are not affected.

## SUMMARY

Pharmacotherapy represents an effective therapeutic procedure for managing the symptomatic behaviors or emotions of children with behavior disorders. The drugs prescribed to manage childhood behavior disorders are referred to as psychotropic drugs. Generally, these drugs are grouped into four categories: major tranquilizers, minor tranquilizers, antidepressants, and stimulants. Major tranquilizers are prescribed to treat psychotic disorders; minor tranquilizers are prescribed to treat anxiety disorders; antidepressants are prescribed to treat childhood depression; and stimulants are prescribed to treat attention-deficit disorders. Although the available reports suggest that these drugs are generally effective in managing behavior disorders, psychotropic drugs may also produce unwanted or toxic side effects. These drug-induced side effects are manifested in physical symptoms or impairments in adaptive functioning.

Among the factors that may influence the severity of these effects are the nature of the drug prescribed, the dosage level, the period of time for which the drug is prescribed, and the number of drugs that are prescribed concurrently. Because of the problems that may occur when psychotropic drugs are prescribed, it is essential that the use of these drugs be carefully monitored. Observing these effects as they are manifested in children's daily lives is a responsibility of the medical community, parents, therapists, and teachers.

## REFERENCES

Agran, M., & Martin, J. E. (1982). Use of psychotropic drugs by mentally retarded adults in community programs. *Journal of the Association for Persons with Severe Handicaps, 7*, 54–59.

Aman, M. G. (1978). Drugs, learning and the psychotherapies. In J. S. Werry (Ed.), *Pediatric psychopharmacology: The use of behavior modifying drugs in children* (pp. 79–108). New York: Brunner/Mazel.

Aman, M. G. (1980). Psychotropic drugs and learning problems—A selective review. *Journal of Learning Disabilities, 13*, 36–46.

Aman, M. G., & Singh, N. N. (1980). The usefulness of thioridazine for treating childhood disorders—Fact or folklore? *American Journal of Mental Deficiency, 84*, 331–338.

Aman, M. G., & Singh, N. N. (1983). Pharmacological interventions. In J. L. Matson & J. A. Mulick (Eds.), *Handbook of mental retardation* (pp. 317–337). New York: Pergamon Press.

Aman, M. G., Field, C. J., & Bridgman, G. D. (1985). City-wide survey of drug patterns among noninstitutionalized retarded persons. *Applied Research in Mental Retardation, 6*, 159–171.

American Psychiatric Association. (1980). *Diagnostic and statistical manual of mental disorders* (3rd ed.—DSM-III). Washington, DC: Author.

Baldessarini, R. J. (1980). Drugs and the treatment of psychiatric disorders. In A. G. Gilman, L. S. Goodman, T. W. Rall., & F. Murad (Eds.), *The pharmacological basis of therapeutics* (6th ed., pp. 391–447). New York: Macmillan.

Barkley, R. A. (1981). *Hyperactive children: A handbook for diagnosis and treatment.* New York: Guilford Press.

Brown, R. T., & Sleator, E. K. (1979). Methylphenidate in hyperkinetic children: Differences in dose effects on impulsive behavior. *Pediatrics, 64,* 408–411.

Burk, H. W., & Menolascino, F. J. (1968). Haloperidol in emotionally disturbed mentally retarded individuals. *American Journal of Psychiatry, 124,* 1589–1591.

Charalampous, K. D., & Keepers, G. A. (1978). Major side effects of antipsychotic drugs. *Journal of Family Practice, 6,* 993–1002.

Davis, K. V., Sprague, R. L., & Werry, J. S. (1969). Stereotyped behavior and activity level in severe retardates: The effect of drugs. *American Journal of Mental Deficiency, 73,* 721–727.

Denhoff, E., Feldman, S., Smith, M. G., Litchman, H., & Holden, W. (1975). Treatment of spastic cerebral-palsied children with sodium dantrolene. *Developmental Medicine and Child Neurology, 25,* 67–80.

DiMascio, A., & Shader, R. I. (1970). Behavioral toxicity: Part 1. Definition; Part 2. Psychomotor functions. In R. I. Shader & A. DiMascio (Eds.), *Psychotropic drug side effects* (pp. 124–141). Baltimore: Williams & Wilkins.

Engelhardt, D. M., & Polizos, P. (1978). Adverse effects of pharmacotherapy in childhood psychosis. In M. A. Lipton, A. DiMascio, & K. F. Killam (Eds.), *Psychopharmacology: A generation of progress* (pp. 1463–1469). New York: Raven Press.

Gadow, K. D. (1983). Effects of stimulant drugs on academic performance in hyperactive and learning disabled children. *Journal of Learning Disabilities, 16,* 290–299.

Gadow, K. D. (1986a). *Children on medication* (Vol. 1). San Diego: College-Hill Press.

Gadow, K. D. (1986b). *Children on medication* (Vol. 2). San Diego: College-Hill Press.

Gadow, K. D., & Kalachnik, J. (1981). Prevalence and pattern of drug treatment for behavior and seizure disorders of TMR students. *American Journal of Mental Deficiency, 85,* 588–595.

Gadow, K. D., & Swanson, H. L. (1985). Assessing drug effects on academic performance. *Psychopharmacology Bulletin, 21,* 877–886.

Gittelman-Klein, R. (1978). Psychopharmacological treatment of anxiety disorders, mood disorders, and Tourette's disorder in children. In M. A. Lipton, A. DiMascio, & K. F. Killam (Eds.), *Psychopharmacology: A generation of progress* (pp. 1471–1480). New York: Raven Press.

Gittelman-Klein, R., & Klein, D. F. (1971). Controlled imipramine treatment of school phobia. *Archives of General Psychiatry, 25,* 204–207.

Gross, M. D., & Wilson, W. C. (1974). *Minimal brain dysfunction.* New York: Brunner/Mazel.

Hill, B. K., Balow, E. A., & Bruininks, R. H. (1985). A national study of prescribed drugs in institutions and community residential facilities for mentally retarded people. *Psychopharmacology Bulletin, 21,* 279–284.

Kauffman, J. M. (1985). *Characteristics of children's behavior disorders* (3rd ed.). Columbus, OH: Merrill.

LaVeck, G. D., & Buckley, P. (1961). The use of psychopharmacologic agents in retarded children with behavior disorders. *Journal of Chronic Diseases, 13,* 174–183.

Leavitt, F. (1982). *Drugs and behavior* (2nd ed.). New York: Wiley.

Lerer, R. J., Lerer, P. M., & Artner, J. (1977). The effects of methylphenidate on the handwriting of children with minimal brain dysfunction. *Journal of Pediatrics, 91,* 127–132.

McNair, D. M. (1973). Antianxiety drugs and human performance. *Archives of General Psychiatry, 29,* 611–617.

Marholin, D., & Phillips, D. (1976). Methodological issues in psychopharmacological research: Chlorpromazine—A case in point. *American Journal of Orthopsychiatry, 46,* 477–495.

Martin, J. E., & Agran, M. (1985). Psychotropic and anticonvulsant drug use by mentally retarded adults across community residential and vocational placements. *Applied Research in Mental Retardation, 6,* 33–49.

Menolascino, F. J., Ruedrich, S. L., Golden, C. J., & Wilson, J. E. (1985). Diagnosis and pharmacotherapy of schizophrenia in the retarded. *Psychopharmacology Bulletin, 21,* 316–322.

Michael, R. L., Klorman, R., Salzman, L. F., Borgstedt, A. D., & Painer, K. B. (1981). Normalizing effects of methylphenidate on hyperactive children's vigilance performance and evoked potentials. *Psychophysiology, 18,* 665–667.

Pomeroy, J., & Gadow, K. E. (1986). Adolescent psychiatric disorders. In K. E. Gadow (Ed.), *Children on medication* (Vol. 2, pp. 132–172). San Diego: College-Hill Press.

Rapoport, J. L., Buschbaum, M., Weingartner, H., Zahn, T. P., & Ludlow, C. (1980). Dextroamphetamine: Cognitive and behavioral effects in normal and hyperactive boys and normal men. *Archives of General Psychiatry, 37*, 933–943.

Ray, O. S. (1978). *Drugs, society, and human behavior.* St. Louis: Mosby.

Reid, M. K., & Borkowski, J. G. (1984). Effects of methylphenidate (Ritalin) on information processing in hyperactive children. *Journal of Abnormal Child Psychology, 12*, 169–185.

Ross, D. M., & Ross, S. A. (1982). *Hyperactivity: Research, theory, and action* (2nd ed.). New York: Wiley.

Safer, D. J., & Allen, R. P. (1975). Stimulant drug treatment of hyperactive adolescents. *Diseases of the Nervous System, 36*, 454–457.

Safer, D. J., & Allen, R. P. (1976). *Hyperactive children: Diagnosis and management.* Baltimore: University Park Press.

Safer, D. J., & Krager, J. M. (1984). Trends in medication therapy for hyperactivity: National and international perspectives. In K. D. Gadow (Ed.), *Advances in learning and behavioral disabilities* (Vol. 3, pp. 125–149). Greenwich, CT: JAI Press.

Safer, D. J., Allen, R., & Barr, E. (1972). Depression of growth in hyperactive children on stimulant drugs. *New England Journal of Medicine, 287*, 217–220.

Safer, D. J., Allen, R., & Barr, E. (1975). Growth rebound after termination of stimulant drugs. *Pediatrics, 86*, 113–116.

Schroeder, S. R., & Gualtieri, C. T. (1985). Behavioral interactions induced by chronic neuroleptic therapy in persons with mental retardation. *Psychopharmacology Bulletin, 21*, 310–315.

Schwartz, S., & Johnson, J. H. (1985). *Psychopathology of childhood.* New York: Pergamon Press.

Shaywitz, S. E., & Shawitz, B. A. (1984). Diagnosis and management of attention deficit disorders: A pediatric perspective. *The Pediatric Clinics of North America, 31*, 429–457.

Singh, N. N., & Aman, M. G. (1981). Effects of thioridazine dosage on the behavior of severely mentally retarded persons. *American Journal of Mental Deficiency, 85*, 580–587.

Singh, N. N., & Millichamp, C. J. (1985). Pharmacological treatment of self-injurious behavior in mentally retarded persons. *Journal of Autism and Developmental Disorders, 15*, 257–267.

Sleator, E. K. (1982). Office diagnosis of hyperactivity by the physician. In K. D. Gadow & I. Bialer (Eds.), *Advances in learning and behavioral disabilities* (Vol. 1, pp. 341–364). Greenwich, CT: JAI Press.

Sleator, E. K., & Ullmann, R. K. (1981). Can the physician diagnose hyperactivity in the office? *Pediatrics, 67*, 13–17.

Sleator, E. K., von Neumann, A., & Sprague, R. L. (1974). Hyperactive children: A continuous long-term placebo controlled follow-up. *Journal of the American Medical Association, 229*, 316–317.

Spiegel, R., & Aebi, H. J. (1983). *Psychopharmacology* (English ed.). New York: Wiley.

Sprague, R. L. (1984). Preliminary report of cross-cultural study and cognitive strategies of ADD children. In L. M. Bloomingdale (Ed.), *Attention deficit disorder: Diagnostic, cognitive, and therapeutic understanding* (pp. 211–219). New York: Spectrum.

Sprague, R. L., & Sleator, E. K. (1975). What is the proper dose of stimulant drugs in children? *International Journal of Mental Health, 4*, 75–104.

Sprague, R. L., & Sleator, E. K. (1977). Methylphenidate in hyperkinetic children: Differences in dose effects on learning and social behavior. *Science, 198*, 1274–1276.

Sprague, R. L., & Ullmann, R. (1981). Psychoactive drugs and child management. In J. M. Kauffman & D. P. Hallahan (Eds.), *Handbook of special education* (pp. 749–766). Englewood Cliffs, NJ: Prentice-Hall.

Sprague, R. L., & Werry, J. S. (1971). Methodology of psychopharmacological studies with the retarded. In N. R. Ellis (Ed.), *International review of research in mental retardation* (Vol. 5, pp. 147–219). Orlando, FL: Academic Press.

Ullmann, R. K., Sleator, E. K., & Sprague, R. L. (1985). Introduction to the use of ACTERS. *Psychopharmacology Bulletin, 21*, 915–930.

Wade, M. G. (1976). Effects of methylphenidate on motor skill acquisition of hyperactive children. *Journal of Learning Disabilities, 9*, 443–447.

Whalen, C. K., & Henker, B. (1984). Hyperactivity and the attention deficit disorders: Expanding frontiers. *Pediatric Clinics of North America, 31*, 399–427.

Whitehouse, D., Shah, U., & Palmer, F. B. (1980). Comparison of sustained-release and standard methylphenidate in treatment of minimal brain dysfunction. *Journal of Clinical Psychiatry, 41*, 282–285.

Wysocki, T., Fuqua, W., Davis, V. J., & Breuning, S. E. (1981). Effects of thioridazine on titrating delayed matching to sample performance of mentally retarded adults. *American Journal of Mental Deficiency, 85,* 539–547.

Zimmerman, R. L., & Heistad, G. T. (1982). Studies of the long term efficacy of antipsychotic drugs in controlling the behavior of institutionalized retardates. *Journal of the American Academy of Child Psychiatry, 21,* 136–143.

# 7     *Psychotherapy*

## Edward J. Nuffield

### Introduction

The purpose of this chapter is to present the theoretical underpinnings of a method of treating children and adolescents exhibiting major psychopathology. The method is psychotherapy, which is based on psychodynamic principles, rather than on learning theories, which in themselves are quite varied (see Chapters 4 and 5 of this book).

This distinction, when fully examined, is unfortunately not water-tight, nor is it as conceptually clear cut as the initial statement suggests. When the process of dynamically based therapy is laid bare and the fact of personality or behavioral change is exposed, it becomes difficult to exclude the fact that learning has taken place and has not acted as a lever producing the change. Nevertheless, there are important semantic differences between the behaviorist and the dynamically oriented therapist; it is the vocabulary of the latter that will be used in this discussion.

In the case of children and adolescents, the psychodynamic theoretician has to be sensitive to the developmental process, which is a critical element. This movement is slow in relation to the usual time frame of therapy, and it may be uneven in its velocity. The developmental movement has to be incorporated into a theoretical matrix whose elements are the dynamic exchanges between the subject and his or her psychological environment, and also between the subject's internal psychological structures, such as desire and conscience. It is the appreciation of these so-called intrapsychic elements that makes psychodynamic theories distinct and separable from other psychological conceptual systems. In the case of children and adolescents, intrapersonal or intrapsychic conflicts seem to play a smaller or perhaps a more subtle role than in the case of adults. Furthermore, members of different "schools" of psychotherapy place different emphases on the relative importance of intrapsychic and interpersonal events; accordingly, their therapeutic strategies are shaped differently. A practical consequence is the preference of individual over group treatments, or vice versa. However, there is much overlap between individual and group therapists as far as theory is concerned. The former do not always stress intrapersonal events, nor do the latter confine themselves to dealing with interpersonal relationships. Nevertheless, the individual practitioners almost always lean toward one side or another. Thus, Slavson (1950), a group therapist, focused on intrapsychic pro-

---

Edward J. Nuffield • Box 57, P.O. Lindfield, 2070 N. S.W., Sydney, Australia.

cesses, whereas Reisman (1973), an individual therapist, laid more stress on interpersonal events. The former was influenced substantially by psychoanalytic theory, and the latter showed more of the influence of Carl Rogers. Those two separate "schools" constitute the main theoretical sources of psychodynamic therapy, although there are other, lesser theoretical contributions, such as theories of play. These conceptual strands are traced here through a historical account of the emergence of child and adolescent psychotherapy.

## HISTORICAL PERSPECTIVES

In tracing the beginning of psychotherapy for children and adolescents, one does not have to go very far back in the history of human civilization. The chief reason is that psychotherapy itself is relatively recent; furthermore, the early psychotherapists focused more on adults than on children and adolescents.

There are some forerunners of child psychotherapy who deserve mention. At the beginning of the 19th century, the French physician Jean-Marc-Gaspard Itard (1806/1962), when undertaking the treatment of Victor, the "wild boy of Aveyron," engaged in an activity that can be labeled either *psychoeducational* or *psychotherapeutic* by modern standards. Another pioneer was Edward Seguin (1866), who used a variety of methods, including training of all the senses, to enhance the development of the idiotic child.

The emphasis on the educational aspects of the treatment of children was continued by the work of Lightner Witmer (1907), whose treatment method was retraining the child who had been subjected to inadequate methods of education. Witmer was more interested in diagnosis than in treatment; the children at his clinic, established in 1896, were subjected to a great deal of physical examination, anthropometric measurement, tests of reaction time, tests of vision, and so on (Reisman, 1966).

The treatment of children by these three pioneers was basically pedagogical. Nevertheless, there were elements of psychotherapy, in that the relationship between the tutor and the child was of some importance, even though it was not stressed in the written accounts. This directive, or tutoring, approach continued into the modern era.

It is traditional to assign the beginning of psychotherapy with children to Sigmund Freud's treatment of little Hans (Carek, 1979). In this classic case, Freud (1959) was asked to deal with a phobic condition in a 5-year-old boy. He chose to treat the boy through the father, without ever seeing the child. This approach tends to be frowned on by most current practitioners, although the method of "filial therapy" closely resembles what Freud actually carried out. The first generation of psychoanalysts was concerned almost exclusively with treating adults. However, the underlying theory of infantile sexual traumata, especially in cases of hysteria and obsessional neurosis, made it inevitable that psychoanalytic intervention and the treatment of younger subjects would sooner or later be practiced.

The first practitioners of the psychoanalytic treatment of children were all women. This should occasion no surprise when one considers the cultural biases during the first third of the 20th century. Because the psychoanalytic method depended heavily on free association and dream analysis, the latter requiring the subject to free-associate to the manifest dream content, the analyst who attempted to treat children was left with no clinical tool to explore the material. A new avenue to the child had to be found, and this was achieved through the activity of play.

The significance of play has been looked at from different perspectives: biological, intrapersonal, interpersonal, and sociocultural (Schaefer & O'Connor, 1983). Biological theories are derived from Darwinism through Herbert Spencer and K. Groos, "the great nineteenth century authority on play" (Slobin, 1964). These authors considered play a release of surplus energy and also a "preexercise" of skills useful in later life, a sort of rehearsal for the future: "Play is the agency employed to develop crude powers and prepare them for life's uses, . . . natural selection will favor those individuals in whom the less elaborated faculties have more chance of being worked out by practice under the protection of parents—i.e., those individuals that play" (Groos, 1901).

The intrapersonal perspective is represented primarily by Sigmund Freud, with later elaborations by Fenichel, Waelder, and especially Erik Erikson. Freud dealt with the phenomenon of repetitive play and considered it a way of achieving mastery over a past traumatic event that had originally been experienced passively. Such repetitions go "beyond the pleasure principle" (1950). Erikson (1950) believed that the child, in play, creates new situations and masters reality through his or her experimenting and planning. This provides a guiding principle of psychoanalytic play therapy.

The interpersonal perspective shifts the focus onto play with others. This social parameter leads to the concept of role in play and the need, in group games, for the child to know the roles of all the others as well as of himself or herself (Slobin, 1964). The child also learns the social rules that regulate behavior; hence, an important element of social learning is involved in group play.

Finally, the sociocultural perspective seeks to explain the different games in different societies, and to reduce these differences to a finite number of common themes.

Hermine von Hellmuth (1921) was the first psychoanalytic worker to use play in therapy with children. She was soon followed by Anna Freud (1928) and Melanie Klein (1932). The approaches of Freud and Klein were very different. It appears that the technique of Klein was more closely tied to the basic canons of psychoanalysis than were the practices of the daughter of the founder of psychoanalysis. Klein (1948) stressed that "consistent interpretations, gradual solving of resistances, and the persistent tracing of the transference to earlier situations—these constitute in children as in adults the correct analytic situation."

On the other hand, Anna Freud viewed the play behavior of the child as not always requiring direct interpretation along the lines that Melanie Klein prescribed. Freud (1964) placed much more emphasis on the development of a positive relationship, an "affectionate tie," between the child and the therapist. She recognized the difficulty that children have with free association, and instead, she used material from daydreams to help the child form mental images that could then be verbalized. Her patients were generally somewhat older than those of Melanie Klein, who described the treatment of a number of pre-school-aged patients. Although Melanie Klein exerted much influence among British child analysts, she made little impact on the practice of American child therapists. Here, Anna Freud's ideas were given much greater weight. There were other theoretical influences at work, however.

Otto Rank (1929) had placed great importance on the psychological effects of birth trauma. Furthermore, he deemphasized the importance of transference and that of other past psychic traumata and laid more emphasis on the patient's current life situation. Though Rank did not work with children himself, his ideas influenced such child therapists as Taft (1933) and Allen (1942).

Whereas this line of thinking led away from exploring the consequences of past traumatic events in the child's life, an opposite approach was taken by Levy (1938), who structured play material in such a way as to facilitate the child's reenactment of the past traumatic event. This caused an abreaction or catharsis, which should, if repeated several times, provide relief from symptoms. Levy called this technique "release therapy."

Somewhat similar was the technique of active play therapy practiced by Solomon (1938), in that abreaction of feelings was also involved. There was special emphasis on the therapist's benign reaction to the child's expression of rage, by which a "corrective emotional experience" is provided. The success of this technique can also be explained in terms of social learning theory.

Another therapist who operated in the adult field but whose influence on child therapists was striking was Carl Rogers (1942). His approach was entirely focused on the here and now, stressing the relationship between therapist and client, and being essentially nondirective. The main protagonists of this approach as applied to play therapy with children were Axline (1947) and Moustakas (1959).

Axline put forward eight basic principles that should guide the therapist in her or his endeavors: warmth, acceptance, establishing an atmosphere of permissiveness, reflecting back feelings, respect for the child's ability to solve problems, nondirectiveness, leisurely pacing of the therapy, and setting only the most necessary limits in therapy. These guidelines were more-or-less accepted by a wide variety of therapists who may or may not have used special techniques or media, such as art, music, or dancing (e.g., Gardner, 1975).

Moustakas (1959) approached the treatment of children from an existentialist position: The therapist "regards every situation as a unique, living experience which contains its own requirements and its own methods and techniques" (p. 3); "Through the process of self-expression and exploration *within a significant relationship*, through realization of the value within, the child comes to be a positive, *self-determining*, and *self-actualizing* individual" (p. 5; italics added). Moustakas also stressed the importance of an atmosphere of harmony, tranquility, and human relatedness in the playroom. He did not avoid the issue of setting limits but dealt with it in a forthright manner. Limits have to be set to avoid real damage to persons or property. When they are broken, the relationship is temporarily suspended but can be resumed at the next encounter. Psychotherapy can be sustained with children who act out in a very primitive way.

The setting of limits not only is necessary to prevent physical damage but can also be therapeutic in itself. This was first pointed out by Bixler (1949). He stressed the fact that limits should be enforced in a nonpunitive manner. He described three steps in the mechanism of limits setting:

1. Reflecting the child's feelings in carrying out the act.
2. Making the limit verbally explicit.
3. Physical control of the child's behavior, if necessary.

Most children desist after Steps 1 or 2, making the last step redundant.

Ginott (1959) likewise stressed the fact that limits are not punitive, nor are they arbitrary or capricious. They need to be stated in a firm, unconditional manner. On the other hand, there should not be a recital of a series of limits at the beginning of a therapeutic session; they are stated when they are about to be broken. When a number of instances of broken limits are analyzed, it becomes evident that the child patient has welcomed the therapist's firmness and control of the situation.

Whereas the emergence of individual psychotherapy with children took place primarily in outpatient clinics (child guidance clinics) or in private offices, group therapy began and flourished originally in residential or inpatient settings. Traditionally, the role of the grandfather of modern group therapy has been assigned to Joseph H. Pratt. Pratt treated severely ill tuberculous adults, in a sanatorium. His treatment consisted of running classes of 20–30 patients; the methods were didactic and supportive. Similar methods were used by E. W. Lazell and L. Cody Marsh with psychiatric patients (Sadock, 1980).

A forerunner in the children's field was J. L. Moreno, who is best known as the inventor of psychodrama. He began a type of group, a "theatre of spontaneity," in Vienna in 1911. This was initially for children, whom he collected in the gardens of the city. He told them improvised stories and arranged them in concentric circles, after which they interacted spontaneously (Moreno, 1947). He moved his spontaneity theater to the United States in 1925; at this time, he may have influenced Slavson, who is considered the father of child and adolescent group therapy. Moreno, however, did not operate in a clinical setting at any time.

At the same time, two other seminal figures in psychiatry had begun group work with youth. Alfred Adler (1930) had opened child guidance clinics in Vienna and Munich immediately after World War I, when the younger generation were generally in turmoil. The treatment there was described as taking place "with the doors wide open," in the presence of strangers, suggesting to the child that his or her problems were not a private affair and hence not of a unique and extraordinary character. There was no focus on child–child interaction and no systematic process of group formation. Group formation was pioneered by August Aichhorn (1935), a student and follower of Sigmund Freud. Beginning in the early 1920s, this therapist applied psychoanalytic knowledge to groups of delinquent and disturbed children and adolescents found in a training school near Vienna. The importance of grouping the children according to certain criteria was recognized for the first time. The main principle was homogeneity according to sex and presenting behaviors. The attitude of the therapists was one of great tolerance and permissiveness. The latitude of the institution's administration evidently allowed Aichhorn and his cotherapist to ride out the most severe storms of aggressive behavior among the children.

Slavson, like Aichhorn, came to group therapy via education. He had organized groups of youngsters into a club as early as 1911 (Rachman & Raubolt, 1984). He worked out a club program consisting of reading literature and poetry, interpretative dancing, discussion of scientific and philosophical subjects, and occasional group attendance at cultural events. The goal of these "treatments," or experiences, was for each student to discover her or his real self. Slavson considered this progressive education a new way of life. He began strictly clinical work in 1934 when he joined the Jewish Board of Guardians in New York City. That institution was to develop a number of group psychotherapists under the influence of Slavson. One of these was Betty Gabriel, who did not publish her work until 1943, but who had begun to conduct groups of adolescent girls considerably earlier (Gabriel, 1944).

Both Slavson (1950) and Redl (1942), who ran therapeutic groups beginning in the early 1940s, paid considerable attention to the proper selection of cases in order to produce properly "composed" groups. One of the parameters that proved to be critical was the toughness versus the shyness dimension, and youngsters were assigned so as to prevent extreme contrasts and not to risk physical hurt to the passive, yielding child.

Although Redl's work was important in advancing the cause of formal group work with delinquent and predelinquent youngsters, it had even greater influence on the structuring of the milieu in which these children and adolescents were being treated (Redl & Wineman, 1951).

The targeting of a particular subsection of the large group of disturbed children and adolescents is seen in the work of Wollan (1941, 1951), who also worked with delinquent adolescent boys in the Boston area. The treatment combined physical activities with verbal discussions, with an emphasis on the former. The groups were conducted in the context of a training program that aimed to produce an increase in the personal responsibility and the emotional maturity of the boys.

The group work of Bender and Woltman (1936) and of Curran (1939) took place in the children's and adolescents' wards of a large psychiatric hospital. Bender and Woltman used puppet shows, more or less as a catalyst, to illuminate the children's psychopathology, which was then dealt with in the discussions that followed. They were struck by the children's ability to become emotionally involved with the puppets and by their close identification with some of the characters. There was relief from tension through catharsis, as well as a change from aggression to love and acceptance, facilitated by the script of the puppet show.

In dealing with an older group of young to mid-adolescent boys, Curran gave his patients the responsibility of authoring their own scripts. The roles of the various characters were often assigned by the boys themselves, and the production was viewed by the rest of the adolescent population, the staff, and some outsiders (i.e., patients from other wards). Again, the performances were followed by group discussion. Apart from the acceptable release of aggressive drive, this form of therapy threw light on the symbolic meaning of the child's behavior and helped the individual therapist in future sessions. Both the work of Bender and Woltman and that of Curran could be described as activity group therapy followed by interview group therapy, and optionally followed by individual therapy.

By the middle 1950s, psychotherapy with children and adolescents seemed to be well established, at least in North America and Britain, and something of a consensus about its psychodynamic foundations was established. However, questions about its efficacy began to be raised. Eysenck (1952, 1955) criticized the claims of adult psychotherapy, and his method of comparing series of treated and untreated subjects was adopted by Levitt (1957). Although the method of combining several studies dealing with different subsets of the treated population and using varying types of psychotherapy over a range of time periods was criticized as having only limited relevance (Heinicke & Goldman, 1960), questions began to be raised about the possibility that psychotherapy might be no better than no treatment, or "inferior" therapy, that is, therapy that uses a behavioral approach. The latter was first attempted by Watson (1921) and Jones (1924) but was not fully developed in the case of children until somewhat later (Graziano, 1975; Ullman & Krasner, 1965; Werry & Woolersheim, 1967). The history of learning theories is discussed elsewhere in this book (Chapter 4); most of the time, there has been a sharp distinction between psychodynamically based psychotherapy and behavioral therapy in the area of child and adolescent therapy. These "schools" have taken up postures that are not only separate but antagonistic.

However, intermittent attempts to mediate between these two approaches can be found (Marks & Gelder, 1966). In the children's field, Blom (1972) described how the two approaches could be integrated practically in a day-care center. Repeatedly, it became clear that, at a clinical level, both psychodynamic and learning theories could be applied, even though they were divided conceptually.

A very important event of recent decades has been the appearance of family systems theory affecting the practice of child and adolescent psychotherapy. Family therapy was pioneered by Nathan Ackerman (1958), a child psychiatrist and analyst, whose therapeutic efforts were still directed toward the child, although they are now seen more clearly in the context of the family. Psychodynamic principles continued to guide the practice of early family therapists, such as Ackerman and Bell. McDermott and Char (1974) felt that a later theoretical basis for family therapy—namely, communication and systems theory—caused an alienation between child psychotherapists and family therapists. The child's pathology and its expression were nothing but a mirror reflecting a disturbance in the family system. The source of the problem was often specified as being marital conflict; hence, any direct intervention with the child was superfluous. Consequently, the participation of children in family therapy was at best peripheral, the therapist's focus was on the parents, and the decision about when and how to include the children became problematic (Satir, 1967). In time, the practice of family therapists became more and more remote from the practice of psychotherapy with children and adolescents, in spite of their common historical roots. The treatment of families is a process that focuses on a metapersonal plane and seeks to effect change by manipulating ecological forces within the family as a system. Although therapists of children and adolescents have to understand those ecological vectors, they concern themselves with producing changes in the internal dynamic system of their individual patients and with improving interpersonal relations between the child and significant others.

Another historically influential development has been the emergence of the community mental health movement, which surfaced more as a result of political and social events than as the product of any scientific theory. The impact of the vast extent of mental illness in society finally produced legislative action in the 1960s that led to the establishment of a network of publically funded treatment facilities for all age groups, namely, the community mental health centers. These structures were a novelty in a society where the bulk of the resources had consisted of public state hospitals, private offices, and clinics; none of these had a mandate to treat a population at risk. Large numbers of previously underserved or unserved children and adolescents became potential patients or clients. After an initial brief period of enthusiasm on the part of child therapists, disillusionment set in (Rafferty, 1975). Paradoxically, children again became one of the underserved groups in the community mental health system. In the meantime, the practical fact remained that, although waiting lists, especially for treatment services, were long, brief psychotherapy was one way to reduce those lists (Proskauer, 1969, 1971; Rosenthal & Levine, 1971). Actually, the practice of brief psychotherapy with children predated the impact of the community mental health movement. H. Witmer (1946) reported several cases treated briefly, and Allen (1942) published a number of such cases. Somewhat later, Shulman (1960) actually proposed "one-visit psychotherapy," which was successful in some cases. A trend away from long-term treatment with indefinite goals had become clearly apparent by the mid-1960s.

A historical account of the practice of psychotherapy with children has to consider the conceptual underpinnings and their evolution, as well as changes in practical application. In terms of the former, a complete description would have to include changes in psychoanalytic theory, learning theory, the epigenetic theories of Piaget (1962) and Werner (1948), ethology (Hess, 1959), and general living systems theory (Miller, 1960), to mention only the more pertinent trends. The influence of those theories can be traced via the understanding of psychopathology that they offer to the shaping of therapeutic practice that has taken such varied forms during this century.

The practical possibilities of the therapeutic situation have also determined what therapists of children have actually done. Social and political forces have played important roles. Although the 20th century has been described as the century of the child, the effect of this viewpoint has fluctuated over the decades. Demographic trends have been important factors in producing changes. The post–World War II baby boom made its impact on society in the late 1950s and the 1960s, and this impact led to a considerable augmentation of interest in and concern about childhood psychopathology (President's Commission on the Mental Health of Children, 1978). With the passing of that boom, one can discern a slackening of this interest, and more attention is being paid to the elderly. It appears that the psychotherapy of children and adolescents is not as fashionable as it was a generation ago. On the other hand, once concern has been raised about the psychological health of children who will be the adults of tomorrow and are therefore potentially productive members of society tomorrow, a strong public demand for services remains. Economic forces have had the effect of limiting sharply the expansion of resources to deal with these demands. The widening gap between the perceived need and the available capacity has exerted great pressure on service providers to come up with innovative and "cost-effective" types of therapy. What was once prescribed routinely (i.e., indefinite-term, psychodynamically based individual psychotherapy) has become a luxury in the present era of austerity.

The previous section described the diversity of the theoretical schools that led to the modern practice of psychotherapy with children and adolescents. Allowing for ideological diversity, it is still possible to postulate some basic principles that meet with a consensus of most practitioners:

1. The child is a living organism, developing continuously, if unevenly, in the areas of thinking, feeling, and behavior.
2. The child's overt behavior is determined, in part, by internal forces, such as needs, wishes, desires, and fantasies; some of these forces are unconscious.
3. The child lives in an interpersonal context, consisting of family, other significant adults, school, and peer group. All these facilitate motivation and action.
4. The child's instrumental behavior is the result of innate disposition or temperament, past experience, and current environmental influences.

For operational purposes, one needs a definition of psychotherapy, not only to specify its essential ingredients, but also to delimit its scope. It should not only be clear what psychotherapy is, but also what it is not. It is easier to begin by describing what it is not. Esman (1983) indicated that child analytic play therapy are not recreation, not education, and not abreaction. Reisman (1973) made a distinction between what is psychotherapy (i.e., a specific procedure) and what is psychotherapeutic (i.e., therapeutically affective). An example of the latter would be the child's watching a football game (which may help her or him). Reisman went on to speak of "professional psychotherapy," the corollary being that there is "non-professional psychotherapy." He excluded "drugs, ridicule, verbal abuse, tutoring and vacation trips" (p. 9) from the ambit of psychotherapy. He also excluded bad techniques, such as the therapist's merely "sitting quietly, and providing a warm, friendly acceptance during the child's play" (pp. 10–11), from psychotherapy, therefore equating bad psychotherapy with what is not psychotherapy.

Of necessity, a definition of psychotherapy includes its goals and purposes. I have defined psychotherapy elsewhere (Nuffield, 1983) as "the formalized exchange between one or more therapists and one or more patients or clients for the purpose of attaining a clinical goal. It is an event that can be described in terms of structure, process and content" (p. 353). The terms *exchange, therapists,* and *events* are crucial to this definition. The first and third terms are broad, so as to include a variety of structural elements and techniques, particularly nonverbal techniques; these are omitted by some other definitions (e.g., Shoben, 1953). The term *therapist* specifies the active agent in this exchange. We can define therapist "as a professional helper." He or she must have certain credentials to be qualified as a professional. A limited number of professions are included in this definition: psychiatry, clinical psychology, psychiatric social work, and psychiatric nursing; they are the four core professions. Others can be added, and their members may also be considered therapists.

The other important ingredient in the definition is the qualifier *formalized,* which excludes chance encounters and unplanned and random contacts between therapist and patient or client.

The term *clinical goal* is both rigorous and open-ended. On the one hand, there can be a variety of understandings about what type of clinical goal is intended to be met; on the other, it specifies the need for defining that goal beforehand. The clinical goal may be the attainment of basic personality change in the child, or the overcoming of a situational crisis, or any other goal of intermediate ambitiousness.

In setting of goals, a certain amount of ideological bias is evident. For example, Carek (1979) sees the goal "for the child to become freer within the experience, to gain a deeper awareness of himself and others, and to find a path to the reasonable expression of emotions" (p. 36). Statements like this have been criticized because they are difficult to put into operation. This is also a problem with the goals of various practitioners of "relationship therapy" (e.g., Rogers, 1962). They see the attainment of a therapeutic relationship as an end in itself, rather than a means to achieving the resolution of a clinical problem.

It is apparent that the assessment and evaluation of the clinical problem is a necessary precursor to psychotherapy with children and adolescents. The application of what has sometimes been deprecated as the "medical model" has not always been accepted. Some treatment facilities have "prescribed" psychotherapy for the child almost routinely, no matter what the presenting problem is or what the underlying pathology may be. Such indiscriminate practices are less common now.

The adequate evaluation of the problem will not be described here in detail. Assessment is sufficiently complex to occupy several volumes for its explication (e.g., Section 3, Volume 1, of *Basic Handbook of Child Psychiatry*, 1970, pp. 485–691; A. Freud, 1965). Suffice it to say that an adequate evaluation has not only to assess the child in the clinical setting, but also to include past history and family functioning and to examine sociocultural factors before a diagnostic formulation can be made. The diagnosis will then lead to a rational treatment plan (see Group for the Advancement of Psychiatry, 1983). The result of a comprehensive assessment is usually the structuring of a treatment plan. Psychotherapy with the child or adolescent is then placed within the context of a number of treatment services. It is useful to consider briefly some of the ingredients of a characteristic treatment plan.

One of the basic circumstances of childhood and adolescence is that the individual lives in considerable dependence on others: either the natural family, a foster family, a group home, or an institution. In these circumstances, the psychological environment contains parents or substitute caretakers. Almost invariably, some positive action will need to be taken in relation to them: counseling, psychotherapy, other psychiatric treatments for parents, or family therapy, unless a personnel change in the caretakers is prescribed. The latter leads to a drastic change in the child's milieu. If it is undertaken, a fresh evaluation of the new psychological changes will then be required, and psychotherapy will be placed in a new context. Apart from those cases that involve administrative and, occasionally, legal steps, treatment of the child or adolescent is a logical consequence of the original assessment and evaluation.

## Selection of Subjects

It is difficult to be certain which children and adolescents, once evaluated, do not require, or are unsuitable for, psychotherapy. If this decision is made, there are two broad possibilities: (1) the problem is so mild and temporary that no intervention is required, or (2) some other form of therapy is indicated. The latter may consist of direct treatment of the child by some other method, such as behavior modification, or by indirect measures, such as marital therapy, milieu therapy, or major environmental manipulations.

Disposition without some form of child psychotherapy is still uncommon. The usual recommendation is to incorporate psychotherapy with the child into an overall treatment plan. The implementation of this direct form of treatment depends on the availability of suitable therapists.

What are the qualities of a suitable therapist? This question has attracted a great deal of attention (see Chapter 4 of *The Process of Child Psychiatry*, 1982, pp. 61–79). A distinction is drawn between the ideal and the actual, that is, what can be described theoretically and sometimes poetically about the quality of a therapist and what therapists are really like and what they actually do. Apart from psychotherapists' behavior, there is the fact of personality traits, which express themselves as stable behavioral patterns. Of these, empathy, warmth, flexibility, and enthusiasm or zeal are often mentioned. One should add humility (realizing one's limitations) and emotional maturity, which enables the therapist to avoid seeking inappropriate gratifications from therapy and precludes positions of bias in the conflicts between child and parents.

The therapist of children and adolescents needs to be in touch with his or her own childhood in order to understand his or her patient's current situation. The therapist's own maturity will preclude any attempt to solve his or her own psychological problems through a relationship with child patients. On a cognitive plane, the therapist has to have a sufficient knowledge of human development and to know some of the technical aspects of therapy.

## GOALS OF PSYCHOTHERAPY

As part of the overall treatment plan, certain goals and objectives need to be selected specifically for psychotherapy. In the case of adults exhibiting evidence of acute psychopathology, the ideal goal is a return to normal health. The underlying supposition is that there was a baseline of more-or-less healthy functioning, which was overlaid by a pathological process; therapy will reverse this process, and the patient or client will function as well as she or he did before becoming ill.

In the case of children and adolescents, it is occasionally possible to conceptualize the situation in this way, for example, in a previously healthy child who develops a simple phobia after a near drowning. The child may be relieved of this symptom fairly simply, so that he or she can function as before the event. Such a clinical problem is more likely to call for behavioral methods rather than psychodynamically based psychotherapy, which considers the developmental dimension as well as dynamic or field factors and aims to propel the child forward along a developmental axis. Progress as a result of such treatment is measured along developmental lines. These lines are not as well calibrated as overt behaviors that can be measured in terms of frequency, duration, and intensity. Any changes brought about by dynamically based psychotherapy are difficult to quantify. When one tries to evaluate the efficacy and efficiency of this form of therapy, this problem becomes very evident.

## PROCESS OF THERAPY

Psychotherapy as a concrete event occupies a series of individual sessions in time and space. As an activity, it must be planned and legitimized. It receives general sanction from the facts that the therapist (or therapists) is considered properly qualified to carry out such a treatment, either autonomously or under supervision, and that the subject or subjects have assumed the position of patient or client in the context of a treatment facility: a hospital, a clinic, or a professional office. It is important to set up a contract before treatment begins. This can be a verbal understanding, which will suffice if there is adequate communication between the affected parties. Communication between therapist and parent(s) can be understood as the transmission of information from adult to adult and is usually a straightforward matter. It can be a problem because of factors in either the therapist or the parent, but a resolution is usually attained. The parent either accepts the therapeutic proposition or rejects it.

When a child or adolescent is the patient or the client, setting up a contract and obtaining consent is much more complicated. In the case of adolescents, the inclusion of the patient in contract making is essential. Janzen and Love (1977) described the utility of involving adolescent patients in the structuring of a token economy plan (i.e., a behavioral form of therapy). Preparation for dynamically based psychotherapy has been reported variously, and its effects have been studied (Hoen-Saric, Frank, Imber, Nash, Stone, & Battle, 1964; Orne & Wender, 1968; Yalom, Houts, Newel, & Rand, 1967). Holmes and Urie (1975) prepared children aged 6–12 for therapy and found that this step reduced the dropout rate. In comparisons of "prepared" children with unprepared ones, preparation did not seem to affect the process or the outcome of therapy.

It is an obvious fact that children referred for treatment to a clinical facility where many will have psychotherapy "prescribed" for them have, for the most part, little positive motivation for participating in such a process. Children, and often adolescents, are referred for treatment because someone else was concerned about their behavior, their emotional functioning, or their appearance (Adelman, Kaser-Boyd, & Taylor, 1984). There is considerable difficulty in conveying the desirability of some change in the child to the subject. Nevertheless, the therapist should state her or his own opinion that such a change is necessary or at least desirable, and that it can be achieved in a foreseeable period of time.

The issue of time-limited versus indefinite or open-ended psychotherapy becomes pertinent before therapy begins. A great deal has been written about the former (Dulcan, 1984; Lester, 1968; Leventhal & Weinberger, 1975; Mackay, 1967; Rhodes, 1973; Rosenthal & Levine, 1971; Turecki, 1982; Williams, Lewis, Copeland, Tucker, & Feagan, 1978). Brief psychotherapy should not be confused with crisis intervention, nor with "trial of therapy." Nor should it be considered time-limited only by necessity; it should be elective, and it requires separate techniques (Turecki, 1982). Although the advocates of brief psychotherapy stress that it should be focused, it can be said categorically that all psychotherapy should focus on relevant content, and not meander aimlessly all over the psychological map. There is, however, a crucial difference between time-limited and nonlimited therapy in the original presentation of the treatment plan to the child and the family. In the former, a specified number of sessions, or a range of sessions, is contracted for. If at the end of the planned block of treatments the problem has not been resolved satisfactorily, a new contract can be negotiated. Obviously, if this process is repeated several times, it will resemble "unlimited" psychotherapy.

Having completed the preliminaries of drawing up a contract between psychotherapist and family, including an agreement on time, place, duration, and the goals to be attained, the process of therapy can begin. A description of this process contains the transactions between therapist and patient, and, in the case of group therapy, between the members of the group as well. The complexity and the number of events taking place are enormous; any observer can select only a finite portion. This will consist of what is perceived as being of primary importance. The therapist has great difficulty in recalling even the critical events in the session afterward unless he or she is totally inactive and functions solely as an observer. However, such a stance is considered nontherapeutic. The therapist needs to be active, though not necessarily directive.

Observations of therapy sessions through one-way screens or by way of videotape enlarge the possibility of capturing events, but still, much that occurs is lost. The observers cannot experience the subjective and intuitive feelings of the therapist who is in the room with the child. Apart from this major exclusion, there are also technical limitations that prevent outside observers from seeing and hearing everything that is taking place.

Having said much about limits and difficulties, we can still draw the broad outlines of the process. A number of stages can be described; the first of these is the beginning of the consolidating of the therapeutic relationship with the child. A great deal of effort is put into this stage, for it is the very ground of therapy; without it, further progress is impossible.

A working relationship is contingent on effective communication between the parties. The therapist must decide which medium will be most effective in this regard. With younger children, the medium of play is of primary utility, as verbal dialogue by itself may not be feasible. (The term *play therapy*, though in common use, is inappropriate. "Psychotherapy through the medium of play" is a preferred phrase.) When play is chosen as a medium, the question becomes what kind of toys are most suitable. The potential list of "props" (which include games as well as toys) is huge: crayons, paper, dolls, a doll house, toy furniture, toy soldiers, toy Indians and cowboys, guns of all varieties, telephones, blocks, Lego sets, nursing bottles, puppets, sand boxes, pots and pans, sieves, water, finger paints, boards, aprons, miniature bowls, basketballs, bop bags, and board games of different degrees of complexity have all been used. Obviously, not everything can be accommodated at once when one is treating an individual child or a group of children. Some of the materials are more suited to preschool children (e.g., nursing bottles and baby dolls). Others are appropriate for the 6- to 12-year-old child (e.g., crayons, drawing paper, and some board games). Much has been written about older children's being "turned off" when presented with toys for preschoolers (e.g., Lebo, 1956), and it has been said that some toys induce regression in the older child. On the other hand, Fishbein (1974) found that it did not seem to matter to either younger and older children whether "appropriate" or "inappropriate" toys were presented to them. They accepted some and rejected some others in each class of toys. It may well be that, initially, a somewhat arbitrary collection of toys will help to "break the ice" with any nonverbal child. As therapy proceeds, however, the selection of toys becomes more critical if the patient is to become involved with the material.

The typical child's posture at the beginning of therapy is often resistance. Although a number of children will express themselves in a revealing manner to the therapist, either verbally or through play, they are in the minority. The therapist's prime objective is to gain a foothold on the child's genuine thoughts and feelings. Above all else, this process requires patience and perseverance. Two main forms of resistance are encountered: the passive and the active.

The novice therapist dreads nothing so much as passive resistance. It presents the therapist with a vacuum, a situation most likely to cause him or her to feel helpless. In the case of passive adult patients, the technique of the therapist's remaining passive himself or herself may be legitimate; however, this is not appropriate when one deals with a totally passive child or adolescent. The therapist must remain active, either verbally or in play, and must attempt to convey his or her own feelings about the situation. Sooner or later, and sometimes it is much later, the patient will break his or her own silence and inactivity.

The active form of resistance is exhibited by acting out on the part of the child. This has to be distinguished from abreaction or catharsis, which is behavior that looks similar but occurs in a different context. The latter is part of a sequence of transactions between therapist and patient and provides emotional relief to the child. The acting-out behavior of the resistant child is provocative and demands a planned and rational response from the therapist. It raises the question of how to set limits. This issue has been much discussed in the literature (Bixler, 1949; Dorfman, 1951; Ginott, 1959, 1961; Moustakas, 1959; Reisman, 1973) already referred to in the previous section. The question is not only when limits should be set, but also how. It is axiomatic that the therapist cannot allow patients to injure themselves or the therapist. The question of property destruction is less easily agreed on. Some materials, like paper, are obviously expendable. Other toys, intended to be used with a number of patients, cannot be allowed to be wasted indiscriminately. Smearing finger paint on walls and urinating or defecating on the floor are also not tolerable by the average therapist. In the technique of imposing limits verbal intervention precedes physical action, unless the child's behavior is sudden and dramatically dangerous. Providing alternative expressions of aggressive feelings is a way of preventing having to set limits. There is good evidence from the experience of many therapists that the imposition of limits can be reassuring to a child who lacks internal controls, and who is basically frightened of her or his own aggressive impulses.

Once a working relationship has been established, the main work of therapy can begin. This middle phase can be subdivided into two subphases. The first of these consists of a liberation of impulses that are more freely expressed in therapy. At this time, there may be a symptomatic worsening of the child's behavior outside therapy. Parents and others usually react negatively to this trend, and the continuation of therapy may be jeopardized. The previously inhibited, so-called neurotic child becomes more expressive and even explosive. This reaction is based not on any new insight or cognitive advance that the child has made, but on the covert message of permissiveness and freedom that has been received in the therapeutic situation.

On the other hand, during this subphase, there may be a rapid disappearance of symptoms, such as the school-phobic child's returning to school without any further anxiety. Such a development has been called a *transference cure*, or a *flight into health*, but both designations are misleading. As far as the former is concerned, no transference has taken place at this stage; with regards to the latter, the assumption that nothing has been gained is unwarranted, and the inevitability of relapse has not been confirmed at follow-up.

Nevertheless, the goals of emotional growth and of strengthening the child's sense of self-worth are not achieved until the next subphase has been completed. The transactions during that time consist of both greater activity on the part of the therapist in guiding the patient toward problem solving and the patient's gains in autonomy and self-assurance. Much of the interaction through play may be replaced by dialogue at this stage.

The last phase of therapy is termination. In long-term psychotherapy, once a decision has been made by the therapist in accordance with the attainment of preset goals, this decision should be communicated to the child in time for the latter to be able to deal with it. With adolescents and some older children, termination may be arrived at through negotiation and mutual agreement. In the case of younger children, the negotiation is with the parent, not the child. Three to four sessions should be devoted to wrapping up the relationship and bringing about a satisfactory conclusion. It is assumed, not always correctly, that a child who has been in psychotherapy for any length of time—say, for more than 6 months—will recapitulate earlier separation and loss experiences and will have to go through a minigrieving process when confronted with termination. The depth of the child's attachment to the therapist can, however, be greater than it has appeared both to the parents and to the therapist.

The preceding description of the process and phases of individual psychotherapy with children may appear to be unduly formal, rigid, and ideal. Unfortunately, it is true that, in many instances, the even progression of therapy comes to an abrupt halt when termination is unplanned and is brought about by nontherapeutic forces. Dulcan (1984) stated that the commonest duration of children's treatment in clinics is four to six sessions, which include assessment of the case. So small a number hardly suggests that the attainment of therapeutic goals is the rule.

When termination occurs abruptly and without planning, it is either because the child refuses to come, because the family no longer sanctions the therapy, or because of some adventitious factor, such as unexpected relocation by the family or the therapist, physical illness in either party, or funds running out. Partly for these reasons, brief psychotherapy has become somewhat popular with child therapists. This model is also favored by some behavior therapists and by some family system therapists (Woodward, Goodman, Levin, & Epstein, 1981). If 8–10 sessions are contracted for (a common range selected), the therapy must be very tightly structured, and the goals must be well demarcated. In terms of content, the issue of termination and therefore of separation pervades the whole series of treatment sessions. It is as if the earlier phases of the process are telescoped into the final phase. This form of treatment requires a great deal of activity and initiative on the part of the therapist, who must confront, interpret, advise, guide, and direct the child, and who gives the family homework. These are tasks they must carry out between sessions (Rosenthal, 1979).

## Group Psychotherapy

Although the basic goals and objectives in group psychotherapy with children and adolescents are broadly similar to those discussed for individual psychotherapy, the process is quite different. As has already been pointed out, the analysis of this process is more complex, involving not only therapist–patient interactions, but also a consideration of what happens between the group members themselves. Additionally, the group as a whole undergoes a certain development. This phenomenon has been studied by means of DiMock's (1971) coding system of task roles, group roles, and individual roles, as displayed by individual group members. Bernfeld, Clark, and Parker (1984) found that, as the group of adolescents progresses, the incidence of individual roles declines, and that of group roles increases. Group roles are largely prosocial: coordinating, harmonizing, facilitating, supporting, encouraging, and following the movement of the group. Individual roles are more antisocial or asocial: digressing, seeking recognition, blocking by arguing, disagreeing persistently, and withdrawing from the field. Task roles seems qualitatively mutual: seeking information, defining the problem, giving information, and seeking and giving opinions (pp. 116–117). The method is derived conceptually from the work of Bales (1950) on the analysis of the interpersonal activities of adults.

The structure of group therapy involves the inclusion of several group members selected according to a set of criteria. These have to do with number, with child or adolescent characteristics such as to age, sex, and clinical presentation, and with group balance. These variables are not entirely independent of each other. Thus, the number may be restricted by child characteristics, such as the excessive motility of the subjects in relation to the available setting. Adult groups of a verbal type, using discussion as their vehicle, are usually composed of six to eight members. Such a number may be too large for certain activity groups composed of latency-aged children.

The grouping according to age is fairly standard. Four brackets are commonly used: preschoolers (aged 3–5); early-latency children (6–10 years old); preadolescents (11–13 years old); and adolescents (from 14 to 19 years old). The latter group may be subdivided further. Mixed-sex groups are the mode as far as the earlier years are concerned; single-sex groups generally appear only in the case of adolescents, although many of these are put into mixed-sex groups also. This procedure follows the lead of Ackerman (1955), who broke away from the practice of single-gender groups of adolescents. Mixing the sexes was found to be constructive and to facilitate the emergence of important psychodynamic material.

Another structural variable is the presence of a cotherapist. There are advantages and disadvantages in this strategem. The advantages include the augmentation of therapeutic skills, the enhanced opportunity for the subjects to relate to one therapist, and the added opportunity for identifications to occur, especially when the therapists are of different sexes. Most important, there is the ability of the therapists to model a healthy relationship, demonstrating mutual respect as well as intimacy. The disadvantages are also quite obvious: the possible display of cognitive dissonance between the therapists and the difficulty of each therapist in assuming a role vis-à-vis the other. Dick (1980) described four stages in the development of cotherapy peer experiences. Stage I is one of getting acquainted and of straightening out of administrative issues. Stage II occupies the phase of working out conflicts between the therapists in actual therapy. Stages III and IV are described as arriving at mutual trust and achieving effortless cotherapy. These last two stages overlap to a large extent. In order to facilitate the process of mutual adjustment, Corder and Cornwall (1978) devised personality- and behavior-rating scales that were considered relevant to the work of the therapists. Each therapist rated himself or herself and the cotherapist on 11 items at the beginning of therapy. After 3 months, it was found that critical issues had arisen in areas where the previous ratings were discrepant and had anticipated future problems. Subsequently, the rating scale was expanded and was used prophylactically with good effect (Corder, Cornwall, & Whiteside, 1984).

Group psychotherapy and individual therapy may be applied to the child at the same time. If they coexist, with the same therapist acting in both, the process is called *combined therapy*. If another therapist carries out the second modality, the term *conjoint therapy* is used (Pfeifer & Spinner, 1985). Most workers prefer the former situation in order to prevent therapist competition and splitting on the part of the patient (Rutan & Alonso, 1982). In practice, the use of two separate therapists is more common because of the division of skills and the different preferences for different treatment modalities among therapists. It is unusual for both therapies to be planned at the outset. More commonly, the second modality is initiated because an impasse has been reached in the first (Rutan & Alonso, 1982). Group psychotherapy as an add-on is often used because the child exhibits social anxiety, poor peer relations, or considerable sibling rivalry. Individual therapy may be "inserted" into a block of group therapy sessions when the child suffers from deep-seated conflicts that she or he cannot bring forward in the group situation. Indeed, some authors (e.g., Slavson & Schiffer, 1975) see such children as being unsuitable for activity group psychotherapy. However, many can be included in activity–interview group therapy.

The question of group balance, though seemingly a matter of great importance, gets relatively little attention in the literature, largely because of the prevalence of pragmatism in a field of clinics with relatively small pools of candidates for group therapy. What one finds is that a child will be placed in a group chiefly because there is a slot available. A certain homogeneity in age bracket and intellectual development is commonly seen. Diversity in terms of a variety of personality style and temperamental characteristics is considered theoretically desirable but is not often attained. A group of exclusively impulsive, highly active 7- to 8-year-old boys creates an unbalanced group; yet, one would not want to place a fearful, inhibited child in such a group. The same caveat applies to putting a sheltered, naive youngster among a collection of street-wise, predelinquent adolescents.

A decision must be made about whether the group will be a closed or an open one. This decision will depend largely on the context and the setting of the therapy. Open groups are almost unavoidable in residential settings where the length of stay is brief or of intermediate duration, such as psychiatric inpatient units. Such settings also predicate short-term therapy (Rosenberg & Cherbuliez, 1979; Williams *et al.*, 1978), which, although probably practiced very widely in such places, is rarely reported in the literature (Scheidlinger, 1984). The open group does complement the therapeutic milieu of residential treatment places. Group psychotherapy also has a large role to play in the overall scheme of partial hospitalization programs.

The process of closed psychotherapy groups resembles that of individual therapies in that a number of concrete phases can be discerned. Anthony (1959) described initial, intermediate, and terminal phases. The intermediate phase, which is the real "working" period, can be subdivided into an early stage, when there is a power struggle between group members and a good deal of anxiety is generated, and a later stage, when group cohesion develops and problems tend to be resolved. The termination phase is monopolized by topics of separation, loss, and the need to "let go." In open groups, these themes are constantly brought up as group members leave intermittently, so that earlier losses are recapitulated by the members.

The qualities required of the effective group therapist are not the same as those of a superior individual psychotherapist; nor does the skilled play-group therapist necessarily constitute an ideal group therapist with adolescents. In group therapy, one must be alert to the interpersonal events between the group members; one must know when to intervene in those interactions, when to comment or interpret, and when to leave the group alone. The task of controlling a group situation that threatens to get out of hand is different from intervening with a child who is about to break limits. Having a cotherapist brings with it its own problems of timing and of collaboration. On the other hand, there is great satisfaction in experiencing the increased cohesiveness of a therapeutic group and its multiplier effect on the group members. The economic principle of treating the largest number of children or adolescents (with a given therapeutic thrust) remains paramount, even if this factor is not regarded very highly by many workers in the field.

## Major Applications

The method of psychodynamically based psychotherapy has broad application in the treatment and management of children and adolescents exhibiting significant psychopathology. Chapters in Part III of this handbook specify and enlarge on applications as they pertain to specific diagnostic categories. The judgment about whether psychological therapy based on psychodynamic principles is more appropriate than therapy based on learning or cognitive theories depends somewhat on the preference of the author. Nevertheless, some diagnoses make the use of dynamically based psychotherapy more likely than in other diagnoses. The anxieties, phobias, and depressions are in the forefront of the cases to which dynamically based psychotherapy is particularly relevant. Some conduct disorders, some attention-deficit disorders, and some eating disorders have also been treated with a measure of success by a form of psychotherapy in which the relationship between therapist and patient is of crucial importance (Bruch, 1970; Giovacchini, 1974; Silver, 1975). In a number of other diagnostic categories, psychotherapy is more effective if based on learning principles: elimination disorders (enuresis and encopresis), infantile autism, and specific learning disorders. In the case of the intellectually limited individual with behavior disorders, behavior-shaping and behavior-modification techniques are generally preferred to a dynamic approach; however, the latter has considerable scope among retarded patients (see Nuffield, 1983; Szymanski, 1980; Szymanski & Rosefsky, 1980) and cannot be totally discounted.

Since the early 1960s, a category of severe psychopathology in children and adolescents has been described as a borderline personality disorder. Although this term is not placed in the Infancy, Childhood and Adolescence Disorders section of the present diagnostic canon (the DSM-III, American Psychiatric Association, 1980), the criteria for the presence of borderline personality disorders (BPD) can be applied to the developing age groups (Fast & Chetick, 1972; Geelert, 1958; Pine, 1974; Rosenfeld & Sprince, 1965). Originally founded on the psychoanalytic developmental theory of Mahler (1948, 1952) which concerned itself with fixation at the stage of individuation and separation, the theory underlying borderline states has been further refined by Kernberg (1967), who "localized" this fixation at the point at which the "good" (loving) self and the "good" (loving) object are still dissociated from the "bad" (aggressive) self and the "bad" (aggressive) external object. This is a black-and-white view of the self and others, a point at which psychological development has been arrested. This "splitting" of the outside interpersonal world leads to unstable interpersonal relationships, which, however, can be very intense and primitive (also to impulsive, unpredictable acting out, and affective instability). The "splitting" of the "good" and the "bad" self expresses itself in identity disturbances, such as a fluctuating, unstable self-image and a gender-identity disturbance.

The form of therapy most commonly applied to these children and adolescents is individual psychotherapy of a psychodynamic type (Chetick, 1979). There are special problems with this therapy in borderline cases, which require different handling from the child who has some intrapsychic conflict (i.e., the so-called neurotic child). Chetick felt that the therapist must enter into the patient's narcissistic world in order to have any beneficial effect. The child tends to manipulate the therapist for her or his own ends and must be gradually helped to integrate her or his illusory world with the real world. Rinsley (1980) describes a similar process with adolescents in a residential setting. Indeed, the practical exigencies of treating these very disturbed patients often require the milieu of a hospital and, at times, even a closed-ward setting. Apart from the therapeutic effects of the milieu, family therapy is also a necessary concomitant in all such cases (Rinsley, 1980).

The application of psychotherapeutic techniques may be determined more by the setting that the child is placed in than by the diagnosis. Examples of such settings are child psychiatric inpatient units, residential treatment centers, and partial hospitalization programs. The aggregation of young patients results in a common preference for group psychotherapy over individual treatment. The types of patients found in such settings vary but tend to have more severe types of psychopathology: aggression; other antisocial behaviors; psychotic symptoms, including loose associations and hallucinations; severe regressions, such as enuresis; and, nearly always, learning problems (Lewis, 1985). The patients in day-treatment or partial-hospitalization programs are also tagged with many diagnoses; conduct disorders, adjustment disorders with mixed disturbance of affect and conduct, and eating disorders are some of the more common ones. Group therapies fit into the milieu and form an important and often essential part of the overall program. The size, structure, and duration of such groups hinge largely on what the overall program provides. For example, a short-term hospital-based inpatient unit will have open-ended groups, probably consisting of a small number of children with a great variety of presenting problems and psychopathological configurations. A large day program for 13- to 18-year-old youngsters, on the other hand, may have more homogeneous groups that last longer, with a mixture of closed and open groups being run. The aims and the techniques will also be different in these two examples. The short-term inpatient group will seek to achieve rapid integration of thoughts and feelings with better impulse control and with the establishment of more effective defenses, as well as the abandonment of severe aggressive maneuvers (Williams *et al.*, 1978). The long-term, day-center-based group will have more extended goals involving a basic reorientation of the adolescent's relationship patterns and will try to advance the child's psychosexual maturation and identity formation (Erikson, 1959).

Group psychotherapy is sometimes used in modern pediatric wards, more as prophylaxis than as treatment. These groups have to be brief because of the children's short hospital stay, but they offer much emotional support to a group of children who are at risk but are not yet identified as psychiatric patients (Cofer & Nir, 1975; Frank, 1978). Apart from its didactic aspects, such as the dissemination of valid information, this therapy allows for the expression of fears and anxiety and the release of other unpleasant feelings. Such events also occur in the treatment of children and adolescents with more serious psychopathology (Scheidlinger, 1984).

Another setting where group psychotherapy has been used extensively is the school (Frank & Zilbach, 1968; Rhodes, 1973; Scheidlinger, 1965). In some cases, the groups attempt to prevent psychopathological manifestations, but for the most part, they include children who have already been identified by school personnel as being disturbed. An example of preventive intervention is a school-based group for children of divorced parents (Cantor, 1977). "Inoculating" a child at risk against future decompensating illness can also be done by individual therapy, but it is achieved more economically by group therapy. The risk factors, such as the presence of a psychotic parent (Anthony, 1972), tend to cause the children to be aggregated by the health care system that treats the parent, and therefore, group therapies become economically feasible and practical.

With the strong emergence of cognitive and behavioral methods in the psychological treatment of children and adolescents, psychodynamically based psychotherapy has retreated somewhat from the center stage. This trend can be expected to continue. Part of the reason for this relative decline lies in the difficulty of evaluating this therapy's worth. Research on outcome has been hampered by a number of factors, which have been discussed in some reviews of the topic (e.g., Rutter, 1982; Shaffer, 1984; Tramontana, 1980). The single-subject design (Kazdin, 1982), which is temptingly economical, will not suffice in this area because the changes brought about by treatment cannot be expected to disappear when treatment is "switched off" (as in an ABAB experimental design).

Another feature militating against any plausible conclusion from outcome studies is the heterogeneity of the subjects studied, as when large cohorts of experimental and control patients are compared. This has been one of the chief criticisms of Levitt's earlier work (1957) by Heinecke and Strassman (1975).

The exact process of psychotherapy is often poorly described, and it is not clear to the outsider what has actually happened (Julian & Kilman, 1979). It is very difficult to standardize psychotherapy with children and adolescents. The aggregation of separate studies does not result in valid generalizations.

A large source of difficulty is the occurrence of intervening variables during the course of treatment and observation. Concurrent therapies can be controlled for with some difficulty, but external contingencies will occur with unforeseen and irregular frequency, so that the matching of treatment and control subjects in terms of their total experience becomes a matter of happenstance and good luck.

The kinds of outcome measures required for rigorous research have not been developed. Symptom counts are generally used, but they often fail to capture changes in the subject that may manifest themselves in improved functioning only later. For that reason, follow-up studies and follow-up reevaluations are universally recommended. Although these are helpful and will increase knowledge, they are also hampered by some of the same problems of measurement and sufficiency in range. Terminal assessments may suffer from global vagueness, on the one hand, or may have too narrow a focus, on the other.

In spite of these pessimistic observations, there is some evidence that the efficacy of psychotherapy can be demonstrated in well-circumscribed groups of subjects treated under tightly controlled conditions. In this connection, the work of Shore and Massimo (1966, 1973) is considered an exemplar (Heinecke & Strassman, 1975). These authors reported on a group of 10 delinquent adolescents who received informal psychotherapy, sometimes 8–10 times per week, for 10 months, while the controls received only remedial education and job placement. The treated group also received those services. At a 10-year follow-up 80% of the treated group and only 20% of the control group were making an adequate adjustment. A criticism must be that the number of subjects was small. However, it is likely that a large number of such well-defined subjects would be difficult to obtain in the first place; treatment by the same therapist and proper matching with an equal number of controls would be a difficult goal to achieve. As the cohorts become larger, the maintenance of proper experimental conditions becomes a larger problem. However, the smaller the groups, the less plausible are the generalizations.

In conclusion, it is important to ask the right questions when attempting to resolve the puzzle of efficacy. It is no longer appropriate to ask: Does psychotherapy for children and adolescents work? Instead, the question should be: Who should be doing what and how to whom and under what circumstances? The variables reside in the therapist, the process and technique of therapy, its context, and the patient. If psychotherapy can help young patients, it can also probably hurt them (McCord, 1978). It may not be as clearly dangerous as pharmacotherapy can be, but it should be undertaken in a planned, judicious manner and should not be used cavalierly.

## REFERENCES

Ackerman, N. (1955). Group psychotherapy with a mixed group of adolescents. *International Journal of Group Psychotherapy, 5,* 249–260.

Ackermann, N. W. (1958). *The psychodynamics of family life.* New York: Basic Books.

Adelman, H. S., Kaser-Boyd, N., & Taylor, L. (1984). Children's participation in consent for treatment and their subsequent response to treatment. *Journal of Clinical Child Psychology, 13,* 170–178.

Adler, A. (1930). *Guiding the child.* New York: Greenberg.

Aichhorn, A. (1935). *Wayward youth.* New York: Viking Press.

Allen, F. (1942). *Psychotherapy with children.* New York: Norton.

American Psychiatric Association. (1980). *Diagnostic and statistical manual of mental disorders* (3rd ed.—DSM-III). Washington, DC: Author.

Anthony, E. J. (1959). The natural history of the therapeutic group. In S. H. Foulkes & E. J. Anthony (Eds.), *Group psychotherapy.* London: Penguin Books.

Anthony, E. J. (1972). Primary presentation with school children. In H. H. Barten, & L. Bellay (Eds.), *Progressive community mental health.* New York: Grune & Stratton.

Axline, V. M. (1947). *Play therapy.* Boston: Houghton-Mifflin.

Bales, R. F. (1950). *Interaction process analysis: A method for the study of small groups.* Reading, MA: Addison-Wesley.

Bender, L., & Woltman, A. (1936). The use of puppet shows as a psychotherapeutic method for behavioral problems in children. *American Journal of Orthopsychiatry, 6,* 341–354.

Bernfeld, G., Clark, L., & Parker, G. (1984). The process of adolescent group psychotherapy. *International Journal of Group Psychotherapy, 34,* 111–126.

Bixler, R. H. (1949). Limits are therapy. *Journal of Consulting Psychology, 13,* 1–11.

Blom, G. F. (1972). A psychoanalytic viewpoint of behavior modification in clinical and educational settings. *Journal of the American Academy of Child Psychiatry, 11,* 675–693.

Bruch, H. (1970). Psychotherapy in primary anorexia nervosa. *Journal of Nervous and Mental Disease, 150,* 51–67.

Cantor, D. W. (1977). School-based groups for children of divorce. *Journal of Divorce, 1,* 183–187.

Carek, D. J. (1979). Individual psychodynamically oriented therapy. In J. D. Noshpitz (Ed.), *Basic handbook of child psychiatry.* New York: Basic Books.

Chetick, M. (1979). The borderline child. In J. D. Noshpitz (Ed.), *Basic handbook of child psychiatry.* New York: Basic Books.

Cofer, D. C., & Nir, I. (1975). Theme-focused group therapy on a pediatric ward. *International Journal of Psychiatry and Medicine, 6,* 541–550.

Corder, B. F., Cornwall, T., & Whiteside, R. (1984). Techniques for increasing effectiveness of co-therapy functioning in adolescent psychotherapy groups. *International Journal of Group Psychotherapy, 34,* 643–654.

Curran, F. (1939). The drama as a therapeutic measure in adolescents. *American Journal of Orthopsychiatry, 9,* 215–231.

DiMock, H. G. (1971). *How to observe your group: Part 2 of leadership and group development series.* Montreal: Concordia University.

Dorfman, E. (1951). Play therapy. In C. Rogers (Ed.), *Client-centered therapy.* Boston: Houghton Mifflin.

Dulcan, M. K. (1984). Brief psychotherapy with children and their families: The state of the art. *Journal of the American Academy of Child Psychiatry, 23,* 544–551.

Erikson, E. (1950). *Childhood and society.* New York: Norton.

Erikson, E. H. (1959). *Identity and the life cycle in psychological issues* (Vol. 1, No. 1). New York: International University Press, Inc.

Esman, A. H. (1983). Psychoanalytic play therapy. In C. E. Schafer & K. J. O'Connor (Eds.), *Handbook of play therapy.* New York: Wiley.

Eysenck, H. J. (1952). The effects of psychotherapy. *Journal of Consulting Psychology, 16,* 319–324.

Eysenck, H. J. (1955). The effects of psychotherapy: A reply. *Journal of Abnormal Social Psychology, 50,* 147–148.

Fast, I., & Chetick, M. (1972). Love aspects of object relationships in borderline children. *International Journal of Psychoanalysis, 53,* 479–484.

Fishbein, C. (1974). *The relationship between age-related toys and therapeutic expression in non-directive play therapy.* Unpublished master's thesis, the Pennsylvania State University, State College, PA.

Frank, J. L. (1978). A weekly group meeting of children in a pediatric ward: Therapeutic and practical functions. *International Journal of Psychiatry and Medicine, 8,* 267–283.

Frank, M. G., & Zilbach, J. (1968). Current trends in group therapy with children. *International Journal of Group Psychotherapy, 18,* 447–460.

Freud, A. (1928). *Introduction to the technique of child analysis* (L. P. Clark, trans.). New York: Nervous and Mental Disease Publishing.

Freud, A. (1964). *The psychoanalytic treatment of children, lectures and essays.* New York: Schocken.

Freud, A. (1965). *Normality and pathology in childhood: Assessment of development.* New York: International University Press.

Freud, S. (1950). *Beyond the pleasure principle.* New York: Liverwright.

Freud, S. (1959). Analysis of a phobia in a five-year-old boy. In E. Jones (Ed.), *Collected Papers* (Vol. 3). New York: Basic Books.

Gabriel, B. (1944). Group treatment for adolescent girls. *American Journal Orthopsychiatry, 14,* 593–602.

Gardner, R. A. (1975). *Psychotherapeutic approaches to the resistant child.* New York: Jason Aronson.

Geleerd, E. (1958). Borderline states in childhood and adolescence. In R. S. Eissler, A. Freud, H. Hartmann, & M. Kris (Eds.), *The psychoanalytic study of the child.* New York: International University Press.

Ginott, H. C. (1959). The theory and practice of "Therapeutic Intervention" in child treatment. *Journal of Consulting Psychology, 23,* 160–166.

Ginnott, H. C. (1961). *Group psychotherapy with children.* New York: McGraw-Hill.

Giovacchini, P. L. (1974). The difficult adolescent patient: Countertransference problems. *Adolescent Psychiatry, 3,* 271–288.

Graziano, A. (1975). *Behavior therapy in children.* Chicago: Aldine.

Groos, K. (1901). *The play of man.* New York: Appleton.

Group for the Advancement of Psychiatry (GAP) (1982). *The process of child therapy* (Vol. 11, Report No. 111). New York: Brunner/Mazel.

Group for the Advancement of Psychiatry (GAP) (1983). *From diagnosis to treatment: An approach to treatment planning for the emotionally disturbed child* (Vol. 8, No. 87). New York: Brunner/Mazel.

Hadden, S. B. (1955). Historic background of group psychotherapy. *International Journal of Group Psychotherapy, 5,* 162–173.

Heinicke, C. M., & Goldman, A. (1960). Research on psychotherapy in children. *American Journal of Orthopsychiatry, 30,* 483–494.

Heinecke, C. M., & Strassman, L. H. (1975). Toward more effective research in child psychotherapy. *Journal of American Academy of Child Psychiatry, 14,* 561–588.

Hess, E. H. (1959). Imprinting: An effect of early experience. *Science, 130,* 133–134.

Hoen-Saric, R., Frank, J. D., Imber, S. D., Nash, E. H., Stone, A. R., & Battle, C. C. (1964). Systematic preparation of patients for psychotherapy. *Journal of Psychiatric Research, 2,* 267–281.

Holmes, D. S., & Urie, R. G. (1975). Effects of preparing children for psychotherapy. *Journal of Consulting and Clinical Psychology, 43,* 311–318.

Hug-Hellmuth, H. (1921). On the technique of child-analysis. *International Journal of Psychoanalysis, 2,* 287–305.

Itard, J. (1962). *The wild boy of Aveyron* (G. Humphrey & M. Humphrey, trans.). New York: Appleton-Century-Crofts. (Originally published, 1806).

Janzen, W. B., & Love, W. (1977). Involving adolescents as active participants in their own treatment plan. *Psychological Reports, 41,* 931–934.

Jones, M. C. (1924). A laboratory study of fear: The case of Peter. *Pedagogical Seminary, 31,* 308–315.

Julian, A., & Kilmann, P. R. (1979). Group treatment of juvenile delinquents: A review of the literature. *International Journal of Group Psychotherapy, 29,* 3–38.

Kazdin, A. E. (1982). *Single case research designs: Methods for clinical and applied settings.* New York: Oxford University Press.

Kernberg, O. (1967). Borderline personality organization. *Journal of the American Psychoanalytic Association, 15,* 641–685.

Klein, M. (1932). *The psycho-analysis of children.* London: Hogarth Press.

Klein, M. (1948). *The psychological principles of infant analysis,* In *Contributions of psycho-analysis, 1921–1945.* London: Hogarth Press and the Institute of Psychoanalysis. (Originally published, 1926.)

Lebo, D. (1956). The question of toys in play therapy: An international problem. *Journal of Education and Psychology, 86,* 375–378.

Lester, E. P. (1968). Brief psychotherapies in child psychiatry. *Canadian Psychiatric Association Journal, 13,* 301–309.

Leventhal, T., & Weinberger, G. (1975). Evaluation of a large-scale brief therapy program for children. *American Journal of Orthopsychiatry, 45,* 119–133.

Levitt, E. E. (1957). The results of psychotherapy with children: An evaluation. *Journal of Consulting Psychologists, 21,* 189–196.

Levy, D. (1938). Release therapy in young children. *Psychiatry, 1,* 387–389.

Lewis, M. (1985). Residential treatment. In H. I. Kaplan & B. J. Sadock (Eds.), *Comprehensive textbook of psychiatry* (4th ed.). Baltimore: Williams & Wilkins.

Lowenfeld, M. (1975). *Play in childhood.* New York: Wiley.

McCord, J. (1978). A thirty year follow-up of treatment effects. *American Psychologist, 33,* 284–289.

McDermott, J. F., & Char, W. F. (1974). The undeclared war between child and family therapy. *Journal American Academy of Child Psychiatry, 13,* 422–436.

Mackay, J. (1967). The use of brief psychotherapy with children. *Canadian Psychiatric Association Journal, 12,* 269–279.

Mahler, M. (1948). Clinical studies in the benign and malignant forms of childhood psychosis. *American Journal of Orthopsychiatry, 19,* 295–305.

Mahler, M. (1952). On childhood psychosis and schizophrenia, autistic and symbiotic infantile psychosis. In R. S. Eissler, A. Freud, H. Hartmann, & M. Kris (Eds.), *The psychoanalytic study of the child.* New York: International University Press.

Marks, I. M., & Gelder, M. G. (1966). Common ground between behavior therapy and psychodynamic methods. *British Journal of Medical Psychology, 39,* 11–23.

Miller, J. G. (1960). Information input overload and psychopathology. *American Journal of Psychiatry, 116,* 695–704.

Moreno, J. L. (1947). *The theater of spontaneity.* New York: Beacon House.

Moustakas, C. F. (1959). *Psychotherapy with children.* New York: Harper & Row.

Noshpitz, J. D. (1979). (Ed.). *Basic handbook of child psychiatry.* New York: Basic Books.

Nuffield, E. J. (1983). Psychotherapy. In J. L. Matson & J. A. Mulick (Eds.), *Handbook of mental retardation.* New York: Pergamon Press.

Orne, M. T., & Wender, P. H. (1968). Anticipatory socialization for psychotherapy: Method and rationale. *American Journal of Psychiatry, 124,* 88–98.

Pfeifer, G., & Spinner, D. (1985). Combined individual and group psychotherapy: An ego developmental perspective. *International Journ Group Psychotherapy, 35,* 11–35.

Piaget, J. (1962). *Play, dreams and imitation in childhood.* New York: Norton.

Pine, F. (1974). On the concept of borderline in children: A clinical essay. In R. S. Eissler, A. Freud, H. Hartmann, & M. Kris (Eds.), *The psychoanalytic study of the child, 29,* 341–367. New York: International University Press.

President's Commission on Mental Health. (1978). Report to the President (Vol. 1). Washington, DC: U.S. Government Printing Office.

Proskauer, S. (1969). Some issues in time-limited psychotherapy with children. *Journal of American Academy of Child Psychiatry, 8,* 154–169.

Proskauer, S. (1971). Focused, time-limited psychotherapy with children. *Journal of American Academy of Child Psychiatry, 10,* 619–639.

Rachman, A. W., & Raubolt, R. R. (1984). The pioneers of adolescent group psychotherapy. *International Journal of Group Psychotherapy, 34,* 387–413.

Rafferty, F. T. (1975). Community mental health centers and the criteria for quality universiality of services for children. *Journal of the American Academy of Child Psychiatry, 15,* 5–17.

Rank, O. (1929). *The trauma of birth.* London: Harcourt Brace Jovanovich.

Redl, F. (1942). Group emotion and leadership. *Psychiatry, 4,* 573–596.

Redl, F., & Wineman, D. (1951). *Controls from within.* New York: Free Press.

Reisman, J. M. (1966). *The development of clinical psychology.* New York: Appleton-Century-Crofts.

Reisman, J. M. (1973). *Principles of psychotherapy with children.* New York: Wiley-Interscience.

Rhodes, S. L. (1973). Short-term groups of latency-age children in a school setting. *International Journal of Group Psychotherapy, 23,* 204–215.

Rinsley, D. R. (1980). *Treatment of the severely disturbed adolescent.* New York: Jason Aronson.

Rogers, C. R. (1942). *Counseling and psychotherapy.* Boston: Houghton Mifflin.

Rogers, C. R. (1962). Theme learnings from a study of psychotherapy with schizophrenics. *Pennsylvania Psychiatric Quarterly,* 8–15.

Rosenberg, J., & Cherbuliez, T. (1979). Inpatient group therapy for older children and pre-adolescents. *International Journal of Group Psychotherapy, 29,* 393–406.

Rosenfeld, S., & Sprince, M. (1965). Some thoughts in the technical handling of borderline children. In R. B. Eissler, A. Freud, H. Hartman, & M. Kris (Eds.), *The psychoanalytic study of the child, 20*, 495–517. New York: International University Press.

Rosenthal, A. J. (1970). Brief psychotherapy with children: A preliminary report. *American Journal of Psychiatry, 127*, 646–651.

Rosenthal, A. J. (1979). Brief focused psychotherapy. In J. Noshpitz (Ed.), *Handbook of child psychiatry*. New York: Basic Books.

Rosenthal, A. J., & Levine, S. V. (1971). Brief psychotherapy with children: Process of therapy. *American Journal of Psychiatry, 128*, 141–146.

Rutan, J. L., & Alonso, A. (1982). Group therapy, individual therapy or both? *International Journal of Group Psychotherapy, 32*, 267–282.

Rutter, M. (1982). Family and school influences: Meanings, mechanisms, and implications. In A. R. Nichols (Ed.), *Practical lessons from longitudinal studies*. Chichester, England: Wiley.

Sadock, B. J. (1980). Group psychotherapy, combined individual and group psychotherapy and psychodrama. In H. I. Kaplan, A. M. Freedman, & B. J. Sadock (Eds.), *Comprehensive textbook of psychiatry* (3rd ed.). Baltimore: Williams & Wilkins.

Satir, V. (1967). Including the children in family therapy. In V. Satir (Ed.), *Conjoint Family Therapy*. Palo Alto: Science & Behavior Books.

Schaefer, C. E., & O'Connor, K. J. (1983). *Handbook of play therapy*. New York: Wiley.

Scheidlinger, S. (1965). Three group approaches with socially deprived latency age children. *International Journal of Group Psychotherapy, 15*, 434–445.

Scheidlinger, S. (1984). Short-term group psychotherapy for children: An overview. *International Journal of Group Psychotherapy, 34*, 573–585.

Seguin, E. (1866). *Idiocy and its treatment by the physiological method*. New York: William Wood.

Shaffer, D. (1984). Notes on psychotherapy research among children and adolescents. *Journal of the American Academy of Child Psychiatry, 23*, 552–561.

Shoben, E. J. (1953). Some observations on psychotherapy and the learning process. In O. H. Mowrer (Ed.), *Psychotherapy theory and research*. New York: Ronald Press.

Shore, M., & Massimo, J. (1966). Comprehensive vocationally oriented psychotherapy for adolescent delinquent boys. *American Journal of Orthopsychiatry, 36*, 609–615.

Shore, M., & Massimo, J. (1973). After 10 years: A follow up study of comprehensive vocationally oriented psychotherapy. *American Journal of Orthopsychiatry, 43*, 128–132.

Shulman, J. L. (1960). "One visit psychotherapy" with children. *Progress in Psychotherapy, 5*, 86–93.

Silver, L. B. (1975). Acceptable and controversial approaches to treating the child with learning disabilities. *Pediatrics, 55*, 406–415.

Slavson, S. R. (1950). *Analytic group psychotherapy with children, adolescents, and adults*. New York: Columbia University Press.

Slavson, S. R., & Schiffer, M. (1975). *Group psychotherapy for children*. New York: International Universities Press.

Slobin, D. I. (1964). The fruits of the first season: A discussion of the role of play in childhood. *Journal of Humanistic Psychology, 4*, 59–79.

Solomon, J. (1938). Active play therapy. *American Journal of Orthopsychiatry, 8*, 479–498.

Szymanski, L. L. (1980). Individual psychotherapy with retarded persons. In S. Szymanski & P. E. Tanguay (Eds.), *Emotional disorders of mentally retarded persons*. Baltimore: University Park Press.

Szymanski, L. L., & Rosefsky, Q. B. (1980). Group psychotherapy with retarded persons. In L. S. Szymanski & P. E. Tanguay (Eds.), *Emotional disorders of mentally retarded persons*. Baltimore: University Park Press.

Taft, J. (1933). *The dynamics of therapy in a controlled relationship*. New York: Macmillan.

Tramontana, M. G. (1980). Critical review of research on psychotherapy outcome with adolescents: 1967–1977. *Psychology Bulletin, 88*, 429–450.

Turecki, S. (1982). Elective brief psychotherapy with children. *American Journal of Psychotherapy, 36*, 479–488.

Ullman, L. P., & Krasner, L. (1965). *Case studies in behavior modification*. New York: Holt, Rinehart & Winston.

Watson, J. B., & Watson, R. R. (1921). Studies in infant psychology. *Scientific Monthly, 13*, 493–515.

Werner, H. (1948). *Comparative psychology of mental development*. New York: Science Editions.

Werry, J. S., & Woolersheim, J. P. (1967). Behavior therapy with children: A broad overview. *Journal of the American Academy of Child Psychiatry, 6*, 348–370.

Williams, J., Lewis, C., Copeland, F., Tucker, L., & Feagan, L. (1978). A model for short-term group therapy on a children's inpatient unit. *Clinical Social Work Journal, 6,* 21–32.

Witmer, H. L. (Ed.). (1946). *Psychiatric interviews with children.* Cambridge: Harvard University Press.

Witmer, L. (1907). Clinical psychology. *Psychological Clinic, 1,* 1–9.

Wollan, K. I. (1941). A new treatment for juvenile delinquents. *Criminal Law and Criminology, 31,* 712–719.

Wollan, K. I. (1951). Application of group therapy principles to institutional treatment of adolescents. *International Journal of Group Psychotherapy, 1,* 356–364.

Woodward, C. A., Goodman, J. T., Levin, S., & Epstein, N. (1981). Client, treatment, and therapist variables related to outcome in brief, systems-oriented family therapy. *Family Process, 20,* 189–197.

Yalom, I. D., Houts, D. S., Newel, G., & Rand, K. H. (1967). Preparation of patients for group psychotherapy: A controlled study. *Archives of General Psychiatry, 17,* 416–427.

# III    Treatment Approaches: Conduct and Anxiety Disorders

This section includes four chapters on the treatment of what are undoubtedly the most commonly observed problems faced by the child practitioner. The first chapter is on conduct disorders. Children evincing this problem are often identified in the school as a major problem for the teacher and the health professional. Considerable new psychological information has emerged recently and is discussed.

Perhaps the most heavily researched of all child problems is hyperactivity. In the next two chapters, pharmacological and psychological interventions are discussed. Although conduct problems have not proved to be easily remediated with pharmacotherapy, hyperactivity is responsive to medication. This is the rationale for including a chapter on both drug and psychological interventions.

The final chapter in this section provides a review of anxiety disorders and phobias and the extensive literature on them. Psychological interventions have been the most widely studied approaches to the treatment of these problems.

Part III, then, constitutes a review of several widespread problems of children.

# 8    *Conduct Disorders*
## *Psychological Therapies*

WILLIAM I. GARDNER AND CHRISTINE L. COLE

## INTRODUCTION

Problems of social conduct are widespread among children and adolescents. These problems include both aggressive and nonaggressive violations of the norms, rules, and laws of acceptable social behavior. When the violations become persistent and of a bothersome magnitude, a number of treatment and management options are available. For example, children may be referred to special education programs, may be treated in community-mental-health clinics, may be treated in inpatient public or private mental hospitals, may be referred to juvenile court, or may be placed in correctional institutions.

The magnitude of the problems associated with conduct disorders is illustrated by data from a variety of sources that emphasize its monetary, social, and personal consequences. Approximately one third to one half of the referrals made by parents and teachers to mental health clinics involve problems of aggressive, oppositional, and antisocial conduct (Herbert, 1978; Robins, 1981). Within the schools, assaultive behavior, property destruction, and general disruptiveness have shown significant increases (Harootunian & Apter, 1983; Lefkowitz, Eron, Walder, & Huesmann, 1977). The results of more serious antisocial acts are illustrated by reported annual school vandalism costs of $600 million, along with some 110,000 serious assaults on teachers and hundreds of thousands of additional ones on students (Harootunian & Apter, 1983; Tygart, 1980). These and related recurring conduct problems in the schools, such as tantrumming, defiance of authority, and profanity, typically result in referral for special education services (Kauffman, 1985). Other children, because of the nature of their antisocial behaviors, have contact with the police and the courts rather than with mental health or special education programs. Violent juvenile crimes and arrests have shown dramatic increases since the mid-1960s (Doke & Flippo, 1983; Strasberg, 1978).

Estimates of the prevalence of conduct disorders, although varying as a result of differences in the sampling procedures and the diagnostic criteria used, range from 4% to 8% and higher. Of significance is the finding that rates among boys are at least three to four times higher than among girls (Graham, 1979;

WILLIAM I. GARDNER AND CHRISTINE L. COLE • Waisman Center on Mental Retardation and Human Development, University of Wisconsin—Madison, Madison, Wisconsin 53706.

Weiner, 1982). In fact, some studies report that 20%–35% of all boys engage in acts of delinquency as defined by police and court contacts (West & Farrington, 1973; Wolfgang, Figlio, & Sellin, 1972).

It is true that most children engage at one time or another in such inappropriate conduct as aggressive, defiant, destructive, disruptive, oppositional, negativistic, or similar reactions in family, school, and neighborhood. The frequency and intensity of these conduct difficulties, however, is within the toleration levels of the social environment, thus necessitating no specific psychological treatment. Further, these difficulties typically occur at a decreasing rate as children grow older. During the socialization process, alternative modes of relating to others, of resolving inter- and intrapersonal conflicts, and of coping with internal and external sources of stress and frustration are developed. As a result, most children acquire both self-regulation and the related personal skills that provide adequate impulse control and a range of socially acceptable behaviors for use under the conditions in which conduct difficulties had previously occurred.

As noted, however, a significant number of children become delayed in social and emotional development, do not learn adequate self-regulation, and continue to engage in socially disruptive behaviors with such frequency, intensity, or duration that specific psychological intervention is required. These children display a lack of control, especially in the presence of provocation resulting in negative emotional arousal, and typically are characterized by a deficit in internalizing the myriad norms of personal and social conduct that represent the standards of behavior expected by society.

Conduct disorder symptomatology that appears early in life, without adequate intervention, is likely to persist. Campbell, Breaux, Ewing, and Szumowski (1986), for example, identified 3-year-old children with persistent problems of aggression and hyperactivity. Follow-up at ages 4 and 6 revealed persistence of the problems, especially among children from lower-class families that experienced recurring stress and disruption and among families in which the mother was negative and directive toward the child.

The long-term durability of conduct disorders in the absence of effective intervention is further emphasized by the finding that the difficulties tend to persist into adolescence and to correlate highly with adult psychopathology (Robins, 1966, 1981). In reviewing 16 longitudinal studies of aggression in males from childhood through adolescence and early adulthood, Olweus (1979) documented the stability of aggression and related conduct difficulties. Across different studies, correlation coefficients ranging from .67 to .98 were found between children's aggression and their aggressive behavior up to 10 years later. This stability rivals that observed in performance on intelligence testing and is greater than the stability observed in most other behavioral pathology (Gersten, Langner, Eisenberg, Simcha-Fagan, & McCarthy, 1976).

The durability of conduct problems supports the notion that enduring personality characteristics are significant contributors to aggressive behavior in older children and adolescents. Variations in levels of aggression in different situations and at different ages also emphasize the interactive influence of environmental variables. As noted later, the psychological treatment programs that are most successful in producing durable change in conduct disorders are those that place a major emphasis on the separate, as well as the interactive, effects of both personal and environmental influences. Thus, chronic childhood problems of conduct present a major and complex challenge to psychological treatment endeavors, especially in view of the observation that traditional psychotherapeutic approaches tend to be less successful with this disorder than with other types of pathology (Yule, 1978). It is also evident, with those children and adolescents who display violent aggression, that the treatment implications must frequently extend beyond the individual and the family and must involve broader community agents, such as the educational, mental health, and legal systems.

This chapter provides a description of the psychological treatment procedures that have been reported to be useful in reducing or eliminating conduct difficulties in children and adolescents. Major attention is given to those treatment procedures derived from various behavior therapy models simply because of the preponderance of the empirical data supporting the efficacy of a range of behavioral treatment approaches. In fact, reports of other approaches typically represent clinical case studies (e.g., Brinich, 1984). In the instances in which data are presented to support the treatment, these are frequently of a preexperimental nature (Curry, Wiencrot, & Koehler, 1984; Kazdin & Frame, 1983). As background for this description of psychological treatment, the topics of definition and terminology, classification systems, concepts of etiology, and clinical assessment are discussed.

## DEFINITION AND TERMINOLOGY

Aggression and related conduct difficulties represent aspects of a wide range of disorders included in formal clinically and empirically based diagnostic and classification systems. The central feature of these disorders is an absence or loss of impulse control and the undesirable acting out of these impulses. These difficulties of conduct violate the rights of others and break the rules or norms of social behavior of family, school, community, and the broader society. The disruptive interpersonal dimensions of the acting-out behaviors are emphasized in such terms as *violent, extreme negativism, destructive, oppositional,* and *verbally and physically assaultive.* Other terms used by various mental health professionals emphasize the disruptive social nature of chronic conduct problems: *sociopathic personality, antisocial,* and *socially aggressive.*

Specific problem behaviors include fighting, punching, hitting, choking, pinching, kicking, and similar displays of aggression toward others; threatening, yelling, demanding, whining, taunting, and similarly annoying verbal behaviors; temper tantrums, especially in younger children and in individuals with developmental disabilities; destruction of property; noncompliance, negativism, and similar acts of objecting to or opposing adult authority; and community rule violations, such as stealing, window breaking, and fire setting. Most characteristically, these behaviors occur in clusters or as a syndrome of interrelated behaviors, rather than in isolation (Forehand & McMahon, 1981; Patterson, 1976; Wahler, 1980).

WILLIAM I. GARDNER
AND CHRISTINE L. COLE

An examination of current diagnostic and classification systems of childhood psychopathology will reveal that conduct difficulties do not represent an isolated or circumscribed disorder. Clinically significant problems of conduct may represent the central feature of a constellation of a child's difficulties (e.g., conduct disorder) or may be only one of a complex of other more central symptomatic features requiring psychological and/or psychopharmacological interventions (e.g., depression). Classification categories included in the DSM-III (American Psychiatric Association, 1980), Quay (1979), and Weiner (1982), in which clinically significant problems of aggression and related difficulties of conduct are, or may be, present, include oppositional disorder, attention-deficit disorder, adjustment disorder with disturbance of conduct, intermittent explosive disorder, psychomotor epilepsy, schizophrenic disorders, specific developmental disorders, mental retardation, depression, pervasive developmental disorders, socialized aggressive disorder, conduct disorder, sociological delinquent, and characterological style.

Current diagnostic and classification systems in psychology and psychiatry that include categories of conduct disorders have been developed either through clinically or empirically based procedures. The DSM-III (American Psychiatric Association, 1980) is currently the most popular example of a clinically derived system. Within the DSM-III, various symptom clusters have been developed from extensive clinical experiences and are conceptualized as diagnostic categories of mental disorders. For each disorder, a set of diagnostic criteria or rules is provided to guide the clinician in arriving at a diagnosis. Thus, the clinician initially identifies the symptoms and then applies the diagnostic rules for selecting a specific mental-disorder category.

Within the DSM-III system, most children and adolescents with persistent and serious acting-out difficulties are provided a diagnosis of *conduct disorder*. The major behavioral characteristic of this disorder is a repetitive and persistent pattern of conduct that violates the basic rights of others or disregards societal norms or rules. The subtypes of *aggressive* and *nonaggressive* violations are included. To meet the diagnostic criteria for the aggressive category, the child or adolescent must demonstrate repetitive and persistent (of at least 6 months' duration) problems of conduct involving physical violence toward other persons (e.g., assault, mugging, or rape) or property (e.g., vandalism, fire setting, or breaking and entering) or thefts outside the home involving confrontation with a victim (e.g., purse snatching, extortion, or the holdup of a store). In contrast, the nonaggressive subtype is characterized by such behaviors as persistent truancy, stealing, substance abuse, or running away, none of which involves confrontation with a victim.

An additional classification of conduct disorders into the subtypes of *undersocialized* and *socialized* is included in the DSM-III. The undersocialized conduct-disordered child does not establish adequate social bonds involving affection or empathy and has no, or only minimal or superficial, relationships with peers. As a result, feelings of guilt or remorse following acting-out behaviors are generally absent. The socialized subtype, in contrast, shows evidence of social attachment to others and does show concern about the welfare of friends and companions.

A distinction is made in the DSM-III system between oppositional disorder (a pattern of disruptive social behaviors involving disobedience, negativism, and provocative opposition to authority figures) and the previously described conduct disorder (in which the basic rights of others or major age-appropriate societal norms or rules are violated). The oppositional attitude is typically shown toward family members and teachers and is exhibited as stubbornness, dawdling, negativism, procrastination, and passive resistance.

A second popular classification system, and one that has special appeal to the behaviorally oriented clinician, is based on a multivariate statistical analysis approach. Quay (1979) described various aggressive and acting-out difficulties as depicting either a *conduct disorder* or a *socialized aggressive disorder*. These empirically derived categories are based on Quay's analysis of a large number of factor-analytic studies of child psychopathology. The conduct disorder factor includes such specific acting-out behaviors as fighting, disobedience, destructiveness, disruptiveness, negativism, rowdiness, irritability, and hyperactivity. The socialized aggressive disorder includes such personal features as having bad company, stealing in the company of others, belonging to a gang, being loyal to delinquent friends, and being truant from school. These disorders may be identified by means of the Behavior Problem Checklist, a rating scale containing a range of problem behaviors (Quay, 1983).

Although not presenting a formal classification system, Weiner (1982) suggested some valuable diagnostic distinctions in the assessment and the subsequent treatment of children and adolescents who engage in repetitive antisocial acts that result in contact with the legal system. The first distinction is made between the *sociological delinquent* and youngsters whose conduct difficulties reflect underlying *psychological problems*. Sociological delinquents have few psychological problems and are well-integrated members of a delinquent subculture that endorses antisocial standards of conduct. They are likely to exhibit conduct difficulties in response to social influences rather than personal psychological problems. These adolescents rarely commit crimes by themselves and seldom keep any illegal acts from their peers. During early life, these conduct-disordered youths typically enjoy good family relationships that provide them the basis for forming interpersonal attachments and for developing judgment and self-control. This category is similar to the DSM-III socialized aggressive conduct disorder.

In contrast, Weiner suggested that conduct difficulties reflecting psychological problems are of three different patterns. The first pattern, *characterological style*, is defined by chronically irresponsible, aggressive, and inconsiderate behavior reflecting a primary asocial personality. Weiner described these conduct difficulties as translating aggressive, acquisitive, and pleasure-seeking impulses into immediate action, with minimal concern about how others may suffer in the process. Antisocial acts occur to express aggression, to satisfy a whim, or to obtain something wanted instead of in response to group pressure or a desire of peer approval and acceptance. In diagnosis, the clinician would find an underdeveloped conscience and related impulse control and motivational features, along with the basic inability to identify with other people.

In a second pattern, antisocial acts represent *neurotic symptoms*. The antisocial acts of youths who are not well-integrated members of a deviant subculture represent an indirect expression of underlying personal concerns. The antisocial behaviors typically contrast sharply with previous life patterns of con-

WILLIAM I. GARDNER
AND CHRISTINE L. COLE

formity and of being well controlled. Further, the antisocial acts follow recurring rejections, losses, or disappointments that intensify the individual's personal need for recognition and attention. As these needs underlying the antisocial acts can be met by others only if detected, the youngster invariably manages to get himself or herself caught. In other youths, the conduct difficulties may represent an appeal for help with other problems, such as depression, that result from feelings of being lonely, isolated, discouraged, or helpless. Treatment would be addressed to the underlying affective and cognitive factors presumed to result in the symptomatic conduct problems.

In a small number of cases, conduct difficulties coexist with *psychotic and organic disorders* and are presumed to be symptomatic of the impairments of judgment, impulse control, and other integrative functions of the personality that result from these underlying conditions. In youngsters with schizophrenia, thought and perceptual disorders impair judgments about the consequences of their behavior. These characteristics, combined with impaired impulse control, may result in aggression and other antisocial behaviors. Youths with temporal lobe epilepsy may engage in episodes of angry, assaultive, antisocial behavior, typically with little or no memory of what has occurred. Obviously, as illustrated in the following section, the type of treatment selected for these conduct difficulties would differ from the approaches used with similar behaviors presumed to reflect a different set of contributing factors.

## FACTORS CONTRIBUTING TO CONDUCT DISORDERS

As noted, conduct difficulties include a variety of behavior problems characterized by their social disruptiveness and thus represent the effects of a range of etiological and maintaining factors. Some psychological treatment models for aggression and related aberrant behaviors, such as those based on psychoanalytic concepts, view these behaviors as overt manifestations of internal drives and instincts. Treatment is thus focused on changing these covert controlling variables (Berman, 1984). Other models, such as those based on social learning theory, conceptualize disorders of conduct as reflecting inappropriate child–environment interactions and controls, and they focus treatment on these external conditions (Kazdin & Frame, 1983).

Factors assumed to contribute to chronic conduct difficulties thus represent both *external* environmental and broader sociological influences (e.g., peers, home and family, community, schools, and social values) and *internal* biological and psychological factors (e.g., genetic, constitutional, organic, and developmental deviations and personality dysfunctions). These various views emphasize that there is neither a single or small cluster of specific causes nor even a unique psychopathology, as might be found in other childhood disorders such as separation anxiety or functional enuresis. In fact, as implied previously, there is ample evidence that conduct difficulties may occur separately from or may accompany a variety of other psychological disorders described in various diagnostic and classification systems. Puig-Antich (1982), for example, report that 33% of a sample of prepubertal boys with major depression also met the DSM-III criteria for conduct disorder. A high correlation between attention-deficit disorder and conduct disorder has been reported for children and adolescents (Loney

& Milich, 1982; Sandberg, Rutter, & Taylor, 1978; Satterfield, Hoppe, & Schell, 1982). Conduct difficulties of clinical significance described in children with specific developmental disorders (Pfeffer, Plutchik, & Mizruchi, 1983), psychoses (Lewis, Shanok, Grant, & Ritvo, 1983), psychomotor epilepsy (Lewis, Pincus, Shanok, & Glaser, 1982), mental retardation (Gardner & Cole, 1984), and pervasive developmental disorders (Johnson & Baumeister, 1981) provide other illustrations of this interrelationship.

When aggression and oppositional behaviors are associated with other disorders, such as psychoses, seizures, or depression, that involve major problems of affect, cognition, or perception, the conduct symptoms often decrease when these underlying clinical conditions are treated. This situation was illustrated by Puig-Antich (1982), who reported, following successful drug treatment (with imipramine) of major depressive disorders in prepubertal boys who also presented conduct disorders, that the conduct problems, in most cases, also abated. Other studies have optimized improvement by a combination of physical and psychological therapies. An example was the successful inpatient treatment of an adolescent with problems of seizure activity and concomitant aggressive outbursts. A combination of antiseizure medication (carbamazepine) and psychological therapy procedures resulted in the control of both seizures and the related acting-out difficulties (Rapport, Sonis, Fialkov, Matson, & Kazdin, 1983). Weiner (1982), in describing the treatment of conduct-disordered delinquents, further illustrated the need to look beyond similarities in observable behaviors and to seek some understanding of why the behaviors are occurring. Conduct difficulties reflecting a psychopathic personality disorder, for example, are unlikely to change unless the child is provided long-term residential care and treatment. In contrast, Weiner noted that the same antisocial behaviors symptomatic of neuroses are "relatively easy to eliminate through numerous kinds of intervention, often on a short-term basis" (p. 421).

In the majority of children and adolescents who display symptoms of conduct disorders, there is no significant correlation with other physical or psychological disorders. Individuals who comprise this larger group, nonetheless, are a remarkably heterogeneous group from a psychological perspective. As a result, individualized child assessment becomes critical in designing the most therapeutically effective treatment program.

## ASSESSMENT FOR TREATMENT

The assessment of conduct difficulties seeks to provide an understanding of the multiple variables that are currently influencing these excessively occurring actions. As there is no single or simple psychological or physical mechanism that underlies conduct difficulties, and as these behaviors are interpersonal and thus must be viewed and treated in the context of social interactions, assessment includes an evaluation of the interpersonal and environmental context of the child's difficulties as well as the child's unique psychological structure and dynamics. The objectives of assessment are threefold: (1) to identify the various internal and external conditions under which the conduct difficulties are likely to occur; (2) to identify the functions served by the problem behaviors (i.e., what the behavior currently contributes to the child or adolescent); and (3) to identify the various child-specific personal characteristics that contribute to the problem

WILLIAM I. GARDNER
AND CHRISTINE L. COLE

behavior. An understanding of these child characteristics is viewed by most therapists as essential if effective and durable therapeutic gains are to be made.

The multicomponent assessment and treatment model of conduct disorders depicted in Figure 1 reflects the classes of variables that serve as the major emphasis of the various treatment approaches. Some psychological therapies focus on changing those environmental and/or personal factors (Class 1, 2, and 3 variables) assumed to be critical to the development and the continued occurrence of various conduct difficulties. Other behavior-change approaches concentrate directly on the problem behaviors by using procedures designed to suppress their continued occurrence (Class 4 factors). Therapies that emphasize Class 4 variables typically conceptualize aggression and related conduct difficulties as operant behavior that may be suppressed or weakened by the presentation of contingent aversive consequences. This treatment approach is typically undertaken without a knowledge of or hypotheses about the personal or environmental factors that may be contributing to the problem behaviors, and it is based on the supposition that the aversive consequences will be sufficient to suppress the problem behaviors by overcoming the effects of whatever may be producing or maintaining them (Foxx, McMorrow, Bittle, & Bechtel, 1986; Rolider & Van Houten, 1985a).

Therapies that focus treatment efforts primarily on Class 2 and Class 3 variables vary widely in their theoretical view of conduct difficulties and in their psychological treatment approaches. As depicted, the Class 2 and Class 3 variables include those internal physical conditions and personal characteristics

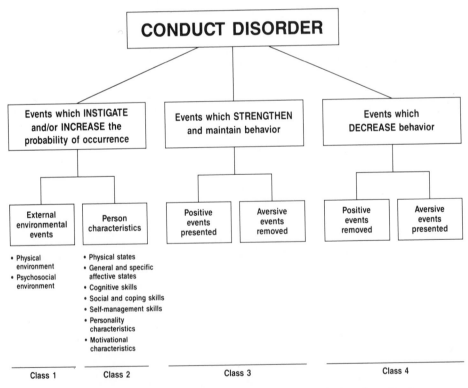

FIGURE 1. Multicomponent assessment and treatment model of conduct disorders.

that, in combination with external stimulus events, instigate and strengthen— that is, increase the likelihood of—specific conduct difficulties such as physical aggression, tantrums, or noncompliance. Examples of these personal characteristics are *physical states* (e.g., pain, fatigue, and drugs), *affective states* (e.g., anger, anxiety, and depression), and *cognitive variables* (e.g., covert verbal ruminations of a provocative nature and paranoid ideation).

Class 2 variables also include *skill areas* and *broader personality characteristics* that, because of their low strength or their absence, increase the likelihood of conduct problems in those inclined to behave disruptively. In illustration, an adolescent, when taunted by peers or criticized by adults, may react aggressively because he does not have alternative interpersonal skills in his repertoire, or if these skills are present, the skills to self-manage them are absent or inefficient (Goldstein, 1983). As a second example, a child may have a poor self-image, limited skills of empathy (Feshbach, 1983), or an underdeveloped ego (Keith, 1984) that increase the likelihood of conduct difficulties.

A final Class 2 child characteristic of significance in understanding and modifying conduct difficulties is the child's *motivational features.* For the behavior therapist, a knowledge of the incentives that are valuable to the person (e.g., adult approval, peer acceptance, or exerting control over others), as well as the variety and the relative influence of the aversive events that influence what the child or adolescent does (e.g., rejection by peers, adult reprimand, or anxiety), is of central importance in designing and providing effective therapeutic experiences. Other psychological therapies may view motivational variables such as aggressive instincts or strong feelings of guilt as relevant to the dynamics of acting-out or oppositional behaviors (Brinich, 1984).

In summary, some Class 2 child characteristics, such as anger, anxiety, or depression, may, *by their presence,* increase the likelihood of conduct difficulties. Other child variables, such as limited conflict-resolution skills, a low motivation to please adults or to abide by the rules of social conduct, or an underdeveloped social conscience, *by their absence or low strength,* render the child more vulnerable to conduct problems under conditions of provocation.

Class 1 variables include both physical and psychosocial environmental conditions that instigate or increase the likelihood that conduct difficulties will occur. These environmental conditions may include such factors as recurring social influences illustrated by sociological delinquency (Weiner, 1982), parental child-management characteristics (Patterson, 1982), or specific stimulation, such as task demands (Carr & Newsom, 1985).

These environmental variables interact with Class 2 variables to produce the problem behaviors on any particular occasion. In illustration of this interaction, an adolescent who is tauted by a peer may respond in a physically aggressive manner if currently in a state of angry emotional arousal. At a later time, when in a positive emotional state, this same adolescent may cope with the taunting and react in an appropriate manner. Treatment based on an assessment of Class 1 variables and the interactions with other influences is designed to eliminate, modify, or rearrange these contributing factors. As illustrated later, the child also may be taught various skills of counteracting the controlling influences of these factors.

Assessment data for each class of variables are obtained by means of a variety of direct observational, interview, and other psychological diagnostic procedures. Regardless of the specific procedures used, the assessment should be sensitive to the context in which the child's problems occur. As noted, conduct difficulties are a function not solely of the child's pathology, but of the child in interaction with various social and physical environments. That the child's problem behaviors can be understood best within this context is illustrated by the success of various family therapies (Forehand & McMahon, 1981; Patterson, 1982).

Assessment data gathered from these various sources are used by the therapist to develop a series of hunches about current factors that contribute to the recurring problem behaviors. Even though the therapist may attempt to reconstruct a previous history in an effort to understand how the current problems have developed over time, this understanding is seldom critical to the development of program hypotheses or to the realization of therapy goals. This assessment strategy is based on the assumption that there is no necessary relationship between those historical factors involved in the initial development of the problem behaviors (their etiology) and those factors that currently instigate and maintain them.

Again, hypotheses are developed about current environmental conditions and child characteristics that increase the likelihood that conduct difficulties will occur (e.g., anger or adult reprimand), as well as about the functions served by the behaviors (e.g., aggression produces peer or adult approval; results in adult distress; mother's demands are removed). Hypotheses are developed relative to Class 1, 2, and 3 influences, as each represents a potential target of therapeutic intervention.

Following the development of hypotheses concerning the factors that serve to instigate and strengthen or maintain the conduct problems, the therapist translates these into treatment program implications and then into specific intervention procedures relevant to each of these hypothesized influential variables. For example, if it were assumed that a child acts out to obtain adult attention with a group of peers, this hypothesis translates into the following program: (1) remove or minimize adult social attention following acting-out behavior; (2) provide adult social attention on frequent other occasions following appropriate behaviors; and, if needed, (3) provide specific skills training to ensure that the child will have appropriate attention-gaining skills for use in group settings.

These program implications are next translated into specific approaches involving (1) extinction and related differential reinforcement procedures (Carr, 1981) and (2) a social-skills training program (Goldstein, 1983). As a second example, the hypothesis may be developed that at least one function served by the highly disruptive behaviors of an adolescent toward a specific teacher is that they produce negative reactions from the teacher and other staff. This hypothesis could be translated into a program of related intervention procedures aimed at removing or reducing the negative reactions of staff, at increasing the positive reinforcement value of the teacher, and at teaching the adolescent other social skills that can be used to more appropriately exert personal influence over his or her teacher or other adults in authority roles.

## Psychological Treatment

Assessments of children and adolescents who present clinically significant problems of aggression and related conduct difficulties indicate wide individual differences in a number of personal characteristics. As noted, of special significance in treatment are the individually unique motivations for aggressive and related difficulties and the specific skills available for coping with internal and external sources of aggravations, frustrations, and negative emotional arousal. Additionally, the environmental contexts in which problems occur differ significantly.

Because of these wide individual differences, no single or best psychological treatment for conduct disorders has been developed. On the contrary, a diversity of psychological treatment approaches are currently available. These differ in (1) the concepts used to account for the development and continued occurrence of the disorder; (2) the therapeutic objectives developed; and (3) the treatment techniques used. In illustration, some behavioral approaches that make primary use of operant reinforcement concepts focus predominately on Class 3 and Class 4 variables (Figure 1). Patterson, Reid, Jones, and Conger (1975) view aggression and noncompliance as social behaviors that have been strengthened and that are currently maintained by the reinforcement that follows these behaviors. Treatment is designed to remove reinforcement for aggressive behavior, to provide reinforcement for prosocial behaviors, and to inhibit aggression through contingent aversive consequences. Other behavioral approaches emphasize Class 2 variables in viewing aggressive behaviors as reflecting social and coping skills deficits and focus therapy on the direct teaching of specific skill alternatives to replace the inappropriate conduct problems (e.g., Gardner & Cole, 1985; Goldstein & Pentz, 1984). Still other behavioral approaches place an emphasis on *both* Class 2 and 3 variables (e.g., Alexander, Barton, Schiavo, & Parsons, 1976). A therapeutic approach based on psychodynamic concepts, although emphasizing Class 2 variables in treatment, would use procedures designed to influence a different set of hypothesized etiological variables from those described above. For example, psychological treatment based on psychoanalytic concepts may focus attention on increasing the ego and superego strength of the child or adolescent (Berman, 1984).

As noted previously, major discussion is provided those treatment approaches associated with various behavior-therapy models because of the evidence supporting their efficacy. Treatments based on various psychodynamic models are typically not empirically validated. Brief illustrations of various psychodynamic approaches are followed here by a discussion of a number of behavior therapy procedures.

## Psychodynamic Approaches

In psychological treatment based on various psychodynamic models, the level of intervention is typically global and indirect. Discrete conduct problems, such as tantrums, noncompliance, or stealing, are seldom the target of treatment. Rather, broader personality structures and dispositions become the focus of treatment. The treatment goal is to alter these more basic or fundamental causal mechanisms, which are believed to influence the series of functionally related conduct difficulties. The specific personality structures or dynamics that become the target of treatment vary, depending on the theoretical perspective of the therapist. Three examples of psychodynamic treatment approaches for conduct-disordered children and adolescents are provided here.

Konstantareas and Homatidis (1984) illustrated the use of a group therapy approach with 12 severely conduct-disordered hospitalized children. The therapeutic intervention incorporated elements of psychodynamic therapy, social learning theory, and educational theory. The overall emphasis was on the use of cognitive and affective processes to assist the children in effectively negotiating everyday demands and expectations. The children were encouraged to evaluate and reflect on the impact of their behavior on others, and to provide support to group members in distress. They were also encouraged to express feelings of frustration appropriately, with an emphasis on assertive rather than aggressive expression.

Junior (6–8 years of age) and senior (10–11 years of age) clinic group members were observed for 8 weeks and again 5 months later for a 4-week period. Following intervention, both groups were more responsive to their peers' social overtures, and aggression in the senior clinic children was reduced. An examination of case files 6 months following treatment revealed that, consistent with these results, the senior clinic-group members were being integrated into regular school, whereas the majority of the junior clinic-group children had not made sufficient gains for such integration.

Brinich (1984) described his 10-year therapy experiences with young aggressive children and their parents. Consistent with Freud's psychoanalytic model (1920), Brinich views a child's aggressive responses as a direct result of his or her difficulties in dealing with aggressive impulses. Once these aggressive impulses and angry feelings emerge in action or words, the therapeutic work has begun. Brinich feels that further effective therapeutic effects occur with these children at the point where the *mothers* are able to take a new look at their children's impulses and to realize how they (the mothers) have responded to these impulses. Brinich considers transference the most difficult challenge encountered in treating young children together with their mothers. This treatment challenge includes transferences that mothers have made onto their children (mothers' seeing their children as representative of traumas or conflicts from the mothers' pasts), projection of the mothers' own aggressive impulses toward the therapist, and the children's attempts to repeat with the therapist aspects of their relationship with their mother. Although a number of case illustrations of successful treatment is provided, no empirical data were reported.

As a final example, Feshbach (1983) described the empathy training program, which was designed to teach aggressive children empathetic skills for the purpose of regulating aggressive behavior and promoting positive social behavior. Empathetic skills were defined as "the capacity to discriminate and identify an emotional state in another, the ability to assume the perspective and role of another, and the ability to respond affectively" (p. 267). This training program was based on data from a number of studies indicating that aggressive, acting-out children either had limited empathetic skills or did not use the available skills in a range of settings. Other studies have demonstrated a reduction in delinquency as perspective-taking skills increased.

Feshbach speculated the following chain of influence, relating empathy to aggression, aggressive drive, and anger. First, the empathetic person, as a result of understanding the other person's point of view, is less likely to become angered because he or she misinterpreted another's behavior. Second, research results suggest that empathy facilitates behaviors that are incompatible with aggression. Thus, theoretically, empathy should inhibit aggression. As aggressive behavior causes pain and distress, an empathetic child's observations of these distress cues should elicit distress responses in the child. As a result, the vicarious affective response of empathy should function to inhibit the child's aggressive inclinations. Use of the empathy training program with children has shown a reduction in aggression and an increase in prosocial characteristics (Feshbach, 1979; Feshbach & Feshbach, 1982). Although this therapeutic approach seems to be useful for some children who display social aggression, additional research is required to demonstrate its applicability to children with varying personal characteristics and types of conduct problems.

## Behavioral Approaches

The effectiveness of behavioral approaches to the treatment of conduct disorders in children and adolescents is well documented (Gardner & Cole, 1985; Kazdin & Frame, 1983; Varley, 1984). Behavioral approaches have been used successfully with such specific conduct problems as disruptive classroom behavior (Buckley & Walker, 1979), noncompliance (Patterson, 1974), and aggressiveness (Bornstein, Bellack, & Hersen, 1980; Schneider, 1974; Wells & Forehand, 1981). Most behavioral procedures are based on operant and social learning concepts that include consideration of the consequences that strengthen appropriate behavior (positive reinforcement procedures) and those that reduce the strength of inappropriate behavior (extinction and punishment procedures). More recently, a number of child characteristics have been considered in the development of cognitive-behavioral treatment strategies. A brief description of the available behavioral procedures is provided here.

### Positive Reinforcement Procedures

Positive reinforcement procedures involve the contingent presentation of consequences (e.g., praise, edibles, toys, activities, or tokens) following the occurrence of socially desired behaviors. The assumption is that, if alternative appropriate behaviors can be strengthened, these will occur and replace the conduct difficulties. The most commonly used positive reinforcement procedures are differential reinforcement, token economies, and contingency contracting.

*Differential Reinforcement.* Differential reinforcement procedures generally involve providing attention or other positive reinforcers contingent on the occurrence of appropriate behavior while ignoring undesired actions. There are various types of differential reinforcement procedures. *Differential reinforcement of other behavior* (DRO) involves specifying the inappropriate behaviors and providing reinforcement following periods of the nonoccurrence of these actions. When the reinforcer is delivered, the child could be doing virtually anything except engaging in the target behavior. Thus, a consideration in the selection of a DRO procedure is whether the child has appropriate behaviors in his or her repertoire that will spontaneously occur during periods of nonoccurrence of the undesired actions. If these behaviors are not present and are not actively taught, less adaptive responses such as inactivity or inattentiveness may be strengthened. Providing reinforcement for positive ways of behaving, rather than for *not* engaging in the undesirable response, may be a more useful approach.

To increase its effectiveness, the DRO procedure has typically been used in combination with other procedures in the treatment of conduct difficulties in children (e.g., Repp & Deitz, 1974; Rolider & Van Houten, 1984). Repp and Deitz, for example, reduced aggressive behaviors in three mentally retarded children by combining DRO with various other techniques. In one case, aggressive behavior in a severely mentally retarded 12-year-old boy was reduced with a DRO (reward provided for periods of no aggression) and a 30-second time-out procedure. In a second study, aggressive classroom behaviors in a moderately mentally retarded 8-year-old boy were decreased by means of a combined verbal reprimand ("No") and DRO (puzzle pieces earned for intervals of no inappropriate behavior) procedure. Finally, exchangeable tokens were provided to a moderately mentally retarded 13-year-old boy after every 15 minutes in which aggressive behavior did not occur, and each inappropriate behavior resulted in the loss of all the tokens accumulated. In each case, the use of the DRO procedure in combination with other techniques successfully reduced the conduct problems.

More specific differential reinforcement procedures have, in fact, been developed as alternatives to reinforcing the nonoccurrence of an inappropriate behavior. With *differential reinforcement of alternative responses* (DRA), reinforcement is provided following the occurrence of specific appropriate behaviors. *Differential reinforcement of incompatible behavior* (DRI) focuses on reinforcing specific behaviors that are appropriate and that are also incompatible with the undesired actions. Leitenberg and colleagues (Leitenberg, Burchard, Burchard, Fuller, & Lysaght, 1977) compared two differential reinforcement procedures, DRO and DRA, in the treatment of sibling conflict in the home. In the DRO condition, children were provided tangible reinforcers for not engaging in conflict during designated 1-minute intervals. The DRA condition involved presenting a reinforcer to each child who engaged in appropriate interactions during 1-minute intervals. Although both procedures were effective in suppressing conflict, DRA resulted in higher rates of positive interactions than DRO.

A final differential reinforcement procedure is *differential reinforcement of low rates of behavior* (DRL), in which children are reinforced for engaging less frequently in an undesired behavior. Typically, reinforcers are provided as long as undesired behaviors do not exceed a specified frequency. For example, Deitz (1977) decreased disruptive classroom behaviors in a 6-year-old first-grade girl. During intervention, the student was informed that for every 5-minute interval in which she engaged in less than two disruptive actions, she would receive a reinforcer. If she engaged in the second disruption, the interval would start over again. Thus, the child received the reinforcer only if she maintained a low rate of disruptive behavior. The DRL procedure was effective in reducing the child's disruptive behavior.

*Token Economies.* Token economies involve the contingent presentation of conditioned reinforcers following specific appropriate behaviors. These conditioned reinforcers, called *tokens*, are objects that have no intrinsic value (e.g., marks, stamps, or poker chips) but that acquire positive reinforcement value by being exchanged for various reinforcing events, referred to as *backup reinforcers*. These may include a wide range of objects, events, activities, and privileges.

Token economies have been used extensively in special-education, remedial, and regular classrooms; in institutional and community-based residential settings; and in vocational and other rehabilitation settings. They are especially valuable in the treatment of chronic conduct disorders in classrooms or institutional settings. In fact, token economies have been demonstrated to be one of the most effective forms of institutional treatment for adjudicated delinquents (Sutker, Archer, & Kilpatrick, 1981). In such programs, a frequently encountered problem is motivating adolescents to participate in desired activities and behaviors. Many are not motivated to engage in appropriate actions merely to obtain adult social attention or approval. Thus, token economies that provide immediate, frequent, and potentially meaningful consequences may be valuable in ensuring participation in potentially therapeutic experiences.

One well-known program for predelinquent youths that has a token economy as an integral component is called Achievement Place. Participants in this program earn points for engaging in specific appropriate behaviors (e.g., being neat and clean, performing chores around the house, and receiving good grades at school) and lose points for engaging in specific inappropriate behaviors (e.g., poor grades, threatening others, lying, stealing, and fighting). Points are exchanged for such privileges as staying up late, going downtown, watching TV, using tools, riding a bicycle, and receiving an allowance. Beneficial effects were demonstrated on such behaviors as social interaction and completion of homework and chores. Additionally, those in the program committed fewer crimes and had fewer contacts with police than delinquents placed on probation or in other settings where the program was not in effect (Kirigin, Braukmann, Atwater, & Wolf, 1982; Kirigin, Wolf, Braukmann, Fixsen, & Phillips, 1979).

Agee (1979) also described the successful use of a token economy system in the treatment of the most incorrigible and disturbed juvenile offenders in a state training school. The program incorporated various levels, from maximum external control, in which staff monitored behavior and delivered immediate consequences, through levels involving both external control and self-control, to a level where the clients graduated out of the point system. Additionally, the treatment emphasis gradually shifted from a focus on institutional adjustment toward behaviors important for a positive adjustment in the community. Various support services, such as staff visits, outpatient therapy, and group therapy, were provided following discharge from the program. In addition to being an effective treatment strategy, Agee's program has been found to be more cost effective than standard institutional programs (Agee, 1979).

*Contingency Contracting.* Contingency contracting involves agreements between change agents and conduct-disordered children or adolescents. The contract specifies the behavioral goals that are to be attained on a regular basis in exchange for predetermined positive reinforcers. Contingency contracting is typically used with older children and adolescents, as it involves mutual negotiation of the terms of the contract.

An advantage of using contingency contracts with individuals who are negativistic or argumentative is the reduced opportunity for confrontations concerning expected behaviors and the associated contingencies. Further, contingency contracts potentially reduce the "controlling" aspects of treatment by dividing responsibilities and consequences equally between the child and the change agent (Ayllon & Skuban, 1973).

WILLIAM I. GARDNER
AND CHRISTINE L. COLE

Bristol (1976) described the use of a contingency contract with an 8-year-old second-grade boy who constantly fought at school. As specified in the contract, the child received signatures from the teacher for no fighting that could be accumulated toward the purchase of a reward. His parents provided praise, posted the cards, and offered extra rewards for signatures received. His fighting was reduced to near-zero levels by means of this contingency contracting procedure.

With more serious problems presented by the conduct-disordered adolescent, however, contingency contracting has its limitations when used as the major treatment approach (Weathers & Liberman, 1975). Its usefulness is increased when it is one component of a larger treatment plan in structured residential settings (Varley, 1984).

## Punishment Procedures

One major behavioral approach to the treatment of conduct problems in children and adolescents involves the use of various types of behavior suppression, or punishment, procedures (Fehrenbach & Thelen, 1982; Gardner & Cole, 1984). These approaches focus directly on the deceleration of specific problem behaviors through the contingent presentation of aversive consequences or the removal of positive consequences following the undesired actions. Although behaviors are assumed to be maintained by a variety of factors, the difficulty in many cases of identifying and modifying these results is a primary emphasis in discovering how the problem behaviors can be most efficiently reduced or eliminated. The implicit assumption underlying this behavior-suppression approach is that once the undesired behaviors are reduced, the child will engage in more appropriate alternative actions. In some instances, additional procedures for teaching or strengthening alternative skills are used in combination with punishment. In fact, a number of studies have demonstrated that a reinforcement program for prosocial behavior is needed to ensure that aggressive and disruptive behaviors will be maintained at a reduced level (e.g., Wahler & Fox, 1980). The punishment procedures discussed here are time-out, response cost, overcorrection, and the presentation of other aversive consequences.

*Time-Out.* Time-out from positive reinforcement (TO) usually refers to a social isolation procedure in which the child is removed from a potentially reinforcing situation for a specific period of time following the undesired behavior. The critical feature of TO is delineating a time period during which reinforcement is unavailable. Calhoun and Matherne (1975) successfully used a social-isolation TO procedure in the classroom with an aggressive, mildly mentally retarded 7-year-old girl who was considered an extreme behavior problem by the training-center directors and teachers. Following target aggressive responses (hitting, kicking, spitting, and throwing), the child was placed in a TO booth until she had been quiet for 2 minutes. The result of this procedure was a significant decrease in aggressive behavior.

For TO to be most effective in suppressing behavior, the environment from which the child is removed must be reinforcing. It has been suggested that the effectiveness of TO may be enhanced if a differential reinforcement procedure is implemented before the TO procedure. Walle, Hobbs, and Caldwell (1984) examined this notion with 25 mothers and their 28 children (2–6 years of age) who engaged in conduct problems. The mothers provided DRI (praise for compliance) and TO (removal of attention and toys for 2 minutes) to their children in various sequences (TO followed by DRI or DRI followed by TO), or they administered both TO and DRI concurrently. TO was observed to produce greater suppression of noncompliance when preceded by DRI. Further, for several children, DRI effectively maintained reductions in noncompliance produced by prior use of TO. Thus, the initial implementation of differential praise appeared to enhance the efficacy of TO, and prior use of TO appeared to enable the differential reinforcement procedure to effectively maintain reductions in noncompliance.

It has been suggested that there is an optimal TO duration for effectively reducing undesired behavior and that additional time spent in TO may be unnecessary or even detrimental. Although one study with aggressive, mildly mentally retarded institutionalized delinquents found 30-minute TO to be more effective than 5-minute TO (Burchard & Barrera, 1972), the data have generally shown no difference in the effectiveness of varying TO durations (e.g., Pendergrass, 1971; White, Nielsen, & Johnson, 1972). However, both White et al. and Kendall, Nay, and Jeffers (1975) reported a contrast effect. Shorter durations were effective unless preceded by TOs of longer duration. The results of a more recent study with psychiatrically hospitalized children and adolescents indicated no additional reduction in frequency of assaults with longer TOs (15 minutes versus 30, 45, 60, and 90 minutes). In addition, the longer the TO duration, the longer the time period required for the children to calm down while in seclusion. These findings suggest that short TOs may be a more therapeutic alternative (Benjamin, Mazzarins, & Kupfersmid, 1983). Forehand and McMahon (1981), in training the parents of young compliant children, suggested that

> the most effective and efficient TO condition is one in which the parent removes the child from all sources of reinforcement rather than just ignoring the child, uses a TO duration longer than 1 minute (but for ethical reasons under 5 minutes), and releases the child from TO when the child is being quiet. (p. 148)

A potential problem in implementing TO procedures with conduct-disordered children is that, when the child is given the instruction to go to the TO location, strong resistance is likely, in the form of tantrum behavior or attempts at escaping the situation (Roberts, 1982). In an effort to attenuate the resistance to chair TOs in children referred for treatment of preschool conduct problems, Roberts (1984) used a procedure of reviewing all TO contingencies with the child just before the child's initial experience with TO. This procedure was based on the hypothesis that preawareness of the contingencies (e.g., tantrumming results in remaining longer on the chair) would decrease resistance to TO. However, this review procedure showed no additional beneficial effects. It appeared that children had to experience at least one TO and/or escape effort before suppressive effects were observed.

A number of variations of TO do not involve removing the children from the situation in which the undesired behavior occurred. One such TO is called *contingent observation*, in which the child is asked to step away from an ongoing activity but may continue watching as peers are reinforced for engaging in the desired actions. Foxx and Shapiro (1978) evaluated this contingent-observation

William I. Gardner
and Christine L. Cole

TO procedure within a classroom reinforcement program for mentally retarded boys. Each child received social and, occasionally, edible reinforcement for performing work and for wearing a colorful ribbon around his neck. Whenever disruptive behavior occurred, the ribbon was removed, and the child was prevented from receiving any reinforcement for 3 minutes. This TO procedure effectively reduced disruptive classroom behavior.

A similar TO procedure was used with an aggressive, mentally retarded, blind and deaf 15-year-old female in a vocational training setting. She was initially provided a small jewelry pin for her blouse. Following periods of no physical aggression (slapping, punching, or scratching), she was reinforced with verbal praise and an edible treat. After each aggressive episode, the teacher removed the pin from the adolescent and terminated interaction for 1 minute. The pin was then replaced with the instruction, "Keep your hands to yourself to keep your pin." The resulting reduction of aggression maintained at near-zero levels at 5-month follow-up (Luiselli, Myles, Evans, & Boyce, 1985).

Another TO variation involves the withdrawal of specific reinforcers, such as music or toys, contingent on inappropriate behavior. The usefulness of this procedure was demonstrated with an profoundly mentally retarded 8-year-old girl (Barmann, Croyle-Barmann, & McLain, 1980). Following each episode of disruptive behavior while riding on the school bus (e.g., screaming, crying, kicking, or falling to floor), music that was being played was interrupted for a brief period. The resulting significant reduction in disruptive behavior was maintained for 8 weeks following program withdrawal.

*Response Cost.* Response cost involves the contingent loss of positive reinforcement following the occurrence of undesired behavior. Generally, a fine is imposed, such as the loss of a priviledge or the loss of points or tokens earned. The most common application of response cost to conduct disorders in children and adolescents is within token economy programs in educational or residential settings. This finding was illustrated by Phillips, Phillips, Fixsen, and Wolf (1971), who used response cost in combination with token reinforcement to reduce a variety of acting-out behaviors in predelinquent boys.

Rapport, Murphy, and Bailey (1982) used a response cost procedure with two second-grade boys who had high rates of disruptive behavior and poor attentiveness, and who did not complete their academic seat work. Each was informed that he would receive 20 minutes of free time for working on his tasks without disruption, but that 1 minute would be lost for instances of inattentive behavior. This contingent withdrawal of minutes of free time improved attentiveness and academic performance in these two boys.

Although response cost may be effective in suppressing a variety of conduct problems in children and adolescents, there are potential disadvantages. For example, the implementation of a response cost procedure may foster negative attitudes toward those administering the fines. Also, experiencing repeated fines may reduce a child's motivation to engage in the desired behaviors. Thus, token economies may, in fact, be more effective when response cost contingencies are eliminated. Hogan and Johnson (1985) evaluated the effects of eliminating the response cost procedure in a token economy program for adolescents with behavior problems. As hypothesized, the elimination of the response cost procedure produced decreases in the frequency of misbehavior reports, use of the TO room, and the number of episodes involving violence. Thus, a shift to a more positive approach may increase the effectiveness of a token economy program that originally used negative contingencies such as response cost. As noted, however, these results may have been related to the initial control gained over the client's behavior by the response cost contingency.

*Overcorrection.* Overcorrection is a combination of procedures designed to punish undesired behaviors while providing opportunities to practice more appropriate behaviors. As this approach was initially developed, the child is required to restore the environment to an improved state (restitution) and repeatedly to practice incompatible behavior in the situation in which the problem behavior occurred (positive practice). If, for example, a child physically injures a peer in school, he or she may be required to accompany the victim to the nurse's office; to assist in cleaning, medicating, and bandaging the wound; to assist in filling out the necessary reports; and to apologize to each person in the classroom. If the child refuses to comply, he or she is physically guided in the corrective responses.

Overcorrection was used by Ollendick and Matson (1976) with an aggressive preschool boy who engaged in frequent hitting and temper tantrums. Each time the child struck his mother, he was required to pat the hit area for 30 seconds and to apologize 10 times. Aggression decreased slightly with this procedure. During the next phase, the boy was required to engage in the above restitution and then raise and lower the arm he had used for hitting 40 times. The child's hitting behaviors were eliminated by this procedure. Foxx and Bechtel (1982) provided a description and critical review of the overcorrection procedure and its use with a variety of aggressive and related behaviors.

*Other Aversive Consequences.* A variety of other types of aversive consequences have been used to suppress conduct problems in children and adolescents. Examples of the aversive stimuli presented contingent on acting-out behavior include verbal reprimands, loud noises, unpleasant tastes, noxious odors, and mild electric shock. Greene and Hoats (1971), for example, described the use of an aversive tickling procedure to reduce physical aggression in a mentally retarded adolescent. Staff approached her from behind and tickled her under the arms "forcefully and somewhat aggressively" for 3–5 seconds following each target behavior.

More recently, aromatic ammonia spirits were applied contingent on the severe aggression of a mentally retarded and behavior-disordered 7-year-old boy in a day treatment program. Aggression included such behaviors as hitting, pushing, or kicking others; throwing objects; and jerking objects away from others. Immediately upon onset of an aggressive response, the teacher-therapist raised an open vial of ammonia to the child's nose and stated, "No, Paul! Don't [specifying the aggressive response]." In addition to abrupt suppression of the target aggressive behaviors, temporary positive effects were noted for untreated inappropriate vocalizations and participation in planned activities (Doke, Wolery, & Sumberg, 1983).

One practical disadvantage of using such punishment procedures is that they cannot always be implemented immediately following inappropriate behavior, such as when a child engages in tantrum behavior in public. One way to

WILLIAM I. GARDNER
AND CHRISTINE L. COLE

overcome this difficulty is to use some type of procedure to mediate the behavior and to present the consequences at a later time. For example, Rolider and Van Houten (1985b) implemented a delayed-punishment procedure mediated by playing audiotape segments to suppress tantrum behavior in four conduct-disordered boys. A short segment of tape-recorded tantrum behavior was played and was immediately followed by punishment (e.g., movement suppression or verbal reprimand), often several hours after the tantrums had occurred. Recreating the tantrum behaviors by playing audiotape segments was an effective mediator for delayed punishment.

Although the presentation of aversive consequences following misbehavior may successfully reduce conduct problems in children, the treatment effects may not generalize to new situations (e.g., Burcher & King, 1971). Further, the intervention may produce negative side effects in some individuals. As one example, electric shock administered contingent on physical aggression in a profoundly mentally retarded 14-year-old boy resulted in his wetting himself, and "when shock was due, Mike ran to a corner of the room, jumped in place, hit himself and yelled" (Birnbrauer, 1968, p. 206). Thus, it cannot be assumed that a particular procedure will automatically produce the same effects in different children. The unique features of each individual must be carefully assessed before the selection and implementation of any aversive procedure.

## Removal of Aversive Events

There is substantial support in the behavioral literature for the notion that conduct disorders in children and adolescents may be maintained by contingent attention delivered by others (Hawkins, Peterson, Schweid, & Bijou, 1966). As a result, the treatment of choice has consisted of procedures designed to minimize or eliminate attention for the undesirable behavior. Although attention remains an important variable to consider, recent research suggests that acting-out behavior, at least in demand situations, may represent a form of escape-motivated behavior rather than an attention-getting response (Carr, Newsom, & Binkhoff, 1980). This interpretation suggests that one possible treatment approach is to make the demand situation less aversive, a change that should result in fewer escape responses (i.e., acting-out behaviors).

Carr and Newsom (1985) evaluated this procedure with three developmentally disabled boys attending a day-school program. Based on the assumption that tantrums served as escape behavior maintained by negative reinforcement, these authors provided strongly preferred reinforcers (e.g., special foods) contingent on compliance with demands. The assumption was that attempted escape from a demand situation containing strongly preferred reinforcers would be less functional than escape from a situation containing only demands. The addition of the strongly preferred food as a reinforcer for compliance not only produced a sharp increase in the rate of compliance but also resulted in the reduction of tantrums to near-zero levels.

In a related study, Carr and Durand (1985) taught functional communication skills to developmentally disabled children who engaged in aggression and other disruptive behaviors under the stimulus conditions of low levels of adult attention or high levels of task difficulty. These newly acquired communication skills, used to alter the controlling antecedent aversive conditions by obtaining the desired social attention or assistance with difficult tasks, resulted in a reduction of the conduct problems. Of related interest is a study by Mace, Page, Ivancic, and O'Brien (1986) that demonstrated wide individual differences in the types of antecedent conditions that would produce aggressive and related disruptive behaviors in conduct-disordered children and adolescents. Social disapproval, adult demands, and reduced social attention produced varying effects on the behaviors of different children. Thus, a treatment program designed to reduce or remove the antecedent aversive conditions presumed to instigate the conduct difficulties must be preceded by a child-specific assessment to identify these conditions.

### Skill-Training Approaches

It is also evident that skill deficits contribute to children's conduct disorders (Clarizio & McCoy, 1983; Patterson *et al.*, 1975). This observation has resulted in a number of recent cognitive-behavioral approaches that put major efforts into reducing deficit social, coping, and self-management skills.

*Social-Skills-Training Approaches.* Goldstein and colleagues (e.g., Goldstein & Pentz, 1984) have developed a multicomponent psychological-skills-training program for use with groups of aggressive individuals, particularly aggressive adolescents (see Goldstein, Sprafkin, Gershaw, & Klein, 1980). This structured-learning approach consists of a number of therapy procedures recommended by Bandura (1973), including modeling, role playing, performance feedback, and transfer training. In *modeling*, each social skill is subdivided into a number of behavioral steps. Therapists portray the steps of the skill being used in a variety of settings relevant to the client's daily life and direct the client's attention to how the actors in each vignette model the behavioral steps. *Role playing* is used to encourage realistic behavioral rehearsal by clients. To enhance realism, the primary actor is asked to choose a peer to play the role of another person who is relevant in his or her life to the skill problem. Finally, clients are encouraged to follow the behavioral steps while role playing.

On the completion of each role play, brief *feedback* is provided. This consists of such information as how well the trainees followed the steps of the skill or in what ways they departed from them, the potential impact of their behavior on others, and encouragement to use the behaviors role-played in real life. Finally, procedures are used to enhance the transfer and the maintenance of the skills learned during training to the client's actual real-life settings. These procedures include the provision of general principles, response availability, identical elements, stimulus variability, and programmed reinforcement (Goldstein, 1981; Goldstein & Kanfer, 1979).

Reviewing 30 studies of the use of psychological skills training with aggressive adolescents, Goldstein and Pentz (1984) concluded that the results for skill acquisition have been consistently positive. Aggressive adolescents are able to learn a variety of new interpersonal, aggressive-management, affect-relevant, and related psychological skills by using this skills-training approach. However, the maintenance and transfer of these newly acquired skills appear to occur only when training procedures explicitly designed to enhance generalization are implemented.

*Coping-Skills-Training Approaches.* A variety of problem-solving and other coping-skills-training approaches have been developed for use with conduct-disordered children and adolescents. Adolescents, for example, may be taught specific skills of interpersonal transaction (problem-solving), assuming another person's point of view (role taking), and inhibiting their own impulses (self-control) (Little & Kendall, 1979). Novaco (1979) described the use of another anger-control procedure referred to as *stress inoculation.* In this approach, the child or adolescent is encouraged to identify circumstances that arouse anger and to discriminate between justified and unjustified anger. Alternative coping skills are then taught through modeling and rehearsal. Finally, the child practices the skills in imagined and role-played interactions. Although this is a promising therapy approach to stress-related conduct difficulties, additional empirical research on this procedure is needed to substantiate its effectiveness with children and adolescents.

Vaughn, Ridley, and Bullock (1984) evaluated the efficacy of an interpersonal problem-solving-skills-training approach for aggressive young children. The skills taught included language concepts, empathy, goal identification, generating alternatives, evaluating consequences, cue sensitivity, and rehearsal. Children trained in these problem-solving strategies were able to generate a greater number of alternative solutions to interpersonal problems with peers than were control group subjects. These children were also less likely to engage in irrelevant talk and were more likely to respond to the problem-solving task with relevant responses and requests for additional information or for time to think about the problem. These gains were maintained 3 months after training was completed. Although this program is promising as a therapeutic procedure for young aggressive children, the effects of the training program on the reduction of aggressive behaviors in naturalistic settings have not been demonstrated.

Other popular coping-skills-training programs include (1) the "think aloud" program, developed for use with aggressive, impulsive children (Camp, Blom, Herbert, & van Doorninck, 1977; Camp & Ray, 1984); (2) the "turtle technique," in which children are taught to use covert problem-solving and to pretend to withdraw into an imaginary turtle shell in provocative situations (Robin, Schneider, & Dolnick, 1976; Schneider, 1974); and (3) a cognitive restructuring procedure in which aggressive children are taught to engage in more adaptive cognitive behaviors in provocative situations (Forman, 1980).

*Self-Management Training Approaches.* Other cognitive-behavioral strategies focus on teaching various skills of self-management. Children may be taught to *self-monitor* (observe, label, and record), *self-evaluate* (assess themselves against a standard), and *self-consequate* (deliver pleasant or unpleasant consequences) following their appropriate and inappropriate actions.

An example of a self-management program for disruptive adolescents in a school setting was described recently by Brigham and colleagues (Brigham, Hopper, Hill, de Armas, & Newsom, 1985). Students who had 12 or more detentions within one quarter for infractions of school rules (e.g., arriving at class late, using foul language, or provoking other students) were required to attend a self-management class. In addition to providing basic concepts of behavior management, the class taught self-management concepts, experimental logic, and specific self-management procedures. Each student was required to successfully complete a self-management project. The program was conducted for three consecutive school years with a total of 103 students. The vast majority of these students reduced their level of disruptive behavior after participation in this self-managment class. Follow-up data for periods of as long as 2 years showed continued lower levels of detentions.

The additional skill of *self-instruction* (verbal mediation) is an integral component of many self-control programs. Meichenbaum's original self-instructional training program involves teaching aggressive children self-verbalizations to direct their own task performance (Meichenbaum & Goodman, 1971). The specific self-instructions taught include identifying the problem, labeling the alternative solutions, evaluating the solutions, choosing one solution, correcting errors, and providing self-reinforcement. The training begins with an adult modeling self-statements while performing a task, and it gradually shifts the responsibility for self-instruction and task performance to the child. The ultimate goal is for the child to perform the task while self-instructing covertly. Research indicates successful use of this approach with hyperactive and impulsive children.

Although various skill-training approaches have been demonstrated to effectively reduce conduct problems in some children and adolescents, the results have been mixed (Camp & Ray, 1984; Hobbs, Moguin, Tryoler, & Lahey, 1980; Kennedy, 1984; Wilson, 1984), and most studies have been conducted with impulsive and hyperactive children (Kazdin & Frame, 1983). However, these approaches are currently undergoing extensive research investigation and should be considered by clinicians in developing treatment programs for conduct-disordered children and adolescents.

## Behavioral Family Therapy

A number of behaviorally oriented therapies are available for use with the families of children and adolescents who have conduct disorders (Griest & Wells, 1983). In each of these, the unit of treatment is the family. Conduct difficulties among young members of the family are viewed in terms of mutually influencing patterns of behaviors and relationships. Behavioral family therapies include operant approaches, cognitive approaches, and approaches that combine both operant and cognitive-behavioral concepts and procedures.

*Operant Approaches.* One group of behavioral family therapies is based on operant and social-learning-theory assumptions that the conduct problems of children and adolescents are learned and maintained by a variety of positive and negative reinforcing consequences provided in the social environment (Forehand & McMahon, 1981; Patterson, 1982; Patterson *et al.*, 1975). In observations of families of aggressive and noncompliant children, Patterson (1982) saw a pattern of coercive interaction in which the parents and the conduct-disordered children were trapped in many different types of negative relationships and life experiences. In this "coercive process," the behavior of one family member is typically reinforced by positive consequences, whereas the behavior of the other is maintained by aversive events. For example, a child may engage in tantrum behavior (e.g., shouting, thrashing about, and crying) followed by the mother's compliance with the child's demand. In this case, the mother's giving in is negatively reinforced by the termination of the aversive tantrum behavior, and the child's tantrum behavior is positively reinforced by having his or her demands met. Patterson hypothesized that both family and school interaction patterns reflect this coercive mechanism.

From this perspective, the treatment objective is to increase the frequency of reciprocal family interactions (i.e., individuals' reinforcing each other positively at an equitable rate) and to decrease coercive interactions. The specific therapy procedures used include (1) teaching the parents the basic principles of reinforcement; (2) identifying, defining, and recording the frequencies of specific child behaviors; (3) parent-training groups in which modeling and role playing are used by the therapists to teach the desired parent behaviors; and (4) providing positive consequences for appropriate child behavior and negative consequences for aggressive or noncompliant behavior. In addition, Patterson (1982) emphasized the importance of family management variables in the disruption and management of families. These include such practices as the establishment of clearly specified house rules, clearly delineated structures and time schedules for individual and family activities, rules for social behavior among family members, parental monitoring of the child's whereabouts, and the child's fulfillment of basic expectations.

Horne and Van Dyke (1983) reported the results of an intervention with 56 families referred to the Oregon Social Learning Center for the treatment of an aggressive child. The target children had a mean age of 8.5 years, and all were male. The average number of treatment sessions provided was 22 (range: 3–85). The observational data from pretreatment to posttreatment showed a significant reduction in the rate of aggression in the target children, their mothers, and their siblings. These positive effects were generally maintained at 12-month follow-up.

There are obviously some families, however, for which this type of treatment is ineffective. In an attempt to identify specific predictors of treatment outcome in 34 families with conduct-disordered children, Webster-Stratton (1985) assessed mothers in terms of socioeconomic variables, depression, attitudes toward their children, number of negative life experiences, and behavioral observations in the home. At 1-year follow-up, the *socioeconomic-disadvantage* and *negative-life-stress* variables were found to correctly classify from 70% to 80% of the families relative to the outcome criteria. Within the variable of socioeconomic disadvantage, the more disadvantaged the family (single-parent, low-income, and low-education), the less likely it was to benefit from family therapy. Coming from a single-parent family was most strongly associated with nonresponse. This finding would suggest that lack of social support is an important predictor of treatment failure. The correlation between the amount of negative life stress experienced and the treatment outcome suggests that those mothers who perceived that they had had more negative life stresses over the previous year also had more negative attitudes toward their children's behaviors. This finding supports the "coercion process" notion described by Patterson and Reid (1970) and by Wahler (1980).

Other investigations have also reported limited succes in using such family therapy procedures with low socioeconomic families (Patterson *et al.*, 1975; Rinn, Vernon, & Wise, 1975), families in which the parents have lower levels of education (Karoly & Rosenthal, 1977), single-parent families (Strain, Young, &

Horowitz, 1981), families maintaining limited levels of positive and functional extrafamilial interactions (Dumas & Wahler, 1983; Wahler, 1980), and families affected by marital conflict (Bernal, Klinnert, & Schultz, 1980; Reisinger, Frangia, & Hoffman, 1976). Thus, although the effectiveness of operant family-therapy procedures in the treatment of children's conduct problems has been demonstrated, the adaptation and generalization of this treatment across family populations have not met with consistent success.

*Cognitive Approaches.* In recent years, expanded behavioral family-intervention models have been suggested as a means of targeting these broader socio-contextual variables. Some of these behavioral approaches attempt to change faulty family communication patterns rather than to modify behavioral contingencies within the family. These approaches use cognitive-behavioral concepts and related intervention procedures and are based on the central assumption that conduct disorders reflect irrational cognitions or deficit cognitive problem-solving skills. The objective of changing family communication patterns is to teach families how to negotiate conflict (Robin, 1981).

Gant and colleagues (Gant, Barnard, Kuehn, Jones, & Christophersen, 1981), for example, used a communication-training procedure with court-referred lower-middle-class families. The treatment, which was held in the families' homes, consisted of therapists' modeling positive communication and teaching parents to monitor their communication patterns. These families also engaged in discussions of family issues that were audiotaped and rated for constructive communication (e.g., approval, encouragement, and validation) and nonconstructive communication (e.g., criticism, nagging, and lecturing). That treated families interacted constructively significantly more than the control families and interacted nonconstructively significantly less. Additionally, the self-report ratings were also slightly better for the treated families.

*Combined Approaches.* A final behavioral family-therapy approach represents a combination of the operant and cognitive models. An analysis of the problem behavior serves as the basis for rearranging problem social contingencies within the family. Additionally, community patterns and problem-solving strategies are taught. A series of studies have been conducted by Alexander, Parsons, and colleagues that represent this combined approach to behavioral family therapy (Alexander & Parsons, 1973; Alexander *et al.*, 1976; Klein, Alexander, & Parsons, 1977). These studies are based on a conceptualization of conduct problems as a function of family system deterioration.

In one example, the subjects studied were court-referred families of adolescents (13–16 years of age) who were generally involved in offenses of "soft" delinquency (e.g., shoplifting). Combined behavioral family therapy involved communication training designed to teach skills conducive to negotiation (e.g., seeking clarification, seeking information, giving feedback, and keeping statements brief and direct) and contingency contracting around specific problem behaviors. The results from posttest audiotapes of parent–child discussions indicated that the behavioral treatment group engaged in more equal communication interactions, less silence, and more clarification-seeking interruptions than families involved in client-centered treatment or no treatment (Alexander & Parsons, 1973).

It is evident that behavioral procedures can be used effectively with families of conduct-disordered children and adolescents. However, it also is apparent that this effectiveness may be restricted to families with certain characteristics (e.g., middle class, intact, and educated). As is the case with other types of treatment, success tends to be lower with disorganized or socially disadvantaged families. Comprehensive treatment packages such as those that combine both operant and cognitive-behavioral procedures may prove to be more effective with families presenting more serious problems. Additionally, an expanded version of the behavioral family intervention model, called *ecobehavioral*, has been suggested (Campbell, O'Brien, Bickett, & Lutzker, 1983; Rios & Gutierrez, 1986). This ecobehavioral perspective is a multidimensional assessment and treatment approach involving behavioral parent training, as well as the treatment of individual and family problems (e.g., marital counseling, intensive job counseling, hygiene management, nutritional instruction, and relaxation training to reduce parental stress). Thus, a need exists for further research aimed at producing effective and durable behavior change in children from families with a variety of characteristics.

## Conclusions

A range of psychological treatment procedures is available for use with children and adolescents with conduct difficulties. Of those that have been evaluated empirically, various behaviorally based therapies have produced the best treatment results. Because of the heterogeneity of the children treated and of the specific problem behaviors that have served as the focus of treatment, only tentative conclusions can be drawn about the general efficacy of any particular procedure or treatment package. It is true that positive changes have been reported to result from a variety of treatment procedures ranging from specific operant ones, such as punishment and differential reinforcement, to complex therapy packages involving multiple operant and cognitive-behavioral techniques. Successful programs have included the family as the unit of treatment in addition to the more frequent focus on the problem behaviors presented by individual children.

A number of restrictions limit the widespread applicability of these positive results. Inadequate descriptions of child characteristics other than the specific target behaviors, inadequate descriptions of the treatment program and the interpersonal and social context of the treatment, limited control of extratreatment factors that may influence the results, limited duration of treatment, and absence of comparisons with other forms of treatment represent some of these restrictions. Of most significance is the finding that, with a few notable exceptions, the durability over time and the transfer across situations and settings of positive therapeutic changes have not been demonstrated consistently. In fact, most studies have not even addressed these problems. This situation is equally true of the more traditional operant treatment procedures that tend to treat the problem behavior directly and of the newer cognitive-behavioral programs that teach deficit skills presumed to influence the conduct problems. An exception to this finding is found in various family therapy studies. Patterson (1982) and Horne and Van Dyke (1983), as examples, have reported follow-up data that are quite promising. Even these findings, however, are tempered by the lack of consistent results with nontraditional families (Rios & Gutierrez, 1986).

As emphasized earlier, there is need for a more individualized assessment of children and of the interpersonal and social contexts in which conduct difficulties occur. Individually tailored treatment programs based on an assessment of the environmental and child variables presumed to influence the development, instigation, and persistence of conduct difficulties hold promise of greater success in the treatment of this socially significant problem. Comprehensive assessment will permit more effective and efficient treatment, as there will be a greater match between the psychological needs of each child and the specific therapeutic experiences provided.

189

CONDUCT DISORDERS:
PSYCHOLOGICAL
THERAPIES

# REFERENCES

Agee, V. L. (1979). *Treatment of the violent incorrigible adolescent*. Lexington, MA: D. C. Heath.

Alexander, J., & Parsons, B. (1973). Short-term intervention with delinquent families: Impact on family process and recidivism. *Journal of Abnormal Psychology, 81,* 219–225.

Alexander, J., Barton, C., Schiavo, R., & Parsons, B. (1976). Systems-behavioral intervention with families of delinquents: Therapist characteristics, family behavior, and outcome. *Journal of Consulting and Clinical Psychology, 44,* 656–664.

American Psychiatric Association. (1980). *Diagnostic and statistical manual of mental disorders* (3rd ed.; DSM-III). Washington, DC: Author.

Ayllon, T., & Skuban, W. (1973). Accountability in psychotherapy: A test case. *Journal of Behavior Therapy and Experimental Psychiatry, 4,* 19–30.

Bandura, A. (1973). *Aggression: A social learning analysis*. Englewood Cliffs, NJ: Prentice-Hall.

Barmann, B. C., Croyle-Barmann, C., & McLain, B. (1980). The use of contingent-interrupted music in the treatment of disruptive bus-riding behavior. *Journal of Applied Behavior Analysis, 13,* 693–698.

Benjamin, R., Mazzarins, H., & Kupfersmid, J. (1983). The effect of time-out (TO) duration on assaultiveness in psychiatrically hospitalized children. *Aggressive Behavior, 9,* 21–27.

Berman, E. (1984). The relationship of aggressive behavior and violence to psychic reorganization in adolescence. In C. R. Keith (Ed.), *The aggressive adolescent: Clinical perspectives*. New York: Free Press.

Bernal, M., Klinnert, M., & Schultz, L. (1980). Outcome evaluation of behavioral parent training and client-centered parent counseling for children with conduct problems. *Journal of Applied Behavior Analysis, 13,* 677–691.

Birnbrauer, J. S. (1968). Generalization of punishment effects—A case study. *Journal of Applied Behavior Analysis, 1,* 201–211.

Bornstein, M., Bellack, A. S., & Hersen, M. (1980). Social skills training for highly aggressive children. *Behavior Modification, 4,* 173–186.

Brigham, T. A., Hopper, C., Hill, B., de Armas, A., & Newsom, P. (1985). A self-management program for disruptive adolescents in the school: A clinical replication analysis. *Behavior Therapy, 16,* 99–115.

Brinich, P. M. (1984). Joint treatment of children and parents. *Psychoanalytic Study of the Child, 39,* 493–508.

Bristol, M. M. (1976). Control of physical aggression through school- and home-based renforcement. In J. D. Krumboltz & C. E. Thoresen (Eds.), *Counseling methods*. New York: Holt, Rinehart & Winston.

Buckley, N. K., & Walker, H. M. (1979). *Modifying classroom behavior: A manual of procedure for classroom teachers*. Champaign, IL: Research Press.

Burchard, J., & Barrera, F. (1972). An analysis of time-out and response cost in a programmed environment. *Journal of Applied Behavior Analysis, 5,* 271–282.

Burcher, B., & King, L. (1971). Generalization of punishment effects in the deviant behavior of a psychotic child. *Behavior Therapy, 2,* 68–77.

Calhoun, K. S., & Matherne, P. (1975). The effects of varying schedules of time-out on aggressive behavior of a retarded girl. *Journal of Behavior Therapy and Experimental Psychiatry, 6,* 139–143.

Camp, B. W., & Ray, R. S. (1984). Aggression. In A. W. Meyers & W. E. Craighead (Eds.), *Cognitive behavior therapy with children.* New York: Plenum Press.

Camp, B. W., Blom, G. E., Herbert, F., & vanDoorninck, W. J. (1977). "Think aloud": A program for developing self-control in young aggressive boys. *Journal of Abnormal Child Psychology, 5,* 167–169.

Campbell, R., O'Brien, S., Bickett, A., & Lutzker, J. (1983). In-home parent training, treatment of migraine headaches, and marital counseling as an ecobehavioral approach to prevent child abuse. *Journal of Behavior Therapy and Experimental Psychiatry, 14,* 47–154.

Campbell, S. B., Breaux, A. M., Ewing, L. J., & Szumowski, E. K. (1986). Correlates and predictors of hyperactivity and aggression: A longitudinal study of parent-referred problem preschoolers. *Journal of Abnormal Child Psychology, 14,* 217–234.

Carr, E. G. (1981). Contingency management. In A. P. Goldstein, E. G. Carr, W. S. Davidson II, & P. Wehr (Eds.), *In response to aggression: Methods of control and prosocial alternatives.* New York: Pergamon Press.

Carr, E. G., & Durand, V. M. (1985). Reducing behavior problems through functional communication training. *Journal of Applied Behavior Analysis, 18,* 111–126.

Carr, E. G., & Newsom, C. (1985). Demand-related tantrums: Conceptualization and treatment. *Behavior Modification, 9,* 403–426.

Carr, E. G., Newsom, C. D., & Binkhoff, J. A. (1980). Escape as a factor in the aggressive behavior of two retarded children. *Journal of Applied Behavior Analysis, 13,* 101–117.

Clarizio, H. F., & McCoy, G. F. (1983). *Behavioral disorders in children* (3rd ed.). New York: Thomas Y. Crowell.

Curry, J. F., Wiencrot, S. I., & Koehler, F. (1984). Family therapy with aggressive and delinquent adolescents. In C. R. Keith (Ed.), *The aggressive adolescent: Clinical perspectives.* New York: Free Press.

Deitz, S. M. (1977). An analysis of programming DRL schedules in educational settings. *Behaviour Research and Therapy, 15,* 103–111.

Doke, L. A., & Flippo, J. R. (1983). Aggression and oppositional behavior. In T. H. Ollendick & M. Hersen (Eds.), *Handbook of childhood psychopathology.* New York: Plenum Press.

Doke, L., Wolery, M., & Sumberg, C. (1983). Treating chronic aggression: Effects and side effects of response-contingent ammonia spirits. *Behavior Modification, 7,* 531–556.

Dumas, J. E., & Wahler, R. G. (1983). Predictors of treatment outcome in parent training: Mother insularity and socioeconomic disadvantage. *Behavioral Assessment, 5,* 301–313.

Fehrenbach, P. A., & Thelen, M. H. (1982). Behavioral approaches to the treatment of aggressive disorders. *Behavior Modification, 6,* 465–497.

Feshbach, N. D. (1979). Empathy training: A field study in affective education. In S. Feshbach & A. Fraczek (Eds.), *Aggression and behavior change: Biological and social processes.* New York: Praeger.

Feshbach, N. D. (1983). Learning to care: A positive approach to child training and discipline. *Journal of Clinical Child Psychology, 12,* 266–271.

Feshbach, N. D., & Feshbach, S. (1982). Empathy training and the regulation of aggression: Potentialities and limitations. *Academic Psychology Bulletin, 4,* 399–413.

Forehand, R. L., & McMahon, R. J. (1981). *Helping the noncompliant child: A clinician's guide to parent training.* New York: Guilford Press.

Forman, S. G. (1980). A comparison of cognitive training and response cost procedures in modifying aggressive behavior of elementary school children. *Behavior Therapy, 11,* 594–600.

Foxx, R. M., & Bechtel, D. R. (1982). Overcorrection. In M. Hersen & R. M. Eisler (Eds.), *Progress in behavior modification* (Vol. 13). New York: Academic Press.

Foxx, R. M., & Shapiro, S. T. (1978). The time out ribbon: A nonexclusionary time-out procedure. *Journal of Applied Behavior Analysis, 11,* 125–136.

Foxx, R. M., McMorrow, M. J., Bittle, R. G., & Bechtel, D. R. (1986). The successful treatment of a dually-diagnosed deaf man's aggression with a program that included contingent electric shock. *Behavior Therapy, 17,* 170–186.

Gant, B., Barnard, J., Kuehn, F., Jones, H., & Christophersen, E. (1981). A behaviorally based approach for improving intrafamilial communication patterns. *Journal of Clinical Child Psychology, 10,* 102–106.

Gardner, W. I., & Cole, C. L. (1984). Aggression and related conduct problems in the mentally retarded: A multicomponent behavioral model. In S. E. Bruening, J. L. Matson, & R. P. Barrett (Eds.), *Advances in mental retardation and developmental disabilities* (Vol. 2). Greenwich, CT: JAI Press.

Gardner, W. I., & Cole, C. L. (1985). Acting-out disorders. In M. Hersen (Ed.), *Practice of inpatient behavior therapy: A clinical guide*. Orlando FL: Grune & Stratton.

Gersten, J. C., Langner, T. S., Eisenberg, J. G., Simcha-Fagan, O., & McCarthy, E. D. (1976). Stability and change in types of behavioral disturbance of children and adolescents. *Journal of Abnormal Child Psychology, 4,* 111–127.

Goldstein, A. P. (1981). *Psychological skill training.* New York: Pergamon Press.

Goldstein, A. P. (1983). Behavior modification approaches to aggression prevention and control. In A. P. Goldstein (Ed.), *Prevention and control of aggression*. New York: Pergamon Press.

Goldstein, A. P., & Kanfer, F. (Eds.). (1979). *Maximizing treatment gains.* New York: Academic Press.

Goldstein, A. P., & Pentz, M. A. (1984). Psychological skill training and the aggressive adolescent. *School Psychology Review, 13,* 311–323.

Goldstein, A. P., Sprafkin, R. P., Gershaw, N. J., & Klein, P. (1980). *Skillstreaming the adolescent.* Champaign, IL: Research Press.

Graham, P. J. (1979). Epidemiological studies. In H. C. Quay & J. S. Werry (Eds.), *Psychopathological disorders of childhood* (2nd ed.). New York: Wiley.

Greene, R. J., & Hoats, D. C. (1971). Aversive tickling: A simple conditioning technique. *Behavior Therapy, 2,* 389–393.

Griest, D. L., & Wells, K. C. (1983). Behavioral family therapy with conduct disorders in children. *Behavior Therapy, 14,* 37–53.

Harootunian, B., & Apter, S. J. (1983). Violence in schools. In A. P. Goldstein (Ed.), *Prevention and control of aggression*. New York: Pergamon Press.

Hawkins, R. P., Peterson, R. F., Schweid, E., & Bijou, S. W. (1966). Amerlioration of problem parent-child relations with the parent in a therapeutic role. *Journal of Experimental Child Psychology, 4,* 99–107.

Herbert, M. (1978). *Conduct disorders of childhood and adolescence.* New York: Wiley.

Hobbs, S. A., Moguin, L. E., Tryoler, M., & Lahey, B. B. (1980). Cognitive behavior therapy with children: Has clinical utility been demonstrated? *Psychological Bulletin, 87,* 147–165.

Hogan, W. A., & Johnson, D. P. (1985). Elimination of response cost in a token economy program and improvement in behavior of emotionally disturbed youth. *Behavior Therapy, 16,* 87–98.

Horne, A. M., & Van Dyke, B. (1983). Treatment and maintenance of social learning family therapy. *Behavior Therapy, 14,* 606–613.

Johnson, W. L., & Baumeister, A. A. (1981). Behavioral techniques for decreasing abberant behaviors of retarded and autistic persons. In M. Hersen, R. M. Eisler, & P. M. Miller (Eds.), *Progress in behavior modification* (Vol. 12). New York: Pergamon Press.

Karoly, P., & Rosenthal, M. (1977). Training parents in behavior modification: Effects on perceptions of family interactions and deviant child behavior. *Behavior Therapy, 8,* 406–410.

Kauffman, J. M. (1985). *Characteristics of children's behavior disorders* (3rd ed.). Columbus, OH: Charles E. Merrill.

Kazdin, A. E., & Frame, C. (1983). Aggressive behavior and conduct disorder. In R. J. Morris & T. R. Kratochwill (Eds.), *The practice of child therapy*. New York: Pergamon Press.

Keith, C. R. (1984). *The aggressive adolescent: Clinical perspectives.* New York: Free Press.

Kendall, P. C., Nay, W. R., & Jeffers, J. (1975). Timeout duration and contrast effects: A systematic evaluation of a successive treatments design. *Behavior Therapy, 6,* 609–615.

Kennedy, R. E. (1984). Cognitive behavioral interventions with delinquents. In A. W. Meyers & W. E. Craighead (Eds.), *Cognitive behavior therapy with children*. New York: Plenum Press.

Kirigin, K. A., Wolf, M. M., Braukmann, C. J., Fixsen, D. L., & Phillips, E. L. (1979). Achievement Place: A preliminary outcome evaluation. In J. S. Stumphauzer (Ed.), *Progress in behavior therapy with delinquents*. Springfield, IL: Thomas.

Kirigin, K. A., Braukmann, C. J., Atwater, J. D., & Wolf, M. M. (1982). An evaluation of teaching-family (Achievement Place) group homes for juvenile offenders. *Journal of Applied Behavior Analysis, 15,* 1–16.

Klein, N., Alexander, J., & Parsons, B. (1977). Impact of family systems intervention on recidivism and sibling delinquency: A model of primary prevention and program evaluation. *Journal of Consulting and Clinical Psychology, 45,* 469–474.

Konstantareas, M. M., & Homatidis, S. (1984). Aggressive and prosocial behaviours before and after treatment in conduct-disordered children and in matched controls. *Journal of Child Psychology and Psychiatry, 25,* 607–620.

Lefkowitz, M. M., Eron, L. D., Walder, L. O., & Huesmann, L. R. (1977). *Growing up to be violent: A longitudinal study of the development of aggression.* New York: Pergamon Press.

Leitenberg, H., Burchard, J. D., Burchard, S. N., Fuller, E. J., & Lysaght, T. V. (1977). Using positive reinforcement to suppress behavior: Some experimental comparisons with sibling conflict. *Behavior Therapy, 8,* 168–182.

Lewis, D. O., Pincus, J. H., Shanok, S. S., & Glaser, G. H. (1982). Psychomotor epilepsy and violence in a group of incarcerated adolescent boys. *American Journal of Psychiatry, 139,* 882–887.

Lewis, D. O., Shanok, S. S., Grant, M., & Ritvo, E. (1983). Homicidally aggressive young children: Neuropsychiatric and experiential correlates. *American Journal of Psychiatry, 140,* 148–153.

Little, V. L., & Kendall, P. C. (1979). Cognitive-behavioral interventions with delinquents: Problem solving, role-taking, and self-control. In P. C. Kendall & S. D. Hollon (Eds.), *Cognitive-behavioral interventions.* New York: Academic Press.

Loney, J., & Milich, R. (1982). Hyperactivity, inattention, and aggression in clinical practice. In M. Wolraich & D. K. Routh (Eds.), *Advances in behavioral pediatrics* (Vol. 3). Greenwich, CT: JAI Press.

Luiselli, J. K., Myles, E., Evans, T. P., & Boyce, D. A. (1985). Reinforcement control of severe dysfunctional behavior of blind, multihandicapped students. *American Journal of Mental Deficiency, 90,* 328–334.

Mace, F. C., Page, T. J., Ivancic, M. T., & O'Brien, S. (1986). Analysis of environmental determinants of aggression and disruption in mentally retarded children. *Applied Research in Mental Retardation, 7,* 203–221.

Meichenbaum, D. H., & Goodman, J. (1971). Training impulsive children to talk to themselves: A means of developing self-control. *Journal of Abnormal Psychology, 77,* 115–116.

Novaco, R. W. (1979). The cognitive regulation of anger and stress. In P. C. Kendall & S. D. Hollon (Eds.), *Cognitive-behavioral interventions: Theory, research, and procedures.* New York: Academic Press.

Ollendick, T. H., & Matson, J. L. (1976). An initial investigation into the parameters of overcorrection. *Psychological Reports, 39,* 1139–1142.

Olweus, D. (1979). Stability of aggressive reaction patterns in males: A review. *Psychological Bulletin, 86,* 852–875.

Patterson, G. R. (1974). Interventions for boys with conduct problems: Multiple settings, treatments, and criterion. *Journal of Consulting and Clinical Psychology, 42,* 471–481.

Patterson, G. R. (1976). The aggressive child: Victim and architect of a coercive system. In E. J. Marsh, L. A. Hamerlynck, & L. C. Handy (Eds.), *Behavior modification and families.* New York: Brunner/Mazel.

Patterson, G. R. (1982). *Coercive family process.* Eugene, OR: Castalia.

Patterson, G. R., & Reid, J. B. (1970). Reciprocity and coercion: Two facets of social systems. In C. Neuringer & T. L. Michael (Eds.), *Behavior modification in clinical psychology.* New York: Appleton-Century-Crofts.

Patterson, G. R., Reid, J. B., Jones, R. R., & Conger, R. E. (1975). *A social learning approach to family intervention* (Vol. 1). Eugene, OR: Castalia.

Pendergrass, V. E. (1971). Effects of length of time-out from positive reinforcement and schedule of application in suppression of aggressive behavior. *The Psychological Record, 21,* 75–80.

Pfeffer, C. R., Plutchik, R., & Mizruchi, M. S. (1983). Predictors of assaultiveness in latency age children. *American Journal of Psychiatry, 40,* 31–35.

Phillips, E. L., Phillips, E. A., Fixsen, D. L., & Wolf, M. M. (1971). Achievement Place: Modification of the behaviors of predelinquent boys within a token economy. *Journal of Applied Behavior Analysis, 4,* 45–59.

Puig-Antich, J. (1982). Major depression and conduct disorder in prepuberty. *Journal of the American Academy of Child Psychiatry, 21,* 118–128.

Quay, H. C. (1979). In H. C. Quay & J. S. Werry (Eds.), *Psychopathological disorders of childhood* (2nd ed.). New York: Wiley.

Quay, H. C. (1983). A dimensional approach to behavior disorder: The Revised Behavior Problem Checklist. *School Psychology Review, 12,* 244–249.

Rapport, M. D., Murphy, H. A., & Bailey, J. S. (1982). Ritalin versus response cost in the control of hyperactive children: A within-subject comparison. *Journal of Applied Behavior Analysis, 15,* 205–216.

Rapport, M. D., Sonis, W. A., Fialkov, M. J., Matson, J. L., & Kazdin, A. E. (1983). Carbamazepine and behavior therapy for aggressive behavior. *Behavior Modification, 7,* 255–265.

Reisinger, J., Frangia, G., & Hoffman, E. (1976). Toddler management training: Generalization and marital status. *Journal of Behavior Therapy and Experimental Psychiatry, 7,* 335–340.

Repp, A. C., & Deitz, S. M. (1974). Reducing aggressive and self-injurious behavior of institutionalized retarded children through reinforcement of other behaviors. *Journal of Applied Behavior Analysis, 7,* 313–325.

Rinn, R., Vernon, J., & Wise, M. (1975). Training parents of behaviorally disordered children in groups: A three-year's program evaluation. *Behavior Therapy, 6,* 378–387.

Rios, J. D., & Gutierrez, J. M. (1986). Parent training with non-traditional families: An unresolved issue. *Child and Family Behavior Therapy, 7,* 33–45.

Roberts, M. W. (1982). Resistance to timeout: Some normative data. *Behavioral Assessment, 4,* 237–246.

Roberts, M. W. (1984). An attempt to reduce time out resistance in young children. *Behavior Therapy, 15,* 210–216.

Robin, A. (1981). A controlled evaluation of problem-solving communication training with parent-adolescent conflict. *Behavior Therapy, 12,* 593–609.

Robin, A., Schneider, M., & Dolnick, M. (1976). The turtle technique: An extended case study of self-control in the classroom. *Psychology in the Schools, 12,* 120–128.

Robins, L. N. (1966). *Deviant children grow up.* Baltimore: Williams & Wilkins.

Robins, L. N. (1981). Epidemiological approaches to natural history research: Antisocial disorders in children. *Journal of the American Academy of Child Psychiatry, 20,* 566–580.

Rolider, A., & Van Houten, R. (1984). The effects of DRO alone and DRO plus reprimands on the undesirable behavior of three children in home settings. *Education and Treatment of Children, 7,* 17–31.

Rolider, A., & Van Houten, R. (1985a). Movement suppression time-out for undesirable behavior in psychotic and severely developmentally delayed children. *Journal of Applied Behavior Analysis, 18,* 275–288.

Rolider, A., & Van Houten, R. (1985b). Suppressing tantrum behavior in public places through the use of delayed punishment mediated by audio recordings. *Behavior Therapy, 16,* 181–194.

Sandberg, S., Rutter, M., & Taylor, E. (1978). Hyperkinetic disorder in psychiatric clinic attenders. *Developmental Medicine and Child Neurology, 20,* 279–299.

Satterfield, J. H., Hoppe, C. M., & Schell, A. M. (1982). A prospective study of delinquency in 110 adolescent boys with attention deficit disorder and 88 normal adolescent boys. *American Journal of Psychiatry, 139,* 795–798.

Schneider, M. (1974). Turtle technique in the classroom. *Teaching Exceptional Children, 8,* 22–24.

Strain, P., Young, C., & Horowitz, J. (1981). Generalized behavior change during oppositional child training: An examination of child and family demographic variables. *Behavior Modification, 5,* 15–26.

Strasberg, P. A. (1978). *Violent delinquents: An investigation to the Ford Foundation from the Vera Institute of Justice.* New York: Monarch.

Sutker, P. B., Archer, R. P., & Kilpatrick, P. G. (1981). Sociopathy and antisocial behavior: Theory and treatment. In S. M. Turner, K. S. Calhoun, & H. E. Adams (Eds.), *Handbook of clinical behavior therapy.* New York: Wiley.

Tygart, C. E. (1980). Student social structures and/or subcultures as factors in school crime: Toward a paradigm. *Adolescence, 15,* 13–22.

Varley, W. H. (1984). Behavior modification approaches to the aggressive adolescent. In C. R. Keith (Ed.), *The aggressive adolescent: Clinical Perspectives.* New York: Free Press.

Vaughn, S. R., Ridley, C. A., & Bullock, D. D. (1984). Interpersonal problem-solving skills training with aggressive young children. *Journal of Applied Developmental Psychology, 5,* 213–223.

Wahler, R. G. (1980). The insular mother: Her problems in parent-child treatment. *Journal of Applied Behavior Analysis, 13,* 207–219.

Wahler, R. G., & Fox, J. J. (1980). Solitary toy play and time out: A family treatment package for children with aggressive and oppositional behavior. *Journal of Applied Behavior Analysis, 13,* 23–39.

Walle, D. L., Hobbs, S. A., Caldwell, H. S. (1984). Sequencing of parent training procedures: Effects on child noncompliance and treatment acceptability. *Behavior Modification, 8,* 540–552.

Weathers, L. R., & Liberman, R. P. (1975). Modification of family behavior therapy. In D. Marholin (Ed.), *Child behavior therapy.* New York: Gardner Press.

Webster-Stratton, C. (1985). Predictors of treatment outcome in parent training for conduct disordered children. *Behavior Therapy, 16,* 223–242.

Weiner, I. B. (1982). *Child and adolescent psychopathology.* New York: Wiley.

Wells, K. C., & Forehand, R. (1981). Childhood behavior problems in the home. In S. M. Turner, K. S. Calhoun, & H. E. Adams (Eds.). *Handbook of clinical behavior therapy.* New York: Wiley.

West, D. J., & Farrington, D. P. (1973). *Who becomes delinquent?* London: Heinemann Educational Books.

White, G. D., Nielson, G., & Johnson, S. M. (1972). Timeout duration and the suppression of deviant behavior in children. *Journal of Applied Behavior Analysis, 5,* 111–120.

Wilson, R. (1984). A review of self-control treatments for aggressive behavior. *Behavioral Disorders, 9,* 131–140.

Wolfgang, M. E., Figlio, R. M., & Sellin, T. (1972). *Delinquency in a birth cohort.* Chicago: University of Chicago Press.

Yule, W. (1978). Behavior treatment of children and adolescents with conduct disorders. In L. A. Hersov and D. Shaffer (Eds.), *Aggression and anti-social behaviour in childhood and adolescence.* New York: Pergamon Press.

# 9     *Attention Deficit Disorder and Hyperactivity*
## Psychological Therapies

ELIZABETH A. SCHAUGHENCY, JASON WALKER, AND
BENJAMIN B. LAHEY

*Attention deficit disorder* (ADD) is the diagnostic term used to describe children with developmentally inappropriate difficulties in attention and impulsivity in the DSM-III (American Psychiatric Association, 1980). It replaced the term *hyperkinetic reaction* of the DSM-II (American Psychiatric Association, 1968) and includes what is commonly referred to as *hyperactivity* as one of two subtypes of the disorder. Thus, according to DSM-III criteria, the child who presents with problems in attention, impulsivity, and motor overactivity would be diagnosed as ADD with hyperactivity (ADD/H), and the child who presents with inattention and impulsivity in the absence of hyperactivity would be diagnosed as ADD without hyperactivity (ADD/WO).

This change in diagnostic nomenclature was based on the clinical observation that a group of children exist who exhibit attention difficulties without concomitant motor overactivity (American Psychiatric Association, 1980; Wender, 1971). It also reflects a shift in focus from motor excess to the cognitive deficits displayed by hyperactive children (cf. Douglas, 1980, 1983). Some professionals have argued that the distinction between the two subtypes is unimportant (e.g., August & Holmes, 1984; Barkley, 1981; Kinsbourne, 1983), and the diagnostic category of Attention Deficit–Hyperactivity Disorder, which has been included in the DSM-III-R (American Psychiatric Association, 1988) eliminated this distinction.

These changing terminology and diagnostic criteria hopefully reflect a growing understanding of ADD/H. To a certain extent, they may also be reminiscent of, and contributory to, the controversy surrounding this diagnostic category. The children described by the term *ADD* in the clinical literature are a diverse population, and such heterogeneity of subject populations introduces potential confounds into the study of ADD, as noted by Schaughency and Hynd (1986).

First, ADD, as specified in the DSM-III, is comprised of two subtypes: with

ELIZABETH A. SCHAUGHENCY • Department of Psychology, University of Oregon, Eugene, Oregon 97403.    JASON WALKER AND BENJAMIN B. LAHEY • Department of Psychology, University of Georgia, Athens, Georgia 30602.

and without hyperactivity. Many articles refer to patients as having ADD without specifying subtype (e.g., Deutsch, Swanson, Bruello, Cantwell, Weinberg, & Baren, 1982; Satterfield, Hoppe, & Schell, 1982; Wright, 1982), and it is only through reading the description of subjects that one learns that the ADD sample is homogeneous with respect to hyperactivity (e.g., Lou, Henriksen, & Bruhn, 1984) or contains both ADD/H and ADD/WO subjects (e.g., Caparulo, Cohen, Rothman, Young, Katz, Shaywitz, & Shaywitz, 1981). Similarly, some practitioners who acknowledge the two subtypes of ADD do not differentiate between the groups with respect to treatment recommendations (e.g., Dulcan, 1985; Shaywitz & Shaywitz, 1984). The DSM-III cautioned, however, that it is not clear whether ADD/H and ADD/WO are dissimilar subtypes of a single disorder or two distinct disorders. Therefore, this practice is of concern because it is not known whether the results of previous research on hyperactive children apply to children diagnosed as ADD/WO.

Research examining the behavioral correlates of children rated as having attentional difficulties with and without hyperactivity suggests that different behavior patterns are associated with the two groups in regular elementary-school (King & Young, 1982; Lahey, Schaughency, Frame, & Strauss, 1985; Lahey, Schaughency, Strauss, & Frame, 1984), learning-disabled (Ackerman, Dykman, & Oglesby, 1983), and outpatient-psychiatric (Edelbrock, Costello, & Kessler, 1984) populations. In general, the results of these studies converge to suggest that children with ADD/H are more impulsive than children with ADD/WO and are more likely to exhibit associated features of an externalizing disorder, whereas ADD/WO has been found to be associated with a slow cognitive tempo and a higher frequency of coexisting internalizing disorders.

Second, there are many other developmental and behavior disorders that co-occur with ADD in greater frequency than in the general population, such as conduct disorder (cf. Lahey *et al.*, in press), learning disability (cf. Ackerman *et al.*, 1983; Caparulo *et al.*, 1981), language disorder (Baker & Cantwell, 1982), and Tourette syndrome (cf. Caparulo *et al.*, 1981; Schaughency, Hurley, & Krahn, 1986), and a careful reading of sample descriptions in the clinical research on ADD suggests the presence of these disorders. Historically. this overlap has led to the suggestion that features of these codiagnoses were characteristic of ADD/H (e.g., conduct disorder: Lahey, Green, & Forehand, 1980; learning disability: Graham, 1979). However, recent research in the area of ADD/H has found distinct subgroups of ADD/H children who also exhibit these disorders and those who do not (conduct disorder: August & Holmes, 1984; August & Stewart, 1983; Lahey *et al.*, in press; learning disability: August & Holmes, 1984; Singer, Stewart, & Pulaski, 1981). Moreover, with respect to conduct disorder, different prognoses in adolescence are associated with hyperactive children who display aggression in childhood and those who do not (August & Holmes, 1984; Loney, Kramer, & Milich, 1981; Weiss, 1983). Such heterogeneity should alert the clinician to conduct a thorough assessment of each individual case so that a comprehensive and appropriate treatment plan may be developed.

## Current Issues in the Treatment of ADD

Given the range of difficulties that may be experienced by children with ADD, a number of professions could be expected to contribute to the management of these children: psychologists, physicians, educators, and other spe-cialists (e.g., those in special education or speech and language pathology) as indicated by the given case. Many writers are currently calling for multifaceted intervention strategies (cf. Bennett & Sherman, 1983; Hughes, Goldman, & Snyder, 1983; Sandoval, Lambert, & Sassone, 1981; Satterfield, Satterfield, & Cantwell, 1980; Shaywitz & Shaywitz, 1984; Walden & Thompson, 1981), and recent research clearly demonstrates the need for such comprehensive manage-ment approaches. In general, the accepted management programs for hyperac-tive children have focused on three major areas: (1) appropriate and specialized educational programming; (2) a selected use of stimulant medications; and (3) individual behavior-modification programs and/or family counseling (Bennett & Sherman, 1983; Sandoval *et al.*, 1981).

Surveys have found that 10% of the cases seen in pediatric clinics involve hyperactivity (O'Leary, 1980), and a study of the management of hyperactivity by primary-care physicians in the state of Washington found that 60% of the pediatricians, 8% of the family physicians, and 9% of the general practitioners followed more than 10 hyperactive children per year (Bennett & Sherman, 1983). Over 90% of all the physicians in the Bennett and Sherman (1983) study reported using stimulant medication for some hyperactive children, and recent school-based studies found that the .6% to 1% of students were currently receiving stimulants (Dulcan, 1985).

It has been well documented that the majority (70%–75%) of children diag-nosed as ADD/H respond well to stimulant medication, for example, whereas the minority show no change or get worse (cf. Dulcan, 1985; Hughes *et al.*, 1983). A long-term follow-up study of the young-adult outcome of children who re-ceived stimulant medication, however, found that, in many areas—school, work, and personal adjustment—stimulant-treated hyperactives did not differ from untreated hyperactives, and both groups were found to be functioning significantly worse than normal controls (Hechtman, Weiss, & Perlman, 1984). Much more promising results were obtained in a two-year follow-up study of individualized multimodality treatment consisting of a combination of medica-tion and relevant psychological interventions, with significant improvements found in behavioral, interpersonal, and academic functioning (Satterfield *et al.*, 1980). Whether the effects of such improvements increase the level of function-ing of hyperactives to that of their normal peers and are maintained into young adulthood awaits further research.

The purpose of this discussion is to illustrate the need for comprehensive intervention with ADD, not to deride the use of stimulant medication. The effects of psychological interventions for ADD have been found to be limited as well. As Sprague (1983) suggested in his chapter on the use of behavioral and educational interventions with ADD, it is unlikely that either stimulant medication or behav-ior therapy, alone or in combination, will ameliorate all the difficulties of the ADD child, and it is unfortunate that the literature evaluating nonpharmacological strategies does so by pitting them against stimulant medication.

Sandoval *et al.* (1981) presented findings suggesting that physicians who treat hyperactive children frequently do combine pharmacotherapy with the recommendation that parents obtain counseling or psychotherapy, as well as help from school personnel for those with learning difficulties, and the findings of the Bennett and Sherman (1983) study also suggest that practicing clinicians were following the recommendations for a combined treatment approach. In our clinical experience, the most significant improvements in some of the most severe cases of children with ADD/H have come from comprehensive approaches including psychological interventions with parents, teachers, and child in collaboration with medical management by the pediatrician.

## MAJOR CLINICAL APPLICATIONS

The ultimate goal of any therapeutic intervention is to improve the child's functioning in his or her natural environment. Consequently, many writers in the field are calling for an assessment of the outcome in important areas of the child's life as the appropriate test of a technique's effectiveness (Hobbs, Moguin, Tyroler, & Lahey, 1980; Lahey, Delamater, Kupfer, & Hobbs, 1978; Lahey & Strauss, 1982; O'Leary, 1980; Sprague, 1983). O'Leary (1980) listed four criteria that should be considered when evaluating treatment effectiveness: (1) the academic performance of the child; (2) behavioral functioning within the family (parent–child interactions and parent perceptions); (3) a cost analysis of the intervention; and (4) consumers' (e.g., parents, and teachers') satisfaction with the treatment. To this list Sprague (1983) added the child's subjective experience of the intervention for an assessment of possible side effects of the treatment as well as consumer satisfaction. Given the findings of disturbed peer relationships in many hyperactive children (Pelham & Milich, 1984), an assessment of social functioning should also be added. Finally, as illustrated by the findings of long-term follow-up studies of stimulant-treated hyperactives conducted by Weiss and colleagues (Hechtman & Weiss, 1983; Hechtman et al., 1984; Weiss, 1983), the evaluation of outcome needs to continue well beyond the termination of the treatment. In sum, the major tests for any intervention used with ADD children are generalization and maintenance of changes in important day-to-day indices of behavior, with the additional considerations of cost-effectiveness and consumer satisfaction.

The intervention strategies to be examined in this chapter are those suggested by the experimental literature to be effective in the sense defined above. These generally fit under the rubric of *behavioral interventions* and will not include individual psychoanalytic or family systems therapies used with ADD children or their families. Individual psychodynamic psychotherapy has generally not been found to be effective in the management of ADD (Heavilon, 1980). Family systems therapy will not be discussed, as there are few studies in the current literature presenting family systems therapy for the child with ADD, and studies of family variables in ADD suggest that not all ADD children come from dysfunctional families (Piacentini, Lahey, & Hynd, 1986; Weiss, 1983). This is not to say, however, that family therapy may not prove to be beneficial to some children with ADD (Heavilon, 1980; Williamson, Anderson, & Lundy, 1980).

## BASIC PRINCIPLES OF THERAPY FOR HYPERACTIVITY

This section presents an overview of the major nonmedical clinical approaches to the management of ADD. These interventions fall into two general treatment strategies (1) contingency management and (2) cognitive-behavioral procedures.

*Contingency Management*

199

ATTENTION DEFICIT
DISORDER:
PSYCHOLOGICAL
THERAPIES

Contingency management has been used both as an alternative and as an adjunct to stimulant treatment of children with ADD/H. Contingency management procedures are derived directly from the principles of operant conditioning. These principles state that an individual's responses are shaped by the consequences that follow them. Positive consequences increase and negative consequences decrease the probability of the recurrence of that response. In negative reinforcement, the response allows the client to escape a negative or aversive situation, so that termination of the aversive situation reinforces the response.

Contingency management procedures use several different reinforcement strategies. The types of reinforcement include material and social reinforcement, which may be used separately or concomitantly, with a gradual fading out of tangible reinforcers. Reinforcement may be delivered by significant adults (e.g., a parent or teacher), by peers, or by the child herself or himself. Self-reinforcement is used in procedures designed to promote self-control, which represents the ultimate goal of behavioral intervention.

Punishment strategies vary as well. The types of punishment procedures include response-cost procedures and time-out. Response cost involves the child's losing some preobtained reward (e.g., tokens) because of inappropriate or negative behaviors. Time-out procedures involve removing the child from the environment that has elicited and maintained the inappropriate responses. The goal of all of these procedures, of course, is to extinguish the inappropriate response(s) by not providing reinforcement. The shortcoming of punishment procedures is that, in isolation, they do not teach the child appropriate responses. For this reason, these strategies should be combined with the positive reinforcement of appropriate responses, so that the child can learn which behaviors are appropriate as well as which are inappropriate.

## Classroom Management Procedures

Classroom management procedures have the goal of helping the ADD child to improve his or her classroom behavior and academic functioning. Early studies documented the short-term effectiveness of feedback alone in decreasing inattentive and disruptive behavior in the classroom (Drabman & Lahey, 1974; Lobitz, 1974), but the results of laboratory studies of children with ADD suggest that they respond differently depending on the type of feedback they receive. Based on the finding that feedback on correct responses led to an increase in impulsive responding (Firestone & Douglas, 1975), Sherman and Anderson (1980) investigated the effects of providing feedback for inattention on the attending behavior and activity level in the classroom of teacher-identified "hyperactive" children in an ABAB between-group design. Each child had a small box mounted to his or her desktop in the regular classroom. The children were told that the experimenters were going to help them by letting them know when they were not paying attention. Then, whenever a child was observed to be not attending to her or his work, the experimenter turned on a light-emitting diode, which remained on until the child returned to work. Both during the second treatment phase and at the 3-week follow-up, the experimental groups significantly decreased their inattentive behavior and displayed less inattention than the nonhyperactive control group.

These results are impressive and demonstrate that the authors did modify the behavior they had set out to change. Unfortunately, they did not assess whether their intervention affected other important aspects of the subjects' functioning. For example, the authors noted that observations were conducted during the independent completion of arithmetic problems but did not report whether decreased off-task behavior resulted in increased accuracy and completion of math problems. Moreover, it should be noted that the "hyperactive" children in the Sherman and Anderson (1980) study were all in regular elementary-school placement and were not receiving stimulant medication. Experimental classification as *hyperactive* had been based on a single informant, rather than on a clinical diagnosis based on all the available information. Thus, the sample in this study may have included children who were not clinically hyperactive.

The effect of feedback on the behavior of a clinically hyperactive boy in an inpatient psychiatric setting was evaluated in a single-case study in conjunction with other intervention strategies (Williamson, Calpin, Dilorenzo, Garris, & Petti, 1981). This child was admitted to the hospital for evaluation of hyperactive behavior, poor peer relationships, and unsatisfactory school achievement. His activity level was assessed by actometers worn on his ankle and wrist and was found to be twice that of a comparison sample of 12 nonhyperactive inpatients in the lunchroom setting. Teacher report indicated that this child's high activity level and inattentiveness impaired his classroom performance. Similarly, a behavioral assessment of his interactions with peers suggested these behaviors led other children to avoid him. Treatment was conducted in an extended ABAB format with the sequential addition of treatment components. The dependent or outcome measures included behavioral observations in the classroom and the lunchroom and during free play, his activity level, and pre- and postmeasures of academic achievement.

The first treatment phase consisted of Dexedrine medication alone, administered twice daily with incremental adjustments until an optimal dosage was reached. Dexedrine medication was reinstituted following a second baseline phase. Behavioral components were then sequentially added as adjuncts to the stimulant medication. The behavioral components included (1) instructions and rationale for decreasing his activity level, provided by a staff member; (2) instructions plus guided practice in decreased movement and appropriate classroom and lunchroom behavior; and (3) instructions, guided practice, feedback, and reinforcement.

In this study, the child was taught how to read a wrist monitor and, thus, to provide his own feedback on his activity level. He was told to limit his checks to four or five within a 30-minute observation period in order to avoid interfering with his ongoing activities. The differential activity count goals for the classroom and the lunchroom were based on the mean activity level of a nonhyperactive comparison sample assessed in those settings. That is, the goal was not to eliminate extraneous movement but to decrease it to a level comparable to that of the subject's peer group. At the end of the observation period, the actometer was read, and the subject was given immediate feedback on whether he had achieved the goal. Reinforcement for achieving the goal consisted of a token entitling him to individual time with a staff member that day.

The most significant behavioral effect of the Dexedrine medication was increased on-task behavior (from 73% to 88%–96%), a finding that is consistent with the results of other studies of the effects of stimulant medication. The results of this case study also indicated that Dexedrine in combination with activity feedback and reinforcement had a broader effect on activity level and appropriate behavior in settings other than the classroom than did Dexedrine alone. Moreover, these effects were found on muscle groups and in settings not targeted in the intervention, findings that imply some degree of generalization. In addition, the results of posttest academic achievement indicated improvements in both spelling and arithmetic performance, although it was impossible to discern the active ingredients effecting this change. Unfortunately, too, no postintervention assessment of peer interventions was included. Clinically, however, as the authors noted, this study does help to elucidate the specific effects of Dexedrine mediation and to document the complementary additive effects of the behavioral intervention.

In general, behavioral interventions emphasizing reinforcement of behavior, whether reinforcement in the classroom or home-based reinforcement (e.g., contingency contracting), have been found to be effective in changing behavior (Carlson & Lahey, 1987; Lahey et al., 1978; O'Leary, 1980). Contingency contracting actively involves the child in selecting the target behavior and the consequences. In essence, the behavioral program is a contract agreed on by all those participating in it (Walden & Thompson, 1981). Contingency contracting may be conducted between student and teacher or may involve the child's parents in a home-based reinforcement program.

In home-based programs, teachers rate the target classroom behavior and communicate it to the parents, frequently in the form of a daily report card, and the parents administer the appropriate consequence, based on the teacher's report. Such home-based programs are becoming increasingly popular. They are acceptable to more teachers and require less extensive teacher involvement than other classroom-based reinforcement programs (Carlson & Lahey, 1987). Moreover, they may facilitate open communication between parents and school regarding the child's functioning, and they foster parental involvement in the child's treatment. A careful parenting evaluation should be conducted before designing a home-based reinforcement system for a given child, however. In order for the program to be successful, the parents must be able to appropriately implement the reinforcement system. If it is suspected that a "bad report card" could be the stimulus for harsh or abusive punishment, a home-based reinforcement system would be inappropriate (Carlson & Lahey, 1987).

A series of studies has been conducted addressing the extent of the effects of a broad behavior-therapy program (Abikoff & Gittelman, 1984), including comparison with stimulant medication (Abikoff & Gittelman, 1985a; Gittelman, Abikoff, Pollack, Klein, Katz, & Mattes, 1980). The behavior therapy program used by Gittelman and colleagues (Abikoff & Gittelman, 1984; Gittelman et al., 1980) included teacher consultation, parent training, and contingency contracting for behavior at home and at school, for which the parents provided backup reinforcement at the end of the school day.

The target behaviors were selected based on a functional assessment of each child and included classroom behaviors such as completion of work and calling out in class. Contracts were amended as appropriate during the course of the treatment. The rewards included tangible reinforcers, privileges, and social reinforcers. Punishments were also used and included loss of privileges and time-out.

In their 1984 study, Abikoff and Gittelman compared the classroom behavior of hyperactive children who had completed the behavior therapy program to that of their normal classmates to determine whether the treatment had brought the behavior of the hyperactive children within normal limits. The results of this study indicated that behavior therapy had been unsuccessful in normalizing behaviors characteristic of ADD/H (inattentiveness, impulsivity, and activity level). Methylphenidate, on the other hand, was found to have had a considerable normalizing effect on many of these behaviors (Abikoff & Gittelman, 1985a). Behavior therapy was found to have been effective, however, in reducing aggressive behavior to within normal limits (Abikoff & Gittelman, 1984).

In their 1980 study, Gittelman et al. compared the effects of behavior therapy and methylphenidate, alone and in combination, on the classroom behavior of hyperactive children. In general, the findings of their more recent work replicated the results from groups treated with either behavior therapy or methylphenidate, with two exceptions. The group receiving behavior therapy alone continued to receive higher teacher ratings of conduct disorder, and the hyperactives treated with methylphenidate alone continued to be disruptive in class. The combined-treatments group, however, were found not to differ from their normal classmates on any behavioral measure at the end of treatment.

Consistent results were reported in another study comparing the effects of a similar behavior-therapy program with those of stimulant medication (Pelham, Schnedler, Bologna, & Contreras, 1980). Pelham et al. (1980) found that, although either stimulant medication or behavior therapy increased on-task behavior, levels of on-task behavior comparable to those of nonhyperactive classmates were reached only with the combination of methylphenidate and behavior therapy.

In sum, these findings suggest that the effects of classroom contingency management may be limited in ameliorating the central features of ADD, but that they may complement the effects of medication, especially in intervening with possible associated behavior problems (e.g., aggression). As noted earlier, a primary goal of classroom management procedures, however, is to improve academic functioning. In general, the results of research examining the effects of interventions that act to directly modify the central behaviors of ADD—whether behavioral (Carlson & Lahey, 1987; Lahey et al., 1978) or pharmacological (O'Leary, 1980; Sprague, 1983; Weiss, 1983)—do not show improved academic achievement. Reviews of the results of studies in which the target behavior was *academic* achievement rather than inappropriate off-task behaviors, on the other hand, suggest that directly reinforcing academic responding results in increases in *both* academic achievement and appropriate classroom behavior (Carlson & Lahey, 1987; Friman & Christopherson, 1983; Heavilon, 1980; Lahey et al., 1978). Together, these results would argue that developers of behavior management programs should target directly the areas of impaired functioning of the ADD child, and in the classroom, these would include academic performance.

The effects of behavioral classroom intervention with ADD also tend to vary with the type of intervention used. Studies comparing strict, direct contingency-management procedures in the classroom to medication typically find stronger effects for the behavioral intervention than do those comparing behavior therapy to medication (Rapport, Murphy, & Bailey, 1982). As Rapport *et al.* noted, there are several plausible methodological explanations for the differences in results. One possibility that emerges from laboratory studies with ADD children suggests that the continuous reinforcement schedules of the direct contingency-management approaches may be more powerful with ADD children than the partial or delayed reinforcement schedules (Friebergs & Douglas, 1969; Parry & Douglas, 1983) usually operating in behavior therapy protocols.

There are obvious drawbacks to strict contingency-management interventions, however, including unrealistic demands on the teacher's time (Rapport, Murphy, & Bailey, 1980; Rapport *et al.*, 1982). An alternative to direct reinforcement programs, which also provides immediate feedback, is response cost. In a series of single-case studies, Rapport and colleagues (1980, 1982) examined the effects of response cost on the hyperactive and academic behaviors in the classroom of hyperactive children.

In the first study, the effects of a response cost procedure using individual and group contingencies were evaluated in a multielement treatment design (Rapport *et al.*, 1980). In the response cost phase, the target behavior was working on individual classroom assignments. The child was told that he could earn up to 30 minutes of free time for working hard during the period for himself or for the whole class. Both the teacher and the child had wooden stands with numbered cards from 30 to 0. The teacher explained to the child that she would occasionally look up from the small group with which she was working to see if he was working on his assignment. If he was not on-task, she would flip down a numbered card from her stand, which indicated that one minute of the child's free time had been lost. He was told to occasionally look at the teacher's stand and then to flip his cards to match hers. During the final condition, the child was told that he could earn the free time, on an all-or-none basis, if all of his assignments were completed within the hour class period.

When the response cost program was implemented, there was an immediate and significant decrease in the child's off-task behavior to within the normal classroom range, accompanied by an increase in the percentage and the accuracy of the assignments he completed. These effects were found under both the individual and the group contingencies, with the effects being strongest in the individual condition. These results were maintained in the final condition and at 1-week follow-up. At the conclusion of the study, questionnaires were administered to the child and his teacher to assess consumer satisfaction; both the child and the teacher viewed the response cost procedure as desirable, effective, and only minimally time-consuming.

In their 1982 study, Rapport *et al.* again used a within-subjects design to compare the effects of methylphenidate to response cost on two hyperactive children's academic and classroom behavior. For one child, the response cost procedures used were essentially the same as those in the previous experiment. For the other, the apparatus was modified in an effort to develop a more easily administered response cost system. This apparatus consisted of a small electronic digital display on the child's desk, which was controlled by a small hand-held counter operated by the teacher. Methylphenidate administration was individually titrated for each child until the optimal dosages were reached. Both the response cost and the methylphenidate were effective in increasing on-task behavior and academic performance; the greatest improvement occurred for both children in the response cost condition.

The possible additive effects of methylphenidate and response cost, however, were not assessed in the Rapport *et al.* (1982) study. In an additive design, Rapport *et al.* (1980) did compare the effects of methylphenidate alone, response cost alone, and methylphenidate plus response cost on the hyperactive and academic classroom behaviors of another child, whose off-task behavior decreased during the medication-alone condition (5 mg methylphenidate) but remained variable. Introduction of the response cost procedure both on and off medication resulted in lower rates of off-task behavior, with the most consistently low rates found with the medication plus the response cost. No clear effects on academic performance were found during the medication-only condition, but performance and accuracy were again found to increase with the introduction of response cost. Consumer satisfaction measures again suggested that the response cost procedure was viewed as fair, effective, and convenient by both student and teacher. It should be noted, however, that the dosage of stimulant medication had not been individually titrated for this child, and therefore, the effects of the stimulant medication may not have been appropriately tested. Taken together, the results of this series of studies suggest that response cost holds promise as a behavioral intervention in the classroom and academic behaviors of ADD children.

Although reinforcement for improving appropriate classroom and academic behavior is the behavior management approach of choice, at times it is necessary to consequate inappropriate behavior that is unacceptable (e.g., aggression). Time-out from positive reinforcement, or simply "time-out," of even a short duration is a method of effectively reducing undesirable behavior. In the school setting, time-out may entail placing the child away from other students, either within the classroom or (e.g., LeBlanc, Busby, & Thompson, 1973) by removing him from the room (e.g., Drabman & Spitalnick, 1973). Another time-out procedure involves removing the opportunity to receive reinforcement rather than actually removing the child from the environment (e.g., Foxx & Shapiro, 1978; Kubany, Weiss, & Slogett, 1971).

In general, reviews of the literature on time-out have found that time-out is an effective procedure for reducing inappropriate behavior in the classroom, and that it can easily be combined with other behavior management techniques (Carlson & Lahey, 1987). However, it is subject to the same criticisms as other punishment procedures, and safeguards must be taken against their misuse (Carlson & Lahey, 1987; Matson & Schaughency, 1988). The potential legal implications of time-out require that it be systematically planned, carefully supervised, and regularly reviewed (Cast & Nelson, 1977).

## Parent Behavior-Management Training

Parent training may be warranted for a number of reasons. First, as noted at the beginning of this chapter, ADD has been associated with disturbances in parent–child interactions. The parents of hyperactive children often report negative attitudes toward their child and report difficulties in child management (Cohen, Sullivan, Minde, Novak, & Keens, 1983). Observational studies of parent–child interactions involving ADD children have found mothers of hyperactive children to be more critical, less positive, and more directive than the mothers of nonhyperactive children (Cohen *et al.*, 1983; Pollard *et al.*, 1984). Moreover, even if the child is on stimulant medication, the drug is typically prescribed only during the school day, and stimulant medication is a fast-acting drug. That is, the effects of medication have worn off by the after-school and evening hours, and the parents may require skills in managing their child's behavior.

Several of the behavior therapy programs reviewed thus far have included a parent-training component (Gittelman *et al.*, 1980; Pelham *et al.*, 1980). Pelham *et al.* (1980), for example, reported on the effects of treatment on parent–child interactions. They found that, during a posttreatment clinic observation of parent–child interactions, the children were found to be on-task more and parents were found to be less aversive and controlling, although reacting no more positively to their children. This study included both behavioral and pharmacological intervention, it will be recalled, and the authors did not report whether the children were on medication at the time of assessment.

In a multiple-baseline across-subjects design, Pollard, Ward, and Barkley (1983) assessed the effects of parent training alone and in combination with methylphenidate on the parent–child interactions of three hyperactive boys. The parent-training program used was parent–child interaction training as outlined by Barkley (1981) and by Forehand and McMahon (1981). It consisted of teaching the parents ways of improving attending to play, compliance, and independent activity, while using time-out for noncompliance and disruptive behavior. Either treatment alone decreased the number of commands given by the mother, sustained the child's compliance with commands, and improved parent ratings of deviant child behavior in the home (Pollard *et al.*, 1983). Only parent training, however, resulted in increases in the mother's use of positive attention following the child's compliance. In addition, the combination of treatments increased the treatment effects in one case, a finding that supports the notion that treatment needs and outcome evaluations should be considered case by case.

## Cognitive Training

Cognitive training has also been used as an alternative or adjunct to the stimulant treatment of hyperactive children. The goals of cognitive training include teaching hyperactive children more effective problem-solving and self-control skills (Abikoff, 1985), which will hopefully facilitate generalization and maintenance effects. The rationale for targeting cognitive strategies is based largely on the theoretical work of Luria (1961) and others who postulated an important role for covert language in the self-control of behavior.

Different treatment approaches and procedures for hyperactive children have been used that fall into the category of cognitive training. Hyperactive children have typically been found to perform impulsively (i.e., to respond quickly and inaccurately) on tasks that require organization and attention to detail. Self-instructional training, modeling, and attentional training are used to teach hyperactive children systematic search and scanning behaviors, methods for remembering important stimulus features, and strategies for comparing stimuli for similarities and differences. Self-monitoring, which requires children to stop and evaluate their performance from time to time, is used to promote greater attention to detail and awareness of the problem-solving process (Abikoff, 1985).

Interpersonal or social problem-solving training has also been used with hyperactive children (e.g., Hinshaw, Henker, & Whalen, 1984a). This strategy uses sequential problem-solving techniques such as those described by Shure and Spivack (1972). The child is taught to recognize and define interpersonal problems when they arise in order to generate alternative solutions to the problem, to consider and evaluate the consequences of the various alternatives, to consider how the chosen solution can be implemented, and to follow through on the chosen solution. Role playing and modeling are frequently used to aid in teaching problem-solving procedures.

From his review of the literature, Abikoff (1985) concluded that the demonstrated effects of cognitive training on the performance of hyperactive children remain equivocal. The studies reviewed suggest that cognitive training facilitates the planning and careful responding needed to perform well on some perceptual-motor tasks, as indicated by fairly consistent findings of improvement in qualitative errors on Porteus mazes. However, in the studies reviewed that examined the effects of cognitive training on cognitive impulsivity, as measured by the Matching Familiar Figures Test (MFFT), the results are less clear. A number of studies reported significant improvement on the MFFT after training, although the significance of these findings is reduced because the MFFT was also used as the training task. In addition, there is no strong evidence that cognitive training enhances memory (e.g., on the Paired Associates Test) or attentional processes (e.g., on the Continuous Performance Test). Even less evidence exists that cognitive procedures are effective in improving academic achievement or classroom behavior.

Some investigators have used multiple training strategies ("multipush") to assess the effects of cognitive training on hyperactive children. Brown and Conrad (1982), for example, examined the effects of self-instructional training, attentional training, and a combination of the two strategies on the cognitive performance of 48 nine-year old hyperactive boys who were randomly selected from special-education classes in a large metropolitan school system. The children in the training groups were individually trained for 10 sessions (length of the training sessions not reported). Training tasks used during self-instructional training were not reported. The MFFT was used in the attentional training and the combination training conditions. The attentional and combined training conditions, but not self-instructional training alone, resulted in improvements in performance ("decreased impulsivity") on the MFFT. Based on these findings, the authors concluded that self-control training alone is insufficient to improve performance. Unfortunately, the use of the MFFT as both training instrument and outcome measure in the attentional and combined training conditions raises the question of whether results obtained in these conditions were due to practice rather than treatment effects.

A number of studies have combined cognitive training with medication to study their effects on cognitive functioning. Brown, Wynne, and Medenis (1985) examined the effects of cognitive training and methylphenidate on the cognitive performance; academic achievement; and teacher, parent, and self-ratings of behavior, of 40 boys (ages 6–11) identified as hyperactive. Thirty boys were randomly assigned to one of three treatment conditions: (1) methylphenidate; (2) cognitive training; and (3) methylphenidate combined with cognitive training. Medication conditions used a 0.3-mg/kg dosage. A no-treatment control group consisted of 10 children who had previously been placed on a waiting list. The four groups did not differ in age, IQ, or Conners teacher-rating scores. The children in the cognitive training groups were trained in individual hour-long sessions twice a week. There were a total of 24 sessions, spanning a 3-month period. Modeling, self-verbalization, and strategy training based on the work of Meichenbaum and Goodman (1971) were used initially, followed by a structured routine similar to the one used by Douglas, Parry, Marton, and Garson (1976; specific training nonspecified). "Superhero thinking cards," which visually modeled the strategies being taught, were used throughout training.

Compared to the no-treatment control group, all three treatment groups made significant gains on the cognitive measures used; these gains had been maintained at 3-month follow-up. The medication and combined conditions resulted in improvements on measures of both attention and listening comprehension and accounted for approximately the same amount of the variance on the dependent measures across pretesting, posttesting, and follow-up testing. The cognitive training alone led to significant improvement only on cognitive measures of attention and accounted for less variance than the other treatment conditions. However, all three conditions accounted for more variance on the dependent measures than no treatment.

Horn, Chatoor, and Conners (1983) examined the additive effects of Dexedrine and self-control training on a 9-year-old boy in a psychiatric inpatient unit who received the codiagnoses of hyperactivity and conduct disorder. Self-instructional training as well as self-reinforcement was used in conjunction with individually titrated medication. The training occurred during two weekly half-hour sessions for 3 weeks (training tasks not reported). Cognitive training was found to have no beneficial effects on cognitive performance. However, significant improvement on the Continuous Performance Test was found with medication alone.

Abikoff and Gittelman (1985b) examined the utility of using cognitive training as an adjunct to stimulant medication. The subjects for the study included 50 boys and girls, between the ages of 6 and 12, who were identified as exhibiting cross-situational hyperactivity and who were receiving maintenance medication treatment. The children were randomly assigned to a cognitive training group, an attention control-group, or a medication-alone group. The groups did not differ significantly in age or degree of academic or behavioral problems while on medication. The training program lasted 16 weeks and emphasized cognitive and interpersonal problem-solving.

During the first 8 weeks, the children were seen individually by their teachers for 1-hour training sessions twice a week. Cognitive modeling and self-instructional training procedures were used to teach reflective problem-solving skills; the training materials consisted of psychoeducational tasks similar to the ones used by Douglas, Parry, Marton, and Garson (1976). To facilitate maintenance and generalization, the parents observed two training sessions and were instructed to encourage and praise the child's use of reflective skills in doing his or her homework. In the final 8 weeks of the training program, the children were seen in small groups of three. Social problem-solving skills were emphasized during this phase of training. Again, the parents were exposed to the social problem-solving techniques and were asked to encourage the use of these skills in the home.

The authors found no significant treatment effects on the Paired Associates Test, the Continuous Performance Test, the Raven Progressive Matrices, or MFFT errors. Response latency on the MFFT was improved significantly for the children who received cognitive training compared to the children in the medication-alone group, but not to the children in the attention control-group. The groups were not found to differ on cognitive performance at 1-month follow-up testing on placebo, however, a finding that indicates that cognitive training did not facilitate maintenance after stimulant treatment.

## Effects of Cognitive Training on Interpersonal Performance

As noted earlier, the difficulties experienced by children with ADD extend beyond the purely cognitive. ADD has been found to be associated with impairments in peer relations in general, and with aggressive behavior problems in particular. The effects of cognitive-behavioral intervention and stimulant medication on the anger control of hyperactive children in a laboratory situation was evaluated in two studies (Hinshaw et al., 1984a).

In the first study, all subjects received brief individual coaching in cognitive-behavioral strategies. In the second study, cognitive self-regulation skills training was contrasted with empathy enhancement and perspective-taking training. Stimulant medication versus placebo was incorporated into both studies to allow an evaluation of possible interactive effects of medication and psychological interventions.

The subjects were hyperactive boys between the ages of 8 and 13 who were recruited for participation in an outpatient intervention program. The selection criteria for participation were reported to be the same in both studies: a primary diagnosis of hyperactivity by the child's physician; average or above-average intellectual functioning; and treatment with a stable dosage of and positive response to methylphenidate for at least 3 months before the start of the program, with no concurrent treatment with other psychotropic medication. Children with signs of mental retardation, severe emotional disturbance, organicity, or acute family distress were excluded.

In Study 1, consecutively enrolled boys were trained in groups of three in six biweekly sessions, co-led by clinical psychology graduate students. The sessions were videotaped for later scoring.

The participants were taught a set of specific problem-solving skills and strategies, which they initially applied to psychoeducational tasks. In Sessions 2–4, interpersonal problem-solving was introduced. In Session 5, an individualized behavioral provocation test was administered to each subject.

The behavioral provocation test was introduced as a way to practice self-control while being teased. The provocations were individualized by having each participant list names or phrases that bothered him. During the assessment, the two remaining group members served as confederates, who attempted to provoke the child being assessed.

Following the assessment, strategies for self-control were reviewed and practiced, and a plan for maintaining self-control in the subsequent provocation was generated. Before the second provocation, each child practiced his plan individually with a group leader.

Medication generally decreased the vigor of behavior, although only the tendency to not respond to provocations reached statistical significance. Following coaching and rehearsal of cognitive-behavioral self-control strategies, the subjects displayed greater levels of self-control, use of purposeful alternatives, and less fidgeting, vocalization, and verbal retaliation. No interactions of medication status and psychological intervention achieved significance.

Although these results appear encouraging, the lack of a control group limits their interpretability. In Study 2, cognitive-behavioral self-regulation training was compared with a control-treatment condition, matched for trainer attention and exposure to cognitive problem-solving techniques, but with no training and rehearsal in specific cognitive-behavioral strategies.

The subjects met daily in groups of four for self-regulation skills training. During the first 2 weeks of treatment, the training was identical in the two conditions. As in Study 1, cognitive self-instructional strategies were initially applied to academic problems, followed by the introduction of interpersonal problems and the generation of an individualized list of problem situations.

Following the behavioral provocation pretest, each group was randomly split, with two boys and one therapist entering the cognitive-behavioral condition and the others entering the control condition. The cognitive-behavioral condition consisted of individualized training in stress inoculation procedures of cue recognition (Novaco, 1979) and specific strategy-training and rehearsal. The control condition included cognitive training in perspective taking and problem solving (see Marsh, Serafica, & Barenboim, 1980). A behavioral provocation posttest was held on Wednesday of Group 3, following administration of the differential interventions.

In sum, the results of these studies suggest that cognitive behavioral approaches hold some promise for interpersonal-skills training. However, many questions remain to be addressed if we are to demonstrate clinical utility: Do treatment effects extend beyond the posttest assessment? Are the effects maintained at follow-up? Are they observed in naturalistic peer interactions, such as on the playground and the neighborhood streets? Do they result in improved sociometric status? These are the types of questions to be addressed by future clinical research. The careful and cogent review conducted by Abikoff (1985) strongly suggests that clinical utility has yet to be demonstrated.

## CONCLUDING REMARKS

The ratio of what is known to what is not known about the psychological treatment of hyperactive children is quite low. At the current level of our clinical science, it is safe only to say that combinations of treatments generally make the greatest clinical sense. Currently, there is substantial evidence to support the individual and combined use of both stimulant medication and home-based and school-based contingency-management programs. To date, there is far less reason to believe that cognitive therapy contributes to the amelioration of hyperactivity. Whereas there is very little evidence to support the use of other forms of psychological therapy with hyperactive children, clinical judgment may certainly call for the use of family therapy in individual cases.

# REFERENCES

Abikoff, H. (1985). Efficacy of cognitive training interventions in hyperactive children: A critical review. *Clinical Psychology Review, 5,* 479–512.

Abikoff, H., & Gittelman, R. (1984). Does behavior therapy normalize the classroom behavior of hyperactive children? *Archives of General Psychiatry, 41,* 449–454.

Abikoff, H., & Gittelman, R. (1985a). The normalizing effects of methylphenidate on the classroom behavior of ADDH children. *Journal of Abnormal Child Psychology, 13,* 33–44.

Abikoff, H., & Gittelman, R. (1985b). Hyperactive children treated with stimulants: Is cognitive training a useful adjunct? *Archives of General Psychiatry, 42,* 953–961.

Ackerman, D. T., Dykman, R. A., & Oglesby, D. M. (1983). Sex and group differences in reading and attention deficit disordered children with and without hyperkinesis. *Journal of Learning Disabilities, 16,* 407–415.

American Psychiatric Association. (1968). *Diagnostic and statistical manual* (2nd ed.). Washington, DC: Author.

American Psychiatric Association. (1980). *Diagnostic and statistical manual of mental disorders* (3rd ed.). Washington, DC: Author.

American Psychiatric Association. (1987). *Diagnostic and statistical manual of mental disorders* (3rd ed., revised). Washington, DC: Author.

August, G. J., & Holmes. C. S. (1984). Behavior and academic achievement in hyperactive subgroups and learning-disabled boys: A six-year follow-up. *American Journal of Disease in Children, 138,* 1025–1029.

August, G. J., & Stewart, M. A. (1984). Familial subtypes of childhood hyperactivity. In S. Chess & A. Thomas (Eds.), *Annual progress in child psychiatry and child development* (pp. 364–377). New York: Brunner/Mazel.

Baker, L., & Cantwell, D. P. (1982). Developmental, social, and behavioral characteristics of speech and language disordered children. *Child Psychiatry and Human Development, 12,* 195–206.

Barkley, R. A. (1981). *Hyperactive children: A handbook for diagnosis and treatment.* New York: Guilford Press.

Bennett, F. C., & Sherman, R. (1983). Management of childhood "hyperactivity" by primary care physicians. *Journal of Developmental and Behavioral Pediatrics, 4,* 88–93.

Brown, R. T., & Conrad, K. J. (1982). Impulse control or selective attention: Remedial programs for hyperactive children. *Psychology in the Schools, 19,* 92–97.

Brown, R. T., Wynne, M. E., & Medenis, R. (1985). Methylphenidate and cognitive therapy: A comparison of treatment approaches with hyperactive boys. *Journal of Abnormal Child Psychology, 13*(1), 69–87.

Caparulo, B. K., Cohen, D. J., Rothman, S. L., Young, S. G., Katz, J. D., Shaywitz, S. E., & Shaywitz, B. A. (1981). Computed tomographic brain scanning in children with developmental neuropsychiatric disorders. *Journal of the American Academy of Child Psychiatry, 20,* 338–357.

Carlson, C. L., & Lahey, B. B. (1987). Behavioral classroom intervention with children exhibiting conduct disorder or attention deficit disorder with hyperactivity. In S. Elliott & F. Gresham (Eds.), *Handbook of behavioral interventions in the classroom.* New York: Plenum Press.

Cast, D. C., & Nelson, C. M. (1977). Timeout in the classroom: Implications for special education. *Exceptional Children, 43,* 461–464.

Cohen, N. J., Sullivan, J., Minde, K., Novak, C., & Helwig, C. (1983). Mother-child interaction in hyperactive and normal kindergarten-aged children and the effect of treatment. *Child Psychiatry and Human Development, 13,* 213–224.

Deutsch, C. K., Swanson, J. M., Bruello, J. H., Cantwell, D. F., Weinberg, F., & Baren, M. (1982). Overrepresentation of adoptees in children with the attention deficit disorder. *Behavioral Genetics, 12,* 231–238.

Douglas, V. I. (1980). Treatment and training approaches to hyperactivity: Establishing internal or external control. In C. K. Whalen & B. Henker (Eds.), *Hyperactive children: The social ecology of identification and treatment* (pp. 283–318). New York: Academic Press.

Douglas, V. I. (1983). Attentional and cognitive problems. In M. Rutts (Ed.), *Developmental neuro-psychiatry* (pp. 250–329). New York: Guilford Press.

Douglas, V. I., Parry, P., Marton, P., & Garson, C. (1976). Assessment of a cognitive training program for hyperactive children. *Journal of Abnormal Child Psychology, 4*(4), 389–410.

Drabman, R. S., & Lahey, B. B. (1974). Feedback in classroom behavior modification: Effects on the target child and classmates. *Journal of Applied Behavior Analysis, 1*, 591–598.

Drabman, R. S., & Spitalnick, R. (1973). Social isolation as a punishment procedure: A controlled study. *Journal of Experimental Child Psychology, 16*, 236–249.

Dulcan, M. (1985). Attention deficit disorder: Evaluation and treatment. *Pediatric Annals, 14*, 383–388.

Edelbrock, C., Costello, A. J., & Kessler, M. D. (1984). Empirical corroboration of the attention deficit disorder. *Journal of the American Academy of Child Psychiatry, 23*, 285–290.

Firestone, P., & Douglas, V. I. (1975). The effects of reward and punishment on reaction times and autonomic activity in hyperactive and normal children. *Journal of Abnormal Child Psychology, 3*(3), 201–215.

Forehand, R., & McMahon, R. J. (1981). *Helping the noncompliant child: A clinician's guide to parent training.* New York: Guilford Press.

Foxx, R. M., & Shapiro, R. T. (1978). A timeout ribbon: A nonexclusionary timeout procedure. *Journal of Applied Behavior Analysis, 11*, 125–136.

Freibergs, V., & Douglas, V. I. (1969). Concept learning in hyperactive and normal children. *Journal of Abnormal Psychology, 74*(3), 388–395.

Friman, P. C., & Christopherson, E. R. (1983). Behavior therapy and hyperactivity: A brief review of therapy for a big problem. *The Behavior Therapist, 6*, 175–176.

Gittelman, R., Abikoff, H., Pollack, E., Klein, D. F., Katz, S., & Mattes, J. (1980). A controlled trial of behavior modification and methyphenidate in hyperactive children. In C. K. Whalen & B. Henker (Eds.), *Hyperactive children: The social ecology of identification and treatment* (pp. 221–243). New York: Academic Press.

Graham, P. (1979). Epidemiological studies. In H. C. Quay & J. S. Werry (Eds.), *Psychopathological disorders of childhood* (2nd ed.). New York: Wiley.

Heavilon, J. C. (1980). A critical evaluation of treatment modalities for hyperkinesis in children. Doctoral dissertation, University of Oregon. (*Dissertation Abstracts International*, 1980, 41, 1915–1916B.)

Hechtman, L., & Weiss, G. (1983). Long-term outcome of hyperactive children. *American Journal of Orthopsychiatry, 53*, 378–389.

Hechtman, L., Weiss, G., & Perlman, T. (1984). Young adult outcome of hyperactive children who received long-term stimulant treatment. *Journal of the American Academy of Child Psychiatry, 23*, 261–269.

Hinshaw, S. P., Henker, B., & Whalen, C. K. (1984a). Self-control in hyperactive boys in anger-inducing situations: Effects of cognitive-behavioral training and of methylphenidate. *Journal of Abnormal Child Psychology, 12*, 55–77.

Hinshaw, S. P., Whalen, C. K., &Henker, B. (1984b). Cognitive-behavioral and pharmocologic interventions for hyperactive boys: Comparative and combined effects. *Journal of Consulting and Clinical Psychology, 52*, 739–749.

Hobbs, S. A., Moguin, L. E., Tyroler, M.. & Lahey, B. B. (1980). Cognitive behavior therapy with children: Has clinical utility been demonstrated? *Psychological Bulletin, 87*, 147–165.

Horn, W. F., Chatoor, I., & Conners, C. K. (1983). Additive effects of dexedrine and self-control training: A multiple assessment. *Behavior Modification, 7*(3), 383–402.

Hughes, M. C., Goldman, B. L., & Snyder, N. F. (1983). Hyperactivity and the attention deficit disorder. *American Family Physician, 27*, 119–126.

King, C., & Young, R. D. (1982). Attentional deficits with and without hyperactivity: Teacher and peer perceptions. *Journal of Abnormal Child Psychology, 10*, 483–495.

Kinsbourne, M. (1983). Toward a model for the Attention Deficit Disorder. *The Minnesota Symposium on Child Development, 16*, 137–166.

Kubany, E. S., Weiss, L. E., & Slogett, B. B. (1971). The good behavior clock: A reinforcement/time out procedure for reducing disruptive classroom behavior. *Journal of Behavior Therapy and Experimental Psychiatry, 2*, 178–179.

Lahey, B. B., & Strauss, C. C. (1982). Some considerations in evaluating the clinical utility of cognitive behavior therapy with children. *School Psychology Review, 11*, 67–74.

Lahey, B. B., Delamater, A., Kupfer, D. L., & Hobbs, S. A. (1978). Behavior aspects of learning disabilities and hyperactivity. *Education and Urban Society, 10*, 477–499.

Lahey, B. B., Green, K. D., & Forehand, R. (1980). On the independence of ratings of hyperactivity, conduct problems, and attention dysfunction children. *Journal of Consulting and Clinical Psychology, 48*, 566–574.

Lahey, B. B., Schaughency, E. A., Strauss, C. C., & Frame, C. L. (1984). Are attention deficit disorders with and without hyperactivity similar or dissimilar disorders? *Journal of the American Academy of Child Psychiatry, 23*, 302–309.

Lahey, B. B., Schaughency, E. A., Frame, C. L., & Strauss, C. C. (1985). Teacher ratings of attention problems in children experimentally classified as exhibiting attention deficit disorder with and without hyperactivity. *Journal of the American Academy of Child Psychiatry, 24*, 613–616.

Lahey, B. B., Schaughency, E. A., Hynd, G. W., Carlson, C., Nieves, N. (in press). Attention deficit disorder with and without hyperactivity: Comparison of behavioral characteristics of clinic-referred children. *Journal of the American Academy of Child Psychiatry.*

LeBlanc, J. M., Busby, K. H., & Thomson, C. (1973). The functions of time out for changing aggressive behavior of a preschool child: A multiple baseline analysis. In R. E. Ulrich, T. S. Stachnik, & J. E. Mabry (Eds.), *Control of human behavior: Behavior modification in education* (Vol. 3, pp. 358–364). Glenview, IL: Scott, Foresman.

Lobitz, W. C. (1974). A simple stimulus cue for controlling disruptive classroom behavior. *Journal of Abnormal Child Psychology, 2*, 143–152.

Loney, S., Kramer, J., & Milich, R. (1981). The hyperactive child grows up: Prediction of symptoms, delinquency and achievement at follow-up. In K. Gadow & J. Loney (Eds.), *Psychosocial aspects of drug treatment for hyperactivity.* Boulder, CO: Westview Press.

Lou, H. C., Henriksen, L., & Bruhn, P. (1984). Focal cerebral hypoperfusion in children with dysphasia and/or attention deficit disorder. *Archives of Neurology, 41*, 825–829.

Luria, A. (1961). *Role of speech in the regulation of normal and abnormal behaviors.* New York: Liveright.

Marsh, D. T., Serafica, F. C., & Borenboim, C. (1980). Effect of perspective-taking training on interpersonal problem solving. *Child Development, 51*, 140–145.

Matson, J. L., & Schaughency, E. A. (1988). Mild and moderate mental retardation. In J. C. Witt, S. Elliott, & F. Gresham (Eds.), *Handbook of behavior therapy in education.* New York: Plenum.

Meichenbaum, D. H. & Goodman, J. (1971). Training impulsive children to talk to themselves: A means of developing self-control. *Journal of Abnormal Psychology, 77*, 115–126.

Novaco, R. W. (1979). The cognitive regulation of anger and stress. In P. C. Kendall (Ed.), *Cognitive-behavioral interventions: Theory, research and procedures*, (pp. 241–285). New York: Academic Press.

O'Leary, K. D. (1980). Pills or skills for hyperactive children. *Journal of Applied Behavior Analysis, 13*, 191–204.

Parry, P. A., & Douglas, V. I. (1983). Effects of reinforcement on concept identification in hyperactive children. *Journal of Abnormal Child Psychology, 11*(2), 327–340.

Pelham, W. E., & Milich, R. (1984). Peer relations in children with hyperactivity/Attention deficit disorders. *Journal of Learning Disabilities, 9*, 560–567.

Pelham, W. E., Schnedler, R. W., Bologna, N. C., & Contreras, J. A. (1980). Behavioral and stimulant treatment of hyperactive children: A therapy study with methylphenidate probes in a within-subject design. *Journal of Applied Behavior Analysis, 13*, 221–236.

Piacentini, J. C., Lahey, B. B., & Hynd, G. (1986). *Personality characteristics of the mothers of conduct disordered and hyperactive children.* Paper presented at the 32nd Annual Meeting of the Southeastern Psychological Association, Kissimmee, FL, March 26–29.

Pollard, S., Ward, E. M., & Barkley, R. A. (1983). The effects of parent training and Ritalin on parent-child interactions of hyperactive boys. *Child and Family Behavior Therapy, 5*, 51–68.

Rapport, M. D., Murphy, H. A., & Bailey, J. S. (1980). The effects of a response cost treatment tactic on hyperactive children. *Journal of School Psychology, 18*, 98–111.

Rapport, M. D., Murphy, H. A., & Bailey, J. S. (1982). Ritalin vs. response cost in the control of hyperactive children: A within-subject comparison. *Journal of Applied Behavioral Analysis, 15*, 205–216.

Sandoval, J., Lambert, N. M., & Sassone, D. M. (1981). The comprehensive treatment of hyperactive children: A continuing problem. *Journal of Learning Disabilities, 14*, 117–118.

Satterfield, J. H., Satterfield, B. T., & Cantwell, D. P. (1980). Multimodality treatment: A two-year evaluation of 61 hyperactive boys. *Archives of General Psychiatry, 37*, 915–919.

Satterfield, J. H., Hoppe, C. M., & Schell, A. M. (1982). A prospective study of delinquency in 110 adolescent boys with attention deficit disorder and 88 normal adolescent boys. *American Journal of Psychiatry, 139,* 119–120.

Schaughency, E. A., & Hynd, G. W. (1986). *Attention and impulse control in attention deficit disorders (ADD): Neural control systems.* Unpublished manuscript, University of Georgia, Athens, Georgia.

Schaughency, E. A., Hurley, L. K., & Krahn, G. L. (1986). *Assessment and differential diagnosis of Tourette's syndrome.* Unpublished manuscript, Oregon Health Sciences University.

Shaywitz, S. E., & Shaywitz, B. A. (1984). Devising the proper drug therapy for attention deficit disorders. *Contemporary Pediatrics, 1,* 12–24.

Sherman, C. F., & Anderson, R. B. (1980). Modification of attending behavior in hyperactive children. *Psychology in the Schools, 17,* 372–379.

Singer, S. M., Stewart, M. A., & Pulaski, L. (1981). Minimal brain dysfunction: Differences in cognitive organization in two groups of index cases and their relative. *Journal of Learning Disabilities, 14,* 470–473.

Shure, M. B., & Spivack, G. (1972). Means–ends thinking, adjustment, and social class among elementary school-aged children. *Journal of Consulting and Clinical Psychology, 37,* 389–394.

Sprague, R. L. (1983). Behavior modification and educational techniques. In M. Rutter (Ed.), *Developmental neuropsychiatry* (pp. 404–421). New York: Guilford Press.

Walden, E. L., & Thompson, S. A. (1981). Review of some alternative approaches to drug management of hyperactivity in children. *Journal of Learning Disabilities, 14,* 213–238.

Weiss, G. (1983). Long term outcome: Findings, concepts, and practical implications. In M. Rutter (Ed.), *Developmental neuropsychiatry* (pp. 422–436). New York: Guilford Press.

Wender, P. (1971). *Minimal brain dysfunction in children.* New York: Wiley.

Williamson, G. A., Anderson, R. P., & Lundy, N. C. (1980). The ecological treatment of hyperkinesis. *psychology in the Schools, 17,* 249–256.

Williamson, D. A., Calpin, J. P., Dilorenzo, T. M., Garris, R. P., & Petti, T. A. (1981). Treating hyperactivity with Dexedrine and activity feedback. *Behavior Modification, 5,* 399–416.

Wright, G. I. (1982). Attention deficit disorder. *Journal of School Psychology,* February 19–120.

# 10 *Attention Deficit Disorder and Hyperactivity*
## *Pharmacotherapies*

### Kenneth D. Gadow

Even though there is an extensive literature about the behavioral effects of psychotropic drugs on hyperactive children, there has been very little research into the effects of specific treatment procedures on therapeutic response and outcome. Numerous "how-to-treat" publications may be found (e.g., Arnold, 1973; Barkley, 1981; Cantwell, 1980; Eisenberg, 1972; Gittelman, 1983; Gross & Wilson, 1974; Katz, Saraf, Gittelman-Klein, & Klein, 1975; Laufer, Denhoff, & Riverside, 1957; Millichap, 1973; Ottinger, Halpin, Miller, Demian, & Hannemann, 1985; Rapoport, 1980; Safer & Allen, 1976; Solomons, 1968, 1971, 1973; Winsberg, Yepes, & Bialer, 1976), but they are based, for the most part, on the author's clinical experience of and/or research into the behavioral effects of psychotropic drugs. Although the literature reveals many differences of opinion about how various treatment situations should be handled, there is general agreement that pharmacotherapy should be carefully monitored and that care providers are an important source of information about the child's response to medication. Nevertheless, data from investigations of "how others have been treated" suggest that there is a marked disparity between the treatment procedures recommended in professional journals and those used in real-world settings (e.g., Brulle, Barton, & Foskett, 1983; Gadow, 1982, 1983; Loney & Ordoña, 1975; Ross, 1979; Sindelar & Meisel, 1982; Solomons, 1973; Weithorn & Ross, 1975).

There are many reasons for this state of affairs, one of the more important being the logistical nightmare of trying to supervise outpatient drug therapy. Partly in response to this situation, researchers are expending considerable effort on the development of clinic-based drug-evaluation procedures that will, in part, free clinicians from labor-intensive and time-consuming interactions with the patient's caregivers. Although this effort is to be lauded, only rigorous scrutiny can reveal its success. Even more troubling than the second-rate status of research on clinical practices and allegations of less than adequate care is the failure to seriously examine the basic assumptions underlying the decision to treat, assumptions that are inextricably linked to the rationale for each treatment

Kenneth D. Gadow • Department of Psychiatry and Behavioral Science, State University of New York at Stony Brook, Stony Brook, New York 11794-8790.

manipulation. Because these assumptions are so fundamental to treatment issues, they warrant some examination—at the very least, some clarification—at the beginning of any discussion of treatment practices.

## Theories of Treatment

Although it is extremely difficult (and possibly abitrary) to classify programs of clinical research and how-to-treat perspectives according to their implicit theory of treatment, an attempt is made here to at least contrast two different viewpoints. Space constraints limit the amount of attention this topic deserves, so only simple examples are presented here. Because theories of treatment generally cannot be reduced to a set of fundamental empirical relationships, they are not amenable to scientific study. For this and other reasons, they are of marginal interest to scientific journals and are rarely discussed publicly. This topic is addressed, however, in social issue journals, the popular media, and occasionally in graduate school seminars. Unfortunately, published discussions are often presented in a way that offends scientists and clinicians and are consequently summarily dismissed as radical press.

One clinical perspective, viewed here as the defective-organism approach, sees the hyperactive child as a patient with an organic disorder and medication responders as being benefited by the drug's ability to reverse or partially correct an aberrant biological process. One treatment prescription that might follow from such a perspective is that short-acting stimulants should be administered several times a day, year-round, so that the patient will receive the maximal benefit from treatment. This argument would seem particularly compelling if the drug is associated with limited risks and the disorder is viewed by the clinician as being a serious social impediment. This approach also embraces any and all associated symptoms as appropriate targets for treatment if they are responsive to medication. For example, if the hyperactive child also exhibits poor handwriting, drug improvement in this symptom could be a major justification for treatment even though poor handwriting in nonhyperactive children is not considered a diagnostic construct. Because symptom suppression and the normalization of aberrant processes is basic to the defective-organism approach, the clinician may feel that undermedication is a serious clinical problem. In other words, symptom suppression can be maximized by exploring the high therapeutic range of the dosage scale. The dose of medication will, of course, be reduced with the appearance of serious somatic complaints, but behavioral toxicity may be considered or evaluated in only a cursory fashion.

Another clinician, however, with a more biopsychosocial perspective, might perceive the same child as having an organic disorder with a relatively favorable prognosis but as nevertheless requiring medication as a therapeutic adjunct for a particular set of symptoms. Exposure to medication would be limited to the periods and settings in which the target symptoms were particularly troublesome. A minimal effective dose would be used, determined in large part by degrees of symptomatic improvement and a systematic evaluation of behavioral and somatic toxicity.

On the basis of these two examples, it should be clear that the researcher-clinician perception of the target and ancillary symptoms and their social significance, risk, etiology, and so on shapes the treatment recommendations. At first blush, it may seem that such issues can be resolved through empirical inquiry, but they cannot; and the failure to grasp the magnitude of this problem can seriously limit one's understanding of the treatment process.

## ROLE OF CARE PROVIDERS

One of the most controversial and least researched areas of drug therapy for hyperactivity concerns who should do what to whom during treatment. The key characters are, of course, the hyperactive child, his or her family, the school personnel, and the physician. The controversy encompasses two broad, interrelated issues. The first is the misuse of drug therapy, specifically the events that lead to treating false positives. The second issue is that the treatment regimens of many medically diagnosed hyperactive children are not managed satisfactorily (Loney & Ordoña, 1975; Solomons, 1973; Sprague & Gadow, 1976).

The effectiveness of psychotropic drug therapy depends on the efforts of a variety of people; it is they, after all, who must recognize the child's problem, make the appropriate diagnosis, prescribe the appropriate medication, adjust the dosage, supervise its administration, monitor the treatment effects, provide the necessary educational and psychological services, and terminate pharmacotherapy when it is no longer warranted, ineffective, or detrimental. Even a casual consideration of these activities will generate an appreciation for the complexity of the treatment process. Whereas for many youngsters and their families taking medication is a fairly straightfoward procedure, many others experience some difficulty with one or more of these activities. Moreover, given the number of people who may become involved in making, or in some way influencing, treatment-related decisions, there are going to be disagreements about what the appropriate course of action should be.

## OBJECTIVES

For purposes of discussion, the drug treatment process can be conceptualized as consisting of three stages: (1) diagnosis; (2) dosage adjustment; and (3) follow-up. Implicit in this trichotomy is a period before referral and diagnosis when the caregivers cope with the child's behavior and may initiate nondrug therapies, as well as a period following the termination of drug treatment when other approaches are used to ameliorate learning and adjustment problems (Sprague & Gadow, 1976). The pre- and postdrug periods have generally been excluded from most scientific investigations, although there is no shortage of discussion on the events that lead to medical referral (Bosco & Robin, 1976).

Given the now vast literature on hyperactivity, it is unrealistic to attempt a review of treatment practices and their empirical support in a single chapter. Therefore, decisions had to be made about which topics were going to receive greater attention than others, and which would be deleted altogether. In keeping with the orientation of the text, it was decided to focus on the specific practices associated with the management of the treatment regimen. Not discussed here is the first phase of the treatment process, diagnosis, but there are several excellent chapters on this topic presented in other books (e.g., Loney, 1983, 1987; Ross & Ross, 1982; Safer & Allen, 1976; Sleator, 1982), and the reader is referred to them for insight into the process that determines candidates for drug therapy. It is noteworthy that the majority of children who do receive a medical diagnosis of hyperactivity are subsequently given psychotropic medication. The topic of clinical efficacy has also been omitted simply because a brief overview of the literature in this area is of questionable value. Again, the reader is referred to comprehensive texts on the subject (Barkley, 1981; Gadow, 1986; Ross & Ross, 1982; Safer & Allen, 1976). The successful implementation of treatment procedures is determined, in part, by a legion of psychosocial variables associated with the dynamics of interpersonal interaction. They are occasionally addressed in how-to-treat publications (e.g., Barkley, 1981; Cantwel, 1980; Rapoport, 1980) but are touched on only lightly here, again because of space limitations.

This chapter describes various recommended treatment practices associated with dosage adjustment and monitoring drug therapy and their empirical support. When available, the findings from studies of treatment practices used in natural settings are also presented in an attempt to give some idea of their actual adoption in real-world settings. Because the assessment of drug effects has become such an important issue in recent years, the application of laboratory tasks to clinical decision-making is given special emphasis.

## STIMULANTS

Information from both the medical literature and various surveys indicates that stimulant drugs are prescribed for people of all ages who are diagnosed as hyperactive. They are used with infants, toddlers, and preschoolers (see Gadow, 1986); elementary-school children (see Ross & Ross, 1982); adolescents (see Reatig, 1985); and adults (Mann & Greenspan, 1976; Wender, Reimherr, Wood, & Ward, 1985). Of the stimulant drugs currently available for the treatment of hyperactivity, three account for the vast majority of all drug prescriptions: methylphenidate (Ritalin), dextroamphetamine (Dexedrine), and pemoline (Cylert).

### Schedule of Drug Administration

Stimulants are relatively short-acting drugs. Their behavioral effects can be observed within a half hour after the medicine is taken orally. A 10-mg tablet of methylphenidate produces a therapeutic effect for approximately 3–4 hours, and a 20-mg tablet lasts for at least an hour longer (Carter, 1956; Safer & Allen, 1976). There is a time-release form of dextroamphetamine (Dexedrine Spansule) that produces a longer lasting effect than the tablets, approximately 12 hours. Also, a long-lasting (8-hour) form of methylphenidate called Ritalin-SR is now available. The *SR* stands for "sustained-release." According to one report, one 20-mg tablet of Ritalin-SR administered at breakfast produces a therapeutic effect equivalent to a 10-mg tablet of regular Ritalin given twice a day (Whitehouse, Shah, & Palmer, 1980). The findings from another study, however, indicate that standard methylphenidate (10 mg of Ritalin b.i.d.) is superior to Ritalin-SR (20 mg) in suppressing certain forms of disruptive behavior (Pelham, Sturges, Hoza, Schmidt, Bijlsma, Milich, & Moorer, 1987).

Children on amphetamine or methylphenidate show their best performance approximately 1.5–2 hours after taking medication (Bradley & Bowen, 1941; Swanson, Kinsbourne, Roberts, & Zucker, 1978). More recent research, however, shows that time-course effects are more complex than previously believed because they differ depending on the dose of medication and the behavioral or biological process being measured (Conners & Solanto, 1984). For example, on a dose of 1.0 mg/kg given once in the morning, children continued to show decreasing activity throughout a 6-hour study interval. (On placebo days, the children became progressively more restless.)

Using behavioral ratings, some researchers have demonstrated that one dose of medication in the morning may be adequate for an entire school day (Safer & Allen, 1973b; Sleator & von Neumann, 1974; Sprague, Christensen, & Werry, 1974). Nevertheless, between 60% and 80% of the hyperactive children treated with methylphenidate or dextroamphetamine are given medication at noon, and some receive an additional dose in the afternoon (Gadow, 1981; Krager & Safer, 1974; Safer & Krager, 1984). Stimulants are also administered late in the day. One survey study of hyperactive preschoolers, for example, found that 28% received methylphenidate or dextroamphetamine in the evening (Gadow, 1977). The parents of these children said the medication helped their child to go to sleep at night. One study that used Dexedrine Spansules found that an evening dose was beneficial for sleep problems in elementary-school-aged hyperactive children (Chatoor, Wells, Conners, Seidel, & Shaw, 1983). Parents noted that the medication made the children more cooperative at bedtime. What may happen is that the rebound effect makes going to bed extremely difficult for some hyperactive children who receive their last dose of medication at noon or in the late afternoon (see also Kinsbourne, 1973).

Pemoline, which is a long-acting stimulant, is typically administered once each day, in the morning. This drug is prescribed infrequently and is relatively understudied, at least in comparison with the research on methylphenidate and dextroamphetamine.

Because stimulants are often administered in divided daily doses, many children must take their medicine during the school day. The percentage of students receiving medicine in school varies from one locale to the next, and this variability is probably due to differences in the extent of drug use, the availability of school nurses, and school policy. For example, Krager, Safer, and Earhart (1979) reported that, during the 1976–1977 school year, 79% of the students treated for hyperactivity (approximately 1.7% of the total public-elementary-school enrollment in Baltimore County, Maryland) received medication in school. In contrast with this finding, Kenney (1976) reported a much lower figure for public elementary schools in Minneapolis during the 1975–1976 school year. He found that 0.42% of the total school enrollment was administered medication in school for hyperactivity. A study of mentally retarded children in public school classes found that two thirds of the treated students received medication in school (Gadow & Kane, 1983).

The administration of medication in school has generated a number of concerns about liability, the storage of medicine, and the possibility of treatment errors. Krager et al. (1979) reported in their survey that school nurses administered the medication, but contrary to what might be expected, classroom teachers and teacher aides often supervise the dispensing of medicine in some areas (Gadow & Kane, 1983). Even though teachers may prefer to have the school nurse handle medication, many school systems have only limited access to a full-time nurse.

Guidelines for the administration of medication in school are available from many sources (e.g., Council for Exceptional Children, 1977), but the extent to which they are used at the school district level is unknown. One set of guidelines promulgated by the American Academy of Pediatrics (1978, 1981) is presented here as an example:

1. Written orders from a physician should detail the name of the drug, dosage, time interval the medication is to be taken, and diagnosis or reason for the medication to be given.
2. Written permission should be provided by the parent or guardian requesting that the school district comply with the physician's order.
3. Medication should be brought to school in a container appropriately labeled by the pharmacy or physician.
4. One member of the staff should be designated to handle medication, ideally a health professional if one is available.
5. A locked cabinet should be provided for the storage of medication.
6. Opportunities should be provided for communication between the parent, school personnel, and physician regarding the efficacy of the medication administered during school hours.

Nonprescription medication (e.g., aspirin, ointments, cold tablets) should not be given without prior written permission of parent or guardian.

There should be close cooperation between school personnel, parents, and the pupil's physician so the medical program can be modified as warranted by changes in the pupil's condition. School districts assuming responsibility for giving medication during school hours should provide liability coverage for the staff, including the nurse, teachers, athletic staff, principal, superintendent, and school board. (1981, pp. 215–216)

## Dosage

There is some disagreement about what is the best dose or dosage range of methylphenidate. Some clinicians (e.g., Sleator & von Neumann, 1974) have found that moderate dosages (0.3 mg/kg to 0.5 mg/kg) are quite effective for many children, whereas other experts (e.g., Klein, Gittelman, Quitkin, & Rifkin, 1980, p. 674) believe that low dosages, such as 0.3 mg/kg, are homeopathic and may account for cases of drug failure. It must be emphasized that children do differ greatly in terms of optimal dosage. Some do quite well on a low dose (0.1 mg/kg), whereas others appear unchanged unless the dose is very high (e.g., 1.0 mg/kg). For this reason, most clinicians start out with a small dose that is gradually increased until the desired effect is achieved. (The figures for milligrams per kilogram given here refer to *individual* doses of medication, which may or may not be administered more than one time per day.) The average daily dose of methylphenidate is usually 20–30 mg, with a morning dose of 10–20 mg and a noon dose of 10 mg (Safer & Allen, 1976). Others have also found that the optimal dose (for paired-associate learning) is 10–15 mg for many, but certainly not all, elementary-school-aged children (Swanson et al., 1978). It is not unusual, however, to find reports that state that the average *daily* dose of Ritalin is 60 mg or that some children are receiving as much as 120–140 mg per day (Gittelman-Klein & Klein, 1976; Renshaw, 1974).

It is common clinical lore that dextroamphetamine is twice as potent as methylphenidate (Safer & Allen, 1976); however, comparisons of the two drugs with regard to performance on a laboratory task suggest that their dose effects may be fairly similar (Sprague & Sleator, 1976). In actual practice, the daily doses of methylphenidate and dextroamphetamine prescribed by physicians appear to be comparable (Gadow, 1981).

The beginning dose of pemoline is usually 37.5 mg, which may be increased to 75 mg per day (Safer & Allen, 1976). The dosage ratio of methylphenidate to pemoline ranges from 1:4 to 1:6 (Pelham, 1983; Stephens, Pelham, & Skinner, 1984). In other words, the behavioral effect produced by 0.3 mg/kg of methylphenidate administered twice a day is similar to the effect produced by 1.2–1.8 mg/kg of pemoline given once a day.

## Assessing Drug Effects

It is the opinion of some clinicians and scientists who work in this area that traditional approaches to the treatment of psychiatric disorders have over-emphasized symptom suppression and have overlooked the psychosocial implications of impairing adaptive behavior. One series of studies, originally initiated in the late 1960s and continued up to the present time, has addressed this issue by studying the dose–response effects of stimulants and neuroleptics on a variety of cognitive, academic, and behavioral measures (e.g., Sprague, 1984; Sprague & Sleator, 1977; Sprague, Werry, Greenwold, & Jones, 1969). The findings from one study are presented here for purposes of discussion.

The relationship between dose of methylphenidate and cognitive performance, classroom behavior, and heart rate is presented in Figure 1. "Learning" (the solid black line) refers to the child's performance (the percentage of correct answers) on a short-term memory (STM) task. The STM task requires the child to sit and study pictures of varying complexity. After exposure to each picture, the child is shown a "test" picture to determine how well he or she remembers the items in the "study" picture. Although short-term memory is one of its important components, classroom learning is obviously a complex process that taps a variety of skills and abilities. Most (65%) hyperactive children gave more correct answers with a 0.3 mg/kg dose than with placebo (10%) or a higher dose of 1.0 mg/kg (25%). It appears that if the dose is increased even more, methylphenidate would cause significantly impaired *group* performance on the STM task. This same dose relationship also holds for latency of response (the amount of time that elapses before responding). In other words, hyperactive children take less time to answer and therefore appear to be less inattentive.

Inappropriate classroom behavior, however, becomes less and less apparent as the amount of medication is increased (the dotted line). Using the Abbreviated Teacher Rating Scale (ATRS; Conners, 1973), teachers rated 72% of the hyperactive children as behaving their best on the highest dose. Only 28% received their best rating on 0.3 mg/kg, and none of the children showed their greatest improvement in behavior on placebo. The optimal dose of methylphenidate for certain classroom behaviors is therefore clearly different from that for concentrating on a laboratory memory task. Although the dose differences for these two behaviors are significant in and of themselves, side effects are also important. As illustrated, heart rate (the dashed line) increases as the dose becomes larger (although the degree of increase may not be clinically important; it must be remembered that these are group averages). The point where teachers

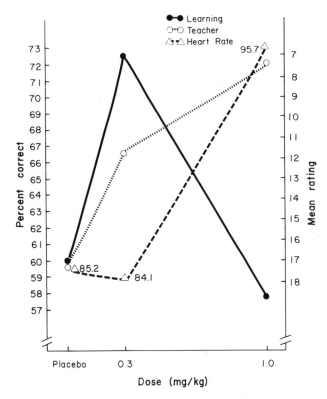

FIGURE 1. Dose–response effects of Ritalin on the short-term memory task with matrix size = 15 (Learning); teacher ratings of classroom behavior (Teacher), where smaller numbers indicate better behavior; and heart rate in beats per minute. (From "Methylphenidate in Hyperkinetic Children: Differences in Dose Effects on Learning and Social Behavior" by R. L. Sprague and E. K. Sleator, 1977, *Science, 198*, p. 1275. Copyright 1977 by the American Association for the Advancement of Science. Reprinted by permission.)

perceive the most improved classroom behavior is also associated with side effects. This does not mean that the teachers actually preferred the higher dose because they also often commented that the child's behavior was too controlled (e.g., overly quiet) with 1.0 mg/kg.

The results of the Sprague and Sleator (1977) study imply that careful consideration should be given to dosage adjustment and to the selection of treatment objectives. If higher doses are required to control severe behavior problems, their side effects should be carefully monitored to include behavioral toxicity. Caregivers should evaluate drug effects on adaptive behaviors such as appropriate social interaction and academic performance.

The traditional and most popular procedure for evaluating drug effects is caregiver reports. As previously noted, teacher ratings (e.g., on the ATRS) are dose-sensitive, and they can be a most useful clinical tool (see Figure 2). In fact, one research team (Sleator & Sprague, 1978) was so impressed by their clinical utility that they commented:

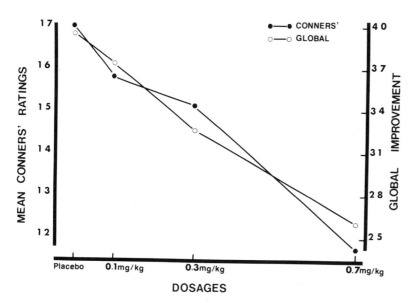

FIGURE 2. Dose–response effects of Ritalin on two different teacher rating scales. Numerical value of both scales decreases with improvement in classroom behavior. (From "Methylphenidate in the Treatment of Hyperkinetic Children" by E. K. Sleator and A. W. von Neumann, 1974, *Clinical Pediatrics, 13*, p. 23. Copyright 1974 by J. B. Lippincott Company. Reprinted by permission.)

> Remarkable sensitivity to drug effects on the part of the teacher has been replicated regularly in our laboratory. No other clinical measure even approaches this sensitivity [and] we recommend strongly that monitoring of drug effects must include reports from the teacher if the physician hopes to effectively treat school children with learning and/or behavior disorders. He must be in active communication with the child's teacher. The physician would not consider treating anemia, for example, without repeated laboratory tests. For the child with learning problems the teacher is the physician's clinical laboratory. (p. 579)

Nevertheless, there is little evidence that teacher rating scales are routinely used in real-world situations to evaluate drug effects or dosage changes (see Table 1).

Teacher ratings are sometimes maligned as being "subjective," the implication being that they do not accurately reflect the child's true behavior. Although this concern is generally directed toward the diagnostic process, it is sometimes used as a justification for corroborating caregiver ratings with laboratory performance tests. Suffice it to say that the track record for teacher ratings (as compared with direct observations) is not bad (see O'Leary, 1981), and they appear to be even more useful for certain purposes than direct observations completed by trained observers under "blind" conditions (e.g., Kazdin, Esveldt-Dawson, & Loar, 1983).

The usefulness of parent evaluations as the primary or sole criterion for determining the efficacy of treatment or for adjusting dosage is controversial. Although earlier studies have not reported encouraging results in parental ability to discriminate between drug and placebo conditions (Denhoff, Davids, & Hawkins, 1971; Rie, Rie, Stewart, & Ambuel, 1976; Sleator & von Neumann, 1974; Waizer, Hoffman, Polizos, & Engelhardt, 1974), investigators have ques-

Table 1. School Involvement in Pharmacotherapy[a]

| Variable | ECSE[b,c] | TMR[b,d] |
|---|---|---|
| Treatment evaluation | ($N = 114$) | ($N = 118$) |
| Report effects of medication | 69(61) | 70(59) |
| Use behavior rating scale | 5( 4) | 11( 9) |
| Report side effects | 45(39) | 46(39) |
| Suggest change in dosage | 32(28) | 37(31) |
| Report effects of dosage alteration | 35(31) | NA |
| Treatment withdrawal | ($N = 23$) | ($N = 16$) |
| Participate in decision to terminate treatment | 11(48) | 6(38) |
| Ask to observe and report evaluation | 8(35) | NA |

[a]Adapted from "School Involvement in Pharmacotherapy for Behavior Disorders" by K. D. Gadow, 1982, *Journal of Special Education, 16*, p. 389. Copyright 1982 by Grune & Stratton. Reprinted by permission.
[b]Numbers in parentheses are percentages. NA = not asked (item was not included in the questionnaire).
[c]ECSE (early childhood special education).
[d]TMR (trainable mentally retarded).

tioned both the appropriateness of the instruments in current use (Gittelman-Klein, Klein, Katz, Saraf, & Pollack, 1976) and the timing of parent ratings (usually completed after the drug's therapeutic effects have dissipated). Regardless of the reason for the conflicting results or for the apparent insensitivity of parent evaluations to treatment effects (a number of possible explanations are cited in the literature), no one has yet empirically documented that parent reports (whatever form they may take) are as useful to the physician as teacher ratings when titrating dosage.

For some time, laboratory tasks have been used by therapists in special clinics to evaluate drug effects. Because there are a number of different types of tasks and different reasons are given for their use, it is very difficult to make anything other than general statements about these tasks here. They have been used to evaluate behavioral toxicity, to assess drug effects on primary symptoms, to corroborate caregiver reports, and to determine spillover effects on associated symptoms. Each use is based on certain assumptions about the nature of the disorder, the symptom complex, and the reason(s) for treatment. Perhaps the single most distinguishing feature of the research on all the laboratory tasks in clinical settings is the failure to compellingly establish their ecological validity. There are, of course, exceptions (e.g., Rapport, Stoner, DuPaul, Kelly, Tucker, & Schoeler, 1988); but until more research is conducted in this area, the applicability of the findings from laboratory tasks to making decisions about drug selection and dosage is somewhat questionable.

There are other aspects of the drug assessment process that should be given more careful consideration in future research protocols for possible application in clinical settings. One is the effect of medication on prominent associated disabilities, such as academic underachievement (see Gadow & Swanson, 1986) and peer aggression (e.g., Pelham & Bender, 1982). A second is the child's perception of the drug effects, including mood, somatic complaints, and therapeutic reactions.

My last comment on drug evaulation procedures pertains to the enormous degree of individual variability in dose–response relations and reactivity on various cognitive and behavioral measures. This variability can best be appreciated by examining the dose–response relations for several hyperactive children treated with methylphenidate; these relations are presented in Figure 3. Even with a fairly broad clinical dosage range, children vary greatly in their response to medication. Findings such as these dramatize the fact that group data inadvertently obscure an important aspect of clinical management, namely, the necessity of conducting systematic drug assessments for each patient.

## Side Effects

Because hyperactivity is commonly associated with academic underachievement and poor peer relations, side effects that exacerbate these problems can seriously limit the significance of any beneficial therapeutic effects. Stimulants, for example, have been reported to (1) alter mood in a manner that simulates depression (Laufer et al., 1957; Ounsted, 1955; Schain & Reynard, 1975; Schleifer, Weiss, Cohen, Elman, Cvejic, & Kruger, 1975); (2) reduce motor activity to an abnormally low level (Laufer et al., 1957; Ounsted, 1955; Rapoport, Buchsbaum, Zahn, Weingartner, Ludlow, & Mikkelsen, 1978); (3) decrease the frequency of social interaction (Schleifer et al., 1975); (4) alter temperament (Ounsted, 1955); and (5) impair performance on certain cognitive tasks (Swanson et al., 1978). In many cases, unwanted side effects can be managed by simply lowering the dosage (E. K. Sleator, personal communication, March 13, 1978; Tec, 1971), whereas other cases require complete drug withdrawal (Schain & Reynard, 1975; Schleifer et al., 1975). Because the behavioral effects of stimulant drugs are relatively short-acting, parents may not observe these side effects when medication is administered only on school days (Sprague & Gadow, 1976). Nevertheless, even when the drug regimen includes dosage administration on weekends, the unique demands of the school environment make it an ideal setting in which to evaluate responses to medication.

Perhaps one of the biggest oversights in the clinical literature is the failure to develop and examine the psychometric properties of practical and cost-effective procedures for obtaining side effects reports on stimulant drugs from care providers. There are, of course, notable examples of how this can be done, such as the Barkley (1981, p. 220) Side Effects Questionnaire. The evidence from studies of treatment practices indicates that parent interview is the standard procedure for obtaining side effects information, to include school reports, which are typically relayed to the doctor via the parent (Gadow, 1982, 1983).

## Placebos

Although placebo controls and double-blind conditions are considered a *sine qua non* for the conduct of empirically valid drug studies, their place in clinical management is less necessary. For many practitioners, comparisons between drug and no-drug conditions are more than adequate, given the established efficacy of the stimulants. Moreover, if a child improved with medication (compared with pretreatment), but not to a marked degree over placebo, medication would have to be rejected; thus, according to some clinicians, a viable treatment option would be eliminated. (In other words, it would be unethical to

KENNETH D. GADOW

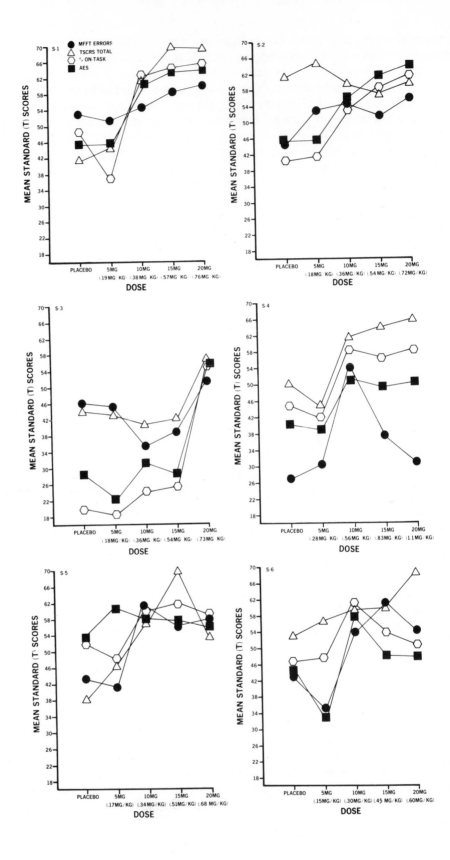

knowingly use a medication that is essentially a placebo.) Much less esoteric is the problem of formulating placebo preparations. Identically matching placebos are again available from the manufacturer, after production was suspended for a brief period (A. Strollor, personal communication, August 12, 1986). Using a gelatin capsule that will hold four 5-mg tablets, it is possible to formulate dosages of 0–20 mg by using various combinations of drug and placebo tablets. With the assistance of a pharmacy service, self-made placebos can be formulated from crushed tablets and filler material (e.g., lactose). As a check for compliance, the capsules (or tablets) can be placed in dated envelopes, at least for the duration of the medication evaluation. At first blush, one may well wonder, given the apparent simplicity of the procedure and its compelling scientific credentials, why it is not used more often. For the busy private practitioner, the procedure is time-consuming and probably not cost-effective. Moreover, the literature on placebo effects in children (see Gadow, White, & Ferguson, 1985), particularly hyperactive patients, is so limited that a question remains in the minds of many about the necessity of placebo use in routine clinical practice. Some clinicians, nevertheless, have shown the utility of placebos in real-world settings (e.g., Ottinger et al., 1985).

## Multiple-Drug Therapy

Children on medication for hyperactivity rarely receive more than one type of drug per day for that condition. An additional drug may be administered in the evening to induce sleep, such as an antianxiety agent (e.g., hydroxyzine or diazepam), diphenhydramine (Benadryl), or a hypnotic. Some children, however, are treated with a combination of (1) methylphenidate and thioridazine (Mellaril); (2) methylphenidate and imipramine (Tofranil), or (3) imipramine and thioridazine (Gittelman-Klein et al., 1976; Katz et al., 1975), but these combinations are used infrequently in everyday practice (Gadow, 1981; Safer & Krager, 1984). Furthermore, a recent report suggests that a combination treatment regimen of methylphenidate and imipramine may lead to severe adverse reactions (Grob & Coyle, 1986).

## Monitoring Drug Therapy

Once a satisfactory drug response has been achieved, it is generally believed that the course of treatment should be carefully monitored. The activities that some clinicians feel should transpire during this phase of therapy are (1) scheduling drug-free periods; (2) evaluating therapeutic progress toward specific

---

FIGURE 3. Dose–response curves of four dependent measures (MFFT error, percent on-task, Academic Efficiency Score [AES], and Teacher Self-Control Rating Scale [TSCRS] total score) for a representative subgroup of six children. Standard ($t$) scores were derived from the performance of the present sample ($N = 22$) aggregated across all conditions (excluding baseline). MFFT errors were inverted so that improvement on all measures is indicated by an upward movement on the vertical axis. (From "Attention deficit disorder and methylphenidate: A multilevel analysis of dose–response effects on children's impulsivity across settings" by M. D. Rapport et al., 1988, Journal of the American Academy of Child and Adolescent Psychiatry, 27, p. 66. Copyright 1988 by the American Academy of Child and Adolescent Psychiatry. Reprinted by permission.

treatment objectives; (3) monitoring the side effects associated with long-term treatment; (4) assessing compliance; and (5) instituting and coordinating psychological and educational therapies.

## Drug-Free Periods

A number of researchers and clinicians have discussed the importance of drug-free periods (e.g., Arnold, 1973; Sleator & Sprague, 1978; Sprague & Gadow, 1976). Such breaks in treatment provide caregivers with an opportunity to evaluate drug efficacy, tolerance of therapeutic response, and the continued need for treatment. These periods also create an opportunity for care providers to observe the child's "real" behavior and to assess educational needs. Some clinicians have suggested that, if possible, hyperactive children should enter school each year off medication; thus, a reevaulation of the need for treatment is allowed for on a yearly basis (Arnold, 1973). A commonly stated practice reported in the literature is to withdraw medication during weekends, holidays, and summer vacations. On such a schedule, drug-free periods are built into the pattern of ongoing care. This schedule also serves to minimize exposure to the drugs, which, in turn, may lessen the probability of the side effects associated with long-term treatment (Safer & Allen, 1976). For children with severe behavior disorders, a break in treatment should probably be preceded by gradual dosage reduction. When drug-free periods are used, consideration must be given to the child's clinical needs (Katz *et al.*, 1975). There are many circumstances (e.g., summer camp) in which a break from therapy may be counterproductive.

Evidence of the utility of this procedure stems primarily from studies that show that the need for medication may dissipate within 1 year (see "Duration of Treatment" below), as well as from caregiver reports of treatment regimens that are ineffective but that are nevertheless maintained (Gadow, 1982, 1983) and from growth rebounds during the off-medication interval (Safer & Allen, 1973a), which may be clinically important for children receiving higher therapeutic doses of stimulant medication (Mattes & Gittelman, 1983). In some cases, clinicians may use homeopathic doses during summers to placate overly concerned parents.

The research literature suggests that drug-free periods are poorly orchestrated and often do not involve standardized drug-assessment procedures (Gadow, 1983). There is some evidence that more severely handicapped children are less likely to receive breaks from treatment during summers or vacations (see Table 2).

## Long-Term Side Effects

At present, the only adverse drug reaction associated with chronic drug administration is growth suppression, evidenced by decreased height and weight (Safer & Allen, 1973a; Satterfield, Schell, & Barb, 1980). The magnitude of this effect, however, is considered quite small and is of little concern, particularly with regard to height (Roche, Lipman, Overall, & Hung, 1979). Nevertheless, this conclusion is based on group averages; individual children do experience clinically significant weight loss, and the risks are greater for young-

TABLE 2. Drug-Monitoring Procedures (%)[a]

| Procedure | ECSE (N = 52) | TMR (N = 48) |
|---|---|---|
| Direct teacher–physician interaction (visit, telephone, letter) | 17 | 8 |
| Drug-free period during school year[b] | 37(30) | 40(19) |
| Parent alters dosage with physician approval | 37 | 44 |
| Parent gives extra medication in special situations | 27 | 25 |

[a]From data present in "Pharmacotherapy for Behavior Disorders" by K. D. Gadow, 1983, *Clinical Pediatrics, 22,* 48–53.
[b]Figure in parentheses is based on teacher reports.

sters treated with higher therapeutic doses. Interestingly, even when this side effect was considered much more serious than it is now, monitoring growth was not always a routine part of medical care (e.g., Loney & Ordoña, 1975).

*Compliance*

The literature on compliance, which has been cogently reviewed by Sleator (1985), indicates that (1) physicians typically cannot judge patient compliance at better than chance levels; (2) noncompliance is a problem mostly for children, for people with psychiatric disorders, and in chronic treatment regimens; and (3) the most valid tests of compliance, such as blood and urine analyses, are not always readily available, as is the case with methylphenidate. Studies of hyperactive children suggest that noncompliance is commonplace (e.g., Brown, Borden, Wynne, Spunt, & Clingerman, 1987; Conrad, Dworkin, Shai, & Tobiessen, 1971; Firestone, 1982; Sleator, Ullmann, & von Neumann, 1982). Interviews with the parents of treated children indicate that many parents adjust the dosage, give extra medication, terminate treatment, and so forth on their own initiative (see Table 2). Although permitting the parents to adjust the dosage may be appropriate in some cases, this is generally considered to be poor clinical practice (Katz *et al.*, 1975; Solomons, 1973). Moreover, whether physicians are capable of determining which parents are competent to be entrusted with this responsibility is questionable. Procedures for improving compliance in hyperactive children and their parents in nonresearch settings have generally received very little attention.

*Concurrent Therapies*

Although there is little well-controlled research into multitreatment approaches for hyperactivity, it is generally believed that drug therapy should be an adjunct to psychological and educational intervention. The latter typically takes the form of school-directed, specialized instructional programs. Psychological therapies include behavior modification programs and counseling for the child, counseling for the parents, marital therapy, and family therapy. Although studies that have examined the added benefit of combining medication and behavioral interventions often show the combination to be superior to medication used alone (Pelham & Murphy, 1986), the difference is generally not statistically significant. Indirect support for the possible superiority of a multiple-therapy approach is also provided in a study by Satterfield, Satterfield, and Cantwell (1981). Evidence that stimulant medication markedly enhances the efficacy of truly effective educational interventions is wanting, at least for short-term intervention periods (Gadow, 1985b).

For those hyperactive children and their families who require multiple therapies, there has been little discussion about who should synchronize all the treatment-related activities. Specialized treatment centers *may* be able to provide coordinated, interdisciplinary service delivery, but it is not always safe to assume that, in such centers, the treatment regimen will be carried out in this fashion (e.g., Loney & Ordoña, 1975). It is unrealistic to expect that many physicians treating hyperactive children are in a position to provide more than medical services except through appropriate referrals to other disciplines.

With regard to behavior modification, teachers and school psychologists have assumed the responsibility of working directly with students and training their parents in administering the appropriate techniques. Family physicians are often called on to advise parents on how to manage discipline problems, and they may be able to offer some helpful suggestions with regard to behavioral approaches (Drabman & Jarvie, 1977). It is doubtful that the majority of doctors who treat hyperactive children know enough about behavior therapy or have the time to train parents in this rigorous procedure.

It is well established that medication-treated hyperactive children receive multiple treatments for their behavioral, academic, and social disabilities. Treatment histories obtained from the parents of children on medication indicate the need for a variety of services as well as the parents' susceptibility to snake oil remedies (see Gadow, 1981). There is little evidence, however, that the administration of multiple treatments is coordinated by a particular therapist, and there is no evidence of routine assessments of the interactive effects.

## Duration of Treatment

How long a particular child will be treated with medication depends on many things. Because stimulants can ameliorate the problems associated with hyperactivity at any age, it is possible that drug therapy could last for many years for some children. Gittelman-Klein *et al.* (1976) reported that 5% of the hyperactive children in their study no longer required medication after 3 months of treatment. In a follow-up study of 42 hyperactive children, Sleator, von Neumann, and Sprague (1974) reported that 26% no longer required medication after 2 years of treatment. Solomons (1973) reported on a follow-up study of 97 hyperactive children who had been treated by family physicians. In that study, the average duration of treatment was 39 months for children still on medication and 27 months for those no longer receiving drug treatment. It is clear that, although some children require drug therapy only for relatively short periods, others are maintained on medication either continuously or intermittently for many years. Pediatricians who treat relatively large numbers of hyperactive children have commented that some of their patients are maintained on medication through high school and into college, if necessary.

Although there is no shortage of discussions of placing a child on medication or making diagnostic decisions, there has been little research into how to terminate treatment. O'Leary and Pelham (1978) conducted a study in which seven hyperactive children receiving stimulants were taken off medication and were subsequently treated with behavior therapy. Before drug treatment was started, each child was placed on placebo for a short time to determine how bad his or her classroom behavior really was. When the study began, medication was either stopped immediately or terminated after gradual dosage reduction. For 4 months, the child's teacher and family were guided by a behavioral therapist while implementing behavior modification techniques. The main focus of the treatment program was the child's social behavior (conduct problems). The following month, both teacher and family carried out the program on their own. At the end of the fifth month, the children were reevaluated. The results showed dramatic improvement in social behavior, to the point where the hyperactive children were not significantly different from their peers. The investigators noted that, although the effects of the drug-withdrawal and behavioral-treatment program were encouraging, "behavior therapy is more expensive than drug treatment and should not be expected to benefit families who are not well motivated to attempt such an alternative to medication" (p. 216).

Very little information is available about how and why medication is terminated in real-world settings. Two studies in which the parents of hyperactive children were interviewed showed that therapeutic improvement was not the major reason for stopping drug therapy (Gadow, 1983). Parents often cited side effects, rebound effects, acquired tolerance in therapeutic response, and failure of the drug to work effectively as reasons for taking their child off medication. One of the major reasons that medication is stopped during adolescence is that teenagers often refuse to take pills because it sets them apart from their peers and contributes to feelings of being "different" (Safer & Allen, 1975; Sleator *et al.*, 1982).

## NONSTIMULANT DRUGS

As previously stated, not all hyperactive children respond favorably to stimulant medication. In such cases, an alternative agent may be given for a trial period. A wide variety of nonstimulant drugs have been used, such as neuroleptics, antidepressants, antianxiety agents, and antiepileptics. These alternative agents are more likely to be prescribed for children who have severe problems, multiple handicaps, or both. For children who are severely overactive and aggressive or who are mentally retarded or emotionally disturbed and have serious behavior problems (which may be accompanied by motor restlessness, impulsivity, and short attention span), neuroleptics are sometimes given when stimulant drugs fail to be clinically useful. In fact, the neuroleptics are the second most frequently prescribed drugs for these children (Gadow, 1985a). Even children who are considered "typical" hyperactives appear to respond favorably to neuroleptic medication (e.g., Gittelman-Klein *et al.*, 1976). The three most commonly prescribed neuroleptics for childhood behavior disorders are thioridazine, chlorpromazine (Thorazine), and haloperidol (Haldol). In general, neuroleptics are prescribed only when necessary because they are associated with a greater risk of side effects than stimulants. Because thioridazine has been reported to have a favorable effect on seizure reduction, this drug can be used with some confidence in the treatment of behavior disorders in epileptic children (Kamm & Mandel, 1967).

There is a considerable range in the reported dosages of neuroleptics across studies with children. The average daily dose of thioridazine and chlorpromazine ranges from 75 to 200 mg per day. Some clinicians prescribe one large dose at night to prevent daytime drowsiness, whereas others divide the total amount into two or three doses during the day (Katz et al., 1975; Winsberg et al., 1976). Most hyperactive children require no more than 50–100 mg three times per day. Relative to body weight, the average dose is 3–6 mg/kg per day. The effective dose of haloperidol ranges from 2 to 5 mg per day, which is divided into three daily doses. It is noteworthy that, in hyperactive boys, significant improvements in cognitive performance have been reported with doses of haloperidol as low as 0.025 mg/kg (Werry & Aman, 1975).

The side effects of neuroleptics in children are similar to those reported in adults. Sedative effects (drowsiness, lethargy, and apathy) are quite common with chlorpromazine, but children usually develop a tolerance for this reaction within several days to a few weeks. Dosage reduction may be necessary in some cases. It is noteworthy that irritability and excitability are also possible. Skin reactions are infrequent. Also reported are diarrhea, upset stomach, dry mouth, blurred vision, constipation, urinary retention, and abdominal pain (Winsberg & Yepes, 1978). A number of studies report increased appetite or weight gain, or both, during drug treatment.

Katz et al. (1975) stated that, in their experience with hyperactive children, the side effects of thioridazine were frequent and severe. Drowsiness was the most common adverse reaction that was difficult to manage. If the dose was reduced, the drowsiness was less severe, but the therapeutic response was weaker. Many children developed enuresis and had to be taken off medication. Increased appetite was also common, as was puffiness around the eyes and mild dry mouth. Stomachache, nausea, and vomiting necessitated dosage reduction in a number of children. Other side effects included nosebleed, mild tremor, and orthostatic hypotension. Some children who reacted well to thioridazine later developed changes in temperament. They became irritable, moody, and belligerent, and medication eventually had to be stopped.

Extrapyramidal syndromes are frequently reported in studies using haloperidol to control behavior disorders in children. Clinicians manage these side effects by administering an anticholinergic agent either at the beginning of drug treatment (a practice that is controversial), after symptoms appear, or after the discontinuation of medication. Although haloperidol is usually not associated with sedative effects, drowsiness has sometimes been reported in studies on children. Other side effects include nausea, ataxia, slurred speech, and weight gain.

Perhaps the most controversial side effect of the neuroleptics is cognitive and academic impairment. This issue is controversial because the studies in this area have not been particularly well designed (see Aman, 1984). Nevertheless, there are good examples of research on the use of neuroleptics for hyperactive (e.g., Sprague, Barnes, & Werry, 1970; Werry & Aman, 1975) and mentally retarded (e.g., Wysocki, Fuqua, Davis, & Breuning, 1981) individuals, which strongly suggest that mental impairment is a definite possibility. It is important, therefore, to monitor adaptive behavior during dosage adjustment and to assess the extent to which desirable behaviors may be adversely affected.

Imipramine is a tricyclic antidepressant drug that has been used to treat behavior disorders in children since 1965 (Rapoport, 1965); it was once considered the drug of second choice for the treatment of hyperactivity on the basis of findings from several studies (e.g., Rapoport, Quinn, Bradbard, Riddle, & Brooks, 1974; Werry, Aman, & Diamond, 1980). The total daily dose ranges from 50 to 180 mg, usually divided into three doses of 50 mg or 75 mg per day (Winsberg *et al.*, 1976). In terms of body weight, the usual starting dose for a hyperactive child is 1 mg/kg, and the upper maximal limit is 2.5 mg/kg per day (Robison & Barker, 1976). The primary side effects are drowsiness, dizziness, dry mouth, profuse sweating, nausea, increased appetite, weight gain, and weight loss. Many children appear to develop a tolerance to the therapeutic response (Quinn & Rapoport, 1975). Some serious side effects have been reported. For example, imipramine may lower the seizure threshold, especially in brain-damaged children (Brown, Winsberg, Bialer, & Press, 1973). Also, one death, possibly due to a cardiotoxic reaction, was reported in the case of a 6-year-old girl who was administered 300 mg (14 mg/kg) of Tofranil in one dose before bed for the treatment of school phobia (Saraf, Klein, Gittelman-Klein, & Groff, 1974).

The antihistamine diphenhydramine is sometimes used with hyperactive children. Fish (1971) found the drug particularly effective with children who had severe behavior problems. It is also administered at bedtime to calm a child down (Arnold, 1973). The dose to induce sleep is 50–100 mg and, for daytime use, is 100–200 mg per day (Safer & Allen, 1976).

Antianxiety agents such as hydroxyzine (Atarax, Vistaril) are used infrequently. Their effectiveness in the management of hyperactivity is questionable, but they may be used in the evening to induce sleep (Greenberg, Deem, & McMahon, 1972).

## SPECIAL CASES

### Mental Retardation

Some of the most commonly prescribed psychotropic drugs for mildly and moderately mentally retarded children are the stimulants (see Gadow, 1985a). Mentally retarded children were often included in early stimulant-drug studies; this was true of all the primary stimulant drugs. In spite of the initial interest in this population, we really know very little about the effect of these drugs on mildly to moderately mentally retarded children. There are many reasons for this, but the most important was the adoption of mental retardation as an exclusion criterion in drug studies with hyperactive children, as one of several measures designed to decrease sample heterogeneity. Although this was understandable and in a certain sense commendable, it has created a glaring gap in our clinical knowledge.

Hyperactive and nonhyperactive educable mentally retarded children appear to respond to stimulant medication in much the same way that nonretarded children respond (Alexandris & Lundell, 1968; Blacklidge & Ekblad, 1971; Blue, Lytton, & Miller, 1960; Molitch & Eccles, 1937; Molitch & Sullivan, 1937; Varley & Trupin, 1982). The results of these studies support this conclusion with regard to a variety of dependent measures, including caregiver ratings and psychological tests. There are a few studies of hyperactive trainable mentally retarded children (Christensen, 1975; Davis, 1971; McConnell, Cromwell, Bialer, & Son, 1964), but they unfortunately do not shed much light on the question of efficacy. Nevertheless, there is some indirect evidence that stimulants may be useful in treating some trainable mentally retarded schoolchildren (Gadow, 1982).

As for severely and profoundly mentally retarded individuals who exhibit overactivity, hyperactivity, or conduct problems, the findings are mixed in the sense that improvement in specific individuals is reported, but group findings are overwhelmingly negative.

Although it is generally assumed that neuroleptics are effective for hyperactivity in mentally retarded people regardless of the level of intellectual ability (see Aman & Singh, 1980, 1983), the research in this area is generally not particularly compelling. Nevertheless, well-designed studies do show a drug effect on hyperactivity (e.g., Singh & Aman, 1981). Studies of intellectually normal hyperactive children (e.g., Gittelman-Klein *et al.*, 1976) have shown that thioridazine does lead to behavioral improvement in some hyperactivity symptoms, particularly in the area of conduct problems.

## Seizure Disorders

Many children with seizure disorders are also hyperactive or exhibit conduct problems. Although stimulant drugs are generally recommended in such cases (e.g., Livingston, 1972; Millichap, 1969), the actual number of studies on this group of children is limited. In one such investigation, Ounsted (1955) found that, whereas dextroamphetamine was very effective for some children, many others responded by becoming withdrawn, depressed, and weepy. Although this reaction is commonly reported in the literature, it is generally considered an indication of excessive medication. Even though mentally retarded epileptic children *may* be less responsive to these agents, treatment prevalence studies (Gadow, 1981; Gadow & Kalachnik, 1981) suggests that many take them with apparent success. Livingston (1978) noted that stimulants are also an effective treatment for barbiturate-induced hyperactivity in epileptic children, but there does not appear to be any research on this practice.

## Preschool-Aged Children

Numerous studies have clearly shown that hyperactivity is a relatively common behavior disorder in preschool-aged children (see Campbell, 1985, and Ross & Ross, 1982, for reviews), and in many cases, severe problems during early childhood continue into the elementary-school years (Campbell, Breaux, Ewing, & Szumowski, 1985). Given the prevalence of behavior disorders and their responsiveness to drug therapy, it is fair to say that a relatively large number of young children receive psychotropic medication (see Gadow, 1986).

Clinicians have described their experience in treating hyperactive infants (Denhoff, 1973; Nichamin, 1972; Oettinger, 1973; Weinberg & Brumback, 1976), toddlers (Denhoff, 1973; Husain, Chapel, & Malek, 1980; Nichamin, 1972; Renshaw, 1974), and preschoolers (numerous reports) with stimulant medication, and there are four published group studies of medication for hyperactive children under 6 years old (Cohen, Sullivan, Minde, Novak, & Helwig, 1981; Conners, 1975; Schleifer *et al.*, 1975; Zara, 1973). There are also at least two group studies of seriously disturbed children (Campbell, Fish, Shapiro, Collins, & Koh, 1972; Fish, 1971). Nevertheless, dextroamphetamine and amphetamine sulfate (Benzedrine) are not approved for children under 3 years old, and methylphenidate and pemoline are not approved by the Food and Drug Administration (FDA) in the United States for children under 6 years old. This situation is interesting because one survey study of early-childhood special-education programs found that approximately 5% of all the children were receiving methylphenidate, and that several had begun treatment before they were 3 years old (Gadow, 1977). To keep this situation in perspective, it must be realized that preschool-aged children have always participated in stimulant drug research. A careful reading of the literature will reveal that a number of early studies of amphetamine (Bender & Cottington, 1942), dextroamphetamine (Ginn & Hohman, 1953; Laufer *et al.*, 1957; Ounsted, 1955), and methylphenidate (Zimmerman & Burgemeister, 1958a,b) included at least a few preschool-aged children in their subject samples.

Stimulant medication appears to affect the behavior of young hyperactive children in much the same way that it does the behavior of older children, with three notable exceptions. First, experimental drug studies do not always find the same degree of therapeutic benefit or improvement in as many different areas with younger children (Conners, 1975; Schleifer *et al.*, 1975). Second, although stimulant drug effects are clearly present, they appear to be "more variable and unpredictable than in similar treatment of older children" (Conners, 1975, p. 74). Third, younger children may be particularly sensitive to the effects of overmedication. Schleifer *et al.* (1975), for example, noted that, although mothers perceived their hyperactive preschoolers as improved on medication, they also observed "that methylphenidate very often had a negative effect on the child's mood and also on his relationship with peers, causing less social behavior and interaction" (p. 49). Interestingly, some of the same children who exhibited social withdrawal after taking medication when younger did not have this reaction to methylphenidate when they were older (G. Weiss, personal communication, September 2, 1980).

The recommended stimulant-drug dosages for infants, toddlers, and preschoolers are presented in Table 3. These figures are based on reports from several sources: methylphenidate (Cohen *et al.*, 1981; Conners, 1975; Hasser, Conners, Denhoff, Millichap, & O'Leary, 1978; Schleifer *et al.*, 1975); dextroamphetamine (Denhoff, 1973; Hasser *et al.*, 1978; Nichamin, 1972; Oettinger, 1973); and amphetamine (Hasser *et al.*, 1978). Because dextroamphetamine is available in liquid form, it may be easier to administer to young children. One survey (Gadow, 1981) of drug use with 3- to 5-year-olds found that the median *daily* dose of methylphenidate was 15 mg (range: 5–45 mg); the figures for dextroamphetamine were similar.

Table 3. Reported Dosages (in Milligrams) of Stimulants
for Infants and Young Children[a]

| Drug | Starting dose | Adjusting dose | Morning dose | Daily dose |
|---|---|---|---|---|
| Benzedrine | | | | |
| 3–5 years | 2.5 | 2.5 | 2.5 | 20.0 |
| Dexedrine | | | | |
| Birth–1 year[b] | | | 2.0 | 4.0 |
| 1–3 years | | | 2.5 | 5.0 |
| 3–5 years | 2.5 | 2.5 | 5 | 10.0 |
| Ritalin | | | | |
| 1–3 years | | | 2.5 | 5 to 10 |
| 3–5 years | 2.5 | 5 | 2.5 to 5 | 5 to 20 |

[a]From *Children on Medication. Vol. 1: Hyperactivity, Learning Disabilities, and Mental Retardation* (p. 197) by K. D. Gadow, 1986. San Diego: College-Hill Press. Copyright 1986 by College-Hill Press. Reprinted by permission.
[b]Reported by Denhoff (1973).

*Neuroleptics*

Although it is true that neuroleptic drugs are prescribed for hyperactivity and aggression in preschool-aged children, there is very little well-controlled research *per se* on the management of these disorders in this age group. In fact, the only condition for which there has been any systematic program of neuroleptic drug research is (early) infantile autism.

Because neuroleptics are the most effective drugs for decreasing severe hyperactivity, aggression, or noncompliance in some children, there is a real need for more information about the use of these agents with this age group. For the present, we have to draw inferences from the findings of studies on older children who have a comparable disorder. The research on autistic children may also be helpful (see Table 4).

Among the neuroleptic drugs currently approved by the Food and Drug Administration in the United States for use with children under 6 years old are thioridazine and chlorpromazine. Dosages for these drugs reported in the *Physicians' Desk Reference* (1985) are as follows: for thioridazine, the dose for children between 2 and 12 years old ranges from 0.5 mg/kg per day to 3.0 mg/kg per day. For chlorpromazine, the dosage for child outpatients with a psychiatric disorder is 0.25 mg per pound, administered every 4–6 hours. Dosage adjustment is a critical procedure whenever one is dealing with a drug whose intended effect is the facilitation of adaptive behavior. For young children receiving special education and other services, neuroleptic medication should be used only when it facilitates cognitive or social development. The side effects reported for neuroleptic treatment in this age group are similar to those reported for older children, including extrapyramidal symptoms such as acute dystonic reaction. One long-term treatment study of the use of haloperidol with autistic children found that 22% developed dyskinesias (like those associated with tardive dyskinesia) either during treatment or when switched to placebo. In a few cases, the dyskinesias were manifested as an aggravation of preexisting stereotypies. The

TABLE 4. Reported Antipsychotic Oral Drug Dosages for Preschool-Aged Children[a]

| Drug | Study | Age (years) | Disorder | Dose (mg/day)[b] | Dose (mean) |
|------|-------|-------------|----------|------------------|-------------|
| Haldol | Campbell et al. (1978) | 2.6–7.2 | Infantile autism | 0.5–4.0 | 1.65 |
| (haloperidol)[c] | Cohen et al. (1980) | 2.1–7.0 | Infantile autism | 0.5–4.0 | 1.78 |
| | Anderson et al. (1984) | 2.3–6.9 | Infantile autism | 0.5–3.0 | 1.11 |
| Lithium carbonate[d] | Campbell et al. (1972) | 3.0–6.0 | Infantile autism | 450–900 | 735 |
| Moban (molindone)[d] | Campbell et al. (1971) | 3–5 | Infantile autism | 1–2.5 | 1.5 |
| Navane (thiothixene)[d] | Campbell et al. (1970) | 3–5 | Infantile autism | 1–6 | 2.0 |
| Stelazine | Fish et al. (1966) | 2–6 | Infantile autism | 2–20 | 8.2 |
| (trifluoperazine)[e] | Fish et al. (1969) | 2–5 | Infantile autism | 2–8 | 4 |
| Thorazine | Fish et al. (1969) | 2–5 | Infantile autism | 30–150 | 75 |
| (chlorpromazine) | Campbell et al. (1972) | 3–6 | Infantile autism | 9–45 | 17.3 |

[a]From *Children on Medication. Vol. 2: Epilepsy, Emotional Disturbance, and Adolescent Disorders* (p. 116) by K. D. Gadow, 1986. San Diego: College-Hill Press. Copyright 1986 by College-Hill Press. Reprinted by permission.
[b]The most current issue of the *Physicians' Desk Reference* (PDR) should be consulted for dosage information.
[c]Not intended for children under 3 years old.
[d]Not recommended for children under 12 years old, because of the limited information on safety and efficacy in this age group.
[e]Dosage information for children under 6 years old is not provided in the *PDR* (1985).

dyskinesias appeared at any time from 5 weeks to 16 months after the onset of treatment. The dyskinesias stopped within 16 days to 9 months after they first began. In some cases, they ceased while the child was on medication and, in others, after the child had been switched to placebo or medication was discontinued.

## Tourette Syndrome

In addition to motor and vocal tics, approximately one half of all diagnosed cases of Tourette syndrome also experience the behavioral symptoms of hyperactivity (attention deficits, motor restlessness, poor concentration, and impulsivity; see Comings & Comings, 1984). Learning disabilities and academic underachievement are common, as are obsessions and compulsions. Many complain of "inner tension" and an inability to relax as others do (Bruun, 1984). The behavioral concomitants of Tourette syndrome may persist into adulthood. At present, neuroleptics such as haloperidol and pimozide (Orap) are the preferred drugs for controlling the tics associated with Tourette syndrome (see Cohen, Leckman, & Shaywitz, 1985; Shapiro & Shapiro, 1981).

It is a well-established fact that stimulant drugs can induce tics and exacerbate the symptoms of Tourette syndrome (Lowe, Cohen, Detlor, Kremenitzer, & Shaywitz, 1982). It is controversial, however, whether stimulants can cause this disorder in children who would not otherwise develop it. For this reason, consideration should be given to the prudence of using stimulants for hyperactivity with children who have a first-degree relative (parent, brother, or sister) with Tourette syndrome. Moreover, drug withdrawal should be seriously considered for children who experience drug-induced tics and who were, before treatment, tic-free. This, too, is controversial because tics may abate with dosage reduction. Imipramine may be a useful alternative for youngsters with stimulant-induced Tourette syndrome (Dillon, Salzman, & Schulsinger, 1985).

## Drug-Induced Hyperactivity

Many psychotropic drugs can cause children to become more restless, irritable, and aggressive as a consequence of treatment, but these are not the common untoward reactions of any particular agent. When they do occur, treatment is typically withdrawn.

Short-acting stimulant drugs occasionally produce a transient increase in the severity of a child's behavior problems, which occurs when the therapeutic benefits of the drug wear off, usually in the late afternoon or early evening. This may also be a problem when drug-free periods are scheduled on weekends. Presumably, the level of the drug in the blood drops, and the child experiences a drug withdrawal reaction, which is referred to as a *rebound effect*. The child may become irritable and even more hyperactive than usual. When the reaction is severe, the clinician may prescribe additional doses of medication to defer the reaction, depending on when and where it occurs.

One side effect of the barbiturate antiepileptic drugs (e.g., phenobarbital) in children is behavior disorder, which may be manifested as irritability, aggressivity, excitability, overactivity, and/or hyperactivity. This side effect has been documented in the clinical literature for many years (e.g., Cutts & Jasper, 1939; Lindsley & Henry, 1941). Livingston (1972) estimated that 15%–20% of the children he treated with phenobarbital experienced this type of reaction. Similarly, Gadow (1977) found that 20% of preschoolers taking phenobarbital for epilepsy exhibited behavior problems as a result of medication. The prevalence of drug-induced hyperactivity, aggressivity, and irritability in children treated for febrile seizures was 25% in one study (Thorn, 1975) and 42% in another (Wolf & Forsythe, 1978). In some cases, the behavior disorder is severe and becomes an even greater problem than the seizures. Wolf and Forsythe (1978) reported that phenobarbital treatment had to be discontinued in half of the children who developed this reaction. They also noted a relationship between this side effect and preexisting behavioral disturbances. Only 20% of the children whose behavior was normal before the seizures began developed a behavioral disturbance on phenobarbital, compared with 80% of those who exhibited behavior disorders before the onset of seizures. In the latter group, phenobarbital seems to aggravate the situation. Not everyone agrees, however, that this side effect is more common in behavior-disordered children (Livingston, 1976). Phenobarbital-induced behavioral disturbances are *not* dose-related; rather, they represent a specific sensitivity to the drug. Livingston (1978) suggested that the physician first see if methylphenidate or dextroamphetamine is effective in controlling the behavior disorder. If they are ineffective, phenobarbital should be gradually replaced with mephobarbital (Mebaral). If the behavior problems still do not abate, mephobarbital should be replaced by primidone (Mysoline).

Another type of behavior disturbance is also associated with antiepileptic drug therapy and has not received much attention (Livingston, 1976). Some behaviorally normal children become profoundly restless, hyperactive, and belligerent and exhibit frequent temper outbursts after their seizures have been controlled by medication, *regardless of the type of drug*. When medication is stopped or the dosage is reduced to the point where the seizures reappear, the child's behavior returns to normal. In many cases, the behavior disorder is a greater problem than the seizures. Livingston noted that "in such cases it is probably best to allow the child to have an occasional seizure and normal interictal behavior than to be completely seizure free but with uncontrolled behavior" (p. 259).

## SUMMARY

Although there is a truly humbling literature on psychotropic drug effects in hyperactive children, research on practical aspects of the treatment process is either woefully inadequate or nonprogrammatic. Furthermore, one would be hard-pressed to identify specific treatment practices that have changed markedly since the mid-1960s. To be sure, our understanding of drug effects, of the natural history of the disorder, and of its diagnostic features has increased measurably, but the payoff for the practitioner has been less impressive. Because (1) most researchers in this area believe that various facets of therapy (e.g., dosage selection, compliance, schedule, and duration of treatment) impact on efficacy and (2) treatment practices research is often perceived as having "lightweight" status (in part because of methodological limitations), a case could be made for the following observation by Nowlis and Nowlis (1956):

> We often wonder if there must always be an inverse relationship between the magnitude and importance of a problem in behavioral science and the adequacy of the scientific methodology by means of which it can be attacked. (p. 345)

With regard to the safety and efficacy of stimulant drug therapy for hyperactivity, five decades of experience in treating children and adolescents have revealed few serious irreversible adverse reactions. Two that have been reported, (seizures and Tourette syndrome) are considered extremely rare and may be manifested only in patients who would have developed these disorders at some time regardless of stimulant drug use. As for efficacy, numerous scientifically rigorous studies have clearly demonstrated the ability of stimulant drugs to suppress the symptoms of hyperactivity and have corroborated the astute clinical observations and the early research findings of Charles Bradley.

Although one can never overemphasize the idiosyncratic nature of stimulant drug response in terms of behavioral effects, dosage, and dose–response relationships, the *general* pattern of treatment with methylphenidate is as follows: The typical dose for elementary-school-aged children is 10–15 mg administered in the morning and at noon. Many (but certainly not all) clinicians believe that individual doses greater than 0.6 mg/kg are generally not necessary for adequate therapeutic response and clinical management. When possible, it is recommended that medication not be given at times when it is unnecessary (e.g., on weekends and during summer vacations). However, such breaks from medication are not in the best interests of some patients. In good responders, treatment may last for several (2–4) years, but periodic drug-free periods (at least once a year) are recommended to ascertain the need for continued treatment. Multiple-drug regimens are almost always ill advised. Drug therapy is typically terminated before the child enters junior high school, but this does not mean that medication is no longer effective. Quite the contrary, stimulants appear to be efficacious for symptom suppression in hyperactive patients of all ages (infancy to adulthood). The probability of success when withdrawing medication can be greatly increased by the concurrent or subsequent implementation of alternative interventions (e.g., behavior therapy).

Stimulant drug therapy is a palliative; to the best of my knowledge, no one has yet demonstrated that medication leads to the permanent alteration of neurological structures, imparts new learning, or is even instrumental in the acquisition of skills that would otherwise not develop had treatment been withheld. Serious, thoughtful consideration must therefore be given to all the patient's clinical needs and those of his or her care providers (if the latter bear on the patient's wellbeing, and they often do). Professionally, we appear to have moved beyond the horse-race mentally of superior interventions and "schools of exclusive salvationism" (Eisenberg, 1975) to the point of appreciating the interactive nature of multiple treatment approaches.

In spite of our vast knowledge about stimulant medication (at least when compared with our knowledge of drugs used for other childhood disorders) and the importance of drug monitoring, there appears to be a marked disparity between the recommended treatment practices and the procedures used in real-world settings. This situation is due, in part, to the logistical problems associated with obtaining drug-response data from caregivers. Although easy-to-use assessment methods are available, they are often not employed. One response to this problem has been to investigate the feasibility of laboratory-based drug-assessment procedures. Whether this will be a completely satisfactory solution remains to be seen. What is certain, however, is that there is a need for improved service delivery.

## REFERENCES

Alexandris, A., & Lundell, F. W. (1968). Effect of thioridazine, amphetamine, and placebo on the hyperkinetic syndrome and cognitive area in mentally deficient children. *Canadian Medical Association Journal, 98,* 92–96.

Aman, M. G. (1984). Drugs and learning in mentally retarded persons. In G. D. Burrows & J. S. Werry (Eds.), *Advances in human psychopharmacology* (Vol. 3, pp. 121–163). Greenwich, CT: JAI Press.

Aman, M. G., & Singh, N. N. (1980). The usefulness of thioridazine for treating childhood disorders—Fact or folklore? *American Journal of Mental Deficiency, 84,* 331–338.

Aman, M. G., & Singh, N. N. (1983). Pharmacological intervention. In J. L. Matson & J. A. Mulick (Eds.), *Handbook of mental retardation* (pp. 317–337). New York: Pergamon Press.

American Academy of Pediatrics. (1978). Medical emergencies and administration of medication in school. *Pediatrics, 61,* 15.

American Academy of Pediatrics. (1981). *School health: A guide for health professions.* Evanston, IL: Author.

Anderson, L. T., Campbell, M., Grega, D. M., Perry, R., Small, A. M., & Green, W. H. (1984). Haloperidol in the treatment of infantile autism: Effects on learning and behavioral symptoms. *American Journal of Psychiatry, 141,* 1195–1202.

Arnold, L. E. (1973). The art of medicating hyperkinetic children. *Clinical Pediatrics, 12,* 35–41.

Barkley, R. A. (1981). *Hyperactive children: A handbook for diagnosis and treatment.* New York: Guilford Press.

Bender, L., & Cottington, F. (1942). The use of amphetamine sulfate (Benzedrine) in child psychiatry. *American Journal of Psychiatry, 99,* 116–121.

Blacklidge, V., & Ekblad, R. (1971). The effectiveness of methylphenidate hydrochloride (Ritalin) on learning and behavior in public school educable mentally retarded children. *Pediatrics, 47*, 923–926.

Blue, A. W., Lytton, G. J., & Miller, O. W. (1960). The effect of methylphenidate on intellectually handicapped children (Abstract). *American Psychologist, 15*, 393.

Bosco, J. J., & Robin, S. S. (Eds.). (1976). *The hyperactive child and stimulant drugs.* Chicago: University of Chicago Press.

Bradley, C., & Bowen, M. (1941). Amphetamine (Benzedrine) therapy of children's behavior disorders. *American Journal of Orthopsychiatry, 11*, 92–103.

Brown, D., Winsberg, B. G., Bialer, I., & Press, M. (1973). Imipramine therapy and seizures: Three children treated for hyperactive behavior disorders. *American Journal of Psychiatry, 130*, 210–212.

Brown, R. T., Borden, K. A., Wynne, M. E., Spunt, A. L., & Clingerman, S. R. (1987). Compliance with pharmacological and cognitive treatments for attention deficit disorder. *Journal of American Academy of Child and Adolescent Psychiatry, 26*, 521–526.

Brulle, A. R., Barton, L. E., & Foskett, J. J. (1983). Educator/physician interchanges: A survey and suggestions. *Education & Training of the Mentally Retarded, 18*, 313–317.

Bruun, R. D. (1984). Gilles de la Tourette's syndrome: An overview of clinical experience. *Journal of the American Academy of Child Psychiatry, 23*, 126–133.

Campbell, M., & Deutsch, S. I. (1985). Neuroleptics in children. In G. D. Burrows, T. Norman, & B. Davies (Eds.), *Drugs in psychiatry (Vol. 3): Antipsychotics* (pp. 213–238). New York: Elsevier Biomedical.

Campbell, M., Fish, B., Korein, J., Shapiro, T., Collins, P., & Koh, C. (1972). Lithium and chlorpromazine: A controlled cross-over study of hyperactive severely disturbed young children. *Journal of Autism and Childhood Schizophrenia, 2*, 234–263.

Campbell, M., Fish, B., Shapiro, T., & Floyd, A., Jr. (1971). Study of molindone in disturbed preschool children. *Current Therapeutic Research, 13*, 28–33.

Campbell, M., Fish, B., Shapiro, T., & Floyd, A., Jr. (1970). Thiothixene in young disturbed children: A pilot study. *Archives of General Psychiatry, 23*, 70–72.

Campbell, M., Fish, B., Shapiro, T., Collins, P., & Koh, C. (1972). Response to triiodothyronine and dextroamphetamine: A study of preschool schizophrenic children. *Journal of Autism and Childhood Schizophrenia, 2*, 343–358.

Campbell, M., Anderson, L. T., Meier. M., Cohen, I. L., Small, A. M., Samit, C., & Sachar, E. J. (1978). A comparison of haloperidol and behavior therapy and their interaction in autistic children. *Journal of the American Academy of Child Psychiatry, 17*, 640–655.

Campbell, S. B. (1985). Hyperactivity in preschoolers: Correlates and prognostic implications. *Clinical Psychology Review, 5*, 405–428.

Campbell, S. B., Breaux, A. M., Ewing, L. J., & Szumoski, F. K. (1985, April). Family characteristics and child behavior as precursors of externalizing symptomatology at school entry. Paper presented at the meeting of the Society for Research in Child Development, Toronto.

Cantwell, D. P. (1980). A clinicians guide to the use of stimulant medication for the psychiatric disorders of children. *Developmental and Behavioral Pediatrics, 1*, 133–140.

Carter, C. H. (1956). The effects of reserpine and methylphenidate (Ritalin) in mental defectives, spastics, and epileptics. *Psychiatric Research Reports, 4*, 44–48.

Chatoor, I., Wells, K. C., Conners, C. K., Seidel, W. T., & Shaw, D. (1983). The effects of nocturnally administered stimulant medication on EEG sleep and behavior in hyperactive children. *Journal of the American Academy of Child Psychiatry, 22*, 337–342.

Christensen, D. E. (1975). Effects of combining methylphenidate and a classroom token system in modifying hyperactive behavior. *American Journal of Mental Deficiency, 80*, 266–276.

Cohen, D. J., Leckman, J. F., & Shaywitz, B. A. (1985). The Tourette syndrome and other tics. In D. Shaffer, A. A. Ehrhardt, & L. L. Greenhill (Eds.), *The clinical guide to child psychiatry* (pp. 3–28). New York: Free Press.

Cohen, I. L., Campbell, M., Posner, D., Small, A. M., Triebel, D., & Anderson, L. T. (1980). Behavioral affects of haloperidol in young autistic children: An objective analysis using a within subjects reversal design. *Journal of the American Academy of Child Psychiatry, 19*, 665–677.

Cohen, N. J., Sullivan, S., Minde, K., Novak, C., & Helwig, C. (1981). Evaluation of the relative effectiveness of methylphenidate and cognitive behavior modification in the treatment of kindergarten-aged hyperactive children. *Journal of Abnormal Child Psychology, 9*, 43–54.

Comings, D. E., & Comings, B. G. (1984). Tourette's syndrome and attention deficit disorder with hyperactivity: Are they genetically related? *Journal of the American Academy of Child Psychiatry, 23*, 138–146.

Conners, C. K. (1973). Rating scales for use in drug studies with children. *Psychopharmacology Bulletin* (Special issue, Pharmacotherapy of children), 24–84.

Conners, C. K. (1975). Controlled trial of methylphenidate in preschool children with minimal brain dysfunction. *International Journal of Mental Health, 4,* 61–74.

Conners, C. K., & Solanto, M. V. (1984). The psychophysiology of stimulant drug response in hyperkinetic children. In L. M. Bloomingdale (Ed.), *Attention deficit disorder: Diagnostic, cognitive, and therapeutic understanding* (pp. 191–204). New York: Spectrum.

Conrad, W. G., Dworkin, E. S., Shai, A., & Tobiessen, J. E. (1971). Effects of amphetamine therapy and prescriptive tutoring on the behavior and achievement of lower class hyperactive children. *Journal of Learning Disabilities, 4,* 45–53.

Council for Exceptional Children. (1977). *Special education and administrative policies for state and local education agencies.* Reston, VA: Author.

Cutts, K. K., & Jasper, H. H. (1939). The effect of benzedrine sulphate and phenobarbital on behavior problem children with abnormal electroencephalograms. *Archives of Neurology and Psychiatry, 41,* 1138–1139.

Davis, K. V. (1971). The effect of drugs on stereotyped and nonstereotyped operant behavior in retardates. *Psychopharmacology, 22,* 195–213.

Denhoff, E. (1973). The natural history of children with minimal brain dysfunction. *Annals of the New York Academy of Sciences, 205,* 188–205.

Denhoff, E., Davids, A., & Hawkins, R. (1971). Effects of dextroamphetamine on hyperkinetic children: A controlled double blind study. *Journal of Learning Disabilities, 4,* 491–498.

Dillon, D., Salzman, I. J., & Schulsinger, D. A. (1985). The use of imipramine in Tourette's syndrome and attention deficit disorder: Case report. *Journal of Clinical Psychiatry, 46,* 348–349.

Drabman, R. S., & Jarvie, G. (1977). Counseling parents of children with behavior problems: The use of extinction and time-out techniques. *Pediatrics, 59,* 78–85.

Eisenberg, L. (1972). Symposium: Behavior modification by drugs: III. The clinical use of stimulant drugs in children. *Pediatrics, 49,* 709–715.

Eisenberg, L. (1975). The ethics of intervention: Acting amidst ambiguity. *Journal of Child Psychology and Psychiatry, 16,* 93–104.

Eisenberg, L., & Conners, C. K. (1971). Psychopharmacology in childhood. In N. B. Talbot, J. Kagan, & L. Eisenberg (Eds.), *Behavioral science in pediatric medicine.* Philadelphia: W. B. Saunders.

Firestone, P. (1982). Factors associated with children's adherence to stimulant medication. *American Journal of Orthopsychiatry, 52,* 447–456.

Fish, B. (1971). The "one child, one drug" myth of stimulants in hyperkinesis. *Archives of General Psychiatry, 25,* 193–203.

Fish, B., Campbell, M., Shapiro, T., & Floyd, A., Jr. (1969). Comparison of trifluperidol, trifluoperazine and chlorpromazine in preschool schizophrenic children: the value of less sedative antipsychotic agents. *Current Therapeutic Research, 11,* 589–595.

Fish, B., Shapiro, T., & Campbell, M. (1966). Long term prognosis and the response of schizophrenic children to drug therapy: A controlled study of trifluoperazine. *American Journal of Psychiatry, 123,* 32–39.

Gadow, K. D. (1977). *Psychotropic and antiepileptic drug treatment with children in early childhood special education.* Champaign, IL: University of Illinois, Institute for Child Behavior and Development. (ERIC Document Reproduction Service No. ED 162 494)

Gadow, K. D. (1981). Prevalence of drug treatment for hyperactivity and other childhood behavior disorders. In K. D. Gadow & J. Loney (Eds.), *Psychosocial aspects of drug treatment for hyperactivity* (pp. 13–76). Boulder, CO: Westview Press.

Gadow, K. D. (1982). School involvement in pharmacotherapy for behavior disorders. *Journal of Special Education, 16,* 385–399.

Gadow, K. D. (1983). Pharmacotherapy for behavior disorders: Typical treatment practices. *Clinical Pediatrics, 22,* 48–53.

Gadow, K. D. (1985a). Prevalence and efficacy of stimulant drug use with mentally retarded children and youth. *Psychopharmacology Bulletin, 21,* 291–303.

Gadow, K. D. (1985b). Relative efficacy of pharmacological, behavioral, and combination treatments for enhancing academic performance. *Clinical Psychology Review, 5,* 513–533.

Gadow, K. D. (1986). *Children on medication: Vol 1. Hyperactivity, learning disabilities, and mental retardation.* San Diego: College-Hill Press.

Gadow, K. D., & Kalachnik, J. (1981). Prevalence and pattern of drug treatment for behavior and seizure disorders of TMR students. *American Journal of Mental Deficiency, 85,* 588–595.

Gadow, K. D., & Kane, K. (1983). Administration of medication by school personnel. *Journal of School Health, 53,* 178–183.

Gadow, K. D., & Swanson, H. L. (1986). Assessing drug effects on academic performance. In K. D. Gadow & A. Poling (Eds.), *Methodological issues in human psychopharmacology (Advances in Learning and behavioral disabilities,* Suppl. 1, pp. 247–279). Greenwich, CT: JAI Press.

Gadow, K. D., White, L., & Ferguson, D. G. (1986). Placebo controls and double-blind conditions: Placebo therapy in experimental design. In K. D. Gadow & A. Poling (Eds.), *Methodological issues in human psychopharmacology (Advances in learning and behavioral disabilities,* Suppl. 1, 41–83). Greenwich, CT: JAI Press.

Ginn, S. A., & Hohman, L. B. (1953). The use of dextroamphetamine in severe behavior problems of children. *Southern Medical Journal, 46,* 1124–1127.

Gittelman, R. (1983). Hyperkinetic syndrome: Treatment issues and principles. In M. Rutter (Ed.), *Developmental neuropsychiatry* (pp. 437–449). New York: Guilford Press.

Gittelman-Klein, R., & Klein, D. F. (1976). Methylphenidate effects in learning disabilities. *Archives of General Psychiatry, 33,* 655–664.

Gittelman-Klein, R., Klein, D. F., Katz, S., Saraf, K., & Pollack, E. (1976). Comparative effects of methylphenidate and thioridazine in hyperkinetic children. *Archives of General Psychiatry, 33,* 1217–1231.

Greenberg, L. M., Deem, M. A., & McMahon, S. (1972). Effects of dextroamphetamine, chlorpromazine, and hydroxyzine on behavior and performance in hyperactive children. *American Journal of Psychiatry, 129,* 532–539.

Grob, C. S., & Coyle, J. T. (1986). Suspected adverse methylphenidate-imipramine interactions in children. *Developmental and Behavioral Pediatrics, 7,* 265–267.

Gross, M. D., & Wilson, W. C. (1974). *Minimal brain dysfunction.* New York: Brunner/Mazel.

Hasser, C. R., Conners, C. K., Denhoff, E., Millichap, J. G., & O'Leary, S. G. (1978). Take a slow approach to hyperkinesis. *Patient Care, 12*(11), 22–73.

Husain, A., Chapel, J., & Malek, A. P. (1980). Methylphenidate, neuroleptics and dykinesia-dystonia. *Canadian Journal of Psychiatry, 25,* 254–258.

Kamm, I., & Mandel, A. (1967). Thioridazine in the treatment of behavior disorders in epileptics. *Diseases of the Nervous System, 28,* 46–48.

Katz, S., Saraf, K., Gittelman-Klein, R., & Klein, D. F. (1975). Clinical pharmacological management of hyperkinetic children. *International Journal of Mental Health, 4,* 157–181.

Kazdin, A. E., Esveldt-Dawson, K., & Loar, L. L. (1983). Correspondence of teacher ratings and direct observations of classroom behavior of psychiatric inpatient children. *Journal of Abnormal Child Psychology, 11,* 549–564.

Kenney, J. B. (1976). Personal communication, December 3.

Kinsbourne, M. (1973). Stimulants for insomnia (correspondence). *New England Journal of Medicine, 288,* 1129.

Klein, D. F., Gittelman, R., Quitkin, F., & Rifkin, A. (1980). *Diagnosis and drug treatment of psychiatric disorders: Adults and children* (2nd ed.). Baltimore: Williams & Wilkins.

Krager, J. M., & Safer, D. J. (1974). Type and prevalence of medication used in the treatment of hyperactive children. *New England Journal of Medicine, 291,* 1118–1120.

Krager. J. M., Safer, D. J., & Earhart, J. (1979). Type and prevalence of medication used to treat hyperactive school children: Follow-up survey results. *Journal of School Health, 49,* 317–321.

Laufer, M. W., Denhoff, E., & Riverside, R. I. (1957). Hyperkinetic behavior syndrome in children. *Journal of Pediatrics, 50,* 463–474.

Lindsley, D. B., & Henry, C. E. (1941). The effects of drugs on behavior and the electroencephalograms of children with behavior disorders. *Psychosomatic Medicine, 4,* 140–149.

Livingston, S. (1972). *Comprehensive management of epilepsy in infancy, childhood and adolescence.* Springfield, IL: Thomas.

Livingston, S. (1976). Behavioral effects of anti-epileptic drugs. *Developmental Medicine and Child Neurology, 18,* 258–259.

Livingston, S. (1978). Medical treatment of epilepsy: 2. *Southern Medical Journal, 71,* 432–447.

Loney, J. (1983). Research diagnostic criteria for childhood hyperactivity. In S. B. Guze, F. J. Earls, & J. E. Barrett (Eds.), *Childhood psychopathology and development* (pp. 109–137). New York: Raven Press.

Loney, J. (1987). Hyperactivity and aggression in the diagnosis of attention deficit disorder. In B. B. Lahey & A. E. Kazdin (Eds.), *Advances in clinical child psychology* (Vol. 10, pp. 99–135). New York: Plenum Press.

Loney, J., & Ordoña, T. T. (1975). Using cerebral stimulants to treat minimal brain dysfunction. *American Journal of Orthopsychiatry, 45,* 564–572.

Lowe, T. L., Cohen, D. J., Detlor, J., Kremenitzer. M. W., & Shaywitz, B. A. (1982). Stimulant medications precipitate Tourette's syndrome. *Journal of the American Medical Association, 247,* 1729–1731.

McConnell, T. R., Cromwell, R. L., Bialer, I., & Son, C. D. (1964). Studies in activity level: 7. Effects of amphetamine drug administration on the activity level of retarded children. *American Journal of Mental Deficiency, 68,* 647–651.

Mann, H. B., & Greenspan, S. I. (1976). The identification and treatment of adult brain dysfunction. *American Journal of Psychiatry, 133,* 1013–1017.

Mattes, J. A., & Gittelman, R. (1983). Growth of hyperactive children on maintenance regimen of methylphenidate. *Archives of General Psychiatry, 40,* 317–321.

Millichap, J. G. (1969). Management of hyperkinetic behavior in children with epilepsy. *Modern Treatment, 6,* 1233–1246.

Millichap, J. G. (1973). Drugs in management of minimal brain dysfunction. *Annals of the New York Academy of Sciences, 205,* 321–334.

Molitch, M., & Eccles, J. P. (1937). Effect of benzedrine sulfate on the intelligence scores of children. *American Journal of Psychiatry, 94,* 587–590.

Molitch, M., & Sullivan, J. P. (1937). Effect of benzedrine sulfate on children taking New Stanford Achievement Test. *American Journal of Orthopsychiatry, 7,* 519–522.

Nichamin, S. J. (1972). Recognizing minimal cerebral dysfunction in the infant and toddler. *Clinical Pediatrics, 11,* 255–257.

Nowlis, V., & Nowlis, H. H. (1956). The description and analysis of mood. *Annals of the New York Academy of Sciences, 65,* 345–355.

Oettinger, L. (1973). Discussion. *Annals of the New York Academy of Sciences, 205,* 345.

O'Leary, K. D. (1981). Assessment of hyperactivity: Observational and rating methodologies. In S. A. Miller (Ed.), *Nutrition and behavior* (pp. 291–298). Philadelphia: Fauklin Institute Press.

O'Leary, S. G., & Pelham, W. E. (1978). Behavior therapy and withdrawal of stimulant medication in hyperactive children. *Pediatrics, 61,* 211–217.

Ottinger, D. R., Halpin, B., Miller, M., Demian, L., & Hannemann, R. (1985). Evaluating drug effectiveness in an office setting for children with attention deficit disorders. *Clinical Pediatrics, 24,* 245–251.

Ounsted, C. (1955). The hyperkinetic syndrome in epileptic children. *Lancet, 2,* 303–311.

Pelham, W. E. (1983). The effects of psychostimulants on academic achievement in hyperactive and learning-disabled children. *Thalamus, 3,* 1–49.

Pelham, W. E., & Bender, M. E. (1982). Peer relationships in hyperactive children: Description and treatment. In K. D. Gadow & I. Bialer (Eds.), *Advances in learning and behavioral disabilities* (Vol. 1, pp. 365–436). Greenwich, CT: JAI Press.

Pelham, W. E., & Murphy, H. A. (1986). Attention deficit and conduct disorders. In M. Hersen (Ed.), *Pharmacological and behavioral treatment: An integrative approach* (pp. 108–148). New York: Wiley.

Pelham, W. E., Sturges, J., Hoza, J., Schmidt, C., Bijlsma, J. J., Milich, R., & Moorer, S. (1987). The effects of Sustained Release 20 and 10 mg Ritalin b.i.d. on cognitive and social behavior in children with attention deficit disorder. *Pediatrics, 80,* 491–501.

*Physicians' Desk Reference* (39th ed.). (1985). Oradell, NJ: Medical Economics.

Quinn, P. O., & Rapoport, J. L. (1975). One-year-follow-up of hyperactive boys treated with imipramine or methylphenidate. *American Journal of Psychiatry, 132,* 241–245.

Rapoport, J. (1965). Child behavior and learning problems treated with imipramine. *International Journal of Neuropsychiatry, 1,* 635–642.

Rapoport, J. L. (1980). The "real" and "ideal" management of stimulant drug treatment for hyperactive children: Recent findings and a report from clinical practice. In C. K. Whalen & B. Henker (Eds.), *Hyperactive children: The social ecology of identification and treatment* (pp. 247–258). New York: Academic Press.

Rapoport, J. L., Quinn, P. O., Bradbard, G., Riddle, K. D., & Brooks, E. (1974). Imipramine and methylphenidate treatments of hyperactive boys. *Archives of General Psychiatry, 30,* 789–793.

Rapoport, J. L., Buchsbaum, M. S., Zahn, T. P., Weingartner, H., Ludlow, C., & Mikkelsen, E. J. (1978). Dextroamphetamine: Cognitive and behavioral effects in normal prepubertal boys. *Science, 199,* 560–563.

Rapport, M. D., Jones, J. T., DuPaul, G. J., Kelley, K. L., Gardner, M. J., Tucker, S. B., & Shea, M. C. (1988). Attention deficit disorder and methylphenidate: A multilevel analysis of dose–response effects on children's impulsivity across settings. *Journal of the American Academy of Child and Adolescent Psychiatry, 27,* 60–69.

Reatig, N. (Ed.). (1985). Pharmacotherapy for ADD-H adolescent workshop. *Psychopharmacology Bulletin, 21,* 169–257.

Renshaw, D. C. (1974). *The hyperactive child.* Chicago: Nelson-Hall.

Rie, H. E., Rie, E. D., Stewart, S., & Ambuel, J. P. (1976). Effects of Ritalin on underachieving children: A replication. *American Journal of Orthopsychiatry, 46,* 313–322.

Robison, D. S., & Barker, E. (1976). Tricyclic antidepressant cardiotoxicity. *Journal of the American Medical Association, 236,* 2089–2090.

Roche, A. F., Lipman, R. S., Overall, J. E., & Hung, W. (1979). The effects of stimulant medication on the growth of hyperkinetic children. *Pediatrics, 63,* 847–850.

Ross, D. M., & Ross, S. A. (1982). *Hyperactivity: Research theory, and action* (2nd ed.). New York: Wiley.

Ross, R. P. (1979). Drug therapy for hyperactivity: Existing practices in physician-school communication. In M. J. Cohen (Ed.), *Drugs and the special child* (pp. 99–109). New York: Gardner.

Safer, D. J., & Allen, R. P. (1973a). Factors influencing the suppressant effects of two stimulant drugs on the growth of hyperactive children. *Pediatrics, 51,* 660–667.

Safer, D. J., & Allen, R. P. (1973b). Single daily dose methylphenidate in hyperactive children. *Diseases of the Nervous System, 34,* 325–328.

Safer, D. J., & Allen, R. P. (1975). Stimulant drug treatment of hyperactive adolescents. *Diseases of the Nervous System, 36,* 454–457.

Safer, D. J., & Allen, R. P. (1976). *Hyperactive children: Diagnosis and management.* Baltimore: University Park Press.

Safer, D. J., & Krager, J. M. (1984). Trends in medication treatment of hyperactive school children. In K. D. Gadow (Ed.), *Advances in learning and behavioral disabilities* (Vol. 3, pp. 125–149). Greenwich, CT: JAI Press.

Saraf, K. R., Klein, D. F., Gittelman-Klein, R., & Groff, S. (1974). Imipramine side effects in children. *Psychopharmacologica, 37,* 265–274.

Satterfield, J. H., Schell, A. M., & Barb, S. D. (1980). Potential risk of prolonged administration of stimulant medication for hyperactive children. *Developmental and Behavioral Pediatrics, 1,* 102–107.

Satterfield, J. H., Satterfield, B. T., & Cantwell, D. P. (1981). Three-year multimodality treatment study of 100 hyperactive boys. *Journal of Pediatrics, 98,* 650–655.

Schain, R. J., & Reynard, C. L. (1975). Observations on effects of central stimulant drug (methylphenidate) in children with hyperactive behavior. *Pediatrics, 55,* 709–716.

Schleifer, M., Weiss, G., Cohen, N., Elman, M., Cvejic, H., & Kruger, E. (1975). Hyperactivity in preschoolers and the effect of methylphenidate. *American Journal of Orthopsychiatry, 45,* 38–50.

Shapiro, A. K., & Shapiro, E. (1981). The treatment and etiology of tics and Tourette syndrome. *Comprehensive Psychiatry. 22,* 193–205.

Sindelar, P. T., & Meisel, C. J. (1982). Teacher-physician interaction in the treatment of children with behavioral disorders. *International Journal of Partial Hospitalization, 1,* 271–277.

Singh, N. N., & Aman, M. G. (1981). Effects of thioridazine dosage on the behavior of severely mentally retarded persons. *American Journal of Mental Deficiency, 85,* 580–587.

Sleator, E. K. (1982). Office diagnosis of hyperactivity by the physician. In K. D. Gadow & I. Bialer (Eds.), *Advances in learning and behavioral disabilities* (Vol. 1, pp. 341–364). Greenwich, CT: JAI Press.

Sleator, E. K. (1985). Measurement of compliance. *Psychopharmacology Bulletin, 21,* 1089–1093.

Sleator, E. K., & Sprague, R. L. (1978). Pediatric pharmacotherapy. In W. G. Clark, & J. del Guidice (Eds.), *Principles of psychopharmacology* (2nd ed., pp. 573–591). Orlando, FL: Academic Press.

Sleator, E. K., & von Neumann, A. (1974). Methylphenidate in the treatment of hyperkinetic children. *Clinical Pediatrics, 13,* 19–24.

Sleator, E. K., von Neumann, A. W., & Sprague, R. L. (1974). Hyperactive children: A continuous long-term placebo controlled follow-up. *Journal of the American Medical Association, 229,* 316–317.

Sleator, E. K., Ullmann, R. K., & von Neumann, A. (1982). How do hyperactive children feel about taking stimulants and will they tell the doctor? *Clinical Pediatrics, 21,* 474–479.

Solomons, G. (1968). Monitoring drug therapy by telephone. *Medical Times, 96,* 205–210.

Solomons, G. (1971). Guidelines on the use and medical effects of psychostimulant drugs in therapy. *Journal of Learning Disabilities, 4,* 470–475.

Solomons, G. (1973). Drug therapy: Initiation and follow-up. *Annals of the New York Academy of Sciences, 205,* 335–344.

Sprague, R. L. (1984). Preliminary report of cross-cultural study and cognitive strategies of ADD children. In L. M. Bloomingdale (Ed.), *Attention deficit disorder: Diagnostic, cognitive, and therapeutic understanding* (pp. 211–219). New York: Spectrum.

Sprague, R. L., & Gadow, K. D. (1976). The role of the teacher in drug treatment. *School Review, 85,* 109–140.

Sprague, R. L., & Sleator, E. K. (1976). Drugs and dosages: Implications for learning disabilities. In R. M. Knights & D. J. Bakker (Eds.), *Neuropsychology of learning disorders: Theoretical approaches.* Baltimore: University Park Press.

Sprague, R. L., & Sleator, E. K. (1977). Methylphenidate in hyperkinetic children: Differences in dose effects on learning and social behavior. *Science, 198,* 1274–1276.

Sprague, R. L., Werry, J. S., Greenwold, W. E., & Jones, H. (1969, November). *Dosage effects of methylphenidate on learning of children.* Paper presented at the meeting of the Psychonomic Society, St. Louis.

Sprague, R. L., Barnes, K. R., & Werry, J. S. (1970). Methylphenidate and thioridazine: Learning reaction time, activity, and classroom behavior in emotionally disturbed children. *American Journal of Orthopsychiatry, 40,* 615–628.

Sprague, R. L., Christensen, D. E., & Werry, J. S. (1974). Experimental psychology and stimulant drugs. In C. K. Conners (Ed.), *Clinical use of stimulant drugs in children* (pp. 141–164). Amsterdam: Excerpta Medica.

Stephens, R. S., Pelham, W. E., & Skinner, R. (1984). The state-dependent and main effects of methylphenidate and pemoline on paired-associates learning and spelling in hyperactive children. *Journal of Consulting and Clinical Psychology, 523,* 104–113.

Swanson, J., Kinsbourne, M., Roberts, W., & Zucker, K. (1978). Time-response analysis of the effect of stimulant medication on the learning ability of children referred or hyperactivity. *Pediatrics, 61,* 21–29.

Tec, L. (1971). An additional observation on methylphenidate in hyperactive children. *American Journal of Psychiatry, 127,* 1424.

Thorn, I. (1975). A controlled study of prophylactic long term treatment of febrile convulsions with phenobarbital. *Acta Neurologica Scandinavica Supplementum, 60,* 67–73.

Varley, C. K., & Trupin, E. W. (1982). Double-blind administration of methylphenidate to mentally retarded children with Attention Deficit Disorder: A preliminary study. *American Journal of Mental Deficiency, 86,* 560–566.

Waizer, J., Hoffman, S. P., Polizos, P., & Engelhardt, D. M. (1974). Outpatient treatment of hyperactive school children with imipramine. *American Journal of Psychiatry, 131,* 587–591.

Weinberg, W. A., & Brumback, R. A. (1976). Mania in childhood: Case studies and literature review. *American Journal of Diseases of Children, 130,* 380–385.

Weithorn, C. J., & Ross, R. (1975). "Who monitors medication?" *Journal of Learning Disabilities, 8,* 458–461.

Wender, P. H., Reimherr, F. W., Wood, D., & Ward, M. (1985). A controlled study of methylphenidate in the treatment of attention deficit disorder, residual type, in adults. *American Journal of Psychiatry, 142,* 547–552.

Werry, J. S., & Aman, M. G. (1975). Methylphenidate and haloperidol in children. *Archives of General Psychiatry, 32,* 790–795.

Werry, J. S., Aman, M. G., & Diamond, E. (1980). Imipramine and methylphenidate in hyperactive children. *Journal of Child Psychology and Psychiatry, 21,* 27–35.

Whitehouse, D., Shah, U., & Palmer, F. B. (1980). Comparison of sustained-release and standard methylphenidate in the treatment of minimal brain dysfunction. *Journal of Clinical Psychiatry, 41,* 282–285.

Winsberg, B. G., & Yepes, L. E. (1978). Antipsychotics (major tranquilizers, neuroleptics). In J. S. Werry (Ed.), *Pediatric psychopharmacology* (pp. 234–273). New York: Brunner/Mazel.

Winsberg, B. G., Yepes, L. E., & Bialer, I. (1976). Pharmacologic management of children with hyperactive/aggressive/inattentive behavior disorders. *Clinical Pediatrics. 15,* 471–477.

Wolf, S. M., & Forsythe, A. (1978). Behavior disturbance, phenobarbital, and febrile seizures. *Pediatrics, 61,* 728–731.

Wysocki, T., Fuqua, W., Davis, V. J., & Breuning, S. E. (1981). Effects of thioridazine (Mellaril) on titrating delayed matching-to-sample performance of mentally retarded adults. *American Journal of Mental Deficiency, 85*, 539–547.

Zara, M. M. (1973). Effects of medication on learning in hyperactive four-year-old children. *Dissertation Abstracts International, 34*, 2407A. (University Microfilms No. 73-27, 620)

Zimmerman, F. T., & Burgemeister, B. B. (1958a). Action of methylphenidylacetate (Ritalin) and reserpine in behavior disorders in children and adults. *American Journal of Psychiatry, 115*, 323–328.

Zimmerman, F. T., & Burgemeister, B. B. (1958b). A new drug for petit mal epilepsy. *Neurology, 8*, 769–775.

# 11    Anxiety and Phobias
## Psychological Therapies

THOMAS R. KRATOCHWILL, ANNA ACCARDI, AND
RICHARD J. MORRIS

Virtually all theoretical models or approaches to human behavior have dealt with children's fears, phobias, or anxieties. Independent of theoretical orientation, fear is generally regarded as a basic human emotion that leads individuals to take protective action and that results in cognitive, behavioral, or physiological responses. All children experience fears that do not interfere with their daily functioning. In fact, these fears are typically viewed as an intregal part of normal development across most major theories of child development (Jersild, 1968; Jersild & Holmes, 1935; Morris & Kratochwill, 1983; Smith, 1979).

Sometimes, fears develop into much more intense or clinically significant problems for children. When children experience intense fears, they are often said to be experiencing a phobic or anxiety reaction (Gittleman, 1986). Since the mid-1960s, a great deal of empirical and theoretical literature has evolved dealing with children's fears, phobias, and anxieties. In this chapter, we provide an overview of some of the normative and prevalence data on children's fears, phobias, and anxiety; thereafter, we provide an overview of some of the major theoretical approaches that have been associated with major therapeutic models and techniques in the practice of child psychotherapy. The chapter is designed to be a broad-based overview and to alert the reader to different schools or models that have evolved in dealing with these problems. In this regard, the interested reader should consult the original sources for a more detailed presentation of the technique or procedure associated with a particular theoretical model.

## DEFINITION

Distinctions are often made among the terms *fear, phobia,* and *anxiety*. Yet, these terms have been used interchangeably in the clinical literature, and one

THOMAS R. KRATOCHWILL AND ANNA ACCARDI • Department of Educational Psychology, School Psychology Program, University of Wisconsin—Madison, Madison, Wisconsin 53706.    RICHARD J. MORRIS • Department of Educational Psychology, University of Arizona, Tucson, Arizona 85721.

often finds such terms as *overanxious*, *stress*, and *avoidant behavior* used in addition to the more traditional *anxiety*, *phobia*, and *fear*. (For an interesting discussion of anxiety as a *construct*, the reader should review Bernstein, Borkovec, and Coles, 1986.)

Some early writers defined a phobia as a special type of fear that is out of proportion to the demands of the situation, that cannot be explained or reasoned away, that is beyond voluntary control, and that leads to the avoidance of a feared situation (Marks, 1969). To this early conceptualization, Miller, Barrett, and Hampe (1974) added that phobias persist over an extended period of time, are maladaptive, and are not specific to any age or stage of the child. Phobias may develop as a function of some traumatic experience or from the child's inability to cope with a particular stressor in the environment.

Attempts have been made to formalize the definition of anxiety through the *Diagnostic and Statistical Manual of Mental Disorders* (3rd edition—DSM-III-R), developed by the American Psychiatric Association (APA, 1987). The DSM-III-R is used widely in both psychiatry and psychology and is generally accepted as being atheoretical, although many individuals associate it with psychodynamic formulations of personality or the medical model view of psychopathology. Within the DSM-III-R, three anxiety disorders are identified: separation anxiety disorder, avoidant disorder of childhood or adolescence, and overanxious disorder. Table 1 provides an overview of the major symptoms associated with these three major types of anxiety within the DSM-III-R.

The DSM-III-R system also provides several other related diagnostic categories in which anxiety may be a prominent feature. Children's and adolescents' disturbances that may have anxiety-based features include obsessive-compulsive disorder, social phobia, simple phobia, and posttraumatic stress disorders. It is possible for these disorders to develop in childhood and adolescence, and to the degree that anxiety is present, a formal diagnosis or subdiagnosis may be made.

The *World Health Organization International Classification of Diseases 9* (WHO-ICD-9) is another clinically derived system that can be used to classify anxiety-related problems in children. Although the system does not provide specific criteria for a diagnosis, broad categories are included. As an example, a child with persistent anxiety not associated with a specific stressor could be regarded as having a *disturbance of emotions* specific to childhood and adolescence, with anxiety and fearfulness. The glossary of the WHO-ICD-9 includes specific disor-

Table 1. Childhood Anxiety Disorders[a]

---

*Separation Anxiety Disorder*

A. Excessive anxiety concerning separation from those to whom the child is attached, as evidenced by at least three of the following:
   (1) unrealistic and persistent worry about possible harm befalling major attachment figures or fear that they will leave and not return
   (2) unrealistic and persistent worry that an untoward calamitous event will separate the child from a major attachment figure, e.g., the child will be lost, kidnapped, killed, or be the victim of an accident

---

TABLE 1. (*Continued*) 251

ANXIETY AND PHOBIAS:
PSYCHOLOGICAL
THERAPIES

(3) persistent reluctance or refusal to go to school in order to stay with major attachment figures or at home
(4) persistent reluctance or refusal to go to sleep without being near a major attachment figure or to go to sleep away from home
(5) persistent avoidance of being alone, including "clinging" to and "shadowing" major attachment figures
(6) repeated nightmares involving the theme of separation
(7) complaints of physical symptoms, e.g., headaches, stomachaches, nausea, or vomiting, on many school days or on other occasions when anticipating separation from major attachment figures
(8) recurrent signs or complaints of excessive distress in anticipation of separation from major attachment figures, e.g., temper tantrums or crying, pleading with parents not to leave
(9) recurrent signs or complaints of excessive distress when separated from home or major attachment figures, e.g., wants to return home, needs to call parents when they are absent or when child is away from home

B. Duration of disturbance of at least two weeks.

C. Onset before the age of 18.

D. Occurrence not exclusively during the course of a Pervasive Developmental Disorder, Schizophrenia, or any other psychotic disorder.

*Overanxious Disorder*

A. Excessive or unrealistic anxiety or worry, for a period of six months or longer, as indicated by the frequent occurrence of at least four of the following:
(1) excessive or unrealistic worry about future events
(2) excessive or unrealistic concern about the appropriateness of past behavior
(3) excessive or unrealistic concern competence in one or more areas, e.g., athletic, academic, social
(4) somatic complaints, such as headaches or stomachaches, for which no physical basis can be established
(5) marked self-consciousness
(6) excessive need for reassurance about a variety of concerns
(7) marked feelings of tension or inability to relax

B. If another Axis I disorder is present (e.g., Separation Anxiety Disorder, Phobic Disorder, Obsessive Compulsive Disorder), the focus of the symptoms in A are not limited to it. For example, if Separation Anxiety Disorder is present, the symptoms in A are not exclusively related to anxiety about separation. In addition, the disturbance does not occur only during the course of a psychotic disorder or a Mood Disorder.

C. If 18 or older, does not meet the criteria for Generalized Anxiety Disorder.

D. Occurrence not exclusively during the course of a Pervasive Developmental Disorder, Schizophrenia, or any other psychotic disorder.

*Avoidant Disorder of Childhood or Adolescence*

A. Excessive shrinking from contact with unfamiliar people, for a period of six months or longer, sufficiently severe to interfere with social functioning in peer relationships.
B. Desire for social involvement with familiar people (family members and peers the person knows well), and generally warm and satisfying relations with family members and other familiar figures.
C. Age at least 2½ years.
D. The disturbance is not sufficiently pervasive and persistent to warrant the diagnosis of Avoidant Personality Disorder.

---

*a*Reprinted from *Diagnostic and Statistical Manual of Mental Disorders, Third Ed.*, Rev. (DSM-III-R) (American Psychiatric Association, 1987).

ders that are subsumed in any given category. For example, overanxious reaction to childhood or adolescence could be included in the above classification. In addition, fear-related disturbances such as separation anxiety, withdrawal reaction of childhood or adolescence, anxiety states, and phobic states are sometimes diagnosed.

A diagnostic approach gaining some respectability among psychologists and others involved in studying psychopathology in children is based on empirically derived categories that use multivariate statistics to organize responses (Achenbach & Edelbrock, 1978; Quay, 1979; Yule, 1981). These approaches typically include standardized rating scales in which dimensional items are completed by parents, teachers, or other care providers. A number of different dimensions of child behavior have been identified, including conduct disorder, anxiety withdrawal, immaturity, and socialized aggression (Quay, 1979). These approaches tend to emphasize an empirical basis for identifying anxiety-related problems in children.

Individuals working in educational settings are often required to use Public Law 94-142, The Education of All Handicapped Children Act (1975), which includes criteria for the diagnosis of serious emotional disturbance. For example, a part of the criteria for emotional disturbance is the tendency for the child or adolescent to develop physical symptoms or fears associated with personal or school problems. School psychologists and others often find that children experience fears and phobias in school settings that interfere with their normal work.

## NORMATIVE AND PREVALENCE DATA

Since the early 1950s, a large number of normative and prevalence data have been collected on children's fears, phobias, and anxieties (Barrios, Hartmann, & Shigetomi, 1981; Graziano, De Giovanni, & Garcia, 1979; Miller, Barrett, & Hampe, 1974; Ollendick, 1979; Smith, 1979). However, many of the incidence data on children's fears are old and suffer from major methodological and conceptual problems (Graziano & Mooney, 1984). Graziano and Mooney speculated that the lack of well-controlled empirical research on the incidence of childhood fears may be based on the notion that the knowledge about adult fears is sufficient for understanding children's fears. However, one can also speculate that, because the constructs under study are ill-defined, it has been very difficult to obtain a quality data base. As Graziano and Mooney (1984) and others have noted, particularly lacking are data on childhood fears of high intensity, long duration, and disturbing content. In terms of normative fear research, some general consistencies have emerged in this area (Graziano & Mooney, 1984, pp. 89–98):

1. Girls generally obtain higher fear scores than boys. However, it should be emphasized that some studies did not find sex differences and that those reporting no differences are more recent, possibly reflecting changes in sex-role stereotyping.

2. Generally, there is a decrease from young childhood to late adolescence in the percentage of children who report one or more specific fears. Although this is not a linear trend, fear patterns change over age.

3. Socioeconomic class (SEC) is one important dimension in children's

fears, in that certain fears tend to be associated with various levels of SEC. For example, lower-SEC children report fears of specific events that may reflect their environment (e.g., violence, whipping, switchblades, drunks, money, rats, or cockroaches), whereas higher-SEC children report fears likely to be more related to the environments in which they function (e.g., car accidents, train wrecks, poisonous insects, or dangerous animals). However, these data are far from conclusive at this point.

4. There are some data that support a positive relation between children's fears and other pathological forms of behavior. It is possible that intense fears are related to other forms of pathological behavior, but this issue has not been empirically examined.

A great deal of criticism has been leveled at the incidence literature, which will not be summarized here. Major problems include the limitations of self-report and/or parent-based or teacher-based fear-rating scales, the type of questions asked, and the limited range of response systems sampled in the incidence research. That is, researchers have not routinely assessed responses in the cognitive, motor, and physiological domains. Generally, research in this area can be regarded as disappointing—a conclusion reached by Berecz (1968) 20 years ago. Despite this paucity of well-controlled normative and incidence research on children's fears and related problems, a great deal of time and effort has been put into treating children's fears, phobias, and anxiety across many different theoretical orientations. These perspectives are reviewed next.

## OVERVIEW OF THEORETICAL APPROACHES TO TREATMENT OF FEARS, PHOBIAS, AND ANXIETY

Numerous theoretical approaches have been advanced on the etiology and treatment of fears, phobias, and anxiety in children. In this section of the chapter, we provide an overview of the etiological theories that have been advanced in the treatment of these childhood problems. Specifically, we discuss the psychoanalytic, Adlerian, biological-organic, and behavioral positions. Each of the theories is reviewed briefly, along with their specific implications for the treatment of fears, phobias, and anxiety.[1] In addition, case examples of treatment are provided where possible to illustrate the various approaches discussed.

### Psychoanalytic Approaches

#### Theoretical Perspectives

Sigmund Freud proposed techniques and a theory that promoted an understanding of infantile sexuality in psychic life (Freud, 1900, 1905, 1909). It is important to emphasize that, although Freud based his theoretical constructs on child and adolescent cases, the theory was, in actuality, formulated to explain neurotic problems in adult clients (O'Connor, Lee, & Schaefer, 1983). Freud's

[1]This section of the chapter is an expanded version of Chapter 1 from Morris and Kratochwill (1983).

conceptualization of phobic disorders had its origins in his famous case of Little Hans (Freud, 1909).

On the basis of the behavioral descriptions associated with this fear and the information revealed during the course of therapy, Freud formulated his theory of the etiology of phobias. Freud's interpretation of the development of Hans's phobia centered on Oedipal conflicts. Hans was said to have had hostile and jealous feelings toward his father and sexual feelings and impulses toward his mother ("premonitions, as it were, of copulation"). Freud maintained that Hans hated his father because he saw him as a rival for the mother and wanted to take "possession" of the mother. Hans also feared punishment from his father in the form of castration because of his hostile feelings toward the father and his sexual attraction to the mother. Freud also noted that Hans repressed these hostile feelings and castration anxiety and "transposed [displaced them] from his father on to the horses."

It is important to emphasize that Freud assumed that only a parent could adequately act as an analyst for a young child (O'Connor et al., 1983). In this regard, Freud thought that the child could not develop a trusting enough relationship with a stranger to permit the normal therapeutic interchange that occurs during psychoanalysis. Thus, Hans's father treated Hans under Freud's direction and supervision. Freud (1909) reported that "it is true that I laid down the general lines of the treatment, and that on one single occasion, when I had a conversation with the boy, I took a direct share in it [i.e., the boy's treatment]; but the treatment itself was carried out by the boy's father" (p. 149).

Several writers (Achenbach, 1974; Elmhirst, 1984; A. Freud, 1974; Marks, 1969; Rachman, 1978) have noted the relative importance of the case of Little Hans and its impact on psychoanalytic theory. Specifically, Anna Freud (1981) stated:

> What the analysis of Little Hans opened up is a new branch of psychoanalysis, more than the extension of its therapy from the adult to the child—namely, the possibility of a new perspective on the development of the individual and on the obsessive conflicts and compromises between the demands of the drive, the ego, and the external world which accompanied the child's laborious steps from immaturity to maturity. (p. 278)

## Therapeutic Applications

Early formulations of psychoanalytic psychotherapy by Freud followed along the lines of the treatment of Little Hans, in which it was believed that only a parent could adequately act as an analyst for his or her child. This view changed, however, as new schools of thought developed regarding child-psychoanalytic therapy. The first school of child psychoanalysis is represented by the work of Anna Freud (1936, 1945, 1965, 1974). In this model, play was regarded as a symbolic representation of the child's life. Within this form of therapy, the child was engaged in a therapeutic relationship with the therapist. The early stages of therapy focused on building the therapeutic alliance. Subsequently, this view was dismissed, and it was assumed that children could experience defense interpretation during early phases of therapy, and that defense interpretation could occur as less threatening than a deeper interpretation of deeper unconscious material (O'Connor et al., 1983). In the second school of child psychoanalysis, Klein (1955) emphasized the direct interpretation of drive material. She placed greater emphasis on a direct interpretation of unconscious and preconscious processes as represented in the child's play.

Despite variations in child psychoanalysis, the approaches share several characteristics, as outlined by Scharfman (1978, p. 48; cited in O'Connor *et al.*, 1983):

> 1. The maintenance of the analytic stance that sets as few limitations as possible on the direction of the treatment. As such, the analyst follows the free expression of the patient's thoughts and actions, attending to those derivatives of the psychic structures as they present in their interaction.
>
> 2. Interpretation is the basic technique utilized to deal with defenses as they impede the flow of material and with transference manifestations as they appear in the course of treatment.
>
> 3. The analyst restricts the use of educative measures or attempts to change the child's environment as much as possible, intervening only where necessary to maintain the continuity of the analytic treatment.
>
> 4. The goal of treatment is to allow individuals to fulfill their development as completely as they can by helping to make conscious those unconscious elements that impede effective functioning.
>
> 5. The presence of the analyst is offered as an object with whom the patient can interact and in whose presence he may experience any thoughts and feelings past, present, and future as may arise. The analyst does not limit the patient's varying perceptions of him, but continuously analyzes them. (p. 544)

According to O'Connor *et al.* (1983), child psychoanalysis generally involves several features, including frequent contacts, involvement with the parents, the use of play materials in a play setting, interpretation, and the development of transference. Typically, there are frequent contacts with the child-client, which may involve five weekly sessions of approximately 1 hour's duration each. The analytic therapist also generally sees the child's parents and especially the mother.

Psychoanalysis has somewhat different goals and techniques, depending on the developmental stage of the child. For example, during the latency age a primary goal is to modify the child's developmental arrest and to reinstate normal development (O'Connor *et al.*, 1983). In this stage, the therapist also attempts to reduce anxiety and depression and to alleviate the major symptoms associated with the referral problem. During the analysis of pre-latency-age children, the primary goal is to remove the obstacles impeding development and to facilitate the child's progress in all areas of psychic growth. Also, the therapist is involved in the interpretation of resistances, transference, and the unconscious aspects of drives, as well as ego and superego functioning. In analysis with adolescents, the therapist clarifies the genital aspects of the individual's development through the revival of visual and affective memories. The primary focus is on the ego ideal and the conscience. It is in this phase that the nature of anxiety and the responses to it are the primary focus for understanding by the adolescent client.

Although there are few writings dealing with the treatment of specific anxiety disorders of childhood, Lewis (1986) discussed how psychoanalytic therapy can be used with children experiencing these problems. He pointed out that intense individual psychotherapy may alone be rarely indicated, and that individual psychotherapy may not be indicated when the problems of the child are more "external" than "internal or internalized." Lewis sees a common theme of individual psychoanalytic psychotherapy's placing a great importance on interpretation (i.e., making the unconscious or preconscious conscious), and especially on the interpretation of transference as the principle therapeutic agent.

Clients experiencing problems with anxiety would be involved in individual psychoanalytic psychotherapy across three major phases: the initial phase, the middle phase, and the termination phase. A major goal of the initial phase is to foster a therapeutic alliance between therapist and child. Generally, the child is offered interpretation that may provide some insight, yet that does not arouse a great deal of anxiety. Typically, the therapist offers interpretations that include setting statements, attention statements, reductive statements, and situational statements (see Lewis, 1986, for a more thorough discussion of these issues).

During the middle phase of therapy, the interpretation of transference or working through occurs. The child must understand that a major goal in psychotherapy is an attempt to gain an understanding of how he or she feels and behaves. Important in this middle phase of therapy are the transference process, reconstruction, further interpretation, countertransference, and working through. Elmhirst (1984) related a case in which the analyst's room also represented the analyst in fantasy and therefore had to be considered a component of transference:

> Children do not only fear being attacked or punished, they can also suffer acute anxiety on behalf of the people they love but to whom they have also had hostile impulses. A three-year-old girl in treatment with me for faecal retention once dared to play with water after we had worked for months studying her fears of it. Unfortunately there was a thunderstorm with torrential rain on the way home. The following session the patient was unable even to go near the side of the room where the sink was. As I began to describe her apparent fear she burst out, "Well you see what happened to me yesterday, I nearly got dead, and are you alright? I thought you'd be blown up and drowned too." (p. 12)

During the final or termination phase, the primary goal is reduced anxiety or some related achievement for the child. During this phase the therapist explores issues of separation (the actions to lose), dependency versus independence, and anxiety about developmental movements of the child. Lewis (1986) noted that it is common to see regression during this phase, in which the original symptoms reappear. The termination phase can vary in length from 6 weeks to 3 months.

Lewis (1986) reviewed little empirical research on specific applications of psychoanalysis with children experiencing severe anxiety disorders.

## Adlerian View[2]

### Theoretical Perspectives

Alfred Adler was one of the charter members of Freud's Vienna Psychoanalytic Society and later became president of the organization. Adlerian theory of personality is regarded as psychodynamic, but it is distinguished from Freudian psychoanalysis on several dimensions (Mosak, 1979). First, in contrast to Freud, who assumed that human behavior is motivated by inborn instincts, Adler argued that human beings are motivated primarily by social factors. Sec-

[2]The authors express appreciation to Dr. Harold Mosak for his comments on an earlier draft of a manuscript on the topic of Adlerian approaches to the treatment of children's fears. The current section is based on that earlier work.

ond, Adler introduced the concept of the creative self, which was perceived as a highly personalized, subjective system that directed experiences for the person. This view contrasts with the Freudian concept of ego, which served the ends of inborn instincts. Third, Adler emphasized the uniqueness of each individual personality. Thus, in contrast to Freud's early views, which held that sexual instincts were central in personality dynamics, Adler stressed that each person is a unique configuration of social factors (e.g., motives, traits, values, and interests). Fourth, in contrast to Freud's heavy emphasis on unconscious processes, Adler made consciousness the center of personality, although there was still an emphasis on the dynamics of personality, where some unconscious processes were said to direct the individual.

In Adlerian theory, deviant behavior is not regarded as a "mental illness." Rather, individuals demonstrating deviant behavior are said to be involved in mistaken ways of living (i.e., the mistaken lifestyle involves mistakes about oneself and the world and about the goals of success, as well as a low level of social interest and activity): "The neurotic by virtue of his ability to choose, creates difficulty for himself by setting up a 'bad me' (symptoms, 'ego-alien' thoughts, 'bad behavior') that prevents him from implementing his good intentions" (Mosak, 1979, p. 46).

Adler noted that the first 4 or 5 years of life laid the foundation for the lifestyle and that pathological behavior can develop during childhood. Adler acknowledged the significance of the mother in positive social development, noting that three negative factors could endanger the process: imperfect organs and childhood diseases, pampering, and neglect. Adler (1964b) also noted that the neglected or unwanted child tries to escape and stay a safe distance from others.

*Therapeutic Applications*

The Adlerian approach to psychotherapy has been characterized as a series of phases, which are not necessarily discrete and often overlap. These phases, described in various sources (e.g., Dinkmeyer, Pew, & Dinkmeyer, 1979; Mosak, 1979), include (1) the establishment and maintenance of a relationship; (2) exploration or analysis of the situation; (3) confrontation of the client with his or her goals; and (4) reorientation.

*Establishment of a Therapeutic Relationship.* Adlerians have emphasized the importance of establishing a positive relationship between therapist and client. Dreikurs (1967) noted:

> The proper therapist relationship as we understand it does not require transference but a relationship of mutual trust and respect. This is more than mere establishment of contact and rapport. Therapeutic cooperation requires an alignment of goals. When the goals and interests of the patient and therapist clash, no satisfactory relationship can be established. Winning the patient's cooperation for the common task is a prerequisite for any therapy; maintaining it requires constant vigilance. What appears as "resistance" constitutes a discrepancy between the goals of the therapist and those of the patient. (p. 65)

A central issue in establishing a therapeutic relationship is the affective factor called *encouragement*. The client is encouraged because inferiority feelings represent the core of psychopathology (Ansbacher & Adler, 1980). To help encourage the client, the therapist expresses concern and support. The therapist also frequently arranges the physical environment (e.g., eliminates a desk or sits facing the client in a chair of the same height) to help ensure a good environment. Such tactics would be considered especially important to use with children because therapeutic relationships may sometimes be difficult to establish with them. Various factors may interfere with the therapeutic relationship, and the therapist must be on guard to eliminate such client problems (Dinkmeyer *et al.*, 1979).

*Exploration or Analysis of the Situation.* The exploration or analysis phase has two primary purposes: an understanding of the lifestyle, and a determination of how the lifestyle affects the client's current functioning in her or his life tasks (Mosak, 1979). Assessment during this phase is both formal and informal. Informal observations are made of the client. For example, in working with a family, the therapist would observe the child and the family closely for verbal and nonverbal interactions. How and when a client says something are important inasmuch as they provide clues to various "scripts" that may be used by the client (Mosak, 1979).

More formalized assessment occurs through the use of the lifestyle investigation. Technically, analysis of the lifestyle begins with the first "psychological" transaction between client and therapist, but various technical aides may also be used. Although there was a paucity of published instruments for the collection of lifestyle data for many years, recent developments have provided some material in this area. For example, Kern (1976) operationalized questions from interview guides into a written Life Style Questionnaire Inventory (LSQI). Also, an "only child" form of the LSQI has been developed. Several other resources have been developed for this endeavor (e.g., Dinkmeyer *et al.*, 1979; Eckstein, Baruth, & Mahrer, 1978; Mosak, Schneider, & Mosak, 1980).

Assessment goes beyond the analysis of the individual in the usual sense. For example, the family is considered an important influence because Adlerians hold as a basic tenet that all behavior must be understood within a social context. An analysis of the family constellation can be made from the responses to a family constellation questionnaire. Adlerians emphasize that siblings influence each other as much as parents influence children. Essentially, in this assessment, the therapist is interested in exploring the conditions prevailing when the child was forming lifestyle convictions (Mosak, 1979).

Although there is an emphasis on the individual's mistakes, some therapists also focus on the client's perceived assets. The Adlerian therapist may also conduct a birth-order analysis in this phase of investigation. Based on birth order, Adler (1964a) made inferences about how a person may have chosen to respond to his or her original position. For example, according to Ansbacher and Adler (1980, p. 737): "A first born, dethroned from his original position as an only child, is often conservative, feeling that those in power should remain in power." On the other hand, "the second child, wanting to equal the first, often does not recognize existing power but wants power to change hands." And the youngest child "is in a favorable position in that he can never be dethroned." Although each individual may manifest behavior differently, within any particular birth order, it is assumed that the birth order becomes a part of lifestyle and must be considered in understanding the client's actions.

Sometimes, the therapist analyzes the child's four goals of misbehavior (Dreikurs, 1971), which are considered the immediate goals of children's misbehavior. The goals of misbehavior, all directed toward adults, are the means by which the child expects to benefit from adults: (1) attention; (2) power; (3) revenge; and (4) hopelessness. The child tries to obtain attention from adults, and if it cannot be obtained through positive means, the child will gain attention through disturbing actions. This activity may lead into the second goal: power. Children go into power struggles with adults, especially when told to do something. The child may also try to pay back the adults for what they do to him or her. This third goal (revenge) purportedly represents the most vicious children, who evoke despair in adults. In an analysis of the four goals of misbehavior, the therapist usually gains insight into the immediate goals of the child. All misbehavior is viewed as discouraged behavior that results from the child's perception of alienation or nonsignificance.

*Goal Confrontation.* Interpretation is done within the context of the purpose of behavior and its consequences. Dreikurs (1971) presented a technique for confronting children with their goal(s). He noted that, if this confrontation is managed properly, the child recognizes his or her goal and responds with the "recognition reflex" (cf. Dreikurs, 1948). A series of questions from Dreikurs (1967) leads to this reflex:

> First we ask the child why he is doing what he is not supposed to do. He either will say he doesn't know, or he will use a rationalization. We know that he doesn't know; but the question "why" is a prerequisite to the next question: "Could I tell you what I think?" And then we can come with the disclosure, but always in a tentative way, never throwing it at the person or accusing him. The key phrase is, "Could it be that. . . ." This phrase has become our trademark. It leads to an explanation of the child's behavior. "Could it be that you want to keep mother busy?" (goal 1). "Could it be that you want to show that nobody can stop or make you?" (goal 2). "Could it be that you want to get even? . . . Or to hurt?" (goal 3). "Could it be that you want to be left alone?" (goal 4). (p. 435)

Although similar techniques may be used by the Adlerian therapist, the interpretation is idiographic, that is, designed to fit the unique lifestyle of each client.

*Reorientation.* Alternative attitudes, beliefs, and actions are considered during this final phase, although this tends to be more the case in adult therapy. Basically, the process is one of changing the child's self-image, which implies an increase in social interest (see the earlier discussion). An important tenet of this phase is also convincing the client that this change is in his or her best interests (Mosak, 1979).

Two major purposes of the reorientation phase are establishing realistic goals and seeing new and functional alternatives (Dinkmeyer *et al.*, 1979). Beyond these aspects, some specific strategies are used to reorient the client. These are usually implemented through interviews. Dreikurs (1967) reviewed several strategies that can be used during this phase. (Other authors have presented a review of some specific strategies: see Dinkmeyer *et al.*, 1979, especially Chapter 7; Dreikurs & Soltz, 1964, presented some principles of child rearing that could be useful in therapy.) One of the first and major strategies is encouragement.

Within the Adlerian framework, "A misbehaving child is a discouraged child" (Dreikurs & Soltz, 1964, p. 36). Thus, encouragement is usually called for in the reorientation phase of therapy. The encouragement is used to help the child work through the misbehavior and is delivered by significant individuals in the environment (e.g., the therapist, the parents, and other adults).

Another procedure is called the *bathroom technique* (see Dreikurs & Soltz, 1964). Dreikurs (1971) noted:

> It was evolved first from the advice that the mother, in a conflict situation, bring a door between herself and the child. Then we suggested that the mother retreat to her bedroom whenever a conflict arises, or—if it gets worse—that she take a walk around the block. It was a mother who brought to our attention that the bathroom is much more effective as a means of disengagement. It has a dramatic effect on children. It is the most powerful method of bringing harmony in the family. The bathroom retreat is a declaration of mother's independence. Every mother, including the psychotic mother, can become more effective, since everyone can go to the bathroom. (p. 442)

The principle involved here is to disengage from a power struggle, and the technique illustrates the principle.

One of the most important procedures for teaching children responsibility is the application of *natural and logical consequences* (e.g., Dreikurs, 1971; Dreikurs & Grey, 1968). Logical consequences permit the parent to remain a "friendly bystander" and do not imply punishment. Natural consequences take place without any action on the part of the parents, whereas logical consequences are initiated by the adult.

### Approach to Treatment of Fears and Phobias

Generally, treatments of fears and phobias remain consistent with Adlerian theory and progress through the four stages of therapy. In this sense, these specific childhood problems are not conceptualized differently from other behavior problems. Although a number of Adlerian writers have discussed childhood fears and phobias, there has been amazingly little empirical work published in this area. Most accounts in the Adlerian literature are case reports from therapy or family counseling.

Within the Adlerian model, fears and phobias are considered a "neurotic" problem. Adler (1964a) discussed several interpretations of phobias and fears in both children and adults. In discussing the case of a 40-year-old man who was afraid of high buildings, Adler related the fear to the goal of superiority, stemming from the person's childhood, during which, it was recollected, he was physically attacked on the first day of school. Thus, it is recognized that early-childhood fear-arousing situations (or the perception of these) can influence adult disturbance. Dreikurs (e.g., Dreikurs, 1971; Dreikurs & Soltz, 1964) has been very consistent in his approach to the interpretation of childhood fears. The approach, best summed up in the title of a chapter devoted to the topic in *Children: The Challenge*, is "Be Unimpressed by Fear." Children are said to develop fears when adults are impressed by them, but children can develop fears through other mechanisms also. Thus, a child may show a particular fear that becomes a serious problem only when the parents provide attention and sympathy. Thus, "children can have a shock reaction, either by sudden noise, falling down, or a threatening experience. But this reaction will not lead to continued fears if the parents do not try to make up for the 'shock'" (Dreikurs, 1971, p. 437). The following case provides an example of the use of fear for its shock value:

> At five, Martha had no fear of grasshoppers. However, one day a very large one jumped on her and surprised her. She gave a small startled yelp and brushed at the grasshopper in such a way that it went inside her dress. The sensation was unpleasant, so she yelled again—but mostly because her cry had made her brother, nine, laugh in ridicule. Her attempts to get rid of the grasshopper appeared to him more and more hilarious. She, in turn, screamed louder and louder, because she was so mad at him. Mother came tearing out of the house, white-faced and shaken by the screams.
> That evening, brother came up to her with his hands closed. "Got something for you." "What?" He opened his hands and a grasshopper jumped out. Martha let out a blood-curdling scream, and both parents responded in haste. They sternly reprimanded brother and scolded Martha for her silliness. From now on, Martha screamed in terror at grasshoppers. But she knew, just underneath, that she wasn't really that scared of them! It was just that her fear had such shock value. (Dreikurs & Soltz, 1964, p. 218)

The purpose of this fear was stated to be its shock value. By being unimpressed by the fear, one could purportedly eliminate its purpose, and hence the fear. It is important to recognize that Dreikurs assumed that the child is aware of the fear and its real intensity. Such an interpretation would also assume that the child is aware, at some level, of the relation between her or his fear behavior and its effects on the parents. Another case provides an example of an analysis of the purpose of fear:

> Mother was trying to help Marcia, three, overcome her fear of the dark. She tucked the child into bed, turned on the hall light, and then turned off the bedroom light. "Mommie, Mommie," Marcia screamed in terror. "That's all right, honey," Mother soothed, "I won't leave you. Come, now, There really isn't anything to be afraid of. See. Mother is right here." "But I want the light on. I'm afraid of the dark." "The hall light is on, baby. And Mother is right here." "You won't leave?" "No, I'll sit right here until you are asleep." She roused frequently to see if Mother was still there. (Dreikurs & Soltz, 1964, p. 220)

In this case, the purpose of the fear was to keep the mother in the girl's service. The treatment implemented here (fading the light) is interpreted as inappropriate. The tactic most useful for this problem would be to put out the bedroom light, leave the hall light on, tuck Marcia in, fail to respond to her fears, and provide encouragement. Important in this process is that the mother must realize that she is not being cruel by leaving the child. In this treatment, the mother must learn (gain insight into) the purpose of the behavior and act accordingly.

Although relatively few reports have appeared in the Adlerian literature on the treatment of fears and phobias, Adlerians have offered some suggestions for the assessment and treatment of "school phobia." Dinkmeyer et al. (1979) recommended that the therapist determine if the phobia is functional or organic. Presumably, during the analysis phase of therapy (see the earlier discussion), the therapist would ask "the question." If the child is reporting abdominal pain, a functional response would lead to social life-task activities (e.g., having more friends, studying better, and getting along at home). If the pain is organic, the answer may be provided without reference to life tasks.

With regard to the specific treatment of school phobia, Baideme and Kern (1979) noted that disclosure of purpose, logical consequences, encouragement, antisuggestion, paradoxical intentions, and parent education were most helpful with a 9-year-old female displaying irregular school attendance and fear of attending school. The authors suggested that involvement of the family and the school personnel were important in this case. Consistent with Adlerian theory, the authors noted that the child was discouraged and was demonstrating helpless attention-getting behaviors.

In summary, fears and phobias in children are interpreted primarily within the context of their purpose. Treatment focuses on being unimpressed by fear and phobic reactions. The available Adlerian literature on fears and phobias is primarily in the form of case studies, with interpretations made within the context of the theory. Adlerian writers on the topic of fears and phobias have suggested that the procedures are quite successful.

## Biological/Organic View

### Theoretical Perspectives

There is a considerable body of literature on the biological/organic origins of fears, phobias, and related problems (see, for example, Delprato, 1980; Gray, 1971; Johnson, Rasbury, & Siegel, 1986, Ch. 6; Marks, 1969; Mathews, Gelder, & Johnston, 1981; Seligman, 1971; Sluckin, 1979). Most writings are typically directed toward adult fears and phobias, to the biological nature of fears in animals (Russel, 1979; Salzen, 1979), or to fears associated with "normal" stages of child development, and little has been written specifically about the etiology of children's clinical fears and phobias (Gray, 1971; Smith, 1979).

Some fears and anxieties seem to be partially genetic. Most likely, the genes have encoded in them a particular predisposition or susceptibility to anxiety disorders, as well as to other neuroses and schizophrenia. Thus, some individuals may be born more susceptible to anxiety disorders than others. Shields (1978) remarked:

> The genes do indeed influence the predisposition of neurotic illness in a number of ways, in particular in their effect on personality and on the kind of disorder an individual is most likely to develop under stress. Neurotics should, therefore, tend to differ from non-neurotics and amongst themselves in biological variables. (p. 166)

Mavissakalian and Barlow (1981a) noted that the biological predisposition to which Shields referred can also be referred to as "anxiety-proneness." Although some research has been reported in the adult phobia literature that supports this anxiety-proneness view (cf. Mavissakalian & Barlow, 1981b), little or no theoretical research on this topic has been conducted with children (e.g., Smith, 1979).

An etiological view was discussed by Seligman (1971). He noted that human phobias are a form of "prepared" classical (Pavlovian) conditioning (i.e., biologically prepared forms of conditioning). Seligman (1971) maintained:

1. Phobias do not extinguish under conventional procedures which reliably extinguish classically conditioned fear in the laboratory. (p. 308)
2. There is a common misconception among clinicians about the extinction of conditioned fear in the laboratory. . . . The misconception arises from a careless interpretation of the avoidance learning literature, a leap from the fact that avoidance responding does not extinguish to the mistaken inference that conditioned fear does not extinguish. (p. 309)
3. Implicit in the general process learning view of phobias is the assumption that they can be learned in one trial. . . . One-trial conditioning of fear is the exception, not the rule, in laboratory fear conditioning. (p. 311)

4. According to Pavlov's view of conditioning, the choice of CS is a matter of indifference. . . . This is the heart of the general process view of learning . . . any CS which happens to be associated with trauma should become phobic. But a neglected fact about phobias is that by and large they comprise a relatively nonarbitrary and limited set of objects . . . events related to the survival of the human species. (p. 312)

Seligman also noted that there is a selectivity associated with the development of fears and phobias, and that this selective learning process has its basis in evolution. That is, he believed that phobias were "prepared" in humans. The degree of a person's or an organism's preparedness for a particular fear or phobia was defined as follows:

The relative preparedness of an organism for learning about a situation is defined by the amount of input (e.g., numbers of trials, pairings, bits of information, etc.) which must occur before that output (responses, acts, repertoire, etc.), which is construed as evidence of acquisition, reliably occurs. (Seligman, 1970, p. 408)

Instinctive responding represents the (extreme) *prepared* end of the preparedness dimension; a response that occurs consistently after only a few pairings is viewed as *somewhat prepared* on the dimension; a response that takes place consistently only after many pairings is viewed as *unprepared*; and finally, if a response occurs only after "very many" pairings or does not occur at all, it is viewed as *contraprepared* (Seligman, 1970). Seligman (1971) maintained that the prepared learning-category provides a good fit for phobias because phobias (1) can be learned in one trial; (2) are selective; (3) show resistance to extinction; and (4) may be noncognitive.

Although some systematic research has been conducted on this model with adults, college-aged students, and laboratory animals, little research has been conducted on the preparedness of children's fears or phobias (see, for example, Clark, 1979; Delprato, 1980; de Silva, Rachman, & Seligman, 1977). Although the research findings (e.g., Hugdahl, Fredrikson, & Ohman, 1977; Ohman, Eriksson, & Olofsson, 1975b; Ohman, Erixon, & Lofberg, 1975a) on adults are interesting, at least one writer (Delprato, 1980) has commented that the research data have "limited" implications "for the inheritance of dispositions to acquire fear" or have "led to evidence in direct conflict with the evolutionary hypothesis" (Delprato, 1980, p. 90). Only a few studies (e.g., McNally & Reiss, 1982) have reported data that are inconsistent with the preparedness-theory position.

*Therapeutic Applications*

Because nervousness and fear are common human emotions that nearly everyone has experienced at one time or another, it is important to differentiate anxiety disorders and phobias from normal fears and anxieties. It is normal, for instance, for a child to feel fearful and anxious on the first day of attending a new school. On the other hand, a child who is still fearful of school after several weeks may have a serious anxiety problem.

It has been known for quite some time that dangerous or life-threatening situations trigger reactions in the parts of the nervous system that govern the level of arousal and that regulate blood flow to the parts of the body that most need it. This reaction prepares the person for a "fight-or-flight" response. To a smaller degree, adults and children experience the same kind of anxiety, triggered by autonomic arousal, in nondangerous situations, such as when giving a speech or taking a test. In these cases, the nervousness and the hyperalertness are normal and adaptive as long as the tension does not become excessive or handicapping. Andreasen (1984) explained that even classic phobias, such as a fear of heights or open spaces, may reflect some primitive adaptive response. In this way, anxiety may be potentially quite useful to human beings in helping them to cope with the stresses and threats of life. Therefore, anxiety should be considered pathological, and thus a symptom of a psychiatric disorder, only when it ceases to be helpful or adaptive and instead becomes crippling or disabling.

One form of treatment for anxiety disorders in children is pharmacological. There is a rapidly growing literature on the biological-psychopharmacological treatment of anxiety in children (see, for example, Algozzine, 1981; Gittleman & Koplewicz, 1986; Gittleman-Klein, 1975, 1978; Gittleman-Klein & Klein, 1973; 1986; Klein, Gittleman, Quitkin, & Rifkin, 1980; Wiener, 1985).

Antihistamines are widely used for developmental anxieties according to clinical anecdotal reports (Wiener, 1985). Benzodiazepines, such as Valium and Librium, have also been used for anxiety in children and adolescents. In a placebo-controlled study by Petti, Fish, Shapiro, Cohen, and Campbell (1982), a benzodiazepine was used with nine hospitalized boys between ages 7 and 11. The results suggest that the drug had a positive effect on the anxious, withdrawn, and mildly depressed children, and a worsening effect on the behavior of severely impulsive-aggressive or schizophrenic children.

Currently, imipramine (a tricyclic antidepressant) is recommended for the treatment of school-phobic children. In a study by Gittelman-Klein and Klein (1973), school-phobic children were placed in a double-blind placebo-controlled study combining placebo and drug with individual and family psychotherapy. The drug group returned to school significantly sooner than the placebo group. This study has not been replicated. Clomipramine is reported to be ineffective in the treatment of school phobia (Berney, Kolvin, Bhate, Garside, Jeans, Kay, & Scarth, 1981). (Because of imipramine's many side effects, such as EKG abnormalities, psychotherapy should be the first consideration for the treatment of school phobia, and imipramine should be reserved only for severe cases.)

The genetic predisposition to anxiety disorders, or "anxiety-proneness," appears to be what Gittleman-Klein and Klein (1973) were referring to in their discussion of one possible etiological view of separation anxiety in school-phobic children. Following Bowlby's position (1969, 1973), they suggested that constitutional variations occur in the threshold of the theorized "biological phenomenon" of separation anxiety. They indicated that

> severe separation anxiety [the type associated with school phobia] may be seen as a pathological manifestation of a normal biological developmental process, around which secondary anxieties may be learned. If such were the case, one would expect relatively little alteration of the biological anxiety threshold via verbal or management therapeutic efforts. (Gittleman-Klein & Klein, 1973, p. 214)

However, the fact that some children are more susceptible to anxiety disorders than others does not mean they will need to depend on drugs to alter the chemical imbalances in their brains. As in the case of the affective disorders, environmental factors play a salient role in producing pathological anxiety and phobias. The relationship between our internal biology and the environment that surrounds us is almost certainly interactive, and it would be foolish to ignore this fact. We need to remember that our brain biology is altered and controlled to some extent by changes in attitude, habits, and behavior. For this reason, it is suggested that drugs be used only in conjunction with some sort of psychological therapy.

In summary, when treating children with anxiety disorders, it is first important to differentiate pathological anxiety and phobias from normal anxiety and fear. The use of any drug in the treatment of children with anxiety disorders should be regarded as investigational at best. Because of the many and varied side effects associated with pharmacological treatment, children being treated with a drug should be monitored closely. Again, it is recommended that drugs be used only in severe and disabling cases, and not without psychological therapy.

## Behavioral View

### Theoretical Perspectives

Behavioral conceptualizations of the development of fears and phobias span several learning-theory positions, including those of Pavlov (1927), Skinner (1938, 1953), Hull (1943), Mowrer (1939, 1960), and Bandura (1969, 1977b; Bandura & Walters, 1963). Generally, most etiological statements regarding fear development include Pavlov's classical conditioning notion in their explanation. Other views are based strictly on an operant-conditioning framework or a social-learning perspective.

Perhaps the most famous study in behavioral psychology that forms the basis for explaining anxiety was conducted by Watson and Rayner (1920) and involved an 11-month-old child called Albert B. These investigators reported that, through classical conditioning, they could teach a child to become afraid of a live white rat, and that this conditioned fear could be generalized to a fear of other animals and furry-like objects (e.g., a white rabbit, a dog, and a piece of cotton). Initially, it was reported that the rat did not elicit any fear reaction from the child, but after its presence was coupled with a loud noise, it elicited fear responses from Albert without the accompanying noise. Although few writers within the behavioral view would question the impact and the relative contribution of Watson and Rayner's findings, a number of theoretical objections to the classical conditioning model have been raised (Shaffer, 1986, pp. 159–160):

1. A number of writers (e.g., Costello, 1970; Harris, 1979; Marks, 1969; Seligman, 1970) have cited later studies by other researchers who were not able to replicate or demonstrate this fear conditioning in young children when more neutral objects (e.g., wooden blocks) were used instead of a furry rat. Delprato (1980), however, questioned such studies on methodological grounds and suggested that sufficient data have not yet been gathered to refute the Watson and Rayner findings.

2. Most phobias occur to a relatively narrow range of stimuli such as spiders, snakes, and heights, but one would not expect this narrowness, given the possibility of an unlimited number of serendipitous pairings. Also, many anxiety-provoking stimuli are commonly encountered, but not all objects are equipotent in fear-eliciting capabilities.

3. Within the classical conditioning paradigm, an unreinforced response should extinguish rapidly when the conditioned stimulus is not followed by the unconditioned stimulus. However, in clinical patients, this finding rarely occurs.

4. Although classical conditioning theory would predict that single-trial learning is the most common source of clinical fears, this rarely occurs in individuals, except under unusual circumstances.

5. Within the classical conditioning paradigm, the acquisition of a conditioned response requires that the CS and the US be paired within a small space in time, yet this rarely happens in natural settings.

Another view that integrated classical and instrumental conditioning theory was developed by Mowrer (1939, 1960) and was called *two-factor learning theory*. Mowrer combined classical conditioning with Hullian instrumental learning to account for the conditioning and maintenance of a fear response. He suggested that fear was a classically conditioned response (CR) that came about by the pairing of an aversive unconditioned stimulus (UCS) with a previous neutral stimulus (CS). The conditioned fear response (CR) motivates avoidance behavior in the organism whenever the CS is present, and this avoidance behavior reduces the CR, which, in turn, reinforces the organism for engaging in the avoidance behavior (Carr, 1979).

Mowrer's view also assisted Wolpe (1958) in conceptualizing his theory of the development and treatment of fears, phobias, and related problems (discussed below). Wolpe maintained that neurotic behavior was a persistent, unadaptive habit that was learned and that therefore could be unlearned. He further wrote that neurotic behavior was learned through a temporal contiguity of the stimulus and the response (classical conditioning) and was maintained by drive reduction (Hullian instrumental learning). Wolpe also supported, in marked contrast to Seligman (1970, 1971), the general-process view toward learning:

> Experimentally it is possible to condition an animal to respond with anxiety to any stimulus one pleases merely by arranging for that stimulus, on a number of occasions, to appear in an appropriate time relation to the evocation of anxiety. . . . In human neuroses one can usually elicit a history of similar kinds of conditioning. (Wolpe, 1964, p. 10)

Mowrer's theory was one of the most prevailing views of fear development up through the 1960s, when writers began critically evaluating and questioning this perspective (e.g., Bandura, 1969; Graziano *et al.*, 1979; Rachman, 1976, 1977). Marks (1969) noted that two-factor theory did not explain the tremendous resistance to extinction found in avoidance responses:

> In theory, as avoidance responses continue the classically conditioned CER is no longer reinforced and should extinguish. This should lead in turn to extinction of the avoidance response. But in practice neither the CER nor the avoidance response are [*sic*] easily extinguished. (p. 59)

Another weakness of the theory has been the finding that avoidance behavior can be learned independent of the presence of a mediating fear; fear is not apparently necessary as an antecedent factor in effecting avoidance behavior (e.g., Carr, 1979; Seligman & Johnston, 1973).

Another behavioral view of the development of fears and phobias is based on operant conditioning (e.g., Skinner, 1938, 1953). Within the operant conditioning paradigm, a number of principles and procedures have been identified as influencing behavior (see, for example, Morris, 1985; Sulzer-Azaroff & Mayer, 1977). One of the most common procedures is reinforcement. An event is regarded as a reinforcer if it increases the probability of the behavior it follows. Reinforcement can be either positive or negative. A reinforcer is said to be positive if an event presented to the child increases some behavior it follows. Negative reinforcement is said to occur when the removal of some event after a target response increases the frequency of responding. Punishment involves the presence of a stimulus (typically aversive) that results in decreased frequency of responding, whereas time-out has the same behavioral effect when some event is removed after a target response. In the use of extinction, no consequences follow the target response. The result of an extinction procedure would be a decreased frequency of the previously reinforced response. In a stimulus control procedure, a response may be followed by a reinforcing or punishing consequence in the presence of one stimulus ($S^D$ or $S^+$), but not in the presence of another ($S$ or $S^-$). In the procedure, a response reinforced in one situation but not in another situation comes under control of the different situations. A situation previously associated with reinforcement of the target response increases the probability that the response will be performed when compared to the situation previously associated with no reinforcement. Thus, when a child has responded differentially to different stimuli, he or she has made a discrimination, and the behavior is said to be under stimulus control. A variety of other operant principles and procedures have been discussed in the professional literature, and the interested reader should consult these sources directly (Sulzer-Azaroff & Mayer, 1977; Wilson & O'Leary, 1980).

Behavior analysts regard such emotional concepts as *fear* and *anxiety* as fraught with difficulties within a scientific analysis (Bijou & Baer, 1978). Bijou and Baer embraced Kantor's views regarding emotion (Kantor, 1966; Kantor & Smith, 1975). In this analysis emotional interaction is regarded as *"a momentary cessation of operant behavior on the occasion of a sudden change in the environment"* (Bijou & Baer, 1978, p. 108), which consists of five phases:

1. The interactions are in progress prior to a sudden change in the environment (a baseline is established).
2. A sudden change in the environment occurs (the emotionalizing event).
3. The cessation of operant interactions and changes in respondent interactions take place (the emotional reaction occurs).
4. The operant interactions follow the cessation of operant interactions (recovery occurs).
5. The predispositions for operant and respondent behaviors persist for some time period following recovery (organismic setting event). (pp. 108–109)

This analysis is consistant with a natural science approach to the study of human emotion.

Extensive empirical support for the operant position of fear and phobia development in children is lacking at present (Morris & Kratochwill, 1983). It seems that most investigators who have conducted research on children's fears and phobias since the mid-1960s have not identified strongly with the operant approach. As a consequence, few etiological studies have been published using humans, although a substantial body of research exists on laboratory animals.

The fourth model involves social-learning-theory approaches to the etiology of fears and phobias in children (e.g., Bandura, 1969, 1977b; Bandura & Walters, 1963). This perspective involves the conditioning of a fear in a person through vicarious learning. The person can acquire a fear or avoidance behavior by directly observing a model being exposed to a traumatic event in a situation and acquiring a *symbolic representation* of the modeled event. The modeling activity is governed by four subprocesses: observer attentional processes; observer retention processes: observer motoric reproduction processes; and reinforcement and motivational processes that regulate the observer's overt expression of the modeled behavior. In 1969, Marks noted that there was experimental evidence of the development of fears through a modeling process in both animals and humans. Indeed, in a study by Bandura and Rosenthal (1966), observers who viewed a model receive shock associated with a buzzer as part of a conditioning experiment showed increased levels of physiological reactivity when the buzzer was presented to them, even though they had had no history of being shocked when the buzzer went on.

More recently, Bandura (1977a) noted that behavior change procedures may serve the function of creating and strengthening "personal efficacy." A distinction is made between outcome expectations that relate to whether a behavior will result in a certain consequence and the efficacy expectations that relate to a personal conviction that the individual can perform a particular behavior. For example, an efficacy expectation would relate to a child's expectation that he or she could enter a darkened area of the house. Outcome expectations could include such factors as reinforcement from the parents and the child's own satisfaction in performing this behavior. More detailed accounts of the self-efficacy construct can be found in Bandura (1977a,b, 1978).

## Therapeutic Applications

A considerable body of literature has developed on the clinical applications of behavior modification or behavior therapy. Indeed, relative to the other models discussed in this chapter, behavior procedures have considerable empirical support despite methodological limitations. Closely related to the above theoretical perspectives, four major behavior-therapy methods have been used to treat children's fears: systematic desensitization (with several variations); contingency management or operant approaches; modeling therapies; and cognitive-behavioral methods. Each of these methods is reviewed in detail in Morris and Kratochwill (1983) and Kellerman (1981). There are also several chapters reviewing behavioral treatment procedures for children's fears, phobias, and anxiety (Carlson, Figueroa, & Lahey, 1986; Graziano & Mooney, 1984; Morris & Kratochwill, 1984).

*Systematic Desensitization.* In the systematic-densensitization treatment-approach developed by Wolpe (1958), it is assumed that anxiety is learned and that it can be inhibited by substituting an activity that is antagonistic to this response. Typically, relaxation or some variation of this procedure is used to inhibit anxiety during treatment. The desensitization procedure involves exposing the child in small graduated steps to some fear stimulus while he or she is performing the actual activity antagonistic to the feelings of anxiety. The graduated exposure to the fear or anxiety event can take place in real life or in an imaginal context.

Systematic desensitization involves three major components (Morris & Kratochwill, 1983): relaxation training, the development of an anxiety hierarchy, and the actual systematic-desensitization treatment-procedure. In the relaxation phase, the student is taught methods of relaxing, usually by relaxing and tensing various muscle groups. In the anxiety-hierarchy-development phase, a hierarchy of various items is constructed, from events that are the least anxiety-provoking to those that would elicit the most intense anxiety in the client. The hierarchies usually differ on a number of dimensions, including the number of people present, particular settings in which the fear occurs, and the actual number of items in the hierarchy. During the formal systematic-desensitization procedure, the therapist pairs relaxation training with the items in the hierarchy. The child is asked to imagine each scene as vividly as possible while maintaining a relaxed state. The hierarchy items developed during the previous phase are subsequently presented in ascending order while relaxation is paired with the item on the hierarchy.

There are at least five variations of systematic desensitization (see Morris & Kratochwill, 1983, for a detailed review). For example, children can often participate in systematic desensitization in a *group format*, in which they proceed at the pace of the slowest member in the group. *In vivo desensitization* involves exposing students to items in the hierarchy in an actual situation rather than through imagination. Such procedures would be advantageous for children (for example, young children) who are unable to imagine or whose treatment needs to be focused on real rather than symbolic representations of the problem. Another variation is called *emotive imagery* and involves having the child listen to the therapist describe particular anxiety-arousing scenes or scenarios that concern the child's favorite hero. The child is requested to imagine a favorite hero, such as Superman, successfully overcoming the anxiety during a particular scene. Other variations of systematic desensitization involve *contact desensitization* and *self-control desensitization*. Contact desensitization combines elements of desensitization and modeling therapeutic approaches. Specifically, the procedure consists of three major components: modeling of the desired behavior, the use of physical and verbal prompts, and the gradual withdrawal of therapist assistance or contact. In self-control desensitization, the treatment is viewed as teaching clients to cope with anxiety so that they can cope with anxiety-provoking situations on their own.

*Contingency Management.* Contingency management procedures are associated with the operant or applied behavior-analysis model of treatment. As noted in the theoretical perspectives section, this model focuses on the environmental consequences of learning and unlearning fear-related responses. A most common therapeutic procedure used within contingency management is positive reinforcement. This procedure has been used alone and in combination with other behavioral procedures to facilitate children's adaptation to settings that were previously deemed fearful by the child. For example, in one project, the effectiveness of a reinforced-practice treatment-program was evaluated by Leitenberg and Callahan (1973). In the project, 14 preschool children were assigned to experimental or control conditions. The experimental group received the reinforced-practice treatment, which involved providing the children with feedback regarding the exact time they spent in the darkened room plus praise reinforcement, repeated practice during each session, and instructions. The authors found that the reinforced-practice procedure produced significant improvement over the control group in the length of time that children remained in both the partially and the completely darkened test rooms.

Other behavioral procedures have been used within the operant approach to treatment, and these procedures are reviewed in greater detail in many child therapy textbooks (see Morris & Kratochwill, 1984; Ollendick & Cerny, 1984).

*Modeling Interventions.* Modeling treatment approaches are affiliated with the social learning theory outlined above. The modeling procedures generally consist of the model, who could be a therapist, a teacher, or a parent, modeling or demonstrating certain coping responses for the child. The child is requested to observe the model engaging in certain behaviors that are fear-provoking, or that result in anxiety for the child. Moreover, the model is typically instructed to approach the target situation gradually and with caution so as to facilitate the modeling effect.

Various aspects of modeling treatments are prerequisites to the successful application of this therapy. The child observer must (1) attend to certain aspects of the modeling situation; (2) retain what has been learned in the modeling situation; (3) motorically reproduce or match what has been observed; and (4) be motivated to perform the observed behavior (Bandura, 1977b). The therapist must also assure the child that the model has not experienced any perceived or unsafe consequences in the anxiety situation.

Modeling can occur in either a live or a symbolic mode. Contact desensitization is sometimes regarded as a modeling treatment (Carlson *et al.*, 1986). In live modeling, individuals may view other children participating in various activities with successful outcomes, such as going to school without any fear. Symbolic modeling, a more common strategy within the modeling research literature, involves children in viewing a tape or film of individuals like themselves participating in an experience. An example study was reported by Melamed and Siegel (1975), who examined the relative effectiveness of symbolic modeling in reducing the anxiety level of children who were facing hospitalization and surgery. The children ranged in age from 4 to 12, were all being hospitalized for the first time, and were scheduled for elective surgery. The childern in the modeling condition arrived at the hospital and viewed a 16-minute film, *Ethan Has an Operation,* a film that depicts a 7-year-old white male who has been hospitalized for a hernia operation. It consists of 15 scenes showing various events that most children encounter when hospitalized for elective surgery, from the time of admission to the time of discharge. It also includes explanations of the hospital procedures provided by the medical staff. Also included are various scenes narrated by the child, describing his feelings and concerns at each stage of the hospital experience. Both the child's behavior and his verbal remarks portray anxiety and apprehension. However, the child is able to overcome his initial fears and to complete each event successfully and without anxiety (Melamed & Siegel, 1975, p. 514). The study demonstrated that the film modeling condition significantly reduced measures of situational anxiety in children compared to a control condition, and that these significant differences were maintained at the follow-up period.

Modeling treatments can be very helpful in working with fearful children. Unfortunately, although modeling procedures have been used extensively with children's non-school-related fears and anxieties, relatively little work has been published on school-related fears and anxieties (Morris & Kratochwill, 1983).

Self-control methods of treatment are typically affiliated with cognitive be-havior-modification procedures (Meichenbaum & Genest, 1980; Ramirez, Kra-tochwill, & Morris, 1987). The basic underlying approach of cognitive self-control therapies is the view that cognitive processes contribute substantially to any behavior change program and that children can regulate their own behavior. Also, the therapist serves as instigator or motivator, but the individual child is primarily responsible for carrying out the intervention program.

Self-control procedures involve several components as a part of the thera-peutic approach: (1) becoming aware of negative thinking styles that impede performance and that lead to an emotional upset and inadequate performance; (2) generating, in collaboration with the therapist, a set of incompatible self-statements, rules, and strategies that the student can use, and (3) learning specific adaptive cognitive-behavioral skills (Meichenbaum & Genest, 1980, p. 403). In order for self-control programs to be effective, the child must be aware of her or his anxiety reactions, possibly across motor, cognitive, and physiological response channels.

In an example study in this area, Kanfer, Karoly, and Newman (1975) com-pared the effectiveness of two types of verbal controlling responses on the reduction of children's fear of the dark. Forty-five children, 5–6 years of age, participated in the study. It was reported that none of these children could stay alone in the dark for more than 27 seconds. The children were then assigned to one of three conditions: (1) a competence group, in which they heard and rehearsed sentences emphasizing their respective competence and active control in the fear situation (e.g., "I am a brave boy (girl). I can take care of myself in the dark"); (2) a stimulus group, in which they heard and rehearsed sentences emphasizing reducing the aversive qualities of the fear situation (e.g., "The dark is a fun place to be. There are many good things in the dark"); or (3) a neutral group, in which they rehearsed sentences related to "Mary Had a Little Lamb" (Kanfer *et al.*, 1975, p. 253). The training took place in a well-lighted room, and assessment took place in a dark one. The pretest and posttest measures consist-ed of the duration of darkness and the terminal light intensity (i.e., the degree of illumination the children needed to stay in the room).

The results showed that from the pretest to the first posttest period, the competence and stimulus groups remained in the darkened room significantly longer than the neutral group, and at the second posttest, the competence group remained in the room significantly longer than either the stimulus or neutral groups. There were no significant differences between the stimulus and the neutral groups at the second posttest period. On the illumination measure, the competence group was also found to be superior to the other two groups. The authors concluded that the training's effectiveness was related to the content of the sentences learned by the three groups.

## SUMMARY

In this chapter, we have provided an overview of four major theoretical approaches to the understanding and treatment of children's fears and phobias.

There appears to be little well-controlled empirical work to support the successful application of psychoanalysis with children. Likewise, the Adlerian literature on the treatment of fears and phobias is primarily in the form of case studies and does not provide strong support for effective treatments. Nevertheless, writers in both theoretical camps have suggested that therapeutic procedures have been used successfully with the fearful child.

In the biological-organic area, the primary mode of treatment has been drugs. Again, there is little well-controlled research on children to argue for the exclusive use of one specific type of medication. Drugs may best be used in very severe cases and along with other forms of psychological therapy. In any case, close monitoring of the child for changes and side effects should be scheduled routinely.

In the behavior therapy area, most of the research on children's fears has centered on systematic desensitization and its variations. Relative to the other therapeutic models, the fear and phobia area has been an active domain of research, both experimental and clinical. However, with the exception of those on modeling treatments, there are actually very few well-controlled experimental studies. Across all behavioral therapies, there is a rather limited data base on intense clinical fears, so that generalizations of the treatment procedures to complex clinical problems are more tentative.

Acknowledgments. This chapter was written while the first author was principal research investigator with the Behavioral and Social Sciences Research Unit of the Wisconsin Center on Mental Retardation and Human Development, which is funded in large part by Grant HD 03352 from the National Institute of Child Health and Human Development.

The authors express appreciation to Ms. Karen Kraemer for her assistance in word-processing the manuscript.

## References

Achenbach, T. M. (1974). *Developmental psychopathology*. New York: Ronald Press.

Achenbach, T. M., & Edelbrock, C. S. (1978). The classification of child psychopathology: A review and analysis of empirical efforts. *Psychological Bulletin, 85,* 1275–1301.

Adler, A. (1964a). *Problems of neurosis*. New York: Harper & Row.

Adler, A. (1964b). *Problems of neurosis: A book of case histories*. New York: Harper & Row.

Algozzine, R. (1981). Biophysical perspective of emotional disturbance. In R. Algozzine, R. Schmidt, & C. D. Mercer (Eds.), *Childhood behavior disorders: Applied research and educational practice* (pp. 83–112). Rockville, MD: Aspen.

American Psychiatric Association. (1980). *Diagnostic and statistical manual of mental disorders (DSM-III)*. Washington, DC: Author.

American Psychiatric Association (1987). *Diagnostic and statisical manual of mental disorders* (3rd ed., revised). Washington, DC: Author.

Andreasen, N. C. (1984). *The broken brain*. New York: Harper & Row.

Ansbacher, H. L., & Adler, A. (1980). In H. I. Kaplan, A. M. Freedman, & B. J. Sadock (Eds.), *Comprehensive textbook of psychiatry/III (Vol. 1)*. Baltimore: Williams & Wilkins.

Baideme, S. M., & Kern, R. M. (1979). The use of Adlerian family therapy in a case of school phobia. *Journal of Individual Psychology, 35,* 58–69.

Bandura, A. (1969). *Principles of behavior modification*. New York: Holt, Rinehart, & Winston.

Bandura, A. (1977a). Self-efficacy: Toward a unifying theory of behavioral change. *Psychological Review, 84,* 191–215.

Bandura, A. (1977b). *Social learning theory*. Englewood Cliffs, NJ: Prentice-Hall.

Bandura, A. (1978). Reflections on self-efficacy. In H. J. Eysenck & S. Rachman (Eds.), *Advances in behavior research and therapy* (Vol. 1), (pp. 139–161). New York: Pergamon Press.

Bandura, A., & Rosenthal, T. (1966). Vicarious classical conditioning as a function of arousal level. *Journal of Personality and Social Psychology, 3,* 54–62.

Bandura, A., & Walters, R. H. (1963). *Social learning and personality development.* New York: Holt, Rinehart, & Winston.

Barrios, B. A., Hartmann, D. P., & Shigetomi, C. (1981). Fears and anxieties in children. In E. J. Mash & L. G. Terdal (Eds.), *Behavioral assessment of childhood disorders* (pp. 259–304). New York: Guilford Press.

Berecz, J. M. (1968). Phobias of childhood: Etiology and treatment. *Psychological Bulletin, 74,* 694–720.

Berney, T., Kolvin, I., Bhate, S. R., Garside, R. F., Jeans, J., Kay, S., & Scarth, L. (1981). School phobia: A therapeutic trial with clomipramine and short-term outcome. *British Journal of Psychiatry, 138,* 110–118.

Bernstein, D. A., Borkovec, T. D., & Coles, M. G. H. (1986). Assessment of anxiety. In A. R. Ciminero, K. S. Calhoun, & H. E. Adams (Eds.), *Handbook of behavioral assessment* (2nd ed.) (pp. 367–428). New York: Wiley.

Bijou, S. W., & Baer, D. M. (1978). *Behavior analysis of child development.* Englewood Cliffs, NJ: Prentice-Hall.

Bowlby, J. (1969). *Attachment.* New York: Basic Books.

Bowlby, J. (1973). *Attachment and loss* (Vol. 2). New York: Basic Books.

Carlson, C. L., Figueroa, R. G., & Lahey, B. B. (1986). In R. Gittelman (Ed.), *Anxiety disorders of childhood* (pp. 203–232). New York: Guilford Press.

Carr, A. T. (1979). The psychopathology of fear. In W. Sluckin (Ed.), *Fear in animals and man* (pp. 199–235). New York: Van Nostrand Reinhold.

Clark, M. A. (1979). *An exploratory investigation of the interaction of internal-external locus of control and therapy type with snake-avoidant preschool children.* Unpublished doctoral dissertation, Syracuse University.

Costello, C. G. (1970). Dissimilarities between conditioned avoidance responses and phobias. *Psychological Review, 77,* 250–254.

Delprato, D. J. (1980). Hereditary determinants of fears and phobias: A critical review *Behavior Therapy, 11,* 805–814.

de Silva, P., Rachman, S., & Seligman, M. E. P. (1977). Prepared phobias and obsessions: Therapeutic outcome. *Behavior Research and Therapy, 5,* 65–77.

Dinkmeyer, D. C., Pew, W. L., & Dinkmeyer, D. C., Jr. (1979). *Adlerian counseling and psychotherapy.* Monterey, CA: Brooks/Cole.

Dreikurs, R. (1948). *The challenge of parenthood.* New York: Duell, Sloan & Pearce.

Dreikurs, R. (1967). The individual psychological approach. In B. B. Wolman (Ed.), *Handbook of child psychoanalysis: Research, theory and practice* (p. 15). New York: Van Nostrand Reinhold.

Dreikurs, R. (1971). *Social equality: The challenge of today.* Chicago: Henry Regnery.

Dreikurs, R., & Grey, L. (1968). *Logical consequences: A new approach to discipline.* New York: Hawthorne Books.

Dreikurs, R., & Soltz, V. (1964). *Children: The challenge.* New York: Hawthorn Books.

Eckstein, D., Baruth, L., & Mahrer, D. (1978). *Life style: What it is and how to do it.* Dubuque, IA: Kendall/Hunt.

Elmhirst, S. I. (1984). A psychoanalytic approach to anxiety in childhood. In U. P. Varma (Ed.), *Anxiety in children* (pp. 1–14). London: Croom Helm.

Freud, A. (1936). *The ego and the mechanisms of defense.* New York: International Universities Press.

Freud, A. (1945). Indications for child analysis. *Psychoanalytic Study of the Child, 1,* 127–149.

Freud, A. (1965). *Normality and pathology in childhood.* New York: International Universities Press.

Freud, A. (1974). *The writings of Anna Freud, 1, 1922–1935: Introduction to psychoanalysis: Letters for child analysts and teachers.* New York: International Universities Press.

Freud, A. (1981). Foreward to 'Analysis of a phobia in a five-year-old boy'. *The writings of Anna Freud (Vol. 3),* 1970–1980. New York: International Universities Press.

Freud, S. (1900). The interpretation of dreams. In J. Strachey (Ed.), *The complete works of Sigmund Freud* (Vols. 4, 5). London: Hogarth.

Freud, S. (1905). Three essays on the theory of sexuality. In J. Strahey (Ed.), *The complete works of Sigmund Freud* (Vol. 7). London: Hogarth.

Freud, S. (1909). The analysis of a phobia in a five-year-old boy. *Standard edition of the complete psychological works of Sigmund Freud* (Vol. 10). London: Hogarth Press, 1963.

Gittleman, R. (Ed.) (1986). *Anxiety disorders in children.* New York: Guilford.

Gittleman, R., & Koplewicz, H. S. (1986). Pharmacotherapy of childhood anxiety disorders. In R. Gittleman (Ed.), *Anxiety disorders of childhood* (pp. 188–203). New York: Guilford Press.

Gittleman-Klein, R. (1975). Pharmacotherapy and management of pathological separation anxiety. *International Journal of Mental Health, 4,* 255–271.

Gittleman-Klein, R. (1978). Psychopharmacological treatment of anxiety disorders, mood disorders, and Tourette's disorder in children. In M. A. Lipton, A. DiMascio, & K. F. Killam (Eds.), *Psychopharmacology: A generation of progress* (pp. 1471–1480). New York: Raven Press.

Gittleman-Klein, R., & Klein, D. F. (1973). School phobia: Diagnostic considerations in the light of imipramine effects. *The Journal of Nervous and Mental Disease, 156,* 199–215.

Gray, J. (1971). *The psychology of fear and stress.* New York: McGraw-Hill.

Graziano, A. M., & Mooney, K. C. (1984). *Children and behavior therapy.* New York: Aldine.

Graziano, A. M., De Giovanni, I. S., & Garcia, K. A. (1979). Behavioral treatments of children's fears: A review. *Psychological Bulletin, 86,* 804–830.

Harris, B. (1979). Whatever happened to little Albert? *American Psychologist, 34,* 151–160.

Hugdahl, K., Fredrikson, M., & Ohman, A. (1977). "Preparedness" and "arousability" as determinants of electrodermal conditioning. *Behaviour Research and Therapy, 15,* 345–353.

Hull, C. (1943). *Principles of behavior.* New York: Appleton-Century-Crofts.

Jersild, A. T. (1968). *Child psychology* (6th ed.). Englewood Cliffs, NJ: Prentice-Hall.

Jersild, A. T., & Holmes, F. B. (1935). Children's fears. *Child Development Monographs,* No. 20.

Johnson, J. H., Rasbury, W. C., & Siegel, L. J. (1986). *Approaches to child treatment: Introduction to theory, research, and practice.* New York: Pergamon Press.

Kanfer, F. H., Karoly, P., & Newman, A. (1975). Reduction of children's fear of the dark by confidence related and situational threat-related verbal cues. *Journal of Consulting and Clinical Psychology, 43.* 251–258.

Kantor, J. R. (1966). Feelings and emotions as scientific events. *Psychological Record, 16,* 377–404.

Kantor, J. R., & Smith, N. W. (1975). *The science of psychology: An interbehavioral survey.* Chicago: Principia Press.

Kellerman, J. (1981). *Helping the fearful child.* New York: Norton.

Kern, R. M. (1976). *Life Style Inventory Questionnaire.* Georgia State University (mimeo).

Klein, D. F., Gittleman, R., Quitkin, F., & Rifkin, A. (1980). *Diagnosis and drug treatment of psychiatric disorders: Adults and children.* Baltimore: Williams & Wilkins.

Klein, M. (1955). The psychoanalytic play technique. *American Journal of Orthopsychiatry, 25,* 232–237.

Leitenberg, H., & Callahan, E. J. (1973). Reinforced practice and reductions of different kinds of fears in adults and children. *Behavior Research and Therapy, 11,* 19–30.

Lewis, M. (1986). Principles of intensive individual psychoanalytic psychotherapy with children. In R. Gittelman (Ed.), *Anxiety disorders in childhood* (pp. 233–255). New York: Guilford Press.

McNally, R. J., & Reiss, S. (1982). The preparedness theory of phobias and human safety-signal conditioning. *Behaviour Research and Therapy, 20,* 153–159.

Marks, I. M. (1969). *Fears and phobias.* New York: Academic Press.

Mathews, A. M., Gelder, M. G., & Johnston, D. W. (1981). *Agoraphobia: Nature and treatment.* New York: Guilford Press.

Mavissakalian, M., & Barlow, D. H. (1981a). An overview. In M. Mavissakalian & D. H. Barlow (Eds.), *Phobia: Psychological and pharmacological treatment* (pp. 1–33). New York: Guilford Press.

Mavissakalian, M., & Barlow, D. H. (Eds.) (1981b). *Phobia: Psychological and pharmacological treatment.* New York: Guilford Press.

Meichenbaum, D., & Genest, M. (1980). Cognitive behavior modification: An integration of cognitive and behavioral methods. In F. H. Kanfer & A. P. Goldstein (Eds.), *Helping people change* (2nd ed., pp. 390–422). Elmsford, NY: Pergamon Press.

Melamed, B., & Siegel, L. (1975). Reduction of anxiety in children facing hospitalization and surgery by use of filmed modeling. *Journal of Consulting and Clinical Psychology, 43,* 511–521.

Miller, L. C. (1983). Fears and anxiety in children. In C. E. Walker & M. C. Roberts (Eds.), *Handbook of clinical child psychology* (pp. 337–380). New York: Wiley.

Miller, L. C., Barrett, C. L., & Hampe, E. (1974). Phobias of childhood in a prescientific era. In A. Davids (Ed.), *Child personality and psychopathology: Current topics.* New York: Wiley.

Morris, R. J. (1985). *Behavior modification with exceptional children: Principles and practices.* Glenview, IL: Scott-Foresman.

Morris, R. J., & Kratochwill, T. R. (Eds.). (1983). *Treating children's fears and phobias: A behavioral approach.* Elmsford, NY: Pergamon Press.

Morris, R. J., & Kratochwill, T. R. (Eds.). (1984). *The practice of child therapy*. New York: Pergamon Press.

Mosak, H. H. (1979). Adlerian psychotherapy. In R. J. Corsini (Ed.), *Current psychotherapies* Itasca, IL: F. E. Peacock.

Mosak, H. H., Schneider, S., & Mosak, L. E. (1980). *Life style: A workbook*. Chicago: Alfred Adler Institute of Chicago.

Mowrer, O. H. (1939). A stimulus-response analysis of anxiety and its role as a reinforcing agent. *Psychological Review, 46*, 553–565.

Mowrer, O. H. (1960). *Learning theory and behavior*. New York: Wiley.

O'Connor, K. O., Lee, A. C., & Schaefer, C. E. (1983). Psychoanalytic psychotherapy with children. In M. Hersen, A. E. Kasdin, & A. S. Bellack (Eds.), *The clinical psychology handbook* (pp. 543–564). New York: Pergamon Press.

Ohman, A., Erixon, G., & Lofberg, I. (1975a). Phobias and preparedness: Phobic versus neutral pictures as conditioned stimuli for human autonomic responses. *Journal of Abnormal Psychology, 84*, 41–45.

Ohman, A., Eriksson, A., & Olofsoon, C. (1975b). One-trial learning and superior resistance to extinction of autonomic responses conditioned to potentially phobic stimuli. *Journal of Comperative and Physiological Psychology, 88*, 619–627.

Ollendick, T. H. (1979). Behavioral treatment of anorexia nervosa: A five year study. *Behavior Modification, 3*, 124–135.

Ollendick, T. H., & Cerny, J. A. (1984). *Clinical behavior therapy with children*. New York: Plenum Press.

Pavlov, I. P. (1927). *Conditioned reflexes* (trans., G. V. Anrep). London: Oxford University Press.

Quay, H. C. (1979). Classification. In H. C. Quay & J. S. Werry (Eds.), *Psychopathological disorders of childhood* (2nd ed., pp. 1–42). New York: Wiley.

Rachman, S. (1976). The passing of the two-stage theory of fear and avoidance: Fresh possibilities. *Behaviour Research and Therapy, 14*, 125–134.

Rachman, S. (1977). The conditioning theory of fear-acquisition: A critical examination. *Behaviour Research and Therapy, 15*, 375–387.

Rachman, S. (1978). *Fear and courage*. San Francisco: Freeman.

Ramirez, S. Z., Kratochwill, T. R., & Morris, R. J. (1987). Cognitive behavioral treatment of childhood anxiety disorders. In L. Michelson & M. Asher (Eds.), *Cognitive-behavioral assessment and treatment of anxiety disorders* (pp. 149–175). New York: Guilford Press.

Russell, P. A. (1979). Fear evoking stimuli. In W. Sluckin (Ed.), *Fear in animals and man* (pp. 86–124). New York: Van Nostrand Reinhold.

Salzen, E. A. (1979). The ontogeny of fear in animals. In W. Sluckin (Ed.), *Fear in animals and man* (pp. 125–163). New York: Van Nostrand Reinhold.

Scharfman, M. (1978). Psychoanalytic treatment. In B. Wolman, J. Egan, & A. Ross (Eds.), *Handbook of treatment of mental disorders in childhood and adolescence* (pp. 47–69). Englewood Cliffs, NJ: Prentice-Hall.

Seligman, M. E. P. (1970). On the generality of the laws of learning. *Psychological Review, 77*, 406–418.

Seligman, M. E. P. (1971). Phobias and preparedness. *Behavior Therapy, 2*, 307–320.

Seligman, M., & Johnston, J. (1973). A cognitive theory of avoidance learning. In J. McGuigan & B. Lumsden (Eds.), *Contemporary approaches to conditioning and learning* (pp. 69–110). New York: Wiley.

Shaffer, D. (1986). Learning theories of anxiety. In R. Gittelman (Ed.), *Anxiety disorders of childhood* (pp. 157–167). New York: Guilford Press.

Shields, J. (1978). Genetic factors in neurosis. In H. M. van Pragg (Ed.), *Research in neurosis* (pp. 155–170). New York: SP Medical & Scientific Books.

Skinner, B. F. (1938). *The behavior of organisms*. New York: Appleton-Century-Croft.

Skinner, B. F. (1953). *Science and human behavior*. New York: Macmillan.

Sluckin, W. (Ed.). (1979). *Fear in animals and man*. New York: Van Nostrand Reinhold.

Smith, P. K. (1979). The ontogency of fear in children. In W. Sluckin (Ed.), *Fear in animals and man* (pp. 164–198). New York: Van Nostrand Reinhold.

Sulzer-Azaroff, B., & Mayer, R. G. (1977). *Applying behavior-analysis proceedings with children and youth*. New York: Holt, Rinehart, & Winston.

Watson, J. B., & Rayner, R. (1920). Conditioned emotional reactions. *Journal of Experimental Psychology, 3*, 1–14.

Wiener, J. (1985). *Diagnosis and psychopharmacology of childhood and adolescent disorders.* New York: Wiley.

Wilson, G. T., & O'Leary, K. D. (1980). *Principles of behavior therapy.* Englewood Cliffs, NJ: Prentice-Hall.

Wolpe, J. (1958). *Reciprocal inhibition therapy.* Stanford, CA: Stanford University Press.

Wolpe, J. (1964). The comparative clinical status of conditioning therapies and psychoanalysis. In J. Wolpe, A. Salter, & L. J. Reyna (Eds.), *The conditioning therapies* (pp. 5–20). New York: Holt.

Yule, W. (1981). The epidemiology of child psychopathology. In B. B. Lahey & A. E. Kazdin (Eds.), *Advances in clinical child psychology* (Vol. 4, pp. 1–51). New York: Plenum Press.

# IV    Treatment Approaches: Severe Mental Disorders

The term *severe* has been used to describe this general area, although there has been recent controversy over whether autism may be a form of psychosis. The popularly held view of researchers to date suggests that it is not. Similarly, depression has been included here although very severe forms of the condition may be manifested, such as suicide or manic-depressive psychosis. Obviously, this subsection and the others within the other treatment sections of the book might have been arranged in some other way. Hopefully, the reader will agree with the logic of the current arrangement.

The severity of these conditions may be reflected by the need for psychological and pharmacology chapters to describe the extensive research available on both topics. Also, it should be emphasized that the combination of both treatment approaches may prove helpful in some cases.

# 12 Infantile Autism and Childhood Schizophrenia
## Psychological Therapies

SANDRA L. HARRIS

## HISTORICAL DEVELOPMENT

Infantile autism, schizophrenia with childhood onset, and other forms of pervasive developmental psychopathology are disorders that pose major challenges for therapeutic intervention. Because of the early onset and the pervasive nature of the disorders, these children typically are severely impaired in multiple domains of functioning: cognitive, affective, social, and so on. Intervention must therefore be of an equally broad-ranging nature, addressing the full gamut of the developmental processes that can go awry.

Strategies for the treatment of severe developmental psychopathology have undergone marked change in the past quarter century. Until roughly the mid-1960s the most respected therapeutic approach for children with autism or schizophrenia was psychoanalytically based, and it was assumed that these disorders were a reflection of a pathological parent–infant relationship. The most prominent proponent of that stance, Bruno Bettelheim, wrote a number of highly readable and often moving books, widely regarded among the educated lay public (e.g., Bettelheim, 1950, 1967, 1974).

The mid-1960s witnessed a significant shift in both our understanding of the possible etiology of many forms of severe developmental psychopathology and our efforts to intervene in these disorders. One source of this change was the writings of Bernard Rimland, an experimental psychologist whose book *Infantile Autism* (1964) presented the first widely disseminated, plausible organic theory of the etiology of autism. That book, which assembled much of what was then known about autism, offered a well-organized, coherent explanation of the possible biological roots of autism and thus highlighted the need to direct research efforts down new paths. Although a number of alternative biologically based explanations for autism have been studied since the mid-1960s, Rimland's work remains significant for its heuristic contribution.

SANDRA L. HARRIS • Graduate School of Applied and Professional Psychology, Rutgers University, Piscataway, New Jersey 08854.

Another important event of the mid-1960s was the publication of a landmark article by Lovaas, Berberich, Perloff, and Schaeffer, (1966) documenting that psychotic children could acquire language through the use of operant conditioning techniques. Ferster (1961), Hewett (1965), Risley (1968), Hingtgen and Churchill (1969), K. Salzinger, Feldman, Cowan, and S. Salzinger (1965), and Wolf, Risley, and Mees (1964) were among the first generation of researchers to explore the potential of behavior modification techniques in the education of children with autism. This work documented persuasively that, through behavior modification techniques, autistic children could learn to speak, to control their disruptive behaviors, and to acquire new and more adaptive modes of dealing with their environment.

In the years that followed that early research, the use of a behavioral approach became widespread among psychologists, speech therapists, special educators, and others who worked with these youngsters. Furthermore, the treatment techniques acquired an increasing sophistication and attempted to answer a broader range of clinical needs. Behavioral techniques grew popular because of their efficacy, and they became more sophisticated with the recognition of the limits inherent in the earlier efforts to use behavioral approaches with this population. Thus, we were forced to continue to grow in response to the as-yet-unmet needs of our clients.

This chapter focuses on current developments in the psychological treatment of autism and related forms of severe developmental psychopathology. One major treatment issue that arose early in the efforts to treat autistic children, and that continues to bedevil clinicians, educators, and researchers alike, is the difficulty that these youngsters have in generalizing newly learned material to other people, places, or stimuli (Handleman, 1979; Powers & Handleman, 1984). Meeting this instructional demand has pervaded much of the research literature since the mid-1970s and so will receive mention throughout the chapter. Although it is impossible to separate current research from its historical context, the focus of this chapter is more on innovative approaches to the treatment of severe developmental psychopathology than on earlier contributions. Space limitations have required that the chapter aim not to be comprehensive in identifying every current major contribution to the field, but to focus on representative efforts.

The chapter is divided into three major sections. The first examines the basic teaching strategies used in educating children with autism and describes changes in the discrete-trial teaching format as it is being used currently. The second section examines the current techniques used to suppress disruptive or dangerous behaviors that threaten to harm the child or others, or that intrude on the learning process. The third section considers the use of behavioral technologies in teaching people with autism new, adaptive skills across a broad range of domains. Data-based case histories are scattered through the chapter to highlight the application of the various techniques under discussion.

## INNOVATIONS IN THE DISCRETE-TRIAL TEACHING FORMAT

There is a long-standing recognition that behavior modification techniques provide the most effective teaching strategies for people with autism. Thus, mastery of the discrete-trial teaching format, in which one presents a discriminative stimulus, prompts as necessary, reinforces the response, and allows a suitable intertrial interval before going on to issue the next command, is an essential skill for the person who teaches autistic individuals (Rincover, Koegel, & Russo, 1978).

In spite of the well-established recognition of the value of this general approach to teaching, a substantial body of recent research has documented that variations on the basic theme of the discrete trial can make a significant difference in the efficiency and generalizability of the teaching process. There are data demonstrating that the qualities of the stimulus material, the kind of prompts provided, the nature of the reinforcer offered, and the duration of the time between trials in a teaching sequence can all impact on the ease of acquisition of the material being taught.

## The Stimulus Material and Use of Prompts

This section examines two broad areas of concern: the presentation of stimulus materials to decrease the overselective responses of people with autism, and other techniques used to vary stimulus and prompt to maintain responding by the autistic student.

### Overselective Responding

One of the problems arising in the preparation of educational materials for people with autism is the tendency of these individuals to respond overselectively. The term *stimulus overselectivity* refers to a tendency to respond to irrelevant or excessively restricted stimulus cues when presented with a stimulus having several components. First identified in subjects with autism some years ago (Lovaas, Schreibman, Koegel, & Rehm, 1971), stimulus overselectively has been shown to occur in both visual and auditory modalities (e.g., Koegel & Wilhelm, 1973; Kovattana & Kraemer, 1974; Lovaas & Schreibman, 1971). A variety of techniques have been explored to help subjects break this pattern of overselective responding and to assist them in recognizing the cue value of several aspects of the stimulus presentation. These techniques have included such strategies as exaggerating the relevant cues (e.g., Schreibman, 1975) and overtraining a discrimination task (Schover & Newsom, 1976; Schreibman, Koegel, & Craig, 1977). Schreibman (1975) and Koegel and Rincover (1976) have reported that extrastimulus prompts—that is, prompts that are not an inherent part of the stimulus material—tend to delay skill acquisition when compared to prompts that are intrinsic in the stimulus.

The importance of avoiding prompts not intrinsic in the stimulus material was illustrated by Nelson, Gergenti, and Hollander (1980) when they compared two procedures for teaching autistic children and adolescents to lace their shoes. One group of subjects learned how to lace their shoes with laces and shoe eyelets that were color-coded red and white and were then tested in a no-prompt condition in which the laces and eyelets were no longer discriminatively colored. A second group of subjects first learned how to lace without the use of the color prompt and were then exposed to the extra color-code prompt. The subjects who first learned in the color-coded condition and then had to transfer to the noncoded condition had more trouble making that transfer than did the subjects who learned without the color prompt and who were then exposed to the colored prompts. On the basis of their study, the authors suggested that teachers avoid the use of highly salient, non-criterion-related prompts as one way to reduce overselective responses.

In another effort to examine classroom-relevant techniques of overcoming the visual overselectivity of children with autism, Hedbring and Newsom (1985) compared an equivalence-training condition that moved subjects from object matching to picture matching in four graduated steps and a functional-use condition in which the subjects were trained in the functional use of the same objects that were presented for matching in the equivalence condition. The study found the equivalence-training condition to be more effective than the functional object use in reducing stimulus overselectivity.

In general, the research on overselective responding in people with autism has highlighted the need to plan carefully the kinds of prompts one uses and to focus on prompts that highlight intrinsic aspects of the stimulus (e.g., Schreibman, 1975) and that thus will remain available to the child as cues in the natural environment.

## Beyond Stimulus Qualities

Curriculum planning requires attention to other details beyond the physical characteristics of the stimulus material. For example, research by Dunlap and Koegel (1980) indicates that children with autism respond better when the tasks are varied during a teaching session. This research compared a constant task condition, in which the subjects were asked to make a single discrimination throughout a session, and a varied task condition, in which the subjects were given several different tasks in the same session. Performance was better and more stable in the condition of varied stimuli than in the constant-stimulus condition. Dunlap and Koegel (1980) suggested that mixing tasks during a teaching session reduces the likelihood of boredom on the part of the student and increases motivation.

Once the discriminative stimulus has been presented, the teacher typically waits a predetermined amount of time (3–10 seconds is common) to allow the child to make a response to the instruction. If the child fails to respond or emits an incorrect response, a prompt is sometimes offered to provide partial guidance in the desired response. The timing and nature of that prompt have been found to influence the autistic person's rate of learning.

In an examination of the effects of teacher verbalizations as prompts, Hughes, Wolery, and Neel (1983) found that general instructions such as "Keep looking" increased the on-task performance of two autistic children when compared to a baseline condition without verbal prompts. Hughes *et al.* did not, however, find maintenance of this improved performance when the verbal prompts were removed. The prompts appear to have had a motivating rather than an instructional function for these subjects. Additional research involving the fading of such prompts would help to determine whether enduring benefits follow from the use of vocal prompts.

One mechanical variation in the use of teacher verbalization to maintain on-task behavior is the use of a "memory pacer," a tiny tape recorder that plays back a message to the listener at predetermined intervals. Browning (1983) used a memory pacer with six autistic and childhood-onset schizophrenic adolescents. The pacer was programmed to tell the subject to "Remember, if you're upset, say 'Will you help?' or 'May I take a break?' and talk quietly." Each subject's message was individualized. Although each adolescent responded in an individual way, the data do show a decrease in negative behaviors when the memory pacer was used. The more cognitively impaired subjects were less responsive to the procedure than the less impaired.

Brief delays between the presentation of the discriminative stimulus and the time when the child is allowed to respond or when a prompt is offered can impact on performance. Dyer, Christian, and Luce (1982) found that simply requiring the child to wait 3 seconds after the presentation of the discriminative stimulus improved performance substantially when compared to a condition in which the child was allowed to respond immediately after the discriminative stimulus was presented. Delaying the teacher's use of prompts while maintaining an expectant expression and manner has also been found to be helpful in increasing the spontaneous responses of autistic children (e.g., Charlop, Schreibman, & Thibodeau, 1985).

When using extrinsic verbal or manual prompts, it is important to insert a sufficient delay to ensure that the student will have an opportunity to respond without aid (e.g., Charlop et al., 1985). Furthermore, it appears helpful to teach the child to delay his or her responses for a few seconds and thereby to decrease impulsive responding (Dyer et al., 1982).

## Reinforcement and Intertrial Interval

Following the individual's correct response, the discrete-trial format requires the delivery of some form of reinforcement, primary or secondary, tangible or symbolic. Here again, research has taught us important things about the kinds of reinforcers that are most likely to be effective for the individual with autism.

Koegel and his colleagues (e.g., Koegel & Williams, 1980; Williams, Koegel, & Egel, 1981) found that autistic children respond better when the reinforcer is inherent in the response chain than when it is extrinsic. For example, a child might be required to pick up the lid of a box to extract the food reward inside rather than to open the box and then receive food from the teacher.

It has also been observed that autistic children respond better when they are offered a variety of reinforcers rather than the same reinforcer after each correct response (Egel, 1981). The range of useful reinforcers for people with autism has been found to include sensory stimulation such as music, vibration, or strobe lights (Murphy, 1982). Ferrari and Harris (1981) observed that sensory reinforcers were effective in maintaining a high rate of responding by children with autism and had reward value comparable to that of food and social reinforcers.

The correct pacing of trials in teaching children with autism also has an impact on learning. Koegel, Dunlap, and Dyer (1980) noted that short intertrial intervals, with the discriminative stimulus for the next trial being given within 1 second after the reinforcer for the previous trial, led to better performance than when a 4-second or longer interval was used.

Thus, the research on reinforcement procedures and intertrial intervals argues for a variety of reinforcers, with primary rewards being intrinsic in the desired target behavior, and the interval between the delivery of a reward and the onset of the next trial being as brief as possible.

### Case Report: Sensory Reinforcement

The following case describes the effect of various sensory, edible, and social reinforcers on the performance of an autistic boy. The full details of this research can be found in Ferrari and Harris (1981).

John, an 8.5-year-old autistic youngster with a tested IQ in the moderate to severely mentally retarded range, exhibited a wide range of self-stimulatory behavior, including body rocking and hand flapping. His communicative speech was limited to single words. In an effort to assess the potential value of a range of reinforcing events for John and some of his classmates, he was selected for participation in an after-school research program to be conducted in his home.

The assessment involved two phases. In the first phase, John was taught how to press the nose on the picture of a scarecrow rigged so that each press on the nose was recorded automatically and yielded reinforcements on a fixed schedule. Then, John was given a maximum of six 15-minute sessions with each of five different reinforcers: food such as candy, fruit, and cereal; a strobe light; popular music; social reinforcement, and vibration delivered with a back massager. In this experimental condition, John showed a clear preference for the vibration; listening to music was his second choice, and food, the strobe light, and social rewards were of less potency.

The next phase of the assessment involved determining the extent to which these reinforcers were also effective in motivating John to learn a discrimination task like the ones he did in school. In this phase, John was presented with two common objects at a time and was asked to touch one ("Touch the truck"). The same reinforcers that had been used in the first phase were offered in the second. In this condition, John continued to show a clear preference for vibration as a reward; music was again a strong second choice, and food, social, and strobe-light reinforcement were less potent in motivating his performance.

The pattern of performance for three of John's classmates showed that each boy had his own pattern of preferences among the five reinforcing events. It is important to note that the sensory stimuli were useful reinforcers for all four youngsters, and that the potency of these events sometimes exceeded that of the traditional food reward. This finding highlights the importance of seeking individualized reinforcers for each child and of recognizing that food may not be the most effective reward for every autistic child.

## SUPPRESSION OF INTERFERING BEHAVIORS

The use of aversive procedures to control dangerous or disruptive behaviors by people with autism has received a great deal of empirical attention since the mid-1960s. Substantial documentation exists of the therapeutic benefits of punishment procedures in coping with self-injury, aggression, self-stimulation, and other difficult-to-manage behaviors.

Although there continues to be a need for punishers, such as aversive odors, bad-tasting liquids, or electric shock, within a very narrow domain of otherwise unmanageable behaviors, an important feature that has marked research in recent years has been the creative movement toward less intrusive punishments. The focus of the present discussion is on innovative, less intrusive procedures for suppressing behavior; this focus does not negate the value of traditional punishment techniques, but these interventions have already been the topic of considerable discussion (e.g., Harris & Ersner-Hershfield, 1978; Matson & Dilorenzo, 1984).

## Overcorrection

Overcorrection procedures are one example of a less drastic alternative to the use of shock and other physically painful punishers (e.g., Azrin, Gottlieb, Hughart, Wesolowski, & Rahn, 1975; Harris & Romanczyk, 1976) for treating self-injury (Azrin *et al.*, 1975), self-stimulation (e.g., Rusch, Close, Hops, & Agosta, 1976), and aggression (Foxx & Azrin, 1972). A demonstration of the efficacy of overcorrection for two of these categories of disruptive behavior is found in the work of W. L. Johnson, Baumeister, Penland, and Inwald (1982), who examined the benefits of the use of overcorrection for the self-injury and self-stimulation of mentally retarded subjects. The results showed that overcorrection was generally more effective than reinforcement procedures for both sets of target behaviors.

### Case Report: Overcorrection

The following case illustrates the use of overcorrection procedures to decrease the self-injury of a visually impaired, deaf, rubella syndrome 8-year-old boy with autistic behavior. The complete details of the study can be found in Harris and Romanczyk (1976).

Robert, whose mother had had German measles during her pregnancy, suffered multiple physical defects and moderate mental retardation along with many symptoms of autism, including a very limited interest in other people, communication skills more impaired than would be expected on the basis of his other handicaps, and some perseverative behaviors. He was admitted to the Douglass Developmental Disabilities Center, in large part because of concern about his severe self-injury.

Robert's self-injury was sufficiently intense so that he had twice broken automobile windshields and left numerous dents on the walls of his family's home. None of the techniques used by his parents, including spankings or ignoring or distracting Robert, had altered this very dangerous behavior. Similarly, none of the nonaversive procedures tried at the center, such as reinforcing appropriate behaviors, had led to important changes in his self-injury.

Shortly after Robert's admission, a complete assessment of his self-injury was conducted. The two categories identified were head banging and chin banging, both appearing to be triggered by a staff demand or intrusion in Robert's ongoing activities. Baseline data were collected both at home and in school. The mean frequency of his self-injury at school was 32 episodes a day and 15.44 at home.

An overcorrection procedure was first introduced at school and then at home, thus creating a multiple baseline across settings. The overcorrection procedure required Robert to move his arms and head in a series of exercises for 5 minutes after each episode of self-injury. Immediately after the introduction of this procedure, his self-injury at school dropped to five episodes a day in the first week, two a day during the second, and then to a near-zero rate for 3 months thereafter. Similarly, the application of the procedure at home led to marked, immediate declines in self-injury.

These dramatic and very important changes in Robert's behavior accomplished the primary objective of his enrollment at the center. Consequently, it was possible the following year to enroll him in a special program for children with visual and auditory handicaps, where he could receive the intensive communication training he required. His progress over the years was monitored. We remained in touch with him, and his condition continued to be excellent and his rate of self-injury remained very low.

## Physical Exercise

Closely related to some forms of overcorrection, in that it requires vigorous physical activity that may be intrinsically beneficial to the child, is the use of contingent or noncontingent physical exercise to reduce unwanted behaviors. For example, Luce, Delquadri, and Hall (1980) required children to engage in a brief interval of contingent exercise each time they emitted verbal or physically aggressive behavior. The result was a dramatic decline in the target behavior. Examining the benefits of noncontingent exercise, Kern, Koegel, Dyer, Blew, and Fenton (1982) produced substantial reductions in the frequency of self-stimulatory behavior among autistic children when the children were required to spend time jogging before work sessions. There were declines in self-stimulation after the jogging periods, as well as increases in play and academic performance. Similar declines in self-stimulation with noncontingent exercise were reported by R. G. Watters and W. E. Watters (1980). Kern, Koegel, and Dunlap (1984) found that the exercise regimen must be vigorous (e.g., running), not mild (e.g., catching a ball).

### Case Report: Contingent Exercise

The following case illustrates the effects of contingent running as a technique of controlling out-of-seat behavior in a 7-year-old autistic boy whose behavior was disruptive for an entire classroom. Complete details of the experimental design can be found in Gordon, Handleman, and Harris (1986).

Mark had been enrolled at the Douglass Developmental Disabilities Center for 3 years. He was in the moderately to severely impaired range of cognitive functioning, and his communication was limited to a few single words. Ever since the time of his initial admission, Mark had posed problems in terms of impulsive, out-of-seat behavior, which included throwing objects and running. A variety of interventions, ranging from reinforcing his quiet sitting to verbal reprimands, brief restraint, and time-out procedures, had failed to improve his appropriate sitting. With the fully informed consent of his parents, Mark's teacher initiated a new program to control his troublesome target behavior: requiring Mark to jog each time he got out of his seat without permission.

Because he was so difficult to control, Mark typically had a one-to-one instructional ratio, and the full-time aide assigned to him continued his educational programming for the duration of the new treatment program. The jogging itself was supervised by Mark's teacher, a master's level special-education teacher who had had more than 3 years' full-time experience working with autistic children.

Following a 5-day baseline condition in which a record was kept of the number of times Mark got out of his seat each day, a contingent running condition was imposed for 5 days, and Mark was required to jog for 3 minutes after each episode of out-of-seat behavior. This procedure was followed by another 5-day baseline, and then 5 days in which Mark was required to run an equivalent amount, but not contingent on his out-of-seat behavior. Finally, there were 11 more days of contingent running. The results of his teacher's intervention were striking: during the first baseline period, Mark's average number of out-of-seat episodes was 77 a day; when the contingent running was introduced, this number declined to a mean of 4. The noncontingent running gave little evidence of therapeutic effect. A follow-up assessment of Mark's behavior 1 year later revealed that his out-of-seat behavior remained at low levels, with an average of 4 episodes during a 6-day observation period.

## Physical Restraint and Protective Equipment

The prolonged use of continuous physical restraint and protective equipment can have serious side effects for a client, including the wasting of muscle tissue and a reduction in social interaction with primary-care staff (e.g., Rojahn, Schroeder, & Mulick, 1980). In contrast, brief periods of contingent restraint have been found to have therapeutic effects on some self-injurious clients. For example, Rapoff, Altman, and Christophersen (1980) used a 30-second physical restraint to decrease the self-injury of a young blind girl, and Singh and Bakker (1984) found a 10-second restraint superior to overcorrection for the reduction of pica.

The most persuasive demonstration of the benefits of brief restraint was by Dorsey, Iwata, Reid, and Davis (1982), who assessed the use of protective equipment in reducing the self-injury of three mentally retarded adolescents. The brief, 2-minute application of protective equipment contingent on the emission of a self-injurious response led to substantial reductions in the target behavior.

Brief contingent restraint has a decided benefit over many other punishing events in that it poses relatively little danger or discomfort to the client. However, it must be noted that, for some clients, restraint may have a reinforcing quality, and one risks having the procedure become a reinforcing event rather than a punisher (e.g., Favell, McGimsey, & Jones, 1978; Favell, McGimsey, Jones, & Cannon, 1981). Careful record-keeping is essential in discriminating the client for whom restraint is reinforcing from the person for whom it is punishing.

## Assessment of the Instructional Context

Changes in environmental complexity, staff demands, and task difficulty may be useful in modifying some disruptive behaviors of children with autism and schizophrenia. For example, the complexity of task demands appears to impact on aberrant behavior (e.g., Carr, Newsom, & Binkoff, 1976, 1980). Weeks and Gaylord-Ross (1981) compared the frequency of difficult-to-manage behaviors in easy versus hard learning tasks and found higher rates of problem behavior when children were confronted with more difficult tasks. These authors suggested that deviant behaviors were maintained through negative reinforcement contingencies: when confronted by a difficult task the child might engage in aberrant behavior and be inadvertently reinforced by the termination of the teacher's demands. Weeks and Gaylord-Ross called for more detailed study of errorless learning as a way to enhance skill acquisition by easing task difficulty and thereby diminishing aberrant behavior on the part of severely handicapped children.

Additional support for the notion that increased demands are related to increases in aberrant behavior was identified by Edelson, Taubman, and Lovaas (1983), who observed the self-injurious behavior of hospitalized autistic, schizophrenic, and mentally retarded children. These authors noted substantial increases in self-injurious behavior by 19 of the 20 children when staff members made demands, denied requests, or punished the behavior of the children. Edelson and his colleagues (1983) suggested that self-injury has a major social component for many children and reflects an interaction between the child and his or her caretaker. Appreciation of this contextual dimension may facilitate behavioral assessment and enhance treatment planning.

In general, the research on the impact of environmental factors indicates a strong relationship between increased demands or more complex tasks and the occurrence of aberrant behavior. This finding argues for the importance of a careful assessment of such demands on a client who is exhibiting troublesome levels of disruptive behavior. Patterns of negative reinforcement leading to increases in unwanted behavior are important to modify, either by changing the demands on the client or by preventing the use of aberrant behavior as an escape response, or both. Furthermore, Carr and Durand (1985) reported that teaching children to solicit adult help with difficult tasks suppresses behavior problems, thus providing additional support for the hypothesis that behavior problems can be viewed as nonverbal communications.

Individual characteristics of clients interact with environmental and task demands to influence whether the suppression of self-stimulatory behavior is necessary for learning to occur. Several studies have suggested that the extent to which self-stimulation intrudes on the child's learning hinges, at least in part, on the child's level of cognitive functioning. After an initial observation by Koegel and Covert (1972) that self-stimulation decreased learning, Klier and Harris (1977) suggested that higher functioning children showed less interference than lower functioning ones. More recently, Chock and Glahn (1983) found that echolalic autistic children were able to master a learning task without external suppression of their self-stimulation, whereas mute children required external suppression before they could learn the new material.

In an interesting examination of the evolution of self-stimulatory behavior over the course of behavioral treatment, Epstein, Taubman, and Lovaas (1985) found that relatively "low-level" motor activities such as rocking, spinning, and twirling were changed into "higher level" behaviors, such as lining up objects, echolalic speech, and a preoccupation with spelling and numbers. They noted that those children who made the greatest gains in behavioral treatment exhibited the highest forms of self-stimulatory behavior after treatment. These authors argued that it may prove beneficial to help clients substitute higher levels of self-stimulation for the lower level behaviors with which they begin treatment. However, these authors did note that their findings were of a correlational nature, and that one cannot base cause-and-effect conclusions on this study.

It should be noted that self-stimulation need not necessarily interfere with learning, and thus, suppression of this behavior may not always be a high priority in a training program. This argument is not intended to diminish the unattractive, and potentially socially aversive, nature of self-stimulation if the client engages in that behavior outside a supportive context; self-stimulation may have to be suppressed for "cosmetic" purposes if not for reasons of skill acquisition. Nonetheless, if the behavior does not intrude on the child's learning, the suppression may be less urgent than if it keeps the child from mastering new material.

## Use of Alternative Activities

One of the most attractive methods of reducing unwanted target behaviors is teaching the client to engage in new, appropriate behaviors that compete with the undesirable behavior. In one effective demonstration of this approach, Eason, White, and Newsom (1982) reinforced appropriate toy play in autistic and mentally retarded children and found a resulting increase in independent, appropriate play and a substantial decline in the children's rate of self-stimulation. Equally important, these authors reported generalized, durable changes in the children's behavior.

Profoundly mentally retarded clients can also be taught to replace self-injury with the use of toys for self-stimulatory behavior and ultimately for play. For example, a client who engaged in pica and hand biting learned to chew on a toy instead (Favell, McGimsey, & Schell, 1982). Furthermore, this move from self-injury to self-stimulation can be shifted to appropriate toy play, with an even greater reduction in self-injury (Favell *et al.*, 1982).

Just as environmental enrichment and increased stimulation may serve to decrease self-stimulation or self-injury in some clients, brief periods of removal of stimulation may produce decreases in unwanted target behaviors for others. McGonigle, Duncan, Cordisco, and Barrett (1982) used a brief visual screening procedure in which the child's eyes were covered by the teacher's hand for 5 seconds contingent on a variety of self-stimulatory behaviors. The authors reported the procedure to be easily used, to require no special equipment, and to be effective and durable in controlling a range of self-stimulatory behaviors. Similar reports have been made on the use of a terry-cloth bib or other object to screen the client's vision for the treatment of self-injury (Lutzker, 1978; Singh, Beale, & Dawson, 1981) and disruptive behavior (Zegiob, Jenkins, Becker, & Bristow, 1976).

## INCREASING APPROPRIATE BEHAVIORS

As time and experience have enabled us to better understand the learning abilities and the potential adaptations of children with autism, our curriculum for teaching new skills has broadened considerably, and our instructional techniques have become increasingly flexible. One can appreciate the changes that have occurred in the conditions for teaching new skills by recalling that, more than a decade ago, Lovaas, Schaeffer, and Simmons (1974) used electric shock to increase the prosocial approach behaviors of two autistic children. In the intervening years, a number of less drastic but very effective procedures have been developed for teaching complex adaptive behaviors to people with autism. This chapter reviews adaptive behaviors in two main areas: life skills and language.

## Teaching Adaptive Life Skills

Life skills can be interpreted as including a broad range of behaviors, such as self-help skills, recreational activities, social skills, and independent living skills. A number of studies have been done in these areas, and this discussion reviews a representative sample to give the reader a sense of the kinds of adaptive skills that have been taught to people with autism and related disorders.

### Social Responsiveness

Although children with autism may rely less on learning through modeling and may appear less responsive to their peers than other children, it is possible to arrange the environment in a way that enhances the likelihood of their learning from their peers (Charlop, Schreibman, & Tryon, 1983). Several studies have explored the use of modeling and peer-mediated instruction to enhance the social behavior of autistic children. For example, Strain, Kerr, and Ragland (1979) taught a normal 11-year-old boy to be a peer trainer for four children with autism. The peer trainer used prompting and reinforcement techniques, as well as initiation of play sequences, with the handicapped youngsters. The outcome of the study showed immediate and dramatic increases in the autistic children's positive social behaviors. The behaviors did not, however, generalize to sessions in which the peer trainer was not present.

In a later study, Strain (1983) examined the benefits of a developmentally integrated setting in modifying the social behavior of four autistic boys aged 7–10. This study was conducted in three different settings, one involved peer-initiated social-interaction training, another was a developmentally integrated generalization setting with normal age-peers, and the third was a segregated generalization setting with autistic peers. Each of the four autistic boys was the focus of peer social initiation with a normal 7-year-old boy for 5 minutes of a 20-minute daily training session. Social behavior in the two generalization settings was assessed each day. The study showed that the peer social-initiation intervention increased positive social behaviors of all four boys, and that the generalization sessions conducted in an integrated setting led to greater generalization than those sessions in the segregated setting. S. L. Odom, Hoyson, Jamieson, and Strain (1985) demonstrated similar findings with preschool handicapped children and their normal peers. Taken as a group, these studies argue for the importance of providing some normalized peer contact as part of the educational experiences of children with autism. Properly trained peers can help the autistic child engage in a greater frequency of prosocial behaviors than would be emitted without such social support.

*Leisure and Recreational Skills*

291

AUTISM AND
SCHIZOPHRENIA:
PSYCHOLOGICAL
THERAPIES

There is often a substantial demand on handicapped people to fill large blocks of leisure time in constructive ways (Wehman, 1983). In years past, the acquisition of leisure-time activities was typically left largely to chance and thus did not occur for many severely impaired people. More recently, there has been an increasing formal emphasis on teaching recreational skills to people with autism and other forms of severe developmental psychopathology.

Research suggests that developmentally disabled people are able to master a variety of leisure-time activities if the equipment, rules, and instructional sequences are adapted to their special needs (Wehman, 1983). Bowling, basketball, pool, card games, cooking, photography, and fishing are all potentially available to the autistic person who is given appropriate instruction. Indeed, research has documented the ability of individuals with marked impairments to master many of these activities (e.g., M. Johnson & Bailey, 1977; Lagomarcino, Reid, Ivancic, & Faw, 1984; Marchant & Wehman, 1979; Schleien, Certo, & Muccino, 1984).

Hawkins (1982) developed a leisure education program for three autistic children. His focus was on increasing the children's participation in gymnasium activities appropriate to 7- and 8-year-old boys. With prompts and praise, he was able to significantly increase the boys' engagement in activities that had previously been low in their hierarchy.

## Independent Living Skills

There has been a long-standing concern with teaching self-help skills to people with autism. For example, toilet training (e.g., Baumeister & Klosowski, 1965; Richmond, 1983) and mealtime behavior (e.g., Barton, Guess, Garcia, & Baer, 1970; van den Pol, Iwata, Ivancic, Page, Neef, & Whitley, 1981) have been the focus of early and continuing concern. Over time, the emphasis in these programs has shifted from the simple acquisition of basic skills to their generalized use in a variety of settings. For example, van den Pol and his colleagues (1981) taught their clients how to order a meal and behave appropriately in a restaurant. Smith and Belcher (1985) documented that programming previously shown to be helpful to mentally retarded adults could be used to teach autistic adults the skills they needed for life in a community-based residential program.

## Acquisition of Language

Major shifts are under way in our curriculum and techniques for teaching speech and language to autistic children. In an excellent discussion of the reasons for this change, Carr (1985) noted that

> it has become obvious to many behaviorally oriented researchers that language intervention efforts are constantly stymied by unanswered questions pertaining to subject differences, choice of curriculum items, problems in generalization, and the lack of communicative use of language by children involved in training. (pp. 37–38)

Repeated confrontations with these kinds of frustrations have demanded that behaviorally oriented researchers and clinicians push the operant model of speech and language instruction to meet a wider range of needs than have been met to date.

Operant conditioning procedures have been documented repeatedly to be effective in establishing basic language skills, such as verbal imitation (Lovaas *et al.*, 1966), and basic grammatical forms, including plural nouns (Guess, Sailor, Rutherford, & Baer, 1968), prepositions (Frisch & Schumaker, 1974), verb tenses (Lutzker & Sherman, 1974), compound sentences (Stevens-Long & Rasmussen, 1974), complex sentences (R. D. Odom, Liebert, & Fernandez, 1969), and interrogative sentences (Twardosz & Baer, 1973). There is little doubt that many previously mute or severely language-impaired children have acquired some basic language through the use of these interventions. Nonetheless, time and experience have demonstrated the continuing limitations of these strategies in establishing generalized, spontaneous speech among the majority of children with autism. As Carr (1985) indicated, we have become acutely aware of our ignorance concerning why some children appear to benefit and others do not, how best to sequence language instruction, and how to enhance the generalization of language skills to novel settings.

### Increasing Spontaneous Speech

One of the interesting problems that researchers have addressed in the past few years has been the challenge of encouraging autistic children to be more spontaneous in their speech. Originally developed to facilitate the language development of disadvantaged preschool children, incidential teaching techniques have provided one vehicle for addressing the problem of spontaneity in children with autism (Hart & Risley, 1975, 1980). These techniques rely on arranging events in the natural environment so that children will be attracted to particular activities and will have to use language to obtain these desirable items. For example, an interesting toy may be put on a shelf beyond the child's reach so that he or she has to ask for help in getting it.

Examples of the use of incidental teaching techniques with children demonstrating severe developmental psychopathology include withholding a food tray until the child asks for it (Halle, Marshall, & Spradlin, 1979), having teachers withhold offers of help until children request assistance (Halle, Baer, & Spradlin, 1981), and teaching receptive language during the course of lunch preparation by requiring the child to present the items necessary to prepare the food (McGee, Krantz, Mason, & McClannahan, 1983). Charlop *et al.* (1985) found that a time delay procedure in which the instructor withheld a modeled response for increasingly longer periods led to spontaneous responses on the part of the child. McGee, Krantz, and McClannahan (1985) compared the use of incidental teaching and traditional training techniques with autistic children and found greater generalization and more spontaneous use of prepositions with the incidental procedures.

### Case Report: Language

The following case illustrates the use of behavioral techniques to teach speech and language to a preschool-aged autistic boy. The complete details of the research and treatment program, in which his parents participated, can be found in Harris (1983).

Alexander, a 3-year-old boy, was diagnosed as autistic on the basis of his lack of interpersonal responsiveness, his failure to develop language, and his unusual responses to the environment, including his resistance to change. He had an estimated IQ of 55, and his communication skills were at the level of a 16-month-old.

Alexander's parents volunteered to participate in an experimental program to teach behavior modification skills to parents of preschool autistic children. Much of their 10-week course focused on methods of encouraging their child to speak through both formal and informal instructional sessions. Thus, in addition to daily formal teaching periods in which they trained Alexander to establish eye contact and to imitate their nonverbal gestures and simple sounds in a discrete-trial format, they were also encouraged to use naturally occurring interactions to facilitate speech.

Among the teaching techniques that Alexander's parents were encouraged to use were ensuring they had their son's attention before they spoke, using simple language, giving him time to comply with their commands, providing labels and descriptions for routine activities around the house and during playtime, repeating back and expanding the things Alexander said to them, requiring him to use whatever speech he had, and rewarding all his efforts to communicate.

The detailed analyses of videotapes made before and after the training program documented the changes in both Alexander and his parents after the program ended. Before the training, his parents rarely made active efforts to encourage Alexander to speak, nor did they reinforce his occasional communicative attempts on any consistent basis. Following the training, they were enthusiastic in their praise of Alexander's modest efforts to speak, using each sound as an opportunity to encourage more speech. Alexander also showed changes in his behavior, in that he made more sounds with communicative intent after treatment than before.

In addition to improving Alexander's speech, his parents also used behavioral procedures to teach him not to climb on top of bookcases and other furniture and to remain in his crib at night instead of wandering around the house. They also had the opportunity to receive considerable social support from the other families who comprised their training group and thus to learn they were not alone in the intensely stressful life of raising an autistic child.

## Manual Signing

In spite of our best efforts, we are not yet able to teach speech to every child. It has therefore been necessary to search for alternative communication modalities, such as manual signs, for these youngsters. Furthermore, there has been some exploration of whether simultaneous communications, in which sign and word are paired, might enhance speech along with the acquisition of signs for speaking as well as mute children.

In a useful review of the research on sign language, Carr (1979) concluded that, although the speech of some children improves with the simultaneous use of sign, for most children speech productions remain minimal. He noted that almost all children, even the very impaired, do, however, acquire some basic signs. He suggested that more cognitively impaired children are likely to learn the signs but not words during simultaneous communication training, whereas echolalic children may show an increase in speech as well as sign during simultaneous training. Empirical support for these observations has been provided by Barrera and Sulzer-Azaroff (1983), Remington and Clarke (1983), and Carr and Dores (1981).

The spontaneous and generalized use of sign language has received recent empirical attention. For example, Carr and Kologinsky (1983) demonstrated that prompting, fading, and differential reinforcement can increase the spontaneous and generalized use of signs by autistic children. Similarly, Schepis, Reid, Fitzgerald, Faw, van den Pol, and Welty (1982) documented that modified incidental teaching techniques facilitated the acquisition of sign by autistic and profoundly mentally retarded youths in a residential setting. These findings parallel those for spontaneous speech as discussed above.

## Outcome Studies

Although this chapter has focused on descriptions of relatively fine-grained analyses of specific intervention procedures, it is also important to know what the impact of a comprehensive treatment package is on the child with autism. One of the earliest follow-up studies of children in a behavioral program was the report by Lovaas, Koegel, Simmons, and Long (1973) concerning the youngsters who had been part of their original research at UCLA. Their findings suggested that, unless the child's environment was a supportive one with well-trained parents or staff, high-quality educational efforts might be lost when the child left an intensive behavioral program. This study was the impetus for much of the parent-training research that followed in the next decade.

More recently, Schopler, Mesibov, and Baker (1982) summarized a series of studies of the children enrolled in Division TEACCH, a statewide service delivery system in North Carolina that has, for many years, been providing state-of-the-art education to autistic young people and their parents. The results of these follow-up studies suggest that the program is useful for a range of child problems, contributes to a low rate of institutional placement, and is evaluated in positive terms by staff and family.

The few studies that have looked systematically at early intervention with very young autistic children argue for early, intensive treatment. Fenske, Zalenski, Krantz, and McClannahan (1985) compared the outcome for nine children who entered their program before age 60 months with nine children who entered after that age and found that the outcome was substantially better for the younger children. In a preliminary report on his early intervention efforts, Lovaas (1980) suggested that an intensive 40-hour-a-week program may be far superior to a less intensive 10-hour-a-week treatment program for young children with autism.

One important measure of treatment effects is the evaluations by parents. Runco and Schreibman (1983) asked parents to rate videotapes of autistic children before and after behavior therapy. The parents socially validated the behavioral treatment, in that they rated the children after treatment as significantly improved. The parents also indicated that they would be more willing to interact with the child shown on the tape after treatment. In an examination of parental response to specific modalities of intervention, Pickering and Morgan (1985) discovered that different reinforcements of other behavior, time-out, and overcorrection were all rated as acceptable treatments, whereas electric shock was unacceptable. Thus, it appears that parents can identify the changes that occur in children as a result of treatment and also have specific ideas about which treatment methods they find most acceptable for the autistic child.

## SUMMARY

The decade from the mid-1970s to the mid-1980s has witnessed important shifts in our treatment of autism, schizophrenia of childhood onset, and other forms of pervasive developmental psychopathology. Coming from firm empirical roots, behaviorally oriented educators, psychologists, and speech therapists have explored a number of important issues that have enhanced our understanding of these disorders and that have increased the effectiveness of treatment.

Both our intervention techniques and our teaching curriculum have grown more sophisticated with accumulating research and clinical experience. For example, extensive detailed study of the discrete-trial teaching format has yielded useful information about the importance of making prompts intrinsic in the stimulus material (e.g., Koegel & Rincover, 1976; Schreibman, 1975), of varying items during an instructional session (Dunlap & Koegel, 1980), of inserting a brief delay between the discriminative stimulus and the child's response (Dyer *et al.*, 1982), and of using varied and intrinsic reinforcers (Egel, 1981; Williams *et al.*, 1981).

Although there continues to be a place for the use of powerful aversive procedures for suppressing very dangerous and difficult-to-treat behavior, recent years have seen the development of a range of mildly aversive or nonaversive measures for reducing unwanted or troublesome client behavior, such as self-injury, self-stimulation, and aggression. These interventions include overcorrection (e.g., Foxx & Azrin, 1972), vigorous exercise (e.g., Luce *et al.*, 1980), and brief physical restraint (e.g., Dorsey *et al.*, 1982). There has also been an appreciation of the value of rearranging task demands (e.g., Weeks & Gaylord-Ross, 1981), of teaching children to ask for help when they are frustrated by a situation (Carr & Durand, 1985), and of reinforcing the use of alternative activities, such as toy play, to reduce inappropriate behaviors (e.g., Eason *et al.*, 1982). Taken as a whole, these studies testify to the creative alternatives that can replace the traditional aversive procedures. They do not, however, eliminate the need for these aversives in exceptional cases.

There is an impressive and growing body of research documenting the broad range of skills that can be acquired by autistic and other developmentally disordered individuals. It has been shown to be possible to increase social responsiveness (e.g., Strain, 1983), to improve recreational skills (e.g., Hawkins, 1982), and to teach independent living skills for use in the wider community (e.g., Smith & Belcher, 1985). Furthermore, our language curriculum is being broadened to encourage the more generalized, spontaneous use of language (e.g., Halle *et al.*, 1981; McGee *et al.*, 1985).

Those of us who work with autistic children and their families can see the results of these advances in treatment not only when we read the research literature, but in our daily dealings with our clients. It is obvious, of course, that there remain many substantial challenges still to be met in the treatment of these disorders. Nonetheless, it is encouraging to observe what the creative efforts of our colleagues have accomplished since the mid-1960s to change the prognosis for these children from a bleak to a brighter one.

## REFERENCES

Azrin, N. H., Gottlieb, L., Hughart, L., Wesolowski, M. D., & Rahn, T. (1975). Eliminating self injurious behavior by educative procedures. *Behaviour Research and Therapy, 13,* 101–111.

Barrera, R. D., & Sulzer-Azaroff, B. (1983). An alternating treatment comparison of oral and total communication training programs with echolalic children. *Journal of Applied Behavior Analysis, 16,* 379–394.

Barton, E. S., Guess, D., Garcia, E., & Baer, D. M. (1970). Improvement of retardate's mealtime behaviors by timeout using multiple baseline techniques. *Journal of Applied Behavior Analysis, 3,* 77–84.

Baumeister, A. A., & Klosowski, R. (1965). An attempt to group toilet train severely retarded patients. *Mental Retardation, 3,* 24–26.

Bettelheim, B. (1950). *Love is not enough.* Glencoe, IL: Free Press.

Bettleheim, B. (1967). *The empty fortress.* New York: Free Press.

Bettleheim, B. (1974). *A home for the heart.* New York: Knopf.

Browning, E. R. (1983). A memory pacer for improving stimulus generalization. *Journal of Autism and Developmental Disorders, 13,* 427–432.

Carr, E. G. (1979). Teaching autistic children to use sign language: Some research issues. *Journal of Autism and Developmental Disorders, 9,* 345–359.

Carr, E. G. (1985). Behavioral approaches to language and communication. In E. Schopler & G. B. Mesibov (Eds.), *Communication problems in autism* (pp. 37–57). New York: Plenum Press.

Carr, E. G., & Dores, P. A. (1981). Patterns of language acquisition following simultaneous communication with autistic children. *Analysis and Intervention in Developmental Disabilities, 1,* 347–361.

Carr, E. G., & Durand, V. M. (1985). Reducing behavior problems through functional communication training. *Journal of Applied Behavior Analysis, 18,* 111–126.

Carr, E. G., & Kologinsky, E. (1983). Acquisition of sign language by autistic children. II: Spontaneity and generalization effects. *Journal of Applied Behavior Analysis, 16,* 297–314.

Carr, E. G., Newsom, C. D., & Binkoff, J. A. (1976). Stimulus control of self-destructive behavior in a psychotic child. *Journal of Abnormal Child Psychology, 4,* 139–153.

Carr, E. G., Newsom, C. D., & Binkoff, J. A. (1980). Escape as a factor in the aggressive behavior of two retarded children. *Journal of Applied Behavior Analysis, 13,* 101–117.

Charlop, M. H., Schreibman, L., & Tryon, A. S. (1983). Learning through observation: The effects of peer modeling on acquisition and generalization in autistic children. *Journal of Abnormal Child Psychology, 11,* 355–366.

Charlop, M. H., Schreibman, L., & Thibodeau, M. G. (1985). Increasing spontaneous verbal responding in autistic children using a time delay procedure. *Journal of Applied Behavior Analysis, 18,* 155–166.

Chock, P. N., & Glahn, T. J. (1983). Learning and self-stimulation in mute and echolalic autistic children. *Journal of Autism and Developmental Disorders, 13,* 365–381.

Dorsey, M., Iwata, B. A., Reid, D. H., & Davis, P. A. (1982). Protective equipment: Continuous and contingent application in the treatment of self-injurious behavior. *Journal of Applied Behavior Analysis, 15,* 217–230.

Dunlap, G., & Koegel, R. L. (1980). Motivating autistic children through stimulus variation. *Journal of Applied Behavior Analysis, 13,* 619–627.

Dyer, K., Christian, W. P., & Luce, S. C. (1982). The role of response delay in improving the discrimination performance of autistic children. *Journal of Applied Behavior Analysis, 15,* 231–240.

Eason, L. J., White, M. J., & Newsom, C. (1982). Generalized reduction of self-stimulatory behavior: An effect of teaching appropriate play to autistic children. *Analysis and Intervention in Developmental Disabilities, 2,* 157–169.

Edelson, S. M., Taubman, M. T., & Lovaas, O. I. (1983). Some social contexts of self-destructive behavior. *Journal of Abnormal Child Psychology, 11,* 299–312.

Egel, A. L. (1981). Reinforcer variation: Implications for motivating developmentally disabled children. *Journal of Applied Behavior Analysis, 14*, 345–350.

Epstein, L. J., Taubman, M. T., & Lovaas, O. I. (1985). Changes in self-stimulatory behaviors with treatment. *Journal of Abnormal Child Psychology, 13*, 281–294.

Favell, J. E., McGimsey, J. F., & Jones, M. I. (1978). The use of physical restraint in the treatment of self-injury and as positive reinforcement. *Journal of Applied Behavior Analysis, 11*, 225–242.

Favell, J. E., McGimsey, J. F., Jones, M. L., & Cannon, P. R. (1981). Physical restraint as positive reinforcement. *American Journal of Mental Deficiency, 85*, 425–432.

Favell, J. E., McGimsey, J. F., & Schell, R. M. (1982). Treatment of self-injury by providing alternate sensory activities. *Analysis and Intervention in Developmental Disabilities, 2*, 83–104.

Fenske, E. C., Zalenski, S., Krantz, P. J., & McClannahan, L. E. (1985). Age at intervention and treatment outcome for autistic children in a comprehensive intervention program. *Analysis and Intervention in Developmental Disabilities, 5*, 49–58.

Ferrari, M., & Harris, S. L. (1981). The limits and motivating potential of sensory stimuli as reinforcers for autistic children. *Journal of Applied Behavior Analysis, 14*, 339–343.

Ferster, C. B. (1961). Positive reinforcement and behavioral deficits of autistic children. *Child Development, 32*, 437–456.

Foxx, R. M., & Azrin, N. H. (1972). Restitution: A method of eliminating aggressive-disruptive behavior of retarded and brain damaged patients. *Behaviour Research and Therapy, 10*, 15–27.

Frisch, S. A., & Schumaker, J. B. (1974). Training generalized receptive prepositions in retarded children. *Journal of Applied Behavior Analysis, 7*, 611–621.

Gordon, R., Handleman, J. S., & Harris, S. L. (1986). The effects of contingent versus non-contingent running on the out-of-seat behavior of an autistic boy. *Child and Family Behavior Therapy, 8*, 337–344.

Guess, D., Sailor, W., Rutherford, G.. & Baer, D. M. (1968). An experimental analysis of linguistic development: The productive use of the plural morpheme. *Journal of Applied Behavior Analysis, 1*, 297–306.

Halle, J. W., Marshall, A. M., & Spradlin, J. E. (1979). Time delay: A technique to increase language use and facilitate generalization in retarded children. *Journal of Applied Behavior Analysis, 12*, 431–439.

Halle, J. W., Baer, D. M., & Spradlin, J. E. (1981). Teachers' generalized use of delay as a stimulus control procedure to increase language use in handicapped children. *Journal of Applied Behavior Analysis, 14*, 389–409.

Handleman, J. S. (1979). Generalization by autistic-type children of verbal responses across settings. *Journal of Applied Behavior Analysis, 12*, 273–282.

Harris, S. L. (1983). *Families of the developmentally disabled: A guide to behavioral intervention.* Elmsford, NY: Pergamon Press.

Harris, S.L., & Ersner-Hershfield, R. (1978). The behavioral suppression of seriously disruptive behavior in psychotic and retarded patients: A review of punishment and its alternatives. *Psychological Bulletin, 85*, 1352–1375.

Harris, S. L., & Romanczyk, R. G. (1976). Treating self-injurious behavior of a retarded child by overcorrection. *Behavior Therapy, 7*, 235–239.

Hart, B., & Risley, T. R. (1975). Incidental teaching of language in the preschool. *Journal of Applied Behavior Analysis, 8*, 411–420.

Hart, B., & Risley, T. R. (1980). In vivo language intervention: Unanticipated general effects. *Journal of Applied Behavior Analysis, 13*, 407–432.

Hawkins, A. H. (1982). Influencing leisure choices of autisticlike children. *Journal of Autism and Developmental Disorders, 12*, 359–366.

Hedbring, C., & Newsom, C. (1985). Visual oversensitivity: A comparison of two instructional remediation procedures with autistic children. *Journal of Autism and Developmental Disorders, 15*, 9–22.

Hewett, F. M. (1965). Teaching speech to an autistic child through operant conditioning. *American Journal of Orthopsychiatry, 35*, 927–936.

Hingtgen, J. N., & Churchill, D. W. (1969). Identification of perceptual limitations in mute autistic children: Identification by use of behavior modification. *Archives of General Psychiatry, 21*, 68–71.

Hughes, V., Wolery, M. R., & Neel, R. S. (1983). Teacher verbalizations and task performance with autistic children. *Journal of Autism and Developmental Disorders, 13*, 305–316.

Johnson, M., & Bailey, J. (1977). The modification of leisure behavior in a half-way house for retarded women. *Journal of Applied Behavior Analysis, 10*, 273–283.

Johnson, W. L., Baumeister, A. A., Penland, M. J., & Inwald, C. (1982). Experimental analysis of self-injurious, stereotypic, and collateral behavior of retarded persons: Effects of overcorrection and reinforcement of alternative activities. *Analysis and Intervention in Developmental Disabilities, 2,* 41–66.

Kern, L., Koegel, R. L., Dyer, K., Blew, P. A., & Fenton, L. R. (1982). The effects of physical exercise on self-stimulation and appropriate responding in autistic children. *Journal of Autism and Developmental Disorders, 12,* 399–419.

Kern, L., Koegel, R. L., & Dunlap, G. (1984). The influence of vigorous versus mild exercise on autistic stereotyped behaviors. *Journal of Autism and Developmental Disorders, 14,* 57–67.

Klier, J. L., & Harris, S. L. (1977). Self-stimulation and learning in autistic children: Physical or functional incompatibility. *Journal of Applied Behavior Analysis, 10,* 311.

Koegel, R. L., & Covert, A. (1972). The relationship of self-stimulation to learning in autistic children. *Journal of Applied Behavior Analysis, 5,* 381–387.

Koegel, R. L., & Rincover, A. (1976). Some detrimental effects of using extra stimuli to guide learning in normal and autistic children. *Journal of Abnormal Child Psychology, 4,* 59–71.

Koegel, R. L., & Wilhelm, H. (1973). Selective responding to the components of multiple visual cues. *Journal of Experimental Child Psychology, 15,* 442–453.

Koegel, R. L., & Williams, J. A. (1980). Direct versus indirect response-reinforcer relationships in teaching autistic children. *Journal of Abnormal Child Psychology, 8,* 537–547.

Koegel, R. L., Dunlap, G., & Dyer, K. (1980). Intertrial interval duration and learning in autistic children. *Journal of Applied Behavior Analysis, 13,* 91–99.

Kovattana, P. M., & Kraemer, H. C. (1974). Responses to multiple visual cues of color, size, and form by autistic children. *Journal of Autism and Childhood Schizophrenia, 4,* 251–261.

Lagomarcino, A., Reid, D. H., Ivancic, M. T., & Faw, G. D. (1984). Leisure-dance instruction for severely and profoundly retarded persons: Teaching an intermediate community-living skill. *Journal of Applied Behavior Analysis, 17,* 71–84.

Lovaas, O. I. (1980). Behavioral teaching with young autistic children. In B. Wilcox & A. Thompson (Eds.), *Critical issues in educating autistic children and youth* (pp. 220–233). Cambridge, MA: Brookline Books.

Lovaas, O. I., & Schreibman, L. (1971). Stimulus overselectivity of autistic children in a two stimulus situation. *Behaviour Research and Therapy, 9,* 305–310.

Lovaas, O. I., Berberich, J. P., Perloff, B. F., & Schaeffer, B. (1966). Acquisition of imitative speech by schizophrenic children. *Science, 151,* 705–707.

Lovaas, O. I., Schreibman, L., Koegel, R. L., & Rehm, L. (1971). Selective responding by autistic children to multiple sensory input. *Journal of Abnormal Psychology, 77,* 211–222.

Lovaas, O. I., Koegel, R., Simmons, J. Q., & Long, J. S. (1973). Some generalization and follow-up measures on autistic children in behavior therapy. *Journal of Applied Behavior Analysis, 6,* 131–165.

Lovaas, O. I., Schaeffer, B., & Simmons, J. Q. (1974). Building social behavior in autistic children by use of electric shock. In O. I. Lovaas & B. D. Bucher (Eds.), *Perspectives in behavior modification with deviant children* (pp. 107–122). Englewood Cliffs, NJ: Prentice Hall.

Luce, S. C., Delquadri, J., & Hall, R. V. (1980). Contingent exercise: A mild but powerful procedure for suppressing inappropriate verbal and aggressive behavior. *Journal of Applied Behavior Analysis, 13,* 583–594.

Lutzker, J. R. (1978). Reducing self-injurious behavior in three classrooms by facial screening. *American Journal of Mental Deficiency, 83,* 510–513.

Lutzker, J. R., & Sherman, J. A. (1974). Producing generative sentence usage by imitation and reinforcement. *Journal of Applied Behavior Analysis, 7,* 447–460.

McGee, G. G., Krantz, P. J., Mason, D., & McClannahan, L. E. (1983). A modified incidental-teaching procedure for autistic youth: Acquisition and generalization of receptive object labels. *Journal of Applied Behavior Analysis, 16,* 329–338.

McGee, G. G., Krantz, P. J., & McClannahan, L. E. (1985). The facilitative effects of incidental teaching on preposition use by autistic children. *Journal of Applied Behavior Analysis, 18,* 17–31.

McGonigle, J. J., Duncan, D., Cordisco, L., & Barrett, R. P. (1982). Visual screening: An alternative method for reducing stereotypic behaviors. *Journal of Applied Behavior Analysis, 15,* 461–467.

Marchant, J., & Wehman, P. (1979). Teaching table games to severely retarded children. *Mental Retardation, 17,* 150–152.

Murphy, G. (1982). Sensory reinforcement in the mentally handicapped and autistic child: A review. *Journal of Autism and Developmental Disorders, 12,* 265–278.

Nelson, D. L., Gergenti, E., & Hollander, A. C. (1980). Extra prompts versus no extra prompts in self-care training of autistic children and adolescents. *Journal of Autism and Developmental Disorders, 10*, 311–321.

Odom, R. D., Liebert, R. M., & Fernandez, L. (1969). Effects of symbolic modeling on the syntactical productions of retardates. *Psychonomic Science, 17*, 104–105.

Odom, S. L., Hoyson, M., Jamieson, B., & Strain, P. S. (1985). Increasing handicapped preschoolers' peer social interactions: Cross-setting and component analysis. *Journal of Applied Behavior Analysis, 18*, 3–16.

Pickering, D., & Morgan, S. B. (1985). Parental ratings of treatments of self-injurious behavior. *Journal of Autism and Developmental Disorders, 15*, 303–314.

Powers, M. D., & Handleman, J. S. (1984). *Behavioral assessment of severe developmental disabilities.* Rockville, MD: Aspen Systems.

Rapoff, M. A., Altman, K., & Christophersen, E. R. (1980). Elimination of a blind child's self-hitting by response-contingent brief restraint. *Education and Treatment of Children, 3*, 231–236.

Remington, B., & Clarke, S. (1983). Acquisition of expressive signing by autistic children: An evaluation of the relative effects of simultaneous communication and sign-alone training. *Journal of Applied Behavior Analysis, 16*, 315–328.

Richmond, G. (1983). Shaping bladder and bowel continence of developmentally retarded preschool children. *Journal of Autism and Developmental Disorders, 13*, 197–204.

Rimland, B. (1964). *Infantile autism.* New York: Appleton-Century-Crofts.

Rincover, A., Koegel, R. L., & Russo, D. C. (1978). Some recent behavioral research on the education of autistic children. *Education and Treatment of Children, 1*, 31–45.

Risley, T. R. (1968). The effects and side effects of punishing the autistic behaviors of a deviant child. *Journal of Applied Behavior Analysis, 1*, 21–34.

Rojahn, J., Schroeder, S. R., & Mulick, J. A. (1980). Ecological assessment of self-protective devises in three profoundly retarded adults. *Journal of Autism and Developmental Disorders, 10*, 59–66.

Runco, M. A., & Schreibman, L. (1983). Parental judgements of behavior therapy efficacy with autistic children: A social validation. *Journal of Autism and Developmental Disorders, 13*, 237–248.

Rusch, F., Close, D., Hops, H., & Agosta, J. (1976). Overcorrection: Generalization and maintenance. *Journal of Applied Behavior Analysis, 9*, 498.

Salzinger, K., Feldman, R. S., Cowan, J. E., & Salzinger, S. (1965). Operant conditioning of two young speech-deficient boys. In L. Krasner & L. P. Ullman (Eds.), *Research in behavior modification* (pp. 84–105). New York: Holt, Rinehart & Winston.

Schepis, M. M., Reid, D. H., Fitzgerald, J. R., Faw, G. D., van den Pol, R. A., & Welty, P. A. (1982). A program for increasing manual signing by autistic and profoundly retarded youth within the daily environment. *Journal of Applied Behavior Analysis, 15*, 363–379.

Schleien, S. J., Certo, N. J., & Muccino, A. (1984). Acquisition of leisure skills by a severely handicapped adolescent: A data based instructional program. *Education and Training of the Mentally Retarded, 19*, 297–305.

Schopler, E., Mesibov, G., & Baker, A. (1982). Evaluation of treatment for autistic children and their parents. *Journal of the American Academy of Child Psychiatry, 21*, 262–267.

Schover, L. R., & Newsom, C. D. (1976). Overselectivity, developmental level and over-training in autistic and normal children. *Journal of Abnormal Child Psychology, 4*, 289–298.

Schreibman, L. (1975). Effects of within-stimulus and extra-stimulus prompting on discrimination learning in autistic children. *Journal of Applied Behavior Analysis, 8*, 91–112.

Schreibman, L., Koegel, R. L., & Craig, M. S. (1977). Reducing stimulus overselectivity in autistic children. *Journal of Abnormal Child Psychology, 5*, 425–436.

Singh, N. N., & Bakker, L. W. (1984). Suppression of pica by overcorrection and physical restraint: A comparative analysis. *Journal of Autism and Developmental Disorders, 14*, 331–341.

Singh, N. N., Beale, I. L., & Dawson, M. J. (1981). Duration of facial screening and suppression of self-injurious behavior: Analysis using an alternating treatments design. *Behavioral Assessment, 3*, 411–420.

Smith, M. D., & Belcher, R. (1985). Teaching life skills to adults disabled by autism. *Journal of Autism and Developmental Disorders, 15*, 163–175.

Stevens-Long, J., & Rasmussen, M. (1974). The acquisition of simple and compound sentences in an autistic child. *Journal of Applied Behavior Analysis, 7*, 473–479.

Strain, P. S. (1983). Generalization of autistic children's social behavior change: Effects of developmentally integrated and segregated settings. *Analysis and Intervention in Developmental Disabilities, 3*, 23–34.

Strain, P. S., Kerr, M. M., & Ragland, E. U. (1979). Effects of peer-mediated social initiations and prompting/reinforcement procedures on the social behavior of autistic children. *Journal of Autism and Developmental Disorders, 9*, 41–54.

Twardosz, S., & Baer, D. M. (1973). Training two severely retarded adolescents to ask questions. *Journal of Applied Behavior Analysis, 6*, 655–661.

van den Pol, R. A., Iwata, B. A., Ivancic, M. T., Page, T. J., Neef, N. A., & Whitley, F. P. (1981). Teaching the handicapped to eat in public places: Acquisition, generalization, and maintenance of restaurant skills. *Journal of Applied Behavior Analysis, 14*, 61–69.

Watters, R. G., & Watters, W. E. (1980). Decreasing self-stimulatory behavior with physical exercise in a group of autistic boys. *Journal of Autism and Developmental Disorders, 10*, 379–387.

Weeks, M., & Gaylord-Ross, R. (1981). Task difficulty and aberrant behavior in severely handicapped students. *Journal of Applied Behavior Analysis, 14*, 449–463.

Wehman, P. (1983). Recreation and leisure needs. A community approach. In E. Schopler & G. B. Mesibov (Eds.) *Autism in adolescents and adults* (pp. 111–132). New York: Plenum, Press.

Williams, J. A., Koegel, R. L., & Egel, A. L. (1981). Response-reinforcer relationships and improved learning in autistic children. *Journal of Applied Behavior Analysis, 14*, 53–60.

Wolf, M. M., Risley, T. R., & Mees, H. (1964). Application of operant conditioning procedures to the behavior problems of an autistic child. *Behaviour Research and Therapy, 1*, 305–312.

Zegiob, L. E., Jenkins, J., Becker, J., & Bristow, A. (1976). Facial screening: Effects on appropriate and inappropriate behaviors. *Journal of Behavior Therapy and Experimental Psychiatry, 7*, 355–357.

# 13 Infantile Autism and Childhood Schizophrenia
## Pharmacotherapies

RICHARD PERRY AND KAREN MEISELAS

## HISTORICAL DEVELOPMENT

In this review, the psychopharmacotherapy of infantile autism and that of child-hood schizophrenia are treated separately. This separation reflects research since the mid-1960s that has led to a consensus in child psychiatry that infantile autism (IA) and childhood schizophrenia (CS) are distinct entities. Whereas the diagnostic criteria in the DSM (American Psychiatric Association—APA, 1952) and DSM-II (APA, 1968) included children with autistic features in its diagnosis of CS, the DSM-III (APA, 1980) subsumed IA in the category of pervasive developmental disorders with its own clinical criteria. CS is not included in the DSM-III. In order for a child to be diagnosed as CS, he or she must conform to the criteria for adult schizophrenia. This practice is criticized by some (Cantor, Evans, Pearce, & Pezzot-Pearce, 1982) who feel that many schizophrenic children do not meet the adult criteria for schizoprenia. In practice, IA has emerged from its separation from CS as a more clearly delineated syndrome relative to CS, and researchers working in the area of IA have found the DSM-III criteria for IA to be useful as the basis for samples of autistic children who have been studied epidemiologically, genetically, clinically, biochemically, neurophysiologically and pharmacologically. From a vast array of data, movement toward a rational psychopharmacology has been made. We are therefore beginning to understand the biochemical abnormalities that coexist with certain symptoms in IA. The aim of a rational psychopharmacology is to treat both the symptoms and the biochemical abnormalities that may underlie the symptoms. This progress has not been made with schizophrenic children. In fact, the muddle in which the diagnosis of CS finds itself is reflected in the paucity of articles dealing with the psychopharmacotherapy of CS.

Even before the DSM-III, there were criteria in use, such as Kanner's (1943) and those of the British Working Party (Creak, 1964), which are similar to those of the DSM-III. Those studies that clearly defined samples or subsamples of

RICHARD PERRY AND KAREN MEISELAS • Department of Psychiatry, New York University Medical Center, New York, New York 10016. Since the time of this research, Dr. Meiselas has accepted an appointment at the University of Medicine and Dentistry of New Jersey at Newark.

autistic children using these criteria often yielded useful information. The result of all this is that, since the mid-1960s, IA has been seriously investigated.

A brief overview follows of the research in the pharmacotherapy of IA since the mid-1960s. The four divisions correspond to the organization in the third section of this chapter, in which the drug studies are detailed:

1. *Various compounds* were tried in the 1960s and 1970s that proved to be of limited or no benefit in the treatment of infantile autism. These include drugs having stimulating qualities such as *d*- and *l*-amphetamine, L-dopa, imipramine, triiodothyronine ($T_3$), methysergide maleate, and the nonstimulants lithium and megavitamins.

2. *Neuroleptics* were studied in the 1970s. It was demonstrated that high-dosage, low-potency, strongly anticholinergic neuroleptics were of little value in treating IA, whereas low-dosage, high-potency, more antidopaminergic neuroleptics were more effective. This approach led to trials in autistic children of haloperidol, which proved effective. Since 1978, Campbell and her associates (Anderson, Campbell, Grega, Perry, Small, & Green, 1984; Campbell, Anderson, Meier, Cohen, Small, Samit, & Sachar, 1978a; Cohen, Campbell, Posner, Small, Triebel, & Anderson, 1980b) have extensively and carefully demonstrated the efficacy of haloperidol in the short- and long-term treatment of IA. Like other neuroleptics, haloperidol treatment can lead to extrapyramidal side effects (dystonias and parkinsonian symptoms) and to dyskinesias, side effects linked to haloperidol's effects on dopamine receptors. Therefore, medications with different mechanisms of action have been pursued.

3. *Fenfluramine* appears to be such a drug in that it is considered primarily a serotonin antagonist and only a weak antidopaminergic agent. Its long-term administration is not associated with tardive dyskinesia. Preliminary studies in the early 1980s reported dramatic improvements in autistic children treated with fenfluramine. More recent studies have yielded more modest results.

4. *Naltrexone*, an opiate antagonist, is now being investigated because of some phenomenological similarities in the presentation of autistic children and opiate-addicted individuals.

Before addressing the various drug studies in IA and CS, some basic principles governing the pharmacotherapy of IA and CS are discussed.

## BASIC PRINCIPLES

Some of the principles guiding the clinician in the pharmacotherapy of IA and CS are as follows:

1. The indication for psychoactive medication in the treatment of IA or CS must be carefully evaluated. Not all patients with IA or CS require medication; the clinician is guided by the nature and severity of the symptoms at home and at school and the degree to which the symptoms interfere with the child's development and functioning. For example, hyperactivity, aggressiveness, self-mutilation, and stereotypies are among target symptoms for pharmacotherapy. All medications carry the risk of side effects, and the potential benefits must outweigh the potential risks.

2. Medication should be targeted toward specific symptoms or problem behaviors, and the effect of drug on these should be monitored closely. One

should not be vague about the desired effects of the drug, as vagueness risks the continuance of ineffective drugs and exposure to side effects.

3. The aims of drug therapy in all patients and particularly in children include the enhancement of prosocial behaviors such as learning and socialization. At a minimum, reduced learning and/or socialization should not overshadow the beneficial effects of the drug in reducing negative behaviors.

4. Psychopharmacological treatment is never used alone, but only as an adjunct to other therapeutic modalities (Irwin, 1968). Children with IA or CS often require special schooling, behavior therapy, psychotherapy, or counseling. Medication can make children more amenable to other psychosocial interventions.

5. Before initiating psychopharmacotherapy, the clinician should carefully observe the child in a drug-free state. The baseline symptoms and their severity should be documented, as should any characteristic that might later be confused with a potential drug side effect. In this vein, it may be necessary to order blood tests or special studies, such as an EEG. If a child is being switched from one medication to another, one should attempt to have a drug-free washout period. This approach is not always possible, as in the case of severe behavioral problems.

6. Medication should be started at a low dosage and gradually increased until the medication has its desired effects on the target symptoms, or until side effects are produced. Beginning at a high dosage results more frequently in side effects, such as sedation with neuroleptics; these, in turn, decrease compliance and can lead to the abandonment of a drug by a patient or the parents before a trial is completed. Once an optimal dosage—the dosage at which there are clear benefits and no significant side effects—is reached, the patient should be seen regularly and should not remain on the drug for an indefinite period. It is generally good practice to withdraw medication every 6 months or so to determine if it is still necessary and, in the case of neuroleptics, to carefully evaluate for the development of abnormal movements.

7. The routine use of anticholinergic drugs, either to treat extrapyramidal symptoms or to prevent them, should be discouraged. If extrapyramidal symptoms occur, it is preferable to treat them by lowering the dosage.

8. Finally, there is no drug that benefits all autistic children. This finding appears to be consistent with the existence of subgroups of autistic children and the lack of success, thus far, in finding a biological marker in IA. As a result, some children may require successive trials on different drugs; some do not show a clear positive response to any drugs, and others consistently experience side effects contraindicating medication.

What evolves from a citation of the guidelines for psychopharmacotherapy are the requirements of drug studies that must generate reliable and valid information for the clinician. One cannot stress too much the need for drug studies to be double-blind and placebo-controlled. One is always surprised at the number of apparent side effects that occur on placebo. The need for control groups is especially important in doing research with children, as maturational changes over time may masquerade as drug effects.

It was emphasized above that clear diagnostic criteria are needed to define homogeneous samples for drug trials. Target symptoms also have to be defined as well as some means of quantification reflecting the intensity of the symptoms before, during, and after drug treatment. In recent years, a number of rating scales have been devised and tested. Scales for cognitive functioning, as well as side effects, are often helpful and should be completed for comparison before, during, and after drug treatment. The data should be submitted for statistical analysis, and the degree of significance of the results should be reported.

Many of the earlier studies of pharmacotherapy in IA, cited below, suffer from one or more methodological problems, for example, the lack of a blind, heterogeneous and/or poorly diagnosed samples, or no use of rating scales.

Some authors have made the important observation that the results of drug studies may be profoundly affected by the setting in which the study was done. Campbell, Geller, and Cohen (1977) cited some data (Christensen, 1973; Werry & Sprague, 1970) in questioning whether drug effects may be lessened or obscured when studies are done in highly structured inpatient settings other than in more naturalistic outpatient settings.

It should also be noted that most of the autistic subjects in drug trials are preschool or school-aged children. A drug may be of proven effectiveness in young children but not in more mature individuals; or the opposite, a drug may not be effective in younger children but may be useful in older subjects. This factor should be kept in mind when the physician is asked to medicate an older autistic patient, whether it be in an institution or in the community.

## MAJOR APPLICATIONS

### Psychopharmacotherapy of Infantile Autism

#### Earlier Studies

The administration of *dextroamphetamine* and *levoamphetamine* (Campbell, Fish, David, Shapiro, Collins & Koh, 1972a; Campbell, Small, Collins, Friedman, David, & Genieser, 1976) resulted in minimal gains, such as slightly reduced hyperactivity and slightly increased attention, which were outweighed by bothersome side effects like increased withdrawal, stereotypies, irritability, and excitability.

Trials of L-*dopa* were carried out because it lowers the levels of blood serotonin, which are elevated in approximately 33% of autistic children (Campbell, Friedman, DeVito, Greenspan, & Collins, 1974; Campbell, Friedman, Green, Collins, Small, & Breuer, 1975; Hanley, Stahl, & Freedman, 1977; Ritvo, Yuwiler, Geller, Ornitz, Saeger, & Plotkin, 1970; Young, Kavanagh, Anderson, Shaywitz, & Cohen, 1982). This finding led to the more recent trials of fenfluramine, a hyposerotonergic agent, which will be discussed later in detail. Ritvo, Yuwiler, Geller, Kales, Rashkis, Schicor, Plotkin, Axelrod and Howard (1971) administered L-dopa to 4 autistic patients ranging in age from 3 to 16. Although the serotonin level dropped significantly in the youngest 3 children, there were behavioral gains. Campbell *et al.* (1976) gave L-dopa to 12 autistic children ages 3–6.9; 5 children improved. In some, negativism and irritability decreased; in others, there was increased play and language production. However, the level of improvements did not reach significance and was not related to a change in serotonin levels. Moreover, L-dopa worsened preexisting stereotypies and caused the emergence of new stereotypies.

In a pilot study (Campbell, Fish, Shapiro, & Floyd, 1971a), *imipramine* was administered to 10 autistic children. The beneficial effects—stimulation and tranquilization—were usually outweighed by the adverse reactions.

Sherwin, Flach, and Stokes (1958) administered $T_3$ to 2 euthyroid autistic children. There were positive stimulating effects, such as increases in alertness, speech, and social contact. These led to a pilot study in which $T_3$ administration benefited some children (Campbell, Fish, David, Shapiro, Collins, & Koh, 1973). This study was poorly controlled. However, a subsequent well-designed, placebo-controlled, double-blind study yielded clear improvement in only 4 of 30 children (Campbell, Small, Hollander, Korein, Cohen, Kalmijn, & Ferris, 1978b).

*Methysergide,* the methylated derivative of D-lysergic acid and diethylamide, was administered to 11 autistic preschool children. The drug produced a mixture of stimulating, sedating, and disorganizing effects. On the one hand, some children showed greater alertness, less withdrawal, more cooperation, and better performance on tasks; on the other hand, there were negative effects such as excessive sedation, hyperactivity, and increased psychotic language. It should be noted that the 2 most retarded patients showed the greatest improvements (Fish, Campbell, Shapiro, & Floyd, 1969).

*Lithium* was ineffective in a sample of 10 autistic children (Campbell, Fish, Korein, Shapiro, Collins, & Koh, 1972b). However, aggressiveness was decreased in 2 of 5 aggressive children, the decrease being dramatic in a chronically explosive, self-mutilating child. The effect of lithium on aggressiveness may result from an increased rate of synthesis of brain serotonin (Perez-Cruet, Tagliamonte, Tagliamonte, & Gessa, 1971). It is known, for example, that lowering brain serotonin in research animals increases aggressiveness.

*Megavitamins* have also received trials in autistic children. Although there is some enthusiasm about the administration of vitamins to autistic children, studies have not yielded results supportive of that enthusiasm. Some studies (Rimland, 1973; Rimland, Callaway, & Dreyfus, 1978) have methodological flaws. In others (Greenbaum, 1970; Roukema & Emery, 1970), the administration of vitamins has been ineffective. Thus, there is little rationale for the administration of megavitamins to autistic children.

## Neuroleptics

This section is divided into three parts. To begin, the earlier studies of the neuroleptic treatment of IA done in the late 1960s and the early 1970s are reviewed. These studies laid the groundwork for several well-designed studies of haloperidol, which are the subject of the second part of this section. Haloperidol has proved to be effective in the treatment of IA. However, it is not universally effective and can cause the appearance of dyskinetic movement disorders, which are the focus of this section's final part. There is now a search for other medications in the treatment of IA which have better benefit-to-risk ratios. The trials of fenfluramine and naltrexone administration in autistic children, which are reviewed later, should be seen in this context.

### Earlier Studies

Various neuroleptics were explored in the treatment of IA in the late 1960s and the early 1970s. The studies suffered from one or more of the following deficiencies: small sample size, heterogeneous samples; poor design, including the lack of placebo control or blind; the absence of rating scales; and absent or insufficient statistical analyses. Nevertheless, the studies indicated that neuroleptics were beneficial in the treatment of at least some autistic children, and that higher potency, less sedative neuroleptics like haloperidol were more effective than lower potency, more sedative drugs. That the higher potency neuroleptics, as compared to those with lower potency, are more specifically anti-dopaminergic in their effects on neurotransmitters raised the possibility that excessive dopaminergic activity was implicated in the etiology of IA in general or in a subgroup of autistic children. Dopamine activity appears to be related to some cerebral functions that are impaired or disordered in autistic children, such as attention, cognition, and motor function (Young *et al.*, 1982).

Supporting evidence for excessive dopaminergic activity contributing to autistic symptomatology comes from biochemical studies (Young *et al.*, 1982). Some autistic children have elevated levels of homovanillic acid (HVA), a metabolite of dopamine, in their cerebrospinal fluid (CSF) (Cohen, Shaywitz, Johnson, & Bowers, 1974; Gillberg, Suennerholm, & Hamilton-Hellberg, 1983). They tend to have lower IQs, more hyperactivity, and more stereotypies than those autistic children with lower CSF-HVA levels (Cohen *et al.*, 1974). Urinary HVA levels have also been reported as being higher in autistic children (Garnier, Comey, Barthelmy, Leddet, Garreau, Muh, & Lelord, 1986). On the other hand, when dopamine agonists (the amphetamines and L-dopa) were administered to children with IA, the side effects often included increased withdrawal, irritability, and excitability and increased stereotypical behavior, including new stereotypies (Campbell *et al.*, 1972a, 1976).

The earlier studies are summarized in Table 1. It should be noted that the number of autistic children in the samples in some studies is an approximation, because of the relative inexactitude of diagnosis prevailing at that time. In Table 1, the results are greatly abbreviated. In general, the studies demonstrated that the higher potency neuroleptics had both tranquilizing and stimulating effects on autistic children. Thus, symptoms such as hyperactivity, stereotypies, and withdrawal were decreased, whereas responsiveness to the environment, attention span, and exploratory behavior were increased. Chlorpromazine, the low-potency neuroleptic that was studied in autistic children, resulted in the same symptomatic improvements, but the effects were much less dramatic. In addition, chlorpromazine caused sedation at therapeutic dosages. Sedation was also reported, but to a smaller extent, with one other neuroleptic at therapeutic dosages: trifluoperazine.

Other side effects were reported in most but not all of the papers dealing with neuroleptic administration to autistic children. In general, the side effects were mild and were outweighed by the benefit of treatment.

*Haloperidol Studies*

From the preceding paragraphs and Table 1, it is clear that haloperidol would present itself as a promising drug to study. The studies by Faretra, Dooher, and Dowling (1970) and Engelhardt, Polizos, Waizer, and Hoffman (1973) support this supposition, as does the earlier study by Fish *et al.* (1969) of trifluperidol, an experimental drug, which like haloperidol is a butyrophenone.

TABLE 1. Early Neuroleptic Studies

| Authors | Year | Drug(s) studied: Generic (brand name) | Sample size: Total/autistic | Ages | Design | Dosage (mg/day) | Findings |
|---|---|---|---|---|---|---|---|
| Fish, Shapiro, & Campbell | 1966 | Trifluoperazine (Stelazine) | 22/22 | 2–6 | Controlled Double-blind | 2–20 | Positive drug effects in the most severely impaired children. |
| Fish, Campbell, Shapiro, & Floyd | 1969 | Trifluoperazine Trifluperidol (Triperidol) Chlorpromazine (Thorazine) | 10/9 | 2–5 | Double-blind Some crossover | 2–8 0.17–0.67 30–150 | Trifluperidol was effective at nonsedating dosage; not true of two other drugs. |
| Campbell, Fish, Korein, Shapiro, Collins, & Koh | 1972 | Chlorpromazine Lithium | 10/7 | 3–6 | Controlled Double-blind Crossover | 9–45 450–900 | Chlorpromazine: slightly effective, toxicity (e.g., sedation) at dosage as low as 9–15 mg. |
| Campbell, Fish, Shapiro, & Floyd | 1972 | Trifluperidol Chlorpromazine d-Amphetamine Chloral hydrate | 15/13 | 2–5 | Double-blind Crossover Acute | 0.2–0.7 2.5–50 1.2–10 500–1500 | Trifluperidol significantly better than chlorpromazine, which is overly sedative. |
| Campbell, Fish, Shapiro, & Floyd | 1970 | Thiothixene (Navane) | 10/9 | 3–7 | Pilot Double-blind | 1–6 | Drug was effective. |
| Waizer, Polizos, Hoffman, Englehardt, & Margolis | 1972 | Thiothixene | 18/18 | 5–13 | Single-blind | 10–24 | Drug was effective. |
| Simeon, Saletu, Saletu, Itil, & DaSilva | 1973 | Thiothixene | 10/3 | 5–15 | Open | 6–30 | 5 of 10: marked to moderate improvement. |
| Campbell, Fish, Shapiro, & Floyd | 1971 | Molindone (Moban) | 10/8 | 3–5 | Pilot Double-blind | 1–2.5 | Promising results. |
| Faretra, Dooher, & Dowling | 1970 | Fluphenazine (Prolixin) Haloperidol (Haldol) | 60/52 | 5–12 | Double-blind Random | 3.75 for most on either drug | 67% of 30 children on fluphenazine improved; 57% of 30 children on haloperidol improved. Haloperidol acted more quickly and brought greater reductions of provocativeness and autism. |
| Engelhardt, Polizos, Waizer, & Hoffman | 1973 | Fluphenazine Haloperidol | 30/19 | 6–12 | Double-blind Random (Fluphenazine) | 10.4 mean dosage | 93% of 15 on fluphenazine much or very much improved; 87% of 15 on haloperidol much or very much improved. Fluphenazine produced more extrapyramidal symptoms. |

Trifluperidol caused a high incidence of extrapyramidal symptoms and was thus withdrawn from use in the United States.

Since the late 1970s, Campbell and her group at Bellevue Hospital have conducted a series of short-term (Anderson *et al.*, 1984; Campbell *et al.*, 1978a; Cohen *et al.*, 1980b) and long-term (Campbell, Grega, Green, & Bennett, 1983a; Campbell, Perry, Bennett, Small, Green, Grega, Schwartz, & Anderson, 1983b; Perry, Campbell, Green, Small, Die-Trill, Meiselas, Golden, & Deutsch, 1985) studies on the efficacy and safety of haloperidol in the treatment of IA. The setting for the short-term studies has been a therapeutic nursery for preschool-aged autistic children located in the child psychiatry unit. The drug trials took place in the context of complete medical and psychological diagnostic workups and a multimodal treatment program. With few exceptions the children were inpatients (a few were in day care), and they were a carefully diagnosed, homogeneous group. The trials were placebo-controlled and double-blind.

Campbell *et al.* (1978a) reported on a group of 40 autistic children. There were 32 boys and 8 girls, with ages ranging from 2.6 to 7.2 and an average of 4.5 years. They had been randomly assigned to one of four treatment groups, depending on whether or not they received haloperidol and/or behavior therapy. Although few of the children had ever been exposed to psychoactive medication, they all began with a 2-week placebo washout period, followed by an 8-week period of continued placebo or haloperidol. After 3 weeks of this 8-week period, the children who were on placebo or haloperidol were exposed to an 8-week course of either behavior therapy or "placebo" (mock) behavior therapy. In the first case, there was reinforcement, contingent on correct replies in such tasks as repeating words or labeling pictures. In the "placebo" behavior therapy, reinforcement was given at set time intervals and was thus noncontingent.

Several rating scales were used by the two blind child psychiatrists. Most of these scales are described and discussed in an issue of the *Psychopharmacology Bulletin* (Vol. 21, 1985), which is a review of the rating scales used in child psychopharmacology research. A specific article in the *Bulletin* deals with the rating scales used in the research on IA (Campbell & Palij, 1985). The scales used in the 1978 haloperidol study were the first 28 items of the Children's Psychiatric Rating Scale (CPRS; *Psychopharmacology Bulletin*, 1985); the Clinical Global Impressions (CGI; *Psychopharmacology Bulletin*, 1985); and the Children's Behavior Inventory (CBI; Burdock & Hardesty, 1964). Nursing staff, also blind, completed the Nurses Global Impressions (NGI; *Psychopharmacology Bulletin*, 1973). Finally, the Dosage Record and Treatment Emergent Symptoms (DOTES; *Psychopharmacology Bulletin*, 1985) and the Treatment Emergent Symptoms Scale Write-In (TESS; *Psychopharmacology Bulletin*, 1985) were completed.

The results showed that haloperidol was significantly superior to placebo in reducing the symptoms of stereotypies and withdrawal (on the CPRS), but only in those children older than 4.5 years. Those children who had received a combination of haloperidol and contingent-reinforcement behavioral therapy had acquired imitative speech at an accelerated pace; this was not so in the three other groups.

The range of optimal dosage for haloperidol, which was individually regulated, was 0.5–4.0 mg/day with a mean optimal dosage of 1.65 mg/day. The side effects were generally mild and transient, and they appeared during the dose regulation period and responded to dose reduction. They were also infrequent except for transient sedation, which occurred in 12 subjects. There were two episodes of dystonic reactions and no extrapyramidal side effects.

The above findings were subsequently replicated in the same setting (Cohen *et al.*, 1980b). Ten preschool subjects (mean age 4.7 years; 6 boys and 4 girls) entered a pilot study of 10 weeks. After a 2-week placebo washout period, each child was blindly given either placebo or haloperidol for a 2-week period. Then there were three crossover periods at 2-week intervals, so that the design was ABAB with each child serving as his or her own control (within-subjects reversal design). Behavioral changes, if any, were noted, as well as each subject's response to the verbal request, made when the child was looking away, of "look at me." The request was repeated 10 times or until the child responded appropriately, with orientation of gaze and establishment of eye contact, three times in a row.

The average individually regulated dosage of haloperidol was 1.65 mg/day during the first medication period and 1.90 mg/day on repeat administration.

Haloperidol was effective in reducing high levels of stereotypies and in increasing the orientating reaction in those children who, at baseline, had tended to orient little. As in the earlier study (Campbell *et al.*, 1978a), there was an effect of age: the older children responded better than the younger ones.

This study did, in fact, replicate some of the findings of the previous study. In addition, it indicated the usefulness of a within-subjects reversal design. It left unanswered the question of how haloperidol improves performance on tasks requiring a response to verbal requests, such as imitating new words as in the 1978 study or orienting to "look at me" in the 1980 study. Does the haloperidol improve attention indirectly by decreasing withdrawal and stereotypies, or does it have a direct effect on attentional mechanisms?

These questions were addressed by the next study (Anderson *et al.*, 1984), in which 40 autistic children (29 boys and 11 girls) were treated with haloperidol. Their ages ranged from 2.3 to 6.9 years (mean: 4.58 years). The study was double-blind and in a crossover design. Following a 2-week placebo washout period, the children were randomly assigned to placebo or haloperidol for 4 weeks, which constituted Condition 1. Following were Conditions 2 and 3, each of 4-week intervals. The possible sequences were therefore haloperidol–placebo–haloperidol or placebo–haloperidol–placebo.

The study focused on the behavioral changes resulting from drug administration, as well as the effects of the drug on attentional learning, which was studied by means of a discrimination-learning task that was completed by 32 of the children (22 boys and 10 girls). The task involved responding to a computer-controlled operant-conditioning apparatus. Each child was seated in front of a console, which at fixed intervals presented a colored pattern on a screen and simultaneously a pure tone (Campbell, Anderson, Small, Perry, Green and Caplan 1982). Thirty-two children could be trained on placebo to press a lever during the presentation of the audiovisual stimulus to acquire an edible reward. Pressing the lever at the presentation of the audiovisual stimulus or indiscriminately was monitored during the three conditions, therefore on and off medication. A score was tabulated that represented the percentage of responses occurring during the stimulus; this score was called the *discrimination index* (DI). A DI of 50% indicated chance; a DI of 100% indicated a perfect performance.

The rating scales used were the CPRS, the CGI, the Conners 10-item Parent

Teacher Questionnaire (PTQ; *Psychopharmacology Bulletin*, 1973), the Timed Behavioral Rating Sheet (TBRS; Cohen *et al.*, 1980b), and the DOTES.

The optimal dosage of haloperidol, which was individually regulated, ranged from 0.5 to 3.0 mg/day (mean: 1.1), which comes to 0.019–0.217 mg/kg per day (mean: 0.05).

The administration of haloperidol resulted in significant improvements in eight symptoms taken from the CPRS: hyperactivity, stereotypies, fidgetiness, withdrawal, abnormal object relationships, angry affect, lability of affect, and negativism. On the CGI, the haloperidol treatment resulted in significant reductions in severity of illness and significantly differed from placebo in causing improvements. The PTQ indicated that the subjects receiving haloperidol showed less severe symptoms than those on placebo.

In discrimination learning, those children receiving haloperidol performed significantly better than those receiving placebo. A simultaneous multiple-regression analysis was performed with discrimination learning as the dependent variable; the independent variables were the Gesell language developmental quotient, the drug, hyperactivity in the laboratory, and stereotypy in the laboratory. The language developmental quotient and the drug were the only two variables that significantly accounted for performance in discrimination learning. Therefore, the improved learning does not appear to have been the result of a decrease in maladaptive behaviors such as hyperactivity and stereotypies but may have resulted from a more direct action on attentional mechanisms.

Concerning the side effects, excessive sedation was, by far, the most frequent, but it occurred either during dosage regulation and/or above optimal dosage. Irritability was a less frequent side effect that also occurred during dosage regulation and/or above optimal dosage. Acute dystonic reactions occurred in 11 of the children during dosage regulation at dosages ranging from 0.5 b.i.d. to 4.0 mg/day. The reactions responded quickly to diphenhydramine hydrochloride (25 mg) given orally or intramuscularly. In all 11 cases, a child experienced only one dystonic reaction, and it was not necessary to permanently discontinue medication.

The finding that haloperidol can enhance cognition is perhaps a surprising one because neuroleptics are generally thought to have deleterious effects on cognitive functioning. This finding was noted above in reference to chlorpromazine, an example of a low-potency, more sedative type of neuroleptic that often does negatively affect cognition in autistic children at the doses necessary for effective behavioral improvement.

In the three haloperidol studies summarized above, a dosage was found for most of the autistic children on which they benefited behaviorally and cognitively, while not being burdened by untoward effects. In fact, in the last study (1984), the parents or guardians of 36 of the 40 children asked that haloperidol be continued at the completion of the study.

It is probable that the effects of haloperidol on cognition are dose-dependent. In another study (Campbell, Small, Green, Jennings, Perry, Bennett, & Anderson, 1984), in which very aggressive nonpsychotic children received haloperidol, the dosage necessary to decrease the target symptoms resulted in more, although slight, adverse effects on cognition (Platt, Campbell, Green, & Grega, 1984). These children generally received higher dosages (mg/per kilogram of weight) than the autistic children in the three haloperidol studies.

The haloperidol studies provide strong evidence of the short-term efficacy and safety of haloperidol in the treatment of preschoolaged autistic children. Given the chronic nature of autism and the association of haloperidol with the potential long-term neuroleptic side effects of dyskinetic movement disorders, it was logical to design a long-term study to explore the long-term efficacy and safety of haloperidol in the treatment of infantile autism.

We are currently engaged in a prospective long-term study of haloperidol in the autistic children who benefited from the drug in our short-term study. The design of the long-term study is detailed elsewhere (Campbell *et al.*, 1983b). In brief, those children who benefited from haloperidol in the short-term study were enrolled, with the approval and the signed consent of their parents or guardians, in the long-term study.

In this study, 6-month periods on medication are followed by 4-week periods on placebo. The child is seen monthly while on haloperidol; on placebo, there are weekly visits in which the assessment of behavior and examination of abnormal movements are videotaped and rated by means of the CPRS, the CGI, the Abnormal Involuntary Movement Scale (AIMS; Guy, 1976), and the Rockland Research Institute Abbreviated Dyskinesia Rating Scale (Simpson, Lee, Zoubok, & Gardos, 1979). During the 6-month drug period, the children receive either haloperidol 7 days a week, or 5 days a week with 2-day drug holidays.

Campbell *et al.* (1983a,b) reported on 36 children who had been in the long-term study from 6 months to 2½ years. Haloperidol retained its therapeutic efficacy at the 6-month rating. One week after switching to placebo, behavioral ratings in the CPRS (hyperactivity, fidgetiness, abnormal object relations, withdrawal, and stereotypies) and the CGI showed significant deterioration.

The long-term study is ongoing, and our more recent data await analysis. The authors of this chapter believe that the above behavioral findings will hold up for the larger sample when the data are analyzed.

The findings from the long-term study as they relate to dyskinetic movements are presented in the next section, after some preliminary remarks on neuroleptic-induced dyskinesias.

*Neuroleptic-Related Dyskinesias*

Neuroleptic-related dyskinesias are defined as abnormal, involuntary movements that frequently have a characteristic buccolingual-masticatory distribution, but that may also involve the neck, the trunk, and the upper and lower extremities. Diaphragmatic involvement can result in respiratory dyskinesia, vocalizations, grunts and dysarthria (Campbell *et al.*, 1983a).

It is important to note that not all abnormal involuntary movements are neuroleptic-related dyskinesias (Granacher, 1981). It is essential to distinguish neuroleptic-related movements from other neurological disorders, such as Huntington chorea, and from movements secondary to the administration of medications such as L-dopa (Campbell *et al.*, 1983a). Another source of confusion is that the populations of children who are frequently treated with neuroleptic medication (e.g., infantile autistics and the mentally retarded) are likely to have preexisting movement disorders. Neuroleptics can suppress stereotypies, and the emergence of an abnormal involuntary movement at the time of drug withdrawal may actually be a stereotypy that is reemerging (Campbell *et al.*, 1983a;

Gualtieri, Barnhill, McGimsey, & Schell, 1980). Finally, movements resembling neuroleptic-related dyskinesia may arise in individuals who have not been exposed to neuroleptics or other psychoactive medication, be they adults (Owens, Johnstone, & Frith, 1982; Varga, Sugerman, Varga, Zomorodi, Zomorodi, & Menkin, 1982) or children. Cohen, Campbell, McCandless, and Posner (1980a) observed autistic children and normal controls and found that, of the 101 controls (ages 2–6), 19.9% had buccolingual-masticatory movements.

The reported prevalence of neuroleptic-related dyskinesias in children ranges from 8% (McAndrew, Case, & Treffert, 1972) to 51% (Engelhardt & Polizos, 1978), based on retrospective studies. This discrepancy in prevalence could be due to differences in the study population, the type of neuroleptic, the duration of drug intake, the assessment methods, the study design, and study populations with high baseline rates of abnormal movements (Campbell *et al.*, 1983a; Campbell, Green, & Deutsch, 1985b).

The reports of neuroleptic-induced dyskinesias in children (Engelhardt & Polizos, 1978; Gualtieri, Quade, Hicks, Mayo, & Schroeder, 1984; McAndrew *et al.*, 1972; Paulson, Rizvi, & Crane, 1975; Polizos, Engelhardt, Hoffman, & Waizer, 1973) suffer from one or more of the following shortcomings: retrospective design, no baseline assessments, diagnostically heterogeneous samples, and children who had received a variety of neuroleptics. The purpose of a prospective study is to avoid some of these problems (Perry *et al.*, 1985). In this ongoing study, 58 children (47 males and 11 females; ages 3.6–7.8 years) diagnosed with IA received maintenance doses of haloperidol. The daily dosage ranged from 0.5 to 3.0 mg (one exception was a boy who received 7.5 mg) for a period of from 3.5 to 42.5 months. The patients were randomly assigned to either a continuous (haloperidol 7 days/week) or a discontinuous (haloperidol 5 days/week, placebo 2 days/week) treatment schedule. Haloperidol was discontinued and replaced with placebo every 6 months for 4 weeks in order to allow an assessment of the child's behavioral status and an examination for withdrawal phenomena. Abnormal movements were documented on a timed stereotypies rating scale, the AIMS, and an abridged Simpson Scale on baseline and at fixed intervals throughout the study. These ratings were videotaped and were rated again in random sequence by two trained raters who were blind to the diagnosis of dyskinesias and the treatment.

Of the 58 children, 13, or 22% (9 male and 4 female; ages 4.1–7.8), developed neuroleptic-related dyskinesias. Continuous or discontinuous drug scheduling did not have a significant effect on the development of the dyskinesias. The topography was as follows: buccal (10); tongue (4); upper extremities (4); lower extremities (2); trunk (2); neck, shoulder, and hip (1); and throaty sounds secondary to laryngeal and diaphragmatic involvement (1). All movements ceased in 16 days to 9 months. The movements ceased spontaneously in 10 children, and they ceased after the reinstitution of haloperidol in 3 children.

The sample size in this study recently grew to include 82 children (66 boys and 16 girls; ages 2.74–11.18 years) (Campbell, Adams, Perry, Spencer, & Overall, 1988). The dosage ranged from 0.25 to 10.5 mg/day. The cumulative exposure to haloperidol was 0.84–74.48 months. The number of children developing dyskinetic movements increased to 24, so that the percentage rose to 29.27%. In the additional 11 children, the movement disorder resolved.

As previously stated, the emergence of neuroleptic-related dyskinesias has increased the interest in using alternative or novel psychopharmacological agents to benefit children with IA. These agents include fenfluramine and naltrexone, which are discussed in the following sections.

## Fenfluramine

Fenfluramine is a sympathomimetic amine that is marketed as an anorectic agent under the brand name of Pondimin. It is chemically related to the amphetamines but differs in that it produces more central nervous system depression than stimulation, and in its mechanism of action, which seems to involve the serotonergic nervous system predominantly. In studies of the rat brain, Garattini, Jori, Buczko and Samanin (1975) determined that fenfluramine, and not amphetamine, decreases brain levels of serotonin (5HT) and 5HIAA and blocks dopamine receptors, causing an increase in homovanillic acid (HVA) levels in the rat striatum. Neither fenfluramine nor amphetamine seems to affect the acetylcholine system, and amphetamine, but not fenfluramine, lowers brain norepinephrine. Both cause anorexia, but by different effects on central biogenic amines.

Serotonergic activity is thought to have modulatory effects on many neuronal systems, including those that regulate sleep, body temperature, sensory perception, sexual behavior, motor functions, neuroendocrine regulation, appetite, learning and memory, and the immune response (Young et al., 1982). However, there is no consistent relationship between specific behaviors and serotonin. As stated above, fenfluramine was first considered as a treatment for autism with the rationale that approximately one third of autistic children are hyperserotonemic (Campbell et al., 1974, 1975; Hanley, et al., 1977; Ritvo et al., 1970). In the study by Campbell et al. (1975), the difference in serotonin levels reached significance in those patients who had more florid symptoms and lower IQs. Hanley et al. (1977) found hyperserotonemia in 50% of his mentally retarded population. Even though the significance of hyperserotonemia as a biological marker is unclear, there are few other conditions in which it occurs (Hanley et al., 1977), so a rationale existed for clinical trials of serotonergic blocking agents. The results of the administration of another antiserotonergic agent, L-dopa, are noted above.

Geller, Ritvo, Freeman, and Yuwiler (1982) reported on three hyperserotonemic autistic males who were treated with fenfluramine. The first child to be given fenfluramine (40 mg/day) was a 3-year-old autistic boy whose blood serotonin decreased by 43%. His platelet counts were unaffected. His behavior improved, as rated by 1 blind and 1 unblind rather during his time on the optimal dose (2 weeks). Two additional boys with hyperserotonemia (ages 3.7 and 5.4) were then studied in a double-blind, placebo-controlled crossover design. The initial placebo phase was 2 weeks long, and the medication phase lasted 11 weeks. During the medication phase, the fenfluramine dosage was adjusted to maintain serotonin levels between 150–200 ng/ml. Fenfluramine decreased the blood serotonin levels, and the authors asserted that this decrease was accompanied by improved behavior and an increase in IQs. Loss of effect was noted 3 months after fenfluramine was discontinued. No untoward effects were noted. The authors noted that it was unclear whether the clinical improvement was related to the decrease in serotonin levels. In addition, the use of serial IQ tests, as in this study, has been questioned, as there is likely to be considerable practice effect. Because these results were based only on three children, further study was warranted.

In 1983, after considerable media attention resulting from the early findings, Volkmar, Paul, Cohen, and Shaywitz cautioned against the use of fenfluramine in autistic children until further studies could clarify its benefits and risks. In a letter to the *New England Journal of Medicine,* they reported on two children who had developed irritability, fearfulness, agitation, and hyperactivity on 40 mg/day of fenfluramine.

Later in 1983, Ritvo, Freeman, Geller, and Yuwiler reported on 14 autistic outpatients (ages 2.10–18 years) who were treated with 1.5 mg/kg per day of fenfluramine. A double-blind, placebo-controlled crossover design was used; the patients were on placebo for 2 weeks, which were followed by 1 month of placebo, 4 months of fenfluramine, and 2 months of placebo. While they were on fenfluramine, their blood serotonin levels fell by 51%. Their platelet counts were unaffected. The therapeutic changes included decreases in restlessness, motility disturbances, and sensory symptoms, as well as improvements in sleep, eye contact, and socialization. Increases in communicative language, affect, and social awareness, as well as a decrease in echolalia, were also reported. There were no significant side effects. One month after the discontinuation of fenfluramine, and while on placebo, all the children were reported to have an increase in symptoms. No relationship seemed to exist between baseline serotonin levels and clinical response. The authors suggested that the relationship between serotonin and behavior is "unlikely to be direct." Again, although IQs increased, a practice effect may have been operative. It should be also noted that the assignment to treatment groups was not randomized, and the patients were heterogeneous with respect to age.

In 1984, Ritvo, Freeman, Yuwiler, Geller, Yokota, Schroth, and Novak published their follow-up study, in which the 14 subjects from the earlier report (Ritvo *et al.,* 1983) continued to receive fenfluramine over a period of 8 months; the same protocol was used. The previous findings were replicated: the serotonin levels in the blood decreased significantly, and so did the behavioral symptoms. There were no clinically significant side effects. As a group, the responders had low serum serotonin levels at baseline and had higher IQs than the nonresponders, perhaps because of "greater cognitive resources, which can emerge when specific symptoms are ameliorated by medication" (Ritvo *et al.,* 1984, p. 827).

A multicenter collaborative study was begun under the leadership of Ritvo in order to further evaluate the efficacy of fenfluramine in a large number of autistic children. They all received a daily dose of 1.5 mg/kg of fenfluramine. The treatment protocol was the same as in the earlier study (Ritvo *et al.,* 1983). The nine patients of August, Raz, and Baird (1985) were ages 6–13 years. Significant decreases in serotonin were associated with marked decreases in hyperactivity and distractibility. No effect on IQ was found, although it was felt that social skills, communication, and learning might develop more readily following a decrease in motor abnormalities. Although "weight loss was noted in most patients, their weight returned to baseline after the discontinuation of medication. Symptoms reemerged when the drug was discontinued and placebo was reinstituted.

It is of interest that, in the multicenter study, Leventhal (1985) reported no beneficial effect on behavior or IQ; his sample consisted of 16 young autistic children with IQs between 40 and 60.

The most recent report from the multicenter collaborative study (Ritvo, Freeman, Yuwiler, Geller, Schroth, Yokota, Mason-Brothers, August, Klykylo, Leventhal, Lewis, Piggott, Realmuto, Stubbs, & Umansky, 1986) included 81 patients (ages 33 months–24 years) from nine centers. Of these children, 33% were considered strong responders, 52% moderate responders, and 15% non-responders. There was a significant correlation between low serotonin levels at baseline, high IQ, and positive clinical response. Beneficial effects noted by parents included decreased restlessness and hyperactivity, decreased repetitive behaviors, increased social responsiveness and eye contact, increased attention span, and improved speech and nonverbal communication. Side effects included mild lethargy, irritability, and insomnia. Anorexia occurred but was not felt to be clinically significant.

In a pilot study, Campbell, Deutsch, Perry, Wolsky, and Palij (1985a) administered fenfluramine to 10 children (7 males and 3 females; ages 3–5.75) over a period of 1–2 months. The dosage was individually regulated. The optimal dose ranged from 15 to 30 mg/day, or 1.093 to 1.787 mg/kg per day; the maximum dose given was 60 mg/day. Untoward effects necessitating a decrease in dosage included drowsiness and lethargy ($N = 9$); weight loss ($N = 7$); irritability ($N = 6$); rigidity, tension, and fidgetiness ($N = 1$); sadness ($N = 2$); increased aggressiveness toward self or others ($N = 2$); insomnia ($N = 1$); and an increase in stereotypies ($N = 1$). In 9 of the 10 children, these untoward effects occurred above optimal dosage during the process of dosage regulation. One child who improved only minimally showed untoward effects at optimal doses. In seven patients, transient weight loss at the end of 1 month of fenfluramine maintenance was followed by weight gain at the end of the second month of treatment. Fenfluramine seemed to have both stimulating effects (increased relatedness and more animated facial expression) and tranquilizing effects (decreases of irritability, temper tantrums, aggressiveness, self-mutilation, and hyperactivity, as well as improved sleep). The most marked effects were seen in patients with low IQs who had failed to respond previously to haloperidol and to special education.

Following this study, Campbell (1988) began a double-blind, placebo-controlled study of fenfluramine in hospitalized, preschoolaged autistic children. A 2-week placebo period was followed by an 8-week fenfluramine or placebo period, which in turn was followed by 2 weeks of placebo. Of the first 24 subjects aged 2.5–6.58 years to complete the study, only 2 of 18 variables in the CPRS, fidgetiness and withdrawal, showed significant decreases on fenfluramine. On a discrimination learning task, children on placebo learned better than those on fenfluramine. Optimal doses of fenfluramine varied from 1.25 to 2.068 mg/kg per day.

## Naltrexone

Endorphins and enkephalins are endogenous opioid peptides produced by the brain. They are "morphinelike" substances that have recently been implicated as underlying a variety of behaviors, including attention, perception, pain appreciation, affect, social behavior, and motor activity. Their abnormalities have been hypothesized in the etiopathogenesis of syndromes such as schizophrenia, affective disorder, and infantile autism (Kalat, 1978; Panksepp, 1979; Vereby, Volavka, & Clouet, 1978). The narcotic antagonists naltrexone (Trexan) and naloxone (Narcan) have been studied in psychiatric patients as a means of testing these hypotheses (Vereby et al., 1978); the results are inconclusive at best.

Kalat (1978) and Panksepp (1979) have forwarded theories on the role of the endogenous opiate system in infantile autism. Kalat (1978) suggested that some behavioral symptoms displayed by autistic children resemble opiate addiction. Examples include social withdrawal, decreased sensitivity to pain, and alternating periods of hyper- and hypoactivity. During periods of intoxication, addicts are likely to ignore sensory stimuli. During periods of withdrawal, they may appear to be "irrationally anxious" with episodes of unprovoked crying. In addition, Kalat drew the parallel that, like children who are born addicted to opiates, autistic children are frequently retarded in height, weight, and bone development; have feeding problems; and are prone to epileptic seizures.

Panksepp (1979) drew on studies that he had performed on animals. He cited features of excess activity of the endogenous opiate system as being similar to features of infantile autism. These features include decreased appreciation of physical pain, decreased ability to cry readily or spontaneously, poor clinging, decreased desire for social companionship, and "unusual learning," or persistence of behavior in the absence of external rewards. The latter was felt to be akin to the insistence on sameness of autistic children. Panksepp noted that the striatum of the prenatal rat brain is rich in B endorphin, but that levels decrease with age and maturation. He proposed that normal infants may have high opiate activity for adaptive purposes (e.g., to decrease motor activity until muscular strength and coordination mature). Autism may represent a failure of the opioid system to decrease with age.

Thus, both Panksepp and Kalat have related the syndrome of infantile autism to the possibility of excessive levels or abnormal activity of the endogenous opioid system and have proposed that this hypothesis could be tested by administering an opiate antagonist, such as naltrexone, to autistic subjects.

In addition to these theoretical constructs, there have been a few case reports of the use of naloxone for the mentally retarded who exhibit self-injurious behavior (Davidson, Kleene, Carroll, & Rockowitz, 1983; Richardson & Zaleski, 1983; Sandman, Datta, Barron, Hoehler, Williams, & Swanson, 1983). These reports have been limited to studies of only one or two patients, but the results have been encouraging, showing decreases in the nature or amount of self-injurious behavior. Such behavior is also a problem in some children with IA, and these reports offer further support for the desirability of studying opiate antagonists in children with IA.

Biochemical support for the role of the endogenous opiate system in self-mutilatory behavior came from Coid, Allolio, and Rees (1983), who found that mean plasma metenkephalin levels were significantly higher in adult psychiatric patients who were self-mutilators than in controls. Metenkephalin levels were corollated with the severity of self-mutilatory behavior. Similarly, Gillberg, Terenius, and Lönnerholm (1985) found that autistic children with symptoms of self-destructiveness and decreased sensitivity to pain tended to have elevated endorphin fraction II levels in their cerebrospinal fluid. However, Weizman, Weizman, Tyano, Szekely, Weissman, and Sarne (1984) found reduced levels of

H-endorphin in 6 of 10 autistic children. Both studies lend support to the notion of a general disruption in the endogenous opioid system in this population.

Naltrexone was administered to 8 autistic boys aged 3.75–6.5 years in an acute-dose tolerance study (Campbell, Adams, Tesch, & Curren, 1988). Following a 2-week baseline, naltrexone was given in a single morning dose, once per week, at dosages of 0.5 mg/kg per day. The first dosage was followed by dosages of 1.0 mg/kg per day and 2.0 mg/kg per day. At all the doses the autistic withdrawal was strongly reduced. At the lowest dose, fidgetiness and negative uncooperative behavior were significantly reduced; at the highest dose, relatedness increased significantly and stereotypies were reduced. Six of the eight children were considered by clinical judgment to be responders. Untoward effects were mild and transient with 5 children showing mild sedation. Campbell is following up this work with a double-blind, placebo-controlled naltrexone/placebo study in a sample of preschoolaged autistic children.

## PRACTICAL CONSIDERATIONS IN THE PHARMACOTHERAPY OF AUTISTIC CHILDREN

Following are some practical suggestions concerning the choice and administration of medication for the individual autistic child. In the section on basic principles above, it was noted that not all children with infantile autism require medication. If an autistic child is a serious management problem and/or the symptoms of autism interfere with learning, medication may be indicated. To date, the best studied medications in the treatment of infantile autism are fenfluramine and haloperidol. For the hyperactive, aggressive, self-injurious autistic child, who may have many stereotypies and who is a serious management problem, a tranquilizer such as haloperidol is perhaps the drug of choice. The biochemical studies cited above (Young *et al.*, 1982) show a clearer association between aggression and dopaminergic activity than between aggression and serotonergic activity. To reiterate, haloperidol is a strong antidopaminergic drug, whereas fenfluramine does not appear to greatly affect the dopamine system.

In our experience with those autistic children who are hyperactive or have periods of hyperactivity alternating with periods of hypoactivity, haloperidol is often effective. Exclusively hypoactive autistic children rarely respond well to haloperidol and may become overly sedated on it.

The starting dosage of haloperidol depends on the age and size of the child. It is usually appropriate to begin with a dosage of 0.5 mg given in the morning or 0.25 mg given twice a day. One can raise the dosage by 0.25 mg or 0.5 mg every 2 or 3 days. The best guides for dosage regulation are the dosages established in the haloperidol studies presented above and the principal that, as the optimal dosage across subjects covers a wide range, one can raise the dosage until haloperidol has its desired effect on the target symptoms or until side effects appear. Transient sleepiness is common as the dosage is being raised. This is handled by either halting increases in the dosage or reducing the dosage; after 1 or 2 days, it is then often possible to raise the dosage without inducing recurrent sleepiness. Many children do best taking their total dosage in the morning or taking two divided dosages during the day. With some children, much trial and error is required in arriving at the optimal regimen. Where sleepiness is a concern, more or all of the dosage can be given at bedtime. It should be noted that many young children will not swallow pills. As haloperidol does not come in an elixir form, pills may have to be crushed in something like applesauce.

Fenfluramine is marketed under the name of Pondimin®. Each scored pill contains 20 mg. The dosage should begin low—at perhaps 10 mg—and should be raised gradually. As shown above, the optimal dosage is usually around 1.5 mg/kg per day in two or three divided dosages. As fenfluramine does not cause tardive dyskinesia, it is reasonable to try it before haloperidol in the autistic child who is not a severe management problem. Because it is used in adults as a diet aid, fenfluramine has an advantage over haloperidol in the treatment of the obese autistic child.

It is difficult to decide on the length of a drug trial. Certainly, if a child has been receiving an appropriate dosage of haloperidol for 2 weeks or longer and there is no positive effect, then it is unlikely that the medication will be effective for that child at that time. Concerning fenfluramine, the length of an adequate trial is less clear, given the more limited experience with the drug. Ritvo et al. (1983) reported continuing improvement during the second to fourth month on the drug. Nonetheless, it is unlikely that a child will respond to fenfluramine if he or she has not begun to respond after 4–6 weeks on medication.

Treatment of the older, larger, and more difficult-to-manage autistic child, adolescent, or adult has not been systematically studied but can present special problems in clinical practice. There are some parents who, for good reasons, do not want to institutionalize their increasingly difficult autistic children and desperately seek help in managing their children. If such a child is not already on medication and then responds well to haloperidol, another neuroleptic, or fenfluramine, then all is well. However, some children are already on one or several medications, including possibly a neuroleptic, an antiparkinsonian drug, and a sleeping pill. Some of these patients can be successfully changed to another, more effective neuroleptic, particularly if they are currently taking a low-potency neuroleptic. Often, antiparkinsonian medication and sleeping pills are then not necessary.

In converting from one medication to another, a drug-free period is indicated during which behavior off medication can be monitored, and an evaluation can be done for the appearance of dyskinetic movements. This drug-free period should last for at least 2–4 weeks because when medication is discontinued, there is sometimes a period of 1–2 weeks when the behavioral difficulties of the child "rebound," to then diminish and stabilize at a level of less severity. Moreover, it often takes time before dyskinetic movements manifest themselves. In this regard, even a 4-week period may be inadequate, but it may be impossible to keep the child off medication for an extended period. It may even be necessary, because of behavioral problems, to begin instituting a new medication while weaning the child from an old one. In those cases in which a child is being changed from one neuroleptic to another neuroleptic or to fenfluramine, the risk of a dyskinetic movement disorder should be discussed or rediscussed with the parents. This is particularly important if there is a switch from one neuroleptic to another, with no drug-free period, as dyskinetic movements can be masked by the new neuroleptic, which may thus contribute to the development of a permanent tardive dyskinesia. Some parents will accept this risk as long as their child is benefited behaviorally and can stay home. Occasionally, a child is withdrawn from a neuroleptic, deteriorates behaviorally, and also begins to experience dyskinetic movements. One must then choose between starting a new neuroleptic, which might help prevent placement but may contribute to the development of a potentially permanent movement disorder and a resulting placement outside the home. The clinician and the parents may decide to start the medication if the parents are informed of and understand the risks. For ethical and legal reasons, discussions about risks should be clearly documented, and consideration should be given to signing an informed consent. In such a situation, very careful following and documentation are needed.

## PHARMACOTHERAPY OF CHILDHOOD SCHIZOPHRENIA

We have previously described the change in the diagnostic criteria for infantile autism and schizophrenia in childhood, which occurred with the publication of the DSM-III in 1980. The DSM-III states that children and adolescents should be diagnosed as having schizophrenia only if they meet adult criteria. This statement reflects the belief that schizophrenia occurring in childhood and adolescence is on a continuum with the syndrome occurring in adulthood. Treatment has followed this line of thought and has proceeded empirically with the use of neuroleptics despite the lack of research in the area.

As a result of the change in diagnostic approach, pharmacotherapy studies of children and adolescents done before 1980 would not be considered relevant to a population that is now diagnosed as schizophrenic. Many of these studies, which contained both autistic and schizophrenic children, have been reviewed above in the section on infantile autism. Some studies contained samples of children having a wide range of diagnoses (Faretra *et al.*, 1970; LeVann, 1969). A notable exception in the literature before 1980 is the study of Pool, Bloom, Mielke, Roniger, and Gallant (1976), which is a double-blind, placebo-controlled study of 75 adolescent patients (ages 13–18) who were hospitalized with a diagnosis of acute schizophrenia or chronic schizophrenia with acute exacerbation. The patients had a minimum of 5 days of washout of previous medication before being randomly assigned to a trial of loxapine, haloperidol, or placebo, which was taken for 4 weeks. Both drugs were found to be superior to placebo on the Brief Psychiatric Rating Scale (BPRS) and the Nurse's Observation Scale for Inpatient Evaluation (NOSIE). On the Clinical Global Impressions scale (CGI), however, there were no significant differences between treatment groups, although there was a trend toward a greater number of improved patients in the haloperidol and loxapine groups of those patients who had been rated "severely ill" or "very severely ill" initially. The symptoms that decreased included hallucinations, delusions, thought disorder, and social withdrawal. The side effects included sedation ($N = 21$ on loxapine and $N = 13$ on haloperidol) and extrapyramidal symptoms ($N = 19$ on loxapine and $N = 18$ on haloperidol).

The recent literature also includes some single-case reports, from which it is difficult to make generalizations. Rogeness and Macedo (1983) published a report on an 11-year-old schizophrenic boy with some symptoms of attention deficit who improved only after methylphenidate was added to his previous regimen of chlorpromazine. Another single-case report is that of Meyers, Tune, and Coyle (1980), who correlated the dose of chlorpromazine with serum levels and the reduction of symptoms in the treatment of a 13.5-year-old "preadolescent" schizophrenic boy.

In contrast to Pool *et al.* (1976), who studied acute schizophrenics, Realmuto, Erickson, Yellin, Hopwood, and Greenberg (1984) studied a chronic population. This study included both a single-blind and a double-blind rater and involved a homogeneous population of 21 chronic schizophrenic adolescents who were randomly assigned to treatment groups of thiothixene or thioridazine. There was no difference between drugs in decreasing anxiety, tension, excitement, and hallucinations as measured by the BPRS and the CGI. Despite improvement in the BPRS scores, nine of the adolescents were only slightly improved, not improved, or worse according to the CGI. This finding was thought by the authors to be due to the selection of the patient population, which was described as a severely impaired group of chronic schizophrenics with traits indicating a poorer prognosis. Drowsiness was the most significant side effect, occurring in 75% ($N = 6$) of the thioridazine group and 54% ($N = 7$) of the thiothixene group, leading the authors to conclude that high-potency neuroleptics may be more sedating in children and adolescents than in adults, but that they may be preferable to low-potency neuroleptics, which cause even greater sedation.

Notwithstanding the limited research regarding the use of neuroleptic medication in children and adolescents with schizophrenia, neuroleptics are the current drugs of choice when psychopharmacological intervention is deemed necessary. With regard to the administration of neuroleptics to this population, Green, Deutsch, Campbell, and Anderson (1985) made the following recommendations, with which we concur:

1. The patient should be given a drug-free period before the initiation of neuroleptic treatment, during which time an adequate behavioral baseline can be established.
2. The starting dose should be low and should be titrated up slowly in order to prevent dystonic reactions. The specific dose depends on the age and size of the child.
3. If dystonic reactions occur, the acute reaction can be treated with Benadryl 25 mg I.M. or P.O. Afterward decreasing the dosage is preferable to the use of anticholinergics or antihistamines.
4. The risk of tardive or withdrawal dyskinesias must be weighed against the potential benefits. This subject was reviewed above in the discussion of the use of neuroleptics in infantile autism.

## CONCLUSION

It seems fitting to conclude by discussing future directions in the use of psychopharmacotherapy for infantile autism and childhood schizophrenia, given the past experience reviewed in this paper. Concerning infantile autism, it is quite possible that more subgroups will be delineated biochemically and pharmacologically. At some point, it seems likely that combinations of two or more drugs may be administered to children who have not shown a good response to any single agent. As for childhood schizophrenia, some resolution of the diagnostic wars is hoped for. Clear diagnostic criteria are a prerequisite to designating samples for psychopharmacological research. As indicated at the beginning of this chapter, some think that the current practice in the DSM-III of diagnosing schizophrenia in childhood by using adult criteria is too restricting (Cantor *et al.*, 1982). Other investigators have diagnosed schizophrenia in childhood by using the adult criteria (Green, Campbell, Hardesty, Grega, Padron-Gayol, Shell, & Erlenmeyer-Kimling, 1984). These two views notwithstanding, the incidence of childhood schizophrenia before puberty, based on the DSM-III criteria, is much less frequent than after puberty (Kydd & Werry, 1982). Therefore, it is hoped that retrospective studies of adult schizophrenic populations and, above all, longitudinal studies of disturbed but not psychotic children and the progeny of schizophrenic adults will yield symptom profiles in childhood of schizophrenics-to-be. It would then be interesting to research such children psychopharmacologically.

Whatever direction psychopharmacological research on infantile autism and childhood schizophrenia takes, one thing is certain: it will continue to be both exhilarating and humbling—exhilarating because technological advances such as biochemical assays and radioisotopic ligand studies have taken us into the age of a more rational psychopharmacotherapy and out of the age of serendipitous discoveries of effective drug treatments in psychiatry; humbling because we appear to be as far from finding cures for infantile autism and childhood schizophrenia as we are from finding specific biological markers in these disorders.

## REFERENCES

American Psychiatric Association, Mental Hospital Service. (1952). *Diagnostic and Statistical Manual (DSM)*. Washington, DC: Author.

American Psychiatric Association. (1968). *Diagnostic and statistical manual of mental disorders (2nd ed.; DSM-II)*. Washington, DC: Author.

American Psychiatric Association. (1980). *Diagnostic and statistical manual of mental disorders (3rd ed.; DSM-III)*. Washington, DC: Author.

Anderson, L. T., Campbell, M., Grega, D. M., Perry, R., Small, A. M., & Green, W. H. (1984). Haloperidol in the treatment of infantile autism: Effects on learning and behavioral symptoms. *American Journal of Psychiatry, 141,* 1195–1202.

August, G., Raz, N., & Baird, T. (1985). Brief report: Effects of fenfluramine on behavioral, cognitive and affective disturbances in autistic children. *Journal of Autism and Developmental Disorders, 15,* 97–107.

Burdock, E. I., & Hardesty, A. S. (1964). A children's behavior diagnostic inventory. *Annual New York Academy of Sciences, 105,* 890–896.

Campbell, M. (1988). Annotations: Fenfluramine treatment of autism. *Journal of Child Psychology and Psychiatry, 29,* 1–10.

Campbell, M., & Palij, M. (1985). Behavioral and cognitive measures used in psychopharmacological studies of infantile autism. *Psychopharmacology Bulletin, 21,* 1047–1053.

Campbell, M., Fish, B., Shapiro, T., & Floyd, A., Jr. (1970). Thiothixene in young disturbed children: A pilot study. *Archives of General Psychiatry, 23,* 70–72.

Campbell, M., Fish, B., Shapiro, T., & Floyd, A., Jr. (1971a). Imipramine in preschool autistic and schizophrenic children. *Journal of Autism and Childhood Schizophrenia, 1,* 267–282.

Campbell, M., Fish, B., Shapiro, T., & Floyd, A., Jr. (1971b). Study of molindone in disturbed preschool children. *Current Therapeutic Research, 13,* 28–33.

Campbell, M., Fish, B., David, R., Shapiro, T., Collins, P., & Koh, C. (1972a). Response to triiodothyronine and dextroamphetamine: A study of preschool schizophrenic children. *Journal of Autism and Childhood Schizophrenia, 2,* 343–358.

Campbell, M., Fish, B., Korein, J., Shapiro, T., Collins, P., & Koh, C. (1972b). Lithium and chlorpromazine: A controlled crossover study of hyperactive severely disturbed young children. *Journal of Autism and Childhood Schizophrenia, 2,* 234–263.

Campbell, M., Fish, B., Shapiro, T., & Floyd, A., Jr. (1972c). Acute responses of schizophrenic children to a sedative and a "stimulating" neuroleptic: A pharmacologic yardstick. *Current Therapeutic Research, 14,* 759–766.

Campbell, M., Fish, B., David, R., Shapiro, T., Collins, P., & Koh, C. (1973). Liothyronine treatment in psychotic and non-psychotic children under 6 years. *Archives of General Psychiatry, 29,* 602–608.

Campbell, M., Friedman, E., DeVito, E., Greenspan, L,, & Collins, P. (1974). Blood serotonin in psychotic and brain damaged children. *Journal of Autism and Childhood Schizophrenia, 4,* 33–41.

Campbell, M., Friedman, E., Green, W. H., Collins, P. J., Small, A. M., & Breuer, H. (1975). Blood serotonin in schizophrenic children: A preliminary study. *International Pharmacopsychiatry, 10,* 213–221.

Campbell, M., Small, A. M., Collins, P. J., Friedman, E., David, R., & Genieser, N. (1976). Levodopa and levoamphetamine: A crossover study in young schizophrenic children. *Current Therapeutic Research, 19,* 70–86.

Campbell, M., Geller, B., & Cohen, I. L. (1977). Current status of drug research and treatment with autistic children. *Journal of Pediatric Psychology, 2,* 153–161.

Campbell, M., Anderson, L. T., Meier, M., Cohen, I. L., Small, A. M., Samit, C., & Sachar, E. J. (1978a). A comparison of haloperidol, behavior therapy and their interaction in autistic children. *Journal of the American Academy of Child Psychiatry, 17,* 640–655.

Campbell, M., Small, A. M., Hollander, C. S., Korein, J., Cohen, I. L., Kalmijn, M., & Ferris, S. (1978b). A controlled crossover study of triiodothyronine in autistic children. *Journal of Autism and Childhood Schizophrenia, 8,* 371–381.

Campbell, M., Anderson, L. T., Small, A. M., Perry, R., Green, W. H., & Caplan, R. (1982). The effects of haloperidol on learning and behavior in autistic children. *Journal of Autism and Developmental Disorders, 12,* 167–175.

Campbell, M., Grega, D. M., Green, W. H., & Bennett, W. G. (1983a). Neuroleptic-induced dyskinesias in children. *Clinical Neuropharmacology, 6,* 207–222.

Campbell, M., Perry, R., Bennett, W. G., Small, A. M., Green, W. H., Grega, D., Schwartz, V., & Anderson, L. (1983b). Long-term therapeutic efficacy and drug-related abnormal movements: A prospective study of haloperidol in autistic children. *Psychopharmacology Bulletin, 19,* 80–83.

Campbell, M., Small, A. M., Green, W. H., Jennings, S. J., Perry, R., Bennett, W. G., & Anderson, L. (1984). Behavioral efficacy of haloperidol and lithium carbonate: A comparison in hospitalized aggressive children with conduct disorder. *Archives of General Psychiatry, 41,* 650–656.

Campbell, M., Deutsch, S. I., Perry, R., Wolsky, B., & Palij, M. (1985a). *Short-term efficacy and safety of fenfluramine in hospitalized preschool-age autistic children: An open study.* Paper presented at the annual NCDEU meeting, Kev Biscayne, Florida, May 1–3, 1985.

Campbell, M., Green, W. H., & Deutsch, S. I. (1985b). *Child and adolescent psychopharmacology.* Beverly Hills, CA: Sage.

Campbell, M., Adams, P., Small, A. M., Tesch, L. M., & Curren, E. L. (1988). Naltrexone in infantile autism. *Psychopharmacology Bulletin, 24,* 135–139.

Campbell, M., Adams, P., Perry, R., Spencer, E. K., & Overall, J. E. (in press). Tardive and withdrawal dyskinesia in autistic children: A prospective study. *Psychopharmacology Bulletin, 24.*

Cantor, S., Evans, J., Pearce, J., & Pezzot-Pearce, T. (1982). Childhood schizophrenia: Present but not accounted for. *American Journal of Psychiatry, 139,* 758–762.

Christensen, D. E. (1973). *The combined effects of methylphenidate (Ritalin) and a classroom behavior modification program in reducing the hyperkinetic behaviors of institutionalized mental retardates.* Ph.D. thesis, University of Illinois at Urbana-Champaign, Urbana.

Cohen, D. J., Shaywitz, B. A., Johnson, W. T., & Bowers, M. B. (1974). Biogenic amines in autistic and atypical children: cerebrospinal fluid measures of homovanillic acid and 5-hydroxyindolacetic acid. *Archives of General Psychiatry, 34,* 561–567.

Cohen, I. L., Campbell, M., McCandless, W., & Posner, D. (1980a). *A timed objective rating scale for autistic children: Comparison of preschoolage patients and normal controls.* Paper presented at the Annual Meeting of the American Academy of Child Psychiatry, Chicago, October.

Cohen, I. L., Campbell, M., Posner, D., Small, A. M., Triebel, D., & Anderson, L. T. (1980b). Behavioral effects of haloperidol in young autistic children: An objective analysis using a within-subjects reversal design. *Journal of the American Academy of Child Psychiatry, 19,* 665–677.

Coid, J., Allolio, B., & Rees, L. H. (1983). Raised plasma metenkephalin in patients who habitually mutilate themselves. *Lancet, 2,* 545–546.

Creak, M. (1964, April). Schizophrenic syndrome in childhood: Further progress report of a working party. *Developmental Medicine and Child Neurology, 6,* 530–535.

Davidson, P., Kleene, B., Carroll, M., & Rockowitz, R. (1983). Effects of Naloxone on self-injurious behavior: a case study. *Applied Research in Mental Retardation, 4,* 1–4.

Engelhardt, D. M., & Polizos, P. (1978). Adverse effects of pharmacotherapy in childhood psychosis. In M. A. Lipton, A. DiMascio, & K. F. Killam (Eds.), *Psychopharmacology: A generation of progress* (pp. 1463–1469). New York: Raven Press.

Engelhardt, D. M., Polizos, P., Waizer, J., & Hoffman, S. P. (1973). A double-blind comparison of fluphenazine and haloperidol. *Journal of Autism and Childhood Schizophrenia, 3,* 128–137.

Faretra, G., Dooher, L., & Dowling, J. (1970). Comparison of haloperidol and fluphenazine in disturbed children. *American Journal of Psychiatry, 126,* 1670–1673.

Fish, B., Shapiro, T., & Campbell, M. (1966). Long-term prognosis and the response of schizophrenic children to drug therapy: A controlled study of trifluoperazine. *American Journal of Psychiatry, 123,* 32–39.

Fish, B., Campbell, M., Shapiro, T., & Floyd, A., Jr. (1969). Schizophrenic children treated with methysergide (Sansert). *Diseases of the Nervous System, 30,* 534–540.

Garattini, S., Jori, A., Buczko, W., & Samanin, R. (1975). The mechanism of action of fenfluramine. *Postgraduate Medical Journal, 51*(Suppl. 1), 27–35.

Garnier, C., Comey, E., Barthelmy, C., Leddet, I., Garreau, B., Muh, J. P., & Lelord, G. (1986). Dopamine-beta-hydroxylase (DBH) and homovanillic acid (HVA) in autistic children. *Journal of Autism and Developmental Disorders, 16,* 23–29.

Geller, E., Ritvo, E. R., Freeman, B. J., & Yuwiler, A. (1982). Preliminary observations on the effect of fenfluramine on blood serotonin and symptoms in three autistic boys. *New England Journal of Medicine, 307,* 1450–1451.

Gilberg, C., Suennerholm, L., & Hamilton-Hellberg, C. (1983). Childhood psychosis and monamine metabolites in spinal fluid. *Journal of Autism and Developmental Disorders, 13,* 383–396.

Gillberg, C., Terenius, L., & Lönnerholm, G. (1985). Endorphin activity in childhood psychosis. *Archives of General Psychiatry, 42,* 780–783.

Granacher, R. P. (1981). Differential diagnosis of tardive dyskinesia: An overview. *American Journal of Psychiatry, 138,* 1288–1297.

Green, W. H., Campbell, M., Hardesty, A. S., Grega, D. M., Padron-Gayol, M., Shell, J., & Erlenmeyer-Kimling, L. (1984). A comparison of schizophrenic and autistic children. *Journal of the American Academy of Child Psychiatry, 23,* 399–409.

Green, W. H., Deutsch, S. I., Campbell, M., & Anderson, L. T. (1985). Neuropsychopharmacology of the childhood psychoses: A critical review. In D. W. Morgan (Ed.), *Psychopharmacology: Impact on clinical psychiatry* (pp. 139–173). St. Louis, Tokyo: Ishiyaku EuroAmerica.

Greenbaum, G. H. (1970). An evaluation of niacinamide in the treatment of childhood schizophrenia. *American Journal of Psychiatry, 127,* 129–132.

Gualtieri, C., Barnhill, J., McGimsey, J., & Schell, D. (1980). Tardive dyskinesia and other movement disorders in children treated with psychotropic drugs. *Journal of the American Academy of Child Psychiatry, 19,* 491–510.

Gualtieri, C. T., Quade, D., Hicks, R. E., Mayo, J. P., & Schroder, S. R. (1984). Tardive dyskinesia and other clinical consequences of neuroleptic treatment in children and adolescents. *American Journal of Psychiatry, 141,* 20–23.

Guy, W. (1976). *ECDEU assessment manual for psychopharmacology* (rev. ed.). Publication (ADM) 76-338. Rockville, MD: Department of Health, Education and Welfare.

Hanley, H. G., Stahl, S. M., & Freedman, D. X. (1977). Hyperserotonemia and amine metabolites in autistic and retarded children. *Archives of General Psychiatry, 34,* 521–531.

Irwin, S. (1968). A rational framework for the development, evaluation, and use of psychoactive drugs. *American Journal of Psychiatry, 124*(Suppl.), 1–19.

Kalat, J. (1978). Letter to the editor: Speculations on similarities between autism and opiate addiction. *Journal of Autism and Childhood Schizophrenia, 8,* 477–478.

Kanner, L. (1943). Autistic disturbances of affective contact. *Nervous Child, 2,* 217–250.

Kydd, R. R., & Werry, J. S. (1982). Schizophrenia in children under 16 years. *Journal of Autism and Developmental Disorders, 12,* 343–357.

LeVann, L. J. (1969). Haloperidol in the treatment of behavioral disorders in children and adolescents. *Canadian Psychiatric Association Journal, 14,* 217–220.

Leventhal, B. L. (1985). *Fenfluramine administration to autistic children: Effects on behavior and biogenic amines.* Paper presented at the 25th NCDEU Annual (Anniversary) Meeting, Key Biscayne, Florida, May 1–4, 1985.

McAndrew, J. B., Case, Q., & Treffert, D. A. (1972). Effects of prolonged phenothiazine intake on psychotic and other hospitalized children. *Journal of Autism and Childhood Schizophrenia, 2*, 75–91.

Meyers, B., Tune, L., & Coyle, J. (1980). Clinical response and serum neuroleptic levels in childhood schizophrenia. *American Journal of Psychiatry, 137*, 483–484.

Owens, D. G., Johnstone, E., & Frith, C. D. (1982). Spontaneous involuntary disorders of movement: chronic schizophrenics with and without treatment with neuroleptics. *Archives of General Psychiatry, 39*, 452–461.

Panksepp, J. (1979). A neurochemical theory of autism. *Trends in Neuroscience, 2*, 174–177.

Paulson, G. W., Rizvi, C. A., & Crane, G. E. (1975). Tardive dyskinesia as a possible sequel of long-term therapy with phenothiazines. *Clinical Pediatrics, 14*, 953–955.

Perez-Cruet, J., Tagliamonte, A., Tagliamonte, P., & Gessa, G. L. (1971). Stimulation of serotonin synthesis by lithium. *Journal of Pharmacology and Experimental Therapeutics, 178*, 325–330.

Perry, R., Campbell, M., Green, W. H., Small, A. M., Die-Trill, M. L., Meiselas, K., Golden, R. R., & Deutsch, S. I. (1985). Neuroleptic-related dyskinesias in autistic children: A prospective study. *Psychopharmacology Bulletin, 21*, 140–143.

Platt, J. E., Campbell, M., Green, W. H., & Grega, D. M. (1984). Cognitive effects of lithium carbonate and haloperidol in treatment-resistant aggressive children. *Archives of General Psychiatry, 41*, 657–662.

Polizos, P., Engelhardt, D. M., Hoffman, S. P., & Waizer, J. (1973). Neurological consequences of psychotropic drug withdrawal in schizophrenic children. *Journal of Autism and Childhood Schizophrenia, 3*, 247–253.

Pool, D., Bloom, W., Mielke, D. H., Roniger, J. J., & Gallant, D. M. (1976). A controlled evaluation of loxitane in seventy-five adolescent schizophrenic patients. *Current Therapeutic Research, 19*, 99–104.

*Psychopharmacology Bulletin* (1973). Special issue: Pharmacotherapy of children.

*Psychopharmacology Bulletin* (1985). Rating scales and assessment instruments for use in pediatric psychopharmacology research. *21*(4).

Realmuto, G. N., Erickson, W. D., Yellin, A. M., Hopwood, J. H., & Greenberg, L. M. (1984). Clinical comparison of thiothixene and thioridazine in schizophrenic adolescents. *American Journal of Psychiatry, 41*, 440–442.

Richardson, J. S., & Zaleski, W. A. (1983). Naloxone and self-mutilation. *Biological Psychiatry, 18*, 99–101.

Rimland, B. (1973). High-dosage levels of certain vitamins in the treatment of children with severe mental disorders. In D. Hawkins & L. Pauling (Eds.), *Orthomolecular psychiatry*. San Francisco: W. H. Freeman.

Rimland, B., Callaway, E., & Dreyfus, P. (1978). The effect of high doses of vitamin $B_6$ on autistic children: A double-blind crossover study. *American Journal of Psychiatry, 135*, 472–475.

Ritvo, E. R., Yuwiler, A., Geller, E., Ornitz, E. M., Saeger, K., & Plotkin, S. (1970). Increased blood serotonin and platelets in early infantile autism. *Archives of General Psychiatry, 23*, 566–572.

Ritvo, E. R., Yuwiler, A., Geller, E., Kales, A. R., Rashkis, S., Schicor, A., Plotkin, S., Axelrod, R., & Howard, C. (1971). Effects of L-dopa in autism. *Journal of Autism and Childhood Schizophrenia, 1*, 190–205.

Ritvo, E. R., Freeman, B. J., Geller, E., & Yuwiler, A. (1983). Effects of fenfluramine on 14 outpatients with the syndrome of autism. *Journal of the American Academy of Child Psychiatry, 22*, 549–558.

Ritvo, E. R., Freeman, B. J., Yuwiler, A., Geller, E., Yokota, A., Schroth, P., & Novak, P. (1984). Study of fenfluramine in outpatients with syndrome of autism. *Journal of Pediatrics, 105*, 823–828.

Ritvo, E. R., Freeman, B. J., Yuwiler, A., Geller, E., Schroth, P., Yokota, A., Mason-Brothers, A., August, G., Klykylo, W., Leventhal, B., Lewis, K., Piggott, L., Realmuto, G., Stubbs, G., & Umansky, R. (1986). Fenfluramine treatment of autism: UCLA-collaborative study of 81 patients at nine medical centers. *Psychopharmacology Bulletin, 22*.

Rogeness, G. A., & Macedo, C. A. (1983). Therapeutic response of a schizophrenic boy to a methylphenidate-chlorpromazine combination. *American Journal of Psychiatry, 140*, 932–933.

Roukema, R. W., & Emery, L. (1970). Megavitamin therapy with severely disturbed children. *American Journal of Psychiatry, 127*, 249.

Sandman, C., Datta, P., Barron, J., Hoehler, F., Williams, C., & Swanson, J. (1983). Naloxone attenuates self-abusive behavior in developmentally disabled clients. *Applied Research in Mental Retardation, 4*, 5–11.

Sherwin, A. C., Flach, F. F., & Stokes, P. E. (1958). Treatment of psychoses in early childhood with triiodothyronine. *American Journal of Psychiatry, 115*, 166–167.

Simeon, J., Saletu, B., Saletu, M., Itil, T. M., & DaSilva, J. (1973). *Thiothixene in childhood psychoses.* Paper presented at the Third International Symposium on Phenothiazines, Rockville, Maryland.

Simpson, G. M., Lee, J. H., Zoubok, B., & Gardos, G. (1979). A rating scale for tardive dyskinesia. *Psychopharmacology* (Berlin), *64,* 171–179.

Varga, E., Sugerman, A. A., Varga, V., Zomorodi, A., Zomorodi, W., & Menken, M. (1982). Prevalence of spontaneous oral dyskinesias in the elderly. *American Journal of Psychiatry, 139,* 329–331.

Vereby, K., Volavka, J., & Clouet, D. (1978). Endorphins in Psychiatry: An overview and a hypothesis. *Archives of General Psychiatry, 35,* 877–888.

Volkmar, F., Paul, R., Cohen, D. J., & Shaywitz, B. A. (1983). Irritability in autistic children treated with fenfluramine. *New England Journal of Medicine, 309,* 187.

Waizer, J., Polizos, P., Hoffman, S. P., Engelhardt, D. M., & Margolis, R. A. (1972). A single-blind evaluation of thiothixene with outpatient schizophrenic children. *Journal of Autism and Childhood Schizophrenia, 2,* 378–386.

Weizman, R., Weizman, A., Tyano, S., Szekely, G., Weissman, B. A., & Sarne, Y. (1984). Humoral-endorphin blood levels in autistic, schizophrenic and healthy subjects. *Psychopharmacology, 82,* 368–370.

Werry, J. S., & Sprague, R. L. (1970). *Some issues in the design of psychopharmacological studies in children.* Paper presented at the meeting of the American Psychiatric Association, San Francisco.

Young, J. G., Kavanaugh, M. E., Anderson, G. M., Shaywitz, B. A., & Cohen, D. J. (1982). Clinical neurochemistry of autism and associated developmental disorders. *Journal of Autism and Developmental Disorders, 12,* 147–165.

# 14    *Depression*
## *Psychological Therapies*

JOHNNY L. MATSON AND MICHAEL CAREY

Since the mid-1970s, the assessment of child and adolescent depression has been studied extensively (Cantwell & Carlson, 1983). However, little attention has been focused on the development and the empirical evaluation of treatments for depression in these age ranges. This chapter is designed to briefly review the conceptual issues, assessment, and differential diagnostic methods used for childhood and adolescent depression. However, the primary emphasis of the chapter is a review of the psychologically based treatments, an area beginning to receive considerable attention. The various theoretical approaches and specific research studies are reviewed. Directions for future treatment research in depression of childhood and adolescence are also discussed.

## CONCEPTUAL ISSUES

Although initial confusion and lack of clarity were evident, researchers and clinicians have now generally agreed that children and adolescents experience a range of depressive behaviors (e.g., sadness, guilt, and sleep disturbance) (Carlson & Strober, 1979; Puig-Antich & Gittelman 1982). However, the existence of depression as a clinical syndrome or disorder (i.e., a response class of depressive behaviors) in childhood and adolescence was an issue of considerable debate in the past, and it was only after considerable discussion that the general nature of the disorder was agreed on (Cyntyn & McKnew, 1974; Kovacs & Beck, 1977; Lefkowitz & Burton, 1978; Puig-Antich & Gittelman, 1982). Four widely cited viewpoints have been identified in the experimental literature. The differences in views of the disorder have lead to much of the confusion that has existed. First, several psychoanalytic clinicians have argued that depression cannot exist in childhood and early adolescence in a form similar to that in adulthood because children lack the ego development necessary to experience a depressive disorder (Rie, 1966). Rie stated that the usual characteristics of adult depression are generally nonexistent in childhood because of the underdevelopment of the superego. Therefore, this orientation has had little involvement in empirical research. Rather, attention has been focused on the effects of early maternal deprivation (Spitz & Wolfe, 1946).

JOHNNY L. MATSON AND MICHAEL CAREY • Department of Psychology, Louisiana State University, Baton Rouge, Louisiana 70803-5501.

A second perspective has been advocated, that depression in childhood exists but has many unique or equivalent features (Arajavi & Huttenen, 1972). Proponents of this approach have advocated that the underlying depression is masked by other overt forms of psychopathology in childhood (e.g., fire setting, hyperactivity, enuresis, conduct disorders, truancy, and headaches). The list of masking symptoms has covered the entire spectrum of child psychopathology. Therefore, this approach has been criticized for the inability of its advocates to differentiate masked depression from other forms of general psychopathology (Kaslow & Rehm, 1983; Kovacs & Beck, 1977). The inclusive nature of the symptoms makes a differential diagnosis extremely difficult. Those who oppose the concept of masked depression have acknowledged that child and adolescent depression can exist and that it may be associated with other problem behaviors not commonly related to adult depression. In fact, it has recently been demonstrated empirically that depressed children and adolescents may suffer from at least one other concurrent disorder (Matson & Nieminen, 1986).

A third perspective has been proposed, that depressive *symptoms* do occur in normal child development, but that a *syndrome* does not exist (Lefkowitz & Burton, 1978). Specifically, Lefkowitz and Burton proposed that depressive symptoms occur so frequently that it would not be prudent to consider them a form of "psychopathology" in children. Moreover, persons who support this perspective have advocated that the depressive symptoms are transient and therefore do not require intervention. Costello (1980) criticized this perspective on three premises. First, he believes that this approach inappropriately focuses on the prevalence of individual symptoms as opposed to a pattern of behaviors (i.e., a response class). Additionally, the premise that depressive symptoms dissipate with increased age has not been supported. Rather, several studies have indicated a poor long-term prognosis for those children with a diagnosed depressive disorder (Eastgate & Gilmour, 1984; Kovacs, Fienberg, Crouse-Novak, Paulauskas. & Finkelstein, 1984a; Kovacs, Fienberg, Crouse-Novak, Paulauskas, Pollock, & Finkelstein, 1984b). Finally, Costello (1980) asserted that treatment of transient problems still has merit if it relieves discomfort, or if it prevents the subsequent development of a more severe problem.

A fourth viewpoint asserts that depression does exist in childhood and that it is similar to adult depression, although there may be some distinguishing characteristics (Kovacs & Beck, 1977). Kovacs and Beck reviewed the literature pertinent to the diagnosis of child and adolescent depression and found that the symptoms listed by various authors bore a surprising resemblance to the major characteristics of adult depression. Among the common symptoms were depressed mood, low self-esteem, lack of energy, and sleep disturbance. Additionally, advocates of this approach have proposed that there are unique features that vary with level of development and chronological age.

In summary, researchers and clinicians have recently asserted that depressive disorders do exist in childhood and adolescence and that they bear considerable resemblance to adult depressive disorders, although distinguishing features may exist (Carlson & Strober, 1979; Puig-Antich & Gittelman, 1982; Reynolds, 1985). Thus, the later perspective has gained prominence, primarily because of the successful application of DSM-III (American Psychiatric Association—APA, 1980) adult criteria of depressive disorders. However, there is a ground swell of support for the opinion that the study of child psychopathology risks "adultomorphism" (Phillips, Draguns, & Bartlett, 1975). Therefore, Rutter, Izard, and Read (1986) have advocated the study of child and adolescent depression, approaching the topic from a developmental psychopathology perspective in order to account for the significant changes in affective disorders associated with increased age.

## ASSESSMENT

Assessment from a behavioral perspective is strongly linked to treatment planning and execution. Specifically, the assessment process is concerned with determining how an individual behaves rather than with assessing the person's underlying personality (Bornstein, Bornstein, & Dawson, 1984). Thus, the behavioral assessment of depression is focused on determining the antecedents, behaviors (i.e., motoric, cognitive, and physiological). and consequences of the youth's depressive behavior across informants (e.g., parents, teachers, and self) and settings (e.g., home, school, and work). Frequently, this goal is accomplished by using information obtained from direct and indirect sources. Direct sources might include an examination of the youth's incomplete or completed school assignments, behavioral observations, archival records (e.g., medical and school records), and physiological recordings, whereas indirect sources might include data collected from self-ratings, behavior checklists, and interviews. Later, data collected by direct and indirect means can be assimilated to provide a comprehensive assessment that directs treatment planning.

Recently, attention has been directed primarily to the development of psychometrically sound measures of the various behaviors associated with depression, by the use of different informants (e.g., self-report and parent report). Generally, the greatest advances have occurred in the development of norm-referenced self-report instruments and structured interviews, although they still require further validation. It is beyond the scope of this chapter to review all the available assessment instruments, particularly given the chapter's focus on treatment. Therefore, the reader is referred to several recent reviews of the measures appropriate for assessing depression in children and adolescents: Kaslow and Rehm (1983); Kazdin and Petti (1982); Rehm, Leventon, and Ivens (1988); and Witt, Cavell, Heffer, Carey, and Marten (1988), as well as to a book devoted to the topic: Frame and Matson (1987). The remainder of this section focuses on finding related to the integration of assessment data on depression.

In general, low to moderate congruence has been obtained between the five most frequently used groups of informants: parents, teachers, peers, clinicians, and self-ratings (Moretti, Fine, Haley, & Marriage, 1985; Reynolds, Anderson, & Bartell, 1986). Additionally, teachers and parents routinely over- or underestimate the level and severity of youths' depressive behaviors (Kazdin, Dawson, Unis, & Rancarello, 1983; Moretti et al., 1985). These findings are not surprising, however, as the various informants spend variable amounts of time with the youths and observe them in different situations (situational specificity). Thus, researchers and clinicians have advocated that information be obtained from several sources.

Another issue is the nature of the behavior being assessed. Specifically, several of the primary components of depression involve behaviors that are not readily observable to teachers, parents, and peers (i.e., dysphoric mood, worry, and suicidal ideation). Thus, parents, teachers, peers, and professionals must rely on the self-reports of the youths. Several investigators have therefore advocated that self-report instruments should routinely be included in the assessment process to assess the subjective experiences of the youths, along with information from other informants and methods (Reynolds *et al.*, 1986; Saylor, Finch, Spirito, & Bennett, 1984), although caution must be exercised when self-ratings are obtained from young or developmentally delayed children. In line with the Behavioral Assessment Grid (Cone, 1978), an added advantage of self-rating instruments is that all three behavioral modalities (i.e., motor, cognitive, and physiological) can be measured by means of self-ratings (Mash & Terdal, 1982).

Also to be considered are less traditional measures of depression and the assessment of ancillary but related areas. Among the depression measures that the clinician and the researcher should consider are standardized interviews such as the Kiddie-SADS and DICA (Witt, *et al.*, 1988). These methods use a branching system in which various responses determine other questions to be asked. Also, biological measures in the form of chemical assays, such as the DEX test and EMG facial readings, have received some attention and are likely to be explored further in the future.

Social skills are perhaps the most frequently studied related area. Helsel and Matson (1985) demonstrated a close relationship between social skills and depression in children. These data expand on the work of Lewinsohn, Antonuccio, Steinmetz, and Teri (1984) with adults. Lewinsohn *et al.* made the identification and treatment of social skills excesses and deficits a major focus of treatment. Moreover, Lewinsohn and Hoberman (1982) have reported significant relations between pleasant and unpleasant events and depression. Thus, clinicians may wish to incorporate a social-skills (Matson, Esveldt-Dawson, Andrasik, Ollendick, Petti, & Hersen, 1980), reinforcement-schedule (Cautela, 1977), or activity checklist (Carey, Kelley, Buss, & Scott, 1986b) in their assessments. Furthermore, considering the demonstrated interrelation of depression and anxiety and their impact on prognosis, clinicians may wish to concurrently assess for anxiety symptoms and syndromes (Weissman, 1985).

In summary, it appears from the available literature that several methods and informants, including self-report, as well as chemical and physiological measures should be used as guides in treatment planning. Moreover, in the spirit of behavioral assessment, the clinician should evaluate these behaviors systematically and continuously in order to monitor the efficacy of the treatment and the maintenance of treatment gains. A clear differential diagnosis and the identification of depression subtypes and specific deficit areas have important implications for choosing treatments. Specific intervention techniques constitute the remainder of our discussion.

## ADULT INTERVENTIONS

A number of intervention strategies have been developed from a behavioral (learning) model of depression in adults. As in most areas of psychopathology, the identification and treatment initially developed with adults have been employed with children. In several instances, variations of these procedures have been used with children and adolescents.

Perhaps one of most extensively researched treatment models was proposed by Lewinsohn, Sullivan and Grosscup (1980) and is behavioral in orientation. Lewinsohn and associates proposed several hypotheses concerning the relation of depression to reinforcement. First, they proposed that a low rate of response-contingent reinforcement is an important antecedent of the occurrence of depression in adults. Additionally, Lewinsohn and associates proposed that high frequencies of unpleasant, aversive, or punishing activities or events are related to depressive disorders. They suggested that these situations play a causal role in the development of depression. These hypotheses have received considerable empirical support (Lewinsohn *et al.*, 1984). However, the correlational nature of the findings makes conclusive causal statements impossible.

Lewinsohn *et al.* (1984) developed a manual for a psychoeducational intervention that has a number of related components in their treatment package for depression. Currently, the intervention package is comprised of 12 sessions of group therapy. Each group is usually composed of six to eight depressed adults and is conducted by a trained instructor. The participants are screened for appropriateness via a comprehensive assessment procedure. This procedure includes the use of a structured interview, the completion of various self-report instruments, an assessment of suicidal behavior, social support, medical and physical health, and the participants' reading ability. Generally, individuals are excluded from participation if they evince acute psychotic symptoms or have serious hearing or visual impairments. Moreover, individuals may be excluded from participation if they evince serious suicidal tendencies and are not receiving additional treatment (e.g., individual or drug therapy).

The intervention is conducted over an 8-week period; two sessions are conducted during each of the first 4 weeks. Generally, the sessions include an agenda and progress with a pep talk, a review of the previous session and homework assignment, a rationale for the current session, a lecture, a preview of the next session, and the assignment of the session's homework. Moreover, follow-up sessions are conducted at 1 and 6 months posttreatment.

During the initial two sessions, the participants become familiar with the session rules, are provided a brief description of the social learning explanation of depression, and are taught self-change skills. The next two sessions are devoted to teaching the participants relaxation training. Sessions 5 and 6 involve teaching the participants the relationship between their engagement in specific activities (i.e., pleasant and unpleasant) and depression. Furthermore, they are instructed to self-monitor their behavior and to plan weekly pleasant activities. The next four sessions involve teaching the participants two methods of constructive thinking as well as assertion training. The two final sessions are devoted to maintaining treatment gains. The intervention package has received substantial empirical support with adults. However, future studies are needed employing direct trials with other psychological and pharmacological interventions (see Lewinsohn, Sullivan, & Grosscup, 1982).

Another treatment approach was proposed by Beck, Rush, Shaw, and Emery (1979). This approach is often referred to as a cognitive approach, although the intervention is probably best termed a *cognitive-behavioral intervention*.

This model stresses the etiological importance of cognitive variables, although behavioral components are acknowledged to have a smaller role in the development and maintenance of depression in adults. Thus, this model evaluates the contents of the "black box." The primary component of the model of Beck *et al.* revolves around the concept of a "cognitive triad," which includes a negative view of the self, the world, and the future. The negative view of the self centers on the individuals' view of themselves as inadequate, worthless, and defective. The second component, the view of the world, focuses on the individuals' perception of their interactions with the environment. Specifically, the client often construes data in favor of self-depreciation and frequently minimizes his or her success in mastery experiences. The third component, the view of the future, results in the individuals' perception of impending doom or hopelessness, increasing their expectations of failure and unpleasant consequences. A treatment package with a detailed treatment manual has been developed by Beck and associates (1979).

Generally speaking, cognitive-behavioral (C-B) therapy is a structured, active, short-term therapy for depression that uses behavioral and cognitive change strategies. Like the Lewinsohn and associates (1984) approach, the cognitive-behavioral treatment has usually been used with unipolar, nonpsychotic adult clients. This therapy approach stresses a collaboration between the client and the therapist toward the goals of treatment. Clients are taught to test the accuracy of their thoughts (beliefs) via their behavior's outcomes. The cognitive-behavioral therapy is limited to 24 sessions spanning a period of 12 weeks.

During the first 2–3 weeks, the client is usually seen twice weekly in order to reduce the risk of premature termination. Usually, the first 5–10 minutes of each session are concerned with collaboratively setting an agenda, reviewing the client's reactions to the previous session and her or his homework assignments. The body of the session is concerned with addressing the issues comprising the agenda in an *a priori* fashion. The final minutes are reserved for the client to summarize the session and to thoroughly discuss any new homework assignments. Generally, this pattern is maintained through the course of therapy. However, the content of the sessions changes as therapy progresses.

In the early sessions, the behavioral techniques are used most frequently, partially because of the clients' inability to engage in complex cognitive examination and the increased severity of depressive symptomatology. Behavioral techniques—such as weekly activity scheduling (hourly), graded task assignments (i.e., getting out of bed, getting dressed, eating, and grooming), self-monitoring of mastery and pleasurable experiences, role play, and, as needed, assertion training—are used to target the clients' idiographic problems. Cognitive techniques such as the self-monitoring of automatic thoughts, hypothesis testing, reattribution training, and searching for alternative solutions are most frequently used in the middle and late stages of therapy. The middle sessions are focused on complex problems that require intense cognitive evaluation. In contrast, the late sessions shift toward a generalization of the treatment effects.

Currently, the effectiveness of the cognitive-behavioral intervention package outlined by Beck *et al.* (1979) is receiving considerable support via well-controlled group-outcome trials (e.g., Blackburn, Bishop, Glen, Whalley, & Christie, 1981; Hollon, Derubeis, Tuason, Evans, Weimer, & Garvey, 1984; Murphy, Simons, Wetzel, & Lustman, 1984; Rush, Beck, Kovacs & Hollon, 1977; Shaw, 1977). On the basis of these studies, cognitive-behavioral treatment appears to be as effective as pharmacological interventions and may aid in the prevention of depressive relapses (Kovacs, Rush, Beck, & Hollon, 1981). A number of investigations have attempted to confirm the assumption that successful treatment outcome is related to changes in the individual's cognitive processes. However, there is no conclusive evidence that Beck's hypotheses, linking faulty cognitive processes to depression, is accurate (Rush & Giles, 1982). Thus, continued research is needed to determine the etiology of affective disorders.

A third treatment approach is the self-control model originally proposed by Rehm (1977). This approach was derived from Kanfer's self-control theory (1970) and incorporates many of the features of Lewinsohn's and Beck's treatment strategies. Self-control is viewed as a process that assists the client in altering the probabilities of a particular response in the absence of immediate external reinforcement (Rehm, 1977). In this model, it is proposed that depression can be conceptualized as deficits in one of the three components that define the process of self-control: self-monitoring, self-evaluation, and self-reinforcement. Self-monitoring involves the individual's making self-observations of the antecedents and consequences of his or her behavior in specific situations. Self-evaluation involves comparing one's estimation of his or her performance with a subjective criterion. Moreover, self-reinforcement assumes that individuals can self-administer reinforcement or punishment to increase or decrease the frequency of their behavior. Thus, Rehm identified several self-control deficits that contribute to the development and maintenance of depression in adults, such as selective attention to negative events or immediate versus long-term events; overly restrictive self-evaluations; a negative attribution style; low rates of contingent positive reinforcement; and high rates of self-punishment.

Self-control therapy has most often been administered in a group format. Like the two previously mentioned therapies, self-control treatment is a highly structured, short-term (i.e., 6- to 12-week) intervention program that uses homework assignments and self-monitoring procedures. The treatment involves teaching clients how to self-monitor their behavior (e.g., positive) and is followed by an examination of the clients' evaluation of their behavior. Moreover, clients are taught to effectively self-reinforce their behavior without any external reward.

Initial outcome trials using a group format have been promising (Fuchs & Rehm, 1977; Rehm, Fuchs, Roth, Kornblith, & Romano, 1979). However, the clients in the initial studies were most often female volunteers from the community. Furthermore, the clients were seen in most cases by graduate students in psychology, an approach limiting the findings generalization to self-referred populations treated by inexperienced clinicians. Therefore, further replications are needed to examine the efficacy of the self-control treatment approach.

In summary, each of the three aforementioned treatment approaches to adult depression have demonstrated some treatment efficacy in comparison to no-treatment conditions; the strongest evidence has resulted from the Beck *et al.* (1979) and the Lewinshon *et al.* (1984) approaches, which have demonstrated treatment efficacy across a series of studies conducted in different settings.

However, only Beck's approach has been systematically evaluated in comparison to pharmacological therapies. All three approaches have obtained equivocal data to support their etiological hypotheses.

## CHILD AND ADOLESCENT INTERVENTIONS

Although an extensive number of treatment outcome studies have been conducted on adults, few intervention studies have examined the efficacy of treatment for depression in children and adolescents. Currently, the majority of investigations have examined antidepressant medications as a treatment for depression in children and adolescents. However, Elkins and Rapoport (1983) indicated that antidepressant medications may not be the treatment of choice with children because they exhibit fewer vegetative symptoms than adults. Additionally, the dosages needed by children often exceed the dosages used by adults and frequently result in side effects and substantial withdrawal effects (Law, Petti, & Kazdin, 1981). Thus, Kaslow and Rehm (1983) suggested that "public concern over the use of psychotropic medications with children may constrain this trend" (p. 33). A more detailed review of this topic, and of the medications and dosages used, is given in Chapter 15.

A number of psychological interventions have been developed for the treatment of child and adolescent depression. Several psychodynamic and family-therapy case studies have appeared in the literature (Bemporad, 1978; Boverman & French, 1979; Furman, 1974; Gilpin, 1976; Sacks, 1979). Though these case studies report improvement, they frequently give scanty descriptions of the client's characteristics, the diagnostic criteria, and the treatment strategy, and there is an overreliance on subjective criteria of success. Moreover, the use of a case study approach, as opposed to an experimental treatment-outcome methodology (i.e., single-case vs. group outcome), makes it unclear whether these interventions actually resulted in a reduction of the depressive symptoms, or whether there was simply a spontaneous remission.

The past decade also has seen a growth in the number of studies using single-case and group-outcome research designs to evaluate behavioral and cognitive-behavioral interventions in child and adolescent depression. The data in these studies are better controlled, and thus, the results are more reliable and valid estimates of treatment efficacy. The approaches used have usually been similar to the treatment packages used with adults (i.e., social skills training, behavioral therapy, cognitive-behavioral therapy, and self-control). Generally speaking, the studies that have used a single-case methodology have examined the effectiveness of social-skills-training interventions for depression in children.

### Single-Case Designs

Our inspection of the literature indicated that five single-case studies were specifically designed to examined social skills interventions with children exhibiting depressive behaviors or a depressive disorder. Calpin and Cincirpini (1978) evaluated the effects of a social-skills-training intervention on two depressed inpatient children. A multiple-baseline design was used to evaluate the efficacy of the social skills intervention. Both children were assessed with the BAT-C (Bornstein, Bellack, & Hersen, 1977) and were found to have social skills deficits. The treatment included instructions concerning appropriate interpersonal interactions, modeling, and feedback on their responses and resulted in improvements in both children. Another study, by Calpin and Kornblith (1978), employed a social skills program using a multiple-baseline design to treat four hospitalized children who met RDC criteria for depression. Additionally, the children also exhibited aggressive behavior and social skills deficits. An intervention similar to that used in the previous study, by Calpin and Cincirpini (1978) was employed and resulted in improvement in the targeted behaviors. However, only three of the children maintained their improvement at follow-up.

In another behaviorally based study, Matson *et al.*, (1980) used a multiple-baseline design across subjects with four emotionally disturbed inpatients. Two males and two females, all between the ages of 9 and 11, served as subjects. The presenting problems of the children included somatic complaints, antisocial behavior, and poor school adaptation. Their social skills were assessed via scenarios that were identified as causing problems for the children and that were later targeted for intervention. Each child evinced several depressive behaviors. The targeted behaviors were appropriate verbal content, appropriate affect, appropriate eye contact, and appropriate body posture. Moreover, a second assessor was present to evaluate the interrater reliability, which averaged 86%. The four targeted behaviors were continuously assessed during baseline, social skills intervention, observation training, and follow-up.

The social skills intervention involved the therapist-provided instructions, information feedback, role-playing, and social reinforcement for appropriate behavior. Specifically, the youths were trained in a group on individual assessment scenes. These scenes were written on 3 × 5 cards and were read to the youths to facilitate a response from the child engaging in the role play. Feedback was provided by the therapist based on the appropriateness of the child's response. When necessary, the therapist modeled the appropriate behavior. The children improved in their responses to training and generalization scenes as well as inward behavior. Furthermore, the treatment gains were maintained at a 15-week follow-up. However, self-ratings by the children indicated low levels of correspondence with the other performance measures and the findings' generalizability to youths with depressive disorders (i.e., major depression and dysthymic disorder) is diminished because the youths were not formally diagnosed as exhibiting a depressive disorder.

A fourth study, conducted by Frame, Matson, Sonis, Fialkov, and Kazdin (1982), evaluated the effectiveness of a behavioral intervention with a 10-year-old male. The child was a psychiatric inpatient with borderline mental ability who had a previous history of suicidal ideation, gestures, temper tantrums, and poor school performance. A multiple-baseline design across phases (baseline, treatment, and follow-up) was used; the assessment interview was videotaped.

The assessment involved having the child's mother, as opposed to the child, complete the Children's Depression Inventory (CDI; Kovacs & Beck, 1977), the Child Behavior Checklist (Achenbach, 1978), and the Bellevue Index of Depression (Petti, 1978). As reported by the mother, the child received high scores on all measures. Moreover, a naive rater scored the videotape interview of the child and also completed the CDI and a depression adjective checklist.

Furthermore, hospital staff identified the following problems, which were later targeted for intervention: inappropriate body position, poor eye contact, poor speech quality, and bland affect.

Treatment involved a videotaped social-skills-training program that included role-play situations, instructions, modeling, and performance feedback. Results were substantial decreases in problem behaviors, with a moderate rebound of problem behaviors at the 8-week follow-up. As stated by Frame *et al.* (1980), one limitation of this study, as of the aforementioned studies, is its inability to demonstrate that the depressive disorder had remitted.

Another single-case study—of three depressed male adolescents—was conducted by Schloss, Schloss and Harris (1984), using a multiple-baseline design. All three youths were diagnosed as exhibiting a schizoaffective disorder. The youths' ages ranged from 15 to 18 years, and they were receiving antipsychotic medication concurrently throughout the course of treatment. The intervention consisted of interpersonal skills training, which focused on teaching the youths to talk politely in their school settings. The goal of the intervention was to increase the youths' frequency of appropriate greetings and goodbyes to other youths and adults. Specifically, the intervention incorporated modeling, behavioral rehearsal, information feedback, and social reinforcement. The authors reported dramatic increases in the frequency of appropriate social skills (i.e., greetings and goodbyes) emitted to other youths and adults. However, it was unclear whether the aforementioned changes substantially decreased the youths' schizoaffective disorder.

In summary, several multiple-baseline single-case designs have been used that show that social-skills-training approaches have considerable promise as viable treatments of depressive behaviors. However, additional studies are needed to replicate and refine these treatment strategies and to determine if social skills interventions similar to the aforementioned treatments can be used to successfully remit depressive disorders (i.e., response classes), as distinguished from discrete depressive behaviors. Furthermore, future studies should incorporate self-ratings of depression at crucial phases (i.e., pretreatment, posttreatment, and follow-up) in order to effectively assess whether the youths experience a significant reduction in depressive behaviors.

## Group-Outcome Studies

In contrast to the large number of controlled group-outcome studies conducted on adults, only three such studies on children and adolescents have been identified. The first controlled group-outcome study to appear in the literature was conducted by Butler, Miezitis, Friedman, and Cole (1980) in the Toronto school system. The investigation compared the efficacy of two active treatments (role play and cognitive restructuring) to an attention placebo and a classroom control condition. The subjects were 56 fifth- and sixth-grade children who were selected from 562 children in five elementary schools through a screening procedure. All children were administered a four-measure test battery, which included the CDI, the Norwicki and Strickland Locus of Control Scale for Children (NSLOC; Norwicki & Strickland, 1973), the Piers-Harris Children's Self-Concept Scale (Piers, 1969), and the Moyal-Miezitis Stimulus Appraisal Questionnaire (MMSAQ; Moyal, 1977). All measures were scored in the direction of maladaption. Specifically, children were selected for inclusion in the treatment study if they received scores 1½ standard deviations above the sample mean on two or more measures or 1½ standard deviations on their summation score. All teachers ($N = 22$) were asked to identify children who displayed low self-esteem and poor academic achievement. However, the children were not formally diagnosed as having a depressive disorder. The selected children were randomly assigned to one of the four conditions. All of the children included in the study were treated in groups at the school for 10 one-hour weekly sessions. A brief review of the components and focus of each of the treatment conditions follows.

The role-play treatment was modeled after the approach advocated by Joyce, Weil, and Wald (1972). Initially, each session included a warm-up phase, followed by a review of the previous session. Next, a problem was identified, and the problem situation was role-played; a discussion followed. This procedure was repeated for a second problem, and the session ended with a summary of the session and the assignment of homework. Specifically, the treatment plan focused on facilitating social interactions, teaching problem-solving skills, and sensitizing the child to the thoughts and feelings of self and others by means of the aforementioned procedure. The cognitive restructuring intervention was reportedly influenced by the Beck (1976), Ellis (1962), and Knaus (1974) approaches. This particular treatment condition was directed toward teaching the children to identify their irrational beliefs, to enhance their listening skills, to adopt logical alternatives to their irrational beliefs, and to discover the relation between thoughts and feelings. The cognitive restructuring sessions included an introduction, exercises, discussion, and homework assignments. Students in the attention-placebo condition were presented with the group-investigation model of teaching (Joyce & Weil, 1972). The final condition, classroom controls, involved children who engaged only in their regular classroom activities and who were later reassessed at posttreatment and follow-up.

Significant differences were obtained in the four conditions on CDI and NSLOC scores; the pretest scores were used as covariates. Unfortunately, no posttests were reported comparing the four conditions. Rather, Butler *et al.* (1980) concluded that the role-play condition was marginally superior to the other active treatment and the two inert conditions on the basis of qualitative changes (teacher report and CDI score changes).

A second group-outcome study, conducted by Stark, Reynolds, and Kaslow (in press) compared the effectiveness of behavior therapy, self-control therapy, and a wait-list control. The behavior therapy approach was based on Lewinsohn's model, and the self-control treatment was based on Rehm's self-control treatment package for adult depression. Both treatments consisted of twelve 45- to 50-minute sessions completed during a 5-week time period. All participants were then randomly assigned to one of the three conditions.

The subjects were 29 children from Grades 4–6 who were initially screened with the CDI from a larger sample of 372 youths. Children who obtained a CDI score greater than 16 on the initial administration and had received parental consent were tested on additional measures: the Children's Depression Scale (CDS; Reynolds, 1988), the Revised-Children's Manifest Anxiety Scale (R-CMAS; Reynolds & Richmond, 1978), and the Coopersmith Self-Esteem Inventory (SEI; Coopersmith, 1975). Furthermore, each child was interviewed in a brief, semistructured depression interview (i.e., using the CDRS; Children's

Depression Rating Scale-Revised, Poznanski, Grossman, Buchsbaum, Banegas, Freeman, & Gibbons, 1984), and the parent completed the CBCL. Children who obtained a CDI score of 13 or higher on the second administration were included in the treatment study.

The self-control and behavior-therapy groups improved on the CDI compared to the wait-list control group, with trends toward significance on the other self-rating and interview measures of depression. However, no significant differences were found between the two active treatments. At the 8-week follow-up, no significant differences were found between the self-control and the behavior-therapy groups on the two self-report measures. However, a significant difference on the child interview scale was found between the two active treatments, with the self-control group faring better than the group in the behavioral condition.

The condition with the largest percentage of subjects evincing depression scores below the recommended cutoff was the self-control condition (78%), followed by the behavioral condition (60%). As expected, only one of the subjects in the wait-list control group (11%) had a score below the recommended CDI cutoff. A similar pattern of results also occurred at follow-up. Furthermore, between-groups comparisons on the R-CMAS and the SEI indicated that no significant differences were found on the R-CMAS, although significant differences were found on the SEI. Specifically, the self-control group reported higher levels of self-esteem than the behavioral groups.

Within-subject comparisons indicated that both active treatments had resulted in decreases in anxiety, whereas only the self-control group reported improvements in self-esteem. Therefore, both treatments showed considerable promise for treating depression in young children. However, as in the Butler *et al.* (1980) study, the subjects represented an analogue population.

A third group-outcome study was conducted by Reynolds and Coats (in press), who compared the relative effectiveness of a cognitive-behavioral intervention, relaxation training, and a wait-list control condition as treatments of depression in adolescents. The subjects were recruited from the school systems by means of a two-stage screening process.

Initially, 800 high-school students were screened with the two most reliable and extensively validated self-report depression screening measures for adolescents: the Beck Depression Inventory (BDI; Beck, Ward, Mendelson, Mock, & Erbaugh, 1961) and the Reynolds Adolescent Depression Scale (RADS; Reynolds, 1988). Individuals who obtained BDI scores $\geq 10$ and RADS scores $\geq 72$ and who had obtained parental consent were then readministered the BDI and the RADS as well as several other measures: the State-Trait Anxiety Inventory (STAI; Spielberger, Gorsuch, & Lushene, 1980), the BDI, and measures of general and academic self-concept. Those students who obtained a BDI score $\geq 12$; a RADS score $\geq 72$; and a BID score $\geq 20$ and who were not currently receiving treatment for depression after the second screening were included in the intervention study. Thus, 29 subjects met all of the aforemention criteria and agreed to participate. These subjects were randomly assigned to the conditions and were treated in groups. Although, this population was also not a self-referred clinical population, the use of such a rigorous screening process increased the generalizability of the findings. Moreover, such a procedure offers an effective procedure for screening large populations (i.e., in schools) for depression (Reynolds, 1985).

The elements common to both active treatments were that the treatments were brief and were conducted in a group format. All subjects were seen for 10 (50-minute) sessions over the course of 5 weeks. The relaxation-training condition was modeled after the procedure reported by Jacobsen (1938). Initially, the subjects were presented with a rationale for the treatment, focusing on the relation between stress and depression. All subjects in the relaxation-training groups were asked to complete homework assignments and to practice their relaxation skills between sessions. The training involved teaching the adolescents to progressively relax specific muscle groups. The later sessions were focused on providing the youths with information and skills that would facilitate generalization across situations.

The cognitive-behavioral treatment focused on training self-control skills by teaching self-monitoring, self-evaluation, and self-reinforcement skills and by employing homework assignments. The intervention was modeled after the treatment approach advocated by Rehm (1977).

Significant differences were found on all three depression measures (the BDI, the RADS, and the BID), and the two treatment groups successfully decreased their levels of depression in comparison to the wait-list control group. However, no differences were found between the two active treatment groups. At 5-week follow-up, significant improvements were found on the BDI and the BID, but not on the RADS. Similarly, both active treatment groups, did better than the wait-list group but not significantly better than each other. An inspection of qualitative changes indicated that 83% of the subjects in the cognitive-behavioral treatment and 75% in the relaxation condition had moved into the normal range on the BDI, whereas no subjects (0%) in the wait-list condition approached normality.

Interestingly, significant differences in anxiety level were obtained only between the relaxation and the wait-list control groups, suggesting some treatment specificity. It appears that the cognitive-behavioral intervention had a more specific effect on levels of depression, whereas the relaxation training may have had a general effect on depression and anxiety. Furthermore, no significant improvement was found in general self-concept, although both active treatments resulted in significant improvements in academic self-concept.

In summary, all three group-outcome studies indicated that various behaviorally oriented interventions can be effective for depression in children and adolescents. All three studies used analogue populations that had not been formally diagnosed as suffering from a major depressive or dysthymic disorder. Thus, their generalization to clinical samples is diminished. In the absence of other firm empirical findings, these studies offer at least potentially viable strategies for treating depressed youths. However, the practicing clinician may need to modify these approaches to suit the specific needs of the client. Furthermore, additional studies are needed to examine the benefits of combining drug and psychosocial interventions.

## Summary and Conclusion

Clinicians and researchers have reached a general consensus that the response class often referred to as depression exists in children and adolescents. Moreover, the rapid rise in parasuicide and suicide in adolescence and the relation of poor academic achievement to depression has prompted a considerable increase in the number of empirical studies examining depression at these age levels (Hawton, 1986; Reynolds, 1985). So far, the majority of the empirical studies have focused on the development of reliable and valid assessments of depression. Rating scales and structured interviews have particularly experienced considerable growth (Carey, Faulstich, Gresham, Ruggiero, & Enyart, 1986a; Witt et al., 1988). Moreover, data concerning the poor long-term prognosis of depressed children and adolescents necessitates the development of effective treatment strategies. Unfortunately, researchers and clinicians have often simply modified adult approaches to suit child and adolescent psychopathology.

For example, the diagnostic criteria for depression in the DSM-III (APA, 1980) have been applied without revision to children and adolescents, although rationally derived age-specific behaviors are also listed. Furthermore, the DSM-III approach yields a decision only about whether the disorder is present or absent and does not account for differences in the level of dysfunctioning of youths diagnosed with the same disorder. Thus, a multidimensional approach that accounts for differences in level of functioning may be more appropriate. Additionally, a similar bias toward "adultomorphism" (Phillips et al., 1975) has also occurred in the development of assessment instruments and interventions.

Several interventions have been developed and subjected to an initial empirical evaluation (i.e., single-case, and controlled group-outcome studies) and appear to be promising. Specifically, in five single-case designs, behaviorally based social-skills training has been demonstrated to be effective in reduce depressive behaviors. However, future studies are needed to determine if social skills interventions can successfully resolve episodes of depression and can prevent future episodes from occurring (Kazdin & Wilson, 1978). Thus, additional single-case studies are needed that use standard diagnostic criteria. These studies must continue to demonstrate generalizability outside role-play situations. For instance, ratings from other informants familiar with the client would be helpful, along with self-ratings at all relevant phases (i.e., pretreatment, postreatment, and follow-up).

Also, the three group-outcome studies have demonstrated that self-control, cognitive-behavioral, and relaxation-training interventions are more effective than no treatment for depressive behaviors in school populations. Specifically, the Reynolds and Coats (in press) controlled group-outcome-study comparisons indicate that relaxation training resulted in a substantially higher percentage of adolescents who moved into the normal range. The recommendations presented for the single-case social-skills interventions also apply to these interventions. Furthermore, future studies are needed comparing other psychological interventions and pharmacological treatments.

Several additional recommendations apply to the intervention studies discussed. Specifically, future studies should use the full range of child and adolescent populations (outpatient, inpatient, school, and detention center) to determine which interventions are most appropriate with specific populations. Also, future studies should assess the response classes related to depression (e.g., acting-out behavior, anxiety, and fears) to determine whether the interventions have treatment-specific effects or result in improvement across a wide range of behavioral response classes.

In sum, it is likely that clinicians will be confronted with increased referrals for depression, particularly among adolescents, and will be asked to intervene. This review has offered some alternatives and techniques that may prove useful in standard clinical practice.

## REFERENCES

Achenbach, T. M. (1978). The Child Behavior Profile: 1. Boys aged 6–11. *Journal of Consulting and Clinical Psychology, 46*, 478–488.

American Psychiatric Association. (1980). *The diagnostic and statistical manual of mental disorders* (3rd ed.—DSM-III). Washington, DC: Author.

Arajavi, T., & Huttenen, M. (1972). Encropresis and enuresis as symptoms of depression. In A. L. Annell (Ed.), *Depressive states in childhood and adolescence*. Stockholm; Almquist & Wiksell.

Beck, A. T. (1976). *Cognitive therapy and the emotional disorders*. New York: International Universities Press.

Beck, A. T., Ward, C., Mendelson, M., Mock, J., & Erbaugh, J. (1961). An inventory for measuring depression. *Archives of General Psychiatry, 4*, 53–63.

Beck, A. T., Rush, A. J., Shaw, B., & Emery, G. (1979). *Cognitive therapy of depression*. New York: Guilford Press.

Bemporad, J. (1978). Manifest symptomatology of depression in children and adolescents. In S. Arieti & J. Bemporad (Eds.), *Severe and mild depression: The psychotherapeutic approach*. New York: Basic Books.

Blackburn, I. M., Bishop, S., Glen, A. I., Whalley, L., & Christie, J. E. (1981). The efficacy of cognitive therapy in depression: A treatment trial using cognitive therapy and pharmacotherapy, each alone and in combination. *British Journal of Psychiatry, 139*, 181–189.

Bornstein, M. R., Bellack, A. S., & Hersen, M. (1977). Social skills training for unassertive children: A multiple baseline analysis. *Journal of Applied Behavior Analysis, 10*, 183–195.

Bornstein, P. H., Bornstein, M. T., & Dawson, B. (1984). Integrated assessment and treatment. In T. H. Ollendick & M. Hersen (Eds.), *Child behavioral assessment*. New York: Pergamon Press.

Boverman, H., & French, A. P. (1979). Treatment of depressed child. In A. French & I. Berlin (Eds.), *Depression in children and adolescents*. New York: Human Sciences Press.

Butler, L., Miezitis, S., Freidman, R., & Cole, E. (1980). The effect of two school-based intervention programs on depressive symptoms in preadolescents. *American Educational Research Journal, 17*, 111–119.

Calpin, J. P., & Cincirpini, P. M. (1978). *A multiple baseline analysis of social skills in children*. Paper presented at Midwestern Association for Behavior Analysis, Chicago, May.

Calpin, J. P., & Kornblith, S. J. (1978). *Training aggressive children in conflict resolution skills*. Paper presented at the Association for the Advancement of Behavior Therapy, Chicago, November.

Cantwell, D. P., & Carlson, G. A. (1983). *Affective disorders in childhood and adolescence: An update*. New York: SP Medical & Scientific Books.

Carey, M. P., Faulstich, M. E., Gresham, F. M., Ruggiero, L., & Enyart, P. (1986a). *The Children's Depression Inventory: Construct and discriminant validity across clinical and normal populations*. Submitted for publication.

Carey, M. P., Kelley, M. L., Buss, R. R., & Scott, O. (1986b). Relationship of activity to depression in adolescents: Development of the Adolescent Activity Checklist. *Journal of Consulting and Clinical Psychology, 54*, 320–322.

Carlson, G., & Strober, M. (1979). Affective disorders in adolescence. *Psychiatric Clinics of North America, 2*, 511–526.

Cautela, J. R. (1977). *Behavior analysis forms for clinical intervention*. Champaigne, IL: Research Press Company.

Cone, J. D. (1978). The Behavioral Assessment Grid (BAG): A conceptual framework and taxonomy. *Behavior Therapy, 9*, 882–888.

Coopersmith, S. (1975). *Self-Esteem Inventory—Form B*. Lafayette, CA: Self Esteem Institute.

Costello, C. (1980). Three basic but questionable assumptions in the Lefkowitz and Burton critique. *Psychological Bulletin, 87*, 185–190.

Cytryn, L. & McKnew, D. H. (1974). Factors influencing the changing clinical expression of the depressive process in children. *American Journal of Psychiatry, 131*, 879–881.

Eastgate, J., & Gilmour, L. (1984). Long-term outcome of depressed children: A follow-up study. *Developmental Medicine and Child Neurology, 26*, 68–72.

Elkins, R., & Rapoport, J. L. (1983). Psychopharmacology of adult and childhood depression: An overview. In D. P. Cantwell & G. A. Carlson (Eds.), *Affective disorders in childhood and adolescence: An update.* New York: Spectrum.

Ellis, A. (1962). *Reason and emotion in psychotherapy.* New York: Lyle Stuart.

Frame, C. L., & Matson, J. L. (1987). *Handbook of assessment in childhood psychopathology: Applied issues in differential diagnosis and treatment evaluation.* New York: Plenum Press.

Frame, C., Matson, J. L., Sonis, W., Fialkov, M., & Kazdin, A. (1982). Behavioral treatment of depression in a prepubertal child. *Behavior Therapy and Experimental Psychiatry, 13*, 239–243.

Fuchs, C. Z., & Rehm, L. (1977). A self-control behavior therapy program for depression. *Journal of Consulting and Clinical Psychology, 45*, 206–215.

Furman, E. A. (1974). *A child's parent dies: Studies in childhood depression.* New Haven, CT: Yale University Press.

Gilpin, D. C. (1976). Psychotherapy of the depressed child. In E. J. Anthony & D. C. Gilpin (Eds.), *Three clinical faces of childhood.* New York: Spectrum.

Hawton, K. (1986). *Suicide and attempted suicide among children and adolescents.* Beverly Hills, CA: Sage.

Helsel, W. L., & Matson, J. L. (1985). The assessment of depression in children: The internal structure of the Child Depression Inventory (CDI). *Behavioral Research and Therapy, 22*, 289–298.

Hollon, S. D., Derubeis, R., Tuason, V. B., Weimer, M. J., Evans, M. D., & Garvey, M. J. (1984). *Combined cognitive-pharmacotherapy versus cognitive therapy alone and pharmacotherapy alone in the treatment of depressed outpatients: Differential treatment outcome in the CPT project.* Unpublished manuscript.

Jacobsen, E. (1938). *Progressive relaxation.* Chicago: University of Chicago Press.

Joyce, B., & Weil, M. (1972). *Models of teaching.* Englewood Cliffs, NJ: Prentice-Hall.

Joyce, B., Weil, M., & Wald, R. (1972). *Three teaching strategies for social studies.* Chicago: Science Research Association.

Kanfer, F. H. (1970). Self-regulation: Research, issues and speculations. In C. Neuringer & J. L. Michael (Eds.), *Behavior modification in clinical psychology.* New York: Appleton-Century-Crofts.

Kaslow, N., & Rehm, L. (1983). Childhood depression. In R. J. Morris & T. R. Kratochwill (Eds.), *The practice of child therapy.* New York: Pergamon Press.

Kazdin, A. E., & Petti, T. A. (1982). Self-report and interview measures of childhood and adolescent depression. *Journal of Child Psychology and Psychiatry, 23*, 437–457.

Kazdin, A. E., & Wilson, T. (1978). *Evaluation of behavior therapy: Issues, evidence and research strategies.* Cambridge, MA: Ballinger.

Kazdin, A. E., Dawson, K., Unis, A. S.. & Rancarello, M. D. (1983). Child and parent evaluations of depression and aggression in psychiatric inpatient children. *Journal of Abnormal Child Psychology, 11*, 401–413.

Knaus, W. (1974). *Rational-emotive education: A manual for elementary school teachers.* New York: Institute for Rational Living.

Kovacs, M., & Beck, A. T. (1977). An empirical-clinical approach toward a definition of childhood depression. In J. G. Shulterbrandt & A. Raskin (Eds.), *Depression in childhood: Diagnosis, treatment, and conceptual models.* New York: Raven Press.

Kovacs, M., Rush, A. J., Beck, A. T., & Hollon, S. D. (1981). Depressed outpatients treated with cognitive therapy or pharmacotherapy: A one year follow-up. *Archives of General Psychiatry, 38*, 33–39.

Kovacs, M., Feinberg, T. L., Crouse-Novak, M. A., Paulauskas, S. L., & Finkelstein, R. (1984a). Depressive disorders in childhood: 1. A longitudinal prospective study of characteristics and recovery. *Archives of General Psychiatry, 41*, 229–237.

Kovacs, M., Feinberg, T. L., Crouse-Novak, M. A., Paulauskas, S. L., Pollack, M., & Finkelstein, R. (1984b). Depressive disorders in childhood: 2. A longitudinal study of risk for a subsequent major depression. *Archives of General Psychiatry, 41*, 643–649.

Law, W., Petti, T. A., & Kazdin, A. E. (1981). Withdrawal symptoms after gradual cessation of imipramine in children. *American Journal of Psychiatry, 138*, 647–650.

Lefkowitz, M. M., & Burton, N. (1978). Childhood depression: A critique of the concept. *Psychological Bulletin, 85*, 716–726.

Lewinsohn, P., & Hoberman, H. M. (1982). Behavioral and cognitive approaches. In E. S. Paykel (Ed.), *Handbook of affective disorders.* New York: Guilford Press.

Lewinsohn, P. M., Sullivan, J. M., & Grosscup, S. J. (1980) Changing reinforcing events: An approach to the treatment of depression. *Psychotherapy: Theory, Research, and Practice, 17*, 322–334.

Lewinsohn, P. M., Sullivan, J. M., & Grosscup, S. J. (1982). Behavior Behavior therapy: Clinical applications. In A. J. Rush (Ed.), *Short term psychotherapies for the depressed patient.* New York: Guilford Press.

Lewinsohn, P., Antonuccio, D.. Steinmetz, J., & Teri, L. (1984). *The coping with depression course.* Eugene, OR: Castalia.

Mash, E. J., & Terdal, L. G. (1982). *Behavioral assessment of childhood disorders.* New York: Guilford Press.

Matson, J. L., & Nieminen, G. S. (1986). *A validity study of measures of depression, conduct disorder an anxiety.* Submitted for publication.

Matson, J. L., Esveldt-Dawson, K., Andrasik, F., Ollendick, T.. petti, T. H., & Hersen, M. (1980). Direct, observation, and generalization effects of social skills training with emotionally disturbed children. *Behavior Therapy, 11*, 552–531.

Moretti, M. M., Fine, M. B., Haley, M. A., & Marriage, M. B. (1985). *Journal of the American Academy of Child Psychiatry, 24*, 298–302.

Moyal, B. (1977). Self-esteem, local of control, stimulus appraisal and depressive symptoms in children. *Journal of Consulting and Clinical Psychology, 56*, 223–240.

Murphy, G. E., Simons, A. D., Wetzel, R. D., & Lustman, P. J. (1984). Cognitive therapy and pharmacotherapy, singly and together, in the treatment of depression. *Archives of General Psychiatry, 41*, 33–41.

Norwicki, S., & Strickland, B. (1973). A locus of control scale for children. *Journal of Consulting and Clinical Psychology, 40*, 148–155.

Petti, T. A. (1978). Depression in hospitalized child psychiatry patients: Approaches to measuring depression. *Journal of the American Academy of Child Psychiatry, 19*, 690–702.

Phillips, L., Draguns, J., & Bartlett, D. (1975). Classification of behavior disorders. In N. Hobbs (Eds.), *Issues in the classification of children.* San Francisco: Jossey-Bass.

Piers, E. (1969). *Manual for the Piers-Harris children's self-concept scale.* Nashville: Counselor Recordings and Tests.

Poznanski, E., Grossman, J., Buchsbaum, Y., Banegas, M., Freeman, L., & Gibbons, R. (1984). Preliminary studies of the reliability and validity of the Children's Depression Rating Scale. *Journal of the American Academy of Child Psychiatry, 23*, 191–197.

Puig-Antich, J., & Gittleman, R. (1982). Depression in childhood and adolescence. In E. S. Paykel (Eds.), *Handbook of affective disorders.* New York: Guilford Press.

Rehm, L. (1977). A self-control model of depression. *Behavior Therapy, 8*, 787–804.

Rehm, L., Fuchs, C. Z., Roth, D. M., Kornblith, S. J., & Romano, J. M. (1979). A comparison of self-control and assertion skills treatments of depression. *Behavior Therapy, 10*, 429–442.

Rehm, L., Leventon, B. G., & Ivens. C. (1988). Depression. In C. L. Frame & J. L. Matson (Eds.), *Handbook of assessment in childhood psychopathology: Applied issues in differential diagnosis and treatment evaluation* pp. 341–364. New York: Plenum Press.

Reynolds, C., & Richmond, B. (1978). What I think and feel: A revised measure of children's manifest anxiety. *Journal of Abnormal Child Psychology, 6*, 271–280.

Reynolds, W. M. (1985). Depression in childhood and adolescence: Diagnosis, assessment, intervention strategies and research. In T. R. Kratochwill (Ed.), *Advances in school psychology* (Vol. 4). Hillsdale, NJ: Erlbaum.

Reynolds, W. M. (1988a). *Assessment of depression in adolescents: Manual for the Reynolds Adolescent Depression Scale (RADS).* Psychological Assessment Resources.

Reynolds, W. (1988b). *Child Depression Scale.* Odessa, FL: Psychological Assessment Resources.

Reynolds, W. M., & Coats, K. I. (in press). A comparison of cognitive-behavioral therapy and relaxation training for the treatment of depression in adolescents. *Journal of Consulting and Clinical Psychology.*

Reynolds, W. M., Anderson, G., & Bartell, N. (1986). Measuring depression in children: A multimethod assessment investigation. *Journal of Abnormal Child Psychology, 13*, 513–526.

Rie, H. E. (1966). Depression in childhood: A survey of some pertinent contributors. *Journal of the American Academy of Child Psychiatry, 5*, 653–685.

Rush, A. J., & Giles, D. E. (1982). Cognitive therapy: Theory and research. In A. J. Rush (Ed.), *Short-term psychotherapies for depression.* New York: Guilford Press.

Rush, A. J., Beck, A. T., Kovacs, M., & Hollon, S. D. (1977). Comparative efficacy of cognitive therapy and pharmacotherapy. *Cognitive Therapy and Research, 1*, 17–38.

Rush, A. J., Beck, A. T., Kovacs, M., Weissenberger, J., & Hollon, S. D. (1982). Comparison of the effects of cognitive therapy on hopelessness and self-concept. *American Journal of Psychiatry, 139,* 862–866.

Rutter, M., Izard, C., & Read, P. (1986). *Depression in young people.* New York: Guilford Press.

Sacks, J. M. (1979). The need for subtlety: A critical session with a suicidal child. *Psychotherapy: Theory, Research, and Practice, 14,* 434–437.

Saylor, C. F., Finch, A. J., Spirito, A., & Bennett, B. (1984). The Children's Depression Inventory: Systematic evaluation of psychometric properties. *Journal of Consulting and Clinical Psychology, 52,* 955–967.

Schloss, P. J., Schloss, C. N., & Harris, L. (1984). A multiple baseline analysis of an interpersonal skills training program for depressed youth. *Behavioral Disorders, 9,* 182–188.

Shaw, B. F. (1977). Comparison of cognitive therapy and behavior therapy in the treatment of depression. *Journal of Consulting and Clinical Psychology, 45,* 543–551.

Spielberger, C., Gorsuch, R., & Lushene, R. (1980). *STAI Manual for the State-Trait Anxiety Inventory.* Palo Alto, CA: Consulting Psychologists Press.

Spitz, R., & Wolfe, K. M. (1946). Anaclitic depression: An inquiry into the genesis of psychiatric conditions in early childhood. *Psychoanalytic Study of the Child, 2,* 313–342.

Stark, K., Reynolds, W., & Kaslow, N. (in press). A comparison of the relative efficacy of self-control and behavior therapy for the reduction of depression in children. *Journal of Abnormal Child Psychology.*

Weissman, M. M. (1985). The epidemiology of anxiety disorders: Rates, risks, and familial patterns. In A. H. Tuma & J. D. Maser (Eds.), *Anxiety and anxiety disorders.* New Jersey: Erlbaum.

Witt, J. C., Cavell, T. A., Heffer, R. W., Carey, M. P., & Marten, B. K. (1988). Child interviewing and self-report. In T. R. Kratochwill & E. S. Shapiro (Eds.), *Behavioral assessment in the schools.* New York: Guilford Press.

# 15    Depression

## Pharmacotherapies

### GABRIELLE A. CARLSON

## INTRODUCTION

The existence and manifestations of depression in children have captured the attention of mental health clinicians and researchers in recent years. No one ever doubted, of course, that children could be unhappy or have a depressed mood state occasionally. The occurrence of a depressive *disorder*, however, is distinguished from merely a depressed mood by its enduring concomitant emotional, cognitive, psychomotor and vegetative symptoms, disabling enough to interfere with a child's social and academic functioning. This has only recently been acknowledged (see review Cantwell & Carlson, 1983). There are a number of issues yet to be clarified, which include (1) the impact of different stages of development on the phenomenology, course, prognosis, and treatment options in childhood depression; (2) the relationship between depressive symptomatology and other child psychiatric disorders; and (3) the continuity or lack of it between childhood and adult depression. If depression in children as it is currently identified appears to be a sufficiently significant entity clinically to warrant evaluation and treatment, the use of psychotropic drugs in children continues to be controversial (Pearce, 1980–1981; Pfefferbaum & Overall, 1984). This factor has handicapped research in the area of antidepressant use. The result is that, although antidepressant drugs have been used in children for almost 30 years, published data that demonstrate unequivocal efficacy or lack of it and that specify the therapeutic effects are surprisingly meager. This situation is even more true for adolescents, although adolescents are occasionally included in adult drug studies, and in my experience, once the diagnosis of a depressive disorder is made in adolescents, there is less resistance to using medication than there is with younger children.

In this chapter three areas will be covered: (1) a brief description of the diagnostic features of major depressive disorder in children; (2) a summary of the components of a good evaluation; and (3) a description of a clinical treatment approach in very practical terms. As there are other sources that exhaustively review the literature on antidepressants in children, this literature is summarized in the context of determining a treatment rationale.

GABRIELLE A. CARLSON • Department of Psychiatry and Behavioral Sciences, State University of New York at Stony Brook, Stony Brook, New York 11794.

Table 1 summarizes the currently used adult criteria (DSM-III; American Psychiatric Association—APA, 1980) for major depression, bipolar disorder (manic-depression), and dysthymic and cyclothymic disorder. One of the challenges in using these criteria, ascertaining symptoms, and making diagnoses, especially in younger children, however, includes deciding which information source should be relied on (parent, child, other, or all) to establish whether a symptom exists. On one hand, it is clear (Kovacs, 1985) that many children, when asked about affective symptoms in a language they can understand, can provide reliable information about their thoughts and feelings. On the other hand, until almost adolescence, they cannot provide the kind of chronology and time frame necessary to distinguish a transiently depressive state from an enduring disorder. Parents, however, although understanding symptom chronology, often focus on the child's misbehavior and sometimes have no insight into his or her underlying distress (Kashani, Orvaschel, Burke, & Reid, 1985).

It has been known since the seminal studies of Rutter and Graham (1968) that information gotten exclusively from either parent, child, or school is inadequate to allow a valid assessment. Hence, it makes sense to acquire information from parent, child, *and* school. In order to minimize inconsistencies, a number of assessment tools have been created that obtain information about children's thoughts and feelings more comprehensively and reliably than the routine "clinical interview." (For review, see Kazdin & Petti, 1982; Orvaschel, 1985.) These instruments seek to obtain specific information from parent(s) and child in either an interview format or a rating-scale format.

Because an accurate diagnosis is the first step in treatment, the interviews that have been developed cover many symptoms and behaviors, so that the inclusionary and exclusionary criteria of major psychiatric disorders are addressed. Some interviews rely more on clinical judgment than others. These structured interviews can be grossly divided into two groups. Those that address lifetime psychopathology, for example, are:

1. The Diagnostic Interview for Children and Adolescents (DICA/DICA-P); Reich, Herjanic, Welner, & Gandhy, 1982).
2. The Diagnostic Interview Schedule for Children (DISC/DISC-P; Costello, Edelbrock, Dulcan, *et al.*, unpublished, 1984).
3. The Schedule for Affective Disorders and Schizophrenia for Children, Epidemilogic Version (K-SADS-E; Orvaschel, Puig-Antich, Chambers, *et al.*, 1982).

And those that assess a presenting problem are:

1. The Interview Schedule for Children (ISC; Kovacs, unpublished, 1983).
2. The Children's Assessment Schedule (CAS; Hodges, McKnew, Cytryn, Stern, & Klein, 1982).
3. The K-SADs, present episode version (Puig-Antich & Chambers, 1978).
4. The Children's Depression Rating Scale (CDRS-R; (Poznanski, Grossman, Buchsbaum, *et al.*, 1984).
5. The Belleview Index of Depression (BID; Petti, 1978).

Major Affective Disorders

Manic Episode

*Diagnostic criteria*

A. One or more distinct periods with a persistent predominantly elevated, expansive, or irritable mood; it may alternate or intermingle with depressive mood.

B. Duration of at least one week (or any duration if hospitalization is necessary), during which, for most of the time, at least three of the following symptoms have persisted (four if the mood is only irritable) and have been present to a significant degree:

   (1) increase in activity
   (2) more talkative than usual or pressure to keep talking
   (3) flight of ideas or subjective experience that thoughts are racing
   (4) inflated self-esteem (grandiosity, which may be delusional)
   (5) decreased need for sleep
   (6) distractibility, i.e., attention too easily drawn to unimportant or irrelevant external stimuli
   (7) excessive involvement in activities that have a high potential for painful consequences which is not recognized, e.g., buying sprees, sexual indiscretions, foolish business investments, reckless driving

C. Neither of the following dominates the clinical picture when an affective syndrome is absent (i.e., symptoms in criteria A and B above):

   (1) preoccupation with a mood-incongruent delusion or hallucination (see definition below)
   (2) bizarre behavior

D. Not superimposed on either Schizophrenia, Schizophreniform Disorder, or a Paranoid Disorder.

E. Not due to any Organic Mental Disorder, such as substance intoxication. (Note: A hypomanic episode is a pathological disturbance similar to, but not as severe as, a manic episode.)

Major Depressive Episode

*Diagnostic Criteria*

A. Prominent and persistent dysphoric mood or loss of interest or pleasure in all or almost all usual activities and pastimes. The dysphoric mood is characterized by symptoms such as the following: depressed, sad, blue, hopeless, low, down in the dumps, irritable. Does not include momentary shifts from one dysphoric mood to another dysphoric mood, e.g., anxiety to depression to anger, such as are seen in states of acute psychotic turmoil. (For children under six, dysphoric mood may have to be inferred from a persistently sad facial expression.)

B. At least four of the following symptoms have each been present nearly every day for a period of at least two weeks (in children under six, at least three of the first four):

   (1) poor appetite or significant weight loss (when not dieting) or increased appetite or significant weight gain (in children under six consider failure to make expected weight gains)
   (2) insomnia or hypersomnia
   (3) psychomotor agitation or retardation (but not merely subjective feelings of restlessness or being slowed down) (in children under six, signs of apathy)
   (4) loss of interest or pleasure in usual activities, or descrease in sexual drive not limited to a period when delusional or hallucinating (in children under six, signs of apathy)
   (5) loss of energy; fatigue
   (6) feelings of worthlessness, self-reproach, or excessive or inappropriate guilt (either may be delusional)
   (7) complaints or evidence or diminished ability to think or concentrate, such as slowed thinking, or indecisiveness not associated with marked loosening of associations or incoherence
   (8) recurrent thoughts of death, suicidal ideation, wishes to be dead, or suicide attempt

C. Neither of the following dominates the clinical picture when an affective syndrome is absent (i.e., symptoms in criteria A and B above):

   (1) preoccupation with a mood-incongruent delusion or hallucination (see definition below)
   (2) bizarre behavior

D. Not superimposed on either Schizophrenia, Schizophreniform Disorder, or a Paranoid Disorder.

E. Not due to any Organic Mental Disorder or Uncomplicated Bereavement.

*(continued)*

TABLE 1. (*Continued*)

Other Specific Affective Disorders

Cyclothymic Disorder

*Differential diagnosis.* Bipolar Disorder, major depressive episode, manic episode.

*Diagnostic criteria*

A. During the past two years, numerous periods during which some symptoms characteristic of both the depressive and the manic syndromes were present but were not of sufficient severity and duration to meet the criteria for a major depressive or manic episode.

B. The depressive periods and hypomanic periods may be separated by periods of normal mood lasting as long as months at a time, they may be intermixed, or they may alternate.

C. During depressive periods there is depressed mood or loss of interest or pleasure in all, or almost all, usual activities and pastimes, and at least three of the following:

During hypomanic periods there is an elevated, expansive, or irritable mood and at least three of the following:

(1) insomnia or hypersomnia

decreased need for sleep

(2) low energy or chronic fatigue

more energy than usual

(3) feelings of inadequacy

inflated self-esteem

(4) decreased effectiveness or productivity at school, work, or home

increased productivity, often associated with unusual and self-imposed working hours

(5) decreased attention, concentration, or ability to think clearly

sharpened and unusually creative thinking

(6) social withdrawal

uninhibited people-seeking (extreme gregariousness)

(7) loss of interest in or enjoyment of sex

hypersexuality without recognition of possibility of painful consequences

(8) restriction of involvement in pleasurable activities; guilt over past activities

excessive involvement in pleasurable activities with lack of concern for the high potential for painful consequences, e.g., buying sprees, foolish business investments, reckless driving

(9) feeling slowed down

physical restlessness

(10) less talkative than usual

more talkative than usual

(11) pessimistic attitude toward the future, or brooding about past events

overoptimism or exaggeration of past achievements

(12) tearfulness or crying

inappropriate laughing, joking, punning

D. Absence of psychotic features such as delusions, hallucinations, incoherence, or loosening of associations.

E. Not due to any other mental disorder, such as partial remission of Bipolar Disorder. However, Cyclothymic Disorder may precede Bipolar Disorder.

Dysthymic Disorder (or Depressive Neurosis)

*Differential diagnosis.* Major Depression; normal fluctuations of mood; chronic mental disorders, such as Obsessive Compulsive Disorder or Alcohol Dependence, when associated with depressive symptoms.

*Diagnostic criteria*

A. During the past two years (or one year for children and adolescents) the individual has been bothered most or all of the time by symptoms characteristic of the depressive syndrome that are not of sufficient severity and duration to meet the criteria for a major depressive episode.

B. The manifestations of the depressive syndrome may be relatively persistent or separated by periods of normal mood lasting a few days to a few weeks but no more than a few months at a time.

C. During the depressive periods there is either prominent depressed mood (e.g., sad, blue, down in the dumps, low) or marked loss of interest or pleasure in all, or almost all, usual activities and pastimes.

TABLE 1. (*Continued*)

349

DEPRESSION:
PHARMACOTHERAPIES

D. During the depressive periods at least three of the following symptoms are present:
   (1) insomnia or hypersomnia
   (2) low energy level or chronic tiredness
   (3) feelings of inadequacy, loss of self-esteem, or self-deprecation
   (4) decreased effectiveness or productivity at school, work, or home
   (5) decreased attention, concentration, or ability to think clearly
   (6) social withdrawal
   (7) loss of interest in or enjoyment of pleasurable activities
   (8) irritability or excessive anger (in children, expressed toward parents or caretakers)
   (9) inability to respond with apparent pleasure to praise or rewards
   (10) less active or talkative than usual, or feels slowed down or restless
   (11) pessimistic attitude toward the future, brooding about past events, or feeling sorry for self
   (12) tearfulness or crying
   (13) recurrent thoughts of death or suicide
E. There are no psychotic features, such as delusions, hallucinations, or incoherence.
F. If the disturbance is superimposed on another mental disorder or a preexisting mental disorder, such as Obsessive Compulsive Disorder or Alcohol Dependence, the depressed mood, by virtue of its intensity or effect on functioning, can be clearly distinguished from the individual's usual mood.

The latter instruments have the advantage of gauging the severity of depressive signs and symptoms and thus lend themselves to studies and estimations of treatment response. In this author's opinion, a major disadvantage of most structured interviews is that they cannot be used *instead* of a clinical interview because one does not get a developmental or historical sequence of events with the environmental pressures that often influence exacerbations. Also, it is necessary to resolve some of the discrepancies that occur between separately obtained parent and child information (Kashani *et al.*, 1985). Finally, structured interviews may overdiagnose psychopathology (Carlson, Kashani, Thomas, Vaidya, & Daniel, 1987). For this reason, in a clinical setting at least, it is recommended that a more open-ended interview be used to obtain a history of present and past problems, and that a structured interview be used subsequently to ensure an accurate recording of all symptoms.

In addition to structured interviews, a number of rating scales have been developed to be completed by parent or child, which try to determine the intensity and severity of the various depressive symptoms (see Petti, 1985, for review). These include adult rating scales that have been used for children and adolescents (Beck Depression Inventory, or BDI; Beck, Mendelson, Mock, & Erbaugh, 1961); adult inventories modified for use by children (Children's Depression Inventory, or CDI; modified from the BDI; Kovacs, 1980–1981), with a parent version developed by Garber (1984); the Center for Epidemiologic Studies Depression Scale for Children (CES-DC; Weissman, Orvaschel, & Padian, 1980); and a Children's Depression Adjective Checklist (C-DACL; Sokoloff & Lubin, 1983). Finally, several scales have been developed *de novo* for children, including the Children's Depression Scale (CDS; Tisher & Lang, 1983) and the Depression Self Rating Scale (DSRS); Asarnow & Carlson, 1985; Birleson, 1981), which are specifically for depression; the Personality Inventory for Children (Lacher, Wirt, Klinedinst, & Seat, 1984); and the Child Behavior Checklist (Achenbach & Edelbrock, 1978), which covers psychopathology in general as well as having depression subscales.

There is a paucity of experience in using interview scales in treatment research, but that is because there is a paucity of treatment research on childhood depression. Any instrument used would have to have good test–retest reliability, as mood and thus score fluctuations are not uncommon in depression. However, the scale also needs to be sensitive to change so that treatment effect can be measured.

Although a history and a mental status exam will provide the information necessary to make a diagnosis of depression, two other factors may increase one's confidence in the diagnosis. The first is a family history positive for major depressive disorder. The second is a positive dexamethasone-suppression test. There is considerable evidence that parents' mental illness increases the risk of general psychopathology in their offspring (see Beardslee, Bemporad, Keller, & Klerman, 1983, for review). In addition, depressive illness in one parent increases the risk of depressive psychopathology in the child (though other disorders also occur), and the risk increases if both parents are depressed (Beardslee, et al., 1983). It is also possible that a heavy familial loading of depressive illness decreases the age of onset of depression (Strober & Carlson, 1982; Weissman, Prusoff, Gammon, Merikangas, Leckman, & Kidd, 1984). Thus, a family history of major depression should stimulate the examiner to consider that diagnostic possibility in a child, though it should be emphasized that the presence of such a history is not conclusive evidence for the diagnosis, nor does its absence negate the possibility of the diagnosis.

When obtaining a family history, it is important to obtain brief psychiatric histories on the subject's sibs, parents, grandparents, aunts, and uncles. If there is a history of depression or bipolar disorder, it is helpful to know the age of onset, the symptoms, the course (i.e., if it is chronic, episodic, or psychotic), the treatment, and the treatment response. If medication has been used, knowing the type, dose, and response can be useful in deciding whether or not to institute pharmacotherapy and what agent to try first.

The dexamethasone suppression test (DST), although not as extensively researched in children as in adults, has been used in children and adolescents (Extein, Rosenberg, Pottash, et al., 1982; Geller, Rogol, & Knitter, 1983; Ha, Kaplan, & Foley, 1984; Hsu, Molcan, Cashman, et al., 1983; Petty, Asarnow, Carlson, & Lesser, 1985; Poznanski, Carroll, Banegas, et al., 1982; Robbins, Alessi, Yanchyshyn, et al., 1983; Targum & Capodanno, 1983; Weller, Weller, Fristad, et al., 1984). The procedure is similar; that is, the dose of dexamethasone is given by mouth at 11 P.M., and cortisol levels are drawn at 4 P.M. and 8 P.M. the following day. Although the issue is not conclusively settled, the data suggest that a 0.5-mg dose of dexamethasone is more sensitive in children (Poznanski et al., 1982), though 1 mg. is used in adolescents. It is not clear whether this dosage change should be based on age, weight, or Tanner stage. Levels of cortisol greater than 5 mg/ml at either 4 or 8 P.M. are considered evidence of nonsuppression. Unfortunately, the test is often normal in children who appear to be clinically depressed (modest sensitivity; 25%–64%), and though the specificity is slightly better (53%–83%), it may be positive in disorders that are difficult to distinguish from depression (e.g., anorexia nervosa and schizophrenia). Thus, the DST cannot substitute for a good clinical examination, although it can add an element of confirmation in some cases.

Not only is obtaining and coordinating information in a thorough evaluation more complicated in children and adolescents than in adults, interpreting the manifestations of the symptoms is not always clear-cut. At the time the DSM-III was formulated (and even now), there were no substantive data to support the notion that depression was grossly different in childhood. Nonetheless, how the various criteria manifest themselves in different age groups of children is the subject of continuing research.

Dysphoric mood and anhedonia, for instance, appear in a variety of ways in children. Although some are articulate enough to admit they feel unhappy or depressed, young children more often demonstrate increased sensitivity. For instance, parents note that the child cries or explodes at the slightest provocation. Thus, tearfulness and/or irritability is a common manifestation, especially when it represents a change in behavior for the child. Another observation frequently made is that the child never smiles. These factors, especially if they represent a change from the child's previous behavior or appearance, are important.

Anhedonia may be pervasive in children, though there is a spectrum ranging from children who seem simply less involved to those who can no longer have fun in anything. Such children describe themselves as bored. Schultz's character Charlie Brown notes, "When you're depressed, all you want to do is nothing. All you want to do is lean your head on your arm and stare into space." Parents or teachers will say that nothing excites the child and may get frustrated when their attempts to get him or her involved are rebuffed.

Some of the next DSM-III criteria are less clear in children than in adults. Regarding psychomotor retardation, for instance, a depressed child may appear listless, may have no energy, and may describe himself or herself as tired all the time. The child may talk in such a quiet voice that he or she is inaudible. In my experience, however, it is unusual to see the kind of psychomotor retardation in a prepubertal child that one sees in a severely depressed adolescent or adult. The response latency verging on mutism and total system slowdown is uncommon.

Children definitely describe agitation and anxiety. The irritability described above, along with increased temper tantrums and fighting, may be a component of agitation. Some of the minor antisocial behaviors seen secondary to depression (Carlson & Cantwell, 1980) seem to arise from the child's feeling sad and angry. As one 6-year-old put it, "When my feelings get hurt, I get sad and mad. Then I do something nasty and get in trouble." The sudden onset of separation problems, fears of illness in self or parents, death fears, worries about school failure or being loved, feeling embarrassed very easily, or encountering new situations are examples of the kinds of anxiety children experience.

School provides the substrate for several expressions of depression. As part of her or his loss of interest, the child is no longer motivated. Because of the irritability, she or he is more sensitive to criticism, and peer and teacher relationships may deteriorate. Like adults, children frequently describe trouble concentrating. This may be preoccupation with one's misery, it may be daydreaming to get one's mind off one's misery, or it may be another aspect of anhedonia. There may be more psychophysiological reasons for the diminished ability to pay attention. The end result is a drop in the child's grades and increased frustration, along with dislike and fear of school.

Some children experience their misery with somatic problems. Headaches, stomachaches, and nonspecific aches and pains are seen in depressed children of all ages and may be even more frequent in younger children (Kashani & Carlson, 1987).

Cognitive symptoms are variably present. Children express feeling like a failure and may feel overly responsible for difficult situations in their environment (especially family strife and family illness). They may describe themselves in negative terms. Finally, suicidal ideation is not uncommon in children, increasing in intensity with the severity of the depression (Carlson & Cantwell, 1982).

Vegetative symptoms in children include insomnia and poor appetite. However, children frequently have initial insomnia and nightmares rather than the more classical terminal insomnia. Appetite changes are similar to those in adults. Parents note that favorite foods no longer please the child.

Often, the most troublesome history to obtain is of when and how the symptoms were first noted. In teenagers, who have had more time for normal development to occur, one can sometimes get a clear history of relatively good premorbid functioning and a clear onset of depressive psychopathology (Carlson, 1984a). The younger the child, the harder it is to ascertain the history. Some children are more temperamental and sensitive than others, and it may be more difficult to delineate an onset of depressive symptoms with such a background. A similar situation that may confound making a diagnosis is the preexistence of other psychopathology. Children with so-called secondary depressions (Carlson & Cantwell, 1980) may have prior histories of attention-deficit disorder, conduct disorder, anxiety disorder, or eating disorders. These disorders share symptoms with depression (e.g., poor attention, irritability, low self-esteem, poor appetite, and insomnia to name), and a careful history is necessary to a diagnosis of a depressive episode. In these cases, the depression may be treated separately from the preexisting disorder. Finally, dysthymic disorder with superimposed major depression occurs in children (Kovacs, Feinberg, Crouse, Novak, Paulauskas, Pollock, & Finkelstein, 1984) as it does in adults (Keller & Shapiro, 1982). This possibility also necessitates a rethinking of the therapeutic modality and is thus of more than theoretical interest.

What happens to children with major depressive disorders? Although there are few follow-up studies, those that exist suggest that this is not a benign disorder (Poznanski, Krahenbuhl, & Zrull, 1976; Kovacs *et al.*, 1984). Although episodes are transient in some children, they last over 6 months in 44% of children and up to a year in 25%. Dysthymic disorder and major depression have a more protracted course. It took 6½ years for 89% of children with dysthymic disorder to remit, and during that time, they were at high risk for superimposed major depression (Kovacs *et al.*, 1984). A comparison of depressed adolescents with an onset in childhood and those having a first episode beginning in adolescence revealed that the earlier onset youngsters had both significantly lower IQs and significantly more academic problems (Carlson, 1984a). This finding suggests that a key area of development can be influenced by this disorder. It has not been possible to measure the cost in family disruption, adult maladjustment, physical illness, or suicide of major depression in children. The

## EXPERIENCE WITH ANTIDEPRESSANT DRUGS IN CHILDREN

### Efficacy

Tricyclic antidepressant (TCA) drugs have been used in adults and children for about 30 years. There has been a plethora of studies demonstrating the efficacy of these drugs in adults. As long ago as 1972, Morris and Beck (1974) found that, in 34 of 56 double-blind studies of imipramine (IMI) or desipamine (DMI), drugs were superior to placebo, and that amitriptyline (AMI) or amitrip-tylinelike antidepressants were superior to placebo in 27 of 37 treatment group comparisons. In general it can be said on the basis of studies in 1,400 subjects that 60%–70% of patients improve on active medication, and 25%–40% on placebo (Klein, Gittelman, Quitkin, & Rifkin, 1980). Given the large sample size, this difference is significant to $p < .0001$.

In contrast to the number and quality of drug studies done on adults, there have been relatively few studies carried out on children, and fewer still whose design has permitted conclusive results. This literature has been thoroughly reviewed by Petti (1983). Briefly, however, among the earlier uncontrolled studies (Frommer, 1967; Kuhn & Kuhn, 1972; Polvan & Cebiroglu 1971; Stack, 1971; Weinberg, Rutman, Sullivan, Penick, & Dietz, 1973), any one or all of the following problems occurred: The diagnostic and/or assessment procedures were unstandardized, or the patient population was diagnostically heterogeneous, the duration of the drug trial was not uniform, or the dosage was not mentioned. Placebos were not used at all. With more sophisticated methodology, more recent reports have incorporated standardized assessment procedures (Pallmeyer & Petti, 1979; Petti, Bornstein, Delameter, & Connors, 1980; Petti & Connors, 1983; Puig-Antich, Blau, Marx, et al., 1978) placebos (Petti & Unis, 1981); and double-blind placebos trials (Kashani, Shekim, & Reid, 1984; Petti & Law, 1982; Puig-Antich, Perel, Lupatkin, Chambers, Tabrizi, King, Goetz, Davies, & Stiller, 1987). It would appear, then, that fewer than 100 children have been reported on with a methodology that would combine diagnostic homogeneity with adequate dose and duration of medication given with placebo. Of those studied with double-blind placebo controls (Kashani et al., 1984; Petti & Law, 1982; Puig-Antich et al., 1987), 47 were given either imipramine or amitriptyline, and 34 responded (72%); 38 were given placebo, to which 17 responded (45%). Although the percentage of response to medication and placebo was similar in children and adults, the small sample size does not rule out the possibility that chance accounted for the conclusion ($p = .09$).

Data demonstrating the efficacy of TCAs in depressed adolescents is even more sparse (Kramer & Feiguine. 1981; Ryan, Puig-Antich, Cooper, Rabinovich, Ambrosini, Davies, King, Torres, & Fried, 1988). In the first study, 10 subjects were given AMI, and 10 were given placebo. Of the drug sample, 80% had moderate to maximum improvement; 60% of the placebo group did as well. In a study by Ryan et al. (1987), no placebo was used, but with adequate duration and monitoring of blood levels, only 44% of the 34 adolescents studied were asymptomatic at the end of the trial. Because of the paucity of studies, it is very difficult to draw meaningful conclusions about whether adolescents with depressive disorders have response patterns like those of children or those of adults.

## Psychopharmacology and Side Effects

Although efficacy has not been demonstrated unequivocally, the need to obtain adequate plasma levels in order to maximize treatment response has. Plasma levels of 150 mg/ml to 225 mg/ml account for a significantly higher percentage of responders than levels below 150 mg/ml (Puig-Antich et al., 1985). It does not appear that specific levels of either imipramine or its pharmacologically active metabolite desipramine are as critical as the combined levels. Unfortunately, the relationship between a given dose and plasma level is extremely variable (Preskorn, Weller, & Weller, 1982), so that body weight provides only a rough guide to dose. The presence or absense of side effects is not particularly helpful in determining adequacy of blood level either. Steady-state plasma level would appear to be the most accurate way of determining whether a child is within therapeutic range. Drug half-life is also quite variable in children, varying anywhere from 4 to 20 hours. Thus, the most reliable time to do plasma levels is about 5 days after the desired dose level has been achieved.

There are controversies in the adult literature about whether the relationship between plasma level and treatment response is linear or curvilinear (i.e., whether levels above a certain range diminish positive treatment outcome). This situation is especially true for nortriptyline, the secondary amine derived from amitriptyline. Levels of this drug greater than 180 mg/ml may be too high (Klein et al., 1980, p. 295), and lowering the level may increase the likelihood of response.

Children are variable in their tolerance of medication side effects and withdrawal effects. Most clinicians choose to start gradually at 1–2 mg/kg, increasing the dosage by 25 mg every few days depending on the severity of the sedative and anticholinergic side effects (Petti, 1983). Drowsiness is certainly the most frequently noted complaint, even when the dose is scheduled for dinnertime and bedtime administration. Anticholinergic effects consist of dry mouth, constipation, nausea, anorexia, sweating, and tremor. More serious effects include cardiovascular and central nervous system changes.

Orthostatic hypotension (feeling dizzy on getting up quickly) is the cardiovascular symptom most frequently complained about. Slight elevations in pulse and blood pressure are quite common, especially as the dose level goes over 3–4 mg/kg. These effects are considered serious enough to warrant stopping treatment only when the heart rate is over 130 beats/minute and the blood pressure is higher than 140/90 mm/mg (Puig-Antich et al., 1987).

Changes in cardiac rhythm occur with tricyclic antidepressants and are also dose-related. These effects are the ones primarily responsible for death in tricyclic overdose. Fortunately, it is easy to monitor such changes with sequential EKGs or rhythm strips (Preskorn & Irwin, 1982). Current guidelines suggest that the PR interval should be kept at less than 0.20 seconds and that the QRS interval should not exceed 130% of baseline (Puig-Antich et al., 1987).

Tricyclic antidepressants may precipitate seizures in seizure-prone children

(Brown, Winsberg, Bialer, & Press, 1973; Petti & Campbell, 1975) as well as in adults. This is not invariable, however, so the presence of a seizure disorder or an abnormal EEG should not preclude the use of TCAs, though one should obviously proceed with caution.

The most notable difference among the currently used TCAs is in the frequency of side effects. Table 2 summarizes the drugs used most in children and their relative effects.

Finally, children have variable responses to the withdrawal of TCAs, and in this author's experience, sensitivity to withdrawal is not necessarily related to the frequency or intensity of side effects. The most frequently reported withdrawal symptoms are gastrointestinal (anorexia, nausea, vomiting, and cramps); tearfulness, agitation, and headache have been reported, too (Law, Petti, & Kazdin, 1981). Vomiting occurs so frequently following abrupt medication withdrawal that, when the parent of a child on a tricyclic calls me to report that the child is vomiting, the first question I ask is whether a dose was inadvertently missed. Almost invariably, this has been the case. The solution is to *gradually withdraw medication,* with the child's subjective symptoms offering a guideline to whether to remain a few days at the next lower dose or to proceed. Some children have no problems when the drug is withdrawn by 25 mg every other day, whereas others have to have the drug withdrawn in 10-mg decrements over several weeks (depending on how much drug they were taking in the first place).

Experience with the newer tricyclics in children is limited. Anecdotally, there does not appear to be any evidence to suggest their greater efficacy, though the frequency of particular side effects may be less. Systematic experience with these drugs in children has not been obtained.

## Suggested Treatment Procedure

The first step when one suspects depression in a child is evaluation and diagnosis. It should be possible during the first interview to decide whether major depression is a strong diagnostic possibility. If that is so, the author begins to educate the family regarding what confirmatory information will be necessary

TABLE 2. Antidepressants Used in Children

| Drug | Trade name | Plasma level | Anticholinergic symptoms | Degree of sedation |
|---|---|---|---|---|
| Imipramine[a] | Tofranil SK-Pramine | 150–240 + ng/ml[c] (IMI + DMI) | 4+ | 2+ |
| Desipramine | Norpramine Pertofrane | 115 ng/ml | 1+ | 1+ |
| Amitriptyline | Elavil Endep | 100–300 ng/ml (AMI + NOR) | 4+ | 4+ |
| Nortriptyline | Aventyl[b] Pamelor | 50–100 ng/ml[c] | 3+ | 2+ |

[a]The only drug approved for children under age 12, though not for depression; the "safety and efficacy" of others have not been determined.
[b]Comes in liquid form.
[c]Based on studies done in children.

and what treatment possibilities exist. In a nonresearch protocol every effort is made to enact any changes in the environmental situation that may be contributing to the child's or the family's problem. Usually, by the time the evaluation is finished over the next couple of weeks, it is possible to get a sense of how fruitful this approach will be. If, however, on the basis of information obtained from the parent, the child, and, if necessary, the school, the child fulfills the criteria for a major depressive disorder, and if he or she has had symptoms for at least a month that interfere with family, social, and/or academic interactions a trial of medication is strongly considered.

At that point, even in a physically healthy child, it is important to obtain a baseline heart rate, blood pressure, and EKG, before a medication trial. As mentioned earlier, the purpose is not so much ruling out heart disease, which is unlikely in children, as obtaining a baseline against which to compare rate and rhythm changes caused by the medication.

The seriousness of the disorder and the major concerns about medication use should be discussed with the family. This author is optimistic about the likelihood of therapeutic response to medication but warns families that different drugs and different dosages may be necessary. In addition to warning about side effects, families should be reassured that the medications, although not addictive, should not be withdrawn precipitously because of rebound symptoms like epigastric pain, nausea, vomiting, and malaise (Law *et al.*, 1981). Although it is useful for the clinician to document that the efficacy and side effects of these medications have been discussed with parents, an actual "informed-consent" document is probably not necessary.

Although imipramine has been used widely in children for enuresis, the reason for its lack of endorsement for children under 12 is mostly that its efficacy in the treatment of depression has not been proved for children.

Because of the high placebo response to medication in children, I begin with a low dose of drug: 25 mg for children under 50 lb or 25 kg. Depending on the urgency of the situation, that dose is continued for a week. Many placebo responders will improve, only to relapse several weeks later. At that time, the author begins to increase the dose. Otherwise, the dose is increased by 25 mg every other day until 3.5 mg/kg is reached or intolerable or serious side effects occur. At that point, it is worth checking pulse, blood pressure, and rhythm strip. If there is no improvement or a contraindication, one may increase the dose gradually to 5 mg/kg. If after 2–3 weeks at that level there is no sign of improvement, it is wise to obtain a plasma determination of imipramine/desimipramine. As mentioned earlier, children, like adults, need to be at combined levels that exceed 150 mg/ml (Puig-Antich *et al.*, 1985) to maximize therapeutic response.

If blood levels are adequate, it is perhaps worth waiting a total of 5–6 weeks before trying another strategy. If blood levels are inadequate at 5 mg/kg, it is wise to repeat the EKG before further increasing the dose. Where there are no changes at all in either the resting heart rate or PR internal, lack of compliance in taking the medication should be suspected and must be addressed.

Where there is no therapeutic response, there is divided opinion on how high the blood level should be allowed to go before deciding to discontinue treatment with imipramine. In Puig-Antich's controlled sample of 30 prepubertal major depressive children (Puig-Antich *et al.*, 1987), 13 responders and 2 nonresponders were found to have IMI/DMI plasma levels greater than 214 ng/ml. In fact, 4 responders had levels higher than 300 ng/ml. The data of Preskorn et al. (1982) largely concur, though these authors stated that none of their subjects responded at plasma levels higher than 225 ng/ml. Until further data are available, the decision on how far to increase the dosage will depend on the presence of untoward effects, the certainty of the diagnosis, the severity of the depression, and the presence of other clinical factors (e.g., a family history of a depression responding to IMI).

Although many of the treatment considerations for children are similar to those for adults (e.g., cardiovascular concerns, similar range of plasma level, and type of side effects), the method of administration may need to be different. With adults and adolescents (Ryan, Puig-Antich, Cooper, Rabinovich, Ambrosini, Fried, Davies, King, Torres, & Suckow, 1987), giving the entire dose of medication at bedtime decreases the problems of compliance and allows the most troubling side effects (drowsiness, dizziness, and dry mouth) to occur at night, when they don't interfere with functioning because plasma levels peak 1–2 hours after the initial dose. As there are suggestions that children may metabolize IMI more rapidly and that EKG abnormalities are highly correlated with plasma concentrations, there has been a general consensus that continuing a divided dose schedule for children is the safest method of administration. Thus, this author gives children their first 75–100 mg at bedtime. Further increments are divided between dinnertime and bedtime (to 150–175 mg), and where necessary, small doses are added in the morning. An effort is made to avoid medication given at school, for practical reasons. Children who do not respond to IMI or who, because of the side effects of cardiovascular changes, cannot reach therapeutic levels have not been systematically studied. As noted above, there is a dearth of information on any other medication treatment. There are scattered reports from the older literature on a number of tricyclic antidepressants, but the absence of assessment procedures to establish proper diagnosis, the absence of controls, and the small sample size render conclusions impossible. Kashani et al.'s data (1984) suggest that amitriptyline may be useful in children, though their small sample size and the high rate of placebo response did not produce dramatic findings. Also Geller, Cooper, Farooki, and Chestnut (1985) published pharmacological studies with nortriptyline in children suggesting that it is a safe drug. Whether amitriptyline or nortriptyline offers advantages over IMI or is efficacious in children who have not responded to IMI has not been studied, nor has the existence of a "therapeutic window" been documented in children. Similarly, there are no controlled studies on the safety or efficacy of monoamine oxidase inhibitors (MAOIs) in children. A study by Frommer in 1967 found that phenelzine and chlordiazepoxide were superior to phenobarbitone in phobic and depressed children. Because phenobarbitone is likely to make most depressed children worse, it is unclear how helpful the phenelzine was in this case. In extrapolating from the adult literature, and what little has been done with children, it makes sense to try other TCAs next.

## Lithium

The use of lithium to treat depression in children and adolescents seems to vary with the alertness of the physician to the possibility of bipolar disorder. In peripubertal children and adolescents, as in adults, the presence of a recurrent disorder characterized by periods of psychomotor slowing, hypersomnia, dysphoric mood, and even mood-congruent psychotic features as, well as one or more periods of accelerated activity, thinking and speaking, elevated or irritable mood, grandiosity, and, again, mood-congruent psychotic features, usually results in the diagnosis of bipolar or manic depressive disorder. The presence of good premorbid adjustment and a strongly positive family history is even more suggestive. The positive effects of lithium carbonate in a high percentage of such patients certainly warrants its trial very early in the treatment plan (see Carlson, 1983, for review).

How much deviation from this classical picture can still be considered bipolar disorder (Davis, 1979)—and by optimistic extention, lithium-responsive—remains to be seen. There are case reports of children with symptomatology resembling attention-deficit disorder (Greenhill, Reider, Wender, Buchsbaum, & Zahn. 1973), conduct disorder (DeLong, 1978), anorexia nervosa (Barcai, 1977), schizophrenia, and atypical psychosis (Annell, 1969) on whom lithium has been tried with success. In these cases, the common denominator has been a strong family history of manic-depressive illness. Similarly, there are reports of lithium use for aggressive behavior (Campbell, Perry, & Green, 1984; DeLong, 1978; Marini & Sheard, 1977) impulsive behavior (Siassi, 1982), and emotionally unstable character disorder (Rifkin, Quitkin, Carrillo, *et al.*, 1972), where nonspecific effects of lithium were purported to be acting. As of this writing, the parameters of the mania and the intensity and duration of the affective episodes, especially in young children, have yet to be delineated and distinguished reliably from other forms of childhood psychopathology. (For a further review of this subject, readers are referred to Carlson, 1984b).

In my view, the indications for a lithium trial (with or without other medications), from most clear-cut to least clear-cut, go as follows:

1. The presence, or a history, of disabling episodes of mania and depression.
2. Episode(s) of severe depression with a possible history of hypomania.
3. The presence of an acute, severe depression characterized by psychomotor retardation, hypersomnia, psychosis, and a positive family history for major or bipolar affective disorder, even without a history of mania (in these cases, it has been found that TCAs may precipitate a manic episode and possibly a rapid cycling course) (Akiskal, Downs, Jordan, Watson, Daugherty, & Pruitt, 1985; Strober & Carlson, 1982).
4. An acute psychotic disorder with affective features.
5. Behavior disorders characterized by emotional lability and aggression, where there is a positive family history of major depression or bipolar disorder.

In the latter two instances, it helps to have good behavioral observations on a daily basis to determine if the target symptoms diminish or increase. In my experience, they rarely completely disappear, and one is left to decide if the benefits of medication outweigh the risks.

For a simple compound, lithium carbonate is wide-reaching in its effects (Lewis, 1982). Although its systematic and controlled use in children and adolescents is limited (see the review in Campbell, Perry, & Green, 1984) there is no reason to believe that children are not vulnerable to the same toxic and long-term effects as adults. However, this means that, in a physically healthy child or adolescent whose serum lithium levels are appropriately monitored, the risks of toxicity are minimal. The most frequently encountered side effects are nausea, stomachache, tremor, weight gain, and polyuria. The long-term effects in adults include hypothyroidism (easily remediated by thyroid supplement) and possible renal impairment. Two reviews (Lewis, 1982; Vestergaard, 1983) provide exhaustive discussions of lithium effects in humans.

Because of the metabolic, renal, and endocrinological effects of lithium, patient evaluations should include a CBC and testing for thyroid hormone (T-4) and thyroid stimulating hormone (TSH), electrolytes, and creatinine, as well as a physical and neurological examination. These tests not only rule out contraindications but provide baselines against which subsequent measures are compared if there are concerns.

Estimating the dosage necessary to obtain therapeutic levels may be done either by beginning at 900 mg/day (300 mg t.i.d.), with the first lithium level drawn 12 hours after the sixth dose, or by following a regimen described by Weller, Weller and Freistad (1986). Their system, based on milligrams per kilogram indicates that children between 25 and 40 kg need 900 mg in divided doses, children between 40 and 50 kg need 1200 mg, and those between 50 and 60 kg need 1500 mg (i.e., about 130 mg/kg per day). The therapeutic range is between 0.6 and 1.2 mg/ml.

The duration of treatment depends on the condition being treated and the degree of therapeutic response. If the medication is stabilizing a youngster with incapacitating mood swings, it should be continued until the mood swings abate (which sometimes occurs past adolescence) or until such time as it makes sense to try a drug holiday. Under these circumstances, a support system should be available to make sure that treatment is resumed promptly if needed. Guidelines for use in more equivocal situations have yet to be determined and are best decided on case by case.

## Conclusions

The success of treatment requires a thorough understanding of the individual patient, the disorder from which he or she is suffering, and the medication with which he or she is being treated. There are limitations in any therapeutic modality, and appropriate expectations for drug regimens are conducive to greater success. In this author's experience, parents' and patients' greatest concerns about medication are (1) that they are habit-forming; (2) that they will take responsibility for any change from the child or family; (3) that they will change the child's personality; (4) that there are likely to be long-term as yet unknown detrimental affects; and (5) that the child will be on the drug forever.

Regarding the points mentioned above it should be noted that:

1. Although there may be withdrawal effects from tricyclics if they are discontinued too rapidly, the tricyclics, the MAO inhibitors, and lithium are not addictive in the usual sense. They do not produce an immediate "high"; in fact, they take several days to weeks to work. Thus, they lack the basic ingredient for addiction.

2. Rather than absolving persons from responsibility, the restoration of optimism, motivation, and the ability to concentrate and a decrease in irritability usually make other forms of therapy (psychotherapy, family therapy, educational remediation, or whatever) easier to implement.

3–5. Questions about personality and long-term effects are harder to answer. It would appear that the long-term effects of untreated depression in children are themselves potentially devastating. Preventing a depressive diathesis from becoming part of a child's basic way of functioning is to his or her benefit. Similarly, one has to weigh the risks of treatment against the risks of no treatment. For families who are opposed to medication, especially if I feel strongly committed to such a recommendation, I suggest a time-limited trial of nonmedication therapy with a decision subsequently to reevaluate.

Although psychopharmacology has made an impact on the treatment of major depression in children, it is safe to say that we have not found a panacea for this disabling condition. Given the complexities of interaction between the individual, the disorder, and the environment, it is unlikely that one magic bullet will cure everything for everyone with this diagnosis. On the other hand, these drugs have made a significant difference for enough seriously depressed children so that, unless they are contraindicated, a medication trial is more useful than speculation about whether or not medication should be undertaken.

## REFERENCES

Achenbach, T. M., & Edelbrock, C. S. (1978). The classification of child psychopathology. *Psychological Bulletin, 85,* 1275–1300.

Akiskal, H. S., Downs, J., Jordan, P., Watson, S., Daugherty. D., & Pruitt, D. B. (1985). Affective disorders in referred children and younger siblings of manic depressives. *Archives of General Psychiatry, 42,* 996–1004.

American Psychiatric Association. (1980). *Diagnostic and statistical manual of mental disorders* (3rd ed.). Washington, DC: Author.

Annell, A. L. (1969). Lithium in the treatment of children and adolescents. *Acta Psychiatrica Scandinavica Supplement, 207,* 19–33.

Asarnow, J. R., & Carlson, G. A. (1985). The Depression Self Rating Scale: Utility with child psychiatric inpatients. *Journal of Consulting and Clinical Psychology, 53,* 491–499.

Barcai, A. (1977). Lithium adult anorexia nervosa: A pilot report on 2 patients. *Acta Psychiatrica Scandinavica, 55,* 97–101.

Beardslee, W. R. (1983). *Children of parents with affective disorder: The pathogenic influence of illness in both parents.* Presented at the American Psychiatric Association Meeting, New York.

Beardslee, W. R., Bemporad, J., Keller, M. B., & Klerman, G. L. (1983). Children of parents with major affective disorder: A review *American Journal of Psychiatry, 140,* 825–832.

Beck, A. T., Mendelson, M., Mock, J., & Erbaugh, J. (1961). Beck Depression Inventory: An inventory for measuring depression. *Archives of General Psychiatry, 4,* 53–63.

Birleson, P. (1981). The validity of depressive disorders and the development of a self rating scale: A research report. *Journal of Child Psychology and Psychiatry, 22,* 73–86.

Brown, D., Winsberg, B. G., Bialer, I., & Press, M. (1973). Imipramine therapy and seizures: Three children treated for hyperactive behavior disorders. *American Journal of Psychiatry, 130,* 210–212.

Campbell, M., Perry, R., & Green, W. H. (1984). Use of lithium in children and adolescents. *Psychosomatics, 25,* 95–105.

Carlson, G. A. (1983). Bipolar affective disorders in childhood and adolescence. In D. P. Cantwell & G. A. Carlson (Eds.), *Affective disorders in childhood and adolescence: An update.* New York: Spectrum.

Carlson, G. A. (1984a). Depression vs. misery in childhood and adolescence. *Journal of Operational Psychiatry, 15,* 46–49.

Carlson, G. A. (1984b). Issues of classification in childhood bipolar disorder. *Psychiatric Developments, 4,* 273–285.

Carlson, G. A., & Cantwell, D. P. (1980). A survey of depressive symptoms, syndrome and disorder in a child psychiatric population. *Journal of Child Psychology and Psychiatry, 21,* 19–25.

Carlson, G. A., & Cantwell, D. P. (1982). Suicidal behavior and depression in children and adolescents. *Journal of the American Academy of Child Psychiatry, 21,* 361–368.

Carlson, G. A., Kashani, J. H., Thomas, M. T., Vaidya, A., & Daniel, A. (1987). Comparison of two structured interviews in psychiatrically hospitalized children. *Journal of the American Academy of Child Psychiatry, 26,* 645–648.

Costello, A. J., Edelbrock, C. S., Dulcan, M. K., et al., (1984). *Report on the NIMH·Diagnostic Interview Schedule for Children.* Unpublished.

Davis, R. E. (1979). Manic depressive variant syndrome of childhood: A preliminary report. *American Journal of Psychiatry, 136,* 702–706.

DeLong, G. R. (1978). Lithium carbonate treatment of select behavior disorders in children suggesting manic-depressive illness. *Journal of Pediatrics, 93,* 689–694.

Extein, I., Rosenberg, G., Pottash. A. L. C., et al. (1982). The dexamethasone suppression test in depressed adolescents. *American Journal of Psychiatry, 139,* 1617–1619.

Frommer, E. A. (1967). Treatment of childhood depression with antidepressant drugs. *British Medical Journal, 1,* 729–732.

Garber, J. (1984). The developmental progression of depression in female children. In D. Achetti & K. Schneider-Rosen (Eds.), *Childhood depression: New directions for child development.* San Francisco: Jossey-Bass.

Geller, B., Rogol, A. D., & Knitter, E. F. (1983). Preliminary data on the dexamethasone suppression test in children with major depressive disorder. *American Journal of Psychiatry, 140,* 620–622.

Geller, B., Cooper, T. B., Farooki, Z. Q., & Chestnut, E. C. (1985). Dose and plasma levels of nortriptyline and chlorpromazine in delusionally depressed adolescents and of nortriptyline in nondelusionally depressed adolescents. *American Journal of Psychiatry, 142,* 336–338.

Greenhill, L. L., Reider, R. O., Wender, P. H., Buchsbaum, M., & Zahn, D. (1973). Lithium carbonate in the treatment of hyperactive children. *Archives of General Psychiatry, 28,* 636–640.

Ha, H., Kaplan, S., & Foley, C. (1984). The dexamethasone suppression test in adolescent psychiatric patients. *American Journal of Psychiatry, 141,* 421–423.

Hodges, K., Mcknew, D., Cytryn, L., Stern, L., & Klein, J. (1982). The Child Assessment Schedule (CAS)-Diagnostic Interview: A report on reliability and validity. *Journal of the American Academy of Child Psychiatry, 21,* 468–473.

Hsu, L. K. G., Molcan, K., Cashman, M. A., et al. (1983). The dexamethasone suppression test in adolescent depression. *Journal of the American Academy of Child Psychiatry, 22,* 470–473.

Kashani, J. H., & Carlson, G. A. (1987). Seriously depressed preschoolers. *American Journal of Psychiatry, 144,* 348–350.

Kashani, J., Shekim, W. O., & Reid, J. C. (1984). Amitriptyline in children with major depressive disorder: A double blind crossover pilot study. *Journal of the American Academy of Child Psychiatry, 23,* 348–351.

Kashani, J., Orvaschel, H., Burk, J. P., & Reid, J. C. (1985). Informant variance: The issue of parent child disagreement. *Journal of the American Academy of Child Psychiatry, 24,* 437–441.

Kazdin, A. E., & Petti, T. A. (1982). Self report and interview measures of childhood and adolescent depression. *Journal of Child Psychology and Psychiatry, 23,* 437–457.

Keller, M. D., & Shapiro, R. W. (1982). "Double depression": Superimposition of acute depressive episodes on chronic depressive disorders. *American Journal of Psychiatry, 139,* 438–442.

Klein, D. F., Gittelman, R., Quitkin, F., & Rifkin, A. (1980). *Diagnosis and drug treatment of psychiatric disorders: Adults and children.* Baltimore/London: Williams & Wilkins.

Kovacs, M. (1980–1981). Rating scales to assess depression in school-aged children. *Acta Paedopsychiatrica, 46,* 305–315.

Kovacs, M. (1983). *The Interview Schedule for Children (ISC): Interrater and parent-child agreement.* Unpublished manuscript.

Kovacs, M. (1985). A developmental perspective on methods and measures in the assessment of depressive disorders: The Clinical Interview. In M. Rutter, G. E. Izard, & P. B. Read (Eds.), *Depression in young people: Developmental and clinical perspectives.* New York: Guilford Press.

Kovacs, M., Feinberg, T. L., Crouse-Novak, M., Paulauskas, S. L., Pollock, M., & Finkelstein, R.

(1984). Depressive disorders in Childhood: 2. A longitudinal study of the risk for a subsequent major depression. *Archives of General Psychiatry, 41,* 643–649.

Kramer, E., & Feiguine, R. (1981). Clinical effects of amitriptyline in adolescent depression. *Journal American Academy of Child Psychiatry, 20,* 636–644.

Kunn, V. E., & Kuhn, R. (1972). Drug therapy for depression in children; indications and methods. In A. Annell (Ed.), *Depressive states in childhood and adolescence.* New York: Halsted Press.

Lacher, D., Wirt, R. D., Klinedinst, R. D., & Seat, P. D. (1984). Multidimensional description of child personality—A manual for the Personality Inventory for Children (PIC). Western Psychological Services. Los Angeles.

Law, W., Petti, T. A., & Kazdin, A. E. (1981, May). Withdrawal symptoms after graduated cessation of imipramine in children. *American Journal of Psychiatry, 138,* 647–650.

Lewis, D. A. (1982). Lithium in internal medicine and psychiatry: An outline. *Journal Clinical of Psychiatry, 43,* 314–320.

Marini, J. L., & Sheard, M. H. (1977). Antiaggressive effect of lithium ion in man. *Acta Psychiatry Scandanavian, 55,* 269–286.

Morris, J. B., & Beck, H. T. (1974). The efficacy of antidepressant drugs: A review of research (1958–1972). *Archives of General Psychiatry, 30,* 667–674.

Orvaschel, H. (1985). Psychiatric Interviews suitable for use in research with children and adolescents. *Psychopharmacology Bulletin, 21,* 737–745.

Orvaschel, H., Puig-Antich, J., & Chambers, W., et al. (1982). Retrospective assessment of child psychopathology with the Kiddie-SADS-E. *Journal of the American Academy of Child Psychiatry, 21,* 392–397.

Pallmeyer, T., & Petti, T. A. (1979). Effects of imipramine on aggression and dejection in depressed children. *American Journal of Psychiatry, 136,* 1472–1473.

Pearce, J. B. (1980–1981). Drug treatment of depression in children. *Acta Paedopsychiatrica, 46,* 317–328.

Petti, T. A. (1978). Depression in hospitalized child psychiatry patients: Approaches to measuring depression. *Journal of the American Academy of Child Psychiatry, 17,* 49–59.

Petti, T. A. (1983). Imipramine in the treatment of depressed children. In D. P. Cantwell & G. A. Carlson (Eds.), *Affective disorders in childhood and adolescence: An update.* New York: Spectrum.

Petti, T. A. (1985). Scales of potential use in the psychopharmacologic treatment of depressed children and adolescents. *Psychopharmacology Bulletin, 21,* 951–956.

Petti, T. A., & Campbell, M. (1975). Imipramine and seizures. *American Journal of Psychiatry, 132,* 538–540.

Petti, T. A., & Conners, K. (1983). Changes in behavioral ratings of depressed children treated with imipramine. *Journal of the American Academy of Child Psychiatry, 22,* 355–360.

Petti, T. A., & Law, W. (1982). Imipramine treatment of depressed children: A double-blind pilot study. *Journal of Clinical Psychopharmacology, 2,* 107–110.

Petti, T. A., & Unis, A. S. (1981). Treating the borderline psychotic child with imipramine: A controlled study. *American Journal of Psychiatry, 138,* 515–518.

Petti, T. A., Bornstein, M., Delamater, A., & Connors, C. K. (1980). Evaluation and multi-modality treatment of a depressed pre pubertal girl. *Journal of the American Academy of Child Psychiatry, 19,* 690–702.

Petty, L. K., Asarnow, J. R., Carlson, G. A., & Lesser, L. (1985). The dexamethasone suppression test in depressed, dysthymic and non-depressed children. *American Journal of Psychiatry, 142,* 631–633.

Pfefferbaum, B., & Overall, J. E. (1984). Decisions about drug treatment in children. *Journal of the American Academy of Child Psychiatry, 23,* 209–214.

Polvan, O., & Cebiroglu, R. (1971). Treatment with psychopharmacologic agents in childhood depressions in Proc. 4th UEP Congress. *Depressive states in childhood and adolescence.* Stockholm: Almquist & Wiksell.

Poznanski, E. O., Krahenbukl, V., & Zrull, J. P. (1976). Childhood depression: A longitudinal perspective. *Journal of the American Academy of Child Psychiatry, 15,* 491–501.

Poznanski, E. O., Carroll, B. J., & Banegas, M. C., et al. (1982). The dexamethesone suppression test in prepubertal depressed children. *American Journal of Psychiatry, 139,* 321–324.

Poznanski, E. O., Grossman, J. A., Buchsbaum, Y., et al. (1984). Preliminary studies of the reliability and validity of the Children's Depression Rating Scale. *Journal of the American Academy of Child Psychiatry, 23,* 191–197.

Preskorn, S. H., & Irwin, H. A. (1982). Toxicity of tricyclic antidepressants, kinetics, mechanism, intervention: A review. *Journal of Clinical Psychiatry, 43*, 151–156.

Preskorn, S. H., Weller, E. B., & Weller, R. A. (1982). Depression in children: Relationship between plasma imipramine levels and response. *Journal of Clinical Psychiatry, 43*, 450–453.

Puig-Antich, J., & Chambers, W. (1978). *Schedule for affective disorders and schizophenia for schoolage children (K-SADS)*. Unpublished manuscript.

Puig-Antich, J., Blau, S., Marx, N., *et al.* (1978). Prepubertal major depressive disorder: A pilot study. *Journal of the American Academy of Child Psychiatry, 17*, 695–707.

Puig-Antich, J., Perel, J. M., Lupatkin, W., Chambers, W. J., Tabrizi, M. A., King, J., Goetz, R., Davies, M., & Stiller. R. L. (1987). Imipramine in prepubertal major depressive disorders. *Archives of General Psychiatry, 44*, 81–89.

Reich, W., Herjanic, B., Welner, Z., & Gandhy, P. R. (1982). Development of a structured psychiatric interview for children: Agreement on diagnosis comparing child and parent interviews. *Journal of Abnormal Child Psychology, 10*, 325–336.

Rifkin, A., Quitkin, F., Carrillo, C., *et al.* (1972). Lithium carbonate in emotionally unstable character disorder. *Archives of General Psychiatry, 27*, 519–523.

Robbins, D. R., Alessi. N. E., Yanchyshyn, G. W., *et al.* (1983). The dexamethasone suppression test in psychiatrically hospitalized adolescents. *Journal of the American Academy of Child Psychiatry, 22*, 467–469.

Rutter, M., & Graham, P. (1968). The reliability and validity of the psychiatric assessment of the child: Interview with the child. *British Journal of Psychiatry, 114*, 563–579.

Ryan, N. D., Puig-Anitch, J., Cooper, T., Rabinovich, H., Ambrosini, P., Davies, M., King, J., Torres, D., & Fried, J. (1986). Imipramine in adolescent major depression: Plasma level and clinical response. *Acta Psychiatrica Scandinavica, 73*, 275–288.

Ryan, N. D., Puig-Antich, J., Cooper, T. B., Rabinovich, H., Ambrosini, P., Fried, J., Davies, M., King, J., Torres, D.. & Suckow. R. F. (1987). The relative safety of single vs divided dose imipramine in adolescent major depression. *Journal of American Academy of Child and Adolescent Psychiatry, 26*, 400–406.

Siassi, I. (1982). Lithium treatment of impulsive behavior in children. *Journal of Clinical Psychiatry, 43*, 482–484.

Sokoloff, R. M., & Lubin, B. (1983). Depressive mood in adolescent, emotionally disturbed females: Reliability and validity of an adjective checklist (C-DACL). *Journal of Abnormal Child Psychology, 11*, 531–536.

Stack, J. J. (1971). Chemotherapy in childhood depression. Proc. 4th UEP Congress. *Depressive states in childhood and adolescence*. Stockholm: Almquist & Wiksell.

Strober, M., & Carlson, G. A. (1982). Bipolar illness in adolescents with major depression. *Archives of General Psychiatry, 39*, 549–555.

Targum, S. D., & Capodanno, A. E. (1983). The dexamethasone suppression test in adolescent psychiatric inpatients. *American Journal of Psychiatry, 140*, 589–591.

Tisher, M., & Lang, M. (1983). The Children's Depression Scale: Review and further developments. In D. Cantwell & G. A. Carlson (Eds.), *Affective disorders in childhood and adolescence*. New York: Spectrum.

Vestergaard, P. (1983). Clinically important side effects of long-term lithium treatment: A review. *Acta Psychiatrica Scandinavica Supplimentum, 305*, 11–36.

Weinberg, W. A., Rutman, J.. Sullivan, L., Penick, E. C., & Dietz, S. G. (1973). Depression in children referred to an educational diagnostic center: Diagnosis and treatment. *Journal of Pediatrics, 83*, 1065–1072.

Weissman, M. M., Orvaschel, H., & Padian, N. (1980). Children's symptom and social functioning self report scales: Comparison of mother's and children's reports. *Journal of Nervous and Mental Disease, 168*, 736–740.

Weissman, M. M., Prusoff, B. A., Gammon, G. D., Merikangas, K. R.. Leckman, J. F., & Kidd, K. K. (1984). Psychopathology in the children (ages 6–18) of depressed and normal parents. *Journal of the American Academy of Child Psychiatry. 23*, 78–84.

Weller, E. B., Weller, R. A., Fristad, M. A., *et al.* (1984). The dexamethasone suppression test in hospitalized prepubertal depressed children. *American Journal of Psychiatry, 141*, 290–291.

Weller, E. B., Weller, R. A., & Fristad, M. A. (1986). Lithium dosage guide for prepubertal children: A preliminary report. *Journal of the American Academy of Child Psychiatry, 25*, 92–96.

# V     Treatment Approaches: Medical Psychology

The largest and perhaps fastest growing new subspecialty is behavioral medicine/medical psychology/pediatric psychology. Whatever title is chosen, it should be evident that the genesis of many problems that have traditionally been presented to the general practitioner, the pediatrician, or the family practitioner may have psychological underpinnings. The most prominent and most frequently studied are the eating disorders and the elimination disorders (enuresis and encopresis). The chapters Part V are devoted to these particular topics. And despite the severity of these problems and their general intractability in the past, much has been done to advance our knowledge of how these problems may be effectively treated. Part V finishes with a more general chapter delineating some of the health issues that have recently come to light in children and how they may be effectively treated.

# 16    Eating Disorders
## Psychological Therapies

DONALD A. WILLIAMSON, RITA C. PRATHER,
ROBERT W. HEFFER, AND MARY L. KELLEY

Problems of eating are very common presenting complaints in outpatient and inpatient pediatric facilities (Christophersen & Rapoff, 1979; Clark & Munford, 1980). The American Psychiatric Association (APA, 1980) lists four eating disorders—anorexia nervosa. bulimia, pica, and rumination disorder of infancy—as psychiatric disorders of childhood and adolescence. Other eating disorders of childhood and adolescence, which have been treated by behavior therapists, are obesity, Prader-Willi syndrome, failure to thrive, and food refusal. This chapter reviews the treatment literature for each of these eating disorders of children and adolescents. Diagnosis and assessment are discussed. For a more comprehensive discussion of diagnosis and assessment. the reader may wish to refer to Williamson, Kelley, Cavell, and Prather (1988). However, it is important to discuss diagnostic issues, and this will be the first area reviewed.

## CHILDHOOD AND ADOLESCENT OBESITY

### Diagnosis

The traditional criterion for a diagnosis of obesity is a weight at least 20% above normal for age and height, based on actuarial tables such as the norms established by the U.S. Department of Health, Education, and Welfare (1973). Early behavioral treatment studies of childhood and adolescent obesity often included subjects less than 20% overweight (e.g., Weiss, 1977). Recent studies, however, have generally adhered to this criterion and thus can be regarded as true clinical studies of childhood obesity. Estimates of the prevalence of obesity in childhood and adolescence have varied widely (from 6% to 15%) (Brownell & Stunkard, 1980). Most studies have found increased prevalence of obesity as a function of age (Coates & Thoresen, 1978) and have found it to be more prevalent among females across all ages in both childhood and adolescence (Brownell & Stunkard, 1980). If a child remains obese at the end of adolescence, the odds are 28 to 1 that he or she will be obese as an adult (Abraham & Nordsieck, 1960).

DONALD A. WILLIAMSON, RITA C. PRATHER, ROBERT W. HEFFER, AND MARY L. KELLEY • Department of Psychology, Louisiana State University, Baton Rouge, Louisiana 70803.

Given the medical and social consequences of obesity (Bellack & Williamson, 1982; Strauss, Smith, Frame, & Forehand, 1985; Stunkard, 1980), there is no question that effective treatment of obesity in childhood is of great significance for a large proportion of the population. Early intervention for obesity is especially important because of the generally negative outcome of the treatment of chronically obese adults (Smith & Fremouw, in press).

The assessment and then the diagnosis of obesity in childhood and adolescence usually involves a comprehensive medical evaluation, behavioral interviews with the child and the parents, the measurement of height and weight, and either self-monitoring or parental monitoring of eating behavior (Williamson *et al.*, 1988). An evaluation of other behavior problems should also be undertaken. Research concerning noneating disordered behavioral problems of obese children has generally found these children to have moderate levels of psychosocial problems, such as social withdrawal, low self-esteem, frequent somatic complaints, and rejection by peers (Israel & Shapiro, 1985; Strauss *et al.*, 1985).

## Treatment

### Basic Treatment Approaches

The first behavioral treatment studies of childhood or adolescent obesity were published by Aragona, Cassady, and Drabman (1975); Rivinus, Drummond, and Hustorf (1976); and Gross, Wheeler, and Hess (1976). Since these first reports, over 20 treatment studies have been published about various behavioral interventions for weight reduction in children and adolescents. Most of the investigations have used group treatment approaches, though individual treatment has also been used (e.g., Coates & Thoresen, 1981; Weiss, 1977). Most programs involve structured didactic presentations and contingency contracting for behavior change. Typically, the group programs involve 10–15 weekly sessions (Brownell & Stunkard, 1980). Specific behavioral interventions that are commonly used in these programs are:

1. Either parental monitoring or self-monitoring of eating behavior, the food consumed, and exercise.
2. Behavioral contracting or contingency management (usually with monetary rewards) for behavior change.
3. Stimulus control procedures in which the subject is instructed to eat only in selected environments and at specified times (cf. Bellack & Williamson, 1982).
4. Modification of eating habits, such as slowing down the pace of eating and breaking the "clean plate habit."
5. Modification of exercise, either aerobic or lifestyle change (e.g., walking up stairs and walking rather than riding in automobiles).

Other methods that have been used include response cost (Aragona *et al.*, 1975), cognitive-behavior therapy (Coates & Thoresen, 1981), and modeling (Rivinus *et al.*, 1976). Generally, these treatment programs have yielded positive results, with mean weight losses to 15 lb. Since these initial studies, controlled investigations of the effects of parental involvement, exercise, and school-based programs have been reported. The sections that follow summarize the results of these studies.

Etiological studies of obesity have consistently found that parental weight status and child weight are positively related (Gara & Clark, 1976). Obese children with obese parents have been found to be at greater risk of maintaining obesity in adulthood (Charney, Goodman. McBride, Lyon, & Pratt, 1976). These findings could be the result of genetics (Foch & McClearn, 1980), the different eating and food storage and buying habits of obese and nonobese parents (Terry & Beck, 1985), or some combination of genetic and behavioral or environmental factors.

Based on the results of these etiological reports, a number of clinical studies have compared behavioral treatment programs involving only the child with programs that incorporated one or both parents in the treatment. These studies have consistently found that involvement of the parents is beneficial for weight loss during the treatment phase, as well as at follow-up as long as 1 year after treatment (Brownell & Stunkard, 1980; Epstein & Wing, 1983; Epstein, Wing, Koeske, Andrasik, & Ossip, 1981; Israel, Stolmaker, & Andrian, 1985; Kingsley & Shapiro, 1977; Kirschenbaum, Harris, & Tomarken, 1984).

Epstein, Wing, Koeske, and Valoski (1986b) reported that after 1-year follow-up, children of nonobese parents lost more weight than children of obese parents. However, this effect disappeared at the 3-year follow-up. In an investigation of the proper role of the parent in the behavioral program, Israel, Stolmaker, Sharp, Silverman, and Simon (1984) compared a program in which one group of parents was in a parallel weight-loss program for themselves and another group served as "helpers" of their children. All the children were in a standard self-control treatment program for obesity. Both approaches were superior to no treatment, but the two programs involving the parents did not differ in effectiveness. Variables that have been found to positively influence long-term treatment outcome are fewer children in the family, female gender, an initial positive response to the treatment program, and an intact family structure (Epstein, Koeske, Wing, & Valoski, 1986a).

To summarize, it is clear that involving family members in the treatment of childhood obesity is beneficial. It does not appear that the type of involvement of the parents is as critical as structuring some type of involvement that promotes parental reinforcement of behavior change and parental modeling of behavior change.

## School-Based Treatment

Two controlled group-outcome studies have evaluated school-based behavioral treatment programs for childhood obesity (Foster, Wadden, & Brownell, 1985) and adolescent obesity (Lansky & Vance, 1983). Both studies found the school-based treatment to be superior to no treatment. Also, Lansky and Vance (1983) found that children whose parents participated in the program lost significantly more weight than those who were in treatment but whose parents were not involved. Neither study reported long-term follow-up, which is significant, as Foster *et al.* (1985) reported a trend toward relapse 18 weeks after the conclusion of treatment.

These studies suggest that school-based interventions may be a viable approach to the treatment of obesity. Furthermore, the results of Lansky and

Vance (1983) suggest that parental involvement may facilitate the weight loss produced by interventions by the school.

## Effects of Exercise

Early behavioral interventions for obesity tended to emphasize the modification of eating habits. Several more recent studies have evaluated the significance of including exercise in a multicomponent treatment package. Epstein, Wing, Koeske, and Valoski (1984) found that diet plus exercise resulted in significantly greater weight loss than diet alone, for parents and children, at 6-month follow-up. At 12-month follow-up, this effect was maintained for the parents, but not for the children. However, both Epstein *et al.* (1984) and Cohen, Gelfand, Dodd, Jensen, and Turner (1980) found that *practice* of regular exercise was associated with the long-term maintenance of weight loss in children. Two studies (Epstein, Wing, Koeske, Ossip, & Beck, 1982; Epstein, Wing, Koeske, & Valoski, 1985) have found that lifestyle-change exercise (e.g., bicycling and walking upstairs) was superior to programmed aerobic exercise (e.g., jogging) when combined with diet. These effects were attributed to better long-term adherence to lifestyle change exercise.

These investigations suggest that exercise is a very important component of successful weight loss in children and adolescents, especially in the promotion of long-term effects. Epstein and colleagues have established that lifestyle-change exercise programs that involve changes in the exercise habits of the entire family seem to yield the best long-term results. These studies have consistently shown that children generally lose approximately 15 lb on the average but remain approximately 20%–30% overweight at the end of treatment and at follow-up periods of 2–3 years. However, many of these children (30%–70%) attain a weight level in the nonobese range (i.e., below 20% overweight). These results are of clinical significance, given the general failure of other approaches to yield results that are this positive.

## Summary

Behavioral treatment of childhood obesity has been intensively studied since the mid-1970s. These studies have been well controlled and have generally yielded positive results. The literature as a whole suggests that comprehensive programs involving eating and exercise modification with family involvement can yield clinically meaningful weight losses that are maintained at long-term follow-up. After treatment, many of these children achieve nonobese status, which is of great significance because it is well established that continuation of obesity from adolescence to adulthood is associated with a very poor long-term prognosis.

## PRADER-WILLI SYNDROME

### Diagnosis

Prader-Willi syndrome (PWS) is a multidimensional congenital disorder that impairs its victims throughout life. The characteristics essential to a diagnosis of

PWS are hypotonia, hypogonadism, obesity after infancy, cognitive dysfunction (e.g., mental retardation), dysmorphic facial features, and short stature for genetic background (Cassidy, 1984; Holm, 1981). During infancy and early childhood, an individual with PWS typically presents with delays in motor development, difficulties in sucking and feeding, and profound muscular hypotonia and with a history of decreased fetal activity, low birth weight, and abnormal delivery (Zellweger, 1981). A second phase of PWS begins between ages 6 months and 6 years, in which features such as hyperphagia, morbid obesity, intellectual impairment, and abnormal sexual development predominate (Hanson, 1981). Obesity is the most life-threatening characteristic of PWS. in that it often produces serious health complications that result in a shortened life expectancy for PWS patients (Laurence, Brito & Wilkinson, 1981; Touquet, Ward, & Clark, 1983).

The etiology and pathogenesis of PWS are not well understood. Many of the physical and behavioral problems observed in PWS patients, however, indicate a hypothalamic dysfunction (Hanson, 1981). Thus, in contrast to obesity in normal children, obesity in a child with PWS is assumed to result from a central nervous system defect. In addition, PWS patients differ from normal obese patients in their body composition and their metabolic processes (Nelson, Huse, Holman, Kimbrough, Wahner, Callaway, & Hayles, 1981). Individuals with PWS have relatively lower rates of energy expenditure and caloric requirements: "Weight maintenance in PWS individuals will occur with 10–11 kcal/cm of height, and 8–9 kcal/cm of height will allow slow weight loss. In normal children weight maintenance is achieved with 12–22 kcal/cm of height" (Cassidy, 1984, p. 19). Furthermore, obesity in PWS is often exacerbated by hyperphagia and an inability to vomit. Individuals with PWS often gorge themselves as long as food is present, steal food to eat in private, eat inedible substances, and engage in violent outbursts when deprived of food (Bray, Dahms, Swerdloff, Fiser, Atkinson, & Carrel, 1983).

In light of the unique nature of PWS, a behavioral and medical assessment of eating behaviors in children with PWS should be conducted collaboratively. The behavioral assessment procedures discussed previously in this chapter and in Williamson *et al.* (1988) with regard to obese children and adolescents may be applied to evaluating obesity in PWS patients.

A behavioral assessment of obesity and feeding problems in a child with PWS usually occurs after, or along with, a medical diagnosis of the disorder. Although PWS is a relatively common disorder with an estimated incidence rate of 1:10,000, no clear clinical marker exists by which physicians can easily identify the syndrome (Cassidy. 1984). Patients with a diagnosis of PWS are a heterogeneous group in which variability in the presence and severity of clinical characteristics hinders diagnosis. Furthermore, the features of PWS change from infancy to childhood, thus increasing the difficulty of medical assessment for the syndrome.

Children are typically identified as having PWS between ages 5 and 10, when obesity is the central presenting problem, rather than in infancy, when feeding difficulties exist and often lead to failure to gain weight properly (Cassidy, 1984). Because of the obstacles to an early diagnosis, some PWS patients are not identified until late adolescence or early adulthood. Clinicians involved in the behavioral assessment of an obese child or an infant with feeding problems should be aware of the features associated with PWS and should recommend a medical evaluation whenever PWS is suspected.

Treatment

As in the assessment of PWS, treatment should be tailored to the specific maladaptive behaviors of the specific child. Some children may present with a full cluster of problem behaviors associated with the disorder, whereas other PWS patients may exhibit a relatively small subset of problems. Furthermore, the treatment of PWS should be multidisciplinary; psychologists, nutritionists, social workers, and physicians should work in concert to ameliorate the difficulties typically encountered by families of children with PWS.

*First Phase of PWS*

If PWS is first identified in infancy, when food refusal may lead to a diagnosis of failure to thrive (i.e., weight for age below the 3rd percentile), treatment should focus on establishing appropriate feeding interactions between parent(s) and child. Zellweger (1981) pointed out that, when food intake and weight gain are poor in the initial phase of PWS, the parents typically become frustrated and worried about feeding difficulties. When the infant begins to show increased appetite, the parents respond by differentially reinforcing (e.g., praising) the infant's eating. Once the hyperphagic phase of PWS begins, however, praise from caregivers for eating only serves to exacerbate a problem of overeating, which is believed to be mediated by a dysfunctional hypothalamus. Among other recommendations for establishing appropriate feeding patterns in the first phase of PWS, Zellweger (1981) proposed that no praise be given for eating and that food not be used as a reward. In addition, "caloric intake [should] be regulated by [a] nutritionist and should be kept to a minimum necessary to ensure adequate weight increase" (p. 66).

*Hyperphagic Phase of PWS*

Excessive somnolence, stealing food, poor self-evaluation, peer rejection, cardiopulmonary disorders, and diabetes mellitus are problems commonly associated with obesity in PWS (Cassidy, 1984). In turn, obesity, the major cause of mortality in PWS patients, is a consequence of hyperphagia and of decreased caloric requirements. The challenge in designing behavioral treatments for children with PWS is to develop a weight loss program that will be resistant over time to what is apparently a biologically determined inclination toward excessive eating. Even medical treatments, such as appetite-suppressant drugs and gastrointestinal surgery, have met with limited success in curbing the insatiable appetite of PWS patients (Bray *et al.*, 1983; Fonkalsrud & Bray, 1981; Soper, Mason, Printen, & Zellweger, 1981).

The nutritional management of obesity in children with PWS typically involves low-calorie diets and control of access to food (Holm & Pipes, 1976; Pipes, 1981). Nelson *et al.* (1981) described a calorie-controlled ketogenic diet for reducing obesity based on the unique manner in which PWS patients metabolize carbohydrates, fats, and proteins. Generally, poor long-term maintenance of weight loss has been found when dietary approaches to treating obesity in PWS were used without specific behavioral procedures as adjuncts.

Marshall and his colleagues described a behavioral weight-reduction program that centered on modifying food-related behavior during and between meals in a hospital setting (Marshall, Elder, O'Bosky, Wallace, & Liberman, 1979; Marshall, Wallace, Elder, Burke, Oliver, & Blackmon, 1981). The components of this behavioral program were (1) shaping, self-monitoring, contingency contracting, and discrimination training to decrease the size of portions and the number of calories eaten; (2) contingency contracting and shaping to increase physical activity; and (3) role playing to train the patients to request positive social reinforcement for weight loss. Although substantial weight loss and increases in exercise were obtained over 80 weeks for the participants of this program, weight gain occurred during home visits. Furthermore, maintenance of treatment results was not achieved across participants even though a generalization phase was incorporated into the program.

Other behavioral researchers have treated obesity in PWS patients on an outpatient basis using self-monitoring and contingency contracting to decrease food intake and to increase exercise, as well as response cost and overcorrection to decrease food stealing (Altman, Bondy, & Hirsh, 1978; Hirsch & Altman, 1981; Thompson, Kodluboy, & Heston, 1980). In addition, fading of contingencies, encouragement of input from family members with regard to treatment, and frequent telephone contact have been reported to enhance the maintenance of treatment gains (Coplin, Hine, & Gormician, 1976; Hirsch & Altman, 1981). Generally, however, behavioral treatments of obesity in PWS have yielded mixed results and have been evaluated by means of poorly controlled case studies using small samples of adolescents or young adults.

## Summary

Obesity and dietary management problems in children and adolescents with PWS often contribute to poor health and a shortened life expectancy. Generally, treatments of obesity in PWS, including surgical, nutritional, and behavioral interventions, have not demonstrated good long-term success in the maintenance of weight loss. Controlled studies are needed in which behavioral treatments designed for children and adolescents with PWS are evaluated. In addition, behavioral treatments for obesity in PWS should address the complex constellation of interrelated problems (e.g., hyperphagia, food stealing, and low intellectual functioning) typically observed in children with PWS.

## FOOD REFUSAL

Food refusal is characterized by children's insistence on eating only a small number of foods or only foods with a particular texture, or by their refusal to eat an amount of food sufficient to produce appropriate weight gain (Kreiger, 1982; Williamson et al., 1988). Restricted eating by children very often begins when parents attempt to switch children from liquids to pureed foods or from soft to solid foods (Siegel, 1983). The behavior also may begin after a period of restricted eating due to illness or surgery. Food refusal may be accompanied by other behavioral problems, including mealtime tantrumming, complaining, dawdling, playing with food, expelling food placed in the mouth, gagging or vomiting food, and protracted periods of chewing.

Eating and mealtime behavior problems are quite common in preschool children and are a frequent source of concern for many parents (Christophersen & Hall, 1978; Hertzler, 1983a,b). As many as 45% of all young children display some degree of eating problems (Bentovin, 1970). Developmentally disabled children are particularly at risk of developing serious feeding difficulties (Riordan, Iwata, Finney, Wohl, & Stanley, 1984).

The consequences of food refusal vary considerably from child to child. Many children outgrow the problem, although serious disturbances in eating may produce significant family conflict, social stigma, malnourishment, retarded growth, or, in rare instances, life-threatening physical consequences.

The assessment of food refusal should be comprehensive and multimodal. It is recommended that a medical evaluation be obtained before treatment, as numerous physical conditions can effect children's eating. Information about the history and the topography of the child's eating behavior can be obtained through interviewing the parents and other adults responsible for providing the child's meals. The interview should include a complete dietary and medical history, with an emphasis on the environmental and developmental variables associated with the onset of restricted eating. Treatment planning can be facilitated by obtaining specific descriptions of interventions used by the parents to correct the child's eating and mealtime problems. The clinical interview also should yield a very specific account of the child's food preferences and the antecedents to and consequences of the child's appropriate and inappropriate eating and mealtime behavior (cf. Williamson *et al.*, 1988). Additionally, the interviewer should obtain information on the presence of other child or family problems. Problems such as noncompliance or significant marital conflict may be associated with the child's eating behavior or may make treatment implementation difficult.

Observation of parent and child interactions during mealtime is important in obtaining a thorough and accurate functional analysis of the child's eating behavior. Videotaping mealtimes can be less obtrusive than direct observation and allows an opportunity to review the interaction, an activity we have found helpful in treatment planning. Essential to the assessment and treatment of food refusal is the daily monitoring of target behavior. Ideally, parents should record the amount and types of food eaten by their children and the relevant situational variables (e.g., the time of day). However, we have found the food-intake-monitoring form (Cavell, 1985) shown in Figure 1 to be adequate, particularly when the child is in the hospital, where standard-sized portions are served.

## Treatment

The treatment of food refusal is tailored to the particular child. Treatment decisions should be guided by the physical status of the child, the degree to which the child's food refusal significantly deviates from that of other children of his or her age, the developmental factors that may have precipitated the disorder, the antecedents and consequences that appear to be maintaining the disorder, and the parents' ability and willingness to implement the treatment recommendations. One must also determine where the treatment will take place. Children whose eating disturbances are serious or life-threatening, or for whom treatment will be difficult to implement, may be best treated in a hospital.

Hospitalizing the child also may be necessary if the parents are unable or unwilling to carry out the treatment during the initial phases, when the child is likely to protest any manipulation of the mealtime environment. In such cases, treatment is often carried out initially by the therapist, and management is transferred to the parent only after improvements in the child's eating have been gained (Linscheid, Oliver, Blyler, & Palmer, 1978).

Severe cases of food refusal appear to require the use of an intervention that is planned, executed, and evaluated very systematically. More minor instances of inappropriate eating and mealtime behavior, which are common in many preschoolers, may be treated or prevented through parent education and the parents' modification of the mealtime routine. The following section discusses parent guidelines for modifying minor mealtime problems and then presents a review of studies where severe, enduring problems of food refusal were treated through the systematic application of behavioral principles.

*Parent Education.* Christopherson and Hall (1978) provide a detailed list of parent guidelines for preventing and modifying minor mealtime problems. The

| Day: | | | | | Day: | | | | | Day: | | | | |
|---|---|---|---|---|---|---|---|---|---|---|---|---|---|---|
| **Breakfast** | | | | | **Breakfast** | | | | | **Breakfast** | | | | |
| Juice | 1/4 | 1/2 | 3/4 | all | Juice | 1/4 | 1/2 | 3/4 | all | Juice | 1/4 | 1/2 | 3/4 | all |
| Milk | 1/4 | 1/2 | 3/4 | all | Milk | 1/4 | 1/2 | 3/4 | all | Milk | 1/4 | 1/2 | 3/4 | all |
| Toast | 1/4 | 1/2 | 3/4 | all | Toast | 1/4 | 1/2 | 3/4 | all | Toast | 1/4 | 1/2 | 3/4 | all |
| Cereal | 1/4 | 1/2 | 3/4 | all | Cereal | 1/4 | 1/2 | 3/4 | all | Cereal | 1/4 | 1/2 | 3/4 | all |
| Egg | 1/4 | 1/2 | 3/4 | all | Egg | 1/4 | 1/2 | 3/4 | all | Egg | 1/4 | 1/2 | 3/4 | all |
| Other | 1/4 | 1/2 | 3/4 | all | Other | 1/4 | 1/2 | 3/4 | all | Other | 1/4 | 1/2 | 3/4 | all |
| Snack | 1/4 | 1/2 | 3/4 | all | Snack | 1/4 | 1/2 | 3/4 | all | Snack | 1/4 | 1/2 | 3/4 | all |
| **Lunch** | | | | | **Lunch** | | | | | **Lunch** | | | | |
| Liquid | 1/4 | 1/2 | 3/4 | all | Liquid | 1/4 | 1/2 | 3/4 | all | Liquid | 1/4 | 1/2 | 3/4 | all |
| Meat | 1/4 | 1/2 | 3/4 | all | Meat | 1/4 | 1/2 | 3/4 | all | Meat | 1/4 | 1/2 | 3/4 | all |
| Starch | 1/4 | 1/2 | 3/4 | all | Starch | 1/4 | 1/2 | 3/4 | all | Starch | 1/4 | 1/2 | 3/4 | all |
| Veg. | 1/4 | 1/2 | 3/4 | all | Veg. | 1/4 | 1/2 | 3/4 | all | Veg. | 1/4 | 1/2 | 3/4 | all |
| Fruit | 1/4 | 1/2 | 3/4 | all | Fruit | 1/4 | 1/2 | 3/4 | all | Fruit | 1/4 | 1/2 | 3/4 | all |
| Bread | 1/4 | 1/2 | 3/4 | all | Bread | 1/4 | 1/2 | 3/4 | all | Bread | 1/4 | 1/2 | 3/4 | all |
| Other | 1/4 | 1/2 | 3/4 | all | Other | 1/4 | 1/2 | 3/4 | all | Other | 1/4 | 1/2 | 3/4 | all |
| Snack | 1/4 | 1/2 | 3/4 | all | Snack | 1/4 | 1/2 | 3/4 | all | Other | 1/4 | 1/2 | 3/4 | all |
| **Supper** | | | | | **Supper** | | | | | **Supper** | | | | |
| Liquid | 1/4 | 1/2 | 3/4 | all | Liquid | 1/4 | 1/2 | 3/4 | all | Liquid | 1/4 | 1/2 | 3/4 | all |
| Meat | 1/4 | 1/2 | 3/4 | all | Meat | 1/4 | 1/2 | 3/4 | all | Meat | 1/4 | 1/2 | 3/4 | all |
| Starch | 1/4 | 1/2 | 3/4 | all | Starch | 1/4 | 1/2 | 3/4 | all | Starch | 1/4 | 1/2 | 3/4 | all |
| Veg. | 1/4 | 1/2 | 3/4 | all | Veg. | 1/4 | 1/2 | 3/4 | all | Veg. | 1/4 | 1/2 | 3/4 | all |
| Fruit | 1/4 | 1/2 | 3/4 | all | Fruit | 1/4 | 1/2 | 3/4 | all | Fruit | 1/4 | 1/2 | 3/4 | all |
| Bread | 1/4 | 1/2 | 3/4 | all | Bread | 1/4 | 1/2 | 3/4 | all | Bread | 1/4 | 1/2 | 3/4 | all |
| Other | 1/4 | 1/2 | 3/4 | all | Other | 1/4 | 1/2 | 3/4 | all | Other | 1/4 | 1/2 | 3/4 | all |
| Snack | 1/4 | 1/2 | 3/4 | all | Snack | 1/4 | 1/2 | 3/4 | all | Other | 1/4 | 1/2 | 3/4 | all |

FIGURE 1. Hospital eating record form (from Cavell, 1985).

authors discuss the importance of introducing pureed and solid foods at the appropriate age and suggest that the premature or delayed introduction of new foods may produce food allergies or behavior problems. These authors also suggest that parents avoid backtracking when a new food texture is introduced.

It is generally recommended that parents work to make mealtime a pleasant experience and a time in which they teach their children appropriate mealtime behavior through shaping. It also is important that parents maintain a certain degree of flexibility about their children's food preferences as children's likes and dislikes fluctuate considerably. Finally, parents should be taught basic developmental information regarding children's eating patterns. For example, many parents become overly concerned when their children's appetite decreases at about one year of age—a phenomena that is normal for most children given their decelerated growth.

Additional guidelines to provide parents in order to prevent or modify minor mealtime problems are presented in Christophersen and Hall (1978).

Although many parents may be able to modify the mealtime environment and minor mealtime problems through the use of such suggestions as those noted by Christophersen and Hall (1978), it is important that a thorough assessment, including a medical evaluation, be conducted. Without complete assessment, therapists risk treating children's food refusal or inappropriate eating in a superficial, ineffective manner and, by doing so, may prolong or perhaps exacerbate the problem. Finally, it is necessary to monitor parents' implementation of suggestions so that behavioral interventions such as children's removal from the table following misbehavior are used appropriately.

### Operant Conditioning Procedures

Severe cases of food refusal have generally been modified through the use of shaping and differential attention procedures. Through the highly structured use of these procedures, substantial increases have been obtained in the amount and variety of foods eaten by both developmentally disabled and normal children (e.g., Bernal, 1972; Linscheid *et al.*, 1978; Riordan *et al.*, 1984; Riordan, Iwata, Whol, & Finney, 1980; Thompson, Palmer, & Linscheid, 1977).

The treatment of children whose restricted patterns of eating are life-threatening or deviate substantially from those of other children their age generally begins by severely restricting the children's intake of preferred foods under the guidance of a physician (Riordan *et al.*, 1984; Thompson *et al.*, 1977).

Increasing children's eating is often accomplished through the use of shaping procedures, in which the child is given a specific number of prompts to eat a bite of a nonpreferred food. Frequently, the therapist begins by offering foods that are likely to be refused but that approximate a preferred food in texture or taste (Linscheid *et al.*, 1978).

Reinforcing food acceptance is typically done by providing the child with praise and bites of preferred foods immediately following compliance. Using liked foods as reinforcers may also function to decrease the expulsion of undesired foods (Riordan *et al.*, 1984). Initially, reinforcement is provided after each instance of appropriate eating; later, it is given only intermittently or at the end of the meal.

Inappropriate mealtime behavior (e.g.. complaining or tantrumming) or refusal to eat a nonpreferred food is generally followed by a brief period of ignoring (Bernal, 1972). Some authors have also placed the child in time-out when inappropriate behavior occurs or at the end of the meal if a specified amount of food was not eaten (Linscheid *et al.*, 1978).

Although increases in appropriate eating have usually been obtained through the use of differential attention procedures, we encountered a situation in which prompts to eat appeared to function as a discriminative stimulus for refusal to eat; a manipulation of environmental consequences produced escalations in disruptive behavior (Heffer, Cavell, & Kelley, 1985). In this study, a 5-year-old child with a growth hormone deficiency was the subject. The mother, who was responsible for implementing the treatment in the hospital, found the use of differential attention too aversive to continue using, given her child's escalation of inappropriate behavior. Consequently, she was instructed to avoid discussing eating during the meal, to eat with the child, and to engage in pleasant mealtime conversation.

The procedure, which emphasized altering the antecedents to eating, resulted in increased eating and decreased disruptiveness and was well received by the mother. However, several methodological shortcomings of the study limit the degree to which definitive statements can be made regarding the treatment's efficacy. The case study does suggest, however, that antecedent control over eating may be an important consideration in the development of an easy-to-implement intervention.

### Classical and Operant Conditioning Procedures

Although operant procedures are often effective in treating food refusal, Siegel (1982) reported that contingency management procedures alone were not effective with a 6-year-old boy who exhibited a strong aversion to table food. The boy frequently gagged or vomited whenever he attempted to eat a new food—a behavior that had apparently developed during an illness. After a contingency management procedure failed to alter the boy's eating, a respondent and operant procedure was implemented. The program involved requiring the child to first smell table foods and then gradually introduced tasting, chewing, and swallowing table foods. In an attempt to decrease the physiological arousal associated with eating, the child was allowed to engage in the target responses while watching TV. The program was effective in remediating the child's food aversion and limited eating.

### Summary

Food refusal and mealtime behavior problems are quite common in preschool children and are a frequent source of concern for many parents. Although many children outgrow mild problems of restricted eating, serious eating disturbances may produce significant, negative environmental and biological consequences. The assessment of food refusal should be comprehensive and multimodal in order to yield an accurate functional analysis of the child's eating behavior. Severe cases of food refusal have been generally modified through the use of operant procedures, including shaping, differential attention, and time-out. These procedures are often administered initially by a professional in a hospital setting, and control is transferred to the child's parent after treatment gains have been obtained.

## FAILURE TO THRIVE

### Diagnosis

Failure to thrive (FTT) is a prevalent pediatric problem, accounting for 1% of hospitalized children (Bithoney & Rathbun, 1983; Schor, 1984). FTT in infants is indicated when weight is persistently below the 5th percentile for age or is less than 80%–85% of the child's ideal weight relative to standardized growth charts. FTT also refers to a failure to maintain an established weight-gain pattern represented by a loss of 2 or more percentiles on an infant's growth curve. An infant whose weight for age is low, but whose rate of weight gain is steady (i.e., tracks his or her "own" growth curve), should not be considered failing to thrive (Accardo, 1982). In addition, FTT is a growth symptom of virtually all serious pediatric illnesses and could be applied to any infant making "suboptimal physical or developmental progress" (Bacon, Spencer, Hopwood, & Kelch, 1982, p. 95).

Traditionally, FTT has been dichotomized into two mutually exclusive categories based on its presumed etiology. In organic FTT, a physical disorder has been diagnosed, whereas in nonorganic FTT (NOFTT), no organic dysfunction has been identified. That is, in the absence of a clear organic etiology, NOFTT is diagnosed by exclusion and is assumed to result from psychosocial variables, such as "emotional deprivation," parental neglect, conditions of poverty, an irritability or passivity, parental psychopathology, and/or feeding problems (Roberts & Maddux, 1982).

Recently, however, some authors have questioned the utility of a dichotomous nosology for FTT (e.g., Krieger, 1982). The identification of an organic etiology for FTT does not preclude the existence of behavioral components in the disease, and biological risks have been implicated in the course of NOFTT (Bithoney & Dubowitz, 1985; Frank, 1985). Homer and Ludwig (1981) have therefore suggested that FTT is best described by means of three etiological categories: (1) organic; (2) psychosocial; and (3) mixed (i.e., having organic *and* psychosocial contributants). Such a nosology accounts for the interactive influences of organic disorders and psychosocial variables on an infant's weight gain.

With regard to FTT in the absence of an organic etiology, Linscheid and Rasnake (1985) proposed two types of NOFTT based on age of onset and behavioral analyses of parent–infant interactions. Type I NOFTT is characterized by dysfunctional parent–infant interactions across multiple situations, which result in failure to gain weight at an early age (i.e., before 8 months). Type I NOFTT, therefore, is similar to what the DSM-III (APA, 1980) refers to as Reactive Attachment Disorder. In contrast, Type II NOFTT typically presents when an infant is 8 months or older and involves weight-gain failure primarily due to poor *feeding* interactions (e.g., food refusal or food selectivity, resulting in conflictual mealtime interactions and inadequate caloric intake).

Because a variety of biological and environmental variables interact to produce the problems associated with FTT, a multidisciplinary team-management approach to assessing this disorder is essential (Berkowitz, 1985; Peterson,

Washington, & Rathbun, 1984). Medical personnel, social workers, psychologists, and nutritionists should work as collaborative consultants to evaluate simultaneously organic and environmental contributants to FTT. Such a comprehensive team approach not only provides invaluable assessment information but also identifies the problems to be targeted in treatment.

The medical information to be obtained includes the current anthropometrics (i.e., weight, height, and head circumference), a history of growth and weight gain, a birth history (e.g., the course of the pregnancy and any perinatal events), a physical exam, family growth patterns, and laboratory tests. Nutritional status and history, as well as information with regard to family ecology (e.g., family size, income, and living conditions), are also integral to an evaluation of FTT (Drotar, Nowak, Malone, Eckerle, & Negray, 1985).

Psychologists are most likely to contribute to an interdisciplinary assessment of FTT by collecting data on an infant's developmental status (e.g., Bayley Scales of Development; Bayley, 1969), a monitoring of food intake, parent psychopathology (e.g., depression or anxiety), and behavioral observations of parent–infant interactions during feeding and nonfeeding situations. Behavioral observations are especially important in an assessment of FTT because they provide information by which a functional analysis of dysfunctional parent–child interaction patterns can be formulated (Finlon, Drotar, Satola, Pallota, Wyatt, & El-Amin, 1985). For a detailed discussion of the assessment issues in FTT, please refer to Williamson *et al.* (1988).

## Treatment

Treatment planning should proceed directly from a multidisciplinary assessment and should target the physical, economic, and behavioral problems identified in the evaluation of a FTT child (Agorb, Pfieffer, & Leichtman, 1979). Organic problems, of course, should be treated by a physician. The difficulties best remediated by psychologists, dieticians, and social workers include problems related to (1) family impoverishment and parental expectations with regard to the child's development; (2) inadequate infant stimulation; and (3) feeding problems.

### Poverty and Lack of Education

In some cases, FTT is the result of inadequate family resources or the parents' lack of appropriate child-rearing information (Frank, Allen, & Brown, 1985). Thus, treatment should center on providing the family access to nutritious food and financial assistance, counseling on the efficient allocation of resources, and education on nutrition and child development. Treatments of this kind have resulted in infant weight gains and improved developmental status (Drotar & Malone, 1985; Ramey, Starr, Pallas, Whitten, & Reed, 1975; Whitten, Pettit, & Fischoff, 1969).

### Inadequate Infant Stimulation

As Linscheid and Rasnake (1985) suggested, infant stimulation in the form of adequate nurturing interactions between parent and infant (e.g., bathing, feeding, cuddling, dressing, and playing) provides the infant with opportunities for learning that his or her behavior influences the environment. Such "contingency experiences" allow the parent and the infant to develop a communication system in which the behavioral cues of the infant elicit appropriate caregiving behaviors from the parent. If infant stimulation is inadequate, a lack of contingency experiences may lead to dysfunctional parent–infant interactions across multiple situations. In turn, the stressed parent–child relationship and the insufficient caloric intake due to ineffective feeding interactions may result in poor weight gain. Such a situation occurs in what Linscheid and Rasnake (1985) referred to as Type I NOFTT.

The treatment of Type I NOFTT should involve intensive stimulation of the infant across a variety of situations and should include all the senses (i.e., visual, auditory, olfactory, tactile, and gustatory). As a result, opportunities for contingency experiences increase, and the infant may develop a repertoire of behaviors that can affect changes in the environment (cf. Field, 1978). Through experiencing contingent interactions with the child, the parent also learns how to effectively "read" the infant's behavior.

Professionals may be used initially to model nurturing behaviors in the hospital or during home visits. The parents should then be faded in as participants in the adult–infant interactions, and feedback and behavioral rehearsal should be used to improve parental performance. In addition, the treatment should address conflicts between family members that may contribute to an infant's failure to gain weight (Drotar, Malone, & Negray, 1979). If parental psychopathology, such as depression or anxiety disorders (cf. T. M. Field, 1984), prevents opportunities for contingency experiences, treatment of the adult should precede, or should be conducted concurrently with, attempts to treat FTT.

## Feeding Problems

If maladaptive behaviors, such as food refusal by a child or ineffective mealtime behaviors by a parent, persist, the feeding situation may become conflictual for both parent and infant. Type II NOFTT is characterized by failure to gain weight because of conflictual feeding interactions (Linschied & Rasnake, 1985). The treatment of Type II NOFTT should target specific parent and infant behavior excesses and deficits. For example, the intervention might focus on increasing a parent's sensitivity to behavioral cues from the child during feeding interactions (Satter, 1986) or on modifying a child's food refusal (Heffer et al., 1985). The treatments discussed previously in this chapter with regard to food refusal may also be applied to cases in which the feeding problems have resulted in FTT (Linscheid & Rasnake, 1985).

A behavioral feeding program designed specifically for FTT infants was described by Larson and Ayllon (1985). Infants aged 4–22 months were treated with a nurturant bonding procedure and a contingency procedure. In the nurturant bonding procedure, the infants were provided with caregiving experiences designed to enhance the attachment between parents and infants. The procedure involved pairing music with affection from an adult and, later, providing music during mealtime contingent on the acceptance of food. A time-out procedure followed instances of food refusal. The contingency procedure was successful, whereas the nurturant bonding procedure did not lead to increased food intake. Although this study needs replication, its unique use of music contingent on food acceptance is interesting and presents an example of how positive reinforcement and time-out procedures may be implemented to increase food intake in children with FTT.

## Summary

Regardless of the etiology (i.e., organic or nonorganic), FTT is a problem of undernutrition (Bithoney & Dubowitz, 1985). The undernutrition in FTT may be attributed to situational variables (e.g., poverty, stress, or perinatal conditions), intraindividual variables (e.g., organic and behavioral deficits of infants or parents), and interindividual variables (e.g., dysfunctional parent–child interactions), which decrease the likelihood that adequate nutrition will be delivered to, or properly metabolized by, an infant. In addition, chronic undernutrition that results in FTT in infancy has been associated with poor developmental outcomes, such as increased health problems and risk of mortality, behavior problems, and cognitive and developmental delays (M. Field, 1984; Galler, Ramsey, & Solimano, 1985; Krieger, 1982; Singer & Fagan, 1984). Given the complexity of FTT, therefore, treatment should be multimodal and comprehensive if the deleterious outcomes of FTT are to be avoided.

## RUMINATION

### Diagnosis

Chronic rumination is the self-induced regurgitation of previously swallowed food (Murray, Keele, & McCarver, 1977). Often, the food is rechewed and reswallowed, although the vomitus may run out of the individual's mouth (Wright & Menolacsino, 1966). Although normal infants sometimes exhibit the behavior, it is seen more commonly in developmentally disabled individuals and in infants with a physical disability, such as gastroesophageal reflux and hiatal hernia (Madison & Adubato, 1984). Numerous medical complications can occur as a result of rumination, such as dehydration, electrolyte disturbances, malnutrition, lowered resistance to infection, and, in some instances, death (Madison & Adubato, 1984; Singh, 1981).

Although rumination is not assumed to be due to a physical abnormality, it is sometimes misdiagnosed as a physical disorder. Singh (1981) suggested that rumination, in contrast to a physical disorder, should be suspected if the child is emaciated, frequently has vomitus on his or her face and clothing, appears to derive pleasure from ruminating, and engages in other self-stimulatory behavior. In addition, vomiting may be a symptom of many childhood infections and disorders. Thus, decisions regarding the diagnosis of rumination should be made in collaboration with a physician.

The behavioral assessment of rumination should include a comprehensive evaluation of the home environment. In some instances, ruminative vomiting may be due partially to a lack of environmental stimulation or to undernourishment (Jackson, Johnson, Ackron, & Crowley, 1975).

Integral to the planning of an appropriate treatment is a thorough evaluation of the antecedents to and the consequences of ruminative behavior. In many instances, individuals may engage in specific, predictable responses just before ruminating. For example, tongue thrusting, stomach rolling, puffed cheeks, gagging, hand in mouth, and lip smacking have been identified as antecedents to ruminative vomiting in individual children (cf. Becker, Turner, & Sajwaj, 1978; Daniel, 1982; Madison & Adubato, 1984). The consequences of rumination may be varied but often include such reinforcers as physical and social attention and avoidance of, or escape from, other activities (Varni, 1983). Also, the act of regurgitating, rechewing, and reswallowing food often appears to be inherently reinforcing.

## Treatment

### Punishment Procedures

Because of the premise that ruminative vomiting is maintained by reinforcing consequences, numerous researchers have attempted to eliminate the behavior through the contingent application of punishing stimuli. Aversive conditioning procedures have included mild electric shock (e.g., Lang & Melamed, 1969; Watkins, 1972), aversive tastes (Becker *et al.*, 1978), and contingent exercise (Daniel, 1982) administered immediately after the occurrence of a ruminative or a preruminative response. The aversive substances have included diluted lemon juice (Sajwaj, Libet, & Agras, 1974) and mouthwash (Singh, Manning, & Angell, 1982). A possibly more socially acceptable substance, which we have found effective in maintaining low levels of ruminative behavior in a profoundly mentally retarded male child, is pickle juice.

Aversive conditioning procedures have been used alone or in combination with other interventions. Although aversion conditioning has been very effective in decreasing ruminative vomiting, ethical regulations and considerations must always be taken into account before their implementation (cf. Singh, 1981).

Overcorrection procedures have also been used to treat rumination. For example, Duker and Seys (1977) substantially decreased the ruminative vomiting exhibited by a 19-year-old female through the contingent use of a restitutional overcorrection procedure. After each instance of vomiting, the woman was shown the results of the act and was required to wash her face, the floor, and the walls for 20 minutes (cf. Singh for a more detailed discussion of the use of overcorrection with ruminators).

### Reinforcement Procedures

Although less frequently used than punishment, reinforcement procedures alone or in combination with ignoring or time-out have been effective in reducing ruminative behavior (Mulick, Schroeder, & Rojahn, 1980b; Munford & Pally, 1979; Sheinbein, 1975). For example, Madison and Adabuto (1984) eliminated ruminative vomiting in a 15-month-old child with gastroesophageal reflux through the use of differential attention. In this study, the parents freely interacted with the child when he did not ruminate and withdrew their attention contingent on rumination. Withdrawal of attention was signaled with a loud click and the word *no*. In another study, two profoundly mentally retarded adults with long histories of ruminative vomiting were successfully treated through the use of a DRO (differential reinforcement of other behavior) procedure in which the nonoccurrence of vomiting was rewarded with small bites of cookie or peanut butter (Conrin, Pennypacker, Johnston, & Rast, 1982).

### Satiation Procedures

Because of the notion that ruminative vomiting is self-reinforcing, several authors have examined the effects of allowing the client to eat until she or he refuses food. This feeding approach is an alternative to many institutional feeding procedures, in which only standard-sized portions are provided. Although satiation procedures have been used only infrequently, severe case studies have reported that the intervention was very effective in reducing ruminative vomiting (Jackson *et al.*, 1975; Rast, Johnston, Drum, Conrin, 1981). Other studies have used the procedure in combination with other behavioral strategies, such as reinforcement for the nonoccurrence of vomiting (Borreson & Anderson, 1982).

### Summary

Chronic rumination is the self-induced regurgitation of previously swallowed food (Murray *et al.*, 1977). The problem is most commonly seen in developmentally disabled children and in children with a physical disability. The behavioral assessment of rumination should include a comprehensive evaluation of the antecedents and the consequences of the behavior. On the supposition that ruminative vomiting is maintained by reinforcing consequences, numerous researchers have eliminated the behavior through the contingent application of aversive stimuli. Although less frequently used than punishment, reinforcement procedures alone or in combination with ignoring or time-out have been effective in reducing ruminative vomiting.

## PICA

### Diagnosis

The characteristics of pica range from the mouthing of objects by older children (i.e., over the age of 18 months; Lourie, Layman, & Millican, 1963) and indiscriminate eating of nonfood and food items (Crosby, 1971; Palmer & Ekvall, 1978) to eating food and objects from floors and walls (Ausman, Ball, & Alexander, 1974; Bucher, Reykdal, & Albin, 1976). The DSM-III (APA, 1980) diagnostic criteria for pica are repeated eating of a nonnutritive substance for a period of at least 1 month that is not due to another disorder, such as infantile autism, schizophrenia, or a physical disorder. These children generally do not show an aversion to food; they simply eat nonnutritive substances in a persistent manner.

Pica is estimated to occur in the normal population at a rate of 9%, with the majority (83%) of children coming from lower-income families who live in older, substandard housing (de la' Burde' & Reames, 1973; Madden, Russo, & Cataldo,

1980b). Reports of pica are generally higher in the mentally retarded population, with prevalence rates ranging from 8% to 26% (Danford & Huber, 1982; Singh & Winton, 1985). Pica usually disappears by the age of 18 months; however, the symptom has been reported to persist past this age in 10%–30% of children (Barltrop, 1966).

Pica can have severe consequences. One of the more serious consequences is lead poisoning, which may lead to neurological impairment (Finney, Russo, & Cataldo, 1982). Nutritional deficiencies have also been linked to pica (Danford, Smith, & Huber, 1982; Kalisz, Ekvall, & Palmer, 1978). There have also been reports of the presence of intestinal parasites and gastrointestinal blockages because of the ingestion of nonnutritive items (Danford & Huber, 1982).

## Treatment

Several studies report the successful elimination of pica by means of overcorrection, combined with differential reinforcement of other behaviors (Finney *et al.*, 1982; Madden, Russo, & Cataldo, 1980a), and by means of overcorrection alone (Foxx & Martin, 1975; Mulick, Barbour, Schroeder, & Rojahn, 1980a; Singh & Bakker, 1984; Singh & Winton, 1985). Physical restraint treatments have also been reported to be useful for quickly reducing pica (Ausman *et al.*, 1974; Bucher *et al.*, 1976; Rojahn, Schroeder, & Mulick, 1980; Singh & Bakker, 1984). One study used the application of a blindfold over the eyes for 1 minute contingent on the eating of nonnutritive substances. Pica was rapidly suppressed, and near-zero occurrences of this behavior were reported at 6-month follow-up (Singh & Winton, 1984). The paucity of long-term follow-up reports has precluded definitive statements concerning the generalization and maintenance of the elimination of pica by means of the above procedures, although these treatments have been shown to have potential efficacy.

## Summary

Pica occurs at a moderate rate in the general population, and it is suggested that this eating disorder occurs at a high rate in the mentally retarded population relative to other groups. Pica carries with it the possibility of severe consequences and should be considered a serious disorder. Behavioral interventions generally use overcorrection, various forms of physical restraint, and the reinforcement of desirable eating and related behaviors. These methods have successfully eliminated pica. However, few long-term follow-up studies have been reported.

## Anorexia Nervosa

### Diagnosis

The DSM-III (APA, 2980) diagnostic criteria for anorexia nervosa include the loss of 25% or more of normal body weight. a refusal to maintain an appropriate weight level, an intense fear of being fat, and a distorted body image, in that anorexics see themselves as being fat when they may, in fact, be emaciated. The anorexic commonly evinces associated psychopathology, such as depression and anxiety. The anorexic individual frequently displays obsessive-compulsive or ritualistic behaviors (Andersen, 1983). Assessment issues and procedures for diagnosing anorexia nervosa are covered more thoroughly in Williamson *et al.* (1988).

Anorexia nervosa occurs most often in females, between the ages of 13 and 20 years; 14½ and 18 years are the most frequent ages of onset (Halmi, 1974; Halmi, Casper, & Eckert, 1979). The prevalence rates are estimated to be around 1%, with 95% of patients being females. It has been proposed that these rates are increasing at a rapid pace (Lucas, Bearn, Kranz, & Kurland, 1983). The physical complications of the anorexic's refusal to eat are abnormal weight loss, amenorrhea, dehydration, lanugo, hair loss, bradycardia, electrolyte imbalances, and deterioration of the heart muscle. Death can occur from cardiac arrest or suicide (Andersen, 1983), and mortality rates have recently been reported to be as high as 6% (Tolstrup, Brinch, Isager, Nielsen, Nystrup, Severin, & Olesen, 1985). Because of their critical low weight and the severe physical complications, these patients are often treated initially as inpatients until a safe weight level has been achieved.

## Treatment

Although there is a wealth of published reports pertaining to anorexia nervosa, most of the treatment literature is based on single-case studies (cf. Christophersen & Rapoff, 1979). Furthermore, treatment methods have not been directly compared. Therefore, it is difficult to determine the successful treatment components. Regardless, it is generally agreed that anorexia nervosa is a complex disorder that requires considerable therapeutic skill and an intervention package that includes both cognitive and behavioral components that address both eating behaviors and the associated psychopathology (Garner, 1986). Much research has also suggested that long-term treatment is needed, and that the patient rarely becomes totally symptom-free (Garner & Bemis, 1982; Hall, Slim, Hawker, & Salmond, 1984; Nussbaum, Shenker, Baird, & Saravay, 1985; Tolstrup *et al.*, 1985). Because anorexics are usually persuaded into treatment, they are often resistant and may deny the disorder. They may seem unable to understand others' concern over their eating habits and weight loss because these features are potently self-reinforcing for anorexics. Recognition and acknowledgment of the anorexic's feelings can be helpful in establishing a therapeutic relationship. She can be reassured that she will not be allowed to become fat, and that self-starvation is not an acceptable option for dealing with fears of weight gain.

Weight stabilization must be addressed immediately with the malnourished anorexic, for obvious physical health reasons, and often, the mental attitudes improve as nutrition is improved (Casper, 1982; Hsu, 1986). A target weight can be established while caloric and nutritional planning to meet the goal weight within a reasonable time limit is begun. Generally, 0.25–0.50 lb/day is an acceptable pace for refeeding weight gain. A goal weight of 10% below average for height and weight is a reasonable level and can be justified, as this weight level has been linked to longer life span (Mayer, 1968). Daily weight measurements aid in determining the caloric needs for the prescribed weight gain. In addition, contracting with the patient often increases compliance. In this way, the anorexic takes an active role in the treatment process. Free time, exercise, and phone calls can often be used as reinforcers for compliance with the behavioral treatment components. In one of the few controlled behavioral studies, Agras, Barlow, Chapin, Abel, and Leitenberg (1974) demonstrated that postitive reinforcement, informational feedback, and offering larger amounts of food to anorexics resulted in increased caloric consumption and weight gain.

It is important to recognize that the restoration of weight is rarely a sufficient treatment for anorexia nervosa. The patient will undoubtedly display a distorted body image and associated psychopathology, such as anxiety and depression. Anxiety is usually apparent before, during, and after eating because of a fear of obesity and loss of control. Relaxation-training sessions may be useful when exposure techniques are used. Teaching the anorexic to identify and challenge irrational or maladaptive cognitions about food and weight gain is instrumental in helping the patient to cope with increased caloric intake. The avoidance of food must be prevented, so that the patient is gradually exposed to the feared stimulus of food and eating. It is also crucial during refeeding to prevent the occurrence of purging, as a poor prognosis is associated with vomiting in anorexics (Hall *et al.*, 1984; Nussbaum *et al.*, 1985; Steinhausen, 1983). Body image therapy can assist the anorexic in being more objective about her body size as she regains weight. Videotaping before, during, and after weight gain is one useful technique that may allow the anorexic to make realistic comparisons of her body size. Behavioral rehearsal that targets events such as people making comments about weight gain, perceived changes in body shape, or numbers increasing on the scale can help the patient to recognize maladaptive cognitions that maintain anorexic behaviors, as well as present opportunities to practice healthier self-statements and behaviors (Garner & Bemis, 1982).

As the anorexic patient often displays depression, a treatment component that addresses the patient's self-esteem and reinforcement in the environment should be considered. It has been noted that depression often improves as weight increases (Casper, 1982; Hsu, 1986); however, social skills or assertiveness training may be required to establish more reinforcing interpersonal relationships and to improve self-esteem (Wetzel, 1984). As weight is restored and the criteria for major depression are evident, the prescription of antidepressants may be warranted (Morgan, Purgold, & Wolbourne, 1983). The use of drugs to improve weight gain has produced inconsistent research results. A recent review by Hsu (1986) suggested that some medications may aid in short-term weight gain when used with behavior therapy or psychotherapy.

It is important to assess whether family therapy is indicated. This approach is particularly important for younger anorexics still living at home (Hsu, 1986). If it is determined that the family environment is providing reinforcement for anorexic behaviors, then counseling may help to develop a relationship with the parents that will enhance their cooperation and participation in treatment following discharge of the patient from the inpatient facility (Nussbaum *et al.*, 1985). Minuchin, Rosman, and Baker (1978) identified five characteristics that were often present in families with anorexic members: overprotectiveness, enmeshment, rigidity, poor conflict resolution, and use of the anorexic patient in parental conflict. The goal of family therapy, according to Sargent (1986), is to change family interactions so as to bring about a healthy balance between independence and the need for supportive relationships.

The treatment of anorexia must be multidimensional in order to address the complex features of this eating disorder. The anorexic patient is often resistant and requires the therapist to be skilled and patient. The treatment is generally long-term, requiring both inpatient therapy for weight restoration and outpatient follow-up for continued work on cognitive processes, body image distortions, anxiety, depression, and dysfunctional family interactions.

Because much of the behavioral-treatment outcome-research is based on case studies and few controlled investigations are available, it is difficult to determine objectively the overall efficacy of behavioral treatment for anorexia nervosa. Although many studies report improvement at the end of treatment, long-term follow-up studies of individual cases have suggested that only 20% of anorexic patients remain symptom-free (cf. Hall *et al.*, 1984), and nearly 50% relapse within 1 year (Hsu, 1980). Another problem is that past treatment improvement is most often defined as weight gained. Controlled research with long-term follow-up that includes the effects of treatment components on cognitive processes, body image, associated psychopathology, family dysfunction, and weight restoration and maintenance is very much needed.

## BULIMIA

### *Diagnosis*

The eating disorder bulimia (DSM-III—APA, 1980) can be divided into two subgroups: binge-purgers and binge eaters. Both groups engage in uncontrolled binge eating, but one subgroup engages in self-induced purgative behaviors (binge-purgers), whereas the other subgroup (binge eaters) does not (Williamson *et al.*, 1988). The primary symptoms of bulimia are frequent binge eating, awareness that the eating pattern is abnormal, and feelings of depression and self-deprecation following binge-eating episodes. Secretive eating, frequent weight fluctuations, self-induced vomiting, and laxative and diuretic abuse to lose or maintain weight may accompany the primary symptoms (APA, 1980). Bulimic binge-purgers also show a distorted perception of their body size (Williamson, Kelley, Davis, Ruggiero, & Blouin, 1985). The reader is referred to Williamson *et al.* (1988) for a more extensive discussion of assessment issues and procedures.

Bulimia occurs predominantly in females and usually begins between the ages of 15 and 18 years, although it is seen in both younger and older females, as well as in males. Estimates of the prevalence rates vary from 1% to 13% (Mizes, 1985). A survey of 1,268 high-school females suggested that 8.3% engaged in frequent binge eating and met the DSM-III criteria for bulimia. and that 4% also self-induced vomiting at least weekly (Johnson, Lewis, Love, Stuckey, & Lewis, 1983a). Several physical complications may accompany bulimia. For example, gastric dilation may result from binging. Fasting, vomiting, and laxative abuse can cause electrolyte imbalances, lethargy, reduced potassium, headaches, and loss of normal bowel peristalsis (Andersen, 1983). Menstrual irregularity and amenorrhea are also often observed (Johnson, Stuckey, Lewis, & Schwartz, 1983b). Vomiting also may lead to sore throats, dental caries, infected parotid glands, and esophagus damage. Given this extensive list of the possible physical side effects of bulimic behavior, it is suggested that treatment be preceded by a thorough medical examination.

## Treatment

Whether treating the bulimic binge-eater or the bulimic binge-purger, intervention programs must target the binging or the binge–purge cycle, its antecedents, and the maintaining factors. These two subgroups differ in treatment requirements in that the binge eater does not evince a distorted body image perception and does not purge. The binge eater may, however, follow binge episodes with fasting.

Although behavioral-treatment outcome-studies for bulimia are sparse, these treatment programs have in common the inclusion of multiple treatment components, including exposure with response prevention (Leitenberg, Gross, Peterson, & Rosen, 1984; Rosen & Leitenberg, 1982) and some type of cognitive restructuring. These elements of treatment are designed to interrupt the binge–fast and the binge–purge cycles and to alter the erroneous and irrational beliefs that the bulimic individual displays concerning food, weight, and perfectionism. Other common treatment components are problem-solving training, assertiveness training, some type of anxiety reduction and relaxation training, and stimulus control methods (Fairburn, 1981; Giles, Young, & Young, 1985; Grinc 1982; Kirkley, Schneider, Agras, & Bachman, 1985; Linden, 1980; Mizes & Fleece, 1984; Mizes & Lohr, 1983; O'Neill, 1982; Ordman & Kirschenbaum, 1985; Prather, Upton, McKenzie, & Williamson, 1985; Williamson, Prather, McKenzie, & Davis, 1986). Recent studies report promising results using these procedures. The results also suggest that, although improvements occur in relatively short treatment lengths of 6 weeks, such as reported by Kumetz and Rush (cited in Kirkley *et al.*, 1985) or Rosen and Leitenberg (1982), longer treatment programs of 16 weeks or more may be required to produce clinically significant results (Kirkley *et al.*, 1985). Periodic booster sessions have been found to be useful for continued reductions in binging, fasting, and purging, as well as for improvements in the associated psychopathology (Prather *et al.*, 1985).

The efficacy of cognitive-behavior-therapy programs for binge-purgers has been demonstrated in two controlled group-outcome studies. Using an individual therapy format, Ordman and Kirschenbaum (1985) reported a reduced frequency of binging and purging behaviors and improvement in depression and psychological adjustment, as well as in attitudes toward food, dieting, and body image. The treatment duration overaged 15.3 weeks. Following the model of Leitenberg *et al.* (1984), the treatment included exposure with response prevention in the clinic and in restaurants. The clients were instructed to use this treatment modality on their own between sessions. Coping self-statements were used when discomfort or guilt was experienced in eating situations. The clients self-monitored binging, purging, and discomfort levels following eating. The consequences of strict dieting and purging were discussed, and behavioral contracting was used to help the clients schedule appropriate eating. The cognitive techniques included identifying and changing unrealistic beliefs and assumptions that maintained the eating disorder. Time was also spent in process-oriented therapy that established rapport and supported the clients, as well as in discussing the functional role of bulimia and addressing problem relationships. In comparison, the control group received only an explanation of self-monitoring and exposure, with response prevention and encouragement to practice these treatment procedures on their own. This group did not show improvement, whereas the cognitive-behavior-therapy group showed substantial improvement, which was statistically and clinically significant.

Using a group therapy format, Kirkley et al. (1985) compared cognitive-behavioral and nondirective approaches to the treatment of bulimic binge-purgers. The treatment duration for both groups was 16 weeks. Both groups self-monitored their eating and related behaviors and graphed their vomiting frequency. The cognitive-behavioral program included specific behavior-change recommendations related to decreasing the eating rate, eating forbidden foods, eating only in nonbinge settings at a table with utensils, using relaxation tapes, delaying vomiting by engaging in incompatible activities following eating, increasing eating regularity and the variety of foods eaten, and changing the vomiting ritual. The nondirective group discussed related topics but received no specific recommendations concerning how to change their behaviors. Although both treatment programs were reported to be highly credible to the bulimics, the cognitive-behavioral group had a lower attrition rate and was found to be significantly more effective in decreasing binging and purging frequency. At 3-month follow-up, 38% of the cognitive-behavioral treatment group had continued to abstain, whereas only 11% of the nondirective treatment group was abstinent. Both treatment modalities, however, resulted in improvements in self-reported depression, anxiety, and associated cognitions.

The use of pharmacological treatment, such as the antidepressants imipramine and the MAO inhibitors, has shown some promise in reducing the frequency of binging (Pope & Hudson, 1982; Pope, Hudson, Jonas, & Yurgelin-Todd, 1983; Walsh, Stewart, Wright, Harrison, Roose, & Glassman, 1982). However, due to the side effects and risks, long-term prescription of these medications with adolescents must be used with caution. This conclusion is especially noteworthy if one considers that at 3-month follow-up a cognitive-behavioral group treatment yielded results comparable to drug treatment. (Kirkley et al., 1985). More studies with long-term follow-up are needed to replicate and extend these findings.

## Summary

Treatment of bulimia is receiving increasing attention by behavioral researchers and two well-controlled outcome studies have recently been published. Most of the research, however, has been with young adults rather than adolescents. These treatment programs have emphasized the interruption of the binge/fast and binge/purge cycle by the use of exposure with response prevention with cognitive therapy to modify maladaptive thinking related to weight, dieting, and foods. Antidepressant medication has also shown some potential for reducing binge eating however results have been inconsistent. Follow-up studies are needed for more definitive statements about the long term effectiveness of behavioral and pharmacological approaches for bulimia. Research to date, however, clearly supports the use of comprehensive cognitive-behavior therapy approaches for this disorder.

CONCLUSION

The treatment of eating disorders in children and rumination, pica, and anorexia nervosa, have been validated by means of a series of single-case studies. These investigations have shown that a variety of behavioral techniques (e.g., reinforcement, punishment, time-out, and DRO) can be used to modify eating or associated behaviors (e.g., vomiting) and can be effective in modifying weight level, by either increasing or decreasing it. Thus, it is clear that behavioral approaches have been used quite successfully for the treatment of eating disorders in children and adolescents and have become established methods in the comprehensive management of these perplexing, and often life-threatening. cases.

## REFERENCES

Abraham, S., & Nordsieck, M. (1960). Relationship of excess weight in children and adults. *Public Health Report, 75,* 263–273.

Accardo, P. J. (1982). Growth and development: An interactional context for failure to thrive. In P. J. Accardo (Ed.), *Failure to thrive in infancy and childhood: A multidisciplinary approach.* Baltimore: University Park.

Agorb, C., Pfeiffer, D., & Leichtman, L. (1979). Treatment of infants with nonorganic failure to thrive. *The International Journal of Child Abuse and Neglect, 3,* 937–941.

Agras, W., Barlow, D. Chapin, H. Abel, G., & Leitenberg, H. (1974). Behavior modification of anorexia nervosa. *Archives of General Psychiatry, 30,* 279–286.

Altman, K., Bondy, A., & Hirsch, G. (1978). Behavioral treatment of obesity in patients with Prader-Willi syndrome. *Journal of Behavioral Medicine, 1,* 403–412.

American Psychiatric Association (1980). *Diagnostic and statistical manual of mental Disorders* (3rd ed.). Washington, DC: Author.

Andersen, A. E. (1983). Anorexia nervosa and bulimia: A spectrum of eating disorders. *Journal of Adolescent Health Care, 4,* 15–21.

Aragona, J., Cassady, J., & Drabman, R. S. (1975). Treating overweight children through parental training and contingency contracting. *Journal of Applied Behavior Analysis, 8,* 269–278.

Ausman, J., Ball, T. S., & Alexander, D. (1974). Behavior therapy of pica with a profoundly retarded adolescent. *Mental Retardation, 12,* 16–18.

Bacon, G. E., Spencer, M. L., Hopwood, N. J., & Kelch, R.P. (1982). *A practical guide to pediatric endocrinology* (2nd ed.). Chicago: Year Book Medical Publishers.

Bayley, N. (1969). *Bayley Scales of Infant Development.* New York: Psychological Corporation.

Barltrop, D. (1966). The prevalence of pica. *American Journal of the Diseases of Childhood, 112,* 116–123.

Becker, J. V., Turner, S. M., & Sajwaj, T. E. (1978). Multiple behavioral effects of the use of lemon juice with a ruminating toddler-age child. *Behavior Modification. 2,* 267–278.

Bellack, A. S., & Williamson, D. A. (1982). Obesity and anorexia nervosa. In D. M. Doleys, R. Meredith, & T. Ciminero (Eds.), *Behavioral psychology in medicine: Assessment and treatment strategies.* New York: Plenum Press.

Bentovin, A. (1970). The clinical approach to feeding disorders of childhood. *Journal of Psychosomatic Research, 14,* 267–276.

Berkowitz, C. (1985). Comprehensive pediatric management of failure to thrive: An interdisciplinary approach. In D. Drotar (Ed.), *New directions in failure to thrive: Implications for research and practice.* New York: Plenum Press.

Bernal, M. E. (1972). Behavioral treatment of a child's eating problem. *Journal of Behavior Therapy and Experimental Psychiatry, 3,* 43–50.

Bithoney, W. G., & Dubowitz, H. (1985). Organic concomitants of nonorganic failure to thrive: Implications for research. In D. Drotar (Ed.), *New directions in failure to thrive: Implications for research and practice.* New York: Plenum Press.

Bithoney, W. G., & Rathbun, J. M. (1983). Failure to thrive. In M. D. Levine, W. B. Carey, A. C. Crocker, & R. T. Gross (Eds.), *Developmental behavioral pediatric*. Philadelphia: W. B. Saunders.

Borreson, P. M., & Anderson, J. L. (1982). The elimination of chronic rumination through a combination of procedures. *Mental retardation, 29*, 34–38.

Bray, G. A., Dahms, W. T., Swerdloff, R. S., Fiser, R. H., Atkinson, R. L., & Carrel, R. E. (1983). The Prader-Willi syndrome: A study of 40 patients and a review of the literature. *Medicine, 62*, 59–79.

Brownell, K. D., & Stunkard, A. J. (1980). Behavioral treatment for obese children and adolescents. In A. J. Stunkard (Ed.). *Obesity*. Philadelphia: W. B. Saunders.

Bucher, B., Reykdal, B., & Albin, J. (1976). Brief physical restraint to control pica in retarded children. *Journal of Behavior Therapy & Experimental Psychiatry, 7*, 137–140.

Casper, R. C. (1982). Treatment principles in anorexia nervosa. *Adolescent Psychiatry, 10*, 431–454.

Cassidy, S. B. (1984; January). *Current problems in pediatrics: Prader-Willi syndrome* (Vol. 14, No. 1). Chicago: Year Book Medical Publishers.

Cavell, T. A. (1985). *Hospital eating record form*. Unpublished manuscript, Louisiana State University, Baton Rouge.

Charney, M., Goodman, H. C., McBride, M., Lyon, B., & Pratt, R. (1976). Childhood antecedents of adult obesity: Do chubby infants become obese adults? *New England Journal of Medicine, 295*, 6–9.

Christophersen, E. R., & Hall, C. L. (1978). Eating patterns and associated problems encountered in normal children. *Issues in Comprehensive Pediatric Nursing, 3*, 1–16.

Christophersen, E. R., & Rapoff, M. A. (1979). Behavioral pediatrics. In O. F. Pomerleau & J. P. Brady (Eds.), *Behavioral medicine: Theory and practice*. Baltimore: Williams & Wilkins.

Clark, D. B., & Munford P. R. (1980). Behavioral consultation to pediatrics. *Child Behavior Therapy, 2*, 25–33.

Coates, T. J., & Thoresen, C. E. (1978). Treating obesity in children and adolescents: A review. *American Journal of Public Health, 68*, 143–151.

Coates, T. J., & Thoresen, C. E. (1981). Behavioral weight changes in three obese adolescents. *Behavior Therapy, 12*, 383–399.

Cohen, E. A., Gelfand, D. M., Dodd, D. K., Jensen, J., & Turner, C. (1980). Self-control practices associated with weight loss maintenance on children and adolescents. *Behavior Therapy, 11*, 26–37.

Conrin, J., Pennypacker, H. S., Johnston, J., & Rast, J. (1982). Differential reinforcement of other behaviors to treat chronic rumination of mental retardates. *Journal of Behavior Therapy and Experimental Psychiatry, 13*, 325–329.

Coplin, S. S., Hine, J., & Gormician, A. (1976). Out-patient dietary management in the Prader-Willi syndrome. *Journal of the American Dietetic Association, 68*, 330–334.

Crosby, W. H. (1971). Food pica and iron deficiency. *Archives of Internal Medicine, 127*, 960–961.

Danford, D. E., & Huber, A. M. (1982). Pica among mentally retarded adults. *American Journal of Mental Deficiency, 87*, 141–146.

Danford, D. E., Smith, J. C., & Huber, A. M. (1982). Pica and mineral status of the mentally retarded. *The American Journal of Clinical Nutrition, 35*, 958–967.

Daniel, W. H. (1982). Management of chronic rumination with a contingent exercise procedure employing topographically dissimilar behavior. *Journal of Behavior Therapy & Experimental Psychiatry, 13*, 149–152.

de la' Burde', B., & Reames, B. (1973). Prevention of pica, the major cause of lead poisoning in children. *American Journal of Public Health, 63*, 737–743.

Drotar, D., & Malone, C. A. (1985, February). From hospital to home: Preventive intervention with the families of failure to thrive infants. In S. Provence (Ed.), *Zero to three: Bulletin of the National Center for Clinical Infant Programs, 5*(3), 17–20. (Available from National Center for Clinical Infant Programs, 733 15th St., N.W., Suite 912, Washington, DC 20005.)

Drotar, D., Malone, C., & Negray, J. (1979). Psychosocial intervention with families of children who fail to thrive. *The International Journal of Child Abuse and Neglect, 3*, 927–935.

Drotar, D., Nowak, M., Malone, C. A., Eckerle, D., & Negray, J. (1985). Early psychological outcome in failure to thrive: Predictions from an interactional model. *Journal of Clinical Child Psychology, 14*, 105–111.

Duker, P. C., & Seys, D. M. (1977). Elimination of vomiting in a retarded female using restitutional overcorrection, *Behavior Therapy, 8*, 225–257.

Epstein, L. H., & Wing, R. R. (1983). Reanalysis of weight changes in behavior modification and nutrition education for childhood obesity. *Journal of Pediatric Psychology, 8*, 97–100.

Epstein, L. H., Wing, R. R., Koeske, R., Andrasik, F., & Ossip, D. J. (1981). Child and parent weight loss in family-based behavior modification programs. *Journal of Consulting Clinical Psychology, 49,* 674–685.

Epstein, L. H., Wing, R. R., Koeske, R., Ossip, D., & Beck. S. (1982). Comparison of lifestyle change and programmed aerobic exercise on weight and fitness changes in obese children. *Behavior Therapy, 13,* 651–665.

Epstein, L. H., Wing, R. R.. Koeske, R., & Valoski, A. (1984). Effects of diet plus exercise on weight change in parents, and children. *Journal of Consulting and Clinical Psychology, 52,* 429–437.

Epstein, L. H., Wing, R. R., Koeske, R., & Valoski, A. (1985). A comparison of lifestyle exercise, aerobic exercise, and calisthenics on weight loss in obese children. *Behavior Therapy, 16,* 345–356.

Epstein, L. H., Wing, R. R., Koeske, R., & Valoski, A. (1986b). Effect of parent weight on weight loss in obese children. *Journal of Consulting and Clinical Psychology, 54,* 400–401.

Epstein, L. H., Koeske, R., Wing, R. R., & Valoski, A. (1986a). The effect of family variables on child weight change, *Health Psychology, 5,* 1–11.

Fairburn, C. G. (1981). A cognitive behavioral approach to the treatment of bulimia. *Psychological Medicine, 11,* 707–711.

Field, T. M. (1978). The three's of infant-adult interactions: Rhythms, repertoires, and responsivity. *Journal of Pediatric Psychology, 3,* 131–136.

Field, T. M. (1984). Early interactions between infants and their postportum depressed mothers. *Infant Behavior and Development. 7,* 517–522.

Finlon, M. A., Drotar, D., Satola, J., Pallota, J., Wyatt, B., & El-Amin, D. (1985). Home observation of parent-child transaction in failure to thrive: A method and preliminary findings. In D. Drotar (Ed.), *New directions in failure to thrive: Implications for research and practice.* New York: Plenum Press.

Finney, J. W., Russo, D. C., & Cataldo, M. F. (1982). Reduction of pica in young children with lead poisoning. *Journal of Pediatric Psychology, 7,* 197–207.

Foch, T. T., & McClearn, G. E. (1980). Genetics, body weight, and obesity. In A. J. Stunkard (Ed.), *Obesity.* Philadelphia: W. B. Saunders.

Fonkalsrud, E. W., & Bray, G. (1981). Vagotomy for treatment of obesity in childhood due to Prader-Willi syndrome. *Journal of Pediatric Surgery, 16,* 888–889.

Foster, G. D., Wadden, T. A., & Brownell, K. D. (1985). Peer-led program for the treatment and prevention of obesity in the schools. *Journal of Consulting and Clinical Psychology, 53,* 538–540.

Foxx, R. M., & Martin, E. D. (1975). Treatment of scavenging behavior (coprophagy and pica) by overcorrection. *Behaviour Research & Therapy, 13,* 153–162.

Frank, D. A. (1985). Biologic risks in "nonorganic" failure to thrive: Diagnostic and therapeutic implications. In D. Drotar (Ed.), *New directions in failure to thrive: Implications for research and practice.* New York: Plenum Press.

Frank, D. A., Allen, D., & Brown, J. L. (1985, February). Primary prevention of failure to thrive: Social policy implications. In S. Provence (Ed.), *Zero to three: Bulletin of the National Center for Clinical Infant Programs,* 5(3), 4–10. (Available from National Center for Clinical Infant Programs, 733 15th St., N.W., Suite 912, Washington, DC 20005.)

Galler, J. R., Ramsey. F., & Solimano, G. (1985). Influence of early malnutrition on subsequent behavioral development: 5. Child's behavior at home. *Journal of the American Academy of Child Psychiatry, 24,* 58–64.

Gara, S. M., & Clark, D. C. (1976). Trends in fatness and the origins of obesity. *Pediatric, 57,* 443–456.

Garner, D. M. (1986). Cognitive-behavioral therapy for eating disorders. *The Clinical Psychologist, 39,* 36–39.

Garner, D. M., & Bemis, K. M. (1982). A cognitive-behavioral approach to anorexia nervosa. *Cognitive therapy and Research, 6,* 123–150.

Giles, T. R., Young, R. R., & Young, D. E. (1985). Case studies and clinical replication series: Behavioral treatment of severe bulimia. *Behavior Therapy, 16,* 393–405.

Grinc, G. A. (1982). A cognitive-behavioral model for the treatment of chronic vomiting. *Journal of Behavioral Medicine, 5,* 135–141.

Gross, I., Wheeler, M., & Hess, K. (1976). The treatment of obesity in adolescents using behavioral self-control. *Clinical Pediatrics, 15,* 920–924.

Hall, A., Slim, E., Hawker, F., & Salmond, C. (1984). Anorexia nervosa: Long-term outcome in 50 female patients. *British Journal of Psychiatry, 145,* 407–413.

Halmi, K. A. (1974). Anorexia Nervosa: Demographic and clinical features in 94 cases. *Psychosomatic Medicine, 36,* 18–36.

Halmi, K. A.. Casper, R. C., & Eckert, E. D. (1979). Unique features associated with age onset of anorexia nervosa. *Psychiatry Research 1.* 209.

Hanson, J. W. (1981). A view of the etiology and pathogensis of Prader-Willi Syndrome. In V. A. Holm. S. J. Sulzbacher, & P. J. Pipes (Eds.), *Prader-Willi syndrome.* Baltimore: University Park Press.

Heffer, R. W., Cavell, T. A., & Kelley, M. L. (1985, November). *Treating food refusal in a 5-year-old with growth hormone deficiency.* Paper presented at the 19th Annual convention of the Association for the Advancement of Behavior Therapy, Houston.

Hertzler, A. A. (1983a). Children's food patterns—A review: I. Food preferences and feeding problems. *Journal of the American Dietetic Association, 83,* 555–560.

Hertzler, A. A. (1983b). Children's food patterns—A review: II. Family and group behavior. *Journal of the American Dietetic Association, 83,* 555–560.

Hirsch, G., & Altman, K. (1981). Maintenance of programmed weight loss in patients with Prader-Willi syndrome. In V. A. Holm, S. J. Sulzbacher, & P. J. Pipes (Eds.). *Prader-Willi syndrome.* Baltimore: University Park Press.

Holm, V. A. (1981). The diagnosis of Prader-Willi syndrome. In V. A. Holm, S. J. Sulzbacher. & P. J. Pipes (Eds.), *Prader-Willi syndrome.* Baltimore: University Park Press.

Holm, V. A., & Pipes, P. L. (1976). Food and children with Prader-Willi syndrome. *American Journal of Diseases of Children, 130,* 1063–1067.

Homer, C., & Ludwig, S. (1981). Categorization of etiology of failure to thrive. *American Journal of Disease of Children, 135,* 848–851.

Hsu, L. K. G. (1980). Outcome of anorexia nervosa: A review of the literature (1954–1978). *Archives of General Psychiatry, 37,* 1041–1046.

Hsu, L. K. G. (1986). The treatment of anorexia nervosa. *American Journal of Psychiatry, 143,* 573–586.

Israel, A. C., & Shapiro, L. S. (1985). Behavior problems of obese children enrolling in a weight reduction program. *Journal of Pediatric Psychology, 10,* 449–460.

Israel, A. C., Stolmaker, L., Sharp, J. P., Silverman, W. K., & Simon, L. G. (1984). An evaluation of two methods of parental involvement in treating obese children. *Behavior Therapy, 15,* 266–272.

Israel, A. C., Stolmaker, L., & Andrian, C. A. G. (1985). The effects of training parents in general child management skills on a behavioral weight loss program for children. *Behavior Therapy, 16,* 169–180.

Jackson, G. M., Johnson, C. R., Ackron, G. S., & Crowley, R. (1975). Food satiation as a procedure to decelerate vomiting. *American Journal of Mental Deficiency, 80,* 223–237.

Johnson, C. L., Lewis, C., Love, S., Stuckey, M., & Lewis. S. (1983a). A descriptive survey of dieting and bulimic behavior in a female high school population. In *Understanding Anorexia Nervosa and Bulimia,* Report on the Fourth Ross Conference on Medical Research. Columbus, OH: Ross Laboratories.

Johnson, C., Stuckey, M. K., Lewis, L. D., & Schwartz, D. M. (1983b). Bulimia: A descriptive study of 316 cases: *International Journal of Eating Disorders, 2,* 3–16.

Kalisz, K., Ekvall, S., & Palmer, S. (1978). Pica and lead intoxication. In S. Palmer & S. Ekvall (Eds.), *Pediatric nutrition in developmental disorders.* Springfield, IL: Thomas.

Kingsley R. G., & Shapiro, J. (1977). A comparison of three behavioral programs for control of obesity in children. *Behavior Therapy, 8,* 30–36.

Kirkley, B. G., Schneider, J. A., Agras, W. S., & Bachman, J. A. (1985). Comparision of two group treatments for bulimia. *Journal of Consulting and Clinical Psychology, 53,* 43–48.

Kirschenbaum, D. S., Harris, E. S., & Tomarken, A. J. (1984). Effects of parental involvement in behavioral weight loss therapy for preadolescents. *Behavior Therapy, 15,* 485–500.

Krieger, I. (1982). *Pediatric disorders of feeding, nutrition, and metabolism.* New York: Wiley.

Lang, P. J., & Melamed, B. G. (1969). Avoidance conditioning therapy of an infant with chronic ruminative vomiting. *Journal of Abnormal Behavior. 74,* 139–142.

Lansky, D., & Vance, M. A. (1983). School-based intervention for adolescent obesity: Analysis of treatment, randomly selected control subjects. *Journal of Consulting and Clinical Psychology, 51,* 147–148.

Larson, K., & Ayllon, T. (1985, November). *A behavioral feeding program for failure to thrive infants.* Paper presented at the meeting of the Association for the Advancement of Behavior Therapy, Houston.

Laurence, B. M., Brito, A., & Wilkinson, J. (1981). Prader-Willi syndrome after age 15 years. *Achives in Diseases m Childhood, 56,* 181–186.

Leitenberg, H., Gross, J., Peterson, J., & Rosen, J. (1984). Analysis of an anxiety model and the process of change during exposure plus response prevention treatment of bulimia nervosa. *Behavior Thrapy, 15,* 3–20.

Linden, W. (1980). Multi-component behavior therapy in a case of compulsive binge-eating followed by vomiting. *Journal of Behaviour Therapy & Experimental Psychiatry, 11,* 297–300.

Linschied, T. R., & Rasnake, L. K. (1985). Behavioral approaches to the treatment of failure to thrive. In D. Drotar (Ed.), *New directions in failure to thrive: Implications for research and practice.* New York: Plenum Press.

Linscheid, T. R., Oliver, J., Blyler, E., & Palmer, S. (1978). Brief hospitalization for the behavioral treatment of feeding problems in the developmentally disabled. *Journal of Pediatric Psychology, 3,* 72–76.

Lourie, R. S., Layman, E. M., & Millican, F. K. (1963). Why children eat things that are not food. *Children, 10,* 143–147.

Lucas, A., Bearn. C., Kranz, J., & Kurland, L. (1983). Epidemiology of anorexia nervosa and bulimia. *International Journal of Eating Disorders, 2,* 85–90.

Madden, N. A., Russo, D. C., & Cataldo, M. F. (1980a). Behavioral treatment of pica in children with lead poisoning. *Child Behavior Therapy, 2,* 67–81.

Madden, N. A., Russo, D. C., & Cataldo, M. F. (1980b). Environmental influences on mouthing in children with lead intoxication. *Journal of Pediatric Psychology, 5,* 207–216.

Madison, L. S., & Adubato, S. A. (1984). The elimination of ruminative vomiting in a 15-month-old child with gastroesophageal reflux. *Journal of Pediatric Psychology, 9,* 231–239.

Marshall, B. D., Wallace, C. J., Elder, J., Burke, K., Oliver, T., & Blackmon, R. (1981). A behavioral approach to treatment of Prader-Willi syndrome. In V. A. Holm, S. J. Sulzbacher, & P. J. Pipes (Eds.), *Prader-Willi syndrome.* Baltimore: University Park Press.

Marshall, B. G., Elder, J., O' Bosky, D., Wallace, C. J., & Liberman, R. P. (1979). Behavioral treatment of Prader-Willi syndrome. *The Behavior Therapist, 2*(2), 22–24.

Mayer, J. (1968). *Overweight: Causes, costs, and control.* Englewood Cliffs, NJ: Prentice-Hall.

Minuchin, S., Rosman, B., & Baker, L. (1978). *Psychosomatic families: Anorexia nervosa in context.* Cambridge: Harvard University Press.

Mizes, J. S. (1985). Bulimia: A review of its symptomatology and treatment. *Advances on Behavior Research and Therapy, 7,* 91–142.

Mizes, J. S., & Fleece, E. L. (May, 1984). *The effect of progressive relaxation on the urge to binge and actual binges in a bulimarexic female.* Paper presented at the 5th Annual Meeting of the Society of Behavioral Medicine, Philadelphia.

Mizes, J. S., & Lohr, J. M. (1983). The treatment of bulmic (binge-eating and self-induced vomiting): A quasi-experimental investigation of the effects of stimulus narrowing, self-reinforcement, and self-control relaxation. *International Journal of Eating Disorders. 2,* 59–65.

Mulick, J. A., Barbour, R., Schroeder, S. R., & Rojahn, J. (1980a). Overcorrection of pica in two profoundly retarded adults: Analysis of setting effects, stimulus and response generalization. *Applied Research in Mental Retardation. 1,* 241–252.

Mulick, J. A., Schroeder, S. R., & Rojahn, J. (1980b). Chronic ruminative vomiting: A comparison of four treatment procedures. *Journal of Autism and Developmental Disorders, 10,* 203–213.

Morgan, H. G., Purgold, J., & Wolbourne, J. (1983). Management and outcome in anorexia nervosa: A standardized prognosis study. *British Journal of Psychiatry, 143,* 282–287.

Munford, P. R., & Pally, R. (1979). Outpatient contingency management of operant vomiting. *Journal of Behavior Therapy & Experimental Psychiatry, 10,* 135–137.

Murray, M. E., Keele, D. K., & McCarver, J. W. (1977). Treatment of ruminations with behavioral techniques: A case report. *Behavior Therapy, 8,* 999–1003.

Nelson, R. A., Huse, D. M., Holman, R. T., Kimbrough, B. O., Wahner, H. W., Callaway, C. W., & Hayles, A. B. (1981). Nutrition, metabolism, body composition, and response to the ketogenic diet in Prader-Willi syndrome. In V. A. Holm, S. J. Sulzbacher, & P. J. Pipes (Eds.), *Prader-Willi syndrome.* Baltimore: University Park Press.

Nussbaum, M., Shenker, I. R.. Baird, D., & Saravay, S. (1985). Follow-up investigation in patients with anorexia nervosa. *The Journal of Pediatrics, 106,* 835–840.

O'Neill, G. W. (1982, November). *A systematic desensitization approach to bulimia.* Paper presented at the 16th Annual Convention of the Association for the Advancement of Behavior Therapy, Los Angeles.

Ordman, A. M., & Kirschenbaum, D. S. (1985). Cognitive-behavioral therapy for bulimia: An initial outcome study. *Journal of Consulting and Clinical Psychology, 53,* 305–313.

Peterson, K. E., Washington, J., & Rathbun, J. M. (1984). Team management of failure to thrive. *Journal of the American Dietetic Association, 84,* 810–815.

Pipes, P. L. (1981). Nutritional management of children with Prader-Willi syndrome. In V. A. Holm, S. J. Sulzbacher, & P. J. Pipes (Eds.), *Prader-Willi syndrome.* Baltimore: University Park Press.

Pope, H. G., & Hudson, J. I. (1982). Treatment of bulimia with antidepressants. *Psychopharmacology, 78,* 176–179.

Pope, H. G., Hudson, J. I., Jonas, J. M., & Yurgelin-Todd, D. (1983). Bulimia treated with imipramine: A placebo-controlled, double-blind study. *American Journal of Psychiatry, 140,* 554–558.

Prather, R. C., Upton, L., McKenzie, S. J., & Williamson, D. A. (1985, November). *A four-component behavioral treatment for bulimics who purge.* Paper presented at the 19th Annual Convention of the Association for the Advancement of Behavior Therapy, Houston.

Ramey, C. T., Starr, R. H., Pallas, J., Whitten, C. F., & Reed, V. (1975). Nutrition, response contingent stimulation, and the maternal deprivation syndrome: Results of an early intervention program. *Merrill-Palmer Quarterly, 21.* 45–53.

Rast, J., Johnston, J. M., Devon, C., & Conrin, J. (1981). The Relation of food quantity to rumination behavior. *Journal of Applied Behavior Analysis, 14,* 121–130.

Riordan, M. M., Iwata, B. A., Wohl, M. K., & Finney, J. W. (1980). Behavioral treatment of food refusal and selectivity in developmentally disabled children. *Applied Research in Mental Retardation, 1,* 95–112.

Riordan, M. M., Iwata, B. A., Finney, J. W., Wohl, M. K., Stanley, A. E. (1984). Behavioral Assessment and treatment of Chronic Food Refusal in handicapped children. *Journal of Applied Behavior Analysis, 17,* 327–340.

Rivinus, T. M., Drummond, T., & Hustorf, A. H. (1976). A group-behavior treatment program for overweight children: The results of a pilot study. *Pediatric and Adolescent Endocrinology, 1,* 212–218.

Roberts, M. C., & Maddux, J. E. (1982). A psychosocial conceptualization of nonorganic failure to thrive. *Journal of Clinical Child Psychology, 11,* 216–226.

Rojahn, J., Schroeder, S. R., & Mulick, J. A. (1980). Ecological assessment of self-protective devices in three profoundly retarded adults. *Journal of Autism & Developmental Disorders, 10,* 59–66.

Rosen, J. C., & Leitenberg, J. (1982). Bulimia nervosa: Treatment with exposure and response prevention. *Behavior Therapy, 13,* 117–124.

Sajwaj, T., Libet, J., & Agras, S. (1974). Lemon juice therapy: The control of life threatening rumination in a six-month-old infant. *Journal of Applied Behavior Analysis, 7,* 557–563.

Sargent, J. (1986). Family therapy for eating disorders. *The Clinical Psychologist, 39,* 43–45.

Satter, E. M. (1986). The feeding relationship. *Journal of the American Dietetic Association, 86,* 352–356.

Schor, D. P. (1984). Failure to thrive. In J. A. Blackman (Ed.), *Medical aspects of developmental disabilities in children birth to three.* Rockville, MD: Aspen Systems Corp.

Sheinbein, M. (1975). Treatment for the hospitalized infantile ruminator: Programmed brief social behavior reinforcers. *Clinical Pediatrics, 14,* 719–724.

Siegel, L. J. (1982). Classical and operant procedures in the treatment of a case of food aversion in a young child. *Journal of Clinical Child Psychology, 11,* 167–172.

Siegel, L. J. (1983). Psychosomatic and psychophysiological disorders. In R. J. Morris & T. R. Kratochwill (Eds.), *The practice of child therapy.* New York: Pergamon Press.

Singer, L. T., & Fagan, J. F. (1984). Cognitive development in the failure-to-thrive infant: A three-year longitudinal study. *Journal of Pediatric Psychology, 9,* 363–383.

Singh, N. N. (1981). Rumination. In N. R. Ellis (Ed.), *International review of research in mental retardation* (Vol. 10). New York: Academic Press.

Singh, N. N., & Bakker, L. W. (1984). Suppression of pica by overcorrection and physical restraint: A comparative analysis. *Journal of Autism & Developmental Disorders, 14,* 331–341.

Singh, N. N., & Winton, A. S. W. (1984). Effects of a screening procedure on pica and collateral behaviors. *Journal of Behavior therapy & Experimental Psychiatry, 15,* 59–65.

Singh, N. N., & Winton, A. S. W. (1985). Controlling pica by components of an overcorrection procedure. *American Journal of Mental Deficiency, 90,* 40–45.

Singh, N. N., Manning, P. J., & Angell, M. J. (1982). Effects of an oral hygiene punishment procedure on chronic rumination and collateral behaviors in monozygous twins. *Journal of Applied Behavior Analysis, 15,* 309–314.

Smith, M. E., & Fremouw, W. J. (in press). A realistic approach to treating obesity. *Clinical Psychology Review.*

Soper, R. T., Mason, E. E., Printen, K. J., & Zellweger, H. (1981). Surgical treatment of morbid obesity in Prader-Willi syndrome. In V. A. Holm, S. J. Sulzbacher, & P. J. Pipes (Eds.), *Prader-Willi syndrome*. Baltimore: University Park Press.

Steinhausen, H. C. (1983). Follow-up studies of anorexia nervosa: A review of research findings. *Psychological Medicine. 13*, 239–249.

Strauss, C. C., Smith, K., Frame, C., & Forehand, R. (1985). Personal and interpersonal characteristics association with childhood obesity. *Journal of Pediatric Psychology, 10*, 337–343.

Stunkard, A. J. (1980). *Obesity*. Philadelphia: W. B. Saunders.

Terry, K., & Beck, S. (1985). Eating style and food storage habits in the home. *Behavior Modification, 9*, 242–261.

Thompson, R. J., Palmer, S., & Linscheid, T. R. (1977). Single subject design and interaction analysis in the behavioral treatment of a child with a feeding problem. *Child Psychiatry & Human Development, 8*, 353–363.

Thompson, T., Kodluboy, S., & Heston, L. (1980). Behavioral treatment of obesity in Prader-Willi syndrome. *Behavior Therapy. 11*, 588–593.

Tolstrup, K., Brinch, M., Isager, T., Nielsen, S., Nystrup, J., Severin, B., & Olesen, N. S. (1985). Long-term outcome of 151 cases of anorexia nervosa. *Acta Psychiatrica Scandinavica, 71*, 380–387.

Touquet, V. L. R., Ward, M. W. N., & Clark, C. G. (1983). Obesity surgery M a patient with the Prader-Willi syndrome. *British Journal of Surgery, 70*, 180–186.

U.S. Department of Health, Education, and Welfare. (1973). *Height and weight of youths 12–17 years*. Rockville, MD: U.S. Public Health Service. (DHEW Publication No. HSW 73-1606.)

Varni, J. W. (1983). *Clinical behavioral pediatrics: An interdisciplinary biobehavioral approach*. New York: Pergamon Press.

Walsh, B. T., Stewart, J. W., Wright, L., Harrison, W., Roose, S. P., & Glassman, A. H. (1982). Treatment of bulimia with monoamine oxidase inhibitors. *American Journal of Psychiatry, 139*, 1629–1630.

Watkins, S. T. (1972). Treatment of chronic vomiting and extreme emaciation by an oversive stimulus: Case study. *Psychological Reports, 31*, 803–805.

Weiss, A. R. (1977). A behavioral approach to the treatment of adolescent obesity. *Behavior Therapy, 8*, 720–726.

Wetzel, J. W. (1984). *Clinical handbook of depression*. New York: Gardner Press.

Whitten, C. F., Pettit, M. G., & Fischoff, J. (1969). Evidence that growth failure from maternal deprivation is secondary to undereating. *Journal of the American Medical Association, 209*, 1675–1682.

Williamson, D. A., Kelley, M. L., Davis, C. J., Ruggiero, L., & Blouin, D. (1985). Psychopathology of eating disorders: A controlled comparison of bulimic, obese, and normal subjects. *Journal of Consulting and Clinical Psychology, 53*, 161–166.

Williamson, D. A., Prather, R. C., McKenzie, S. J., & Davis, C. J. (1986, November). *Inpatient versus outpatient treatment of bulimia*. In J. S. Mizes (Chair), symposium conducted at the 20th annual convention of the Association for the Advancement of Behavior Therapy, Chicago.

Williamson, D. A., Kelley, M. L., Cavell, T. A., & Prather, R. C. (1988). Eating and eliminating disorders. In C. L. Frame & J. L. Matson (Eds), *Handbook of assessment in child psychopathology: Applied issues in differential diagnosis and treatment evaluation*. New York: Plenum Press.

Wright, M. M., & Menolacsino, F. J. (1966). Nurturant nursing of mentally retarded ruminators. *American Journal of Mental Deficiency, 71*, 451–459.

Zellweger, H. (1981). Diagnosis and therapy in the first phase of Prader-Willi syndrome. In V. A. Holm, S. J. Sulzbacher, & P. J. Pipes (Eds.), *Prader-Willi syndrome*. Baltimore: University Park Press.

# 17  Enuresis and Encopresis
## Psychological Therapies

ROBERT D. LYMAN, JAMES P. SCHIERBERL, AND
MICHAEL C. ROBERTS

Disorders of elimination (urination and defecation) are among the most common presenting problems in pediatric-clinical child psychology practices as well as in pediatric and medical practices. In a summary of three pediatric psychology services, Roberts (1986) found that between 5% and 10% of referrals were for toileting difficulties, one of the higher rates in any problem category. The two major diagnostic categories for these problems are enuresis and encopresis. These are problems of too little and too much retention of body waste products—each affecting a different system. Each of these conditions is generally considered a clinical problem when inappropriate elimination occurs after the age at which the child should be toilet-trained.

*Enuresis* refers to the child's urinating at the wrong time or place, typically in bed or clothing when the child is old enough to have achieved better control. Enuresis is also known as *urinary incontinence*. *Encopresis* refers to the passing of bowel movements in inappropriate places (usually into clothing) and sometimes the withholding of feces for periods of time. Encopresis, with a variety of presenting symptoms, also passes under the other labels of *fecal incontinence, functional* or *psychogenic megacolon, psychological constipation, stool holding,* and *soiling*.

Before turning to the clinical disorders of enuresis and encopresis, we want to note that there are several approaches to establishing proper toilet habits before any problems develop. Toilet training is a major milestone of child development, and parents may attempt to train toileting behaviors in a variety of ways (Christophersen & Rapoff, 1983). The clinician is well-advised to become familiar with these various orientations and techniques, not only because referrals will be made for assistance in normal toilet training, but also because parents may have unsuccessfully attempted a procedure before coming to a health professional. A knowledge of proper and improper application can aid in diagnosis and treatment. In the past, and too frequently in the present, parents have resorted to punishment, coercion, and scolding in order to "break" children of eliminating in a diaper. In contrast, over the years, many parents have relied on Dr. Benjamin Spock's book on children's health care. The toileting recommenda-

ROBERT D. LYMAN • Department of Psychology, The University of Alabama, Tuscaloosa, Alabama 35486.    JAMES P. SCHIERBERL • St. Vincent Health Center, Erie, Pennsylvania 16544.    MICHAEL C. ROBERTS • Department of Psychology, The University of Alabama, Tuscaloosa, Alabama 35486.

tions in the early editions of the Dr. Spock book and others emphasized children's *readiness* to be trained as being critical, thus allowing them to "become trained of their own free will" (Spock & Rothenberg, 1985, p. 317). This approach lets the child gain a sense of mastery as the parents trust the child's natural desire to mature and become trained (Brazelton, 1962). Other popular-press publications also carry this attitude of leaving a child alone to develop an unpressured awareness of bladder and bowel control (e.g., Ross Laboratories, 1975). Many such recommendations include putting the child on a potty when the parent thinks the child is going to urinate or defecate and praising him or her when elimination occurs. The latest edition of the Spock book (Spock & Rothenberg, 1985) continues with this emphasis, that the child should progress through the stages of toilet training at an individual pace.

More structured procedures for toilet training have been formulated by behavioral psychologists, using behavioral rehearsal or practice and reinforcement for proper toileting. Azrin and Foxx (1974) published validated and popular techniques for parents to use in *Toilet Training in Less Than a Day*. This intensive training procedure may be more difficult for parents to implement without professional overview (Butler, 1976; Matson & Ollendick, 1977), but it can be successfully used, especially if one ignores the "less than a day" mandate. Christophersen and Rapoff (1983) outlined a "dry pants" sequential process of toileting training that relies on behavioral techniques as well. Many parents and professionals adopt more middle-of-the-road approaches by combining an "easy-going" Spock orientation while using rewards with the child for appropriate toileting. These various techniques for normal toilet training usually work; maturation and development also aid in the acquisition of acceptable toileting habits. However, in some cases, toilet training is not achieved, or inappropriate toileting habits are developed after seemingly successful training. In these cases, the clinician needs to consider the clinical disorders of enuresis and encopresis, as discussed in the following sections.

## ENURESIS

Enuresis, or the repeated inappropriate and involuntary passage of urine after an age at which continence is expected, is one of the most commonly occurring childhood behavioral disorders, with estimates that 3–7 million school-aged children are suffering from enuresis in the United States (Schaefer, 1979). Estimates of the percentages of American children who are enuretic range from 2.2% (Halverstadt, 1976) to 25% (Michaels & Goodman, 1954). Approximately twice as many boys as girls are enuretic (White, 1971). A major problem in the definition of enuresis is identifying the age at which continence should be expected. By age 4, 75% of all children are essentially bladder-trained; by age 6, 85% are; and by age 10, 95% are (Oppel, Harper, & Rider, 1968). The *Diagnostic and Statistical Manual of Mental Disorders III* (DSM-III) of the American Psychiatric Association (APA, 1980) arbitrarily sets 5 years as the lower age cutoff for a diagnosis of enuresis; other practitioners and researchers would consider such a diagnosis for children as young as 3 (DeJonge, 1973). Another difficulty in the definition and diagnosis of enuresis is the frequency of inappropriate urination necessary to justify the clinical diagnosis. Oppel *et al.* (1968) reported, for instance, that 30% of all 5-year-olds and 15% of all 9-year-olds have occasional lapses in bladder control. The DSM-III requires "at least two such events per month for children between the ages of five and six, and at least one event per month for older children" (APA, 1980, p. 80) to diagnose enuresis.

Another significant differentiation to be made in any consideration of enuresis is between nocturnal (nighttime) and diurnal (daytime) enuresis; nighttime bladder control is usually achieved a year or more later than daytime control. Fewer than 10% of enuretics experience frequent involuntary diurnal voiding (Breckenridge & Vincent, 1966).

Enuresis can also be classified as primary or secondary: primary enuretics have never achieved bladder control, and secondary enuretics have achieved bladder control for at least a year before the onset of involuntary voiding. Primary enuretics make up 85% of all cases of enuresis (DeJonge, 1973).

Many children experiencing enuresis become continent by adolescence, even without treatment. Forsythe and Redmond (1974) found that spontaneous remission rates averaged 14% per year between ages 5 and 9, 16% per year between ages 10 and 14, and 16% per year between ages 15 and 19. According to the DSM-III, only 1% of 18-year-old males and almost no 18-year-old females are enuretic (APA, 1980).

## Historical Development

According to Glicklich (1951), enuresis was identified as a medical problem by the Egyptians as early as 1550 B.C. Over the centuries, such folk remedies as raising the foot of the bed, restricting fluid intake, potions, special diets, massage, and circumcision were implemented (Mowrer & Mowrer, 1938). These approaches had varying degrees of success, in some cases benefiting greatly from spontaneous remission.

Until recently, emotional factors were considered a primary cause of enuresis; psychotherapy (often psychoanalysis) was viewed as the appropriate treatment. Freud (1916) interpreted enuresis as an ejaculation analogue and, therefore as a way of expressing repressed sexual feelings. Fenichel (1946) viewed enuresis as indicative of regression and gender-identity confusion, and Inhof (1956) regarded it as a symbolic expression of an unmet need for love ("weeping through the bladder"). Robertiello (1956) also viewed enuresis as symbolic, representing a "cooling off" of the genitals and thus a diminishment of sexual drives.

## Basic Principles

Although there are a number of theories explaining enuresis, none are completely satisfactory, and some are directly contradicted by experimental evidence. It now appears that enuresis is a condition with multiple causes, often with more than one causal mechanism operating in an individual case. This complex pattern of causality dictates comprehensive and sophisticated assessment procedures.

### Physical Causes

Although enuresis is defined as a functional disorder by the DSM-III, a number of medical conditions can also cause involuntary voiding. It is imperative that these factors be adequately considered and assessed before intervention, even though the research literature suggests that no more than 10% of cases of urinary incontinence are caused by physical factors (Arena, 1969; Geppert, 1953; Martin, 1966; Pierce, 1972; Stewart, 1946). Some of the possible physical causes for urinary incontinence are discussed in the following paragraphs.

*Urogenital Tract Obstructions and Dysfunctions.* A number of structural problems in the urogenital tract may cause enuresis, including weakness of the external sphincter muscle, urethral fistulas, obstructions of the urethral valves, and an abnormally short urethra (Brock & Kaplan, 1980). Often, other symptoms are present along with enuresis, such as painful or frequent urination and irregular urine stream. Chronic bladder obstruction can result in myogenic bladder, in which urinary retention causes the bladder to overdistend and the detrusor muscle to decompensate (Walker, Milling, & Bonner, 1988). A problem known as vaginal reflux, caused by a short urethra, can cause urinary dribbling and can also predispose a girl to vaginal infections (Schmitt, 1982a). Surgical procedures are available for the correction of many of these conditions, although frequently, remedial bladder training is necessary even after surgery.

*Urinary Tract Infection.* A high percentage of enuretic children, particularly girls, have urinary tract infections. One study found that 1 out of 10 girls with nightly enuresis had such an infection (Taylor & Turner, 1975). However, the direction of causality is unclear, as incontinence can both predispose a child to urinary tract infection (Galdston & Perlmutter, 1973) and be caused by such infections. One study found that only 1 of 18 enuretic children with urinary tract infections was cured of enuresis after successful treatment of the infection (Forsythe & Redmond, 1974). The symptoms of urinary tract infections include fever, painful or difficult urination, dribbling, and excessive urinary frequency. Antibiotics are often effective in treating these infections.

*Nervous System Dysfunctions.* Grand mal seizures may often be accompanied by involuntary voiding, and if such seizures occur exclusively at night, as is sometimes the case, the cause for the enuresis will not be readily apparent. Petit mal seizures are not usually associated with incontinence, but on occasion, voiding may occur in conjunction with these periods of absence. Waking and sleep EEGs may be necessary to diagnose a seizure disorder. The treatment usually consists of one or more antiseizure medications and varies widely in effectiveness. Even in children without observable seizures, EEG abnormalities are more commonly found in enuretics than in nonenuretics, with abnormal patterns seen in 22% (Pierce, Lipcan, McLary, & Noble, 1956) to 77% (Gunnarsen & Melin, 1951) of enuretics and only 2% (Pierce *et al.*, 1956) of nonenuretics. Spinal cord lesions, demyelinating diseases, and peripheral neuropathy due to such causes as diabetes can also cause urinary incontinence.

*Bladder Capacity.* It has long been asserted by a number of researchers and practitioners (Hallman, 1950; Muellner, 1960, 1963; Starfield, 1967) that small bladder capacity is a common cause of enuresis in children. Many children with small bladder capacities are not enuretic, however, and Doleys (1978) showed that not all enuretics have small bladder capacity. Therefore, it appears that bladder capacity alone is insufficient to explain enuresis. Urinary retention training is often recommended to help enuretic children increase their bladder capacity and will be discussed later.

*Sleep Arousal Disorders.* Anecdotal evidence suggests that enuretics may be more difficult to arouse while sleeping than nonenuretics; however, there has been conflicting empirical evidence on this issue. Bostock (1958) found that enuretic children did take longer to awaken to a buzzer than nonenuretics. Finley and Besserman (1973) also found enuretics to be more difficult to awaken. However, Boyd (1960) found that they awakened more quickly to shaking and calling their name than nonenuretics, as did Dittman and Blinn (1955). Finley and Wansley (1977) stated emphatically that a high threshold of arousability is the primary cause of enuresis. There does not, however, appear to be any reliable association between enuresis and specific stages of sleep (Mikkelsen *et al.*, 1980), although several studies have found overall differences between enuretics' and nonenuretics' sleep patterns (Broughton & Gastaut, 1964; Strom-Olson, 1950).

*Heredity.* Researchers have found that there is a higher incidence of enuresis in the relatives of enuretic children, with approximately 50% of parents or close relatives having experienced this problem as children (Baller, 1975). Bakwin and Bakwin (1972) noted higher enuresis concordance rates for monozygotic (67.9%) than for dizygotic (35.7%) twins and a higher incidence of enuresis in children of two parents who were enuretic as children (77.3%) than in children of one parent who was enuretic as a child (approximately 43%). Despite this evidence supporting a genetic basis for enuresis, therapeutic interventions have proved to be effective even with children who have a positive family history for enuresis.

## Psychological-Behavioral Factors

*Intelligence.* Although enuresis is more common among severely mentally retarded children than among children with average intelligence, there does not appear to be any relationship between intelligence and enuresis in the average range (Hallgren, 1957; Harnach, 1953), and most of the severely mentally retarded can learn bladder control with sufficient remedial training (Azrin, Sneed, & Foxx, 1973). Intellectual capability, therefore, does not appear to be a primary causal mechanism in enuresis.

*Toilet-Training Practices.* It has been suggested that toilet training begun too early and conducted too strictly is responsible for enuresis (Despert, 1944; Powell, 1951). One study found that 35 of 41 enuretic children had experienced "early" toilet training, and the parents of 29 of these children described the training as "rigidly strict" (Bindelglas, Dee, & Enos, 1968). Other researchers, however, have found no relationship between toilet-training practices and enuresis (Dimson, 1959; Klackenberg, 1955; Lovibond, 1964). It appears that parental toilet-training practices may be only a secondary cause of enuresis, interacting with other variables.

*Emotional Disturbance.* Approximately 20% of enuretic children show indications of emotional disturbance (Rutter, Yule, & Graham, 1973; Taylor & Turner, 1975). Although this figure is somewhat higher than the incidence of emotional disturbance reported in nonenuretic populations, it has been criticized as biased and unreliable (Shaffer, 1973). It is also possible that such emotional disturbances may be a product of enuresis rather than a cause. Several studies have found no relationship between childhood enuresis and emotional disturbance (Cullen, 1966; Lapouse & Monk, 1959; MacFarlane, Allen, & Honzik, 1954; Tapia, Jekel, & Domke, 1960). Other researchers, however, have found that stress and anxiety in children can be associated with enuresis (Galdston & Perlmutter, 1973; Jehu, Morgan, Turner, & Jones, 1977), particularly secondary enuresis. It appears, therefore, that emotional disturbance is not a primary cause of enuresis and is not even a strong correlate. Stress and anxiety may be associated with secondary enuresis, but even here, the direction of causality is unclear.

### Treatment

In addition to the folk remedies mentioned earlier, there is a time-honored tradition of parental punitiveness toward enuresis that continues even today. Such measures as spanking, public humiliation, and withdrawal of privileges have proved to be largely ineffective in treating the condition. Environmental manipulations such as restricting fluids and periodically wakening and toileting the child throughout the night are also commonly tried by parents. The first of these procedures has only limited effectiveness (Doleys, 1979), but random wakening (rather than wakening at fixed times) has been demonstrated to have significant treatment efficacy (Creer & Davis, 1975; Young, 1964). Simply having a child record the frequency of enuresis has also been demonstrated to result in some improvement (Collins, 1973), as has wakening the child on finding the bed wet (Catalina, 1976). Such commonsense approaches result in improvement in approximately one third of all enuretics (McGregor, 1937), although spontaneous remission may be responsible for a sizable portion of this figure. A number of more formal treatment approaches are commonly implemented by medical and mental health professionals.

*Psychotherapy.* Even though there is little evidence that emotional disturbance is a primary cause of enuresis, verbal psychotherapy has been among the most often implemented courses of treatment. There is little evidence to support the superiority of psychotherapy to spontaneous remission in the treatment of enuresis (Lovibond, 1964; Werry & Cohrssen, 1965). However, hypnotherapy has been reported to be effective in treating enuresis; hypnotic suggestions are usually made that the child will wake to use the toilet during the night (Collison, 1970; Kohen, Olness, Cornwell, & Heimel, 1984; Olness, 1975).

*Medication.* The most commonly prescribed medication for enuresis is imipramine (Tofranil), a tricyclic antidepressant, given in the afternoon or before bed. Its mechanism of action is not known. Of children treated with imipramine, 10%–40% show a significant reduction in bed-wetting (Forsythe & Redmond, 1974), but relapses occur at a rate of over 50% when the drug is withdrawn, and complete dryness is uncommon (Ack, Norman, & Schmitt, 1985). The resulting "cure rate" of no higher than 25% is not compelling when compared with the 15% per year spontaneous remission rate. In addition, even slight imipramine overdoses can be fatal, and the drug has a number of potentially harmful side effects.

Stimulant medication (methylphenidate or dextroamphetamine sulfate) is also commonly prescribed for enuresis, with the presumed goal of lightening the child's level of sleep. The efficacy and relapse rates roughly parallel those of imipramine, and there are also significant negative side effects with prolonged use (Schaefer, 1979). Oxybutinin (Ditropan) was demonstrated to have considerable effectiveness with enuretics who did not respond to imipramine (Schmitt, 1982b), but its long-term efficacy remains unproven.

In summary, medication may result in some short-term improvement in enuresis but has proved largely ineffective over extended periods of time. In addition, the drug treatment of enuresis carries significant risks.

*Behavior Therapy.* Generally, behavioral approaches have proved to be the most effective interventions with enuresis. As stated earlier, even merely having a child record the occurrence of wetting incidents (or conversely, dry nights) consistently produces some improvement (Collins, 1973; Doleys, 1977). Simple reward and/or punishment programs have also been shown to be effective. Popler (1976) found that coupons earned by dry nights and redeemable for cash were effective within 24 weeks in eliminating primary enuresis in a 14-year-old male. The boy was still dry at a 6-month follow-up. Similarly, Bach and Moylan (1975) used modest monetary rewards (10–25 cents) for appropriate toileting and dry nights to control enuresis and encopresis in a 6-year-old boy. Benjamin, Serdahely, and Geppert (1971) found that social reinforcers (hugging, kissing, and praise) were more effective than social punishment (shaming, spanking, and name calling) in initially training nocturnal continence in children. Allgeier (1976) found that, along with self-monitoring, making access to liquids after dinner contingent on 21 consecutive dry nights was effective in eliminating enuresis in two sisters, aged 8 and 11. The mild punishment of having to change their own sheets also appears to decrease enuresis in some children (Doleys, 1977). In addition to these fairly simple approaches, more complex applications of behavioral technology have been developed that are effective in treating enuresis.

## Major Applications

### Retention-Control Training

The theory behind retention-control training is that having a child refrain from urinating for progressively longer periods of time after feeling the urge to do so will result in increased functional bladder capacity and improved sphincter control. Muellner (1960) found that following such a procedure did result in increased bladder capacity (as measured by urine output), and that when children were able to retain 10–12 ounces of urine during the daytime, their nocturnal enuresis disappeared. He found that it took 3–6 months for most children to achieve this level of bladder capacity. Starfield and Mellits (1968) asked 83 enuretic children to refrain once a day from urinating for as long as possible (to a maximum of 40 minutes) after feeling the need to do so. These authors found that the enuresis of 85% of the children decreased, although only 20% were cured.

Kimmel and Kimmel (1970) used retention-control training in conjunction with reinforcement procedures. On the first day of training, they asked the children to tell their parents when they had to urinate and then to refrain from actually urinating for 5 minutes. Successful delay of urination resulted in tangible rewards, such as candy, cookies, and soda. As training continued, the required retention interval was gradually increased, eventually to as long as 30 minutes in many cases. This procedure resulted in a decrease in the frequency of both daytime urination and nocturnal enuresis in many cases, often within 2 weeks. Paschalis, Kimmel, and Kimmel (1972) replicated the above procedure and found similar results. They gradually increased the required retention interval until urination could be delayed for 45 minutes, with tokens and praise awarded after the successful delay of urination. The tokens could be exchanged for a variety of toys and games. The children were also responsible for recording their retention time. The training lasted 20 days, with follow-up 3 months later. At that time, 48% of the children were cured, and 74% were substantially improved.

Stedman (1972) combined self-monitoring and the Kimmel and Kimmel procedure with a 13-year-old female who was a primary enuretic. She was asked to record bladder distention cues, frequency of daytime urination, and incidents of nocturnal enuresis. She was also asked to refrain from urinating for 30 minutes after she felt a strong need to. Daytime urination and nocturnal enuresis both decreased significantly, and within 12 weeks, the child was no longer enuretic. A 3-month follow-up found only a few incidents of enuresis. Miller (1973) asked his subjects, two institutionalized adolescents, to record their frequency of daytime urination and the number of incidents of nocturnal enuresis. They were instructed over a 3-week period to refrain from urinating for an increasing period of time (from 10 to 30 minutes) following the onset of the urge to do so. In addition, during this training period, the subjects were told to increase their daily fluid consumption. Both subjects' enuresis was cured after 11 weeks of treatment, with continued success at a 7-month follow-up. Rocklin and Tilker (1973) also used the Kimmel and Kimmel procedure but found only a 30% cure rate, as opposed to the approximate 50% cure rate cited by Paschalis *et al.* (1972). Doleys and Wells (1975) implemented a 21-day retention-control training program with a 3-year-old girl and found no decrease in nocturnal enuresis until nighttime wakening and toileting were initiated, despite an increase in functional bladder capacity as measured by urine output. Similarly, Doleys, Ciminero, Tollison, Williams, and Wells (1977a) found no relationship between bladder capacity changes and frequency of enuresis. Harris and Purohit (1977) also found that retention-control training resulted in increased functional bladder capacity but no decrease in frequency of enuresis.

In addition to retention-control training, sphincter-control training has been implemented by some researchers. Such training involves having the child practice starting and stopping the flow of urine once urination has begun. Miller (1973), Chapman (1974), and Walker *et al.* (1988) have reported some success in using this technique in conjunction with retention control training.

In summary, the preponderance of evidence suggest that there is some value in the utilization of retention-control training in the treatment of enuresis, even though the relationship between bladder capacity and the disorder is unclear. A realistic estimate of the proportion of enuretic children who may benefit from such training is probably 50%–75%, with 30%–50% becoming completely nonenuretic. It appears that the children most likely to benefit from retention-control training are those with demonstrated small functional bladder capacity, as indicated by reduced urinary output and frequent daytime urination.

## Enuresis Alarm

In the early 1900s, Pflaunder (1904) used electrical alarms that rang a bell when the child wet the bed; these alarms were placed in the beds of children hospitalized on a pediatric ward. Although the intent was merely to alert the nursing staff that the child needed changing, Pflaunder noted a decrease in incidents of enuresis. Later, Mowrer and Mowrer (1938) demonstrated the efficacy of a similar device in treating 30 enuretic children. Since that time, numerous studies have been done to evaluate the enuresis alarm. Young (1969) found that, in 19 studies using enuresis alarms, the success rates ranged from 68% to 100%, with a mean of 71%. Doleys (1977) reviewed the literature on enuresis alarms between 1960 and 1975 and found that 75% of all cases were treated successfully in 5–12 weeks. However, he did note a 41% relapse rate; two thirds of these relapsed enuretics were successfully reconditioned. Other researchers have also noted high relapse rates. Baller and Schalock (1956) found that 15% of successfully treated cases had relapsed at a 2½-year follow-up, and DeLeon and Sacks (1972) reported a 20% relapse rate 4 years after successful treatment. Lovibond (1964) reported 30% relapses, and Young and Morgan (1972) reported an initial relapse rate of 35%, which was later reduced to 13% through the use of overcorrection procedures.

There are a number of different types of enuresis alarms, all of which function to turn on an alarm (a buzzer or light) when urine completes an electrical circuit. The most commonly used model is available from several large retail and catalog stores and consists of two metal sheets (the top one with holes in it) separated by a fiber insulating sheet. When urine wets this middle sheet, it becomes conductive, and a buzzer (and in some models, a light) is turned on. Unfortunately. this device requires approximately 10 ml of urine to activate it, and therefore, the response time is slow. The apparatus is also difficult to dry sufficiently so that it may be reset for children who wet more than once a night. False alarms are fairly common because of inadvertent touching of the two metal sheets. Newer versions of the enuresis alarm include models with small sensors that attach to the front of the child's underpants or pajama pants and a buzzer unit that is attached to the shoulder area of an undershirt or a pajama top. These alarms are sensitive to a few drops of urine and therefore have much quicker response times than the older models. In addition, they are easier to dry and are much less prone to false alarms.

There is considerable debate concerning the theoretical rationale by which enuresis alarms produce therapeutic effects. Originally, it was suggested (Mowrer & Mowrer, 1938) that a classical conditioning paradigm was at work, with the conditioned stimulus (bladder distension cues) gradually gaining the ability to produce wakefulness (the conditioned response) through pairing with the unconditioned stimulus (the buzzer or light). More recently, however, this interpretation has been criticized as representing backward conditioning, which has been shown to be an ineffective conditioning model. In addition, this interpretation fails to explain why children treated with the enuresis alarms usually do not learn to get up and urinate at night; instead, they begin to sleep through the night without wetting (White, 1971). More recent interpretations (Azrin, Sneed, & Foxx, 1974) have emphasized the operant conditioning aspects of the procedure, with the sound of the buzzer and subsequent abrupt awakening functioning as an unpleasant consequence that can be prevented by learning not to urinate during sleep.

Effective use of the enuresis alarm usually requires professional guidance (Schaefer, 1979). The apparatus should be fully explained and demonstrated to both parents, other family members, and the enuretic child. It should be explained to all parties that it usually takes as long as 12 weeks for the procedure to eliminate enuresis, and that, initially, there may be no reduction in wetting frequency. The need for accurate record-keeping regarding the date, time, and magnitude (size of wet spot) of enuretic incidents should also be explained. Usually, there is a baseline period of 2 weeks or more, during which data are gathered but no interventions are initiated. When the enuresis alarm is put into operation, the parents are told to take their child into the bathroom when the alarm sounds, to make sure that he or she is awake (splashing cold water in the child's face, if necessary), and to have him or her attempt to urinate, even if the bed is already significantly wet. It is also important that the child be given the responsibility of immediately remaking the bed with dry sheets and that the alarm be reset. The parents must also be instructed regarding the duration of use of the enuresis alarm. Schaefer (1979) and Taylor and Turner (1975) have recommended that it be used until there have been 28 consecutive nights with only one enuretic incident. Forsythe and Redmond (1974) found that keeping the child on the alarm 2–4 weeks after achieving dryness reduces the chance of relapses.

A number of modifications in the standard enuresis alarm procedure have been developed in an attempt to improve its effectiveness. An overcorrection procedure, consisting of having the child drink large quantities of liquids immediately before bedtime after the enuresis episodes have been initially controlled through use of the alarm, has been found to be effective in reducing relapse rates (Jehu *et al.*, 1977; Morgan, 1978; Taylor & Turner, 1975; Young & Morgan, 1972). Periodically removing the alarm for a night has not been shown to be effective (Lovibond, 1964; Turner, Young, & Rachman, 1970), but using a modified enuresis alarm, which sounds the alarm according to an intermittent rather than a continuous schedule, has been shown to be effective in reducing relapse rates (Finley, 1971; Finley, Besserman, Bennett, Clapp, & Finley, 1973; Finley & Besserman, 1973). A schedule in which 70% of enuretic incidents trigger alarms appears to be optimal (Finley, Rainwater, & Johnson, 1982).

The use of cold baths as an aversive stimulus following alarms does not appear to be any more effective than the standard enuresis-alarm procedure (Tough, Hawkins, McArthur, & Van Ravensway, 1971). The delivery of electric shock on urination also does not produce results superior to those obtained with the buzzer alarm alone (McKendry, Stewart, Jeffs, & Mozes, 1972). McConaghy (1969) found that use of the enuresis alarm in conjunction with imipramine was more effective initially than use of the alarm alone and resulted in lower relapse rates than use of the medication alone.

In summary, the use of the enuresis alarm appears to be the most efficacious method extant. It has been found to be more effective than psychotherapy (DeLeon & Mandel, 1966), retention-control training (Fielding, 1980), and medication (Wagner, Johnson, Walker, Carter, & Wittner, 1982). The problem of high relapse rates appears solvable through the use of overcorrection and intermittent reinforcement procedures, and the technique has none of the dangers of the possible side effects of medication. The use of the enuresis alarm does require a considerable time commitment and disruption of sleep for the parents and the child, however, and it does not offer an immediate cure.

## Dry Bed Training

Azrin *et al.* (1974) combined the use of the enuresis alarm with a number of reinforcement and training procedures in a highly structured program that they call "dry bed training." They found that the procedure eliminated enuresis (14 consecutive dry nights) in all 24 children in their initial experimental group, with no relapses after six months. This success was achieved with an average of only two enuretic incidents per child following the initial night-training session. Doleys *et al.* (1977b), however, reported only a 62% success rate after a 6-week training period, with a 37% relapse rate. Bollard and Woodroffe (1977) found that parent-supervised dry-bed training eliminated enuresis in all 14 of their subjects within an average of 12 days, with only two relapses after 6 months. Griffiths, Medrum, and McWilliam (1982) were also able to eliminate enuresis in 100% of their subjects, although it took as long as 20 weeks and there was a 27% relapse rate after 9 months.

Dry bed training consists of an initial intensive training session during which parents and child review the entire procedure (with a therapist or by themselves). The child is then encouraged to drink fluids and, whenever she or he has to urinate, attempts to delay urination as long as possible. One hour before bedtime 20 practice trials are conducted, during which the child gets up from bed, goes to the bathroom, and attempts to urinate. At bedtime, the child drinks more fluids and reviews the procedure. Each hour during the night, the parents wake the child and ask him or her if he or she can delay urination for another hour. If the reply is yes, the child is returned to bed. If the reply is no, the child is taken to the bathroom and praised for appropriate toileting. More fluids are given, and the child is returned to bed. If the enuresis alarm sounds, the child is mildly reprimanded and taken to the bathroom to finish urinating. The child must then change clothes, remake the bed, and practice correct toileting 20 times.

After this initial training session, the child is asked to practice correct toileting 20 times at bedtime if she or he has been enuretic the previous night. The parents waken and toilet the child at their bedtime each night, with the time of this toileting advancing by 30 minutes (until it occurs only 1 hour after the child's bedtime, at which time it is discontinued) following dry nights. Enuresis alarms result in the same procedure as during the initial training night. Dry nights result in praise and other reinforcement. After seven consecutive dry nights the enuresis alarm and parental wakening are discontinued, and the child's bed is inspected each morning. A wet bed results in the child's remaking it and having 20 practice trials of correct toileting at bedtime that night. A dry bed produces praise and reinforcement from parents. Two enuretic incidents within 1 week result in reinstitution of the enuresis alarm and parental wakening until seven consecutive dry nights are achieved again.

Azrin and Thienes (1978) modified dry bed training to make it less invasive by eliminating the enuresis alarm and stopping parental wakenings after 1:00 A.M. on the initial training night. These authors reported that dry bed training without the enuresis alarm was more effective than use of the alarm alone and yielded results roughly equivalent to those of the original procedure. However, Nettelbeck and Langeluddecke (1979) found that dry bed training with the enuresis alarm was far more effective than the same procedure without the alarm, as did Bollard, Nettelbeck, and Roxbee (1982). Bollard and Nettelbeck (1981) found that the enuresis alarm alone was superior to dry bed training without the alarm, which was no better than the no-treatment control condition. Dry bed training with the enuresis alarm was the most effective intervention. Bollard (1982) found no differences between dry bed training with the enuresis alarm and the alarm alone in treatment effectiveness. Bollard and Nettelbeck (1982), however, found that dry bed training did add to the enuresis alarm's effectiveness.

In summary, the dry-bed-training procedure appears to add to the effectiveness of the enuresis alarm but to have limited usefulness when used without the alarm. It is extremely important to note, however, that this is an extremely invasive procedure that can be aversive to both children (Matson & Ollendick, 1977) and parents (Butler, 1976).

## ENCOPRESIS

Encopresis is one of the more frequent, and certainly one of the most challenging, childhood disorders encountered by health care professionals. It is probably safe to say that it is also one of the least understood disorders. Historically, there has been widespread disagreement regarding whether it is primarily a medical or a psychological problem, with associated disagreements regarding its etiology and appropriate treatment modalities. Unfortunately, a much more basic lack of agreement on definition and terminology has contributed to the long-standing confusion and controversy. The primary issues of dispute and inconsistency among different authors regarding definition (and therefore also diagnosis) include the age beyond which incomplete continence is defined as a disorder; the frequency of "accidents"; the inclusion versus the exclusion of organically based bowel dysfunctions; the so-called typical etiological factors; and the various patterns of toileting behavior and stool characteristics differentiating "encopresis" (as a syndrome) from other variations and distortions of the normal toilet-training process.

The DSM-III (APA, 1980) provides a good general definition that avoids theoretical complexities and seems to offer the closest thing to a consensus point of view currently available on this disorder. The DSM-III criteria include (1) the repeated voluntary or involuntary movement of feces in inappropriate places; (2) at least one inappropriate passage of feces per month after age 4; and (3) physical disorder must be ruled out. By the use of these criteria, an incidence rate of 1% has been established for 5-year-old children. Depending on the particular definition used, various authors have estimated the incidence of functional encopresis at between 0.4% (Weissenberg, 1926) and 5% (Olatawura, 1973). Wright, Schaefer, and Solomons (1979) noted that 1.5% seems to be the figure mentioned most frequently in the literature. However, many professionals believe that encopresis is seriously underreported. Whatever the overall incidence, encopretic conditions are much more common in males than in females. Estimates of the male-to-female ratio range from 3:2 (Lifshitz & Chovers, 1972) to 6:1 (Wright, 1975; Young, 1973).

## Historical Development

Encopresis has been recognized as unacceptable—and therefore, as some type of a disorder—since the beginnings of civilized society. The first mention of an involuntary soiling disorder in the recorded medical literature was in 1881 by Henock (Wright *et al.*, 1979). The term *encopresis* was not coined until years later, however, and there is even disagreement in the literature regarding who first used the term. Most authors credit Weissenberg (1926) with the original use, though Wright *et al.* (1979) noted an earlier usage by Pototsky in 1925. Additional historical perspectives on encopresis are available in Fisher (1979).

Encopresis was initially viewed as directly analogous to enuresis, and the result was a similarity in the early efforts at both conceptualization and treatment. As with most behavioral abnormalities, the primary orientation was psychoanalytic until the popularization of behavioral approaches during the 1970s. Psychoanalytic viewpoints emphasized the standard psychosexual issues, as well as prolongation of the mother–child power struggle surrounding toilet training (Hilbun, 1968), symbolic ventilation of hostility toward a domineering mother (Hushka, 1942), reaction to a lack or loss of parental love (Halpern, 1977), or reaction to more general family stress (Amsterdam, 1979). Psychodynamic perspectives on encopresis remain very prevalent and popular today and are described in more detail below. However, the primacy of this orientation appears to have declined steadily in recent years, in favor of either a more straightforward medical intervention approach, behavioral approaches, or a combination of the two. Indeed, as is the case with so many complex medical disorders with substantial psychological complications, the coordinated application of both medical and behavioral approaches has resulted in truly major strides in effectively treating this notoriously treatment-resistant disorder (Roberts, 1986).

Yet there exists a continuing widespread impression among health care practitioners (in both medical and mental health settings) that encopresis treatment programs almost invariably meet with minimal success. The contrast between this prevalent point of view and the very high rates of successful treatment reported by leading authorities, using combined pediatric and behavioral intervention strategies (e.g., Levine, 1982; Wright & Walker, 1977), indicates a great need for both further education of practitioners and further case consultation among practitioners of varying professions (physicians and psychologists in particular).

## Basic Principles

Although primary therapeutic procedures may vary widely depending on the individual practitioner's orientation and preferences, somewhat greater consensus exists regarding the general guidelines for the initial phases of treatment for the encopretic child. Most of these have to do with the assessment process.

Beyond this opening phase, a large number of specific therapeutic techniques are available, with which some fundamental familiarity is important. Some of these are reviewed here, and there is more extensive description of the more scientifically substantiated of these techniques in the final section of this chapter.

### Assessment

The value of a thorough physical examination of encopretic children is critical, perhaps more than for the many other childhood disorders for which such a medical exam is routinely recommended as an initial starting point. The two critical issues to be resolved are whether an organic disease process is responsible for the encopresis (e.g., Hirschsprung disease) and whether constipation or impaction is present as a complicating physiological condition. Excellent guidelines to the thorough evaluation of all possible physical causes and concomitants of encopresis have been provided by Fleisher (1976) and Gabel (1981). Some recently developed procedures increasing the detail and sophistication of the physical examination are a technique for more precisely measuring the degree of stool retention (Barr, Levine, & Wilkinson, 1979) and the use of anal manometry to assess the anal sphincter dysfunction associated with chronic constipation (Loening-Bauke, 1984).

Next, a thorough history is in order, covering both physical and psychosocial considerations. The principal value of this assessment procedure centers on the concept of specific subtypes of encopresis. There seem to be almost as many schemes for conceptualizing and classifying encopretic subtypes as there are authors addressing the topic. However, there is general agreement that such classification serves a valuable purpose in guiding an optimal formulization of an individualized treatment plan. It should be mentioned at the outset, however, that support for the value of such differential treatment programming based on specific subtypes remains currently at the theoretical and anecdotal levels (Roberts, 1986). Empirical research documenting such value is not currently available.

Probably the most established and useful dimension for differentiating encopretic subtypes has been "primary" versus "secondary" encopresis. The former, also labeled *continuous encopresis* by some authors, refers to the child who has never been successfully toilet-trained. Secondary, or discontinuous, encopresis refers to the child presenting with fecal incontinence who was satisfactorily continent at some point in his or her earlier development. The second dimension for dichotomizing different subtypes of encopresis concerns the degree of conscious awareness and/or control that the child experiences regarding her or his soiling behavior. There is obviously something very different about the child whose soiling episodes represent true "accidents" in spite of sincere efforts to overcome this difficulty (probably the largest subpopulation of encopretics) and children who either deliberately defecate in their clothing (or elsewhere) as an expression of hostility, or who simply do not care enough about the social ramifications of soiling to interrupt ongoing activities for a trip to the bathroom.

Anxiety-related considerations also provide a useful basis for subclassifying cases of encopresis. The two most common scenarios here are of very young children who are truly fearful of the toilet and therefore either soil their clothes continuously or else develop problem stool-retention habits, and the older, chronically anxious child whose anxiety results in constant loose stools and/or frequent diarrhea. The pattern of frequent minor accidents exhibited by the latter child is often referred to in the literature as *irritable bowel syndrome*.

Probably the single most useful dimension for classifying encopretic subtypes is the presence or absence of constipation as a major component of the symptom picture (Kohlenberg, 1973). Particularly where the constipation is chronic, resulting in substantial fecal impaction, this factor has a major bearing on the likelihood of success of the various treatment approaches. Specifically, any approach failing to provide for medical evacuation (or cleaning out by enema or suppository) of the impacted colon will be doomed to failure, especially if the condition has progressed to the point of functional megacolon (or enlarged, distended colon), where normal functioning of the colon has been seriously compromised. Large-scale studies have shown stool impaction to be present in between 80% (Levine, 1975) and 95% (Fitzgerald, 1975) of childhood encopretics. The specific procedures for confronting such cases are outlined below.

Some psychodynamically oriented authors, most notably Anthony (1957) and Bemporad, Kresch, and Asnes (1980), have attempted to subclassify different types of encopresis on the basis of personality and/or family dynamics. Such dimensions have proved somewhat more unreliable than those just discussed, however, as shown by the lack of success in research aimed at correlating the specific patterns of dynamics with their hypothesized symptom patterns (e.g., Olatawura, 1973).

Various authors have attempted more comprehensive classification schemes for subtypes of encopresis, using various combinations of the dimensions just reviewed (Berg & Jones, 1964; Easson, 1960; Gavanski, 1971). The most useful of these schemes appears to be that of Walker (1978), whose framework includes three broad categories: manipulative soiling, chronic diarrhea and irritable bowel syndrome, and chronic constipation with impaction and resulting diarrhealike seepage of feces around the impaction.

Beyond the search for useful, clinically familiar subtypes, obtaining a thorough history provides two additional advantages. First, the relative contribution of wider ranging psychopathology—either in the patient or in the family system—can be assessed. Some of the more common family dynamics of relevance here include the neglectful, undersocializing family that simply does not sufficiently prioritize and attend to the toilet-training process and the family with major (though often submerged) interpersonal conflicts in which the child's soiling serves either a controlling or a stabilizing function (e.g., manipulating parents to get attention or detouring attention and energy onto the child as a means of preventing possibly more severe, even violent, conflicts among other family members). A more commonly encountered scenario involves the child whose soiling serves an indirect (i.e., passive-aggressive) hostility-venting function, though this is not as common as many practitioners, and especially parents, believe. Indeed, the misattribution of involuntary soiling (e.g., constipation or impaction with fecal seepage) as a deliberate communication of hatred or resentment for the parent(s) is a frequent complicating factor in many cases that might otherwise respond to a basic medical intervention. It therefore becomes one of the clinician's greatest challenges in the assessment process to address such concerns on the part of the parents and to accurately determine if and when such interpretations of "willfulness" actually apply. In such cases, treatment then focuses on training the child in the use of more appropriate (i.e., assertive) means of communicating anger or dissatisfaction with his or her lot in the family (Kellerman, 1976).

The infinite possible variety of patterns of family dysfunction surrounding encopresis (as both precipitants of and reactions to) calls for considerable sensitivity and skill in interviewing the encopretic child and the family. The necessary familiarity with certain "classic" dysfunctional communication and relationship patterns underlines the value of psychological expertise on a treatment team, even in a primarily medical setting. One of the more common such patterns, which has been commented on frequently in the literature, is the family with an absent or underinvolved father. Bemporad, Pfeifer, Gibbs, Cortner, and Bloom (1971) studied the families of a large group of encopretics and found that, in addition to a 50% divorce rate among the parents, the father was absent from the home in an additional 33% of the cases. In the remaining, "intact" families, the authors found that, in every case, the father either held two jobs or was otherwise busy with activities outside the home. It would therefore appear important to devote somewhat more than the average time to evaluating the father's role in the family, and the father–patient relationship in particular, in cases of childhood encopresis.

Recent research contrasting historical and other variables in "treatment-resistant" versus more successfully treated cases of encopresis (Levine & Bakow, 1976) points the way toward other important factors to explore during the assessment process. The basic issue of symptom severity (both of the soiling behavior itself and of the underlying constipation) is highly predictive of treatment outcome, particularly the variable of whether the child soils while in school or after getting ready for bed. Second, children with many behavioral, developmental, or academic problems in addition to their encopresis have a poorer prognosis for overcoming their encopresis than children who have no such concomitant difficulties. In a related finding, the parents' demonstrated capacity for conscientious and consistent compliance with the treatment program to be implemented primarily in the home setting is closely related to the degree of success obtained in treatment. Finally, cases of severe resistance to treatment are usually associated with reports of substantial difficulty with early bowel training. Therefore, a careful assessment of these factors is a means of adjusting the treatment or anticipating slow or inconsistent progress. A more recent follow-up study by Levine and his associates added the differentiating factor of less stool retention in the resistant cases, along with an associated tendency by the parents in these cases to emphasize emotional and motivational causation more than physiological variables (Landman, Levine, & Rappaport, 1983).

As in the case of the very effective "bell-and-pad" method of treating enuresis, many otherwise treatable cases may be lost to treatment because of the clinician's failure to help the family realistically anticipate the length of time required to obtain a successful outcome. The exact timetable will vary widely, depending on many variables, such as the skills of the clinician and the parents, the motivation of the child and the parents, the number of complicating psychosocial variables, and the frequency of therapeutic contact. It is generally true, however, that the longer the child has been experiencing abnormalities of bowel function, the longer it will take to restore the digestive system to smooth functioning.

Levine (1982) provided an excellent description of the multiple and interacting determinants leading to the development of encopresis. By use of the concept of *potentiation,* virtually all possible factors capable of adversely affecting normal digestive and toileting functions are delineated and integrated. Although some behavioral practitioners may protest that effective treatment does not require such etiological conceptualization, families and patients (and many practitioners as well) may feel more satisfied with, and perhaps more motivated toward, the often detailed and somewhat intrusive treatment programs for encopresis when they have such a meaningful understanding of the roots and complexities of the disorder. Levine (1982) also provided useful guidelines for transmitting this developmental perspective to the child.

## Treatment

Encopresis has been treated by the full gamut of traditional psychotherapies for children, with varying degrees of success. Kellerman (1976) pointed out how just the basic procedure of the parents bringing the child to a professional for an initial consultation often leads to a fairly dramatic interruption in long-standing encopretic symptom patterns. Of course, such improvement is usually short-lived if it is not followed by an appropriate treatment program. But this phenomenon, whether due to placebo effect or other factors, has probably led to many mistaken impressions and exaggerated claims regarding the efficacy of various approaches. In addition, the failure of many authors to specify the details of the symptom pattern (subtype) in the case being reported may lead some to the mistaken conclusion that the specific treatment used in that case will be equally effective for any encopretic child. Despite the paucity of research documenting the relative value of specific treatment strategies geared toward specific subtypes, both basic theoretical logic and clinical experience strongly support the pragmatic benefits of such an orientation. To take a few extreme examples, consider the absurdity of prescribing frequent enemas for the encopretic child presenting without constipation or impaction, who is soiling because of an irritable bowel syndrome; or treating the child with a long history of impaction with play therapy only; or setting up a behavior-modification program offering stars or points for appropriate toileting as the sole approach with a child whose soiling represents a deliberate act of revenge against an over-controlling mother. These not-unheard-of scenarios underscore the importance for the practitioner to have at least a basic familiarity with a wide variety of therapeutic approaches, even though one or two basic "treatments of choice" will probably suffice for the majority of the cases encountered.

*Psychotherapy.* Traditional psychotherapy, of either the nondirective, supportive or the psychodynamic, insight-oriented variety, was the most commonly reported form of treatment reported in the literature through the 1960s. Under the assumption that the encopresis is a symptom of more pervasive underlying disturbances in personality functioning, the therapist meets with the child regularly, usually for weekly 1-hour sessions, and explores with the child the issues currently troubling him or her. Play materials and/or artistic expression may be used to facilitate the uncovering and discharge of the disturbing emotions. From the child's direct verbal and indirect symbolic communications, the therapist discerns the intrapsychic (or possibly the interpersonal and family) dynamics contributing to the encopresis and assists the child in resolving these. Through the trusting relationship developed between therapist and child, the child becomes "freed up" from problem conflicts and concerns and learns new ways of dealing with her or his feelings and communicating her or his needs. This result may be accomplished by facilitating the symbolic expression of troubling issues in play or art and then gradually interpreting these to the child, or perhaps simply by allowing the child "free rein" to discharge unacceptable emotions and impulses in a supportive atmosphere of respect and acceptance, so that the child gradually grows beyond a previous preoccupation with them.

More specific guidelines to the techniques of individual therapy with encopretic children can be derived from basic references on child psychotherapy (Freedheim & Russ, 1983; Sandler, Kennedy, & Tyson, 1980; Schaefer & O'Conner, 1983) and are not detailed here. Numerous case studies are also available describing this approach in more detail (e.g., Segall, 1957; Shane, 1967; Warson, Caldwell, Warineer, Kirk, & Jensen, 1954).

Very few reports of the successful treatment of encopresis using individual psychotherapy have appeared in recent years; thus, this approach is probably of limited usefulness in the majority of cases. The few controlled, or even uncontrolled, large-scale studies of the effectiveness of this approach have yielded unimpressive results. Berg and Jones (1964) followed up 70 children treated for encopresis and found no difference in rates of remission for those who had received psychotherapy and those who had not. Lifshitz and Chovers (1972) conducted a study of psychodynamic therapy in cases of encopresis and reported the discouraging finding that the untreated control group actually showed greater improvement that those receiving psychotherapy. Somewhat more positive results were reported by Pinkerton (1958), using verbal psychotherapy with 30 encopretic children. Seventeen were reported as being in complete remission at follow-up several years after the termination of therapy. McTaggert and Scott (1979) used play therapy as a primary technique and reported 7 of 12 cases cured and 3 others "improved."

An increasingly popular form of psychotherapy with much potential applicability to encopretic children is family therapy. Based on a "systems" perspective, such approaches conceptualize encopresis (like other individual psychopathology) as being indicative of family dysfunction (Sheinbein, 1975). The specific problems in family relationships thus become the primary focus of psychotherapy sessions, and other family members are encouraged, or even required, to attend all treatment sessions. Baird (1974) and Bemporad *et al.* (1980) have provided elaborate descriptions of some of the more commonly encountered variants of maladaptive family relationship and communication patterns frequently seen in the families of encopretic children. Guidelines and case examples regarding specific therapeutic procedures using the family therapy approach have been provided by Andolphi (1978), Dreman (1977), and Rydzinski and Kaplan (1985). At present, there is too little research available regarding the effectiveness of family therapy with encopretic children to adequately judge the value of this approach. However, the continued growth of family therapy in the wider mental-health field, coupled with the frequent observation that disturbed family relationships are a common correlate and complicating factor in most cases of encopresis, suggests that this is an approach with considerable promise, if not as the primary treatment modality, then at least as an adjunctive therapy.

*Medication.* Simply because of the prevailing view in medicine that en-

copresis is essentially a medical problem, many cases are still treated exclusively
from a medical management standpoint. This arrangement is due both to parental reluctance to consider possible psychological problems affecting their child
and to a lack of familiarity with behavioral approaches on the part of most
physicians (Heins & Beerends, 1978). Sometimes referred to as the *Davidson
approach* (Davidson, 1958, 1980), the standard pediatric treatment method consists of various combinations of enemas and laxatives for initial evacuation of the
colon, followed by mineral oil and stool softeners (e.g., Dulcolax, Metamucil, or
Colace) to facilitate continuing smooth bowel function, and modification of diet
to increase the child's awareness of stool build-up and to prevent constipation
(Davidson, Kugler, & Bauer, 1963; Nisley, 1976). This approach also calls for
increased encouragement and reminders from parents regarding more regular
toileting efforts. However, an insufficient emphasis on the complications attendant on this single "behavioral" component of the pediatric approach has probably been the primary reason for its limited and inconsistent effectiveness (Landman & Rappaport, 1985; Schaefer, 1979). A more comprehensive medical
approach to encopresis is presented in the "Major Applications" section later in
this chapter.

*Behavior Therapy.* Therapies using behavioral technologies have been shown
to be potentially powerful tools for ameliorating encopretic symptoms (Johnson
& Van Bourgondien, 1977). The primary advantage of behavior therapy over
traditional psychotherapy for treating encopresis (as for treating most other
disorders) is the much shorter length of time usually required to obtain a significant impact on the problem. A major reason is the standard provision for parent-
mediated ongoing treatment procedures in the home on a daily basis, as opposed to the traditional 1 hour per week of psychotherapy, where the bulk of the
therapeutic procedures is confined to the therapy hour. An additional advantage
is that physicians seem to be much more comfortable with the focus on observable symptoms, the shorter term pragmatic orientation, and the deemphasis of
esoteric theoretical concepts; thus, these techniques are readily incorporated
into treatment plans.

Positive reinforcement for appropriate toileting behavior is the most frequently reported behavioral technique applied to encopresis. The typical program provides for the child to be rewarded with secondary reinforcers such as
stars on a chart, stickers, tokens, or points for each incident of defecation in the
toilet (or possibly simply for sitting on the toilet and attempting to defecate). The
secondary reinforcers are cumulatively applied to earning more meaningful rewards, such as toys or special privileges. Though sometimes effective in itself,
such a positive reinforcement program usually needs to be combined with other
approaches targeting other complicating aspects of the child's condition if maximal effectiveness is to be achieved. Examples would include family therapy for
cases in which soiling serves a manipulative or communication function, medical treatments such as specialized diets, or enemas for cases in which constipation is a major component of the clinical picture.

If such complicating variables are not present, the more simple reward
program may often be the treatment of choice. Young and Goldsmith (1972)
reported the successful treatment of an 8-year-old boy with chronic soiling of a

year's duration, by rewarding the boy with a small toy car at the end of each day of no soiling and at least one bowel movement in the toilet. It is important to be careful not to make the absence of soiling the sole criterion for reward, as the child may accomplish this simply by withholding feces, and the result may be even more impaction.

Another basic reward-based procedure was described by Ayllon, Simon, and Wildman (1975) in their successful treatment of a 7-year-old boy with chronic encopresis. These authors advised the boy's mother to award him a star on a chart at the end of each day in which there was no soiling. Seven stars were set as the criterion for earning the primary reinforcer of an outing with the psychologist. A supplemental procedure used here and in many other case reports was a requirement that the child wash his own soiled clothing on the few occasions when he did not remain continent through the day. Within 4 weeks, the encopresis had been completely eliminated, at which point the special reinforcement procedures were gradually faded out by having the mother use extensive praise in place of the stars, taking the child on the earned outings herself, and gradually reducing the regularity and frequency of these outings to an informal arrangement (Ayllon *et al.*, 1975).

Parental praise and monetary reward were used as reinforcers by Plachetta (1976) in eliminating a 6-year-old boy's habit of soiling his clothes twice a day for several months before treatment. The child was instructed to sit on the toilet on four scheduled occasions each day, with the reinforcer being a penny earned for each 10-minute period he remained on the toilet, plus a nickel for each bowel movement there. Several additional components of the treatment package make this case less an example of a "pure" positive-reinforcement approach and more a typical example of multiple behavioral procedures serving to combat the symptoms from a number of different "angles." Specifically, the parents ignored any soiling that did occur and discontinued their previous use of spankings for this problem. The child was required to wash out his own clothes when soiling did occur. Finally, there was a strong emphasis on self-monitoring, in which the child charted his own progress by recording stars on a chart whenever he was successful in toileting. Additional illustrations of primarily reward-based operant approaches to encopresis have been reported by Bach and Moylan (1975), Neale (1963). Pedrini and Pedrini (1971), and Tomlinson (1970).

Additional behavioral procedures that supplement the basic positive-reinforcement approach, such as self-monitoring, differential attention, and logical consequences (washing soiled clothes), have already been mentioned. Other recently developed variations of the operant conditioning approach include the use of a negative reinforcement paradigm (Rolider & Van Houten, 1985), "paradoxical" interventions (Jacob & Moore, 1984), and variable-ratio reinforcement schedules for toileting behavior (Bornstein, Balleweg, McLellarn, Wilson, & Sturm, 1983).

Punishment approaches are sometimes combined with reward procedures to strengthen the treatment package. Time-out from positive reinforcement, imposed contingent on incidents of soiling, has been the most frequently reported (e.g., Barrett, 1969; Edelman, 1971). Ferinden and Van Handel (1970) used a more aversive punishment, washing soiled clothes in cold water using a mildly abrasive soap, as the negative consequence of soiling (in combination with other procedures, including counseling). Doleys's full cleanliness training, described later, also makes use of some aversive consequences, but again, as part of a comprehensive package of interventions (Doleys, 1978, 1979). Because of the long-standing impression of many clinicians that encopresis is somehow related to a sense that toileting is an aversive experience or else is related to issues of aggression and hostility and resentment of perceived parental harshness, the use of punishment as an exclusive or even a primary treatment strategy is widely regarded as contraindicated. As only one of several treatment procedures, however, and with the advice that such punishment be administered calmly and matter-of-factly by the parents, some punishment procedures may hold value in strengthening the impact of a treatment program in certain cases (Houle, 1974).

Other techniques are psychologically based through behavioral techniques. These less familiar but potentially powerful treatment techniques involve the use of biofeedback (Cerulli, Nikoomanesh, & Schuster, 1979; Engel. Nikoomanesh, & Schuster, 1974; Kohlenberg, 1973; Lowery, Srour, Whitehead, & Schuster, 1985; Olness, McFarland, & Piper, 1980). Developed primarily for patients with fecal incontinence due to neurological disorders (Wald, 1981; Whitehead, Parker, Masek, Cataldo, & Freeman, 1981), these fairly complex retraining procedures appear to be useful in treating some other types of encopresis as well, especially in treatment-resistant cases and in those where lengthy histories of impaction have disrupted the normal functioning of the bowel. Similarly, despite its relative unfamiliarity and the widespread impression that it is an esoteric or nonscientific method, the creative application of hypnotism also deserves consideration as an effective approach when more traditional methods have failed (Goldsmith, 1962; Kohen et al., 1984; Olness, 1975, 1976).

## Major Applications

### Pediatric Approaches

Levine (1982) gradually evolved a modified version of the standard pediatric approach that has been shown to be much more successful than the traditional Davidson approach (as noted in the section on medication). Levine delineated the specific procedures guiding the use of enemas, laxatives, mineral oil, and dietary modification, with particular attention to the suggested timetable for the implementation of each phase. Levine stressed the value of such psychologically based approaches as the use of charts and stars for monitoring and reinforcing progress and supplemental counseling for psychosocial complications.

Perhaps the primary advantage of Levine's approach over other pediatric methods in his strong psychoeducational emphasis. Specifically, much attention is devoted to "demystifying" the various factors involved in the development of encopresis, particularly the physiological dysfunction underlying the chronic symptomatology. By the use of diagrams and pictures, the child (and often the parents as well) is shown exactly which organs are not functioning properly and how this occurs. In addition, much reassurance and relieving of guilt and shame are provided by the physician by an explanation of the frequency and normality of this problem, even among "cool kids." Using an analogy of coaching, the physician provides ongoing support and guidance to the child in what is represented as essentially a (bowel) muscle-building program. The increased amount of time devoted to the child by the physician and the emphasis on a "strong trusting alliance" between them, along with the stressing of a standard positive reinforcement program, make Levine's approach more of a combined pediatric-psychological approach than a purely medical one (Levine & Bakow, 1976). In contrast to many of the behavioral approaches, Levine strongly recommended against requiring the child to wash out the soiled clothing, though he did indicate that the child should wash his or her own body. The treatment thus remains firmly grounded in the traditional medical model, conferring the sick role on the child and providing the sympathy and relief from responsibilities typically afforded to a child suffering from other medical disorders.

### Psychological Approaches

Probably the most popular treatment method in use today, and certainly the one with the most proven track record, is that devised by Logan Wright (1973, 1975; Wright & Walker, 1977). Under a physician's overview, the child's colon is first thoroughly evacuated via enema(s). A behavior contract between parents and child is then arranged, formally establishing expectations regarding acceptable toileting and the criteria for earning rewards. Then, on rising each morning (or occasionally at some other agreed-on time later in the day), the child goes to the bathroom to attempt a bowel movement voluntarily. If the child is able to defecate a predetermined amount of feces (e.g., 0.25–0.50 cup), the parent gives the child a small reward (e.g., money, a toy, or candy). If the child does not have a bowel movement, no reward is given at that point, and the parent instead inserts a glycerine suppository to assist the child in defecating. In the meantime, the child eats breakfast, gets dressed and ready for the day's activities (usually school), and then attempts to defecate again. If the child is successful with the aid of the suppository, a smaller reward is provided. If the child is unsuccessful, an enema is given, and no reward is provided. Caution is obviously required at this point in severely resistant cases, to prevent the physiological hazards associated with the excessive frequency of enemas. Wright suggested 10 consecutive daily enemas as a limit, beyond which their use should be limited to every 2 or 3 days.

A second opportunity for reward is provided at the end of the day, at which point the child's clothing is examined for evidence of soiling. If none has occurred, a reward is delivered. If at this point (or any other time earlier in the day) the child is noted to have soiled his or her pants, then a mild punishment is used (e.g., no TV that evening or sitting in a "time-out" chair for 15 minutes). The combined package of medical and behavioral techniques focuses on inducing the child to defecate regularly, so that a habit is established, muscle tone is returned to the colon, and a high-probability behavior is provided for the parents to reward and thereby strengthen.

In contrast to the relatively minor emphasis on the use of star charts and other rewards in Levine's multicomponent program (1982), Wright considered the use of rewards the most essential component of his approach. Careful interviewing of the parents and the child regarding the selection of the most appealing reinforcers is stressed as being critical to the chances of success. A particularly motivating reward for such children has been found to be special play time with a parent, during which the parent agrees to play whatever the child wants.

This procedure affords the additional therapeutic advantage of promoting pleasant interactions and a deeper relationship between parent and child, as well as a substitute means of controlling or obtaining attention from the parent in those cases where such manipulation is a factor. Although one of the principal advantages of the Wright method is the standardized, step-by-step procedure applied exactly in accordance with fairly rigid guidelines, the selection of meaningful rewards and punishments must be highly individualized (and subject to revision over time) if maximum effectiveness is to be achieved. Consideration must also be given to the practicality of sustaining a frequent delivery of rewards over the average 4 months required to obtain full continence. In most cases, the child is gradually weaned from the most powerful rewards originally provided by the use of secondary reinforcers such as marks on a chart or points, which apply toward earning the desired rewards with slowly decreased frequency.

An additional important component of the Wright method is strict requirements for detailed record-keeping by the parents and frequent communication with the therapist by mailed progress reports and phone calls. Following 2 consecutive weeks of no soiling, the cathartics are gradually phased out to 1 day per week (i.e., they are not used even if the child does not have a bowel movement). Any further soiling results in "backing up" one step by again making cathartics applicable for an additional day per week. Wright and Walker (1977) also suggested adding an enema the morning following such soiling during the phasing out, as further avoidance motivation and also to ensure prevention of the early stages of constipation. About 10%–15% of parents appear to be incapable of following through on the rigorous procedures involved in this approach. In those cases where full parental compliance is obtained, Wright and Walker (1977) reported a 100% success rate. Although Wright (1975) found a range of 10 to 38 weeks' duration necessary for a complete "cure," the dramatic reduction in the frequency of soiling usually obtained in the first few weeks was typically sufficient to motivate the parents to stick with the program through completion.

Several interesting variants of Wright's approach have been reported in the literature (cf. Christophersen & Rapoff, 1983). Ashkenazi (1975) used glycerine suppositories and positive reinforcement to successfully treat 16 out of 18 encopretic cases. Illustrating the importance of subtype considerations, Ashkenazi's sample of Israeli children were apparently not significantly constipated, so that enemas were not needed, whereas a large subgroup were described as having a serious toilet phobia which was successfully deconditioned via rewarding the child for successive approximations to the toilet. Likewise developed independently from Wright's efforts, Young's "gastroileal reflex training" (1973) used a similar combination of requirements for toileting efforts on a regular basis after meals, positive reinforcement for successes, and a "medical" intervention to facilitate defecation, in this case administration of the drug Senekot just before bedtime. Christophersen and Rainey (1976) used enemas and suppositories in combination with positive reinforcement, plus an added emphasis on hygiene training, in a series of successful case studies.

The requirement that the encopretic child wash out his or her soiled clothing has been noted as a frequent component of several different treatment packages reviewed here and elsewhere. Capitalizing on the obvious effectiveness of this procedure, several authors have expanded the approach into an overcorrection procedure. Directly analogous to the use of such procedures in treating enuresis (reviewed earlier in this chapter), children have been required to wash the clothes for extended periods of time, or to wash other clothes or rags in addition to the soiled clothing (Crowley & Armstrong, 1977). Very few treatment programs, however, have used overcorrection exclusively as primary treatment modality (e.g., Leon, 1975). More typically, it is used as one of several primary components in more comprehensive approaches.

One particularly notable example of such an approach was reported by Crowley and Armstrong (1977) in a combined report of three case studies of severely encopretic boys. The other central elements of their procedure were positive reinforcement (praise) for successful toileting, behavioral rehearsal (role-playing the procedures for excusing oneself from ongoing social activities to go to the toilet), positive practice (1-hour periods imposed following each instance of soiling, during which the child was required to alternate between 10 minutes sitting and doing nothing and 10 minutes sitting on the toilet attempting to defecate), and "habit-training" sessions. The latter consisted of talking with a counselor about the sensations and responses involved in the act of defecating, and then practicing these. Specifically, the child was encouraged to practice "squeezing" and "pushing," first with the counselor and then on a regular basis at home. The multimodal approach reportedly led to a complete cure of all three children in 5–9 weeks, verified by follow-up after a few months and again at 18 months. Butler (1977) and also Freeman and Pribble (1974) have reported similar successful results with the use of various combinations of overcorrection and positive practice techniques.

A particularly impressive and rather unique application of these same two procedures, in combination with a stronger emphasis on punishment than most approaches advise, is the full cleanliness training developed by Doleys and his colleagues (Doleys & Arnold, 1975; Doleys, McWhorter, Williams, & Gentry, 1977b). Adapted from the dry bed training program of Azrin *et al.* (1974) for the treatment of enuresis, Doleys's approach calls for frequent parental prompting to attempt toileting in the initial phase, along with a substantial use of positive reinforcement (mainly praise) for sincere efforts at defecation on the toilet and frequent (i.e., hourly in the beginning) "pants checks" to detect any soiling that has occurred. Noting that the major disruption in preferred activities required by this procedure is in itself highly motivating to the children, and stressing the importance of the positive reinforcement for clean pants and successful toileting as well, these authors have suggested that it is primarily the unique aversive consequences involved in the full cleanliness training following "accidents" that are responsible for the high rate of success obtained in this approach. This training consists of parental expressions of disappointment, followed by the child's being required to scrub both the underwear and the pants for 20 minutes each, and then to take a bath in "cool" water for another 20 minutes. The typical length of time required for the elimination of soiling was reportedly between 9 and 16 weeks (Doleys, 1978).

## CONCLUDING REMARKS

The clinical problems of enuresis and encopresis account for relatively frequent referrals, especially if the clinician works in a medical practice or a hospital. Because these disorders, when properly diagnosed and treated, are most amenable to psychological interventions, the clinician must be cautious in assuming that all presenting problems with these symptoms are psychologically based. A careful consideration of physical causes, as outlined in this chapter, must be pursued. This consideration required consultation with pediatricians, especially to rule out physical causation (Roberts, 1986).

Treatment of enuresis and encopresis often requires a reliance on the parents to implement the techniques outlined by the clinician. A careful assessment is needed of their willingness and ability to conduct the program for either disorder. Additionally, the clinician will need a grounding of knowledge in child development and an ability to communicate it to the parents in order to deal with their perceptions of and expectations for their child. Sometimes instruction in child development alone can remove unreal expectations and pressures on parents and children and will allow more appropriate elimination behaviors to develop. One of the authors of this chapter once had a referral of a 9-month-old child who was considered enuretic by the mother's "in-laws" because the child was not toilet-trained at the time he could crawl. Reassurance and information provision on normal child development and toileting, rather than psychotherapy or behavioral interventions, were the treatment of choice. The clinician also needs to be alert to the difficulties of implementing the procedures outlined here for both enuresis and encopresis and to the sometimes long-term requirements of successful treatment. These cautions notwithstanding, psychological involvement in the diagnosis and treatment of elimination disorders can be effective and efficient in enhancing children's development.

## REFERENCES

Ack, M., Norman, M. E., & Schmitt, B. D. (1985). Enuresis: Alarms and drugs. (P. D'Epiro, Ed.). *Patient Care*, 1.

Allgeier, A. R. (1976). Minimizing therapist supervision in the treatment of enuresis. *Journal of Behavior Therapy and Experimental Psychiatry, 7*, 371–372.

American Psychiatric Association. (1980). *Diagnostic and statistical manual of mental disorders* (3rd ed.). Washington, DC: Author.

Amsterdam, B. (1979). Chronic encopresis: A system-based psychodynamic approach. *Child Psychiatry and Human Development, 9*, 137–144.

Andolphi, M. (1978). A structural approach to a family with an encopretic child. *Journal of Marriage and Family Counseling, 4*, 25–29.

Anthony, E. J. (1957). An experimental approach to the psychopathology of childhood: Encopresis. *British Journal of Medical Psychology, 30*, 156–174.

Arena, J. M. (Ed.). (1969). *Compleat pediatricani*. Philadelphia: Lea & Febiger.

Ashkenazi, Z. (1975). The treatment of encopresis using a discriminative stimulus and positive reinforcement. *Journal of Behavior Therapy and Experimental Psychiatry, 6*, 155–157.

Ayllon, T., Simon, S. J., & Wildman, R. W. (1975). Instructions and reinforcement in the elimination of encopresis: A case study. *Journal of Behavior Therapy and Experimental Psychiatry, 6*, 235–238.

Azrin, N. H., & Foxx. R. M. (1974). *Toilet training in less than a day*. New York: Simon & Schuster.

Azrin, N. H., & Thienes, P. M. (1978). Rapid elimination of enuresis by intensive learning without a conditioning apparatus. *Behavior Therapy, 9*, 342–354.

Azrin, N. H., Sneed, T. J., & Foxx, R. M. (1973). Dry bed: A rapid method of eliminating bed-wetting (enuresis) of the retarded. *Behavioral Research and Therapy, 11*, 427–434.

Azrin. N. H., Sneed, T. J., & Foxx, R. M. (1974). Dry-bed training: Rapid elimination of childhood enuresis. *Behaviour Research and Therapy, 12*, 147–156.

Bach, R., & Moylan, J. J. (1975). Parents administer behavior therapy for inappropriate urination and encopresis: A case study. *Journal of Behavior Therapy and Experimental Psychiatry, 6,* 239–241.

Baird, M. (1974). Characteristic interaction patterns in families of encopretic children. *Bulletin of the Menninger Clinic, 38,* 144–153.

Bakwin, H., & Bakwin, R. M. (1972). *Behavior disorders in children.* Philadelphia: W. B. Saunders.

Baller, W. R. (1975). *Bed-wetting: Origin and treatment.* New York: Pergamon Press.

Baller, W. R., A Schalock, H. D. (1956). Conditioned response treatment of enuresis. *Exceptional Children, 22,* 233–236, 247–248.

Barr, R. G., Levine, M., & Wilkinson, R. H. (1979). Occult stool retention: A clinical tool for its evaluation in school-aged children. *Clinical Pediatrics, 18,* 674.

Barrett, B. H. (1969). Behavior modification in the home: Parents adapt laboratory-developed tactics to bowel-train a 5½ year old. *Psychotherapy: Theory, Research, and Practice, 3,* 172–196.

Bemporad, J. R., Pfeifer, C. M., Gibbs, L., Cortner, R. H., & Bloom, W. (1971). Characteristics of encopretic patients and their families. *Journal of the American Academy of Child Psychiatry, 10,* 272–292.

Bemporad, J. R., Kresch, R. A., & Asnes, R. S. (1980). Treatment of encopresis. In G. P. Sholevar, R. M. Benson, & J. Barton (Eds.), *Treatment of emotional disorders in children and adolescents.* Jamaica, NY: Spectrum.

Benjamin, L. S., Serdahely, W., & Geppert, T. V. (1971). Night training through parents' implicit use of operant conditioning. *Child Development, 42,* 963–966.

Berg, I., & Jones, K. V. (1964). Functional fecal incontinence in children. *Archives of Diseases in Childhood, 39,* 465–472.

Bindelglas, P. M., Dee, G. H., & Enos, F. A. (1968). Medical and psychosocial factors in enuretic children treated with imipramine hydrochloride. *American Journal of Psychiatry, 124*(3), 125–130.

Bollard, J. (1982). A 2-year follow-up of bedwetting treated by dry-bed training and standard conditioning. *Behaviour Research and Therapy, 20,* 571–580.

Bollard, J., & Nettelbeck, T. (1981). A comparison of Dry-Bed Training and standard urine-alarm conditioning treatment of childhood bedwetting. *Behaviour Research and Therapy, 19,* 215–226.

Bollard, J., & Nettelbeck, T. (1982). A component analysis of Dry-Bed Training for treatment for bedwetting. *Behaviour Research and Therapy, 20,* 383–390.

Bollard, J., & Woodroffe, P. (1977). The effect of parent administered dry-bed training on nocturnal enuresis in children. *Behaviour Research and Therapy, 15,* 159–165.

Bollard, J., Nettelbeck, T., & Roxbee, H. (1982). Dry-Bed Training for childhood bedwetting: A comparison of group with individually administered parent instruction. *Behaviour Research and Therapy, 20,* 209–217.

Bornstein, P. H., Balleweg, B. J., McLellarn, R. W., Wilson, G. L., & Sturm, C. A. (1983). The "bathroom game": A systematic program for the elimination of encopretic behavior. *Journal of Behavior Therapy and Experimental Psychiatry, 14,* 67–71.

Bostock, J. (1958). Exterior gestation, primitive sleep, enuresis and asthma: A study in aetiology. *Medical Journal of Australia, 149,* 185–192.

Boyd, M. M. (1960). The depth of sleep in enuretic school children and in nonenuretic controls. *Journal of Psychosomatic Research, 44,* 274–281.

Brazelton, T. B. (1962). A child-oriented approach to toilet training. *Pediatrics, 29,* 121–128.

Breckenridge, M. E., & Vincent, E. L. (1966). *Child development: Physical and psychological growth through adolescence.* Philadelphia: W. B. Saunders.

Brock, W. A., & Kaplan, G. W. (1980). Voiding dysfunction in children. *Current Problems in Pediatrics, 10,* 1–63.

Broughton, R. J., & Gastaut, H. (1964). Polygraphic sleep studies of enuresis nocturna. *Electroencephalography and Clinical Neurophysiology, 16,* 625–629.

Butler, J. F. (1976). The toilet training success of parents after reading "Toilet training in less than a day." *Behavior Therapy, 7,* 185–191.

Butler, J. F. (1977). Treatment of encopresis by overcorrection. *Psychological Reports, 40,* 639–646.

Catalina, D. A. (1976). Enuresis: The effects of parent contingent wake-up. *Dissertation Abstracts, 37,* 28025.

Cerulli, M. A., Nikoomanesh, P., & Schuster, M. M. (1979). Progress in biofeedback conditioning for fecal incontinence. *Gasteroenterology, 76,* 742–746.

Chapman, A. H. (1974). *Management of emotional problems in children and adolescents.* Philadelphia: Lippincott.

Christophersen, E. R., & Rainey. S. K. (1976). Management of encopresis through a pediatric outpatient clinic. *Journal of Pediatric Psychology, 4*, 38–41.

Christophersen, E. R., & Rapoff, M. A. (1983). Toileting problems of children. In C. E. Walker & M. C. Roberts (Eds.), *Handbook of clinical child psychology*. New York: Wiley.

Collins, R. W. (1973). Importance of the bladder-cue buzzer contingency in the conditioning treatment for enuresis. *Journal of Abnormal Psychology, 82*, 299–308.

Collison, D. R. (1970). Hypnotherapy in the management of nocturnal enuresis. *Medical Journal of Australia, 1*, 52–54.

Creer, T. L., & Davis, M. H. (1975). Using a staggered wakening procedure with enuretic children in an institutional setting. *Journal of Behavior Therapy and Experimental Psychiatry, 6*, 23–25.

Crowley, C. P., & Armstrong, P. M. (1977). Positive practice, overcorrection, and behavior rehearsal in the treatment of three cases of encopresis. *Journal of Behavior Therapy and Experimental Psychiatry, 8*, 411–416.

Cullen, K. J. (1966). Clinical observations concerning behavior disorders in children. *Medical Journal of Australia, 2*, 533–543.

Davidson, M. (1958). Constipation and fecal incontinence. *Pediatric Clinics of North America, 5*, 749–757.

Davidson, M. (1980). Constipation. In S. Gellis & B. Kagan (Eds.), *Current pediatric therapy*. Philadelphia: Saunders.

Davidson, M., Kugler, M. M., & Bauer, C. H. (1963). Diagnosis and management in children with severe and protracted constipation and obstipation. *Journal of Pediatrics, 62*, 261–275.

DeJonge, G. A. (1973). Epidemiology of enuresis: A survey of the literature. In I. Kolvin, R. C. MacKeith, & S. R. Meadow, (Eds.), *Bladder control and enuresis*. Philadephia: Lippincott.

DeLeon, G., & Mandel, W. (1966). A comparison of conditioning and psychotherapy in the treatment of functional enuresis. *Journal of Clinical Psychology, 22*, 326–330.

DeLeon, G., & Sacks, S. (1972). Conditioning functional enuresis: A four-year follow-up. *Journal of Consulting and Clinical Psychology, 39*, 299–300.

Despert, J. (1944). Urinary control and enuresis. *Psychosomatic Medicine, 6*, 294–307.

Dimson, S. B. (1959). Toilet training and enuresis. *British Medical Journal, 2*, 666–670.

Dittman, K. S., & Blinn, K. A. (1955). Sleep levels in enuresis. *American Journal of Psychiatry, 12*, 913–920.

Doleys, D. M. (1977). Behavioral treatments for nocturnal enuresis in children: A review of the recent literature. *Psychological Bulletin, 84*, 30–54.

Doleys, D. M. (1978). Assessment and treatment of enuresis and encopresis in children. In M. Hersen, R. Esler, & P. Miller (Eds.), *Progress in behavior modification* (Vol. 6). New York: Academic Press.

Doleys, D. M. (1979). Assessment and treatment of childhood encopresis. In A. J. Finch, Jr., & P. C. Kendall (Eds.), *Clinical treatment and research in child psychopathology*. New York: Spectrum.

Doleys, D. M., & Arnold, S. (1975). Treatment of childhood encopresis: Full cleanliness training. *Mental Retardation, 13*, 14–16.

Doleys, D. M., & Wells, K. C. (1975). Changes in functional bladder capacity and bed-wetting during and after retention control training: A case study. *Behavior Therapy, 6*, 685–688.

Doleys, D. M., Ciminero, A. R., Tollison, J. W., Williams, C. L., & Wells, K. C. (1977a). Dry-bed training and retention control training: A comparison. *Behavior Therapy, 8*, 541–548.

Doleys, D. M., McWhorter, A. Q., Williams, S. C., & Gentry, R. (1977b). Encopresis: Its treatment and relation to nocturnal enuresis. *Behavior Therapy, 8*, 105–110.

Dreman, S. B. (1977). Secrecy, silk gloves and sanctions: A family therapy approach to treating an encopretic child. *Family Therapy, 4*, 171–177.

Easson, W. M. (1960). Encopresis—Psychogenic soiling. *Canadian Medical Association Journal, 82*, 424–630.

Edelman, R. F. (1971). Operant conditioning treatment of encopresis. *Journal of Behavior Therapy and Experimental Psychiatry, 2*, 71–73.

Engel, B. I., Nikoomanesh, D., & Schuster. M. M. (1974). Operant conditioning of rectospheric responses in the treatment of fecal incontinence. *New England Journal of Medicine, 290*, 646–649.

Fenichel, O. (1946). *The psychoanalytic theory of neurosis*. London: Routledge & Kegan Paul.

Ferinden, W., & Van Handel, D. (1970). Elimination of soiling behavior in an elementary school child through the application of aversive techniques. *Journal of School Psychology, 8*, 267–279.

Fielding, D. (1980). The response of day- and night-wetting children and children who wet only at night to retention control training and the enuresis alarm. *Behaviour Research and Therapy, 18,* 305–317.

Finley, W. W. (1971). An EEG study of sleep of enuretics at three age levels. *Clinical Electroencephalography, 1,* 35–39.

Finley, W. W., & Besserman, R. L. (1973). Differential effects of three reinforcement schedules on the effectiveness of the conditioning treatment for enuresis nocturna. *Proceedings of the American Psychological Association, 8,* 923–924.

Finley, W. W., & Wansley, R. A. (1977). Auditory intensity as a variable in the conditioning treatment of enuresis nocturna. *Behaviour Research and Therapy, 15,* 181–185.

Finley, W. W., Besserman, R. L., Bennett, L. F., Clapp, R. K., & Finley, P. M. (1973). The effect of continuous, intermittent and "placebo" reinforcement on the effectiveness of the conditioning treatment for enuresis nocturna. *Behaviour Research and Therapy, 11,* 289–297.

Finley, W. W., Rainwater, A. J., & Johnson. G. (1982). Effect of varying alarm schedules on acquisition and relapse parameter in the conditioning treatment of enuresis. *Behaviour Research and Therapy, 20,* 69–80.

Fisher, S. M. (1979). Encopresis. In J. D. Noshpitz (Ed.), *Basic handbook of child psychiatry* (Vol. 2). New York: Basic Books.

Fitzgerald, J. F. (1975). Encopresis, soiling, constipation: What's to be done? *Pediatrics, 56,* 348–349.

Fleisher, D. R. (1976). Diagnosis and treatment of disorders of defecation in children. *Pediatric Annals, 5,* 71–101.

Forsythe, W. I., & Redmond, A. (1974). Enuresis and spontaneous cure rate. *Archives of Diseases of Childhood, 49,* 259.

Freedheim, D. K., & Russ. S. W. (1983). Psychotherapy with children. In C. E. Walker & M. C. Roberts (Eds.), *Handbook of clinical child psychology.* New York: Wiley.

Freeman, B. J., & Pribble, W. (1974). Elimination of inappropriate toileting by overcorrection. *Psychological Reports, 35,* 802.

Freud, S. (1916). *Three contributions to the theory of sex.* New York: Nervous and Mental Disease Publishing.

Gabel, S. (1981). Fecal soiling, chronic constipation, and encopresis. In S. Gabel (Ed.), *Behavioral problems in childhood: A primary care approach.* New York: Grune & Stratton.

Galdston, R., & Perlmutter, A. D. (1973). The urinary manifestations of anxiety in children. *Pediatrics, 52,* 818–822.

Gavanski, M. (1971). Treatment of non-retentive secondary encopresis with imipramine and psychotherapy. *Canadian Medical Association Journal, 104,* 46–48.

Geppert, T. V. (1953). Management of nocturnal enuresis by conditioned response. *Journal of the American Medical Association, 152,* 381–383.

Glicklich, L. B. (1951). An historical account of enuresis. *Pediatrics, 8,* 859–876.

Goldsmith, H. (1962). Chronic loss of bowel control in a nine year old child. *American Journal of Clinical Hypnosis, 4,* 191–192.

Griffiths, P., Medrum, C., & McWilliam, R. (1982). Dry-bed training in the treatment of nocturnal enuresis in childhood: A research report. *Journal of Child Psychology and Psychiatry, 23,* 485–495.

Gunnarsen, S., & Melin, K. A. (1951). The electroencephalogram in enuresis. *Acta Paediatrica, 40,* 496–501.

Hallgren, B. (1957). Enuresis: A clinical and genetic study. *Acta Psychiatrica et Neurologica Scandinavica, 114*(Supplement), 1–159.

Hallman, N. (1950). On the ability of enuretic children to hold urine. *Acta Paediatrica, 39,* 87.

Halpern, W. I. (1977). The treatment of encopretic children. *Journal of the American Academy of Child Psychiatry, 16,* 478–499.

Halverstadt, D. (1976). Enuresis. *Journal of Pediatric Psychology, 1,* 13–14.

Harnach, G. A. von (1953). Wesen and soziale Bedingtheit fruhkundlicher Verhaltensstorungen. *Bibliotheca Paediatrica,* fasc. 55, Basel.

Harris, L. S., & Purohit, A. P. (1977). Bladder training and enuresis: A controlled trial. *Behaviour Research and Therapy, 15,* 485–490.

Heins, H. A., & Beerends, J. J. (1978). Who should accept primary responsibility for the encopretic child? *Clinical Pediatrics, 17,* 67–70.

Hilbun, W. B. (1968). Encopresis in childhood. *Journal of the Kentucky Medical Association, 66,* 978.

Houle, T. A. (1974). The use of positive reinforcement and aversive conditioning in the treatment of encopresis. *Devereaux Forum, 9,* 7–14.

Hushka, M. (1942). The child's response to coercive toilet training. *Psychosomatic Medicine. 4*, 301–308.

Inhof, B. (1956). Bettnasser in der erziehingsberatung. *Heilpaedagogische Werkblaetter, 25*, 122–127.

Jacob, R. G., & Moore, D. J. (1984). Paradoxical interventions in behavioral medicine. *Journal of Behavior Therapy and Experimental Psychiatry, 15*, 205–213.

Jehu, D., Morgan, R. T., Turner, R. K., & Jones, A. (1977). A controlled trial of the treatment of nocturnal enuresis in residential homes for children. *Behaviour Research and Therapy, 15*, 1–16.

Johnson, J. H., & Van Bourgondien, M. E. (1977). Behavior therapy and encopresis: A selective review of the literature. *Journal of Clinical Child Psychology, 6*, 15–19.

Kellerman, J. (1976). Some comments on Ayllon, Simon, and Wildman's Instructions and Reinforcement in the Elimination of Encopresis. *Journal of Behavior Therapy and Experimental Psychiatry, 7*, 307–308.

Kimmel, H. D., & Kimmel, E. (1970). An instrumental conditioning method for the treatment of enuresis. *Journal of Behavior Therapy and Experimental Psychiatry, 1*, 121–123.

Klackenberg. G. (1955). Primary enuresis: When is child dry at night? *Acta Paediatrica, 44*, 513.

Kohen, D. P., Olness, K. N., Cornwell, S. D., & Heimel, A. (1984). The use of relaxation-mental imagery (self-hypnosis) in the management of 505 pediatric behavioral encounters. *Journal of Developmental and Behavioral Pediatrics, 5*, 21–25.

Kohlenberg, R. J. (1973). Operant conditioning of human anal sphincter pressure. *Journal of Applied Behavior Analysis, 6*, 201–208.

Landman, G. B., & Rappaport, L. (1985). Pediatric management of severe treatment-resistant encopresis. *Journal of Developmental and Behavioral Pediatrics, 6*, 349–351.

Landman, G. B., Levine, M. D., & Rappaport, L. (1983). A study of treatment resistance among children referred for encopresis. *Clinical Pediatrics, 23(8)*, 449–452.

Lapouse, R., & Monk, M. A. (1959). Fears and worries in a representative sample of children. *American Journal of Orthopsychiatry, 29*, 803–818.

Leon, J. (1975). The use of overcorrection to eliminate functional encopresis: A case study. *Research and the Retarded, 2*, 1–5.

Levine, M. D. (1975). Children with encopresis: A descriptive analysis. *Pediatrics, 56*, 412–416.

Levine, M. D. (1982). Encopresis: Its potentiation, evaluation, and alleviation. *Pediatric Clinics of North America, 29(2)*, 315–329.

Levine, M. D., & Bakow, H. (1976). Children with encopresis: A study of treatment outcome. *Pediatrics, 58*, 845–852.

Lifshitz, M., & Chovers, A. (1972). Encopresis among Israeli Kibbutz children. *Israel Annals of Psychiatry and Related Disciplines, 4*, 326–340.

Loening-Bauke, V. A. (1984). Abnormal rectoanal function in children recovered from chronic constipation and encopresis. *Gastroenterology, 87*, 1299–1304.

Lovibond, S. H. (1964). *Conditioning and enuresis.* New York: Pergamon Press.

Lowery, S. P., Srour, J. W., Whitehead, W. E., & Schuster, M. M. (1985). Habit training as treatment of encopresis secondary to chronic constipation. *Journal of Pediatric Gastroenterology and Nutrition, 4*, 397–401.

McConaghy, N. (1969). A controlled trial of imipramine, amphetamine, pad-and-bell conditioning and nocturnal awakening in the treatment of nocturnal enuresis. *Medical Journal of Australia, 2*, 237–239.

MacFarlane, J. W., Allen, L., & Honzik. M. P. (1954). *A developmental study of the behavior problems of normal children between 21 months and 14 years.* Berkley: University of California Press.

McGregor, H. G. (1937). Enuresis in children: A report of 70 cases. *British Medical Journal, 1*, 1061–1063.

McKendry, J. B. J., Stewart, D. A., Jeffs, R. D., & Mozes, A. (1972). Enuresis treated by an improved waking apparatus. *Canadian Medical Association Journal. 106*, 27–29.

McTaggart, A., & Scott, M. A. (1979). A review of twelve cases of encopresis. *Journal of Pediatrics, 54*, 762–768.

Martin, C. R. A. (1966). *A new approach to nocturnal enuresis.* London: H. K. Lewis.

Matson, J. L., & Ollendick, T. H. (1977). Issues in toilet training normal children. *Behavior Therapy, 8*, 549–553.

Michaels, J. J., & Goodman, S. E. (1954). Disorders of character: Persistent enuresis, juvenile delinquency and psychopathic personality. *Archives of Neurology and Psychiatry, 72*, 641–643.

Mikkelsen, E. J., Rapoport, J. L., Nee, L., Gruenau, E., Mendelson, W., & Gillin, J. L. (1980).

Childhood enuresis: Sleep patterns and psychopathology. *Archives of General Psychiatry, 37,* 1139–1145.

Miller, P. M. (1973). An experimental analysis of retention control training in the treatment of nocturnal enuresis in two institutionalized adolescents. *Behavior Therapy, 4,* 288–294.

Morgan, R. T. T. (1978). Relapse and therapeutic response in the conditioning treatment of enuresis: A review of recent findings on intermittent reinforcement, overlearning, and stimulus intensity. *Behaviour Research and Therapy, 16,* 273–279.

Mowrer, O. H., & Mowrer, W. M. (1938). Enuresis: A method for its study and treatment. *American Journal of Orthopsychiatry, 8,* 436–459.

Muellner, S. R. (1960). Development of urinary control in children: A new concept in cause, prevention and treatment of primary enuresis. *Journal of Urology, 84,* 714–716.

Muellner, S. R. (1963). Primary enuresis in children. *Biochemical Clinic, 2,* 161.

Neale, D. H. (1963). Behavior therapy and encopresis in children. *Behaviour Research and Therapy, 2,* 239.

Nettelbeck, T., & Langeluddecke, P. (1979). Dry-Bed Training without an enuresis machine. *Behaviour Research and Therapy, 17,* 403–404.

Nisley, D. D. (1976). Medical overview of the management of encopresis. *Journal of Pediatric Psychology, 4,* 33–34.

Olatawura, M. O. (1973). Encopresis. *Acta Pediatrica Scandinavia, 62,* 358–364.

Olness, K. (1975). The use of self-hypnosis in the treatment of childhood nocturnal enuresis: A report on 40 patients. *Clinical Pediatrics, 14,* 273–279.

Olness, K. (1976). Autohypnosis in functional megacolon in children. *American Journal of Clinical Hypnosis, 19,* 28–32.

Olness, K., McFarland, F. A., & Piper, J. (1980). Biofeedback: A new modality in the management of children with fecal soiling. *Journal of Pediatrics, 96,* 505–509.

Oppel, W. C., Harper, P. A., & Rider, R. V. (1968). The age of attaining bladder control. *Pediatrics, 42,* 614–626.

Paschalis, A. P., Kimmel, H. D., & Kimmel, E. (1972). Further study of diurnal instrumental conditioning in the treatment of enuresis nocturna. *Journal of Behavior Therapy and Experimental Psychiatry, 3,* 253–256.

Pedrini, B. C., & Pedrini, D. T. (1971). Reinforcement procedures in the control of encopresis: A case study. *Psychological Reports, 28,* 937–938.

Pflaunder, M. (1904). Demonstration of an apparatus for automatic warning of the occurrence of bedwetting. *Verhandlungen der Gesellschaft fur Kinderheilpundl, 21,* 219–220.

Pierce, C. M. (1972). Enuresis. In A. M. Freedman & H. I. Kaplan (Eds.), *The Child* (Vol. 1). New York: Atheneum.

Pierce, C. M., Lipcan, H. H., McLary, J. H., & Noble, H. F. (1956). Enuresis: Psychiatric interview studies. *United States Armed Forces Medical Journal, 7(9),* 1–12.

Pinkerton, P. (1958). Psychogenic megacolon in children: The implications of bowel negativism. *Archives of Diseases in Childhood, 33,* 371–380.

Plachetta, K. E. (1976). Encopresis: A case study utilizing contracting, scheduling, and self-charting. *Journal of Behavior Therapy and Experimental Psychiatry, 7,* 195–196.

Popler, K. (1976). Token reinforcement in the treatment of nocturnal enuresis: A case study and six month follow-up. *Journal of Behavior Therapy and Experimental Psychiatry, 7,* 83–84.

Pototsky, C. (1925). Die enkopresis. In O. Schwartz (Ed.), *Psyhogenic and psychtherapie korperlicher symptome.* Berlin: Springer-Verlag.

Powell, N. B. (1951). Urinary incontinence in children. *Archives of Pediatrics, 68,* 151–157.

Robertiello, R. C. (1956). Some psychic interrelations between the urinary and sexual systems with special reference to enuresis. *Psychiatric Quarterly, 30,* 61–62.

Roberts, M. C. (1986). *Pediatric psychology: Psychological interventions and strategies for pediatric problems.* New York: Pergamon Press.

Rocklin, N., & Tilker, H. (1973). Instrumental conditioning of nocturnal enuresis: A reappraisal of some previous findings. *Proceedings of the American Psychological Association, 8,* 915–916.

Rolider, A., & Van Houten, R. (1985). Treatment of constipation-caused encopresis by a negative reinforcement procedure. *Journal of Behavior Therapy and Experimental Psychiatry, 16,* 67–70.

Ross Laboratories. (1975). *Developing toilet habits.* Columbus, OH: Author.

Rutter, M., Yule, W., & Graham, P. (1973). Enuresis and behavioral deviance. In I. Kolvin, R. C. MacKeith, & S. R. Meadow (Eds.), *Bladder control and enuresis.* London: Heinemann.

Rydzinski, J. W., & Kaplan, S. L. (1985). A wolf in sheep's clothing? Simultaneous use of structural family therapy and behavior modification in a case of encopresis and encopresis. *Journal of Clinical Psychiatry, 7,* 71–81.

Sandler, J., Kennedy, H., & Tyson, R. L. (1980). *The technique of child psychoanalysis: Discussions with Anna Freud.* Cambridge: Harvard University Press.

Schaefer, C. E. (1979). *Childhood encopresis and enuresis: Causes and therapy.* New York: Van Nostrand Reinhold.

Schaefer, C. E., & O'Conner, K. J. (Eds.). (1983). *Handbook of play therapy.* New York: Wiley.

Schmitt, B. D. (1982a). Daytime wetting (diurnal enuresis). *Pediatric Clinics of North America, 29,* 9–20.

Schmitt, B. D. (1982b). Nocturnal enuresis: An update on treatment. *Pediatric Clinics of North America, 29,* 21–30.

Segall, A. (1957). Report of a constipated child with fecal withholding. *American Journal of Orthopsychiatry, 27,* 819–825.

Shaffer, D. (1973). The association between enuresis and emotional disorder: A review of the literature. In I. Kolvin, R. C. MacKeith, & S. R. Meadow (Eds.), *Bladder control and enuresis.* Philadelphia: J. B. Lippincott.

Shane, M. (1967). Encopresis in a latency-age boy. *The Psychoanalytic Study of the Child, 22,* 296–314.

Sheinbein, M. (1975). A triadic behavioral approach to encopresis. *Journal of Family Counseling, 3,* 58–61.

Spock, B., & Rothenberg, M. B. (1985). *Dr. Spock's baby and child care.* New York: Pocket Books.

Starfield, B. (1967). Functional bladder capacity in enuretic and nonenuretic children. *Journal of Pediatrics, 70,* 777–781.

Starfield, B., & Mellits, E. D. (1968). Increase in functional bladder capacity and improvements in enuresis. *Journal of Pediatrics, 72,* 483–487.

Stedman, J. M. (1972). An extension of the Kimmel treatment method for enuresis to an adolescent: A case report. *Journal of Behavior Therapy and Experimental Psychiatry, 3,* 307–309.

Stewart, C. B. (1946). Enuresis. *Canadian Medical Association Journal, 55,* 370–372.

Strom-Olson, R. (1950). Enuresis in adults and abnormality of sleep. *Lancet, 2,* 133–135.

Tapia, F., Jekel, J., & Domke, H. (1960). Enuresis: An emotional symptom. *Journal of Nervous and Mental Disorders, 130,* 61.

Taylor, P. D., & Turner, R. K. (1975). A clinical trial of continuous, intermittent and overlearning "Bell and Pad" treatment for nocturnal enuresis. *Behaviour Research and Therapy, 13,* 281–293.

Tomlinson, J. R. (1970). The treatment of bowel retention by operant procedures: A case study. *Journal of Behavior Therapy and Experimental Psychiatry, 1,* 83–85.

Tough, J. H., Hawkins, R. P., McArthur, M. M., & Van Ravensway, S. V. (1971). Modification of enuretic behavior by punishment: A new use for an old device. *Behavior Therapy, 2,* 567–574.

Turner, R. K., Young, G. C., & Rachman, S. (1970). Treatment of nocturnal enuresis by conditioning techniques. *Behavior Research and Therapy, 8,* 367–381.

Wagner, W., Johnson, S. B., Walker, D., Carter. R., & Wittner, J. (1982). A controlled comparison of two treatments for nocturnal enuresis. *Journal of Pediatrics, 101,* 302–307.

Wald, A. (1981). Usc of biofeedback in treatment of fecal incontinence in patients with meningomyelocele. *Pediatrics, 68,* 45–49.

Walker, C. E. (1978). Toilet training, enuresis, encopresis. In P. E. Magrab (Ed.), *Psychological management of pediatric problems* (Vol. 1). Baltimore: University Park Press.

Walker, C. W., Milling, L., & Bonner, B. (1988). Enuresis, encopresis, and related disorders. In D. K. Routh (Ed.), *Handbook of pediatric psychology.* New York: Guilford Press.

Warson, S. R., Caldwell, M. R., Warineer, A., Kirk, A. J., & Jensen, R. A. (1954). The dynamics of encopresis. *American Journal of Orthopsychiatry, 24,* 402–415.

Weissenberg, S. (1926). Uber enkopresis. *Zietschrift für Kinderheilkunde, 40,* 674–677.

Werry, J. S., & Cohrssen, J. (1965). Enuresis: An etiologic and therapeutic study. *Journal of Pediatrics, 67,* 423–431.

White, M. (1971). A thousand consecutive cases of enuresis: Results of treatment. *Child and Family, 10,* 198–209.

Whitehead, W. E., Parker, L. H., Masek, B. J., Cataldo, M. F., & Freeman, J. M. (1981). Biofeedback treatment of fecal incontinence in patients with myelomeningocele. *Developmental Medicine and Child Neurology, 23,* 313–322.

Wright, L. (1973). Handling the encopretic child. *Professional Psychology, 4,* 137–145.

Wright, L. (1975). Outcome of a standardized program for treating psychogenic encopresis. *Professional Psychology, 6,* 453–456.

Wright, L., & Walker, C. E. (1977). Treatment of the child with psychogenic encopresis: An effective program of therapy. *Clinical Pediatrics, 16,* 1042–1045.

Wright, L., Schaefer, A. B., & Solomons, G. (1979). *Encyclopedia of pediatric psychology.* Baltimore: University Park Press.

Young, G. C. (1964). A staggered-wakening procedure in the treatment of enuresis. *Medical Officer, 111,* 142–143.

Young, G. C. (1969). The problem of enuresis. *British Journal of Hospital Medicine, 2,* 628–632.

Young, G. C. (1973). The treatment of childhood encopresis by conditioned gasto-ileal reflex training. *Behavior Research and Therapy, 11,* 499–503.

Young, G. C., & Morgan, R. T. T. (1972). Overlearning in the conditioning treatment of enuresis: A long term follow-up study. *Behaviour Research and Therapy, 10,* 409–410.

Young, I. L., & Goldsmith, A. O. (1972). Treatment of encopresis in a day treatment program. *Psychotherapy: Theory, Research, and Practice, 9,* 231–235.

# 18 *Pediatrics*
## *Psychological Therapies*

FRANK ANDRASIK, ELISE KABELA,
AND DUDLEY DAVID BLAKE

## INTRODUCTION

*Pediatric psychology* has been defined as that field of research and practice concerned with "a wide variety of topics in the relationship between the psychological and physical well-being of children, including behavioral and emotional concomitants of disease and illness, the role of psychology in pediatric medicine, and the promotion of health and prevention of illness among healthy children" (Roberts, Maddux, & Wright, 1984, pp. 56–57). The need for such a merging of pediatrics and psychology was aptly demonstrated years ago in a survey of patient patterns in pediatric practice. Here, it was found that only 12% of patients presenting to pediatricians had problems exclusively of a physical nature. The remaining problems were either largely psychological (36%) or such that physical and psychological factors were both of importance (52%) (Duff, Rowe, & Anderson, 1973).

Surveys of profiles of patients presenting to pediatric psychology practices (e.g., Kanoy & Schroeder, 1985; Ottinger & Roberts, 1980; Walker, 1979) reveal a diverse array of presenting problems. Wright, Schaefer, and Solomons (1979) cataloged over 100 problems dealt with in pediatric practice in their *Encyclopedia of Pediatric Psychology*. Many more problems have surfaced and have been found to be amenable to pediatric psychology approaches since publication of this encyclopedia nearly a decade ago. The various problem entities run the gamut and are too great in number to be addressed individually here. Several problems germane to pediatric psychology are covered elsewhere in this book (problems of conduct, anxiety, developmental delay and disability, learning, eating, and eliminating), so that it is unnecessary to give them additional coverage here. Still, we can only scratch the surface of the remaining areas and must restrict our focus to selected topics. In the pages to follow, we sample some of the exciting work being done with children and adolescents in the management of certain chronic medical conditions, preparation for stressful medical procedures, the

FRANK ANDRASIK • Department of Psychology, University of West Florida, Pensacola, Florida 32514-5751.     ELISE KABELA • Center for Stress and Anxiety Disorders, State University of New York at Albany, Albany, New York 12203.     DUDLEY DAVID BLAKE • Psychology Service, Veterans Administration Medical Center, Boston, Massachusetts 02130.

promotion of positive health behaviors and prevention of medical problems, and the management of child abuse and neglect. Treatment strategies in these areas are most useful when designed to be flexible, practical, and time-efficient (Roberts, 1986b). The reviews that follow have been prepared with an eye toward these criteria.

## MANAGEMENT OF CHRONIC MEDICAL CONDITIONS

### Pain

Pediatric pain has been categorized into four types: (1) pain occurring in the absence of a well-defined or specific disease state or injury (e.g., vascular and tension headaches and recurrent abdominal pain); (2) pain accompanying a disease state (e.g., hemophilia, arthritis, and sickle-cell anemia); (3) pain accompanying physical trauma (e.g., burns and fractures); and (4) pain associated with medical or dental procedures (e.g., bone marrow aspirations, lumbar punctures, surgery, and injections) (Varni, 1983).

Pain, in children and adults, is a complex condition, with multiple interacting components that serve to complicate assessment and treatment. Work with pediatric pain patients is, ideally, interdisciplinary, exploring psychological (cognitive, behavioral, and self-report), medical-biological, and socioenvironmental factors (Varni, 1983). The clinician working with children faces further difficulties because of children's varied knowledge and understanding of pain and their expressive language abilities. Research on health and illness conceptualizations, for example, reveals that children below the age of 11 are not likely to comprehend either physiological or psychophysiological explanations of illness or pain (Bibace & Walsh, 1981; Perrin & Gerrity, 1981; Whitt, Dykstra, & Taylor, 1979). Thus, the utility of cognitive-behavioral treatment procedures, widely and effectively used with adult chronic-pain patients (McCarran & Andrasik, 1987; Turk, Meichenbaum, & Genest, 1983), is likely to be of diminished value with younger children. Further, children between the ages of 7 and 10 view most illness as being caused externally, and most have only a rudimentary understanding of internal organs, functions, and state. The Pediatric Pain Questionnaire (Varni & Thompson, 1985) is an instrument developed specifically for children and constructed to allow measurement of these multiple dimensions of pain, in a format appropriate to children of various ages. Separate forms for children and their parents allow the therapist to look for commonalities and divergences in report that provide a comprehensive picture that will be useful in treatment planning. McGrath, Cunningham, Goodman, and Unruh (1986a) reviewed various options for collecting measures of pain from pediatric patients of varied ages.

In working with pediatric pain patients, it is helpful to keep in mind the nine guidelines that McGrath, Dunn-Geier, Cunningham, Brunnette, D'Astous, Humphreys, Latter, and Keene (1986) developed from their extensive work, and that apply to medical as well as psychological practitioners (see Table 1). The overall intent of the guidelines is to encourage practitioners to construe a recurrent pain problem as arising from ineffective coping strategies. Such a focus lays the groundwork for a broader based assessment (which includes familial and

TABLE 1.  Guidelines for Helping Children Cope
with Chronic, Benign Intractable Pain[a]

1. Include psychosocial assessment early in the clinical course.
2. Avoid the organic–psychogenic dichotomy.
3. Establish the context and meaning of the pain.
4. Emphasize coping rather than curing.
5. Focus on family strengths.
6. Investigate the school situation.
7. Teach coping skills.
8. Do not blame the patient or the family.
9. Understand without pitying.

[a]From McGrath et al. (1986).

school factors, along with a contextual view of pain), makes the search for the definitive organic or psychological cause less important, and promotes active patient involvement.

Space limitations do not permit us to review all four of the types of pain problems mentioned above. Our review here is confined to the disorder having received the most research attention to date (headache). Recent reviews of treatment efforts with the remaining pain conditions can be found in McGrath and Feldman (1986), Varni (1983), and Varni, Jay, Masek, and Thompson (1986).

*Headache*

By the age of 7, headache is already a familiar symptom to a substantial number of children. Of the 40% or so of children experiencing headache by age 7, approximately 5% are troubled on a recurring basis. By the age of 15, the percentage of adolescents experiencing frequent, recurrent headache climbs to approximately 20% (Bille, 1962; Deubner, 1977; Sillanpaa, 1983b). Headache is distributed equally across gender through about age 10, at which point females begin to predominate. Contrary to past beliefs, recently completed longitudinal studies indicate that continuation rather than remission best characterizes the long-term prognosis of headaches that start early in life (Bille, 1981; Sillanpaa, 1983a). Headache can be quite disabling to children, creating a great deal of physical discomfort and distress, leading them to seek repeated medical care, and ultimately causing them to miss activities important to their development (e.g., school and social events). For example, Egermark-Eriksson (1982) found that approximately 70% of the schoolchildren in his sample who missed 4 or more days of school suffered from recurrent headache.

The majority of headaches appear to fall into the categories of migraine (due to paroxysmal aberrations of cerebral blood flow and subsequent biochemical changes), tension (believed to be due to increased contractures of shoulder, neck, and skeletal muscles), or a combination of both, in the absence of underlying structural defects or diagnosable physical conditions. Rothner (1978) provided a helpful description of the clinical features and a listing of the criteria for distinguishing various forms of headache in children. Basically, migraine is experienced as an episodic, sudden-onset, intensely throbbing pain. In adults, the focus is usually one-sided; in young children, the focus is more often bilateral and frontal. In adults, the duration of a migraine attack is extended, often continuing into the next day. In children, episodes may be of briefer duration but may occur with greater frequency. Abdominal pain, nausea, and vomiting are common accompaniments. A small percentage of children experience neurological prodromes (primarily of the visual type), and these are termed *classic migraine*. Migraines in the absence of aura are labeled *common*. In contrast, tension headache is experienced as a dull, bilateral pain or ache, which is insidious in onset and resolution; gastrointestinal symptoms are rare but may occur after a prolonged episode. Children with combined headache experience features of both types.

Headaches can be triggered and/or exacerbated by a variety of biopsychosocial events, and it is held by some that socioenvironmental factors can serve to maintain or intensify headache (Andrasik, Blake, & McCarran, 1986). Stress is recognized as a common precipitant of headache; experiencing recurrent, unremitting headache for a protracted period can produce a stressful state for the headache sufferer as well and can lead to a further intensification of pain (Bakal, 1982). Psychological approaches attempt to deal with both aspects of the stress response.

Medical treatments are well studied in adult patients and serve palliative, abortive, and/or prophylactic functions (Diamond & Dalessio, 1986). The efficacy of these adult-derived medication regimens seems to have been assumed with child forms of migraine and tension headache; experimental evaluation of their clinical utility with children is not extensive. Most practitioners remain cautious in the use of many of these medications because of uncertainty about the negative side effects arising from administering medication during a child's critical growth periods. Children's reduced incidence of headache "warning signs" limits the utility of abortive preparations as well (Andrasik *et al.*, 1986). Also, recent research suggests that overuse of certain prescribed palliative and abortive medications can, over time, serve paradoxically to increase headache pain because of habituation and tolerance phenomenona (Kudrow, 1982; Saper, 1987). Regular reliance on these medications at a young age would seem to place children at increased risk for subsequent medication "rebound" headaches. It is not surprising that psychological, or nondrug, treatment approaches have begun to be explored with pediatric headache patients.

Psychological treatment approaches (for all pain disorders) fall into one of two types (Varni, Jay, Masek, & Thompson, 1986). The first is regulation of pain perception, which is accomplished via a host of self-regulatory procedures (guided imagery, progressive muscle relaxation, meditation, hypnosis, and cognitive restructuring). The second is regulation of pain behavior via an identification and modification of the socioenvironmental reinforcement contingencies. Most studies conducted to date have focused on the regulation of pain perception through the use of relaxation, autogenic, and biofeedback (electromyographic and thermal) approaches (see Andrasik *et al.*, 1986, for a more complete review). Typical treatment effects fall within the neighborhood of 50%–90% symptom improvement over the short run. Thus far, no one pain-regulation procedure has been shown to be superior to another. The high level of improvement found in children exceeds that typically seen when similar procedures are applied to adults (see Holroyd, 1986, for a quantitative review of treatment effects). These encouraging results suggest that children may be especially good candidates for self-regulatory procedures and that treatment during childhood may prevent subsequent adult symptomatology. Children's increased enthusiasm, quicker rate of learning, enhanced confidence in "special abilities," fewer prior treatment failures, reduced chronicity, and reduced skepticism about self-control procedures are among the factors speculated to account for the increased responsiveness found in them (Attanasio, Andrasik, Burke, Blake, Kabela, & McCarran, 1985). Long-term follow-up evaluations are very limited, but those available suggest that the treatment gains endure.

Cognitive restructuring therapy has received only minimal attention to date, but existing evidence indicates its use leads to similar levels of improvement (Richter, McGrath, Humphreys, Goodman, Firestone, & Keene, 1986). One small-scale investigation found cognitive therapy to be more effective than biofeedback at brief follow-up (Kabela & Andrasik, 1987). Analyses conducted thus far have yielded no consistent predictors of response to treatment. With such favorable results, this may not be surprising. Most comparative treatment outcome investigations, however, have not taken into account significant differences among children regarding familial, situational, and emotional factors associated with headache and this may account, in part, for a lack of significant effects (McGrath, 1987).

Nearly all of the investigations of the self-regulatory treatment of headache have involved the administration of treatment in the traditional one-to-one, in-office delivery format. For these treatments to have their greatest impact, alternative delivery models will need exploration. Sallade (1980) found that a multicomponent treatment package (dietary management, relaxation, and client-centered therapy), delivered in a group format, was effective for the 8 children receiving it. Larsson and Melin (1986) similarly found group-administered relaxation to be efficacious and superior to both an information-only placebo and a self-monitoring procedure, all administered at school. Burke and Andrasik (1987) recently pilot-tested two ways to administer biofeedback treatment with reduced therapist contact. In one condition, the parents served as therapists; in the other, the children attempted to administer most of the treatment on their own. Both treatments were conducted under the supervision of a therapist, but with markedly reduced contact (3 hours of therapist time versus 10). The follow-up data collected through one year revealed a similar effectiveness for both home-based treatment procedures; this effectiveness rivaled that obtained by children treated in a standard, office-based procedure that was conducted for purposes of comparison. The results from these investigations of ways to deliver psychological treatments in a more economical, time-efficient manner are encouraging and warrant further research attention.

Learned pain behaviors are often seen in children with recurrent pain syndromes (McGrath, 1987). Three case study reports describe the successful use of the contrasting treatment approach: focusing directly on modifying pain behavior. Contingency management incorporating punishment procedures effectively alleviated the symptoms of a 6-year-old migraineur (Ramsden, Friedman, & Williamson, 1983), selective attention and modification of consequent events improved the school attendance of an 11-year-old migraineur (Lake, 1981), and a response-cost contingency successfully reduced headaches in a 14-year-old adolescent (Yen & McIntire, 1971). Although the punishment component of Ramsden *et al.* (1983) appeared to contribute to the observed treatment effect, the potential for abuse and unpleasant emotional side effects are likely to limit widespread use of this procedure (Andrasik *et al.*, 1986).

Most of the research reviewed here has been conducted with migraine patients, and the results to date are highly encouraging. Few reports have addressed tension headache, probably the more common form of headache in children and adolescents. Why this is so is unclear. We expect increased attention to this headache type in the future. If these initial promising findings continue to hold up to subsequent replication and are shown to endure during long-term follow-up, then psychological treatment approaches may soon be judged to be legitimate treatment alternatives to medical care for pediatric headache patients.

## Asthma

Asthma is an intermittent, variable, and reversible obstruction of the airway (Scadding, 1966). Attacks, which can be terrifying for children and parents alike, are characterized by edema of the bronchial mucosa, airway obstruction by mucous secretion, and changes in bronchial musculature. Most researchers acknowledge that psychological factors are "inextricably interwoven" with physical factors in asthma, and therefore, frequent collaboration between medicine and psychology is necessary during treatment (Creer, 1982). It is estimated that between 5% and 15% of all children under the age of 12 experience asthma (American Lung Association, 1975). Before age 5, male asthmatics outnumber female asthmatics by 1.5 to 2.0. The incidence rates become more equivalent for ages 5–9, at which age females begin increasingly to outnumber males. The probability of a child's continuing with symptoms beyond puberty is in wide disagreement, with estimates ranging from 26% (Rackemann & Edwards, 1952) to 78% (Johnstone, 1978). The prognosis appears to be enhanced, however, in cases with an early onset (Creer, Renne, & Chai, 1982). A significant number of absences from school are attributed to this condition, and the costs associated with its treatment are sometimes staggering (Creer *et al.*, 1982).

A diagnosis of asthma is confirmed by (1) the existence of a functional abnormality of bronchial smooth muscle (usually in response to a series of physical challenges); (2) the partial or complete reversibility of the physiological abnormality (which distinguishes asthma from other chronic respiratory disorders, such as emphysema or bronchitis); and (3) a chronic but intermittent course (Creer & Winder, 1986). Clinicians have traditionally distinguished between extrinsic and intrinsic asthma when designing treatment programs. Individuals with extrinsic or "allergic" asthma suffer attacks primarily during times when provoking stimuli are abundant and are probably best treated by short-term medical interventions. Intrinsic, or idiopathic, asthma lacks clearly defined precipitating or initiating factors, and attacks occur perennially, so that these individuals are better suited to broad-based interventions that take into account psychological procedures (Creer & Winder, 1986). Creer and Winder (1986), noting the problems inherent in this typology, recommended the use of a newer approach (by Reed & Townley, 1978) that classifies patients according to (1) the stimuli provoking the airway obstruction; (2) the variables linking the stimuli to the response; and (3) the physiological and pathological responses that constitute the airway obstruction.

The dominant treatment is medication, consisting chiefly of bronchodilators, corticosteroids, sympathomimetics, and immunotherapy. Some of these medications must be carefully titrated and monitored because the range between therapeutic effectiveness and toxicity is narrow, and children show wide variations in rates of metabolism (Alexander, 1983).

Psychological intervention follows one of three basic approaches. The first is traditional psychotherapy aimed at resolving the universal conflicts presumed to underlie the condition (infantile dependent attachments that lead to inhibited suppressed cries experienced as attacks of asthma). Evidence of the utility of this approach, however, is nonexistent (Creer, 1982). The two remaining approaches concern more direct means and attempt either to alter the abnormal pulmonary functioning or to alter maladaptive asthma-related behaviors (Alexander, 1983); treatment often uses both in concert.

*Alteration of Pulmonary Physiology*

During an asthma attack, the rate and volume of airflow decrease, and airway resistance increases. Electromyographic biofeedback from the forehead area and progressive muscle-relaxation training seek to modify these respiratory events by indirect means and assume that changes in muscle tone will lead to concomitant changes in these events. A second variety of biofeedback studied involves feedback of airflow or airway resistance variables as a more direct means of controlling the symptoms of asthma. Although the treatment rationale for airway biofeedback is clear and straightforward, the measurement technology used to accomplish this type of biofeedback is exceedingly complex, and this complexity has hampered research progress.

Early investigations of frontal EMG biofeedback typically combined it with relaxation therapy as well and found the combination to have some effect on respiratory parameters and symptoms (e.g., Davis, Saunders, Creer, & Chai, 1973; Scherr, Crawford, Sergent, & Scherr, 1975). Subsequent work by Kotses, Glaus, and associates (Kotses, Glaus, Crawford, Edwards, & Scheer, 1976; Kotses, Glaus, Bricel, Edwards, & Crawford, 1978) isolated and examined the effects on respiratory functions of forehead EMG biofeedback alone, again with promising findings. Kotses and Glaus (1981) speculated that relaxing the forehead muscles may lead to concomitant changes in pulmonary tone because of a neural reflex comprising trigeminal and vagal components.

One of the more interesting biofeedback treatment approaches (Khan, 1977; Khan, Staerk, & Bonk, 1973) uses airflow biofeedback in a counterconditioning paradigm. A child first receives biofeedback for the level of forced expiratory volume, in order to relax the bronchial tubes. Once this response is acquired, bronchoconstriction is induced by a variety of procedures (e.g., hyperventilation, recall of past attacks, or inhalation of a bronchoconstrictor) to the point of wheezing, at which time the child uses his or her biofeedback skills to abort the bronchospasms. The initial results of this procedures were very promising, but subsequent attempts to replicate have not always been as successful (Danker, Miklich, Pratt, & Creer, 1975).

Feldman (1976) piloted an alternative airway-biofeedback procedure that involves continuous monitoring of total respiratory resistance (TRR) by a forced-oscillation technique. In this procedure, a small-amplitude pressure of a known and well-calibrated quantity is directed into the subject's airway through a tightly sealed mouthpiece. TRR can be measured with each exhalation by clipping the subject's nostrils together. This information is then fed back to the subject via an external speaker as a tone whose pitch is directly proportional to TRR. An advantage of this procedure is that it requires only that subjects breathe normally; therefore, effort and motivational biases exert a minimal influence. Normal breathing sounds were presented to subjects by headphones, and during biofeedback training-trials subjects attempted to match their breathing patterns, as reflected by the external speaker, to the pattern heard over the earphones. A detailed study of this technique with four male asthmatics (ages 10–16) revealed that changes on certain parameters rivaled those occurring as a result of medication, the first biofeedback procedure to do so. The elaborate nature of this treatment and the high associated equipment costs appear to be limiting further exploration of the treatment boundaries.

### Alteration of Asthma-Related Behaviors

The intent of the treatments in this category is to modify the behavioral excesses and deficits related to asthma. Common behavioral excesses include anxiety-induced hyperventilation, "asthma panic," malingering, and inappropriate coughing (Alexander, 1983). Awareness, education, relaxation (as an alternative behavioral response), and occasionally systematic desensitization have been used effectively to treat hyperventilation. An asthma attack can be life-threatening and extremely frightening, leading to conditioned anxiety and fear. In such cases, systematic desensitization (imaginal or *in vivo*) and implosion have been reported to be effective. Malingering behavior has been treated successfully by time-out and satiation procedures. Cough is a common symptom of asthma, but in exaggerated forms, it can be disruptive socially and can even promote further bronchospasms. Conceptualizing excessive coughing as either attention-getting or an inappropriate habit pattern has led to the use of extinction, negative reinforcement, and punishment as the primary treatments (see Alexander, 1983, and Creer, 1979, for further details and supporting case evidence).

Behavioral (compliance difficulties and inappropriate use of therapy equipment), social, and educational deficits commonly occur in child asthmatics. Many of the medications used for symptom management must be administered with precision. Positive reinforcement combined with educative techniques have resulted in enhanced compliance with prescribed medication regimens. The presence of recurrent attacks of asthma can lead to a host of interpersonal and social deficits, such as lowered self-concept, restriction of social activities and outlets, and passivity. Education about the cause, nature, and course of the problem, specific training in how to recognize or discriminate attack onset and to react appropriately, and individual and family therapy have all been found to be useful (Alexander, 1983; Creer, 1982).

In recent years, a number of educational programs have been developed to teach asthmatics self-management skills. These programs typically include a simplified presentation about the etiology of asthma, a discussion of the physiology and mechanics of breathing, and instruction in problem-solving and decision-making skills. Such self-management programs have been used successfully in classrooms (Parcel & Nader, 1977), hospital outpatient departments (Hindi-

Alexander & Cropp, 1981), physicians' offices (Fireman, Friday, Gira, Vierthaler, & Michaels, 1981), and residential treatment centers (Creer, 1979; Creer & Leung, 1981). The American Lung Association has even initiated a national self-management project (Weiss, 1981). Self-administered programs have also resulted in success (Rakos, Grodek, & Mack, 1985). Rubin, Leventhal, Sadock, Letovsky, Schottland, Clemente, and McCarthy (1986) suggested that a computer-based instructional format can facilitate educative efforts. McNabb, Wilson-Pessano, and Jacobs (1986) have conducted a detailed analysis of the behaviors critical to the prevention and amelioration of acute asthma episodes in children. Their "self-management competency assessment" can be helpful in designing an effective education program for a given child.

Attempts to aid in the regulation of asthma through biofeedback and relaxation training are promising, but by no means definitive. Further, until the equipment costs and the technical requirements decrease, biofeedback treatments may remain experimental. Efforts aimed at teaching asthmatics to better manage their condition and the behavioral responses to and the consequences associated with asthma are increasingly being viewed as important, legitimate adjuncts to medical care. Here is where pediatric psychologists can have a sizable impact on both the child's quality of care and the child's quality of life.

## Diabetes

Defined by some investigators as chronic hyperglycemia (high blood-glucose concentration; Pohl, Gonder-Frederick, & Cox, 1984), diabetes mellitus is a widespread health problem that may affect up to 5% of the American population. Briefly, this complex disorder occurs when the pancreas produces insufficient amounts of the hormone insulin. Insulin carries glucose from the blood stream into muscle and fat cells, thereby providing vital nutrients for body use or storage; this insufficiency creates, in effect, a state of starvation, leaving the body to metabolize its own muscle and fat cells. With too much insulin, blood glucose levels become high (i.e., because normal glucose metabolism does not take place), and unmetabolized glucose is expelled into the urine. Diabetes is classified into two categories: Type I (insulin-dependent or juvenile-onset diabetes) and Type II (non-insulin-dependent diabetes). The majority of diabetics fall in the latter class; the former, which typically has an onset before age 30, requires a more rigorous self-care regimen. As many as 150,000 American children and adolescents suffer from insulin-dependent diabetes.

Diabetes carries with it several serious health risks, such as those related to microangiopathy, macroangiopathy, and neuropathy; these systemic problems translate into dramatically increased risk for blindness, kidney failure, gangrene of the lower extremities, and early death. As a result of these risks, both Type I and Type II diabetics are advised to adhere to a complex and rigorous health program. Psychological factors and stress figure prominently in the course of this medical disorder (Chase & Jackson, 1981; Evans, 1985; Fisher, Delamater, Bertelson, & Kirkley, 1982; Johnson, 1980; Surwit & Feinglos, 1984), further complicating attempts to predict and control it.

Although the health program varies from individual to individual, the basic elements usually involve (1) daily blood-glucose self-monitoring via urine or blood sampling; (2) insulin administration daily or twice-daily and at times when blood glucose levels are excessive; (3) adherence to a prescribed diet; and (4) exercise (Wing, Epstein, Nowalk, & Lamparski, 1986). Child compliance with the diabetic self-care regimen has been shown to be difficult to achieve (Simonds, 1979). To maximize children's compliance, numerous treatments have been designed (for detailed reviews, see Hobbs, Beck, & Wansley, 1984, and Varni, 1983).

Using writing prompts and a home token system, Lowe and Lutzker (1979) improved a 9-year-old female diabetic child's adherence to a self-care regimen that included urine testing, proper diet, and daily foot inspection and care. Her nearly flawless performance of these behaviors had been maintained at a 10-week follow-up. However, her glucose measures were not reported, so it is unknown whether this skill acquisition was reflected in greater metabolic control.

Epstein, Beck, Figueroa, Farkas, Kazdin, Daneman, and Becker (1981a) reported a comprehensive training program of 20 families of diabetic children. The training program involved instruction in seven topics: (1) glucose and acetone monitoring; (2) insulin dose adjustment; (3) diet; (4) exercise; (5) shot administration; (6) stress; and (7) hypoglycemia warning signs and care. In addition, the family members were instructed in techniques of motivating adherence, from point (token) economies to parental praise. The program proved extremely successful in helping the children adhere to their self-care programs.

Schafer, Glasgow, and McCaul (1982) reported their use of goal setting and goal setting plus behavioral contracting to promote the self-care compliance of three diabetic adolescents (targeting three of the following: urine testing, insulin injections, exercise, wearing diabetic identification, and/or home blood-glucose testing). Substantial improvements were seen in two of the subjects' adherence, along with marked decreases and stabilization in their blood and urine glucose levels. The failure of the third individual was attributed to poor subject follow-through on therapist instructions and to family problems. Thus, except in cases of child unreliability and family turmoil, child diabetics may benefit from relatively simple behavioral techniques for promoting medical compliance.

More recently, Gross (1982) taught four insulin-dependent diabetic boys behavioral self-modification skills in an attempt to improve adherence to their medical self-care regimen. The children showed significant improvements in their self-care skills; however, only half of the children had maintained their gains at a 2-month follow-up.

To promote generalization of the self-modification training, Gross, Magalnick, and Richardson (1985) added parental participation to their training package. Seven children and their parents participated in separate once-per-week training classes. While the children learned self-modification skills and implemented their own personal self-change projects, the parents were taught to praise their children for displays of the health-care behaviors; the children, in turn, were instructed to acknowledge this parental praise. Compared to a control group of children and parents, the self-modification subjects showed increased compliance with the medical regimen, as well as a decrease in diabetes-related family arguments. Furthermore, these gains had been maintained at 2- and 6-month follow-up.

Other investigators have reported attempts to help child diabetics gain control by teaching them ways to better mediate ongoing stresses (Fowler,

Budzynski, & VandenBergh, 1976; Rose, Firestone, Heick, & Faught, 1983).
Fowler *et al.* (1976) used EMG biofeedback (forehead) and relaxation training
with a 20-year-old woman described as being a poorly controlled diabetic; emotional and physical stressors appeared to throw the woman into ketoacidosis,
and as a result, she had been hospitalized seven times in the previous 2 years.
Following treatment, her daily insulin units had been nearly halved, and she
rated herself as being less emotional and as having fewer diabetic fluctuations.

Rose *et al.* (1983) taught five poorly controlled female diabetic adolescents
relaxation-based anxiety-management training (AMT). The daily mean urine
glucose values were significantly reduced in all subjects following AMT. Two
hypotheses were offered to explain these positive findings: (1) better subject
adherence to the medical regimen, instilled by the self-monitoring promoted by
the program, and (2) the direct influence of relaxation on the psychophysiological mechanisms controlling diabetes. From these positive findings, AMT
appears to be a useful adjunct in the health care of pediatric diabetes.

Several tactics appear to be of value in working with child diabetics. Diabetic
children can be taught to adhere to their complex medical regimens through a
variety of instructional, prompting, and incentive programs. The effects of these
efforts appear to be enhanced by involving the parents in the training program.
Relaxation training, as well as other stress-reduction efforts, also appears to be
of use in assisting child diabetics to better manage this oftentimes handicapping
condition.

Several points are worth raising, to serve as cautions against premature
conclusions and to help direct future research efforts in this area. First, it is
apparent that, particularly in self-care adherence interventions, we need to understand more fully the interplay between diet, exercise, stress, and biochemical
control. For example, Epstein *et al.* (1981a) found that glucose levels *increased* in
their successful subjects. Gross *et al.* (1985) found that the glucose levels of the
experimental and control subjects, though both showing decreases, were equivalent at follow-up, even though only the experimental subjects had adequately
adhered to the self-care regimen. Other studies have failed to report data on
glucose levels (Gross, 1982; Lowe & Lutzker, 1979). This information is essential
to gaining a more complete understanding of diabetes processes and to finding
an optimal self-care regimen.

Metabolic control appears to be related to a variety of biological, psychological, health-care-behavior, familial, extrafamilial, and health-care-system variables (Hanson & Henggeler, 1984; Johnson, 1980). Disruptions may occur across
any or all systems, which may explain why metabolic control is difficult to
achieve. The multifactorial nature of diabetes is highlighted by studies where
diabetic children/adolescents are trained in self-regulatory skills rather than to
adhere to health care regimens. Efforts in this regard can be seen in recent work
by Gross and colleagues using social (Gross, Heimann, Shapiro, & Schultz, 1983)
and coping (Gross, Johnson, Wildman, & Mullet, 1981) skills training to child
and adolescent diabetics. Both efforts have yielded promising returns, with
significant changes in the individual's life functioning.

Diabetes is a complex phenomenon that may be further understood in a
behavioral-systems framework. Adopting an encompassing conceptualization
may be more fruitful than continuing with the relatively molecular approaches
that have been used in the past. Naturally, the first step in this endeavor should

begin with expanding the level of assessment, going from the one or two dependent measures typically used to several that can address the many facets of diabetes. In sum, the time seems ripe for extending our sphere of inquiry regarding pediatric diabetes.

## Epilepsy

*Epilepsy* refers to chronically recurrent episodes of abnormal neural activity, or seizures, that dramatically disrupt brain functioning, with resulting motor, sensory, and cognitive disturbances. Seizures have been categorized into four main types, according to the presenting picture and the specific neurological activity (see Parker & Cincirpini, 1984), but the two most recognized classes are grand mal and petit mal seizures. *Grand mal* refers to seizures that often result in complete loss of consciousness, tonic and clonic movements, and incontinence; *petit mal* refers to a milder change of consciousness, sometimes mistaken for "daydreaming," which is usually accompanied by myoclonic jerks and an akinetic seizure pattern. The other recognized seizure types are focal and psychomotor seizures.

To date, anticonvulsant drugs have been the treatment of choice for seizures (Johnson & Freeman, 1981). Nonmedical or psychological treatments have been largely aimed at manipulating the contingencies under which seizures occur or at modifying the epileptic's physical response to stress or behavior during a seizure.

Gardner (1967) taught behavioral principles to the parents of a 10-year-old girl hospitalized for seizures. Just before and after the girl's discharge, the parents were instructed to become "deaf and dumb" to her seizure behaviors and somatic complaints and, at the same time, to start attending to her displays of appropriate behavior. Her seizure activity dropped to zero. After 26 weeks with no seizures, the parents were instructed to reverse the contingencies so that they again paid attention to the girl's somatic complaints; shortly thereafter, she had a seizure, and the parents reinstated the more fruitful contingency. One year later, the girl continued to be seizure-free. Unfortunately, the data were collected informally over the phone, so their reliability and validity may be questioned. Furthermore, the girl's seizures appeared to be atypical and could not be verified medically (including by EEG), so the generality of these findings to bona fide pediatric seizure patients may be limited.

Balaschak (1976) used a classroom contingency-management system to reduce the seizure activity of an 11-year-old girl with epilepsy. The teacher was instructed to pay as little attention to the seizure behaviors as possible, and the girl earned a check mark on a "good times chart" for seizure-free periods. At the end of each seizure-free week, the girl received candy and verbal reinforcement. Seizure activity showed marked reductions in the classroom and later in the home, where the child's mother initiated an information-incentive system. Unfortunately, seizure activity returned to baseline levels after the teacher declined to continue the contingency system.

Cataldo, Russo, and Freeman (1979) used a time-out procedure ("contingent rest") to reduce the seizure activity of a 5-year-old girl. The girl experienced both myoclonic and grand mal seizures, which were refractory to several major anticonvulsant medications and to a ketogenic diet. The girl experienced hundreds of myclonic seizures on the ward each day and was placed in contingent rest if her rate of seizures reached or exceeded 1.5 per minute for two consecutive 5-minute blocks. At these times, she was removed from the ongoing activity and was instructed to sit on a chair in her room with her eyes closed for a 10-minute period. The procedure resulted in a dramatic reduction in seizures, an improvement that was maintained for 16 weeks after her discharge from the hospital. The investigators reported that this procedure provided "effective and ethical treatment from both the medical and psychological perspective" (p. 421).

Zlutnick, Mayville, and Moffat (1975) reduced the daily seizures of five epileptic children by using behavioral procedures to eliminate those behaviors found to reliably precede seizure activity (i.e., the "aura" and its accompaniments). Essentially, the intervention required the change agent, on noticing previously identified preseizure activity, to (1) "shout, 'No!' loudly and sharply, and (2) grasp the subject by the shoulders with both hands and shake him once vigorously" (p. 2). One of the children was instead provided an alternative interruption procedure involving manual guidance and differential reinforcement for nonseizure activity. These interventions produced reductions in the seizure activity of four of the subjects.

Other investigators have examined the value of teaching physical self-regulation and control to the epileptic child (Ince, 1976; Lubar & Bahler, 1976; Seifert & Lubar, 1975). Ince (1976) used systematic desensitization to reduce the anxiety that a 12-year-old epileptic boy experienced in school, social, and medical situations. When the treatment began, the boy was reportedly having daily seizures, with approximately three grand mal and nine petit mal seizures per week. After he no longer felt nervous on visualizing the most anxiety-arousing step of each desensitization hierarchy, the boy was instructed to use cue-controlled relaxation (saying, "Relax" to himself) whenever he felt a seizure starting. For the next 9 months, the boy reportedly did not experience any seizure activity, either at home or at school.

Recently, attention has shifted to attempts to modify brain-wave activity to reduce seizure activity. Specifically, neuromotor inhibitory processes have been linked to the sensorimotor rhythm (SMR), a waveform between 12 and 14 Hz in the absence of 4–7 Hz activity and recorded over the Rolandic area. This brain wave has also been found to correspond to attentional processes. Work by Lubar and colleagues (Lubar & Bahler, 1976; Seifert & Lubar, 1975) has shown that SRM-feedback training can be effective in reducing children's and adults' epileptic seizures. Eight poorly controlled epileptics between the ages of 12 and 26 received SMR feedback; as our concern is with children, only the findings from the subjects below age 18 ($N = 4$) are considered here. Three of these children showed reductions in seizure activity concomitant with either EEG normalization or evidence of increased SMR activity. SMR training has a potential for use with child epileptics, but the complex technology required to implement this form of biofeedback treatment and the extensive number of training sessions needed for an effect limit its widespread use at present (Andrasik & Attanasio, 1985). Further research is needed to help ascertain the specific value of SMR feedback training.

Investigators have recently examined the use of nonmedical procedures to help epileptic children and adolescents. Notable success has been achieved with contingency management, relaxation, and biofeedback. Although the reports reviewed in this section reveal much promise for pediatric psychologists, future study should help to promote the clinical application of these procedures.

## PREPARATION FOR STRESSFUL MEDICAL PROCEDURES: HOSPITALIZATION AND SURGERY

A substantial literature has evolved regarding the preparation of children for surgery, hospitalization, and other medical procedures (e.g., Elkins & Roberts, 1983; Johnson, 1979; Siegel, 1976). A variety of approaches have been used in this endeavor, including puppet therapy (Linn, Beardslee, & Patenaude, 1986), play therapy (Ellerton, Caty, & Ritchie, 1985), and the provision of reassurance and support (Fosson & deQuan, 1984). Two other approaches that have shown particular promise are stress-point preparation (Visitainer & Wolfer, 1975; Wolfer & Visitainer, 1975, 1979) and modeling (Ferguson, 1979; Klinzing & Klingzing, 1977; Melamed & Siegel, 1975; Peterson & Shigetomi, 1981; Vernon & Bailey, 1974). For purposes of illustration, work using these latter two approaches is now reviewed. More extension discussion may be found in Anderson and Masur (1983), Elkins and Roberts (1983), and Lambert (1984).

### Stress-Point Preparation

*Stress-point preparation* refers to supportive care "to remove or minimize sources of stress and assist the child in coping with unavoidable stress through the provision of information, instruction, rehearsal, and support by a single nurse at critical times" (Visitainer & Wolfer, 1974, p. 191). "Critical times" are those circumstances in which the child's anxiety is expected to be high. For example, for surgical (tonsillectomy) pediatric patients, Visitainer and Wolfer (1975) used this preparation at six points: (1) at hospital admission; (2) before blood testing; (3) on the day before the operation; (4) shortly before administering the preoperative medications; (5) just before transporting the child to the operating room; and (6) after the child returned from the operation.

Wolfer and Visitainer (1975) used stress-point preparation with a group of 45 hospitalized children. Compared to a second group of children, who went through the routine hospital procedures, the experimental subjects were found to be less upset, more cooperative, and better adjusted at posthospitalization; the parents of these children were less anxious and more satisfied with the hospital care provided their child. Visitainer and Wolfer (1975) reported similar findings in a group of 84 hospitalized children; they also found the preparation to be superior to single-session preparation provided at the beginning of the child's hospitalization. In a more recent study of 163 children, Visitainer and Wolfer (1975) found that home preparation (written materials, pictures of hospital settings and apparatus, and a "hospital kit" sent to the parent and the child) added little or nothing to hospital stress-point preparation.

Although the above applications are specific to children admitted to hospitals for surgery, it seems likely that a similar approach can be applied to other pediatric health-service settings. Other advantages of this stress-point preparation are that it is personalized and individualized, and its actual content and the manner in which it is given depend on the child's intellectual and cognitive development (according to Piagetian formulations; Visitainer & Wolfer, 1975). Stress-point preparation is also time-efficient, as nurses or other service providers can deliver the preparation within the procedural constraints of hospital routine. In addition, this approach involves the parents, a tactic that itself has been successfully used as a preparation aid (Knox & Hayes, 1983; Skipper & Leonard, 1968).

## Modeling Approaches

In an innovative program, Melamed and Siegel (1975) used filmed modeling with a group of 4- to 12-year-old hospitalized children. Thirty children, scheduled for minor surgery, viewed a 16-minute film ("Ethan Has an Operation") that shows a 7-year-old boy preparing for a hernia operation. The film covers a wide range of hospital experiences between the time of the child's admission to his time of discharge. In addition, portions of the film include narratives by the child, in which he expresses his feelings and concerns about the impending operation but successfully overcomes his apprehensions at each stage of the hospitalization. The children who viewed the coping-model film showed significant improvements in psychological, physiological, and behavioral indices of distress over children who viewed a neutral film.

Ferguson (1979) compared prehospital home contact by a nurse to the use of a filmed peer-modeling sequence ("Yolanda and David Have Their Tonsils Out") in preparing 82 young children for surgery. The children who received a preadmission visit had lower fear at pre- and posthospitalization. Compared to the mothers of the children in a control group, the mothers of the children in both experimental groups showed lower anxiety and greater satisfaction with the care that they and their child received; significantly less negative posthospital behavior was also seen in the two experimental groups. Finally, children who saw the peer model evidenced lower behavioral and physiological (trapezius muscle EMG) signs of anxiety.

Twardosz, Weddle, Borden, and Stevens (1986) compared individual nurse preparation with a preoperative class (which included modeling procedures) and a videotape of that class. Children in the *in vivo* preparation group exhibited fewer negative reactions than the children in the two other groups. Demarest, Hooke, and Erickson (1984) used an *in vivo* slide show to prepare 16 children for minor surgery. The *in vivo* preparation was found to be superior to both the slide presentation and a control (neutral) procedure, in terms of reducing the children's hospital fears.

More recently, Peterson, Schultheis, Ridley-Johnson, Miller, and Tracy (1984b) worked with 44 children aged 2 to 11 who had been hospitalized for oral surgery. These investigators found that modeling, filmed or live, was superior to an informal preparation offered by the hospital staff. Peterson, Ridley-Johnson, Tracy, and Mullins (1984a) compared a standard hospital tour to a tour plus either modeling or modeling and coping-skills training. Both modeling groups were superior to the tour-alone group on indices of child distress and parental calmness, confidence, and satisfaction, as well as on one child posthospital adjustment measure. Thus, further support was provided for modeling versus traditional hospital preparation, and adding coping-skills training was found to have no advantage.

In formalized preparatory programs such as these, one important issue is the context of the intervention. Typically, these interventions are provided under relatively controlled conditions with low-distressed children and parents. Unfortunately, in practice, this ideal state may be difficult to achieve, and children and parents seen during emergency admissions may present an altogether different picture (Eberly, Miles, Carter, Hennessey, & Riddle, 1985; Roskies, Bedard, Gauvreau-Guilbault, & LaFortune, 1975). Relatedly, since many children's first experience with the hospital is the emergency room, an often hectic place with its own anxiety producing stimuli, the implementation of a formal preparation program may not be feasible. Furthermore, while the hospital-based programs have shown promise, some have argued that their limitations call for other preparatory tactics (Trawick-Smith & Thompson, 1984). For instance, many hospitals do not provide these programs and those that do may lack the funding to provide training to all the children served. Due to these and other limitations, community and school-based hospital preparatory programs seem advised (Trawick-Smith & Thompson, 1984).

Peterson and Ridley-Johnson (1984) provided hospital education in a school setting to a group of 131 fourth- and fifth-graders. One third of the children were given a lecture on hospital routine and a demonstration of hospital equipment; one third viewed a commercially available film ("Ethan Has an Operation"; Melamed & Siegel, 1975) showing a child model coping with and preparing for a hernia operation; and the remaining children listened to a neutral presentation (on the space shuttle *Columbia*). The results of the study showed that the hospital-relevant conditions significantly reduced children's general and hospital-related fear and increased their knowledge of hospital procedures and instrumentation. Unexpectedly, the lecture demonstration was superior to the filmed modeling (consistent with the findings of Demarest *et al.*, 1984 and Twardosz *et al.*, 1986). One implication of this finding is that less costly preparatory interventions may, in fact, work as well as or better than the less readily available options. Continued research in this area will help to determine the optimal cost-efficiency of preparatory interventions.

Elkins and Roberts (1984) reported an evaluation of the "Let's Pretend Hospital" (LPH) with 50 first-graders. The LPH is described as an "experiential and information program wherein a mock hospital is set up for children to visit" (p. 31). The results of the program showed that the children who had gone through the LPH program had fewer medically related fears and greater medical knowledge than the children who had not.

Elkins and Roberts (1985) tested the relative efficacy of three peer-modeling procedures (two commercially available films or videotapes and a slide and audiotape program) with 80 third- and fifth-grade children. The children who saw the slide and audiotape program showed significant increases in their medical knowledge. Unfortunately, none of the modeling procedures significantly affected the children's hospital-related fears. This result may have been based on the (nonhospitalized) children's fears not being high in the first place, so improvements may have been more difficult to show than in a more fearful population. In support of this suggestion was the finding that the children who had been most fearful at pretreatment did show significant decreases in medically related fear, across all three modeling programs.

The two approaches described have been shown to be of substantial value in preparing pediatric patients for hospitalization and surgery. A natural question at this point regards which of the two is more effective. As both stress-point preparation and modeling appear to be effective, perhaps research examining which procedure works best with what type of pediatric patient (e.g., along the lines of age, gender, and medical condition) would be most productive. Future work might involve a careful collection and analysis of data about the subjects themselves as well as about the interventions. Knowledge of this type would enable pediatric psychologists to weigh cost with efficiency. The timing of the preparation also appears to be worthy of study. For example, Melamed, Meyer, Gee, and Soule (1976) found that filmed modeling 1 week before surgery produced optimal benefits for older children, whereas preparation the day before worked best with younger children.

# PROMOTION OF HEALTH AND PREVENTION OF ILLNESS

Health promotion has two goals: (1) improving the well-being of children during their childhood and (2) improving the later health status of the child as an adult (Maddux, Roberts, Sledden, & Wright, 1986). The importance of health promotion as a prevention strategy becomes very clear from data outlining the problems afflicting young people and the causes of death in this age group. For children aged 1–14, the leading cause of death is "accidents" (e.g., motor vehicle collisions, drownings, falls, fires, and poisoning), and the leading causes of death for adolescents and young adults (ages 15–24) are motor vehicle collisions, homicides, other accidents, and suicides. Additional health threats to this latter age group are alcohol and drug abuse, sexually transmitted diseases, and unwanted pregnancies. For adults (ages 25–65 years), one third of all deaths are due to cardiovascular disease, and another large proportion is due to cancer. Clear relationships exist between these causes of death and behavior such as smoking, diet, exercise, and coping with stress (Roberts, 1986a). Because many adverse health-related behaviors are initially learned during childhood and adolescence (Hamburg & Brown, 1978; Marks, 1980), it seems logical that pediatric psychologists may contribute significantly to the prevention of cardiovascular disease and cancer.

In this section, prevention efforts in the areas of substance abuse, obesity, and accident or injury are discussed. For a review of prevention and intervention efforts involving other cardiovascular and cancer-risk factors, see Varni (1983).

## Substance Abuse

Consumption rates of tobacco, alcohol, and other drugs among children and adolescents are unacceptably high (MacDonald, 1984), and longitudinal data suggest that early substance use can lead to later serious abuse (Schinke & Gilchrist, 1985). The risks associated with chronic smoking are well documented (e.g., coronary heart disease and cancer of the lung, the larynx, the mouth, the esophagus, and the bladder), as are those associated with the abuse of alcohol and other drugs (e.g., heart, lung, brain, liver, and stomach damage). Compared to nonsmokers, smokers spend over one third more time away from their jobs because of illness. Excessive drinking is involved in a major portion of car accidents and fatalities, of other accidents at home and at the job, and of suicides. Half of those killed in alcohol-related car accidents are teenagers (Schaefer & Millman, 1981), and teenage alcohol use has been related to low self-esteem, poor grades, absenteeism, and vandalism in school (Oster, 1983).

Cigarette smoking and drinking often begin in junior high school. Among teenage drinkers, beer is the beverage of choice, most drinking is done at home, and peers are the most common drinking companions. Relative to other drugs (except perhaps tobacco), alcohol is less expensive and easier to get, and its use is more acceptable to adults (Schaefer & Millman, 1981). For these reasons, this review focuses primarily on cigarette and alcohol abuse.

In light of the risks associated with chronic smoking and alcohol abuse and the generally disappointing results of cessation programs, prevention programs appear to be of clear value. Substance-abuse prevention-programs have focused on the agent substances, the environment (the settings where abuse originates), and the hosts (those who will use the interventions). This section selectively examines examples of environment and host interventions; see Schinke and Gilchrist (1985) for a review of agent intervention programs (e.g., technological and social controls).

Environmental prevention programs (based in schools, homes, and communities) involve attempts to change everyday influences on youngsters' substance abuse by creating climates supporting nonabusive behavior. Many of these programs can also be viewed as host prevention programs, as they attempt to teach children and adolescents cognitive and behavioral skills for avoiding substance use (Schinke & Gilchrist, 1985). Initial prevention efforts, primarily through school-based health education, positively affected children's and adolescents' knowledge and attitudes, but few such efforts significantly reduced their actual substance abuse (Snow, Gilchrist, & Schinke, 1985). The interventions that have most influenced substance abuse rates have enlisted peer leaders, because peer pressure contributes significantly to smoking and drinking. For example, Evans (1976) used older, well-respected peers to teach entering seventh-graders to recognize and cope with peer, parental, and media pressure to smoke. The seventh-graders were also shown the relationship between smoking and increases in nicotine and carbon dioxide. This program was successful in reducing the smoking incidence among the participating students.

McAlister, Perry, Killen, Slinkard, and Maccoby (1980) also used peer leaders to train students (sixth- and seventh-graders) to resist social pressure to use tobacco and included alcohol and other drug use as well. For example, the students were taught to say, "I would be a chicken if I smoked just to impress you" after being called a "chicken" for not trying a cigarette. When later compared to nontrained students (who were exposed to an intensive course on health education), the students with resistance training began smoking at less than one half the rate of those who did not receive this training. Alcohol and marijuana use were also less prevalent among the group receiving the resistance training.

Although peer leaders may enhance program credibility, school-based programs using other methods have also been effective. This effectiveness seems to be largely due to a targeting of variables that directly promote initial drug use (e.g., lack of assertiveness in the face of peer pressure) rather than simply educating youth about long-term health hazards. Assertion-training techniques that entail effective alternative responses to peer pressure are part of many of these successful school-based preventive programs (Anderson Johnson, Hansen, Collins, & Graham, 1986; Englander-Golden, Elconin, & Satir, 1986a).

One program, known as "Say It Straight," showed significantly fewer alcohol- and drug-related school suspensions and referrals of sixth- to eighth-graders (middle-school children) than in two control middle schools in the same city that had not been given such training (Englander-Golden, Elconin, & Miller, 1985). The students learned to recognize how they responded in different interactions (via role playing and guided imagery) and received peer feedback concerning their effectiveness. When two shorter versions of this 10-day program (7- and 5-day models) were later compared to the earlier model, they, too, produced significant changes toward more assertive attitudes. Moreover, alcohol- and drug-related school suspensions were significantly lower among the 1,564 students who received such training than among the 1,295 who did not (Englander-Golden, Elconin, Miller, & Schwarzkophf, 1986a).

Anderson Johnson and colleagues (Anderson Johnson et al., 1986) compared training in social pressure resistance skills to health education in an attempt to deter cigarette smoking among high school students. Health education prevented initial experimentation most effectively among those students who hadn't smoked before study participation. For those students who had previously experimented with cigarettes, social influence/resistance training was most effective in deterring higher cigarette use.

Other environment-based preventive programs include home- and community-based interventions. Home-based prevention programs include television-mediated family intervention (Flay, 1985) and several parent interventions. Parental interventions for preventing smoking include modeling (parents not smoking themselves) and drug education at home. Examples of the latter include (1) letting the child know that the parents care about him/her and will help him/her to make an informed decision about smoking; (2) focusing on the immediate consequences of smoking (e.g., shortness of breath, greater likelihood of sickness); and (3) letting children know that some adult smokers don't like it but find it very difficult to quit smoking (Schaefer & Millman, 1981). Oei and Fea (1987) concluded in their recent review of smoking prevention programs for children that parent-implemented programs targeting children younger than 12 years of age may be more effective than the school-based, peer-led health education programs.

Schaefer and Millman also suggested several ways in which parents can help prevent their children from abusing alcohol: (1) appropriate parental example; (2) discussing alcohol facts; (3) teaching children to abstain or to drink moderately; (4) supervising initial use; and (5) providing alternatives (e.g., sports, yoga, or mediation). As with cigarette smoking, these clinicians believe that it's best to talk to children about alcohol before they enter seventh grade, to avoid exaggerated "scare" tactics, and to objectively point out the dangers of abuse. Teaching moderate drinking includes teaching children to sip alcohol slowly, to avoid drinking on an empty stomach, and not to use alcohol to escape (when physically or emotionally upset, lonely, or in need of solace). The supervision of initial use includes consumption of small quantities of diluted alcoholic beverages at home.

Although schools appear to be the most effective sites for conducting these programs, more research integrating school, family, and media prevention programs is needed. Chassin, Presson, and Sherman (1985) suggested that prevention programs may deter initial smoking by decreasing the perceived salience of smoking cues in adolescents' social environments (e.g., reducing smoking advertisements and eliminating smoking areas in schools), by developing messages aimed at deviance-prone adolescents (those more likely to smoke in order to project an image of toughness, precocity, and sociability), and by providing compensatory social-skills training to help adolescents attain the perceived social-image benefits of smoking. Methodologically, evaluations of smoking prevention programs should assess other substance use (particularly smokeless tobacco use) to ensure that other substances are not being substituted for cigarettes and should conduct longer-term follow-up studies (4–5 years postintervention).

## Obesity

Obesity (defined as being 20% or more above the average weight) is a serious problem that frustrates its victims and afflicts a sizeable portion of the population. With increasing body weight, a person is at an increased risk of developing hypertension, diabetes, and hyperlipidia, as well as social and psychological problems (e.g., school and employment discrimination and difficulties with social and sexual situations; Brownell & Foreyt, 1985). Almost one third of children under age 18 become overweight adults. Childhood obesity is also positively correlated with the family incidence of obesity (e.g., 45% chance with one obese parent and 80% chance with two obese parents; Coates & Thoresen, 1978). Moreover, although there are promising short-term results with dieting, counseling, exercise programs, and behavior therapy for adults, reports of significant and maintained weight loss are disappointingly rare. These results compellingly suggest that obesity must be prevented rather than coped with by lifelong dieting.

Childhood obesity stems from several factors, including distinctive eating styles (such as eating food quickly, preferring fattening foods, and eating too much food) and a less active lifestyle than nonobese peers. Psychologically, overeating may sometimes be seen as a consolation source (e.g., to ward off anxiety-provoking interactions or to deal with boredom and loneliness). Overeating may be learned, for example, when parents ignore the child's ability to self-regulate and overestimate how much food he or she needs. Obese parents may also be imitated in their consumption of excess or fattening foods, snacking on high-calorie foods, and/or eating in response to external (visible food) cues rather than internal (hunger) cues. Obese siblings can also model poor eating and exercise habits. Peer modeling has been shown to influence both food preference (Birch, 1980) and eating topography (Perry, Lebow, & Buser, 1979). Family patterns also affect exercise patterns. Parents of obese children are more likely to limit their children's activity (see Epstein, Koeske, Wing, & Valoski, 1986) and are less likely to engage in regular exercise (e.g., walking, jogging, and swimming; Schaefer & Millman, 1981).

A number of clinic-based and school-based pediatric weight-intervention programs have been reported for overweight children and adolescents. Brownell and Stunkard (1978) reviewed several clinic-based studies that look promising in managing pediatric obesity. These studies illustrate the potential of behavioral techniques in controlling infant, childhood, and adolescent obesity by changing eating, exercise, and diet patterns.

Epstein et al. (1986) recently summarized the results of a series of standardized family-based behaviorally oriented treatment programs (Epstein, Wing, Steranchak, Dickson, & Michelson, 1980; Epstein, Wing, Koeske, Andrasik, & Ossip, 1981b; Epstein, Wing, Koeske, Ossip, & Beck, 1982; Epstein, Wing, Koeske, & Valoski, 1984). In all, families were given an education program based on a "traffic light" diet and an aerobic or lifestyle exercise program. In this diet, foods were divided into red, yellow, and green groups, which respectively corresponded to high, medium, and low calorie-density. The consumption of these foods was explained in relation to traffic light colors: "green" foods could be eaten freely, "yellow" foods required caution, and "red" foods signaled "stop." Social reinforcement and contracts negotiated between parent and child were used to promote behavior change. Parents and children (aged 8–12) were seen separately once a week for 8–12 sessions, and then monthly for at least 6 months. The programs were based on parental management of the child's eating and exercise behavior, with regular home meetings to assess behavior change and parent–child-determined reinforcers to motivate behavior change. No differences in weight change in programs emphasizing parent versus child management were seen over 3 years. Moreover, the three studies' respective mean overweight percentage changes after 6 months of treatment were −17.5%, −17.1%, and −18.2%.

When Epstein et al. (1986) later assessed the effect of family variables on the weight change in the above three studies' child subjects, they found that the more successful children lost more weight initially, had fewer siblings, and were female. They suggested further that family size may interact with the treatment to deter weight change, so that, in larger families, the parent has less time to spend with the child in promoting behavior change. Likewise, increased family size may be stressful, which would make effective management of the children more difficult.

Coates and Thoresen (1981) taught two 16-year-old adolescents (a 15-year-old was a control subject) the use of self-monitoring, stimulus control, the selection of lower calorie foods, self-instructions, and self-reinforcement; the family members were taught ways to support and encourage the subjects' appropriate eating behaviors. After 14 weeks, the treated subjects had lost 20 and 11.5 lb, and the control subject had gained 11.5 lbs. However, each treated subject showed different patterns of behavior change, even though both received identical instructions. The differential changes indicated the importance of systematically assessing therapeutic adherence.

Coates, Jeffery, Slinkard, Killen, and Danaher (1982) randomly assigned 38 obese adolescents to one of four treatment groups in a 2 × 2 factorial design. The factors examined were reinforcement for weight loss versus caloric change and frequency of therapeutic contact (five times versus once per week). All subjects participated in classes for 15 weeks to learn behavior self-management skills, which included self-observation and caloric goals, stimulus control procedures, exercise, self-talk, imagery, social control, and general problem-solving skills. Only the group that received rewards for weight loss and that went to the clinic five times per week showed significant decreases in the percentage that they were overweight. Furthermore, these gains were maintained at 6-month follow-up. Changes in cardiovascular risk factors were also reported; clinically and statistically significant changes in the recommended directions in blood pressure, total cholesterol, high-density and low-density lipoproteins, and triglycerides were correlated with the weight changes.

Compared to programs in clinical settings, school-based programs for obese children generally produce smaller weight losses (e.g., less than 1 kg or a 2%–5% decrease in percentage overweight for 8–12 weeks of treatment; Foster, Wadden, & Brownell, 1985). However, a program reported by Brownell and Kaye (1982) did produce clinically significant weight losses (4.4 kg), and Dietz (1983) reported that, if even the smaller losses are maintained for a year or more while height increases, weight will become normalized in mildly obese youngsters.

Foster *et al.* (1985) assessed the efficacy of parental involvement and the feasibility of using older peers as counselors for 48 obese children in Grades 2–5. Unlike previous school-based programs, this program also included follow-up (18-week) data. The treated children participated in a 12-week program involving contacts with eighth-grade counselors three times per week. The counselors weighed the children, examined their lunchboxes for nutritious foods, and recommended changes in eating and exercise habits. The children were rewarded with stickers and verbal praise for having appropriate foods in their lunchboxes and for minimal levels of weight loss. They also were instructed in record keeping, stimulus control, slowed eating, lifestyle activity, and attitude change, and they participated in a weekly exercise class. In contrast, a control group of 41 similarly aged peers received only three weigh-ins. Finally, one half of the subjects' parents were invited to attend the first and last meetings, and the other half of the parents were invited to attend five meetings.

Results indicated that the positive short-term changes in weight, self-concept, and food selection were only partially maintained. Compared to pretreatment, the treated subjects were still significantly less obese at 18-week follow-up than the controls, but the size of the group differences had decreased by that time. Moreover, relatively small losses were reported (a 5.3% decrease in percentage overweight for the treated subjects and a 0.3% increase for controls). From these (and past) findings, the authors suggested that weight stabilization (rather than weight loss) should be the goal of school programs, and that weight stabilization is likely to be achieved only if the treatment is followed by a weight-loss-maintenance program.

Several important issues should be considered when examining and/or engaging in pediatric obesity research. First, Weil (1977) noted the importance of considering the measurement of weight relative to each child's height and age status; Dwyer (1980) advocated the close supervision of diet change to ensure the proper nutrition of the rapidly growing child or adolescent. Clearly, these two factors pertain to the issue of ensuring the most beneficial interface between the pediatric intervention and the child's physical development. Second, the assessment and management of adherence by the children and their parents to the prescribed eating, exercise, and diet regimens require further attention, as two major features of weight control programs (regimens that are both complex and long-term) have been associated with the greatest noncompliance (Varni, 1983). Third, Varni (1983) suggested that both weight loss and behavioral parameters must be systematically assessed, as weight loss measured at the clinic visit may still result from inappropriate behaviors, such as fasting, excessive exercise, unhealthy diet, or even self-induced vomiting and the use of cathartics.

Fourth, Epstein *et al.* (1986) suggested that other familial and individual difference variables that influence child weight loss should also be investigated, and that their family-based behavioral treatment programs should be replicated with younger and older children to establish some generalization parameters. Fifth, the results of Coates *et al.* (1982) suggest that future studies might try contingencies other than money (such as tokens or raffle tickets) or might change their program to benefit greater numbers of children (e.g., by using weigh-in centers at schools). Finally, Foster *et al.* (1985) suggested that the role of social support in school-based programs needs more investigation, as their manipulation of parental involvement may not have been sufficiently strong. They also suggested the need to compare the efficacy of peer counselors with adult instructors, as the latter were employed in the more successful Brownell and Kaye (1982) study.

## Accident and Injury Prevention

Accident prevention is of unsurpassed importance to children's health, as accidents remain the number one killer of children (Gratz, 1979). Successful accident prevention requires intervention at both the societal and the family levels; the goals most difficult to achieve involve lifestyle changes for children and their caretakers (Peterson & Mori, 1985). The epidemiological data suggest that the common agents of child injury are automobile mishaps, drowning, burns, the ingestion of harmful substances, and falls (Gratz, 1979), and that the home and the automobile are the two most frequent locations for accidental injury (Dershewitz & Williamson, 1977). Inappropriate adult supervision is a major contributor to children's accidents (Peterson & Mori, 1985).

Boys are generally more at risk than girls, as are those children who are more extraverted, daring, aggressive, competitive, inattentive, impulsive, temperamental, and disobedient and/or have a low frustration tolerance (e.g., Langley, McGee, Silva, & Williams, 1983; Manheimer & Mellinger, 1967). Children from single-parent families, teenage mothers, and large families are also at increased risk (Wadsworth, Burnell, Taylor, & Neville, 1983). Matheny (1986) reported that injury-liable toddlers were more likely to have less educated mothers of lower SES who saw themselves as more emotionally overwhelmed and less energetic. Matheny also suggested that the correlates of injury liability change with developmental progress. For example, with age, the contributions of the parents and the home environment may become less salient, whereas community attributes become more salient.

Most preventive interventions concerning the harmful agents are legislated and rely on passive rather than active prevention (e.g., one-time changes, such as a company's making a safer bicycle, vs. progressively more effort-intensive responses, ranging from installing and periodically checking a smoke alarm to using a safety seat each time the child enters a car) (Peterson & Mori, 1985). Harmful agent-related interventions are also more likely to use a population-wide approach (e.g., regulations regarding the safe construction of infant cribs) and are quite effective. In contrast, prevention programs directed toward the caretaker are not often legislated, and even where they are legislated, they are often poorly enforced.

More common interventions targeting the caretaker (and the child) involve educational and persuasive methods, such as brief messages on television or in brochures and instructions given by pediatricians. Unfortunately, these methods are relatively ineffective. Of greater effectiveness are interventions that target high-risk groups and "milestone" educational interventions with caretakers (e.g., parents of newborn children are more easily influenced to acquire child safety restraints). Such interventions have at times effectively used behavioral techniques targeting children's skills. Examples of high-risk-group interventions include changing children's responses to a potential child molester (Poche, Brouwer, & Swearingen, 1981; Saslawsky & Wurtele, 1986), training in pedestrian safety skills (Yeaton & Bailey, 1978), training in safe reactions to a fire (Hillman, Jones, & Farmer, 1986; Jones, Kazdin, & Haney, 1981) and safety training for latchkey children (e.g., Peterson & Mori, 1985).

A perusal of several of the above studies reveals certain notable findings. For example, in teaching children fire-emergency skills (Hillman et al., 1986), providing a rationale for each skill produces greater retention of learned skills than does not providing a rationale. These results are consistent with those of Jones et al. (1981) and Hillman et al. (1986), who reported that subjects who become more cognitively involved in learning produce superior performance. Moreover, subjects in the more recent study who received behavioral practice of fire safety skills (three 20-minute sessions) performed better than did subjects exposed to verbal skills practice.

Teaching safe responding to latchkey children has become increasingly important, given the rapidly growing number of young children left unsupervised as an expanding number of primary caretakers join the work force (Belsky & Steinberg, 1978). In addition to a significant relation between many home injuries and the absence of parental supervision (Rivara, 1982), this training is also important because of a disturbing gap between what parents and children think children know and what children actually know when left unsupervised at home. One study found that children were unaware of their parents' rules and did not appear to be well prepared to be left at home unsupervised. Not only were they unable to recall their parents' rules, but they didn't recognize which behaviors were acceptable even when the behavioral rules were presented (Peterson, Mori, & Scissors, 1986).

One example of home safety training for latchkey children was provided by Peterson and Mori (1985). Two groups of four children (ages 7–10) were trained once per week for 8 consecutive weeks in several domains involving daily concerns (e.g., after-school activities, selection and preparation of food, and coming home during a rainstorm), interacting with strangers (answering phone and door), and responding to emergencies (e.g., fire or a serious cut or burn). Both groups involved modeling and differential reinforcement for correct answers; small tangible items (stickers or small stuffed animals) were given to reward effort at each sessions's end. One of the groups was also given training in problem-solving skills. At 5-month follow-up, both groups of children similarly recalled a large variety of safety responses and required booster training of less than 1 hour to restore safe behavior to very high levels. Moreover, the trained behaviors generalized from the assessment trials to safe responding in the real world (e.g., volunteers, in the parents' absence, called each child and came to the door posing as a repairman). Unfortunately, neither training method led to generalization to untrained problem areas.

Peterson and Mori's study (1985) is noteworthy because it demonstrated both cost-effectiveness (through the use of paraprofessional trainers and a small number of training sessions) and generalization, although the latter finding was less strong. These authors suggested that even lower cost training might be obtained by training whole classrooms of children or by having parents train their own children. Using teachers and parents to provide booster sessions to strengthen maintenance should also be investigated, as should ways of promoting greater generalization.

In addition to the issues of cost-effectiveness, maintenance, and generalization, Peterson and Mori (1985) more generally suggested that psychologists' skills in affecting human behavior are relevant to influencing both legislation and education, to designing effective populationwide communications, and to influencing high-risk populations. Prevention efforts should also attend to encouraging safety adherence and to altering judgments of self-efficacy. Increasing the child's cognitive involvement (e.g., by promoting the recall of safety measures) may be one way to increase safety adherence.

Coppens (1986) recommended that safety education programs help children to identify preventive measures by encouraging the understanding of cause–effect relationships between potential accident agents and potential injury. Videotaping children in multiple environments may guide experiences in preventive thinking and may make concrete the abstract concepts of safety and prevention. Environments (e.g., street, playground, and home) could be scanned with close-ups of critical features that make situations safe or unsafe. Child models could first be shown in unsafe situations, with safe actions then demonstrated. Coppens (1986) also noted that pediatric well-child visits give a good opportunity to screen for children's understanding of causal relationships, safety, and prevention, and to present an injury prevention program directed toward the children's cognitive abilities. Pediatric psychologists could also help children already injured to view accidents as learning situations by identifying the environmental elements critical in producing risk and by explaining how any resulting injury might have been prevented.

Finally, it is important to gear interventions to the youngsters' developmental level (and concurrent abilities). Commendably, most of the successful prevention programs described have carefully considered developmental status, and Roberts (1986a) provided other noteworthy examples (e.g., anticipatory guidance training, which uses a knowledge of child development to anticipate the abilities and the potential accidents seen at different ages). A consideration of developmental level may improve program impact because the information presented will be better integrated into the youngsters' schema.

## Management of Child Abuse and Neglect

The physical and psychological abuse of children by their parent(s) is an infrequent but all-too-common phenomenon. Not only are abused children at risk for immediate or short-term complications stemming from the maltreatment itself, but the probability is multiplicatively enhanced for later aggressivity

(Hoffman-Plotkin & Twentyman, 1984; Howes & Eldridge, 1985; Reidy, 1977), juvenile delinquency (McCord, 1983), noncompliance (Oldershaw, Walters, & Hall, 1986), and suicide (Deykin, Albert, & McNamara, 1985). Because problems occur in attempts to define this phenomenon, the following discussion is limited to those children who receive "non-accidental physical injury(ies) as a result of acts/or omissions on the part of [their] parent or guardians that violates [*sic*] community standards regarding the treatment of children" (Kempe & Helfer, 1972, p. 1).

One widely held view of the causes of child abuse involves the parents' having inadequate child management skills and largely relying on coercion and physical punishment. During stressful times and/or extreme child misbehavior, punishment may fail or may have only short-term effects. The parents then escalate the intensity and frequency of their punishment, and abuse is the eventual result. Evidence in support of this view can be found in observations by Burgess and Conger (1977, 1978), in which abusive parents, when compared to nonabusive parents, showed lower levels of interaction, overall, and higher levels of negative, coercive behavior toward their child(ren). Accordingly, numerous investigators have implemented programs for ameliorating the suspected skill deficits of abusive parents (Gambrill, 1983; Isaacs, 1982; Smith, 1984). Some of this work is described here.

Sandler, Van Dercar, and Milhoan (1978) used reading and practice assignments, role playing, and contingent reinforcement in teaching behavior management skills to two parents (mothers) identified as child abusers. This training resulted in decreases in negative parental commands in one family and in increases in approval, talking, and laughing in both families. These gains were maintained over the 3-month follow-up periods. Similarly, Crozier and Katz (1979) taught behavior management principles to two families in which child abuse had occurred. In both families, parent and child behavior became less aversive and/or more positive after treatment; no incidents of abuse were reported in the 7-month period from baseline to follow-up. Wolfe and Sandler (1981) provided parent training and implemented contingency contracting for three abusive families. The training resulted in notable decreases in composite measures of parent and child total aversive behaviors, along with increases in child compliance with parental commands.

Wolfe, St. Lawrence, Graves, Brehony, Bradlyn, and Kelly (1982) trained an abusive mother in behavior management and also used an electronic "bug-in-the-ear" microphone to help the woman reduce abuse-related behaviors displayed toward her three children (hostile verbal and physical prompts). Improvements in the mother's positive behavior and in parent–child interactions were observed, and these positive changes had been maintained at 2-month follow-up. Thus, this approach appears to be useful for parents who are overtly hostile and punitive with their children. The bug-in-the-ear microphone has also been used successfully to increase the positive verbal and physical attention of an inattentive and neglectful mother of a 4-year-old boy (Crimmin, Bradlyn, St. Lawrence, & Kelly, 1984). These behaviors had been maintained at 4-month follow-up.

In what is perhaps the most comprehensively documented report to date on the treatment of child-abusive parents, Smith and Rachman (1984) provided further support for the behavior management training. Six families received and reported positive changes from the training. Interestingly, however, two of four control families also reported improvement (though one of these successful families had inadvertently received behavioral training). No incidents of abuse occurred throughout the treatment and up to a 3-year follow-up. Smith and Rachman argued that behavioral treatments can make a contribution if provided from a supportive (professional-helper) relationship over an extended period of time. Furthermore, the investigators suggested that, in working with abusive families, a detailed functional analysis be conducted to identify all the systems within the family that will affect the change. This advice seems consistent with that of recent investigators.

Although it appears especially worthwhile to help parents to learn effective and positive behavior-management techniques, it is important to acknowledge that child-abusing parents often have a multitude of problems. In fact, several investigators have contended that more attention should be given to the other problems exhibited by the abusing parent or family (e.g., marital dysfunction, drug or alcohol abuse, social insularity, and parental depression), perhaps even before addressing child discipline issues (Koverola, Elliot-Faust, & Wolf, 1984; Smith, 1984; Smith & Rachman, 1984).

Consistent with this more contextualist view is the "ecobehavioral" approach espoused by Lutzker and colleagues (Lutzker, 1984; Lutzker, Frame, & Rice, 1982; Lutzker & Rice, 1984; Lutzker, Wesch, & Rice, 1984). In this approach, child abuse is not viewed as stemming solely from parental problems in child discipline and deficits in handling stress. Rather, training is provided that includes nutrition, home safety, assertiveness and social support, job placement, marital counseling, alcoholism referral, and money management. Evidence that supports this multifaceted approach to a multifaceted problem is mounting (Lutzker & Lamazor, 1985).

Parent training in behavior management appears to be an effective intervention approach for psychologists working with child-abusive families. At the same time, it is clear that focusing entirely on ameliorating parenting-skill deficits may be inadequate. An ecobehavioral strategy appears to be a promising alternative to the uni- and bidimensional approaches found in most reports of behavioral parent-training interventions.

A more extensive discussion of these treatments, with related problems, is presented elsewhere. Obviously, however, the broad range of conditions that we have reviewed, many of which have been viewed as traditional medical problems, have an important psychological side as well.

# REFERENCES

Alexander, A. B. (1983). The nature of asthma. In P. J. McGrath & P. Firestone (Eds.), *Pediatric and adolescent behavioral medicine: Issues in treatment.* (New York: Springer.

American Lung Association. (1975). *Introduction to lung diseases.* (6th ed.). New York: Author.

Anderson, K. O., & Masur, F. T., III. (1983). Psychological preparation for invasive medical and dental procedures. *Journal of Behavioral Medicine, 6,* 1–40.

Anderson Johnson, C., Hansen, W. E., Collins, L. M., & Graham, J. W. (1986). High-school smoking prevention: Results of a three-year longitudinal study. *Journal of Behavioral Medicine, 9,* 439–452.

Andrasik, F., & Attanasio, V. (1985). Biofeedback in pediatrics: Current status and appraisal. In M. L. Wolraich & D. K. Routh (Eds.), *Advances in developmental and behavioral pediatrics* (Vol. 6). Greenwich, CT: JAI.

Andrasik, F., Blake, D. D., & McCarran, M. S. (1986). A biobehavioral analysis of pediatric headache. In N. A. Krasnegor, J. D. Arasteh, & M. F. Cataldo (Eds.), *Child health behavior: A behavioral pediatrics perspective.* New York: Wiley.

Attanasio, V., Andrasik, F., Burke, E. J., Blake, D. D., Kabela, E., & McCarran, M. S. (1985). Clinical issues in utilizing biofeedback with children. *Clinical Biofeedback and Health, 8,* 134–141.

Bakal, D. A. (1982). *The psychobiology of chronic headache.* New York: Springer.

Balaschak, B. A. (1976). Teacher-implemented behavior modification in a case of organically based epilepsy. *Journal of Consulting and Clinical Psychology, 44,* 218–223.

Belsky, J., & Steinberg, L. D. (1978). The effects of day care: A critical review. *Child Development, 49,* 929–949.

Bibace, R., & Walsh, M. E. (1981). Childen's conception of illness. In R. Bibace & M. E. Walsh (Eds.), *Children's conceptions of health, illness and bodily functions.* San Francisco: Jossey-Bass.

Bille, B. (1962). Migraine in school children. *Acta Paediatrica Scandinavica, 51,* 1–151.

Bille, B. (1981). Migraine in childhood and its prognosis. *Cephalalgia, 1,* 71–75.

Birch, L. L. (1980). Effects of peer models' food choices and eating behaviors on preschoolers' food preferences. *Child Development, 51,* 489–496.

Brownell, K. D., & Foreyt, J. P. (1985). Obesity. In D. H. Barlow (Ed.), *Clinical handbook of psychological disorders.* New York: Guilford Press.

Brownell, K. D., & Kaye, F. S. (1982). A school-based behavior modification, nutrition education, and physical activity program for obese children. *American Journal of Clinical Nutrition, 35,* 277–283.

Brownell, K. D., & Stunkard, A. J. (1978). Behavioral treatment of obesity in children. *American Journal of Diseases of Children, 132,* 403–412.

Burgess, R. L., & Conger, R. D. (1977). Family interaction patterns related to child abuse and neglect: Some preliminary findings. *Child Abuse and Neglect, 1,* 269–277.

Burgess, R. L., & Conger, R. D. (1978). Family interaction in abusive, neglectful and normal families. *Child Development, 49,* 1163–1173.

Burke, E. J., & Andrasik, F. (1987). *Home versus clinic-based treatments for pediatric migraine headache: Results of treatment through one year follow-up.* Manuscript under review.

Cataldo, M. F., Russo, D. C., & Freeman, J. M. (1979). A behavior analysis approach to high-rate myoclonic seizures. *Journal of Autism and Developmental Disorders, 9,* 413–427.

Chase, H. P., & Jackson, G. G. (1981). Stress and sugar control in children with insulin-dependent diabetes mellitus. *Journal of Pediatrics, 98,* 1011–1113.

Chassin, L. A., Presson, C. C., & Sherman, S. J. (1985). Stepping backward in order to step forward: An acquisition-oriented approach to primary prevention. *Journal of Consulting and Clinical Psychology, 53,* 612–622.

Coates, T. J., & Thoresen, C. E. (1978). Treating obesity in children and adolescents: A review. *American Journal of Public Health, 68,* 143–151.

Coates, T. J.. & Thoresen, C. E. (1981). Behavior and weight changes in three obese adolescents. *Behavior Therapy, 12,* 383–399.

Coates, T. J., Jeffery, R. W., Slinkard, L. A., Killen, J. D., & Danaher, B. G. (1982). Frequency of contact and monetary reward in weight loss, lipid changes, and blood pressure reduction with adolescents. *Behavior Therapy, 13,* 175–185.

Coppens, N. M. (1986). Cognitive characteristics as predictors of children's understanding of safety and prevention. *Journal of Pediatric Psychology, 11,* 189–201.

Creer, T. L. (1979). *Asthma therapy: A behavioral health care system for respiratory disorders.* New York: Springer.

Creer, T. L. (1982). Asthma. *Journal of Consulting and Clinical Psychology, 50,* 912–921.

Creer, T. L., & Leung, P. (1981). The development and evaluation of a self-management program for children with asthma. *Self-management educational programs for childhood asthma* (Vol. 2). Bethesda, MD: National Institute of Allergy and Infectious Disease.

Creer, T. L., & Winder, J. A. (1986). Asthma. In K. A. Holroyd & T. L. Creer (Eds.), *Self-management of chronic disease: Handbook of clinical interventions and research.* Orlando, FL: Academic.

Creer, T. L., Renne, C. M., & Chai, H. (1982). *The application of behavioral techniques to childhood asthma.* In D. Russo & J. Varni (Eds.), *Behavioral pediatrics: Research and practice.* New York: Plenum Press.

Crimmins, D. B., Bradlyn, A. S., St. Lawrence, J. S., & Kelly, J. A. (1984). A training technique for improving the parent-child interaction skills of an abusive-neglectful mother. *Child Abuse and Neglect, 8,* 533–539.

Crozier, J., & Katz, R. C. (1979). Social learning treatment of child abuse. *Journal of Behavior Therapy and Experimental Psychiatry, 10,* 213–220.

Danker, P. S., Miklich, D. R., Pratt, C., & Creer, T. L. (1975). An unsuccessful attempt to instrumentally condition peak expiratory flow rates in asthmatic children. *Journal of Psychosomatic Research, 19*, 209–213.

Davis, M., Saunders, D., Creer, T. L., & Chai, H. (1973). Relaxation training facilitated by biofeedback apparatus as a supplemental treatment in bronchial asthma. *Journal of Psychosomatic Research, 17*, 121–128.

Demarest, D. S., Hooke, J. F., & Erickson, M. T. (1984). Preoperative intervention for the reduction of anxiety in pediatric surgery patients. *Children's Health Care, 12*, 179–183.

Dershewitz, R. A., & Williamson, J. W. (1977). Prevention of childhood household injuries: A controlled clinical trial. *American Journal of Public Health, 67*, 1148–1180.

Deubner, D. C. (1977). An epidemiologic study of migraine and headache in 10–20 year olds. *Headache, 17*, 173–180.

Deykin, E. Y., Albert, J. J., & McNamara, J. J. (1985). A pilot study of the effect of exposure to child abuse or neglect on adolescent suicidal behavior. *American Journal of Psychiatry, 142*, 1299–1303.

Diamond, S., & Dalessio, D. J. (Eds.). (1986). *The practicing physician's approach to headache* (4th ed.). Baltimore: Williams & Wilkins.

Dietz, W. H. (1983). Childhood obesity: Susceptibility, cause, and management. *Journal of Pediatrics, 10*, 676–684.

Duff, R. S., Rowe, D. S., & Anderson, F. P. (1973). Patient care and student learning in a pediatric clinic. *Pediatrics, 50*, 839–846.

Dwyer, J. (1980). Diets for children and adolescents that meet the dietary goals. *American Journal of Diseases of Children, 134*, 1073–1080.

Eberly, T., Miles, M. S., Carter, M. C., Hennessey, J., & Riddle, I. (1985). Parental stress after the unexpected admission of a child to the intensive care unit. *Critical Care Quarterly, 8*, 57–65.

Egermark-Eriksson, I. (1982). Prevalence of headache in Swedish school-children. *Acta Paediatrica Scandinavica, 71*, 135–140.

Elkins, P. D., & Roberts, M. C. (1983). Psychological preparation for pediatric hospitalization. *Clinical Psychology Review, 3*, 275–295.

Elkins, P. D., & Roberts, M. C. (1984). A preliminary evaluation of hospital preparation for nonpatient children: Primary prevention in a "Let's Pretend Hospital." *Children's Health Care, 13*, 31–36.

Elkins, P. D., & Roberts, M. C. (1985). Reducing medical fears in a general population of children: A comparison of three audio-visual modeling procedures. *Journal of Pediatric Psychology, 10*, 65–75.

Ellerton, M., Caty, S., & Ritchie, J. A. (1985). Helping young children master intrusive procedures through play. *Children's Health Care, 13*, 167–173.

Englander-Golden, P., Elconin, J., & Miller, K. J. (1985). SAY IT STRAIGHT: Adolescent substance abuse prevention training. *Academic Psychology Bulletin, 7*, 65–79.

Englander-Golden, P., Elconin, J., Miller, K. J., & Schwarzkopf, A. B. (1986a). Brief SAY IT STRAIGHT training and followup in adolescent substance abuse prevention. *Journal of Primary Prevention, 6*, 219–230.

Englander-Golden, P., Elconin, J., & Satir, V. (1986b). Assertive/leveling communication and empathy in adolescent drug abuse prevention. *Journal of Primary Prevention, 6*, 231–243.

Epstein, L. H., Wing, R. R., Steranchak, L., Dickson, B., & Michelson, J. (1980). Comparison of family-based behavior modification and nutrition education for childhood obesity. *Journal of Pediatric Psychology, 5*, 25–36.

Epstein, L. H., Beck, S., Figueroa, J., Farkas, G., Kazdin, A. E., Daneman, D., & Becker, D. (1981a). The effects of targeting improvements in urine glucose on metabolic control in children with insulin dependent diabetes. *Journal of Applied Behavior Analysis, 14*, 365–375.

Epstein, L. H., Wing, R. R., Koeske, R. R., Andrasik, F., & Ossip, D. (1981b). Child and parent weight loss in family-based behavior modification programs. *Journal of Consulting and Clinical Psychology, 49*, 674–685.

Epstein, L. H., Wing, R. R., Koeske, R., Ossip, D. J., & Beck, S. (1982). A comparison of lifestyle and programmed aerobic exercise on weight and fitness changes in obese children. *Behavior Therapy, 13*, 651–665.

Epstein, L. H., Wing, R. R., Koeske, R., & Valoski, A. (1984). The effects of diet and diet plus exercise on weight change in parents and children. *Journal of Consulting and Clinical Psychology, 52*, 429–437.

Epstein, L. H., Koeske, R., Wing, R. R., & Valoski, A. (1986). The effect of family variables on child weight change. *Health Psychology, 5*, 1–11.

Evans, M. B. (1985). Emotional stress and diabetic control: A postulated model for the effect of emotional distress upon intermediary metabolism in the diabetic. *Biofeedback and Self-Regulation, 10,* 241–254.

Evans, R. I. (1976). Smoking in children: Developing a social-psychological strategy of deterrence. *Journal of Preventive Medicine, 5,* 122–127.

Feldman, G. M. (1976). The effect of biofeedback training on respiratory resistance of asthmatic children. *Psychosomatic Medicine, 38,* 27–34.

Ferguson, B. F. (1979). Preparing young children for hospitalization: A comparison of two methods. *Pediatrics, 64,* 656–664.

Fireman, P., Friday, G. A., Gira, C., Vierthaler, W. A., & Michaels, L. (1981). Teaching self-management skills to asthmatic children and their parents in an ambulatory care setting. *Pediatrics, 68,* 341–348.

Fisher, E. B., Jr., Delamater, A. M., Bertelson, A. D., & Kirkley, B. G. (1982). Psychological factors in diabetes and its treatment. *Journal of Consulting and Clinical Psychology, 50,* 993–1003.

Flay, B. R. (1985). What do we know about the social science approach to smoking prevention? In C. S. Bell (Ed.), *Prevention research: Deterring drug abuse among children and adolescents.* Washington, DC: U.S. Government Printing Office.

Fosson, A., & deQuan, N. M. (1984). Reassuring and talking with hospitalized children. *Children's Health Care, 13,* 37–44.

Foster, G. D., Wadden, T. A., & Brownell, K. D. (1985). Peer-led program for the treatment and prevention of obesity in the schools. *Journal of Consulting and Clinical Psychology, 5,* 538–540.

Fowler, J. E., Budzynski, T. H., & VandenBergh, R. L. (1976). Effects of an EMG biofeedback relaxation program on the control of diabetes. *Biofeedback and Self-Regulation, 1,* 105–112.

Gambrill, E. (1983). Behavioral interventions with child abuse and neglect. In M. Hersen, R. M. Eisler, & P. M. Miller (Eds.), *Progress in behavior modification* (Vol. 15). New York: Academic Press.

Gardner, J. E. (1967). Behavior therapy treatment approach to a psychogenic seizure case. *Journal of Consulting Psychology, 31,* 209–212.

Gratz, R. R. (1979). Accident injury in childhood: A literature review on pediatric trauma. *Journal of Trauma, 19,* 551–555.

Gross, A. M. (1982). Self-management training and medication compliance in children with diabetes. *Child and Family Behavior Therapy, 4,* 47–55.

Gross, A. M., Johnson, W. G., Wildman, H., & Mullet, N. (1981). Coping skills training with pre-adolescent diabetics. *Child and Family Behavior Therapy, 3,* 141–153.

Gross, A. M., Heimann, L., Shapiro, R., & Schultz, R. M. (1983). Children with diabetes: Social skill training and hemoglobin Ac levels. *Behavior Modification, 7,* 151–164.

Gross, A. M., Magalnick, L. J., & Richardson, P. (1985). Self-management training with families of insulin-dependent diabetic children: A controlled long-term investigation. *Child and Family Behavior Therapy, 7,* 35–50.

Hamburg, D. A., & Brown, S. S. (1978). The science base and social context of health maintenance: An overview. *Science, 200,* 847–849.

Hanson, C. L., & Henggeler, S. W. (1984). Metabolic control in adolescents with diabetes: An examination of systemic variables. *Family Systems Medicine, 2,* 5–16.

Hillman, H. S., Jones, R. T., & Farmer, L. (1986). The acquisition and maintenance of fire emergency skills: Effects of rationale and behavioral practice. *Journal of Pediatric Psychology, 11,* 169–176.

Hindi-Alexander, M., & Cropp, G. J. A. (1981). Community and family programs for children with asthma. *Annals of Allergy, 46,* 143–148.

Hobbs, S. A., Beck, S. J., & Wansley, R. A. (1984). Pediatric behavioral medicine: Directions in treatment and prevention. In M. Hersen, R. M. Eisler, & P. M. Miller (Eds.). *Progress in Behavior Modification* (Vol. 16). New York: Academic Press.

Hoffman-Plotkin, D., & Twentyman, C. T. (1984). A multimodal assessment of behavioral and cognitive deficits in abused and neglected preschoolers. *Child Development, 55,* 794–802.

Holroyd, K. A. (1986). Reccurent headache. In K. A. Holroyd & T. L. Creer (Eds.), *Self-management of chronic disease: Handbook of clinical interventions and research.* New York: Academic.

Howes, C., & Eldridge, R. (1985). Responses of abused, neglected, and non-maltreated children to the behavior of their peers. *Journal of Applied Developmental Psychology, 6,* 261–270.

Ince, L. P. (1976). The use of relaxation training and a conditioned stimulus in the elimination of epileptic seizures in a child: A case study. *Journal of Behavior Therapy and Experimental Psychiatry, 7,* 39–42.

Isaacs, C. D. (1982). Treatment of child abuse: A review of the behavioral interventions. *Journal of Applied Behavior Analysis, 15,* 273–294.

Johnson, M. R. (1979). Mental health interventions with medically ill children: A review of the literature 1970–1977. *Journal of Pediatric Psychology, 4,* 147–163.

Johnson, M. V., & Freeman, J. M. (1981). Pharmacological advances in seizure control. *Pediatric Clinics of North America, 28,* 179–194.

Johnson, S. B. (1980). Psychosocial factors in juvenile diabetes: A review. *Journal of Behavioral Medicine, 3,* 95–116.

Johnstone, D. E. (1978). A study of the natural history of bronchial asthma in children. *American Journal of Diseases of Children, 115,* 213–216.

Jones, R. T., Kazdin, A. E., & Haney, J. I. (1981). Social validation and training of emergency fire safety skills for potential injury prevention and life saving. *Journal of Applied Behavior Analysis, 14,* 249–260.

Kabela, E., & Andrasik, F. (1987). *A process analysis of thermal biofeedback and cognitive coping training for pediatric migraine.* Unpublished manuscript.

Kanoy, K. W., & Schroeder, C. S. (1985). Suggestions to parents about common behavior problems in a pediatric primary care office: Five years of follow-up. *Journal of Pediatric Psychology, 10,* 15–30.

Kempe, H. C., & Helfer, R. E. (1972). *Helping the battered child and his family.* New York: Lippincott.

Khan, A. U. (1977). Effectiveness of biofeedback and counter-conditioning in the treatment of bronchial asthma. *Journal of Psychosomatic Research, 21,* 97–104.

Khan, A. U., Staerk, M., & Bonk, C. (1973). Role of counter-conditioning in the treatment of asthma. *Journal of Psychosomatic Research, 17,* 389–392.

Klinzing, D. R., & Klinzing, D. G. (1977). Communicating with young children about hospitalization. *Communication Education, 26,* 307–313.

Knox, J. E., & Hayes, V. E. (1983). Hospitalization of a chronically ill child: A stressful time for parents. *Issues in Comprehensive Pediatric Nursing, 6,* 217–226.

Kotses, H., & Glaus, K. (1981). Applications of biofeedback to the treatment of asthma: A critical review. *Biofeedback and Self-Regulation, 6,* 573–593.

Kotses, H., Glaus, K. D., Crawford, P. L., Edwards, J. E., & Scheer, M. S. (1976). Operant reduction of frontalis EMG activity in the treatment of asthma in children. *Journal of Psychosomatic Research, 20,* 453–459.

Kotses, H., Glaus, K. D., Bricel, S. K., Edwards, J. E., & Crawford, P. L. (1978). Operant muscular relaxation and peak expiratory flow rate in asthmatic children. *Journal of Psychosomatic Research, 22,* 17–23.

Koverola, C., Elliot-Faust, D., & Wolfe, D. A. (1984). Clinical issues in the behavioral treatment of a child abusive mother experiencing multiple life stresses. *Journal of Clinical Child Psychology, 13,* 187–191.

Kudrow, L. (1982). Paradoxical effects of frequent analgesic use. In M. Critchley, A. P. Friedman, S. Gorini, & F. Sicuteri (Eds.), *Advances in neurology: Headache: Physiopathological and clinical concepts* (Vol. 33). New York: Raven Press.

Lake, A. E. (1981). Behavioral assessment considerations in the management of headache. *Headache, 21,* 170–178.

Lambert, S. A. (1984). Variables that affect the school-age child's reaction to hospitalization and surgery: A review of the literature. *Maternal-Child Nursing Journal, 13,* 1–18.

Langley, J., McGee, R., Silva, P., & Williams, S. (1983). Child behavior and accidents. *Journal of Pediatric Psychology, 8,* 181–189.

Larsson, B., & Melin, L. (1986). Chronic headaches in adolescents: Treatment in a school setting with relaxation training as compared with information-contact and self-registration. *Pain, 25,* 325–336.

Linn, S., Beardslee, W., & Patenaude, A. F. (1986). Puppet therapy with pediatric bone marrow transplant patients. *Journal of Pediatric Psychology, 11,* 37–46.

Lowe, K., & Lutzker, J. R. (1979). Increasing compliance to a medical regimen with a juvenile diabetic. *Behavior Therapy, 10,* 57–64.

Lubar, J. F., & Bahler, W. W. (1976). Behavioral management of epileptic seizures following EEG biofeedback training of the sensorimotor rhythm. *Biofeedback and Self-Regulation, 1,* 77–104.

Lutzker, J. R. (1984). Project 12-ways: Treating child abuse and neglect from an ecobehavioral perspective. In R. F. Dangel & R. A. Polster (Eds.), *Parent training: Foundations of research and practice.* New York: Guilford Press.

Lutzker, J. R., & Lamazor, E. A. (1985). Behavioral pediatrics: Research, treatment, recommendations. In M. Hersen, R. M. Eisler, & P. M. Miller (Eds.), *Progress in behavior modification* (Vol. 19). New York: Academic Press.

Lutzker, J. R., & Rice, J. M. (1984). Project 12-ways: Measuring outcome of a large-scale in-home service for the treatment and prevention of child abuse and neglect. *Child Abuse and Neglect, 8,* 519–524.

Lutzker, J. R., Frame, R. E., & Rice, J. M. (1982). Project 12-ways: An ecobehavioral approach to the treatment of child abuse and neglect. *Education and Treatment of Children, 5,* 141–155.

Lutzker, J. R., Wesch, D., & Rice, J. M. (1984). A review of Project "12-ways": An ecobehavioral approach to the treatment and prevention of child abuse and neglect. *Advances in Behaviour Research and Therapy, 6,* 63–73.

McAlister, A., Perry, C., Killen, J., Slinkard, L. A., & Maccoby, N. (1980). Pilot study of smoking, alcohol, and drug abuse prevention. *American Journal of Public Health, 70,* 719–721.

McCarran, M. S., & Andrasik, F. (1987). Migraine and tension headaches. In L. Michelson & L. M. Ascher (Eds.), *Anxiety and stress disorders: Cognitive-behavioral assessment and treatment.* New York: Guilford Press.

McCord, J. (1983). A forty year perspective on effects of child abuse and neglect. *Child Abuse and Neglect, 7,* 265–170.

MacDonald, D. I. (1984). *Drugs, drinking, and adolescents.* Chicago: Year Book Medical Publishers.

McGrath, P. A. (1987). The multidimensional assessment and management of recurrent pain syndromes in children. *Behaviour Research and Therapy, 25,* 251–262.

McGrath, P. J., & Feldman, W. (1986). Clinical approach to recurrent abdominal pain in children. *Developmental and Behavioral Pediatrics, 7,* 56–61.

McGrath, P. J., Cunningham, S. J., Goodman, J. T., & Unruh, A. (1986a). The clinical measurement of pain in children: A review. *Clinical Journal of Pain, 1,* 221–227.

McGrath, P. J., Dunn-Geier, J. D., Cunningham, S. J., Brunette, R., D'Astous, J., Humphreys, P., Latter, J., & Keene, D. (1986b). Psychological guidelines for helping children cope with chronic benign intractable pain. *Clinical Journal of Pain, 1,* 229–233.

McNabb, W. L., Wilson-Pessano, S. R., & Jacobs, A. M. (1986). Critical self-management competencies for children with asthma. *Journal of Pediatric Psychology, 11,* 103–117.

Maddux, J. E., Roberts, M. C., Sledden, E. A., & Wright, L. (1986). Developmental issues in child health psychology. *American Psychologist, 41,* 25–34.

Manheimer, D. E., & Mellinger, G. D. (1967). Personality characteristics of the child accident repeater. *Child Development, 38,* 491–513.

Marks, A. (1980). Aspects of biosocial screening and health maintenance in adolescents. *Pediatric Clinics of North America, 27,* 153–161.

Melamed, B. G., & Siegel, L. J. (1975). Reduction of anxiety in children facing hospitalization and surgery by use of filmed modeling. *Journal of Consulting and Clinical Psychology, 43,* 511–521.

Melamed, B. G., Meyer, R., Gee, C., & Soule, L. (1976). The influence of time and type of preparation on children's adjustment to hospitalization. *Journal of Pediatric Psychology, 1,* 31–37.

Oei, T. S., & Fea, A. (1987). Smoking prevention programs for children: A review. *Journal of Drug Education, 17,* 11–42.

Oldershaw, L., Walters, G. C., & Hall, D. K. (1986). Control strategies and noncompliance in abusive mother-child dyads: An observational study. *Child Development, 57,* 722–732.

Oster, R. A. (1983). Peer counseling: Drug and alcohol abuse prevention. *Journal of Primary Prevention, 3,* 188–199.

Ottinger, D. R., & Roberts, M. C. (1980). A university-based predoctoral practicum in pediatric psychology. *Professional Psychology, 11,* 707–713.

Parcel, G. S., & Nader, P. R. (1977). Evaluation of a pilot school health education program for asthmatic children. *Journal of School Health, 47,* 453–456.

Parker, L. E., & Cincirpini, P. M. (1984). Behavioral medicine with children: Applications in chronic disease. In M. Hersen, R. M. Eisler, & P. M. Miller (Eds.), *Progress in behavior bodification* (Vol. 17). New York: Academic Press.

Perrin, E. C., & Gerrity, P. S. (1981). Clinician's assessments of children's understanding of illness. *American Journal of Diseases of Children, 137,* 874–878.

Perry, R. P., LeBow, M. D., & Buser, M. M. (1979). An exploration of observational learning in modifying selected eating responses of obese children. *International Journal of Obesity, 3,* 193–199.

Peterson, L., & Mori, L. (1985). Prevention of child injury: An overview of targets, methods, and tactics for psychologists. *Journal of Consulting and Clinical Psychology, 53,* 586–595.

Peterson, L., & Ridley-Johnson, R. (1984). Preparation of well children in the classroom: An unexpected contrast between the academic lecture and filmed modeling methods. *Journal of Pediatric Psychology, 9*, 349–361.

Peterson, L., & Shigetomi, C. (1981). The use of coping techniques to minimize anxiety in hospitalized children. *Behavior Therapy, 12*, 1–14.

Peterson, L., Ridley-Johnson, R., Tracy, K., & Mullins, L. L. (1984a). Developing cost-effective presurgical preparation: A comparative analysis. *Journal of Pediatric Psychology, 9*, 439–455.

Peterson, L., Schultheis, K., Ridley-Johnson, R., Miller, D. J., & Tracy, K. (1984b). Comparison of three modeling procedures on the presurgical and postsurgical reactions of children. *Behavior Therapy, 15*, 197–203.

Peterson, L., Mori, L., & Scissors, C. (1986). Mom or dad says I shouldn't: Supervised and unsupervised children's knowledge of their parents' rules for home safety. *Journal of Pediatric Psychology, 11*, 177–188.

Pohl, S. L., Gonder-Frederick, L., & Cox, D. J. (1984). Diabetes mellitus: An overview. *Behavioral Medicine Update, 6*, 3–7.

Rackemann, F. M., & Edwards, M. D. (1952). Medical progress: Asthma in children: Follow-up study of 688 patients after 20 years. *New England Journal of Medicine, 246*, 815–858.

Rakos, R. F., Grodek, M. V., & Mack, K. K. (1985). The impact of a self-administered behavioral intervention program on pediatric asthma. *Journal of Psychosomatic Research, 29*, 101–108.

Ramsden, R., Friedman, B., & Williamson, D. (1983). Treatment of childhood headache reports with contingency management procedures. *Journal of Clinical Child Psychology, 12*, 202–206.

Reed, C. E., & Townley, R. G. (1978). Asthma: Classification and pathogenesis. In E. Middleton, Jr., C. E. Reed, & E. F. Ellis (Eds.), *Allergy: Principles and practice*. St. Louis: C. V. Mosby.

Reidy, T. J. (1977). The aggressive characteristics of abused and neglected children. *Journal of Clinical Psychology, 33*, 1140–1145.

Richter, I. L., McGrath, P. J., Humphreys, P. J., Goodman, J. T., Firestone, P., & Keene, D. (1986). Cognitive and relaxation treatment of pediatric migraine. *Pain, 25*, 195–203.

Rivara, F. P. (1982). Epidemiology of childhood injuries. *American Journal of Diseases of Children, 136*, 399–405.

Roberts, M. C. (1986a). Health promotion and problem prevention in pediatric psychology: An overview. *Journal of Pediatric Psychology, 11*, 147–161.

Roberts, M. C. (1986b). *Pediatric psychology: Psychological interventions and strategies for pediatric problems*. New York: Plenum Press.

Roberts, M. C., Maddux, J. E., & Wright, L. (1984). The developmental perspective in behavioral health. In J. D. Matarazo, N. E. Miller, S. M. Weiss, & J. A. Herd (Eds.), *Behavioral health: A handbook of health enhancement and disease prevention*. New York: Wiley.

Rose, M. I., Firestone, P., Heick, H. M. C., & Faught, A. K. (1983). The effects of anxiety management training on the control of juvenile diabetes mellitus. *Journal of Behavioral Medicine, 6*, 381–395.

Roskies, E., Bedard, P., Gauvreau-Guilbault, H., & LaFortune, D. (1975). Emergency hospitalization of young children: Some neglected psychological considerations. *Medical Care, 8*, 570–581.

Rothner, A. D. (1978)., Headaches in children: A review. *Headache, 18*, 169–175.

Rubin, D. H., Leventhal, J. M., Sadock, R. T., Letovsky, E., Schottland, P., Clemente, I., & McCarthy, P. (1986). Educational intervention by computer in childhood asthma: A randomized clinical trial testing the use of a new teaching intervention in childhood asthma. *Pediatrics, 77*, 1–10.

Sallade, J. B. (1980). Group counseling with children who have migraine headaches. *Elementary School Guidance and Counseling*, 87–89.

Sandler, J., Van Dercar, C., & Milhoan, M. (1978). Training child abusers in positive reinforcement practices. *Behavior Research and Therapy, 16*, 169–175.

Saper, J. R. (1987). Ergotamine dependency: A review. *Headache, 27*, 435–438.

Scadding, J. G. (1966). Patterns of respiratory insufficiency. *Lancet, 1*, 701–704.

Schaefer, C. E., & Millman, H. L. (1981). *How to help children with common problems*. New York: Van Nostrand Reinhold.

Schafer, L. C., Glasgow, R. E., & McCaul, K. D. (1982). Increasing the adherence of diabetic adolescents. *Journal of Behavioral Medicine, 5*, 353–362.

Scherr, M. S., Crawford, P. L.. Sergent, C. B., & Scherr, C. A. (1975). Effects of biofeedback techniques on chronic asthma in a summer camp environment. *Annals of Allergy, 35*, 289–295.

Schinke, S. P., & Gilchrist, L. D. (1985). Preventing substance abuse with children and adolescents. *Journal of Consulting and Clinical Psychology, 53*, 596–602.

Seifert, A. R., & Lubar, J. F. (1975). Reduction of epileptic seizures through EEG biofeedback training. *Biological Psychology, 3*, 157–184.

Siegel, L. J. (1976). Preparation of children for hospitalization: A selected review of the research literature. *Journal of Pediatric Psychology, 1*, 26–30.

Sillanpaa, M. (1983a). Changes in the prevalence of migraine and other headaches during the first seven school years. *Headache, 23*, 15–19.

Sillanpaa, M. (1983b). Prevalence of headache in prepuberty. *Headache, 23*, 10–14.

Simonds, J. F. (1979). Emotions and compliance in diabetic children. *Psychosomatics, 20*, 544–551.

Skipper, J. K., Jr., & Leonard, R. C. (1968). Children, stress, and hospitalization: A field experiment. *Journal of Health and Social Behavior, 9*, 275–287.

Smith, J. E. (1984). Non-accidental injury to Children: 1. A review of the behavioural interventions. *Behaviour Research and Therapy, 22*, 331–347.

Smith, J. E., & Rachman, S. J. (1984). Non-accidental injury to Children: 2. A controlled evaluation of a behavioural management programme. *Behaviour Research and Therapy, 22*, 349–366.

Snow, W. H., Gilchrist, L. D., & Schinke, S. P. (1985). A critique of progress in adolescent smoking prevention. *Children and Youth Services Review, 7*, 1–19.

Surwit, R. S., & Feinglos, M. N. (1984). Stress and diabetes. *Behavioral Medicine Update, 6*, 8–11.

Trawick-Smith, J., & Thompson, R. H. (1984). Preparing young children for hospitalization. *Young Children, 39*, 57–63.

Turk, D. C., Meichenbaum, D., & Genest, M. (1983). *Pain and behavioral medicine: A cognitive-behavioral perspective.* New York: Guilford Press.

Twardosz, S., Weddle, K., Borden, L., & Stevens, E. (1986). A comparison of three methods of preparing children for surgery. *Behavior Therapy, 17*, 14–25.

Varni, J. W. (1983). *Clinical behavioral pediatrics: An interdisciplinary biobehavioral approach.* New York: Pergamon Press.

Varni, J. W., & Thompson, K. L. (1985). *The Varni/Thompson Pediatric Pain Questionnaire.* Unpublished manuscript.

Varni, J. W., Jay, S. M., Masek, B. J., & Thompson, K. L. (1986). Cognitive behavioral assessment and management of pediatric pain. In A. D. Holzman & D. C. Turk (Eds.), *Pain management: A handbook of psychological treatment approaches.* New York: Pergamon Press.

Vernon, D. T. A., & Bailey, W. C. (1974). The use of motion pictures in thepsychological preparation of children for induction anesthesia. *Anesthesiology, 40*, 68–72.

Visitainer, M. A., & Wolfer, J. A. (1975). Psychological preparation for surgical pediatric patients: The effects on children's and parents' stress responses and adjustment. *Pediatrics, 56*, 187–202.

Wadsworth, J., Burnell, I., Taylor, B., & Neveille, J. (1983). Family type and accidents in preschool children. *Journal of Epidemiology and Community Health, 37*, 100–104.

Walker, C. E. (1979). Behavioral interventions in a pediatric setting. In J. R. McNamara (Ed.), *Behavioral approaches to medicine: Applications and analysis.* New York: Plenum Press.

Weil, W. B. (1977). Current controversies in childhood obesity. *Journal of Pediatrics, 91*, 175–187.

Weiss, J. H. (1981). Superstuff. *Self-management educational programs for childhood asthma* (Vol. 2). Bethesda, MD: National Institute of Allergy and Infectious Diseases.

Whitt, J. K., Dykstra, W., & Taylor, C. A. (1979). Children's conception of illness and cognitive development. Implications for pediatric practice. *Clinical Pediatrics, 18*, 327–335.

Wing, R. R., Epstein, L. H., Nowalk, M. P., & Lamparski, D. M. (1986). Behavioral self-regulation in the treatment of patients with diabetes mellitus. *Psychological Bulletin, 99*, 78–89.

Wolfe, D. A., & Sandler, J. (1981). Training abusive parents in effective child management. *Behavior Modification, 5*, 320–335.

Wolfe, D. A., St. Lawrence, J., Graves, K., Brehony, K., Bradlyn, D., & Kelly, J. A. (1982). Intensive behavioral parent training for a child abusive mother. *Behavior Therapy, 13*, 438–451.

Wolfer, J. A., & Visitainer, M. A. (1975). Pediatric surgical patients' and parents' stress responses and adjustment as a function of psychological preparation and stress-point nursing care. *Nursing Research, 24*, 244–255.

Wolfer, J. A., & Visitainer, M. A. (1979). Prehospital psychological preparation for tonsillectomy patients: Effects on children's and parents' adjustment. *Pediatrics, 64*, 646–655.

Wright, L., Schaefer, A. B., & Solomons, G. (1979). *Encyclopedia of pediatric psychology.* Baltimore: University Park Press.

Yeaton, W. H., & Bailey, J. D. (1978). Teaching pedestrian safety skills to young children: An analysis and one-year follow-up. *Journal of Applied Behavior Analysis, 11,* 315–329.

Yen, S., & McIntire, R. W. (1971). Operant therapy for constant headache complaint: A simple response-cost approach. *Psychological Reports, 28,* 267–270.

Zlutnick, S., Mayville, W. J., & Moffat, S. (1975). Modification of seizure disorders: The interruption of behavioral chains. *Journal of Applied Behavior Analysis, 8,* 1–12.

# VI    Treatment Approaches:
# Physical and Learning Disabilities

No book on childhood problems would be complete without a thorough discussion of mental retardation, learning disabilities, and sensory and physical handicaps. Mental retardation in particular has received a great deal of empirical study, particularly with respect to psychological interventions. Drug studies have been less frequent with mental retardation and learning disabilities than with many other problems. Thus, one pharmacotherapy chapter is included for both topics. It should be emphasized that such a presentation should not be viewed as an endorsement of need or effectiveness. Rather, this approach reflects our current state of knowledge.

Perhaps the most understudied of the many groups covered in this book are the sensory and physically handicapped, who represent a highly underserved population. It should be underscored that this group of children deserves greater attention in the future. However, there is currently some valuable information that will highlight the need for researchers and practitioners to study this area more extensively.

# 19

# *Mental Retardation*
## *Psychological Therapies*

## Johannes Rojahn and Jennifer Burkhart

## Introduction

The human condition of mentally retarded persons has historically lingered in the shadow of society's attention. The relative concern about these people has increased considerably in many countries, specifically since the end of World War II. However, a number of problems remain to be addressed. One problem area is mental health care for mentally retarded children and adolescents, which has only recently become duly recognized (e.g., Matson, 1985b; Matson & Barrett, 1982; Menolascino & Stark, 1985).

Psychological therapies have played a significant role in the habilitation and treatment of mentally retarded children and adolescents in recent years. The following pages focus on various treatment techniques for emotional and behavioral problems among the mentally retarded that have shown therapeutic value or at least have demonstrated some potential. This chapter summarizes the basic principles of the different treatment modalities and briefly describes their procedures, along with some illustrations from the scientific literature. Some areas of treatment application are also highlighted. The selected treatment studies are examples of many other good studies, and we make no claim to an exhaustive literature review. Where possible, references are provided for those who are looking for a more detailed or comprehensive picture in certain areas. There is a clear focus on those forms of therapy that have been subjected to the scrutiny of empirical evaluations. Before different psychological treatments and their applications are discussed, however, a few key terms must be defined.

## *Psychological Therapies*

Psychological therapies are intervention procedures for a goal-directed change of a person's behaviors or emotions; they are based primarily on psychological theories. The main treatment variables are psychological in nature, which means that they operate through experience. The following psychological treatment approaches are presented:

*Behavior modification*, derived from learning theories of operant and classical

---

Johannes Rojahn and Jennifer Burkhart • Western Psychiatric Institute and Clinic, University of Pittsburgh School of Medicine, Pittsburgh, Pennsylvania 15213.

JOHANNES ROJAHN AND
JENNIFER BURKHART

conditioning, has been the most influential treatment approach used with mentally retarded clients. It has been adapted for a number of different problem areas and has resulted in a variety of different treatment procedures. In fact, some forms of behavioral treatment, such as overcorrection, were originally developed with mentally retarded persons. We will also concentrate on a relatively new and promising area of treatment research, namely, the interaction of *behavior modification* and *pharmacotherapy*.

*Biofeedback* techniques and instrumentation have been under-researched in this population but are also briefly addressed.

*Cognitive-behavior modification* was discovered to be of great benefit for some kinds of problems in mentally retarded persons, but it has generally been restricted to higher functioning, verbal clients (Whitman, Burgio, & Johnston, 1984).

Various forms of *psychotherapy* have also been tried with mentally retarded patients. Their effectiveness and utility, however, are more difficult to evaluate because empirical assessments of treatment outcome are rarely performed in this field.

## Mental Retardation

Mental retardation (MR) is defined as significantly subaverage general intellectual functioning that is accompanied by deficits in adaptive behavior, and that becomes manifest during the developing period (set between birth and the 18th birthday). This MR definition was adopted by the *American Association on Mental Retardation* (AAMR; Grossman, 1977). The important aspects of this definition are that it defines mental retardation without reference to any specific theory of etiology and implies no notions about its prognosis. Intellectual functioning is generally viewed vis-à-vis sociocultural standards. Retarded intellectual performance is statistically defined by a score of more than two standard deviations below the test mean for a certain age level on a standardized general intelligence test. The classification of the degree of mental retardation also follows AAMR guidelines, with mild, moderate, severe, and profound levels of mental retardation. These levels correspond to 2, 3, 4, and 5 standard deviations below the mean score of an IQ test, respectively. The IQ tests most commonly used with mentally retarded persons are the Stanford Binet (Thorndike, Hagen, & Sattler, 1986) and the Wechsler Scales (WISC-R, WPPSI, WAIS). The interested reader is referred to Sattler (1982) or Morgenstern (1983) for a more detailed account of IQ assessment in mental retardation.

*Adaptive behavior* refers to the degree of personal and social independence. It is usually assessed by standardized rating scales that measure levels of personal effectiveness, independence, and social responsibilities in comparison to sociocultural expectations or norms. Adaptive behavior scales frequently include an assessment of adaptive behavior as well as maladaptive behavior. The most commonly used scales are the AAMR Adaptive Behavior Scale (Nihira, Foster, Shellhaas, & Leland, 1974) and the revised Vineland Social Maturity Scale (Sparrow, Balla, & Cicchetti, 1984). For a more comprehensive discussion of the assessment of adaptive behavior, see Leland (1983), Sattler (1982), or Spreat, Roszkowski, and Isett (1983).

The term *psychopathology* in mental retardation is somewhat troublesome. First, there is a definition problem. Psychopathology is a descriptive category that requires a distinction between normality and pathology. This distinction, however, is extremely difficult to make in a globally satisfactory manner because normality and pathology are somewhat arbitrary concepts. They vary with the distinction criteria applied; in other words, defining pathology involves a value judgment (Rutter, Tizard, & Whitmore, 1981).

Second, determining what is "normal" or "abnormal" in a mentally retarded person is even more complicated than in the nonretarded population because of the diagnostic overshadowing (Reiss & Szyszko, 1983) caused by a confound of phenomena that are associated with retarded development and those that are considered psychopathological (Costello, 1982). A good example is abnormal movements, which could potentially be stereotypical behavior, seizure-related activity, or another form of dyskinetic movement. Also, certain forms of psychopathology may appear to be phenomenologically very different in a mentally person and in a normal-IQ individual. A theoretical conceptualization of psychopathology in mental retardation is therefore necessary, on the basis of which data can be collected that will refine the diagnostic criteria and that will improve treatment decisions (Matson, 1985a).

Third, the term *psychopathology* is a term associated with medicine and the medical model of disease. Thus, behavioral and emotional problems are considered symptoms of an underlying disease or pathology. Consequently, the underlying disease becomes the primary treatment target. This, for example, is the presumed rationale for the administration of psychotropic drugs by the physician. The management and control of "symptoms," as attempted by some treatment forms, are therefore, from this point of view, considered less than therapeutic. However, to date, neither the medical disease model in general nor drug treatment specificly have contributed substantially to a *rational* treatment of the most prevalent behavioral or emotional problems in the mentally retarded population, such as aggression or self-injury. The adoption of the medical disease model as the primary conceptualization of psychopathology in mental retardation is therefore, at this point, unwarranted. Behavior modification, for instance, which has achieved quite remarkable treatment success in some areas of psychopathology with mentally retarded persons, follows quite a different disease model. In fact, the term *psychopathology* has been avoided for a long time in the behavior modification and assessment literature, presumably because of these connotations. From a behavioral standpoint, the determining factors maintaining aberrant behavior are assumed to lie in the interaction of the individual with his or her environment, rather than in an undetected biological defect. Systematic control of the targeted "behavior problem" is therefore a legitimate treatment goal for the behavior analyst, and it is achieved by systematic changes of these environmental conditions. Cognitive-behavior modification usually adheres to yet another model of disease, which is based on changing the maladaptive thought processes assumed to mediate aberrant behavior.

Hence, the term *psychopathology* will be used here descriptively without reference to any etiological model or specific school of thought. For the purpose of this chapter, *psychopathology* refers pragmatically to psychiatric syndromes, such as affective disorders, psychotic disorders, or anxiety disorders, as listed in the American Psychiatric Association's *Diagnostic and Statistical Manual of Mental Disorders, Third Edition—Revised* (DSM-III-R; APA, 1987), as well as to other problem behaviors that are found primarily among mentally retarded persons, such as stereotypical, self-injurious, and aggressive behavior. The terms *psychopathology, psychiatric disorder, emotional disorder*, and *mental illness* are used interchangeably in this chapter.

## Dual Diagnosis

It is important to recognize that psychopathological disorders are not a constituting part of mental retardation. They are conditions that can occur in mentally normal as well as in mentally retarded persons. Psychopathology in mental retardation has been ignored for a long time. In fact, it was believed that mental illness could not occur in a mentally retarded person because a certain intellectual level, with the potential for reasoning and complex thought, was a prerequisite of emotional disorders (Lewis & McLean, 1982). Most epidemiological and other survey studies, however, have clearly and consistently indicated that such psychopathological conditions do exist in mentally retarded persons, and that their prevalence is, in fact, much higher in the mentally retarded than in the nonretarded population (Chazan, 1964; Chess & Hassibi, 1970; Corbett, 1985; Dewan, 1948; Phillips & Williams, 1975; Pollack, 1944; Rutter, Graham, & Yule, 1970). This lack of recognition has presumably resulted in the limited access of mentally retarded persons with emotional problems to mental health services, which have been traditionally separated from mental retardation services in the United States. In addition, mental-health treatment modalities for mentally retarded individuals living in the community are rarely the focus of research (Reatig & Raskin, 1985), so that funding from the National Institute of Mental Health (NIMH) and other mental-health research-funding agencies has been scarce for the retarded population. As a consequence, mentally retarded persons with mental health problems have been referred to as *dually diagnosed*. Although this term has been criticized by some concerned experts as representing a greater disservice than a benefit to those labeled dually diagnosed (Szymanski & Grossman, 1984), it does at least emphasize the multiple handicap of mentally retarded persons with mental health problems.

## Assessment and Diagnosis

The clinical assessment and diagnosis of psychopathology in mentally retarded children and adolescents, specifically in the more severely mentally retarded persons, are limited by population characteristics, such as handicapped communication skills. Typically, assessment and diagnosis rest on repeated *clinical observations* over time, which are recommended to be performed in as many settings as possible (Costello, 1982). Psychiatric and behavioral *interviews* with the patient or with significant others are another important source of diagnostic information (Matson & Frame, 1983).

*Standardized assessment instruments* for mentally retarded children and adolescents are generally lacking. There are either psychopathology scales for nonretarded children, such as the Child Behavior Checklist (Achenbach, 1978; Achenbach & Edelbrock, 1979), or instruments for mentally retarded adults. The Aberrant Behavior Checklist (ABC) by Aman, Singh, Stewart, and Field (1985a,b), for instance, is an empirically developed informant-rated scale with 58 items in five different dimensions (irritability, stereotypy, hyperactivity, excessive speech, and lethargy). The ABC has fairly good psychometric properties, as far as internal consistency, test–retest reliability, and validity are concerned (Aman, Richmond, Stewart, Bell, & Kissel, 1987 ) . Part II of the Adaptive Behavior Scale also solicits ratings on psychopathological behavior such as aggression, destruction, stereotypy, and self-injury. Matson, Kazdin, and Senatore (1984) empirically developed the Psychopathology Instrument for Mentally Retarded Adults (PIMRA), which assesses seven types of pathology on the basis of DSM-III-R (schizophrenic, affective, psychosexual, adjustment, anxiety, somatoform, and personality disorder). Kazdin, Matson, and Senatore (1983) used the PIMRA and modified versions of self-rating instruments of depression with mostly borderline to moderately retarded adults (e.g., the Beck Depression Inventory, the Zung Self-Rating Depression Scale, and the MMPI Depression Scale) and compared these results with ward personnel ratings on the Hamilton Rating Scale. They found that mildly and moderately retarded adults can readily report on their depressed mood. The Beck, Zung, and Hamilton scales, with simplified language for maximum comprehension, were particularly useful. These modified instruments correlated well with other measures and discriminated patients with and without a diagnosis of depression.

The primary purpose of *behavioral assessment* is evaluation of the treatment effectiveness of behavior modification techniques. Particularly in the MR population, behavioral assessment relies almost entirely on *systematic behavior observation* (Rojahn & Schroeder, 1983). With systematic behavior observation, target and collateral behaviors are usually operationally defined for each individual. *Global ratings* of the frequency, duration, or intensity of specific behavior problems are relatively inexpensive, easy to implement, and therefore frequently used in clinical assessment. However, global ratings are usually not very reliable. *Self-monitoring* has also been demonstrated to be a useful and low-cost assessment procedure for higher functioning mentally retarded persons (Matson & Frame, 1983).

## PSYCHOLOGICAL THERAPIES

### Behavior Modification

#### Historical Development

The history of behavior modification began in the 1920s with the work of Watson (1924) and his colleagues (Jones, 1924; Watson & Rayner, 1920). This work was extended during the next decade by Mowrer and Mowrer (1938), and behaviorism continued to receive much attention in experimental psychology. The popularity of the behavioristic approach received a boost in clinical psychology in the 1950s, when the therapeutic basis of the previously popular psychotherapy approach began to fall into disrepute. The efficacy of psychotherapy was questioned by both emerging behaviorists (Eysenck, 1960, 1966; Skinner,

1953; Ullman & Krasner, 1965) and child clinicians (Levitt, 1957, 1963), who
pointed to the lack of data to support this approach.

Behavior therapy became a predominant treatment approach for psychiatric
problems during the latter part of the 1950s and the early 1960s. Presumably, the
earliest studies on the successful treatment of psychopathological behavior in
severely disordered children involving behavior modification techniques were
published in the mid-1960s. These studies had a considerable impact on treatment research. Among the first studies was a paper by Wolf, Risley, and Mees
(1964), who were able to reduce tantrums and self-injurious behavior (SIB) in a
3½-year-old boy by a combination of time-out and extinction. Shortly after that,
Lovaas, Freitag, Gold, and Kassorla (1965) demonstrated the functional relationship of self-injurious behavior in a schizophrenic girl to specific environmental events. Sympathetic attention contingent on SIB was shown to increase its
rate. In addition, SIB covaried as a function of the reinforcement–extinction rate
of other behaviors. In a third paper, Tate and Baroff (1966) reported the successful reduction of SIB in a 9-year-old blind boy, using two different forms of
aversive control. The main contributions of these early studies were (1) that even
seemingly uncontrollable, bizarre, and psychotic behavior, such as SIB, is systematically related to environmental variables; (2) that such behaviors can be
altered by behavior modification techniques through systematic changes of
some of these environmental variables; (3) that social attention, which appears
to be a very natural and almost unavoidable response for naive parents and
caretakers, may be counterproductive, and that it may, in fact, even add to the
deterioration of these behavior problems; and (4) that the behavior of severely
and profoundly mentally retarded persons is amenable to behavior modification. These surprising and encouraging reports sparked a wave of treatment
research by applied behavior analysts, which, in turn, resulted in a variety of
treatment methods for aberrant behaviors in mentally retarded persons.

### Definition and Terms

*Behavior modification* and *behavior therapy* are terms that are used synonym-
ously throughout this chapter. There have been attempts to distinguish between
behavior therapy and behavior modification (Kazdin, 1982), but these discussions are not relevant to the current context. They refer to a variety of treatment
modalities, which are historically and conceptually rooted in the experimental
psychology of learning. The central treatment elements of behavior modification
techniques are interpreted in terms of principles of learning, such as reinforcement, punishment, and extinction. Treatment selection is supposed to be based
on systematic behavior analysis, in which the maintaining conditions, or the
motivational factors of the target behavior, are identified. Behavior modification
treatment is usually accompanied by objective assessment procedures according
to the methodology of single-subject experimental design (e.g., Hersen & Barlow, 1984).

### Basic Principles and Application

Learning principles were originally discovered in learning laboratories.
They are descriptive statements of operations that produce many of the known

forms of individual behavior (Baer, Wolf, & Risley, 1968). According to the paradigms used in their discovery, they were divided into classical and operant conditioning. This distinction is primarily a historical one, and it is generally agreed that this division is artificial. The basic elements involved in conditioning are stimuli and responses and their functional relationship to each other.

A *stimulus* can be a physical, chemical, organismic, or social event, and it can come from within the individual or from external sources. Stimuli that have some systematic effect on a response are called *functional stimuli*. Functional stimuli either precede or follow a response. The classical conditioning paradigm concentrates mainly on the stimulus–response sequence. It focuses on stimuli as response-preceding events, or on stimuli that *elicit* a response. In operant conditioning, both preceding and consequent stimuli are of importance. Preceding functional stimuli in an operant paradigm are called *discriminative stimuli*. They do not elicit responses, but they function as signals to the individual, indicating what kind of consequent event can be "expected" for which behaviors. Positive discriminative stimuli set the occasion for the occurrence of an operant response that has previously been reinforced in its presence; negative discriminative stimuli are signals for withholding a response that has previously been punished in its presence. However, it is the consequent stimuli, or the stimuli that occur *contingent on* (i.e., immediately after) the behavior, that control the behavior, according to the operant paradigm.

A *behavior* or a *response* can be a motor movement, a visceral response, or even a cognitive element. Classical conditioning has been concerned with so-called respondent behaviors (respondents), which are controlled by a preceding, or eliciting, stimulus. In humans, these are usually inherited responses to certain environmental events, like the eye-blink reflex elicited by a blow of air to the open eye. Their occurrence is usually not affected by consequent stimuli. Functional stimuli in the classical paradigm *produce* respondent behavior. Operant conditioning deals with operant behaviors (operants), which are mainly controlled by stimuli that occur contingent on the operant. In other words, operants *produce* stimuli. Most of the behavior modification procedures used with the mentally retarded are based on principles of operant conditioning. The learning mechanisms of operant conditioning can be described in terms of their effects on the future rates of behavior. The probability of the occurrence of a behavior can be strengthened or decreased.

*Positive Reinforcement.* Positive reinforcement is a mechanism that strengthens or increases the probability of occurrence of an operant response. This is accomplished by the presentation of a reinforcer contingent on the performance of that response, which over time is aimed at increasing future response rates. Technically, a stimulus can be called a reinforcer only if it actually increases the future rate of a response. This, of course, is a circular definition. Although this circularity may represent epistemological problems, it has practical utility. Namely, it points out that a stimulus can never be a reinforcer independent of the respective individual, behavior, and the other situational variables involved. Therefore, it is always important to empirically derive those stimuli that are effective reinforcers for a given individual. Although, for instance, sweets or other edibles are generally found to be very effective reinforcers for mentally retarded children, this generality can never be taken for granted. *Primary* reinforcers, such as food or a drink, are unconditioned and are usually of biological significance. *Secondary,* or conditioned, reinforcers gain their behavior-controlling qualities through learning.

Another form of reinforcement was described by Premack (1965). He found that higher probability behavior (given the free choice of the individual) can reinforce lower probability behavior. In other words, preferred activities, such as watching television, could be used as a reinforcer for less preferred activities, such as doing schoolwork.

For the acquisition of new behaviors in a person's response repertoire, two reinforcement principles are important. *Shaping* is the first of these techniques, and it is a process of the selective reinforcement and nonreinforcement of simple reponses, which are gradually modified into a new response. Shaping procedures have also been used in the treatment of phobias and fears in the form of a procedure known as *successive approximation* (or *reinforced praxis*). This technique represents the most widely used operant treatment procedure for phobic behavior (e.g., Leitenberg, 1976), and it has been occasionally used with mentally retarded subjects (Matson, 1981a,b). The development of behavioral sequences is established by *chaining*. In this second approach, responses are gradually linked together by the reinforcement of the last link. Reinforcement can be produced only by the display of the complete chain in correct order.

Positive reinforcement has played an important role in the treatment of pathological behavior in mentally retarded individuals. Reinforcement procedures have been implemented mostly to indirectly reduce the problem behaviors by strengthening desirable behaviors. For example, Mulick, Hoyt, Rojahn, and Schroeder (1978) systematically reinforced toy play in a profoundly mentally retarded blind adult in order to eliminate mild self-injurious behavior (finger picking and nail biting). Biting and picking were ignored, whereas toy manipulations were prompted and reinforced; the result was a concomitant decrease in self-injury and an increase in toy contact.

There are other reinforcement procedures, which are time-based. For example, in a *differential reinforcement of other behavior* (DRO) program, reinforcement for any behavior at the end of a given time interval is provided if the target behavior has not occurred during that interval. DRO has also been called *omission training.* Repp, Deitz, and Deitz (1976) were able to demonstrate that a DRO procedure alone effectively reduced stereotypical responding in three severely mentally retarded persons. *Differential reinforcement of incompatible behavior* (DRI) also holds a dual requirement for the client, but here, it is the occurrence of a certain incompatible behavior and the absence of the target behavior during a given time period. Incompatible responses are chosen mostly so that they cannot be exhibited simultaneously with the target behavior. For example, playing with toys is usually incompatible with stereotypical or self-injurious behavior. In a direct comparison between DRO and DRI procedures used on three profoundly mentally retarded head-bangers, Tarpley and Schroeder (1979) found that DRI suppressed self-injurious behavior more than DRO, which, in turn, was more effective than extinction (see below). Although DRO and DRI procedures have been demonstrated to be effective in reducing problem behaviors in mentally retarded persons, they have mostly been employed in combination with other procedures, such as punishment (LaGrow & Repp, 1984).

In *token economy programs*, reinforcers are given contingent on specified behaviors, in form of tokens, such as chips or stars. These tokens can later be traded in for backup reinforcers (e.g., edibles and tangibles) at certain times (Kazdin, 1977).

There are various *schedules of reinforcement*. A response is most rapidly strengthened if every single occurrence of that response is reinforced. This is called *continuous reinforcement. Intermittent* schedules of reinforcement, which provide reinforcement for specified occurrences of the response only, can also increase the response rate; yet, this happens more slowly than with continuous reinforcement. Behavior that is intermittently reinforced, however, tends to be more resistant to extinction than continuously reinforced behavior. In building up new behaviors, it is therefore often useful to start out with continuous reinforcement, and then to switch over to an intermittent schedule as a method of maintaining behavior under more natural reinforcement conditions.

*Negative Reinforcement.* Another mechanism that strengthens a response is negative reinforcement. This term refers to the termination of the presence of an "aversive" stimulus (a negative reinforcer). Negative reinforcement (or escape training) is usually not used as a treatment strategy by itself. However, it is presumably an active ingredient in some treatment programs, such as time-out (see below). Also, negative reinforcement is considered an important motivational variable in the development of problem behaviors (Carr, 1977). For example, if a child does not like to engage in certain tasks in the classroom (i.e., is in an aversive situation), he or she may become angry and may throw the teaching materials to the floor. If the teacher does not request the child to continue the task, allowing the child to *escape* the demands, throwing materials may be negatively reinforced and may eventually develop into a maladaptive strategy. *Escaping* refers to the termination of a negative reinforcer, and *avoiding* refers to postponing a negative reinforcer.

*Punishment.* Punishment is a response-suppressing mechanism. It refers to the presentation of a noxious stimulus contingent on the occurrence of a maladaptive response. Whether a stimulus is an aversive stimulus (a punisher) or not is defined by its response-decreasing effect. There are, at least in terms of the clinically justifiable range of stimuli, no punishers *per se*, just as there are no guaranteed reinforcers. The functional property is defined on the basis of its effect on the future response rate. The most frequently used stimuli in punishment programs with psychopathological behaviors in the mentally retarded are electric shock, aromatic ammonia, water mist, and slaps. Punishment programs are usually very effective in their rapid and complete response suppression. This prompt suppression is the main advantage of punishment as compared to other treatment approaches. However, a number of serious problems are related to the administration of punishment that have to be considered. Matson and DiLorenzo (1984) listed nine arguments against the use of punishment. The most important ones are that undesirable emotional states and aggressive behavior are likely to be produced in the client; that social interruption may occur because of punishment, leading to escape from or avoidance of the therapist; that the suppression is likely to be only temporary; and that there is a great potential of abuse. Punishment can also suppress desirable behaviors that happen to coincide with the punished response; and behavioral side effects have also been observed as a result of punishment procedures. In some cases, however, the benefit of punishment can clearly outweigh its disadvantages. Punishment procedures are particularly warranted with highly dangerous behaviors, such as severe self-injurious behavior or interpersonal aggression, as an initial breakthrough, before less intrusive treatment techniques can be implemented (e.g., Foxx, McMorrow, Bittle, & Bechtel, 1986).

*Response Cost.* Response cost (or negative punishment) is also a response-decreasing mechanism. It consists of the response-contingent withdrawal of a positive stimulus. Response cost is frequently used within the context of token economy systems. The clients are provided with a specified number of tokens at the outset of the treatment sessions; these tokens are then taken away by the therapist—one or more at a time—contingent on the display of the targeted behavior. Shapiro, Kazdin, and McGonigle (1982), for example, compared the relative effect of response cost and of a token reinforcement procedure on five mentally retarded children with various psychiatric diagnoses. The treatment sessions were divided into 18 short time intervals of varying lengths. During the token reinforcement condition, those children in the classroom who were on-task when the intervals started received a poker chip. In the response cost condition, the children were given the maximum number of tokens that could be earned during the token reinforcement condition (18) before the session started. Whenever the interval started, those children who were not on-task had a token removed. Both procedures improved on-task behavior. However, the differences between response cost and time-out were difficult to determine unequivocally because of multiple treatment interferences in the design. Contingent *sensory-blocking* is a response reduction technique, based on the assumption that blocking sensory input can be punishing in a response cost paradigm. So far, only visual blocking has been reported on in the literature. Zegiob, Jenkins, Becker, and Bristow (1976) used a "facial screening" procedure, in which a terry-cloth bib was used to cover a client's face for 10 seconds contingent on disruptive behavior. Screening was also demonstrated to be effective with an eye screen (Winton, Singh, and Dawson, 1984). Winton *et al.* (1984) demonstrated that the effect of "facial screening" can be attributed to the visual blocking involved in the procedure. In "visual screening," the client's eyes are covered with the therapist's palm rather than with a piece of cloth. This approach has been successfully implemented to reduce stereotypical behavior (McGonigle, Duncan, Cordisco, & Barrett, 1982) and compulsive rituals (Barrett, Staub, & Sisson, 1983).

*Extinction.* If reinforcement is withheld from an operant response, its rate decreases and it finally extinguishes. This process is called *extinction.* Before the response rate starts to decrease, however, it frequently shows a short-term initial increase (*extinction burst*). Extinction programs in applied settings often involve the withholding of social contact and attention (i.e., ignoring), if there is reason to believe that this constitutes the relevant reinforcer of a problem behavior. The main advantage of extinction by withholding social reinforcers is that it is probably the least intrusive response-reducing procedure. The disadvantage is that the process of reduction is relatively slow, and that the selection of behaviors chosen for extinction should usually be limited to behaviors that are not overly dangerous.

Other forms of extinction are the *sensory extinction* procedures that prevent sensory reinforcement. These are administered for behaviors that are seen as being motivated by sensory reinforcement (Rincover, 1978; Rincover, Cook, Peoples, & Packard, 1979; Rincover & Devany, 1982; Rincover, Newsome, & Carr, 1979). In order to reduce stereotypical plate-spinning behavior, for example, which was assumed to be reinforced by the sound of the spinning plate, Rincover (1978) carpeted the table top; the result was a significant reduction in that behavior. Similarly, the proprioceptive stimulation of finger tapping was masked by a vibrator stimulation on the child's hand, and visual stimulation was eliminated by a blindfold. Other successful implementations of sensory extinction of stereotypical behaviors were also reported. The difference between sensory-blocking procedures and sensory extinction is the contingent versus the noncontingent application of sensory deprivation. The attenuation or elimination of sensory input during sensory extinction is administered continuously independent of the occurrence of the target behavior.

*Time-Out from Positive Reinforcement.* The necessity of reducing problem behavior in the mentally retarded and the reluctance to use noxious stimuli for punishment led to the use of alternative response reduction techniques, which have often been called *mild punishment procedures.* One of the most prominent procedures used for the management of maladaptive behavior in mentally retarded persons is *time-out from positive reinforcement.* A variety of different time-out procedures have been reported in the literature. The short-term denial of specific reinforcers is the common component of these various approaches (Sulzer-Azaroff & Mayer, 1977). Time-out has its ancient, ubiquitous, nonbehavioristic precursors in some child-rearing practices (such as standing in the corner), and in penal law (jail terms). In behavior analysis, time-out was originally developed with animal subjects, in the highly controlled environment of learning laboratories, where the response, the reinforcer, and the setting variables were not only clearly defined but could also be manipulated at the discretion of the experimenter. When time-out is applied in clinical settings, the situation is usually more complex, and the variables involved are often confounded.

Presumably, the least intrusive form of time-out is *cued time-out*, in which a cue is displayed contingent on the target behavior, which indicates that the client is temporarily excluded from reinforcement. Spitalnik and Drabman (1976), for example, used a cued time-out procedure with 10 institutionalized mentally retarded children. Whenever a child misbehaved, the teacher would place an orange card on the child's desk for a 10-minute period, during which the child was not to receive a reinforcer. A similar procedure was described by Foxx and Shapiro (1978), in which all students wore a ribbon that served as a discriminative stimulus for reinforcement. When the child misbehaved, the ribbon was removed. While the ribbon was removed, reinforcement dispensed by the teacher and participation in activities were withheld. Another form of time-out consists of the *removal of a present reinforcer,* or the reinforcement dispenser. Mansdorf (1977) successfully reduced tantrums and disruptive behaviors in a moderately mentally retarded girl by the contingent withdrawal of TV, music, personal items, and other sources of reinforcement. The prototype of time-out is *isolation time-out,* or *seclusionary time-out,* in which the client is removed from the setting and from the ongoing activities to a designated location, contingent on exhibiting the target behavior. Time-out seclusion has been performed in special areas within the "time-in" area, in which the target behavior occurred (Williams, Schroeder, Eckerman, & Rojahn, 1983), often involving standing in a corner or sitting in a time-out chair; other programs involve separate time-out rooms, such as the bedroom (Wolf *et al.*, 1964), bathrooms, or special seclusion rooms (Calhoun & Matherne, 1975).

*Physical Restraint.* Another type of response-reducing procedure that has some similarities to time-out is contingent physical restraint (Spreat & Stepansky, in press). Bitgood, Crowe, Suarez, and Peters (1977), for example, used a procedure that they called "immobilization" to reduce self-stimulatory behavior by contingent physical restraint. Immobilization consisted of grasping the client's forearms and holding them at the side of the body with the minimal required effort for 15 seconds. Other restraint procedures involve some mechanical restraint device, such as a restraint chair (e.g., Hamilton, Stephens, & Allen, 1967). Spreat and Stepansky (in press) noted that most of the successful treatment studies involving contingent physical restraint deal with stereotypical or self-injurious behavior.

Occasionally, combinations of time-out and physical restraint procedures are used, such as physical restraint and isolation time-out. Rolider and Van Houten (1985) used a technique they called "movement suppression time-out." Their clients were instructed to go to the corner of the room immediately on engaging in self-injurious behavior; they had to stand there with the chin against the wall, with both hands behind the back, and both feet close together. As soon as the children moved during time-out, they were physically held in the corner by the therapist (or parent). For the treatment of four subjects with self-injurious behaviors, Williams, *et al.* (1983) used for time-out, a narrow, open-topped, waist-high box (standing chair), which was situated within the treatment setting. When self-injurious behavior continued in time-out, the clients' arms were strapped in leather handcuffs that were attached to the chair.

*Overcorrection.* Another complex "mild" punishment procedure, which was specifically developed with and for developmentally disabled persons by Foxx and Azrin (1972), is *overcorrection*. The rationale of overcorrection is having the client take the responsibility for the consequences of his or her own misbehavior, and providing the educative practice of appropriate behaviors related to that misbehavior. This approach involves two sequential steps. *Restitution* is usually the first step. It requires the client first to repair the situation that was disrupted by the client's behavior, and then to improve it beyond its original state. During *positive practice*, the client is made to repeatedly practice overly appropriate behaviors or behaviors that are incompatible with the target behavior. For instance, Foxx (1976) treated public disrobing with an overcorrection procedure in a profoundly mentally retarded woman. Whenever the client was discovered nude, she first had to pick up her discarded clothing. Then, she was given repeated training in dressing herself (restitution). After that, the client was required to assist other residents in improving their appearance (positive practice). The individual overcorrection steps are accompanied by verbal instructions and manual guidance to ensure that the person will carry out the desired movements. Generally, the least amount of physical force is recommended (Foxx, 1978).

*Setting Events.* Most of the procedures described so far are based primarily on the manipulation of consequent stimuli. Altering stimulus conditions has not been the focus of applied behavioral research. An important stimulus concept in this regard is the setting event, defined as the environmental context in which a stimulus–response interaction occurs, and which influences the stimulus–response function (Bijou & Baer, 1978). The physical environment, the social context, or the current physiological conditions of the organism can all be conceptualized as setting events. For example, aggressive behaviors in institutionalized mentally retarded patients were demonstrated to depend on the individual space available per person (Rago, Parker, & Cleland, 1978). The functional relationship between specific stimuli (represented by the peers) and a response (aggressive behavior) was altered by changes in the setting events (the available space per individual). The influence of space on aggressive behavior between peers represents a physical setting event. Kern, Koegel, and Dunlap (1984) gave an example of a successful manipulation of the physiological setting events, as it were, for the control of stereotypical behavior. They found that 15 minutes of continuous vigorous jogging reduced levels of stereotypical responding in subsequent 90-minute observation periods. It was hypothesized that the altered physiological arousal, or the release of certain neurotransmitters because of the physical exercise, was the organic basis of this change in stereotypical responding. Alternating the physiological "setting event" through vigorous exercise changed the stimulus–stereotypy relationship. An example of the relevance of environmental setting events was presented by Solnick, Rincover, and Peterson (1977). They found that the effectiveness of a time-out program for self-injurious behavior and spitting in a 16-year-old severely mentally retarded Down syndrome boy was related to the environmental conditions of the treatment setting. Time-out was initially effective in an "enriched" setting only, in which new toys and rewarding social interaction were provided.

The concept of the setting event can be important in research on the prevention of maladaptive behavior and in the interaction research on behavioral and nonbehavioral treatment variables, such as psychoactive medication. Such an approach, which attempts to identify setting-event variables and to incorporate them into applied treatment analyses, is the *ecobehavioral analysis* proposed by Rogers-Warren and Warren (1977). Schroeder, Rojahn, and Mulick (1978), for instance, followed an ecobehavioral approach to applied research on self-injurious behavior in mentally retarded people.

## Interaction of Behavior Modification and Medication

It has been widely recognized that the interaction of behavior modification and psychoactive drugs may be a promising therapeutic synthesis for different clinical populations and problems (Hersen, 1986; Marks, 1982; Schroeder, Lewis, & Lipton, 1983). In fact, behavior modification techniques and pharmacotherapy have frequently been used in clinical practice with the mentally retarded population. Radinsky (1984), for instance, reported that 38% of mentally retarded persons receiving psychotropic drugs were simultaneously treated with some behavior modification program for some maladaptive behavior. Considering this extensive use of conjoint behavioral and pharmacological treatments, much too little clinical research has been done in this area (Sprague & Baxley, 1978).

There are a few clinical studies in which *neuroleptic drugs* and behavior modification techniques have been researched. McConahey (1972) investigated the multiple effects of *chlorpromazine* (of the phenothiazine class) and *token economy* systems involving 51 severely to profoundly mentally retarded, institutionalized women over several months. It was found that the token programs achieved overall positive results, whereas drug effects were almost undetectable. Chlorpromazine failed to show any consistent behavioral effects. McConahey, Thompson, and Zimmermann (1977) concluded that chlorpromazine—and presumably other phenothiazines as well—may be unwarranted as a medical treatment to control maladaptive behavior in mentally retarded persons. Sandford and Nettlebeck (1982) reported similar effects in two single-case studies involving four mildly to moderately mentally retarded subjects with behavior problems. They studied the effects of a *token program* and two low to moderately dosed phenothiazines (two subjects on *thioridazine* and two on *fluphenazine*). The token program elicited immediate improvements in appropriate behaviors, whereas the phenothiazines did not have a significant impact on either appropriate or inappropriate behaviors. The token reinforcement program also suppressed psychoticlike behaviors in one subject, which were unaffected by 5.0 mg fluphenazine. Burgio, Page, and Capriotti (1985) presented experimental single-subject data on three mentally retarded subjects. The effects of *thioridazine* and *dextroamphetamine* were compared to the effects of behavior management techniques (*time-out, DRO,* and *visual screening*) on aggressive and other behaviors. The drug effects turned out to be variable across subjects, settings, behaviors, and dosages, whereas the behavior modification consistently decreased the inappropriate behavior. Because of some shortcomings in the designs, however, these results must be considered preliminary.

The effects of a combination of *haloperidol* (of the butyrophenone class) treatment and a *mild punishment* technique (an arm squeeze contingent on self-hitting) were compared to each of these treatment modalities alone for SIB in a profoundly mentally retarded adult, who was treated over 12 months (Durand, 1982). The procedure involved a withdrawal design with single-blind conditions (therapists and reliability observers were blind to the drug manipulations), but no placebo control. The data suggested that neither the medication nor the behavioral intervention alone effectively reduced SIB, whereas a combination of the two treatment modalities turned out to be highly effective. Durand hypothesized, on the basis of the clinical observations, that haloperidol may have increased the sensitivity of the subject to pressure. Haloperidol may have acted as a setting event, in which the drug influenced the stimulus function of the arm squeeze.

Campbell, Anderson, Meier, Cohen, Small, Samit, and Sachar (1978) studied the effect of individually titrated dosages of *haloperidol* on a decrease in psychiatric symptoms and a *reinforcement* program for the acquisition of imitative speech. Forty autistic children, two of them with normal IQ, ranging from 2.6 to 7.2 years of age, participated in this randomly assigned, double-blind, placebo-controlled study. The study featured a four-group factorial design with two levels of drugs (haloperidol vs. placebo) and two levels of language training (response-contingent vs. response-independent reinforcement). The optimal dosage of haloperidol ranged from 0.5 to 4.0 mg/day. As measured by the Children's Psychiatric Rating Scale, haloperidol was found to decrease stereotypical and withdrawal behavior in the children who were older than 4.5 years. The effectiveness of behavioral language training was significantly improved by the medication. These results confirm Durand's conclusions (1982), that a combination of behavior modification techniques and psychoactive medication could be potentially beneficial.

A number of studies have been published on the effects of behavior modification in combination with *anticonvulsant medication* on seizure-disordered children. Although not considered a mental disorder, epileptic seizures represent a severe problem for a large percentage of mentally retarded children and manifest themselves in a variety of behavioral disturbances. Zlutnick, Mayville, and Moffat (1975) used a *behavior chain interruption* procedure and *differential reinforcement* to reduce seizure activity. Five subjects, who had diagnoses of major or minor motor seizures, were all on anticonvulsant medication throughout the study. Seizures were conceptualized as the final link in a behavioral chain. The treatment was based on the interruption of early behavior elements in the chain. Seizure frequency was successfully reduced in four of the subjects, and parents and teachers were reported to be effective change agents. Unfortunately, however, information on the type of anticonvulsant medication and the dosage levels was scarce. It appeared that the medication was held constant across the withdrawal design demonstrations.

In another study Rapport, Sonis, Fialkov, Matson, and Kazdin (1983) observed the effects of *carbamazepine* (1200 mg/day) with and without a behavior treatment program on seizure-related aggressive behavior. The subject was a 13-year-old mentally retarded girl. Carbamazepine was administered throughout the study. A behavior program was introduced in an ABAB withdrawal fashion (Hersen & Barlow, 1984). The behavioral program consisted of a 15-minute *DRO* procedure for continuous periods without aggressive behavior and an *interruption–redirection* procedure implemented after each incident of aggressive behavior. It was demonstrated that the combination of anticonvulsant medication and the behavioral program kept the level of aggressive outbursts at a consistently lower level than medication alone, and that these treatment effects generalized to settings outside the hospital.

Krafft and Poling (1982) reviewed 11 studies on behavioral treatments of epilepsy in addition to anticonvulsant medication. They concluded that, although the majority of these studies suggested a potentially beneficial effect of behavioral treatment procedures in combination with anticonvulsant medication for epileptic seizures, the obvious methodological inadequacies do not permit strong conclusions.

## Automatic Cuing Devices

Biofeedback training provides the patient with signals informing him or her about the state of certain body functions that are to be brought under voluntary control. This goal is achieved by biofeedback instruments, which can measure the relevant body function and inform the patient by means of visual or auditory signals. There have been no studies reported in the literature about biofeedback training with mentally retarded persons. Biosignal instruments, however, have been used in a few studies to alert the therapist early to an upcoming response. For example, Schroeder, Peterson, Solomon, and Artley (1977) used EMG technology with two severely mentally retarded head-bangers. The treatment involved contingent restraint and differential reinforcement for relaxation of the right trapezius muscle. Other devices have also been used. Leboeuf and Boeverts (1981) implemented a cuing device for the treatment of nocturnal rectal digging in a 16-year-old profoundly mentally retarded girl. The device, consisting of a plastic belt with a copper foil strip situated just above the client's buttocks, as well as copper foil electrodes taped to the subject's forearm, activated an alarm whenever the electrode touched the cooper strip. Rectal digging was almost impossible for the patient without activating the alarm. Aqueous ammonia was used as a punisher contingent upon 30 seconds of alarm to successfully eliminate digging.

## Cognitive-Behavior Modification

### Historical Development

Behavior therapy underwent significant changes in the 1970s that eventually contributed to the development of cognitive-behavior modification. A number of factors were responsible for these changes. These contributions included research on and implementation of operant procedures that revealed limitations of the behavior modification techniques, including results showing lack of total suppression, difficulty in maintenance, and poor generalization (Bellack & Hersen, 1977). In addition, the assumed behavioral rationale underlying specific behavioral techniques was not being supported by empirical research (Kazdin & Wilcoxon, 1976). Another influence was the development and expansion of cognitive research in the areas of information processing and psycholinguistics. The increase in the application of behavior modification to less severely disturbed children resulted in a greater concern with internal thought processes as both targets and mechanisms of change (Meyers & Craighead, 1984). Furthermore, several behavioral psychologists began to adopt the concepts of social learning and self-control (Bandura, 1977; 1978) and to acknowledge the complex interrelationship between the individual and the environment, which was difficult to interpret in behavioral terms. Bandura's concept of reciprocal determinism (1969, 1978), for example, which views the individual as an active participant in events rather than as a passive product of environment influences, found increasing recognition among behavioral psychologists. With the publication of *Control of Coverants: The Operations of the Mind* (Homme, 1965) and *Principles of Behavior Modification* (Bandura, 1969), researchers reappraised behaviorism's neglect of "covert" events and began to address covert cognitive concepts (e.g., thoughts, feelings, and images) as well as the cognitive symbolic mechanisms that govern behavior.

### Definition

The central purpose of cognitive-behavior modification is to establish the internal locus of control of the client's behavior and to enhance self-regulatory functions (Whitman et al., 1984). It is assumed that behavior is determined by cognitive processes and that the goal of therapy is therefore to evaluate and alter these cognitive processes and their behavioral correlates (Mahoney & Arnkoff,

1978). The distinguishing characteristic of cognitive-behavior modification, as compared to the traditional behavioral approach, is its attention to cognitive activities such as beliefs, self-statements, expectancies, and problem solving. Definitions of cognitive-behavior therapy tend to differ according to the emphasis placed on either cognition or overt behaviors. At one extreme is the premise that cognitive-behavior therapy focuses primarily on changes in cognition rather than in behavior, a premise that clearly separates it from traditional behavior modification (Ledwidge, 1978). Others believe that the final target of cognitive-behavior modification is still observable behavior, and that there is no need for a dintinction between cognitive-behavior therapy and traditional behavior therapy (Wilson, 1978). The remaining concern with overt behavior in terms of treatment targets differentiates cognitive-behavior modification from pure cognitive, insight-oriented therapies (Kendall & Braswell, 1985).

Cognitive-behavior modification is seen as a particularly appealing technique for mentally retarded children, who are generally viewed as being unable to control their own behavior (Kurtz & Neisworth, 1976), as being outer-directed in their problem-solving mechanisms (Balla & Zigler, 1979), and as being dependent on ongoing supervision (Mahoney & Mahoney, 1976).

## Cognitive Treatment Strategies

*Self-Regulation and Self-Control.* The goal of self-regulation is to teach self-control skills. Self-control procedures have been part of the behavioral literature since Skinner's proposal (1953) that individuals control their own behavior in the same way that they control others' behavior. There are several components in this technique. They include increasing the child's awareness of the behavior targeted for modification through *self-observation* and *self-monitoring;* thus, the child learns to identify and record information on his or her behavior. This approach is followed by the introduction of a self-change strategy involving alteration in either the antecedents or the consequences of the behavior. Appropriate goals for behavioral change are based on clinical concerns and/or the child's own performance. The child is then taught to evaluate his or her performance relative to the set goals and to provide *self-reinforcement* for appropriate performance relative to this standard.

A fair amount of research has been devoted to investigating certain components of self-control. For instance, several studies have been aimed at assessing children's capacity to *delay gratification* in favor of more long-term rewards; this capacity considered a major prerequisite of self-regulation. The initial findings were negative (e.g., Morena & Litrownik, 1974). However, research with moderately mentally retarded adolescents revealed that they can be trained to delay gratification at increasingly greater intervals (Litrownik, Franzini, Geller, & Geller, 1977), that their choices are determined in part by the reward options (Franzini, Litrownik & Magy, 1978), and that the self-control behaviors increased when the subjects had prior exposure to delay intervals (Litrownik *et al.,* 1977).

Initial research on mentally retarded children's abilities to *self-monitor* their behaviors were also discouraging (Nelson, Lipinski, & Black, 1976; Zegiob, Klukas, & Junginger, 1978). However, several studies have shown that moderately mentally retarded children can monitor their behaviors while being en-

JOHANNES ROJAHN AND
JENNIFER BURKHART

gaged in a variety of different tasks (Litrownik & Freitas, 1980; Litrownik, Freitas, & Franzini, 1978b; Mahoney, & Mahoney, 1976). A number of studies have indicated that *self-monitoring* can be used to effect behavioral change in various applied settings (Litrownik & Freitas, 1980; Nelson *et al.*, 1976; Nelson, Lipinski, & Boykin, 1978; Zegiob *et al.*, 1978). For instance, Nelson *et al.* (1976) found that, despite initially low accuracy, mentally retarded adolescents and adults could be taught to reliably record both positive and negative behaviors, and that, through these recordings, positive behavior (talking) increased while negative behavior (face touching) was not significantly affected. Other studies have shown that self-monitoring, even when implemented inaccurately, has increased appropriate verbalizations (Nelson *et al.*, 1978) and has decreased socially maladaptive behaviors (Zegiob *et al.*, 1978) in mentally retarded adolescents. In attempting to delineate the differential effects of self-assessment and self-reinforcement training, Shapiro, McGonigle, and Ollendick (1980) found that some children could adequately engage in self-regulation following self-monitoring training alone. Other children required training in both self-monitoring and self-reinforcement, and still other children were incapable of learning any of the necessary components of successful self-regulation. Thus, the authors were led to conclude that individual differences play a major part in mentally retarded children's abilities to learn self-control skills.

*Setting performance standards* and evaluating behavior have been shown to improve performance in both mentally retarded (Rosen, Diggory, & Werlinsky, 1966; Warner & de Jung, 1971) and intellectually average children (Rosen *et al.* 1966). Although researchers (Rosen, Diggory, Floor, & Nowakiwska, 1971) were initially skeptical about mentally retarded children's ability to be trained to set appropriate performance standards, others have reported positive results in this area. The successful studies of performance evaluations in mentally retarded children include those that have used models to set performance standards (Litrownik, Cleary, Lecklitner, & Franzini, 1978a), experimenter-administered feedback (Brodsky, LePage, Quiring, & Zeller, 1970; Campione & Brown 1977), and the administration of self-reinforcement (Litrownik *et al.*, 1978). Overall, research on the self-regulation of mentally retarded children and adolescents reveals that the components of self-regulation, including the delay of gratification, self-monitoring, the setting of performance standards, self-evaluation, and self-reinforcement, can be taught reliably to individuals who lack a high degree of verbal skills or abstract conceptualization (Urbain & Kendall, 1980).

Self-control strategies can be successfully applied to a variety of subjects and a wide range of behaviors (Mahoney & Thoresen, 1974; Thoresen & Mahoney, 1974). Based on a series of experimental probes across a period of 4 years, Mahoney and Mahoney (1976) reported the effective implementation of behavioral self-control techniques by mentally retarded individuals in developing a number of self-regulatory skills in the areas of personal hygiene, aggression, and academic performance. Several studies have used self-regulation to maintain performance following behavioral change initiated through externally controlled techniques (Frederiksen & Frederiksen, 1975; Nelson *et al.*, 1978; Robertson, Simon, Pachman, & Drabman, 1979). Research in this area has focused on maintaining newly acquired on-task behavior and reduced disruptive behaviors through children's self-evaluation and continued reinforcement by the teachers (Frederiksen & Fredrikson, 1975) or by the child (Robertson *et al.*, 1979; Shapiro

Nelson *et al.* (1976) found that self-evaluation increased the appropriate behaviors (e.g., tidiness, participation and conversation) of mentally retarded adults beyond the levels achieved with an externally controlled token system.

*Self-Instructional Training.* Self-instructional training is based on the notion that individuals can be trained to produce internally generated self-statements to guide their behavior (Meichenbaum, 1974). This technique was developed through research with schizophrenics and was influenced by rational emotive therapy (Ellis, 1977), behavior therapy, and the language development models of Luria (1961) and Vygotsky (1962). Self-instructional training, like correspondence training, uses an individual's verbal behavior to direct his or her nonverbal behavior. In a series of studies, Meichenbaum and Goodman (1969, 1971) established a self-instructional training program for impulsive children. The training sequence of this program consisted of (1) a model's performing a task while describing his or her performance; (2) the child's performing the task assisted by the model's directions; (3) the child's performing the task while repeating the instructions aloud; (4) the child's rehearsing the task while whispering self-instructions; and (5) the child's completing the task while using covert self-instruction (Whitman *et al.*, 1984). Unlike correspondence training, which generally focuses on fairly basic skills, self-instructional training is usually used in complex activities that require multiple problem-solving strategies. However, self-instruction has some advantages over other techniques because it can be matched to the individual's needs. Tailored to specific tasks, it incorporates clear teaching methods and goals, along with the processes as well as the product of problem solving, while making the child the locus of control (Whitman *et al.*, 1984).

A considerable number of studies have been published indicating that self-instructional training can be successfully used with mentally retarded persons. In the majority of studies, however, it has been implemented mainly to improve work-related behavior. Again, its usefulness for severe behavior problems in mentally retarded children and adolescents has not been adequately explored.

*Problem Solving.* Problem solving refers to overt or covert processes in which an individual generates a variety of possible solutions to a problem situation and learns to recognize and use the most effective response (Goldfried & Davison, 1976). Once the most productive response has been identified and implemented, it may be maintained through self-control techniques. The steps in this process usually include (1) a general orientation, which familiarizes the client with the rationale of the treatment; (2) the definition of the problem and its formulation as a problem that can be solved; (3) the generation of alternative ways to respond and an examination of the appropriateness of these options; (4) the selection of one of the alternative responses, which is then carried out for verification; and (5) the maintenance or revision of the solution (Goldfried & Davison, 1976).

Little attention has been given to developing problem-solving skills in mentally retarded children. The available research suggests that mentally retarded individuals in general are deficient in problem-solving skills (Miller, Hale, & Stevenson, 1968; Smith, 1967; Stevenson, Hale, Klein, & Miller, 1968). Based on the hypothesis that mentally retarded children's inability to problem-solve is related to deficits in attending to and/or discriminating between the relevant and the irrelevant components of a problem, Ross and Ross (1979) developed a different approach to problem-solving training. This method featured the presentation of stories of social conflict in which mildly mentally retarded children were encouraged to discuss and recognize the relevant and irrelevant features of a problem by using peer modeling, repetition, and reinforcement. The results of paper-and-pencil tests showed that the trained children were more successful in recognizing the relevant and irrelevant dimensions than untrained children.

Most studies on mentally retarded children focus on developing specific dimensions of the problem-solving approach. For example, Ross and Ross (1973) developed a program to improve children's ability to (1) *listen to* and *understand* the problem statement; (2) *identify the relevant elements* to help solve problems; (3) recognize that many problems have *alternative solutions;* and (4) have confidence in their ability to develop adequate solutions to problems. The trained children offered more problem-solving solutions than those in a control group, and these results generalized to the classroom setting.

Several investigators have explored the possibility that mentally retarded children who have been provided with several solutions to a problem can be trained to choose the best solution. Budoff and Corman (1976) taught mentally retarded children to improve their performance on the Raven Colored Progressive Matrices Test by training them to select the best alternative from the solutions provided. Ross and Ross (1978) trained EMR children to select the best alternative by using an actual social situation requiring a decision in problem solving, group discussion in a gamelike atmosphere, and the provision of tokens for appropriate performance. Although the trained children produced both better alternatives and better rationales for their choices, the training required 40 training sessions, reflecting the difficulty that retarded children have in acquiring these skills.

Problem-solving techniques have also been used in combination with other procedures to form training packages (Allen, Chinsky, Larcen, Lachman, & Selinger, 1976; Gesten, Flores de Apodaca, Rains, Weissberg, & Cowen, 1979). Schneider (1974) used problem-solving techniques as a component of a treatment package (e.g., the turtle technique) devised to teach impulse control to aggressive mentally retarded children. The problem solving was aimed at helping the children to think of alternative responses to and consequences of aggressive behavior.

Although the research on problem solving in mentally retarded children and adolescents is in its initial stages, the overall preliminary results suggest that these individuals can be taught to generate several solutions to problem situations and to choose the best options from a series of alternatives provided. However, further research is needed to assess the ability to implement the chosen alternative and to generalize these skills to other settings.

*Cognitive Strategy Training.* Cognitive strategy training refers to procedures devised to teach children to learn (Brown & French, 1979). These involve helping children to become aware of their own thought processes in order to modify or compensate for cognitive deficits and to facilitate optimal cognitive performance. The theoretical basis of cognitive strategy training is closely linked to cognitive theories of mental retardation, intelligence models, and cognitive development.

Turnure, Buium, and Thurlow (1976) proposed that instruction deficiency is a result of researchers' frequent failure to provide mentally retarded children with effective strategies for accomplishing tasks. These investigators found that when mentally retarded children are provided with effective cognitive strategies, their performance on various tasks improves (Turnure et al., 1976). For instance, questioning strategies were found to be instrumental in stimulating young children of average intelligence and mildly retarded children to produce verbal responses that were effective in enhancing the acquisition and recall of paired associates (Kendall, Borkowski, & Cavanaugh, 1980; Turnure et al., 1976).

The Instrumental Enrichment Program (IEP; Feuerstein, Rand, & Hoffman, 1979; Feuerstein, Rand, Hoffman, & Miller, 1980) represents the most comprehensive cognitive-strategy training-program developed for mildly retarded children. This program is based on mediational and cognitive delivery models in which deficiencies are conceptualized as occurring in one of three phases: input, elaboration, and output. The IEP is devised to compensate for these deficits by exposing children to tasks that stimulate cognitive functions that are deficient. The training involves instruction in a topic and important concepts, reinforcement, and feedback. The results of the preliminary data show an increase in general intellectual functioning and performance on cognitive tasks (e.g., spatial concepts and analytic perception), academic achievement, and classroom interactions (Whitman et al., 1984). Similarly, Arbitman-Smith and Haywood (1980) reported a significant increase in the scores of mildly retarded children on the Lorge Thorndike IQ test following a 1-year exposure to the IEP. Research on cognitive strategy training is fairly new, and systematic investigations are rare. Its potential for ameliorating psychopathological problems has not yet been widely examined.

*Correspondence Training.* Correspondence training refers to the relationship between what individuals say and what they do and is based on the premise that nonverbal behavior can be altered and controlled by modifying the verbal behavior. This technique is particularly efficacious in maintaining behavior in situations where direct reinforcement may be inconvenient or impractical (Israel, 1978). Three forms of correspondence training have been reported in the literature. One type, the *say-do* program, requires the child to state what he or she is going to do and features reinforcement for behavior that corresponds to the stated interaction (Israel, 1978). A second type of correspondence training, the *do-say* program, features reinforcement for statements that accurately describe previous behavior (Risley & Hart, 1968). Research has shown that these two procedures produce similar results (Israel & O'Leary, 1973). The third type of correspondence training program is the *show-do* sequence (Whitman, Scibak, Butler, Richter, & Johnson, 1982), in which an instructor describes the correct performance of a target behavior and the child is then required to correctly enact the behavior. If the child performs the target behavior as it would appear in the setting in which it should occur, he or she is reinforced. If the incorrect response is exhibited, reinforcement is withheld, and the child receives feedback on his or her response.

Correspondence training evidently involves some degree of both receptive and expressive language skills. In order to address the role of language in the correspondence training program, Whitman et al. (1982) assessed the effectiveness of the show-do procedure in nonverbal mentally retarded children. The results were an increase in on-task behavior during training, maintenance, and transfer conditions. Research on correspondence training with mentally retarded children and adolescents is still rare, and its usefulness in the treatment of psychopathological problems remains to be tested. Future research is also needed to address the effective components of this behavior, including self-monitoring, reinforcement, and overt and covert verbalizations.

## Psychotherapy

Defining *psychotherapy* is a difficult task, and the typically available definitions vary widely. To cover the variety of theories and the procedures related to the resulting treatment techniques, which are usually referred to as *psychotherapy*, requires a very broad definition (Matson, 1984). In this chapter, *psychotherapy* refers loosely to nonbehavioral forms of psychological treatment, with a theoretical basis and a historical background in psychodynamic approaches. Some forms of psychotherapy have also been used, although infrequently, with mentally retarded children. Apparently, psychotherapy lost some of its popularity for use with the mentally retarded population with the advances in behavioral and cognitive-behavioral therapies.

Accounts of the use of psychotherapeutic techniques with mentally retarded individuals date back to the early 1960s (see Chess, 1962; Kanner, 1964). However, they were applied even earlier in state institutions and schools (e.g., Ackerman & Menninger, 1936; Chidester & Menninger, 1936; Freeman, 1936; Leland, Walker, & Toboada, 1959). Outpatient clinics serving mentally retarded children also incorporated psychotherapy into their treatment programs (Cooley, 1945; Glassman, 1943; Wegman, 1944).

The methods of psychotherapy used with mentally retarded individuals include individual and group therapies. These techniques usually involve an expression of emotions in conjunction with emotional control, release and catharsis, reassurance, attainment of insight, and positive self-actualization. *Play therapy* has become the predominant psychotherapeutic technique used with mentally retarded children (Axline, 1949). This approach includes nondirective play, in which the child is required to "work through" difficulties in play (Moustakas, 1966) and role playing by the use of puppets (Kelly, 1981) and adult role models (Ollendick, Shapiro, & Barrett, 1982). Leland and Smith (1962, 1965) provided a comprehensive play therapy model for mentally retarded children, which conceptualizes the therapeutic process as a learning experience involving variations in structure imposed by both the therapist and the materials. Other psychotherapeutic approaches used with mentally retarded children and adolescents include *art therapy* (Roth & Barrett, 1980) and *music therapy* (Heimlich, 1960; Joseph, & Heimlich, 1959; Nordoff & Robbins, 1965; Weigl, 1959), as well as the combination of these techniques (Cantalapiedra, Deweerdt, & Frederick, 1977). *Counseling* has also been used (Blohm, 1978; Deblassie, & Lebsock, 1979; Eldridge, Witmer, Barcikowski & Bauer, 1977), particularly with mentally retarded adolescents on both an individual (Selan, 1979; Walker, 1977) and a group basis (Cotzin, 1948; Fine & Dawson, 1965; Fisher & Wolfson, 1953; Wilcox & Guthrie, 1957). More detail about the use of psychotherapy with the mentally retarded can be found in a review by Nuffield (1983).

Criticisms of psychotherapeutic techniques have been made, particularly with regard to methodological problems, lack of rigorous empirical evaluations of treatment effectiveness, and the uncertainty about treatment generalization outside the therapy setting (Bialer, 1967; Crowley, 1965; Li, 1981). The reader is directed to Matson (1984) for a critical summary of the measurement techniques used to assess treatment effectiveness.

## AREAS OF APPLICATION

The traditional areas of the psychological treatment of the mentally retarded have been severe problem behaviors such as self-injury, stereotypical behaviors, and aggression. The successful, empirically evaluated treatment or management techniques for these maladaptive behaviors have been almost exclusively behavior modification procedures. More recently, other forms of psychopathology, such as phobic and depressed behavior, have also been subject to psychological treatment, with promising results. Some selected areas of application are briefly reviewed here, with an emphasis on empirically tested treatment techniques.

### Self-Injurious Behavior

Self-injurious behavior (SIB) often presents a serious clinical problem. It refers to a number of different forms of repetitive behavior that actually or potentially cause physical damage to the individual's own body. SIB is a descriptive term often used for heterogeneous forms of behavior, such as self-hitting, biting, scratching, gouging, vomiting or rumination, and the ingestion of non-nutritive substances (pica). The estimates of SIB prevalence vary from 1.7% among noninstitutionalized retarded persons to 8%–23% among institutionalized persons living in public residential facilities (Rojahn, 1986). A wide variety of approaches have been tried to the management of SIB, including such desperate attempts as brain surgery and electroconvulsive treatment (ECT). Noncontingently applied mechanical restraints, such as camisoles, arm splints, helmets, and face masks, or antipsychotic medications are frequently the last resort for SIB control often encountered in residential facilities. The administration of neuroleptic medication is a very popular form of intervention, although there is basically no scientific justification in terms of its effectiveness or therapeutic rationale (Singh & Millichamp, 1985). The problem is that either form of restraint—physical or chemical—tends to lower the person's level of functioning and restricts the opportunity to learn (Rojahn, Schroeder, & Mulick, 1980). So far, the most promising results in SIB management have been reported with behavior modification. Numerous behavioral procedures have been used to control SIB, ranging from relatively intrusive forms of punishment to the reinforcement of appropriate behaviors. A number of SIB review articles are available (Baumeister & Rollings, 1976; Favell, Azrin, Baumeister, Carr, Dorsey, Forehand, Foxx, Lovaas, Rincover, Risley, Romanczyk, Russo, Schroeder, & Solnick, 1982; Horner & Barton, 1980; Schroeder, Schroeder, Rojahn, & Mulick, 1981; Singh, 1981).

*Punishment* procedures have been among the first techniques used with SIB. Tate and Baroff (1966) reported the implementation of brief contingent electric stimulation (approximately 130 V) for head banging and other SIBs, delivered by a hand-held stock prod. A number of other studies have been published on the use of electric stimulation (e.g., Baroff & Tate, 1968; Browning, 1971; Bucher &

Lovaas, 1968; Corte, Wolfe, & Locke, 1971; Duker, 1976; Lovaas & Simmons, 1969; Romanczyk & Goren, 1975). Ethical objections, however, have frequently been raised against electric stimulation, and its use has been disallowed in many facilities. Alternative noxious stimuli have been used, such as aromatic ammonia (Altman, Haavik, & Cook, 1978; Baumeister & Baumeister, 1978; Rojahn, McGonigle, Curcio, & Dixon, 1987; Singh, Dawson, & Gregory, 1980; Tanner & Zeiler, 1975) and water mist (Dorsey, Iwata, Ong, & McSween, 1980; Rojahn et al., 1987). Punishment procedures are frequently paired with reinforcement procedures, such as DRO, in order to reduce the potential side effects of punishment (e.g., Corte et al., 1971; Jenson, Rovner, Cameron, Peterson, & Kesler, 1985). A few studies have reported the use of response cost procedures (e.g., Nunes, Murphy, & Ruprecht, 1977). "Mild" punishment techniques, such as time-out (e.g., Wolf, Risley, Johnston, Harris, & Allen, 1967) and overcorrection (e.g., Harris & Romanczyk, 1976), have also been used quite extensively with SIB. Extinction alone was used in early experimental studies (e.g., Lovaas et al., 1965), but it is not warranted for the treatment of severe self-injurious behavior because of its slow rate of behavior reduction and its possible side effects (Singh, 1981). Reinforcement techniques such as DRO (Repp et al., 1976) and DRI (Tarpley & Schroeder, 1979) are also occasionally implemented alone. With more severe forms of self-injurious behavior, DRO and DRI are usually combined with suppressive techniques such as punishment.

## Stereotypical Behavior

Stereotypical behavior is repetitive, developmentally inappropriate, and invariant motor movement, without any apparent function. The most frequently treated forms of stereotypy are body rocking, mouthing, and complex hand and finger movements (LaGrow & Repp, 1984). Stereotypy is found in about two thirds of the institutionalized severely mentally retarded population (Berkson, & Davenport, 1962), where it occurs between 7% and 47% of the time (Repp & Barton, 1980). Survey data among noninstitutionalized retarded persons indicate a stereotypy prevalence of 65% in persons with concomitant SIB, and of 62% in individuals without SIB (Rojahn, 1986). Repp, Barton, and Gottlieb (1983) reported stereotypical behavior as occurring 13% of the time among community-based persons. The elimination of stereotypical behavior is considered an important treatment goal, as it has been demonstrated to interfere with learning and the acquisition of new skills (Koegel & Covert, 1972), as it represents "abnormal" behavior that is socially undesirable and unacceptable, and as it may be a basis for the development of self-injurious behavior through accidental learning (Baumeister & Forehand 1973).

The most widely used forms of treatment for stereotypical behaviors have been behavior modification techniques (Burkhart, 1988; LaGrow & Repp, 1984). These included punishment via electrical stimulation (Baumeister & Forehand, 1972), slaps (Koegel & Covert, 1972), and vigorous shaking (Risley, 1968); physical restraint (Bitgood et al., 1977); or mild forms of punishment overcorrection (Luiselli, Pemberton, & Helfen, 1978; Matson, Ollendick, & Martin, 1979; Rollings & Baumeister, 1981) and time-out (Pendergrass, 1972). Extinction (Rincover, 1978), DRO (Repp et al., 1976) and DRI (Berkson & Mason, 1964) have also been successfully implemented. For a critical review of the treatment procedures for stereotypical behaviors, see LaGrow and Repp (1984).

Aggressive behavior is one of the most prevalent forms of maladaptive behavior in mentally retarded persons who are placed in or readmitted to restrictive public residential facilites (Hill & Bruininks, 1984). Again, behavior modification techniques have been demonstrated to be potentially very effective in controlling aggressive behavior. Punishment, time-out, overcorrection, and response cost have also been demonstrated to be effective. Increasing the repertoire of social skills and other adaptive behavior should receive increased attention in future applied research (Mulick & Schroeder, 1980). Golden and Consorte (1982) used a cognitive treatment package consisting of rational-emotive therapy, coping self-statements, relaxation training, biofeedback, coping imagery, behavioral rehearsal, and assertiveness training in treating aggressive responding in four mildly retarded adults. The results were a reduction in anger outbursts in all subjects and total suppression of violent behavior in the form of hitting, kicking, and property destruction. Critical review papers by Matson and Gorman-Smith (1986), Mulick and Schroeder (1980), and Repp and Brulle (1981) provide an excellent overview of the treatment of aggressive behavior in mentally retarded persons.

## Depression

Only a few empirical studies have been published on the treatment of depression in the mentally retarded. One of the major reasons for this unfortunate lack of treatment research may be the difficulty involved in the conceptualization and diagnosis of depression in this population (Matson, 1983).

Matson (1982) treated behavioral characteristics of depression in four mildly to moderately mentally retarded adults. He identified eight behaviors that are commonly judged to be related to depression: The number of words spoken, somatic complaints, irritability, grooming, negative self-statements, flat affect, eye contact, and speech latency. The treatment took place in individual sessions in which the clients had to answer 20 questions regarding somatic complaints and negative self-statements. Appropriate responding in each of these areas of depression was modeled for the client and was reinforced by tokens; inappropriate responding was corrected by the therapist. Social validity criteria were established with nondepressed retarded persons to show the levels of performance that can be expected on each of these items. All four subjects were reported to have significantly improved on these target behaviors. Improvement was also demonstrated with pre-, post-, and follow-up measures on the Self-Rating Scale and the Beck Depression Inventory. A similar combination of token reinforcement, performance feedback, instructions, and modeling was also demonstrated to be a useful procedure in the treatment of somatic complaints in three mildly retarded adults (Matson, 1984).

A similar study was reported by Frame, Matson, Sonis, Fialkov, and Kazdin (1982), who treated a 10-year-old borderline retarded boy diagnosed as having childhood depression. Four categories of depressive manifestation were identified, (eye contact, bland affect, poor speech, and inappropriate body position). These target categories were then systematically altered in individual skill-training sessions. The treatment sessions consisted of instructions in the respective appropriate skills to be trained, modeling, role playing by the child with performance feedback, and praise for appropriate responses.

JOHANNES ROJAHN AND
JENNIFER BURKHART

Several studies have used variations of self-instructional training with children lacking social skills, who were variously labeled as impulsive, hyperactive, or non-self-controlled, or as having behavior problems. In a comparative study of 48 moderately retarded institutionalized adults, Bramston and Spence (1985) found that the subjects involved in behavioral social-skills training showed a significant increase in social skills performance compared to subjects assigned to either a cognitive social-problem-solving group, an attention-placebo control group, or a no-treatment control group. The subjects assigned to the cognitive problem-solving training, on the other hand, showed a significant increase in their generation of alternative solutions over the behavioral social-skills group and the two control groups. However, neither training approach resulted in skills maintenance or in changes in global ratings of social competence.

## Fears and Phobias

The treatment of fears or phobias is rarely reported in mentally retarded persons. Matson (1981b) treated fear of going to a grocery store in 24 adults in the mild and moderate range with successive approximation and participant modeling. The treatment consisted of tasks structured in a graduated hierarchy, which slowly approximated the highly fear-causing shopping situation. Verbal reinforcement was provided for the appropriate performance of therapist-prompted tasks. In another study, Matson (1981a) reported using participant modeling for the reduction of long-standing fears of strangers in three moderately mentally retarded females. The clients had refused to talk to or be around adults other than their parents and their teachers. The training trials were performed in a treatment setting, and probe sessions were conducted in the children's homes. The training involved participant modeling by the mothers (which consisted of modeling the correct response), role play by the children with prompts, reinforcements for appropriate trials, and fading. The treatment procedure proved to be effective, and the gains had been maintained at 6-month follow-up.

## Other Forms of Psychopathology

Other psychopathological syndromes in mentally retarded persons that have been treated by psychological therapies are *exhibitionism* (Lutzker, 1983), *public masturbation* (Cook, Altman, Shaw, & Blaylock, 1978), *hypochondrias* (Matson, 1984), and *compulsions* (Barrett *et al.*, 1983; Cuvo, 1976). They were all treated by behavior modification techniques.

## CONCLUDING REMARKS

This chapter has attempted to briefly describe the most prominent psychological therapies that have been implemented for the treatment of various forms of psychopathology in mentally retarded children and adults. It becomes apparent that the patient population characteristics, in terms of specific handicaps, determine the choice of the treatment modality to some degree. It is therefore not surprising that behavior modification techniques, which generally do not require language skills or a high level of cognitive functioning, have been found to be by far the most widely used and most effective treatments for behavioral and emotional problems in this population. With the lower functioning clients, they are about the only form of treatment with well-documented success. The main problems with behavior modification are the frequently encountered lack of maintenance, the difficulty of transferring treatment gains to the natural environment of the client, and their high cost in terms of work intensity for the therapists. In fact, the generalization problems of behavior modification are primarily associated with the lack of the necessary time commitment and sophistication of therapists, which are most frequently an issue of cost rather than a theoretical problem. Only relentless consistency of programming and continuing behavioral analysis with program adaptations can bring about the generalization of treatment gains. In clinical settings, these efforts are often unavailable.

Cognitive-behavior modification, on the other hand, appears to be more useful for mildly mentally retarded persons. With these clients, cognitive techniques have been mainly applied for the development of social skills, learning techniques, and work-related behavior, rather than for the treatment of severe psychopathological problems. So far, there is not enough evidence in the research literature to make specific clinical recommendations with regard to cognitive therapy in this earea.

Other treatment options, such as the combination of behavior modification and psychotropic or anticonvulsant drugs, or the application of automated response-detection technology, seem promising and should be further explored in future clinical research.

Despite these limitations and problems, however, it must be recognized that highly effective psychological treatment forms are already available for most psychopathological problems in the retarded population.

ACKNOWLEDGMENT. The authors wish to thank Dr. William J. Helsel for his critical reading of drafts of this manuscript.

REFERENCES

Achenbach, T. M. (1978). The Child Behavior Profile: 1. Boys aged 6–11. *Journal of Consulting and Clinical Psychology, 46*, 478–488.

Achenbach, T. M., & Edelbrock, C. S. (1979). The Child Behavior Profile: 2. Boys aged 12–16 and girls aged 6–11 and 12–16. *Journal of Consulting and Clinical Psychology, 47*, 223–233.

Ackerman, N. W., & Menninger, C. F. (1936). Treatment techniques for mental retardation in a school for personality disorders in children. *American Journal of Orthopsychiatry, 6*, 294–312.

Allen, G. J., Chinsky, J. M., Larcen, S. W., Lochman, J. E., & Selinger, H. (1976). *Community psychology in the schools.* Hillsdale, NJ: Erlbaum.

Altman, K., Haavik, S., & Cook, J. W. (1978). Punishment of self-injurious behavior in natural settings using contingent aromatic ammonia. *Behavior Research and Therapy, 16*, 85–96.

Aman, M. G., Richmond, G., Stewart, A. W., Bell, J. C., & Kissel, R. C. (1987). The Aberrant Behavior Checklist: Factor structure and the effect of subject variables in American and New Zealand facilities. *American Journal of Mental Deficiency, 91*, 570–578.

Aman, M. G., Singh, N. N., Stewart, A. W., & Field, C. J. (1985a). The Aberrant Behavior Checklist: A behavior rating scale for the assessment of treatment effects. *American Journal of Mental Deficiency, 89*, 485–491.

Aman, M. G., Singh, N. N., Stewart, A. W., & Field, C. J. (1985b). Psychometric characteristics in the Aberrant Behavior Checklist. *American Journal of Mental Deficiency, 89*, 492–502.

American Psychiatric Association. (1987). *Diagnostic and statistical manual of mental disorders* (3rd ed. rev.; DSM-III-R). Washington, DC: Author.

Arbitman-Smith, R., & Haywood, A. C. (1980). Cognitive education for learning disabled adolescents. *Journal of Abnormal Child Psychology, 8*, 51–64.

Axline, V. M. (1949). Mental deficiency: Symptom or disease? *Journal of Consulting Psychology, 13*, 313–327.

Baer, D. M., Wolf, M. M., & Risley, T. R. (1968). Some current dimensions of applied behavior analysis. *Journal of Applied Behavior Analysis, 1*, 91–97.

Balla, D.. & Zigler, E. (1979). Personality development in retarded persons. In N. R. Ellis (Ed.), *Handbook of mental deficiency, psychological theory and research.* Hillsdale, NJ: Erlbaum.

Bandura, A. (1969). *Principles of behavior modification.* New York: Holt, Rinehart & Winston.

Bandura, A. (1977). *Social learning theory.* Englewood Cliffs, NJ: Prentice-Hall.

Bandura, A. (1978). The self system in reciprocal determinism. *American Psychologist, 33*, 344–358.

Baroff, G. S., & Tate, B. G. (1968). The use of aversive stimulation in the treatment of chronic self-injurious behavior. *Journal of the American Academy of Child Psychiatry, 7*, 454–470.

Barrett, R. P., Staub, R. W., & Sisson, L. A. (1983). Treatment of compulsive rituals with visual screening: A case study with long-term follow-up. *Journal of Behavior Therapy and Experimental Psychiatry, 14*, 55–59.

Baumeister, A. A., & Baumeister, A. A. (1978). Suppression of repetitive self-injurious behavior by contingent inhalation of aromatic ammonia. *Journal of Autism and Childhood Schizophrenia, 8*, 71–77.

Baumeister, A. A., & Forehand, R. (1972). Effects of contingent shock and verbal command on body rocking of retardates. *Journal of Clinical Psychology, 28*, 586–590.

Baumeister, A. A., & Forehand, R. (1973). Stereotyped acts. In N. R. Ellis (Ed.), *International review of research in mental retardation* (Vol. 6). New York: Academic Press.

Baumeister, A. A., & Rollings, J. P. (1976). Self-injurious behavior. In N. R. Ellis (Ed.), *International review of research in mental retardation* (Vol 8). New York: Academic Press.

Bellack, A. S., & Hersen, M. (1977). *Behavior modification: An introductory textbook.* Baltimore, MD: Williams & Wilkins.

Berkson, G., & Davenport, R. K. (1962). Stereotyped movements of mental defectives: 1. Initial survey. *American Journal of Mental Deficiency, 66*, 849–852.

Berkson, G., & Mason, W. (1964). Stereotyped movements of mental defectives: 4. Situation effects. *American Journal of Mental Deficiency, 68*, 511–524.

Bialer, I. (1967). Psychotherapy and other adjustment techniques with the mentally retarded. In A. A. Baumeister (Ed.), *Mental retardation, appraisal, education and rehabilitation.* Chicago: Aldine.

Bijou, S. W., & Baer, D. M. (1978). *Behavior analysis of child development.* Englewood Cliffs, NJ: Prentice-Hall.

Bitgood, S. C., Crowe, M. J., Suarez, Y., & Peters, R. D. (1977). Immobilization: Effects and side effects on stereotyped behavior in children. *Behavior Modification, 4*, 187–208.

Blohm, A. L. A. (1978). Group counseling with moderately mentally retarded and hearing disabled elementary school children. *Dissertation Abstracts International, 39* (6A), 3362.

Bramston, P., & Spence, S. H. (1985). Behavioral versus cognitive social skills training with intellectually handicapped adults. *Behavior Research and Therapy, 23*, 239–246.

Brodsky, G., LePage, T., Quiring, J., & Zeller, R. (1970). Self-evaluative rersponses in adolescent retardates. *American Journal of Mental Deficiency, 74*, 792–795.

Brown, A., & French, L. (1979). The zone of potential development: Implications for intelligence testing in the year 2000. *Intelligence, 3*, 253–271.

Browning, R. M. (1971). Treatment effects of a total behavior modification program with five autistic children. *Behaviour Research and Therapy, 9*, 319–327.

Bucher, B., & Lovaas, O. I. (1968). Use of aversive stimulation in behavior modification. In M. R. Jones (Ed.), *Miami symposium on the prediction of behavior. 1976: Aversive Stimulation.* Coral Gables, FL: University of Miami Press.

Budoff, M., & Corman, L. (1976). Effectiveness of a learning potential procedure in improving problem-solving skills of retarded and nonretarded children. *American Journal of Mental Deficiency, 81*, 260–264.

Burgio, L. D., Page, T. G., & Capriotti, R. M. (1985). Clinical behavioral pharmacology: Methods for evaluating medications and contingency management. *Journal of Applied Behavior Analysis, 18*, 45–59.

Burkhart, J. E. (in press). Theories on the etiology and maintenance of sterotypic behavior. In R. P. Barrett, & J. L. Matson (Eds.), *Advances in Developmental Disorders.*

Calhoun, K. S., & Matherne, P. (1975). The effects of varying schedules of time-out on aggressive behavior of a retarded girl. *Journal of Behavior Therapy and Experimental Psychiatry, 6*, 139–143.

Campbell, M., Anderson, L. T., Meier, M., Cohen, I. L., Small, A. M., Samit, C., & Sachar, E. J. (1978). A comparison of haloperidol and behavior therapy and their interaction in autistic children. *Journal of the American Academy of Psychiatry, 12*, 640–655.

Campione, J. C., & Brown, A. L. (1977). Memory and metamemory development in educable mentally retarded children. In R. W. Kail, & J. W. Hagen (Eds.), *Perspectives on the development of memory and cognition*. Hillsdale, NJ: Erlbaum.

Cantalapiedra, M. A., Deweerdt, C., & Frederick, F. (1977). Le role psychotherapique de l'educateur dans un externat pour jeunes enfants. *Revue de Neuropsychiatrie Infantile, 25*, 787–811.

Carr, E. G. (1977). The motivation of self-injurious behavior: A review of some hypotheses. *Psychological Bulletin, 84*, 800–816.

Chazan, M. (1964). The incidence and nature of maladjustment among children in schools for the educationally subnormal. *British Journal of Educational Psychology, 34*, 292–304.

Chess, S. (1962). Psychiatric treatment of the mentally retarded child with behavior problems. *American Journal of Orthopsychiatry, 32*, 863.

Chess, S., & Hassibi, M. (1970). Behavior deviations in mentally retarded children. *Journal of the American Academy of Child Psychiatry, 9*, 292–297.

Chidester, L., & Menninger, K. A. (1936). The application of psychoanalytic methods to the study of mental retardation. *American Journal of Orthopsychiatry, 6*, 616–625.

Cook, J. W., Altman, K., Shaw, J., & Blaylock, M. (1978). Use of contingent lemon juice to eliminate public masturbation by a severely retarded boy. *Behavior Research and Therapy, 16*, 131–134.

Cooley, J. M. (1945). The relative amenability of dull and bright children to child guidance. *Smith College Studies in Social Work, 16*, 26–43.

Corbett, J. A. (1985). Mental retardation: Psychiatric aspects. In M. Rutter & L. Hersov (Eds.), *Child Psychiatry: Modern approaches* (2nd ed.). Oxford: Blackwell.

Corte, H. E., Wolf, M. M., & Locke, B. J. (1971). A comparison of procedures for eliminating self-injurious behavior of retarded adolescents. *Journal of Applied Behavior Analysis, 4*, 201–213.

Costello, A. (1982). Assessment and diagnosis of psychopathology. In J. L. Matson & R. P. Barrett (Eds.), *Psychopathology in the mentally retarded*, New York: Grune & Stratton.

Cotzin, M. (1948). Group therapy with mentally defective problem boys. *American Journal of Mental Deficiency, 53*, 268–283.

Crowley, F. J. (1965). Psychotherapy for the mentally retarded: A survey and projective consideration. *Training School Bulletin (Vineland), 62*, 5–11.

Cuvo, A. J. (1976). Decreasing repetetive behavior in an institutionalized mentally retarded resident. *Mental Retardation, 14* (1), 22–25.

Deblassie, R. R., & Lebsock, M. S. (1979). Counseling with handicapped children. *Elementary School Guidance and Counseling, 13*, 199–206.

Dewan, J. G. (1948). Intelligence and emotional stability. *American Journal of Psychiatry, 104*, 548–554.

Dorsey, M. F., Iwata, B. A., Ong, P., & McSween, T. E. (1980). Treatment of self-injurious behavior using a water mist: Initial response suppression and generalization. *Journal of Applied Behavior Analysis, 13*, 343–353.

Duker, P. C. (1976). Remotely applied punishment versus avoidance conditioning in the treatment of self-injurious behavior. *European Journal of Behavior Modification. 3*, 179–185.

Durand, V. M. (1982). A behavioral/pharmacological intervention for the treatment of severe self-injurious behavior. *Journal of Autism and Developmental Disorders, 12*, 243–251.

Eldridge, M. S., Witmer, J. M., Barcikowski, R., & Bauer, L. (1977). The effects of a group counseling program on the self-concepts of EMR children. *Measurement and Evaluation in Guidance, 9*, 184–191.

Ellis, A. (1977). The basic clinical theory of rational emotive therapy. In A. Ellis & G. Grieger (Eds.), *Handbook of rational emotive therapy*. New York: Springer.

Eysenck, H. J. (1960). *Behavior therapy and neurosis*. New York: Pergamon.

Eysenck, H. J. (1966). *The effects of psychotherapy*. New York: International Science Press.

Favell, J. E., Azrin, N. H., Baumeister, A. A., Carr, E. G., Dorsey, M. F., Forehand, R., Foxx, R. M., Lovaas, O. I., Rincover, A., Risley, T. R., Romanczyk, R. G., Russo, D. C., Schroeder, S. R., & Solnick, J. V. (1982). The treatment of self-injurious behavior. *Behavior Therapy, 13*, 529–554.

Feuerstein, R., Rand, Y., & Hoffman, M. (1979). *The dynamic assessment of retarded performers*. Baltimore, MD: University Park Press.

Feuerstein, R., Rand, Y., Hoffman, M., & Miller, R. (1980). *Instrumental enrichment: An intervention program for cognitive modifiability*. Baltimore, MD: University Park Press.

Fine, R. H., & Dawson, J. C. (1965). A therapy program for the mildy retarded adolescent. *American Journal of Mental Deficiency, 69*, 23–30.

Fisher, L. A., & Wolfson, I. N. (1953). Group therapy of mental defectives. *American Journal of Mental Deficiency, 57*, 463–476.

Foxx, R. M. (1976). The use of overcorrection to eliminate the public disrobing (stripping) of retarded women. *Behavior Research and Therapy, 14*, 53–61.

Foxx, R. M. (1978). An overview of overcorrection. *Journal of Pediatric Psychology, 3*, 97–101.

Foxx, R. M., & Azrin, N. H. (1972). Restitution: A method of eliminating aggressive-disruptive behavior of retarded and brain damaged patients. *Behavior Research and Therapy, 10*, 15–27.

Foxx, R. M., & Shapiro, S. T. (1978). The time-out ribbon: A nonexclusionary time-out procedure. *Journal of Applied Behavior Analysis, 11*, 125–136.

Foxx, R. M., McMorrow, M. J., Bittle, R. G., & Bechtel, D. R. (1986). The successful treatment of a dually-diagnosed deaf man's aggression with a program that included contingent electric shock. *Behavior Therapy, 17*, 170–186.

Frame, C., Matson, J. L., Sonis, W. A., Fialkov, M. J., & Kazdin, A. E. (1982). Behavioral treatment of depression in a prepubertal child. *Journal of Behavior Therapy and Experimental Psychiatry, 13*, 239–243.

Franzini, L. R., Litrownik, A. J., & Magy, M. A. (1978). Immediate and delayed reward preferences of TMR adolescents. *American Journal of Mental Deficiency, 82*, 406–409.

Frederiksen, L. W., & Frederiksen, C. B. (1975). Teacher-determined and self-determined token reinforcement in a special education classroom. *Behavior Therapy, 6*, 310–314.

Freeman, M. (1936). Drawing as a psychotherapeutic intermedium. *American Journal of Mental Deficiency, 41*, 182–187.

Gesten, E. L., Flores de Apodaca, R., Rains, M. H., Weissberg, R. P., & Cowen, E. L. (1979). Promoting peer related competence in young children. In M. W. Kent, & J. E. Rolf (Eds.), *The primary prevention of psychopathology: Social competence in children*. Hanover, NH: University Press of New England.

Glassman, L. A. (1943). Is dull normal intelligence a contraindication for psychotherapy? *Smith College Studies in Social Work 13*, 275–298.

Golden, W. L., & Consorte, J. (1982). Training mildly retarded individuals to control their anger through the use of cognitive behavior therapy techniques. *Journal of Contemporary Psychotherapy, 13*, 182–187.

Goldfried, M. R., & Davison, G. C. (1976). *Clinical behavior therapy*. New York: Holt, Rinehart, & Winston.

Grossman, H. J. (Ed.). (1977). *Manual on terminology and classification in mental retardation*. Washington, DC: American Association on Mental Deficiency.

Hamilton, H., Stephens, L., & Allen, P. (1967). Controlling aggressive and destructive behavior in severely retarded institutionalized residents. *American Journal of Mental Deficiency, 71*, 852–856.

Harris, S. L., & Romanczyk, R. G. (1976). Treating self-injurious behavior of a retarded child by overcorrection. *Behavior Therapy, 7*, 235–239.

Heimlich, E. P. (1960). Music as therapy with emotionally disturbed children. *Child Welfare, 39*, 3–7.

Hersen, M. (Ed.). (1986). *Pharmacological treatment—An integrative approach*. New York: Wiley.

Hersen, M., & Barlow, D. H. (1984). *Single case experimental design* (2nd ed.). New York: Pergamon Press.

Hill, B. K., & Bruininks, R. H. (1984). Maladaptive behavior of mentally retarded individuals in residential facilities. *American Journal of Mental Deficiency, 88*, 380–387.

Homme, L. (1965). Perspectives in psychology. *Psychological Record, 15*, 501–511.

Horner, R. D., & Barton, E. S. (1980). Operant techniques in the analysis and modification of self-injurious behavior. *Behavior Research of Severe Developmental Disabilities, 1*, 61–91.

Israel, A. C. (1978). Some thoughts on correspondence between saying and doing. *Journal of Applied Behavior Analysis, 11*, 271–275.

Israel, A. C., & O'Leary, K. D. (1973). Developing correspondence between children's words and deeds. *Child Development, 44*, 575–581.

Jenson, W. R., Rovner, L., Cameron, S., Petersen, B. P., & Kesler, J. (1985). Reduction of self-injurious behavior in an autistic girl using a multifaceted treatment program. *Journal of Behavior Therapy and Experimental Psychiatry, 16*, 77–80.

Jones, M. C. (1924). The elimination of children's fears. *Journal of Experimental Psychology, 7*, 382–390.

Joseph, H., & Heimlich, E. P. (1959). The therapeutic use of music with "treatment resistant" children. *American Journal of Mental Deficiency, 64,* 41–49.

Kanner, L. (1964). *A history of care and study of the feebleminded.* Springfield, IL: Thomas.

Kazdin, A. E. (1977). *The token economy: A review and evaluation.* New York: Plenum Press.

Kazdin, A. E. (1982). History of behavior modification (pp. 3–32). In A. S. Bellack, M. Hersen, & A. E. Kazdin (Eds.), *International handbook of behavior modification and therapy.* New York: Plenum Press.

Kazdin, A. E., & Wilcoxon, L. A. (1976). Systematic desensitization and non-specific treatment effects: A methodological evaluation. *Psychological Bulletin, 83,* 729–758.

Kazdin, A. E., Matson, J. L., & Senatore, V. (1983). Assessment of depression in mentally retarded adults. *American Journal of Psychiatry, 140,* 1040–1043.

Kelly, J. A. (1981). Using puppets for behavior rehearsal in social skills training sessions with young children. *Child Behavior Therapy, 3,* 61–64.

Kendall, C., Borkowski, J. G., & Cavanaugh, J. C. (1980). Metamemory and the transfer of an interrogative strategy by EMR children. *Intelligence, 4,* 255–270.

Kendall, P. C., & Braswell, L. (1985). *Cognitive behavioral therapy for impulsive children.* New York: Guilford Press.

Kern, L., Koegel, R. L., & Dunlap, G. (1984). The influence of vigorous versus mild exercise on autistic stereotypic behavior. *Journal of Autism and Developmental Disabilities, 14,* 57–67.

Koegel, R., & Covert, A. (1972). The relationship of self-stimulation to learning in autistic children. *Journal of Applied Behavior Analysis, 5,* 381–387.

Krafft, K. M., & Poling, A. D. (1982). Behavioral treatments of epilepsy: Methodological characteristics and problems of published studies. *Applied Research in Mental Retardation, 3,* 151–162.

Kurtz, P. D., & Neisworth, J. T. (1976). Self-control possibilities for exceptional children. *Exceptional children, 42,* 212–217.

LaGrow, S. L., & Repp, A. C. (1984). Stereotypic responding: a review of intervention research. *American Journal of Mental Deficiency, 88,* 595–609.

Leboeuf, A., & Boeverts, M. (1981). Automatic detection and modification of aberrant behaviors: Two case studies. *Journal of Behavior Therapy and Experimental Psychiatry, 12,* 153–157.

Ledwidge, B. (1978). Cognitive behavior modification.: A step in the wrong direction? *Psychological Bulletin, 85,* 353–375.

Leitenberg, H. (1976). Behavioral approaches to treatment of neuroses. In H. Leitenberg (Ed.), *Handbook of behavior modification and behavior therapy.* Englewood Cliffs, NJ: Prentice-Hall.

Leland, H. (1983). Adaptive behavior scales. In J. L. Matson & J. A. Mulick (Eds.), *Handbook of mental retardation.* New York: Pergamon Press.

Leland, H., & Smith, D. (1962). Unstructured material in play therapy for emotionally disturbed, brain damaged mentally retarded children. *American Journal of Mental Deficiency, 66,* 621–627.

Leland, H., & Smith, D. (1965). *Play therapy with mentally subnormal children.* New York: Grune & Stratton.

Leland, H., Walker, J., & Taboada, A. N. (1959). Group play therapy with a group of post-nursery male retardates. *American Journal of Mental Deficiency, 63,* 848–851.

Levitt, E. (1957). The results of psychotherapy with children: An evaluation. *Journal of Consulting Psychology, 21,* 189–196.

Levitt, E. (1963). Psychotherapy with children: A further evaluation. *Behavior Research and Therapy, 1,* 45–51.

Lewis, M. H., & McLean, W. E. (1982). Issues in treating emotional disorders. In J. L. Matson & R. P. Barrett (Eds.), *Psychopathology in the mentally retarded.* New York: Grune & Stratton.

Li, A. (1981). Play and mentally retarded child. *Mental Retardation, 19,* 121–126.

Litrownik, A. J., & Freitas, J. L. (1980). Self-monitoring in moderately retarded adolescents: Reactivity and accurracy as a function of valence. *Behavior Therapy, 11,* 245–255.

Litrownik, A. J., Franzini, L. R., Geller, S., & Geller, M. (1977). Delay of gratification: Decisional self-control and experience with delay intervals. *American Journal of Mental Deficiency, 82,* 149–154.

Litrownik, A. J., Cleary, C. P., Lecklitner, G. L., & Franzini, L. R. (1978a). Self-regulation in retarded persons: Acquisition of standards for performance. *American Journal of Mental Deficiency, 83,* 86–89.

Litrownik, A. J., Freitas, J. L., & Franzini, L. R. (1978b). Self-regulation in retarded persons: Assessment and training of self-monitoring skills. *American Journal of Mental Deficiency, 82,* 499–506.

Lovaas, O. I., & Simmons, J. Q. (1969). Manipulation in self-destruction in three retarded children. *Journal of Applied Behavior Analysis, 2,* 143–157.

Lovaas, O. I., Freitag, G., Gold, V. J., & Kassorla, I. C. (1965). Experimental studies in childhood schizophrenia. *Journal of Experimental Child Psychology, 2*, 67–84.

Luiselli, J. K., Pemberton, B. W., & Helfen, C. S. (1978). Effects and side-effects of a brief overcorrection procedure in reducing multiple self-stimulatory behavior: A single case analysis. *Journal of Mental Deficiency Research, 22*, 187–293.

Luria, A. R. (1961). *The role of speech in the regulation of normal and abnormal behavior.* New York: Liverwright.

Lutzker, J. R. (1983). Reinforcement control of exhibitionism in a profoundly retarded adult. *Proceedings of the 81st Annual Convention of the American Psychological Association.*

McConahey, O. L. (1972). A token system for retarded women: behavior modification, drug therapy, and their combination. In T. Thompson & J. Grabowski (Eds.), *Behavior modification for the mentally retarded* (1st ed.). New York: Oxford University Press.

McConahey, O. L., Thompson, T., & Zimmermann, R. (1977). A token system for retarded women: Behavior therapy, drug administration, and their combination. In T. Thompson & J. Grabowski (Eds.), *Behavior modification for the mentally retarded* (2nd ed.). New York: Oxford University Press.

McGonigle, J. J., Duncan, D., Cordisco, L., & Barrett, R. P. (1982). Visual screening: An alternative method for reducing stereotypic behaviors. *Journal of Applied Behavior Analysis, 15*, 461–467.

Mahoney, M. J., & Arnkoff, D. B. (1978). Cognitive and self-control therapies. In S. L. Garfield & A. E. Bergin (Eds.), *Handbook of psychotherapy and behavior change: An empirical analysis* (2nd ed.). New York: Wiley.

Mahoney, M. J., & Mahoney, K. (1976). Self-control techniques with the mentally retarded. *Exceptional Children, 42*, 338–339.

Mahoney, M. J., & Thoresen, C. (1974). *Self-control: Power to the person.* Monterey, CA: Brooks/Cole.

Mansdorf, I. J. (1977). Reinforcer isolation: An alternative to subject isolation in time-out from positive reinforcement. *Journal of Behavior Therapy and Experimental Psychiatry, 8*, 391–393.

Marks, I. (1982). Drugs combined with behavioral psychotherapy. In A. S. Bellack, M. Hersen, & A. E. Kazdin (Eds.), *International handbook of behavior modification and therapy.* New York: Plenum Press.

Matson, J. L. (1981a). Assessment and treatment of clinical fears in mentally retarded children. *Journal of Applied Behavior Analysis, 14*, 287–294.

Matson, J. L. (1981b). A controlled outcome study of phobias in mentally retarded adults. *Behavior Research and Therapy, 19*, 101–107.

Matson, J. L. (1982). The treatment of behavioral characteristics of depression in the mentally retarded. *Behaviour Therapy, 13*, 209–218.

Matson, J. L. (1983). Depression in the mentally retarded: Toward a conceptual analysis of diagnosis. In M. Hersen, R. Eisler, & P. Miller (Eds.), *Progress in behavior modification* (Vol. 15). New York: Academic Press.

Matson, J. L. (1984). Behavioral treatment of psychosomatic complaints of mentally retarded adults. *American Journal of Mental Deficiency, 88*, 638–646.

Matson, J. L. (1985a). Biosocial theory of psychopathology: A three by three factor model. *Applied Research in Mental Retardation, 6*, 199–227.

Matson, J. L. (1985b). Emotional problems in the mentally retarded: The need for assessment and treatment. *Psychopharmacology Bulletin, 21*, 258–261.

Matson, J. L., & Barrett, R. P. (1982). *Psychopathology in the mentally retarded.* New York: Grune & Stratton.

Matson, J. L., & DiLorenzo, T. M. (1984). *Punishment and its alternatives.* New York: Springer.

Matson, J. L., & Frame, C. (1983). Psychopathology. In J. L. Matson & S. E. Breuning (Eds.), *Assessing the mentally retarded.* New York: Grune & Stratton.

Matson, J. L., & Gorman-Smith, D. (1986). A review of treatment research for aggressive and disruptive behavior in the mentally retarded. *Applied Research in Mental Retardation, 7*, 95–103.

Matson, J. L., Ollendick, T. H., & Martin, J. E. (1979). Overcorrection revisited: A long-term follow-up. *Journal of Behavior Therapy and Experimental Psychiatry, 10*, 11–14.

Matson, J. L., Kazdin, A. E., & Senatore, V. (1984). Psychometric properties of the psychopathology instrument for the mentally retarded. *Applied Research in Mental Retardation, 5*, 81–89.

Meichenbaum, D. (1974). *Cognitive behavior modification.* Morristown, NJ: General Learning.

Meichenbaum, D., & Goodman, J. (1969). The developmental control of operant motor responding by verbal operants. *Journal of Experimental Child Psychology, 7*, 553–565.

Meichenbaum, D., & Goodman, J. (1971). Training impulsive children to talk to themselves: A means of developing self-control. *Journal of Abnormal Psychology, 77*, 115–126.

Menolascino, F. J., & Stark, J. A. (1985). *Handbook of mental illness in the mentally retarded.* New York: Plenum Press.

Meyers, A. W., & Craighead, W. E. (Eds.). (1984). *Cognitive behavior therapy with children.* New York: Plenum Press.

Miller, L. K., Hale, G. A., & Stevenson, H. W. (1968). Learning and problem solving by retarded and normal Ss. *American Journal of Mental Deficiency, 72,* 681–690.

Morena, D. A., & Litrownik, A. J. (1974). Self-concept in educable mentally retarded and emotionally handicapped children: Relationships between behavioral and self-report indices and an attempt at modification. *Journal of Abnormal Child Psychology, 2,* 281–292.

Morgenstern, M. (1983). Standard intelligence tests and related assessment techniques. In J. L. Matson & J. A. Mulick (Eds.), *Handbook of mental retardation.* New York: Pergamon Press.

Moustakas, C. (1966). *The child's discovery of himself.* New York: Ballantine.

Mowrer, O. H., & Mowrer, W. M. (1938). Enuresis—A method for its study and treatment. *American Journal of Orthopsychiatry, 8,* 436–459.

Mulick, J. A., & Schroeder, S. R. (1980). Research relating to management of antisocial behavior in mentally retarded persons. *The Psychological Record, 30,* 397–417.

Mulick, J. A., Hoyt, P., Rojahn, J., & Schroeder, S. R. (1978). Reduction of a "nervous habit" in a profoundly retarded youth by increasing toy play. *Journal of Behavior Therapy and Experimental Psychiatry, 9,* 381–385.

Nelson, R. O., Lipinski, D. P., & Black, J. L. (1976). The reactivity of adult retardates' self-monitoring: A comparison among behaviors of different valances and a comparison with token reinforcement. *Psychological Record, 26,* 189–201.

Nelson, R. O., Lipinski, D. P., & Boykin, R. A. (1978). The effects of self-recorders training and the obtrusiveness of the self-recording device on the accuracy and reactivity of self-monitoring. *Behavior Therapy, 9,* 200–208.

Nihira, K., Foster, R., Shellhaas, N., & Leland, H. (1974). *AAMD adaptive behavior scale: Manual.* Washington, DC: American Association on Mental Deficiency.

Nordoff, P., & Robbins, C. (1965). *Music therapy for handicapped children: Investigations and experiences.* Blauvelt, NJ: Rudolph Steiner.

Nuffield, E. J. (1983). Psychotherapy. In J. J. Matson & J. A. Mulick (Eds.), *Handbook of mental retardation.* New York: Pergamon Press.

Nunes, D. L., Murphy, R. J., & Ruprecht, M. L. (1977). Reducing self-injurious behavior of severely retarded individuals through withdrawal of reinforcement procedures. *Behavior Modification, 1,* 499–516.

Ollendick, T. H., Shapiro, E. S., & Barrett, R. P. (1982). Effects of vicarious reinforcement in normal and severely disturbed children. *Journal of Consulting and Clinical Psychology, 50,* 63–70.

Pendergrass, V. E. (1972). Timeout from positive reinforcement following persistent, high-rate behavior in retardates. *Journal of Applied Behavior Analyis, 5,* 85–91.

Phillips, I., & Williams, N. (1975). Psychopathology and mental retardation: A study of 100 mentally retarded children: 1. Psychopathology. *American Journal of Psychiatry, 132,* 1265–1271.

Pollack, H. M. (1944). Mental disease among mental defectives. *American Journal of Psychiatry, 191,* 361.

Premack, D. (1965). Reinforcement theory. In D. Levine (Ed.), *Nebraska symposium on motivation.* Lincoln: University of Nebraska Press.

Radinsky, A. M. (1984). *A descriptive study of psychotropic and antiepileptic medication use with mentally retarded persons in three residential environments.* Dissertation, University of Pittsburgh.

Rago, W. V., Parker, R. M., & Cleland, C. C. (1978). Effect of increased space on the social behavior of institutionalized profoundly retarded male adults. *American Journal of Mental Deficiency, 82,* 554–558.

Rapport, M. D., Sonis, W. A., Fialkov, M. J., Matson, J. L., & Kazdin, A. E. (1983). Carbamazepine and behavior therapy for aggressive behavior. *Behavior Modification, 7,* 255–265.

Reatig, N., & Raskin, A. (1985). Introduction: Pharmacotherapy and mental retardation workshop. *Psychopharmacology Bulletin, 21,* 257.

Reiss, S., & Szyszko, J. (1983). Diagnostic overshadowing and professional experience with mentally retarded persons. *American Journal of Mental Deficiency, 87,* 396–402.

Repp, A. C., & Barton, L. E. (1980). Naturalistic observations of institutionalized retarded persons: A comparison of licensure decisions and behavioral observations. *Journal of Applied Behavior Analysis, 13,* 333–341.

Repp, A. C., & Brulle, A. R. (1981). Reducing aggressive behavior of mentally retarded persons. In J. L. Matson & J. R. McCartney (Eds.), *Handbook of behavior modification with the mentally retarded.* New York: Plenum Press.

Repp, A. C., Deitz, S. M., & Deitz, D. E. D. (1976). Reducing inappropriate behaviors in classrooms and in individual sessions through DRO schedules of reinforcement. *Mental Retardation, 14,* 11–15.

Repp, A. C., Barton, L. E., & Gottlieb, J. (1983). Naturalistic studies of institutionalized retarded persons: 2. The effects of density on the behaviors of profoundly or severely retarded persons. *American Journal of Mental Deficiency, 87,* 441–447.

Rincover, A. (1978). Sensory extinction: A procedure for eliminating self-stimulatory behavior in developmentally disabled children. *Journal of Abnormal Child Psychology, 6,* 299–310.

Rincover, A., & Devany, J. (1982). The application of sensory extinction procedures to self-injury. *Analysis and Intervention in Developmental Disabilities, 2,* 67–81.

Rincover, A., Cook, A. R., Peoples, A.. & Packard, D. (1979). Sensory extinction and sensory reinforcement principles for programming multiple adaptive behavior change. *Journal of Applied Behavior Analysis, 12,* 221–233.

Rincover, A., Newsome, C. D., & Carr, E. G. (1979). Use of sensory extinction procedures in the treatment of compulsive-like behavior of developmentally disabled children. *Journal of Consulting and Clinical Psychology, 47,* 695–701.

Risley, T. R. (1968). The effects and side effects of punishing the autistic behaviors of a deviant child. *Journal of Applied Behavior Analysis, 1,* 21–34.

Risley, T., & Hart, B. (1968). Developing correspondence between the nonverbal and verbal behavior of preschool children. *Journal of Applied Behavior Analysis, 1,* 267–281.

Robertson, S. J., Simon, S. J., Pachman, J. S., & Drabman, R. S. (1979). Self-control and generalization procedures in a classroom of disruptive retarded children. *Child Behavior Therapy, 1,* 347–362.

Rogers-Warren, A., & Warren, S. F. (Eds.). (1977). *Ecological perspectives in behavior analysis.* Baltimore: University Park Press.

Rojahn, J. (1986). Self-injurious behavior and stereotypic behavior in noninstitutionalized mentally retarded people. *American Journal of Mental Deficiency, 91,* 268–276.

Rojahn, J., & Schroeder, S. R. (1983). Behavioral assessment. In J. L. Matson & J. A. Mulick (Eds.), *Handbook of mental retardation.* New York: Pergamon Press.

Rojahn, J., Schroeder, S. R., & Mulick, J. A. (1980). Ecological assessment of self-protective devices in three profoundly retarded adults. *Journal of Autism and Developmental Disorders, 10,* 59–66.

Rojahn, J., McGonigle, J. J., Curcio, C., & Dixon, J. (1987). Suppression of pica by water mist and aromatic ammonia: A comparative analysis. *Behavior Modification, 11,* 65–74.

Rolider, A., & Van Houten, R. (1985). Movement suppression time-out for undesirable behavior in psychotic and severely developmentally delayed children. *Journal of Applied Behavior Analysis, 18,* 275–288.

Rollings, J. P., & Baumeister, A. A. (1981). Stimulus control of stereotypic responding: Effects on target and collateral behaviors. *American Journal of Mental Deficiency, 86,* 67–77.

Romanczyk, R. G., & Goren, E. R. (1975). Severe self-injurious behavior: The problem of clinical control. *Journal of Consulting and Clinical Psychology, 43,* 730–793.

Rosen, M., Diggory, J. C., & Werlinsky, B. E. (1966). Goal-setting and expectancy of success in institutionalized and non-institutionalized mental subnormals. *American Journal of Mental Deficiency, 71,* 249–255.

Rosen, M., Diggory, J. C., Floor, L., & Nowakiwska, M. (1971). Self-evaluation, expectancy, and performance in the mentally subnormals. *Journal of Mental Deficiency Research, 15,* 81–95.

Ross, D. M., & Ross, S. A. (1973). Cognitive training for the EMR child: Situational problem-solving and planning. *American Journal of Mental Deficiency, 78,* 20–26.

Ross, D. M., & Ross, S. A. (1978). Cognitive training for EMR children: Choosing the best alternative. *American Journal of Mental Deficiency, 82,* 598–601.

Ross, D. M., & Ross, S. A. (1979). Cognitive training for the EMR child: Language skills prerequisite to relevent-irrelevant discrimination task. *Mental Retardation, 17,* 3–7.

Roth, E. A., & Barrett, R. P. (1980). Parallels in art and play therapy with a disturbed retarded boy. *The Arts in Psychotherapy, 7,* 19–26.

Rutter, M., Graham, P., & Yule, W. (1970). *A neuropsychiatric study in childhood.* London: Heinemann/SIMP.

Rutter, M., Tizard, J., & Whitmore, K. (Eds.). (1981). *Education, health, and behavior.* Huntington, NY: Krieber.

Sandford, D., & Nettlebeck, T. (1982). Medication and reinforcement within a token program for disturbed mentally retarded residents. *Applied Research in Mental Retardation, 3,* 21–36.

Sattler, J. (1982). *Assessment of children's intelligence and special abilities* (2nd ed.). Philadelphia: W. B. Saunders.

Schneider, M. R. (1974). Turtle technique in the classroom. *Teaching Exceptional Children, 6*, 22–24.

Schroeder, S. R., Peterson, C. R., Solomon, L. J., & Artley, J. J. (1977). EMG feedback and the contingent restraint of self-injurious behavior among the severely retarded: Two case illustrations. *Behavior Therapy, 8*, 738–741.

Schroeder, S. R., Rojahn, J., & Mulick, J. A. (1978). Ecobehavioral organization of developmental day care for the chronically self-injurious. *Journal of Pediatric Psychology, 3*, 81–88.

Schroeder, S. R., Schroeder, C. S., Rojahn, J., & Mulick, J. A. (1981). Self-injurious behavior: An analysis of behavior management techniques. In J. L. Matson & J. R. McCartney (Eds.), *Handbook of behavior modification with the mentally retarded*. New York: Plenum Press.

Schroeder, S. R., Lewis, M. H., & Lipton, M. A. (1983). Interactions of pharmacotherapy and behavior therapy among children with learning and behavioral disorders. In K. Gadow & I. Bialer (Eds.), *Advances in learning and behavioral disabilities* (Vol. 2). Greenwich, CT: JAI Press.

Selan, B. H. (1979). Psychotherapy with the mentally retarded. *Social Work, 24*, 263.

Shapiro, E. S., & Klein, R. D. (1980). Self-management of classroom behavior with retarded /disturbed children. *Behavior Modification, 4*, 83–97.

Shapiro, E. S., McGonigle, J. J., & Ollendick, T. (1980). An analysis of self-assessment and self-reinforcement in a self-managed token economy with mentally retarded children. *Applied Research in Mental Retardation, 1*, 227–240.

Shapiro, E. S., Kazdin, A. E., & McGonigle, J. J. (1982). Multiple-treatment interference in the simultaneous- or alternating-treatments design. *Behavioral Assessment, 4*, 105–115.

Singh, N. N. (1981). Current trends in the treatment of self-injurious behavior. In J. A. Barness (Ed.), *Advances in pediatrics* (Vol. 28). Chicago: Year Book Medical Publishers.

Singh, N. N., & Millichamp, C. J. (1985). Pharmacological treatment of self-injurious behavior in mentally retarded persons. *Journal of Autism and Developmental Disorders, 15*, 257–267.

Singh, N. N., Dawson, M. J., & Gregory, P. R. (1980). Self-injury in the profoundly retarded: Clinically significant versus therapeutic control. *Journal of Mental Deficiency Research, 24*, 87–97.

Skinner, B. F. (1953). *Science and human behavior*. New York: Free Press.

Smith, R. M. (1967). Creative thinking abilities of educable mentally handicapped children in the regular grades. *American Journal of Mental Deficiency, 71*, 571–575.

Solnick, J. V., Rincover, A., & Peterson, C. R. (1977). Some determinants of the reinforcing and punishing effects of time-out. *Applied Behavior Analysis, 10*, 415–424.

Sparrow, S. S., Balla, D. A., & Cicchetti, D. V. (1984). *Vineland adaptive behavior scales*. Circle Pines, MN: American Guidance Service.

Spitalnik, R., & Drabman, R. (1976). A classroom time-out procedure for retarded children. *Journal of Behavior Therapy and Experimental Psychiatry, 7*, 17–21.

Sprague, R. L., & Baxley, G. B. (1978) Drugs used for the management of behavior in mental retardation. In J. Wortis (Ed.), *Mental retardation* (Vol. 8). New York: Brunner/Mazel.

Spreat, S., & Stepansky, D. (in press). The effectiveness of contingent restraint on aggression, self-injury, and property destruction of institutionalized mentally retarded persons. *Behavioral Residential Treatment*.

Spreat, S., Roszkowski, & Isett, R. D. (1983). Assessment of adaptive behavior in the mentally retarded. In S. E. Breuning, J. L. Matson, & R. P. Barett (Eds.), *Advances in mental retardation and developmental disabilities*. Greenwich, CT: JAI.

Stevenson, H. W., Hale, G. A., Klein, R. E., & Miller, L. K. (1968). Interrelations and correlates in children's learning and problem solving. *Monographs of the Society for Research in Child Development, 33* (7, Serial No. 123).

Sulzer-Azaroff, B., & Mayer, G. R. (1977). *Applying behavior analysis procedures with children and youth*. New York: Holt, Rinehart & Winston.

Szymanski, L., & Grossman, H. (1984). Dual implications of "dual diagnosis." *Mental Retardation, 22*, 155–156.

Tanner, B. A., & Zeiler, M. (1975). Punishment of self-injurious behavior using aromatic ammonia as the aversive stimulus. *Journal of Applied Behavior Analysis, 8*, 53–57.

Tarpley, M. D., & Schroeder, S. R. (1979). Comparison of DRO and DRI on rate of suppression of self-injurious behavior. *American Journal of Mental Deficiency, 84*, 188–194.

Tate, B. G., & Baroff, G. S. (1966). Aversive control of self-injurious behavior in a psychotic boy. *Behavior Research and Therapy, 4*, 281–287.

Thoresen, C. E., & Mahoney, M. J. (1974). *Behavioral self-control*. New York: Holt, Rinehart, & Winston.

Thorndike, R. L., Hagen, E., & Sattler, J. (1986). *Stanford-Binet*. Chicago: Riverside.

Turnure, J. E., Buium, N., & Thurlow, M. L. (1976). The effectiveness of interrogatives for promoting verbal elaboration productivity in young children. *Child Development, 47,* 851–855.

Ullman, L. P., & Krasner, L. (1965). *Case studies in behavior modification*. New York: Holt, Rinehart & Winston.

Urbain, E. S., & Kendall, P. C. (1980). Review of social-cognitive problem-solving interventions with children. *Psychological Bulletin, 88,* 109–143.

Vygotsky, L. (1962). *Thought and language*. New York: Wiley.

Walker, P. W. (1977). Premarital counseling for the developmentally disabled. *Social Casework, 58.* 475–479.

Warner, D. W., & deJung, J. E. (1971). Effects of goal setting upon learning in educable retardates. *American Journal of Mental Deficiency, 75,* 681–684.

Watson, J. B. (1924). *Behaviorism*. Chicago: University of Chicago Press.

Watson, J. B., & Rayner, R. (1920). Conditioned emotional reactions. *Journal of Experimental Psychology, 3,* 1–14.

Wegman, B. S. (1944). Intelligence as a factor in the treatment of problem children. *Smith College Studies in Social Work, 14,* 244–245.

Weigl, V. (1959). Functional music, a therapeutic tool in working with the mentally retarded. *American Journal of Mental Deficiency, 63,* 672–678.

Whitman, T., Scibak, J., Butler, K., Richter, R., & Johnson, M. (1982). Improving classroom behavior in mentally retarded children through correspondence training. *Journal of Applied Behavior Analysis, 15,* 545–564.

Whitman, T., Burgio, L., & Johnston, M. B. (1984). Cognitive behavioral interventions with mentally retarded children. In A. E. Meyers & W. E. Craighead (Eds.), *Cognitive behavior therapy with children*. New York: Plenum Press.

Wilcox, G. T., & Guthrie, G. M. (1957). Changes in adjustment of institutionalized female defectives following group psychotherapy. *Journal of Clinical Psychology, 13,* 9–13.

Williams, J. L., Schroeder, S. R., Eckerman, D. A., & Rojahn, J. (1983). Time-out from positive reinforcement with mentally retarded persons: An ecological review and analysis. In S. E. Breuning, J. L. Matson, & R. P. Barrett (Eds.), *Advances in mental retardation and developmental disabilities* (Vol. 1). Greenwich, CT: JAI.

Wilson, G. T. (1978). Cognitive behavior therapy: Paradigm shift or passing phase? In J. P. Foreyt & D. P. Rathjen (Eds.), *Cognitive behavior therapy: Research and applications*. New York: Plenum Press.

Winton, A., Singh, N. N., & Dawson, M. J. (1984). Effects of facial screening and blindfold on self-injurious behavior. *Applied Research in Mental Retardation, 5,* 29–42.

Wolf, M. M., Risley, T. R., & Mees, H. L. (1964). Application of operant conditioning procedures to the behavior problems of an autistic child. *Behavior Research and Therapy, 1,* 305–312.

Wolf, M. M., Risley, T., Johnston, M., Harris, F., & Allen, E. (1967). Application of operant conditioning procedures to the behavior problems of an autistic child.: A follow-up and extension. *Behavior Research and Therapy, 5,* 103–111.

Zegiob, L. E., Jenkins, J., Becker, J., & Bristow, A. (1976). Facial screening: Effects on appropriate and inappropriate behaviors. *Journal of Behavior Therapy and Experimental Psychiatry, 7,* 355–357.

Zegiob, L., Klukas, N., & Junginger, J. (1978). Reactivity of self-monitoring procedures with retarded adolescents. *American Journal of Mental Deficiency, 83,* 156–163.

Zlutnick, S., Mayville, W. J., & Moffat, S. (1975). Modification of seizure disorders: The interruption of behavioral chains. *Journal of Applied Behavior Analysis, 8,* 1–12.

# 20 *Mental Retardation and Learning Disability*

## *Pharmacotherapies*

### Maria de Fatima Thomas

## Introduction

To discuss the pharmacological treatment of learning disabilities and mental retardation simultaneously is a difficult task. Even though both have in common learning difficulties, these two conditions are quite different, having distinct diagnostic characteristics, treatment approaches, and outcomes. Whereas the mentally retarded child functions below his or her chronological age in many areas of development because of impaired ability, the learning-disabled child underachieves in school despite normal or above-normal intelligence. On the other hand, in both conditions, pharmacological intervention, when used, is aimed at treating the underlying or associated psychiatric, emotional, or behavioral problems. In other words, medications may be used either to suppress undesired behaviors or to facilitate and enhance desired behaviors and, incidently, to facilitate learning.

The term *mental retardation* implies significant developmental delays and deficits in cognitive ability, resulting in significantly subaverage intellectual functioning and impairment in adaptive behavior. In other words, the term is applied to individuals who, from very early in life, whether from biological, psychosocial, or both factors, have been functioning below their chronological age in many areas of development. The level of intellectual functioning is usually measured by tests that give an intelligence quotient (IQ).

It is well accepted that the IQ of $70 \pm 5$ represents the borderline between low average intelligence and high-functioning, mild mental retardation. Subtypes of mental retardation are classified according to IQ as follows: mild (50–70), moderate (35–49), severe (20–34), and profound (below 20). However, IQ alone is not enough for the diagnosis of mental retardation, especially in the upper limits of IQ scores (IQs between 60 and 70). The level of adaptive behavior has to be considered an important factor in determining whether mental retardation is present or not. Adaptive behavior is assessed primarily by clinical judgment, with the help of the available quantitative scales. These scales measure

Maria de Fatima Thomas • Department of Psychiatry, University of Missouri—Columbia, Columbia, Missouri 65212.

how well an individual meets the standards of personal independence and social responsibility expected for his or her age and cultural group.

Whereas mental retardation is diagnosed in children who have learning problems and who fit the above described criteria, regardless of the causation (organic or brain-based, or not), the diagnosis of learning disability is depends on its causation.

The term *learning disability* implies a marked discrepancy between ability and academic achievement. This definition is very broad and includes a multitude of possible etiologies. A discrepancy between ability and school achievement can result from (1) an inappropriate school environment, that is, unstimulating instruction, inappropriate expectations of the child, and stressful relationship with teachers or with other students; (2) the family's attitude and behavior toward education, that is, illiteracy, negativism, and obstructive behavior toward the school; and (3) problems inherent in the child, that is, emotional and behavioral problems affecting the acquisition of information and processing problems affecting the use of the acquired information. Only the processing problem fulfills the American Psychiatric Association's DSM-III (APA, 1980) and the U.S. Department of Education (USDHEW, Public Law 94–142, 1977) definition of learning disability.

## HISTORICAL DEVELOPMENT

### History of Psychopharmacology in Learning Disabilities

A review of the literature on pharmacotherapy for learning disabilities revealed that most studies address the use of stimulants to treat hyperactive children. Claims of enhanced academic performance due to the use of stimulants goes back to Bradley (1937) and his original paper on the use of amphetamine (Benzedrine) in behaviorally disordered children. Since then, more than five decades of accumulated research on the use of stimulants have passed. To this date, there have been only three published studies on the use of stimulants in nonhyperactive learning-disabled children (Aman & Werry, 1982; Gittelman, Klein, & Feingold, 1983; Gittelman-Klein, Klein, Saraf, & Pollack, 1976). These studies have failed to show the effectiveness of Ritalin in treating reading deficits in nonhyperactive children.

The earlier studies of the 1950s, the 1960s, and the early 1970s, with claims of improved academic performance due to stimulant medications, had several methodological problems. First, they all failed to differentiate isolated, true learning disability from attention-deficit disorder, a difficult task, as academic underachievement is a very common problem in hyperactive children with or without an associated learning disability. Second, the studies did not control for the effect of other interventions (such as remedial instruction) on the outcome. Third, most of the studies used standardized achievement tests as the only measure of improvement, excluding measures of academic achievement in the classroom environment. Fourth, most of the studies were of short duration. Better designed studies in the mid-1970s–1980s failed to demonstrate specific drug-treatment effects on learning. Long-term studies have been almost uniformly negative, as stimulant medications seem to improve school performance by increasing on-task behavior, leading to greater output and accuracy *but* only in hyperactive learning-disabled children.

Increased reading performance, improved completion of and performance on classroom arithmetic assignments, better spelling, and neater, more legible handwriting were the findings of studies addressing the use of stimulants in a mixed-bag population of children. Improved expressive language—increases in the amount and the complexity of speech—has been reported with the use of stimulants in children with attention-deficit disorder (ADD) and learning disability (LD).

Based on the available data, it is safe to conclude that there is no real indication for the use of stimulant medications to treat learning disability *per se*. However, these medications can make attention-deficit-disordered children, with or without an associated learning disability, more responsive to instruction, thus enhancing the effectiveness of their education.

Thus far, we have focused only on the effect of stimulant medications on the treatment of learning problems. This has been so because all other medications used to treat psychopathology that interferes with the learning process have not yet been well studied with respect to their effect on learning. No specific beneficial effect on academic achievement has been attributed to any other class of drugs, except for the stimulants and, lately, to some nootropic substances, such as gamma-aminobutyric acid (GABA) and its derivative piracetam. We will discuss these two later in the chapter. On the other hand, a negative effect on learning has been attributed to all sedating medications used in children, especially when used in high therapeutic doses. These include the major tranquilizers such as Thorazine, the minor tranquilizers or anxiolytics such as Valium, the antidepressants such as Tofranil, and the antiepileptics such as phenobarbital.

## History of Psychopharmacology in Mental Retardation

Institutions for the mentally retarded began to use drugs such as chloral hydrate and bromides to control disturbing behaviors around the turn of the century. The antiepileptic drugs were introduced about 50 years ago. However, the "drug revolution" did not begin until impressive results were obtained by using phenothiazines to treat the mentally ill. The introduction of chlorpromazine into the treatment of the mentally ill and the "feebleminded" in the 1950s had a great impact on the medical community. The so-called snake pits, warehouses, and asylums were nearly emptied within 15 years.

After the pioneering use of chlorpromazine in children in 1953, widespread enthusiasm, based on unsound research, resulted in the unbridled use of the phenothiazines for a variety of problems in the pediatric disturbed population. Soon, it became evident that research was needed to give guidelines for clinical use. The 1960s fostered extensive research on new-drug development and the biological aspects of mental illness. After the prototype phenothiazine, chlorpromazine (Thorazine), new phenothiazine compounds, such as thioridazine (Mellaril), fluphenazine (Prolixin), trifluoperazine (Stelazine), and mesoridazine (Serentil), were developed and were quickly followed by the butyrophenones, such as haloperidol (Haldol), and the thioxanthenes (Navane).

Questions regarding the significance of the effectiveness of the psychotropics motivated scientific research into the pharmacological action of these drugs in the central nervous system (CNS). The identification of responders and nonresponders and the correlation of the responders with diagnostic grouping, neurophysiological parameters, and behavioral criteria represented a leap forward. Attention began to be paid to the side effects, and a push was made for the judicious use of these drugs. The newly discovered psychoactive drugs, such as lithium, the tricyclic antidepressants, and the monoamine oxidase inhibitors, effective in treating very different and specific patient profiles, put an end to the indiscriminate use of the psychoactive drugs in children. However, it was not so true for the subgroup of mentally retarded, behaviorally disordered children.

Literature addressing psychopharmacological development specific to the mentally retarded child is scant. The early efforts in pediatric psychopharmacological research appropriately focused on the use of the phenothiazines to treat "childhood schizophrenia." However, it is important to point out that, because of the poorly defined diagnostic criteria and the inconsistent terminology, the term *childhood schizophrenia* was used to define a group of children with very disturbing behaviors. This catch-all terminology included not only schizophrenic but also autistic and behaviorally disordered, mentally retarded children.

After Freedman *et al.* (1955) conducted their chlorpromazine placebo-controlled study with a group of "schizophrenic" children, several other studies followed, proving the efficacy of the antipsychotic medications in treating the population of children so labeled. As an example, Fish (1960), after treating "schizophrenic" children with various antipsychotic medications, reported that drug therapy was a "safe and useful adjunct" in the treatment of such children. However, she noted that a subgroup of children with mental retardation, hyperactivity, and features of early infantile autism became easily sedated by even low doses of chlorpromazine (1 mg/kg), whereas those treated with trifluoperazine showed a response in very small doses (0.02 mg/kg) with little or no sedation. The distinction between high-potency–low-sedation and low-potency–high-sedation antipsychotics began to be made clinically. Fish's uncontrolled study was rapidly followed by other equally uncontrolled or poorly controlled studies that claimed improvement in "childhood schizophrenia" symptoms.

Although the effectiveness of the antipsychotic drugs continued to be demonstrated by better designed studies during the late 1960s and throughout the 1970s, the diagnostic terminology used still referred to a mixed-bag population of children with severe behavior disorders and mental retardation. However, studies began to suggest that autistic children responded better to the more potent, less sedating antipsychotic medications. This finding is relevant to the pharmacological research on mental retardation because about 70% of the autistic children are also mentally retarded.

Although many drugs have been tried in the treatment of behaviorally disordered mentally retarded children, the sedating phenothiazines, especially chlorpromazine (Thorazine) and thioridazine (Mellaril), are the most commonly used. This finding was demonstrated by Lipman (1970) in his survey of medication use in institutions for mentally retarded persons and by Sprague (1977) and by Cohen and Sprague (1977). Despite the lack of more recent data, we can speculate that this finding is still valid.

The literature on the specific use of psychoactive medications with mentally retarded populations can be briefly discussed by a look at only the more relevant studies. In 1955, Bair and Harold conducted a matched controlled study of chlorpromazine on 10 institutionalized children with severe behavior problems, concluding that 90% of the drug-treated group showed improvement. In 1957, Craft found that chlorpromazine was better than placebo in decreasing hyperactivity and improving the social behavior of mentally retarded children. Hunter and Stephenson (1963) used chlorpromazine and trifluoperazine in a placebo-controlled study and reported significant improvement in the hyperactivity and abnormal behavior of severely mentally retarded children. Later, LeVann (1971) found that chlorpromazine was significantly less effective than haloperidol in treating mildly to moderately mentally retarded children.

In 1963, Allen, Shannon, and Rose conducted a thioridazine–placebo-controlled study with 30 mentally retarded individuals, finding global improvement of behavior in 50% of the thioridazine-treated group compared to 4% improvement observed in the placebo group. More improvement was observed in patients with higher IQs. In yet another study a double-blind comparison of thioridazine and haloperidol was made by Ucer and Kreger (1969). They found thioridazine to be less effective than haloperidol in improving global behavior and the target symptoms (hyperactivity, anxiety, aggressivity, and impulsivity). However, the doses used were not equivalent; thus, the findings were muddled. In 1968, Alexandris and Lundell conducted a placebo-controlled study comparing thioridazine and amphetamines in children with IQs between 55 and 85. Thioridazine was found to be significantly better than placebo in all measured areas (hyperkinesis, concentration, attention, aggressiveness, sociability, interpersonal relations, comprehension, mood, work interest, and work capacity), except for reading, spelling, and arithmetic. Amphetamine was superior to placebo only in comprehension and work interest, but it was never superior to thioridazine. Thioridazine was also found by Davis, Sprague, and Werry (1969) to be effective in reducing stereotypical behaviors.

Trifluoperazine has been studied by several investigators and has been found to be useful in controlling several behavior problems in mentally retarded persons, including head banging, assaultiveness, self-injury, and hyperactivity. Fluphenazine has not been as well studied as the other drugs.

Haloperidol has been studied by Burk and Menolascino (1968), LeVann (1971), and the already-mentioned Ucer and Kreger (1969). It has been found to be much better than placebo, somewhat better than chlorpromazine, and questionably better than thioridazine in reducing behavior problems and in improving the general level of functioning of the mentally retarded with behavior problems.

Almost all of the researches on the use of neuroleptics with mentally retarded persons were conducted in institutions, such as hospitals and residential institutional facilities, on severely disturbed children. In this population, very few psychotropics other than neuroleptics have ever been tried. However, non-institutionalized mentally retarded children, with less severe behavior problems or more accepting parents and community, have also been treated with medications. Because their problems are different, either in quality or in severity, from the ones encountered in the institutionalized population, the profile of the drugs used with them is more varied. Although most of the research has shown that between 51% and 31% of institutionalized mentally retarded children were taking medications (Cohen and Sprague, 1977; Hill *et al.*, 1983, 1986; Lipman, 1970), only 19% of mentally retarded children in community residential placements such as foster homes and group homes were taking psychotropic medications (Hill, 1984). This figure is very representative of what has been found by several other investigators in different locations. Of course, the children placed in community residential facilities have less severe behavior problems and higher IQs than the children placed in institutions.

As for the children able to remain in their homes and to attend public-school special-education programs, they have a different pharmacological profile. Gadow and Kalachnik (1981) found that 4.9% of the trainable mentally retarded children (TMR; IQ scores between 30 and 55) whom they studied in Illinois were taking medication for behavior disorder, and that an additional 1.8% were taking drugs for both behavior problems and seizures. Stimulants accounted for 45% and neuroleptics for 37% of the psychotropic drugs used. In regard to the use of medication with educable mentally retarded (EMR) children (IQ scores between 50 and 80), Epstein *et al.* (1985), in a pilot study of 294 children enrolled in EMR programs in northern Illinois, found that 13.3% of the EMR children were receiving medication for behavior disorders. Stimulants were the most frequently used medications.

In summary, the use of psychoactive medications with mentally retarded children is very different according to IQ level, the severity of the behavior problems, and the placement setting. Institutionalized severely to profoundly mentally retarded individuals are being treated primarily with neuroleptic medications, especially the low-potency–high-sedation drugs such as chlorpromazine (Thorazine) and thioridazine (Mellaril). Children in community placements and special-education programs are being treated primarily with stimulants, followed closely by the neuroleptics. Trainable mentally retarded (TMR) children are, comparatively, taking more medication than the educable mentally retarded (EMR) and much less than the severely to profoundly mentally retarded.

Despite the generally negative view taken by some nonmedical professionals of the use of medication with the mentally retarded population, drugs have helped a great many children, enabling them to be more easily managed by their parents and teachers and, in some cases, even preventing institutionalization. In other cases, pharmacotherapy has made institutionalized children easier to work with. Of course, this therapeutic tool has been abused and is still being abuse in some settings. However, as the interest in the treatment of the mentally retarded grows, and professionals as well as parents become active in protecting these children's rights, forcing protective legislation and allocation of resources, this adjunct form of treatment will be more judiciously used.

## BASIC PRINCIPLES

### Rationale for the Use of Psychoactive Medications with the Learning-Disabled Child

Before treating children with learning problems, it is very important to conduct a comprehensive evaluation to identify, as clearly as possible, all the possible etiologies of the child's problems, the associated conditions, and the available resources.

The differential diagnosis of learning problems begins with ruling out low cognitive ability (mental retardation). Then, the differential diagnosis should focus on distinguishing between problems extrinsic and intrinsic in the child. This approach is sometimes difficult because, in many cases, several factors are interacting and contributing to the child's underachievement. However, the closer one gets to the main cause, the better for treatment. When the problem is identified as being inherent in the child, the next step is to differentiate "true learning disability" from emotional and behavior problems affecting the learning process. It is well accepted that true learning disability is usually limited to one aspect of cognitive ability, such as reading or mathematics. On the other hand, underachievement because of anxiety, depression, and inattention is global and affects all areas of cognitive ability. The child with learning disability is able to concentrate appropriately but experiences an unusual amount of difficulty in grasping certain concepts or in remembering certain types of information because of brain-based, uneven cognitive skills.

Children who are learning-disabled often have associated organic, emotional, or behavioral problems. Thus, in the learning-disabled population, learning difficulties can be aggravated by underfocused attention, poor concentration, an inability to filter distracting stimuli, impulsivity, and purposeless overactivity (DSM-III Attention Deficit Disorder with or without hyperactivity). In fact, stimulant medications that treat attention-deficit disorders are the pharmacological agents most frequently used in children with learning disabilities. Overfocused attention on details, worries, and preoccupations due to anxiety, as well as inability to concentrate, indecisiveness, and psychomotor retardation due to depression, can interfere with academic work. If present in a learning-disabled child, these symptoms might be the focus of pharmacological intervention with antidepressants and anxiolytic medication. Learning-disabled children may also be treated with the major tranquilizers and lithium for excess aggression and psychotic symptoms, and with the anticonvulsant medications for seizure disorders. Figures 1 and 2 illustrate the differential diagnosis, assessment, and pharmacological interventions described above.

## Rationale for the Use of Psychoactive Medications with the Mentally Retarded Child

As with learning-disabled children, associated organic, behavioral, and emotional problems are the reasons for using medication in mentally retarded individuals. Most often, mentally retarded persons are treated with sedating medications, such as the major tranquilizers and anxiolytics, to suppress aggression and disruptiveness. These medications, or "chemical restraints," are very effective in controlling these undesirable behaviors. However, when these medications are overused, rather than facilitating learning they interfere with the learning process by decreasing alertness and causing excessive sedation.

Epidemiological studies have indicated that there is a greater prevalence of psychiatric disorder among the mentally retarded than in the general population (Rutter, Graham, & Yule, 1970). However, there is a lack of interest in the medical and psychiatric community in treating these individuals. This situation reflects not only the obvious difficulties in evaluating the mentally retarded but also the poor training received by physicians in this area. Psychopathology among mentally retarded persons often goes unnoticed and untreated, as the

510

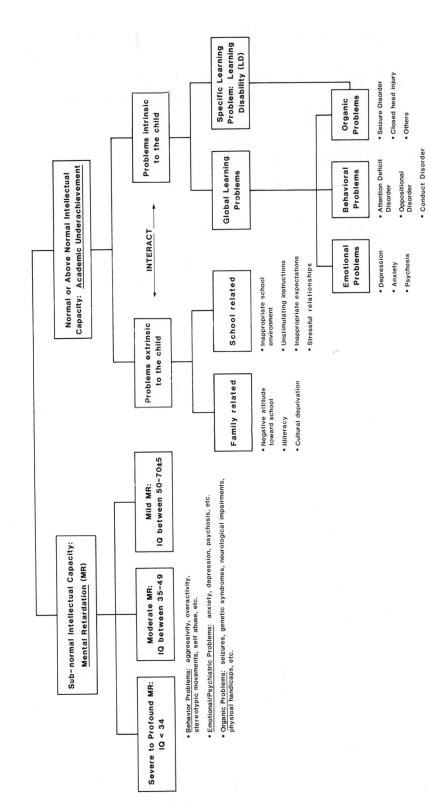

FIGURE 1. Differential diagnosis of children with learning problems.

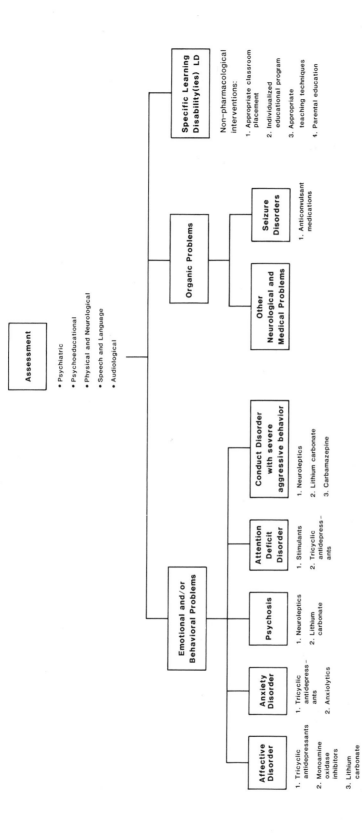

FIGURE 2. Assessment and pharmacotherapy of children underachieving academically despite normal or above-normal intelligence.

training of professionals working with the mentally retarded tends to focus on disorders of cognitive development without attention to emotional disturbances. Psychiatric disorders, including attention-deficit disorder, depression, anxiety, and even psychosis, are underdiagnosed in the mentally retarded, and their manifestations are mislabeled as being "due to the mental retardation." When the major tranquilizers (antipsychotic medications) are used, they are often used for behavior control and not to treat identified psychotic symptoms. When anxiolytics are used, it is often because of their sedating effect and not because an anxiety disorder has been diagnosed. Whereas the stimulants are frequently prescribed for the hyperactive mentally retarded child placed in the public-school special-education program, the neuroleptics (major tranquilizers) are largely used in institutional settings for children with similar behavior problems. The antidepressants are rarely used in the MR population.

Psychopathology in the mentally retarded goes largely unnoticed—and undertreated—and psychoactive medications are sometimes misused. On the other hand, medical and neurological problems, especially seizures, are readily diagnosed, and anticonvulsant medications are often appropriately used in this population. This situation reflects the fact that most mentally retarded individuals are evaluated and treated by primary-care physicians, with minimal or no involvement of psychiatrists. Primary-care physicians are well trained and qualified to diagnose and treat medical conditions. On the other hand, they are not as familiar with psychopathology and psychoactive medications as psychiatrists.

The differential diagnosis of, assessment of, and use of psychopharmacological intervention with children with subnormal intellectual capacity are illustrated in Figures 1 and 3. After a child has been found to have an IQ below 70 $\pm$ 5 and a level of adaptive functioning below his or her chronological age, the diagnosis of mental retardation is made. A comprehensive assessment of such a child must include a complete physical and neurological evaluation, which usually includes laboratory studies (e.g., complete blood count, serum chemistries, chromosomal studies, various hormone and enzyme tests, an electroencephalogram, skull X rays, and computerized tomography of the brain, or CT scan). This work is followed by a detailed psychological and behavioral assessment. The psychiatric evaluation (the longitudinal family history, a psychiatric history, and a mental status evaluation), although very important, is often neglected.

A comprehensive assessment of the mentally retarded child will result in his or her classification in one of the following groups: mild mental retardation, also called educable mentally retarded (EMR); moderate mental retardation, or trainable mentally retarded (TMR); and severe to profound mental retardation. The assessment will also identify associated behavioral, emotional, and/or organic problems in need of special interventions. When an associated behavior problem is identified, it is important to determine whether it is secondary, or due to mental retardation *per se*, or whether it reflects an underlying psychopathology.

It is not easy to differentiate between mental retardation with behavior problems "requiring attention and treatment and that are not part of another disorder" (DSM-III terminology) and mental retardation with behavior problems that are due to an underlying psychopathology. However, a developmental approach can help a great deal. Some behaviors are "immature," that is, inappropriate and troublesome for a child, considering his or her chronological age.

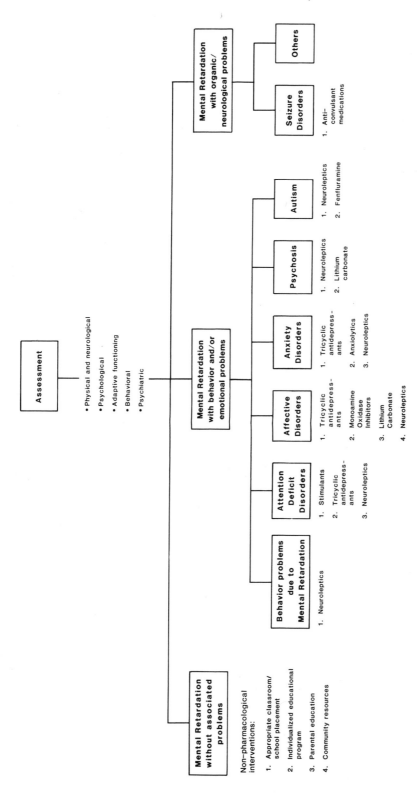

FIGURE 3. Assessment and pharmacotherapy of mentally retarded children.

But these behaviors are developmentally appropriate considering his or her mental age. For example, immature behaviors, such as negativism, temper tantrums, an inability to share, and an oppositional attitude, in a 12-year-old with a mental and developmental age of 2–3 years are not pathological *per se* and should be regarded as being due to mental retardation. Other behaviors, such as withdrawal and excessive aggression, on the other hand, usually represent an underlying psychopathology in need of treatment.

For obvious reasons, a differential diagnosis of the various psychopathologies is particularly difficult in mentally retarded persons with low IQs (below 50). The clinician has to rely on data from many sources and from his or her own observations. Many times, drug trials are conducted to aid in the diagnosis and reveal the appropriate pharmacological agent. Unfortunately, many drug trials are poorly controlled and thus fail to help the clinician and the patient. Systematic, well-conducted trials should be carried out to help in difficult cases. Careful attention should be paid to the choice of the drug, the dosage, and the administration. Detailed documentation of response and side effects should be carried out by the individuals most familiar with the patient. The ultimate goal of a drug trial is to obtain the maximum response with the lowest dose and minimal side effects. In other words, costs and benefits should always be ascertained, and medication should be continued only if the gains far outweigh the side effects.

## MAJOR APPLICATIONS

In Tables 1 and 2, the classes of medication used with both the learning disabled and the mentally retarded child have been listed. Also, throughout the text, a variety of pharmacological terms have been used to describe medications. Table 1 will help readers, especially those less familiar with the pharmacological terminology, to understand the terms and to conceptualize the classification of the psychoactive drugs mentioned.

All the psychoactive medications listed are used to treat underlying psychopathology in the population of children being discussed. This section briefly reviews the medications, focusing on their application with the two defined populations.

### Pre- and Postmedication Assessment

When, after a comprehensive evaluation of a child, medication is deemed necessary, the physician must document a predrug status. A baseline assessment is extremely helpful in determining the response and the emergence of side effects. Different classes of drugs affect the organism differently, depending on their site of action. It is important to obtain the baseline status of all different functions that may be affected by the drugs. In general, the workup for children who are candidates for pharmacological intervention includes the following: a physical and neurological examination documenting weight and height, vital signs, baseline behavior and mood ratings and observations, and laboratory work (complete blood count and differential, urinalysis, kidney and liver function tests, and a pregnancy test for sexually active female adolescents). Other baseline parameters are discussed along with the specific medications.

TABLE 1. Psychoactive Medications *Most Commonly Used* with Mentally Retarded and Learning-Disabled Children

A. Neuroleptics (major tranquilizers, antipsychotics)
   1. Phenothiazines
      Chlorpromazine (Thorazine)
      Thioridazine (Mellaril)
   2. Butyrophenone
      Haloperidol (Haldol)
   3. Thioxanthene
      Thiothixene (Navane)
B. Tricyclic antidepressants
   Amitriptyline (Elavil)
   Imipramine (Tofranil)
   Desipramine (Norpramine)
   Nortriptyline (Aventyl)
C. Lithium
   Lithium carbonate (Eskalith, Lithobid)
D. Anxiolytics (minor tranquilizers, antianxiety agents)
   1. Benzodiazepines
      Alprazolam (Xanax)
      Chlordiazepoxide (Librium)
      Diazepam (Valium)
E. Sedative-hypnotics
   1. Benzodiazepines
      Flurazepam (Dalmane)
      Temazepam (Restoril)
   2. Barbiturates
      Phenobarbital (Luminal)
      Secobarbital (Seconal)
      Amobarbital (Amytal)
   3. Antihistamines
      Diphenhydramine (Benadryl)
      Hydroxyzine (Vistaril, Atarax)
   4. Miscellaneous
      Chloral hydrate (Noctec)
      Meprobamate (Equanil)
G. Stimulants
   Dextroamphetamine (Dexedrine)
   Methylphenidate (Ritalin)
   Pemoline (Cylert)
H. Anticonvulsants (antiseizure medications)
   Carbamazepine (Tegretol)
   Clonazepam (Clonopin)
   Ethosuximide (Zarontin)
   Phenobarbital (Luminal)
   Phenytoin (Dilantin)
   Primidone (Mysoline)
   Valproic acid (Depakene)

TABLE 2. Neuroleptic Medications Used in Mentally Retarded
and Learning-Disabled Children

| Generic name (trade name) | Doses (in mg) | Indications (diagnosis: target behavior) | Common side effects |
|---|---|---|---|
| Chlorpromazine (Thorazine)[a] | 10–300 | Schizophrenia, reactive psychosis, organic psychosis: delusions, hallucinations, thought disorder, agitation, aggression, withdrawal. | Autonomic nervous system: sedation. |
| Thioridazine (Mellaril)[a] | 10–300 | | Anticholinergic: dry mouth, constipation, blurring of vision, orthostatic hypotension, urinary retention. |
| Trifluoperazine (Stelazine) | 1–20 | | |
| Fluphenazine (Prolixin) | 1–15 | Mental retardation, pervasive developmental disorder/infantile autism: stereotypical behaviors, self-stimulation, agitation, aggression. | Extrapyramidal: acute dystonic reactions (muscular spasms), akathisia (agitation), Parkinsonism (tremors, muscular regidity, dradykinesia, gait problems). |
| Haloperidol (Haldol)[a] | 1–16 | | |
| Thiothixene (Navane) | 2–20 | | |
| Molindone (Moban) | 10–50 | | |
| Loxapine (Loxitane)[b] | 5–60 | Conduct disorder: severe aggression. | Endocrine: gynecomastia (breast enlargement), weight gain, menstrual irregularity. Hypersensitivity: rashes, blood dyscrasia (decreased white blood cells), liver toxicity. CNS: decrease seizure threshold, tardive dyskinesia. |

[a]Approved by FDA for children under 12 years of age.
[b]Not FDA-approved for children under 16 years of age.

The effectiveness of medications can be assessed by measuring the behaviors targeted for treatment before and after medication use to establish the risks–benefits ratio and the clinical significance of the changes. Target behaviors can be measured by the physician's global clinical impression, by the global impression of an independent observer, by self-report, by rating scales, by measuring severity, by a tally of the frequency of behavior, and by laboratory studies.

## Clinical Applications: Neuroleptics

### Mechanism of Action

All neuroleptic drugs inhibit dopamine function in the brain. Dopamine is a chemical brain messenger, or neurotransmitter. It is present in the nigrostriate, the mesolimbic, and the hypothalamic areas of the brain. The neuroleptics' effect on the nigrostriate dopamine pathway is responsible for the extrapyramidal (EPS) or Parkinsonian side effects. Its action on the hypothalamic dopamine pathway is responsible for the endocrine side effects. The action of the neuroleptics in the mesolimbic dopamine system results in the antipsychotic as well as the behavioral effects of the drugs.

The neuroleptics also block the effects of acetylcholine, another neu-

rotransmiter, in the CNS and the peripheral nervous system (PNS). This block-
ade is responsible for the anticholinergic side effects of these drugs.

### Classification

The neuroleptics are classified according to their chemical structure as follows: (1) the phenothiazines—chlorpromazine (Thorazine), thioridazine (Mellaril), trifluoperazine (Stelazine), fluphenazine (Prolixin), and perphenazine
(Trilafon); (2) the butyrophenones—haloperidol (Haldol); (3) the thioxanthenes—thiothixene (Navane); (4) the dibenzoxazepines—loxapine (Loxitane);
and (5) the dihydroindolones—molindone (Moban).

Of all these medications, only a few are FDA-approved for children under
12 years of age (see Table 2). This is not to say that the other medications are not
or should not be used in children. Drugs are many times chosen on their side-
effect profiles, to achieve the best possible risks–benefits ratio. For some children, systematic drug trials are necessary to achieve this goal, and the drug of
choice can turn out to be the one not yet FDA-approved for the child's age. In
this case, good documentation justifying the choice of drug is necessary. The
neuroleptics are also classified according to their dopaminergic and cholinergic
actions. The drugs with more mesolimbic dopaminergic activity also seem to
have high extrapyramidal activity and less anticholinergic properties. They are
the so-called high-potency–low-sedation neuroleptics, such as haloperidol,
fluphenazine, and thiothixene. They have more antipsychotic activity, high extrapyramidal side effects, moderate endocrine side effects, and comparatively
low anticholinergic side effects. The opposite is true of the drugs with a less
specific mesolimbic (antipsychotic) site of action. They tend to have less extrapyramidal but more endocrine and anticholinergic affects. They are the so-called
low-potency–high-sedation neuroleptics, such as chlorpromazine and thioridazine. The other neuroleptics, such as trifluoperazine, loxapine, and molindone, fall somewhere between these two groups. However, they have specific
characteristics worth mentioning. Trifluoperazine is highly anticholinergic. Loxapine is much less likely to cause tardive dyskinesia. Molindone causes the least
endocrine side effects of all the neuroleptics.

### Indications

The neuroleptics' primary indication is the treatment of schizophrenia or
psychotic symptoms such as hallucinations, delusions, agitation, and thought
disorder. However, in children, their primary indication also includes the target
symptoms of several other disorders, such as agitation, stereotypical behaviors,
aggression, and social withdrawal. Tourette disorder is a formal indication for
the use of haloperidol.

Table 2 contains information regarding the neuroleptics' indications, dose,
and side effects. It is important to add, however, that the doses listed represent
the usual range, from the smallest effeclive dose to the highest dose used to
obtain a clinically significant response. The amount of medication used is highly
individualized. Some children show good response on small doses, and others
need a much higher dose to show the same response. Also, mentally retarded or
not, autistic children seem to do better with the high-potency–low-sedation

drugs. The same is true of mildly to moderately retarded children, in whom sedation is to be avoided. However, the very aggressive, agitated mentally retarded, with a variety of other behavior problems, seem to need the sedating properties of the low-potency neuroleptics. When using neuroleptics, it is particularly important to be aware of the potential for inducing seizures in otherwise well-controlled seizure-disorder patients, and to be aware of the potential for tardive dyskinesia after prolonged use.

## Clinical Applications: Stimulants

### Mechanism of Action

The stimulant medications act as general nonspecific stimulators of the central nervous system (CNS) by increasing neuroamines in the brain. These psychostimulant drugs increase the release of both norepinefrine (NE) and dopamine (DA) in the brain from storage sites. In addition, they are potent blockers of NE and DA reuptake in the adrenergic terminals, and inhibit the breakdown of these neurotransmitters by the monoamine oxidase enzyme. The psychostimulants seem to affect the arousal state in the reticular activating system of the brain. Malmo (1959) has suggested that there is a U-shape relationship between physiological state of arousal and behavior efficiency. If arousal is too low there is very little behavior, and when the optimum level of arousal is exceeded there is a resulting general disruption in behavior. Also, stimulants seem to work as a filter to sensory stimulation, thus decreasing off-task behavior. Therefore, stimulants' clinical usefullness in treating attention deficit disorder is probably related to their effects on the arousal state and also to their effects on the discriminative control of sensory stimulation over behavior.

The psychostimulants' effects on the CNS striatum system is responsible for the motor tics and Tourette's syndrome induced in vulnerable children by these drugs. The release of hypothalamic NE is thought to be responsible for the appetite suppressant side effect and perhaps for the debatable adverse effect on growth. Their effect on the reticular activating system is responsible for the insomnia. The dopaminergic potentiating action of stimulants in the neurolimbic system is probably responsible for precipitating psychosis in children at risk.

### Classification

There are three classes of psychostimulants available in this country to treat children with attention deficit disorder: methylphenidate (Ritalin), dextroamphetamine (Dexedrin), and magnesium pemoline (Cylert).

Dextroamphetamine reaches peak plasma levels between 2 to 4 hours following an oral dose. It is easily absorbed and distributed throughout the body. It is poorly bound to plasma protein and rapidly metabolized. It's plasma elimination half life is 2–4 hours. There is no correlation across individuals in behavioral response plasma levels of amphetamines. Therefore, doses are highly individualized. Dextroamphetamine is also available in sustained release form which has a later and longer peak plasma level.

Methylphenidate is a piperidine derivative structurally related to amphetamine. It is rapidly absorbed and distributed, reaches peak plasma level within

1–3 hours and is poorly protein bound and rapidly converted to its inactive metabolite, ritalinic acid. Its plasma elimination half-life is 6–10 hours. Methylphenidate is also available in sustained-release (SR) preparation, but as with dextroamphetamine, there is no evidence of significant prolongation of behavior response with the SR preparation. On the other hand, SR preparation may avoid the rebound phenomena observed in some children.

Pemoline is a milder CNS stimulant as compared to the other two drugs described. Its structure is different from amphetamine. Its peak plasma level is at 1–3 hours after oral administration, however it has a prolonged half-life of about 12 hours, and its onset of therapeutic effect is delayed. It is reported to lag 3–4 weeks, with maximum effect at 6–8 weeks of regular administration. Also, children show considerable individual variability in pemoline elimination half-life.

*Indications*

The stimulants' primary pediatric indication is for the treatment of Attention Deficit Disorder (ADD), with or without hyperactivity. They are used similarly in the mentally retarded, and learning disabled children with the ADD syndrome. Figure 6 provides information regarding psychostimulant doses, and presentations. In general, indication for the use of stimulant medication is the presence of inattention, impulsivity, and hyperactivity, of sufficient severity and duration to cause impairment of function at school, home, and in social situations. The choice of drug is based on the physician's individual preference, as well as other factors. Methylphenidate is the most commonly used stimulant, and physicians feel more comfortable adjusting the dosage. However, because of its short half-life, it has to be given twice per day, and in some cases, three times per day. It is more liable to cause rebound hyperactivity. However, it interferes less with growth and is also much less likely to be abused than dextroamphetamine. Pemoline is preferable in older children with potential for drug abuse, however it is important to educate the family and patient about its delayed onset of action. If taking medication at school is seen as objectionable or difficult, sustained release preparations or pemoline are preferable.

Assessment of response to the medication is done by close follow-up with input from the school. Side effects need to be monitored closely by physical examination approximately every 3 months, documenting height, weight, blood pressure, heart rate, and neurological functioning.

The common side effects reported with the stimulants are nausea, abdominal discomfort, anorexia, and insomnia. Adverse effect on growth is reported primarily with dextroamphetamine use in very young children. Precipitation of psychosis in children at risk (with positive family history of schizophrenia, and/or a previous psychotic state) is seen with all the stimulants. Movement disorders (tics, Tourette's syndrome) can be precipitated in children who are vulnerable (with positive family history for movement disorders and/or a preexisting movement disorder). Pemoline may cause liver dysfunction, including elevated liver enzymes, hepatitis, and jaundice. Palpitations, tachycardia, and elevation of blood pressure have been reported with both dextroamphetamine and methylphenidate. Rebound overexcitability, irritability, hyperactivity is reported more with methyphenidate than with dextroamphetamine. This side effect can be minimized with sustained release preparation. All the other side effects can be minimized by "drug holidays," if the child's condition permits.

Maria de Fatima
Thomas

## Other Medications

### Antidepressants

The tricyclic antidepressant medications are seldom used with mentally retarded populations of children with the exception of imipramine (Tofranil). Imipramine's pediatric indications are for the treatment of enuresis, childhood depression, attention deficit disorder, and separation anxiety disorder (school phobia). The daily doses used ranges are 25–125 mg for enuresis, 25–200 mg for ADD, and 100–300 mg for depression and separation anxiety. Response is seen within days for the former two conditions, while it lags 3–4 weeks for the latter two. Blood levels are important in the treatment of depression. There is evidence to support the existence of a therapeutic window for imipramine and desipramine plasma level, below which there is no significant clinical response, and above which there is no significant gain and more toxicity. The therapeutic plasma level for imipramine is between 146–200 ng/ml of both the parent drug and its metabolite, desipramine. Common side effects are dry mouth, orthostatic hypotension, blurring of vision, constipation, tachycardia, and urinary retention. The cardiac side effects are alteration of cardiac conduction and repolarization, seen on the electrocardiogram as prolongation of PR and QRS intervals and even arrhythmias. The cardiotoxic side effects are mostly seen in higher than therapeutic doses. Children on antidepressants need very close psychiatric follow up. A baseline physical examination and electrocardiogram should be obtained prior to treatment, and monitored thereafter.

### Lithium

Lithium carbonate (Eskalith or Lithobid) can be used in the mentally retarded pediatric population to treat a diagnosable affective disorder (mania, bipolar disorder, or recurrent depression). However, it is mostly used in this population to treat aggressivity, overactivity, or self-injurious behavior. In prepubertal children, dosage ranges from 100 to 2,000 mg per day to achieve therapeutic levels. Lithium has many potentially serious side effects and requires very close monitoring of blood levels. Levels of 0.6 to 1.6 mEq/liter are within therapeutic range, but some children require up to 1.8 to 2.0 mEq/liter to show clinically significant response. The most common side effects of lithium are nausea, vomiting, diarrhea, abdominal discomfort, tremors, fatigue, increased thirst and urinary output due to its kidney toxicity, and hypothyroidism and goiter potential. The follow-up of children on lithium includes measurement of weekly lithium plasma levels until a therapeutic level is achieved, then monthly lithium plasma levels. Also, renal, endocrine, and cardiac functions are to be monitored at regular intervals.

### Anxiolytics and Sedative-Hypnotics

The medications such as chlordiazepoxide (Librium), diazepam (Valium), and alprazolam (Xanax) are called anxiolytics because they are used to treat anxiety states in adults. However, in children, these drugs have not yet been proven effective and safe, and the medication of choice for children with anxiety disorders is imipramine. However, in adolescents, small doses of a benzodiazepine for a limited period of time can be helpful as an adjunct to individual therapy in the treatment of anxiety that is interfering with daily functioning. Diazepam (Valium), given in small doses at bedtime, can be useful in the treatment of night terrors in young children.

The benzodiazepines are sometimes used to control agitation in mentally retarded children. However, neuroleptics are safer and more effective than the benzodiazepines for the treatment of agitation. The benzodiazepines can cause a paradoxical reaction in children, aggravating the agitation, causing excessive sedation, and a confusional state. They can also cause dependence and severe withdrawal reactions. When sedation is needed to control agitation, and the neuroleptics are contraindicated, it is better to use the antihistamine rather than the benzodiazepine medications.

Antihistamine drugs like diphenhydramine (Benadril) and hydroxazine (Vistaril) are useful in treating agitation, as well as sleep disturbances and excessive fearfulness in children and adolescents.

For children with sleep disorders, chloral hydrate is a safe and effective hypnotic. Other hypnotic medications, such as flurazepam (Dalmane) and temazepam (Restoril), are sometimes used with adolescents needing nighttime sedation.

### Anticonvulsants

Anticonvulsants are frequently used in the MR population to control seizures. The most widely used anticonvulsants are phenobarbital (Luminal), phenytoin (Dilantin), and carbamazepine (Tegretol). Phenobarbital should be well-known by those treating children because of its side effects, especially mood disturbance. effects. It can cause irritability, depressed affect, hyperactivity, and mimic psychiatric illness. Phenytoin (Dilantin) also causes mood disturbances similar to phenobarbital, but to a lesser degree. Therefore, in children taking these medications, a drug-free baseline assessment, if at all possible, should be done before psychiatric diagnosis is given. Carbamazepine (Tegretol) is an important drug because it is used to treat partial complex (temporal lobe) seizures. These seizures are manifested as behavioral or psychiatric abnormalities. carbamazepine is sometimes also used to treat severe aggressivity in children with neurological problems.

### Nootropics

Nootropics are drugs said to have selective cognitive effects. Piracetam (Normabrain, Euviflor, Nootropyl), a substance structurally related to gamma aminobutyric acid (GABA), is currently the focus of an intense multicenter study involving several countries. Ianni et al. (1985) in their paper on the use of piracetam in children with dyslexia have summarized various research on the use of piracetam in children and adults with cognitive deficiencies and in normal volunteers. The data presented suggests that piracetam improves performance on tasks associated with left hemisphere brain functioning, such as short-term memory, arithmetic, verbal learning, and reading speed and accuracy. Several studies with children have reported modest treatment effects, such as increased speed in reading and writing, decreased spelling errors, improved ability to read single words, and to remember words and pictures. However, much needs to be learned about this drug before it can be FDA-approved and recommended for the treatment of learning disabilities.

## CONCLUSIONS

Pharmacological interventions with the learning disabled and mentally retarded children are restricted to the treatment of underlying or associated psychopathology, manifested either as behavior or emotional problems. The cognitive deficits of the mentally retarded and the learning problems of the learning disabled children are not the reasons for the use of medications. However, medications can facilitate the learning process by supressing interfering undesired behaviors, by controlling disruptive emotional states, and by facilitating desired behaviors.

Before medication is introduced in the treatment of children with cognitive deficits and learning problems, a comprehensive psychiatric and psychoeducational evaluation needs to be conducted. After a diagnosis of the underlying psychopathology is made, careful consideration has to be given to the choice of medication. Baseline physical and neurological status need to be assessed and monitored thereafter for the emergence of possible side effects. Target behaviors need to be identified before treatment, and monitored thereafter, to evaluate the effectiveness of the treatment.

The ultimate goal of pharmacological therapy is to achieve clinically significant response with the lowest possible medication dose, and with minimal or no side effects.

Despite some clinicians' negative attitude toward the use of medication with the mentally retarded population, pharmacological intervention has made a significant difference in the lives of many mentally retarded individuals.

## REFERENCES

Alexandris, A., & Lundell, F. W. (1968). Effect of thioridazine, amphetamine, and placebo on the hyperkinetic syndrome and cognitive area in mentally deficient children. *Canadian Medical Association Journal, 98,* 92–96.

Allen, M., Shannon, G., & Rose, D. (1963). Thioridazine hydrochloride in the behavior disturbances of retarded children. *American Journal of Mental Deficiency, 68,* 63–68.

Aman, M. G., & Singh, N. N. (1982). Methylphenidate in severely retarded residents and the clinical significance of stereotypic behavior. *Applied Research in Mental Retardation, 3,* 345–358.

Aman, M. G., & Werry, J. S. (1982). Methylphenidate and diazepam in severe reading retardation. *Journal of the American Academy of Child Psychiatry, 1,* 31–37.

Aman, M. G., Field, C. J., & Bridgman, G. D. (1985). City-wide survey of drug patterns among non-institutionalized retarded persons. *Applied Research in Mental Retardation, 6,* 159–171.

American Psychiatric Association (Task Force on Nomenclature and Statistics) (1980). *Diagnostic and statistical manual of mental disorders,* third ed., DSM-III. Washington, DC: American Psychiatric Association.

Bair, H. V., & Harold, W. (1955). Efficacy of chlorpromazine in hyperactive mentally retarded children. *Archives of Neurology and Psychiatry, 74,* 363–364.

Bradley, C. (1937). The behavior of children receiving benzedrine. *American Journal of Orthopsychiatry, 94,* 577–585.

Breuning, S. E., & Pling, A. D. (1982). Pharmacotherapy. In J. L. Matson & R. P. Barrett (Eds.), *Psychopathology in the mentally retarded.* New York: Grune & Stratton.

Burk, H. W., & Menolascino, F. J. (1968). Haloperidol in emotionally disturbed mentally retarded individuals. *American Journal of Psychiatry, 124,* 1589–1591.

Cantwell, D. P. (1983). The Use of Psychotropic Medications in the Pediatric Population. In C. E. Hollingsworth (Ed.), *Coping with pediatric illness.* New York: SP Medical and Scientific Books.

Coffey, B. J. (1986). Therapeutics III: Pharmacotherapy. In K. S. Robson (Ed.), *Manual of clinical child psychiatry* (pp. 149–184). Washington, DC: American Psychiatric Press.

Cohen, M. N., & Sprague, R. L. (1977, March). *Survey of drug usage in two midwestern institutions for the retarded.* Paper presented at the Gatlinburg Conference on Research in Mental Retardation, Gatlinburg, TN.

Craft, M. (1957a). Tranquilizers in mental deficiency: Chlorpromazine. *Journal of Mental Deficiency Research, 1,* 91–95.

Davidson, P. W., Kleene, B. M., Carroll, M., & Rockowitz, R. J. (1983). Effects of naloxone on self-injurious behavior: A case study. *Applied Research in Mental Retardation, 4,* 1–4.

Davis, K. V., Sprague, R. L., & Werry, J. S. (1969). Stereotyped behavior and activity level in severe retardates: The effect of drugs. *American Journal of Mental Deficiency, 73,* 721–727.

Durand, V. M. (1982). A behavioral/pharmacological intervention for the treatment of severe self-injurious behavior. *Journal of Autism and Developmental Disorders, 12,* 243–251.

Fish, B. (1960). Drug Therapy in Child Psychiatry: Pharmacological aspects. *Comprehensive Psychiatry, 1,* 212–227.

Freedman, A. M., Effron, A. S., and Bender, L. (1955). Pharmacotherapy in children with psychiatric illness, *Journal Nervous & Mental Disorder., 122,* 479–486.

Gadow, K. D. (1985). Prevalence and efficacy of stimulant drug use with mentally retarded children and youth. *Psychopharmacology Bulletin, 21,* 291–303.

Gadow, K. (1986). Hyperactivity, learning disabilities, and mental retardation. *Children on Medication,* Vol. 1. San Diego, CA: College-Hill Press.

Gadow, K. D., & Kalachnik, J. (1981). Prevalence and pattern of drug treatment for behavior and seizure disorders of TMR students. *American Journal of Mental Deficiency, 85,* 588–595.

Gittelman-Klein, R., Klein, D. F., Katz, S., Saraf, K., & Pollack, E. (1976). Comparative effects of methylphenidate and thioridazine in hyperkinetic children. *Archives of General Psychiatry, 33,* 1217–1231.

Gittelman, R., Klein, D. F., & Feingold, I. (1983). Children with reading disorders–II. Effects of methylphenidate in combination with reading remediation. *Journal of Child Psychology and Psychiatry, 24,* 193–212.

Hill, B. K., Balow, E. A., & Bruininks, R. H. (1983). *A national study of prescribed drugs in institutions and community residential facilities for mentally retarded people* (Brief no. 20). Minneapolis: University of Minnesota, Department of Educational Psychology.

Hill, B. K., & Bruininks, R. H. (1984). Maladaptive behavior of mentally retarded individuals in residential facilities. *American Journal of Mental Deficiency, 88,* 380–387.

Hill, B. K., & Lakin, K. C. (1986). Classification of residential facilities for individuals with mental retardation. *Mental Retardation, 24,* 107–115.

Hunter, H., & Stephenson, G. M. (1963). Chlorpromazine and trifluoperazine in the treatment of behavioral abnormalities in the severely subnormal child. *British Journal of Psychiatry, 109,* 411–417.

Ianni, M. D., Wilsher, C. R., Blank, M. S., Conners, C. K., Chase, C. H., Funkenstein, H. H., Helfgott, E., Holmes, J. M., Lougee, L., Maletta, G. J., Milewski, J., Pirozzolo, F. J., Rudel, R. G., & Tallal, P. (1985). The effects of Piracetam in children with dyslexia. *Journal of Clinical Psychopharmacology, 5,* 272–278.

Kinsbourne, M.. & Caplan, P. J. (1979). *Children's learning and attention problems.* Boston, MA: Little, Brown and Company.

LeVann, L. J. (1971). Clinical comparison of haloperidol with chlorpromazine in mentally retarded children. *American Journal of Mental Deficiency, 75,* 719–723.

Lipman, R. S. (1970). The use of psychopharmacological agents in residential facilities for the retarded. In F. J. Menolascino (Ed.), *Psychiatric approaches to mental retardation,* (pp. 387–398). New York: Basic Books.

Livingston, S. (1972). *Comprehensive management of epilepsy in infancy, childhood, and adolescence.* Springfield, IL: Charles C. Thomas.

Rutter, M., Graham, J. P., & Yule, W. (1970). A neuropsychiatric study in childhood. *Clinics in Developmental Medicine, Nos. 35/36.* London: Heinemann.

Singh, N. N., & Millichamp, C. J. (1985). Pharmacological treatment of self-injurious behavior in mentally retarded persons. *Journal of Autism and Developmental Disorders, 15,* 257–267.

Sprague, R. L. (1977). Overview of psychopharmacology for the retarded in the United States. In P. Mittler (Ed.), *Research to practice in mental retardation* (Vol. 3, pp. 199–202). Baltimore: University Park Press.

Ucer, E., & Kreger, K. C. (1969). A double-blind study comparing haloperidol with thioridazine in emotionally disturbed, mentally retarded children. *Current Therapeutic Research, 11,* 278–283.

U.S. Department of Health, Education, and Welfare (August, 1977). *Public Law 94-142,* The Education for All Handicapped Children Act, 42 Federal Register 42474.

# 21 Learning Disabilities
## Psychological Therapies

NIRBHAY N. SINGH AND IVAN L. BEALE

## INTRODUCTION

The major purpose of this chapter is to provide an evaluative survey of the treatments used in the remediation of learning disabilities (LD) or, as they are sometimes called, specific learning disabilities. Before this survey can sensibly be attempted, it is first necessary to discuss the historical antecedents of the current definitions of LD and to describe some working classifications of LD typology. Because the theoretical antecedents of various treatment approaches to LD are widely disparate, we have included some discussion and classification of these, both as an indication of their current status and as a basis for our organization of treatment methods.

Although our main concern is with treatment, rather than with definition, theory, and diagnosis, some coverage of the controversies involving these aspects of LD is essential to an adequate appreciation of some of the treatment issues and has been included for this reason.

## DEFINITION OF LEARNING DISABILITY

Analyses of the historical antecedents of the current LD field (Kavale & Forness, 1985; Radencich, 1984; Weiderholt, 1974) describe the strong influence of "medical" etiological models of learning problems, in which the underlying causes were either brain damage or related anomalous neurological processes. Examples include poorly established cerebral dominance (Orton, 1937), maturational lag in brain development (Bender, 1957), and incomplete "patterning" of the brain (Doman, Spitz, Zucman, Delacato, & Doman, 1960). The use of the term *learning disability* to refer to a diagnostically useful group of behavioral disorders was first proposed by Kirk and Bateman (1962) and was adopted in the United States in 1963 by the Association of Children with Learning Disabilities. Most workers in the LD field have since retained one or another medical model

NIRBHAY N. SINGH • Educational Research and Services Center, Inc., DeKalb, Illinois 60115.
IVAN L. BEALE • Department of Psychology, University of Auckland, Auckland, New Zealand.

525

of LD, largely through the strong influence of Strauss and Kephart (1955), Werner (1948), and their colleagues.

According to the "Strauss and Werner paradigm," as Kavale and Forness (1985) have called it, LD is associated with neurological abnormality manifested in disorders of specific basic psychological processes, but not caused by a generally handicapping condition such as underlies mental retardation. In the view of some, this paradigm places undue emphasis on assumed underlying neurological impairment, which is difficult to establish by independent criteria and which suggests a medical rather than an educational approach to remediation (Kavale & Forness, 1985).

In 1981, the National Joint Committee for Learning Disabilities (NJCLD) adopted the following definition of LD, now widely (but not unanimously) accepted in the field:

> Learning disabilities is a generic term that refers to a heterogeneous group of disorders manifested by significant difficulties in the acquisition and use of listening, speaking, reading, writing, reasoning, or mathematical abilities. These disorders are intrinsic to the individual and presumed to be due to nervous system dysfunction. Even though a learning disability may occur concomitantly with other handicapping conditions (e.g., sensory impairment, mental retardation, social and emotional disturbance) or environmental influences (e.g., cultural differences, insufficient/inappropriate instruction, psychogenic factors), it is not the direct result of those conditions or influences. (Hammill, Leigh, McNutt, & Larsen, 1981, p. 336)

The rationale for and the advantages of this definition are fully described by Hammill *et al.* (1981). It shares with the older, legal definition passed by the U.S. Congress (*Federal Register,* 1977) some terms that are capable of diverse interpretation, and critics have argued for alternative definitions comprised of terms that are operationally defined or, at least, amenable to such a definition (Chalfant & King, 1976; Schere, Richardson, & Bialer, 1980). Such operational definitions make no reference to presumed etiologies, on the grounds that these have no proven implications for remedial interventions. In addition, a reference to "basic psychological processes" underlying LD is tied to a set of processes defined by certain test procedures. The definition offered by Schere *et al.* (1980) is as follows:

> Learning disability refers to an academic deficit accompanied by a disorder in one or more of the basic psychological processes involved in understanding or in using language—spoken or written—in a child whose intellectual, emotional, and/or physical status allows participation in a traditional academic curriculum. (p. 9)

There are probably two major obstacles to the widespread adoption of operational definitions of LD. First, the discovery of neurological correlates of LD syndromes remains, for many psychologists, a real possibility that has useful implications for treatment. The diagnosis of abnormality or damage of the brain need not imply a poor prognosis for educational treatment, a fact well attested to by the literature on the rehabilitation of victims of acquired brain damage (e.g., Gardner, 1975). Second, insistence on specific operational definitions of psychological processes is not likely to be accepted until there is a general agreement on what the critical processes are.

## Behavioral Approaches

Behavioral approaches to the remediation of academic deficits involve the direct use of stimulus-control and reinforcement-control procedures to produce the desired academic behaviors. Based on the methods of experimental and applied behavior analysis, these techniques arise from a model that emphasizes environmental variables as controllers of behavior, and that eschews the use of intervening variables, such as psychological processes, as explanatory or heuristic tools (Skinner, 1950). Subject variables have been accorded little importance in this model, and the assessment of children with academic deficits is typically restricted to a functional analysis of those deficits in relation to their antecedents and consequences for the child's behavior in the learning situation (e.g., Nelson & Hayes, 1979). Diagnosis of the disorder as to cause or classification is often regarded as unimportant and may be omitted altogether, with the result that little is known about the generalizability of behavioral approaches from one diagnostic group to another. Essentially, the same approaches are used whether the academic deficit is associated with cultural, educational, or emotional deprivation, with a genetic disorder, mental retardation, or a specific learning disability. The basic approach is to "suck it and see" in the context of a flexible experimental design and the use of repeated measures that permit an ongoing evaluation of the effectiveness of the intervention (e.g., Kazdin, 1982).

## Psychological-Process Approaches

Although many consider the behavioral approach sufficient for the design and implementation of remedial procedures for LD children, much of the research and writing in the area is concerned with the "basic psychological processes" that may underlie learning problems. Widely accepted definitions of LD place an emphasis on the existence, in LD children, of deficits in basic psychological processes. This emphasis appears to be based on an implicit belief that remedial techniques will be effective only to the extent that they are based on a knowledge of what deficits in psychological processes underlie the behavioral problem. Presumably, many of the children demonstrating specific academic deficits, who are otherwise normal, have already been exposed to the same instruction that was effective for their peers; yet, for them, it was insufficient. It might be argued that the LD child may simply have missed out on some critical step in the instructional process and may consequently have failed to understand all that followed. But such pupils would be atypical of the LD population and would actually be excluded from it by most accepted definitions. It must be taken as axiomatic that LD children, as defined, do not make adequate progress under normal teaching conditions.

Proponents of the psychological-processes approach to LD (e.g., Torgesen, 1979) have argued that this approach fosters research aimed at identifying those process deficiencies that can be modified by remedial training and those, perhaps related to structural abnormality, that may not be modifiable and must therefore be circumvented in any effective remedial program. Another suggested advantage of the process approach is that any modification of a process deficiency should result in a general improvement in the learning of all skills involving that process, whereas remediation of a specific academic deficit by a strictly behavioral intervention may not generalize beyond the actual tasks used in training. This may, of course, be an unwarranted assumption, as many behavioral programs incorporate generalization training procedures that may turn out to be sufficient for this purpose (Stokes & Baer, 1977).

The range of psychological processes implicated in LD is as broad as those implicated in learning generally. Most derive from cognitive, social learning, or neuropsychological models, although behavioral models of learning have also made a contribution (Heal & Johnson, 1970; Evans, 1982). The processes thought to be relevant include perceptual-motor organization, selective attention, sustained attention, encoding into or decoding from memory, short-term memory, long-term memory, sequential processing, the cerebral lateralization of function, the transient visual system, the lateralization of eye movements, and binocular dominance. Abnormalities in one or more of these and other processes have been implicated in various categories of LD.

Some investigators have stressed the value of interpreting behavioral and process deficiencies in terms of the underlying neurological functions (Barkley, 1981; Cruickshank, 1967; Gaddes, 1981; Orton, 1937). It is noted that, for many developmental learning problems, there are analogous acquired disorders known to result from damage to specific brain structures. A mutual explanatory framework for both acquired and developmental disorders must have advantages for both. However, critics of this approach have pointed to the danger that, if learning disorders are generally regarded as being symptomatic of brain dysfunction, there may be many educators who will feel that educational remediation is doomed to failure.

A somewhat stronger neurological model has been proposed that regards LD and some other developmental disorders as being best interpreted as resulting from "minimal brain damage" (Wender, 1971). But this view, emphasizing research on the correlations between behavioral disorders and physiological measures of neural function, has not been substantiated by the experimental evidence to date (see Lahey, 1976, for review).

It is sometimes suggested that LD can originate in a delayed development of certain neurological processes, so that the cognitive strategies used by the learner are inappropriate for the normal development of skills (Bakker, Teunissen, & Bosch, 1976; Witelson, 1976). Other evidence of delay in the development of psychological processes has been presented by Ross (1976) for selective attention and by Satz and Friel (1973) for left-hemispheric maturation. The delay models may be different from a deficit model if it is assumed that the delay in development will eventually be eliminated in the course of growth, and it presumably leads to a better prognosis and a different treatment orientation. Such *developmental lag* models are generally unsupported by outcome studies, which show that LD children typically fail to catch up with their normal peers on either academic or process-oriented measures (Horn, O'Donnell & Vitulano, 1983; Rourke, 1975). It seems more likely that differences between LD and normal learners will persist over time, even in the face of intervention, and remedial efforts should not be delayed in the hope of spontaneous remission.

What is the status of the psychological-process theory of the origins of LD? Educators (e.g., McLeod, 1983) have pointed out that LD children are usually an educational responsibility, and that remediation nearly always has an educational character. Even if it is assumed that neuropsychological factors are causative of LD, there remains the question of whether suitable assessment is available and whether it leads to a more effective treatment than would otherwise be prescribed.

Unfortunately, reviews of the LD field have reported many limitations on the current utility of the neuropsychological-process approach. Satz and Fletcher (1981), for example, pointed out the mistake of *assuming* brain dysfunction in LD, noting the need for studies of differences in neuropsychological processes between children with *known,* and children with *assumed,* cerebral dysfunction (see also Kavale & Forness, 1985; Torgesen, 1979). A conservative view is that the approach holds much promise, but much research has yet to be done before there is a level of understanding from which remedial and assessment procedures will flow that can be applied by those at the chalk face with confidence in a positive outcome.

## CLASSIFICATION

Primary classifications of LD are usually based on the nature of the behavioral deficit(s) demonstrated by the child. For example, the American Psychiatric Association's DSM-III (APA, 1980), under *specific developmental disorders,* lists reading, arithmetic, language, articulation, mixed and atypical. In the DSM-III, as in the National Joint Committee on Learning Disabilities (Hammill *et al.*, 1981) definition, these disorders may not be diagnosed in a child where they are due to another, more general, disorder, such as mental retardation or infantile autism. Of the categories listed, the most prevalent is reading, perhaps because this skill is the most complex. Reading disability has also attracted the most research, both on the psychological processes involved and on remedial procedures.

There have been numerous suggestions of useful subclassifications of LDs, usually on the basis of the diagnosis of the neuropsychological processes responsible for the behavioral deficit. The suggested classifications of children with reading disability include dysphonetic, dyseidetic, or mixed (Boder, 1973); and audiophonic or visuospatial (Ingram, Mason, & Blackburn, 1970). These and other classifications are reviewed elsewhere (e.g., Barkley, 1981). There is little information on the reliability and validity of the tests used for these differential classifications, and therefore, there is little basis for choosing between them. They are intended to provide a functional classification that leads to the selection of an effective treatment; that is, they are meant to provide a basis for diagnostic-prescriptive treatment. Analyses of diagnostic-prescriptive programs based on early classifications of LD suggest that these diagnoses are ineffective in providing a functional basis for treatment (e.g., Hartlage & Telzrow, 1983). It remains to be seen whether current neuropsychological research will provide more effective classifications.

NIRBHAY N. SINGH AND
IVAN L. BEALE

It is usually advocated that the choice of an appropriate remedial procedure should be based on a thorough assessment of the LD child's deficiencies and strengths, his or her available resources, environmental expectations, a good knowledge of alternative remedial methods, and anything else that might be relevant. However, it is probably more typical for the choice of treatment to reflect mainly the orientation and training of the professional responsible for the intervention. A variety of procedures have been advocated for use in the treatment of LD, representing different views of the etiology of LD, different emphases on behavioral or process deficits, and different philosophies concerning the aims of treatment.

This chapter encompasses a broad range of treatment methods, with the intention of providing a useful, structured guide to most of the methods that have been advocated. Critical comment is based on an appraisal of evaluative research on the effects of treatment, where it exists, rather than on an analysis of the theories on which the treatments are purportedly based. In our view, the effectiveness of a treatment may bear little relation to the properties of its underlying theory. The space devoted here to the different treatments varies according to the availability of previous reviews of similar material and the amount of evaluative research on each method.

## Behavioral Treatments

Behavioral approaches have been used in the acquisition and remediation of reading in LD children. The majority of studies have focused on the enhancement of reading proficiency through the reinforcement of accuracy and the correction of errors during oral reading. In these studies, the children had progressed beyond the elementary stage of reading, although proficient decoding of words was still their major problem. A small but important set of studies have also evaluated behavioral strategies for increasing comprehension in LD children. However, the acquisition of an initial vocabulary of sight words by LD children has been totally neglected by behavioral researchers.

We will consider three main classes of behavioral methods in this section: stimulus control, cognitive-behavior modification, and behavior modification. The aim is not to provide an exhaustive review of the literature but to alert the reader to the variety of treatment methods that are available for remediating reading deficits in LD children.

### Stimulus Control

A majority of children do not have any problems in learning to read basic sight words through traditional teaching methods, such as trial-and-error learning (Etzel & LeBlanc, 1979; McGee & McCoy, 1981). In the typical trial-and error learning situation, the teacher models the pronunciation of a new word and then reinforces the child's correct responses to the word. All incorrect responses are corrected but not reinforced. For those children who have difficulty learning through this method, the teacher has to use alternative teaching procedures.

One such class of procedures, usually termed *stimulus control,* is derived from basic studies in discrimination learning. *Stimulus control* refers "to the extent to which the value of an antecedent stimulus determines the probability of occurrence of a conditioned response" (Terrace, 1966, p. 271). Although studies using stimulus control methods have not usually employed LD children, the procedures used are applicable across children with a variety of disabilities. In addition, it has been noted that "the actual definition of learning disability employed by different investigators is variable [and] many of the children who were not labeled as learning disabled in behavioral studies would probably meet the criteria for learning disability" (Gadow, Torgesen & Dahlem, 1983, p. 313).

A number of errorless discrimination learning procedures are available that can be used to teach learning-disabled children basic sight words. In all of these procedures, the subjects are initially provided training on an easy discrimination that is gradually made more difficult or complex by systematically changing the discriminative stimuli. Procedures pertinent to the present discussion include stimulus fading, stimulus shaping, superimposition and fading, and prompting.

*Stimulus Fading.* Stimulus fading is derived from the work of Terrace (1963), who showed that difficult discriminations could be taught virtually without errors by the gradual shifting of control from one dimension to another. For example, Sidman and Stoddard (1966) taught children to discriminate between a circle and an ellipse. In a two-stage training procedure, they first presented an illuminated circle and seven dark keys. Gradually, they increased the intensity of the dark keys to the same level as the circle. The children were thus taught to discriminate between the circle and the illuminated blank keys. Then, an ellipse was slowly faded in on the blank keys until they were of the same intensity as the circle. Because the children were required to respond only to the circle during successive stages of training, an errorless circle–ellipse discrimination resulted. An alternative training format would be to begin the circle–ellipse discrimination by initially having an enlarged circle as the training stimulus (but a criterion-size ellipse) and then systematically fading its size until it is the same as that of the ellipse (Etzel & LeBlanc, 1979).

Stimulus fading can be used to teach both letters and words to learning-disabled children. For example, in letter-discrimination, training the criterion letter (e.g., the letter *A*) can be presented at full intensity, and then, a second letter (e.g., *B*) can be systematically faded in until an *A-B* discrimination is established. An alternative format would be to enhance the size (i.e., the salience) of letter *A,* but not *B,* during initial training and then to systematically fade *A* to criterion size.

Rincover (1978) taught a *J-S* discrimination to autistic children by increasing the salience of *J* but not *S.* The salience of *J* was increased by exaggerating the crossbar on the *J,* and when the discrimination between the two letters was established, the exaggeration was faded. Furthermore, Rincover (1978) taught the children to discriminate between three-letter words (e.g., *JAR–SON*) by initially exaggerating the first letter of the target word (i.e., the crossbar on *J*) and then fading the exaggeration on subsequent trials. Egeland and Winer (1974) and Egeland (1975) reported that, when compared to a trial-and-error method, children made fewer errors on letter discrimination when using a fading procedure. In another study, Lancioni, Ceccarani, and Oliva (1981) taught words by initially increasing the salience of the first letter of each word, which was faded once the discrimination between the words was established.

*Stimulus Shaping.* In stimulus-fading procedures, there is no change in the topography of the training or the criterion stimulus. On the other hand, stimulus shaping involves critical changes in the topography of the stimulus. That is, the initial training stimulus, which may not resemble the criterion stimulus but is easily discriminated by the subject, is gradually shaped over successive training trials to form the criterion stimulus.

There are several examples of the use of stimulus shaping in the literature. For example, Touchette (1968) shaped a black rectangle to a black square, and Bijou (1968) shaped mirror images in a left–right discrimination. In addition, stimulus shaping has been used to teach motor (Stoddard & Gerovac, 1981) and visual-motor responses (Gold & Barclay, 1973; Mosk & Bucher, 1984).

Stimulus shaping can be used to teach simple sight words to children (Le Blanc, Etzel, & Domash, 1978). Initially, a pictorial stimulus is presented, which is gradually shaped to form a word. For example, to teach the word *LOG,* a line drawing of a log is initially presented, and then, in successive phases, the letters *L, O,* and *G* are shaped from the line drawing of *LOG.* In a variation of this procedure, Miller and Miller (1968, 1971) used a stimulus-shaping procedure (termed "symbol accentuation" by the authors) to teach sight words to mentally retarded children. In addition, Miller and Miller (1971) found stimulus shaping to be more effective than a trial-and-error procedure in teaching sight words to children. Jeffree (1981) provided further confirmation of the efficacy of this approach. Finally, Smeets, Lancioni, and Hoogeveen (1984) demonstrated the superiority of stimulus shaping over fading and nonfading procedures in sight word recognition by mentally retarded children.

*Superimposition and Fading.* Another procedure that can be used to teach words to children involves the superimposition of two stimuli (a training stimulus and a prompt), followed by the fading of the prompt. For example, a word (e.g., *APPLE*) and a picture prompt (i.e., a picture of an apple) are presented together as a complex stimulus, and the child is told what the word is. Typically, the picture controls the child's response because it is the easier stimulus to discriminate. In successive trials or sessions, the picture is gradually faded out of the complex stimuli, and only the word is left. Once the picture is faded, the control is shifted from the picture to the word, and the child responds to the word.

A number of studies have used this technique to teach sight word vocabulary to children. Corey and Shamow (1972) compared the effects of superimposition alone or paired with fading of the prompt on the acquisition and retention of sight words. They found that young children learned and retained more words when both procedures were used. Similar results were reported by Dorry and Zeaman (1973, 1975) in mentally retarded children. In another study, Dorry (1976) found that fading the prompt alone was just as effective as simultaneously fading out the picture prompt and fading in the word. In an extension of this line of research, Walsh and Lamberts (1979) compared the efficacy of the fading procedure with a stimulus-shaping reading program (Edmark Reading Program). Although children learned sight words in both procedures, they performed better in stimulus shaping.

*Delayed Prompting.* Delayed prompting is similar to the Dorry and Zeaman (1973, 1975) procedure of presenting a complex stimulus consisting of two dimensions and then fading one of them. In delayed prompting, a complex stimulus is presented, but in successive trials or sessions, the presentation of the second stimulus (i.e., the prompt) is systematically delayed or faded on a temporal dimension (Touchette, 1971). In a variation of this procedure, the training stimulus (e.g., the word *APPLE*) is presented, and after a delay, a prompt (e.g., a picture of an apple) is presented. The subject's response is under the control of the word if she or he responds before the prompt is provided, and it is under the control of the picture if the response comes after the prompt.

In the Touchette (1971) study, each correct response delayed the onset of the prompt in the following trial by 0.5 seconds, and each error reduced the delay by 0.5 seconds. Variations of the delayed prompting procedure have been successfully used to teach instruction-following skills (Striefel, Bryan, & Aikins, 1974; Striefel, Wetherby, & Karlan, 1976); sign language (Smeets & Striefel, 1976a,b); spontaneous speech (Charlop, Schreibman, & Thibodeau, 1985; Halle, Baer, & Apradlin, 1981; Halle, Marshall, & Spradlin, 1979); and assembly tasks in a workshop (Walls, Haught, & Dowler, 1982).

Two studies have used delayed prompting procedures to teach letter and word recognition skills to children. McGee and McCoy (1981) compared the effectiveness of trial-and-error, fading, and delayed-prompting procedures in teaching oral reading responses to mentally retarded children. Greater acquisition and retention were evident with both fading and delayed prompting than with the trial-and-error procedure. In the other study, Bradley-Johnson, Sunderman, and Johnson (1983) compared the effectiveness of delayed prompting and fading techniques in teaching easily confused letters to young children. Delayed prompting was found to be more effective than fading in this study.

*Extra- and Intrastimulus Prompting.* An added or extrastimulus prompt can be used to facilitate a child's reading. For example, a picture, an object, or pointing by the teacher can be used to facilitate a child's learning of a new word. Stimulus prompts that are additional to the training stimulus are termed extrastimulus prompts, and it is assumed that the child will continue to respond correctly when the extrastimulus prompt is withdrawn (Schreibman, 1975; Schreibman, Charlop, & Koegel, 1982). Intrastimulus prompts are those that involve increasing the salience of the training stimulus itself.

Extrastimulus prompts in the form of pictures are typically used in basal readers for young children (Samuels, 1967, 1970). However, the current research literature suggests that using extrastimulus prompts may have detrimental effects on the reading performance of some children. These children fail to transfer from the extrastimulus prompt to the training stimulus (Saunders & Solman, 1984). Similar findings have been reported with autistic children (Koegel & Rincover, 1976). The problem is compounded in those children who are overselective in their response to multiple stimuli. Such overselectivity has been found to be a characteristic of some children who are autistic (Lovaas, Koegel, & Schreibman, 1979); mentally retarded (Gersten, 1983; Huguenin, 1985; Wilhelm & Lovaas, 1976); learning-disabled (Bailey, 1981); and normal (Eimas, 1969). Comparative studies of intra- and extrastimulus prompting show that children perform better when intrastimulus prompts are used (Schreibman, 1975; Wolfe & Cuvo, 1978).

Nirbhay N. Singh and
Ivan L. Beale

Cognitive-behavior-modification procedures have had a huge impact on the field of learning disabilities since the mid-1960s. The procedures have been derived from cognitive and behavioral approaches, focusing on both covert and overt behaviors. The main impetus for this approach was provided by Donald Meichenbaum of the University of Waterloo (see Craighead, 1982; Meichenbaum, 1977, for reviews), who was influenced by the theories of Luria (1961) and Vygotsky (1962) on the effects of language and thought on behavior. The growing interest in cognitive-behavior modification is attested to by the large number of recent reviews of the literature (e.g., Abikoff, 1985; Craighead, 1982; Craighead-Wilcoxon & Meyers, 1978; Craighead, Meyers, & Craighead, 1985; Hallahan, Kneedler, & Lloyd, 1983; Meyers & Craighead, 1984; Whalen, Henker, & Hinshaw, 1985) and special issues on the topic in journals (e.g., *Exceptional Education Quarterly*, 1980, Vol. 1, No. 1; *Journal of Abnormal Child Psychology*, 1985, Vol. 13, No. 3).

There are a number of reasons that cognitive-behavior modification has proved to be a very popular alternative to the traditional treatment approaches used with LD children. For example, it has been suggested that other approaches are not totally effective and that their limitations in this field are now apparent (see Kauffman & Hallahan, 1979; Whalen & Henker, 1980). One of these problems pertains to the maintenance and generalization of behavior change. It has been suggested that, although behavior change can be produced by using operant procedures, its maintenance and generalization in LD children are immensely difficult. The problem is that operant procedures do not teach children effective ways of regulating their own behavior, as behavior change is achieved through external control.

Cognitive-behavior modification is used to teach skills to the child that enhance self-control and problem-solving strategies. In comparison to the operant approach, behavior change is not externally controlled by a therapist or a significant other (e.g., a parent, a teacher, or a peer). Rather, behavior change skills are internalized by the child, enabling the child to use these skills in a variety of situations and places over time. It is the internalization of the skills that leads to the maintenance and generalization of behavior change. Thus, this approach appears to be particularly attractive for children who are characterized as having an external locus of control and deficits in self-regulation, problem solving, or inhibition (Harris, 1982). A later section in this chapter deals more generally with locus of control as a secondary effect of LD.

A number of terms have been used to describe cognitive-behavior-modification procedures, including *self-instruction, self-verbalization, self-observation, self-monitoring, self-evaluation, self-reinforcement, verbal mediation, verbal rehearsal, verbal control, cognitive control, cognitive training, problem solving,* and *cognitive restructuring.* Although these procedures vary somewhat, they share three major characteristics (Hallahan *et al.,* 1983). The subject is (1) given direct instruction, which may or may not be supplemented by modeling; (2) taught to use some form of verbalization, which eventually internalizes his or her skills and assists in behavior change; and (3) required to assume responsibility for the intervention through one or more of the "self-" strategies, such as self-instruction, self-evaluation, and self-reinforcement.

A majority of the studies using this approach with LD children have focused on behavior problems; only a limited literature is available on academic problems. We will briefly review the self-instructional and self-monitoring studies on academic behavior in LD. For more general reviews, the interested reader should consult Abikoff (1979, 1985). Kauffman and Hallahan (1979), Harris (1982), Hallahan *et al.* (1983), Meichenbaum and Asarnow (1979), and Craighead, Meyers, and Craighead (1985).

*Self-Instruction.* Self-instruction is "the use of self-verbalized directions designed to guide an individual through a series of steps that will result in the solution of a problem" (Hallahan *et al.*, 1973). One of the best examples of the use of self-instruction comes from two laboratory studies by Meichenbaum and Goodman (1969, 1971). In these studies, self-instructional strategies were used to gain verbal control over motor tasks (e.g., pushing a foot pedal and finger tapping). In a comparison of impulsive with reflective children, Meichenbaum and Goodman (1969) found that the reflective children were better able than the impulsive children to use verbal self-instructions to gain control over their motor behavior. In the other study, Meichenbaum and Goodman (1971) used a self-instructional strategy with hyperactive subjects. They found self-instruction plus modeling to be superior to the modeling-alone, the assessment-only, and the control conditions on a number of dependent measures.

The self-instruction format used in the 1971 study served as a model for subsequent research. Basically, it involves the experimenter modeling the solution to the problem and verbalizing self-instructions while the subject observes. Then, the roles are reversed, and the client performs the task, initially using overt self-instructions but gradually changing to covert self-instructions. Harris (1982) has suggested that a four-step training procedure is used in these studies, involving cognitive modeling (experimenter models and talks aloud while client observes); overt guidance (roles are reversed, and experimenter provides graduated guidance); faded self-guidance (client gradually reduces self-instructions from aloud to a whisper); and covert self-instruction (client performs the task using covert self-instruction).

*Collateral Changes in Academic Behavior.* In the early laboratory studies with LD children, self-instruction was used for behavior problems or for changing cognitive style. However, collateral measures were often taken of academic behavior, and some studies showed positive changes on some of these measures. For example, Egeland (1974) showed that impulsive children improved on tests of reading vocabulary and comprehension as a consequence of self-instructional training on the systematic use of a scanning strategy. However, other studies did not find any changes in collateral academic behaviors (e.g., Epstein, Hallahan, & Kauffman, 1975). It should be noted that, because laboratory studies focus on tasks that have little direct relationship to academic behavior, it is not surprising that positive changes are not generally found.

Other nonlaboratory studies have also presented data on collateral academic behaviors, and a few have shown positive changes. For example, Camp, Blom, Hebert, and Van Doorninck (1977) used a "think-aloud" self-instruction procedure with aggressive boys and reported that, in addition to reduced levels of aggression, there was a significant increase in the boys' reading scores as measured on a standardized test. Improvements in oral reading and oral comprehension were reported in a study using self-instruction with hyperactive children (Douglas, Parry, Marton, & Garson, 1976). Like the laboratory studies, some nonlaboratory studies have also reported no changes in academic behavior (e.g., Glenwick & Barocas, 1979; Varni & Henker, 1979).

*Direct Changes in Academic Behavior.* The results are more positive when academic behaviors have been targeted for change through self-instruction (with or without modeling). For example, improvements due to self-instruction have been reported in handwriting (e.g., Graham, 1983; Kosiewicz, Hallahan, Lloyd, & Graves, 1981; Robin, Armel, & O'Leary, 1975); reading (Brown & Alford, 1984); reading comprehension (Bommarito & Meichenbaum, cited in Meichenbaum & Asarnow, 1979; Knapczyk & Livingston, 1974; Wong & Jones, 1982); written language (Harris & Graham, in press); arithmetic (Leon & Pepe, 1983); and study skills (Greiner & Karoly, 1976).

Although only a few studies have used self-instruction techniques to produce changes in academic behavior in LD children, a number of operant studies have evaluated the effects of self-verbalizations on academic achievement (e.g., Grimm, Bijou, & Parsons, 1973; Lovitt & Curtiss, 1968). These studies suggest that the efficacy of operant procedures can be enhanced by the addition of self-verbalization.

No strong conclusions can be reached from the limited number of studies that have used self-instructions to enhance academic achievement. However, if taken in their best light, these studies suggest that self-instruction may be a potentially useful procedure for producing academic behavior change in LD children.

*Self-Monitoring.* Self-monitoring requires the child to engage in self-assessment and self-recording during the performance of a specific task. Thus, the child is required to slow down, reduce impulsive responding, and evaluate his or her performance. The child is required to identify and record each occurrence of the behavior.

A number of studies have evaluated the effects of self-monitoring of attention on the on-task and academic behavior of LD children (see Hallahan & Sapona, 1983, for a review). In self-monitoring studies, the subject is first taught to monitor his or her attending behavior through self-assessment. Often, this is aided by an experimenter-provided cue (e.g., an audiotape recorder that emits a periodic signal), which informs the child when to self-assess and record whether or not he or she was attending to the task.

The best studies on self-monitoring in LD children come from the ongoing research program at the University of Virginia. The self-monitoring procedures used in these studies were adapted from Glynn and Thomas (1974) and Glynn, Thomas, and Shee (1973). In these studies, the self-monitoring procedure was administered by the children's class teacher or teacher aide, and no backup reinforcers were used. The children were taught to self-monitor their on- and off-task behavior by using an audiotape recorder to cue their self-recording.

The first study showed that an LD child's on-task behavior increased dramatically with self-monitoring during both math and handwriting sessions (Hallahan, Lloyd, Kosiewicz, Kauffman, & Graves, 1979). Subsequent studies examined the contribution of various aspects of the self-monitoring procedure (e.g., self-recording, provision of audio cues, and self-assessment vs. teacher assessment of on- and off-task behavior). Although these studies have not been published, the interested reader is referred to Hallahan *et al.* (1983) for a brief description of each. In a final study, Hallahan, Marshall, and Lloyd (1981) evaluated the effectiveness of a self-monitoring procedure in a small-group setting while the teacher aide instructed the children using the SRA (Science Research Associates) Corrective Reading Program (Engelmann, Becker, Hanner, & Johnson, 1979). As in other studies, clear treatment effects were demonstrated in terms of increased on-task behavior.

Although changes in academic behavior (e.g., changes in math proficiency) were not formally monitored in these studies, informal teacher reports suggested that positive changes had occurred. This is an important omission, as changes in academic behavior are an important goal for LD children. However, at least one study has shown that LD children can improve their academic performance by self-monitoring academic behavior (Rooney, Polloway, & Hallahan, 1985). This study suggested that increasing on-task behavior may not necessarily increase academic achievement and that individual subject areas (e.g., math and reading) may have to be targeted for improvement.

In sum, the few studies on self-monitoring with LD children now available show that the behavior that is monitored increases dramatically as a consequence of intervention. However, this conclusion must be viewed cautiously, as virtually all the studies have focused on on- or off-task behavior and not on academic behavior *per se*. It remains to be demonstrated whether the initially promising results of this procedure will be borne out by studies on academic behavior change.

### Behavior Modification

Behavioral procedures have been used in the direct instruction of LD children in reading. The behavioral approach views the learning-disabled child as having skills deficits in reading that can be remediated through the manipulation of antecedent events (e.g., instructional materials and setting and teacher variables) and consequent events (see Treiber & Lahey, 1983). In this section, we discuss a number of behavioral procedures that have been used in the remedial reading instruction of LD children.

*Antecedent Strategies.* Although a majority of studies have used response-contingent error-correction procedures, antecedent strategies have proved to be effective in producing behavior change in educational contexts (Glynn, 1982). A number of antecedent strategies have been used to increase LD children's proficiency in oral reading and comprehension.

*Antecedent Modeling.* In the antecedent modeling of basic sight words, the teacher presents a word to the child and says, "This word is . . . ," and then asks, "What word is this?" Hendrickson, Roberts, and Shores (1978) used this procedure to teach basic sight words to two LD children. In addition, they found that antecedent modeling was more effective than a contingent modeling procedure. A similar strategy has been used to improve children's oral reading of basal readers (Smith, 1979), and a variation of the procedure (using tape recordings of the words) was used by Freeman and McLaughlin (1984).

*Phonics Instruction.* Phonics instruction can be used either as an antecedent strategy or as a consequent (error) correction strategy. Lovitt and Hurlburt (1974) evaluated the effects of prior phonics instruction on the oral reading of LD children. They found that phonics instruction enhanced the children's performance on five phonics tasks and increased their oral reading proficiency.

*Previewing.* A number of studies have shown that children's reading accuracy can be improved if they are allowed to preview the text before oral reading. The commonly used previewing procedures either require the teacher to introduce and highlight significant aspects of the story or have the child silently read the passage before reading it aloud. The efficacy of a number of previewing procedures in improving oral reading accuracy has been demonstrated in several studies (Rose & Sherry, 1984; Sachs, 1984; Singh & Singh, 1984; Wong & McNaughton, 1980).

The effects of previewing difficult short stories on both LD and high-ability children's comprehension has been investigated by Graves and his colleagues (Graves & Cooke, 1980; Graves, Cooke, & LaBerge, 1983; Graves & Palmer, 1981). These studies clearly showed that previewing facilitates students' comprehension. Similar facilitative effects of previewing on LD children's comprehension have been reported by Sachs (1983). Finally, Chang, Williams, and McLaughlin (1983) reported that comprehension can be improved if LD children are required to read the target text orally to the teacher, who simply corrects mispronunciations or word substitutions.

*Question Prompts.* In two related studies, Wong (1979, 1980) demonstrated the efficacy of question prompts in increasing LD children's comprehension. Question prompts require the teacher to provide the children with the questions before they read the target text. It appears that previewing the questions has a facilitative effect on the children's comprehension. In another study, Clark, Deshler, Schumaker, Alley, and Warner (1984) found that LD children could improve their comprehension if they engaged in self-questioning during the reading of the target text. In addition, comprehension was facilitated if the children were able to visualize the contents of the target text.

*Study Skill Training.* It has been found that teaching children study skills techniques, such as the Survey, Question, Read, Recite, and Review (SQ3R) procedure (Robinson, 1941), can improve their reading comprehension. In an evaluation of the SQ3R procedure, Alexander (1985) found that LD children were able to increase their story-retelling scores through the use of this procedure.

In summary, it is clear that a number of empirically validated procedures can be used to improve LD children's oral reading and comprehension skills. However, our impression of the literature is that the number of methodologically sound studies of LD children is very limited and that further evaluative studies are necessary. In addition, there is a paucity of comparative studies that evaluate the effects of two or more procedures on LD children.

*Consequent Strategies.* Several consequent strategies have been used to increase oral reading and comprehension skills in LD children. In addition, other procedures used with children who have other mildly handicapping conditions may be equally applicable to LD children. Because there are a number of descriptive and evaluative reviews of this literature (e.g., Hansen & Eaton, 1978; Hansen & Lovitt, 1977; Lahey, 1977; Rose, Koorland, & Epstein, 1982a; Ross, 1981; Singh & Singh, 1986c), we present here only a brief discussion of the procedures that can be used with LD children.

*Feedback.* Simply providing feedback often results in increased performance. For example, Thorpe, Chiang, and Darch (1981) provided group and individual feedback for oral reading accuracy in LD children. It was found that simply providing a graphic display of their performance increased the accuracy of their oral reading in both individual and group conditions.

*Reinforcement.* Various studies have shown that tokens or tangible reinforcement procedures can be used to increase oral reading accuracy (e.g., Billingsley, 1977; Jenkins, Barksdale, & Clinton, 1978; Lahey & Drabman, 1974; Lahey, McNees, & Brown, 1973). In addition, Swanson (1981) found that comprehension can be increased when it is targeted for reinforcement but not when oral reading accuracy is targeted for reinforcement. This study confirmed and extended earlier research (e.g., Jenkins *et al.*, 1978; Roberts & Smith, 1980) which suggested that reinforcement has specific effects on the behavior that is reinforced without producing concommitant changes in other behaviors. That is, when oral reading accuracy is reinforced, little or no improvement occurs in comprehension and vice versa.

*Attention to Errors.* It has been shown that teacher attention to errors increases the accuracy of oral reading of LD children (McNaughton & Delquadri, 1978). However, other studies have shown that delaying teacher attention may be more effective than immediate attention to errors (McNaughton & Glynn, 1981; Singh, Winton, & Singh, 1985).

*Drill.* Drill is a procedure that has been used to enhance decoding skills in children. A number of alternative drill procedures can be used, including flash cards and word lists. In a comparative study, Jenkins and Larson (1979) found isolated word drill to be more effective than other error-correction procedures (e.g., word meaning, sentence repeat, word supply, and end-of-page review) in increasing the oral reading accuracy of LD children. In another study, drill (flash cards) was used in addition to other procedures in a cross-age tutoring program (Chiang, Thorpe, & Darch, 1980). The procedures were effective in increasing the word recognition skills of LD children. O'Shea, Munson, and O'Shea (1984) found word drill and phrase drill to be superior to word supply in increasing children's recognition of words in isolation, but that phrase drill was more effective than word drill in increasing the children's recognition of words in context. In another study, drill and modeling procedures were used to increase the oral reading accuracy and the comprehension of LD children (Roberts & Smith, 1980).

*Word Analysis and Word Supply.* These two error-correction procedures are used with beginning readers extensively in elementary schools. Word analysis requires the teacher to direct the child's attention to the phonetic elements of the error word and to "sound out" the word. Word supply requires the teacher to "supply" or tell the child the correct word following an error. Comparative studies of the use of these two procedures with LD children have produced mixed results: one study reported word supply to be more effective in increasing oral reading accuracy (Rose, McEntire, & Dowdy, 1982b), and another (Meyer, 1982) showed no difference. To complicate matters further, Singh and Singh (1985) found word analysis to be more effective than word supply with mentally retarded children.

*Overcorrection.* Overcorrection, a package of procedures originally devised for decreasing maladaptive behavior, has been found to be effective in enhancing a number of academic behaviors (Singh, 1985). Singh, Singh, and Winton (1984) used overcorrection to increase the oral reading accuracy of mentally retarded children. In this procedure, each incorrectly read word is repeated five times, and the sentence in which the word occurs is correctly repeated once. Overcorrection has been found to be effective in both individual (Singh *et al.*, 1984) and group training formats (Singh, 1987), and to be more effective than isolated word drill (Singh & Singh, 1986b) in increasing oral reading accuracy in mentally retarded children. Whether overcorrection is as effective with LD children as with the mentally retarded remains to be demonstrated.

The efficacy of consequent strategies for enhancing oral reading accuracy and comprehension appears to be well established with LD children. Although the earlier studies were methodologically flawed in several respects (see Gadow *et al.*, 1983), more recent and better controlled studies provide the basis for this conclusion. In addition to the studies reviewed above, there are others that have used a combination of antecedent and consequent strategies to facilitate oral reading and comprehension in children with reading problems, including those with learning disabilities (e.g., Limbrick, McNaughton, & Glynn, 1985; Schumaker, Deshler, Alley, Warner, & Denton, 1982; Scott & Ballard, 1983; Singh & Singh, 1986a). These studies suggest that behavioral procedures can be used to produce significant gains in the oral reading accuracy and the comprehension of LD children.

## Process-Oriented Treatments

### Perceptual-Motor Therapy

A variety of treatments are subsumed under this heading, including those described by Delacato (1959), Getman and Kane (1964), Kephart (1971), and Frostig and Horne (1964). The theories and treatments vary considerably, but all are based on a view that perceptual development is a function of the central nervous system and follows an orderly series of developmental steps requiring particular sensorimotor interaction with the environment. LD is seen as resulting from inadequate or anomalous perceptual-motor development, and treatment is directed at perceptual-motor organization using exercises usually unrelated to the academic deficiencies leading to the LD diagnosis.

Evaluative reviews of perceptual-motor therapies for LD have concluded that there is little evidence of their effectiveness in remediating either academic deficiencies or, perhaps more surprisingly, deficits in perceptual-motor skills (Balow, 1971; Hammill, 1972; Keogh, 1978). Hammill (1972), for example, reviewed 13 studies of the effectiveness of visual-perceptual training programs that used adequate experimental design and methodology. The programs used included those of Barsh, Cratty, Delacato, Frostig, Getman, and Kephart, as well as combinations of these and some specially designed treatments. Only three studies found beneficial effects of training on perceptual-motor skills, the remainder showing no differences between perceptually trained and nontrained subjects. Hammill (1972) also reviewed 25 intervention studies in which perceptual training (usually Frostig-Horne or Kephart programs) was used in an attempt to remediate reading problems. Most of these studies (21) concluded that perceptual-motor training did not improve reading ability. Kavale and Mattson (1983) conducted a meta-analysis of 180 studies of perceptual-motor intervention in LD and found such training to be ineffective in improving academic, cognitive, or perceptual-motor performance. Analyses of subsets of studies based on programs, subjects, school grade, and design variables returned essentially the same negative result.

These investigators supported the conclusion of Myers and Hammill (1976) that perceptual-motor training cannot be assumed to be beneficial relative to no treatment because it may waste valuable resources and divert efforts from the implementation of more effective programs.

*Preferred-Modality Instruction*

LD children can be divided into subtypes on the basis of their apparent preferences of sensory modalities, usually measured by relative performance levels on tests requiring primarily visual or auditory discriminations (see the section on classification). Some researchers (e.g., Wepman, 1967) have regarded such preferences as reflecting the relative strengths of underlying psychological processes, indicating strengths and weaknesses that should be taken into account when selecting appropriate remedial measures. Some writers have recommended teaching to the child's strengths or preferences, at least in the first instance (Sabatino & Hayden, 1970; Wepman, 1967), and others feel that remediation should be "deficit-oriented" (Hallahan & Cruickshank, 1973), as this approach addresses the weaknesses that underlie the LD child's deficits. A middle road is also offered (e.g., Kirk & Kirk, 1971), advocating both the use of strengths and the treatment of deficits, with an emphasis on intersensory integration.

Reviews of aptitude–treatment interactions and diagnostic-prescriptive training have generally been unenthusiastic about the relevance of sensory strengths and weaknesses to the effectiveness of treatments (Arter & Jenkins, 1977; Hartlage & Telzrow, 1983; Sabatino, Ysseldyke, & Woolston, 1973; Tarver & Dawson, 1978). However, a meta-analysis of research in this area is made difficult by problems of inadequate experimental design, methodological weaknesses, and poor generalizability (Chronbach & Snow, 1977). An additional problem is the wide range of aptitude variables that have been considered and the variety of dependent variables used to measure them. Some of the major difficulties were discussed by Hartlage and Telzrow (1983), who advocated a model for choosing aptitude variables that have a sound neuropsychological basis in current research on learning processes. As has already been intimated, the neuropsychology of learning disabilities must still be regarded as a research area in which there are more questions than answers, and the neuropsychological processes critical to academic skills are still a matter of debate and experimental investigation (Corballis & Beale, 1983; Knights & Bakker, 1976). It may be that basic neuropsychological research is the best source of concepts and methods for measuring an LD child's strengths and weaknesses, but the source is best approached in a conservative and experimental spirit.

If the alternative remedial approaches are teaching to strengths, circumventing weaknesses, or teaching to overcome weaknesses, it may be desirable to know the extent to which the weaknesses are modifiable by instruction. At the simplest level of sensory preference or aptitude, there is some evidence of modifiability in LD students. Koorland and Wolkerling (1982) showed that reinforcement of stimulus control by stimuli of the nonpreferred modality can result in a reversal of relative control by competing stimulus modalities, a result that supports the idea that remediation can be approached by the strengthening of areas of weakness. This view is supported by studies of the modifiability of stimulus-modality preferences in mentally retarded and autistic children. Selective control by particular modalities or dimensions of compound discriminative stimuli, often found to be characteristic of these populations (Lovaas *et al.*, 1979; Zeaman & House, 1963), can be reduced or eliminated by appropriate stimulus-reinforcement relations (Allen & Fuqua, 1985). It is emphasized, however, that evidence of modifiability is confined to the learners' preferences of stimulus modalities or dimensions and should not be taken to apply generally to "aptitudes," especially those that are closely identified with neuropsychological processes.

## Psycholinguistic Training

Language disorders occur more often in conjunction with mental retardation than as a type of LD, where their incidence is estimated at about 1:1,000 (APA, 1980). For this reason, most evaluations of remedial programs for language deficits have used mentally retarded children as subjects. There is little specific information on the efficacy of these programs with LD children.

Studies of psycholinguistic training have usually revolved around the use of the Illinois Test of Psycholinguistic Abilities (ITPA; Kirk, McCarthy, & Kirk, 1968) as a diagnostic instrument. This test has served as the basis for several widely used remedial programs (e.g., Karnes, 1968; Minskoff, Wiseman, & Minskoff, 1972) that attempt to train psycholinguistic abilities diagnosed as weak by the ITPA or similar tests.

A meta-analysis of numerous experimental evaluations of psycholinguistic training have not yielded clear-cut results. Hammill and Larsen (1974) reviewed 38 studies that had used the ITPA as a dependent measure and concluded that the effectiveness of psycholinguistic training was not supported. A subsequent meta-analysis (Kavale, 1981) of 34 studies (excluding several included in Hammill and Larsen's 1974 study) reached a more favorable conclusion. For example, they found that the average child receiving training performed better than 65% of untrained children. Larsen, Parker, and Hammill (1982) reported the results of a further meta-analysis that included six studies not analyzed by Kavale. They showed that the expected increase in score following some 50 hours of training was only about one quarter of the standard error of measurement. It is difficult to imagine a cost–benefit analysis that would find such a gain worthwhile.

Too few of the studies analyzed used LD children to enable a differential analysis of the effectiveness of training in this group. However, an evaluative study of the effects of a training program devised by Minskoff *et al.* (1972), with intellectually normal children, again found psycholinguistic training to be ineffective (Sowell, Parker, Poplin, & Larsen, 1979). In summary, the effectiveness of the psycholinguistic training of LD children has yet to be established.

## Treatment of Secondary Disorders

The chronic failure experienced by the LD child in affected academic areas, often prolonged over many years, must often give rise to additional, secondary problems both at school and at home. Often cited are problems of anxiety, poor self-esteem, and low expectancy of ability to achieve success by one's own efforts (Henker, Whalen, & Hinshaw, 1980).

The use of cognitive-behavior modification to help the child achieve self-control of behavior changes was described in a previous section. Other suggested remedial methods are outlined below. Some are advocated as sufficient in themselves to bring about improvement in academic performance, and others are suggested for use in conjunction with additional procedures that specifically address the academic disabilities.

### Art and Dance Therapies

Dance therapy (Leventhal, 1980) is supposed to "directly affect the child's perceptual-motor and sensorimotor development" (p. 33). Emotional benefits and improvements in interpersonal skills are also claimed, although no hard evidence has been presented on the effects of dance therapy on any of these variables. Art therapy has been claimed to give better results than "traditional training" in visual alertness, motor coordination, word recognition, linguistic ability, spatial relations, and perceptual age (Carter, 1979). Again, no experimental evidence has been put forward in support of this claim. It is probably true that LD children receive emotional and other benefits from activities in areas in which their academic deficits are not a disadvantage, and that such benefits may conceivably improve motivation on academic tasks. But such benefits have not been proved, and there remains the cost–benefit question of whether resources could be expended more profitably in other directions.

### Hypnosis and Suggestion

Both hypnosis and suggestion have been used as a means of increasing both academic performance and self-esteem in LD children. Although some practitioners have claimed that these methods are effective (Mutke, 1967; Oldridge, 1982), studies comparing control groups with groups given hypnotic training (Jampolsky, 1975; Johnson, Johnson, Olson, & Newman, 1981) suggest that hypnotic techniques may be effective in improving self-esteem but not academic performance.

## Relaxation Training

Relaxation training has been used with LD children as a means of reducing levels of anxiety thought to interfere with learning and academic performance. Russell and Carter (1978) used electromyographic feedback training to induce arm muscle relaxation and obtained both a substantial reduction in muscle activity and improved performance on several academic tasks. However, other studies of the effects of progressive relaxation training on academic measures suggest that this approach is ineffective (Luiselli, Steinman, Marholin, & Steinman, 1981; Spillios & Janzen, 1983). In the absence of more positive evidence on this type of treatment, it is concluded that the usefulness of relaxation training for LD has not yet been established.

## Modification of Locus of Control

Dudley-Martling, Snider, and Tarver (1982) reviewed several studies of the locus of control in LD children and concluded that there is strong evidence that an external locus of control is generally characteristic of LD children; that is, they tend to attribute successes and failures to factors outside their own control. However, there is some evidence that the external locus of control in LD children is confined to success and that they have an internal locus of control for failure. As internal control is associated with academic failure, efforts by LD children toward success may only follow a change toward external control. Possible treatments arising from this point of view include those that teach self-control of behavior and the efficient application of problem-solving strategies (Henker et al., 1980). Some research on the effectiveness of these procedures has been reviewed above, under the heading "Cognitive-Behavior Modification." Other research has focused on the relevance of a diagnosis of internal or external locus of control to the choice of learning programs for LD students (Bendell, Tollefson, & Fine, 1980; Gajara, Cohen, & Tarver, 1978). For example, Bendell et al. (1980) found that LD adolescents with internal control performed better on a spelling task when given no instructions on strategy than when they were given detailed instructions. For students with external control, the reverse effect was obtained.

A different approach to the modification of external control was reported by Omizo and Williams (1982), who taught LD students "self-control" by electromyographic biofeedback training. In addition, progressive relaxation training was given. The effects were measured in impulsivity, attention to task, and locus of control. Only on the first two variables, however, was there a significant improvement, a finding suggesting that this treatment may be ineffective for the modification of external control.

Some additional approaches have been suggested (e.g., Fuller & Fuller, 1982; Grimes, 1981), but have not yet been tested by evaluative research. Overall, it appears that locus of control is a useful concept to include in the assessment of the LD child. Its modification may be more readily achieved by cognitive-behavior modification than by procedures further removed from academic instruction (e.g., biofeedback training).

Finally, we should recognize that, although we have treated attributes such as anxiety, poor self-esteem, and external locus of control as being secondary to LD, there may be some children in whom this implied causality is reversed, that is, in whom LD arises as a result of the prior existence of the other problems. No difference in treatment is suggested in these cases, save for some consideration of the determinants of the prior conditions, which may themselves need to be a subject of intervention.

## CONCLUSIONS

In this chapter we discussed psychological therapies for learning disabled children in terms of behavioral and psychological process approaches. Some exciting new developments have been witnessed with the behavioral approach in the amelioration of academic deficits. While we cannot conclude that all learning disabled children's academic problems can be overcome with good teaching, especially with the use of appropriate behavioral procedures, we strongly believe that a majority would benefit from such an approach (see Singh & Beale, 1988). The success obtained with psychological process approaches has generally been limited as far as academic remediation of learning disabled students is concerned. While these approaches may hold some promise, much of this remains unfulfilled.

## REFERENCES

Abikoff, H. (1979). Cognitive training interventions in children: Review of a new approach. *Journal of Learning Disabilities, 12,* 123–135.
Abikoff, H. (1985). Efficacy of cognitive training interventions in hyperactive children: A critical review. *Clinical Psychology Review, 5,* 479–512.
Alexander, D. F. (1985). The effect of study skill training on learning disabled students' retelling of expository material. *Journal of Applied Behavior Analysis, 18,* 263–267.
Allen, K. D., & Fuqua, R. W. (1985). Eliminating selective stimulus control: A comparison of two procedures for teaching mentally retarded children to respond to compound stimuli. *Journal of Experimental Child Psychology, 39,* 55–71.
American Psychiatric Association. (1980). *Diagnostic and Statistical Manual of Mental Disorders* (3rd ed.—DSM-III). Washington, DC: Author.
Arter, J. A., & Jenkins, J. R. (1977). Examining the benefits and prevalence of modality considerations in special education. *The Journal of Special Education, 11,* 281–298.
Bailey, S. L. (1981). Stimulus overselectivity in learning disabled children. *Journal of Applied Behavior Analysis, 14,* 239–248.
Bakker, D. J., Teunissen, J., & Bosch, J. (1976). Development of laterality—Reading patterns. In R. M. Knights & D. J. Bakker (Eds.), *The neuropsychology of learning disorders.* Baltimore, MD: University Park Press.
Balow, B. (1971). Perceptual-motor activities in the treatment of severe reading disability. *The Reading Teacher, 24,* 513–542.
Barkley, R. A. (1981). Learning disabilities. In E. J. Marsh & L. G. Terdal (Eds.), *Behavioral assessment of childhood disorders.* Chichester: Wiley.

Bendell, D. B., Tollefson, N., & Fine, M. (1980). Interaction of locus-of-control orientation and the performance of learning disabled adolescents. *Journal of Learning Disabilities, 13,* 32–35.

Bender, L. A. (1957). Specific reading disability as a maturational lag. *Bulletin of the Orton Society, 7,* 9–18.

Bijou, S. W. (1968). Studies in the experimental development of left-right concepts in retarded children using fading techniques. In N. R. Ellis (Ed.), *International review of research in mental retardation* (Vol. 3). New York: Academic Press.

Billingsley, F. F. (1977). The effects of self- and externally-imposed schedules of reinforcement on oral reading performance. *Journal of Learning Disabilities, 10,* 549–555.

Boder, E. (1973). Developmental dyslexia: A diagnostic approach based on three atypical reading patterns. *Developmental Medicine and Child Neurology, 15,* 663–687.

Bradley-Johnson, S., Sunderman, P., & Johnson, C. M. (1983). Comparison of delayed prompting and fading for teaching preschoolers easily confused letters and numbers. *Journal of School Psychology, 21,* 327–335.

Brown, R. T., & Alford, N. (1984). Ameliorating attentional deficits and concomitant academic deficiencies in learning disabled children through cognitive training. *Journal of Learning Disabilities, 17,* 20–26.

Camp, B. W., Blom, G. E., Hebert, F., & Van Doorninck, W. J. (1977). "Think aloud": A program for developing self-control in young aggressive boys. *Journal of Abnormal Child Psychology, 5,* 157–169.

Carter, J. L. (1979). Art therapy and learning disabled children. *Art Psychotherapy, 6,* 51–56.

Chalfant, J. C., & King, F. S. (1976). An approach to operationalizing the definition of learning disabilities. *Journal of Learning Disabilities, 9,* 228–243.

Chang, S. Q., Williams, R. L., & McLaughlin, T. F. (1983). Differential effects of oral reading to improve comprehension with severe learning disabled and educable mentally handicapped students. *Adolescence, 18,* 619–626.

Charlop, M. H., Schreibman, L., & Thibodeau, M. G. (1985). Increasing spontaneous verbal responding in autistic children using a time delay procedure. *Journal of Applied Behavior Analysis, 18,* 155–166.

Chiang, B., Thorpe, H. W., & Darch, C. B. (1980). Effects of cross-age tutoring on word-recognition performance of learning disabled students. *Learning Disability Quarterly, 3,* 11–19.

Chronbach, L. J., & Snow, R. E. (1977). *Aptitudes and instructional methods.* New York: Irvington.

Clark, F. L., Deshler, D. D., Schumaker, J. B., Alley, G. R., & Warner, M. M. (1984). Visual imagery and self-questioning: Strategies to improve comprehension of written material. *Journal of Learning Disabilities, 17,* 145–149.

Corballis, M. C., & Beale, I. L. (1983). *The ambivalent mind: The neuropsychology of laterality.* Chicago: Nelson-Hall.

Corey, J. R., & Shamow, J. (1972). The effects of fading on the acquisition and retention of oral reading. *Journal of Applied Behavior Analysis, 5,* 311–315.

Craighead, W. E. (1982). A brief clinical history of cognitive-behavior therapy with children. *School Psychology Review, 11,* 5–13.

Craighead, W. E., Meyers, A. W., & Craighead, L. W. (1985). A conceptual model for cognitive-behavior therapy with children. *Journal of Abnormal Child Psychology, 13,* 331–342.

Craighead, W. E., Wilcoxon-Craighead, L. & Meyers, A. W. (1978). New directions in behavior modification with children. In M. Hersen, R. M. Eisler, & P. M. Miller (Eds.), *Progress in behavior modification* (Vol. 6, pp. 159–201). New York: Academic Press.

Cruickshank, W. M. (1967). *The brain-injured child in home, school, and community.* New York: Syracuse University Press.

Delacato, C. H. (1959). *The treatment and prevention of reading problems: The neurological approach.* Springfield, IL: Thomas.

Doman, R. J., Spitz, E. B., Zucman, E., Delacato, C. H., & Doman, G. (1960). Children with severe brain injuries: Neurological organizations in terms of mobility. *Journal of the American Medical Association, 174,* 257–262.

Dorry, G. W. (1976). Attentional model for the effectiveness of fading in training reading-vocabulary with retarded persons. *American Journal of Mental Deficiency, 81,* 271–279.

Dorry, G. W., & Zeaman, D. (1973). The use of a fading technique in paired-associate teaching of a reading vocabulary with retardates. *Mental Retardation, 11,* 3–6.

Dorry, G. W., & Zeaman, D. (1975). Teaching a simple reading vocabulary to retarded children: Effectiveness of fading and nonfading procedures. *American Journal of Mental Deficiency, 79,* 711–716.

Douglas, V. I., Parry, P., Marton, P., & Garson, C. (1976). Assessment of a cognitive training program for hyperactive children. *Journal of Abnormal Child Psychology, 4,* 389–410.

Dudley-Marling, C. C., Snider, V., & Tarver, S. G. (1982). Locus of control and learning disabilities: A review and discussion. *Perceptual and Motor Skills, 54,* 503–514.

Egeland, B. (1974). Training impulsive children in the use of more efficient scanning techniques. *Child Development, 45,* 165–171.

Egeland, B. (1975). Effects of errorless training on teaching children to discriminate letters of the alphabet. *Journal of Applied Psychology, 60,* 533–536.

Egeland, B. & Winer, K. (1974). Teaching children to discriminate letters of the alphabet through errorless discrimination training. *Journal of Reading Behavior, 6,* 143–150.

Eimas, P. D. (1969). Multiple-cue discrimination learning in children. *The Psychological Record, 19,* 417–424.

Englemann, S., Becker, W. C., Hanner, S., & Johnson, G. (1979). *Corrective reading series.* Chicago: Science Research Associates.

Epstein, M. H., Hallahan, D. P., & Kauffman, J. M. (1975). Implications of the impulsivity-reflectivity dimension for special education. *Journal of Special Education, 9,* 11–25.

Etzel, B. C., & LeBlanc, J. M. (1979). The simplest treatment alternative: The law of parsimony applied to choosing appropriate instructional control and errorless-learning procedures for the difficult-to-teach child. *Journal of Autism and Developmental Disorders, 9,* 361–382.

Evans, P. L. C. (1982). Inhibition and individual differences in inhibitory processes in retarded children. In N. R. Ellis (Ed.), *International Review of Research in Mental Retardation* (Vol. 11). New York: Academic Press.

*Federal Register* (1977, Thursday, December 29). Vol. 42, No. 250.

Freeman, T. J., & McLaughlin, T. F. (1984). Effects of a taped-words treatment procedure on learning disabled students' sight-word oral reading. *Learning Disability Quarterly, 7,* 49–54.

Frostig, M., & Horne, D. (1964). *The Frostig program for the development of visual perception.* Chicago: Follett Educational.

Fuller, G. B., & Fuller, D. L. (1982). Reality therapy: Helping LD children make better choices. *Academic Therapy, 17,* 269–277.

Gaddes, W. H. (1981). An examination of the validity of neuropsychological knowledge in educational diagnosis and remediation. In G. W. Hynd & J. E. Obrzut (Eds.), *Neuropsychological assessment and the school-age child: Issues and procedures.* New York: Grune & Stratton.

Gadow, K. D., Torgesen, J. K., & Dahlem, W. E. (1983). Learning disabilities. In M. Hersen, V. B. Van Hasselt, & J. L. Matson (Eds.), *Behavior therapy for the developmentally and physically disabled.* New York: Academic Press.

Gajara, D. P., Cohen, S., & Tarver, S. (1978). Selective attention and locus of control in learning disabled and normal children. *Journal of Learning Disabilities, 11,* 47–52.

Gardner, H. (1975). *The shattered mind.* New York: Knopf.

Getman, G. N., & Kane, E. R. (1964). *The physiology of readiness: An action program for the development of perception for children.* Minneapolis: Programs to Accelerate School Success.

Glenwick, D. S., & Barocas, R. (1979). Training impulsive children in verbal self-control by use of natural change agents. *Journal of Special Education, 13,* 387–398.

Glynn, E. L., & Thomas, J. D. (1974). Effect of cueing on self control of classroom behavior. *Journal of Applied Behavior Analysis, 7,* 299–306.

Glynn, E. L., Thomas, J. D., & Shee, S. K. (1973). Behavioral self-control of on-task behavior in an elementary classroom. *Journal of Applied Behavior Analysis, 6,* 105–118.

Glynn, T. (1982). Antecedent control of behavior in educational contexts. *Educational Psychology, 2,* 215–229.

Gold, M. W., & Barclay, C. R. (1973). The learning of difficult visual discriminations by the moderately and severely retarded. *Mental Retardation, 11,* 9–11.

Graham, S. (1983). The effects of self-instructional procedures on LD students' handwriting performance. *Learning Disability Quarterly, 6,* 231–234.

Graves, M. F., & Cooke, C. L. (1980). Effects of previewing difficult short stories for high school students. *Research on Reading in Secondary Schools, 6,* 38–54.

Graves, M. F., & Palmer, R. J. (1981). Validating previewing as a method of improving fifth and sixth grade students' comprehension of short stories. *Michigan Reading Journal, 15,* 1–3.

Graves, M. F., Cooke, C. L., & LaBerge, M. J. (1983). Effects of previewing difficult short stories on low ability junior high school students' comprehension, recall, and attitudes. *Reading Research Quarterly, 18,* 262–276.

Greiner, J. M., & Karoly, P. (1976). Effects of self-control training on study activity and academic performance: An analysis of self-monitoring, self-reward, and systematic-planning components. *Journal of Counselling Psychology, 4,* 179–197.

Grimes, L. (1981). Learned helplessness and attribution theory: Redefining children's learning problems. *Learning Disability Quarterly, 4,* 91–100.

Grimm, J. A., Bijou, S. W., & Parsons, J. A. (1973). A problem-solving model for teaching remedial arithmetic to handicapped young children. *Journal of Abnormal Child Psychology, 1,* 26–39.

Hallahan, D. P., & Cruickshank, W. M. (1973). *Psychoeducational foundations of learning disabilities.* Englewood Cliffs, NJ: Prentice-Hall.

Hallahan, D. P., & Sapona, R. (1983). Self-monitoring of attention with learning-disabled children: Past research and current issues. *Journal of Learning Disabilities, 16,* 616–620.

Hallahan, D. P., Lloyd, J., Kosiewicz, M. M., Kauffman, J. M., & Graves, A. W. (1979). Self-monitoring of attention as a treatment for a learning disabled boy's off-task behavior. *Learning Disability Quarterly, 2,* 24–32.

Hallahan, D. P., Marshall, K. J., & Lloyd, J. W. (1981). Self-recording during group instruction: Effects on attention to task. *Learning Disability Quarterly, 4,* 407–413.

Hallahan, D. P., Kneedler, R. D., & Lloyd, J. W. (1983). Cognitive behavior modification techniques for learning disabled children: Self-instruction and self-monitoring. In J. D. McKinney & L. Feagans (Eds.), *Current topics in learning disabilities* (Vol. 1). Norwood, NJ: Ablex Publishing.

Halle, J. W., Marshall, A. M., Spradlin, J. E. (1979). Time delay: A technique to increase language use and facilitate generalization in retarded children. *Journal of Applied Behavior Analysis, 12,* 431–439.

Halle, J. W., Baer, D. M., & Spradlin, J. E. (1981). Teacher's generalized use of delay as a stimulus control procedure to increase language use in handicapped children. *Journal of Applied Behavior Analysis, 14,* 389–409.

Hammill, D. D. (1972). Training visual perceptual processes. *Journal of Learning Disabilities, 5,* 552–559.

Hammill, D. D., & Larsen, S. C. (1974). The effectiveness of psycholinguistic training. *Exceptional Children, 41,* 5–15.

Hammill, D. D., Leigh, J. E., McNutt, G., & Larson, S. C. (1981). A new definition of learning disabilities. *Learning Disability Quarterly, 4,* 336–342.

Hansen, C. L., & Eaton, M. D. (1978). Reading. In N. G. Harring, T. C. Lovitt, M. D. Easton, & C. Hansen, (Ed.), *The fourth R: Research in the classroom.* Columbus: Charles E. Merrill.

Hansen, C. L., & Lovitt, T. (1977). An applied behavior analysis approach to reading comprehension. In J. T. Guthrie (Ed.), *Cognition, curriculum and comprehension.* Newark, DE: International Reading Association.

Harris, K. R. (1982). Cognitive-behavior modification: Application with exceptional students. *Focus on Exceptional Children, 15*(2), 1–16.

Harris, K. R., & Graham, S. (in press). Improving learning-disabled students' composition skills: A self-control strategy training approach. *Learning Disability Quarterly.*

Hartlage, L. C., & Telzrow, C. F. (1983). The neuropsychological basis of educational intervention. *Journal of Learning Disabilities, 16,* 521–528.

Heal, L. W., & Johnson, J. T. (1970). Inhibition deficits in retardate learning and attention. In N. R. Ellis (Ed.), *International review of research in mental retardation* (Vol. 4). New York: Academic Press.

Hendrickson, J. M., Roberts, M., & Shores, R. F. (1978). Antecedent and contingent modeling to teach basic sight vocabulary to learning disabled children. *Journal of Learning Disabilities, 11,* 524–528.

Henker, B., Whalen, C. K., & Hinshaw, S. P. (1980). The attributional contexts of cognitive intervention strategies. *Exceptional Education Quarterly, 1,* 17–30.

Horn, W. F., O'Donnell, J. P., & Vitulano, L. A. (1983). Long-term follow-up studies of learning-disabled persons. *Journal of Learning Disabilities, 16,* 542–555.

Huguenin, N. H. (1985). Attention to multiple cues by severely mentally retarded adults: Effects of single-component pretraining. *Applied Research in Mental Retardation, 6,* 319–335.

Ingram, T. T. S., Mason, A. W., & Blackburn, I. (1970). A retrospective study of 82 children with reading disability. *Developmental Medicine and Child Neurology, 12,* 271–281.

Jampolsky, G. G. (1975). Unpublished paper cited by Johnson *et al.,* 1981.

Jeffree, D. (1981). A bridge between pictures and print. *Special Education: Forward Trends, 8,* 28–31.

Jenkins, J. R., & Larson, K. (1979). Evaluating error-correction procedures for oral reading. *Journal of Special Education, 13,* 145–156.

Jenkins, J. R., Barksdale, A., & Clinton, L. (1978). Improving reading comprehension and oral reading: Generalization across behaviors, settings and time. *Journal of Learning Disabilities, 11,* 607–617.

Johnson, L. S., Johnson, D. L., Olson, M. R., & Newman, J. P. (1981). *Journal of Clinical Psychology, 37,* 291–299.

Karnes, M. B. (1968). *Activities for developing psycholinguistic skills with preschool disadvantaged children.* Washington, DC: Council for Exceptional Children.

Kauffman, J. M., & Hallahan, D. P. (1979). Learning disability and hyperactivity (with comments on minimal brain dysfunction). In B. B. Lahey & A. E. Kazdin (Eds.), *Advances in clinical child psychology* (Vol. 2). New York: Plenum Press.

Kavale, K. (1981). Functions of the Illinois Test of Psycholinguistic Abilities (ITPA): Are they trainable? *Exceptional Children, 47,* 496–510.

Kavale, K. A., & Forness, S. R. (1985). Learning disability and the history of science: Paradigm or paradigm? *RASE, 6*(4), 12–23.

Kavale, K., & Mattson, P. D. (1983). "One jumped off the balance beam": Meta-analysis of perceptual-motor training. *Journal of Learning Disabilities, 16,* 165–173.

Kazdin, A. E. (1982). *Single-case research designs.* New York: Oxford University Press.

Keogh, B. K. (1978). Noncognitive aspects of learning disabilities: Another look at perceptual-motor approaches to assessment and remediation. In L. Oettinger, Jr., & E. V. Majovski (Eds.), *The psychologist, the school, and the child with MBD/LD.* New York: Grune & Stratton.

Kephart, N. (1971). *The slow learner in the classroom.* Columbus, OH: Merrill.

Kirk, S. A., & Bateman, B. (1962). Diagnosis and remediation of learning disabilities. *Exceptional Children, 29,* 73–78.

Kirk, S. A., & Kirk, W. D. (1971). *Psycholinguistic learning disabilities.* Chicago: University of Illinois Press.

Kirk, S. A., McCarthy, J. J., & Kirk, W. D. (1968). *Illinois Test of Psycholinguistic Abilities.* Urbana: University of Illinois Press.

Knapczyk, D. R., & Livingstone, G. (1974). The effects of prompting question asking upon on-task behavior and reading comprehension. *Journal of Applied Behavior Analysis, 7,* 115–121.

Knights, R. M., & Bakker, D. J. (Eds.). (1976). *The neuropsychology of learning disorders.* Baltimore: University Park Press.

Koegel, R. L., & Rincover, A. (1976). Some detrimental effects of using extra stimuli to guide learning in normal and autistic children. *Journal of Abnormal Child Psychology, 4,* 59–71.

Koorland, M. A., & Wolkering, W. D. (1982). Effect of reinforcement on modality of stimulus control in learning disabled students. *Learning Disability Quarterly, 5,* 264–273.

Kosiewicz, M. M., Hallahan, D. P., Lloyd, J., & Graves, A. W. (1981). The effects of an LD student's treatment choice on handwriting performance. *Learning Disability Quarterly, 4,* 281–286.

Lahey, B. B. (1976). Behavior modification with learning disabilities and related problems. In M. Hersen, R. M. Eisler, & P. M. Miller (Eds.), *Progress in behavior modification* (Vol. 3). New York: Academic Press.

Lahey, B. B. (1977). Research on the role of reinforcement in reading instruction: Some measurement and methodological deficiencies. *Corrective and social psychiatry and Journal of Behavior Technology Methods, 23,* 27–32.

Lahey, B. B., & Drabman, R. S. (1974). Facilitation of the acquisition and retention of sight-word vocabulary through token reinforcement. *Journal of Applied Behavior Analysis, 7,* 307–312.

Lahey, B. B., McNees, M. P., & Brown, C. C. (1973). Modification of deficits in reading for comprehension. *Journal of Applied Behavior Analysis, 6,* 475–480.

Lancioni, G. E., Ceccarani, P., & Oliva, D. (1981). Avviamento alla lettura tramite insegnamento programmato. *Psicologia e Scuola, 7,* 16–27.

Larsen, S. C., Parker, R. M., & Hammill, D. D. (1982). Effectiveness of psycholinguistic training: A response to Kavale. *Exceptional Children, 49,* 60–66.

Le Blanc, J. M., Etzel, B. C., & Domash, M. A. (1978). A functional curriculum for early intervention. In K. E. Allen, V. A. Holm, & R. L. Schiefelbusch (Eds.), *Early intervention: A team approach.* Baltimore: University Park Press.

Leon, J. A., & Pepe, H. J. (1983). Self-instructional training: Cognitive behavior modification for remediating arithmetic deficits. *Exceptional Children, 50,* 54–60.

Leventhal, M. B. (1980). Dance therapy as treatment of choice for the emotionally disturbed and learning disabled child. *Journal of Physical Education and Recreation, 51,* 33–35.

Limbrick, E., McNaughton, S., & Glynn, T. (1985). Reading gains for underachieving tutors and tutees in a cross-age tutoring programme. *Journal of Child Psychology and Psychiatry, 26,* 939–953.

Lovaas, O. I., Koegel, R. L., & Schreibman, R. L. (1979). Stimulus overselectivity in autism: A review of research. *Psychological Bulletin, 86,* 1236–1254.

Lovitt, T. C., & Curtiss, K. A. (1968). Effects of manipulating an antecedent event on mathematics response rate. *Journal of Applied Behavior Analysis, 1,* 329–333.

Lovitt, T. C., & Hurlburt, M. (1974). Using behavior-analysis techniques to assess the relationship between phonics instruction and oral reading. *Journal of Special Education, 8,* 57–72.

Luiselli, J. K., Steinman, D. L., Marholin, D., & Steinman, W. M. (1981). Evaluation of progressive muscle relaxation with conduct-problems, learning-disabled children. *Child Behavior Therapy, 3,* 41–55.

Luria, A. (1961). *The role of speech in the regulation of normal and abnormal behaviors.* New York: Liveright.

McGee, G. G., & McCoy, J. F. (1981). Training procedures for acquisition and retention of reading in retarded youth. *Applied Research in Mental Retardation, 2,* 263–276.

McLeod, J. (1983). Learning disability is for educators. *Journal of Learning Disabilities, 16,* 23–25.

McNaughton, S., & Delquadri, J. (1978). Error attention tutoring in oral reading. In T. Glynn & S. McNaughton (Eds.), *Behavior analysis in New Zealand.* Auckland, New Zealand: University of Auckland.

McNaughton, S., & Glynn, T. (1981). Delayed versus immediate attention to oral reading errors: Effects on accuracy and self-correction. *Educational Psychology, 1,* 57–65.

Meyer, L. A. (1982). The relative effects of word-analysis and word-supply correction procedures with poor readers during word-attack training. *Reading Research Quarterly, 17,* 544–555.

Meichenbaum, D. (1977). *Cognitive-behavior modification: An integrative approach.* New York: Plenum Press.

Meichenbaum, D., & Asarnow, J. (1979). Cognitive-behavioral modification and metacognitive development: Implications for the classroom. In P. C. Kendall & S. D. Hollon (Eds.), *Cognitive-behavioral interventions: Theory, research, and procedures.* New York: Academic Press.

Meichenbaum, D. M., & Goodman, J. (1969). Reflection-impulsivity and verbal control of motor behavior. *Child Development, 40,* 785–797.

Meichenbaum, D. M., & Goodman, J. (1971). Training impulsive children to talk to themselves: A means of developing self-control. *Journal of Abnormal Psychology, 77,* 115–126.

Meyers, A. W., & Craighead, W. E. (1984). *Cognitive behavior therapy with children.* New York: Plenum Press.

Miller, A., & Miller, E. A. (1968). Symbol accentuation: The perceptual transfer of meaning from spoken to printed words. *American Journal of Mental Deficiency, 73,* 200–208.

Miller, A., & Miller, E. A. (1971). Symbol accentuation, single-track functioning and early reading. *American Journal of Mental Deficiency, 76,* 110–117.

Minskoff, E., Wiseman, D. E., & Minskoff, J. G. (1972). *The MWM program for developing language abilities.* Ridgefield, NJ: Educational Performance Associates.

Mosk, M. D., & Bucher, B. (1984). Prompting and stimulus shaping procedures for teaching visual-motor skills to retarded children. *Journal of Applied Behavior Analysis, 17,* 23–34.

Mutke, P. H. (1967). Increased reading comprehension through hypnosis. *The American Journal of Clinical Hypnosis, 9,* 262–266.

Meyers, A. W. & Craighead, W. E. (1984). Cognitive behavior therapy with children. New York: Plenum Press.

Myers, P. I., & Hammill, D. D. (1976). *Methods for learning disorders* (2nd ed.). New York: Wiley.

Nelson, R. O., & Hayes, S. C. (1979). The nature of behavioral assessment: A commentary. *Journal of Applied Behavior Analysis, 12,* 491–500.

Oldridge, O. A. (1982). Positive suggestion: It helps LD students learn. *Academic Therapy, 17,* 279–287.

Omizo, M. M., & Williams, R. E. (1982). Biofeedback-induced relaxation training as an alternative for the elementary school learning disabled child. *Biofeedback and self-regulation, 7,* 139–148.

Orton, S. T. (1937). *Reading, writing, and speech problems in children.* New York: Norton.

O'Shea, L. J., Munson, S. M., & O'Shea, D. J. (1984). Error correction in oral reading: Evaluating the effectiveness of three procedures. *Education and Treatment of Children, 7,* 203–214.

Radencich, M. C. (1984). The status of learning disabilities: The emergence of a paradigm or a paradigm shift? *Learning Disabilities, 3,* 79–89.

Rincover, A. (1978). Variables affecting stimulus fading and discriminative responding in psychotic children. *Journal of Abnormal Psychology, 87,* 541–553.

Roberts, M., & Smith, D. D. (1980). The relationship among correct and error oral reading rates and comprehension. *Learning Disability Quarterly, 3,* 54–64.

Robin, A. L., Armel, S., & O'Leary, K. D. (1975). The effects of self-instruction on writing deficiencies. *Behavior Therapy, 6,* 178–197.

Robinson, F. P. (1941). *Diagnostic and remedial technique for effective study.* New York: Harper & Brothers.

Rooney, K., Polloway, E. A., & Hallahan, D. P. (1985). The use of self-monitoring procedures with low IQ learning disabled children. *Journal of Learning Disabilities, 18,* 384–389.

Rose, T. L., & Sherry, L. (1984). Relative effects of two previewing procedures on LD adolescents' oral reading performance. *Learning Disability Quarterly, 7,* 39–44.

Rose, T. L., Koorland, M. A., & Epstein, M. H. (1982a). A review of applied behavior analysis interventions with learning disabled children. *Education and Treatment of Children, 5,* 41–58.

Rose, T. L., McEntire, E., & Dowdy, C. (1982b). Effects of two error-correction procedures on oral reading. *Learning Disability Quarterly, 5,* 100–105.

Ross, A. O. (1976). *Psychological aspects of learning disabilities and reading disorders.* New York: McGraw-Hill.

Ross, A. O. (1981). *Child behavior therapy.* New York: Wiley.

Rourke, B. P. (1975). Brain behavior relationships in children with learning disabilities: A research program. *American Psychologist, 30,* 911–920.

Russell, H. L., & Carter, J. L. (1978). Biofeedback training with children. *Journal of Clinical Child Psychology, 7,* 23–25.

Sabatino, D. A., & Hayden, D. L. (1970). Prescriptive teaching in a summer learning disabilities program. *Journal of Learning Disabilities, 3,* 220–227.

Sabatino, D. A., Ysseldyke, J. E., & Woolston, J. (1973). Diagnostic-prescriptive perceptual training with mentally retarded children. *American Journal of Mental Deficiency, 78,* 7–14.

Sachs, A. (1983). The effects of three prereading activities on learning disabled student's reading comprehension. *Learning Disability Quarterly, 6,* 248–251.

Sachs, A. (1984). The effects of previewing activities on oral reading miscues. *RASE, 5*(3), 45–49.

Samuels, S. J. (1967). Attentional processes in reading: The effects of pictures on the acquisition of reading responses. *Journal of Educational Psychology, 58,* 337–342.

Samuels, S. J. (1970). Effects of pictures on learning to read, comprehension, and attitudes. *Review of Education Research, 40,* 397–407.

Satz, P., & Fletcher, J. M. (1981). Emergent trends in neuropsychology: An overview. *Journal of Consulting and Clinical Psychology, 49,* 851–865.

Satz, P., & Friel, J. (1973). Some predictive antecedents of specific learning disability: A preliminary one-year followup. In P. Satz & J. J. Ross (Eds.), *The disabled learner.* Rotterdam: Rotterdam University Press.

Saunders, R. J., & Solman, R. T. (1984). The effect of pictures on the acquisition of a small vocabulary of similar sight-words. *British Journal of Educational Psychology, 54,* 265–275.

Schere, R. A., Richardson, E., & Bailer, I. (1980). Toward operationalizing a psychoeducational definition of learning disabilities. *Journal of Abnormal Child Psychology, 8,* 5–20.

Schreibman, L. (1975). Effects of within-stimulus and extra-stimulus prompting on discrimination learning in autistic children. *Journal of Applied Behavior Analysis, 8,* 91–112.

Schreibman, L., Charlop, M. H., & Koegel, R. L. (1982). Teaching autistic children to use extra-stimulus prompts. *Journal of Experimental Child Psychology, 33,* 475–491.

Schumaker, J. B., Deshler, D. D., Alley, G. R., Warner, M. M., & Denton, P. H. (1982). Multipass: A learning strategy for improving reading comprehension. *Learning Disability Quarterly, 5,* 295–239.

Scott, J. M., & Ballard, K. D. (1983). Training parents and teachers in remedial reading procedures for children with learning difficulties. *Educational Psychology, 3,* 15–30.

Sidman, M., & Stoddard, L. T. (1966). Programming perception and learning for retarded children. In N. R. Ellis (Ed.), *International review of research in mental retardation.* New York: Academic Press.

Singh, J., & Singh, N. N. (1985). Comparison of word-supply and word-analysis error-correction procedures on oral reading by mentally retarded children. *American Journal of Mental Deficiency, 90,* 64–70.

Singh, N. N. (1985). Overcorrection of academic behavior. In C. Sharpley, A. Hudson, & C. Lee (Eds.), *Proceedings of the eighth annual conference of the Australian Behavior Modification Association.* Melbourne: ABMA.

Singh, N. N. (1987). Overcorrection of oral reading errors: A comparison of individual and group training formats. *Behavior Modification, 11,* 165–181.

Singh, N. N., & Beale, I. L. (1988). Learning disability. In M. Hersen & C. G. Last (Eds.), *Child behavior therapy casebook*. New York: Plenum Press.

Singh, N. N., & Singh, J. (1984). Antecedent control of oral reading errors and self-corrections by mentally retarded children. *Journal of Applied Behavior Analysis, 17*, 111–119.

Singh, N. N., & Singh, J. (1986a). A behavioural remediation program for oral reading: Effects on errors and comprehension. *Educational Psychology, 6*, 105–114.

Singh, N. N., & Singh, J. (1986b). Increasing oral reading proficiency: A comparative analysis of drill and positive practice overcorrection procedures. *Behavior Modification, 10*, 115–130.

Singh, N. N., & Singh, J. (1986c). Reading acquisition and remediation in the mentally retarded. In N. R. Ellis & N. W. Bray (Eds.), *International review of research in mental retardation* (Vol. 14). New York: Academic Press.

Singh, N. N., Singh, J., & Winton, A. S. W. (1984). Positive practice overcorrection of oral reading errors. *Behavior Modification, 8*, 23–37.

Singh, N. N., Winton, A. S. W., & Singh, J. (1985). Effects of delayed versus immediate attention to oral reading errors on the reading proficiency of mentally retarded children. *Applied Research in Mental Retardation, 6*, 283–293.

Skinner, B. F. (1950). Are theories of learning necessary? *Psychological Review, 57*, 193–216.

Smeets, P. M., & Striefel, S. (1976a). Acquisition and cross modal generalization of receptive and expressive signing skills in a retarded deaf girl. *Journal of Mental Deficiency Research, 20*, 251–260.

Smeets, P. M., & Striefel, S. (1976b). Acquisition of sign reading by transfer of stimulus control in a retarded deaf girl. *Journal of Mental Deficiency Research, 20*, 197–205.

Smeets, P. M., Lancioni, G. E., & Hoogeveen, F. R. (1984). Effects of different stimulus manipulations on the acquisition of word recognition in trainable mentally retarded children. *Journal of Mental Deficiency Research, 28*, 109–122.

Smith, D. D. (1979). The improvement of children's oral reading through the use of teacher modeling. *Journal of Learning Disabilities, 12*, 172–175.

Sowell, V., Parker, R., Poplin, M., & Larsen, S. (1979). The effects of psycholinguistic training on improving psycholinguistic skills. *Learning Disability Quarterly, 2*, 69–77.

Spillios, J. C., & Janzen, H. L. (1983). Anxiety and learning disabilities. *School Psychology International, 4*, 141–152.

Stoddard, L. T., & Gerovac, B. J. (1981). A stimulus shaping method for teaching complex motor performance to severely and profoundly retarded individuals. *Applied Research in Mental Retardation, 2*, 281–295.

Stokes, T. F., & Baer, D. M. (1977). An implicit technology of generalization. *Journal of Applied Behavior Analysis, 10*, 349–367.

Strauss, A. A., & Kephart, W. C. (1955). *Psychopathology and education of the brain-injured child: Vol. 2. Progress in theory and clinic*. New York: Grune & Stratton.

Striefel, S., Bryan, K. S., & Aikins, D. A. (1974). Transfer of stimulus control from motor to verbal stimuli. *Journal of Applied Behavior Analysis, 7*, 123–135.

Striefel, S., Wetherby, B., & Karlan, G. R. (1976). Establishing generalized verb-noun instruction-following skills in retarded children. *Journal of Experimental Child Psychology, 22*, 247–260.

Swanson, L. (1981). Modification of comprehension deficits in learning disabled children. *Learning Disability Quarterly, 4*, 189–202.

Tarver, S. G., & Dawson, M. M., (1978). Modality preference and the teaching of reading: A review. *Journal of Learning Disabilities, 11*, 17–29.

Terrace, H. S. (1963). Discrimination learning with and without "errors." *Journal of the Experimental Analysis of Behavior, 6*, 1–27.

Terrace, H. S. (1966). Stimulus control. In W. K. Honig (Ed.), *Operant behavior: Areas of research and application*. New York: Appleton-Century-Crofts.

Thorpe, H. W., Chiang, B., & Darch, C. B. (1981). Individual and group feedback systems for improving oral reading accuracy in learning disabled and regular class children. *Journal of Learning Disabilities, 14*, 332–334, 367.

Torgesen, J. K. (1979). What shall we do with psychological processes? *Journal of Learning Disabilities, 12*, 16–23.

Touchette, P. E. (1968). The effects of graduated stimulus change on the acquisition of a simple discrimination in severely retarded boys. *Journal of the Experimental Analysis of Behavior, 11*, 39–48.

Touchette, P. E. (1971). Transfer of stimulus control: Measuring the moment of transfer. *Journal of the Experimental Analysis of Behavior, 15*, 347–354.

Treiber, F. A., & Lahey, B. B. (1983). Toward a behavioral model of academic remediation with learning disabled children. *Journal of Learning Disabilities, 16,* 111–115.

Varni, J. W., & Henker, B. K. (1979). A self-regulation approach to the treatment of three hyperactive boys. *Child Behavior Therapy, 1,* 171–192.

Vygotsky, L. (1962). *Thought and language.* New York: Wiley.

Walls, R. T., Haught, P., & Dowler, D. L. (1982). Moments of transfer of stimulus control in practical assembly tasks by mentally retarded adults. *American Journal of Mental Deficiency, 87,* 309–315.

Walsh, B. F., & Lamberts, F. (1979). Errorless discrimination and picture fading as techniques for teaching sight words to TMR students. *American Journal of Mental Deficiency, 83,* 473–479.

Wender, P. (1971). *Minimal brain dysfunction in children.* New York: Wiley.

Wepman, J. (1967). The perceptual basis for learning. In E. C. Frierson & W. B. Barbe (Eds.), *Educating children with learning disabilities.* New York: Appleton-Century-Crofts.

Werner, H. (1948). *Comparative psychology of mental development.* New York: International Universities Press.

Whalen, C. K., & Henker, B. K. (1980). *Hyperactive children: The social ecology of identification and treatment.* New York: Academic Press.

Whalen, C. K., Henker, B., & Hinshaw, S. P. (1985). Cognitive-behavioral therapies for hyperactive children: Premises, problems, and prospects. *Journal of Abnormal Child Psychology, 13,* 391–410.

Wiederholt, J. L. (1974). Historical perspectives on the education of the learning disabled. In L. Mann & D. Sabatino (Eds.), *The second review of special education.* Philidelphia: JSE Press.

Wilhelm, H. & Lovaas, O. I. (1976). Stimulus overselectivity: A common feature in autism and mental retardation. *American Journal of Mental Deficiency, 81,* 26–31.

Witelson, S. F. (1976). Abnormal right hemisphere specialization in developmental dyslexia. In R. M. Knights & D. J. Bakker (Eds.), *The neuropsychology of learning disorders.* Baltimore: University Park Press.

Wolfe, V. F., & Cuvo, A. J. (1978). Effects of within-stimulus and extra-stimulus prompting on letter discrimination by mentally retarded persons. *American Journal of Mental Deficiency, 83,* 297–303.

Wong, B. Y. L. (1979). Increasing retention of main ideas through questioning strategies. *Learning Disability Quarterly, 2,* 42–48.

Wong, B. Y. L. (1980). Activating the inactive learner: Use of questions/prompts to enhance comprehension and retention of implied information in learning disabled children. *Learning Disability Quarterly, 3,* 29–37.

Wong, B. Y. L., & Jones, W. (1982). Increasing metacomprehension in learning-disabled and normally-achieving students through self-questioning training. *Learning Disability Quarterly, 5,* 228–240.

Wong, P., & McNaughton, S. (1980). The effects of prior provision of context on the oral reading proficiency of a low progress reader. *New Zealand Journal of Educational Studies, 15,* 169–175.

Zeaman, D., & House, B. J. (1963). The role of attention in retardate discrimination learning. In N. R. Ellis (Ed.), *Handbook of mental deficiency.* New York: McGraw-Hill.

# 22 Sensory and Physical Handicaps
## Psychological Therapies

Vincent B. Van Hasselt, Robert T. Ammerman, and
Lori A. Sisson

## Introduction

Sensory-impaired children and youth have been the focus of increased clinical and investigative endeavors over the past several years. This heightened interest is largely attributable to a burgeoning body of research documenting social and emotional adjustment problems in a disproportionately high number of visually impaired and hearing-impaired children (cf. Ammerman, Van Hasselt, & Hersen, 1986; Helsel, 1988; Matson & Helsel, 1986; Van Hasselt, 1983a, 1987). These difficulties are not surprising given the critical roles that vision and audition play in our everyday functioning. For example, as Warren (1981) pointed out, the effects of a visual disorder "may extend far beyond the visual system itself to affect every area of development, both perceptual and nonperceptual" (p. 195). The deleterious effects of blindness and severe visual problems on perceptual, conceptual, and social development have been discussed at length (see reviews by Warren, 1981, 1984). Audition is involved in the location of sound sources within the environment and is important in orientation and information processing (Morax, Bates, & Barrett, 1965). The negative implications of a hearing impairment for cognitive and social functioning as well as overall life adjustment have been the focus of considerable study (see Hoemann & Briga, 1981; Stein, Mindel, & Jabaley, 1981).

An examination of the extant literature concerning the psychological and psychiatric aspects of sensory impairment reveals a variety of social, behavioral, and vocational handicaps associated with these disorders. Such problems are compounded in individuals with dual sensory impairments, like the deaf-blind. Indeed, Schein (1975) and others contend that a second disability results in *multiplicative* rather than additive effects on performance and functioning across

VINCENT B. VAN HASSELT • Department of Psychiatry and Human Behavior, University of California—Irvine, Medical Center, Orange, California 92668.    ROBERT T. AMMERMAN • Western Pennsylvania School for Blind Children, Pittsburgh, Pennsylvania 15213.    LORI A. SISSON • Department of Psychiatry, University of Pittsburgh School of Medicine, Pittsburgh, Pennsylvania 15213.

a number of areas. This is clearly illustrated by deaf-blind individuals who also are mentally retarded and display chronic and pervasive behavioral disturbances (e.g., self-injury, aggression, and self-stimulation) that often are highly resistant to even the most intensive remedial strategies. With continuing advancements in medical technology, the reduction of infant mortality through improved medical and surgical care, and further investigation of the etiology and treatment of infant diseases, the number of dually and multiply diagnosed disabled children is expected to rise substantially (Mulliken & Buckley, 1983; Sisson, Van Hasselt, & Hersen, 1987b).

The purpose of this chapter is to review the psychological treatment approaches that have been used with children who have sensory impairments. Specifically, we will examine the use of interventions with children who are (1) visually impaired; (2) hearing-impaired; and (3) visually impaired and hearing-impaired (i.e., the deaf-blind). Included is an examination of both clinical and experimental efforts with each group across a number of categories. This chapter also discusses several case studies in each of the respective sections. Though lacking experimental rigor, they constitute a large portion of the publications in this area. Their exclusion would represent an incomplete presentation of the field. Further, some of these reports represent pioneering efforts in the use of psychological interventions with the sensory-impaired. Finally, conclusions and suggestions are offered for directions that future research might take.

## VISUAL IMPAIRMENT

Applications of psychological assessment and treatment strategies to the problems of the blind and the visually impaired have proliferated in recent years (see Biglan, Van Hasselt, & Simon, 1988; Matson & Helsel, 1986; Van Hasselt, 1987). Part of the reason for the heightened activity with this population is the fact that nearly 11.5 million persons in the United States have some form of visual impairment (National Society to Prevent Blindness, 1980). Approximately 500,000 of these individuals are legally blind (i.e., their degree of corrected vision in the better eye is 20/200 or worse, or there is a severe restriction in the visual field). Further, it is estimated that almost 37,000 children in this country carry this diagnosis.

Another reason for the increased attention to the visually impaired is the convergence of evidence attesting to social and emotional maladjustment in many of these children and youth (see Ammerman *et al.*, 1986; Van Hasselt 1983b). For example, data have been accrued that show maladaptive response patterns and problems in social adaptation in a subgroup of this population (Jan, Freeman, & Scott, 1977; Petrucci, 1953; Van Hasselt, Kazdin, & Hersen, 1986b).

In addition to mental health issues, professionals working with visually impaired children have expressed concern about their deficiencies in the skills requisite for independent functioning (e.g., mobility, emergency safety responses, self-dressing, and self-feeding). In this section, we review the psychological interventions used to ameliorate some of these difficulties in blind and visually impaired children. Endeavors in each of the following categories are presented: (1) social skills; (2) maladaptive behavior; (3) adaptive living skills; and (4) family interactions.

Initial research on the social functioning of visually impaired children was conducted nearly a half century ago (Bradway, 1937; McKay, 1936; Maxfield & Fjeld, 1942). These investigations used global assessment measures such as the Vineland Social Maturity Scale or some variant. The results of these studies consistently revealed deficits or lags in social maturity in samples of blind or visually impaired children. For example, Maxfield and Fjeld (1942) administered a form of the Vineland Scale for blind children ranging in age from 9 months to 7 years. The Social Quotient for blind children was 83.5 in comparison to the norm of 100 for sighted children. Also, blind children appeared to be more introverted and docile, and to have less initiative than partially sighted children. More recently, Van Hasselt, Kazdin, Hersen, Simon, and Mastantuono (1985) conducted finer-grained analyses of social skills in visually impaired children. These investigators developed a role-play test to assess levels of interpersonal effectiveness. They found that this instrument discriminated between samples of blind and sighted children on a number of verbal and nonverbal skill components (e.g., posture, direction of gaze, and hostile tone), with the former group exhibiting numerous skill deficits.

As a result of assessment research showing social skills deficiencies in blind and visually impaired children, several social skills training programs have been implemented. One effort in this area was reported by Petersen *et al.* (1979), who used verbal praise and teacher prompts to increase rates of social behaviors such as toy sharing and touching in three severely and profoundly retarded blind adolescents. Greater peer-directed social behavior was noted as a function of the training. An innovative procedure described by Farkas, Sherick, Matson, and Loebig (1981) involved the administration of braille-coded tokens (exchangeable for backup reinforcers) for reduced rates of stereotypical responses (tapping, rocking, and hand flapping) and poor motoric orientation in a 12½-year-old blind girl. The results of a multiple-baseline analysis demonstrated the efficacy of this program in modifying her maladaptive behaviors and enhancing her social functioning.

Van Hasselt and his colleagues have carried out a series of social skills training investigations with visually impaired and multihandicapped children (Ammerman, Van Hasselt, & Hersen, 1985; Sisson, Van Hasselt, Hersen, & Strain, 1985; Van Hasselt, Hersen, Kazdin, Simon, & Mastantuono, 1983; Van Hasselt, Simon, & Mastantuono, 1982). In one study, Van Hasselt *et al.* (1983) used a social skills training package (direct instructions, behavior rehearsal, modeling, performance feedback, and manual guidance) to improve behavioral components of assertion (e.g., direction of gaze, voice tone, posture, and requests for new behavior change) in four visually handicapped adolescents (14–20 years old). Role plays of interpersonal situations requiring assertive responses were used as the primary vehicle for assessment and training. Each subject received 3–4 weeks of assertion training consisting of five 15- to 30-minute sessions per week. A multiple-baseline analysis across behaviors demonstrated the controlling effects of treatment in all cases, and gains were still evident at a 10-week follow-up.

Sisson *et al.* (1985) adapted the peer-mediated intervention approach developed by Strain and his associates (e.g., Ragland, Kerr, & Strain, 1978, 1981;

Strain, Kerr, & Ragland, 1978) for use with blind multihandicapped children. These investigators trained two nonhandicapped peers to direct social initiations to two male and two female multihandicapped children (age 9 years 3 months to 11 years 7 months) during free play. All of the handicapped children were mentally retarded as well as legally blind. The results of a multiple-baseline analysis of the two female subjects are shown in Figure 1. These data indicate increased rates of social behaviors in multihandicapped children as a function of play facilitation by nonhandicapped peer trainers. Generalization probes conducted during situations in which no treatment occurred showed a moderate transfer of treatment effects. As the figure indicates, the durability of the intervention was apparent at a 4-month follow-up.

More recently, Sisson, Babeo, and Van Hasselt (in press) modified the procedure employed by Sisson *et al.* (1985) for use in a group training format. Five multihandicapped boys (9–12½ years old) were trained to initiate social interactions, to respond to initiations by others, and to maintain social interactions during social skills "lessons" that were incorporated into the ongoing classroom curriculum. Direct observations in free-play settings revealed higher rates of social responses, and lower rates of isolative behaviors with training. In a social validation of the treatment effects, the levels of social behavior displayed by the

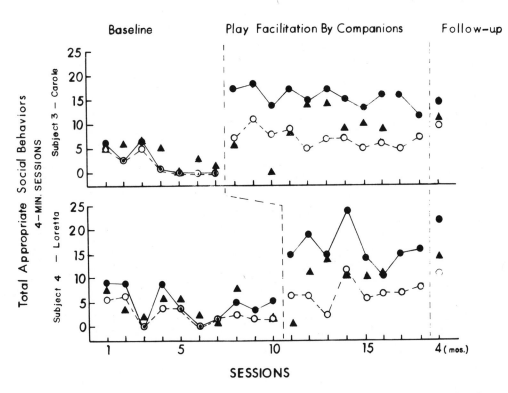

FIGURE 1. Frequency of appropriate social behaviors and social initiations emitted by two female subjects. (Figure 3, p. 313, from L. A. Sisson, V. B. Van Hasselt, M. Hersen, & P. S. Strain (1985). Peer Interventions: Increasing Social Behaviors in Multihandicapped Children. *Behavior Modification, 9,* 293–321. Copyright 1985 by Sage. Reproduced by permission.)

handicapped subjects were found to closely approximate those of nonhandicapped peers in similar situations.

## Stereotypic, Self-Injurious, and Disruptive Behavior

Heightened clinical and investigative activity has been directed toward the
elimination or reduction of various forms of aberrant behaviors in visually handicapped children (see reviews by Van Hasselt, 1983b, 1987). Historically, the
term blindism has been used in the vision literature to refer to the high frequency
of stereotypical acts (e.g., rocking, head weaving, and hand flapping) exhibited
by many blind or visually impaired children (Carroll, 1961; Smith, Chethik, &
Adelson, 1969). The negative impact of such responses was articulated by Hoshmand (1975), who stated, "Once established in the blind child's repertoire, they
would continue to interfere with most, if not all, functional interactions with the
environment and effective learning. The consequences can be very serious without appropriate and timely intervention" (p. 57).

Of even greater concern are the self-injurious behavior (SIB) and aggressive
behavior more commonly displayed by many blind multihandicapped individuals. Table 1 presents studies that have attempted to remediate these difficulties as well as other serious behavior problems. These efforts have generally
involved the application of various behavior therapy techniques.

A large number of the subjects in these investigations had a disability in
addition to the visual impairment (e.g., mental retardation). Further, suppression of self-injury was the primary goal of most (70%) of these reports. Also, as
the table illustrates, a wide variety of behavioral interventions were used. Overcorrection, either alone or in combination with other treatment techniques (usually positive reinforcement), has frequently been used to suppress stereotypic
acts (Caetano & Kauffman, 1975), self-injurious behavior (Conley & Wolery,
1980; Kelly & Drabman, 1977; Luiselli & Michaud, 1983; Measel & Alfieri, 1976;
Wesolowski & Zawlocki, 1982), and self-induced vomiting (Rotatori, Kapperman, & Schryven, 1979). A number of aversive control strategies also have been
used, including the presentation of electric shock (Lovaas & Simmons, 1969;
Tate & Baroff, 1966), sounds of screeching chalk (Blasch, 1978), the placement of
an ice cube in the child's mouth (Drabman, Ross, Lynd, & Cordua, 1978), and
aversive tickling (Greene & Hoats, 1971).

Generally, behavioral interventions have been successful in eliminating or
suppressing the disparate maladaptive response classes that have been targeted.
Unfortunately, an evaluation of the maintenance and generalization of the treatment gains has been lacking or sporadic. Follow-up intervals have ranged from
no follow-up at all to 12 months. Only 20% of the studies had a follow-up
interval of 6 months or more. Also, except for the work of Drabman and his
colleagues (Drabman et al., 1978; Kelly & Drabman, 1977), there has been a lack
of attention to the generalization of gains beyond the treatment setting.

## Adaptive Living Skills

The acquisition of adaptive and independent living skills is requisite to the
adequate functioning of handicapped individuals. Persons who are blind or
visually impaired are unable to learn such skills via the observational processes

TABLE 1. Behavioral Treatment of Stereotypic, Self-Injurious, and Disruptive Behaviors in Visually Handicapped and Multihandicapped Persons

| Reference | Subject(s) | Target behavior(s) | Treatment(s) | Outcome | Follow-up(s) |
|---|---|---|---|---|---|
| Belcher *et al.* (1982) | 19-yr.-old severely retarded, visually handicapped male | Violent and disruptive tantrums | Behavioral interruption (verbal prompt and 360° guided turn) | Decrease in frequency and duration of target behavior to near zero levels; increased sociability | 9 months |
| Blasch (1978) | 4 female and 2 male visually handicapped adolescents (16–20 yrs.) | Rocking, head rolling, eye poking | Punishment (recording of screeching chalk) and positive reinforcement | Decrease in rate of stereotypical acts and SIB; some reduction in untreated responses and generalization to nontreatment setting | 10 days |
| Caetano and Kauffman (1975) | 2 visually handicapped females (9 and 10 yrs.) | Rocking | Elements of overcorrection (feedback and reminders) and positive reinforcement | Reduction of rocking with some generalization to nontreatment setting | Intervals not reported |
| Conley and Wolery (1980) | 7-yr.-old mentally retarded, blind female and 5-yr.-old mentally retarded, blind male | Eye gouging | Overcorrection and positive reinforcement | Rapid deceleration in SIB in both subjects | 3 weeks for female and 7 weeks for male; treatment resumed for male after 9-month follow-up |
| Drabman *et al.* (1978) | 2½-yr.-old profoundly retarded, blind male | Sucking and chewing on fingers | Punishment (icing procedure) and hands down (carried out by mentally retarded peers) | Decrease in targeted responses in treatment sessions; generalization across time with specific programming | None reported |
| Greene and Hoats (1971) | Two, 13-yr.-old mentally retarded, blind adolescent females | Head banging, aggressive behavior | Punishment (aversive tickling) | General reduction in target behaviors although considerable variability in re- | None reported |

| Study | Subject | Target behavior | Treatment | Response rate during treatment | Follow-up |
|---|---|---|---|---|---|
| Greene et al. (1970) | 15-yr.-old mentally retarded, blind male | Rocking, hand shaking | Punishment (music distortion) | Rapid deceleration of rate of target behaviors | None reported |
| Kelly and Drabman (1977) | 3-yr.-old visually handicapped male | Eye poking | Overcorrection and positive reinforcement (verbal praise) | Reduced rate of SIB in treatment and generalization settings | None reported |
| Lovaas and Simmons (1969) | 8-yr.-old mentally retarded, visually handicapped female | Self-hitting and scratching of face and body | Punishment (electric shock) | Immediate suppression of SIB, although effects specific to trainer and setting | None reported |
| Luiselli and Greenridge (1982) | 12-yr.-old mentally retarded, visually handicapped female | Slapping and punching others | Three time-out procedures and positive reinforcement | Rapid elimination of target behavior with isolation time-out | 7 months |
| Luiselli and Michaud (1983) | 19- and 11-yr.-old mentally retarded, visually handicapped females | Self-biting of arm, face and head hitting, aggression toward others | Overcorrection and positive reinforcement | Decrease in SIB for both subjects | 4 months for first subject and 1 month for second child |
| Martin and Iagulli (1974) | 4-yr.-old mentally retarded, visually handicapped female | Middle-of-the-night tantrums | Extinction, keeping child awake until midnight | Elimination of tantrums | 3 and 6 months |
| Measel and Alfieri (1976) | 14- and 16-yr.-old mentally retarded, visually handicapped males | Head slapping and banging | Overcorrection and positive reinforcement | SIB eliminated when overcorrection and reinforcement applied to first subject; reinforcement alone and in combination with overcorrection led to increased SIB in second subject | 4 months for first subject only |
| Miller and Miller (1976) | 13-yr.-old visually handicapped female | Head wagging | Positive reinforcement, modeling, self-monitoring, and peer feedback | Reduction in head wagging with multiple treatments | 4 and 11 months |

(continued)

Table 1 (*Continued*)

| Reference | Subject(s) | Target behavior(s) | Treatment(s) | Outcome | Follow-up(s) |
|---|---|---|---|---|---|
| Myers and Deibert (1971) | 11-yr.-old mentally retarded, visually handicapped male | Head hitting | Positive reinforcement, time-out, and shaping of incompatible feeding response | Decrease in frequency of SIB | 9 months |
| Rapoff *et al.* (1980a) | 7-yr.-old mentally retarded, visually handicapped male | Head hitting | Response-contingent brief restraint | Elimination of SIB; increased compliance in classroom | 2 months |
| Rotatori *et al.* (1979) | 33-yr.-old mentally retarded, visually handicapped male | Self-induced vomiting | Overcorrection, physical guidance, and positive reinforcement | Significant decrease in frequency of SIB | 5 weeks |
| Simpson *et al.* (1982) | 7-yr.-old visually handicapped male | Eye gouging and head weaving | Time-out and positive reinforcement | Reduction in both target behaviors to near-zero levels; improved social and academic performance | None reported |
| Tate and Baroff (1966) | 9-yr.-old visually handicapped, psychotic male | Head banging and face slapping | Time-out from physical contact and punishment (electric shock) | Both treatments effective in reducing SIB and stereotypic acts | 6 months |
| Wesolowski and Zawlocki (1982) | 6-yr.-old mentally retarded, visually handicapped twin females | Eye gouging | Time out from auditory stimuli; response interruption; auditory time-out plus DRO; overcorrection plus DRO | Substantial decrease in SIB for both subjects with multiple treatments; overcorrection plus DRO effective in reducing SIB 1 year after initial treatment | 2 and 12 months |

generally used by the sighted. A vital area for the visually impaired, given its role in environmental adaptation and integration into the community, is mobility. Although most schools and rehabilitation centers serving the visually impaired offer some form of orientation and mobility instruction (Welsh & Blasch, 1980), little information is available regarding the actual training methods. Experimental analyses of the efficacy of these strategies are scarce. Of the published work that is available, most investigations include visually impaired adults who have additional handicapping conditions (Burleson, 1973; Kennedy, 1982; McGlinchey & Mitala, 1975). One of the few reports on mobility instruction with a child was provided by Gallagher and Heim (1974), who used a multiple-component intervention to increase mobility skills in a 15-year-old blind male. The training (social reinforcement, instructions, performance feedback, and manual guidance) was carried out on a 104-yard path resembling a question mark. The results of the BAB design indicated a mean travel time of 10 minutes 5 seconds in the initial treatment phase. Withdrawal of the intervention led to an increase in travel time to 17 minutes 12 seconds. The reintroduction of training significantly reduced the time required to cover the course ($\bar{X}$ = 6 minutes 3 seconds).

Another area of import for visually impaired children is their ability to respond to emergency situations. Although the value of training in emergency safety skills (e.g., accident prevention, and fire evacuation) has been documented with both developmentally disabled and nondisabled children (e.g., Haney & Jones, 1982; Jones & Kazdin, 1980; Matson, 1980), preliminary activities with the visually impaired have only recently been conducted. Yet, their inability to use visual cues, along with their decreased mobility, puts this population particularly at risk in emergency situations.

In response to the need for intervention in this area, Jones, Van Hasselt, and Sisson (1984b) developed a fire-emergency evacuation-program to teach emergency safety skills to four visually handicapped children aged 17–19. The training consisted of social and external reinforcement, performance feedback, behavior rehearsal, and instruction in self-control strategies (self-evaluation and self-reinforcement). The subjects were trained to respond correctly to a series of simulated fire-emergency situations. The results of a multiple-baseline design across subjects revealed improved emergency fire-safety responses in three of the four subjects. However, the generalization of the behaviors to actual nighttime fire drills was minimal. Consequently, Jones, Sisson, and Van Hasselt (1984a) devised a group-training approach in which three of the subjects from the initial study were taught to provide cues and instructions concerning appropriate fire-safety responses to their roommates. This strategy led to a generalization of emergency skills to nighttime fire drills for six of the eight participants.

## Family Adjustment

Several clinical case studies have described disturbed interactions and adjustment problems in the families of visually impaired children. For example, numerous mental-health professionals have discussed the initial reaction of parents to the diagnosis of blindness in their child. The responses typically include shock, grief, and disappointment (Catena, 1961; Froyd, 1973). A visually handicapped child may also place increased social, physical, and economic demands on the family. The complexity of teaching basic self-care skills (e.g., toileting, feeding, and dressing) alone is considerable. Froyd (1973) contended that the physical, cognitive, and emotional needs of the blind child may be so great that the parents eventually become overwhelmed. Further, many parents of visually impaired children have been characterized as insular, socially withdrawn, overly cohesive, and psychiatrically vulnerable (Lambert & West, 1980; Sarason, 1959; Schaffer, 1964; Solnit & Stark, 1961).

Also, there is increasing evidence of problem parent–child interactions occurring as early as in the blind child's infancy (see Van Hasselt, 1987; Williams, 1968). Lairy and Covello (1973) stated that, at this point, it is particularly important for parents to stimulate the child. However, early findings attest to the neglect and rejection of some blind infants on their parents' realization of their impairment (Barry & Marshall, 1953; Blank, 1959). Typically, the parents' sustained anxiety, depleted energy level, and feelings of guilt have been implicated in such responses. Irrespective of the cause, there are likely to be deleterious short- and long-term effects of negative parental responses to the blind or visually impaired child. Most notably, formation of the attachment bond (i.e., the relationship that infants develop in the first year of life with the primary caregiver) is disrupted. In light of experimental findings showing an association between quality of attachment and later problem-solving ability and competence with peers (e.g., Matas, Arend, & Sroufe, 1978) the prognosis for the later socialization of many blind children is poor (Van Hasselt, 1983a).

As part of an ongoing program of research on blind and multihandicapped children and their families, Van Hasselt and his associates (Klein, Van Hasselt, Trefelner, Sandstrom, & Snyder, 1988; Van Hasselt, Ammerman, Moore, & Hersen, 1987; Van Hasselt, Hersen, Moore, & Simon, 1986a) have developed family assessment and treatment programs specifically geared to the unique problems and issues in families with these children. One of these endeavors is the Parent and Toddler Training (PATT) project (Klein *et al.*, 1988). PATT is an early intervention program designed to (1) enhance the social responsivity of visually impaired and multihandicapped infants; (2) increase parenting skills; and (3) implement specific interventions with parents to improve their overall psychological adjustment and the quality of family life. To accomplish these goals, information and training are provided on a wide range of topics: early child development, family reactions to a handicapped child, social development, behavior management techniques, methods of enhancing infant development, and conflict-resolution and problem-solving skills. Training in these areas is carried out over the course of 18–20 weekly family treatment sessions. Although Klein *et al.* (1988) contend that PATT should provide both immediate and long-term benefits for the participating children and families, the efficacy of this program awaits empirical verification.

In an extension of this work, Van Hasselt *et al.* (1986a) are currently examining interactions and psychopathology in families with a visually handicapped adolescent. In this effort, the children and parents are evaluated on problem-solving and conflict-resolution skills, social skills, family discord, and psychiatric symptomatology. For example, a recently completed study assessed interaction and marital adjustment in the parents of visually handicapped adolescents (Van Hasselt *et al.*, 1987). Specifically, the parents of visually handicapped (VH) adolescents (aged 10–17) were contrasted with the parents of adolescents with spina bifida (SB) and the parents of nonhandicapped (NC) adolescents ($N$ = 25 per group). The Marital Interaction Coding System (MICS-III; Hops, Wills, Patterson, & Weiss, 1972) was used to evaluate the problem-solving discussions of husband–wife dyads. Self-reports of marital satisfaction were also obtained from the participants.

The results indicated that parents in the VH and SB conditions exhibited increased communication deviance (e.g., blaming, complaining, and criticizing) and marital dissatisfaction relative to the NC group. Interestingly, marital disharmony appeared to be greatest in the SB parents. Analyses of parent–child interaction and other assessment data are being completed. These findings will be used to determine the elements in a family treatment regimen.

## HEARING IMPAIRMENT

Current incidence estimates indicate that there are nearly 2 million persons with hearing impairments in the United States today. Further, as many as 12 million individuals have some form of milder hearing impairment (Neisser, 1983). A 1974 survey by Adler and Williams revealed that the number of school-aged children with hearing impairments totaled approximately 90,000; two thirds of this population were in elementary school.

As with the visually impaired, mental health professionals have become more attuned to the needs of hearing-impaired persons, partly because of the burgeoning population with this disorder. However, here again, the accelerated activity is also a function of the numerous reports showing relatively high levels of psychopathology and behavior disturbances in many hearing-impaired children and youths. For example, early investigations by Springer (1938) and Myklebust and Burchard (1945) found greater evidence of psychoneurotic tendencies in hearing-impaired children than in nonimpaired children. More recently, psychiatric problems, primarily neurosis and personality disorders, have been described in samples of hearing-impaired children (e.g., Altshuler, 1974; Meadow & Schlesinger, 1971). High rates of aggression, impulsivity, and emotional immaturity have also been reported with some consistency (see reviews by Goetzinger & Proud, 1975; Helsel, 1988; Matson & Helsel, 1986).

Although there has been considerable discussion of the emotional problems of the hearing-impaired, few treatment studies focusing on the remediation of the various difficulties have been carried out. An issue common to work with the visually impaired is that many intervention strategies are used by clinicians and special educators in nonresearch contexts (e.g., the clinic and the classroom). Although many of these approaches may be effective, there is a lack of emphasis on an empirical determination of their utility. The following sections review studies involving the use of psychological approaches with hearing impaired children. The areas covered include (1) social skills; (2) behavior management; (3) family adjustment; and (4) communication skills.

### Social Skills

Numerous clinicians, researchers, and educators have commented on the problems of social adjustment in many hearing-impaired children and youths

(Bradway, 1937; Brill, 1960; Freeman, Malkin, & Hastings, 1975; Matson, Macklin, & Helsel, 1985). In a review on deafness and psychiatric illness, Cooper (1976) discussed the social isolation experienced by many of these individuals:

> Isolation results primarily from sensory defect which directly impedes communication and social interchange, but is also the inevitable consequence of social withdrawal which so frequently accompanies the feelings of inferiority and social inadequacy associated with this particular form of physical disability. (p. 220)

Despite recommendations to develop and implement social skills intervention with the hearing-impaired (Hummel & Schirmer, 1984; Koetitz, 1976), the remedial strategies used with this population have been minimal. In one of the few available reports, gaze aversion (i.e., the absence of eye-to-eye contact) in a 19-year-old institutionalized deaf girl was targeted for modification (Brooks, Morrow, & Gray, 1968). This response interfered significantly with the subject's normal social interaction and required treatment before the enhancement of other social skills could proceed. Twenty-six daily experimental sessions (averaging 30 minutes each) consisted of providing positive reinforcement (M&M's) for a visual attention response in which the subject made eye contact with the experimenter for 2 seconds. Further, the investigators tested the relative efficacy of continuous (reinforcement of every response) and variable-ratio (reinforcement administered intermittently, on the average of 20 responses per reinforcement) reinforcement schedules. The cumulative response records showed that positive reinforcement increased the subject's visual attention responses relative to baseline and extinction phases. Further, the highest and most stable response rates were obtained under the variable-ratio schedule.

Beene and Beene (1980) designed a positive-reinforcement (counselor-attention) program to increase social and recreational activities in eight deaf adolescents and young adults residing in a halfway house facility. Five of the eight participants (six males and two females) had additional handicapping conditions (cerebral palsy, epilepsy, or mental retardation) and displayed low rates of social interaction. To determine treatment efficacy, the number of the subjects' social interactions for three successive weekends before reinforcement were contrasted with their interaction frequency on the same number of weekends after the interventions. A significant increase in weekend social activities was seen after the behavioral intervention was instituted.

Barton and Osborne (1978) devised a teacher-assisted positive-practice strategy to train a kindergarten class of five hearing-impaired children (5½–6½ years old) in initiation and reciprocation of sharing. Two types of sharing responses were targeted: (1) physical sharing, that is, close proximity to another child and conjoint toy use, and (2) verbal sharing, that is, verbal requests to share, verbal compliance, and acceptance of invitations to share. Positive practice involved instructions, modeling, and rehearsal, in which a nonsharing student practiced verbally the role of initiator (the person who asked another to share a toy) or the acceptor (the person who agreed to share). The training was carried out in a regular classroom during a free-play period in which toys were available. An experimental analysis revealed a threefold increase in the subjects' physical sharing of toys as a function of positive practice. Verbal sharing, however, was minimally affected. These gains had been maintained at a 15-week follow-up. Further, sharing appeared to generalize to a new teacher, a different class with untrained peers, and new toys.

Citing the need to ameliorate specific skill deficits in hearing-impaired children, Lemanek, Williamson, Gresham, and Jensen (1986) applied a social-skills-training "package" (instructions, performance feedback, modeling, behavior rehearsal, and social reinforcement) to increase social skills in four hearing-impaired children and adolescents (11 years 7 months to 18 years 3 months of age). All participants received eight skills-training sessions consisting of two 45-minute sessions per week, with role-play test items used in assessment and treatment. These role-play scenarios depicted disparate categories of social behaviors, including assertiveness and giving and accepting help and praise. The behaviors targeted for behavior change included speech duration, response latency, content, and smiles. In a multiple-baseline design across subjects, the skills training led to improved social behavior during role play for all subjects. Further, the effects generalized to novel (untrained) role-play scenes and a 5-minute social interaction with a confederate. These improvements had been maintained at a 2-month follow-up.

An area that has recently become a topic of study for social skills researchers is social perception and its relationship to overall interpersonal functioning (Bellack & Morrison, 1982). Morrison and Bellack (1981) defined social perception as the ability to accurately identify, label, and reflect different emotional or affective states. This skill is considered crucial for adequate social effectiveness. However, there are some indications that hearing-impaired children may have social perception deficiencies.

Two investigations have examined empathy, a subcategory of social perception, in samples of hearing-impaired children. In the first study, Odom, Blanton, and Laukhuf (1973) asked 15 deaf 7- to 8-year-olds and 30 hearing control subjects to sort faces portraying nine affective categories and to match those faces with drawings of appropriate emotion-arousing situations. The hearing-impaired subjects were able to perform the first part of the task at a level commensurate with the hearing children. However, they were less accurate than their hearing peers on matching the faces with the situations. Odom et al. (1973) concluded that the deaf children had deficits in their ability to analyze and interpret emotion-arousing events.

Another study (Bachara, Raphael, & Phelan, 1980) involved the administration of the Borke Test of Emphathy (Borke, 1971) to 21 preadolescents and adolescents between the ages of 9 and 14 years, equally divided into three groups: congenitally deaf, prelingually deaf (birth to 18 months), and postlingually deaf (18 months to 6 years). The Borke test is a series of 16 visual and signed presentations in which the subject is required to choose an emotion (happy, sad, afraid, or angry) that corresponds to a particular stimulus situation. As an example, the examiner says, "Show me how Nancy would feel if she were eating the food she liked best," while showing the subject a picture of a girl without a head eating ice cream. The child is asked to select a picture with a face depicting the emotion that would be appropriate, and to place it on the picture. Comparisons with norms of hearing children indicated that the deaf group had significantly more difficulty with empathy development. Also, postlingual onset of deafness was less detrimental to a child's ability to recognize emotions than other forms of the disorder. Bachara et al. (1980) contended that, given the contribution of poor empathic ability to "social isolation, withdrawal, and the attendant deficiencies in social skills and interpersonal relationships" (p. 71), many hearing-impaired children face deleterious social consequences without intervention.

## Behavior Management

Behavior management techniques have been used for a wide range of problems in hearing-impaired children (see reviews by Belcastro, 1979; Matson & Helsel, 1986; Webster & Green, 1973). The potential of the use of behavioral strategies with this population was first discussed by Osborne and Wageman (1969) nearly two decades ago. Their overview of the successful use of operant conditioning procedures for hearing-impaired children included several case examples with a number of treatment targets (e.g., task completion, appropriate classroom behavior, and improved penmanship). Unfortunately, most of these case illustrations were unpublished reports and anecdotal accounts. Yet, they provided preliminary evidence of the value of behavior management techniques in dealing with maladaptive response patterns of hearing-impaired children.

Several investigators have designed behavior management programs to reduce problem behaviors in the classroom. Osborne (1969) used time free from schoolwork as a reinforcer for remaining seated in the classroom. Six females (ages 11 years 8 months to 13 years 8 months), grouped in one class at a school for the deaf because of poor academic achievement and below-average intelligence, were told that, for each of several 15-minute segments in which they all remained seated, they would be given 5 minutes of free time. The baseline data revealed that, before the reinforcement contingency, the students engaged in slightly more than one out-of-seat response per 15-minute observation period. With the introduction of the contingency, inappropriate responding decreased to near-zero levels. A shift to a noncontingent free-time phase resulted in a minimal change in the already-lowered response rate. An extension of the in-seat contingency to reinforcement for 25-minute segments of in-seat behavior, along with a corresponding reduction in the number of free-time periods provided, did not diminish the procedure's effectiveness.

Three studies have focused on increasing task attention as part of programming for hearing-impaired and multihandicapped children. Benassi and Benassi (1973) used positive reinforcement (small portions of breakfast, smiles from the experimenter, and rubbing of the face) to train attending behavior and discriminative vocal responses in a 6-year-old nonverbal boy diagnosed as deaf, cerebral-palsied, and severely mentally retarded. A three-phase procedure was followed over the course of 52 sessions lasting between 13 and 15 minutes each. First, because the child did not reliably attend to others, looking at the experimenter's face was targeted for change. Once this change was well established, reinforcement was provided when the child emitted a vocalization while maintaining eye contact for at least 5 seconds. In the third phase, the child was reinforced for looking at the experimenter, vocalizing an "ah" sound, and holding it for 5 seconds. After these behaviors were trained, reinforcement shifted from a continuous to a fixed-ratio (FR2) and eventually a variable-ratio (VR2) schedule. The results documented the efficacy of this treatment approach. Further, anecdotal reports by the subject's mother and physical and occupational therapists indicated that newly acquired attending behaviors generalized to the home and to the child's physical and occupational therapy sessions.

Garrard and Saxon (1973) applied a multiple-component behavioral intervention (positive reinforcement, extinction, and time-out) to increase attending and sitting behavior and to decrease screaming and crying behavior in a 2½-year-old female with severe hearing loss and numerous maladaptive responses that precluded her participation in therapeutic and educational programs. Through a series of AB single-case designs, the investigators provided evidence of the utility of their strategy in reducing problem behaviors. For example, the child's percentage of time spent crying at a speech clinic decreased from 96% during baseline to zero after five treatment sessions. Also, her attending behaviors increased from approximately 5% in baseline to nearly 95% following 11 treatment sessions. Finally, the use of a time-out procedure by the mother substantially reduced the child's screaming at home.

Van Houten and Nau (1980) also attempted to enhance the attention skills and suppress the disruptiveness of three boys and two girls (ages 6–9) in an adjustment class for deaf students. To accomplish this, they examined the relative efficacy of fixed-ratio (FR) and variable-ratio (VR) schedules of reinforcement. Under FR, the subjects received checks (exchangeable for a grab-bag prize) if they were attentive and nondisruptive. During the VR condition, they earned a draw from the grab bag as in the VR schedule, with a mean ratio equal to the value of the prior FR schedule. The students attended more and exhibited less disruptive behavior in the VR condition. Their productivity on classroom tasks was also higher when the VR schedule was in effect.

Two investigations examined strategies to facilitate the acquisition of self-help and independent living skills. In one of these, six multihandicapped students (aged 15–22) with severe hearing loss were taught to put on their own hearing aids by use of the following graded sequences of trainer assistance: (1) no help; (2) verbal instruction; (3) demonstration and verbal instruction; and (4) physical guidance and instruction (Tucker & Berry, 1980). All "verbal" instructions or prompts were given either vocally, vocally with manual sign, or with manual sign alone, depending on each student's level of communication. The sequence of assistance was used for each step in a hearing-aid chain that was determined via task analysis. Also, correct performance at each step was consequated with praise.

The data showed rapid skill acquisition for all subjects. However, because two students showed limited generalization of abilities to other environments, a second experiment was conducted to evaluate the transfer of behavior across settings and to replicate the effectiveness of the intervention. A multiple-probe baseline design revealed that the skills generalized to other locales without direct training in these settings.

A drawback of most behavior-management programs in classroom settings is that teachers are typically instructed in their use by an experimenter. This strategy may be beneficial for the modification of distinct difficulties in certain contexts. However, without training in more general principles or behavioral methods, teachers may become proficient in the implementation of a few procedures that may not apply across all situations. In an innovative approach to dealing with this problem, Hundert (1982) trained two special-education teachers at a school for the deaf both to write and to implement behavior-modification treatment-plans. The teachers taught classes of three multihandicapped (hearing-impaired, mentally retarded, and autistic) pupils, each consisting of two boys and one girl (ages 8–10½), who had been excluded from regular classes at a school for the deaf because of severe learning and behavior problems (e.g., self-injury and tantrums). The first part of the study involved "measurement" training, in which the teachers were taught to set behavioral objectives and to measure the subjects' performance. In the "programming" phase, a training manual was used to teach general problem-solving approaches to developing behavior modification programs. Experimenter feedback was provided to the teachers after each training condition for their application of treatment to one focal behavior in the child (e.g., on-task, head shaking, or writing).

Hundert (1982) found that "measurement" training had little impact on teacher or student behavior. However, "programming" training led to increased program writing and the correct use of behavioral strategies by the teachers. Further, the teachers generalized this training across students and target behaviors. Significant improvements in student behaviors were concurrently observed.

### Family Adjustment

The effects of a child's deafness on his or her parents and family have been examined (Stein & Jabaley, 1981). In an overview of the development of reciprocal family relationships, Altshuler (1974) pointed out the negative effects of severe hearing loss on early spontaneous mimicry and learning of verbal language. Deficiencies in these areas are likely to impede the adequate expression of emotion and, consequently, to disrupt the formation of attachment between child and parent. According to Altshuler (1974), "when such communication is interfered with, the bond between parent and child is altered, and along with it the quality of closeness and the clarity of identification of feelings" (p. 368).

Possible negative parental reactions (depression, denial, anger, and guilt) to the diagnosis of a severe hearing impairment in their child have also been discussed in the literature (Cantor & Spragins, 1977; Fuller, 1962; Lax, 1972; Stein & Jabaley, 1981; Vernon, 1972). Because of these difficulties, and because of the potentially harmful short- and long-term effects of such parental responses on the children themselves, many clinicians have recommended parent or family intervention (Altschuler, 1974; Belcastro, 1979; Northern & Downs, 1974). Cantor and Spragins (1974) contended that "The parents need guidance in dealing with child care, the special needs of the hearing impaired child, developing independence and responsibility in the child, and specific techniques for changing behavior" (p. 334).

An early family-oriented training program was reported by Mira (1972), who instructed the parents of deaf children in the application of behavior modification techniques to deal with child behavior problems. In one of a series of case studies, attempts by the mother to discipline her daughter led to aggressive outbursts and hitting. During a 10-day baseline phase, the mother recorded three to four hits per day. However, results of an AB design showed that, after a week of extinction, in which aggressive episodes were followed by the mother's turning her back and walking away, the rates of the targeted behavior decreased and reached zero levels within 4 weeks. This improvement was still observed at a 3-month follow-up.

A second case involved a 3½-year-old boy who refused to wear his hearing aid. The positive-reinforcement strategy initiated for this child consisted of allowing him to watch his favorite TV shows or play his record player once each day contingent on his wearing his hearing aid for a specified time period. Increased aid-wearing occurred within a week. When the approach was modified so that reinforcement was provided every 3 hours for wearing the aid during the previous 3 hours, the child wore the aid the entire day.

Another case example presented by Mira (1972) involved an attempt to reduce gaze aversion that interfered with the acquisition of communication in a 3-year-old autistic child. Here, the child's father was instructed to increase eye-to-eye contact by immediately providing hugs and kisses whenever the child looked directly at him. An AB design revealed an increase in the child's rate of eye contact from a median rate of .025 per minute to .3 per minute, a 10-fold increase in response rate.

In two more cases, "negative reactions" (noncompliance and tantrums) were exhibited by a male and a female preschooler from different families. Their parents were trained in the use of time-out, which required each child to stay in his or her room for a 10-minute period, with 2 minutes of quiet time required for release. The data showed a significant reduction in noncompliance and tantrum behaviors with the implementation of the treatment procedure. Also, a 100-day follow-up of the female indicated that the gains had been maintained.

Citing the need to shift from the targeting of individually deviant child behaviors to more general parent-management competencies, Forehand, Chaney, and Yoder (1974) examined the effects of a program designed to modify parent–child interactions. The child in this study was a 7-year-old deaf male referred for treatment because of noncompliance (running or turning away, tantrums, and physical resistance) in response to maternal commands. The parental training consisted of instructing the mother to be a "more effective reinforcing agent" by expanding the range and frequency of her social rewards. In addition, an attempt was made to reduce parental questions and commands that were incompatible with rewards. Nine sessions of a multiple-component intervention (discussion, modeling, behavior rehearsal, and role playing), in which the mother learned reinforcement techniques not dependent on hearing (e.g., affectionate physical contact and smiling), resulted in an increase in the mother's rate of rewards and a diminished use of questions and commands. The final four treatment sessions of this study involved the application of a time-out procedure for noncompliance. The institution of this strategy affected improved percentages of child compliance and parental rewards relative to the number of child compliances. Forehand et al. (1974) reported that all gains were still evident 3 months after the formal termination of the training. Further, these investigators concurrently found that the mother's post-treatment scores on the Parents Attitude Test (Cowen, Huser, Beach, & Rappaport, 1970) reflected her perceptions of her child as being generally better adjusted after the treatment.

## Communication

The deaf child's lack of audition results in a limited or impaired ability to communicate with others. Such difficulties are apparent as early as infancy, when, because of hearing loss, modeling, mimicry, and spontaneous learning of verbal language are impeded (Altshuler, 1974). Further, studies of communication in deaf and hearing-impaired children indicate that their speech is often difficult to understand even after several years of conventional methods of speech training (Carr, 1953; Eveslage & Buchmann, 1973; Heider, Heider, & Sykes, 1941). Consequently, the enhancement of various forms of communication skills is a critical element of the deaf child's psychoeducational program.

Several investigators have examined methods of improving communication in hearing-impaired children. In a multiphase study by Bennett and Ling (1972), a behavioral intervention was used with a 3-year-old hearing-impaired girl who had previously never used the article *the* nor the auxiliary verb *is* in a sentence. In this approach, token reinforcers (exchangeable for candy) were initially administered, combined with verbal praise contingent on her inclusion of the article *the* when imitating the experimenter in response to a picture of a girl swimming (e.g., "*the* girl swimming"). The next phase involved reinforcement (praise only) for including all of the required words ("*the* girl *is* swimming"). Eventually she was able to emit complete sentences in response to the command, "Tell me about this" (picture). Further, she was able to use other sentences in the present progressive form to describe additional pictures for which no training had been provided.

Another investigation tested the efficacy of performance feedback and positive reinforcement in increasing the percentages of intelligible speech in three boys and four girls (ages 9 years 4 months to 10 years 8 months) in a first-grade classroom at a school for the deaf. Here, the teacher passed a basket containing word cards to the children, who each drew a card and then read the word on it without allowing the teacher to see the word. The teacher then wrote down what she heard and compared her response to the word card. When the cards matched the teacher's response, the child received a penny. The results indicated substantially improved percentages of intelligible verbal emissions with reinforcement in comparison to phases in which the responses were not reinforced.

Pirreca and Fitch (1973) used a behavioral chaining strategy to increase the mean length of response (MLR) in two male and two female deaf preschoolers. Individual treatment sessions were carried out four times a week over a 10-week period. They initially consisted of the administration of reinforcement for a subject's imitation (through appropriate signs) of a two-word phase describing a picture. Gradually, increased MLR was required for reinforcement. The results of a series of withdrawal designs indicated substantially elevated MLRs during reinforcement conditions in comparison to baseline levels.

Lipreading or speech reading is an important aspect of receptive language skills in educational programming with hearing-impaired children. Johnson and Kaye (1976) addressed deficits in this area in a 9-year-old deaf boy who was also emotionally disturbed and mentally retarded. In the first of two experiments, positive reinforcement (tokens and praise) was delivered contingent on his correctly pointing to one of six fruits (plastic imitations) after the therapist pronounced one of them. The second experiment involved the experimenter's pronunciation of the names of nine colors, each of which was printed on a card. Reinforcement was again provided for correct stimulus identification. The results of the reversal and multiple-baseline designs in Experiments 1 and 2 showed essentially that tokens and social reinforcement presented either simultaneously or separately were effective in shaping lipreading. Further, the child learned to lipread both voiced and nonvoiced names of objects.

Over the last decade, several definitions of deaf-blindness have emerged (Jensema, 1980; Kramer & Rosenfeld, 1975; Meyers, 1981). Most emphasize the multiplicative effects of dual handicapping conditions (DuBose, 1976). Indeed, factors related to each condition affect conceptual, motoric, and social development both singly and in combination, to cause impediments to normal growth that are more detrimental than either impairment alone (Kennedy, 1974). Regulations related to the implementation of Public Law 94-142 (The Education of All Handicapped Children Act) provide these general guidelines for identifying deaf-blind children and youth:

> Deaf-blind means concomitant hearing and visual handicaps the combination of which causes such severe communication and other developmental and educational problems that [such children] cannot be accommodated in special education programs solely for deaf or blind children. (Sec. 300.5 (b) (2))

No accurate estimate of the deaf-blind population in the United States is available, because of (1) inconsistent definitions of deaf-blindness; (2) difficulties in assessing sensory functioning in persons with severe cognitive and behavioral deficits; and (3) the inappropriate placement of many deaf-blind persons in programs designed for other severely handicapped populations. However, relatively recent estimates indicate that there are approximately 10,000 individuals with this disability in the United States (5,400 adults and 4,600 children; Seligson, 1983).

More is known about the causes of deaf-blindness. Several diseases and conditions can have a dramatic effect on both vision and hearing. Maternal rubella, heredity (e.g., Usher syndrome), and bacterial meningitis are the leading known etiologies of deaf-blindness in school-aged children and youths (Sims-Tucker & Jensema, 1984). Deaf-blindness rarely occurs in isolation because congenital etiologies are usually organismically devastating and cause other handicaps as well. For example, expectant mothers infected with rubella, especially during the first 3 months of pregnancy, are at risk for bearing infants who are afflicted with deafness, congenital heart disease, cataracts, and/or gross mental retardation (Campbell, 1961; Guldager, 1969; Vernon, 1967; Vernon & Hicks, 1980).

Although there is considerable variability in the cognitive capacities of deaf-blind persons, evidence has accrued showing that the majority suffer from significant deficits in cognitive and adaptive functioning (see Sisson, Van Hasselt, & Hersen, 1987). For example, the deaf-blind are repeatedly described as functioning at very low levels across communicative modalities (Curtis, Donlon, & Tweedie, 1974a, 1975b; Tweedie, 1974a,b,c). Further, teachers, parents, and various professionals working with deaf-blind children and youths have articulated concerns about their persistent and pervasive maladaptive behaviors (Blea & Overbeck, 1977; Curtis *et al.*, 1975a; Moersch, 1977). The most notable of these are self-stimulation (e.g., loud repetitive vocalizations and light filtering); self-injury (e.g., face slapping, head banging, and hand biting); and aggression (e.g., temper tantrums, hitting and biting others, and destroying property). These behaviors are common among low-functioning deaf-blind persons (Sims-Tucker & Jensema, 1984). In addition, hyperactivity and distractibility have frequently been observed (Thomas, 1970). Many investigators have also commented on the failure of these individuals to acquire social and self-help skills and their inability to function adequately in academic and vocational environments (Curtis & Donlon, 1984; Sims-Tucker & Jensema, 1984).

Of the populations covered in this chapter, the deaf-blind have received the least attention from mental health professionals and researchers. This lack of attention is due to a host of factors, including their (1) low incidence and unavailability; (2) primary participation in special-education programs; and (3) lack of responsiveness to behavior change strategies. The following sections examine the work that has been carried out with deaf-blind children and youths to date. These reports are primarily program descriptions, case narratives, or position papers by workers in the field in the areas of behavior management, social skills, and vocational competence.

## Behavior Management

Reduction of maladaptive responses has been the focus of the majority of empirical studies that have addressed the treatment of deaf-blind individuals. The emphasis on behavior management is a function of the priority afforded to remediation of self-injury and/or aggression because of the potential for harm to the individual or others (Luiselli & Michaud, 1983). Further, severe behavior problems interfere with the acquisition of skills and therefore must be controlled before other training programs are implemented (Calvert, Reddell, Jacobs, & Baltzer, 1972).

Three reports used interventions to reduce self-stimulatory behaviors. In the first, McDaniel, Kocim, and Barton (1984) attempted to eliminate hand mouthing in three young children with varying degrees of visual and auditory deficits, as well as mental retardation. Each child received one of the following consequences for hand mouthing: (1) a verbal cue ("No!") plus manual turning of the head from side to side; (2) the presentation of a bitter substance (e.g., lemon juice); or (3) the "No" headshake condition combined with the bitter substance. The three procedures appeared to reduce hand mouthing and to increase toy play in relation to baseline levels.

Two studies tested the efficacy of behavioral treatments to reduce high rates of eye gouging. Luiselli, Myles, Evans, and Boyce (1985) used the differential reinforcement of other behavior (DRO) and verbal redirection with a 10-year-old female who was deaf-blind and severely to profoundly mentally retarded. In this strategy, the child gained access to a favorite toy for 1 minute contingent on the absence of eye gouging for increasing durations of time. In addition, the cue "Stop touching your eye" followed instances of eye gouging. The use of a multielement experimental design established the efficacy of this treatment package over verbal redirection alone in reducing the frequency of the target behavior. Reinforcement was systematically faded from 1- to 25-minute intervals. The treatment gains had been maintained at a 3-month follow-up evaluation.

Slifer, Iwata, and Dorsey (1984) also targeted eye gouging. Their subject was a 6-year-old male who was deaf-blind and profoundly mentally retarded. Manual prompting and praising of toy play occurred every 15 seconds across baseline and treatment conditions. The treatment entailed interrupting eye gouging with a verbal prompt ("No") and physical restraint (manual restraint of the child's hands for 10 seconds). A multiple-baseline design across settings (individual session and group activity) indicated that the rates of eye gouging were significantly suppressed as a result of the treatment. Generalization programming included training the child's teacher and mother in the intervention. The maintenance of treatment gains was evident up to 5 months in the home and 9 months in the classroom.

Overcorrection has been shown to be effective in reducing self-injurious behavior displayed by deaf-blind children and youths. In one investigation, Harris and Romancyk (1976) modified head and chin banging in an 8-year-old male who was deaf-blind and who functioned in the moderately mentally retarded range. The treatment involved following every instance of head or chin banging with 10 minutes of manually guided head and arm movements. A systematic replication in two settings (the treatment center and the home) demonstrated the efficacy of this intervention. Anecdotal reports regarding maintenance of the treatment gains were positive. They also suggested that academic and social progress correlated with the declines in maladaptive behavior.

A subsequent study (Barton & LaGrow, 1983) expanded these results by using a similar treatment to diminish self-injurious behaviors exhibited by three females (5, 9, and 21 years old), who suffered from varying, but unspecified, degrees of visual, auditory, mental, and behavioral impairments. Although their rates of self-injurious behavior decreased when the treatment was introduced, experimental control was demonstrated in only one case, using a multiple-baseline design across behaviors (aggression and self-injury). For this subject, a 14-week follow-up probe demonstrated the durability of the treatment effects.

More recently, Luiselli (1986) evaluated an innovative treatment for face hitting and head banging in a 16-year-old boy who was deaf-blind and developmentally delayed. The intervention consisted of the application of a protective helmet and mittens for a predefined duration whenever self-injurious responses were emitted. Protective equipment plus DRO (edibles delivered after 15 minutes of noninjury) was shown to be effective in a withdrawal design. In addition, reinforcement was gradually faded and discontinued. Follow-up probes for up to 6 months showed further decreases in self-injurious responding.

Aggressive behaviors have been targeted in four investigations. In a series of reports, Luiselli and his colleagues (Luiselli & Greenidge, 1982; Luiselli, Myles, & Littman-Quinn, 1983; Luiselli et al., 1985) used reinforcement plus time-out to reduce hitting, punching, and scratching by adolescents who were deaf-blind and moderately to severely mentally retarded. The results showed essentially that DRO (praise, edibles, or tokens delivered contingent on increasing periods without aggression) alone was ineffective in managing these maladaptive behaviors (e.g., Luiselli et al., 1983). However, when DRO was combined with the removal of teacher attention (Luiselli et al., 1985) or with isolation time-out (Luiselli & Greenidge, 1982; Luiselli et al. 1983), the aggression was reduced to clinically nonsignificant levels. Two of the three studies established the controlling effects of treatment in withdrawal designs (Luiselli et al., 1985) or multiple-baseline designs (Luiselli et al., 1983). Further, in both reports, reinforcement was systematically faded across the latter stages of the study, and the treatment gains were still observed at 4 months (Luiselli et al., 1983) and 5 months (Luiselli et al., 1985).

Finally, Lawrence and Drabman (1984) used multiple behavioral approaches to diminish chronic high-frequency spitting in a 15-year-old male who was deaf-blind and severely to profoundly mentally retarded. The subject's recalcitrant spitting was eliminated with a behavioral intervention and facial screening (towel covering the face) for spitting. Experimental control was demonstrated by means of a multiple-baseline design across settings (three instructional tasks). Anecdotal follow-up reports suggested that the frequency of spitting remained at low levels for 1 year. Further, improvements in academic and social skills were noted as spitting was eliminated.

## Social Skills

Although many centers serving deaf-blind and other severely handicapped groups implement some form of social competency training, their dissemination of information concerning the implementation and utility of this training tends to be minimal (Blea & Overbeck, 1977; Lenske, Rotatori, & Kapperman, 1980). Consequently, the treatment literature in this area is sparse. A number of clinicians have simply highlighted the need of increased social exposure of interactions with nonhandicapped individuals *per se* (Simpson, 1981; Smithdas, 1981; Wilson, 1974). Others have called for the development of more formal social-skill assessment and training programs specifically for the deaf-blind (e.g., Bourgeault, Harley, DuBose, & Langley, 1977). In some reports, interpersonal skills having potential utility for deaf-blind children and adults have been delineated. For example, Netick (1977) discussed the utility of arranging social behaviors along a skill hierarchy. In this conceptualization, the social skills warranting intervention range from "very simple recognition activities all the way to communication with peers and teachers in the appropriate way" (p. 42). Other behaviors in the hierarchy are basic attending and self-care skills, play activities, and the indication of preferences.

Recently, increased attention has been directed to an area closely related to social skills: the recreation and leisure skills needs of severely handicapped individuals. With regard to selecting appropriate activities, it has been recommended that only skills that are chronologically age-appropriate and that are used by the nonhandicapped population be considered. Also, leisure activities should provide the deaf-blind individual with enhanced sensory input and should minimize motoric and speed requirements for operation. Adaptations of materials may include (1) the use of permanent tactile prompts, such as a raised plastic tape attached to the flipper buttons of a pinball machine; (2) the stabilization of materials with bolts, hooks, or suction cups; (3) the enhancement of visual or auditory input by the use of large print or stereo headphones; and (4) the simplification of task requirements.

Hamre-Nietupski, Sandvig, Sandvig, and Ayres (1984) described a program of systematic leisure-skills instruction with deaf-blind young adults in a residential setting. The subjects were two males (17 and 19 years old), who functioned in the severe to profound range of mental retardation. One had additional physical disabilities. The subjects were taught to operate an eight-track tape player by means of backward chaining through the steps of a task analysis, a graduated hierarchy of assistance, and positive reinforcement (praise and music) for performing the task requirements correctly. The subjects acquired these leisure skills and maintained them over a 2-month period.

Vocational skills training endeavors with deaf-blind individuals are severely limited and essentially nonempirical. The most informative reports merely describe prevocational and vocational training programs (Busse, Romer, Fewell, & Vadasy, 1985; Freedman, 1978). A major emphasis in these articles is on the importance of incorporating techniques used by vocational rehabilitation counselors into classroom activities in preparation for eventual placement in community settings. These techniques include the use of "assembly line-type tasks that require sequencing, left-right orientation, on-task behaviors, high rate productivity, completion of piecework, and self-correction" (Sims-Tucker & Jensema, 1984, p. 310). Lockett and Rudolph (1981) argued that effective prevocational and vocational training for severely mentally retarded deaf-blind individuals should be provided according to a continuum of functional skills. The initial areas in need of remediation are personal care, basic communication, and motor skills. Later, daily living skills and behaviors needed for adequate work performance in simulated or actual work settings are taught. By age 18, the focus of training is on community living, recreation, and work in appropriate settings. This approach has goals quite different from the previous goals of educational programs that have attempted to slowly move deaf-blind youth along the sequential stages of development demonstrated by normal children, regardless of the student's age (Busse *et al.*, 1985; Orlansky, 1981).

Although little research has been carried out in the area of vocational skills training with deaf-blind individuals, Yarnall (1980) shaped a prerequisite behavior in a 21-year-old woman who was deaf-blind and mentally retarded. This woman was trained to "wait" by (1) manually signaling "wait"; (2) delivering social and tangible reinforcers for sitting quietly; and (3) providing a verbal cue ("No!") and manual guidance (turning her chin back and forth) for moving from the "wait" position. Waiting was increased from zero to 2 seconds over the 2-week study.

## SUMMARY AND FUTURE DIRECTIONS

The purpose of this chapter has been to review the psychological treatment approaches used with sensory-impaired children and youths. Relevant work was examined for each of three types of handicapping conditions: visual impairment, hearing impairment, and deaf-blindness. For each disorder, the major difficulties that have been the targets of intervention by mental health professionals were covered. Psychological interventions were directed toward the remediation of maladaptive response patterns (e.g., stereotypic acts, self-injury, and disruptiveness) and social skill deficits in all three groups. Other areas receiving remedial work included family adjustment (for the visually and hearing impaired), adaptive living skills (for the visually impaired only), and communication skills (for the hearing impaired only).

Research concerning the psychological treatment of sensory-impaired children is clearly in the nascent stage. Although some significant strides have been made in certain areas, a number of problems and issues warrant greater consideration in future research. For example, training in adaptive living skills is seriously needed to enhance life adjustment in sensory-impaired persons. Yet, few investigators have attempted to improve the wide range of skills required for independent functioning in these individuals. Many programs for teaching various self-help behaviors (e.g., transportation use, self-feeding, and clothing selection) to the mentally retarded have proved successful (Watson & Uzzell, 1981). Such approaches may have direct applicability to sensory-impaired persons, particularly those who are visually impaired or multihandicapped.

With regard to social skills, heightened investigative activity is required for each of the three sensory-impaired groups. Indeed, there has been a convergence of data attesting to the poor socialization of many of these children. In light of the large body of research documenting the relationship between impaired social functioning in childhood and long-term maladjustment (e.g., Cowen, Pederson, Babigian, Izzo, & Trost, 1973; Roff, Sell, & Golden, 1972), sensory-impaired children would appear to be at high risk for psychological problems later in life. A direction that future research might take in this area is the extension of treatment into more diverse categories under the rubric of social skills. For example, training in making friends, in conversation, and in heterosocial skills may serve to reduce the social isolation prevalent in all too many visually impaired and hearing-impaired children. Enhancement of the basic interpersonal and communication behaviors useful for participation in social, recreational, and leisure activities would be worthwhile goals of comprehensive program efforts for deaf-blind children, especially those functioning at low cognitive levels. Also deserving further study and intervention are emotional problems (e.g., schizophrenia and depression) in sensory-impaired children. Investigations of severe forms of psychopathology in these groups are virtually nonexistent.

We strongly agree with Matson and Helsel (1986) that there is an inadequate number of qualified professionals to serve the sensory-impaired. According to these investigators:

> It is typically the case that in clinical and school psychology, and in child psychiatry, the professionals working with these people have little or no understanding of special considerations in assessment or treatment. Such problems have made the provision of proper care in the realm of emotional problems outmoded and poorly implemented. A change in this situation is long overdue. (p. 378)

To correct this deficiency, graduate programs in clinical psychology, child psychiatry, child development, and special education should offer coursework in developmental and physical disabilities that deals with the unique and special problems and issues encountered by these populations. Such instruction should include information on the etiology and characteristics of sensory impairments, along with training in relevant forms of communication (e.g., braille and sign language). Background in these areas should promote more effective mental-health services.

Finally, but hardly least of all, there is a need for greater methodological rigor in treatment research with the sensory-impaired. Van Hasselt (1987) pointed out that interpretations of the results of intervention studies on these individuals are obfuscated by serious methodological flaws (e.g., unvalidated assessment instruments and inadequate experimental controls). This is partly a result of the wide range of professional groups (e.g., psychologists, special educators, speech pathologists, and audiologists) that have considered themselves the primary service providers for the sensory-impaired. Consequently, the quality and the nature of the available studies have been quite variable. Here again, improved professional training with a stronger emphasis on research methods is called for to bring investigative efforts with the sensory-impaired up to a level commensurate with other areas of child psychopathology and adjustment.

ACKNOWLEDGMENTS. Preparation of this chapter was facilitated by grant number G008530258 (Special Education Programs) and contract number 300-82-0368 (Early Childhood Research Institute) from the U.S. Department of Education. However, the opinions expressed here do not necessarily reflect the position or policy of the U.S. Department of Education, and no official endorsement by the Department should be inferred. The authors wish to thank Judith A. Kowalski for her technical assistance on this manuscript.

# REFERENCES

Adler, E. P., & Williams, B. R. (1974). Services to deaf people in the seventies. In R. E. Hardy & J. G. Cull (Eds.), *Educational and psychosocial aspects of deafness.* Springfield, IL: Thomas.

Altshuler, K. Z. (1974). The social and psychological development of the deaf child: Problems, their treatment and prevention. *American Annals of the Deaf, 119,* 365–376.

Ammerman, R. T., Van Hasselt, V. B., & Hersen, M. (1985). Social skills training for visually handicapped children: A treatment manual. *Psychological Documents, 15*(2684).

Ammerman, R. T., Van Hasselt, V. B., & Hersen, M. (1986). Psychological adjustment of visually handicapped children and youth. *Clinical Psychology Review. 6,* 67–85.

Bachara, G. H., Raphael, J., & Phelan, W. J. (1980). Empathy development in deaf preadolescents. *American Annals of the Deaf, 25,* 38–41.

Barry, H., & Marshall, F. E. (1953). Maladjustment and maternal rejection in retrolental fibroplasia. *Mental Hygeine, 37,* 570–580.

Barton, E. J., & Osborne, J. G. (1978). The development of classroom sharing by a teacher using positive practice. *Behavior Modification, 2,* 231–250.

Barton, L. E., & LaGrow, S. J. (1983). Reducing self-injurious and aggressive behavior in deaf-blind persons through overcorrection. *Journal of Visual Impairment and Blindness, 77,* 421–424.

Beene, G., & Beene, L. (1980). Behavior modification of social interaction with deaf clients in a halfway house facility. *Journal of Rehabilitation of the Deaf, 14,* 15–18.

Belcastro, F. P. (1979). Use of behavior modification with hearing-impaired subjects. *American Annals of the Deaf, 124,* 820–824.

Belcher, T. L., Conetta, C., Cole, C., Iannotti, E., & McGovern, M. (1982). Eliminating a severely retarded blind adolescent's tantrums using mild behavioral interruption: A case study. *Journal of Behavior Therapy and Experimental Psychiatry, 13,* 257–260.

Bellack, A. S., & Morrison, R. L. (1982). Interpersonal dysfunction. In A. S. Bellack, M. Hersen, & A. E. Kazdin (Eds.), *International handbook of behavior modification and therapy.* New York: Plenum Press.

Benassi, B. J., & Benassi, V. A. (1973). Behavioral strategies for a deaf and cerebral palsied child. *Journal of Communication Disorders, 6,* 165–174.

Bennett, C. W., & Ling, D. (1972). Teaching a complex verbal response to a hearing-impaired girl. *Journal of Applied Behavior Analysis, 5,* 321–327.

Biglan, A., Van Hasselt, V. B., & Simon, J. (1988). Visual impairment. In V. B. Van Hasselt, P. S. Strain, & M. Hersen (Eds.). *Handbook of developmental and physical disabilities.* New York: Pergamon Press.

Blank, H. R. (1959). Psychiatric problems associated with congenital blindness due to retrolental fibroplasia. *New Outlook for the Blind, 53,* 237–244.

Blasch, B. B. (1978). Blindisms: Treatment by punishment and reward in laboratory and natural settings. *Journal of Visual Impairment and Blindness, 72,* 215–230.

Blea, W. A., & Overbeck, D. (1977). Research needs in the area of the deaf-blind. In E. L. Lowell & C.

C. Rouin (Eds.), *State of the art: Perspectives on serving deaf-blind children.* Sacramento: California State Department of Education.

Borke, H. (1971). Interpersonal perception of young children; Egocentrism or empathy? *Developmental Psychology, 5,* 263–269.

Bourgeault, S. E., Harley, R. K., DuBose, R. F., & Langley, M. B. (1977). Assessment and programming for blind children with severely handicapped conditions. *Journal of Visual Impairment and Blindness, 71,* 49–53.

Bradway, K. P. (1937). Social competence of exceptional children: 3. The deaf, the blind, and the crippled. *Exceptional Children, 4,* 64–69.

Brill, R. G. (1960). A study in the adjustment of three groups of deaf children. *Exceptional Children, 26,* 464.

Brooks, B. D., Morrow, J. E., & Gray, W. F. (1968). Reduction of autistic gaze aversion by reinforcement of visual attention responses. *The Journal of Special Education, 2,* 307–309.

Burleson, G. (1973). Modeling: An effective behavior change technique for teaching blind persons. *New Outlook for the Blind, 67,* 443–441, 469.

Busse, D. G., Romer, L. J., Fewell, R. R., & Vadasy, P. F. (1985). Employment of deaf-blind rubella students in a subsidized work program. *Journal of Visual Impairment and Blindness, 79,* 59–64.

Caetano, A. P., & Kauffman, J. M. (1975). Reduction of rocking mannerisms in two blind children. *Education of the Visually Handicapped, 7,* 101–105.

Calvert, D. R., Reddell, R. C., Jacobs, U., & Baltzer, S. (1972). Experiences with preschool deaf-blind children. *Exceptional Children, 38,* 415–421.

Campbell, M. (1961). Peace of maternal rubella in the etiology of congenital heart disease. *British Medical Journal, 1,* 691–696.

Cantor, D. W., & Spragins, A. (1977). Delivery of psychological services to the hearing-impaired child in the elementary school. *American Annals of the Deaf, 122,* 330–336.

Carr, J. (1953). An investigation of speech sounds of five year olds. *Journal of Speech and Hearing Disorders, 18,* 22–29.

Carroll, T. J. (1961). *Blindness: What it is, what it does, and how to live with it.* Boston: Little Brown.

Catena, J. (1961). Pre-adolescence: The caseworker and the family. *New Outlook for the Blind, 55,* 297–299.

Conley, O. S., & Wolery, M. R. (1980). Treatment by overcorrection of self-injurious eye gouging in preschool blind children. *Journal of Behavior Therapy and Experimental Psychiatry, 11,* 121–125.

Cowen, E. L., Huser, J., Beach, D. R., & Rappaport, J. (1970). Parental perceptions of young children and their relations to indexes of adjustment. *Journal of Consulting and Clinical Psychology, 34,* 97–103.

Cowen, E. L., Pederson, A., Babigian, H., Izzo, L. D., & Trost, M. A. (1973). Long-term follow-up of early detected vulnerable children. *Journal of Consulting and Clinical Psychology, 41,* 438–446.

Curtis, W. S., & Donlon, E. T. (1984). A ten-year follow-up study of deaf-blind children. *Exceptional Children, 50,* 449–455.

Curtis, W. S., Donlon, E. T., & Tweedie, D. (1974a). Communicative behavior of deaf-blind children. *Education of the Visually Handicapped, 6,* 114–118.

Curtis, W. S., Donlon, E. T., & Tweedie, D. (1975a). Adjustment of deaf-blind children. *Education of the Visually Handicapped, 1,* 21–26.

Curtis, W. S., Donlon, E. T., & Tweedie, D. (1975b). Learning behavior of deaf-blind children. *Education of the Visually Handicapped, 7,* 40–48.

Drabman, R. S., Ross, J. M., Lynd, R. S., & Cordua, G. D. (1978). Retarded children as observers, mediators, and generalization programmers using an icing procedure. *Behavior Modification, 2,* 371–385.

DuBose, R. F. (1976, April). *The multiply handicapped child: The diagnostician's challenge.* Paper presented at the Annual International Convention of the Council for Exceptional Children, Chicago.

Eveslage, R. A., & Buchmann, A. V. (1973). The effects of consequences delivered contingent upon intelligible speech of deaf children. *American Annals of the Deaf, 118,* 46–453.

Farkas, G. M., Sherick, R. B., Matson, J. L., & Loebig, M. (1981). Social skills training of a blind child through differential reinforcement. *The Behavior Therapist, 4,* 24–26.

Forehand, R., Chaney, T., & Yoder, P. (1974). Parent behavior training: Effects on the non-compliance of a deaf child. *Journal of Behavior Therapy and Experimental Psychiatry, 5,* 281–283.

Freedman, S. (1978). Support services and alternatives to institutionalization for deaf-blind children. *Journal of Visual Impairment and Blindness, 72,* 249–254.

Freeman, R. F., Malkin, S. F., & Hastings, J. O. (1975). Psychosocial problems of deaf children and their families: A comparative study. *American Annals of the Deaf, 120,* 391–405.

Froyd, H. E. (1973). Counseling families of severely visually handicapped children. *New Outlook for the Blind, 67,* 251–257.

Fuller, C. W. (1962). Your child, maturity and you: A talk with parents. *American Annals of the Deaf, 107,* 320–328.

Gallagher, P. A., & Heim, R. E. (1974). The classroom application of behavior modification principles for multiply handicapped blind students. *New Outlook for the Blind, 68,* 447–453.

Garrard, K. R., & Saxon, S. A. (1973). Preparation of a disturbed deaf child for therapy: A case description in behavior shaping. *Journal of Speech and Hearing Disorders, 38,* 502–509.

Goetzinger, C. P., & Proud, G. O. (1975). The impact of hearing impairment upon the psychological development of children. *Journal of Auditory Research, 15,* 1–60.

Greene, R. J., & Hoats, D. L. (1971). Aversive tickling: A simple conditioning technique. *Behavior Therapy, 2,* 389–393.

Greene, R. J., Hoats, D. L., & Hornick, A. J. (1970). Music distortion: A new technique for behavior modification. *Psychological Record, 20,* 107–109.

Guldager, L. (1969). The deaf-blind: Their education and their needs. *Exceptional Children, 36,* 203–206.

Hamre-Nietupski, J., Sandvig, R., Sandvig, M. B., & Ayres, B. (1984). Leisure skills instruction in a community residential setting with young adults who are deaf/blind severely handicapped. *The Journal of the Association for the Severely Handicapped, 9,* 49–54.

Haney, J. I., & Jones, R. T. (1982). Programming maintenance as a major component of a community-centered preventive effort: Escape from fire. *Behavior Therapy, 13,* 47–62.

Harris, S. L., & Romanczyk, R. G. (1976). Treating self-injurious behavior of a retarded child by overcorrection. *Behavior Therapy, 7,* 235–239.

Heider, F., Heider, G. M., & Sykes, J. L. (1941). A study of the spontaneous vocalizations of fourteen deaf children. *The Volta Review, 43,* 10–14.

Helsel, W. J. (1988). Assessing exceptional populations: Hearing-impaired. In C. L. Frame & J. L. Matson (Eds.), *Handbook of assessment in childhood psychopathology: Applied issues in differential diagnosis and treatment evaluation.* New York: Plenum Press.

Hoemann, H. W., & Briga, J. I. (1981), Hearing impairments. In J. M. Kauffman & D. P. Hallahan (Eds.), *Handbook of special education.* Englewood Cliffs, NJ: Prentice-Hall.

Hops, H., Wills, T., Patterson, G., & Weiss, R. (1972). *Marital Interaction Coding System.* Unpublished manuscript, University of Oregon Research Institute.

Hoshmand, L. T. (1975). ''Blindness'': Some observations and propositions. *Education of the Visually Handicapped, 7,* 56–60.

Hummel, J. W., & Schirmer, B. E. (1984). Review of research and description of programs for the social development of hearing-impaired students. *The Volta Review, 86,* 259–266.

Hundert, J. (1982). Training teachers in generalized writing of behavior modification programs for multihandicapped deaf children. *Journal of Applied Behavior Analysis, 15,* 111–122.

Jan, J. E., Freeman, R. D., & Scott, E. P. (Eds). (1977). *Visual impairment in children and adolescents.* New York: Grune & Stratton.

Jensema, C. K. (1980). A profile of deaf-blind children within various types of educational facilities. *American Annals of the Deaf, 125,* 896–900.

Johnson, C. M., & Kay, J. H. (1976). Acquisition of lipreading in a deaf multihandicapped child. *Journal of Speech and Hearing Disorders, 41,* 226–232.

Jones, R. T., & Kazdin, A. E. (1980). Teaching children how and when to make emergency telephone calls. *Behavior Therapy, 11,* 509–521.

Jones, R. T., Sisson, L. A., & Van Hasselt, V. B. (1984a). Emergency fire-safety skills for blind children and adolescents: Group training and generalization. *Behavior Modification, 8,* 267–286.

Jones, R. T., Van Hasselt, V. B., & Sisson, L. A. (1984b). Emergency fire-safety skills: A study with blind adolescents. *Behavior Modification, 8,* 59–78.

Kelly, J. A., & Drabman, R. S. (1977). Generalizing repsonse suppression of self-injurious behavior through an overcorrection punishment procedure: A case study. *Behavior Therapy, 8,* 468–472.

Kennedy, A. (1974). Language awareness and the deaf-blind child. *Teaching Exceptional Children, 31,* 99–102.

Kennedy, A. B. (1982). The effects of three reinforcers on the mobility of a severely retarded, blind women. *Education and Treatment of Children, 5,* 337–346.

Klein, B., Van Hasselt, V. B., Trefelner, M., Sandstrom, D. J., & Snyder, P. B. (1988). The Parent and Toddler Training (PATT) Project: Early intervention for visually handicapped children and their families. *Journal of Visual Impairment and Blindness.*

Koetitz, L. E. (1976). Cognitive and psycho-social development in deaf children: A review of the literature. *Education and Training of the Mentally Retarded, 11*, 66–72.

Kramer, L., & Rosenfeld, J. (1975). Speech and communication techniques with adult deaf-blind. *Journal of Rehabilitation of the Deaf, 8*, 27–34.

Lairy, G. C., & Covello, A. H. (1973). The blind child and his parents: Congenital visual defect and the repercussion of family attitides on the early development of the child. *Research Bulletin, American Foundation for the Blind, 25*, 1–24.

Lambert, R., & West, M. (1980). Parenting styles and the depressive syndrome in congenitally blind individuals. *Journal of Visual Impairment and Blindness, 74*, 333–337.

Lawrence, J. S., & Drabman, R. S. (1984). Suppression of chronic high frequency spitting in a multiply handicapped and mentally retarded adolescent. *Child and Family Behavior Therapy, 6*, 45–55.

Lax, R. F. (1972). Some aspects of the interaction between mother and impaired child: Mother's narcissistic trauma. *International Journal of Psychoanalysis, 53*, 339.

Lemanek, K. L., Williamson, D. A., Gresham, F. M., & Jensen, B. J. (1986). Social skills training and hearing-impaired children and adolescents. *Behavior Modification, 10*, 55–71.

Lenske, B. J., Rotatori, A. F., & Kapperman, G. (1980). The use of behavior modification with deaf-blind persons. *Journal for Special Educators, 17*, 86–91.

Lockett, T., & Rudolph, J. (1981). Prevocational programming for deaf-blind/profoundly handicapped. *Viewpoint in Teaching and Learning, 57*, 33–42.

Lovaas, O. I., & Simmons, J. Q. (1969). Manipulation of self-destruction in three retarded children. *Journal of Applied Behavior Analysis, 2*, 143–157.

Luiselli, J. K. (1986). Modifications of self-injurious behavior: An analysis of the use of contingently applied protective equipment. *Behavior Modification, 10*, 191–204.

Luiselli, J. K., & Greenidge, A. (1982). Behavioral treatment of high-rate aggression in a rubella child. *Journal of Behavior Therapy and Experimental Psychiatry, 13*, 152–157.

Luiselli, J. K., & Michaud, R. L. (1983). Behavioral treatment of aggression and self-injury in developmentally disabled, visually handicapped students. *Journal of Visual Impairment and Blindness, 77*, 388–392.

Luiselli, J. K., Myles, E., & Littman-Quinn, J. (1983). Analysis of a reinforcement time-out treatment package to control severe aggressive and destructive behaviors in a multihandicapped, rubella child. *Applied Research in Mental Retardation, 4*, 65–78.

Luiselli, J. K., Myles, E., Evans, T. P., & Boyce, D. A. (1985). Reinforcement control of severe dysfunctional behavior in blind, multihandicapped students. *American Journal of Mental Deficiency, 90*, 328–334.

Martin, J. A., & Iagulli, D. M. (1974). Case reports: Elimination of middle-of-the-night tantrums in a blind, retarded child. *Behavior Therapy, 5*, 420–422.

Matas, L., Arend, R. A., & Sroufe, L. A. (1978). Continuity of adaptation in the second year: The relationship between quality of attachment and later competence. *Child Development, 49*, 547–556.

Matson, J. L. (1980). Preventing home accidents: A training program for the retarded. *Behavior Modification, 4*, 397–410.

Matson, J. L., & Helsel, W. J. (1986). Psychopathology of sensory impaired children. In B. B. Lahey & A. E. Kazdin (Eds.), *Advances in clinical child psychology* (Vol. 9). New York: Plenum Press.

Matson, J. L., Macklin, G. F., & Helsel, W. J. (1985). Psychometric properties of the Matson Evaluation of Social Skills with Youngsters (MESSY) with emotional problems and self concept in deaf children. *Journal of Behavior Therapy and Experimental Psychiatry, 16*, 117–123.

Maxfield, K. E., & Fjeld, H. A. (1942). The social maturity of the visually handicapped preschool child. *Child Development, 13*, 1–27.

McDaniel, G., Kocim, R., & Barton, L. E. (1984). Reducing self-stimulatory mouthing behaviors in deaf-blind children. *Journal of Visual Impairment and Blindness, 78*, 23–26.

McGlinchey, M. A., & Mitala, R. F. (1975). Using environmental design to teach ward layout to severely and profoundly retarded blind persons. *New Outlook for the Blind, 69*, 168–171.

McKay, B. E. (1936). Social maturity of the preschool blind child. *Training School Bulletin, 33*, 146–155.

Meadow, K. P., & Schlesinger, H. S. (1971). The prevalence of behavioral problems in a population of deaf school children. *American Annals of the Deaf, 115*, 346–348.

Measel, C. J., & Alfieri, P. A. (1976). A treatment of self-injurious behavior by a combination of reinforcement for incompatible behavior and overcorrection. *American Journal of Mental Deficiency, 81,* 147–153.

Meyers, S. O. (1981). A general overview of disabilities and handicaps. In S. Walsh & R. Holzberg (Eds.), *Understanding and educating the deaf-blind severely and profoundly handicapped.* Springfield, IL: Thomas.

Miller, B. S., & Miller, W. H. (1976). Extinguishing "blindisms": A paradigm for intervention. *Education of the Visually Handicapped, 8,* 6–15.

Mira, M. (1972). Behavior modification applied to training young deaf children. *Exceptional Children, 38,* 225–229.

Moersch, M. S. (1977). Training the deaf-blind child. *The American Journal of Occupational Therapy, 31,* 425–431.

Moray, N., Bates, A., & Barnett, T. (1965). Experiments on the four-eared man. *Journal of the Acoustical Society of America, 38,* 196–201.

Morrison, R. L., & Bellack, A. S. (1981). The role of social perception in social skill. *Behavior Therapy, 12,* 69–79.

Mulliken, R. K., & Buckley, J. J. (1983). *Assessment of multihandicapped and developmentally disabled children.* Rockville, MA: Aspen Publication.

Myers, J. J., & Deibert, A. N. (1971). Reduction of self-abusive behavior in a blind child by using a feeding response. *Journal of Behavior Therapy and Experimental Psychiatry, 2,* 141–144.

Myklebust, H. R., & Burchard, E. M. L. (1945). A study of the effects of congenital and adventitious deafness on intelligence, personality, and social maturity of school children. *Journal of Educational Psychology, 34,* 321–343.

Neisser, A. (1983). *The other side of silence: Sign language and the deaf community in America.* New York: Knopf.

Netick, A. (1977). Programming for consistency in training for deaf-blind in a residential center. *Education of Visually Handicapped, 9,* 41–44.

Northern, J. L., & Downs, M. P. (1974). *Hearing in children.* Baltimore: Williams & Wilkins.

Odom, P. B., Blanton, R. L., & Laukhuf, C. (1973). Facial expressions and interpretation of emotion-arousing situations in deaf and hearing children. *Journal of Abnormal Child Psychology, 1,* 139–151.

Orlansky, M. D. (1981). The deaf-blind and the severely/profoundly handicapped: An emerging relationship. In S. R. Walsh & R. Holzberg (Eds.), *Understanding and educating the deaf-blind/severely and profoundly handicapped.* Springfield, IL: Thomas.

Osborne, J. G. (1969). Free-time as a reinforcer in the management of classroom behavior. *Journal of Applied Behavior Analysis, 2,* 113–118.

Osborne, J. G., & Wageman, R. M. (1969). Some operant conditioning techniques and their use in schools for the deaf. *American Annals of the Deaf, 114,* 141–153.

Petersen, G. A., Austin, G. J., & Lang, R. D. (1979). Use of teacher prompts to increase social behavior: Generalization effect with severely and profoundly retarded adolescents. *American Journal of Mental Deficiency, 84,* 82–86.

Petrucci, D. (1953). The blind child and his adjustment. *New Outlook for the Blind, 47,* 240–246.

Pirreca, M. S., & Fitch, J. L. (1973). Increasing mean length of response by application of reinforcement principles. *Journal of Communication Disorders, 6,* 175–183.

Ragland, E. U., Kerr, M. M., & Strain, P. S. (1978). Behavior of withdrawn autistic children: Effects of peer social initiations. *Behavior Modification, 2,* 565–578.

Ragland, E. U., Kerr, M. M., & Strain, P. S. (1981). Social play of withdrawn children: A study of the effects of teacher-mediated peer feedback. *Behavior Modification, 5,* 347–359.

Rapoff, M. A., Altman, K., & Christophersen, E. R. (1980a). Elimination of a retarded blind child's self-hitting by response-contingent brief restraint. *Education and Treatment of Children, 3,* 231–236.

Rapoff, M. A., Altman, K., & Christophersen, E. R. (1980b). Suppression of self-injurious behaviour: Determining the least restrictive alternative. *Journal of Mental Deficiency and Research, 24,* 37–46.

Roff, M., Sell, B., & Golden, M. M. (1972). *Social adjustment and personality development in children.* Minneapolis: University of Minnesota Press.

Rotatori, A. F., Kapperman, G., & Schryven, J. (1979). The elimination of self-induced vomiting in severely retarded visually impaired female. *Education of the Visually Handicapped, 11,* 60–62.

Sarason, S. (1959). *Psychological problems in mental deficiency.* New York: Harper.

Schaffer, H. R. (1964). The too-cohesive family: A form of group pathology. *International Journal of Social Psychiatry, 10,* 266–275.

Schein, J. D. (1975). Deaf students with other disabilities. *American Annals of the Deaf, 120,* 92–99.

Seligson, J. L. (1983). Problems of psychiatric care of a deaf-blind population. *International Journal of Psychiatry in Medicine, 13,* 85–92.

Simpson, F. (1981). Prevocational/vocational programming. In S. R. Walsh & R. Holzberg (Eds.), *Understanding and educating the deaf-blind/severely and profoundly handicapped.* Springfield, IL: Thomas.

Simpson, R. L., Sasso, G. M., & Bump, N. (1982). Modification of manneristic behavior in a blind child via a time-out procedure. *Education of the Visually Handicapped, 14,* 50–55.

Sims-Tucker, B. M., & Jensema, C. K. (1984). Severely and profoundly auditorially/visually impaired students. In P. J. Valetutti & B. M. Sims-Tucker (Eds.), *Severely and profoundly handicapped students: Their nature and their needs.* Baltimore: Paul H. Brooks.

Sisson, L. A., Van Hasselt, V. B., & Hersen, M. (1987). Psychological approaches with deaf-blind persons: Strategies and issues in research and treatment. *Clinical Psychology Review, 7,* 303–328.

Sisson, L. A., Van Hasselt, V. B., Hersen, M., & Strain, P. S. (1985). Peer interventions: Increasing social behaviors in multihandicapped children. *Behavior Modification, 9,* 293–321.

Sisson, L. A., Babeo, T. J., & Van Hasselt, V. B. (in press). Group training to increase social behaviors in young multihandicapped children. *Behavior Modification,*

Slifer, K. J., Iwata, B. A., & Dorsey, M. J. (1984). Reduction of eye gouging using a response interruption procedure. *Journal of Behavior Therapy and Experimental Psychiatry, 15,* 369–375.

Smith, M. A., Chethik, M., & Adelson, E. (1969). Differential assessments of "blindisms." *American Journal of Orthopsychiatry, 39,* 807–817.

Smithdas, R. J. (1981). Psychological aspects of deaf-blindness. In S. R. Walsh & R. Holzberg (Eds.), *Understanding and educating the deaf-blind/severely and profoundly handicapped.* Springfield, IL: Thomas.

Solnit, A. J., & Stark, M. H. (1961). Mourning and the birth of a defective child. *Psychoanalytic Study of the Child, 16,* 523–537.

Springer, N. A. (1938). A comparative study of the psychoneurotic responses of deaf and hearing children. *Journal of Educational Psychology, 29,* 459.

Stein, L. K., & Jabaley, T. (1981). Early identification and parent counseling. In L. K. Stein, E. D. Mindel, & T. Jabaley (Eds.), *Deafness and mental health.* New York: Grune & Stratton.

Stein, L. K., Mindel, E. D., & Jabaley, T. (Eds.). (1981). *Deafness and mental health.* New York: Grune & Stratton.

Strain, P. S., Kerr, M. M., & Ragland, E. U. (1978). Effects of peer-mediated social initiations and prompting reinforcement procedures on the social behavior of autistic children. *Journal of Autism and Developmental Disorders, 9,* 41–54.

Tate, B. G., & Baroff, G. S. (1966). Aversive control of self-injurious behavior in a psychotic boy. *Behaviour Research and Therapy, 4,* 281–287.

Thomas, E. O. (1970). Medical aspects of deaf-blind children: A five-year diary. In E. D. Thomas (Ed.), *Behavior modification for deaf-blind children* (pp. 27–47). Dallas: Callier Hearing and Speech Center.

Tucker, D. J., & Berry, G. W. (1980). Teaching severely multihandicapped students to put on their own hearing aids. *Journal of Applied Behavior Analysis, 13,* 65–75.

Tweedie, D. (1974a). Behavioral change in a deaf-blind multihandicapped child. *The Volta Review, 76,* 213–219.

Tweedie, D. (1974b). Demonstrating behavioral change of deaf-blind children. *Exceptional Children, 40,* 510–512.

Tweedie, D. (1974c). Observing the communication behavior of deaf-blind children. *American Annals of the Deaf, 119,* 343–347.

Van Hasselt, V. B. (1983a). Social adaptation in the blind. *Clinical Psychology Review, 3,* 87–102.

Van Hasselt, V. B. (1983b). Visual impairment. In M. Hersen, V. B. Van Hasselt, & J. L. Matson (Eds.), *Behavior therapy for developmentally and physically disabled persons.* New York: Academic Press.

Van Hasselt, V. B. (1987). Behavior therapy for visually handicapped persons. In M. Hersen, P. Miller, & R. M. Eisler (Eds.), *Progress in behavior modification* (Vol. 21). New York: Sage.

Van Hasselt, V. B., Simon, J., & Mastantuono, A. K. (1982). Social skills training for blind children: A program description. *Education of the Visually Handicapped, 14,* 34–40.

Van Hasselt, V. B., Hersen, M., Kazdin, A. E., Simon, J., & Mastantuono, A. K. (1983). Training blind adolescents in social skills. *Journal of Visual Impairment and Blindness, 77,* 199–203.

Van Hasselt, V. B., Kazdin, A. E., Hersen, M., Simon, J., & Mastantuono, A. K. (1985). A behavioral-analytic model for assessing social skills in blind adolescents. *Behaviour Research and Therapy*, *23*, 395–405.

Van Hasselt, V. B., Hersen, M., Moore, L. E., & Simon, J. (1986a). Assessment and treatment of families with visually handicapped children: A project description. *Journal of Visual Impairment and Blindness*, *80*, 633–635.

Van Hasselt, V. B., Kazdin, A. E., & Hersen, M. (1986b). Assessment of problem behavior in visually handicapped adolescents. *Journal of Clinical Child Psychology*, *15*, 134–141.

Van Hasselt, V. B., Ammerman, R. T., Moore, L. E., & Hersen, M. (1987). *Interactions and marital adjustment in parents of visually handicapped adolescents*. Unpublished manuscript, Western Pennsylvania School for Blind Children.

Van Houten, R., & Nau, P. A. (1980). A comparison of the effects of fixed and variable ratio schedules of reinforcement on the behavior of deaf children. *Journal of Applied Behavior Analysis*, *13*, 13–21.

Vernon, M. (1967). Psychological, educational and physical characteristics associated with post-rubella deaf children. *The Volta Review*, *69*, 176–185.

Vernon, M. (1972). Psychodynamics surrounding the diagnosis of a child's deafness. *Rehabilitation Psychology*, *19*, 127–134.

Vernon, M., & Hicks, D. (1980). Relationship of rubella, herpes simplex, cytomegalovirus, and certain other viral disabilities. *American Annals of the Deaf*, *125*, 529–534.

Warren, D. H. (1981). Visual impairments. In J. M. Kauffman & D. P. Hallahan (Eds.), *Handbook of special education*. Englewood Cliffs, NJ: Prentice-Hall.

Warren, D. H. (1984). *Blindness and early childhood development* (2nd ed., rev.). New York: American Foundation for the Blind.

Watson, L. S., & Uzzell, R. (1981). Teaching self-help skills to the mentally retarded. In J. L. Matson & J. R. McCartney (Eds.), *Handbook of behavior modification with the mentally retarded*. New York: Plenum Press.

Webster, L. M., & Green, W. B. (1973). Behavior modification in the deaf classroom: Current applications and suggested alternatives. *American Annals of the Deaf*, *18*, 511–518.

Welsh, R. L., & Blasch, B. B. (Eds.). (1980). *Foundations of orientation and mobility*. New York: American Foundation for the Blind.

Wesolowski, M. D., & Zawlocki, R. J. (1982). The differential effects of procedures to eliminate an injurious self-stimulatory behavior (digito-ocular sign) in blind retarded twins. *Behavior Therapy*, *13*, 334–345.

Williams, C. E. (1968). Behavior disorders in handicapped children. *Developmental and Medical Child Neurology*, *10*, 736–740.

Wilson, D. A. (1974). Teaching multiply handicapped blind persons in a state hospital. *The New Outlook for the Blind*, *68*, 337–343.

Yarnall, G. D. (1980). Teaching a deaf-blind women to "wait" on command. *Journal of Visual Impairment and Blindness*, *74*, 24–27.

# Index